JS
1228
.S37

D0948902

Lander College Library
Lander College
Greenwood, S. C.

STATEMENT CONCERNING PUBLICATIONS OF RUSSELL SAGE FOUNDATION

Russell Sage Foundation was established in 1907 by Mrs. Russell Sage "for the improvement of social and living conditions in the United States of America." While the general responsibility for management of the Foundation is vested in the Board of Trustees, the responsibility for facts, conclusions, and interpretations in its publications rests with the authors and not upon the Foundation, its Trustees, or its staff. Publication under the imprint of the Foundation does not imply agreement by the organization with all opinions or interpretations expressed. It does imply that care has been taken that the work on which a manuscript is based has been thoroughly done.

GOVERNING NEW YORK CITY

Politics in the Metropolis

WALLACE S. SAYRE
Eaton Professor of Public Administration
Columbia University

HERBERT KAUFMAN
Associate Professor of Political Science
Yale University

30912

Lander College Library
Lander College
Greenwood, S. C.

RUSSELL SAGE FOUNDATION
New York · 1960

352.07471
S 275 g

© 1960
RUSSELL SAGE FOUNDATION
Printed in the United States
of America

Library of Congress
Catalog Card Number: 60-8408

WM. F. FELL CO., PRINTERS
PHILADELPHIA, PA.

Contents

Part Two

Strategies of the Contestants:
Efforts to Determine Who Gets Public Office
and Employment

Part Three

Strategies of the Contestants:
Shaping Governmental Decisions

Part Four

Conclusions

Charts

Tables

Preface

THERE ARE PROBABLY A HUNDRED WAYS to write about the government and politics of New York City. Each has its own advantages, its own shortcomings, its own champions, its own critics. Each serves the purposes of some observers and students of the city, and each is less useful to some than one or another of the alternatives.

We have chosen to write primarily about the *process* by which the city is governed. Broadly speaking, we have tried to answer three sets of general questions: (1) What is politics in New York about? What do the participants in the city's government and politics get in return for the time, energy, and money they invest in governmental and political activity? (2) Who are the participants? (3) How do the participants go about getting what the system offers? In other words, what strategies do they use?

Thus viewed, the process takes on the characteristics of a contest. Part One of this volume is an outline of the background and setting of the contest: a description of the city as the over-all environment, a definition of the stakes and prizes of political action in the city, a classification of the contestants for the stakes and prizes, and a summary of the rules according to which the contest is conducted. Parts Two and Three deal with the strategies of the contestants as they pursue the stakes and prizes. In Part Two we examine their efforts to determine who gets public office and employment; here, nominations, elections, appointments, and removals are discussed. In Part Three we turn to the strategies adopted by the contestants to influence the decisions of governmental officers and employees since most stakes and prizes not distributed in the form of office or employment are dispensed in the form of governmental decisions, large and small. All contestants employ similar strategies, but each category of contestants has its distinctive strategies determined by its position in the contest and its special relationships with other contestants. Part Three therefore consists of studies of each major category of participants: administrators of line agencies, special authorities, and overhead agencies; leaders of the organized city bureaucracies, the parties, and non-governmental groups; the courts; the officials of other governments; and the three central institutions of the city government, namely, the Council, the Board of Estimate, and the Mayor. Approaching the system from these many

I

angles reveals both the common and the unique strategies of the contestants. It also brings to light the ties among the contestants, the autonomy of many contestants or groups of contestants, and a number of traits of the entire governmental system of the city. These general aspects are taken up in Part Four, in which the system and the leading proposals for change are appraised.

We have aimed to maintain a clinical detachment toward the data, even in our final appraisals. Our objective was simply to describe what we saw as we examined the system. We did not set ourselves up as judges; we did not seek to apply the standards of value urged by the most articulate participants in the contest, or even those propounded by the writers of textbooks on munici-pal government. Our sympathies and prejudices have doubtless cropped out in places. As citizens who have spent most of our lives in the city, who feel great admiration and affection for it, and who are therefore delighted with its achievements and sometimes outraged by its abuses, we could not hope to be invariably clinical. Nevertheless, we have tried to attain an approxima-tion of the objectivity of medical researchers who hope their investigations may in the long run improve health and vanquish disease, but who know that they contribute more to such endeavors by performing their work in a neutral, disinterested fashion than by devoting themselves to denunciations, encomi-ums, or exhortations. We hope we have succeeded in avoiding most of the distortions and biases of personal preferences.

Our professional colleagues will understand our efforts best, perhaps, if we describe this volume as a set of propositions and hypotheses about the gov-ernment and politics of the city. James G. March and Herbert A. Simon[1] have recently distinguished between three types of propositions: (1) those that state the dependence of one variable on one or more other (independent) variables; (2) qualitative descriptive generalizations (comparable to, "A man has a heart that contracts periodically."); (3) assertions that a particular structure or process performs a particular function. Only occasionally do our propositions take the first form; they are far more often of the second or third type. While a rigorous theory would consist of a set of interlocking proposi-tions of all three kinds, we do not pretend to have constructed such a "model" of New York City government and politics. We are convinced, though, that valid propositions of the second and third kinds make it possible to under-stand and explain much that happens in the government and politics of the city, and even to make limited kinds of predictions about what will happen under specified conditions. Astute politicians have long been doing this as a matter of course, but the somewhat more explicit and systematic description of the contest presented here may make it possible for many more people to do so—and perhaps to modify some misconceptions and superstitions that have governed the behavior of some contestants. Such an analysis may also

[1] In their book, *Organizations.* John Wiley and Sons, New York, 1959, pp. 7-9.

advance slightly the struggle to develop more rigorous and accurately predictive theories in social science.

We plead for more research. As the bibliography for each chapter reveals, scholarly studies of New York City and its politics are relatively sparse and usually specialized. Much of the additional available material consists of exposés and accusations of alleged irregularities or corruption or inefficiencies, and with special prescriptions for political reform or managerial betterment. Many other items are autobiographies, or biographies, or partisan "histories" that are really personal defenses or apologies, or condemnations and denunciations of political opponents. Most of them emphasize the dramatic and spectacular personalities and events in the city's history at the expense of equally important but less sensational aspects of the city's life. There is as yet no broad base of primary research on which comprehensive studies can confidently rely.

We have treated the sensational and partisan materials as raw data rather than as dependable secondary sources to be accepted at face value. In addition, necessarily, we turned to original sources for much of our basic information. For a number of reasons, however, these sources do not occupy in our bibliography an amount of space proportionate to their importance; if sheer number of references were taken as a measure of their qualitative, or even quantitative, contribution to the volume, the original sources would be underrepresented.

The official documents—the New York State Constitution, state statutes, the New York City Charter, the Administrative Code, the rules and regulations of administrative agencies, the annual reports of officials and agencies, the decisions of courts, and others—are identified as entities rather than by individual sections and paragraphs. Initially, we had hoped to cite them in detail, but the volume of references promptly threatened to reach such proportions as to make them unwieldy and of dubious utility to other researchers checking on our work or pursuing particular points in greater depth. We have therefore employed blanket references to entire statutes and pieces of local legislation, to whole series of reports, to general bodies of administrative issuances. This compression disproportionately reduced their prominence in the bibliography compared to the other sources.

We were compelled for similar reasons to abandon our initial plan of citing each newspaper item that helped us. Several of the city's newspapers were read and clipped systematically during the three years this book was in preparation and were tapped more selectively for many preceding years. Detailed citations of this enormous mass of material would have burdened the general reader unduly without providing assistance of compensatory value to researchers. Our great debt to it, consequently, is not reflected in the bibliography.

We acknowledge in the section that follows, without citation in the bibliography, the help given us by more than a score of party leaders, officials and ex-officials, civic and other group leaders, journalists, and other informed observers who gave freely of their time and knowledge, and by an even larger number of experts who read all or parts of the manuscript and commented critically upon its factual accuracy, and on the validity, completeness, and insightfulness of the analysis.

Our research assistants sifted and organized vast quantities of material. Their research reports and memoranda were exceptionally rich sources of information not included in the bibliography.

Finally, we drew heavily on our own experiences and observations. One author was a city official for more than four years of the LaGuardia administration and has for over twenty-five years been active in the civic life of New York. The other author is a native New Yorker, a product of the city's schools and universities, and an author of several studies of its governmental processes.

We hope our identification of sources is sufficiently full, despite our economies and compressions, to furnish substantial aid to future research on New York City government and politics, and to indicate on what grounds we have reached our conclusions about the system. Little scholarly analysis has been done on the government and politics of New York. Much remains to be done. Why the city has been thus neglected is difficult to say. We hope it will not remain neglected.

Events are quicker than the pen. Many authors are faced with the unhappy choice between trying to cover all the latest developments in their fields, which means they may never finish because there are always new developments before a manuscript goes to press, or arbitrarily selecting a cut-off date for coverage, which means significant recent events may be omitted. In order to complete this book we decided to include developments only up to the early part of 1959. Since then a number of noteworthy things have occurred. Nothing that has happened since the cut-off date, however, would compel us to alter significantly anything we have said in the book; indeed, recent events tend to corroborate our analysis.

Since it is impossible to be up-to-the-minute in writing about a dynamic city in a rapidly moving world, we can only hope that we succeeded in not being out-of-date. Events and details in the city's political and governmental system change often and rapidly. The system itself is surprisingly stable.

WALLACE S. SAYRE
HERBERT KAUFMAN

November, 1959

Acknowledgments

ALL BOOKS ARE THE PERSONAL RESPONSIBILITY of their authors, and we fully accept the responsibility for this one. The blame for its shortcomings not only will, but should, fall on us alone. Nevertheless, we wish to acknowledge that this volume is the product of a collective effort. We are not only indebted to the people whose contributions to this enterprise were as vital to its completion as our own efforts, but that debt is greater than we can adequately state. In taking this opportunity to express our profound appreciation for their help, we do not pretend to repay them, or even to suggest the value of their assistance. Only they and we can possibly know the full extent of our dependence upon them.

To none are we more indebted than to Russell Sage Foundation. It was Foundation support that made the project possible. We are grateful for the financial aid, and for the vote of confidence that this aid implied.

We owe very special debts, too, to Theodore J. Lowi, Theodore Diamond, Murray Silberman, and Frederick Shaw. Mr. Lowi did research for us on a full-time basis for a year and, despite the heavy burden of his own work, gave us further assistance from time to time for two more years. While there is scarcely a chapter of the study that does not in some way reflect the products of his labors, his contributions to the chapters on nominations, elections, and appointments are particularly extensive. Mr. Diamond worked with us full time for two summers, and part time at various intervals, collecting data on a wide range of subjects but, most importantly, gathering and analyzing the information that provided the foundations for the chapter on the courts. Mr. Silberman prepared highly useful biographies of each of the mayors of New York from 1898 to the present, and assembled a preliminary general bibliography. The materials for the final bibliography, however, and the inventory of special libraries and other collections of New York City materials were compiled largely by Dr. Shaw, whose services, because of his exceptional qualifications for this task, we were most fortunate to obtain.

Repeatedly, in the course of preparing our manuscript, we found ourselves in need of additional data for particular purposes, data not available in convenient form from any readily accessible source. In such cases, we called on Pearl Handshuh Hack, Joseph K. Roberts, Janet Cutting Feldman, or Allan

5

Schechter for assistance. The special research projects they did for us helped us over what would otherwise have constituted troublesome and perhaps serious obstacles.

Nor could we have done this job without the assistance of those participants in, and expert observers of, the political scene who gave us a great deal of time from their busy schedules for extended (and sometimes repeated) consultations, or to read and comment on most of the manuscript, or both. This cooperation was invaluable to us; from it we acquired much of our information and many of our ideas, and it saved us from a number of errors of fact and interpretation. For all this, the following stand high on our list of "creditors": Erwin W. Bard, John E. Bebout, William N. Cassella, Jr., Edward N. Costikyan, Lyle C. Fitch, Frank P. Grad, Luther Gulick, George H. Hallett, Louis Harris, Stanley M. Isaacs, Edward M. Kresky, Daniel L. Kurshan, Maxwell Lehman, John M. Leavens, Joseph D. McGoldrick, Robert J. Mangum, Mrs. Rita Morris, H. Douglas Price, Robert H. Schaffer, Harold Stein, Ludwig Teller, John J. Theobald, David B. Truman, and Robert C. Wood.

In addition, for their immensely helpful suggestions and criticisms regarding the chapters they were kind enough to review for us, and for other assistance, we extend our warm thanks to Lewis Abrahams, Herbert E. Alexander, Morton S. Baratz, John Bartky, Robert A. Dahl, John A. Davis, Stanley Feingold, Abraham J. Gellinoff, Arthur H. Goldberg, Samuel Hendel, Roger J. Herz, Mark D. Hirsch, Victor Jones, Dr. Roscoe P. Kandle, Richard C. Lee, Louis J. Lefkowitz, Norton E. Long, Arthur W. Macmahon, Arthur Mann, Richard E. Neustadt, James H. Scheuer, Allan P. Sindler, Samuel D. Smoleff, Sterling D. Spero, Samuel F. Thomas, Clement E. Vose, T. T. Wiley, Louis E. Yavner, and William H. Zucker.

For several decades, in the closing year of each ten-year period, the Institute of Public Administration has published a brief pamphlet describing the structure of the New York City government. Comprehensive despite its brevity, the pamphlet has long been of service not only to those in need of a quick, authoritative introduction to the city's government, but also to many active participants in, and students of, the city. Dr. Luther Gulick, president of the Institute, has generously consented to the inclusion in this volume of the forthcoming edition of the pamphlet and its accompanying charts. They appear as Appendix C and may also be obtained separately from the Institute.

This statement of our obligations would be incomplete without emphasis on another source of information and insight: the city's daily newspapers. Their news items, their feature stories, their editorials, their columns, even their letters-to-the-editors, are indispensable to the student of New York's government and politics. No other record of the city's political events and personalities is so searching and complete. It is no exaggeration to admit that we would not have attempted to write this book had we not known that we could depend for much of our data on the aggressive, probing, thorough reporting by the daily press. Our experience confirmed that expectation, and we made full use of the great volume of material the newspapers furnish day by day. To them, too, therefore, we should like to declare our appreciation.

Producing the manuscript became a substantial office operation that might well have overwhelmed us but for the extraordinary diligence, devotion, and skill of Miss Florence Perry. Although aiding us in this study was only one of her responsibilities, she typed most of two drafts of the manuscript, handled our correspondence, kept our accounts, maintained our files, and even found time to do spot research on more than one occasion. We thank her heartily, not only for all she did for us, but also for what she spared us when she took upon herself the combined burdens of secretary, office manager, and administrative assistant.

We have, in short, enjoyed the benefits of extensive cooperation and support which we are happy to acknowledge. But the point of view of the book, and the use made of the materials and services available to us, are our own. That is why we add a prayer that the penalties for our sins will not be visited upon our innocent benefactors.

W. S. S.
H. K.

PART ONE
BACKGROUND AND SETTING

CHAPTER I

Birth and Growth of the Greater City

THE POLITICAL AND GOVERNMENTAL CITY

THE CENSUS OF 1890 did more than mark the end of the frontier in the United States. It disclosed also that the nation's three largest cities were closely crowding each other for the coveted honor of first place: New York City with a million five hundred thousand people, Chicago with a million one hundred thousand, Philadelphia with a million fifty thousand. Chicago was coming up fast; no one could predict how the census of 1900 might rank the urban giants.

But two years before the census takers of 1900 began their canvass, a new urban phenomenon had been created. "Greater" New York had a population of 3,437,202 to match, two-to-one, Chicago's 1,698,575. For six decades that ratio of population leadership has been maintained. "Consolidation" in 1898 had placed New York City beyond challenge as the nation's first city. In that process the fourth largest city in the United States (Brooklyn, with an 1890 population of 838,547) had been "consolidated," along with the first city and additional communities (the latter containing about 150,000 people), into the new "Greater City." The resulting metropolis was to have many consequences for urbanization in the United States—and for the politics of New York City, of New York State, and of the nation. A new dimension, in scale and quality, had been added to the government and politics of urban America.

The Road to Consolidation

The enlarged city which began its governmental life on January 1, 1898, had been long in the making. Many forces—economic, social, and political— contributed to the incentives, the hesitations, and the bargaining which eventually led to an almost sudden and surprising culmination in 1897. As early as 1833, New York's Mayor and aldermen opposed the incorporation of Brooklyn as a separate city, on the grounds that it should be joined with Manhattan; but Brooklyn was not to be denied, becoming a city in 1834. More than twenty years later the idea assumed a different form: governmental necessities and political party strategies combined in 1857 to produce a metropolitan Police Board, a state agency with a geographical jurisdiction approximating that of the Greater City established in 1898. In 1866 a Board of Health was similarly established, as was also a Board of Excise. These regional governmental institutions were regarded by many as pointing emphatically toward the logic and necessity of complete consolidation.

The most general and sustained drive for consolidation, however, was supplied by the leadership of Andrew Haswell Green, who for thirty years made the creation of the Greater City the prime object of his active career. While a member of the New York Park Board, he presented in 1868 a carefully developed proposal and design for an "imperial city," requiring the governmental and political integration of New York City, Brooklyn, and surrounding territories. Thereafter, Green worked ceaselessly for his ideal (his proposal evoking from his opponents the label of "Green's hobby"). He found many opportunities to advance his cause. The New York press gave him wide support in the seventies and eighties, a Municipal Union Society agitated in behalf of his plan, and the state legislature was pressed with petitions and bills. A small step was taken by the 1874 annexation of three western townships in The Bronx, while in 1883 the opening of the Brooklyn Bridge gave Green and his friends an additional impetus. In 1890 Green's "hobby" became an official goal. The Governor and the legislature joined in the creation of "a commission to inquire into the expediency of consolidating the various municipalities of the State of New York occupying the several islands in the harbor of New York." Green was appointed chairman, and no strong opponents were named as members. The commissioners drafted a bill for immediate consolidation.

The legislature spent four years in the search for a formula which could muster a majority among the legislators. In 1894 a popular referendum was decided upon. Thus in the November, 1894, general election—when the voters were choosing a Governor, congressmen and state legislators, Mayors in New York and in Brooklyn, and voting upon the recommendations of the 1894 State Constitutional Convention—the voters in the metropolitan region were also asked to approve or disapprove consolidation. The Consolidation League led the expansionist forces to a narrow victory: 176,170 for, 131,706 against; in Brooklyn, the margin was only 277 votes—64,744 for, 64,467 against. The legislature of 1895 was uncertain of its mandate; confronted by Brooklyn opposition, and by second thoughts in Manhattan, the legislature wavered, and at adjournment had merely authorized the annexation of the eastern towns and villages in The Bronx to New York City. Green and his associates had acquired territory on the "mainland" for the city, but not the "islands in the harbor."

Thus matters stood at stalemate in the closing months of 1895. For the next two years, confusion, uncertainty, cross-purposes, and shifting opinions were to characterize the battle over consolidation. Long-range aspirations for a

Greater City, the sentiment for an "independent" Brooklyn, the social and economic interdependence of the metropolitan district all became inextricably interwoven with the short-range incentives of the main actors in the contest. In the end, it was the party leaders and the public officials who brought the tangled issues to decision—and among these the central and crucial actor was Thomas C. Platt, long the leader of the Republican state party organization. In 1895 Platt faced more than his usual share of problems as the state party leader. The State Constitutional Convention of 1894 had been more "reformist" than "regular"; it had written a strong merit system requirement into the state's basic law, separated city elections from state elections, imposed strict limitations upon state and city finances, and in other ways made the life of party leaders more difficult. The 1894 city elections in New York and Brooklyn had brought the victories of "independent" Mayors (Strong and Wurster) who were not responsive to Platt's leadership. The national and state elections of 1896 were just over the horizon, and the aspirations of such "mavericks" as Theodore Roosevelt in that contest were unpredictable. In the midst of these dilemmas, Platt became a determined consolidationist, although his exact motivations for doing so still remain uncertain.

Events now moved rapidly. Governor Morton asked the 1896 legislature to expedite consolidation; the legislature appointed a joint committee, the committee held hearings and received petitions for and against consolidation, and then proposed the creation of a charter commission to establish a government for Greater New York, which under the joint committee's proposal was to be established on January 1, 1898. This proposal had a stormy course in the legislature; Platt needed, and received, some Tammany votes for its first passage. Then Mayors Strong and Wurster vetoed the bill (under a new "home-rule" provision of the 1894 constitution) and Platt was compelled to use all his resources to secure the required second enactment by the state legislature. In early May, 1896, Governor Morton was empowered to appoint the charter commission. He named as president Benjamin F. Tracy (who had been Harrison's Secretary of the Navy and was now a law partner of Platt's son); Green was a member, as were Seth Low (former mayor of Brooklyn and now president of Columbia University), Mayor Strong and Mayor Wurster, and ten others. The commission was able to present its first draft "as a gift to the city" on Christmas morning, 1896. The legislature adopted the charter in February, 1897. Brooklyn quickly acquiesced with the signature of Mayor Wurster. But now New York City had its doubts about the concrete terms and prospects of consolidation, and Mayor Strong (although as a member of the charter commission he had approved the charter) vetoed it. Platt again secured its passage in the legislature, and on May 4, 1897, Governor Black signed the charter into law. The thirty-year drive led by Andrew Green and the party organization led by Thomas Platt had together brought the Greater City into being. The question now was: what forces would govern the new metropolis?

First Consequences of Consolidation

Consolidation became a legal fact in May, 1897; thereafter the boundaries of the new city were not in question. The debate now shifted to criticism of the new charter (a hastily assembled document of some 600 pages and 1,620 sections) and its distribution of the powers of government. The new government of the new city was to be strongly centralized; power was to be concentrated in City Hall, although the five boroughs (Brooklyn, The Bronx, Manhattan, Queens, Richmond) were each to have a President and some governmental functions. At City Hall, the Mayor was to have great formal powers (he would serve four years, have an extensive appointing power, as well as unusually effective veto powers over the municipal assembly), but there were

CHART 1. TERRITORIAL EXPANSION OF NEW YORK CITY

numerous boards and commissions whose autonomy threatened to reduce the Mayor's control over administration. The bicameral legislative body was to be large in numbers but uncertain in powers. Charter revision, however, obviously had to wait until after the first city elections.

To the state and city party leaders, and to the other leaders in the city's political life, it was clear that a new political force had been created. A government for a city of almost three and a half million people was something new in the nation and in the state. The key to this new power structure, everyone agreed, was the mayoralty. All those who sought power and influence in the city government turned to the capture of that prize at the first election in November, 1897.

Platt immediately encountered trouble. He had been one of the main architects of the consolidation and of the charter, but he could not transfer his power at Albany to the city, where the nominations for Mayor were to be decided. His need was for a Republican candidate who was "regular" enough for Platt's taste and who could also muster wide support from the independents and the reformers. Benjamin Tracy was his choice, but he was not acceptable to the forces which in 1894 had elected Mayor Strong in New York and Mayor Wurster in Brooklyn. These groups, led by the Citizens Union, wanted Seth Low. Neither Platt and his Republican party leaders nor the Citizens Union and its followers would concede to the other. Tracy became the Republican candidate; Seth Low, the candidate of the Citizens Union. Thus the anti-"Tammany" forces in the city's first election were divided against themselves, as they were often to be thereafter.

In the Democratic party Richard Croker, the New York County (Manhattan) leader, who had watched the course of consolidation from his semi-retirement in England, had fewer difficulties. He came home to persuade his Brooklyn and other party colleagues to nominate Robert Van Wyck, a relatively unknown regular Democrat and the bearer of an old and distinguished Knickerbocker name. Out of power at Albany, and at New York and Brooklyn City Halls since 1894, the Democratic leaders were more than ordinarily anxious and determined to win the new prizes of power in the Greater City.

Van Wyck won. The vote, in round numbers, was: Van Wyck, 234,000; Low, 151,000; Tracy, 100,000; Henry George (who died during the campaign), 22,000. Croker and his associates had won the first chance at leadership of the "imperial city." But the measure of their future troubles was to be seen in Van Wyck's 45 per cent plurality.

Further Consequences of Consolidation

These troubles came soon. The Republican leaders had power at Albany, and the independents and reformers had no difficulty in agreeing with them upon the use of that power to supervise the Van Wyck administration. Legislative investigation was the first power of supervision to be used. In 1899 the Mazet committee explored the city's government, discovering and emphasizing the irregularities and corruption which Lincoln Steffens was soon to find endemic in all of America's large cities. The second weapon was charter revision by the state legislature in 1901, as the Van Wyck term neared its end. The third assault was a coalition in the city election of 1901: Seth Low, as the "Fusion" candidate of Republicans and independents, won the mayoralty. The Republican leaders, the independents, and the reformers had rediscovered the tripartite formula for their successful participation in the city's political contest—state legislative investigation, charter revision from Albany, and Fusion in the city election.

The charter revision of 1901, however, was more than a stratagem in the political and governmental contest. It also sharply redistributed power in the city's political and governmental system, with lasting effect upon the opportunities and liabilities of all the main participants in that system. The Mayor was reduced in power, the borough governments were enhanced at the expense of power at City Hall, and the party organizations were confirmed as five county-borough systems, precluding the growth of integrated citywide party organizations. The key institutional instrument in producing these changes was the creation of a newly designed Board of Estimate and Apportionment, with the Mayor, the President of the Board of Aldermen, the Comptroller, and the five Borough Presidents as members, the Board being endowed with generous powers which were to be steadily increased during the following decades. The Mayor was thus put "in commission," while the borough officials and their party-leader associates were moved into full partnership in the city government's most powerful single institution. Many clues to the subsequent political life of the city are imbedded in this transformation set in motion by the charter of 1901.

The charters of 1897 and 1901 were framed in the midst of, and as products of, a complex political contest involving not merely the creation of the Greater City but the stakes of the political system of New York State and of the nation as well. The long-range goals and short-term necessities of the leading actors, their perceptions (myopic or clear-sighted) and their motivations (self-centered or selfless), were the mixed ingredients of the public debate accompanying the decision to consolidate and the subsequent decisions making the formal distribution of power under the two charters. If the charter makers were distracted by the contradictions and inconsistencies of the debaters, and if they did not correctly anticipate all the major consequences of their actions, they did succeed in building a viable system of politics and government for the city which succeeding generations have changed only in detail.

The reformers of 1897–1901 were most sharply disappointed over the refusal of the charter drafters to introduce "nonpartisan" government into the charter of the Greater City. Instead, the charter commissions accepted the political party as a valued, if not indispensable, institution in the governance of the city. They gave more attention to, but ultimately rejected, proposals from the reformers to provide assured representation for minority parties (a plan which was to be tried from 1937 to 1947). The charters of 1897 and 1901 emerged free from almost all doctrines of nonpartisan or bipartisan city government, thus removing New York City from the tendencies which were to become so pronounced in Boston, Detroit, and Los Angeles. At the same time, and perhaps somewhat inadvertently, the 1901 charter, by creating a powerful Board of Estimate, confirmed the tendencies toward five separate party systems in the city (one for each of the five boroughs or counties). As the boroughs of The Bronx, Queens, and Richmond grew in population (and so also in voters), the party system of the city became increasingly, within both the Democratic and the Republican parties, a system of struggle, bargaining, and accommodation among borough power centers. The boroughs quickly became the equivalent of large cities (by 1930, four of them exceeded a million people each, and Richmond had almost 160,000). The resulting "borough politics" of New York City offers many contrasts to the "ward politics" of Chicago and Philadelphia. A Borough President is not an alderman; a county party leader is not a ward leader. The borough-county constituencies are large and diverse; Borough Presidents and County Leaders must respond to a wider array of forces than do aldermen and ward leaders. They are more visible, more vulnerable, and in that sense more responsible.

New York City's political and governmental system, then, is unusual even though it may not be described as unique. The charters of 1897 and 1901, confirmed by the charter of 1938, kept the parties and the party leaders on the list of principal actors in the city's political contest. The ambiguities and low visibility of nonpartisan city government have, as a consequence, been largely avoided. By constructing a system of borough politics, the charter commissions enabled the city to escape much of the parochialism and low visibility of a system of ward politics. And while many other forces in the life of the city have contributed to the nature of its political and governmental system, the commitment of a prominent role to parties and to party leaders, and to a system built around a few large boroughs rather than numerous small wards, has played a significant part in developing the main characteristics of New York City government and politics to be described in the following pages: a system of "open" politics, the absence of a single dominant ruling elite, a pattern of competition and bargaining from which no group is for long alienated or excluded, a system inherently conservative but not incapable of innovation.

THE SOCIAL AND ECONOMIC CITY

The political and governmental city and the social and economic city are reciprocal in their influences upon each other. The size, diversity, and wealth of the city affect the size and worth of its political stakes; the political and governmental system in turn affects the growth and character of the city. Much of the special quality of New York City as a social, economic, and political center flows from its status as the "First City" in the United States—first in population, in economic wealth, in cultural resources, and in first place among the nation's burgeoning metropolitan regions at mid-century. These cherished "firsts" are the direct and indirect gifts of the political and governmental system which established the Greater City in 1898 and which has maintained and nurtured its growth for six decades. The social, economic, and political concerns of the city are in a very real sense indistinguishable from each other, meshed together inextricably.

Population Growth

To a large extent, New York's population growth is the result of fortunate geography. New York Bay is a magnificent natural harbor—large, well sheltered, deep enough to accommodate the largest ships, shallow enough to afford convenient anchorage. Moreover, the natural waterways of the region provide several hundred miles of excellent waterfront and expedient means of

TABLE 1. POPULATION OF NEW YORK CITY
AND ITS BOROUGHS, 1890–1957

	1890[a]	1900	1910	1920
The Bronx	88,908	200,507	430,980	732,016
Brooklyn	838,547	1,166,582	1,634,351	2,018,356
Manhattan	1,441,216	1,850,093	2,331,542	2,284,103
Queens	87,050	152,999	284,041	469,042
Richmond	51,693	67,021	85,969	116,531
Entire city	2,507,414	3,437,202	4,766,883	5,620,048
	1930	1940	1950	1957
The Bronx	1,265,258	1,394,711	1,451,277	1,424,367
Brooklyn	2,560,401	2,698,285	2,738,175	2,602,433
Manhattan	1,867,312	1,889,924	1,960,101	1,794,069
Queens	1,079,129	1,297,634	1,550,849	1,762,582
Richmond	158,346	174,441	191,555	212,020
Entire city	6,930,446	7,454,995	7,891,957	7,795,471

[a] The Greater City had not yet been formed at this time. New York City consisted of Manhattan and about half of The Bronx. Brooklyn was a separate city, and Queens, Richmond, and half of The Bronx were separate counties containing small villages.

SOURCE: *Statistical Abstract of the United States;* 1957 figures based on special census as reported in *The World Almanac,* New York World-Telegram Corporation, New York, 1959, p. 240.

moving goods inside the area. These natural advantages made New York a center of economic activity and opportunity. People flocked to it in such numbers that it was already the largest city in the United States by 1790 (with a population of about 33,000), and its population had almost doubled when the census of 1800 was taken. The growth of the city was further encouraged by the opening of the Erie Barge Canal in 1825, since this permitted shipping goods in bulk relatively quickly and cheaply between the interior and the East. The Appalachian Mountain range was for decades a towering barrier blocking land communications with other ports, which meant that when railroads came, rail service in and out of New York on the water-level route paralleling the Hudson-Mohawk and Erie Canal system also long enjoyed a competitive advantage. New York experienced a virtual revolution in commerce as it became the primary transportation center for

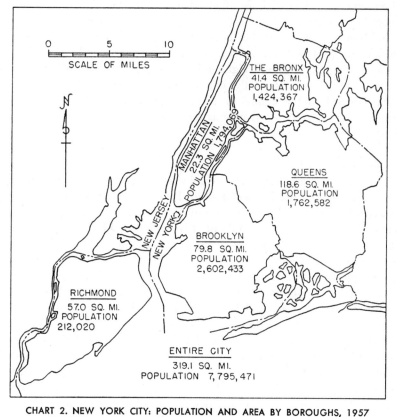

CHART 2. NEW YORK CITY: POPULATION AND AREA BY BOROUGHS, 1957

SOURCES: *The World Almanac*, New York World-Telegram Corporation, New York, 1959; area data from *Official City Directory*, New York, 1959.

the exchange of raw materials from the West for the finished products of Europe and the Eastern Seaboard. Its miles of waterfront permitted it to handle this explosive growth with ease. By 1855 the city had almost 630,000 inhabitants, roughly ten times its population at the start of the century.

It was the industrialization of the United States, though, that produced the greatest jump in the population of New York City. Floods of people from foreign lands poured into the country to take advantage of the burgeoning opportunities. Most of these immigrants passed through New York because the principal lines of transportation radiated from it, and enough of the recent arrivals remained to swell the ranks of New Yorkers rapidly. Rural and small town America sent its thousands also. These migrations created a great pool of comparatively cheap labor, much of it skilled, which accelerated further industrial and commercial expansion, and in turn attracted new enterprises and additional immigration. By 1880 the population of the city had passed the million mark. By 1898, when the Greater City was established, its population exceeded three million. By 1920 it had more than five and a half million people. Even the termination of free immigration by federal statute in 1924 did not stop its growth; there were seven million residents in the city in 1930, and almost eight million in 1950, as natural increase and influxes from other parts of the country continued to feed it. As the city looked forward to the census of 1960, a stabilization of population was expected—but the city stood now as the vital "central city" of the nation's largest metropolitan region.

Economic Growth

The financial and commercial preeminence of the city are products of the same forces that built its population—its strategic location, its position athwart the transportation and communication channels of the world, the stream of goods that flows in and out of it every day. Moreover, the concentration of population itself adds to the city's economic power, for property values are directly related to the intensity of use, and the local populace is both a huge market and an abundant supply of manpower. Money early accumulated here (money made by trade, money borrowed against the security of valuable land and improvements) and became available for investment in new ventures—for the development of the West, for railroads, for industry. It is not at all surprising that before the end of the eighteenth century Alexander Hamilton founded the Bank of New York, and that the beginnings of the stock exchange were already discernible. Men with ideas came to the place where financial backing was to be found; men with money came to the city where opportunities for venture capital abounded. The process was self-reinforcing, and the cycle that was to make Wall Street a worldwide symbol of finance capitalism was set in motion. Today, over $500 billion a year clears through the banks of New York, an amount roughly equal to the total clearings of the next highest 37 cities in the country, and about ten times the bank clearings in Philadelphia, which is next in line. The shares traded on an average day in the New York and American Stock Exchanges constitute over 87 per cent of the nation's total by volume and 96 per cent of the national total by dollar value. New York is one of the great money markets of the world, and the leading one in the United States for foreign currency transactions. It is the busiest seaport in the world. The real

TABLE 2. THE CAPITAL PLANT OF NEW YORK CITY, 1958–1959: ASSESSED VALUATIONS OF REAL ESTATE, 1958–1959

In millions of dollars

Area	Land	Total
Taxed property		
Manhattan	$3,896	$9,585
The Bronx	747	2,661
Brooklyn	1,392	4,995
Queens	1,180	4,758
Richmond	134	451
Total, Taxed	$7,349	$22,450[a]
Tax-exempt property, 1958–1959		
City of New York		$4,621
New York City Housing Authority		1,030
New York City Transit Authority		1,206[b]
Triborough Bridge and Tunnel Authority		392
Port of New York Authority		418
State and federal		501
Religious		507
All other		1,205
Total, Tax exempt		$ 9,880
Grand total		$32,330

[a] Property is assessed at less than "full value." "Full value" is $25,031 million.

[b] Property administered by Transit Authority although owned by city.

SOURCE: Adapted from Citizens Budget Commission, *Pocket Summary of New York City Finances*, October, 1958.

property within the city's borders is assessed at $32 billion. In all these respects the city towers, and its influence, felt everywhere, lends to its politics a widespread interest that lesser cities cannot match.

New York City is an industrial town, too. It has forty thousand manufacturing establishments, with the largest factory work force in any American city (nearly a million industrial workers) and the largest manufacturing payroll (close to $3 billion a year). The garment industry is the dominant one, but printing and publishing are also huge (one fifth of all the printing and

TABLE 3. GROWTH OF LARGEST UNITED STATES CITIES, 1880–1950

City	1880	1890	1900	1910	1920	1930	1940	1950
1. New York, N. Y.	1,911,698	2,507,414	3,437,202	4,766,883	5,620,048	6,930,446	7,454,995	7,891,957
2. Chicago, Ill.	503,185	1,099,850	1,698,575	2,185,283	2,701,705	3,376,438	3,396,808	3,620,962
3. Philadelphia, Pa.	847,170	1,046,964	1,293,697	1,549,008	1,823,779	1,950,961	1,931,334	2,071,605
4. Los Angeles, Calif.	11,183	50,395	102,479	319,198	576,673	1,238,048	1,504,277	1,970,358
5. Detroit, Mich.	116,340	205,876	285,704	465,766	993,678	1,568,662	1,623,452	1,849,568
6. Baltimore, Md.	332,313	434,439	508,957	558,485	733,826	804,874	859,100	949,708
7. Cleveland, Ohio	160,146	261,353	381,768	560,663	796,841	900,429	878,336	914,808
8. St. Louis, Mo.	350,518	451,770	575,238	687,029	772,897	821,960	816,048	856,796
9. Washington, D. C.	147,293	188,932	278,718	331,069	437,571	486,869	663,091	802,178
10. Boston, Mass.	362,839	448,477	560,892	670,585	748,060	781,188	770,816	801,444
11. San Francisco, Calif.	233,959	298,997	342,782	416,912	506,676	634,394	634,536	775,357
12. Pittsburgh, Pa.	235,071[a]	343,904[a]	451,512[a]	533,905	588,343	669,817	671,659	676,806
13. Milwaukee, Wis.	115,587	204,468	285,315	373,857	457,147	578,249	587,472	637,392
14. Houston, Texas	16,513	27,557	44,633	78,800	138,276	292,352	384,514	596,163
15. Buffalo, N.Y.	155,134	255,664	352,387	423,715	506,775	573,076	575,901	580,132
16. New Orleans, La.	216,090	242,039	287,104	339,075	387,219	458,762	494,537	570,445
17. Minneapolis, Minn.	46,887	164,738	202,718	301,408	380,582	464,356	492,370	521,718
18. Cincinnati, Ohio	255,139	296,908	325,902	363,591	401,247	451,160	455,610	503,998
19. Seattle, Wash.	3,533	42,837	80,671	237,194	315,312	365,583	368,302	467,591
20. Kansas City, Mo.	55,785	132,716	163,752	248,381	324,410	399,746	399,178	456,622

[a] Includes Allegheny City.

SOURCE: *The World Almanac*, New York World-Telegram Corporation, New York, 1959, p. 304.

publishing in the United States is done here), and machinery and metal products, scientific instruments, chemical products, leather goods, paper products, furniture and wood products, and textile products are turned out in substantial quantities by the city's plants.

The national headquarters of many nationwide and worldwide companies are located in New York, and the concentration of managerial personnel has been increasing since World War II. With them come ancillary services—the major law firms, accounting houses, consulting engineers, management consultants. Some 70 per cent of the national advertising agencies of the country locate their central offices here. Wholesalers in New York do more than $42 billion worth of business a year—18 per cent of the national total, three times as much as Chicago, the second largest wholesale center. Each activity, each service, attracts others; all make the city's government a matter of general rather than purely local concern.

Cultural Resources

The economic greatness of the city brought it still other sources of greatness. The United Nations came to New York because this was a convenient place for it to be—and because the city had become the home of the Rockefeller family, who had the resources and the generosity to give the UN a home. The city is a great intellectual center. Over forty institutions of higher learning with students from all over the globe, and one fifth of all students doing postgraduate work in the United States, are here. And in an area "on Broadway north of Times Square or in the adjoining side streets, . . . bounded by Eighth Avenue to the west and the Avenue of the Americas (Sixth Avenue) to the east," writes Brooks Atkinson, drama critic of *The New York Times*, "in this compact, shabby neighborhood, where cheap souvenir booths and penny arcades abound, where the traffic is angry and nervous and the sidewalks are jammed, where the honky-tonk atmosphere prevails—in this decaying neighborhood, about seventy or seventy-five productions are put on the stage every season and most of the theatrical history of America is inadvertently written."[1] A visitor seeking to attend all the musical events in New York in the course of a single week was amazed and exhausted to discover this included "performances by four world-famous orchestras, by the Metropolitan Opera, by violinists and pianists, by ballet companies and an operetta troupe. . . . For quantity and quality," Howard Taubman, the *Times* music critic observes, "New York as a musical center has no peer anywhere in the world. . . . For better or worse," he adds, "we set standards. New York has become a showcase for the nation, and its imprimatur of approval is influential not only throughout the country but in

[1] Atkinson, Brooks, "Theatre: Fascinating and Fabulous," *The New York Times Magazine*, April 29, 1956, Part 2, p. 35.

TABLE 4. UNITED STATES CITIES WITH METROPOLITAN AREAS[a]

Rank	Standard metropolitan area		Total population		In central cities Number	Per cent
1	New York-N.E. New Jersey	April, 1957	12,911,994	(14,186,000[b])	8,629,750	66.8
2	Chicago, Ill.		5,495,364		3,620,962	65.9
3	Los Angeles, Calif.		4,367,911		1,970,358	45.1
4	Philadelphia, Pa.		3,671,048		2,071,605	56.4
5	Detroit, Mich.		3,016,197		1,849,568	61.3
6	Boston, Mass.		2,369,986		801,444	33.8
7	San Francisco-Oakland, Calif.		2,249,767		1,159,932	51.8
8	Pittsburgh, Pa.		2,213,236		676,806	30.6
9	St. Louis, Mo.	Jan., 1956	1,681,281	(1,892,000[b])	856,796	51.0
10	Cleveland, Ohio		1,465,511		914,808	62.4
11	Washington, D.C.	Jan., 1956	1,464,089	(1,884,000[b])	802,178	54.8
12	Baltimore, Md.		1,337,373		949,708	71.0
13	Minneapolis-St. Paul, Minn.		1,116,509		833,067	74.6
14	Buffalo, N.Y.		1,089,230		580,132	53.3
15	Cincinnati, Ohio		904,402	(975,000[b])	503,998	55.7
16	Milwaukee, Wis.	Jan., 1956	871,047		637,392	73.2
17	Kansas City, Mo.		814,357		456,622	56.1
18	Houston, Texas	Jan., 1956	806,701	(1,077,000[b])	596,163	73.9
19	Providence, R.I.	July, 1956	737,203	(771,000[b])	248,674	33.7
20	Seattle, Wash.		732,992		467,591	63.8

[a] A standard metropolitan area must contain at least one city having a population of 50,000 or over. The largest city is the principal central city for which the area is named, although there may be several cities in the area with a population of 50,000 or over. Metropolitan areas have been specifically defined to identify large concentrations of population in and around cities of 50,000 population or more. One exception exists to this rule. In the case of the standard metropolitan area centering on New York City, the central cities are New York City, Newark, N.J., and Jersey City, N.J.

[b] According to results of censuses and estimates of the Bureau of the Census taken after April 1, 1950.

SOURCE: *The World Almanac*, New York World-Telegram Corporation, New York, 1959, p. 305.

other lands."[1] "Any one of New York's twenty-odd museums would be a matter of single-minded civic pride elsewhere," says one art critic;[2] and many of the museums have special exhibitions in addition to their permanent collections, while there are over 1,600 shows a year in more than a hundred commercial galleries. All these things enhance the city's distinction, and this distinction, whether its people and politicians wish it or not, give New York's government a special significance everywhere.

Diversity and Variety

But probably nothing makes the government of the city so interesting as the diversity of its population. No major city in America—nor in the world, for that matter—boasts so varied a populace, such an assemblage of different interests. Alec Waugh, the British novelist, comments:

In Copenhagen, Paris, Tangier, Baghdad, and Rome, I have searched in order to understand the city's central core, but not in New York. . . . There is no such thing as . . . a common basic of New York life. Everyone's New York is different. When I lived in London as a young man, I lived the same life as many thousand others. I prided myself on being "a real Londoner." Today I pride myself on being by adoption "a real New Yorker," yet I am very well aware that there are not a dozen people in Manhattan whose routine is the same as mine.

Yet, he adds, for all the differences among the people of the city, they are *all* New Yorkers:

You have to have been born in London to be a Londoner, you have to be a Dane to be a Copenhagener. Could anyone born in Missouri become a real Bostonian? But New York is different. It is a city where the unrooted can take root. You do not need to have been born in New York, you do not, I believe, even need to be an American, to feel yourself a New Yorker. The basic difference surely lies in this, that whereas London, Paris and Vienna have grown as England, France and Austria have grown, expanding outward from a center, New York has been a magnet drawing to itself from East, North, South, West, from every state of the Union and from every European country, the restless, the dissatisfied and the ambitious, who have demanded more from life than the circumstances of their birth offered them.[3]

The city is fascinating in that it does afford each individual a realistic hope of fulfilling himself in his own way. It is important as a social experiment in that it manages to provide these opportunities despite the enormous number

---

[1] Taubman, H., "Music: A Great, Endless Festival," *op. cit.*, p. 49.
[2] Saarinen, A. B., "Art: Something for Everybody," *op. cit.*, p. 53.
[3] Waugh, Alec, "Rivals: 'New York Is Unique,' " *op. cit.*, pp. 24, 70.

of different values and patterns of living that must somehow be accommodated with each other. If New York were administered like a military camp—with standardized clothing, diet, architecture, living routines, types of work, recreation, and so on, and with tight control over the movement and disposition and interrelations of personnel—the technological operation of feeding, sheltering, clothing, amusing, and keeping order among eight million people crammed into a little over 300 square miles of land area would constitute a remarkable achievement. New York City accomplishes all this without sacrificing the variety, the multifarious customs, the divergent interests, or the competing objectives of its people.

Something of the diversity of the city is suggested by the many national cultures represented in it. One and three-quarter million of its inhabitants were born abroad, and three million more are the children of immigrants. Consequently, the New York Bible Society distributes to New Yorkers Bibles printed in more than 80 languages; libraries house collections not only in the most widely used tongues of the world, but in Arabic, Albanian, Bohemian, Bulgarian, Finnish, Hebrew, Hungarian, Lettish, Lithuanian, Norwegian, Portuguese, Rumanian, Ukranian, and many others as well; 240 publications, including 28 dailies, in scores of languages appear regularly; radio stations broadcast programs in well over a dozen languages; dozens of motion picture theaters (not counting the "art" houses that show foreign films primarily to English-speaking audiences) specialize in foreign pictures for particular language groups. Without leaving New York, one can enjoy meals in restaurants featuring the cuisine of all nations, including Indonesian, Indian-Pakistanian, Japanese, Persian-Assyrian, and patronized heavily, in some cases almost exclusively, by customers of the corresponding national stock. Hundreds of nationality-group organizations flourish in the city. The numerically predominant ones are of Austrian, English, German, Hungarian, Irish, Italian, Polish, and Russian origin or descent, but many other nationalities are represented in substantial numbers.

There are also more than a hundred religious denominations in the city. Three faiths comprise the vast majority of New Yorkers: Roman Catholic, with about three and a half million adherents (45 per cent of the total population); Protestant, with some two million (25 per cent); and Jewish, with roughly two million (25 per cent). But even small percentages, for all other religious persuasions, are far from negligible in absolute numbers when the base is a community the size of this metropolis. (For all religions, however, most adherence is nominal; it has been estimated that only a tenth of the adherents are active in their churches or synagogues.)

Over three quarters of a million residents of the city are nonwhite. Most of these are native American Negroes, but included in the total are persons of Oriental or other birth or descent.

TABLE 5. NEW YORK CITY POPULATION, BY AGE, RACE, SEX, BOROUGH: ANALYSIS OF SPECIAL CENSUS OF APRIL 1, 1957[a]

Age and borough	Total	White		Nonwhite			
				Negro		Other races	
		Male	Female	Male	Female	Male	Female
All ages	7,795,471	3,302,599	3,511,621	434,038	514,158	21,505	11,550
Under 5	650,053	274,010	263,127	55,022	54,811	1,593	1,490
5 to 9	620,458	262,850	253,392	50,149	50,362	1,877	1,828
10 to 14	555,754	246,909	238,498	33,936	35,108	693	610
15 to 19	450,108	194,441	200,397	24,450	29,541	682	597
20 to 24	481,313	192,058	222,393	25,551	39,293	1,117	901
25 to 29	568,475	237,196	246,194	34,273	47,894	1,516	1,402
30 to 34	584,333	234,104	252,736	40,642	53,546	1,968	1,337
35 to 39	596,308	234,121	268,057	40,510	50,647	1,945	1,028
40 to 44	596,054	240,034	277,921	34,599	40,725	2,001	774
45 to 49	572,115	243,279	266,955	27,521	31,959	1,860	541
50 to 54	551,544	245,308	254,977	23,228	25,754	1,884	393
55 to 59	454,905	206,646	211,759	16,530	18,154	1,544	272
60 to 64	405,067	184,749	194,142	11,519	13,271	1,211	175
65 to 69	319,271	141,526	158,507	7,899	10,433	811	95
70 to 74	200,391	88,872	100,210	4,447	6,319	479	64
75 to 79	105,888	45,155	54,866	2,238	3,392	211	26
80 to 84	56,076	21,692	31,437	1,009	1,847	78	13
85 and over	27,358	9,649	16,053	515	1,102	35	4
Under 21	2,368,024	1,015,076	998,236	167,886	177,177	5,004	4,645
21 and over	5,427,447	2,287,523	2,513,385	266,152	336,981	16,501	6,905
Median age	34.9	35.2	36.5	29.1	30.0	38.4	26.2
Boroughs							
Bronx	1,424,367	621,796	665,273	62,412	72,355	1,458	1,073
Brooklyn	2,602,433	1,118,396	1,172,257	141,133	166,663	2,359	1,625
Manhattan	1,794,069	669,553	721,659	172,787	208,281	15,125	6,664
Queens	1,762,582	791,052	850,861	53,577	62,616	2,392	2,084
Richmond	212,020	101,802	101,571	4,129	4,243	171	104

[a] The U.S. Bureau of the Census conducted a special census of New York, N. Y., as of April 1, 1957. The final count, released October 8, 1957, indicated a population of 7,795,471, a drop of 96,486, or 1.2%, from 1950. The 1957 special census was conducted under residence rules identical with those used in the 1950 Census. Several special factors contributed to the decline between 1950 and 1957.

In 1950 about 50,000 transients enumerated in other parts of the country who reported their usual residence of New York City were added to its population. In 1957 such additions were not possible because the census was not taken on a country-wide basis. Another factor contributing to the decline in population between 1950 and 1957 was the increase in the size of the Armed Forces in this period. In both 1950 and 1957, members of the Armed Forces stationed in New York City were included in the count but former residents of New York City serving elsewhere in the Armed Forces were not. The latter number exceeds the former, and owing to the over-all increase in the size of the Armed Forces between 1950 and 1957, this net loss is estimated to have increased by about 40,000 in this period.

SOURCE: *The World Almanac*, New York World-Telegram Corporation, New York, 1959, p. 260,

Nationality differences, religious differences, and ethnic differences often mean differences in folkways, differences in social position, differences in political strength. So, too—and perhaps more emphatically—do economic differences. New York is, as many writers and screen scenarists have repeatedly pointed out, a city of extreme contrasts; it has some of the richest people in the world in its midst, and some of the poorest in the United States, and these are often found side by side with each other, the slum tenements of the latter leaning against the exclusive apartment skyscrapers of the former. (The extremes capture most attention; the large middle class seems less dramatic.) New York is the headquarters of many of the country's largest and wealthiest corporations, whose executives abound; and it has a huge white-collar work force; but it also has a million industrial workers, a huge number of small and independent factory owners, and a large population of small shopkeepers. There is a large reservoir of unskilled laborers and domestics, but there is probably nowhere in the world such a collection of practitioners of the skilled trades as may be found here, nor such a concentration of professional manpower—legal, medical, engineering, scientific, teaching, and the like. Indeed, with relatively few exceptions—farming, ranching, mining, for instance—one is likely to find in New York somebody routinely producing precisely the goods or performing exactly the services one needs, no matter how specialized or unusual. In this single metropolis, in these 300 square miles, physically close to each other and often geographically intermingled, the rich and the poor, the big and the little, the distinguished and the disreputable, the managers and the workers, the powerful and the helpless, live with each other, depend on each other. Social cleavages run deep, but no social class in the city can live unaware of the others, and no group can avoid its interdependence with the others.

The diversity of New York is geographical as well as social; the city contains hundreds of neighborhoods, each with unique characteristics as distinctive as those of separate cities. Neighborhoods develop individually because people of the same national, ethnic, social, and economic background tend to congregate and thus give each area, each subcommunity, its special flavor. Greenwich Village, Flatbush, Harlem, Yorkville, Riverdale, Forest Hills, St. George, the Lower East Side, and Washington Heights, for example, are little worlds of their own, while Wall Street, the garment center, Times Square, Fifth Avenue, Radio City, and scores of other areas are special concentrations of particular kinds of business and industry. But the gregariousness of people with common culture patterns or mutual interests is not the whole explanation; the history and geography of the city are significant factors in the growth of neighborhoods.

Most of New York, after all, is in a technical sense not even on the continental mainland. It is divided into five boroughs (each coterminous with a county): Manhattan (New York County) is an island, with bedrock just below its surface capable of supporting skyscrapers; Richmond (Richmond County) occupies another island, Staten Island; Brooklyn (Kings County) and Queens (Queens County) together occupy the western end of Long Island; only The Bronx (Bronx County) is on the mainland. Long Island Sound separates The Bronx from Queens; the Harlem River, which connects East River and the Hudson River, flows between The Bronx and Manhattan; the East River, not a river at all, but a salt-water strait, separates Manhattan and The Bronx, on one side, from Brooklyn and Queens on the other; Upper New York Bay stands between Manhattan and Richmond; the Narrows, the thin passage of water connecting the Upper Bay with the Lower Bay and the sea, is between Richmond and Brooklyn. The Hudson flows to the west of the city, touching Manhattan and The Bronx, and separating them from New Jersey. "The City on Many Waters," one author[1] appropriately called New York. No other city in the world is so crisscrossed by broad, navigable streams. The waters, including a number of creeks and canals, were the making of New York in giving access by ship and barge to almost every part of the city, thus reducing transportation costs. The railroads still use carfloats and lighters and barges to transfer freight instead of building huge marshaling yards comparable in number and size to those of Chicago. The waters have been the binders as well as the dividers of the city; for a long period, however, they encouraged the subdivisions of the city to develop independently, and the character of these separate communities that grew up in earlier times has not yet totally disappeared.

Each area added to Manhattan had a long history of its own. Brooklyn itself had absorbed a number of separate communities, such as Williamsburg, Flatbush, New Utrecht, and Gravesend. Queens contained a large number of suburban, residential villages as well as some larger communities—Flushing, Astoria—and some industrial centers—Long Island City, Jamaica. St.George, Stapleton, Port Richmond, and Tottenville on Staten Island are old communities. In The Bronx, old settlements like West Farms, Wakefield, Williamsbridge, Morrisania, High Bridge, and Riverdale have left their names, a measure of neighborhood consciousness, and their imprints. Even in Manhattan, the neighborhoods recall the sites of the original settlements—Greenwich Village, Murray Hill, Lenox Hill, Harlem, Yorkville, Fort George. As people poured into New York and spilled out into the environs of Manhattan, the surrounding sections began to change. But they often preserved an awareness of themselves as communities, and newcomers tended to adapt to the locally prevailing standards as well as to modify those standards, so that the city has not yet turned into a homogeneous collection of uniform subdivisions. There are many areas reminiscent of small towns; about 684,000 families live

[1] Berger, Meyer, and Fritz Busse, *New York: City on Many Waters*. Arts, New York, 1955.

in private homes, and Brooklyn is still sometimes called the City of Homes. The early isolation of the communities eventually brought into the city thus had a lasting effect, and many of them resist vigorously changes or encroachments that they believe would alter their character even though they have in fact been changing all the time.

Changes in the City

Writing of *The United States in 1800*, Henry Adams declared: "Innovation was the most useful purpose which New York could serve in human interests, and never was a city better fitted for its work."[1] Change has continued to be a hallmark of the city. The rapidity and extent of change helps to keep the diversity of the city from declining. On the basis of logic alone, one might expect the city to move in the direction of greater standardization, for technology has standardized many other aspects of modern life—as, indeed, many observers, viewing the drab sameness of vast housing projects, have feared it is already doing. While it is not impossible that even New York may one day succumb to pressures toward conformity, the past record of the city indicates it has powerful built-in forces making for continued variety. Sections alter with rapidity, and by the time a new section resembling an established neighborhood is completed, chances are the original one will already have been transformed into something else.

Three generations ago Harlem was a fashionable residential area of the upper middle class. In a few decades it became one of the city's worst slums as its initial residents moved away and landlords took advantage of discrimination against Negroes in other parts of New York to extract exorbitant rentals from these housing-short people for flats that were quickly overcrowded and inadequately maintained. Today Harlem is again changing with massive slum-clearance programs that may restore some of its former attractiveness.

Greenwich Village is an old section that deteriorated when it became a temporary stopping place for newly arrived immigrants, who moved to newer and more comfortable quarters as soon as they were able. The cessation of immigration further depressed the dilapidated neighborhood, and the declining rents and food prices in the area attracted struggling artists without much in the way of capital or income, but with a great desire to be in New York. The growth of its reputation as an artistic, intellectual, and bohemian center drew more well-to-do people to it, and rents and prices began to rise until it became what it is today—not a refuge for artists, but an expensive district in which a comparatively substantial and steady income is usually a necessity. Meanwhile, across Manhattan, in another depressed area, the process may be starting again as the "East Village" takes shape.

[1] Adams, Henry, *The United States in 1800*. Cornell University Press, Ithaca, N. Y., 1955, p. 80.

On Park Avenue and Fifth Avenue above Fifty-ninth Street, what were once private mansions are now occupied largely by nonprofit (and therefore tax-exempt) institutions, or by the diplomatic establishments of foreign governments. Many of the lavish old structures have given way to luxury apartment buildings. In Riverdale, the section of The Bronx facing the Hudson River, rambling houses have yielded to twenty-story apartment buildings. But on upper Riverside Drive, the luxury apartment buildings of an earlier day have been cut up into small flats, and the deterioration of the structures has reached an advanced stage. Third Avenue was a grim and

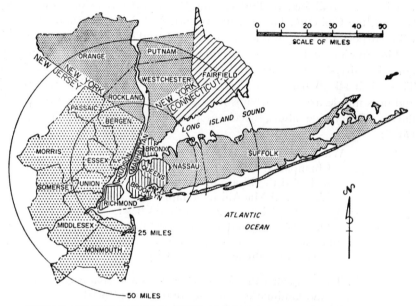

CHART 3. THE NEW YORK-NEW JERSEY-CONNECTICUT METROPOLITAN REGION
SOURCE: *Third Annual Report* of Mayor Robert F. Wagner, 1956.

stark slum as long as the shadow of the city's oldest elevated rapid transit line fell across it, but the demolition of the "El" in 1955 has turned it into one of the city's fastest-growing boulevards.

Neighborhoods bloom, decline, come back (or are brought back), probably to decline and return again. The cycles, however, are not uniform in speed or character; hence, at any given moment, it is almost inevitable that the city will encompass very different kinds of districts. Change here does not necessarily make for uniformity. It is true that there has been a rather consistent trend toward more intensive land use; rarely is the reverse true, and larger structures are not often razed to make way for smaller ones. Yet since 1940 most of the growth in the metropolitan region has taken place in the suburbs, and the city, although it has grown at a rate greater than the average for the country as a whole, has not increased so spectacularly as its surrounding areas. Moreover, 27 per cent of the land within New York's borders is still vacant. So even the one consistent tendency may not continue. Patterns of future development may well be at variance with those of the past; the process of differentiation of the parts of the city from each other can be expected to go on unabated.

The most dramatic index of change in New York is the number of landmarks constructed since 1925. Yankee Stadium, the Chrysler Building, the Empire State Building, Radio City, the Waldorf-Astoria Hotel, the United Nations, the Coliseum, La Guardia Airport, New York International (Idlewild) Airport, the George Washington Bridge, and dozens of other nationally and internationally famous edifices that have become symbols of the city did not exist thirty-five years ago. Other equally famous symbols have vanished. Through it all, though, New York remains New York; change is part of it and does not destroy but sustains the city, reinforces its nature, preserves its flavor. "Everything alters," declares poet Phyllis McGinley, "except the City":

> When the Murray Hill wore its stately honors
>   Champagne came served in a satin shoe.
> Now it and the El are phantoms, goners,
>   Like Ward MacAllister's happy few.
> At the Hippodrome, once, trapezes flew.
>   Once organs ground us an April ditty.
> Once we could sail to Coney, too.
>   Everything alters except the City.
>
> They swarm with rivets and cranes and spanners
>   And landmarks go while we're saying "Boo!"
> We change our minds as we change our manners.
>   For Harrison (Rex) we swap John Drew.
> But while on some ultimate Avenue
>   The great voice roars and the air is gritty,
> Always the Town comes bursting through.
>   Everything alters except the City.[1]

GOVERNMENT AND THE CITY

Government is the city's central agency of change and conservation. It is the city's prime rule-maker, the omnipresent supervisor. Its officials are always important actors in the negotiations, the bargaining, and the numerous settlements which comprise the decisions by which the city lives. Equally

---

[1] McGinley, Phyllis, "Ballade: Eccentric for an Egocentric Town," *The New York Times Magazine*, April 29, 1956, Part 2, p. 20.

important, the government is often the innovator and the provider of indispensable facilities and services for the city and its people.

Many of its piers that serve world shipping, for example, were built by the city. During the nineteenth century a large number were sold to private interests—shipping companies and railroads—but this led to difficulties in accommodating all the vessels seeking to enter the port, and the city subsequently bought back as many piers as it could, to manage them on a coordinated basis. Because the railroads were reluctant to relinquish the advantages of their own facilities, the Port of New York Authority was eventually created by New York State and New Jersey in 1921 to help these companies develop joint operations so as to reduce the number of piers they would need and thus to free the piers for ships. The Port Authority's program was not successful in this regard, but it later did acquire a grain terminal in Brooklyn and a section of the Brooklyn waterfront and renovated these, as well as instituting a large-scale port-promotion program, while the city began to improve its own waterfront properties under the pressure of competition from other Atlantic seaports. Water-borne commerce in the port owes a great deal to governmental action.

The same is true of air-borne commerce. Floyd Bennett Field was constructed by the city in 1931, its first response to air traffic at a time when the airplane was still an experimental and uncertain vehicle. In 1939 air-minded Mayor La Guardia was responsible for the completion of the airport later to bear his name, and in 1941 he initiated work on the mammoth air terminal in the Idlewild district of Queens. (Ultimately, Floyd Bennett Field was purchased by the Navy, and the other two air fields were leased to the Port of New York Authority for development and operation.) It was inevitable that the new medium of transportation should converge on New York, but New York's leadership in air commerce could not have asserted itself had there not been imaginative and resourceful government officials to encourage it and to take the necessary action.

Governmental accomplishments in the realm of ground transportation in New York City are even more dramatic. There are 6,000 miles of streets, virtually all publicly built, illuminated, and maintained. Thousands of traffic lights and other traffic engineering devices keep the colossal stream of traffic moving. Ten major vehicular bridges connect Manhattan and The Bronx; one joins Manhattan, The Bronx, and Queens; another runs from The Bronx to Queens directly; four bridges and two vehicular tunnels span the waters between Manhattan and Long Island (Brooklyn and Queens); there are three Hudson River crossings between Manhattan and New Jersey, and three between Staten Island and New Jersey; and there are many lesser bridges and tunnels scattered elsewhere through the city. The original subways were built by the city, although they were initially leased to private companies for operation; today, all the subways—241 route miles of them—as well as a large number of bus lines are city owned and operated. The Port of New York Authority built and runs a truck terminal and a union bus terminal in Manhattan. A network of limited-access parkways and highways, free of grade crossings and traffic lights, speeds express motor traffic into, out of, and through New York. Without all these, the city's commerce would have strangled itself, and population and commerce could not have grown to their present dimensions.

It takes more than commerce and transportation to sustain the city's population and a large portion of these other things is provided by public agencies. It takes two billion gallons of pure water a day, removal of four

TABLE 6. LARGEST CITIES OF THE WORLD, 1957[a]

City[b]	Population
New York	7,795,471
Tokyo	7,161,513
Shanghai	6,204,417
Moscow	4,847,000
Buenos Aires	3,673,575
Chicago	3,620,962
London	3,273,000
Bombay	3,211,000
Sao Paulo	3,149,504

[a] *The New York Times*, using a different definition of the term "city" and its own estimates of current populations, reports Tokyo and London as larger than New York. The *Times* list of the seven largest cities in the world includes, in order of size, Tokyo, London, New York, Shanghai, Moscow, Mexico City, and Peiping. See the issue of September 20, 1959, section 4. The figures in the table above are the official UN statistics.

[b] City proper only.

SOURCE: *United Nations Demographic Yearbook, 1957.* Statistical Office of the United Nations in collaboration with the Department of Economic and Social Affairs, pp. 152–160.

million tons of refuse, thousands of miles of sewers and huge sewage disposal plants, regulation and inspection of food and food handlers and processors, disease control to prevent epidemics, air pollution control to prevent the poisoning of the atmosphere, and a fire-fighting organization capable of handling every kind of blaze from small home fires to immense conflagrations in tenements, skyscrapers, industrial structures, and the waterfront. The basic physical and biological requirements of urban life are either provided or guaranteed by government.

So are some of the fundamental social conditions. People would flee the city if they could not educate their children here, and at a cost within reason. The city provides free education from kindergarten through college. For recreation the city furnishes one of the most extensive municipal park systems in the world, hundreds of playgrounds and ball fields and golf courses and even archery ranges, and eight beaches with a total of 17 miles of salt-water surf. The city subsidizes or supports (at least in part) the principal museums, three zoos, botanical gardens, and the aquarium, and maintains an extensive free public library system. It strives to set a floor under living standards for everyone by providing health, hospital, and welfare services for those in need. It protects its residential areas by land-use regulation (which also serves to guide the growth and development of the city). It regulates a great many types of business, either to assure satisfaction of at least minimum standards of quality or to prohibit the kind of destructive competition that might deprive the people of some needed goods and services altogether. Over

TABLE 7. LARGEST REPORTED METROPOLITAN
REGIONS OF THE WORLD, 1957[a]

Metropolitan areas[b]	Population
New York	14,066,000
Tokyo	8,471,637
London	8,270,430
Paris	6,436,296
Chicago	4,920,816

[a] *The New York Times,* employing its own definitions of metropolitan areas, or adopting definitions of planning groups, reports Tokyo as the largest metropolitan area in the world with a population of 20 million, New York as second largest with a population of 16.5 million, and London as third with a population of 10.4 million. See the issue of September 20, 1959, section 4. The figures in the table above are the official UN statistics.

[b] Core city and environs.

SOURCE: *United Nations Demographic Yearbook, 1957.* Statistical Office of the United Nations in collaboration with the Department of Economic and Social Affairs, pp. 152–160.

84,000 families live in public housing, and urban redevelopment, slum clearance, and enforcement of housing codes have been applied to the fight against urban blight. City agencies combat prejudice and discrimination against minority groups; wage a continuing struggle against juvenile delinquency; furnish protection against crime and disorder. All these things combined help make the city habitable, satisfying, and even reasonably comfortable. And they therefore help it hold together its prime source of greatness: its people.

GOVERNMENT AND POLITICS IN THE CITY

Much depends on the decisions and actions of governmental organs and agencies in the city; some group or groups always have a stake in the outcome of a particular governmental action or decision. Because the city is diverse and constantly changing, rarely do all interests coincide; unanimous approval or disapproval or total indifference with respect to a decision almost never occurs. In the quest for the stakes imbedded in what governmental officials and employees decide and do, competition is the usual state of affairs. Government and politics thus have many attributes of a contest.

The interactions of all those engaged in government and politics have a fascination of their own. There is drama and tension in the conflicts and clashes, the alliances and coalitions, the negotiations and accommodations, the bargains, the surrenders, the victories and defeats comprehended in the outward manifestations of public policy. In the end, however, the most fascinating, and perhaps the most amazing, aspect of this complex of phenomena is that it works. The stakes involved are extraordinarily high; the incentives to acquire them are consequently unusually strong; the opportunities, the risks, and the contestants are numerous; the magnitude of the stresses and strains on the political system is correspondingly great. Yet the system does work. Rarely has the capacity of men of many backgrounds, many statuses, many outlooks, many interests, to live together in peace and mutual respect been put to a severer test. Rarely have men responded as successfully as have the people and the politicians of New York City in devising their political institutions and practices.

BIBLIOGRAPHY

SOCIAL, ECONOMIC, AND CULTURAL FEATURES OF NEW YORK TODAY
(See also bibliography for Chapter II)

Beggs, Donald, editor, *New York: The City That Belongs to the World.* New York City Dept. of Commerce and Public Events, New York, 1956.

Brown, Henry Collins, *From Alley Pond to Rockefeller Center.* E. P. Dutton and Co., New York, 1936.

Daily News, *New York City Guide and Almanac, 1957–58.* New York University Press, New York, 1957.

Hawkins, Stuart, *New York, New York.* Wilfred Funk, New York, 1957.

Look Magazine, *New York City.* Houghton Mifflin Co., Boston, 1946. A handbook for the vacationist, the traveler, and the stay-at-home.

The New York Times, "New York—Coliseum City," *The New York Times,* sec. 6, part 2, April 29, 1956. Descriptions and paeans of praise on the occasion of the opening of the Coliseum in Columbus Circle convey some of the flavor of, and many facts about, the city.

Rothery, Agnes E., *New York Today.* Prentice-Hall, New York, 1951.

Simon, Kate, *New York Places and Pleasures.* Meridian Books, New York, 1959.

U.S. Works Progress Administration, Federal Writers Project, *New York Panorama.* Random House, New York, 1938.
New York Guide. Random House, New York, 1939.

DESCRIPTIONS AND APPRECIATIONS OF THE CITY

Berger, Meyer, *The Eight Million*. Simon and Schuster, New York, 1942.

Berger, Meyer, and Fritz Busse, *New York: City on Many Waters*. Arts, Inc., New York, 1955.

Klein, Alexander, editor, *Empire City*. Rinehart and Co., New York, 1955.

Markey, Morris, *Manhattan Reporter*. Dodge Publishing Co., New York, 1935.

Morris, Lloyd, *Incredible New York*. Random House, New York, 1951.

Stokes, Isaac N. P., *New York Past and Present*. Plantin Press, New York, 1939. New York history and landmarks, 1524–1939, in 100 views reproduced and described.

Ulmann, Albert, *A Landmark History of New York*. Appleton-Century-Crofts Co., New York, 1939.

Werner, Morris Robert, *It Happened in New York*. Coward-McCann, New York, 1957.

White, E. B., *Here Is New York*. Harper and Bros., New York, 1949.

FORMATION OF THE GREATER CITY

Alexander, De Alva Stanwood, *Four Famous New Yorkers*, vol. 4 of *A Political History of New York State, 1882–1905*. 4 vols. Henry Holt and Co., New York, 1923. A detailed political history of New York City at the turn of the century.

Bogard, Milo T., editor, *The Redemption of New York*. P. F. McBreen and Sons, New York, 1902. A review of the election of 1901 by New Yorkers who contributed to the victory of Seth Low.

Breen, William H., *Thirty Years of New York Politics Up-to-Date*. The Author, New York, 1899. New York politics prior to and at the time of the city's consolidation.

The Brown Book: A Biographical Record of Public Officials of the City of New York for 1898–99. M. B. Brown and Co., New York, 1899. A brief description of the scope and functions of the major city departments under the original charter of the consolidated city, followed by brief descriptions of city officials in executive, administrative, and legislative positions.

Coler, Bird S., *Municipal Government as Illustrated by the Charter, Finances, and Public Charities of New York*. D. Appleton and Co., New York, 1900. The Comptroller of the city discusses the problems of the consolidated City of New York under its first charter.

Conkling, Alfred R., *City Government in the United States*. D. Appleton and Co., New York, 1899. A former member of the Board of Aldermen touches on some aspects of city government in New York.

Durand, Edward Dana, *The Finances of New York City*. Macmillan Co., New York, 1898. Discusses the fiscal story of New York City from 1830 to 1897, just prior to consolidation.

Eaton, Dorman B., *The Government of Municipalities*. Columbia University Press, New York, 1899. Chapter 18 treats the charter of Greater New York.

Fitch, Charles E., editor, *Official New York from Cleveland to Hughes*. 4 vols. Hurd Publishing Co., New York, 1911. Chapter 1 of vol. 4 is a summary of the formation of Greater New York.

Foord, John, *The Life and Public Services of Andrew Haswell Green*. Doubleday, Page Co., Garden City, N. Y., 1913. A biography of the foremost champion of consolidation.

Gosnell, Harold F., *Boss Platt and His New York Machine*. University of Chicago Press, Chicago, 1924. A biography of the state Republican leader in power at the time of the formation of the Greater City.

Hall, Edward H., *A Short Biography of Andrew Haswell Green*. New York, 1904. Excerpted from *Ninth Annual Report* of American Scenic and Historic Preservation Society, of which it forms Appendix A. This biography of the "Father of Greater New York" traces the steps in the consolidation of the city.

Hirsch, Mark D., *William C. Whitney: Modern Warwick*. Dodd, Mead and Co., New York, 1948. The biography of a prominent figure whose life touched on many important aspects of the city's affairs just prior to consolidation.

Howe, Wirt, *New York at the Turn of the Century: 1899–1916*. The Author, Toronto, 1916. Republican politics in the newly consolidated city.

Ivins, William M., *Machine Politics and Money in Elections in New York City*. Harper and Bros., New York, 1887. An authoritative and incisive volume which reveals much about politics in the city prior to consolidation.

McGurrin, James, *Bourke Cockran: A Free Lance in American Politics*. Charles Scribner's Sons, New York, 1948. Biography of a notable figure in Tammany circles at the turn of the century.

Morris, Lloyd, *Incredible New York*. Random House, New York, 1951. A graphic portrait of the city at the time of its consolidation.

Nevins, Allan, and John A. Krout, editors, *The Greater City: New York, 1898–1948*. Columbia University Press, New York, 1948. The story of the city's consolidation, its early years, and its development.

O'Connor, Richard, *Hell's Kitchen*. J. B. Lippincott Co., Philadelphia, 1958.

Parkhurst, Charles H., *My Forty Years in New York*. Macmillan Co., New York, 1923, pp. 106–145. The Rev. Charles Parkhurst's own story of his "successful assault upon the Tammany interest," 1892–1894.

Patton, Clifford W., *The Battle for Municipal Reform: Mobilization and Attack, 1875 to 1900*. American Council on Public Affairs, Washington, 1940. Contains much on New York and Brooklyn on the eve of consolidation.

The Republic Press, *The Second City of the World*. New York, 1898. Details of events leading to consolidation of the Greater City.

Rodgers, Cleveland, and Rebecca S. Rankin, *New York: The World's Capital City*. Harper and Bros., New York, 1948. A broad view of the history of the city including the period of consolidation.

Shaw, Frederick, *History of the New York City Legislature*. Columbia University Press, New York, 1954. Includes discussion of the old Board of Aldermen before consolidation and under city's first charter.

Shepard, Edward M., "Political Inauguration of Greater New York," *Atlantic Monthly*, vol. 81, 1958, pp. 104–120. Describes the municipal election of 1897.

Sherman, Phileman T., *Inside the Machine: Two Years in the Board of Aldermen, 1898–1899*. Cooke and Fry, New York, 1901. A description of the functioning of the city government directly after consolidation, with the emphasis on the Board of Aldermen and the Council.

Smith, Ray B., editor, *History of the State of New York, Political and Governmental*. 6 vols. Syracuse University Press, Syracuse, N. Y., 1922. The political development of New York City at the time of consolidation is treated in vol. 4.

Steffens, Lincoln, *Autobiography*. Literary Guild, New York, 1931. An outstanding commentator in municipal government tells his story, touching upon New York City at the turn of the century.

The Shame of the Cities. Sagamore Press, New York, 1957. A famous muck-raking book, which deals in part with the government of New York City in the opening years of the century.

Syrett, Harold C., *The City of Brooklyn, 1865–1898: A Political History*. Columbia University Press, New York, 1944. The story of Brooklyn on the eve of consolidation.

Townsend, John D., *New York in Bondage*. The Author, New York, 1901. An unfriendly view of Tammany and its operations at the turn of the century.

Van Wyck, Frederick, *Recollections of an Old New Yorker*. Boni and Liveright, New York, 1932. Recollections of a cousin of the first Mayor of the Greater City.

CHAPTER II

The Stakes and Prizes
of the City's Politics

NEARLY EVERYONE IN THE CITY takes some part in the city's political and governmental system. Taking part in "politics"—that is, engaging in deliberate efforts to determine who gets public office (whether elective or appointive) and to influence what public officials and employees do—is an almost universal vocation among New Yorkers. Not all participate to the same extent or with the same intensity, and many of them are unaware that they are participating in politics at all, except as voters on Election Day. But in fact they are engaging in the city's political process in many other ways— as leaders or members of "civic" groups, neighborhood associations, professional associations, economic interest groups, ethnic and racial and religious associations, and not infrequently as individuals seeking directly to influence governmental action in specific instances.

The more continuous, extensive, and intensive participation in the city's governmental and political process is delegated, so to speak, by the citizens of the city to several main categories of actors in the political contest, who are rarely permitted to forget that their role is representative and temporary, subject to change and redefinition. The general electorate retains its rights as critic and customer. Thus the five main categories of leading participants in the city's politics—the party leaders, the city's public officials, the city bureaucracies, the nongovernmental groups and the communication media, and the officials and bureaucracies of the state and national governments, all of whom will be discussed more fully in later chapters—are constantly aware not only of their competitive relationships with each other, but also of their needs for a popular base of support. The principal actors are incessantly seeking to explain and justify their actions to a wider audience, as a way of maintaining their base and recruiting allies. Few citizens remain for long unsolicited or uninvited to participate.

The city presents a rich variety of goals, stakes, rewards, and prizes—all offered by and serving as strong incentives for participation in its political and governmental system. Agreement upon the true nature of the stakes and prizes the participants *seek* is difficult, bound up as the seeking is in the

39

inscrutable and complex motivations of human beings and the strategic vocabularies in which goals are stated by the participants, but it is possible to identify the types of rewards they *get* through political action. Participation in the political and governmental process of the city yields ideological and other "intangible" rewards, public office or employment, economic rewards, and desired governmental services. Whatever their stated objectives and whatever their perceptions and motives, those who take part in the city's political contest receive their observable rewards—or the hope and promise thereof—in these media of exchange.

THE FUSION OF PRIZES

If an observer attempts to analyze New York City politics and government without taking ideological and other "intangible" factors into account, the behavior of some of those involved will seem inexplicable. If he tries to find a political participant who never claims any material reward, he will look a long time and reap a small harvest. All the stakes are so intertwined in reality that they seldom appear separately. A single appointment may mean ideological victory, office, prestige, income, and power to the appointee, the appointer, and to some or many intermediaries. A single provision of a law may make scores of people richer or poorer. A decline in the quality or quantity of service may result in unseating officials and a redistribution of stakes. Every action and transaction involves several—not infrequently, all—of the currencies of reward: ideology, office, money, service, and less tangible benefits. The proportions and combinations of prizes sought and achieved by the contestants vary, but the blending of prizes for all contestants is virtually universal.

The prizes of local political action are not exclusively local; they are often state and federal as well. Thus, for instance, in terms of public office, on the elective side are the seats in the state Assembly and Senate with districts entirely within the boundary of the city, the congressional seats in the city, and a large number of positions in the judiciary of the state. In addition, New Yorkers commonly are represented liberally on the lists of candidates of the political parties for statewide elective office (the governorship, the lieutenant governorship, the comptrollership, and the attorney generalship of the state; the United States senatorships; judgeships on the Court of Appeals of New York; and the presidency itself, with its statewide slates of electors), for the city contains a large proportion of the state's voting population and of the machinery of each of the political parties. On the appointive side, federal and state judgeships, administrative posts in Albany and Washington and in the field services of both governments, and positions in the service of the state legislature and of Congress are often filled by men and women from the city. The two highest paid nonjudicial employees of the state (with the sole exception of the Governor) were recently revealed to be aides of the minority leaders of the Assembly and the Senate, all four being from New York City. City residents seeking state or federal office, as well as municipal office, in any branch of government, therefore pursue their goals a good deal of the time by participating in the politics of the city; conversely, those who participate in municipal politics are often rewarded with state or federal positions.

In much the same way, influence over city officials, party leaders, and electorates can be employed to shape state and federal decisions with regard to spending, borrowing, regulation, franchises and licenses, land use, and service—and, consequently, affect the distribution of these tangible rewards. Through city people placed in strategic positions in both higher levels of government by election and appointment, and through others who owe their elections at least in part to city votes, those who are politically active in the city are able to register their preferences on the laws, administrative rules, and the actions of the state and federal governments. Ideological rewards as well as others may be sought and sometimes secured through these channels. These, then, are also among the stakes of city politics, although requiring extension of the participation into the systems of other levels of government.

At the same time, it should be recognized that groups with direct access to state and federal officials and party leaders may often, in turn, employ such influence as a lever to move the city government in the directions they want it to go. The struggle for the prizes of political action in the city government may in this way also involve the higher governmental levels.

For many—perhaps for most—purposes, the three levels of government may be conveniently treated as relatively discrete entities, closely related but distinguishable. However, in considering the rewards of politics, and the tactics and strategies of participants in the political process, the distinctions tend to vanish. All the contestants attempt to get their rewards for their efforts wherever the rewards are to be had, and they make their efforts from whatever sources of strength and through whatever channels are available to them. From this point of view, although there are three rings, there is only one arena.

IDEOLOGICAL AND INTANGIBLE REWARDS

For many participants, the city's political system offers opportunities for rewards which are primarily ideological. Particular policies, specific programs, or procedural changes in governmental operations become goals, the championship or the accomplishment of which provide powerful incentives to those who are dedicated to these policies or procedures. The participants identified with these ideological goals are frequently allied with others seeking more tangible and self-centered rewards for themselves, but the ideological

30912

rewards nevertheless have a separate and important function in the city's political system.

For example, the goal of a "master plan" to guide the physical and esthetic development of the city represents an important ideological stake for several articulate groups involved in the city's political life. For others, there are goals with high moral or religious content: the Protestant opposition to off-track betting, the Catholic resistance to birth control services in the city's hospitals and health clinics, the Jewish fear of sectarian teachings in the city's public schools. Other participants are dedicated to egalitarian and humanitarian goals in public policy: the eradication or limitation of ethnic, racial, or religious discrimination, the provision of special services to the underprivileged, the improved care of children, changes in the treatment of prisoners, and a hundred other similar goals in public policy or governmental programs. Still other participants in the city's political life find opportunities to seek or secure rewards which to them represent objective improvements in governmental or political procedures: permanent personal registration, the proportional representation voting system, competitive bidding for governmental contracts, a performance system of city budgeting, a "clean city" or an "anti-noise" campaign, and scores of other long-range or short-term goals. Another category of participants identify their efforts with national political and party stakes; participation in the political life of the city represents to them the rewards of strengthening the Democratic party, or the Republican party, in the state and in the nation, and so increasing the chances of realizing wider policy goals with which these parties are associated.

The city's political system offers other rewards which are less objective and impersonal but no less attractive to many participants. Social recognition, prestige, and community respect are often the rewards of active participation in the city's politics—whether in the political party, in public office, in the bureaucracy, or in the nongovernmental associations. The size and variety of the city's total political system, the sense of being associated with great events and prominent persons, even at a great distance from the center of the stage, presents rewards which are a magnet to many groups and individuals. Few citizens of the city are wholly immune to its pull. For many, these rewards have a great and special significance. Immigrants who have felt the whiplash of contempt, minorities encountering occupational and other barriers, and groups denied status in other ways, find in the city's political system an escalator out of the social cellar. They use it. They use it to state their aspirations and their discontents, to win recognition as spokesmen for a constituency, to win office for themselves or those they endorse, to win career opportunities in a bureaucracy for their groups, and to secure public policies which meet their needs as they see them. Even when participation achieves few of these things, or secures them but slowly, those who are even slightly influential in the political system acquire rewards of prestige and recognition in their own group and sometimes in the community at large. For them, this is usually a prize to be sought energetically.

The ideological and the intangible stakes in the city's political system give it ferment and movement. Much of the content of the city's public debate is provided by those who seek these goals. They produce some of the sharpest clashes between the forces of innovation and the defenders of the *status quo*. Other stakes of the system are more familiar and more easily measured, but the stakes of ideology in policy and procedure and the prizes of recognition and prestige are distinctive features of New York City politics.

THE PRIZES OF OFFICE

Much political action in the city revolves around the acquisition of public office. For many participants, office is often a means to other ends. It may mean money, service, prestige. It may convey influence—the ability to determine who gets other positions, to make or at least to help shape governmental decisions, and to climb to still higher office. For the most active and persistent seekers after public office, it means a career in a series of offices, each representing advancement up the ladder of officialdom, which is the most valued prize. From this point of view, a public office is instrumental for the office seeker.

For some, however, a particular public office is an end in itself. For there are seekers after office who seem to gain little else from success in their quest. They grow no richer. They enjoy no service they could not otherwise have. They do not enhance—and sometimes they risk—their reputations. Their influence is increased only slightly. Yet they strive for public office. When due allowance is made for the instrumental aspects of such office, and for the chance factors that draw people into it, and even for the inertia that keeps them in once they find themselves there, there is still a residue of contributory elements that can only be explained as the value placed on office *qua* office. Public office, in and of itself, must be regarded as one of the stakes of politics.

But public office is not a stake merely for those who personally seek or achieve it for themselves. It is also a crucial stake in the city's political system for those who groom the prospective candidate, sponsor him when the competition is at its sharpest, and rely upon him in office for fulfillment of those expectations which prompted their choice of him over alternative candidates. Every major participant in the city's politics—party leaders, the city's public officials themselves, the bureaucracies, the nongovernmental groups, the communication media, the officials and the bureaucracies of the state and federal governments—has a high stake in the prizes of public office within the gift or influence of the city's political system. These public offices stand at the center of the whole system of rewards in the political contest; the powers of public officials are most often the key to the whole range of prizes for which the participants compete.

The range of public offices available through the city's political system represents a hierarchy of prizes. The most valued, both for those who seek office and those who aspire to determine or influence the choices, are those high offices which lie outside the direct gift of the city but which the city's leading participants may make realistic targets of their political action: the President of the United States (because the city's electorate is a major element in determining which presidential candidate gets New York's 45 electoral votes), membership in the President's cabinet, and many federal judgeships; the offices of Governor of New York State, its two United States Senators, the Lieutenant Governor, the Comptroller, the state Attorney General, the judgeships on the state Court of Appeals, and the major appointments made by the Governor. For these great prizes, the participants in the city's political system must compete and bargain with the leading participants in other political systems, but no other city has so many assets as does New York with which to bargain in these larger arenas.

The second order of prizes of public office are those provided by the city's political system within its own jurisdiction. Among these, in the approximate order of value assigned to them by the leading participants, are the offices of Mayor, the higher judicial posts, the Comptroller, the President of the Council, congressmen, the heads of the major city departments, the lesser judicial posts, state senators, assemblymen, councilmen, the deputy commissioners, and other executive officers of the city government. The total number of elected officials with constituencies wholly inside the city is about 350. The number of key appointive offices in the city government, apart from the posts in the permanent bureaucracies, is about a thousand. These elective and appointive offices are impressive both in their number and in their separate and collective impact upon the other stakes of the city's political contest.

The governmental bureaucracies in the city represent another kind of political stake. There are approximately 382,000 civilian government employees who work in the city.[1] About 250,000 are city employees; the remainder work in the city for the state and federal governments. Most of them are employed under the selection and tenure provisions of various types of "merit" systems, and so are more or less protected against the interventions of party leaders. But their offices and their actions constitute an important stake in the city's political system. Their offices represent careers, in the opportunities of which many of the city's political participants have a continuing and important interest (for example, the nongovernmental professional associations, on behalf of their members and the profession; the party leaders, on behalf of their constituents). The bureaucracies are also policy makers, and

[1] See Table 15, p. 74; Table A, Appendix C.

thus are the object of constant attention from the city's interest groups and others affected by the wide-ranging decisions of the bureaucracies. Finally, many of the bureaucracies are organized to participate directly in the city's political contest, and as such their alliances represent important political stakes to the other contestants.

Not all the bureaucratic positions are under the merit systems. These several thousand positions represent substantial stakes to some of the participants in the city's politics, especially to the party leaders. The residue of the once universal patronage systems, these jobs—city, state, federal—are the small change as well as some of the larger units of the currency of rewards distributed mainly through the party organizations but often traded by the party leaders in their negotiations for alliance and support from other participants.

ECONOMIC STAKES

Money, like public office, is both an end in itself and a means with which to obtain the other stakes of political action. Some participants in the city's political process are concerned with millions; some seem satisfied with steady, secure, though modest incomes; a great many get nothing more than small sums now and then. Whether large or small, pecuniary payoffs—legal or in violation of the law, open or clandestine, moral or tainted—obviously play a large role in the city's politics, and some of the battles over small sums occasionally rival in intensity those involving huge amounts.

Virtually every decision made by any government affects somebody's pocketbook. Collectively, all the units of government in the United States spend an annual total exceeding $100 billion, or roughly one quarter of the gross national product. There is keen competition for shares in this vast market for goods and services, and the competition is at least as political as economic. The bill for these expenditures falls upon the public at large, but not with equal force on all segments of the population. Perhaps the most furious and continuous political battles of all, especially at the state and local level, rage around the question: Who will pay the governmental bill? Many governmental decisions neither directly put public money into anybody's pocket nor remove it to fill the public treasuries, but their economic impact is enormous because they affect the rate of return on investment and the competitive positions of individuals and firms. Large numbers of people show little interest in getting public office or employment for themselves, or even in the decisions about who does get them. But the proportion of the population directly and profoundly affected by governmental decisions affecting their incomes is far greater, and, correspondingly, the percentage displaying lack of interest in these decisions is much smaller. Governmental actions having financial aftermaths are mighty stimuli to political action. In New York City these stimuli are particularly numerous and strong.

Who Will Get What the City Spends?

Each year, for example, the City of New York spends $2 billion for operating expenses and some $400 million additional for capital improvements. Of this amount, $900 million a year goes into wages and salaries of the city government's employees and officials; as an *employer*, the city's magnitude is matched or exceeded only by the federal government and by a handful of corporate giants. Pressed by inflation, city officials and the organized bureaucracies may demand wage increases, buttressing their demands with all the political force they can muster. But to other participants, higher salaries for the city's employees mean higher taxes or, alternatively, diminished service. Taxpayers can usually be counted upon to object strenuously to higher levies, while the beneficiaries of municipally provided services protest vehemently against reduced services. The political awareness of all these contestants for financial advantage—or, at least, for the avoidance of financial deprivation—is highly developed in New York City, and, as later discussion will demonstrate, their knowledge of political strategies and tactics is both extensive and profound. Consequently, the wages and salaries of public servants are among the salient stakes of political action; one consequence is that pay scales and fringe benefits, being the results of adjustments and compromises among the contestants and reflecting the unequal power of various

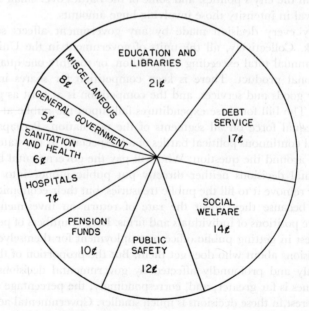

CHART 4. THE NEW YORK CITY EXPENSE DOLLAR: ADMINISTERING AND OPERATING EXPENSES OF THE CITY AND COUNTY GOVERNMENTS

SOURCE: *Annual Report* of the Comptroller of New York City, 1957–1958, Part I, chart 7.

segments of the city bureaucracy, are something less than orderly and symmetrical. Decisions made by the city in its capacity as employer distribute some of the money stakes of politics; inevitably, therefore, these decisions are foci of political contention.

So, too, are the decisions of the city government in its capacity as *consumer* of products. New York City spends millions of dollars a year on items of every conceivable kind. Steel, bricks, concrete, asphalt, and other materials for its buildings, bridges, streets, and other parts of the city's great physical plant loom large in its purchases. There are, too, the usual office supplies and equipment, which it consumes in enormous quantities. But there are large amounts of other items—food, soap, towels, electric light fixtures and lamps, beds and bedding for hospitals, shelters, and prisons. And it buys automobiles and trucks and mechanical street sweepers and snow removers for sanitation, fire, police, and other services. Substantial amounts of radio equipment for police and emergency cars, fire trucks, and for its radio station are among the city's purchases. Replacement parts, tires, fuel, and oil must be furnished. There are firearms and ammunition for the police force; rakes and shovels and lawn mowers for its acres of parks; spraying apparatus and pruning saws and ladders for its trees; bats and balls and games for its playgrounds; coal and oil and electric power to operate all its facilities; vast quantities of printing; and thousands of other things.

TABLE 8. EXPENSES FOR ADMINISTERING AND OPERATING THE CITY AND COUNTY GOVERNMENTS

Department or purpose	Amount		Per cent of total	Per capita[b]
Education and libraries		$416,407,522.94	20.80	$52.00
Debt service[a]		348,915,379.86	17.42	43.55
Social welfare		279,950,938.07	13.98	34.95
Public safety		239,695,895.33	11.97	29.92
Pension funds		194,314,897.48	9.70	24.25
Hospitals		132,805,059.39	6.63	16.57
Sanitation and health		122,598,369.92	6.12	15.30
General government and legislature		92,695,284.38	4.63	11.58
Miscellaneous:				
Public enterprises	$49,872,570.05			
Parks, cultural, and recreational	34,109,211.12			
Correction and judicial	29,440,984.06			
County expense	22,069,445.34			
General Fund Stabilization Reserve Fund	9,859,437.00			
Tax deficiency	7,298,680.00			
Other	22,466,516.47	175,116,844.04	8.75	21.88
Total expenses		$2,002,500,191.41	100.00	$250.00

[a] Excludes $3,500,000 of budget notes.

[b] The population of the city as of July 1, 1958, is estimated by the Department of Health to be 8,010,000.

SOURCE: *Annual Report* of the Comptroller of New York City, 1957–1958, p. 13.

For all these items, there are prospective sellers anxious to get the city's business. To be sure, a great deal of this business is handled by fixed administrative procedure. Nevertheless, dealers and manufacturers strive to preserve part of this market for themselves, and this generally involves them in political strategies. Thus, for example, it is a matter of front-page news when the Fire Department decides to reject a bid by a fire-equipment manufacturer, a matter which may eventually be aired before the City Council. The placement of orders, the division of business among competing firms, are decisions to which retailers, wholesalers, and manufacturers bend their efforts to win the competition or at least to secure adoption of procedures that improve their chances. The purchases and sales and the rules governing them are, in short, political stakes.

TABLE 9. CITY EXPENDITURES ON CURRENT EXPENSES, IN CURRENT AND CONSTANT DOLLARS, IN SELECTED YEARS

	City expenditures, current expenses			
	Current dollars		Constant dollars[a]	
Fiscal year	Amount (millions)	Per cent increase over previous figure	Amount (millions)	Per cent increase over previous figure
1934	551	..	939	..
1939–1940	586	6.4	978	4.2
1944–1945	726	23.9	944	(3.5)[b]
1949–1950	1,184	61.7	1,152	22.0
1954–1955	1,596	34.8	1,393	20.9
1957–1958	2,003	25.5	1,666	19.6
Over-all Increase	1,452	265.3	672	77.4
Ratio 1957–1958 TO 1934	3.64	..	1.77	..

[a] 1947–1949 = 100 in terms of consumer purchasing power of the dollar.
[b] Per cent decrease.

SOURCES: *Statistical Abstract of the United States*, U.S. Dept. of Commerce, Washington, 1958, Table 418, p. 331; *Annual Reports* of the Comptroller of New York City.

The municipal government is also one of the largest *builders, tenants,* and *landlords* in the city. Every year several hundred million dollars are expended through contracts for the construction of schools and other public buildings, piers and wharves, bridges, street lights and traffic signals, roads and highways, playgrounds and swimming pools and beaches, and many other projects. These activities make the city also a large buyer and seller of land and other properties. It rents piers to shipping companies and railroads, and rents space for concessions on its other properties. Millions of dollars of insurance are carried on facilities owned by the city. Shortage of space in public buildings, and the need to institute services in areas in which there are an insufficient number of public buildings and in which additional construction is unwarranted, compel many city agencies to rent space in privately owned buildings. As in the case of purchases, tight statutory restrictions and other rules govern the handling of these contracts, sales, and leases. Nevertheless, contractors strive vigorously to get as much of the city's construction business as they can, concessionaires compete for space on city property and for favorable rental charges, and landlords are generally delighted to sign long-term leases with city agencies for substantial rentals. A great deal of political negotiation is centered on the capture of all these valuable prizes.

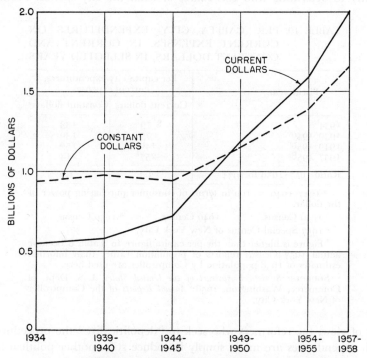

CHART 5. CITY EXPENDITURES ON CURRENT EXPENSES, IN CURRENT AND CONSTANT DOLLARS, IN SELECTED YEARS

The city is also a *benefactor*. Almost $200 million a year (much of this being supplied by the state government) is spent on welfare payments and other health and welfare services for city residents in urgent need of assistance. Here again, legislative specifications tend to reduce the administration of welfare assistance to the level of routine, but much political action is aimed at decisions defining eligibility for assistance, and the size and duration of welfare benefits. Indeed, great storms have been generated by allegations of denial of benefits to deserving and needy persons, and of provision of service to persons not in need of it. It is not unusual for attempts to be made outside formal administrative channels to influence the disposition of such benefits, even of occasional individual applications for help. In any event, it was political action by many groups that made the city (and other levels of government) the benefactor it is, and that continues to influence the extent of its generosity.

In all these ways, and in all these capacities, the government of the city makes its huge expenditures. The object of many engaged in politics is apparently to determine who gets shares of what the city spends. From this

TABLE 10. PER CAPITA CITY EXPENDITURES ON CURRENT EXPENSES, IN CURRENT AND CONSTANT DOLLARS, IN SELECTED YEARS

Fiscal year	Per capita city expenditures, current expenses	
	Current dollars	Constant dollars[a]
1934[b]	$ 79	133
1939–1940[c]	79	130
1949–1950[d]	146	150
1957–1958[e]	257[f]	214
Ratio 1957–1958 to 1934	3.3	1.6

[a] 1947–1949 = 100 in terms of consumer purchasing power of the dollar.

[b] 1930 Census.   [c] 1940 Census.   [d] 1950 Census.

[e] 1957 Special Census of New York City.

[f] Figure is higher than the per capita figure in Table 8 because actual 1957 Census reports of population rather than informal estimates of 1958 population by Comptroller are used here.

SOURCES: *Statistical Abstract of the United States*, U.S. Dept. of Commerce, Washington, 1958; *Annual Reports* of the Comptroller of New York City.

point of view, the reformers who seek to "depoliticalize" the procedures by which expenditures are made simply introduce still another political factor into the contest over the distribution of this money. This does not alter the central argument that money in the form of municipal spending is one of the main issues in municipal politics.

Who Will Pay the Governmental Bill?

Similarly, one decision about methods of raising money to pay the costs of city government may impose a heavy fiscal burden on some elements of the population and a light one on others, while another decision may distribute the load quite differently. Probably no issue arouses stronger passions than the question: Into whose purse will the city reach? People fight hard to keep it out of their own.

For example, the state constitution contains provisions establishing certain tax and debt limits for local units of government in the state; under its terms, New York City is prohibited from imposing property taxes producing an excess of 2.5 per cent of a five-year average of the full valuation of taxable real estate in the city, and from incurring funded and bonded debts totaling over 10 per cent of the same base. One consequence of this is the protection of property owners from more than a stated maximum of taxation. Another is a guarantee to bondholders that their loans to the city will be secure. These restrictions have become great stakes in the city's politics, one group of contestants defending them, another seeking exemptions from the ceilings.

At the same time, the city has been compelled to resort increasingly to other taxes—taxes on sales, on hotel rooms, on gross payrolls, on the use of automobiles, on theater tickets, and on a host of other transactions, each of which produces relatively small revenues and arouses a great deal of irritation—to finance its operations; or, alternatively, to reject demands for service which it might otherwise satisfy. The city sales tax (the chief money maker for the city government after the property tax, although first adopted in 1934 as a "temporary, emergency" measure for the relief of the unemployed) has been tripled in rate in a generation. The city has been slow to grant increases in

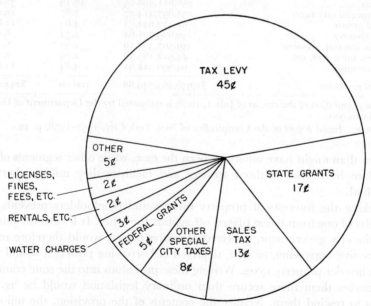

CHART 6. THE NEW YORK CITY REVENUE DOLLAR: SOURCES FROM WHICH THE CITY REVENUE IS DERIVED

SOURCE: *Annual Report* of the Comptroller of New York City, 1957–1958, Part I, chart 6.

wages to city employees because of the difficulty in paying for such raises; in a sense, then, the employees have involuntarily subsidized a lightened load on payers of property and other taxes. The city government has had to curtail investments in capital property—in schools, hospitals, streets, and parks, for example—because it was pressing on its debt ceiling. It has transferred some of its responsibilities to special public authorities which charge fees for the services they render or has itself levied charges and earmarked the revenues for specific bond issues (which are then exempted from the debt limit) because it was not allowed to borrow more, with the result that the users of the facilities rather than the entire community (to which the benefits are presumed to accrue) pay today for structures once charged against all. Owners of real property and city bonds are thus protected, but hotel guests, businesses, wage-earners, public servants, theatergoers, motorists, consumers, subwayriders, and others have consequently borne a larger proportion of the fiscal

TABLE 11. SOURCES FROM WHICH CITY'S REVENUE WAS DERIVED

Source of revenue	Amount	Per cent of total	Per capita[a]
Tax levy	$875,187,154.06	44.74	$109.27
State grants	337,096,131.85	17.23	42.08
Sales tax	256,811,398.25	13.13	32.07
Other special city taxes	153,897,414.57	7.87	19.22
Federal grants	94,473,942.33	4.83	11.80
Water charges	49,669,701.64	2.54	6.20
Rentals, interest, services	49,507,329.19	2.53	6.18
Licenses, fines, fees, etc.	44,924,165.38	2.29	5.59
Other revenue	94,696,512.61	4.84	11.82
Total revenue	$1,956,263,749.88	100.00	$244.23

[a] The population of the city as of July 1, 1958, is estimated by the Department of Health to be 8,010,000.

SOURCE: *Annual Report* of the Comptroller of New York City, 1957–1958, p. 12.

burden than might have otherwise been the case, while other segments of the populace have done without services and facilities they might otherwise have had.

Linking the interests of property owners and bondholders prevents the interests of one from being played off against the other. It lessens the danger that the city government, deprived of taxing power, would therefore resort to excessive borrowing, or that, deprived of borrowing power, it would levy much heavier property taxes. Writing these provisions into the state constitution makes them more secure than ordinary legislation would be against efforts to rescind them. Neither the contents of the provision, the union of lenders of money and property taxpayers, nor the imbedding of the provisions in the solid framework of the constitution, was an accident; these are the outcomes of consciously used political tactics. That is not to say the policies are necessarily unsound; on the contrary, a great deal can be said in their defense, both in economic and moral terms. But sound or not, they illustrate how determined groups, alert to the possibilities of political action, can adjust the fiscal policies of governments in their own favor. For them, this means financial gain—or, at least, avoidance of financial loss. Money is a political stake or reward, even for many in the city who never think of themselves as "in politics."

Whose Economic Interests Will Be Furthered?

Setting Standards of Performance. Decisions regarding minimum standards of health, safety, morals, and welfare, though they do not directly affect the flow of cash into or out of the city treasury, increase or decrease the rate of return by wholly private investments. Mandatory criteria of cleanliness for restaurants and markets and other establishments that store and sell un-packaged food, for example, may add considerably to the cost of doing that kind of business. Building codes effectively prohibiting prefabricated struc-tures and fixtures or other new methods of construction may raise building costs and therefore rentals paid by tenants, but they may also protect plumb-ers, electricians, and other skilled laborers against technological unemploy-ment and reduction to the ranks and pay scales of unskilled labor. Insistence, for reasons of safety, that every legitimate theater be a free-standing structure (rather than part of a commercial edifice) is alleged to have made the erection of new theaters unprofitable, restricting the growth of the legitimate theater, driving up the rates charged by older theaters (which are in short supply), and reducing actors' and producers' and directors' opportunities for money-making ventures and employment. Merchants and bus companies fight bit-terly against the introduction of one-way streets, claiming that this practice cuts down their volume of business. Determination to reduce air pollution produces rules and regulations compelling many companies to install expen-sive smoke-abatement apparatus. Laws forbidding stores to operate seven days a week increase overhead costs by forcing expensive installations to stand idle at least 13 per cent of the time. Reserving curb space on streets for com-mercial loading and unloading diminishes time loss and inconvenience in business operations, but it drives private cars into parking lots and garages, to the advantage of these businesses and at the expense of the motorists. In these and hundreds of other ways, what the city does to protect some or many of its citizens may incidentally—and occasionally by design—put money into someone's bank account or, by the same token, take it out. As might be expected, a large proportion of political action revolves around decisions about these stakes.

Enforcement of Standards. Once a standard is set formally—that is, pro-mulgated as a law or an administrative regulation—the focus of political tactics by the affected groups shifts to the level and intensity of enforcement. If an individual or a firm or an industry can in practice ignore a requirement, it may escape the costs it imposes and thereby enlarge its margins of profit. If one group can evade provisions competitors observe, it may also gain a considerable competitive advantage. And if an illegal operation can avoid suppression by enforcement officers, the operators may enjoy large incomes—especially if competing violators are driven out of business.

Sometimes these tactics take the form of an organized challenge to the discretion of enforcement officers—an argument, for instance, that a particular floor-load limit has been set too low, or that glasses at soft-drink stands are really no more hazardous than disposable paper cups, or that gas-operated refrigerators are in fact no more dangerous than electric ones. Having failed to defeat the enactment of a law or regulation, its opponents attempt to soften the economic blow by attacking its administration. All sides mobilize all the potential strength at their command to make their respective interpretations prevail.

Frequently, there are efforts to encourage selective nonenforcement. The practice ranges from arrangements among some residents of downtown apartment buildings, their doormen, and patrolmen on the beat to "protect" the illegally parked cars of the residents (which costs the residents less than garages and brings an increment of income to both doormen and policemen who are parties to these arrangements), through underassessment of taxes or overlooking violations of the Sanitary Code, all the way to permitting bookmakers and other gamblers to ply their trades in security and allowing brothels to flourish. No function is too trivial, and none too important, to be immune to this kind of manipulation. It is not very surprising that a rigorous enforcement campaign by the Commissioner of Health in 1951 revealed hundreds of eating and food-handling establishments in violation of the law; or that a more recent joint survey of tenements and apartment buildings by the Departments of Buildings, Health, and Fire disclosed breaches of legal requirements by landlords neglecting maintenance and service in order to cut costs; or that a "ring" of policemen was found selling tickets whose holders were automatically released when stopped for traffic offenses; or that a magazine could point out dozens of unlawfully parked cars permitted to stand all day in restricted zones. Nor is it difficult to explain why organized gambling and prostitution continue despite prohibitions. Admittedly, even the best enforcement system cannot be totally effective; in addition, enforcement is often blunted by group and political action designed specifically to take the edge off it.

There are also demands *for* enforcement as well as for *non*enforcement. For years, regulations of the Police Department forbade overnight parking in the streets. However, garage operators in some neighborhoods would occasionally complain about flagrant violation of the overnight parking ban, and local campaigns against the practice would drive more motorists to rent garage space. Eventually, a newly created Department of Traffic bowed to the inevitable (as well as to the protests of the Automobile Club of New York) and rescinded the regulation in many areas. There are more determined automobile drivers than garage men, and, anyway, the ever-increasing number of cars has filled both garages and streets.

The city government itself does not grow significantly richer or poorer as an immediate result of enforcement or nonenforcement; revenues from this source are lower than the expenses of administration. But the large and influential groups affected by decisions to compel compliance to the letter, or to take action against only the most egregious violators, or to wink at requirements, may gain or lose a good deal. The appropriations and the size and quality and behavior of the staff invested by the city in enforcement is for this purpose one of the stakes of politics.

Franchises and Licenses. A license is a permit to do what is otherwise prohibited—to operate a barbershop, for example, or a cabaret, or to erect a building. Literally hundreds of activities are licensed by the city. Some are issued in unlimited numbers; the applicants need merely demonstrate they have complied with laws and regulations. Issuance of others ceases at a point, as is the case with limits on the number of "medallions" or permits to operate taxis. This restricts the number of people engaged in the activity, thus restrains the intensity of competition, and simultaneously turns the medallions into capital assets of considerable value (which may be sold, and which currently change hands at prices in excess of $15,000 each).

Franchises are exclusive licenses. That is, they confer a monopoly on the person or corporation to whom they are awarded (for instance, to operate the only bus line on a given route). To an even greater extent than licenses issued in limited quantity, franchises suspend the operation of the competitive market. For this reason the activities they authorize are usually subject to relatively close supervision and regulation by public officials.

Supervised or not, limited in quantity or not, franchises and licenses are worth money to those to whom they are granted. Since they are issued by public officers, these officials are therefore objects of political pressure. Indeed, some of the bitterest and most sordid episodes in New York's history were battles over streetcar, subway, and bus franchise rights. In these battles, millions were at stake. Even today a few private traction companies have expressed interest in buying the franchises and equipment of several publicly owned and operated bus lines. But it is not only the gigantic prizes that generate political action; so, too, do the permits to engage in more modest enterprises, such as running drive-in theaters (there is only one in the city), parking lots, private refuse collection, "going-out-of-business" sales, and peddling from pushcarts in open-air markets, to name but a few of the hundreds of kinds. Many permits are handled routinely, but administrative denial does not ordinarily end the matter. Applicants often resort to political pressure to gain their ends. Where a city license or franchise means money or the loss of it, political action will occur.

Land-Use Regulation. Finally, regulations governing use of land in the city have profound consequences for property values and business opportunities. A block zoned for business in a residential area may prove immensely valuable, for businesses in that location will be easily accessible to the residents of

TABLE 12. NEW YORK CITY EXPENDITURES FOR CAPITAL IMPROVEMENTS, FISCAL YEAR 1957–1958

Purpose	Amount
Docks	$ 6,608,178.94
Education	121,368,211.21
Hospitals and allied buildings	9,291,380.51
Low rent housing[a]	5,011,959.81
Sewage treatment works	6,761,571.64
Slum clearance	5,074,935.85
Transit	105,806,651.29
Water	484,098.19
Other	113,534,740.00
Total	$373,941,727.44

[a] Does not include expenditures by the New York City Housing Authority for low rent housing facilities.

SOURCE: Compiled from *Annual Report* of the Comptroller of New York City, 1957–1958.

the neighborhood and will thus prove exceedingly profitable to the property owners who sell or rent, and to businessmen who can afford to buy or rent, the space. By the same token, permitting the construction of commercial buildings near an established business center will present new competition.

Displacement of residents and stores from an area to make way for new projects is invariably costly and inconvenient to the people forced to move. The erection of a cultural center in Lincoln Square met with vehement—and politically organized—opposition; battles have been fought over the Brooklyn approaches to the proposed Narrows bridge; automobile expressway routes have been altered to placate objecting groups. An airport, a sewage disposal plant, a prison, a firehouse, a leather tannery, an oil refinery, or a factory can depress land values in nearby sections, losses that come out of the resources of property owners. On the other hand, a neighboring park or school can enhance real estate values, and authorizations to open parking lots can improve retail business. A decision to allow the building of tall apartment structures permits intensified land use and hence higher returns, but it may destroy the character of a neighborhood of small houses and drive down the prices they command on the market. In short, when the city decides how a piece of land may be used, it may thereby enable some people to net a financial windfall and/or reduce the capital assets or the return on investment for someone else. Many such decisions brew political storms.

The Politics of Economics. In a "perfectly free" economy, if such a thing is conceivable—one in which the government keeps order but takes no other actions affecting prices—the market place would presumably determine all economic values. In fact, values are very greatly modified by many governmental decisions, decisions which do not directly relate to the raising or spending of public moneys. This being the case, substantial numbers of people

TABLE 13. TOTAL CITY EXPENDITURES, FISCAL YEAR
1957–1958

Total current expenses	$2,002,500,191.41
Total capital expenditures	373,941,727.44
Total expenditures for year	$2,376,441,918.85

SOURCE: Compiled from *Annual Report* of the Comptroller of New York City, 1957–1958.

in the city who stand to gain or lose by such governmental decisions devote considerable time, money, and energy to selecting and influencing the officials who promulgate and enforce the decisions. For economic purposes they enter the political arena. And money is therefore one of the prime stakes of city politics.

STAKES OF GOVERNMENTAL SERVICE

The fourth type of stakes sought by the contestants for influence over the municipal government is service by the city government. Groups demand that the city do things *for* them and *to* others. In one respect, it must be admitted, this category of rewards overlaps the quest for money, for when the city undertakes to furnish a service it relieves some individuals or groups of the cost of doing it for themselves and spreads the burden over the entire community; and when it regulates or constrains an activity, those already engaged in it have less to fear from competition, both legitimate and unfair. But, though the pursuit of money and that of service often coincide, they are not identical. The struggle for one is not always the same as the struggle for the other, and frequently they lead in different directions and involve different contestants altogether.

The City Government Is One Service Organization Among Many

Practically no service rendered and no regulation imposed by the city lacks a counterpart performed by private persons in their private capacities at private expense, with the exception of imprisonment of criminal offenders or accused.

Banks and department stores and warehouses and armored trucking companies employ their own uniformed special police, and detective agencies furnish private detectives for a fee. Some large industrial plants have their own auxiliary fire-fighting forces. The Department of Sanitation does not remove industrial and commercial waste; this is handled by private carters for a price. Health associations (such as the Heart Fund, the Tuberculosis and Health Association of New York, and The National Foundation, to mention but a few), voluntary and proprietary hospitals and labor union health centers, parallel in many ways the work of the Departments of Health and Hospitals, while both secular and sectarian charitable societies supplement the efforts of the Department of Welfare. One fourth of the elementary and high-school students of the city attend parochial and private institutions. Commercial amusement parks offer alternatives to city playgrounds, and there is at least one private park in the city. There are even private streets, ceremoniously roped off once each year to protect the title of the owners. Some avenues are served by city-owned bus lines, others by private companies. Until the city took over all the subways in 1939, the Interborough Rapid Transit Company and the Brooklyn-Manhattan Transit Company (the IRT and the BMT) operated their underground railroads at the same time that the city ran its own Independent (IND) Subway. In appearance and management, and sometimes even in rentals, some of the large privately built (though publicly subsidized) housing projects in New York are indistinguishable from those constructed and managed by the New York City Housing Authority.

The activities of the Regional Plan Association, a privately endowed organization, are very similar to some of the functions of the City Planning Commission. The Honest Ballot Association helps the Board of Elections protect the integrity of the electoral process. There are privately owned airports, privately run museums, privately operated piers in the city. Private, special, and university libraries complement the public library system. The famous Forty-second Street Library is maintained by private funds, only the circulation system and the branches being supported by the city. The city runs its own ferries to Staten Island, but some of the few remaining ferry lines across the Hudson are private. Owners of patents often license competitors to manufacture products that would otherwise be prohibited to them, much as the city licenses activities that may not be engaged in without a permit. Grievance and arbitration machinery in labor relations is not dissimilar to judicial and administrative justice. The Better Business Bureau enforces honest commercial practices. *Good Housekeeping*, Underwriters Laboratories, Inc., and Consumers Union check the quality and safety of manufactured and food products. In short, it is difficult to name anything the city government does that is exclusive, although there are many fields it has not entered at all and other areas in which it is overwhelmingly dominant even if not alone.

Defined in terms of what it *does* rather than in legal terms, the city is but one of the institutions that provide the people of New York with the things and services they want. Why, then, do they turn to the city government?

Why the People Turn to the City Government

Its Vulnerability. One reason that demands are made on the city government is its vulnerability to pressure. This is a difference in degree. Customers may express displeasure with the leadership of a company by withholding their patronage, and employees may do so by withholding their labor, but they cannot often expel the leadership from its position. In the political arena, on the other hand, officials may lose their political heads if they incur the hostility of a sufficient number of voters to push the vote for their party below the plurality needed for election. Both kinds of leadership develop a sensitivity to the preferences of their respective constituencies, but the problem of assembling a voting majority and holding it together makes popularly elected officers especially receptive, or at least accessible, to comparatively small groups requesting particular courses of action. Upsets at the polls are sufficiently frequent in New York to keep even the most strongly entrenched machines from becoming excessively complacent. So, when groups in the city cannot get what they want in the market place at a price they are willing to pay, or when they find or believe they can obtain through governmental action economic advantages they are unable to extract from their competitors or suppliers or customers, they exercise the leverage upon city officials and employees afforded by the designed insecurity of these officials, and seek through political channels what they were unable to secure elsewhere. Frequently, maneuvers on the part of one group to procure municipal services precipitates countermeasures by opposed factions, and political battle is joined.

Therein lies a partial explanation of the unsymmetrical, sometimes illogical, pattern of city functions. There are heavy city commitments in some activities, peripheral involvement in others, and a complete abstention from still others. Being the outcome of a process of give and take among the members of the community who have discovered their political effectiveness vis-à-vis their government, the pattern of city service is neither neat nor always rational. Nor is it likely to be so long as it is shaped by the interaction of many groups with a municipal government vulnerable to the people's discontent.

Its Resources. No less important as a factor in the proneness of the people of New York City to look to their government for services is the vastness of its fiscal resources and its capacity by taxation and borrowing to spread over the

TABLE 14. FUNDED DEBT OUTSTANDING BY PURPOSE FOR WHICH ISSUED

	Funded debt outstanding July 1, 1957	Bonds issued 1957–1958	Maturities 1957–1958	Funded debt outstanding June 30, 1958
FUNDED DEBT ISSUED FOR PUBLIC ENTERPRISES				
Transit	$1,440,926,088.77	$100,250,000.00	$22,620,325.18	$1,518,555,763.59
Transit—Deficiency pensions	7,185,000.00	. . .	7,185,000.00	. . .
Transit—B.M.T. and I.R.T. pensions	3,100,000.00	4,050,000.00	1,100,000.00	6,050,000.00
Water supply	723,772,225.00	40,000,000.00	18,107,600.00	745,664,625.00
Docks and piers	161,632,938.07	6,350,000.00	13,973,913.05	154,009,025.02
Municipal airports	36,988,531.19		2,090,356.00	34,898,175.19
Municipal ferries	16,300,426.12	693,711.06	3,107,302.23	13,886,834.95
Public markets	17,568,156.52	55,183.35	408,058.65	17,215,281.22
Sewage treatment works	101,697,828.37	7,089,830.96	4,569,691.37	104,217,967.96
Off-street parking	861,550.43	399,622.27	302,799.43	958,373.27
Parking meters	1,515,815.19	736,929.68	105,228.19	2,147,516.68
Total, Public enterprises	$2,511,548,559.66	$159,625,277.32	$73,570,274.10	$2,597,603,562.88
FUNDED DEBT ISSUED FOR GENERAL CITY PURPOSES				
Educational:				
Schools including Housing	$502,348,759.49	$146,275,000.00	$55,952,362.43	$592,671,397.06
Colleges	26,199,650.35	6,600,000.00	3,122,878.00	29,676,772.35
Libraries	15,682,531.65	904,701.21	1,909,186.78	14,618,046.08
Recreation, Science, and Art:				
Museums	9,197,754.52	369,019.20	1,478,223.52	8,088,550.20
Gardens	1,526,382.39	121,570.84	198,749.73	1,449,203.50
Parks including Housing	52,238,350.85	3,704,443.82	7,227,029.54	48,715,765.13
Social Welfare:				
Public Baths	1,819,353.18		498,764.19	1,320,588.99
Correction	9,378,733.79	534,816.27	567,999.47	9,345,550.59
Welfare	12,108,434.60	1,197,783.36	1,539,269.77	11,766,948.19
Slum clearance	21,300,000.00	1,050,000.00	2,400,000.00	19,950,000.00

Public Safety:			
Armories	3,101,296.99		276,441.08	2,824,855.91
Fire	10,265,831.60	312,255.57	1,425,721.96	9,152,365.21
Police	7,746,707.51	1,147,231.95	1,044,552.49	7,849,386.97
Sanitation and Health:			
Health	7,042,334.43	117,201.28	515,449.52	6,644,086.19
Hospitals	175,557,160.94	10,711,010.46	17,198,551.22	169,069,620.18
Sanitation	37,310,054.93	4,203,079.77	6,323,628.16	35,189,506.54
Highways and Bridges:			
Bridges	70,520,278.24	6,086,826.52	12,231,618.26	64,375,486.50
Tunnels	18,590,177.88		684,151.00	17,906,026.88
Streets, roads, and sewers	71,530,593.03	4,152,561.22	10,157,492.56	65,525,661.69
Miscellaneous	18,048.10		3,156.82	14,891.28
Public Buildings and offices:			
Borough and county	28,534,730.32	367,798.67	1,495,043.87	27,407,485.12
Courts	36,478,857.84	3,848,696.41	1,487,440.29	38,849,113.96
Miscellaneous:			
Judgments and claims	19,600,000.00	18,500,000.00	7,175,000.00	30,925,000.00
Repaving	7,000,000.00	7,700,000.00	1,400,000.00	13,300,000.00
Demolition unsafe buildings	65,195.44	266,726.13	13,039.44	318,882.13
Social Security		29,500,000.00	..	29,500,000.00
Various purposes—undistributed		41,958,000.00	..	41,958,000.00
Deficiency in taxes	14,062,500.00		..	14,062,500.00
Total, General city purposes	$1,159,223,718.07	$288,728,722.68	$136,385,750.10	$1,311,566,690.65

FUNDED DEBT ISSUED FOR ASSESSABLE IMPROVEMENTS

Parks, parkways, and streets	$7,650,000.00		$2,250,000.00	$5,400,000.00
Streets, roads, and sewers	91,350,000.00	$60,000,000.00	32,600,000.00	118,750,000.00
Total, Assessable improvements	$99,000,000.00	$60,000,000.00	$34,850,000.00	$124,150,000.00
Total, Funded debt	$3,769,772,277.73	$508,354,000.00	$244,806,024.20	$4,033,320,253.53

SOURCE: *Annual Report* of the Comptroller of New York City, 1957–1958, p. 337.

entire community the cost of programs that would otherwise fall only upon entrepreneurs or users. If fire or police protection, or sanitation and health services, or education were paid for by immediate users alone, the cost would be beyond the reach of most of the population, and many who benefit from these services both directly and indirectly would escape their share of the burden. New York could not continue on this basis, and neither could any other city. But there are $32 billion worth of real property in New York, billions of dollars of manufacture and sales and services, billions of dollars of payrolls. These make the city possible, it is true, but the city government also makes them possible. So these resources are tapped to help pay for the public functions of the municipal government that enable the city as a community to continue. By taxing them, and by borrowing on the basis of the power to tax them, the city government compels everybody to pay some part of the governmental bill. And because the city government can do this, people who live here and want some service, a service unavailable at an economic price in the market place, often turn to their government for help (not always for themselves, incidentally, for some of the most ardent advocates of welfare programs do not benefit from them personally unless the community as a whole benefits). The government thus gets pushed into activities that, as a general rule, cannot pay for themselves, and is often pushed out again as soon as someone scents the possibility of personal gain. Thus, the over-all pattern of municipal governmental services will differ with respect to scope and quality over time.

Its Powers. People turn to government, third, because it is the chief social institution empowered to invoke force legitimately in support of its programs. Every organization has penalties at its disposal (discharge from a job, for example, or expulsion from a union, or withdrawal of business and transfer of accounts elsewhere), and some do not hesitate to use force illicitly. But only agents of the government are commonly regarded as having the "right" to take life, liberty, or property. What would be homicide, abduction, or larceny if done by others may be simple duty when performed by them. In fact, it is to agents of the government that one turns for protection of one's rights and property against infringement by others, for the use of force by private citizens even for admittedly justifiable ends will not ordinarily be tolerated. At bottom, these powers of government are based on the possession of the necessary instruments of force by governmental agents, and on a widespread feeling that it is proper for them to have and to exercise these instruments. For both reasons, most people will abide by governmental commands that they would immediately reject if the commands came from some other source.

Many times the city government does depend on this special capacity to elicit obedience. Anyone can buy land on which to put up a building, but the city can take land over the objections of the owners and compensate them later. Anyone can charge prices for a commodity or service, but the city can levy taxes unrelated to any *specific* work it performs. Buyers can bargain with sellers over the price and quality of goods and services, but the city can regulate both. When it appears to the supporters of a plan that the plan will fail unless this authority stands behind it, they usually try to get public officials to assume the responsibility.

Competing Demands for City Services

So the people of the city want services; they seek them wherever they can get them. Very often they do obtain them in the market place; but they also induce the city government to provide them when its vulnerability, resources, and powers make it the most convenient or logical choice. That is why service is one of the major goals of political action. Groups and individuals strive to influence the city to institute new services in the welfare, mental health, and public housing fields. They seek help for the aging, centers for the care of children of working mothers, and assistance to more limited clienteles (such as the hay fever sufferers, by the destruction of ragweed). The city is asked to inaugurate new programs of regulation. It clamped down on ticket brokers when scalping of theatergoers and sports fans reached scandalous proportions, and it began an investigation of private refuse collectors after complaints that this function had been taken over by racketeers. There are campaigns to expand existing services—efforts to get new schools, new playgrounds, traffic signals and police crossing-guards at dangerous intersections, heavier police protection, more subway trains—and to prevent the contraction of familiar operations—a sentiment which stymied the recommendations of the Mayor's Committee on Management Survey in 1952 that the number of firehouses in the city be reduced. At the same time, there have often been equally strenuous endeavors to induce the city to reject pleas for additional programs and to curtail existing services.

The quality of service is sometimes a bone of contention, too. How often will the sanitation trucks visit a given neighborhood? How often will a police officer patrol a particular street? How frequently will buses or subway trains operate over a route? Will a neighborhood have a full branch library with twenty or thirty thousand volumes and day and evening service, or a sub-branch open only twenty-five or thirty hours a week to administer a collection of four or five thousand books? There are people who care about these things, and they fight for them. The budget of the City of New York, large as it is, is not without limit, so every year the partisans of particular departments and programs mobilize their energies to get a greater share than they got before, or at least to keep their part from shrinking. Service is one of the series of great prizes at stake in the contest for influence over the city government.

Demands for Services by Other Governments

The participants in the city's politics are by no means confined merely to the city government in their search for governmental services. The state government represents an alternative or complementary set of opportunities, as does the federal government. The major contestants in the city's political system often compete with each other in these higher governmental arenas for the services which the city government lacks the money, the powers, or the disposition to perform, and the contestants use the resources they have in the city to aid them in these other battles for services. The services of the three separate levels of government are thus intertwined as stakes and prizes in the city's political contest.

THE STAKES OF POLITICS AS INCENTIVES

The rich variety of prizes, the wide range and high value of rewards, and the gravity of the stakes involved help explain why so many and such varied participants engage so continuously and so intensively in the city's politics. They are attracted by ideological stakes, public office, economic reward, and governmental services. Most participants strive simultaneously for combinations of these stakes and prizes, seeking them at whatever level of government seems strategically relevant.

The variety and richness of rewards available through the city's political system evoke and sustain a commensurate variety and energy in the contestants who participate competitively and cooperatively in the system. The vigor of the city's politics, and the measure of its democratic quality, are reflected in the number, variety, and strength of the groups that have a strong commitment to participate actively and regularly in the political process.

BIBLIOGRAPHY

GENERAL

The stakes of politics are discussed generally by Harold D. Lasswell in *Politics: Who Gets What, When, How*, Whittlesey House, New York, 1936, and in Harold D. Lasswell and Abraham Kaplan, *Power and Society*, Yale University Press, New Haven, 1950. No specific references cover all the stakes of politics in New York City; the sources cited at the end of chapters in this volume may all be regarded as relevant to this topic. However, for an overview of the objectives of political action in the city, consult the following:

GOVERNMENT AND ADMINISTRATION OF THE CITY
(arranged chronologically)

The Brown Book: A Biographical Record of Public Officials of the City of New York for 1898–99. M. B. Brown and Co., New York, 1899. A brief description of the scope and functions of the major city departments under the original charter of the consolidated city, followed by brief descriptions of city officials in executive, administrative, and legislative positions.

Bureau of Municipal Research, *Municipal Year Book of the City of New York, 1913.* J. W. Pratt Co., New York, 1913. For *1915*, Brooklyn Eagle Press, Brooklyn, N. Y., 1915. For *1916*, *1917*, Municipal Reference Library, New York. Detailed expositions of the principal organs of city government and their incumbents at the periods specified.

New York City Commissioners of Accounts and New York Bureau of Municipal Research, *Government of the City of New York: A Survey of Its Organization and Functions.* J. J. Little and Ives Co., New York, 1915. A survey of the city's governmental machinery.

Carman, Harry J., *The Street Surface Railway Franchises of New York City.* Columbia University Press, New York, 1919.

Arent, Lenora, *Electric Franchises in New York City.* Doctoral dissertation, Columbia University, 1919.

Caccavajo, Joseph, *Guide to the Municipal Government of New York.* Brooklyn Daily Eagle, Brooklyn, N. Y., 1924. A résumé of the salient features of the government of the period.

New York State, Constitutional Convention Committee, *New York City Government: Functions and Problems,* vol. 5 of *Reports and Studies.* Burland Printing Co., New York, 1938. A summary of the organization, functions, and problems of the city government.

Rankin, Rebecca B., editor, *New York Advancing: World's Fair Edition.* Municipal Reference Library, New York, 1939. Describes the functioning of the municipal government of the City of New York from 1934 through the first quarter of 1939, the first five years of the La Guardia administration.

New York Advancing: Victory Edition. Municipal Reference Library, New York, 1945. Describes the operations of the several branches of municipal government in the City of New York during the years 1939 through 1945, the last seven years of the La Guardia administration.

Guide to the Municipal Government of the City of New York. Record Press, New York, 1952. "The purpose of this book is to present in a concise and intelligible form the more important facts relating to New York's city government. It may be used as an authoritative and up-to-date manual of the governmental organization and administration of the city."

Institute of Public Administration, *Governmental Organization within the City of New York.* 5th ed. The Institute, New York, 1949. A brief but authoritative analysis of the city government.

New York City, Mayor's Committee on Management Survey, *Modern Management for the City of New York.* 2 vols. The Committee, New York, 1953. These volumes summarize the findings and conclusions of the Mayor's Committee on Management Survey and cite the special studies on which this report is based.

New York State, Temporary State Commission to Study the Organizational Structure of the Government of the City of New York, *Four Steps to Better Government of New York City: A Plan for Action.* 2 vols. The Commission, New York, 1953. Findings and recommendations of a body appointed by the Governor, concentrating on managerial, budgeting, and personnel problems.

Robson, William A., *Great Cities of the World.* Macmillan Co., New York, 1955. Contains an essay, "New York in Perspective," by Rexford Guy Tugwell, former head of the Department of City Planning.

Smith, Thelma, *Guide to the Municipal Government of the City of New York.* Record Press, New York, 1959. An authoritative presentation by an associate editor of the *Municipal Reference Library Notes.*

New York City, The City Record, *Official Directory.* The City Record, New York. This little volume (known unofficially as "The Green Book"), issued annually, contains basic information about agencies of all levels and all branches of government, the incumbents of the major offices, the licenses issued in the city, and so forth.

The City Record: Official Journal. Published daily except Sunday and legal holidays, this journal constitutes an official record of the offices, regulations, and services of the city government.

The New York Red Book. J. B. Lyon Co., Albany, N. Y. An illustrated, annual state manual, published since 1892. Information on elections, officeholders, and so forth.

WITH RESPECT TO FINANCES

Bird, Frederick L., *The Municipal Debt*. Mayor's Committee on Management Survey, New York, 1951. A description, analysis, and appraisal of debt policy and administration of the city.

Citizens Budget Commission, *Fiscal Facts Concerning the City of New York*. The Commission, New York, 1940. A twenty-year statistical summary of the city's finances.

Fiscal Facts Concerning the City of New York. The Commission, New York, 1947, vol. 2. A statistical summary of the city's finances.

Coler, Bird S., *Municipal Government as Illustrated by the Charter, Finances, and Public Charities of New York*. D. Appleton and Co., New York, 1900. The Comptroller of the city discusses the problems of the consolidated City of New York under its first charter.

Dun and Bradstreet, Inc., *The Finances of New York City*, New York, 1934.

Durand, Edward D., *The Finances of New York City*. Macmillan Co., New York, 1898.

Haig, Robert M., and Carl S. Shoup, *The Revenue Problem of the City of New York and a Proposed Program*. Mayor's Committee on Management Survey, New York, 1951. A broad survey of the fiscal position of the city. See also the technical monographs that accompany it.

Haig, Robert M., Carl S. Shoup, and Lyle C. Fitch, *The Financial Problem of the City of New York*. Mayor's Committee on Management Survey, New York, 1952. A comprehensive analysis of New York City finances.

Hauser, Hugo E., *Transit Unification and the Credit of New York City*. Gertler and Co., New York, 1935. The rapid transit situation on New York City and the effect of unification on the future financial position of the city.

Lehman, Herbert H., *The Finances and Financial Administration of New York City: Recommendations and Report of the Sub-Committee on Budget, Finance, and Revenue, of the City Committee on Plan and Survey*. Columbia University Press, New York, 1928. A report that preceded creation of the Bureau of the Budget.

Ma, Yin Ch'u, *The Finances of the City of New York*. Columbia University Press, New York, 1914. Doctoral dissertation, Columbia University. A comprehensive description of the taxing, budgeting, spending, and auditing processes of the city in 1914.

McGee, Cushman, *The Finances of the City of New York*. R. W. Pressprich and Co., New York, 1940.

New York City, Bureau of the Budget, *Budget*. The Mayor's annual recommendations for expenditures for current expenses and for taxes. The accompanying Mayor's Budget Message summarizes the main points of the budget.

New York City, Planning Commission, *Proposed Capital Budget [for each year] and the Capital Program for the Next Succeeding Five Calendar Years*. The Commission's recommendations for short-range and longer-range outlays for capital improvements by the city. Published annually.

New York City, *Annual Report of the Comptroller*. The official record of the city's fiscal operations.

Pound, Arthur, *The Golden Earth*. Macmillan Co., New York, 1935. The story of Manhattan's landed wealth.

CHAPTER III

Contestants for the Prizes
of the City's Politics

As ONE MIGHT EXPECT from the nature of the stakes, there is, within the context of agreement that unites the people of the city, a steady and vigorous competition for the rewards of political action.

The contestants fall into five groups: the party leaders, the public officials, the bureaucracies, the nongovernmental groups (including the press and the other mass media of communication), and the officials and bureaucracies of the state and federal governments involved in city affairs.

None of these categories is monolithic. Each has several components, and each component functions with considerable autonomy, although some categories have a nominal unity of mission and leadership. Nevertheless, because the elements here grouped into categories share many common attributes, they may be treated as classes for the purpose of organizing the discussion.

PARTY LEADERS

Efforts are made in some cities to operate the electoral system on a non-partisan basis. New York City, by contrast, has always been committed to the political party as a central institution in its governing processes. Party leaders, in consequence, are major participants in the city's politics.

A political party as an institution consists of two main elements: its members and its officers or functionaries. Party members may be dedicated partisans, or usually loyal members, or persons only lightly attached to their party. The main business of the parties is conducted by its officers, who make up the party organization. The party leaders are the contestants with whom we are here concerned.

The Functions of Party Leaders

The services that city party leaders perform are fourfold. First, by their controls over nominations, thus presenting in the general election only one candidate for each office, they reduce to manageable proportions the number of choices each voter is called upon to make. If the party organizations did not winnow out aspirants to office, and if their nominees did not ordinarily stand a better chance than independent candidates of emerging victorious, there might well be dozens of names for each post. Not only might such a situation overwhelm the electorate, but it would also increase the probability of a city government splintered into fragments without majority support.

Second, the leaders of the party organizations serve the city electoral system by keeping it competitive. In New York City they produce candidates even when the chances of winning seem slight. There is always an element of risk for anybody in or seeking office. In New York City even the strongest bastions have occasionally fallen, even the safest constituencies have sometimes been captured by the opposition. This uncertainty keeps candidates and officials more responsive to popular demands than they would be otherwise. The party organizations sometimes function as recruiters as well as filters and in so doing help create an atmosphere in which elections fulfill their many purposes.

Third, the party leaders serve candidates by providing the machinery needed to win votes. Even candidates for positions with the smallest constituencies—seats in the state Assembly, the lower house of the state legislature—must make their appeals to at least fifteen thousand voters in the smallest districts and from two to four times as many in more populous districts, while candidates whose constituencies comprise the entire city (for example, Mayor, President of the City Council, Comptroller; for statewide offices, including Governor and United States Senator; and for President and Vice President of the United States) must think in terms of electorates of two to three and a half million city voters. Sometimes, in a safe district, a nominee may not have to campaign at all; his party's label may be all he needs to win even though he himself, as a person, is virtually unknown. At other times, and invariably for the more prominent elective offices, candidates who fail to make their names and affiliations, if not their programs, familiar to the people run serious risks of being defeated even in areas regarded as almost certain.

Since every electoral contest in the city involves such large numbers of voters, acquainting electorates with candidates requires the services of an organization skilled and experienced in this kind of campaigning. Even a candidate with a great deal of money, a candidate with supporters who can afford to buy publicity and hire many people to help him, may be at a disadvantage in a struggle with a party unit that has been functioning as a team over a long period, knows its area intimately and has established lines of access and contact with the voters, and can, if necessary, enlist the support of prominent and influential ticket leaders of their own party to assist in their local cause. Organization itself, no less than money and manpower, is a valuable resource in the conduct of electoral campaigns. It is this resource, and often the others as well, that the party leaders put at the disposal of their candidates.

Fourth, in thus serving their candidates, the party organizations also serve the city's voters. In carrying the appeals of nominees to the public, party workers make it possible for voters to gain some familiarity with the personalities and issues in elections with little or no effort by the voters. They also familiarize the public with their respective party emblems and the programs with which the parties are associated. Thus, if an individual voter has for some reason not been reached by the parties' propaganda efforts, or has paid no attention to the candidates in the course of the campaigning, he can still form some reasonably reliable expectations about the behavior of the several candidates should they be elected to office. Without party organizations in a city the size of New York, voters would be deprived of many clues to the future actions of the candidates on which electoral choices presumably rest. To be confronted with the obligations to make selections among total unknowns is tantamount to having no option at all. The party leaders help to rescue the voters from this possible futility.

In New York City the services performed by the party organizations for candidates and electorate are by no means confined to contests for local office. On the contrary, it is the same organizations, the same party workers, who do the basic campaign jobs whether city, county, state, or federal positions are at stake. Their ranks may be swelled by temporary volunteers when major offices are to be filled, and their operations may be paralleled by various kinds of citizens' associations and similar groups of more or less amateur politicians, but the backbone of every campaign conducted in the city for every office from state assemblyman to President of the United States is the regular organizations of the established parties. It is on these regular, frontline troops of party warfare that every candidate who hopes to win votes in the city is compelled to depend, regardless of the office he seeks.

Although elections are the chief business of the party leaders, elective office is not the only prize of politics with which they are connected. Because of their influence over voters—that is, their vote-getting capabilities—party officials can make claims upon the elected officials whose victories they were instrumental in engineering, and such claims will almost always be heard and often satisfied. The claims extend to the selection of personnel to fill appointive positions and to the wide range of governmental decisions through which the other rewards of the political system are distributed. In part, these demands are asserted on behalf of party supporters, particularly for those leaders of groups whose help has been significant in votes, financial contributions, or useful public endorsement. Claims are also made by the party leaders for themselves, and they are often the recipients in the distribution of rewards.

Who the Party Leaders Are

The party leaders in the city's politics include, most importantly, the County Leaders (five in each major party), the Assembly District Leaders (usually one for each party in each of the city's 62 Assembly Districts, unless a party divides a district in order to recognize two or even three leaders), and the Election District Captains. If a party were staffed in each of the city's Election Districts, it would have about four thousand captains. Each party has also recognized woman suffrage by establishing for women the positions of co-leaders and co-captains, thus, in, effect doubling the number of party workers in the city. If both the major parties were fully organized, and if the leading minor party (the Liberal party) were assumed to be at half the organizational strength of a major party, then the total number of active party workers in the city would be about twenty thousand. Perhaps only in closely contested citywide elections would the number approach this level.

The party leaders who count most as participants in the city's governmental and political system are the County Leaders and the Assembly District Leaders—numbering about three hundred men and women in the two major parties combined. These are the party leaders who play important parts in the contest for, and the distribution of, the prizes in the city's politics.

The Party Leaders Compete with Each Other

The three hundred party leaders live in a highly competitive political system. Within each party, the five County Leaders compete and bargain with each other for citywide nominations and for City Hall appointments for their respective supporters. In statewide nominations, and for state and federal appointments, they compete and bargain also with party leaders of other counties. Within each county, each Assembly District Leader encounters similar competition and the necessities for bargaining and alliances with other leaders of his party for prizes outside the borders of his district. Unity is purchased by continuous bargaining and accommodation among the leaders.

Across party lines the party leaders are, of course, even more continuously competitive. The stakes of the contest are high and the incentives for victory correspondingly compelling. Alliances and accommodations across party lines are infrequent although not altogether absent. Party leaders find some currency of exchange across party boundaries in legislation, in influencing the decisions of executive and judicial officials, and in the exercise of compassion for some professional colleagues who have lost office in the contest. But the basic relationship across party lines is one of competition. It is in large part because they are the managers of conflict and competition in the city's politics that the party leaders have their distinctive part in the contest.

PUBLIC OFFICIALS

Public officials do not, once they have achieved office, cease their quest for the prizes of political action. On the contrary, they often intensify their efforts. They seek to consolidate or broaden their constituencies. They aspire to increase their own autonomy and bargaining power in the political system. They seek favorable alliances with other participants. They utilize their positions as springboards to higher positions, in the fashion common to members of all large organizations. They exert influence on governmental decisions dealing with public moneys—sometimes to further the agencies in which they serve, sometimes to promote programs to which they are psychologically and materially committed, sometimes to advance their own rates of compensation or other personal interests. They figure significantly in the formulation of decisions about governmental services, for these affect their prestige, their promotional opportunities, their work, their bargaining power. They seek many of the ideological and intangible rewards connected with governmental action, such as the satisfactions of public service and status in the community. All the stakes of politics, in short, are goals of those officials who are "in" the government as much as they are the objectives of those who manage the political parties or serve as members of the bureaucracies or who as "outsiders" are served or regulated by government.

The Distinctive Role of Public Officials

Public officials, however, are in a special position in the political process. They promulgate the official decisions of government and supervise the performance of the acts that translate the words of the formal decisions into deeds and objects. They are thus distributors of the rewards of politics as well as beneficiaries of the system and, therefore, are the targets of all who are interested in shaping public policy. They occupy the center of the governmental arena.

Statements of general policy binding on the people of the community take the form of duly authenticated constitutional amendments, statutes, executive orders, administrative regulations and directives, and other documents emanating formally from officialdom. And in them are imbedded decisions concerning the sharing of the prizes of politics—decisions about governmental services and regulations, about taxation and spending and borrowing, about organs of government and their powers and procedures, about individual citizen rights and privileges, about public employee appointments, promotions, punishments, and dismissals.

A Group of Many Parts

Although public officials as a group occupy a unique position in the governmental process, they are not a homogeneous group. They do not constitute a monolithic organization. On the contrary, they are divided into many segments having different loyalties, different perspectives, different aspirations, different—sometimes competing—objectives, different sources of influence, different jurisdictions. Seldom, if ever, do they function as a single unit.

Division by Branches of Government. Executives, legislators, and judges all are public officials, but their separation into comparatively independent organs makes for differences among them. They are subject to divergent pressures. Different expectations as to their roles on the part of the public and of their specific constituencies exert influence. The separate branches are sometimes rivals for control of public policy, and they are generally touchy about infringements on their powers. As individuals, they are unequally visible, chief executives being constantly in the limelight, most legislators, judges, and lesser executives operating in relative anonymity compared to the chief executives. Their functions and traditions vary. Executives have tended to assume the mantle of initiative in government, legislators the role of suspicious and restraining guardians, judges the posture of impartial referees. Necessarily, they often work cooperatively with each other and sometimes even slip into each other's roles. But the establishment of three branches of government separates the members of each from the members of the others in important respects treated in detail later on. The distinctions manifest themselves in the relations of the Mayor with the Board of Estimate of the city, and with the City Council; the relations of the Governor with the chambers of the state legislature; the contacts between the President and Congress. All these divisions have significant consequences for the roles of the officials and for the government and politics of New York City.

Mode of Accession and Tenure. Government officials are further classified according to whether they are elected or appointed, and whether their tenure in office is uncertain or stable. The manner in which they come to office and their job security produce disparate values and perceptions. Their own expectations and the expectations of others concerning their roles differ, and these differences produce competition as well as cooperation.

The number of elective officers is not large—less than four hundred; counting all elective officials voted for in the city, from state assemblyman to President of the United States. These officials have widely varied constituencies, and their terms of office range from two years for assemblymen and United States Representatives to fourteen years for some judges.

The number of appointed officials is much larger. Their total is in the thousands. They range from high-ranking executives and judges to minor functionaries of temporary significance. Some appointive officers serve at the pleasure of those who appoint them, some have fixed terms. Federal judges are appointed for life. Insofar as tenure may be a factor in the capacity of officials to ignore pressures from all sources, the federal judges are in the strongest position; they stay on while elected officials, and many appointed ones, come and go.

Functional Differences. Public officials are further differentiated by the kinds of services they perform, and the kinds of people for whom they perform them. Life for officials in the line agencies is different from that in the overhead or staff agencies. The officials who lead these different lives do not always display complete harmony with each other.

What is more, the agencies, whether line or overhead, have become highly specialized.[1] In the city government alone, more than fifty bureaus serve the public in a variety of ways, and some ten overhead agencies guide and supervise their operations. Public officials who head these agencies must often deal with clusters of fairly autonomous bureaus, each organized around a specialty. The officials heading these organizations must usually develop strong attachments to their agencies and to the programs they conduct. They become jealous of their jurisdictions, aggressive in their leadership against the competing claims of other officials heading other agencies.

Public Officials as a Heterogeneous Class. In sum, while it is useful to speak of "government" as an institution from which decisions emerge, each decision is promulgated and supervised by particular sets of officials. These officials are not a solid, undifferentiated, tightly integrated body; they are an aggregation of many parts, of many kinds. In the contest for the stakes of politics, it is the specific sets and combinations of officials, rather than the general class, that must be observed. But public officials are nevertheless major participants in the city's politics.

THE ORGANIZED BUREAUCRACIES

The employees who work in the city, whether for the federal, state, county, or city governments, are employed, for the most part, under some type of merit system—that is, a personnel system providing for entrance by examination, advancement by seniority and performance, wages and salaries under a job classification plan, and tenure during satisfactory service. In the six decades since the establishment of the Greater City and under the protections offered by the merit systems, the many separate bureaucracies in the city have slowly but steadily enhanced their claims to autonomy and have acquired status as major participants in the city's political life.

Their combined numbers are great—about 382,000 at the three levels of government in the city. Like the public officials, the bureaucrats have a special position in the political process. As individual employees and as the staffs of governmental bureaus they initiate small and great proposals for the formal signatures of officials, and in carrying out these and other policies and decisions they ordinarily possess great discretionary power. Like the officials,

[1] See Appendix C.

too, they are in the government and their agreement is usually essential to the goals of other major participants that require governmental action. As Luther Gulick has observed,

> Much of the actual discretion used in administration is used at the very bottom of the hierarchy, where public servants touch the public. The assessor who walks into the home and sees the furniture and the condition of the house, the policeman who listens to the motorist's story, the health inspector who visits the dairy, the income tax auditor who sees the return and interviews the taxpayer—all these people are compelled to exercise discretion, and more important discretion from the point of view of the citizen, than many other functionaries much farther up in the organization.[1]

In these ways the bureaucracies play key parts in setting the quality, the direction, and the intensity of governmental service and regulation, function-

TABLE 15. GOVERNMENT OFFICIALS AND EMPLOYEES, ALL LEVELS OF GOVERNMENT, IN NEW YORK CITY, 1958

Governmental jurisdiction	Number of personnel
New York City[a]	246,316
Port of New York Authority	4,335
New York State	20,400
Federal government	111,000
Total	382,051

[a] Includes the New York City Transit Authority, the Triborough Bridge and Tunnel Authority, and the New York City Housing Authority, with 46,111 employees.

SOURCES: Mayor's *Annual Report*, 1957; Port of New York Authority *Annual Report*, 1958; New York State Department of Labor.

ing not simply as claimants seeking satisfaction of their own demands, but also as dispensers of rewards or penalties.

But it is as organized, self-conscious, and cohesive groups that the bureaucracies have achieved status as participants in the city's political system. These associations are quite numerous. The membership of some of them is large. The power of others is measured by unusual cohesiveness or by strategic location in the city's governmental or political process. Thus, the associations of teachers, policemen, firemen, transit workers, and sanitation workers represent numbers which have great political significance, while the social workers, lawyers, engineers, accountants, and other relatively small groups depend for influence upon their professional unity and their strategic roles in the administration of public agencies. All seek allies inside or outside

[1] Gulick, Luther, "Politics, Administration, and 'the New Deal,' " *Annals of the American Academy of Political and Social Science*, vol. 169, September, 1933, p. 62.

the government itself. Their skills as contestants in the city's politics have steadily increased. In many situations their power is a crucial factor in determining how the prizes are distributed.

The Bureaucracies Are Not Monolithic

The bureaucracies share an important characteristic with the categories of party leaders and the public officials. Like them, the bureaucracies are not a monolithic category. Instead, like the public officials, they are separated by governmental levels, by functional differences, by a variety of closed personnel systems. Although they are found primarily in the executive branch of each of the three levels of government, the individual departments and bureaus tend to become strongholds of particular professions and trades.

As a result, there is not one large, unified bureaucracy in the city, but a number of separate bureaucracies. From time to time, some of them join with one another in a cooperative endeavor to achieve some common goal. Far more frequently, however, they function without much reference to one another, or in competition or conflict with one another.

The ranks of the bureaucracies are intersected by the many kinds of associations and societies into which they group themselves, or with which some among them affiliate. The workers in some departments and agencies—in the Sanitation Department and the New York City Transit Authority, for example—are strongly unionized and are affiliated with the labor movement. Professional personnel—doctors, lawyers, engineers, nurses, social workers, and others—are, on the other hand, generally members of the separate associations that speak for their specialties. Cutting across departmental lines are other types of organizations, the public service unions—the Civil Service Forum, the American Federation of State, County, and Municipal Employees. Still another type is represented by the Patrolmen's Benevolent Association. Associations of police officers from sergeant to captain function in the Police Department in much the same fashion as labor unions. Similar associations are found in the Fire Department. Indeed, it was even customary, during the depression decade, for eligibles—those who had passed civil service examinations and were registered on civil service eligible lists—to form numerous separate associations to promote their interests. In many of the larger agencies there are also religious fraternities—Catholic Holy Name Societies, Protestant St. George Societies, and Jewish Shomrim Societies—made up of employees of the same faith. These, too, often have political goals.

The bureaucracies are thus crisscrossed by all manner of groupings. There are groups whose functions derive from the existence and nature of the public bureaucracies—associations of public personnel administrators, civil service specialists and lawyers, labor relations lawyers specializing in governmental employee relations, civil service newspapers, civil service examination "cram" schools. Though not themselves part of the machinery of government in many cases, such groups promote the self-consciousness of bureaucrats as a segment of government and society, and stimulate the self-identification of parts of the bureaucracies as separate and distinct entities.

In the city's political contest, the several organized bureaucracies have come of age as leading and influential participants. They are divided and often competitive among themselves, but each major grouping has the capacity and inclination to assert its own separate and autonomous bargaining power, to offer inducements to allies, and to claim the privileges of its role as a member of the third category of major participants in the political life of the city.

NONGOVERNMENTAL GROUPS

Each of the thousands of governmental decisions reached yearly by party leaders, public officials, and the bureaucracies affects a possible interest of some New Yorkers. This is true not only of decisions impinging directly on the public—laws and ordinances, executive orders, judicial decisions, rules, regulations, adjudications and orders of administrative agencies—but also of many kinds of action often described as "internal" or "managerial"—budget directives, personnel directives, organization and reorganization plans. It is a rare piece of duly authenticated official paper that does not lead somebody to the conclusion that he, as a result of it, has either lost or gained ground in the struggle for political prizes. Concern with who get public office or employment and what they do when they have it is thus not confined exclusively to officials and employees themselves, or to party leaders. Private citizens, by definition not in the government, are deeply interested in what governments do. Though not often themselves seekers of public office, they may organize to intervene energetically in the decisions of who will occupy these positions. Though these organizations are not political parties, they are not far removed in tactics or accomplishments. Though not so large as the city electorate, and incapable by themselves of turning out government officials as an electorate can and does, they probably wield greater influence on the day-by-day activities of public officials and the bureaucracies than does the electorate as such. Though most of these groups do not think of themselves as political, they are often deeply involved and actively participant in the political process. No discussion of government and politics is complete without an analysis of these nongovernmental groups as contestants for the rewards of political action.

Spokesmen for Legitimate Interests

More than a century ago de Tocqueville commented on the tendency of Americans to form associations for every purpose; he was struck by the plenitude and variety of voluntary groups in American society and politics. Were he to return today and survey New York City, he would discover not only that the tendency still flourishes, but that it has, if anything, intensified over the years. No careful census of these nongovernmental groups in the city has ever been made, but the number seems to run at least to tens of thousands. This estimate comprises only those groups sufficiently well organized to have letterheads, telephones, and/or to appear in some published directory. Just these visible and respectable groups add up to an impressive total.

They are not all alike, of course. Some of them have a long history and have had a reputation of power and influence for decades; others are clearly transient and limited in power. They vary in membership from a few score to many thousands. To finance their activities, some nongovernmental groups depend on contributions by a limited number of sponsors, others on donations from the general public, and still others upon dues levied on their members. Their operating budgets range from a few hundred to several hundred thousand dollars a year. The work of smaller, less well-financed groups is generally performed by part-time, volunteer, and amateur workers. Some of the larger, or the more affluent, associations employ permanent, full-time, highly paid professional staffs and provide them with research and secretarial and clerical assistance. The differences among these organizations seem endless; no two groups are identical.

Many groups at one time or another attempt to exert influence on the selection of public officials and bureaucrats, on particular governmental programs, on individual governmental decisions and actions, or on any combination of these. Only a handful, however, are concerned primarily with government. The overwhelming majority are mobilized around other central interests, and active participation in the city's political process is merely one subsidiary phase of much broader sets of activities. Many organizations in the city are established as occupational groups to protect and promote the common interest of those engaged in particular kinds of work. These are the business and professional associations and the labor unions, of which there are thousands. Many others are organized on status lines, building their memberships on the basis of what people are rather than what they do. The most prominent and numerous of these are associations of persons of the same religion, national origin, or race, and the veterans' organizations. Others are territorial in character, some being identified with particular streets (the Fifth Avenue Association, the Twenty-third Street Association), others with particular neighborhoods. Some concentrate on individual governmental or social functions—for instance, health (usually a single disease), welfare (including a host of private charities), or education.

In addition, *ad hoc* groups spring up in relation to specific issues, such as fluoridation of water supplies, hazards to children, and the so-called baby-carriage brigades of mothers who throw road blocks across busy intersections of the city to compel the installation of traffic signals or the assignment of traffic patrolmen. Such groups may also force the modification of local conveniences, typified by the outraged birdwatchers who successfully prevented the destruction of a grove in Central Park favored by migrating birds, as well as by the indignant parents who stopped the transformation of a Central Park lawn from a play area used by their children into a parking lot.

At most, only a handful of associations can be identified as groups whose chief orientation is toward government and whose activities are confined almost exclusively to studying and influencing the conduct of government. The others intervene in the city's political process only when their special interests are at stake, devoting most of their energies to the relations of their members with each other and with other nongovernmental institutions.

This classification of the many kinds of interests of the legitimate nongovernmental groups in the city suggests the reason why every official decision and action, no matter how trifling it may seem, arouses a response from some element of the population. It suggests also the myriad patterns of coalition and conflict that can be expected to develop over time. Most nongovernmental groups can be classed as logically in one category as another. Borough-wide business associations and professional societies, for example, stress their territorial nature at some times and their occupational nature at others. Religious, welfare, and labor agencies behave now as status groups and now as functional groups. Many groups that make common cause with respect to one policy may end up on opposite sides of the fence when another is involved. In fact, it is often difficult to predict which stand a given group will take because one of its interests may lead it in one direction, another in a contrary direction. The context of the city's politics and its governmental decision-making is therefore always complicated and volatile.

Another useful way of looking at the city's nongovernmental groups is to examine the scope of their interests and the degree of persistence with which they pursue those interests. The groups can thus be plotted on a chart formed by the intersection of two scales (see Chart 7): a horizontal scale of scope of political interest ranging from narrow to broad, and a vertical scale of degree of persistence ranging from high to low.

In the first quadrant fall those groups with a wide range of interests and a record of continual intervention in the formulation of political and governmental decisions. This quadrant is sparsely populated, for it is confined primarily to the city's civic groups and the communication media. The second quadrant comprises the groups displaying high persistence in relatively narrow segments of the whole spectrum of political action. While it contains groups of every kind, the most prominent class is those groups defined above as having functional interests. The second quadrant is more heavily populated than the first, but far less so than the third. The third quadrant includes all those groups that participate only intermittently in the political or governmental process, and only in relation to decisions that impinge directly and heavily on their special interests. The great bulk of the nongovernmental groups in the city are found here. The fourth quadrant is almost empty, for there are few groups that have a broad range of political interests yet intervene only intermittently in governmental decisions.

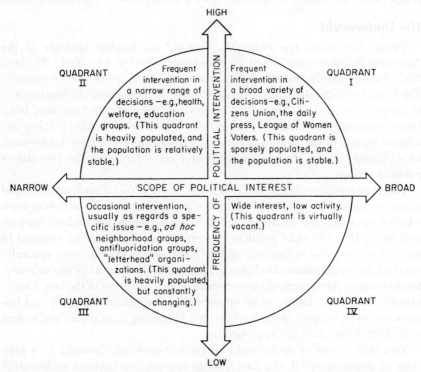

HIGH

QUADRANT II — Frequent intervention in a narrow range of decisions —e.g.,health, welfare, education groups. (This quadrant is heavily populated, and the population is relatively stable.)

QUADRANT I — Frequent intervention in a broad variety of decisions—e.g., Citizens Union, the daily press, League of Women Voters. (This quadrant is sparsely populated, and the population is stable.)

POLITICAL INTERVENTION

NARROW ← SCOPE OF POLITICAL INTEREST → BROAD

FREQUENCY OF

Occasional intervention, usually as regards a specific issue — e.g., *ad hoc* neighborhood groups, antifluoridation groups, "letterhead" organizations. (This quadrant is heavily populated, but constantly changing.)

Wide interest, low activity. (This quadrant is virtually vacant.)

QUADRANT III

QUADRANT IV

LOW

CHART 7. CLASSIFICATION OF NONGOVERNMENTAL GROUPS BY SCOPE OF POLITICAL INTEREST AND FREQUENCY OF POLITICAL INTERVENTION IN GOVERNMENTAL DECISION-MAKING

Any single group in the first quadrant is likely to have a greater impact on a larger number of governmental decisions than any single group in the other quadrants. Similarly, any single group in the second quadrant is likely to affect a larger number of decisions than any single group in the third quadrant. It may well have greater influence on a particular decision within its special area of competence than any group in any quadrant, but it will normally play a role in fewer decisions than any group in the first quadrant. A group in the third quadrant may occasionally be exceedingly influential in an individual instance, but the number of such instances is likely to be low. Groups in the fourth quadrant rarely exercise much influence at all.

Some political issues bring out large numbers of groups, most bring out a few who are directly interested, a few bring out only the civic groups, and the civic groups may well turn up to take sides on any issue. The most significant fact for the city's politics, perhaps, is that there are few enduring alliances uniting any substantial number of these groups. They are incurably pluralistic, competitive, specialized in their interests, jealous of their separate identities.

The Underworld

Twenty-five years ago Denis W. Brogan,[1] an English observer of the American political scene, noted the importance of what he called "the three B's"—betting, booze, and brothels—in state and local politics in this country. The repeal of prohibition has greatly reduced the importance of bootlegging, although some still continues by evaders of liquor tax and customs laws. Illegal gambling, organized prostitution, and narcotics sales remain significant factors in the politics of the city, and organizers of these trades must be reckoned among the nongovernmental contestants for the rewards of political action.

The gross business of these three "trades" in New York City is often alleged to run to hundreds of millions of dollars annually. Since the activities from which these revenues, whatever their actual magnitude, are derived are proscribed by law, the chief political concern of the organizations engaged in them is to ease the stringency of law enforcement. While they naturally conduct their operations clandestinely, they cannot afford to be too secretive, for they might thus escape their customers as well as agents of the law. Consequently, they must induce some appropriate governmental officials and bureaucrats to be tolerant of them while they are plying their trades and lenient with them when they are apprehended.

Two other types of underworld enterprise seemingly brought to a high stage of development in the past quarter century are business racketeering and labor racketeering. The "business" groups often assume the guise of trade associations of the kind that regulate conditions in an industry and defend the interests of the industry both economically and politically. Under this protective coloration, some alleged business associations have taken to providing "services" for their members, which often means nothing more than that they will refrain from committing violence upon their victims if the victims join the association and contribute regularly to it. In the same fashion the "labor" gangs often disguised as unions threaten work stoppages and violence in order to exact tribute from employers. In trucking and on the waterfront these methods have been employed to prevent action by employers

[1] *Government by the People.* Harper and Bros., New York, 1933, pp. 240–245.

and insurance companies against organized and large-scale pilferage. Both kinds of racketeers have been known to use their gains to influence some party leaders, public officials, and bureaucrats, particularly to safeguard themselves against suppression by law enforcement. Strenuous efforts are made by business associations, labor unions, and law enforcement agencies to eliminate these illegitimate organizations. But stamping out criminal elements masquerading as legitimate groups has proved not to be an easy task; they continue to exist and to wield an influence in some sections of the political arena.

These underworld groups concentrate a very high proportion of their energies and resources on mitigating the severity of law enforcement. There are some political tactics and strategies these groups cannot use because they are anxious to stay out of the public eye, but, in trying to get friendly people into office and affecting the behavior of those already in office, their practices are not fundamentally different from those of other nongovernmental groups. Many respectable individuals and nongovernmental groups resort to techniques in their endeavors to sway the behavior of public servants (such as inspectors, tax assessors, and law-enforcement officers) that are hardly distinguishable in kind from those of underworld groups. Legitimate groups and underworld groups can be distinguished from each other, but nongovernmental groups of all types share many characteristics in connection with their strivings for the rewards of political action.

THE SPECIAL ROLE OF THE PRESS

Like the other institutions of the city, the mass communication media are often profoundly affected by governmental actions and decisions. In this respect, they are classed with other nongovernmental groups.

In other respects, however, they are special and a class apart. In the first place, they are not merely contestants in the great game of the city's politics, they are also the principal channel through which all other contestants reach the general public; hence, they have a great impact—usually deliberately, sometimes inadvertently—on some governmental and party decisions. In the second place, the popular image of government and politics depends heavily on the information supplied by the communication media. The whole tenor, the atmosphere, of political contest is colored by their presentations and portrayals. While it perhaps cannot be said that the mass media are more powerful than other nongovernmental participants in the political and governmental process, it is clear that they occupy a unique position.

Among the various media, the daily newspapers undoubtedly play a larger role than any other. As compared with radio and television, their coverage is more complete; more of their total output is devoted to news reporting and commentary, which is their chief function rather than a subsidiary one. As compared with news magazines, news of special interest to

New York City, whether it happens in New York, Albany, Washington, or elsewhere, receives fuller attention in the city's press. The magazines are addressed primarily to national audiences and are consequently unable to give as much play to issues of local concern. In addition, the newspapers maintain staffs at City Hall and Albany as well as in Washington, and they have subject-matter specialists—in real estate, finance, civil service, traffic management, ship and port news, and other fields—who pick up and follow items that radio and television networks, and even magazines, are not so well equipped to handle. Finally, the newspapers allocate much space to columns, feature stories, letters to the editor, and editorials which take public position

TABLE 16. MAJOR ENGLISH-LANGUAGE DAILY NEWS-
PAPERS WITH CITYWIDE CIRCULATION IN
1901 AND 1959

1901	1959
Evening Journal	Daily Mirror
Evening Telegram	Daily News
New York American	Journal-American
New York Evening Post	New York Herald Tribune
New York Evening Sun	New York Post
New York Herald	New York World-Telegram and Sun
New York Tribune	The New York Times
New York World	
The New York Times	

SOURCE: N. W. Ayer and Sons, *Directory of Newspapers and Periodicals*, New York, 1959.

on local issues and candidates. Admittedly, parties and candidates have been putting increasing emphasis on purchased time on television and radio to carry their messages to mass audiences, but the newspapers are still far ahead in regular news coverage. Although television has shown signs of becoming a strong competitor in this respect, special political programs on New York State and New York City having been recently introduced, it has still not seriously challenged the predominance of the press. As influences on the nature and outcome of the city's contest for the stakes of government power, the daily newspapers are still the preponderant medium of mass communication in New York City politics.

In common with the other categories of nongovernmental contestants seeking to influence the choice and behavior of party leaders, public officials, and bureaucrats, newspapers do not constitute a solid, unified bloc. They do share certain common attributes—the tendency to give greater prominence to stories about wrongdoing and inadequacy than to reports of positive accomplishment, to stress conflict and contradiction in government and politics more than harmony and cooperation, to cast party leaders in a less flattering light than people who allegedly stay "out of politics." This consensus is important, for it presents a virtually unanimous characterization of the political and governmental process to the people of the city. In the handling of specific issues, however, in balance of coverage between competing viewpoints and groups and parties, in sensationalism or suffocation in the treatment of particular events, in editorial stands and political alignments, the newspapers differ widely.

They differ partly because they reflect the personal preferences of their publishers and partly because they have different audiences. The two factors are related, but they are also distinguishable. With regard to the former, the editorial position and manner of news presentation in the chief newspapers

TABLE 17. WEEKDAY CIRCULATION OF MAJOR
ENGLISH-LANGUAGE DAILIES IN NEW YORK, 1958[a]

Newspaper	Circulation
Daily Mirror	880,000
Daily News	2,057,000
Journal-American	564,000
New York Herald Tribune	335,000
New York Post	344,000
New York World-Telegram and Sun	454,000
The New York Times	600,000

[a] Does not include essentially trade journals (for example, *The Wall Street Journal, Women's Wear Daily*).
SOURCE: N. W. Ayer and Sons, *Directory of Newspapers and Periodicals*, New York, 1959.

of the city—the seven English-language, secular dailies—are shaped in large measure by their owners. The political tone of the *Daily Mirror* and the *New York Journal-American* mirror the conservative Republican leanings of the Hearst family, of whose newspaper empire they are a part. The *Daily News* embodies the rather similar views of the Patterson-McCormick interests which also own *The Chicago Tribune*. The *New York World-Telegram and Sun* speaks for the Scripps-Howard chain, whose principal owner is emphatically Republican, though somewhat less conservative. The liberal Republicanism of the Reid family (and of its new owner, John H. Whitney) is consistently evident in the *New York Herald Tribune*. Arthur Hays Sulzberger's middle-of-the-road predilections can be seen in the journalistic and editorial policies of *The New York Times*. The *New York Post* exhibits the political predisposition toward the liberal wing of the Democratic party and toward the Liberal party of its publisher, Mrs. Dorothy Schiff. Under other ownerships, each of these journals would probably follow other patterns of news coverage and analysis and adopt other editorial positions.

The three tabloids—the *Mirror*, the *News*, and the *Post*—and the *Journal-American* rely extensively on sensationalism, and often a lurid sensationalism, to attract readers. As a result, a great deal of political news in general, and local news in particular, is relegated to the inside pages, although each has a weekly column devoted exclusively to local political affairs. In their simplified style, their sensational subject matter, and the dominance of popular features over extended news coverage, these papers seem to appeal to audiences seeking entertainment as eagerly as information. The *World-Telegram and Sun* appears in many ways to have patterned itself after the small-city, family newspaper, giving a great deal of its space to family features and local affairs. In contrast, *The Times* and the *Herald Tribune* stress their information function and apparently strive for reporting that is both broad and intensive, for

TABLE 18. CIRCULATION OF MAJOR BOROUGH-ORIENTED ENGLISH-LANGUAGE DAILIES IN NEW YORK, 1958[a]

Newspaper	Circulation
Brooklyn Daily	32,000
Long Island Advocate	18,000
Long Island Press	275,000
Long Island City Star-Journal	92,000
Queens Evening News	10,000
Staten Island Advance	47,000

[a] Dozens of less frequent neighborhood papers appear throughout the city.

Source: N. W. Ayer and Sons, *Directory of Newspapers and Periodicals*, New York, 1959.

balance and sobriety, and for education in their articles and columns. Since no systematic studies of the newspaper-reading habits of New Yorkers have been published, not much is known about the overlap of the audiences of the several journals. But it would appear that the readers of *The Times* and the *Herald Tribune*, on the average, have more formal schooling, higher incomes, and clerical, managerial, or professional jobs.

Circulation is the lifeblood of a newspaper; without it, there are no revenues of any kind. Having established their audiences, the newspapers of New York City are more or less compelled to continue to appeal to them, since a drastic change in the nature of a newspaper may cost it its own regular readers without winning away readers of other papers in the field it attempts to invade. Thus, a newspaper's readership is determined in part by what the newspaper itself becomes. At the same time, once a newspaper is established, what it can become is limited by the composition of its following. Moreover, the kind and quantity of advertising the newspapers attract—advertisers are the other component of their constituencies—is a function of the number and status of their readers. For this reason, although those that compete for the same readers imitate and resemble one another, they are not altogether alike. While it is useful to consider newspapers a category, the category cannot be regarded as homogeneous.

What has been said of the seven major journals applies even more force-fully to the other newspapers published in the city. While all occupy the special position of the press on the political stage, there is great variation among them growing out of differences in the opinions of their owners and publishers and differences in their audiences. Dozens of newspapers, not counting the house organs of many companies and trade unions and trade

TABLE 19. WEEKDAY CIRCULATION OF MAJOR DAILY
NEWSPAPERS PRINTED IN FOREIGN LAN-
GUAGES, IN NEW YORK CITY, 1958

Language	Number of newspapers	Combined circulation of all newspapers published in each language[a]
Arabic	1	3,000
Chinese	4	39,000
Slovak	1	20,000
German	1	21,000
Greek	2	32,000
Italian	1	Not given[b]
Polish	1	25,000
Russian	3	31,000
Spanish	2	69,000
Yiddish	3	133,000

[a] In addition, some 35 other foreign-language newspapers appear weekly, biweekly, or triweekly, three Negro newspapers appear weekly, and many other foreign, Negro, or religious publications appear monthly.
[b] 61,000 in 1956.
SOURCE: N. W. Ayer and Sons, *Directory of Newspapers and Periodicals*, New York, 1959.

TABLE 20. CIVIL SERVICE NEWSPAPERS (WEEKLIES)
IN NEW YORK CITY, 1958

Newspaper	Circulation
The Chief	42,000
The Civil Service Leader	86,000

SOURCE: N. W. Ayer and Sons, *Directory of Newspapers and Periodicals*, New York, 1959.

associations but including all commercial newspaper enterprises, appear in New York City. Most of them are relatively obscure neighborhood weeklies and bimonthlies, but the roster also includes the *Wall Street Journal*, many distinguished foreign-language papers, several trade journals of note, and a few significant religious newspapers. Many of these exhibit little interest in the government and politics of New York City, and none compares in influence on the local scene with the major dailies. In connection with specific governmental or party decisions—frequently as specific as an individual administrative action—they will occasionally employ as much influence as they can muster to affect the course of events.

The communication media, and particularly the newspapers, are like the political parties in the sense that they are instruments on which the democratic governmental system depends but are not part of the official machinery of that system. At the same time, being business enterprises, they resemble in status and behavior other nongovernmental groups. In this dual capacity they are not only able to claim some of the rewards of political action for themselves, but they also figure prominently in the process by which the rewards of other contestants are distributed.

OFFICIALS AND BUREAUCRATS OF THE STATE AND FEDERAL GOVERNMENTS

As we have seen earlier, the public officials and the organized bureaucracies of the city are each an important class of participants in the city's politics. So, too, are many of the public officials and the bureaucracies of the state and federal governments. These officials and bureaucracies are, of course, primarily participants in their own separate political and governmental systems, but the intervention of many of them in the city's political system is sufficiently frequent and important to give them the status of major participants in the city system.

Almost every federal and state governmental agency has an office in the city. Several state agencies have their main offices here. State and federal courts are located in the city. More than 130,000 members of state and federal bureaucracies work in the city. Since the public officials who direct these activities and the bureaucracies who perform them make a multitude of decisions concerning governmental services to be provided, the governmental regulations to be imposed, the spending and collecting of public money, the distribution of public office and employment, they become perforce major participants in the city's political system, dealing continuously or frequently as the case may be with city officials, bureaucracies, party leaders, the leaders of the city's nongovernmental groups and the press, as well as directly with the citizens to whom they provide services or whose behavior they regulate.

The city's political system also has representatives in the state and federal systems. There are the city's delegation in the United States House of Representatives, the claims the city has upon the two United States Senators from New York, and the federal executives and judges whose appointments depend upon their connections with the city's political system. There are, further, the city's delegations to the two houses of the state legislature, the claims of the city upon the statewide elected executives (the Governor and others) and upon the state's elected judges whose electoral constituencies include the city, and the appointed state executives and judges whose selection and tenure is connected with its political system.

The officials and bureaucracies of the state and federal governments become major participants in the city's government and politics in several important ways. They distribute some of the prizes of office and employment for which the other contestants compete—for example, federal judgeships, postmasterships, state executive posts. They provide governmental services to the people of the city, in competition with or in addition to services provided by the city government—for example, postal service, highway construction. They initiate, administer, and exercise discretion under numerous statutes and rules governing many opportunities and liabilities of the city's residents. They grant or refuse to grant large sums of money for the support of city government activities (for example, federal aid in urban renewal, state aid for general governmental support, education, and many other city government programs). They supervise city officials and bureaucrats in many ways: through state legislative statutes, the regulations and rules of state executive and administrative agencies, the power to investigate, to criticize, and even to remove city officials. These are the ever-present, powerful levers with which federal or state officials and bureaucracies exercise their influence as participants in the city's political and governmental contest.

The officials and the bureaucracies of the state and federal governments, as contestants in local politics, share many of the characteristics of the other participants. They are not a monolithic group. Party lines often divide them. Function separates them. Differences in mode of selection and conditions of tenure introduce additional divisions among them. The degree of their dependence upon, or relative autonomy from, the city's political system produces different behavior. Their separate career aspirations are another source of differing attitudes and actions among both officials and bureaucrats. In short, like the other major categories of contestants, they are also pluralistic in composition, competitive with each other, playing their roles in the city's politics as many separate sets of officials and bureaucrats, each relating its strategy to the particular environment in which it finds itself. But, as a distinguishable category of participants, the state and federal officials and bureaucrats constitute a set of important contestants in the city's political life.

THE ELECTORATE

In the last analysis, the whole pattern of the distribution of the stakes of city politics is shaped by the electorate of the city.[1] Every electoral contest for

---

[1] As will be seen later, voters can be regarded as a number of electoral constituencies rather than as one. Elective government offices, party posts, and nominations made in primary elections all have different constituencies. Different numbers of voters appear in different years, when different offices are at stake, and, in any given election or primary, the number of ballots cast for different offices in any given election district also will vary.

government or party office, or for a nomination, is decided ultimately by the relevant constituency of voters. They thus determine who will fill the key positions in the political system, and they thereby determine which office seekers and officeholders will be rewarded. Moreover, their electoral choices profoundly affect the selection of appointive personnel and the lines of access and communication and pressure carefully developed over the years between elections by all the contestants—nongovernmental as well as party and official—for the stakes of political power. The preferences and behaviors of the electorate change often enough to keep the entire system highly fluid. By their actions, the voting constituencies can work more drastic transformations in the disposition of the stakes of politics than any other participants in the political process.

Party leaders, officials, candidates, and others envisage and solicit the support of a great variety of constituencies within the electorate: borough-conscious constituencies, ethnic constituencies, racial constituencies, religious constituencies; home-owning constituencies, rent-paying constituencies, tax-conscious constituencies; partisan constituencies and "independent" constituencies; and so on through a seemingly endless series. These are usually, to the extent they exist at all, amorphous sets of forces. They influence the stakes of politics largely as indirect factors in the calculations and strategies of other contestants.

Only in the most general sense, then, can these specialized electorates be said to share in those stakes. Their claims are so diffuse, their heterogeneity so pronounced, their tolerance for the neglect of campaign promises so generous, and the connection between their nebulous mandates and the day-to-day decisions and activities of governmental officials and party officers so tenuous, that it is difficult to identify anything that might meaningfully be called a reward. The city's voters speak in a thunderous voice, but largely in generalities. Yet whatever any contestant gets, or is denied, can be traced in the end to what the electoral constituencies do.

The loose-knit organizations of party leaders, the multitude of officeholders and office seekers, the numerous organized and specialized bureaucracies, the plethora of nongovernmental groups, the media of mass communication (especially the press), and the many-faceted city electorate constitute the dramatis personae of the vast and intricate spectacle that is the government and politics of New York City. Each category is itself immensely complicated, and the interactions among them are exceedingly complex. The stakes they pursue are high, as befits the first city of the nation and of the world, a city created by the competitive as well as the cooperative efforts of eight million people.

THE BROAD CONTEXT OF AGREEMENT

Portraying the city's politics as a contest among individuals and groups focuses attention on its most exciting and dynamic elements—the rivalry, competition, conflict, bargaining, and maneuvering; the alliances and coalitions; the victories and defeat—out of which public policy emerges. Even in totalitarian societies, where the opportunities for ordinary citizens to assert their demands and to organize to press for them without the sanction of the ruling cliques are tightly circumscribed, there are some evidences that this bargaining process occurs. In a democratic polity such as New York City enjoys, prevailing political values not only tolerate such a contest, they encourage it. Most New Yorkers doubtless regard it not as a privilege, but as a *right*, and many consider it a *duty*, to participate. Widespread contest over office and over governmental decisions is thus not a pathology of democratic government, but a sign of its vigor. The study of opposing forces in New York City politics is in this sense an inquiry into the operation of a democracy.

But the analogy of the contest must not be carried too far. The city is not an example of a Hobbesian "war of all against all." The contest takes place in an environment of agreement, within a matrix of accepted rules and a context of cooperation. The observer who lifts his eyes to the broader scene can hardly fail to be struck also by the degree of concord, mutual accommodation, and good will characteristic of the city. Bargaining and mutual concession, not stubborn rigidity, are also hallmarks of its politics.

BIBLIOGRAPHY

THE DIVERSITY OF PARTICIPANTS IN THE POLITICAL CONTEST

Bercovici, Konrad, *Around the World in New York*. Century Co., New York, 1924.

Bomar, W. Melmoth, *I Went to Church in New York*. Graymond Publishers, New York, 1937. Churches of all faiths in New York.

Bone, Hugh A., *American Politics and the Party System*. McGraw-Hill Book Co., New York, 1949, chaps. 3, 5, 6, 8, 9, 16, 17. This basic party text describes some broad categories of participants in politics.

Common Council for American Unity, *Around the World in New York: A Guide to the City's Nationality Groups*. The Council, New York, 1950.

Dworkis, Martin B., *The Impact of Puerto Rican Migration on Government Services in New York City*. New York University Press, New York, 1957.

Glazer, Nathan, "New York's Puerto Ricans," *Commentary*, vol. 26, December, 1958, pp. 469–478.

Herring, Pendleton, *The Politics of Democracy*. Rinehart and Co., New York, 1940. The role of the public bureaucracy is examined in Chapter 28, Can Officials Be Neutral?

Key, V. O., Jr., *Politics, Parties and Pressure Groups*. 4th ed. Thomas Y. Crowell Co., New York, 1958. Although this is a general textbook, its excellent treatment of the participants in politics is directly relevant to the discussion here. See especially chaps. 3–6, 13, 25.

Kranzler, George, *The Jewish Community of Williamsburg, Brooklyn, New York*. Doctoral dissertation, Columbia University, 1954.

McKean, Dayton D., *Party and Pressure Politics*. Houghton Mifflin Co., Boston, 1949. The multiplicity of pressure groups, treated generally, is discussed in chaps. 6, 11–13, 20–28.

Morsell, John A., *The Political Behavior of Negroes in New York City*. Doctoral dissertation, Columbia University, 1951.

The New York Times, "New York—Coliseum City," *The New York Times*, sec. 6, part 2, April 29, 1956. Articles on the variety of activities and groups—economic, religious, cultural—in the city, each constituting a separate "interest."

Rand, Christopher, *The Puerto Ricans*. Oxford University Press, New York, 1958.

Truman, David B., *The Governmental Process*. Alfred A. Knopf, New York, 1955. Groups in the political process.

Zeller, Belle, *Pressure Politics in New York*. Prentice-Hall, New York, 1937. A study of group representation before the state legislature.

Zink, Harold, *Government of Cities in the United States*. Macmillan Co., New York, 1949. Chapter 14 treats municipal pressure groups.

THE PRESS AND POLITICS IN NEW YORK CITY

Barnes, Joseph, "Reminiscences." Columbia University Oral History Collection, Special Collections, Butler Library. Mass media assessed by an editor and co-owner of the *New York Star* and reporter on the *New York Herald Tribune*.

Berger, Meyer, *The Story of The New York Times*. Simon and Schuster, New York, 1951. A reporter's history of a newspaper whose editorials and news columns have repeatedly affected the politics and policies of the city.

Blankenhorn, Heber, "Reminiscences." Columbia University Oral History Collection, Butler Library. Includes appraisals of the work and influence of several New York newspapers.

Carlson, Oliver, and Ernest S. Bates, *Hearst: Lord of San Simeon*. Viking Press, New York, 1936. A biography of a famous publisher who was prominent in the politics of the city for many years.

Davis, Elmer, *History of The New York Times: 1851–1921*. The New York Times, New York, 1921. Contains many examples of how a newspaper can influence municipal government.

Duffus, Robert L., "Reminiscences." Columbia University Oral History Collection, Special Collections, Butler Library. An eminent journalist's recollections, including appraisals of newspapers in the life of the city.

Lundberg, Ferdinand, *Imperial Hearst: A Social Biography*. Equinox Co-operative Press, New York, 1936. The work and influence of the famous newspaper publisher who played a large part in the governing of the city.

McClaim, Russell Harding, *The New York Express: Voice of Opposition*. University Microfilms, Publication no. 12,065. Ann Arbor, Mich. Doctoral dissertation, Columbia University, 1955. The history and influence of one of the predecessors of the present *World-Telegram and Sun*.

Nevins, Allan, *The Evening Post: A Century of Journalism*. Boni and Liveright, New York, 1922. A history of a New York newspaper by a famous historian who was a newspaperman before becoming a teacher.

O'Brien, Frank M., *The Story of the Sun: 1833–1928*. D. Appleton and Co., New York, 1928. A history of an influential city newspaper.

Prendergast, William A., "Reminiscences." Columbia University Oral History Collection, Special Collections, Butler Library. Recollections about William Randolph Hearst and the influence of his newspapers in the early years of the century.

Regier, C. C., *The Era of the Muckrakers*. University of North Carolina Press, Chapel Hill, N. C., 1932. The power of the press to influence public affairs in New York City, among other places.

Rodgers, Cleveland, "Reminiscences." Columbia University Oral History Collection, Special Collections, Butler Library. A memoir that includes recollections of the Brooklyn *Eagle*, 1906–1937.

Stern, J. David, "Reminiscences." Columbia University Oral History Collection, Special Collections, Butler Library. Reflections on the *New York Post* by a former owner.

Tebbel, John, *The Life and Good Times of William Randolph Hearst*. E. P. Dutton and Co., New York, 1952. A biographical study of the newspaper publisher who exerted great influence on city politics.

Thacher, Thomas D., "Reminiscences." Columbia University Oral History Collection, Special Collections, Butler Library. The Chairman of the Charter Revision Commission that drafted New York City's present charter evaluates the effect of mass communication media on the campaign for adoption in 1936.

Walker, Stanley, *City Editor*. Frederick A. Stokes Co., New York, 1934. Contains evidence of the influence of a newspaper (*New York Herald Tribune*) on city and national affairs.

Winkler, John K., *William Randolph Hearst*. Hastings House, New York, 1955. A biography of a publisher influential in the politics of New York City.

VICE AND THE UNDERWORLD IN NEW YORK CITY

Arm, Walter, *Pay-Off! The Inside Story of Big City Corruption*. Appleton-Century-Crofts, New York, 1951. The "unholy alliance" between gamblers and law enforcement agencies discussed by a newspaperman who became a city police official.

Asbury, Herbert, *The Gangs of New York: An Informal History of the Underworld*. Blue Ribbon Books, Garden City, N. Y., 1939. Politics and law enforcement emerge as interests of the New York City underworld in this study of criminal gangs.

Bell, Daniel, "Crime as an American Way of Life," *The Antioch Review*, Summer, 1953, pp. 131–154.

Combs, George H., "Reminiscences." Columbia University Oral History Collection, Special Collections, Butler Library. Includes reflections on the "Kefauver Committee" and its disclosures of friendly working relationships between the underworld and New York City officials.

Katcher, Leo, *The Big Bankroll*. Harper and Bros., New York, 1959. The life and times of Arnold Rothstein.

Kefauver, Estes, *Crime in America*. Doubleday and Co., New York, 1951, pp. 283–307. Describes contacts between organized crime and officials of New York City.

The Kefauver Committee Report on Organized Crime. Didier Co., New York, 1952. A complete reprinting of the several reports of the Special Senate Committee to Investigate Organized Crime in Interstate Commerce, which found links between racketeers and public officials in New York and other American cities.

Kneeland, George J., *Commercialized Prostitution in New York City*. Century Co., New York, 1917. Includes material on the relationship of commercialized prostitution and law enforcement.

Lavine, Emanuel H., *Secrets of the Metropolitan Police*. Garden City Publishing Co., Garden City, N. Y., 1937. Describes links between criminals and the police.

Lynch, Dennis T., *Criminals and Politicians*. Macmillan Co., New York, 1932. How criminals have attempted to influence municipal officeholders in New York City.

Mockridge, Norton and Robert H. Prall, *The Big Fix*. Henry Holt and Co., New York, 1954. A survey of evidence of close ties between a giant gambling syndicate and city officialdom.

New York Committee of Fifteen, *Social Evil: With Special Reference to Conditions Existing in the City of New York*. G. P. Putnam's Sons, New York, 1912. A report on the white-slave traffic in the city in the early years of the century.

Reid, Edward, *The Shame of New York*. Random House, New York, 1953. Exposes connections between crime and politics in New York City.

U. S. Senate, Special Committee to Investigate Organized Crime in Interstate Commerce, 82nd Congress, First Session, *Hearings*, Part 18: New York and New Jersey, July 6–August 17, 1951. Government Printing Office, Washington, 1957. Official transcripts of the hearings of the Kefauver Committee, which uncovered links between the underworld and New York City officialdom.

Committee to Investigate Organized Crime in Interstate Commerce, *Third Interim Report*. Government Printing Office, Washington, 1951, pp. 109–144. Summarizes the findings and conclusions of the committee hearings in New York City; reports ties between organized crime and municipal officials.

CHAPTER IV

Rules of the Contest

THE STAKES OF THE CITY'S POLITICS are high, the contestants plentiful and determined. Consequently, despite the broad consensus under which the quest for the stakes of politics is conducted in the city, the contest might deteriorate into a shapeless, even violent, free-for-all if it were not for the existence and wide acceptance by the participants of rules that give form and order to the processes of the city's government and politics.

The rules governing the city's political contest are a complex web. Constitutional provisions, federal and state statutes, the city charter, the city's Administrative Code, numerous executive orders and administrative regulations, and party rules are all interwoven in such an intricate maze that even the best informed and most sure-footed participants are expert only in their own areas of interest and special competence. The rules found in state statutes and the Administrative Code are particularly difficult to unravel, being characterized by duplication, ambiguity in their relationship to each other, and rich in opportunities for the obfuscation of the less experienced contestants. Complexity and ambiguity in the rules are in part the product of their inclusive scope and their step-by-step evolution, in part due to a lack of incentive to simplify them.

Despite these and other shortcomings, the rules provide form and order in at least five important ways. First, they establish and identify the offices of government and party, thereby defining the structure of these central institutions of the city's political and governmental system. Second, they describe the powers and the limits on the powers of the occupants of these offices, setting forth what they must do, what they may do, what they are forbidden to do, and prescribing the procedures they are to follow in formulating and promulgating their decisions. Third, they spell out the procedures by which the aspirants to these offices may legitimately come to occupy them and to wield their powers, and ways in which the occupants may legitimately be removed. Fourth, they restrict the methods by which contestants may attempt to influence the decisions of officeholders and electorates. Finally, they specify the procedures by which formal changes in the formal rules may legitimately be effected.

In form, the range is from fundamental statements of the most general rules (constitutions and charters), through those more detailed rules issued by elected or appointed officers (statutes, executive and administrative orders and regulations, court decisions and orders), through political party rules, to those rules found mainly in custom and usage. There is a fluidity of function among the various forms: any one of the five functions may appear in two or more forms, or the form may be changed (from party rule to statute, for example, or from statute to constitutional provision), and each form contains provisions applicable to all five functions.

Constitutions, charters, statutes, administrative regulations, custom, and the other forms in which rules are issued or arise (except the rules of the political parties) also deal with more than the rules of political contest alone. That is, in addition to their treatment of the organization and powers and procedures in government and party, these documents also contain a greater number of provisions governing the relations of citizens and groups to each other. Generally speaking, these latter provisions are not *rules* of the contest for the stakes of political action; they are more accurately seen as end products—some of the *prizes*—of the contest. Although the rules and the prizes thus appear in the same documents, the distribution of the prizes is left for later discussion. It is to the rules only that this chapter is addressed.

FUNCTIONS OF THE FORMAL RULES

Defining the Central Institutions in the Contest

The Constitution of the United States. The Constitution of the United States is a major element of the rules of the contest for the stakes of politics in New York City. It establishes the structure of the federal government, creating political prizes (including the offices of President and Vice President, Senator, Representative, and others) and centers of political decision-making which are of great significance to the political process in the city. Its silences leave the organization of the state and the city's governments largely to the state, a factor that plays an important part in the strategies of participants in the city's government and politics, and it leaves to the state the governing of political parties with minimal reference to federal law.

The State Constitution. Thus the national Constitution makes the state constitution, the city charter, and both state and city legislation, the chief vehicles for the rules which define the central institutions for two levels of government. The state constitution defines the structure of the government at Albany, a government that contains not only some of the largest political stakes at issue in city politics but also determines how much weight the city will carry in the state's decisions. The state constitution, moreover, includes explicit provisions governing the judiciary and local governments of the state, as well as some dealing with the administration of particular functions (for example, elections, housing, civil service, criminal prosecution).

State Statutes. Many state constitutional provisions are expressed in greater detail by state statutes, which name the offices of the state government and of the parties and other political groups in the state, and determine—by legislation concerning New York City alone, or by more general legislation— the structure of some segments of the city government, such as those concerned with education, health, and rapid transit.

The City Charter. The city charter, in turn, is roughly akin in legal status to state legislation, although duly authorized and enacted state laws take precedence when the charter conflicts with them. Indeed, until the present charter went into force in 1938, the city charters were state statutes. Under the terms of a 1923 home rule provision of the state constitution, and of a Home Rule Act and a later Home Rule Law (all to be examined more fully later), it became possible for the city to have its own Charter Commission draft a proposed charter, and for the charter to take effect when approved by the voters of the city in a referendum. This option was exercised in 1936, and the new charter became operative in 1938. With subsequent amendments, it grew to 49 separate chapters totaling 85 pages. In the charter, the offices and powers of the mayoralty, the Board of Estimate, the City Council, and all the major city departments and agencies are established, and, in many cases, their organization prescribed.

The City's Administrative Code. The provisions of the charter are paralleled, chapter by chapter, in the Administrative Code of the city, which, in the course of its three thousand pages, refines and adds to the organizational specifications of the charter; in fact, some important city offices (City Construction Coordinator being the prime example) have their basis only in the Code. The Code, in essence, is the standing body of local law adopted by the city government as provided in the charter and may be described as roughly analogous, in form and scope at least, to the United States Code and the codified New York State laws.

Agency Rules. These rules are supplemented by still others expressed in the orders and regulations of executive and administrative agencies. To a considerable extent, the rules of federal, state, and city agencies concern only the organization of their own agencies, but federal and state administrative decisions and actions often have important repercussions in the organization of city agencies as well. Because these federal and state agencies are often themselves targets of political action in the city, and because they affect the agencies of the city, the structural regulations of all three levels of governmental administration become parts of the rules of the political contest in New York City.

Election Law and Party Rules. Political party organization in New York State and thus in the city also is governed in great detail by the state Election

Law, supplemented in important respects by the rules of the national and state conventions and committees, and of county committees. The national party machinery is established primarily by party rules; within the state, party rules operate only to the extent that the Election Law confers authority on them to do so. Fundamentally, then, party structure throughout New York State—including the city—is a product of state legislation.

Qualifications for voting in general elections, and, by judicial extension, in party primaries, are defined by the Constitution of the United States (Article I, Sections 2 and 4; Amendments XIV, XV, XVII, and XIX) and by federal civil rights statutes; by the state constitution (Article II); and by the state Election Law, which also sets the requirements for party membership. Taken together with all constitutional, statutory, and charter provisions describing the methods of election of various federal, state, and city officials, and with the legislation drawing the boundaries of various electoral constituencies, these rules may be said to establish the electorate of the city (which here means all those eligible to vote).

Summary. The organizing rules of the contest thus establish some of the chief categories of participants in the governmental and political processes in New York City: the parties, the officials and bureaucracies of the city, and the officials and bureaucracies of other governments. In so doing, the rules describe the major outlines of the contest. The other contestants (nongovernmental groups and the media of mass communication) may, subject to very few formal rules, organize themselves as they like and find many rewards and prizes in a wide variety of activities not covered by the rule books of government and politics. When they seek the rewards of political action, however—that is, action directed toward influencing the selection of public officeholders or the decisions and behavior of officeholders—they are brought at once into the framework constructed by the rules. Their targets and methods are by and large defined for them.

Defining Powers and Procedures

The contest for the stakes of politics in the city is further shaped by rules defining the legal roles of officeholders, party functionaries, and the electorate. The rules not only name some of the main players; they also announce what these players are required to do, are authorized (that is, permitted, in their discretion) to do, and are forbidden to do, and identify the procedures by which their actions are to be taken as well as the substance of their jurisdiction and responsibilities. In sheer volume, the proportion given to this function of the rules probably outweighs all the others combined.

Federal Rules. The Constitution of the United States is largely a statement of the powers and duties of the three branches of government and of limits on their authority with respect to each other, the states, and the people. Grants of power, in a sense, contain their own limits, since what is not expressly or implicitly granted is presumably not possessed. In addition, there are in the Constitution many express limitations on each branch individually and on all collectively, the most sweeping being the Bill of Rights. Moreover, the Constitution contains a number of sections imposing explicit restrictions on the states as well as on the federal government, and several provisions of the Bill of Rights—which originally applied to the federal government alone—have been applied to the states by the Supreme Court of the United States since the adoption of the Fourteenth Amendment. Since New York City is, like all local governments within the borders of any state, a "creature" or subdivision of the state, the provisions of the United States Constitution that bind the state government are also binding upon city officials. Thus, despite the Constitution's silence on local government, its provisions dealing with the powers of, and restraints on, public officers play a vital part in ordering the political contest in New York City—first, by their effects on federal and state offices and actions (for these are also among the stakes of politics in New York City); second, by their application to city offices and actions directly.

Under the "national supremacy" clause of the Constitution, authorized and duly enacted federal laws and treaties take precedence over the enactments of the states (and, by extension, the subdivisions of the states) whenever there is any conflict between the actions of the various levels of government. Consequently, whenever the federal government enters into an area of activity, it may modify, or in rare cases eliminate, state and local action in that area. Thus, what all the officeholders—federal, state, and city—about whom the political contest in New York turns, are permitted to do is partly, and in some instances importantly, the result of some federal statutes. And, of course, many other federal statutes that confer power on, and/or circumscribe, federal officers from the President down, without significantly affecting state and city officials, will often be of deep concern to many people engaged in the city's political life. Consequently, although much federal legislation is not so obviously a part of the rules as is the Constitution, the effects of the legislation are much the same as the Constitution.

State Rules. The state constitution and state legislation loom larger in the day-by-day conduct of the contest in New York City because their provisions concerning powers, and limits on the powers, of state and city officials and party functionaries affect a larger number of people immediately involved in the struggle, and in a greater variety of contexts. In part, this impact results from the extensive interrelationships of the state and the city (see Chapter XV). The provisions of the state constitution and the statutes conferring and limiting the powers of the Governor, the legislature, administrative agencies, and the courts touch all the contestants in the city in many ways. In part, the impact also stems from the detail with which the state constitution and laws treat of city officers. The constitution contains articles on local finances, local governments, education, public officers, taxation, social welfare, and housing, some of which contain sections naming New York City explicitly, and all of which are amplified by more detailed legislation. In addition, many of the seventy volumes of state laws (legislation on rapid transit, for example, and on public property, public health, legal penalties, and many other subjects) affect the powers of both state and local officials and employees, and one— the Election Law—describes the rule-making powers of party functionaries. City officers and employees, no less than the officials and bureaucrats in state employ, also find sources and restraints of power in other state documents— in home rule provisions mentioned earlier and in the general laws on munici-palities. Similarly, all judicial officers in the state operate under grants of authority and specifications of duties and responsibilities set forth in the constitution and laws of the state. A Bill of Rights of 18 sections—10 printed pages long—is a detailed guarantee to private citizens and groups, a guaran-tee that circumscribes the sphere of official action at both state and local levels.

City Rules. The discretion of city officers and employees is defined and channeled by the city charter and the Administrative Code as well as by all the foregoing forms of rules of the contest. With greater specificity than is usually found anywhere else, these spell out what the holders of city office and employment are permitted or required to do; they seldom contain limitations on powers because the courts tend to construe their powers narrowly, which, in combination with the implied and expressed restraints in state and federal organic and ordinary law, renders superfluous most additional safeguards against abuses.

In the city's administrative agencies, administrative personnel get their authority from and are restricted by executive and administrative orders as well as by constitutional and statutory specifications. These rules are numer-ous and complex.

In a special category are the officers and employees of the City Depart-ments of Sanitation and Health, for their powers and procedures and assign-ments derive from the Sanitary Code of New York City as well as from the more usual sources. The Sanitary Code is enacted by the New York City Board of Health, a body appointed by the Mayor and invested by state legislation and the charter with authority to adopt regulations on all matters of health and sanitation, including the processing, handling, and storage of foods, drugs, and cosmetics; the regulation of offensive industries and trades; the licensing of many businesses and occupations; and on many other matters in addition to disease prevention and suppression, the activities commonly associated with public health. The regulations of the Board—that is, the Sanitary Code—have the effect of state or city legislation within the city; the

Board is thus really a unifunctional legislative organ. The Board of Education and the Board of Hospitals are somewhat similar institutions.

Procedural Rules. Many of the rules—constitutional, statutory, and administrative—stipulate not only *what* government officers, employees, and party functionaries may do but *how* they may do it. The United States Constitution, the Constitution of New York State, and the New York City Charter, for example, particularize the steps by which legislation (at each level of government, respectively) may be enacted. Important aspects of judicial procedure are spelled out in the state constitution. The rules of state and county party units, under the terms of the Election Law, specify procedures for the adoption of party rules. Statutes, local laws, court rulings, and orders establish the methods of issuing administrative regulations and orders and the modes of proceeding in judicial actions. Legislation also forbids certain abuses of official authority—for example, by establishing penalties for soliciting or receiving bribes, for taking unlawful reward for omitting or delaying official acts, for selling the right to official powers, for neglect of duty, for misconduct in nominating or election procedures, for corrupt use of position or authority, and for other things. These procedural requirements are as important as substantive rules in structuring the quest for the stakes of politics.

Summary. While it is customary to view provisions describing jurisdiction and procedure as impinging primarily upon those in public or party office or employment, they also affect profoundly the positions and strategies of nongovernmental contestants. Such rules set up opportunities and methods for nongovernmental participants in the political process to challenge, and perhaps to modify or overthrow, promulgated decisions, or even to intervene in the process of their formulation. These rules also fix the patterns in which officeholders and party functionaries at any given level of government deal with each other and with their counterparts at other levels. They thus elaborate the configuration of the political process whose broad outlines are established by the creation—or, more accurately, by the naming and ordaining—of governmental and party offices.

Delineating Accession and Removal

How one legitimately ascends to the positions set up, in order to exercise whatever authority these positions confer, is also described in the rules of the contest.

Filling Elective Offices. The methods of filling elective offices at each level of government are set forth in the respective organic laws—the Constitution of the United States, the state constitution, and the city charter. The organic laws stipulate qualifications of the officeholders, the boundaries of their constituencies (or the bodies that may fix the constituency boundaries), the terms of office, the conditions under which a successor to any incumbent will be chosen, the method of selection and the term of the successor, and the manner in which each elected officer may be removed. Legislation by Congress and, to a much larger extent, by the state legislature fill in the details. Ordinary city legislation with respect to elections is negligible.

Methods of nominating candidates for elective office are spelled out chiefly in state legislation. With but one exception, all candidates for elective office for which the voters of New York City cast ballots (which means all offices from state assemblyman and city councilman up to and including presidential electors) are nominated according to procedures mandated by the state Election Law. Where state or county party units, or judicial conventions, make rules governing any aspect of nominations, it is only in those areas in which the Election Law specifically confers this power on them. The only exception to the almost exclusive sway of the state Election Law in matters of nomination is the method of selecting presidential candidates; the presidential nominating conventions make their own rules. Thus, the rules of nomination are contained either in a state statute or, to a lesser extent, in the rules of the parties.

Appointments to Office. Appointments to office are also subjected to procedural requirements. Constitutional provisions at the federal and state levels specify that some appointments by the President and the Governor, respectively, must be made with the advice and consent of their respective Senates. In addition, procedures governing appointments to offices created by legislation are designated in legislation, so that the procedures for filling many positions not mentioned in the two constitutions are under the same restrictions as some constitutional offices, or under other equally limiting provisions. As a matter of fact, even the freedom of the chief executives to make appointments without necessarily obtaining advice or consent from any source stems often from explicit constitutional or statutory provisions, although it has been interpreted as inhering in the office when such provisions are absent or ambiguous. At the city level, the charter expressly confers broad freedom of this kind on the Mayor (subject to "other provisions of law"). Requirements are not very restrictive, either, as regards offices to be filled by Congress (such as congressional staff and the staff of the Library of Congress), the state legislature (analogous positions), the City Council (the City Clerk and others), and by judges and court clerks.

Below the chief executives, appointing power derives virtually completely from legislation and from executive and administrative orders issued under the authority of enabling statutes. In the federal, state, and city governments, civil service procedures obtain widely, and appointments are made only after the specified steps have been taken. At the federal level, these steps are characterized in legislation, presidential orders, and rules and regulations of the United States Civil Service Commission. At the state level, there are constitutional as well as statutory, executive, and Civil Service Department provisions. At the city level, many state provisions apply, and are supplemented by the rules and regulations of the city's Personnel Department.

A substantial proportion of the rules of the contest for the stakes of politics in New York City is thus given over to the filling of public office and employment. A great deal of attention is focused on introducing order into this phase of the contest—the phase that has, in the history of government, provoked bitter and often violent struggle.

Filling Party Offices. Procedures for filling party office are found exclusively in the Election Law and the rules of the parties. In general, the statute provides for the methods of choosing the members of all party committees and conventions within the state, and allows specified alternative practices among which the committees may opt according to their preferences. Whether Assembly District Leaders are elected directly by rank-and-file party members in primaries or by the county committeemen in each Assembly District, for example, is a decision left to the county committees themselves. The modes of selection of state executive committeemen, and of national committeemen, are fixed in the rules of the state and national party units, respectively. Battles for control of party machinery can often be as intense as the battles for nomination and election; here, too, the rules of the political contest render these competitions reasonably orderly.

Removal of Officers and Employees. Finally, there are specified methods of removing all government officials and employees. Generally speaking, challenges of the legal qualifications of any incumbent, or of the legal validity of the procedures by which an incumbent ascended to his position, fall to the courts (assuming, in the case of an appointed officeholder, the appointment is not rescinded or declared void by administrative action upon issuance of the challenge). However, power of removal of *validly* installed officers is vested in a number of institutions. Impeachment is an instrument available to the Congress for use against the President, Vice President, and federal judges; the manner of impeachment is set forth in the Constitution. The state legislature, under the state constitution, enjoys similar powers, and similar restraints, with respect to the highest elected officers of the state government, other than legislators. Every legislative body possesses the authority to judge the qualifications of its own members and may unseat members without resort to impeachment proceedings.

The state constitution and legislation create a body of high-ranking judges authorized to remove judges of all but the highest court, the Court of Appeals, under certain conditions and by specified processes. The constitution, legislation, and the city charter provide for the removal by the Governor of the Mayor and other members of the Board of Estimate of the city, of certain appointed city department heads and commission or board members, and of District Attorneys, but there are procedural safeguards for the incumbents of each office. The City Council may, in its discretion, expel its own members. Officers appointed by the Mayor to positions other than those in which they serve at his pleasure may be dismissed only after explicit procedural requirements—contained in the state constitution, legislation, the city charter, or the Administrative Code—have been met. Civil service appointees are protected by procedural specifications in the Civil Service laws and the regulations of Civil Service Commissions.

In addition, the rules establish procedures for settling disputes over the results of filling office in government and parties. For the most part, these procedures call for appeal to the courts from the decisions of the administrative and party functionaries entrusted with the responsibility for certifying incumbents. In the case of civil service appointments, however, preliminary steps—appeals within the machinery of the civil service system—are also required.

In all these ways the rules of the contest establish not only the offices and powers of government and parties, but the pathways into, and out of, those positions.

Limiting the Modes of Influence

The rules that structure the contest for the stakes of politics in New York City tend to discourage or prevent the use of some strategies and to encourage the use of others by the various contestants. Furthermore, the rules specifically prohibit some modes of influence.

Influencing Voters and Officials. Some prohibitions concern the methods of influencing the electorate. The Penal Law of the state, for example, forbids furnishing money or entertainment to induce attendance at the polls; giving or receiving consideration for votes; duress and intimidation of voters. The recently enacted federal Civil Rights Law also contains prohibitions of certain discriminatory tactics against voters. Federal and state legislation place limitations on campaign expenditures by all groups and individuals, except political parties.

Some prohibitions relate to the raising of money for political purposes—that is, to influencing donors. In particular, political assessments upon public officers and employees by other public officers and employees are forbidden at the federal level by federal law, at the state and local levels by state law. The state Penal Law also bars soliciting candidates by any organizations other than those to which the candidates belong. Solicitation of candidates as a condition of newspaper support is specifically covered in a separate section.

Other prohibitions, such as the provision of the state Penal Law establishing penalties for making corrupt bargains for appointment, apply to the manner of influencing appointing officers. Additional prohibitions apply to the techniques of influencing the decisions of public officers and employees. These range from penalties for various kinds of fraud and conspiracy, designed to skew decisions by misinformation or similar devices, through penalties for bribery and resisting an officer.

Along with all the other rules of the political contest, these give shape to the order and processes of government and party activity. The rules treated in this section, however, have an added characteristic that gives them a rather special function: they are the only ones that deal explicitly with the actions of nongovernmental groups and private individuals as well as with those of public officials and employees, party leaders, and the electorate. Since they confer sweeping governmental and political powers on government, parties, and the electorate, the rules are proliferated in efforts to confine the powers to the desired channels, and therefore refer primarily to these three categories of contestants. Nevertheless, the few provisions concerned particularly with nongovernmental participants in the contest point up a noteworthy feature of the contest: the occupants of public office and employment, the inner cores of the parties, and the voters are under more restrictions in the use of their broad powers than the nongovernmental groups are in the exercise of the powers they possess. Except for the requirements and limitations summarized in this section of the discussion, and for the imperatives imposed by the machinery of government and politics, the nongovernmental contestants are free to fashion virtually whatever instruments of influence they can conceive and to wield those instruments in practically any way they see fit.

Protecting Public Officials and Employees. In earlier days, public officials were not publicly paid. The effect was to exclude from public office those who did not possess independent means and to render many officeholders vulnerable to influence. The introduction of compensation admitted to the political arena many contestants who had formerly been debarred and rendered them somewhat less susceptible to temptation than previously. At the same time, opportunities to control the formal rewards of office placed an important instrument of influence in the hands of the exercisers of control. Hence, although *remuneration* itself may be considered one of the substantive *prizes* of politics, the *procedures* for setting and changing remuneration are among the *rules* according to which the contest for the city's political stakes is conducted.

Salary scales are set by legislation at the federal level, by constitutional and legislative provision at the state level, and by charter and local legislation at the city level. Administrative regulations dealing with classification also affect many civil servants. Fringe benefits—ranging from dwellings for chief executives through expense allowances and paid assistants to retirement allowances—constitute significant forms of remuneration. "Conflict of interest" provisions, which affect the sources of income over and above public compensation, of public officials and employees, complete the picture.

For the most part, the decisions about remuneration are matters of legislative, executive, judicial, or administrative discretion. A number of restrictions, however, have been imposed on ordinary legislation and administrative action. The salaries of the President, Vice President, and federal judges may not be reduced for any incumbents of these positions in the course of their tenures. State judges are similarly shielded. At the federal level, the Supreme Court has interpreted the constitutional prohibition against congressional bills of attainder as preventing enactment of laws forbidding payment of the salaries of named individuals. At the state level, retirement systems for public employees have been held under a state constitutional provision to be contractual arrangements, and therefore protected against alterations unfavorable to the employees. Where salaries are written into sections of a constitution (as is the case with the salary of the Governor and other high state officers) or the charter (as is the case with the Mayor and other high city officers), the effect is to safeguard them from reduction (and, on the other hand, increase) by any process but the relatively slow and cumbersome one of formal amendment. Administrative classification and pay decisions are normally appealable, under legislation and administrative regulation, to the appropriate personnel agencies, and, ultimately, to the courts.

These rules of the contest constitute a small part of the machinery of the city's political process. Nevertheless, if they were deleted from the corpus of formal rules, the changes would eventually have important effects on the behavior of many contestants and on the character of the contest itself.

Permitting Changes in the Rules

One of the main functions of the formal rules is to establish orderly procedures by which the formal rules themselves may be changed. When the rules are expressed as statutes, executive or administrative regulations or orders, judicial decisions or findings, or party regulations, they may be altered by an action of the same kind, and by the same authority that promulgated them, or by a duly authenticated stronger form of law (for example, an administrative decision by a statute). In such cases, the methods of change are simply the methods of original issuance, the ordinary kind of governmental action. In the case of changes in organic law—the constitutions of the United States and of New York State, and the New York City Charter—the situation is a little more complex because the methods of original adoption are somewhat different from the usual methods of subsequent amendment.

The contents of the rules of the city's political contest are sometimes changed even when the wording remains unaltered; the words are reinterpreted. In a broad sense, this is permitted by the structure of government, which implicitly set up the courts as arbiters of uncertainties about the meaning of rules—or so the system has worked out in practice. Judicial construction thus must be included among the techniques of formal change, the Supreme Court of the United States being the ultimate interpreter whenever any federal questions are involved, the Court of Appeals of New York State having the final interpretative role in all other cases in the state.

The formal rules, then, keep the city's political contest orderly, but not static. They contain arrangements for growth and adjustment of the rules themselves, and therefore of the character of the contest itself, so the contest may remain a suitable instrument for the governance of a democratic city.

CUSTOM AND USAGE

The formal rules of the city's political contest are supplemented, and occasionally sharply amended, at many points by custom and usage. These appear most visibly in the familiar procedures for filling governmental office: "balancing" tickets ethnically, religiously, and geographically; spreading appointments of officials in similar fashion; the allocation of certain official posts to "career" appointees; joint party nomination of satisfactory "sitting judges"; casting the state's electoral college votes for the presidential candidate who wins a popular majority in the state; and "senatorial courtesy" in both federal and state governments are illustrations of customary practices in operation and importantly affecting the character of the contest for the stakes of city politics.

But custom makes itself felt with respect to the other functions of the rules, too; there are positions in government that clothe their incumbents with power and eminence almost entirely on the basis of custom—such as the development of Grover Whalen into the "official greeter" of distinguished visitors to New York City, the emergence of the office of executive secretary to the Mayor for a time as the main patronage-dispensing and -arbitrating center of the city government, the former use of the Postmaster Generalship for much the same purpose at the federal level, and the "kitchen cabinets" and "palace guards" with which Presidents, Governors, and Mayors have frequently surrounded themselves. Thus the powers, the limits on powers, and the procedures of officials and employees are frequently defined by custom—sometimes more broadly, sometimes more narrowly—than by the formal rules.

Custom and usage so pervade the city's political process that the practices easily isolated as illustrative are doubtless only the peaks of the iceberg. If there were no regularities of behavior other than those spelled out in writing, it is most unlikely that the machinery of the city government could continue to function as satisfactorily as it does. Traditional and informal "settlements" are certainly no less important than the formal rules in many areas of the city's politics and government. The chapters which follow will frequently emphasize their significance.

STRATEGIC USES OF THE RULES

The Rules as Instruments of the Contestants

The rules govern the behavior of the participants in the contest for the stakes of city politics, but the participants also determine the contents of the rules. In one way or another, the contestants seek the rewards of political action not only within the established political framework but also by altering the rules prescribing the framework in ways which will improve their chances of success.

But changing the rules always represents differential advantages to the several major participants in the city's political contest. Creation of new positions, for example, means new opportunities for some, more cost for others, and more stringent regulation for still others. Addition of policemen to the police force offers the promise of advancement to the men of the Department and of employment to applicants. At the same time it may result in better protection (demanded by many), more rigorous enforcement (protested by few), and allocation of scarce funds to this one agency rather than to any of the others competing for the appropriations. Establishment of a Department of Traffic took traffic regulation from the hands of the police, removed parking meter and off-street parking facilities and their revenues from the jurisdiction of a Parking Authority, opened new fields of advancement and higher status and pay for traffic engineers, and eventually produced one-way traffic on the main north-south thoroughfares of Manhattan over the strenuous objections of the major bus companies. Added judgeships open new channels for aspirants to places on the bench, and, in some cases, for judges waiting for advancement to higher judicial posts. A new Youth Board focuses the attention of a specialized group on a particular problem and creates problems of relationships between the new body and other departments. The introduction of the City Administrator into the top ranks of the city government provided a resource for the Mayor, a source of anxiety and rivalry for the Director of the Budget, a more receptive point of contact for management-oriented groups, a new source of directives and inquiries for the line agencies, and a group of specialists to concentrate on the technical problems of organization and procedures in the city government.

The list could be extended almost indefinitely. Every time a new position or agency is established, it immediately appears as a job opportunity, or a series of job opportunities, to those contestants seeking office, a possible medium of exchange for party functionaries, a painful adjustment of jurisdiction for other officeholders and agencies, a path of access to the governmental decision-making machinery for some nongovernmental groups and a weakening of influence for others, and an augury of greater emphasis on a particular program supported and opposed by various contestants. Similarly, the elimination of a post or an agency, whether by incorporation into another or by outright deactivation, concerns many participants in the political contest. When the rules establish or abolish offices in party or government, they often do more than influence the behavior of the contestants; they may also increase or reduce the share of the prizes a given contestant or groups of contestants will obtain.

Changing Powers or Procedures

In like fashion, the rules of power and procedure in connection with any office—the definitions of what the incumbents are directed to do, permitted to do, the manner in which they are to do these things, and the specification of what they are forbidden to do—are not neutral matters for the contestants. One set of definitions will benefit some, another set, sometimes if only slightly different, may be to the advantage of others. When one agency rather than another is given an assignment[1] the substantive decisions with respect to the function involved are often quite different—sometimes because different groups have access to the different agencies, sometimes because the orientations of the departments are dissimilar (as a result of their different over-all missions), and sometimes because one pattern of work division produces more intense interagency rivalries than another.

When a function is lodged in the city government (fire protection, refuse collection, and traffic management, for example), those groups well organized at the city level (including the city bureaucracies) often prove especially influential. City groups may be less effective when they must compete on a larger stage with groups from other parts of the state or the nation with respect to functions controlled tightly by the state government (as is education) or functions in which the federal government has taken a hand (as in welfare and urban redevelopment). State constitutional limitations on city taxation and indebtedness have a profound impact on the distribution of the fiscal burdens imposed by the city and on the pattern and volume of services rendered by the city. The federal and state bills of rights are important factors in checking the tendencies of government officials and employees to ride roughshod over their opponents. Consequently, provisions governing powers and procedures, as these are set forth in the rules of the city's political contest, are not merely abstract exercises in political architecture and processes. The kinds of decisions that emerge are directly related to the participants favored or disadvantaged by such rules.

[1] For example, when certain variations from zoning regulations are made the province of the Board of Standards and Appeals rather than the City Planning Commission, when the Department of Licenses rather than the Department of Sanitation is given jurisdiction over regulation of private refuse collectors, or when inspection of buildings is divided among the Departments of Buildings, Health, Fire, and Water Supply, Gas, and Electricity rather than being centralized in a single unit.

Changing the Rules on Appointments or Removal

Determining who will secure public or party office or public employment, and how they exercise the authority they thus acquire, depends to a large extent on the rules for filling these positions and for removing incumbents. The people who can win elective office are generally different from those who would occupy the same positions if the positions were made appointive. They are vulnerable to different pressures, responsive to different groups, often pursue different objectives, and enjoy different opportunities. Those who are elected from large (statewide or citywide) constituencies tend to behave differently with respect to demands upon them from those who come from small constituencies. When the New York City Council was elected by proportional representation, some minority groups obtained a forum and a degree of access to the city's governmental decision-making machinery that were less readily available to them when the city returned to a single-member district system. Adoption of the direct primary system for many nominations and for choosing the occupants of party offices gave party insurgents a greater chance than previously to place their own men in key places.

If the appointing power is limited by the requirement of confirmation, the men installed in office may be of a different type from those appointed by an officer having full discretion. Still others may be appointed if there are professional or experience or residential requirements and if qualifying or competitive examinations are required. The loyalty of the appointees—to their appointing officers, to the party leaders, to the professions, to the agencies, to programs, to their own careers, to their clienteles—will vary according to the kind of rules imposed. Similarly, officials subject to removal at the pleasure of some higher officers will often have different loyalties and degrees of responsiveness from those guaranteed notice and hearings by the removing officers, while officials and employees protected against removal except with the consent of a civil service commission are likely to behave differently from both other categories. In short, the kinds of rules promulgated to describe the paths into, and out of, government and party service can be expected to play an important part in the distribution of the prizes of political action among the city's contestants.

Using Rules on Modes of Influence

So, too, with the rules on the modes of influence. Low salary scales, for instance, may prevent people without wealth from accepting full-time government or party work, may make the incumbents vulnerable to economic influence, and may handicap governments and parties in their competition with the private sector of the economy for able and technically qualified personnel. Prohibitions against "buying" votes and intimidating voters, even if only partly effective, tend to inhibit practices that give advantages to certain groups. Limitations on contributions to parties and campaign funds, or requirement of public reports on contributions, sometimes encourage illicit donations in cash, and thus assist groups with large amounts of ready cash and no obligation to account for their use of it—an opportunity especially attractive to illegitimate groups.

Stakes in the Methods of Change

The modes of formally changing the rules affect differentially the chances of success of the participants in the contest for the stakes of city politics. If a particular set of provisions favors the influence of one set of participants and disadvantages another in the struggle, the disadvantaged group may be expected to seek to change the rules. If the methods of changing the rules are complicated and difficult, the currently favored contestants are benefited; if the changes are simple and easy, the challengers are aided. The modes of changing the rules are rarely ends in themselves, but they are often controversial subjects for contestants capable of looking three stages ahead: first, to facilitating rule changes by easing the requirements for change; second, to securing, by the easiest means, the adoption of rules more favorable to them; third, to using the new rules to obtain the installation of personnel, or the selection of governmental or party policies, congenial to them. Their opponents, aware of the objectives, usually fight any such strategy of change.

Summary

Thus, in all their functions, the rules of the contest help determine the sharing of the rewards of political action among the contestants in the city's political system. For this reason, the contestants do not simply abide by them passively, nor are the rules left static. On the contrary, the rules are constantly in flux as a result of maneuvers by each group to get provisions or interpretations that enhance their chances of securing the office or the decisions they want. The rules lend order and method to the contest; they are also instruments in the hands of the contestants; simultaneously, they are products of the contest. Manipulating them is one of the common strategies of the participants in the city's politics.

THE GROWTH OF FORMAL RULES

Over the years an increasing proportion of the rules of the city's political contest has been set down in formal documents; less is left to custom or even to precedent. The trend of the times is toward explicit and detailed statement. That is not to say that all, or even most, of the practices of the city's government and politics have been reduced to formal rules, but their extension relative to practices governed by custom has grown markedly over the years.

In part, this is a result of the expansion of governmental activity. Each time the city government embarks upon a new program, each time a new agency is created and invested with power to issue regulations of its own, each time an additional phase of relationships among private citizens is subjected to legal definition, the body of prevailing rules grows. The twentieth century has been a period of extraordinarily rapid governmental expansion in all these regards. Technological development, population increase and more intensive land use, greater interdependence of segments of the city's population upon each other, popular insistence on governmental assumption of new responsibilities, and many other factors have combined to generate new public services, public agencies, public regulation. These innovations tend to be expressed in formal rules; the exigencies of the modern era have produced many innovations and therefore many new formal rules.

Expansion of government is not sufficient by itself to account for the rapid relative increase of formal rules. For this increase has taken place even in fields in which the city government has long been involved. The New York State Civil Service Law, for example, was originally a scant half-dozen pages long when it was enacted in 1884; today, it is over 150 pages long, and is supplemented by several hundred pages of rules and regulations of the state and city Civil Service Commissions. Similarly, the structure of political parties and their procedures for filling party posts and nominating candidates were initially left to the discretion of party members, as voluntary associations of voters. Today, the state Election Law covers these topics in minute detail, and written party rules fill in much that the law omits. In the courts, although the common law is still an important part of substance and procedure, statutory provisions covering many substantive and procedural aspects of the law have become more extensive and more controlling. Virtually no phase of the governmental and political process has been immune to the growth of the formal rules.

Causes of the Growth of Formality

The explanation may be found in the special demands of an age of rapid change upon the city's political and governmental system. The alternative to formal rules is the slow growth of custom, but in a time of rapid change the contestants cannot wait for the slower process of informal adjustment and accommodation. This is perhaps the basic condition which now accelerates the transition from custom to formality that has long been under way in the city and other governments.

There have been at least four special sources of this long-term trend: distrust of men in government and parties; strict judicial construction of the powers of municipal corporations; strategic and tactical advantages of formalization; and the requirements of technology.

The Distrust Factor

The distrust of public officials, employees, and party leaders engenders complete and explicit rules to make sure that the boundaries of their jurisdiction are unmistakably demarcated and that the procedures they are to follow are clearly laid out. Generally speaking, the greater the faith of the rule-formulators in the men who will occupy the offices the rules establish, the broader the discretion entrusted to the occupants, and the shorter and more general the rules tend to be. When each grant of authority is carefully framed to avoid the possibility of abuse, and then surrounded by restrictions until little discretion is left to public and party officials, the volume of formal rules increases.

The reform movements culminating in the Progressive era have been a fertile source of formal restrictive rules. Thus, the introduction into the state constitution of provisions naming the departments of the state government, requiring a merit system in the civil service, limiting local taxation and indebtedness, guaranteeing that the state forest preserve shall be "forever kept wild," making "membership in any pension or retirement system of the state or of a civil subdivision thereof . . . a contractual relationship, the benefits of which shall not be diminished or impaired," and many similar items, reflects the apparent conviction that state legislators and city officials cannot be trusted to use their judgment in these matters. In the same way, much state legislation reducing city agencies to appendages of state departments, or otherwise confining the discretion of officers and employees of the city, exhibits a lack of confidence in the personnel of the city government. The Election Law shows much distrust of party leaders and attempts to fix in statutory form what could be—and once was, seemingly with not altogether happy results—the province of party rules. The Civil Service Law sprang from the failings of appointing officers of an earlier day and now circumscribes the discretion of present officers in the exercise of their appointing powers. Confidence in the wisdom, justness, and integrity of the officials involved might lead to less restrictive rules. But the faith being by no means complete, elaboration of the rules of the contest is the result.

Judicial Construction

At the same time, the tendency of the courts to view municipal corporations with some suspicion has compelled drafters of state legislation and the city charter to be quite specific in their descriptions of the powers granted to city organs and agencies. It is usually assumed by the rule makers that any uncertainty about the power of the city to take an action is likely to be resolved against the city by the courts if the power is challenged. The courts have ruled that there is no inherent legal right to local self-government in the city and have construed narrowly the doctrine of implied powers as this applies to the city. Consequently, every city action must be tied to some particular and comparatively unambiguous provision of the state constitution or of authorized state legislation, and the city charter must leave no grants of authority to be inferred. Therefore, state enactments dealing with the city tend to grow long and numerous. The Charter of New York City is more than five times as long as the Constitution of the United States, including all constitutional amendments. Circumstances have thrust new responsibilities upon the city. The attitude of the judiciary has, under these conditions, led to the proliferation of many formal rules.

Advantages of Formal Rules to Some Contestants

In all probability, however, the formal rules would have multiplied even if this were not an age of rapid change, if there were no distrust of officialdom and of party leaders, and if there were a far broader construction of city powers by the courts. For there are, for some participants in the contest for the stakes of city politics, advantages in formalization of rules. Officials in Albany, for example, prefer to grant power to the city piecemeal, in specific terms, and subject to detailed restrictions, because this compels city officers to return to the capital in quest of new authority or the lifting of restrictions, an occasion which gives the state officials bargaining opportunities they would not otherwise have. With the state legislature often in the hands of a party different from the party in power in the city, the incentives of the former to make the rules detailed and limiting add to the number and length of the rules. Moreover, unwritten rules may often be altered by those who stand to gain by such manipulation, which usually means by those already in public or party office. Challengers who might have won victories under the customary rules may suddenly find their efforts rendered futile; explication of the rules may at least stabilize them sufficiently for contestants to plan and execute their strategies.

Requirements of Technology

Technological complexity in the city government's activities adds to the growth of formal rules in detail and length. The control of air pollution, for example, calls for more explicit regulations than did earlier regulations for the maintenance of clean streets. Traffic rules in the motor age need to be more elaborate than did regulation of horse-drawn vehicles. Building regulations for skyscrapers and tall apartment houses are necessarily more involved than those for small office buildings or one- and two-family homes. Statutes and other rules controlling land-use in a technological era respond to similar necessities. In an even broader sense, the growth and elaboration of the formal rules not merely are consequences of the entry of the city government into many new fields of action, but also of the growing social, economic, and technological complexity of both old and new functions.

COMPETITION WITHOUT CHAOS

When the stakes of a struggle are as high as they are in the political contest in New York City, the relationships among the contestants require the stability and certainties provided by rules to which all participants are committed, at least until they can be changed by methods which the contestants also accept as binding upon each of them. On the whole, the struggle does take place in a context of agreement that makes it meaningful to speak of rules, and therefore to speak of a contest rather than of a no-holds-barred melee. In trying to determine who gets office, and to sway the decisions of party leaders, officeholders, bureaucracies, and the electorate, most contestants operate within the rules most of the time and make their efforts to change the rules primarily by the designated and accepted procedures. As the formal rules gain in importance, the system becomes even more ordered and symmetrical (although whether at the expense of flexibility is debatable). The strategies and tactics of the contestants certainly shape the system of rules. Indeed, shaping the system is one of the strategies all the contestants use. But the system shapes their strategies and tactics, too. The following chapters describe the way the strategies and the rules interact as the contestants in the politics of New York City attempt to influence the choice of personnel and the contents of governmental decisions.

BIBLIOGRAPHY

FEDERAL SOURCES

The Constitution of the United States

Corwin, Edward S., editor, *The Constitution of the United States of America: Analysis and Interpretation*. Government Printing Office, Washington, 1953. See especially Art. I, Secs. 2, 3, 4, 10; Art. II, Sec. 1; Art. III, Secs. 1, 2; Art IV, Secs. 1, 2; Art. IV, Sec. 4; Art. VI; Amendments I–X, XI, XII, XIV, XV, XVII, XIX, XX, XXII.

Federal Statutes and Administrative Regulations

Code of Federal Regulations. Government Printing Office, Washington. Contains a codification of the rules in force of federal administrative agencies. In structure, the Code roughly parallels the U.S. Code.

Federal Code Annotated. Bobbs-Merrill Co., Indianapolis, 1952. Another edition of the U.S. Code.

The Federal Register. Government Printing Office, Washington. Published five days a week, contains rules and regulations of general application issued by federal executive and administrative agencies and officers.

Government Organization Manual. Government Printing Office, Washington. Issued regularly to describe organization and functions of federal agencies.

United States Code. Government Printing Office, Washington, 1953, and *Supplements.* There is little in the 50 titles of this codification of federal statutes in force that does not impinge in one way or another on government and politics in New York City. Examples of provisions of particular relevance and importance as "rules" of the contest in New York City are contained in Title 2 (the Congress), Title 3 (the President), Title 5 (Executive Departments and Government Officers and Employees), Title 20 (Education), Title 23 (Highways), Title 28 (Judiciary and Judicial Procedure), Title 29

(Labor), Title 33 (Navigation and Navigable Waters), Title 39 (The Postal Service), Title 40 (Public Buildings, Property, and Works), Title 41 (Public Contracts), Title 42 (The Public Health and Welfare), Title 46 (Shipping).

United States Code Annotated. West Publishing Co., St. Paul, 1952. Parallels the official U.S. Code, but adds some material not found in the official edition. The 50 titles and annotation occupy 84 volumes. Kept up to date with supplements.

Federal Court Reports

United States Reports, Federal Reporter, Federal Rules Decisions, and *Federal Supplement,* all published by the government, contain the decisions of federal courts at all levels.

STATE SOURCES

The Constitution of New York State

New York State Constitution. Issued annually by the Secretary of State, Albany. (May also be found in New York State, Department of State, *Manual for the Use of the Legislature of the State of New York;* and in *McKinney's Consolidated Laws of New York,* Book 2, Parts 1 and 2.) Of special pertinence to this study are Arts. I (Bill of Rights), II (Suffrage), V (Officers and Civil Departments), VI (Judiciary), VIII (Local Finances), IX (Local Governments), XI (Education), XIII (Public Officers), XVI (Taxation), XVII (Social Welfare), and XVIII (Housing). New York City is mentioned specifically in Arts. VI, VIII, and IX. Other portions of the constitution, however, also have effects on the government and politics of New York City, but less directly and forcefully.

Breuer, Ernest H., compiler, *Constitutional Developments in New York: 1777–1958.* State Education Department Bibliography Bulletin 82, Albany, 1958.

New York State Statutes and Administrative Regulations

Bohm, Edwin M., *Bradbury's Lawyers' Manual.* Baker Voorhis and Co., New York, 1953. A standard work on the New York Civil Practice Act as it applies to state and municipal courts in New York City.

Clevenger's Annual Practice of New York. Matthew Bender and Co., Albany, contains the Civil Practice Act, Rules of Civil Practice, Court of Claims Act, Surrogates' Court Act, New York City Court Act, New York Municipal Court Code, Justice Court Act, Court Rules, and annotation, which constitute the procedures for civil practice in the courts of New York State.

McKinney's Consolidated Laws of New York, annotated. Edward Thompson Co., Brooklyn, N. Y., 1944. Kept up to date with annual supplements. Particularly important as "rules" of the political contest in New York City are Books 7A (City Home Rule), 8 (Civil Rights), 9 (Civil Service), 9A (Condemnation), 10B (Correction), 11 (County), 16 (Education), 17 (Elections), 20 (General City), 21 (General Construction), 23 (General Municipal), 29 (Judiciary), 30 (Labor), 33 (Local Finance), 35A (Multiple Dwellings), 35B (Multiple Residence), 39 (Penal), 42 (Public Authorities), 43 (Public Buildings), 44 (Public Health), 44A (Public Housing), 46 (Public Officers), 47 (Public Service), 47A (Public Works), 48A (Rapid Transit), 59 (Tax), 62A (Vehicle and Traffic). Other volumes, however, also contain sections of some relevance.

Medina, Harold R., *Important Features of Pleading and Practice Under the New York Civil Practice Act.* Baker, Voorhis and Co., New York, 1922. A scholarly exposition of the New York Civil Practice Act, written not long after it was originally passed.

New York State, Secretary of State, *Official Compilation of Codes, Rules and Regulations of the State of New York.* A collection of the rules and regulations of the administrative agencies of the state government. Kept up to date with supplements.

New York State Court Reports

New York Appellate Division Reports. Williams Press, Albany. Covering cases decided in the Appellate Division of the Supreme Court.

New York Miscellaneous Reports. Williams Press, Albany. Covering cases decided in New York courts other than the Court of Appeals and the Appellate Division of the Supreme Court.

New York Reports. Williams Press, Albany. Covering cases decided in the Court of Appeals.

New York Supplement. West Publishing Co., St. Paul. Covering decisions of the courts of record in New York State.

Rules and Regulations of Courts
See bibliography for Chapter XIV.

CITY SOURCES

New York City Charters, 1897 to Date, arranged chronologically

Ash, Mark, editor, *The Greater New York Charter as Enacted in 1897.* Weed-Parsons, Albany, 1897. An authoritative edition.

Ash, Mark, and William Ash, editors, *The Greater New York Charter as Enacted in 1897 and Amended in 1901.* Baker Voorhis and Co., New York, 1901. The charter under which the city was governed, 1902–1937.

Birdseye, Clarence F., *The Greater New York Charter, Constituting Chapter 378 of the Laws of 1897.* Baker Voorhis and Co., New York, 1897. The report of the Committee which drafted the charter and the report of full Charter Commission to the legislature are included.

Lee, Henry J., editor, *The Charter of the City of New York, with Amendments to May 1, 1930; Also the Home Rule Law, Chapter 363, Laws of 1924, with Amendments to May 1, 1930.* Brooklyn *Eagle* Library, Brooklyn, N. Y., 1930.

Savona, Francis, editor, *Amendments to the Eagle Library Edition of the Charter of the City of New York from May 1, 1930, to the Close of the Extraordinary Sessions of the 1934 State Legislature.* Brooklyn *Eagle* Library, Brooklyn, N. Y., 1934. The versions of the charter employed by the Thacher Charter Commission.

Tanzer, Lawrence A., *The New York City Charter Adopted November 3, 1936.* Clark Boardman Co., New York, 1937. The charter that went into effect in 1938, published by the associate counsel to the Charter Commission.

Viertel, William, editor, *New York City Charter Adopted at the General Election Held November 3, 1936.* City Record, New York, 1958. Issued periodically by this official source, this document is an authoritative text of the city charter, with amendments passed by local legislation and state law up to the date of publication.

Charter Commission Reports and Documents, arranged chronologically

Report of the Charter Revision Commission to the Governor of the State of New York, with Proposed Amendments to the Greater New York Charter. M. B. Brown and Co., New York, 1900. Report of a commission appointed by Governor Theodore Roosevelt. This charter was in effect from 1902 through 1937.

Report of the Charter Revision Commission of 1907 to the Governor of the State of New York, November 30, 1907. J. B. Lyon Co., Albany, 1908. Report of the Ivins Commission.

Report of the New York Charter Commission to the Legislature, 1909. J. B. Lyon Co., Albany, 1909. Report of a commission whose work did not bear fruit.

An Act Constituting the Charter of the City of New York. State of New York, Senate Print 1253, April 25, 1910. The so-called Gaynor Charter, which was rejected.

Bruère, Henry, *A Plan of Organization for New York City: A Mayor, A Board of Directors, A City Manager.* M. B. Brown and Co., New York, 1917. Personal report of one member of a Charter Commission, appointed by Mayor Mitchel, which issued no official report.

Report of the New York Charter Commission with a Draft of Charter for the City of New York, March 5, 1923. M. B. Brown and Co., New York, 1923. Report of the Baldwin Commission.

Minority Report of the New York Charter Commission Created by Chapter 343 of the Laws of 1921, with Proposed Home Rule Charter. New York, March 21, 1923. A report by Charles L. Craig, Comptroller of the City of New York.

New York City Charter Commission, 1922–1923 (The Baldwin Commission). Correspondence, documents, and papers. Columbia University Oral History Collection, Special Collections, Butler Library.

Preliminary Report of Charter Revision Commission Appointed by Hon. John P. O'Brien, Mayor. New York, January 2, 1933. Document issued by a committee whose purpose was to stave off genuine charter revision.

Preliminary Report and Draft of the Proposed Charter for the City of New York. New York City Charter Revision Commission, New York, 1936.

Proposed Charter for the City of New York, Filed with the City Clerk on August 16, 1936, and Report of the New York Charter Revision Commission. New York City Charter Revision Commission, New York, 1936. Reports of the Thacher Charter Commission, before and after public hearings.

New York Charter Commission, *Public Hearings, May 7–22, 1936.* New York Public Library, Astor Branch. Records of the Thacher Commission's public hearings.

Thacher, Thomas D., "Notes on the Work of the New York City Charter Revision Commission, Appointed 1936." Columbia University Oral History Collection, Special Collections, Butler Library, microfilm. These papers and documents tell part of the story of the commission that drafted a home rule charter.

New York City Charter Revision Commission, *Records of Public Hearings and Minutes of Executive Meetings, February 18, 1935–August 4, 1936.* 4 vols., mimeographed. New York Public Library, Astor Branch. Official records of the Thacher Commission.

Documents. 10 vols. Kent Hall, Columbia University. The papers and documents of the Thacher Commission, prepared by its counsel.

Commentaries on the City's Charters, arranged chronologically

Pryor, James W., "The Greater New York Charter," *Annals of the Academy of Political and Social Science*, vol. 10, 1897, pp. 23–28, 32. An authoritative description of the first charter of the Greater City.

Goodnow, Frank J., "The Charter of the City of New York," *Political Science Quarterly*, vol. 17, 1902, pp. 1–23. An expert analysis of the city's original charter, which went into effect in 1898, and of the changes introduced by the charter of 1902.

Dougherty, J. Hampden, *The Proposed New York City Charter, 1911.* The City Club, New York, 1911. A denunciation of the so-called Gaynor charter by a member of the Ivins Commission.

City Club of New York, *The So-Called Gaynor Charter: What It Is and What It Does.* The Club, New York, 1911. An unfavorable analysis of a proposed and eventually rejected charter.

Citizens Union, "How Ripper Charter Rips," *The Searchlight*, vol. 1, August 9, 1911. This special charter number presents the Citizens Union view of the city charter proposed that year.

Tanzer, Lawrence A., "The Defeat of the Tammany-Gaynor Charter," *National Municipal Review*, vol. 1, January, 1912, pp. 61–68. A charter expert, who later served as associate counsel to the Thacher Commission, describes the rejection of a proposed City Charter.

Appelby, Frances S., *Amendments to the New York City Charter During the Years 1918, 1919, 1920, and 1921.* Master's thesis, Columbia University, 1923, unpublished.

Forbes, Russell, "Charter Reform in New York City," *National Municipal Review*, vol. 21, April, 1932, pp. 168–171. Explains the need for redesigning the city's government.

McGoldrick, Joseph D., "Is the City Manager Plan Suitable for New York?" *National Municipal Review*, vol. 21, May, 1932, pp. 289–292. This article foreshadowed the rejection of the city-manager plan by the Thacher Charter Commission, of which Dr. McGoldrick was a member.

"Proposals for the Reorganization of the City of New York," *American Political Science Review*, vol. 27, April, 1933, pp. 336–340. Summarizes a spate of recommendations for charter revision, following the Seabury report.

Forbes, Russell, and others, *Charter Revision for the City of New York*. Department of Government, Washington Square College, New York University, New York, 1934. A plan, prepared by the Department's Division of Research in Public Administration, which suggested changes needed in the city charter.

Hallett, George H., "Charter Commission for New York City," *National Municipal Review*, vol. 23, May, 1934, pp. 268–270. A discussion of an abortive Commission headed by former Governor Alfred E. Smith.

Earle, Genevieve, "Papers Relating to the Charter Revision Commission of 1935–36." Columbia University Oral History Collection, Special Collections, Butler Library. Documents and other pieces written while Mrs. Earle was a member of the Charter Commission.

Proskauer, Joseph M., *A Segment of My Times*. Farrar, Straus and Co., New York, 1950, pp. 172–177. A member of the Charter Revision Commission of 1935 reviews his experiences on that body.

Olmstead, H. M., "New York City's Charter Revision Commission Reports," *National Municipal Review*, vol. 25, May, 1936, pp. 289–290. Comments on the charter drafted by the Thacher Commission.

Citizens Union, *The Searchlight*, Special Charter Number, vol. 26, July, 1936. An analysis of the important changes in the charter prepared by the Thacher Commission. This appraisal presents the Citizens Union viewpoint.

Allen, William H., *Why Tammanies Revive: La Guardia's Mis-Guard*. Institute for Public Service, New York, 1937, pp. 111–117. Charter revision during the first La Guardia administration.

Earle, Genevieve, "Reminiscences." Columbia University Oral History Collection, Special Collections, Butler Library. A member of the Charter Revision Commission tells how the charter adopted at the polls in 1938 was drafted.

Tanzer, Lawrence A., *The New York City Charter*. Clark Boardman Co., New York, 1937. The Thacher Charter Commission's Associate Counsel describes its work.

Thacher, Thomas D., "Reminiscences." Columbia University Oral History Collection, Special Collections, Butler Library. The Chairman of the Charter Revision Commission, which drew up the instrument that went into effect in 1938, tells his story.

Shaw, Frederick, *History of the New York City Legislature*. Columbia University Press, New York, 1954, pp. 8–9, 12–14, 121–122, 152–170. Notes on charter commissions and proposals.

New York Chamber of Commerce, "A Charter Commission for New York City," *New York Chamber of Commerce Bulletin*, February, 1959, pp. 355–358. Discusses the Mayor's proposals for charter revision.

New York City Administrative Code

Administrative Code of the City of New York. J. B. Lyon Co., Albany, 1938. On December 30, 1937, the old Code of Ordinances of New York City, revised to conform to the new charter and enacted (Chapter 929 of the Laws of 1937) as "An Act to provide an administrative code for the city of New York in harmony with and supplemental to the New York City Charter," took effect in its new form. This is the original code, which has been brought up to date as noted in the next citation.

Charter and Administrative Code, Annotated. Williams Press, Albany, 1957, 6 vols. A complete and authoritative edition of both documents, checked against relevant statutes, local laws, and court decisions.

Lazarus, Reuben, "A New Administrative Code for New York City," *National Municipal Review*, vol. 27, February, 1938, pp. 93–99. The preparation of the city's administrative code, which went hand-in-hand with charter revision.

Health (Sanitary) Code

New York City Health Code, Preliminary Drafts. Columbia University, Legislative Drafting Research Fund, New York Sanitary Code Revision Project, mimeographed, 1956. Preliminary drafts of the revision of the Sanitary Code prepared for the Board of Health, by the Legislative Drafting Research Fund took effect in 1959.

Board of Health, *The Sanitary Code of New York City.* City Record Office, New York. (Superseded by New York City Health Code in 1959; see page 116.) Legislation of the Board of Health covering a variety of subjects ranging from Diseases, Drugs and Cosmetics, and Food and Drink, to Buildings, Street Conditions, Railroad Cars, and Aircraft. Kept current with supplements. Contains Regulations of the Board of Health, which have the same force and effect as provisions of the code. Appendices include relevant provisions of state law.

Board of Hospitals, *Hospital Code of New York City.* Legislation applying to proprietary hospitals, nursing homes and other similar institutions.

Other City Codes

Parts of the Administrative Code of the city are entitled "codes," two major ones being the Building Code and the Electrical Code. They have no separate standing apart from the Administrative Code, however, as does the Sanitary Code, but are chapters of the broader document. Technically speaking, the great bodies of local law are the Administrative Code and the Sanitary Code.

Administrative Rules and Regulations of New York City Agencies

Department of Buildings, *Building Laws of the City of New York.* City Record Office, New York. "Laws, Rules, Regulations, Etc., Applicable to the Erection, Construction, Maintenance and Alteration of Structures and Buildings in the City of New York." Provisions of the charter, the Administrative Code, state law, and state and city administrative agency regulations. Kept up to date with supplements.

Law Department, *Rules and Regulations of New York City Agencies, 1938–1946; Supplement to Rules and Regulations of New York City Agencies, 1946–1952; Rules and Regulations of New York City Departments, since 1952.* The Department, New York, 1946, 1952. Collected by Municipal Reference Library.

SPECIAL AUTHORITIES

For materials on the special public authorities, see the bibliography for Chapter IX.

PARTY RULES

The rules of the parties are not published in any systematic way, nor are they regularly compiled and filed in public places. Consequently, the usual way of obtaining copies of these rules is to communicate with the committee of each party for each county, the state, and the nation.

PART TWO

STRATEGIES OF THE CONTESTANTS: EFFORTS TO DETERMINE WHO GETS PUBLIC OFFICE AND EMPLOYMENT

CHAPTER V

The Structure and Operation
of Nominating Machinery

NOMINATIONS AND THE STAKES OF POLITICS

OCCUPANTS OF ELECTIVE PUBLIC OFFICE are, as noted earlier, among the chief factors determining who gets what stakes of politics. The formal powers of elected officials place them in a position to exercise considerable influence in the formulation of major public decisions, and they appoint or control officers and employees influential in the formation of lesser policies. Hence, one of the more obvious strategies of contestants for the prizes of political action is to get elective office for themselves when they can, or at least to use all the strength they can summon to secure the election of persons whose official behavior is likely to be favorable to them.

The struggle for control of elective office is not exclusively an interparty phenomenon nor is it confined to elections proper. Rather, it goes on actively within the parties prior to elections in the form of negotiations among factions, each seeking to secure the nomination of its party for its own favored choice. Factions able to select party leaders normally have the upper hand in such negotiations, for party leaders possess formal rule-making powers and special powers of nomination that give them crucial strategic advantages in picking nominees. Efforts to dominate the structure and operation of nominating machinery therefore constitute one of the principal strategies of contestants concerned about who gets public office and employment and what they do when they have it.

THE MACHINERY FOR NOMINATIONS BY PARTIES

The Legal Definition of a Party

Nomination is the process by which the names of candidates are selected to appear on the official ballots in elections for public offices. Nominating as well as election procedures in New York City, whether for federal, state, county, or city office, are governed by the New York State Election Law. It is not necessary to be nominated by a party in order to appear on an election ballot, but the law provides different procedures for the selection of party

candidates as contrasted with independent candidates. The procedures prescribed for party candidates apply to "any political organization which at the
last preceding election for governor polled at least 50,000 votes for governor."

Party Structure

Party Members. Practically everyone who takes the trouble to vote in New
York State enrolls in a party; roughly 95 out of every 100 registrants for any
city election normally declare themselves to be members of one party or
another.

For it is just as easy to enroll as not to enroll. Every voter, when he appears
at his polling place or at his borough office of the Board of Elections to register, is handed an enrollment blank. All he need do is fill in his name and
address, sign a certificate that he is a qualified voter in the Election District
in which he has been registered, and "that I am in general sympathy with the
principles of the party which I have designated by my mark hereunder; and
that it is my intention to support generally at the next general election, state
or national, the nominees of such party for state or national offices," and
make a mark next to the party of his choice; the names and emblems of all
the recognized parties appear on the face of the enrollment blank. A voter
may decline to enroll in a party by returning the blank to the registration
inspectors unmarked, or by executing it but failing to indicate his party
preference; in either case, almost as much time and effort are required for
declination as for enrollment. Since party membership thus costs nothing,
creates no personal liabilities, incurs only a moral obligation to support the
party, and does bring with it some advantages, the pressures in favor of
enrollment are generally stronger than those against it. Many of those who
refuse to enroll in any of the parties listed are actually identified with those
small groups called independent bodies in the Election Law—parties unable
to attract at least 50,000 votes in a gubernatorial election. So only a very small
percentage of the total voting population actually rejects affiliation with any
political association as a way of asserting political independence.

The benefits of membership in a party constitute a second reason for enrollment. For one thing, only enrolled party members are permitted to participate (the following year) in the primaries in which the candidates for
elective office are nominated and the occupants of *party* office are chosen. For
another thing, when official channels prove unyielding, any individual who
wants a personal favor from any level of government—that is, who wants a
share in the stakes of politics—frequently finds it to his advantage to enlist the
aid of an officer of his party. Naturally, the leverage of adherents of the party
in power in the city is normally somewhat greater than is the influence of the
supporters of the opposition. The claims of the minority party (which, however weak it may be locally, generally has considerable strength in Albany

TABLE 21. REGISTRATION AND PARTY ENROLLMENT, 1948–1958

Numbers (in thousands) and percentages[a]

Election year	Total number registered voters	Total number enrolled in all parties	Number enrolled in Democratic party	Per cent of all enrollees who chose Democratic party	Number enrolled in Republican party	Per cent of all enrollees who chose Republican party	Number enrolled in Liberal party	Per cent of all enrollees who chose Liberal party	Number enrolled in American Labor party	Per cent of all enrollees who chose American Labor party
1948 Presidential	3,316	3,075	1,939	63	843	27	93	3	200	7
1949 Mayoral	2,776	2,581	1,819	70	485	19	113	4	164	6
1950 Gubernatorial and special mayoral	2,809	2,597	1,825	71	566	22	108	3	98	3
1951 Off year	1,913	1,586	1,227	77	206	13	97	6	56	4
1952 Presidential	3,529	3,238	2,132	66	963	29	90	3	53	2
1953 Mayoral	2,397	2,238	1,606	72	507	23	93	4	33	1
1954 Gubernatorial	2,466	2,306	1,709	74	516	22	59	3	22	1
1955 Off year	1,691	1,610	1,211	75	360	22	39	3	...	...
1956 Presidential	3,291	3,077	2,087	68	923	30	67	2	...	...
1957 Mayoral	2,443	2,282	1,677	73	549	25	56	2	...	...
1958 Gubernatorial	2,665	2,502	1,833	73	607	24	62	2	...	...

[a] Figures may not add to totals because of rounding.

SOURCE: Annual Reports of the New York City Board of Elections.

and/or Washington) and the claims of the third parties also tend to win more
sympathetic attention as a rule than do the claims of those rugged individ-
ualists who disclaim connection with any political organization.

Under these circumstances, the overwhelming verdict for party enrollment
among the city's voters is hardly unexpected. However, total enrollment in
all the parties, and in each of them individually, has fluctuated greatly from
year to year. For enrollment in any year has depended on the number of
people who registered to vote in the preceding general election. Under the
system of annual, personal registration in effect in New York City until very
recently, the volume of registration was directly related to the prominence of
the offices at stake each year. The number of registrants invariably reached
its peaks in presidential years, dropped to about two thirds of this maximum
in mayoral and gubernatorial years, and dropped to less than one half of the
presidential-year figures in the odd years immediately preceding presidential
elections, when almost the only offices to be filled were judicial. The adoption
of a system of permanent, personal registration by New York City in 1957,
under the authority of an amendment to the state Election Law enacted by
the legislature two years earlier, will doubtless greatly reduce these fluctua-
tions. Under this system, the voter need register only once, and his name will
then be maintained on the voting and party lists indefinitely as long as he

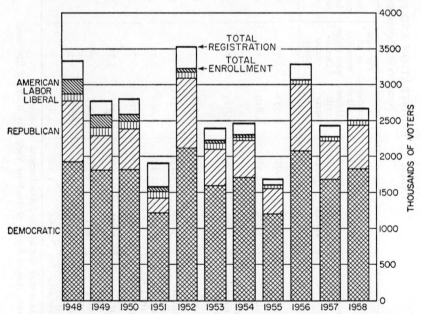

CHART 8. REGISTRATION AND PARTY ENROLLMENT IN NEW YORK CITY IN SELECTED YEARS
Source: Compiled from *Annual Reports* of the New York City Board of Elections.

remains in the same Election District, continues to vote in general elections at least every other year, and does not apply for a change in enrollment. Eventually, this may well stabilize registration figures, although it will not end variations altogether because there are many thousands of people who turn out to vote only for presidential candidates. The spread between the highest and lowest points of party enrollment should decrease correspondingly.

Invariably, the vast majority of the enrollees in the city select the Democratic party. The size of the Democratic enrollment varies inversely with the size of the total enrollment in all parties; the greater the number of people who register and enroll in parties, the smaller the *percentage* of the total (but not, of course, the absolute figure) who enroll as Democrats. Nevertheless, even in presidential years, when registration and total enrollment figures reach their zeniths, the Democrats normally capture two thirds of all the enrollees. In the years when a Governor or Mayor is to be elected, over 70 per cent of all the enrollees list themselves as Democrats. In the off years, when enrollment drops to its lowest point, Democrats normally constitute three quarters of the total.

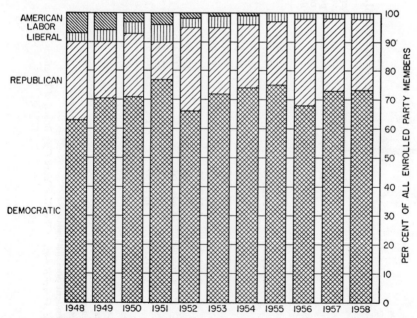

CHART 9. PER CENT OF ALL ENROLLED PARTY MEMBERS ENROLLED IN EACH PARTY IN NEW YORK CITY, 1948–1958

SOURCE: Compiled from *Annual Reports* of the New York City Board of Elections.

TABLE 22. TOTAL AND PARTY VOTES IN GENERAL ELECTIONS, NEW YORK CITY, 1948–1958[a]

Year	Total ballots cast	Democratic votes	Democratic votes as per cent of total ballots	Republican votes	Republican votes as per cent of total ballots	Liberal votes	Liberal votes as per cent of total ballots	American Labor votes	American Labor votes as per cent of total ballots
1958[b]	2,393,167	1,116,617	47	1,011,814	43	205,251	9	22,859[f]	1
1957[c]	2,224,054	1,284,856	57	585,768	26	217,941	10	..	..
1956[d]	3,221,178	1,383,092	43	1,553,298	48	231,784	7	..	..
1955[e]	1,458,624	863,391	59	382,533	26	110,416	8	..	..
1954[b]	2,308,464	1,260,426	54	765,464	33	203,693	9	39,768	2
1953[c]	2,244,146	1,022,626	46	661,591	25	428,688	19	53,045	3
1952[d]	3,461,706	1,517,982	44	1,495,491	43	336,948	10	56,647	2
1951[c]	1,724,082	665,574	38	470,690	27	360,475	21	113,905	7
1950[b]	2,705,236	1,033,198	38	1,119,450	41	244,831	9	176,202	7
1949[c]	2,656,324	1,266,512	48	570,713	21	373,287	14	356,626	13
1948[d]	3,216,438	1,403,379	44	1,108,218	34	193,166	6	422,355	13

ᵃ Figures may not add to totals because of unrecorded votes and scattered votes not reported here.
ᵇ Figures are votes for Governor.
ᶜ Figures are votes for Mayor.
ᵈ Figures are votes for President.
ᵉ Figures are sum of votes for Supreme Court justices.
ᶠ Independent Socialist party.
SOURCE: *Annual Reports* of the New York City Board of Elections.

For the Republicans, the reverse is true. Their best years are those in which the presidency is to be filled, and they make their poorest showings in the off years. But they rarely capture a third of the total enrollment in the city even under conditions that are for them the most favorable, and they attract less than a quarter in the lean years. The Liberal party can generally count on from 3 to 4 per cent of the total enrollment in any year, and the American Labor party, which failed in 1954 to win sufficient votes to retain its status as an official party and which therefore dissolved itself the following year, fell to a bare 1 per cent of the total enrollment.

Enrollment, however, is not a reliable index of party strength in elections. Consistently a far smaller number of the voters in any election in New York City cast Democratic ballots than enroll in the Democratic party, while the number of people who vote for candidates of the Republican or other parties almost always exceeds the number who enroll in those parties.

The excess of Democratic enrollment over Democratic voting is explained largely by the fact that Democratic candidates normally win most of the elective offices in the city. In the first place, in virtually every area of the country in which such one-party dominance obtains, primary contests are far more common in the majority organization than in the opposition. In New York City, such contests are four to six times as common in the Democratic party as in the Republican party and fights for the nomination in Liberal

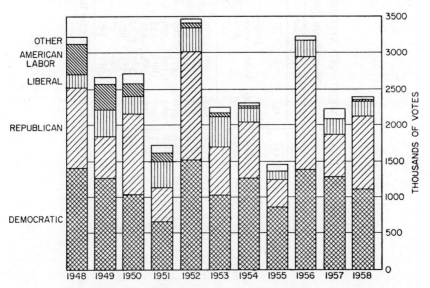

CHART 10. TOTAL AND PARTY VOTES IN GENERAL ELECTIONS, NEW YORK CITY, 1948–1958
SOURCE: Compiled from *Annual Reports* of the New York City Board of Elections.

TABLE 23. ENROLLMENT AND VOTING PATTERNS IN NEW YORK CITY, 1948-1958

Numbers (in thousands) and percentages

Year	Democrats				Republicans				Liberals				American Laborites			
	(1) Enroll-ment	(2) Vote	(3) Differ-ence (2)−(1)	(4) Per cent change (3)÷(1)	(5) Enroll-ment	(6) Vote	(7) Differ-ence (6)−(5)	(8) Per cent change (7)÷(5)	(9) Enroll-ment	(10) Vote	(11) Differ-ence (10)−(9)	(12) Per cent change (11)÷(9)	(13) Enroll-ment	(14) Vote	(15) Differ-ence (14)−(13)	(16) Per cent change (15)÷(13)
1948	1,939	1,403	−536	−27.6	843	1,108	265	31.4	93	193	100	107.5	200	422	222	111.0
1949	1,819	1,267	−552	−30.3	485	571	86	17.7	113	373	260	230.1	164	357	193	117.7
1950	1,825	1,033	−792	−43.4	566	1,119	553	99.6	108	245	137	126.8	98	176	78	79.6
1951	1,227	665	−562	−45.8	206	471	265	128.6	153	360	207	135.3	56	114	58	103.6
1952	2,132	1,518	−614	−28.8	963	1,495	532	55.2	90	337	247	273.3	53	57	4	7.5
1953	1,606	1,023	−583	−35.7	507	662	155	30.6	93	429	336	361.3	33	53	20	60.6
1954	1,709	1,260	−449	−26.2	516	765	251	40.4	59	204	145	245.8	22	40	18	81.8
1955	1,211	863	−348	−28.7	360	383	23	6.4	39	110	71	197.4	...	...	...	...
1956	2,087	1,383	−704	−33.7	923	1,553	630	68.3	67	232	165	246.3	...	...	...	...
1957	1,677	1,285	−392	−23.4	549	586	37	6.7	56	218	162	311.5	...	...	...	...
1958	1,833	1,117	−716	−39.1	607	1,012	405	66.7	62	205	143	230.6	...	...	...	...

SOURCE: Compiled from *Annual Reports* of the New York City Board of Elections.

party primaries are even more infrequent than in the Republican. Consequently, any voter who wishes to make his weight felt in the selection of nominees as well as of officials will usually have a far greater opportunity to do so if he is enrolled as a Democrat. In the second place, the hand of any individual who anticipates that he may one day seek favors from the government through political channels is likely to be strengthened if he makes his demand as a member of the party in power; in New York City, this generally means the Democratic party. To secure these advantages, large numbers of voters who have little expectation of voting for Democratic candidates nevertheless list themselves as members of the Democratic party. This practice of enrolling in the dominant party is not confined to New York City; in other areas throughout the state it is equally common. It makes no difference which party predominates; in one-party sections like the Democratic deep South and the Republican Midwest, and in so-called modified one-party regions like New York City (regions in which one party consistently wins most of the elections, but is defeated just often enough to introduce a strong element of uncertainty), the dominant party tends to attract a larger proportion of the enrollees than of the actual ballots.

Some New York City residents demonstrate the depth of their loyalty to the Democratic party by turning out for every election, regardless of the importance of the office at stake. This is what accounts for the extraordinarily high proportion of Democratic enrollment and voting in the years when the voting is light, and for the smaller Democratic margins when the voting is heavy. The solid core of devoted adherents is overwhelmed by the numbers of the intermittent and less dependable party supporters in elections which produce heavy voting, but it continues to stand firm in the off years when the seeming inconsequence of the elections fails to stimulate most voters and induces them to leave the field to the regulars. The Republicans, on the other hand, boast a smaller reliable core and depend more heavily on the irregulars to rally to their standard in disproportionately large numbers whenever they do turn out; hence the higher Republican proportion of both enrollment and voting when the turnout is heavy.

Party membership in New York State is thus nominal and, at bottom, ephemeral. It is only loosely related to voting behavior. Up to now, it has gone through regular cycles of expansion and contraction, oscillations the new system of permanent registration is likely to diminish in magnitude but not to eliminate entirely. Yet this is the base on which the framework and processes of party life have been erected.

Committees. In a loose, rhetorical sense, party members may be said to constitute the parties, just as the whole body of citizens "is" the government. In a more restricted legal sense, the parties are essentially equivalent to their governing bodies as defined by statute. In a practical sense, the parties are the relatively small organized groups of party officers who dominate their decision-making processes; the actual managers overlap, but are not identical with, the statutory governing bodies.

The statutory bodies are committees prescribed by law for the county and state level. No citywide governing body is established by legislation. Under the state Election Law each constituency smaller than a county (with the sole exception of Judicial Districts of the State Supreme Court, discussed later) — state Assembly Districts, state Senatorial Districts, Congressional Districts, and Municipal Court Districts — also has a party committee, but this committee consists simply of the members of the county committees who reside within the lesser jurisdiction. And only the committees at the county and state levels have rule-making authority.

At both county and state levels, the law requires each party to have a full committee and an executive committee. A full county committee consists of members elected in party primaries in each Election District within the several counties. (Election Districts, often called precincts in other states, comprise up to about 900 voters and are set up primarily for the registration of voters and the conduct of elections.) County committees may provide in their rules for either annual or biennial election; all in the city have opted for the latter, some in even-numbered years, some in odd-numbered years. By law, each Election District is entitled to at least two county committeemen, and may, depending on the rules of the state committees, be allotted additional ones for a particularly heavy party vote. The number of Election Districts in the city averages 4,000, ranging from over 1,200 in Kings County (Brooklyn) to roughly 100 in Richmond County (Staten Island). The largest county committee (the Democratic one in Kings) has some 4,000 members, the smallest (the Democrats in Richmond) about 300.

Partly because the county committees are such unwieldy bodies, and partly because the men who write state party rules and draft state electoral legislation are anxious to keep control of the parties in the hands of relatively small governing cliques, all the powers of the full county committees are delegated, without limitation between meetings of the county committees, to county executive committees. Since the county committees normally meet for a brief time within twenty days after their election in order to comply with the requirements of the Election Law, and do not ordinarily reassemble for the remainder of their two-year terms, it is the county executive committees that wield their powers for all practical purposes.

Each county committee makes its own rules about the composition and mode of selection of its own executive committee, so the executive committees differ from county to county and party to party. All, however, consist primarily of Assembly District Leaders and coleaders (discussed below), although many of the ten (one for each party in every county) major-party executive committees have additional members who hold their places automatically by virtue of occupying other party positions. (Most of the members of the county executive committees are also members of the full county committees, although this is not mandatory in all cases.) No county executive committee exceeds 75 members.

Broad discretion in the internal management of party affairs is lodged by law in the state committees, which are the parties' highest legislative organs in the state. The Election Law confers on the state committee of each party the authority to adopt for its own composition whatever units of representation it prefers and to make its own rules as to the number of representatives from each unit, subject only to the requirement that the number of representatives from all units of representation must be the same. The state committees of both major parties have enacted rules providing for two members—one man and one woman—from each Assembly District in the state to be elected every even-numbered year by the registered party members of each such district in party primaries. There being 150 Assembly Districts in the state (65 of them in New York City), the state committees consist of at least 300 members, and they normally include roughly 50 additional members—chiefly members of the state executive committees described in the next paragraph—who are appointed rather than elected to their positions. In practice, the overwhelming majority of the members of the state executive committees of the major parties are Assembly District Leaders or coleaders; thus, the managerial personnel of the parties' district, county, and state organs overlap extensively and form an interlocking directorate.

When the state committees are not in session, the rules of both major parties provide that all their powers shall be exercised by their respective state executive committees. The state executive committee of each party is appointed by its state chairman (a party functionary elected by the full state committee). The rules of the Democratic party provide that a majority of the members of the Democratic state executive committee must be elected members of the full state committee, but place no other restrictions on the chairman. Republican party rules make the elected officers of the full state committee, the two national committeemen from the state, and the president of the Young Republicans of New York State *ex officio* members of the state executive committee, and require also that the membership of the executive committee include at least two representatives from each of the Judicial Districts of the state Supreme Court selected by those state committeemen residing in each such district; beyond this, the Republican state chairman has great freedom. Furthermore, the state chairmen of both parties are empowered to name the chairmen of all the subcommittees of their respective executive committees. These procedures clearly make it possible for a determined state chairman to dominate the executive committees, and, in fact,

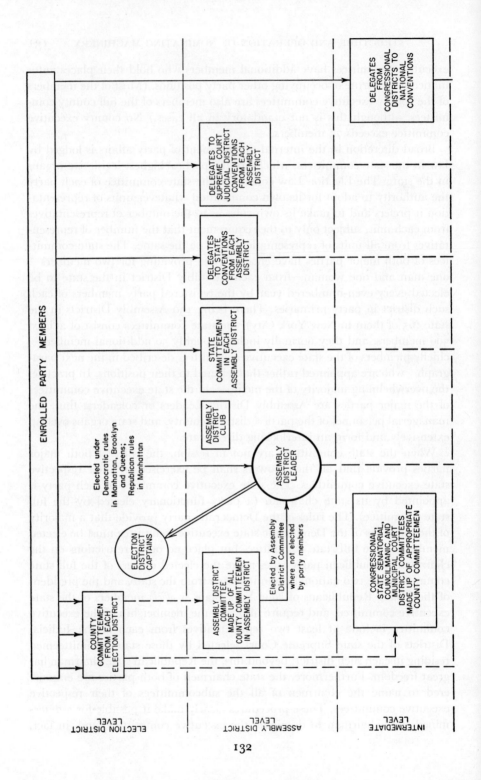

ENROLLED PARTY MEMBERS

DELEGATES FROM CONGRESSIONAL DISTRICTS TO NATIONAL CONVENTIONS

DELEGATES TO SUPREME COURT JUDICIAL DISTRICT CONVENTIONS FROM EACH ASSEMBLY DISTRICT

DELEGATES TO STATE CONVENTIONS FROM EACH ASSEMBLY DISTRICT

STATE COMMITTEEMEN IN EACH ASSEMBLY DISTRICT

ASSEMBLY DISTRICT CLUB

Elected under Democratic rules in Manhattan, Brooklyn and Queens; Republican rules in Manhattan

ASSEMBLY DISTRICT LEADER

ELECTION DISTRICT CAPTAINS

Elected by Assembly District Committee where not elected by party members

COUNTY COMMITTEEMEN FROM EACH ELECTION DISTRICT

ASSEMBLY DISTRICT COMMITTEE MADE UP OF ALL COUNTY COMMITTEEMEN IN ASSEMBLY DISTRICT

CONGRESSIONAL, STATE SENATORIAL, COUNCILMANIC, AND MUNICIPAL COURT DISTRICT COMMITTEES MADE UP OF APPROPRIATE COUNTY COMMITTEEMEN

ELECTION DISTRICT LEVEL

ASSEMBLY DISTRICT LEVEL

INTERMEDIATE LEVEL

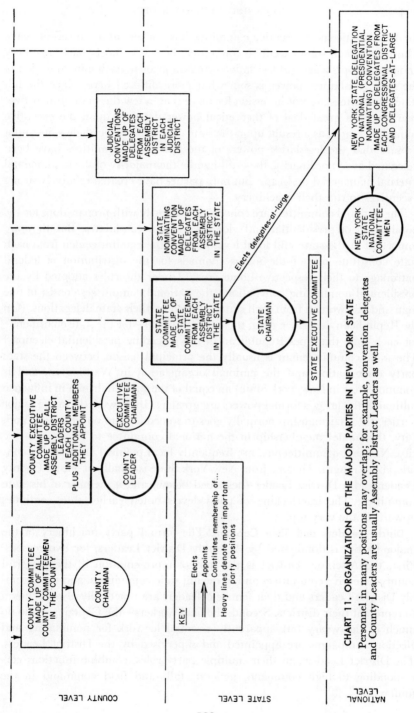

CHART 11. ORGANIZATION OF THE MAJOR PARTIES IN NEW YORK STATE

Personnel in many positions may overlap; for example, convention delegates and County Leaders are usually Assembly District Leaders as well.

COUNTY COMMITTEE MADE UP OF ALL COUNTY COMMITTEEMEN IN THE COUNTY

COUNTY CHAIRMAN

COUNTY EXECUTIVE COMMITTEE MADE UP OF ALL ASSEMBLY DISTRICT LEADERS IN EACH COUNTY PLUS ADDITIONAL MEMBERS THEY APPOINT

COUNTY LEADER

EXECUTIVE COMMITTEE CHAIRMAN

STATE COMMITTEE MADE UP OF STATE COMMITTEEMEN FROM EACH ASSEMBLY DISTRICT IN THE STATE

STATE CHAIRMAN

STATE EXECUTIVE COMMITTEE

STATE NOMINATING CONVENTION MADE UP OF DELEGATES FROM EACH ASSEMBLY DISTRICT IN THE STATE

JUDICIAL CONVENTIONS MADE UP OF DELEGATES FROM EACH ASSEMBLY DISTRICT IN EACH JUDICIAL DISTRICT

Elects delegates-at-large

NEW YORK STATE DELEGATION TO NATIONAL (PRESIDENTIAL NOMINATING) CONVENTION MADE UP OF DELEGATES FROM EACH CONGRESSIONAL DISTRICT AND DELEGATES-AT-LARGE

NEW YORK STATE NATIONAL COMMITTEE-MEN

KEY

—— Elects
↑ Appoints
— Constitutes membership of...
Heavy lines denote most important party positions

COUNTY LEVEL

STATE LEVEL

NATIONAL LEVEL

the Democratic state executive committee has not met at all in recent years. The Republican state executive committee, however, meets fairly regularly and even adopts a general legislative program prior to each annual session of the state legislature; power is somewhat more diffused here. Since the full state committees are not in session for more than a few days out of their two-year terms, a great deal of theoretical power devolves upon the executive committees, and, as a result, upon the state chairmen. Nevertheless, it cannot be said that the legislative powers of the full state committees have been delegated away; ordinarily, they still handle the majority of the fundamental internal managerial problems. But both parties have created relatively strong executives to run their machinery.

The national committees are concerned primarily with preparations for the nomination of presidential and vice presidential candidates. But they are important at the state and local level because the committeemen from each state constitute one of the major channels for the distribution of federal patronage to their respective home areas. Under the rules adopted by the presidential nominating conventions, the national committees consist of one man and one woman from each state, selected by their state delegations. (On the Republican side, since 1952, there is a third seat—for the state chairmen— for each state that goes Republican in the preceding presidential election.) The male committeeman is usually the principal liaison between the state party organization and the national organization in Washington, and is commonly (as in New York State) an equal of the state chairman in influence (although the latter's formal powers are greater). In New York, in the major parties, the chairmanship normally goes to someone from outside New York City, the (male) membership in the national committee to someone in the city. National committeemen are frequently local political chieftains of considerable strength. The one from New York State is usually at least a County Leader and a District Leader (described below) and a member of his state committee. The interlocking of party levels noted earlier thus continues upward to the very top.

District Leaders and Their Captains. The formal party machinery of the major parties is dominated by Assembly District Leaders, for two reasons. First, the Assembly District is the unit of representation in the powerful county executive committees and in the full state committees, and the Assembly District Leaders and their female coleaders are practically always chosen to represent their districts. Second, the field workers—the Captains—who do much of the weary but apparently essential legwork for nominating and election campaigns are appointed and supervised by the District Leaders. The District Leaders, in their multiple party roles, combine functions corresponding to high command, general staff, and field command in the military.

The development of state Assembly Districts as the units of representation on the county executive committees and the state committees is an interesting and rather curious phenomenon on which practically no research has been done. A number of factors, however, taken together, suggest a plausible explanation. One is that Assembly Districts have long been the smallest political subdivisions in the state in which there are contests for elective office. At one time the wards in New York City (abolished with the adoption of the charter of 1936) of the old Board of Aldermen (supplanted by the City Council in 1936) were perhaps slightly smaller, but not significantly so. Assembly Districts could thus be easily managed from a political clubhouse (described below) and were thus highly convenient units for party organization.

Another factor underlying the development of the Assembly District as a unit of party representation is that until 1938 state assemblymen were elected annually. Consequently, the party units in their districts were almost constantly ready for action. They had a continuity, a cohesion, a steady state of preparedness, in contrast with the campaign organizations for less frequently contested offices, that made them the most effective and natural shock troops for candidates from all constituencies to employ. It seems natural, then, that they should have become the primary building blocks for party organization.

Third, when Richard Croker became the leader of Tammany Hall, the Democratic county organization of New York County (Manhattan), then the entire City of New York, he found it convenient to delegate or surrender to his District Leaders power over all municipal offices in their districts. This practice freed him for other business, but it also made the District Leaders more influential figures than they had ever been. Conceivably, this helped establish beyond question the importance of the Assembly District organizations of his party and set an example for others.

The factors that made Assembly Districts the fundamental constituencies of the parties' governing bodies also made them the basis of party field organization. Each Assembly District Leader is empowered by party rule to appoint a male Captain and a female cocaptain in each Election District within his territory. (Generally, the Captains are county committeemen, too.) The basic function of the Captains and cocaptains is to get out the party vote in their territories. In addition, as the points of contact between the parties and the public, Captains and cocaptains are sometimes called upon by the constituents of their respective parties to get favors of a personal nature from governmental officials—favors extending all the way from "fixing" parking tickets to recommendations for public employment, for various kinds of licenses and permits, and similar kinds of special considerations. Since it is the duty of the Captains to establish personal liaison with as many voters as possible, these party functionaries are often the first ones many people think of when they seek help or special privilege in their relations with officialdom. At the same time, many people sophisticated enough to employ the machinery of the parties for such purposes are also well enough informed about and acquainted with party machinery to press their claims higher in the party or the official hierarchies. So although representation of the interests of party supporters in the election districts is one of the responsibilities discharged by Captains, it is overshadowed in importance, and in the amount of time and energy required, by the function of getting the members of their respective parties to go to the polls and cast their ballots for the appropriate candidates.

District Leaders recruit, mobilize, deploy, supervise, and encourage their Captains and keep them under control by holding out the promise of reward (and by threat of deprivation of expected rewards). The Leaders thus manage the manpower with which primary and general election campaigns are conducted, which gives them a powerful instrument for repulsing challengers and for bargaining with other party officers and candidates and officeholders who want and need the votes the district organizations seem to be able to carry.

The center of political gravity in the parties, therefore, is located in the Assembly District Leaders. These positions (and the positions of the women coleaders, with equally formal prerogatives, but usually with far less influence) are defined by party rule rather than by law. Consequently, they are not identical everywhere. Some (Democrats in Manhattan, Queens, and Brooklyn; Republicans in Brooklyn) are chosen every other year by party members in primary elections. All others are named by the biennially elected county committeemen in their respective Assembly Districts (who constitute the Assembly District committees). Usually, District Leaders are themselves county committeemen, but the Manhattan Democratic organization is the only one to require this as a qualification for leadership.

Some of the county executive committees have divided up Assembly Districts and permitted each subdivision to choose a Leader and coleader. (These subdivisions are *party* units only. They need not be the same for both parties. And no matter what the parties do with respect to their own internal organization, only one assemblyman comes from any Assembly District.) The leaders of the subdivisions of any district have almost all the same powers, privileges, and responsibilities as the leaders of full districts. However, the Election Law permits only one vote on county executive committees for each Assembly District, and the leaders and coleaders of each division in an Assembly District share equal fractions of the district's one vote; the larger the number of divisions, the smaller the fractional vote of each Leader and coleader. Furthermore, only two representatives go to the state committees from each Assembly District no matter how many subdivisions are established by county executive committees. The subdivisions thus complicate intraparty relations and intensify internal bargaining. But they also make it possible for the dominant clique in a county executive committee to eliminate subdivisions that fall into insurgent hands and to create a new leadership for a displaced loyal member of the clique. The subdivisions also permit Leaders to concentrate their efforts on smaller areas and members of voters than they would otherwise have to deal with. Hence, in both major parties, there are more Leaders and coleaders than there are Assembly Districts. These differences from one county and party to another, however, are minor variations; the overriding features of all the District Leaders are their central position and power. Regardless of the variations among them, this is their outstanding common attribute. They are the channels through which many of the stakes of politics—particularly elective offices—are dispensed.

Political Clubs. The position of a District Leader rests in large degree on his command of a political club, which is a voluntary association of party members, an unofficial, self-governing society of individuals. A club is forbidden by the Election Law to identify itself publicly with a party unless authorized to do so by the party's county executive committee. The county executive committees recognize only one in each Assembly District or subdivision, and these are the "regular" clubs. (In Queens some coleaders also head recognized clubs of their own, but this is unusual.) There is nothing to prevent clubs from forming and operating vigorously without recognition and without the use of the party labels, but such independent or insurgent clubs normally seek official recognition as their first target.

For recognition symbolizes the acknowledgment by those higher in the parties of the claims of the club upon the rewards and resources of the parties. It normally goes to the club in any district or subdivision that succeeds in securing the election of its own choice as District Leader, either by carrying him to victory in a direct primary or by capturing control of the Assembly District committee at the primaries in those county organizations that provide for indirect selection of leaders. To the regular clubhouse—particularly of the winning party in the district—come those who seek special help or advice, those who hope for political careers, those who want appointments. From these, the organization is built, and through the organization, the electorate is served. The club is the District Leader's source of strength, and the District Leader's strength is the source of reward. This holds the clubs together, and keeps them more or less loyal to the Leaders, who ordinarily are the presidents. Thus, although the clubs are not statutory parts of the party hierarchies, they are pivotal components of party structure and activity.

Since the major parties—the Democrats more than the Republicans—have subdivided some Assembly Districts for party purposes, there are more regular clubs in each party than there are districts. With 65 Assembly Districts in the city, the Democrats have about 80 regular clubs, the Republicans perhaps 70.

Third parties have only scattered clubs in the areas of their greatest strength. But there are, in many districts, associations of party followers seeking to dislodge the established clubs and to install themselves in their place. Their composition varies; some are organized primarily to promote reform or policy changes or preferred candidates, while others are dissident groups of regular party workers disgruntled by the distribution of rewards, dissatisfied with repeated defeats in general elections, or trying to speed their own advancement. No matter what their objectives, they always face an uphill battle because the county executive committees tend to fear insurgents and use their rule-making powers to hurl obstacles in the path of challengers. Moreover, the legal injunction against use of the party label puts most insurgent groups at a disadvantage. Nevertheless, insurgents do succeed now and again, in one district or another. One remarkable attribute of the system is that they then become the regulars; the system manages not only to accommodate insurgency, but even to transform it into regularity. Whether insurgent or regular, however, the first objective of any faction seeking control of a major party is to capture and retain the Assembly District leaderships, and the clubs are the principal instruments in this strategy.

County Leaders. The county executive committees of each party choose the County Leaders every other year. Like the position of District Leader, the County Leader's post is established by party rule rather than by law. But the County Leaders spend little of their time in direct contact with the voting public. They are executives who devote themselves to relations with their counterparts in other counties in deciding on city and state nominations and appointments, with their District Leaders regarding nominations and appointments for the members of the various clubs, and with fund raisers for their respective parties.

State nominating machinery in New York tends to be dominated by County Leaders; nominations for statewide offices are normally decided by understandings among them. Much of the state's patronage is also distributed through them (although District Leaders also exert influence on appointing officers directly through their assemblymen and state senators). County Leaders also stand out in the state delegations to the presidential nominating conventions and exercise considerable authority in deciding the actions of the delegations.

At the city level, there is no established party mechanism for choosing candidates for citywide office; consequently, this is done essentially by agreement among the five County Leaders of each party. While the Manhattan (New York County) leaders of both the Democrats and the Republicans are always very strong in these negotiations, they by no means rule their colleagues. Meetings are truly bargaining sessions, with the Queens and Brooklyn Republicans playing especially large roles in their party, and the Bronx and Brooklyn Democrats presenting heavy counterweights to their New York County (Tammany Hall) opposite numbers. City tickets usually represent compromises among these major forces, and appointments at the city level commonly reflect these understandings.

Probably the greater part of the time of the County Leaders, however, is spent in managing party affairs within their respective jurisdictions. This means satisfying the claims of their District Leaders with respect to county, borough, and judicial nominations, and with respect to appointments at every level of government and in all branches. It also means settling disputes among District Leaders regarding nominations for offices with constituencies embracing more than one such leader's territory. By and large, in their home areas, the County Leaders are adjudicators, arbiters, and mediators. They command great respect within the parties, but they reconcile conflicting proposals by their District Leaders as often as they advance proposals of their own.

As a matter of fact, since the County Leaders are chosen (and removed) by the county executive committees, and the county executive committees are essentially collections of District Leaders, the County Leaders depend for their tenure on their nominal subordinates. This is why County Leaders as well as District Leaders look suspiciously on insurgents in any Assembly District, and rally to the support of threatened regulars. It is why County Leaders are usually careful to placate their District Leaders, giving them time and attention generously and fighting to get for them the rewards they ask for. And it is why they must negotiate with their District Leaders rather than command them. County Leaders have been unseated by coalitions of rebellious District Leaders. The Democrats in Queens have had internal factional struggles for their county leadership. And in a brief but bitter struggle, the self-selected candidate to succeed Thomas Curran, long-time Republican leader in Manhattan who died in 1958, was defeated. Important and powerful as the County Leaders are, they are not so autonomous, so politically self-contained, as the District Leaders and their district clubs.

The top management structure of county-level party organizations includes, in addition to the County Leaders, the county chairmen (chosen by the full county committees) and the chairmen of the county executive committees (chosen by the executive committees), offices defined in general terms by the Election Law and in detail by party rules. In most cases the offices of County Leader, county chairman, and chairman of the county executive committee are separated. Occasionally, however, two of these positions may be formally joined by the party rules in a particular county. The New York County Republican chairman, for example, is County Leader *ex officio*. Or a single individual may hold two posts simultaneously (as Carmine De Sapio, who served as both county chairman and County Leader).

In any event, it is normally the County Leaders who exercise the greatest influence by virtue of the support they command among their District Leaders. When the chairmanships are not occupied by the County Leaders themselves, the occupants are almost invariably their staunch allies and are overshadowed in prominence and power by the leaders. As long as a firm majority of the Assembly District Leaders are solidly behind them, County Leaders are among the most powerful officers in their party hierarchies.

Convention Delegates. There are three types of nominating conventions to which party members in New York elect delegates: state Supreme Court Judicial District conventions, state conventions, and national conventions. These delegates are thus part of party structure. In practice, however, delegacies are minor posts indeed; if a delegate is influential, it is ordinarily by virtue of another party office or official position. If a delegate has no additional place in his party hierarchy, he normally counts for little in party affairs. Coalitions of District and County Leaders run the conventions; dilettante delegates are part of the machinery but not part of the inner cores.

Unpaid Service. Party positions are unpaid, in the ordinary sense of the term. They bring their incumbents no regular, stipulated salaries from party or public treasuries, except that party workers on Election Day usually get small stipends. By and large, party leaders and workers depend on jobs in government, contributions by candidates and by party supporters and beneficiaries, and on their businesses, professions, or trades for their incomes. At election time, the higher levels of the party organizations give the lower ones modest financial help; for the most part, however, each party unit learns to shift for itself.

A Feudal Pattern and Its Internal Bonds. Clearly, party organizations in New York City are not monolithic in character. Each Assembly District unit is virtually an independent principality. Several Manhattan Republican District Leaders, for example, and their county committeemen nominated Representative Adam Clayton Powell, a Democrat temporarily read out of his party, to run for Congress from their Congressional District although the County Leader objected vehemently to this choice. In the Democratic party, a bloc of District Leaders of Italian descent rebelled against County Leader De Sapio's candidate for Surrogate, and forced him to accept the man they favored. Governor Harriman and other state officers of the Democratic party brought heavy pressure to bear on the Democratic County Leader in Queens, and on his District Leaders, to persuade them to repudiate a bargain with their Republican counterparts, but the local party leaders, for their own reasons, insisted on abiding by the terms of the agreement. There is little that "superior" officers in a major party can do to discipline "subordinates." Only the third parties tend to display a substantial degree of centralization.

A number of factors hold these loose associations together. One is a web of personal allegiances. Another is their shared interest in victory over organized opposition. The third is the possibility that political rewards will be cut off from above—a possibility minimized by the fact that the higher levels depend on the district organizations more heavily for field work (as later discussions of sabotage and defection will show) than the District Leaders do on the higher levels for rewards (for District Leaders can by-pass the higher party echelons in quest of benefits). Fourth is the interlocking of party components noted earlier; Captains are normally county committeemen, District Leaders are county executive committeemen and state committeemen, most County Leaders are also District Leaders, national committeemen are almost always County Leaders, and other party committees and conventions are ordinarily composed in large measure of various combinations of these functionaries. To put it another way, one man may be a county committeeman, a District Leader, a county executive committeeman, a County Leader, a state committeeman, a national committeeman, and a delegate to many conventions; this, in fact, is a list of the party offices occupied by Carmine De Sapio, who is somewhat unusual, perhaps, but not extremely so in this regard. The number of individual party positions is many times greater than the number of individual persons who actually fill them. The potential independence of, and possible mutual disregard of each other by, party units and bodies is held in check by overlapping personnel. The parties are aggregations of segments rather than organic entities. They are decentralized and fragmented and undisciplined, but they achieve sufficient unity of purpose and action and leadership to identify them as organizations.

The Primaries

What They Are. In the summer or fall of every year (save the years when a President is to be elected, and then in the spring), all the parties, as defined by the Election Law, in New York State hold primaries. A primary is an election open only to enrolled members of the legally defined parties, regulated by state law, and conducted at public expense. At these primary elections, the rank and file of the parties officially select the parties' nominees for offices, delegates to conventions at which their parties' nominees for other offices will be selected, and the party officers and committees constituting the legally recognized party hierarchies.

The Names on Primary Ballots. Any enrolled party member entitled to vote in a primary can have his name placed on the primary ballot of his party in a try for a nomination, a delegacy, membership on some committee, or (where these are elected by the rank and file) a leadership, or any combination of these. The procedure by which names are certified to appear on such ballots is termed "designation" in the state Election Law, and consists of the collection on petitions of a specified minimum number of signatures of enrolled party members residing within the constituency of the public or party office to be filled.

In most of the state, to run in a primary for nomination for public office the aspirant is required to obtain the signature of at least 5 per cent of the enrolled members in the appropriate unit. In New York City, the population density would greatly overburden the signature-gathering machinery of all the parties, so the Election Law states the actual *number* of signatures required for designation for each office rather than a percentage. For citywide office, it is 5,000 valid signatures; for county (including all judgeships elected from coun- tywide constituencies) and borough offices, 2,500; for United States Repre- sentative, state senator, city councilman, and Municipal Court Justice (that is, for all offices with constituencies smaller than a county but larger than an Assembly District), 750; and for state assemblyman, 350. Designating peti- tions must be signed between the eleventh and the fifth Tuesdays preceding the primaries, which means there is no time for waste motion; the signature- collecting machinery must be ready to roll promptly when the period for signing begins. An individual may seek designations for as many offices as he likes, but he must circulate separate petitions for each. A petition must con- tain the names of a committee of at least three enrolled party members residing in the appropriate constituency who are to pick a replacement in case a designee withdraws or dies before the primary.

Similarly, persons seeking election by the parties' rank and file to party offices must have their names placed on the primary ballots by designation. Those who want to be state committeemen, or Assembly District Leaders or coleaders where these are elected directly by party members, or delegates to state or judicial conventions, must secure at least 350 signatures of enrolled party members in their respective Assembly Districts in order to appear on primary ballots. Those who want to run for county committeemen must col- lect the signatures of at least 5 per cent of the enrolled party members in their respective Election Districts. Those who want to be delegates to a national convention must acquire the signatures of 750 enrolled party members in their Congressional Districts (or, as described later, get appointed as dele- gates at large). Occasionally, there are competing aspirants to these party positions as different factions battle for control of an area; usually, however, the "regular" slate is unopposed in the primaries.

Until 1960, primaries had to be held whether or not there were contests for any of the nominations or party posts at stake. And the process of designation had to be completed for each primary by (or on behalf of) each individual who desired a place on any primary ballot even if he were unopposed.

Conducting the Primaries. When the city voter in the primary turns up at his polling place, public election inspectors representing all parties check his qualifications just as they do at general elections and hand him the ballot of the party in which he is enrolled. He marks it in secret and deposits it in the ballot box. Although the use of voting machines where they are applicable to primary elections was authorized by the state legislature in 1954, they are still not employed in the city.

Participation in a primary election is no more burdensome for the individual voter than participation in a general one but only a small fraction of those eligible take part in the primaries of their parties. Even an exciting contest between rival wings of the Democratic party for the mayoralty nomination (the most important office for which nominees are directly elected by the rank and file of the party in New York City) fails to bring out much more than one quarter of the eligibles, and often as few as 15 per cent may exercise their right to vote in a primary when lesser issues are involved.

In part, low turnout may be due to the relative infrequency of open competition for party nominations in the city. Four out of every five persons desiring to be named as their parties' candidates will normally appear unopposed on the primary ballots even in even-numbered years, when the number of nominees to be selected by direct primary in each party may run as high as 150. (See Table 25.) For the thousands of county and state committee and convention delegate positions in the parties, opposition is virtually nonexistent, making the ratio of contests to total number of offices in any primary even smaller than this. The motivations to vote when there are no choices to be made are slight indeed. In this respect, enrolled Republicans have even less incentive to take part in their party primaries than do Democrats. Since the Republicans stand little chance of capturing most of the lesser offices, there is less intense competition for these Republican nominations, and primary contests in the Republican party are far fewer than Democratic contests. As a matter of fact, although the Republicans put up just as many candidates for election as the Democrats, seldom do more than three or four Republican aspirants have opposition in the primary. Opposition is even more unusual in the Liberal primaries. But, although contests in Democratic primaries are far more common than in the other parties in the city, they are still the exception rather than the rule.

Thus, voter nonparticipation in primaries engendered by lack of choice is intensified by the fact that the individual party member, unless he is closely associated with the "regular" wing of his party, must rely on his own alertness and ingenuity to find out whether one of the few primary contests taking place is in his district. The odds are generally against it, and it is only the person with a special interest who makes the effort to keep abreast of these things. It is not enough to have contests to move the rank and file of the parties to action; the contests must be widely known, which is not the case for many offices. Moreover, unless the party member has followed the internal

TABLE 24. PARTICIPATION IN THE DEMOCRATIC PRIMARY FOR CITYWIDE OFFICES, 1953

	Mayor	President of the City Council	Comptroller
Number of eligible voters	2,132,000	2,132,000	2,132,000
Primary ballots cast	Wagner 350,474 Impelliterri 181,295 Blaikie 9,317 Sullivan 5,300 Total 546,386	Stark 300,337 Helfand 180,565 Total 480,902	Gerosa 275,258 Keegan 202,234 Total 477,492
Vote cast as percentage of number of eligibles	25.6	22.6	22.4

SOURCE: *The New York Times*, September 17, 1953, p. 24.

TABLE 25. POSSIBLE AND ACTUAL PRIMARY CONTESTS FOR NOMINATIONS IN SELECTED YEARS

Year	Total possible primary contests in the three parties[a]	Actual number of primary contests in the three major parties			Total	
		Democratic	Republican	Liberal	Number	Per cent
1956	402	23	3	1	27	6.7
1955	84	3	0	1	4	4.7
1954	387	39	2	0	41	10.6
1953	159	17	5	0	22	13.8
1952	363	12	6	0	18	5.0
Total	1,395				112	8.3

[a] Republican, Democratic, and Liberal. These numbers were computed by multiplying by three the total numbers of elective offices for which the party nominations would be determined by primary elections.

SOURCES: *Annual Reports* of the New York City Board of Elections, 1952–1956; *The New York Times*, June 6, 1956, p. 22; September 14, 1955, pp. 1, 32; September 15, 1954. p. 30; September 17, 1953. p. 24; August 21, 1952, p. 14.

maneuverings within his organization with exceptional interest, he is apt to be at a loss when he finally does turn up at a primary in which there is opposition and in which he has to make a choice. There is nothing on the ballot comparable to the party emblems in a general election to identify candidates and issues for him. All that appears is the list of nominations or party posts at stake and the names of those who seek them. Unless the voter is informed, he must, in effect, choose between two unknowns. Apparently, few people will go out of their way to put themselves in this discouraging situation.

The designee for each candidacy who receives the highest number of votes becomes the candidate of his party for the office sought. The turnout at primaries being low, even on the rare occasions when contests occur, the issue is normally decided by a small percentage of the eligible party members. The relatively disciplined followers of the inner cores commonly make up the majority of this small group. It is this fact that disappointed many sponsors of the direct nominating primary, for, although the necessity to go to the membership to put forward candidates presents some risks and uncertainties to the inner cores, it has not seriously challenged their dominion over party machinery and the choice of nominees.

Nominations by Party Members

Nominations for city, county, and borough elective offices; for United States Representative, state senator, and state assemblyman; and for all elective judgeships, save the state Supreme Court and Court of Appeals, are made by the rank and file of the parties in primaries. Candidates for Mayor, President of the City Council, and Comptroller; District Attorney of each county; Borough President; and city councilman are chosen in the year following a United States presidential election (which is when the terms of these offices expire). Candidates for congressman, state senator, and assemblyman are selected every even-numbered year. The judicial candidates mentioned are picked as vacancies occur. Thus there are primaries every year, but for different offices in each year of the regular four-year cycle. All primaries for all offices and all parties are conducted on the same day; the ballot of each party in each Election District contains the names of aspirants to candidacy for every office with a constituency that includes the district. Selection by party members voting in primaries is the only means of nomination (except in emergencies discussed later) of party candidates for the offices named above.

Nominations by Conventions

Party conventions choose party candidates for all nationwide and statewide offices, and for seats on the New York Supreme Court. Nominations for

President and Vice President are made by national conventions; for Governor, Lieutenant Governor, United States Senator, state Comptroller, state Attorney General, and Justice of the Court of Appeals by state conventions; for Justice of the Supreme Court of the state by judicial conventions in each Judicial District of the Supreme Court. The delegates to these conventions are elected by party members voting in primaries, but the official candidates for public office are named by the conventions. The delegates are not legally bound to specific individuals by the primaries and can choose whomever they want.

The provisions of the state Election Law governing the selection of delegates to national conventions are brief and general, investing broad discretion in the parties themselves to operate through party rules. The national rules of the Democratic party provide for a total of 1,521 votes at the 1960 convention, with 114 allotted to the New York State delegation; the Republicans have 1,331 votes, with 96 for New York. The Election Law requires only that the state's delegates and alternates shall be chosen either entirely from Congressional Districts or partly from Congressional Districts and partly from the state at large; that all delegates and alternates must be enrolled party members; and that the district delegates shall be elected at the spring primary in presidential years. Both major parties in New York have lodged the power to choose delegates at large in their respective state committees. In past years, about half of the delegations have normally come from the city, the remainder from the rest of the state, and most delegates and alternates have usually been party leaders.

In the case of state conventions, delegates and alternates must, under the Election Law, be selected from Assembly Districts, and "the number of delegates from each assembly district shall be substantially in accordance with the ratio which the number of votes cast for the party candidate for governor at the last preceding general state election in such unit bears to the total vote cast in such election for such candidate in the entire state, and the number of alternates from any assembly district shall not exceed the number of delegates therefrom." Delegates and alternates are chosen in summer or fall primaries in the years in which statewide offices are to be filled. Beyond these requirements, the composition and operation of the state conventions are set by the rules adopted by the state committee of each party. Both major parties allot one delegate and alternate to each Assembly District, and one additional delegate and alternate to each Assembly District for every 2,500 votes or major fraction thereof cast in it for the party's candidate for Governor in the last preceding general state election. Generally, there are between a thousand and 1,200 delegates and alternates at a state convention of a major party; like the New York delegations to the national conventions, they are uninstructed.

Judicial District conventions are constituted under party rules in the same way as the state conventions, with delegates coming from each of the Assembly Districts within the Judicial District boundaries. (There are 10 Judicial Districts in the state, in each of which a panel of Supreme Court justices is elected for fourteen-year terms. New York City voters are concerned with three of these districts. Two are entirely within the city, while the Borough of Queens is a part of the third.) The number of members of judicial conventions in the three Judicial Districts with which New York City voters are concerned varies from about 135 to perhaps 275. Like their counterparts in state and national conventions, the legal discretion of the delegates to judicial conventions is exceedingly broad.

Nomination by convention in New York State has had an erratic history. Prior to 1911, when the first comprehensive election law was adopted, nominations were made by various combinations of caucuses and conventions. The 1911 statute abolished these practices, and required nomination for all elective offices (with the exception, of course, of the President and Vice President of the United States) by direct primary. For a decade, these provisions continued in force. Then, in 1921, the convention system was reintroduced to the extent noted above. Thus, today, both methods are in use at the same time, though for different offices.

Nominations by Party Committees

When circumstances prevent completion of the procedure for nomination by direct primary or by convention, the power to name party candidates for public office passes, under the Election Law, to the party committees in the jurisdictions affected. The committees thus exercise nominating authority as well as the rule-making authority previously described.

Authority to nominate candidates for public office devolves upon the party committees under three special conditions: One is when there is too little time to go through the whole regular nominating process (that is, if a nominee dies or withdraws after nomination but prior to general election, or if a vacancy unexpectedly occurs in a public office too late for designating petitions to be circulated). The second is when there is a tie vote in a primary, in which case the appropriate party committee chooses one of the high candidates. The third is for special elections, which the Governor must call if a vacancy occurs in an elective office for which no automatic succession is established and no interim appointment is authorized, and the next general election is not scheduled for a "substantial" period of time. The only candidates who are *regularly* chosen by party committees are those for presidential elector, who are nominated by the state committees.

In all these special circumstances, by party rules authorized under the Election Law, the nominations are made by the state committees for statewide offices; by joint meetings of the five County Leaders (Democrats) or the five county committees (Republicans) for citywide office; by the county committees for all county or borough offices; and by Judicial District committees, Congressional District committees, state Senatorial District committees (which are also the committees for the coterminous Councilmanic Districts), and Assembly District committees—all the foregoing consisting of the county committeemen from each constituency—for their respective jurisdictions.

Thus the Election Law is drawn to permit parties to present candidates for every office to be filled in an election; it covers every conceivable emergency. But the statute and the rules of the parties, with respect to all modes of nomination, also produce another effect: the inner cores of the parties are given the key roles in the process.

THE KEY ROLE OF THE INNER CORES IN THE NOMINATING PROCESS

Their Sources of Influence

Inner-core Organization Versus Public Quiescence. The present system of nomination of candidates for elective office by the rank and file of the parties, or by representatives elected by the rank and file to sit in on conventions or party committees, was devised to permit ordinary voters to take part in both the choice of candidates and in the governance of their parties. And groups of party members dissatisfied with the way their party units perform can and do occasionally seize control from the ascendant party functionaries and install replacements more congenial to the insurgents.

Nevertheless, the inner cores of the parties—particularly, the party functionaries recognized by law and party regulation—still dominate the process by which candidates are selected. For they are comparatively well organized, strongly motivated, and reasonably disciplined, while ordinary members of the parties, even when they become indignant about the quality of candidates and party functionaries and party management, are not usually able or willing to mobilize the strength—that is, to invest the time, energy, and money—to seize the reins from those they oppose. The potential power of the rank and file under the law is immense, but it is diffused, and the appearance of leaders who can focus it sharply and persistently enough to make it felt is not an everyday occurrence.

It takes leadership and organization to get designating petitions circulated, properly signed, and legally filed. It takes leadership and organization, too, to get party members to the polls on primary day to win party office and nominations when there are primary contests. These functions the Assembly District Leaders and their Election District Captains perform. It is the Captains who trudge from door to door with their designating petition forms, soliciting signatures from enrolled party members whose names appear on the official lists the Captains carry with them. And it is the Captains who personally contact party members known to be loyal to their factions of their respective parties and urge them to vote in primaries whenever a contest occurs. County Leaders and District Leaders raise money or dip into their reserves built up during previous general elections to finance the work and publicity for regular aspirants to party office or candidacy who must fight dissident elements of their own party to win the places they seek. For the members of the inner cores, control of party machinery and of nominations is a matter of bread and butter; they depend on it to validate their claims on government officials and employees. Their incentives are strong, their labor neatly divided, their responsibilities clearly drawn, their assignments sharply defined. There are pitfalls that can nullify painstakingly assembled lists of signatures. Amateurs often fall into these traps, the professionals are trained to avoid them. Insurgents must find out by trial and error which party members belong to the opposing factions and which can be recruited to their own banners; the entrenched factions generally know precisely who their friends are, and concentrate their energies on bringing out these friends in solid blocs. It takes time and tradition to weld an aggregate of individuals into a drilled, coordinated team. This advantage the regulars almost always have on their side, and it is generally enough to offset the enthusiasm and sense of mission of those who rebel against them. This does not mean the insurgents never win; rather, it means they are generally the ones who have the uphill fight.

Control of nominations by the inner cores is substantially furthered by the general nonparticipation of the public. Since not more than one eligible voter in three casts a ballot in the most hotly contested primary struggles for nomination even to the most important offices, and since even this low maximum figure is not frequently attained, a relatively small number of dependable followers is all a faction needs to win. Indeed, with nothing more than the personal followers, friends, and relatives of the Captains and cocaptains, incumbent factions in most Election Districts can usually beat off the attacks of rivals, whose well-intentioned endeavors come to naught because they simply cannot persuade a large enough section of the rank and file to turn out. If Captains grow careless or lazy and fail to maintain dependable bands of loyal followers, or if the opposition happens to be led by exceptionally skilled amateurs or disaffected professionals, the insurgents may achieve victory in the primaries with only a small percentage of the voters. Normally, however, the low turnouts in the primaries tend to favor the organized, knowledgeable, incumbent inner cores and their comparatively small, but unfailingly solid, groups of followers. In the majority of cases, therefore, the regular party choices win the nominations decided by the membership of the parties in direct primaries. This fact alone, in turn, discourages many potential insurgents, so that the inner-core choices of individuals to be party officers, or party candidates for elective office, are not only seldom defeated, but are relatively seldom challenged. In short, in spite of the system of nominations through party primaries open to all party members, the supremacy of the inner cores with respect to nominations and to party machinery is still very much in evidence.

Control of Conventions and Committees. Given their ascendancy in the primaries generally, it is hardly surprising that the Leaders and Captains virtually control delegates to conventions and members of party committees and executive committees. Moreover, since there is no barrier to holding many party offices by a single individual, the Leaders and Captains not only *control* the delegates and committeemen, they *are* the delegates and committeemen, for theirs are the names presented to the rank and file of the parties in the primaries. So they run the conventions and committees.

Inner-core ascendancy is further protected by provisions of the state Election Law that confer on the members of state or county party committees and executive committees the authority to fill until the next primary any vacancies in their ranks, provided only that each replacement they select must be "an enrolled voter of the party qualified for election from the unit of representation as to which such vacancy shall have occurred." This saves the state the cost of special primaries, and it also keeps under control this minimal threat to the dominance of the inner cores.

Consequently, the nominations of party candidates for elective public office made by conventions and committees are almost completely in the hands of these inner-party circles. Direct nominations by party members through the primary did not shatter the hold of these inner circles; indirect nominations through delegates and representatives certainly could not do so.

As a matter of fact, though insurgents may capture the machinery of Assembly Districts, or defeat "regular" candidates for seats on county committees from individual Election Districts, they have never won so many Assembly Districts that they took over all at once all the committees and conventions of their party in their county. Factional changes in the parties thus tend to be piecemeal and gradual. The ruling faction, having lost a battle and a stronghold, has not necessarily been dislodged from its position; its control of conventions and committees remains undisturbed. Insurgent triumphs must be widespread to be complete.

Control of the Election Law. It is obvious that domination of party machinery leads to domination of both party rules and nominations. As things have worked out in New York State, it leads also to control of the Election Law. Each major party in the state has a party counsel whose job it is to know the details of election law and procedure, and to be able to interpret the details from the point of view of the welfare of his particular party. Volunteers generally able to call upon the services of other attorneys (who abound in both parties) as needed, both parties' counsel are the draftsmen of virtually all legislation dealing with party organization and electoral procedure. They formulate legislative proposals on these topics that spring from within their own parties, and review for their parties proposals advanced from any other sources. The legislative delegations in Albany of each party take their cues from their respective party counsel on questions of election law. When the counsel of both parties agree on a measure, as they often do on matters affecting the security of their respective inner cores against insurgency or inroads by third parties, the measure is usually adopted routinely. The Wilson-Pakula Law, for example, requiring the assent of county executive committees to allow candidates of one party to be nominated by another party as well, was enacted by agreement to block Congressman Vito Marcantonio of the American Labor party, whose supporters penetrated both major parties in his district and prevented those parties from putting up candidates to oppose him.

When the parties differ on the Election Law, they usually manage to work out some compromise, although the Republicans, who occasionally capture both houses of the state legislature and the governorship as well, can sometime override Democratic opposition. Even then, however, they often find some basis of agreement because the Democrats could raise such a hue and cry about alleged violations of the sanctity of the two-party system that the Republicans would be embarrassed. When the Democrats hold the governorship, they have no trouble blocking changes in the Election Law proposed by the Republican legislative majority. In 1957, for example, the Republicans were thwarted in their efforts to halt the practice of the Liberal party of putting up candidates who then withdrew, leaving the choice of replacements to party committees, which almost always endorsed Democrats. The Republicans thought Liberal party *members* would endorse Republicans more often than would Liberal party *committees*. But they got nowhere with their measures to change the procedures. Very infrequently, a wave of reform or of nonpartisan pressure sweeps both parties unwillingly along in its current. It was in this fashion that primaries were introduced in 1911, and that permanent, personal registration (replacing the statutory provision for annual registration of voters) was adopted in 1955. But, in the main, the party counsel, by agreement, are largely responsible for the contents of the Election Law. Inevitably, the law tends to support the inner cores, and though it by no means guarantees the predominance of the factions in power at any given moment, it makes their position a great deal more secure than would be the case if other participants in the political process were equally successful in manipulating the contents of that crucial statute.

To sum up, the inaction of the rank and file of the parties as contrasted with the organization and knowledge of the inner cores, and the consequent control by inner cores of party conventions and committees and of the Election Law as well, give the party leaders a greater role in the management of party machinery and in the choice of candidates for elective office than any other category of contestants for the prizes of political action.

Dilemmas of the Inner Cores

Internal Competition and Bargaining. To say that the inner cores have the upper hand in making nominations is not to say they are not rent by serious internal divisions, or that other contestants are utterly without influence in the process. In the major parties, most party decisions, including nominating decisions, are characterized by intense bargaining among the segments of the inner circles and between the inner cores and "outsiders."

In the first place, many, if not most, of the party functionaries strive for their share of the nominations for public office. District Leaders must placate their Captains and other club members. County Leaders must see that all their District Leaders get some share of the nominations for offices with countywide constituencies. District Leaders, lumped together in Congressional Districts, state Senatorial Districts, Judicial Districts, Councilmanic Districts, and Municipal Court Districts, must work out understandings with each other and with their County Leaders regarding the selection of candidates for these posts. County Leaders must negotiate with each other to agree on candidates for the three citywide offices. That is, every geographic subdivision of every party demands some recognition of its work in the form of a nomination of one of its members for office. No party officer can afford to have too many disgruntled subordinates, for those subordinates might work less energetically for their party's candidates in the general elections than they otherwise would, and they might even throw in their lot with a rebellion against the established leadership. On the other hand, subordinates fear to alienate their superiors lest this result in diminution of the flow of offices and other benefits to their units. Hence, decisions are reached by bargaining and negotiation among subordinates, coequals, and superiors in a highly fluid manner. Sometimes, for instance, a County Leader will try to impose a selection of his own on some of his District Leaders, and will succeed in the attempt. At other times, District Leaders will agree among themselves on the partitioning of nominations in their territory, and their County Leaders are almost compelled to accept their choices. Yet County Leaders may also be called upon to mediate disputes among District Leaders unable to arrive at mutually agreeable solutions. County Leaders treat with one another like ambassadors from independent nations when they choose candidates for the citywide offices. Most of the Mayors since the formation of the Greater City have come from Manhattan or Brooklyn (for a long time the two most populous boroughs), and each of their running mates has usually come from other boroughs. County Leaders of the city also negotiate with other County Leaders throughout the state to obtain for their followers as many statewide nominations as they can. There is no fixed formula for balancing off the claims of the territorial units of each of the parties. Each year, the bargaining starts anew, and the intricate calculus by which settlements are made changes from year to year with variations in the strength and the past concessions of each claimant. On the whole, when the inner cores come to an agreement, their selections are ratified through the formal mechanics of nomination, whether this be a party committee, a convention, or a direct primary. But the procedure by which their own decisions are made is one of pulling and hauling, of give and take, of trading and compromising among the functionaries from all the areal subdivisions of the organization. The bargaining is always vigorous and sometimes bitter.

Geographical considerations in the distribution of nominations, complicated though they are, constitute only one factor in the delicate process of putting forward "balanced tickets." Members of the inner cores also demand nominations on religious and ethnic grounds. Catholic, Protestant, and Jewish Captains and Leaders insist that the roster of candidates in any general election include individuals of their own faiths. Negro party functionaries demand recognition for themselves and other members of their race. With the heavy influx of Puerto Ricans since World War II, Puerto Ricans have taken their places in the machinery of all the parties, and, increasingly, Spanish names blossom proudly on the faces of voting machines. Nationality groups—Irish, Italian, Greek, and Polish—also assert claims to nomination. Women demand women candidates. In the calculations and negotiations behind the selection of candidates for elective office, the weight of all these claims is felt. No group of any size has long been kept out of the inner circles of the parties once that group began to exercise the franchise—chiefly, it appears, because its representatives are presumed to be more effective in working among their own people, but also, perhaps, because someone from outside a relatively cohesive group would probably lose a primary fight for party office against a member of the group. At any rate, once they become part of the regular party machinery, the representatives of the various groups tend to insist on recognition of their groups in the distribution of nominations and appointments.

Another complicating element in ticket-balancing is its mythology. It is by no means certain that all the "claims" and "demands" to which party leaders respond are in fact exerted. Nor is it clear that failure to respond to them, even if they are real and accurately assessed, would have the consequences attributed to such a failure. The assumptions about the expectations and reactions of party workers, party members, and voters are not demonstrated, for party leaders are hesitant to test them when so much is at stake. So the process of employing traditional techniques to satisfy ambiguous require-ments based on untested hypotheses (all perhaps manipulated at times for personal ends by shrewd strategists) continues as though it rested on demon-strated truth.

The complexity of balancing claims, both real and imagined, is somewhat eased by the fact that a single nomination, all by itself, may satisfy a number of demands. Just one adroit choice, for instance, might quiet a restless Assem-bly District Leader, appease women party workers clamoring for recognition through nomination, partially gratify the desires of Negro inner-core mem-bers, and answer some of the pointed queries of Protestant insiders. Fiorello La Guardia not only took advantage of his obvious Italian descent, but he emphasized proudly to selected audiences that his mother was Jewish, and he let it be known that he was a Protestant. The multiple memberships of virtually every individual thus decrease the need for computation by ticket "balancers." Moreover, people of like backgrounds tend to congregate; many neighborhoods in the city are highly homogeneous in many respects, and claims on candidacy based on area, religious conviction, ethnic identification, and national origin or descent in German Yorkville, Jewish Flatbush, Negro Harlem, Puerto Rican East Harlem, "Little Italy," the heavily Irish areas of Manhattan, and in similar heavy concentrations of comparatively uniform populations throughout the city, can often be satisfied in the person of one individual. The tensions of ticket-balancing are further relieved by the gen-eral willingness of members of the inner cores of all the parties to wait pa-tiently for the satisfaction of their demands. They know the problems involved in dividing the honors, so they tend to be tolerant. They are also inclined to place high value on appointment to choice nonelective offices, which reduces internal pressures still further. All these mitigating circumstances simplify the calculus of placation.

Consequently, the various factions of each party manage to reconcile their differences long before the primaries take place each year. Potentially, every nomination by every party can precipitate some kind of primary fight. Ac-tually, it is a rare year when as many as one third of those that can theo-retically occur do actually take place. In the five-year period from 1952 to 1956, inclusive, 465 elective offices were voted on by electorates in New York City, and there could logically have been a primary contest in each of the legally recognized parties (Democratic, Republican, Liberal) for each office, or a total of just under 1,400 battles. Only 112 primary fights ultimately materialized in all three parties over the whole interval. However, two or more persons filed designating petitions in 168 cases; the difference between this figure, representing instances in which preparations were made for primary contests, and 112, the number of actual contests, is mainly the number of compromises regarding nominations reached by factions inside each of the three parties. If one makes the assumption that an even larger number of compromises prevented many additional rivalries from getting even as far as the designating-petition-circulating stage, it would appear that the bargaining process with respect to nominations is both active and highly successful in the avoidance of overt internal warfare. Nevertheless, gifted as they are with great talent for negotiation and mutual accommodation, the professional politicians are still confronted with a hard core of conflict that cannot be resolved except at the polls in primary elections. In all likelihood, the occasional primary fights persuade members of the inner cores to make concessions to one another and even to insurgents from time to time because they can normally reserve more for themselves and their followers through compromise than through all-or-nothing struggles; at the same time, the hard core cases indicate to all concerned that bluffs will sometimes be called. Consequently, party activists, whether of an insurgent or a "regular" stripe, often pursue the strategy of threatening to make independent runs in the primaries, going as far as circulating their designating petitions if their initial threats are of little avail, and actually going into the primaries only as a last resort. Most of the time, things are settled in the earlier stages.

Looking at the legal machinery and the heterogeneous components of the parties, one might anticipate they would produce far more than they do in the way of defections and rebellions. In later chapters it will be seen that these do occur. But, compared to the volume of theoretical opportunities, they are surprisingly infrequent. Somehow, the system distributes rewards in proportions that keep the inner cores firmly in control and reasonably unified.

Concessions to People Outside the Inner Cores. Despite their unity, the inner cores are forced to make concessions to individuals and groups who are not, strictly speaking, members of the inner leadership circles. It is abundantly clear from the behavior of party functionaries that they regard nomination for public office as a reward for toil in the vineyards of their respective parties. On the whole, they obviously prefer to see a nomination go to one of their own number than to anyone else. But they have also learned the lesson of what retailers call the loss leader—that is, the item that may lose money for the storekeeper but which lures customers in and thereby leads to increases in purchases of profitable merchandise. Similarly, in politics, the inner circles of the parties often agree that their candidates for the most prominent positions at stake in any general election may have to be "outsiders"—meaning individuals who did not begin their careers in politics at the Election District level, who have not been active workers in political clubs, and who did not work their way up through the party ranks and through the less desirable elective positions in government before making their claims upon some of the highest honors a party can bestow. The regulars usually make this sacrifice only if it appears to them that no one in their own circle has the same vote-getting capacity as a particular outsider, stands as good a chance of victory as the outsider, or can draw as many uncommitted votes and opposition party members to the organization line on the voting machines. For these strategic and tactical reasons, an outsider can win a nomination for a major office much desired by party functionaries. Many candidates for offices with statewide or citywide constituencies are not members of the inner cores (as this phrase is used here) of their parties, and some whose influence within their parties eventually became extensive. Democrats Herbert Lehman and Averell Harriman and Republicans Thomas Dewey and Nelson Rockefeller, for example, did not begin their political careers by climbing up the levels of their respective party hierarchies.

What makes a man a vote getter is hard to say. In part, of course, it is a matter of personality. It is also a matter of reputation for both competence and incorruptibility, which is a product of actual performance and of evaluation by respected nongovernmental groups, esteemed public figures, and the press. Many politicians believe that it depends, too, on belonging to a large religious or ethnic group. They assume, although the evidence is by no means conclusive, that the members of these groups tend to vote for candidates who are their coreligionists or are in the same ethnic category. Whether or not any of these factors is as important as the inner cores of the parties seem to think, the fact that these considerations enter into the deliberations on the selection of regular nominees indicates how outsiders participate indirectly in the nominating process, at least as far as ticket leaders are concerned. The inner cores try to anticipate the behavior of the electorates, which means that voters in general elections are not only choosing their governing officials, but are also unwittingly furnishing instructions governing the choice of future candidates. Thus, even if there were no primaries, it is possible, if not highly probable, that the composition of party tickets would not be significantly different from what now obtains. Nongovernmental groups, in general, have been able to exercise little influence upon nominations when the parties put forward candidates the nongovernmental groups consider mediocre or even mildly distasteful, but they have demonstrated now and then that they can be roused to bitter and vehement opposition to candidates who are demonstrably unqualified, tainted with corruption, or unfriendly to the interests of the objecting group. Both major parties have elder statesmen, chiefly politicians no longer in the competition for public office, to whose opinions many members of the inner circles defer when nominees are being chosen. Officials, elected and appointive, who owe their positions to a party, may offer recommendations on nominations to the inner core, and may back up their suggestions with the influence of their offices. The personal entourage of officials

—the campaign managers, advisers, aides, and others—are also heard by the inner cores when candidates are being chosen. As for the press, although it has never been shown that newspapers' support or opposition can itself determine the outcomes of elections, it is manifestly better to have standard bearers whose calibre wins at least grudging admiration and deferential coverage even from unsympathetic reporters, editors, and publishers.

In recent years, members of the inner cores of all the parties have been responsive to those outside forces as well as to their own desires to nominate one of their own for each available elective office. As a matter of fact, some party leaders systematically consult with outsiders about the selection of candidates. Both parties have employed public opinion research organizations to make attitude surveys among the general populace. In 1953 leaders of the New York County Democrats conducted a postcard survey of their own among enrolled Democrats to help them plan their nomination strategy. Party leaders often confer informally with the representatives of those non-governmental groups whose support they are anxious to obtain or retain. As a result of this practice of making nomination selections for major offices with one eye cocked on people beyond the boundaries of the inner cores, it is not unusual to have an outsider spearheading a ticket at the state or city level, and, less commonly, in constituencies smaller than the city as a whole.

Another factor entering into the choice of nominees is money. Party leaders display a marked preference for persons who can pay their own campaign expenses. In a limited sense, nominations are thus for sale. While many members of the inner cores are able to guarantee payment of a substantial part or even all of their election expenses, and while the parties themselves will undertake to finance some of their less wealthy workers in recognition of service rendered, the pecuniary demands of political battle are sometimes so heavy as to offer opportunities for party members with monetary reserves or support to advance themselves more rapidly than would otherwise be probable, and for wealthy backers of candidates for nomination to push their friends ahead. Fiscal resources are especially important when there are primary contests to be fought, for the Election Law forbids expenditures on primary contests by party committees, thereby placing the costs of primary campaigns chiefly on the seekers after nomination and their friends. Some contributors to parties are thus able to influence party decisions as to which inner-core member will be nominated for office, and to add inducements for the inner cores to accept outsiders for the loss leader places on the ballot.

From the point of view of the inner core of any particular party the leaders of other parties, though professional politicians, are outsiders. Yet it sometimes happens that these outsiders influence the nominations of their rivals. In the first place, if one party so "balances" its ticket as to make a special appeal to some area, religious group, or ethnic group, the others try to offset this possible advantage by achieving an appropriate counterbalance in the composition of their own slates. This, for example, is one of the reasons all the parties had Negro candidates for Borough President of Manhattan in 1953. In the second place, the estimated vote-getting capacity of opposition standard bearers helps determine whether a party needs a proven vote getter of its own, regardless of whether he is a regular party worker or not, or can hope to win with virtually anybody it puts up. In the third place, there have been times when both major parties either carried the state or the city or a smaller constituency, or could have carried them, only with third-party support. Consequently, the inner cores of the major parties sometimes solicit the endorsement of third parties for some or all of their candidates, which means that the inner cores of the third parties so approached may use the leverage thereby placed at their disposal to persuade the major party in question to nominate candidates acceptable to the third party. Indeed, third parties have sometimes been successful in getting a major party to nominate some third-party candidates in return for third-party nomination of major-party candidates. In the fourth place, both major parties, it will be seen later, occasionally jointly nominate the same individuals for a given office. Usually, joint nominations of this kind represent efforts by both inner cores to avoid the uncertainties of electoral battle with each other; in a couple of cases, however, they joined hands to beat back a strong bid by a third party. In any event, whenever there are joint nominations, it is clear that the nominee must be acceptable not only to his own party but to the concurring party as well.

For all these reasons, despite the tight hold of the inner cores on the nominating procedures and practices of their respective parties, other contestants for the prizes of political action do have an impact on the selection of candidates for elective public office. That is not to say the outsiders represent a serious challenge to the power of the inner cores. They do, however, impose some of the premises on which inner-core decisions are based.

Differences Among the Parties

Although the major outlines of the nominating process, and of the strategies of participants in the process, are similar for the three political organizations that currently meet the qualifications for parties as defined by the Election Law—that is to say, the Democrats, the Republicans, and the Liberals—they are by no means identical. The Democrats, as noted in the next chapter, win most of the electoral contests in which voters of the city participate. The Republicans can be fairly certain only of several pockets of Republican strength, while the Liberals try by and large to prove that they hold the balance of power. Under these circumstances, differences among the parties have quite naturally arisen.

Since the Democrats win so many elective offices, Democratic nominations are highly prized and vigorously pursued by office seekers. The competition for nominations inside the Democratic party, and the jockeying for position to control Democratic nominations, is more intense than in either of the other parties in New York City. This is reflected in the fact that there are five to six times as many contests in Democratic primaries, on the average, as in Republican primaries (and eight or more times as many Republican primary contests as Liberal primary contests). The Democratic problem is to screen out aspirants to nomination, and outsiders have a hard time in the midst of such keen fighting among the members of the inner circles.

The Republicans, by contrast, have to screen applicants for nomination only in those constituencies in which they have a proven capacity to win. Elsewhere, they must often search for candidates rather than sift applicants. Consequently, the Republicans make somewhat more use of outsiders as nominees than do the Democrats.

In the Liberal party even more than in the Republican party, the expectations of independent victory are generally low, and nominating practices are designed as much to influence the choice of nominees by the major parties, and to extract policy commitments from the major parties, as to win office. To be sure, the Liberals have run candidates of their own for statewide and citywide offices as well as for lesser constituencies, and once (1951) even won a special election for President of the City Council. Most of the time, though, the purpose of an independent campaign is clearly to demonstrate to the inner cores of the major parties that the Liberals can draw enough votes to constitute the margin of victory, and to remind the leaders of the major parties that the Liberals will not employ their power on behalf of candidates uncongenial to them. Most of the time they end up endorsing Democratic candidates, but there is always a small number of Republican candidates almost every year who are also nominated by the Liberals. To strengthen their hand in negotiations, the Liberals often nominate candidates of their own, then have these candidates withdraw if they are satisfied with the results of their threat to make an independent stand, and have their party committees endorse the major-party candidates who are acceptable to them. In 1956, for example, 52 Liberal candidates withdrew from the election and were replaced by Democrats, whose names thus appeared on two different party lines on the voting machines. In the rare primary contests that develop in the Liberal party, the fight is far more likely to be between a faction favoring an independent Liberal candidate and a faction working to nominate a Republican or Democratic candidate rather than between two independent Liberal aspirants to a nomination. Strategic considerations practically force the Liberals to deal with both major parties and to run independently from time to time, for they would otherwise have no threat to hold over the head of either the Democrats or the Republicans. Nevertheless, it is quite clear that the inner core of the Liberal party, which is more unified than its major-party counterparts and in fuller control of the nominating process, is more closely linked to the Democratic party in New York City by ideology, sentiment, and the probability that Liberal voters would turn to the Democrats rather than to the Republicans if the Liberal party were not on the scene.

Another difference among the parties is the kind of outsider to whom their respective inner cores make concessions in choosing nominees. Both major parties are sensitive to a much wider band of the political spectrum than the Liberals. The Republicans, it is true, are somewhat closer to the business community than the Democrats, but the Democrats also have many businessmen among their supporters. The Democrats, on the other hand, are somewhat more intimately associated with labor leaders in the city, but the Republican party sometimes gets important labor support, particularly from some of the craft unions. The Liberal party receives its chief financial support and leadership from the International Ladies' Garment Workers Union, and its policies and strategies are hardly distinguishable from those of the union.

In all the parties, then, the inner cores dominate the nominating process. In all the parties, the influence of the inner cores in this respect springs from the same sources—their organization as contrasted with the inaction and relative disorganization of the rank and file, their control of conventions and committees, and their control of the Election Law. At the same time, they are all beset by internal competition and bargaining and by the necessity to make concessions to outsiders. The ardor of the internal competition, it is true, is not the same in all the parties, nor do they have identical bargaining policies. Moreover, the outsiders to whom they make concessions vary, but there is a great deal of overlap among their bodies of supporters. Since the positions of the parties in the struggle for the stakes of politics in New York City are not identical, the strategies and tactics they follow in nominating their candidates for elective public office are not the same either. It is perhaps accurate to say that they are of the same genus, but not of the same species.

NOMINATIONS BY INDEPENDENT BODIES

Independent bodies are a different *genus*. They are those political organizations whose respective candidates for Governor did not receive at least 50,000 votes in the state at the last general election (including organizations without gubernatorial candidates at that time). For one thing, their internal structure is not governed by statute in the same manner as parties. For another, their candidates for elective public office are nominated by petition rather than by primary or convention.

For statewide offices (including presidential electors), the minimum number of signatures required by the Election Law for nomination is 12,000, with at least 50 in every county in the state. For offices with smaller constituencies, the requirements are as follows: 7,500 signatures for any office voted upon by all the voters of the city; 5,000 for county or borough offices; 3,000 for any Municipal Court District, Congressional District, or state Senatorial District; and 1,500 for Assembly Districts. For offices with constituencies embracing more than one county (Judicial Districts of the Supreme Court), the figure is equal to the aggregate of the signatures required for either of the counties so contained. These amounts are much higher than those decreed for *designating* petitions, but the *nominating* petitions actually secure a place on the general *election* ballot for the candidate, while designating petitions merely admit him to a party *primary*. As in the case of designating petitions, the signatures on nominating petitions must be collected in six weeks (but ending on the fourth Tuesday before the election) for general elections, and sometimes (but not necessarily) in a shorter time for special elections. To cover situations in which a candidate nominated by the petitions of some independent body dies or withdraws, the petitions must include the names of a committee of at least three persons authorized by the signers to fill such vacancies.

The name of any person whose petitions have been signed by the requisite number of voters appears on the ballot as a candidate for the appropriate office. Other than the fact that parties are listed first, no distinction of any kind between "parties" and "independent groups" is drawn on the ballot. Collecting and filing the signatures properly is all the latter have to do to nominate.

Actually, the task is much more difficult than it sounds. Gathering signatures is not easy for an organization that is not well established, and has only a small, scattered following and no regular organization in the field. Yet in every general election in which a major office is at stake, there are usually several independent bodies with candidates on the ballot. Several— for example, the Socialist party, the Socialist Worker party, and the Industrial Government party—regularly enter slates for national and state offices. Some, such as the Recovery party (1933), the No Deal party (1945), the Experience party (1950), and the City Fusion party (intermittently for many years) vie only for city offices, often on an *ad hoc* basis. A few put candidates in the field for only one or a few positions instead of presenting full slates. As a result, residents of New York City have had the opportunity to vote for the candidates of over 50 different independent bodies whose nominees have had lines on the voting machines in one or more elections since 1920.

A few of these independent organizations have had profound effects on New York City government and politics. Consisting of discontented reformers or factions of the major parties who could not obtain their choices of candidates in the party primaries, who would not accept the candidates who did win the nominations, and who therefore made independent runs in the elections as independent bodies, they affected the outcomes of some elections (see the following chapter). Even when they did not actually alter the election results, their shows of strength built up their bargaining power in succeeding nomination contests within the regular parties. But the great majority of the remaining four dozen or so independent bodies that have appeared in elections in New York City are small groups fervently, almost religiously, devoted to a cause or ideology. Without hope of victory, uninterested in compromise with the established parties, they are apparently more concerned with evangelism than with the immediate question of selecting personnel for public office.

Finally, a few are instruments of the major parties, and nominate major-party candidates in order to capture the votes of people who like the nominees but dislike the parties whose banners they carry.

The members of virtually all the independent bodies are more homogeneous in outlook than those of the parties. Though dissenters themselves, they are not tolerant of dissidence in their own ranks. Challengers of the prevailing orthodoxy often must defect and run their own candidates if they would be heard. Some independent bodies hold together in spite of raging factional disputes; most are left with a solid cadre in mutual agreement. In all of them, the small clique that organizes the campaign to get on the ballot is in solid control.

Some observers have protested that the difficulties in the way of independent bodies trying to get on the ballot are indefensibly high, imposed by the major parties to protect their own domination of the electoral process and to discourage insurgents in their own ranks. Moving from the status of independent body to the status of party is particularly arduous, for it requires putting up a candidate for Governor, and this, in turn, means getting people in every county of the state to sign his petitions. To do this within the time limits established by law calls for a degree of advance organization and a network of statewide contacts. Moreover, within the city, administration of the nominating process is entrusted to a Board of Elections composed of two Republicans and two Democrats who are not notably friendly to independent bodies. Others argue it is already so easy to get on the ballot that any further easing of requirements would weaken the two-party system. A procedure that avoids both dangers must fall in a very narrow area of general satisfaction. The present system can probably benefit from some changes, but the fact remains that it has neither prevented independent nominations nor caused the disintegration of the parties.

ADMINISTRATION OF THE NOMINATING PROCESS

The system of nominations is governed by the general provisions of the state constitution and the detailed provisions of the Election Law of the state;

the city charter is, therefore, silent on nominating procedures and on their administration. Responsibility for administering and supervising nominations is invested in two state agencies, the Secretary of State of New York State and the New York City Board of Elections, and in the courts. Except for the facts that the expenses of overseeing and validating nominating procedures are mandated upon the city, that the City Council appoints the four members of the bipartisan Board of Elections (described more fully in the next chapter), and that city police keep order at the polls in primaries as well as in general elections, the nominating process is a state rather than a municipal responsibility.

Most of the business connected with the administration of nominations in the city falls to the Board of Elections, for it has jurisdiction over every phase of the process for all offices whose constituencies are entirely within the city limits—namely, for Mayor, Comptroller of the city, President of the City Council, United States Representative, city councilman, state senator, state assemblyman, and all locally elected judges—and for all party officers elected by New York City party members in primaries. For all of these, the Board receives and approves or rejects all petitions, both designating and nominating; certifies names to appear on primary ballots; tallies primary returns; receives reports of judicial conventions in the city; and certifies the names of individuals to appear as candidates on election ballots or to serve as party functionaries. For statewide offices (and for nominations for the Supreme Court in the Tenth Judicial District, which includes one county in the city and two outside it), these functions are performed by the Secretary of State.

The Board of Elections also fixes the number and boundaries of Election Districts and engages personnel to man all polling places for registration, primaries, and general elections. Its other duties—providing and maintaining voting machines; printing forms for petitions and ballots for primaries; procuring and distributing equipment, materials, and supplies for polling stations; placing election notice advertisements in newspapers—are essentially ministerial.

It is the discretionary powers of the Board that are most important—and most controversial—in the contest for the stakes of politics in New York City. It has been charged that the Board is rather arbitrary in its decisions regarding acceptance or rejection of the designating petitions submitted by insurgent groups endeavoring to challenge the incumbent party leaders in primary contests within the major parties, and cavalier in its treatment of nominating petitions submitted by independent bodies whose appearance on the election ballot might seriously threaten the dominant position of the major parties.

There is a logical appeal in this contention, growing out of the open and strong distaste of professional politicians for insurgency. Like the executives of all organizations, they regard evidence of disharmony as a breakdown of normal processes. Further, professional politicians on both sides of the political fence join forces against newcomers in the field. There is also an impressive body of empirical evidence to lend credence to the allegation. Provisions of the election statute are drawn in great detail to prevent election officials from skewing nominating and election results by manipulation of the size and print on ballots, of color variations to violate ballot secrecy, or of introducing technical pitfalls in the language of petitions. Minor technicalities, such as failure to number pages properly, have sometimes been seized upon by the Board of Elections to disqualify parts of some petitions, and similar small deviations have been used as grounds for disallowing individual signatures. Relatively insignificant defects in the required signatures of witnesses to petitions have been offered as reasons for disqualifications. When even such trifling technical excuses cannot be found, even more cavalier arguments for rejection are offered—such as one disqualification of insurgent papers on the ground that it is impossible legitimately to prepare so perfect a set of petitions. Ordinarily, whole sheafs of petitions are very quickly approved or disapproved, clearly on the basis of cursory examinations at best and apparently in the light of decisions already made.

There is thus no denying that the administration of the nominating process makes the way rough for insurgents and independents, both inside the parties and in competition with the parties as independent bodies. On the other hand, there are always a number of contests in every primary, sometimes for high offices. And, as noted above, defectors from the parties as well as small ideological associations show up frequently in general elections. Consequently, while the criticisms of the way nominations are handled are not without justification, it is equally true that the obstacles placed in the path of those who choose to battle the established leaders of the parties can be surmounted by determined and persistent groups. Of course, they may have to appeal to the courts to get satisfaction, but they can and do make their weight felt in the end.

The Election Law confers on the Supreme Court broad powers of review with respect to nomination and election questions, both as to law and fact. Its jurisdiction—"which," provides the statute, "shall be construed liberally"— is sweeping, comprising every facet of the process. Proceedings of this kind may be instituted under somewhat more informal and speedy rules than apply to other types of legal action, and "shall have preference over all other causes in all courts." The court is even empowered to "direct a reassembling of any convention or the holding of a new primary election where a convention or primary election has been characterized by such frauds or irregularities as to render impossible a determination as to who rightfully was nominated or elected. . . ."

Rulings of the Board of Elections may be appealed by petitioners affected by a ruling, by counsel for other parties, or even by individual voters. As might be expected, this leads to a great deal of litigation. From time to time, court rulings shake the Board thoroughly (as did one judgment by the Court of Appeals, the highest court in the state, which awarded a petitioner damages against the administrative agency); more often, it suffers simple reversals in the courts. However, the impressive volume of lawsuits over nomination involves only a fraction of all decisions made by the Board. Furthermore, the Board is far more often upheld than overruled. Its findings are final most of the time. Since judicial determinations constitute precedents for administrative findings, and since it is clear that administrative findings are shaped by the anticipation of judicial reactions, court influence reaches a good deal further than statistics alone can tell. The result has been to wipe out the worst discrimination against party rebels and independents and to keep both primaries and elections reasonably open.

NOMINATION IS A PRELUDE

It takes a lot of politicking in New York City just to get into a position to run for elective public office. All categories of contestants for the prizes of political action do what they can to influence the selection of nominees, some because they want nominations for themselves or their friends and followers, others (including good-government people and reformers as well as representatives of special interests) because they want the candidates of all parties to be receptive to their suggestions. This leads to battles for control of party machinery, that is, to the pursuit of party office. The process gets quite complicated and its ramifications quite extensive.

The inner cores play the stellar roles in the selection of candidates. Other contestants participate, but the party functionaries stand out in this phase of the political process. As a result, candidates who survive the preelectoral sifting emerge with commitments and obligations to party leaders, who in turn have commitments and obligations to others. At the same time, the candidates often incur their own moral or material debts to other contestants. Not only is this stage of government a step in deciding *who* will occupy elective office, but, in the course of it, conditions are attached to what they will *do* in office if and when they win it. That is why the struggles over nomination and party machinery reach the feverish pitch they often attain. Even if one does not get office himself, even if one does not *want* office himself, astute bargaining at this time can lead to other political rewards. For when candidates obtain nominations, they have merely obtained passports from one (the nominating) arena to another (the electoral arena). Here, they face new struggles, struggles that once again help decide not only who get public office but, at least in part, how they perform in office. For demands based on old obligations incurred during the quest for nomination will often be intensified during election campaigns, and new ones added.

Whether a nomination is strongly contested or easily won, and whether an election campaign is hard fought or almost automatically successful, the candidate contracts liabilities. All this affects his subsequent behavior. In a double sense, then, nomination is a prelude—to the election, and to claims to be made after election.

BIBLIOGRAPHY

See references at the end of Chapter VI, page 206.

CHAPTER VI

Elections

THE KEY ROLE OF THE ELECTORATE

ONLY THE ELECTORATE can formally and legitimately decide who will occupy the elective seats of government. Parties and "independent bodies" merely offer candidates; the electorate makes the final choices among the candidates. Even in the sections of the country where there is only one party to speak of, this ritual of democratic practice is preserved. Where an element of competition exists, the practice is far more than mere ritual. It is a real exercise of substantial power. Parties, candidates, and groups of every kind can entreat, implore, deceive, and even coerce voters, but only the voters can decide the outcome of elections in a legally and morally binding sense. The authority of the electorate is an authority no one else can wield.

The role of the electorate is not confined to deciding elections. As noted in the previous chapter, nominations, though dominated by the party inner cores, are usually made partly on the basis of anticipated voter behavior. In the same way, governmental decisions, though often controlled by relatively few contestants, are reached after consideration of possible electoral repercussions. There is a constant feedback, through the medium of past elections and expected future action, from the electorate of the city to those who are especially prominent and influential in the formulation of any personnel or policy decision. The precise effects of this feedback defy existing measuring techniques; it appears at times to be unnecessarily inflated and at others to be less adequate than some would like. The effect depends largely on the highly subjective, personal judgments of the most active participants in each decision and on the extent to which those most directly affected by the reaction of the electorate can impress their anxieties and assessments of their situation upon other participants not so vulnerable to electoral sanctions. Consequently, no general patterns are found. All that can be said with confidence is that the electorate does have some influence on who get office and what they do when in office, and that this influence extends beyond Election Day choices among candidates. If the "will" of the electorate in these respects is ambiguous and subject to varied interpretations, it is nevertheless a significant factor in the contest for the stakes of politics. It hovers dimly and vaguely in

167

the background, its intent and future action shrouded in mystery, but it is seldom totally ignored and totally ineffective.

Nonvoters, it should be stressed, also play a part in the decision-making process. Even for presidential elections, only a fraction of those eligible actually vote. The calculations of party functionaries and of other contestants normally include estimates of nonparticipation, and strategies are formulated accordingly. Furthermore, many voters pull the levers for some offices, but not for others. Stay-at-homes and selective nonvoters help shape the results of elections and the behavior of other contestants, although they themselves do not always seem aware of it.

All those *eligible* to vote, then, must be regarded as factors in the contest for the stakes of politics. Their presence intrudes itself at many points in the contest. They can never be neglected because only they can gratify the aspirations of parties and candidates and other groups with respect to legitimate elevation of individuals to elective public office.

The exclusiveness of the electorate's authority means that all other contestants concerned with the outcome of elections can affect the results only by influencing the voters' behavior or by falsifying the count of the votes. The first of these strategies has produced the familiar practices of election campaigns. The second has given rise to machinery for the prevention of election fraud.

EFFORTS TO INFLUENCE THE ELECTORATE

The Conduct of Campaigns

Election campaigns are built around two strategies: personal contact with voters and publicity. The first is largely the preserve of the parties through their Captains and cocaptains in each Election District. The second is employed by other contestants and by candidates as well as by the parties.

Personal contact frequently takes the form of "ringing doorbells"—visits to the homes of voters. Over time, only the parties have proved capable of consistently putting an effective force in the field for these purposes. Volunteer aides may assist during presidential campaigns, but the bulk of the burden falls on regular party workers. Party workers sometimes work more energetically for the smaller, less visible offices than for prominent ones with large constituencies.

Publicity is another matter. Except for the comparatively inexpensive practice of direct mail appeals to voters, it must be purchased. Because it is costly, only the largest constituencies—the nation, the state, the city as a whole—produce enough party revenue to support it. Finally, because party revenues are attracted to the heads of tickets, public relations campaigns, managed by their aides, usually focus on those candidates. In any event, the mass media of communication are not efficient or economical for reaching small audiences. Public relations consequently focus on the highest offices and are directed from Washington, Albany, or the headquarters of mayoral candidates. When no major offices are at stake, an election is apt to be conducted in relative obscurity. The lower echelons of the parties do little publicity work beyond billboard notices and placards.

Top-echelon party public relations, supplemented from time to time by parallel programs by volunteer organizations, constitute the main publicity effort in political campaigns. The advertisements, the broadcasts, the huge rallies and campaign tours are sustained and arranged by party leaders and by the personal aides of the candidates. Candidates may bid for news coverage by their claims, charges, promises, and appeals to various groups, but the candidates do so principally from forums provided for them through high-level party expenditures.

The parties, however, do not have a monopoly on this as they do, for all practical purposes, on personal contact. The press itself is in a position to influence electorates, and most newspapers do so, partly by editorial comment, but, more importantly, by the amount of coverage and kind of treatment they give the candidates. The Citizens Union rates the qualifications of candidates (although it does not express preferences between equally qualified candidates) for many locally filled offices, and several associations of lawyers do the same for judicial candidates. These ratings are fairly widely circulated and receive some notice in the press. Occasionally, a group of citizens will, on their own, place advertisements supporting their choices.

In addition, some organizations conduct limited campaigns aimed at narrow segments of the city electorates. Labor leaders, for example, often work for the parties they support by appealing to their union members through the union news organs and administrative organizations. Religious leaders have frequently succeeded in making their preferences unmistakably clear to their congregations, although explicit endorsements are rarely announced from the pulpits. The hierarchical structure and unity of the Roman Catholic Church, as contrasted with the decentralized and divided character of the Protestant and Jewish faiths, makes the informal support of diocesan and archdiocesan officers especially valuable to candidates. Some ethnic and nationality groups and lay religious organizations also let their wishes be known.

Nevertheless, while the parties are not the only organizations engaged in public relations work designed to influence electoral behavior, their efforts in this direction tower over those of other groups. Election campaigning in the city by means of publicity as well as by personal contact is largely a function of the parties. Others do what they can, but their activities are not so sustained or intensive.

Financing Campaigns

Nobody knows exactly how much is spent on election campaigns in the city. To be sure, the state Penal Law puts a ceiling on contributions to, and expenditures by, candidates and voluntary organizations working for particular candidates (namely, $20,000 for gubernatorial candidates; $12,000 for all other elective statewide offices, other than judicial; $8,000 for United States Representative or presidential elector; $4,000 for state senator; $2,000 for assemblyman; and for any other office, $1,000 for the first 5,000 voters in the constituency in the last preceding gubernatorial contest, plus $6.00 for each additional hundred voters). But official *party* committees are not limited, thus ensuring that their central roles in elections will not be seriously threatened. Moreover, so many legal ways of evading the technical limits have been devised, and so many of the contributions take the form of clandestine cash donations, that the total amounts have never been accurately calculated. Some suggestion of the magnitude of the expenditures is provided by a report from an authoritative source that the Democrats commonly invest in the neighborhood of half a million dollars on battles for the entire city, whether for citywide, statewide, or nationwide office. In addition, smaller sums are spent on contests for lesser offices. Whatever the exact dimensions of the effort, it is certainly of substantial proportions.

Much of the money goes for material expenses: rentals of office space and telephones, purchase of office equipment and supplies and postage; hiring of halls and sound trucks; printing; advertising; television and radio time; catering for luncheons and dinners. A large sum also goes into small stipends for Election District Captains, flowing from campaign headquarters through the Assembly District Leaders. Some excess cash is apparently siphoned off by District Leaders, and County Leaders are wont to hold some in reserve for future emergencies.

The money for the major offices is obtained mainly by means of direct solicitation and 25, 50, and 100 dollars-a-plate luncheons and dinners, organized by party fund-raising committees set up by agreement among the County Leaders to avoid repeated approaches to their main sources of revenue, and attended by officeholders, benefactors, and other supporters of the parties. High elected and appointed officials also contribute in proportion to their salaries, and some bureaucrats, though now protected by the state Penal and Civil Service Laws against forced assessments, make substantial donations. Cash contributions are made by the underworld, contractors, suppliers, and other special interest groups. County and/or District Leaders make their own arrangements to collect these, working through trusted lieutenants (no records are kept) whose reliability is maintained by devotion to their employers and by the possibility of exposure by donors claiming their due. Candidates are also expected to finance part of their campaign costs.

For lesser offices, the candidates bear most of the expense. Their scale of operation, however, is modest, and most of them are able to finance campaign activities personally or with the help of friends. They turn their funds over to their District Leaders (who will not tolerate direct dealings with their Captains, and who may direct the Captains to drag their feet if a parallel volunteer field organization is established). This pays for special efforts on behalf of the candidates for the minor posts. Some District Leaders have been known to extract contributions from each candidate needing their services, though all candidates will be served by the same work force in a single concerted campaign. The candidates in one area, on the other hand, are reported to have united, pooled their resources, and presented a single contribution to their Leader to avoid the high costs of duplicate donations in excess of requirements. Higher party headquarters only occasionally show a financial interest in the minor candidates, but District Leaders tend to use for local purposes some of the money passed down from above to help carry their districts for major candidates. Fiscal controls, if the loose practices of the parties may be called that, are too weak to counteract the decentralization of party structure and procedure.

Logic would seem to dictate the conclusion that generous donors, given the nature of our economic system, must enjoy great material returns on their investments. There is little empirical evidence to support or refute this proposition, particularly as it applies to those who contribute to local party units. It is by no means clear that most contributors have well-formed political objectives in giving to the parties. Donations at this level come from such diverse sources that it seems almost impossible to accede to any set of claims without alienating a large number of donors on the other side of the questions at issue. Habit, tradition, principle, desire to mingle with public figures, and many similar factors are unquestionably as important as expectations of material benefits in keeping the party coffers filled. One can only speculate on the effect of political money-raising on who gets office and what they do with their authority; probative data are yet to be gathered.

Campaigns and the Voters

Do the attempts to sway electorates actually do so? Again, the evidence is inconclusive; so many factors figure prominently in voting behavior that the results of campaign efforts of parties and other groups have not been isolated or measured. Later sections of this chapter will point out how defections of components of parties have been followed by splits in the expected votes for the regular candidates, but even these events, though strongly suggestive, do not demonstrate that field workers actually carry their districts, for many other elements also play parts in these splits.

The campaigns for the candidates of one major party are probably offset by the campaigns for their opponents. True, all campaign efforts are probably not equal in magnitude or intensity, though which candidates receive more campaign support in the city is uncertain since the expenditure figures are unreliable and heavier expenditures for one may be counterbalanced by more voluntary labor for the other. But both parties do try to influence the electorates, so that the campaign factors tend to neutralize each other, which may well be all that is expected of them. As a result, social and economic conditions in the city, the changing composition of electorates, controversial issues (state, national, and international, as well as municipal), the records of the parties in Albany and Washington as well as in City Hall, and many other things probably influence electoral behavior as much as deliberate striving to win votes.

TABLE 26. THE ELECTION CYCLE: OFFICES VOTED ON IN NEW YORK CITY, AND THE SEQUENCE OF REGULARLY SCHEDULED GENERAL ELECTIONS

	Number	Presidential year	Mayoral year	Gubernatorial year	Off year
Presidential electors	45	x			
U.S. Senators	2		See note ᵃ below.		
U.S. Representatives	22	x		x	
Governor	1			x	
Lieutenant Governor	1			x	
Comptroller	1			x	
Attorney General	1			x	
State senators	25	x		x	
Assemblymen	65	x		x	
Mayor	1		x		
Comptroller	1		x		
President of the Council	1		x		
Borough Presidents	5		x		
Councilmen	25		x		
District Attorneys	5		See note ᵇ below.		
Subtotal	201				
Justices and judges	190		See note ᶜ below.		
Total	391				

Note in right margin (spanning Off year column): Some judicial offices are the only ones regularly filled in the off years. Most other off-year elections are to fill vacancies occurring in the course of a term of office.

ᵃ Elected separately in different even-numbered years. Thus, every third even-numbered year, there is no regularly scheduled election of a U.S. Senator. Ignoring special elections to fill out remainders of terms, the dates of the last nine U.S. senatorial elections in New York State were 1958, 1956, 1952, 1950, 1946, 1944, 1940, 1938, 1934.

ᵇ Elected for four years. When vacancies occur, they are filled by the Governor until the next general election. If the election occurs in an odd-numbered year, the office is filled for a full term of four years; if in an even-numbered year, for the remainder of the unexpired term. As a result, the terms of three of the current incumbents (Bronx, Queens, and Richmond Counties) will expire in 1959, the other two (New York and Kings Counties) in 1961.

ᶜ Terms vary. Elections for each court staggered. Vacancies filled for full term (or until mandatory retirement age) as they occur. From 1948 to 1957, inclusive, the smallest number of judicial offices at stake in the city was 14, the maximum 33, for an average of 24.

SOURCES: New York State *Election Law* and *Annual Reports* of the New York City Board of Elections.

ELECTIONS   173

TABLE 27. NUMBER OF ELECTED OFFICES VOTED ON IN NEW YORK CITY IN GENERAL ELECTIONS, 1915–1958

Year	Total Offices	National Offices[a]	State Offices[b]	City Offices[c]	Judicial Offices[d]	County Offices[e]
1958	148	23	94	..	31	..
1957	58	..	2	33	21	2
1956	145	24	90	1	30	..
1955	40	..	2	2	33	3
1954	149	22	94	..	33	..
1953	61	..	4	33	21	3
1952	130	24	92	..	14	..
1951	30	..	2	2	24	2
1950	145	25	96	1	23	..
1949	67	2	2	33	27	3
1948	132	25	92	1	14	..
1947	30	1	4	1	22	2
1946	139	25	96	2	16	..
1945[f]	63	..	2	31	26	4
1944	132	26	92	..	14	..
1943	47	..	6	17	22	2
1942	128	26	89	..	12	1
1941	64	..	1	34	20	9
1940	135	28	85	2	20	..
1939	59	..	3	21	31	4
1938	128	28	89	..	9	2
1937	80	1	..	34	35	10
1936[g]	137	27	89	1	19	1
1935	156	2	63	65	18	8
1934	135	27	89	1	17	1
1933	167	..	63	73	19	12
1932	138	28	89	1	15	5
1931	158	1	63	66	26	2
1930	139	24	89	2	20	4
1929	186	1	62	73	35	15
1928	128	26	89	2	10	1
1927	165	..	63	65	31	6
1926	140	25	89	4	18	4
1925	162	..	62	73	15	12
1924	131	25	92	1	8	5
1923	156	3	62	65	19	7
1922	135	25	92	5	11	2
1921	159	..	63	73	12	11
1920	146	26	92	3	21	4
1919	166	..	64	68	29	5
1918	130	24	92	3	9	2
1917	183	..	64	75	32	12
1916	135	26	92	4	11	2
1915	162	1	63	74	15	9

[a] Presidential electors, U.S. Senators, U.S. Representatives.

[b] Governor, Lieutenant Governor, Comptroller, Attorney General, state senators, state assemblymen. Also, prior to 1925, state Secretary of State, Treasurer, and Engineer.

[c] All members of Board of Estimate and City Council (Board of Aldermen prior to 1936).

[d] All elective judicial offices, including Court of Appeals.

[e] District Attorneys, and, prior to 1942, County Sheriffs, Registers, and Clerks.

[f] Four-year term for councilmen begins.

[g] Last year of annual election of assemblymen. Biennial from this year on.

SOURCE: *Annual Reports* of the New York City Board of Elections.

THE ELECTORAL BEHAVIOR OF THE METROPOLIS

A Continuing Democratic Preference

The Democrats Win Elections. One factor in winning an election is the continuing Democratic predilection of the people of the city. They decide in favor of Democratic candidates most of the time. In the four-year electoral cycle from 1952 to 1955, inclusive, the people of the city voted to fill 379 vacancies created by expiration of terms, resignations, and deaths of national, state, and municipal officers, including a large number of short-term positions which were filled twice in this interval. Of the 379 contests, 321, or approximately 85 per cent, resulted in majorities or pluralities for Democratic candidates or candidates with Democratic and other endorsements. Since a number of these were for offices having statewide constituencies—presidential electors, United States Senator, Governor, and so on—majorities or pluralities within the city did not always guarantee election. Nevertheless, it is significant that Democratic candidates could count on securing majorities or pluralities in New York or in districts within it in all but 15 per cent of the electoral contests in this interval.

There have been four-year cycles in which the Democrats were not quite so successful, securing local majorities in as few as 75 per cent of the competitions, but they have also done better in some periods, winning as many as 90 per cent of all possible victories. In single years, when the Republican tide was running unusually high in the state and nation, Republicans have managed to win as many as 39 per cent of all the electoral contests in the city, but these upsurges of minority strength are remarkable because they are so rare. Even in good years for the Republicans, they are not likely to enjoy local victories in as many as 25 per cent of the contests. By contrast, in the off years preceding presidential elections, when there are no prominent Republican candidates for citywide, statewide, or nationwide office to enhance the strength of the rest of the Republican ticket, and when a great many candidates for judicial office are jointly nominated by both parties in extensive and intricate trades, all winners of local majorities may be Democrats or have Democratic and other endorsements. From this standpoint, the outlook for the minority parties in New York City is discouragingly bleak.

Legislative seats in Congress, the state legislature, and the City Council provide the bedrock upon which the Democratic edifice has been erected. Over the years since 1920, the Democrats have consistently won more than 85 per cent of the seats of the city's delegation to the United States House of Representatives. Through 1950, this meant an average of 20 out of 24 Representatives; several times, the figure was 22 or 23 out of 24. Even in 1946, a year when the Democrats suffered heavy legislative losses all over the country, they managed to hold more than two thirds of the 24 seats in New York City.

TABLE 28. DEMOCRATIC POPULAR VOTE FOR CHIEF EXECUTIVES COMPARED WITH DEMOCRATIC LEGISLATIVE SEATS WON IN NEW YORK CITY, 1920–1958

Year	Per cent of the city's legislative seats won by Democrats				Per cent of popular vote cast in New York City for Democratic candidates for		
	State Assembly[a]	State Senate	City Council[b]	U.S. House of Representatives	Mayor	Governor	President
1920	42	43	..	67	..	56	27
1921	81	..	77	..	64	..	..
1922	90	100	..	83	..	68	..
1923	89	..	88	..	..	..	..
1924	87	91	..	79	..	67	35
1925	90	..	95	..	66	..	..
1926	94	100	..	92	..	67	..
1927	92	..	89	..	..	..	..
1928	90	96	..	88	..	59	60
1929	94	..	94	..	61	..	..
1930	97	96	..	96	..	66	..
1931	98	..	98	..	..	..	..
1932	97	96	..	96	52	70	65
1933	79	..	75	..	27	..	..
1934	97	96	..	79	..	69	..
1935	95	..	92	..	..	..	..
1936	97	100	..	96	..	65	74
1937	..	..	54	..	40	..	..
1938	92	87	..	92	..	65	..
1939	..	..	67	..	..	..	..
1940	87	83	..	83	..	..	61
1941	..	..	65	..	46	..	..
1942	87	79	..	92	..	42	..
1943	..	..	65	..	..	..	..
1944	73	68	..	88	..	..	61
1945	..	..	65	..	57	..	..
1946	55	52	..	67	..	54	..
1947	..	..	..	..	..	..	..
1948	84	80	..	71	..	..	44
1949	..	..	96	..	49	..	..
1950	85	88	..	88	36	49	..
1951	..	..	..	..	..	..	..
1952	72	72	..	73	..	..	54
1953	..	..	92	..	46	..	..
1954	86	92	..	73	..	56	..
1955	..	..	..	..	..	..	..
1956	75	80	..	73	..	..	51
1957	..	..	96	..	68	..	..
1958	80	84	..	73	..	47	..

[a] Elected annually until 1935, biennially thereafter.

[b] Board of Aldermen prior to 1937. Elected biennially until 1945, quadrennially thereafter.

SOURCE: *Annual Reports* of the New York City Board of Elections.

Since 1950, when the city's representation in Congress was reduced to 22 as a result of the 1950 census, but not because of this, the Democrats have not fared so well as they had for a third of a century earlier; they have been reduced to roughly three quarters (16 or 17) of the city's congressional seats. But it is only by the standards set in previous years that this proportion looks like a sign of weakness; by any other measure it is an impressive demonstration of overwhelming strength and a firm foundation upon which to build a party.

The Democrats in the city fared just about as well with the city's delegations to both houses of the state legislature. Of the 25 state senators (23 prior to 1944) from New York City, only once since 1920 have fewer than two thirds been Democrats. Normally, the Democrats can be expected to win at least three quarters of these places, have occasionally triumphed in the contests for 90 per cent of them, and several times (1922, 1926, 1936) won all of them. Similarly, in only two general elections after 1920 did the Democrats fail to capture at least three quarters of the 67 state Assembly seats (62 before 1944; 67 from 1944 to 1954; 65 after 1944) in New York City. The median Democratic proportion for this period is roughly 85 per cent, and it has exceeded 95 per cent a number of times. It is a good year for the Republicans in New York City when they can send as many as a dozen assemblymen and seven or eight senators to Albany.

Still more striking is the degree of Democratic domination of the City Council, and of its predecessor, the Board of Aldermen. In eight elections from 1921 to 1935, inclusive, for the old 65-man Board, the Democrats took 60 or more (90 per cent or better) of the 65 positions in four cases, more than 55 (over 85 per cent) twice, and dropped to a mere two-thirds majority (45 seats) or a little better on two occasions. The replacement, in 1937, of the Board of Aldermen by a City Council of relatively small size elected by the Hare system of proportional representation hit the Democrats hard. In 1937, when the new system went into effect for the first time, they took only 14 seats, while the Republican-Fusion coalition won 6 and the American Labor party independently took 5. In the next four elections under proportional representation, the Democrats regained a good deal of lost ground, their share of the Council hovering around the two-thirds mark. Proportional representation was abandoned after the 1945 election, which was also the first election of city councilmen for four- instead of two-year terms. In the three councilmanic elections since then, with one councilman being elected in each of the state Senatorial Districts, the Democrats have recovered their old crushing majority; 24 of the 25 councilmen elected in 1949 ran on the Democratic ticket, 23 in 1953, and 24 in 1957. Thus, even when the Democratic party suffered its worst councilmanic defeats, its control of the city's legislative body was never upset, it managed to hold its combined opposition

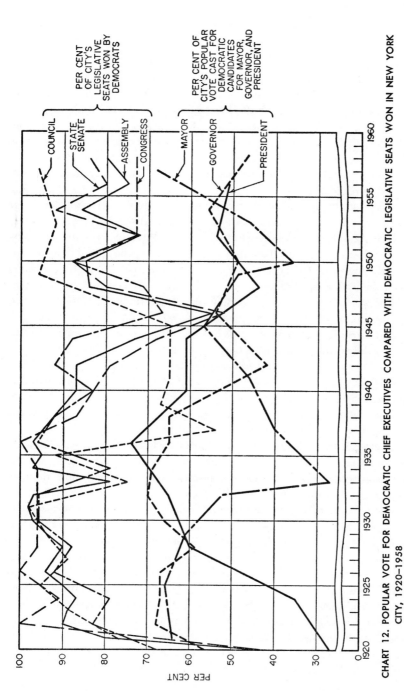

CHART 12. POPULAR VOTE FOR DEMOCRATIC CHIEF EXECUTIVES COMPARED WITH DEMOCRATIC LEGISLATIVE SEATS WON IN NEW YORK CITY, 1920–1958.

SOURCE: Compiled from *Annual Reports* of the New York City Board of Elections.

177

to roughly a third of the available positions even during the period of proportional representation, and it has now resumed its role of overpowering dominance.

In like fashion, the city has favored Democratic candidates for President in eight out of ten elections since 1920—every Democratic candidate from 1928 on, although these candidates have not always carried the entire state. Since 1920, every Democratic candidate for Governor, without exception, and most of their running mates on the statewide ticket, have also won the city. In 14 races for seats in the United States Senate in the same period, only twice (in 1920 and 1952) did the city fail to give a majority to the Democratic standard bearer.

The Democratic organization has fared worst at the citywide level, for reasons to be discussed presently. In 12 general and special mayoralty elections since 1920, the Democrats lost 4 (including three in a row to La Guardia). They lost the comptrollership 3 times out of 11; they were defeated for the presidency of the City Council in 4 elections out of 11. In the same interval, including special elections, there were 58 contests for borough presidencies; slightly under three quarters of these, or 43 (including two candidates endorsed by both major parties), were won by Democrats. The Democratic record for these offices is less impressive than that for legislative posts, but the verdict was still heavily in favor of the majority party.

It is somewhat more difficult to evaluate the record with respect to judges because of the longstanding and widespread practice of joint renomination of candidates for these positions by both major parties and often by third parties as well. Consequently, many candidates for these offices run unopposed. Nevertheless, it is significant that less than 10 per cent (62) of all candidates elected between 1920 and 1956 (632) succeeded without Democratic endorsement, and that 410 Democrats running without Republican endorsement (though sometimes with third-party support) have triumphed more than six times as often as Republicans who have not been jointly nominated. Of 57 elections for District Attorney in the same period, 48 went to Democrats (some with support of third parties), 6 were won by candidates jointly nominated, and in only 3 (about 5 per cent) did Republicans triumph.

In short, gauged by the proportion of Democratic triumphs in electoral contests for offices at all levels and in all branches (with special emphasis on the legislative branch) of government, the Democratic proclivities of New Yorkers would seem to be sufficiently pronounced to dishearten the opposition were it blessed with the resources of Hercules and the patience of Job.

Republican Submission to the City's Democratic Leanings. Not very surprisingly, some Republican party leaders have occasionally succumbed to discouragement. With most of the reins of city government firmly in the hands of the opposition, with the prizes of politics so consistently beyond the grasp of the continuing minority, one can understand those leaders who lose heart at the prospect of waging expensive, exhausting campaigns for comparatively limited rewards, particularly since they can often get as much or more by negotiating with the opposition as by waging all-out war. Under these conditions, it could well be argued by those who have labored long and hard in the minority camp that the survival of their organization as well as the personal interests of their followers and supporters depend on the considerations they can extract from their adversaries by bargaining, since there is so little else to distribute. To some devout defenders of the faith, negotiated peace invariably means collusion and betrayals; to others, it is the dictate of reason and realism. However such a policy may be evaluated, there are some Republicans in the New York City units of the party who advocate it—and who practice it.

While it might appear that the majority party, virtually assured of sweeping victories, has no need to negotiate, politicians show a marked tendency to reduce risks to a minimum, and candidates in the safest constituencies are often driven by momentary failures of nerve to seek additional assurances of victory. In New York, as we shall see shortly, the anxieties of many Democrats are not entirely groundless. Hence, many of them are receptive to, and even solicit, approaches by Republicans and leaders of the third parties.

What these Democrats seek is reduced opposition. This may mean nothing more than that the Republican organization in specified areas will put up only a token fight, thus cutting down the energy and financial investments required by the Democrats and swelling the probabilities of Democratic victory. Local politicians operate on the assumption that the dedication and vigor of precinct units are always among the most important factors in carrying districts for any candidate, and, by this standard, it is good strategy to bargain with the enemy in order to weaken his grass-roots offensive. When such deals are made, word is passed through the ranks of the minority party that there is no enthusiasm in the party leadership for specified candidates, and the campaign for them then never gets out of low gear.

But deals can go further than this. The minority may agree to put up a weak candidate for a given office instead of its strongest possibility, thus reassuring the Democratic nominee. Or it may agree to joint nomination, thus eliminating competition for particular positions. This has been particularly true for judgeships and district attorneyships, but it has occurred in connection with many other offices as well. Indeed, in 1937 there were rumors and even strong public intimations of such maneuvers aimed at excluding La Guardia from the mayoralty itself. If the benefits derived from such arrangements were not sufficient to induce the Democrats to bargain with the Republicans at election time, Republican influence in the state legislature, in the Governor's office when it is in Republican hands, and in Washington when the Republicans are ascendant there, often melts the aloofness of the local majority party. The underdogs are not without their levers for bargaining purposes, and awareness of this leverage convinces some Republican politicians they are better off using it at the negotiating table for as much as they can get in this fashion than they would be by making strenuous efforts to win the votes of a population that seems persistently unfriendly. Waging war might win a few additional offices for them, but it might at the same time cost them everything they are now able to extract from the Democrats by mutual accommodation.

What they extract from the Democrats are all those things we have called the stakes of politics. They obtain elective offices by insisting that some Republican candidates as well as Democratic nominees receive joint nominations, and they sometimes succeed in getting the Democrats to weaken their campaign efforts in pockets of Republican strength just as some Republicans do where the Democrats are predominant. Some of their claims to appointive office are also honored. Generally, the choicest, most powerful, most lucrative offices are not available to them, but enough lesser posts are put at their disposal to enable them to hold their organization together and thus to make bargaining worthwhile. Supporters of the Republican party seeking material advantages, relief from rigorous enforcement of the letter of the law, or improvements in governmental services are sometimes granted their requests if they make them through Republican District and County Leaders whose negotiations have kept open the lines of access to Democratic party officers and governmental officials. In similar fashion, third parties and even independent bodies have their own and their followers' demands satisfied. Collaboration with the prevailing party thus benefits minority organizations. It is also to the advantage of the Democrats because it channels opposition and protest into known, predictable courses, and fortifies the controlling influence that has so long rested in their hands.

This collaboration is always an unstable process, surrounded by intimations of illegitimacy and subject to abrupt breakdown in particular instances. It is inhibited by the fact that the Republicans cannot afford to reduce their strength in statewide contests. Despite this, it continues year after year.

Continuing Democratic Hazards

With the Democrats so solidly in the saddle, and their opponents partially demoralized and often visibly debilitated, many observers of the New York scene have quite understandably concluded that victory for the Democrats in the city is virtually automatic. This oversimplified characterization is misleading. It conceals a number of tendencies in the electoral behavior of the metropolis that introduce elements of uncertainty and great anxiety into the lives of Democratic party leaders and candidates. The situation as they see it is far from cut and dried, and a second look at the figures tells why. There are important evidences of opposition strength and of Democratic vulnerability.

Republican Victories. For twelve out of the twenty-four years between 1933 and 1957, the mayoralty of New York was in the possession of the Republicans—or, to be more precise, of Fiorello H. La Guardia. Each of the three times La Guardia was elected, it took a coalition to bring him the prize. In 1933 an alliance of the Republicans with the City Fusion party gave him the margin of victory. They were later joined in 1937 and 1941 by the American Labor party, whose support turned out to be essential to the triumph of the coalition, and a couple of small independent groups. Nevertheless, the defeat of the Democrats in the heart of their own fortress demonstrated that they were not invincible, and that the forces of protest and reform, with luck, willingness to cooperate, determination, hard work, and an able candidate, could beat them on their home ground. Moreover, every time La Guardia was victorious, he carried with him his running mates for Comptroller and President of the City Council, which, even without the borough presidencies taken by the alliance he headed, was enough to assure the Republicans and their friends of control of the powerful Board of Estimate (although his control in his first term was upset by the deaths of the Comptroller and the President of the City Council and the victory of Democrats in special elections to replace them). As a matter of fact, La Guardia always carried at least two Borough Presidents with him, and four of them came in with him in 1937. Indeed, from 1925 to 1957 the Democrats were never able to capture all five borough presidencies, and their difficulties since the end of World War II in Queens and Richmond suggest that these areas are likely to give them trouble from now on.

There are indications that the Republicans in the city can make inroads on the city's delegations to the state legislature when national sentiment runs heavily in favor of the Republicans. In 1946, a year of severe setbacks for the Democrats throughout the country, the Republicans captured 12 of the city's 25 state senators and 35 of its 67 assemblymen. Similarly in 1920, another year of sweeping Republican victories following the conclusion of a war, the GOP won 12 of 23 seats in the state Senate and 33 of 62 places in the Assembly. These Republican highwater marks were, it is true, quite extraordinary and accomplished under the most unusual circumstances, but they remind the Democrats that their fortunes locally may be tied to the fortunes of their party on the national scene and that their municipal dominance may be sharply challenged and perhaps overthrown. While the disasters that befell the Democrats in 1920 extended to the city's Representatives in Congress—16 of the 25 Congressional Districts in the city went Republican, and one returned a Socialist—they came through the 1946 reverses in better shape, losing only 8 of the 24 seats to the Republicans. Superficially, this would seem to suggest that the Democrats' hold on the congressional delegation became almost unassailable, but whereas the Republicans could expect generally to win only three or four of these positions prior to World War II, they appear to have a fairly firm grip on six or seven since the war, a figure not great enough to cause panic in Democratic ranks but sufficient to serve as a disquieting straw in the wind, particularly since the city has had only 22 Representatives since 1950.

Bearing in mind that to these developments must be added Republican judges (and an occasional District Attorney) elected with the endorsement of both parties as a result of the understandings between the party leadership groups, as well as the handful of such posts won by the Republicans over Democratic electoral opposition, it is clear that the minority party in New York, despite its seeming weakness, continually presents a real threat to the Democrats which they cannot ignore. There is a relatively small but solid base from which the Republicans can operate.

The Prevalence of Pluralities. Still more unsettling to the Democrats is the frequency with which their candidates are carried into office by pluralities rather than majorities. In spite of the large number of offices they win, the Democrats can hardly be unaware that less than half the voters of New York vote Democratic in most competitions for major offices, and in a great many contests for less prominent positions. Were the opposition not divided among a number of parties, were the Liberals more inclined to endorse Republicans or run independent candidates of their own instead of nominating Democrats, and were there fewer joint nominations, it is conceivable that the Democrats of New York City might find themselves in serious trouble.

In only one of the four presidential elections since 1940 has the Democratic candidate for President obtained on the Democratic line 50 per cent of the popular vote within the city. Even Franklin D. Roosevelt could not do so in 1944. (In all four of these instances, votes cast for the Democratic candidate on third and minor party lines gave the city to him with varying degrees of decisiveness. It is highly significant that hundreds of thousands of voters apparently took pains to indicate that they liked the Democratic nominee but preferred not to support the Democratic party in the city.) In 1952, on the Democratic line in the city, Adlai E. Stevenson drew but 44 per cent of the votes cast in New York for President; Dwight D. Eisenhower won 43 per cent on the Republican line. In 1956, the vote for President Eisenhower on the Republican line was actually greater than the vote for Governor Stevenson on the Democratic line, 45 per cent to 43 per cent, and the Democratic nominee would have failed to have carried the city for the first time since 1924 had the Liberal vote for him not provided a large enough increment to give him the small lead with which he ultimately emerged.

The same is true of gubernatorial elections between 1938 and 1957. In this interval, there were five races for the governorship. In only one of them (1954) did a Democratic candidate get a clear Democratic majority in the city, and two actually fell below their Republican rivals, polling only 33 per cent in 1946, 38 per cent in 1950. They managed to eke out a slight lead in the city—but not in the state—only with third-party support.

These observations apply also to United States senatorial elections. After 1940, only one Democratic candidate (Robert F. Wagner, Jr., in 1956) in six elections attracted sufficient votes to the Democratic line in the city to get a majority. In 1946, only 37 per cent of the ballots cast for Senator were Democratic—the Republicans did better—and the Democrats would have been defeated in the city as well as losing the statewide office had it not been for the third-party vote. Indeed, the city did go for the Republican candidate for Senator in 1952, when the Liberals ran their own nominee.

The Democrats have not won any office having a statewide constituency in the last quarter century without piling up, with third-party support when necessary, a margin of at least 650,000 votes in the city to offset Republican leads upstate. Even if the Republicans cannot attain majorities in the city for these offices, they can swing the state into the Republican column by cutting Democratic leads. Far from having a mere *pro forma* existence, then, the Republicans in New York City play a major role in determining who will occupy the executive mansion in Albany and the White House in Washington, and who will represent the state in the United States Senate. These circumstances have also placed the Liberal party, which can muster from 250,000 to more than 400,000 votes, mostly within New York City, in a peculiarly strategic position and has enlarged its impact on elections in the state far beyond expectation in view of the comparatively modest size of the party and its following.

The election results for statewide offices are paralleled by the record for citywide positions. Between the special mayoral election of 1932 and the regular one of 1957, not a single Democratic candidate for Mayor received on one line a majority of the votes cast. In 1933, the Democratic votes for Mayor dropped to a low of 26 per cent of the total; the Democrats lost that fight. They lost others, too, and even dropped below the 30 per cent mark again in the special election in 1950, but this was their low ebb. Even when they won—in 1945, 1949, and 1953—they did so without attracting to their own line a majority of the votes cast. Robert Wagner's victory in 1957, when he polled on the Democratic line almost 57 per cent of the total vote for Mayor, was the first mayoral election in eight in which any candidate received such a majority. In general, the balloting for Comptroller and President of the City Council follow the same pattern, although the Democratic candidates for these offices in 1949 outdrew the leader of their ticket and secured a majority that eluded him, indicating that the voters of New York City split their tickets. Two years later, however, in a special election to fill a vacancy in the presidency of the City Council, the Democratic candidate fell back to approximately 28 per cent of the vote cast (in spite of the fact that the vote was low that year), ran well behind the Liberal candidate (who won), and was almost overtaken by the Republican. In bad years, in short, the Democrats, with somewhat surprising frequency in the past few decades, have revealed unanticipated weakness. Even when they have emerged victorious, their victories several times appeared to rest on rather shaky foundations.

The Democratic hold on the borough presidencies is a good deal firmer, but even here, for the two decades from 1933 to 1953, out of a total of 32 contests the Republicans managed to take 13. Most of the races were close, with third and splinter parties so numerous that neither the Republicans nor the Democrats could win clear majorities by themselves. So many people failed to vote for these offices that 45 per cent of the voters frequently sufficed to choose the winner. However, Democratic fortunes soared in 1957, when Democratic candidates captured all five posts, including three by clear majorities. The Democrats have the advantage, but their record gives them no cause for complacency.

Legislators alone commonly obtain definite majorities. Situations in the various districts vary so extensively that generalizations are difficult to draw and must be advanced cautiously, but many congressmen, state legislators, and councilmen of both parties do receive on single lines more than 50 per cent of the votes cast for their offices within their constituencies. Overwhelming victories are not extremely common, the winners' percentages tending to cluster in the low and middle fifties. The Republicans lose most of these contests, but the margin of Democratic victory within each district is smaller than the *number* of defeats might appear to imply.

So the facts qualify the popular picture of New York as a firmly Democratic town. Admittedly, most Democratic politicians are in stronger positions than their Republican counterparts. Yet the Republicans' role is not a futile one. The constancy of their challenge to the Democrats on every front helps keep the incumbents sympathetic to the demands of their constituents and generally responsive to the needs and desires of the community. Nor is the position of the Republicans hopeless. They have scored important triumphs, and there are signs that time may be on their side.

Divisions and Coalitions. Adding to the hopes of the minority parties, and to the vexation of the Democrats, is the dissension within Democratic ranks, the opportunism of the third parties, and the unpredictability of some of the small city groups, such as the City Fusion party, which sometimes spring to life with unanticipated energy and amass followings that astound and confound professional politicos.

The specter of a "split" haunts the Democrats at every mayoral election. A split occurs when a faction within a party decides not to support the party's candidate for a particular office, and to back the faction's own selection for that office in opposition to the party's choice, entering the faction's candidate under the label of either a party or an independent body already in existence or of an independent body especially created for this purpose. Whenever this happens, segments of the electorate that normally support the nominee of the regular party organization break away and throw their weight behind the candidate of the disaffected faction. A division of this kind in a situation in which pluralities elect may be fatal to a party's chances.

Since 1913 splits of this kind in mayoral races have occurred four times in the Democratic party and twice in the Republican. With the sole exception of the revolt against the regular Republican candidate for the presidency in 1912 that produced the Bull Moose party and divided Republicans in New York just as it divided them in the nation, almost all the splits in the sense in which the term is used here, that have taken place in the two major parties in New York City in the twentieth century have concerned only municipal, including borough, offices. Offices with statewide constituencies have been totally immune, and, while dissidents in both parties have occasionally put up their own candidates for offices with smaller-than-borough districts (particularly judicial posts), revolts at the lower echelons have been rather rare and ineffectual. Noteworthy major-party splits are phenomena involving citywide positions.

One plausible explanation is that the city and borough levels are the only ones at which rebellious factions have any real hope of scoring victories. A statewide split in either of the major parties assures almost absolutely the triumph of its adversaries. At the lower levels, Democratic strength is great enough virtually to guarantee the defeat of defectors without hurting the chances of the regular Democratic candidates in any material way. In either case, the defectors stand to gain very little by breaking away; there is little incentive to open a breach. Only at the intermediate levels, particularly because of election by pluralities, does revolt by a faction really pay off.

In three of the four Democratic defections mentioned, the insurrectionists gained substantially by their strategies. In 1913 John Purroy Mitchel, a lifelong Democrat himself and the scion of a family long influential in Democratic politics, but a vigorous opponent of Charles Francis Murphy (the powerful leader of the New York County Democratic organization—that is, the "boss of Tammany Hall"), accepted the nomination of the Fusion party and beat the champion of the Democratic party. (Fusion comprised a coalition of Republicans, reformers, anti-Tammany Democrats, and other anti-

Tammany elements; Mitchel was encouraged to lead this group by Woodrow Wilson, who had not forgotten that Murphy opposed him in the presidential nominating convention of 1912 and who wanted to keep the city in friendly hands while taking it away from Murphy.) In 1933 Bronx County Democratic Leader Edward J. Flynn organized the Recovery party to support his candidate for the mayoralty, Joseph V. McKee, against the regular Democratic nominee, John P. O'Brien. McKee, who had been President of the Board of Aldermen and served as Acting Mayor when James J. Walker resigned the mayoralty late in 1932, lost to Fiorello H. La Guardia, but he ran ahead of O'Brien and managed to carry to victory the candidates of his party for a number of important county and borough positions in The Bronx at a time when the Democrats lost most of these to the Republican-Fusion union elsewhere in the city. These local victories helped Flynn achieve dominance in New York City Democratic councils, a position of particular importance while the Democrats were out of power in the city but in power in Albany and Washington, so the insurgency must be counted a success even though it did not win the major office at stake. Finally, in the special election of 1950, Vincent R. Impellitteri, former Democratic President of the City Council and Acting Mayor after the resignation of William O'Dwyer, organized a party of his own, the Experience party, and, with himself as the only candidate on the whole ticket, made a run against the regular Democratic nominee. Supported by a substantial number of Democratic District Leaders who had grown dissatisfied with the way they had been treated by the party leadership under O'Dwyer, and apparently enjoying impressive financial and other backing, Impellitteri won. Three times in less than 50 years, in three mayoral elections out of 14, the city's Democrats had been defeated because parts of their organization went over to some form of opposition. Democratic leaders therefore face every new mayoral campaign with some trepidation.

They have seen the effects of similar divisions among the Republicans. In 1917 the Republican-Fusion alliance that had put Mitchel in office at the previous mayoral election broke up (although, peculiarly, it held together for the comptrollership and the presidency of the Board of Aldermen) as Mitchel ran on the Fusion ticket against a Republican, a Democrat, and a strong Socialist. The Democrats won easily against this fragmented opposition, but presumably the lesson was not lost upon them. They were again reminded of it in 1945, when Newbold Morris, a Republican from a staunch Republican family and a former President of the City Council under Mayor La Guardia, refused to endorse the Republican nominee for Mayor and ran against him at the head of his own hastily organized No Deal party, polling more than the regular Republican candidate.

Only one defection in this period failed to make any difference at all to the party deserted or the party joined by the discontented faction. This was the bolt from the Democrats to the Republicans by Jonah J. Goldstein, a judge on the Court of General Sessions, who had long been active in Tammany Hall. Goldstein was nominated for Mayor by the Republicans in 1945, but their strategy, which was apparently based on the hope that Goldstein would carry with him a great many Democratic votes just as Mitchel had done in 1913, backfired badly. Not only did he fail to attract Democratic voters, but it was his nomination that provoked many hitherto loyal Republicans into mobilizing the No Deal party protest vote against him. That year, the Republican nominee ran a poor third.

But against this one case in which a split did not injure the party in which it occurred, and may have redounded to the disadvantage of both the defectors and the groups with which they joined, stand five instances of damage to the divided organization, three of which occurred among the Democrats and led them to defeat. There may be a continuing Democratic preference among the voters in New York City, but the Democrats have cause for uneasiness.

Their uneasiness has been heightened by the rise of the third parties. Since 1936, when the leaders of the garment workers' unions rejected the admonition of Samuel Gompers to stay clear of political parties and decided to organize the American Labor party, either the ALP or the Liberals (led by labor leaders who opposed the left-wing ALP leadership and broke away in 1944 to establish their own political organization) or both have had a pronounced impact on the outcome of many elections. In three of the six presidential elections from 1936 to 1956, the third parties demonstrated that they might be able to hurt the Democrats in the state if they chose. Although, as previously noted, the Democrats won at least a plurality every time and a majority a couple of times inside the city, their margins of victory on the Democratic line alone were too small to give them the state. Had the ALP vote in 1940 and the combined ALP and Liberal votes in 1944 gone to someone other than the Democratic nominees, then New York State, with its massive bloc of electoral votes, would have swung into the Republican column. In 1948, if the heavy ALP vote for Henry A. Wallace had gone to Harry S. Truman, the Republicans would not have taken the state. Similarly, in the same twenty-year period, the Democrats would have lost three more United States senatorial races than they did had the ballots cast for their candidates on the third-party lines been given to someone else. Indeed, the Democrats received a stern warning in 1946, when the Republican candidate for Senator not only won the seat but would have carried the city itself had it not been for the Liberal votes for the Democratic standard bearer. Third-party endorsements of the Democratic candidates for Governor in 1938 and 1954 drew large enough numbers of votes to have brought defeat to these individuals had they gone to someone else. Moreover, in both 1946 and 1950, the third parties demonstrated the strategic nature of their position by giving the

TABLE 29. GROWTH OF JOINT NOMINATIONS BY DEMOCRATS AND OTHER PARTIES IN ELECTIONS HELD IN NEW YORK CITY, 1920–1958

Year	Number of offices at stake	Victorious candidates nominated by Democrats alone		Victorious candidates nominated by Democrats and other parties					Total victorious candidates with Democratic nominations	
		Number	Per cent of all offices	Democrats and Republicans only	Democrats and third parties only	Democrats, Republicans, and third parties	Total joint endorsements		Number	Per cent of all offices
							Number	Per cent of all offices		
1920	146	50	34.2	6	..	2	8	5.5	58	39.7
1921	159	120	75.5	11	..	..	11	6.9	131	82.4
1922	133	122	91.7	3	..	..	3	2.3	125	94.0
1923	156	134	85.9	3	..	2	5	3.2	139	89.1
1924	131	113	86.3	1	..	..	1	.7	114	87.0
1925	162	150	92.6	2	..	..	2	1.2	152	93.8
1926	140	130	92.9	4	..	..	4	2.8	134	95.7
1927	165	142	86.1	9	1	..	10	5.0	152	91.1
1928	128	116	90.6	..	1	..	1	.8	117	91.4
1929	186	171	91.9	5	..	1	6	2.7	177	94.6
1930	139	127	91.4	4	..	..	4	2.8	131	94.2
1931	166	134	80.7	22	..	..	22	13.3	156	94.0
1932	138	128	92.8	5	..	1	6	4.3	134	97.1
1933	167	34	20.2	..	90	5	95	57.0	129	77.2
1934	135	86	63.7	1	32	9	42	31.1	128	94.8
1935	156	133	85.3	7	10	..	17	10.9	150	96.2

1936	137	119	86.7	11	3	..	14	8.2	133	94.9
1937	80	21	26.3	2	19	4	25	31.2	46	57.5
1938	128	65	50.8	1	50	3	54	46.9	119	97.7
1939	59	40	67.8	7	3	2	12	20.3	52	88.1
1940	135	87	64.4	3	22	5	30	22.3	117	86.7
1941	64	25	39.1	1	5	6	12	34.3	47	73.4
1942	128	62	48.4	6	43	1	50	39.1	112	87.5
1943	47	21	44.7	3	5	10	18	38.3	39	83.0
1944	132	31	23.5	..	65	5	70	53.0	101	76.5
1945	63	23	36.5	1	15	15	31	49.2	54	85.7
1946	139	29	20.9	..	47	7	54	38.8	83	59.7
1947	30	6	20.0	3	6	15	24	80.0	30	100.0
1948	132	15	11.4	22	51	12	85	64.4	100	75.8
1949	67	35	52.2	3	13	14	30	44.8	65	97.0
1950	145	52	35.9	..	66	8	74	51.0	126	86.9
1951	30	4	13.3	15	2	5	22	73.4	26	86.7
1952	130	28	21.5	1	61	3	65	50.0	93	71.5
1953	61	39	64.0	2	6	11	19	31.0	58	95.0
1954	148	35	23.6	4	85	6	95	64.2	130	87.8
1955	40	7	18.5	1	22	10	33	81.5	40	100.0
1956	145	26	17.9	..	78	9	87	60.0	113	77.9
1957	58	22	37.9	..	26	9	35	60.4	57	98.3
1958	148	23	15.5	7	74	15	96	64.9	119	80.4

SOURCE: *Annual Reports* of the New York City Board of Elections.

Democratic gubernatorial candidates enough additional votes to swing New York City behind them even though they could not build up large enough majorities to deliver the state. There are so many imponderables at work in these situations that it would be exceedingly rash to draw any sweeping conclusions. But it is not difficult to understand why Democratic leaders do not treat elections in New York as foregone conclusions, and act as though they have almost as much to fear from the defections of some of their allies as they do from splits within their own ranks. Assembling a winning team in a highly pluralistic community can be a trying, and, for those deeply involved, a nerve-wracking experience.

Even in those Democratic strongholds, the legislatures, the weight of the third parties is making itself felt to a larger and larger extent. Up to the mid-thirties, legislative delegations were normally composed of men running beneath a single banner. When the labor-backed parties appeared on the scene, the new organizations intervened in only a handful of legislative contests. But the scope of their participation increased steadily over the years until now a minority of candidates—sometimes a very small minority—bears only a single label. For example, more than half of the members of the city's delegation elected to the House of Representatives have run for office with two or more endorsements in every congressional election since 1936 save one (1940, when 18 out of 26 were nominated by one party only). Once, in 1944, only 3 out of 24 ran on just one line on the ballot, but the figure today hovers between 9 and 10 out of 22. Roughly the same proportion holds true for the city's delegation to the state Assembly, and the ratio of candidates with multiple endorsements to the total number of candidates for the state Senate tends to be even higher. Only in the City Council is joint nomination still a relatively unusual thing.

By far the majority of the major-party candidates endorsed by the third parties are Democrats. At every election, a few Republican candidates for legislative positions have enjoyed ALP or Liberal support; on the whole, however, probably between 80 and 95 per cent of the major-party candidates endorsed by the third parties are Democrats. This is true even though the Bronx Democratic organization, certain of its position, steadfastly refused Liberal endorsements of any of its candidates until very recently. To be sure, it is still relatively uncommon for third-party support to make the difference between victory and defeat for legislative candidates, and third parties very infrequently garner enough votes when they run their own candidates against both major parties to demonstrate that they hold the balance of power. But since the end of World War II, there has scarcely been a legislative election (excluding the City Council) in which the vote on the third-party line (or lines) has not amounted to the margin of victory for a few seats—one or two congressional seats, an equal number of state senatorial seats, and from three to as many as half a dozen or more Assembly seats. Occasionally, it has been the Republicans who have benefited from third-party endorsements or suffered the consequences of separate third-party candidacies, but the beneficiaries (or victims) have much more often been Democrats. So the Democrats have shown a tendency to get nervous even about those contests in which they are more secure than anywhere else, and to seek third-party support with ever-increasing frequency.

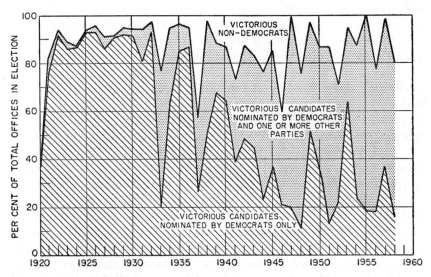

CHART 13. GROWTH OF JOINT NOMINATIONS BY DEMOCRATS AND OTHER PARTIES IN ELECTIONS HELD IN NEW YORK CITY, 1920–1958

Source: Compiled from *Annual Reports* of the New York City Board of Elections.

Both the American Labor and Liberal parties have shown the highest degree of independence from the Democrats in mayoral elections, which is at once a result of the Democrats' vulnerability at this level and a cause of it. Both third parties have endorsed Republican mayoral nominees or run their own candidates independently about as often as they have joined with the Democrats. Moreover, they have shown great power here. In 1937, for example, by which time the Democrats had healed the split that helped bring them down to resounding defeat in 1933, Mayor La Guardia would not have been reelected without the more than 480,000 American Labor votes that were added to his 675,000 Republican ballots. It required the same GOP-ALP union to reelect him again in 1941. In 1945, the year of the Republican split, the political forces in the city realigned themselves drastically and somewhat peculiarly. The American Labor party teamed up with the Democrats, the Liberals got behind the Republicans, and a large number of Republicans followed Newbold Morris out of their party. Under these conditions, the Democratic plurality was enough to carry the party through even without ALP support, but the combined Republican-No Deal-Liberal vote exceeded the Democratic vote alone and indicates that the Democrats would have needed the ALP had the opposition been unified.

The Liberals again allied themselves with the Republicans in 1949, while the ALP now ran independently, the three parties together winning enough of the vote to have defeated the Democrats had they been united. Again, it was the fragmentation of the opposition that opened the door for the Democrats. In the special election of a Mayor in 1950, the Liberals were on the side of the Democrats, the Experience party of Impellitteri stood alone, and the Republicans and the American Laborites each ran candidates of their own, too. In spite of this, Impellitteri won, but if this gave any Democratic leaders the idea that the Liberals made no difference to them, the Liberal capture of the presidency of the City Council in the special election of the following year (when all four parties had their own candidates) quickly disabused them of it. The Liberal party displayed great vitality and proved that its fate would be different from that of the waning American Labor party. The Democrats easily came in first again in 1953, when the Republicans, Liberals, and remnants of the American Labor party each ran candidates of their own. Had the Liberals and the Republicans been united on this occasion as they had been in the past, and assuming that each of them would have received the same number of votes under this condition as they did running separately, they would have beaten the Democrats. The Democratic victory, however gratifying it might have been to the party's leaders, did little to increase their sense of security.

Their insecurity must have been intensified by the continual shifts and realignments at the borough level. In 1945, for example, the Republicans and the ALP teamed up against the Democrats in Richmond; the Democrats and the ALP allied against the Republicans and the Liberals in Manhattan, Brooklyn, and Queens; and all four parties ran separate candidates in The Bronx. In a special election in Queens in 1951, each party had its own nominee. In 1953, each party had its own nominee in four of the five boroughs, but the Democrats and Republicans teamed up in the face of a strong Liberal challenge in Brooklyn. In 1955, on the other hand, a special election in Richmond produced a Democratic-Liberal coalition against the Republicans. In very few of these cases did the third party possess the balance of power, but the bewildering game of political musical chairs suggests that neither of the major parties feels particularly safe in any of these constituencies. The borough presidencies have changed hands often enough in the last twenty years to make these apprehensions understandable.

If all this were not enough to drive politicians to distraction, there is one more thing that might: the fact that the names of over fifty parties ("independent bodies" in the language of the Election Law) have appeared since 1920 on the ballots voted by New York City residents. Included among these are a wide variety of associations. Many of them are organized by well-meaning, but often politically unsophisticated, amateur reformers. A large number are left-wing parties, including small splinter groups that have broken away from their parent bodies in schisms based on ideological differ-

TABLE 30. "INDEPENDENT BODIES" THAT HAVE APPEARED ON NEW YORK CITY VOTING MACHINES SINCE 1920[a]

Anti-Communistic	Law Preservation
Assurance	No Tammany
American	No Boss
Benjamin Gitlow	No Deal
Both Emblems	People's Rights
Bronx County Party	Progressive
Citizens Independent	Prohibition
Citizens Nonpartisan	Public Interest
City Fusion	Recovery
Commonwealth Land	Reunion
Communist	Richmond County Independent
Conservative	Rock
Experience	Single Tax
Farmer-Labor	Social Labor
Five-cent Fare	Socialist
Fusion	Socialist Worker
Honest Government	Square Deal
Independent	Taxpayer
Independent Citizens	Trades Union
Independent League	Trotskyist
Independent Progressive	Trotsky-Anti-War
Industrial Government	United City
Industrial Union	Vigilant
Jefferson	Veteran's Victory
John F. X. Masterson	Worker
Joseph V. McKee	Worker's League

[a] Some were short-lived organizations with little success; some, however, have continuously run candidates (for example, Industrial Government and Socialist Worker), a few, such as City Fusion, with occasional considerable success.

SOURCE: *Annual Reports* of the New York City Board of Elections.

ences. Some were created to capture a single office, or to publicize a single issue, such as the 5-cent subway fare. Some are the personal instruments of a single individual. A few are actually adjuncts of the major parties set up to attract the votes of people who would like to protest against the major parties as organizations but not against their principal candidates, and who innocently suppose that they accomplish this end by pulling the lever for the group with the moral name (such as Honest Government, Law Preservation, No Tammany, Independent Citizens, No Boss). For the most part, these parties collect a few hundred, or, if they are lucky, a few thousand votes, or practically never enough to make much difference to the major or third parties. But some do occasionally explode into temporary prominence and upset many political calculations in individual elections. For example, in the mayoral election of 1929, the Socialists drew 175,000 votes and they climbed to 250,000 in 1932. They went steadily downhill to a low of 3,400 in 1949, after which they stopped entering candidates. The City Fusion party, which comes to life intermittently, polled over 420,000 votes in 1933, when it backed

TABLE 31. ELECTIONS IN WHICH THIRD PARTY VOTES WERE IMPORTANT FACTORS IN THE RESULTS, 1938–1958

Year and office	Total vote for victor	Total vote for loser	Margin of victory	Third-party vote for victor	Vote for separate third-party candidate
1938[a] Governorship	2,391,286 Lehman	2,326,892 Dewey	64,394	419,979 ALP	..
1940[a] Presidential	3,251,916 Roosevelt	3,027,478 Willkie	224,438	417,416 ALP	..
1941[b] Mayoralty	1,103,859 LaGuardia	1,054,235 O'Dwyer	49,624	435,374 ALP	..
1948[a] Presidential	2,841,163 Dewey	2,557,642 Truman	283,121	..	509,559 Wallace
1948[c] Surrogate, N.Y. County	305,122 Republican	303,972 Democrat	1,150	62,963 Liberal	96,856 ALP
1951[b] Council President	659,311 Liberal	495,011 Democrat 435,699 Republican	(Liberal was victorious)	659,311 Liberal and other	..
1953[b] Mayoralty	1,022,626 Wagner	661,591 Republican	361,035	..	467,105 Halley
1954[a] Governorship	2,560,738 Harriman	2,549,613 Ives	11,125	264,093 Liberal	39,768 ALP
1958[a] State Comptroller	2,778,485 Levitt	2,730,177 Lundy	48,308	267,497 Liberal	..

[a] Statewide figures.   [b] Citywide figures.   [c] Countywide figures.

La Guardia, but it temporarily retired from the field when it declined to 12,000 in 1949, and it drew fewer than 7,000 votes when it returned to endorse Wagner in 1957. In 1953 the Independent party endorsed the Liberal candidate for Mayor and received more than 38,000 votes on its line. To be sure, except for Fusion in 1933, none of these happened to be crucial despite the fairly substantial numbers involved. Nevertheless, because the city's voting pattern is often so fractionized, it is not inconceivable that some political group appearing very suddenly on the political horizon and then disappearing almost as suddenly as it came could prove costly to the larger, more permanent parties. By itself, perhaps, this possibility would probably not cause any deep concern to the leaders of the Democratic party, but added to all the other uncertainties they face, it builds up the forebodings with which they approach Election Day.

The Rise of Queens. One new hazard has developed in recent years to dismay the Democrats still further. That is the rise of Queens in population and voting strength. In 1952 the total registration and the total number of votes cast in Queens County for the first time exceeded those in New York County

TABLE 32. THE RISE OF QUEENS: POPULATION OF CITY BY BOROUGHS, 1940, 1950, 1957

Borough	Population			Net gain or loss			Per cent gain or loss,
	1940	1950	1957	1940–1950	1950–1957	1940–1957	1940–1957
Queens	1,297,634	1,550,849	1,762,582	253,215	211,733	464,948	+35.8
Richmond	174,441	191,555	212,020	17,114	20,465	37,579	+21.5
The Bronx	1,394,711	1,451,277	1,424,367	56,566	− 26,910	29,656	+ 2.1
Brooklyn	2,698,285	2,738,175	2,602,433	39,890	−135,742	−95,852	− 3.5
Manhattan	1,889,924	1,960,101	1,794,069	70,177	−166,032	−95,855	− 5.2
Entire city	7,454,995	7,891,957	7,795,471	436,962	− 96,476	340,476	+ 4.5

SOURCES: *Statistical Abstract of the United States*, U.S. Dept. of Commerce, Washington, 1958; *The World Almanac*, New York World-Telegram Corporation, New York, 1959.

TABLE 33. REGISTRATION IN CITY BY BOROUGHS, 1940, 1948, 1956

Borough	1940		1948		1956	
	Registration, all parties	Per cent of city total	Registration, all parties	Per cent of city total	Registration, all parties	Per cent of city total
Queens	634,022	18.7	666,763	20.1	813,546	24.7
Brooklyn	1,196,597	35.3	1,138,309	34.4	1,054,072	32.0
Manhattan	829,330	24.4	783,565	23.6	712,864	21.7
The Bronx	650,688	19.2	651,111	19.6	624,210	19.0
Richmond	79,823	2.4	76,081	2.2	86,477	2.6
Entire city	3,390,460	100.0	3,315,829	100.0	3,291,169	100.0

SOURCE: *Annual Reports* of the New York City Board of Elections.

—the traditional seat of Democratic strength—and have remained ahead ever since. It is now second only to Brooklyn and far ahead of the strongly Democratic Bronx. The Republicans have found a new base of municipal power here, for this borough's voting pattern varies from a fairly equal division between the two major parties when the Democrats are having a good year to thumping Republican majorities when Republican candidates are running well. Richmond County, though small in population, behaves in much the same way. Not only does this augment the instability that marks municipal politics and grows ulcers in Democratic stomachs, not only does it make it increasingly difficult for the Democrats to roll up the overwhelming majorities that offset Republican majorities upstate when statewide offices and presidential electors are at stake, not only does it often assure the Republicans of a place on the public forum of the Board of Estimate and a fulcrum they can use to exert leverage upon the Democrats, but it strikes fear into the hearts of Democratic leaders because these are the areas of future growth within the city. The burgeoning of Queens from a region of small homes and suburban living to one of massive apartment house developments and huge shopping centers after the extension of the Independent subway, and the tendency of the new residents to follow at least in part the Republican traditions of the earlier inhabitants, have already altered the political complexion of the city. Since the growth of Queens is likely to continue for a number of years, it is difficult to foretell with any confidence what the future holds, but the disquiet of the Democrats clearly is not unjustified. If Richmond should follow the Queens pattern when the construction of a bridge across The Narrows provides a fast, inexpensive vehicular route to Manhattan, the political balance in the city will undergo further adjustment. To the Democrats, the years ahead seem fraught with danger to their grip on the city.

While there is no disputing the existence of a continuing Democratic preference on the part of New Yorkers, as evidenced by the number of electoral battles the Democrats win consistently and by the discouragement evinced by some Republican leaders in the city, it is equally true that the Democratic position is less secure than the proportions of their victories suggest. The frequency with which the Democrats come to power on the basis of pluralities rather than majorities, the recurrence of splits in the Democratic ranks, the increasing significance of the Liberal party to the Democrats, the number of times the Republicans have won important offices in the last quarter-century, and the rising star of Republican power in Queens and Richmond combine to present continuing hazards that keep the Democrats constantly on edge.

Differential Hazards. It is the offices with the larger constituencies that present the greatest uncertainties to the Democrats. In most constituencies smaller than a county, they win steadily. In battles to carry a county (or borough), the risks of defeat are somewhat higher. In the city as a whole, they often win by pluralities rather than majorities, and the frequency of Republican victories is higher than is the case for lesser offices.

The way constituency boundaries are drawn is a major factor in producing a pattern of this kind. If the pockets of strength of one party are carefully bounded, that party's strength can be isolated so that it carries some districts by overwhelming margins but cannot apply its excess strength to other districts. Only in the larger constituencies of which the pockets are part does the

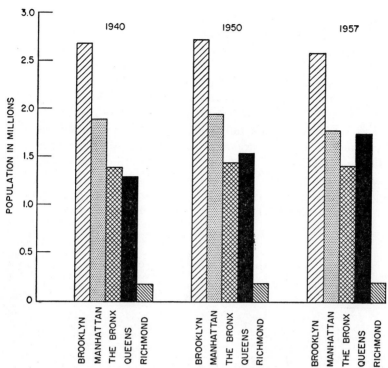

CHART 14. POPULATION OF NEW YORK CITY BY BOROUGHS IN SELECTED YEARS

SOURCES: *Statistical Abstract of the United States*, U.S. Dept. of Commerce; *The World Almanac*, New York World-Telegram Corporation, New York.

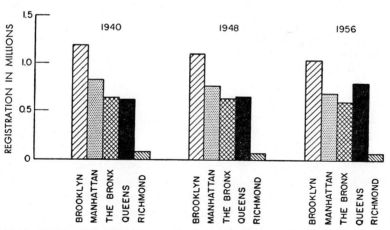

CHART 15. TOTAL REGISTRATION IN ALL PARTIES IN NEW YORK CITY BY BOROUGHS IN SELECTED YEARS

SOURCE: *Annual Reports* of the New York City Board of Elections.

large size of the local majorities offset less emphatic opposition majorities else-where. Under these conditions one party may amass on the whole nearly as many votes as another, but its power, being concentrated, is contained within a few districts and is a threat to the opposition outside those areas only when higher offices are at stake. So the lesser offices remain largely in the hands of one party while the higher offices change hands from time to time.

Chances are this "gerrymander" factor is at work in New York City and helps account for some of the differential hazards noted. It is not possible to say how much of the difference may thus be explained, because the required painstaking analysis of voting records in the various districts over time has

TABLE 34. PERCENTAGE OF DEMOCRATIC VOTES IN NEW YORK CITY COMPARED WITH PERCENTAGE OF DEMOCRATIC VOTES IN QUEENS

Year	Total ballots cast in city	Democratic votes in city	Democratic votes in city as per cent of total ballots in city	Total ballots cast in Queens	Democratic votes in Queens	Democratic votes in Queens as per cent of total ballots in Queens
1958[a]	2,393,167	1,116,617	47	604,355	247,124	41
1957[b]	2,224,054	1,284,856	57	562,096	300,399	53
1956[c]	3,221,178	1,383,092	43	798,683	275,304	34
1955[d]	1,458,624	863,391	59	359,760	185,112	51
1954[a]	2,308,464	1,260,426	54	528,658	244,672	46
1953[b]	2,244,146	1,022,626	46	511,731	207,918	41
1952[c]	3,461,706	1,517,982	44	798,283	281,735	35
1951[d]	1,724,082	665,574	38	387,594	135,183	35
1950[a]	2,705,236	1,033,198	38	558,595	184,509	33
1949[b]	2,656,324	1,266,512	48	515,898	270,062	52
1948[c]	3,216,438	1,403,379	44	648,640	249,863	39

[a] Figures are votes for Governor.   [b] Figures are votes for Mayor.
[c] Figures are votes for President.
[d] Figures are the sum of votes for Supreme Court justices.
SOURCE: *Annual Reports* of the New York City Board of Elections.

never been made. It is doubtful that gerrymandering is the whole explana-tion. The boundaries of Congressional and state Senatorial Districts, for ex-ample, are prescribed by the state legislature, and the state legislature is generally controlled by the Republicans. It seems unlikely that this body, even allowing for its willingness to make bargains with Democratic Governors and legislators, would manipulate the lines to the advantage of the Demo-crats. Moreover, while the City Council draws Assembly District lines within counties in the city, the state constitution enjoins it to set up every Assembly District within a Senate District, and to have the same number of Assembly Districts (with one exception) in each Senate District. The opportunities for the Democrats in the city to guarantee their almost total control of the lesser offices by gerrymander are consequently limited.

It seems reasonable to infer, therefore, that some added factor is operative —something about the behavior of individual voters as well as the way they are grouped. What suggests itself at once is the practice of some voters of refraining from voting straight party tickets. There is no party-ticket lever on New York State voting machines to encourage ticket voting. Each office must be voted on separately. This facilitates selective nonvoting (voting on some offices, but not on others) and ticket-splitting (voting for the candidates of one party for some offices, candidates of other parties for other offices). There is evidence that both types of discrimination occur.

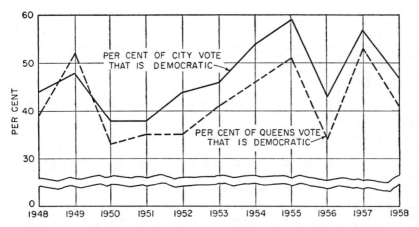

CHART 16. PERCENTAGE OF DEMOCRATIC VOTES IN NEW YORK CITY COMPARED WITH THE PERCENTAGE OF DEMOCRATIC VOTES IN QUEENS

SOURCE: Compiled from *Annual Reports* of the New York City Board of Elections.

The evidence of selective nonvoting is the number of what is officially termed "unrecorded votes" in every constituency for every office. Invariably, more people vote in an election than cast ballots for any given office. The difference between the total number of voters and the number of votes cast for a particular office is the unrecorded vote for that office. In some Assembly Districts, the unrecorded votes for an individual office sometimes exceeds 10 per cent of the total number of voters. Clearly, a substantial portion of the population discriminate not only among candidates and parties but among offices as well. By and large, the percentage of unrecorded votes tends to be greater in the case of minor offices than for major offices. As a result, the straight-ticket voters apparently dominate the choice of lesser officials, while the selective nonvoters introduce additional variables and uncertainties into the election of higher officials. So the total party vote for lower offices is more stable than for higher offices. And there are more Democratic than Republican straight-ticket voters in the city, keeping the lower offices relatively safe for the Democratic party.

TABLE 35. EVIDENCE OF TICKET-SPLITTING AND SELECTIVE NONVOTING

Year and offices compared	Number of Assembly Districts in which candidates for chief executive ran *behind* their legislative running mates				Number of Assembly Districts in which candidates for chief executive ran *ahead* of their legislative running mates				Total number of Assembly Districts
	Dem.	Rep.	Lib.	ALP	Dem.	Rep.	Lib.	ALP	
1948 (ASSEMBLYMAN/PRESIDENT)									
The Bronx	8	0	7	3	5	13	6	10	13
Brooklyn	15	1	15	7	9	23	9	17	24
Manhattan	7	0	9	4	9	16	7	12	16
Queens	12	0	12	2	0	12	0	10	12
Richmond	2	0	2	0	0	2	0	2	2
Whole city	44	1	45	16	23	66	22	51	67
1949 (COUNCILMAN/MAYOR)									
The Bronx	10	2	0	0	3	11	13	13	13
Brooklyn	14	1	3	1	10	23	21	23	24
Manhattan	8	1	2	0	8	15	14	16	16
Queens	5	5	1	0	7	7	11	12	12
Richmond	0	2	2	0	2	0	0	2	2
Whole city	37	11	8	1	30	56	59	66	67
1950 (ASSEMBLYMAN/GOVERNOR)									
The Bronx	13	0	1	7	0	13	12	6	13
Brooklyn	24	0	17	18	0	24	7	6	24
Manhattan	7	0	8	4	9	16	8	12	16
Queens	12	0	8	6	0	12	4	6	12
Richmond	2	0	1	2	0	2	1	0	2
Whole city	58	0	35	37	9	67	32	30	67
1952 (ASSEMBLYMAN/PRESIDENT)									
The Bronx	12	0	5	13	1	13	8	0	13
Brooklyn	19	0	5	24	5	24	19	0	24
Manhattan	2	0	7	16	14	16	9	0	16
Queens	10	1	8	12	2	11	4	0	12
Richmond	2	0	2	2	0	2	0	0	2
Whole city	45	1	27	67	22	66	40	0	67
1953 (COUNCILMAN/MAYOR)									
The Bronx	10	0	0	0	3	13	13	13	13

Brooklyn	19	2	0	2	5	22	24	22	24
Manhattan	0	2	0	0	16	14	16	16	16
Queens	7	3	0	12	5	9	12	0	12
Richmond	2	0	0	1	0	2	2	1	2
Whole city	38	7	0	15	29	60	67	52	67
1954 (Assemblyman/Governor)									
The Bronx	3	0	1	0[a]	9	12	11	5[a]	12
Brooklyn	12	2	10	1[a]	10	20	12	12[a]	22
Manhattan	0	1	3	0[a]	16	15	13	12[a]	16
Queens	9	2	6	0[a]	4	11	7	5[a]	13
Richmond	2	0	2	2	0	2	0	0	2
Whole city	26	5	22	3[a]	39	60	43	34[a]	65
1956 (Assemblyman/President)									
The Bronx	12	0	5	:	0	12	7	:	12
Brooklyn	21	0	13	:	1	22	9	:	22
Manhattan	11	0	7	:	5	16	9	:	16
Queens	13	0	13	:	0	13	0	:	13
Richmond	2	0	2	:	0	2	0	:	2
Whole city	59	0	40	:	6	65	25	:	65
1957 (Councilman/Mayor)									
The Bronx	1	1	9	:	11	11	3	:	12
Brooklyn	11	5	19	:	11	17	3	:	22
Manhattan	0	6	10	:	16	10	6	:	16
Queens	3	10	7	:	10	3	6	:	13
Richmond	0	2	2	:	2	0	0	:	2
Whole city	15	24	47	:	50	41	18	:	65
1958 (Assemblyman/Governor)									
The Bronx	12	0	5	:	0	12	7	:	12
Brooklyn	21	0	18	:	1	22	4	:	22
Manhattan	15	1	12	:	1	16	4	:	16
Queens	12	0	11	:	0	12	2	:	13
Richmond	2	0	2	:	0	2	0	:	2
Whole city	62	1	48	:	3	64	17	:	65

[a] ALP did not run candidates in every district in these years.

Source: *Annual Reports* of the New York City Board of Elections.

A further indication of selective nonvoting is the fact that in most Assembly Districts Democratic candidates for Mayor, Governor, or President usually do not receive *as many* votes as candidates for lesser offices, while Republican candidates for chief executive posts receive *more* than their running mates. This could be the result of selective nonvoting alone if selective Democratic voters tend to vote for lesser candidates of their party but not the major ones, while selective Republican voters support only their leaders but not the lesser lights. It could, however, also be produced by ticket-splitting, with voters choosing ticket leaders on the basis of personality or program (these candidates being the visible ones) and voting for the minor and relatively unknown candidates on the basis of party label. The Democratic bias of the populace would then display itself on the lower levels, while the higher candidates would encounter greater uncertainty. The major Democratic nominees would lose votes to their Republican opponents while the minor ones did not, causing the top Democrats frequently to run behind their Democratic colleagues and the top Republicans frequently to run ahead of their Republican fellows. Ticket-splitting may not be the most common voting pattern, but it is doubtless not uncommon.

For all these reasons, Democratic chances of defeat rise with the importance of the offices to be filled. Democratic chieftains may perhaps take comfort from the sureness of their grip on smaller positions. They must also suffer agonies when they survey their situation and realize that the greatest doubts attend the largest stakes. The continuing Democratic preference of the city is pronounced; the continuing Democratic hazards are real and significant.

ELECTION ADMINISTRATION

For many years, it was not certain whether election returns reflected the wishes of the city's electorates or the machinations of party officers. Unquestionably, elections were stolen. Neither side had a monopoly on fraud: both employed "floaters" and "repeaters"; both sent out squads to intimidate voters; both tried to falsify records. For a generation, however, these practices have been all but eliminated. At no time in the last twenty-five years has anyone alleged that fraudulent votes reached such proportions as to affect the outcome of any election. Today, election returns in New York are honest and accurate.

The Board of Elections

All elections within the city are administered by the Board of Elections, a body of four Commissioners established by the state constitution and the Election Law. The Commissioners are appointed for four-year terms by the City Council on recommendation of the Manhattan and Brooklyn county chairmen of those parties that cast the highest and second-highest votes for Governor at the last preceding general election. Thus, the Board of Elections always consists of a Democrat and a Republican from each of these two counties. They are removable by the Governor after a hearing.

The powers and duties of the Board are of five kinds: (1) ensuring that only those who meet the requirements of the law (age, citizenship, residence, literacy, no criminal convictions) vote in primary, special, and general elections; (2) providing the personnel (on a bipartisan basis), public announcements, space, equipment, and supplies for the conduct of the elections; (3) certifying the names of designees to appear on primary ballots and of nominees (whether nominated by petition, convention, or primary) to appear on election ballots, including canvass of primary votes; (4) canvassing election returns and transmitting to the winners certified declarations of their election, or for offices with constituencies extending beyond the boundaries of the city, canvassing the returns and reporting them to the Secretary of State; and (5) receiving and keeping records of elections and reports on campaign receipts, expenditures, and contributions, the latter on forms requisitioned from the Secretary of State in Albany.

The Secretary of State

For nominations and elections to all offices with constituencies extending beyond the city limits and to the office of United States Representative, and for certification of the fate of proposed amendments to the state constitution, the Secretary of State has official responsibility. His province includes presidential electors, United States Senators, the Governor and all other elective state officers other than legislators, and all Supreme Court justices save those elected wholly within New York City. He also receives from the Board of Elections reports on nominations, elections, and election finances in the city. A state Board of Canvassers (the Attorney General, two members of the Senate, and two members of the Assembly, the legislators being divided between the two largest parties) reviews all results and reports its findings to the Secretary of State, who officially proclaims them.

The Police Department

The New York City Police Department is specifically charged by the Election Law to assist election officers, check the qualifications of certain voters, take custody of certain official election records, and collect and report election returns. There was a time when many police officers took advantage of these powers to forge mutually beneficial alliances with the dominant party. Police partisanship then became an important factor in the electoral fate of many candidates. Things changed when it became clear that the police were losing more by collusion than they could hope to gain. Like all public employees, they wanted benefits from Albany, and the party that controls the state legislature is generally different from that controlling the city. Investigations by the legislature hurt the force. Its appropriations were endangered, its leaders shifted, its members dismissed or prosecuted when apprehended. Twelve years of a reform administration under La Guardia demonstrated the inexpediency of an alliance with one party. The rise of strong third parties—the Labor American party in 1936, the Liberal party in 1944—made such coalitions even riskier, the dangers of discovery and exposure even greater. Civic groups and the press kept a steady glare of publicity on the police. The rise of literacy and political sophistication as immigrants became familiar with local institutions and, as their children reached maturity, made the crude practices of an earlier period unacceptable and ineffective. The Department had more to gain by nonpartisanship and scrupulous adherence to a neutral course than by connivance in election frauds. Under conscientious commissioners, its security was built up by development of professional expertise and ethics. Today, it seems to follow a rule of strict nonentanglement, free of favoritism to any party in the management of elections.

The Board of Regents

Since 1922 ability to read and write English has been a qualification for voting in New York. Proof of schooling through the eighth grade or of honorable military service is accepted as evidence of this by the Board of Elections. Otherwise, the prospective voter must procure a certificate of literacy from the Board of Regents.

The Board of Regents is the overseer of all education, both public and private, in the state. Under the Election Law and the Regents' regulations, the Board of Education of the city details teachers to serve as examiners at literacy testing centers during every registration period. Thus literacy tests are not employed for partisan purposes.

Official Checks on Election Administrators

The state Attorney General and the courts provide additional deterrents to election irregularities. The Attorney General is empowered by the Executive Law to appoint a special deputy to investigate charges arising under the Election Law and the Penal Law provision on crimes against the elective franchise, and to employ special Assistant Attorneys General to enforce the Election Law anywhere in the state. These officers have all the powers of peace officers, and a corps of them stand by at every election.

The courts have sweeping powers in election matters. The Election Law authorizes voters, candidates, or specified party officers to institute suit against designated election officials. The Supreme Court may rule on almost any aspect of election procedures and practices, including canvasses and finances. Individual Supreme Court justices and county judges may decide questions of voter registration, party enrollment, and eligibility. There is no corner of the electoral process into which the powers of the courts do not reach. Election proceedings take preference over all other causes and are summarily determined in the first instance.

Unofficial Checks on Election Administrators

Over and above the bipartisanship of the Board of Elections and its field clerks, parties and independent bodies keep close watch on election administration through their own watchers and challengers. The Election Law confers on these certified party representatives powers and privileges with regard to surveying the operation of the polls, recording the returns, and challenging prospective voters. In this way, third parties are able to join in supervising the elections. The theory is that the competitors will scrutinize each other more suspiciously and jealously than any neutral agency can.

Nevertheless, a nonprofit civic organization, the Honest Ballot Association, has taken part in the protection of the integrity of New York City elections since 1909. To this end, it has secured evidence against and pressed prosecution of dishonest officials and fraudulent voters; it has helped in revising election laws; it has led the fight for installation of voting machines in New York City. At election time, its staff advises voters of their rights, alerts them to detect fraud, conducts training sessions for watchers, and runs widespread information and education programs on the essentials of election law. Most important of all, the Association maintains a staff of lawyers at its own headquarters in Manhattan and, by invitation of the Police Commissioner, at Police Headquarters, every election and primary day. They handle inquiries from all over the city, and, if necessary, send roving squads out to visit polling places from which complaints have been received. For about thirty years, at every general election, Association officers serving without compensation have been deputized by the Attorney General of the state to help police elections. Moreover, many qualified watchers of the various parties are selected as representatives of the Honest Ballot Association and have powers of arrest.

Honest Elections

Small wonder, then, that elections in New York City today are honest—honest in the sense that few votes are bought or sold, compelled or prevented by intimidation or duress, or miscounted. The machinery, it would seem, has become too intricate for these modes of fraud to survive.

It would be a mistake, however, to ascribe the decline of election dishonesty entirely to the mechanics of administration. The machinery has existed for a long time; it is the use of it that has changed. Public tolerance has narrowed. New kinds of men have entered the political arena. The role of government in modern life has expanded. Professionalism and specialization have introduced new factors into politics. The environment in which elections are conducted has been transformed. It is to this, rather than to procedural arrangements, that the integrity of today's elections in the city must be attributed.

Whatever the explanation, it is clear that the probity of New York City elections is no longer in question. The victorious candidates are the ones selected by the voters from among the nominees presented.

THE NEXT ARENA

Before the candidates elected on Election Day can be inaugurated some two months later, the contestants for the stakes of political action are already at work trying to tell them what to do in office. In nominations and elections, the parties and electorates predominate. In the day-to-day decisions of government officials and employees, the other participants in politics become more prominent. But they do not wait for the election winners formally to assume office before exerting influence on them. They start to press their demands as soon as the results are known.

The first pressures officers-elect have to face concern the use of their appointing powers. No sooner has the hectic process of nomination and election produced the top government officials than the new, and scarcely less harrowing, process of appointment begins.

BIBLIOGRAPHY

GENERAL

Among the many general treatments of American parties and politics, the following are especially suggestive:

Key, V. O., Jr., *Politics, Parties, and Pressure Groups.* 4th ed. Thomas Y. Crowell Co., New York, 1958.
　American State Politics. Alfred A. Knopf, New York, 1956.

Leiserson, Avery, *Parties and Politics.* Alfred A. Knopf, New York, 1958.

Penniman, Howard K., *Sait's American Parties and Elections.* 5th ed. Appleton-Century-Crofts, New York, 1952.

Ranney, Austin, and Willmoore Kendall, *Democracy and the American Party System.* Harcourt, Brace and Co., New York, 1956, especially Part Three.

Schattschneider, E. E., *Party Government.* Rinehart and Co., New York, 1942.

PARTY ORGANIZATION, NOMINATING PROCEDURES, AND ELECTIONS

Abrahams, Lewis, *Digest of Election Law Decisions.* William C. Chanler, New York, 1942. Court decisions relating to the structure of political parties and nominating and election procedures in New York State.
　New York Election Law Manual. H. Wolff, New York, 1939. Party organization, and nominating and election procedures, in New York State.

Alexander, Jack, "District Leader: Profile of James J. Hines," *The New Yorker*, vol. 12, July 25, 1936, pp. 21–26; August 1, 1936, pp. 18–23; August 8, 1936, pp. 18–24. A study of a district leader in Manhattan that reveals much about ward politics in New York City.

Almond, Gabriel A., *Plutocracy and Politics in New York City*. Microfilmed doctoral dissertation, University of Chicago, 1939.

Bone, Hugh A., "Political Parties in New York City," *American Political Science Review*, vol. 40, April, 1946, pp. 272–282. A description of the political parties in the metropolis in 1946.

Caldwell, Lynton K., *The Government and Administration of New York*. Thomas Y. Crowell Co., New York, 1945, pp. 45–49. The processes of nominating and electing candidates in New York.

Citizens Union, "Party Organization in New York City," *The Searchlight*, vol. 41, May, 1951. A brief summary and evaluation of the structure and functioning of party organizations in Greater New York, as viewed by the Citizens Union.

Clark, Harry Wilcox, *Political Parties, Politics and Government*. Master's thesis, Columbia University, 1948, unpublished. Political parties and elections in New York City.

Colville, Lorraine, *A Comparison and Evaluation of the Organization and Techniques of the Major Political Parties in New York City and the Reaction of the Electorate to the Organizations (1929–1949)*. University Microfilms, Publication no. 10,624, Ann Arbor, Mich., 1956. Doctoral dissertation, New York University, 1954. Describes the structure, operation, and effectiveness of political parties in New York City from 1929 to 1949.

Curran, Henry H., *John Citizen's Job*. Charles Scribner's Sons, New York, 1924. Some observations on political campaigning in New York City elections by a veteran of the game.

Democratic Party, *Rules* (county, state, national). See bibliography for Chapter IV.

Feldman, Justin N., "How Tammany Holds Power." Reprinted from the *National Municipal Review*, July, 1950, in Richard S. Childs, *Civic Victories: The Story of an Unfinished Revolution*. Harper and Bros., New York, 1952, pp. 309–314. How the Democratic party in Manhattan uses the primary laws to remain in power and battle insurgents.

Flournoy, Houston I., *The Liberal Party in New York State*. University Microfilms, Publication no. 20,115, Ann Arbor, Mich., 1957. An important minor party in New York City.

Flynn, Edward J., *You're the Boss*. Viking Press, New York, 1947, pp. 219–235. How political parties select their candidates for office.

Forman, Seymour B., *Silk Stocking Politics: A Study of Two Political Clubs in a New York County Assembly District*. Master's thesis, Columbia University, 1954, unpublished.

Frankel, Max, *Robert B. Blaikie and His Irregular Democratic Club*. Master's thesis, Columbia University, 1953, unpublished.

Gassman, Benjamin, *The ABC of the Direct Primary Law*. Primary Publications, New York, 1940. An annotated explanation of direct primaries in New York State.

Gittell, Marilyn, *Administration and Organization of Political Parties in New York City*. Master's thesis, New York University, 1953, unpublished.

Glasser, Israel, *An Analysis of Differential Voting Participation in the 1953 Democratic Mayoralty Primary Election in New York City*. University Microfilms, Ann Arbor, Mich., 1958. Doctoral dissertation, New York University, 1957. A study of the socioeconomic and political elements that prompt voters to cast ballots or not to participate in a New York City mayoralty primary campaign.

Herlands, William B., *Administration of the Election Law in New York City*. Department of Investigation, New York, 1940. The Commissioner of Investigations reports on the functioning and operation of the Election Law.

Ivins, William M., *Machine Politics and Money in Elections in New York City*. Harper and Bros., New York, 1887. A graphic description of political nominating conventions and election practices in New York City before consolidation.

Lavine, Emanuel H., *"Gimme": Or How Politicians Get Rich*. Vanguard Press, New York, 1931, pp. 66–74. Election frauds, violence, and use of "floaters" in elections.

League of Women Voters of New York, *Direct Primary Systems in the United States*. The League, New York, 1953. A comparison between the New York State primary system and the primary systems of other states.

Luthin, Reinhard H., *American Demagogues: Twentieth Century*. Beacon Press, Boston, 1954. How Vito Marcantonio controlled nominations in the American Labor party (pp. 229–230); the effects of the Wilson-Pakula Law (p. 232).

Merriam, Charles Edward, and Louise Overcracker, *Primary Elections*. University of Chicago Press, Chicago, 1928. Although a generalized work, this volume makes frequent reference to primaries in New York.

Morsell, John A., *The Political Behavior of Negroes in New York City*. Doctoral dissertation, Columbia University, 1951.

Moscow, Warren, *Politics in the Empire State*. Alfred A. Knopf, New York, 1948. This description of New York State politics by a journalist and public official deals extensively with many aspects of New York City government and politics.

New York City Board of Elections, *Annual Reports*, for the year ended December 31, 1909 to date. These reports, with slight variations in title, cover the elections for all offices, federal, state, and local, held within the City of New York each year. They indicate registration, party enrollment, and votes cast in general elections (including absentee voting). Results of primary elections are not printed, but the figures may be obtained from the Board of Elections.

New York City Charter. Permanent Personal Registration, provided in chap. 50 (as added by Local Law 80, 1956).

New York State *Constitution*. The state constitution provides for municipal elections in odd-numbered years in Art. IX, Sec. 15, as renumbered and amended by the Constitutional Convention of 1938 and approved by vote of the people, November 8, 1938.

New York State Constitutional Convention Committee, *Problems Relating to Home Rule and Local Government*. J. B. Lyon Co., Albany, 1938, vol. 11 of *Reports and Studies*. Chapter 7, The Right to Vote in New York State, pp. 139–225; chap. 8, Permanent Registration, pp. 226–237. Reviews the constitutional provisions relating to suffrage in New York State and collates the facts on the system of permanent personal registration.

New York State Legislature. *Statutory Provisions Governing Parties, Nominations and Elections*. Elections in New York City, in general, are governed by the following: The Election Law (chap. 100, Laws of 1949), chap. 17 of the Consolidated Laws; sec. 69 of the Executive Law (chap. 800, Laws of 1951); art. 74 of Penal Law (chap. 88, Laws of 1909, as amended).

New York State Superintendent of Elections for the Metropolitan Elections District, *Annual Reports*, 1898–1901. For 1898, Wynkoop Hallenbeck Crawford, Albany, 1899; for 1899–1904, J. B. Lyon Co., Albany, 1900–1905; for 1905, Brandon Printing Co., Albany, 1906; for 1906–1908, J. B. Lyon Co., Albany, 1907–1909. Prior to the organization of the Board of Elections for New York City, elections were conducted and reports made for the counties of New York, Kings, Queens, Richmond, and Westchester by a Metropolitan Elections District, established by the state legislature in 1898. Unfortunately, election results are not recorded in these volumes. The volumes are concerned largely with the efforts of election officials to prevent fraud.

Peel, Roy V., *The Political Clubs of New York City*. G. P. Putnam's Sons, New York, 1935. The classic work on this subject.

Republican Party, *Rules* (county, state, national). See bibliography for Chapter IV.

Saxe, John Godfrey, *A Treatise on the New York Laws Relating to Elections*. J. B. Lyon Co., Albany, 1918. Election law and administration in 1918.

Spinrad, William, *New Yorkers Cast Their Ballots*. University Microfilms, Ann Arbor, Mich., 1955. Doctoral dissertation, Columbia University. This study indicates the relationship between voting in local and national elections and traces the changes in voting between two mayoralty elections. It is based on the mayoralty elections in New York City in 1941 and 1945, the gubernatorial election of 1942, and the presidential election of 1944.

Thomas, Norman, and Paul Blanshard, *What's the Matter with New York? A National Problem*. Macmillan Co., New York, 1932. Machine control of nominations and elections.

SPECIFIC NOMINATIONS AND ELECTIONS IN NEW YORK CITY

(See also bibliographies for Chapters I, XII, and XVIII; also Appendix A.)

Individual Elections, arranged chronologically

Bryce, James, "The Mayoralty Election in New York," *Contemporary Review*, vol. 72, November, 1897, pp. 751–760. Importance of the municipal election of 1897.

Shepard, Edward M., "Political Inauguration of Greater New York," *Atlantic Monthly*, vol. 81, 1898, pp. 104–120. Some observations on the first election in Greater New York City.

Alexander, De Alva Stanwood, *Four Famous New Yorkers*, vol. 4 of *A Political History of New York State, 1882–1905*. 4 vols. Henry Holt and Co., New York, 1923. How the campaign slates for the elections of 1897 (pp. 292–299), 1901 (pp. 360–366), and 1903 (pp. 395–410) were made up.

Bogard, Milo T., editor, *The Redemption of New York*. P. F. McBreen and Sons, New York, 1902. A review of the election of 1901 by New Yorkers who contributed to the victory of Seth Low.

Republican County Committee, *Honest Government for New York: Campaign Book of the Republican Party, October, 1901*. The Committee, New York, 1901. A plea by the New York County Committee for the election of Republican candidates in the municipal elections of 1901.

Shepard, Edward M., "The Second Mayoralty Election in Greater New York," *Atlantic Monthly*, vol. 89, February, 1902, pp. 192–208. A thorough discussion of the issues and men in the municipal election of 1901.

Citizens Union of New York, "Shepard-Low Campaign, Fall of 1901." New York Public Library, Astor Branch. A scrapbook of handbills, notices, campaign literature, and so forth for the municipal campaign of 1901.

Hodder, Alfred, *A Fight for the City*. Macmillan Co., New York, 1903. A contemporary account of the election campaign for William Travers Jerome, candidate for District Attorney of the County of New York in 1901.

Robinson, Beverly, "Reminiscences." Columbia University Oral History Collection, Special Collections, Butler Library. Recollections of the mayoralty campaign of 1905.

Citizens Union of New York, "Citizens Union Pamphlets and Campaign Literature for 1909." Columbia University, Citizens Union Collection. A scrapbook that contains a great deal of information on the municipal campaign of that year.

Bennett, William S., "Reminiscences." Columbia University Oral History Collection, Special Collections, Butler Library. A full-scale description of the municipal campaign of 1909, written by the campaign manager for the Republican candidate for Mayor.

Durstine, Roy S., "Reminiscences." Columbia University Oral History Collection, Special Collections, Columbia University. A reporter on the New York *Sun* offers his recollections of the municipal campaign of 1909.

Leonard, Ira, *The New York City Mayoralty Election of 1909: A Study in the Realities of Reform Politics*. Master's thesis, City College, 1959, unpublished. A well-documented survey of the municipal elections of 1909.

Welling, Richard, *Papers of Richard Welling*. Manuscript Division, New York Public Library. Papers on the Committee of 100, which spearheaded the Fusion movement of 1909, contain original material on the negotiations that preceded the nominations for municipal office in that year.

New York Historical Society, *Charles L. Bemheimer Papers*. Charles L. Bemheimer was Treasurer of the Fusion Committee that nominated Mitchel for Mayor in 1913.

Pink, Louis H., "Reminiscences." Columbia University Oral History Collection, Special Collections, Butler Library. Recollections and observations on the municipal campaign and election in 1913.

Friedman, Jacob A., *The Impeachment of Governor William Sulzer*. Columbia University Press, New York, 1939. How the impeachment and removal of the Governor affected the municipal election of 1913.

Klein, Henry H., *Politics, Government, and the Public Utilities in New York City*. The Author, New York, 1933, pp. 101–140. Some issues in the municipal campaign of 1917.

Amberg, Eda, and William H. Allen, *Civic Lessons from Mayor Mitchel's Defeat*. Institute for Public Service, New York, 1921. This pamphlet attempts to analyze the reasons for the downfall of the Fusion ticket in 1917.

Price, Joseph M., "Fusion Mistakes and a Way Out," *National Municipal Review*, vol. 7, March, 1918, pp. 183–186. An analysis of the Fusion movement in the municipal campaign of 1917.

Hillquit, Morris, *Loose Leaves from a Busy Life*. Macmillan Co., New York, 1934. The Socialist candidate for Mayor in 1917 recalls the municipal campaign.

Hard, William, "The New York Mayoralty Campaign," *The New Republic*, vol. 12, October 6, 1917, pp. 270–273; October 13, 1917, pp. 291–294. The issues and personalities in the election.

Democratic-Fusion Committee, *Restore the City to the People*. The Committee, New York, 1917. A Democratic campaign document in the election of 1917.

Ingersoll, Raymond V., "The Recent New York City Fusion Campaign," *National Municipal Review*, vol. 7, March, 1918, pp. 189–198. An adherent of Fusion offers his views of the municipal election of 1917.

Weinstein, James, "Anti-War Sentiment and the Socialist Party, 1917–1918," *Political Science Quarterly*, vol. 74, June 1959, pp. 215–239. Considers the mayoralty campaign of 1917 in New York City in the context of the antiwar campaign waged by the Socialists.

Curran, Henry H., *Van Tassel and Big Bill*. Charles Scribner's Sons, New York, 1923, pp. 42–54. A fictionalized account of how a candidate for alderman was chosen in a "smoke-filled room."

Macmahon, Arthur, "Municipal Elections in 1925," *National Municipal Review*, vol. 15, April, 1926, pp. 218–227. A political scientist describes the municipal election of that year.

Gilford, Duff, "La Guardia," *Plain Talk*, vol. 5, October, 1929, pp. 415–420. Issues in the municipal campaign of 1929.

Pringle, Henry F., "The Italian Table D'Hote: Profile of Fiorello La Guardia," *The New Yorker*, vol. 5, August 31, 1929, pp. 26–29. Written during the mayoralty election of 1929, this article gives a good insight into the campaign and its issues.

Schieffelin, William J., "Reminiscences." Columbia University Oral History Collection, Special Collections, Butler Library. The Chairman of the Committee of a Thousand, which sparked the Fusion movement in the 1933 mayoralty election, offers his recollections of the campaign.

Blanshard, Paul, "La Guardia vs. McKee," *The Nation*, vol. 137, October 25, 1933, pp. 474–477. The municipal election of 1933 and its importance.

Childs, Richard S., "New York City Elections as a Problem in Political Science," *National Municipal Review*, vol. 24, January, 1935, pp. 23–26. How the city Fusion party named its ticket in the municipal election of 1933.

McCaffrey, George H., "New York's 1937 Election and Its Results," *National Municipal Review*, vol. 27, January, 1938. The municipal election of 1937.

"New York Election of 1949." Columbia University Oral History Collection, Special Collections, Butler Library. A series of interviews that recorded the story of the election, before and after, including all major candidates and parties.

Garagon, Joseph A., "Reminiscences." Columbia University Oral History Collection, Special Collections, Butler Library. The municipal election of 1950.

Combs, George H., "Reminiscences." Columbia University Oral History Collection, Special Collections, Butler Library. The New York election of 1950.

President of the City Council, *Election of 1951*. 2 vols. In Municipal Archives. Scrapbook of newspaper clippings relating to this election.

Materials Spanning Several Elections, arranged chronologically

Earle, Genevieve, "Reminiscences." Columbia University Oral History Collection, Special Collections, Butler Library. The part Fusion played in electing Mitchel mayor in 1913; issues of the mayoralty campaign of 1917; mayoralty election of 1945.

Gibbons, Edward R., *Mayoralty Nominations in New York*. Master's thesis, Columbia University, 1930, unpublished.

Isaac, Julius, "Reminiscences." Columbia University Oral History Collection, Special Collections, Butler Library. A review of the mayoralty elections of 1929, 1933, 1945, and 1949 by a prominent public figure.

Klein, Henry H., *My Last Fifty Years*. The Author, New York, 1935. Some aspects of the mayoralty election of 1909 (pp. 27–34); the mayoralty election of 1917 (pp. 157–167); and the municipal campaign of 1933 (pp. 435–460.)

McAneny, George, "Reminiscences." Columbia University Oral History Collection, Special Collections, Butler Library. Descriptions of the municipal mayoralty campaigns of 1901, 1909, 1913, and 1917.

Prendergast, William A., "Reminiscences." Columbia University Oral History Collection, Special Collections, Butler Library. Reflections on the municipal elections of 1897, 1901, 1905, 1907, 1909, 1913, and 1917.

Tanzer, Lawrence A., "Reminiscences." Columbia University Oral History Collection, Special Collections, Butler Library. Recollections of the mayoralty campaigns of 1897, 1945, and 1949.

CHAPTER VII

Appointments and Removals

THE APPOINTMENT PROCESS

MORE OFFICIALS ARE APPOINTED TO OFFICE—some of them by elected officials, some by other higher-ranking appointed officials—than are elected. All those positions occupied by the people usually described as "employees" of the governments in the city are also filled by appointment. Thus the process of appointment to public office or to public employment pervades the politics and government of the city.

The appointing officers see the offices and positions which they are dispensing from one angle of vision; the groups seeking to influence the appointing process see the offices and positions from a quite different perspective; and the individual who seeks the office or position for himself has still another view. For the appointing officer, the office or position for which he must choose an incumbent is an asset to be expended to meet past commitments (perhaps acquired during his own efforts to secure nomination, election, or appointment to his present position), or to strengthen the hand of the appointing officer in carrying out his present responsibilities, or to improve the appointing officer's own future career prospects. To the extent that the appointment may involve him in the risks of greatly displeasing some groups while pleasing others, the appointing officer may also regard it as a painful choice between his several opportunities and competing costs and perhaps as more of a liability than an advantage. To the parties and other groups seeking to influence the appointing officer, the office or position is seen as an opportunity to secure preferred access to the official or the employee when future decisions of importance to the group are to be made, or to prevent the appointment of an unfriendly candidate, or to reward friends and allies and supporters, or to enhance the general prestige of the group by a display of influence in the appointment process. To those who are themselves candidates for the office or position, the appointment is significant in terms of salary and tenure, its usefulness as a rung in the career ladder, its prestige and utility.

The appointing officers make their choices of the appointees under pressures from the full range of the participants in the city's political process.

Some choices are more hotly contested than others. Some are the object of attention from a great number of participants; others are the concern of only a few, while others may be the focus of a single almost monopolistic influence. Still other appointments are closely hedged in by formal rules, devised to narrow the discretion of the appointing officer. Only in rare instances is the appointing officer allowed to regard an appointment as an act of his own uninhibited judgment. In almost all instances an appointment is the result of bargaining between the appointing officer and other strategically placed participants, a bargaining which takes place under rules or practices which confer differing advantages upon the participants.

Appointing Officers and Appointive Positions

Constitutional and statutory appointing powers are widely distributed among and within the governments of the city. There are numerous appointing officers, and the rules under which they exercise the appointing power vary greatly. This multiplicity and variety increase the number of participants in the process (since each appointing officer and set of rules is surrounded by a distinct constellation of forces) as well as the range of their methods of exerting influence on appointments.

The Mayor as Appointing Officer. The Mayor is the most important single appointing officer in the city government. He appoints, with but few exceptions, the heads of all departments, the members of all city boards and commissions, and (as the charter puts it) "all other [city] officers not elected by the people, except as otherwise provided by law," including, of course, the assistants and other members of the staff in the Office of the Mayor. The Mayor also appoints the City Magistrates, Special Sessions justices, justices of the Domestic Relations Court, and has the power to appoint judges, who serve until the next election, when vacancies occur in the Municipal Court. In addition, the Mayor has the power, which is frequently exercised, to appoint advisory or *ad hoc* committees composed of officials, citizens, or both.

In the exercise of these appointing powers, the Mayor's formal act of appointment is final; the formal approval of no other body is required. Unlike most important appointments by the Governor or the President, which must be approved by the upper houses of the state legislature and Congress, respectively, the Mayor is not required to seek the formal approval of either the Council or the Board of Estimate for his appointments.

The Mayor is also able, by virtue of his position as the city's chief executive, to supervise and control in considerable degree the appointments made by certain other appointing officers. He ordinarily requires department heads to discuss with him in advance, and secure his approval of, their nominees (or to accept his nominees) for appointment to such positions as

TABLE 36. THE APPOINTING POWER OF THE MAYOR OF NEW YORK CITY
IN 1959

I. APPOINTMENTS AT THE PLEASURE OF THE MAYOR

    A. Authorized by the city charter:

        1. Deputy Mayor
        2. Division of Administration—City Administrator
        3. Tax Department—President of the Tax Commission
        4. Department of Finance—Treasurer
        5. Police Department—Commissioner
        6. Fire Department—Commissioner
        7. Department of Parks—Commissioner
        8. Hospitals Department—Commissioner
        9. Welfare Department—Commissioner
      10. Department of Correction—Commissioner
      11. Department of Buildings—Commissioner
      12. Department of Public Works—Commissioner
      13. Department of Marine and Aviation—Commissioner
      14. Department of Sanitation—Commissioner
      15. Department of Licenses—Commissioner
      16. Department of Purchase—Commissioner
      17. Department of Personnel—President of the Civil Service Commission
      18. Department of Markets—Commissioner
      19. Art Commission—3 members
      20. Department of Traffic—Commissioner
      21. Department of Labor—Commissioner
      22. Bureau of the Budget—Director
      23. Board of Assessors—3 members
      24. Department of Water Supply, Gas, and Electricity—Commissioner

    B. Authorized by state and local laws:

        1. Office of the Mayor—11 assistants and aides
        2. City Construction Coordinator—nonsalaried
        3. New York City Youth Board—18 members, nonsalaried
        4. Office of Civil Defense—Director
        5. Slum Clearance Committee—6 members, nonsalaried
        6. Department of Commerce and Public Events—Commissioner, non-
           salaried
        7. Commission on Intergroup Relations—15 members, nonsalaried
        8. New York City Housing Authority—Chairman
        9. Teachers' Retirement Board—2 members, nonsalaried

                      Number of such appointments: 84

II. APPOINTMENTS RESTRICTED BY JOB-EXPERIENCE REQUIREMENTS

    A. Authorized by the city charter:

        1. Law Department—Corporation Counsel
        2. Health Department—Commissioner
        3. Department of Investigation—Commissioner
        4. Art Commission—4 members, nonsalaried
        5. Department of Air Pollution Control—Commissioner

                      Number of such appointments: 8

III. APPOINTMENTS TO POSITIONS WITH RESTRICTIONS ON REMOVAL

    A. Authorized by the city charter:

        1. City Planning Commission—7 members (8-year terms)
        2. Board of Health—2 members, nonsalaried (8-year terms)
        3. Board of Standards and Appeals—1 member (6-year term)
        4. Board of Hospitals—5 members, nonsalaried (5-year terms)

TABLE 36. THE APPOINTING POWER OF THE MAYOR OF NEW YORK CITY
IN 1959 (Continued)

B. Authorized by state and local laws:
  1. Board of Correction—9 members, nonsalaried (6-year terms)
  2. Mental Health Board—5 members, nonsalaried (4-year terms)
  3. New York City Housing Authority—4 members (5-year terms)
  4. New York Transit Authority—1 member (6-year term)
  5. Parole Commission—3 members (10-year terms)
  6. Triborough Bridge and Tunnel Authority—3 members, nonsalaried (6-year terms)
  7. Board of Water Supply—3 members (life term)

  Number of such appointments: 43

IV. APPOINTMENTS WITH RESTRICTIONS ON SELECTION AND REMOVAL
  A. Authorized by the city charter:
  1. Board of Health—2 members,[a] nonsalaried
  2. Board of Standards and Appeals—4 members[a] (6-year terms)
  3. Department of Personnel—Civil Service Commission—2 members[b] (6-year terms)
  4. Board of Education—9 members,[c] nonsalaried (7-year terms)
  5. City Record—Supervisor[a]
  6. City Sheriff[a]
  7. City Register[a]
  8. Chief Medical Examiner[a]
  9. Board of Hospitals—5 members,[a] nonsalaried (5-year terms)
  10. City Marshals—83,[c] fees only.
  11. Tax Department—6 Tax Commissioners[d]

  B. Authorized by state and local laws:
  1. Board of Higher Education—21 members,[c] nonsalaried (9-year terms)
  2. Commission for the Foster Care of Children—15 members,[e] nonsalaried (6-year terms)
  3. Mental Health Board—2 members,[a] nonsalaried (4-year terms)

  Number of such appointments: 153

V. JUDICIAL APPOINTMENTS[f]   97
  Grand total[g]   385

---

[a] Job-experience restrictions.   [b] Partisan restrictions.   [c] Geographic restrictions.
[d] Geographic restrictions on appointment; no restrictions on removal.
[e] Geographic and religious restrictions.
[f] See Chapter XIV.
[g] This list does not include: several *ad hoc* Mayor's committees, and several *ex officio* committees whose members are designated by the Mayor.

deputy commissioner and departmental secretary, and, less frequently, for other positions "exempt" from civil service selection procedures, positions being filled by "provisional" appointees (pending establishment of a civil service eligible list), and even for such key "competitive" positions as bureau chief.

Other City Appointing Officers. The Comptroller, Borough Presidents, and the President of the Council severally exercise the appointing power within their own departments and staffs. They are under no formal obligation to discuss these appointments with the Mayor. Jointly, as the Board of Estimate, they appoint the chiefs of the Board's four bureaus (Secretary, Franchises, Engineering, Retirement and Pensions), the bureau staffs, and, from time to time, special consultants and experts.

The City Council appoints the City Clerk and Clerk of the Council, the staff of the City Clerk, and the "attachés" of the Council (Chief Clerk, committee clerks, legislative clerks, and sergeant-at-arms). The Council also appoints the four Commissioners of Elections upon the recommendations of the two major political party organizations in New York and Kings counties.

Each of the five District Attorneys elected within the city appoints his own staff.

Both the elected and appointed judges have authority to appoint their own law assistants and law secretaries. The various courts appoint their staffs and attendants. The County Clerks are appointed by the Appellate Division. The Public Administrators are appointed by the Surrogates, who also appoint guardians, and executors and administrators of estates under certain circumstances. A Commissioner of Records is appointed by the Chief Justice of the City Court. Several of the courts appoint referees.

Heads of administrative agencies, including department heads and the members of boards and commissions and special authorities, though themselves appointees, are appointing officers for their own staffs. Collectively, the appointments which they make outnumber by far the appointments of all other appointing officers. But their importance in the appointing process is reduced by three factors: (1) each of them acts separately in the appointment process; (2) the Mayor can and usually does closely supervise their exercise of the appointment powers for the higher positions in many of these agencies; and (3) civil service statutes and rules sharply limit their discretion in most other appointments.

The Governor and Other State Officials. The Governor, the state Comptroller, the Attorney General, and the heads of state departments and agencies are important participants in the appointment process, who in various ways affect the city's politics and government. The Governor, for example, makes interim appointments when vacancies occur in certain offices and judgeships in the city. Even more importantly, the Governor and his state government colleagues make many appointments to state government positions located within the city, and appoint many city residents to state government positions located in Albany or elsewhere in the state. All these appointments tend to affect, and some to be intimately involved with, the appointment process of the city government. Sometimes a state position represents a step up the career ladder for a city official; sometimes a city position is an advancement for a state official. Both state and city positions are therefore frequently included in some of the intricate bargaining among party organizations, public officials, and nongovernmental groups.

The President and Other Federal Officials. The President, United States Senators and Representatives, and federal agency heads as appointing officers also have significant influence in the city's politics and government. The President nominates and appoints, with the advice and consent of the Senate, a considerable number of officials to positions of importance to the city's government and politics. United States District judgeships, United States District attorneyships, city postmasterships, and other federal positions located in the city, as well as federal positions outside the city filled by city residents are presidential appointments. Since, under the federal government's appointment practices, the President delegates considerable initiative to Senators and Representatives of his party, those from New York are in essence *de facto* appointing officers for many federal government positions in New York City.

Influencers and Would-be Influencers of Appointing Officers

Other Officials. The appointing officer is almost invariably the object of attention and advice from one or more other officials when he makes an appointment. The Mayor exercises greater or less "supervision" over department heads in their choice of subordinates, and the department heads, in turn, are likely to watch their subordinates' choice of their subordinates. But participation by other officials in the decisions of appointing officers is a still broader practice. Some officials, especially elected officials, have their own "following" or protegés, and for these they tend to seek appointments whenever feasible from any appointing officer to whom they have access. Other officials have jurisdictional interests which impel them toward participation in the choices of appointing officers, as when a District Attorney advises the Mayor on the selection of a Police Commissioner or of a Chief Magistrate, or when the Traffic Commissioner offers advice to the Police Commissioner on the choice of the Police Inspector to be in charge of the Police Traffic Division. Still other officials see in the appointment process an opportunity or a necessity for bargaining and trading in which a series of appointments, perhaps involving several appointing officers, are linked together, as when the recognition of one ethnic, racial, religious, geographical, or factional group in one appointment must be "balanced" by the recognition of another or several competing groups in the actions of other appointing officers. Most appointing officers thus become accustomed to the intervention of other officials in some number and degree whenever an appointment is pending.

Party Organization Leaders. Influencing the choices of appointing officers is one of the historic functions of party organization leaders. In the era of uninhibited patronage practices, the party leaders were alleged to have a virtual monopoly on such influence. They are still perhaps the most systematic participants in the business of influencing the appointment process, and their attention to appointing officers is more extensive in its range than is that of any other participant. All other interveners are more specialized in their attention than are the party leaders, whose interest and scrutiny include federal, state, and local positions, whether executive, legislative, or judicial, and at all levels of salary and status.

TABLE 37. MAYORAL CABINET APPOINTMENTS, 1898–1957, SHOWING PARTY ACTIVITY OF APPOINTEES

| Mayor | All cabinet appointees | | | | | | |
| | Party activity[a] | | No party activity[b] | | Not ascertained | | Total |
	Number	Per cent	Number	Per cent	Number	Per cent	number
Van Wyck	48	77	5	8	9	15	62
Low	37	40	13	14	43	46	93
McClellan	84	52	26	16	51	32	161
Gaynor	40	42	21	22	34	36	95
Mitchel	26	28	27	28	41	44	94
Hylan	73	61	18	15	28	24	119
Walker	60	56	12	13	18	31	90
O'Brien	39	78	2	4	9	18	50
LaGuardia	37	22	70	41	63	37	170
O'Dwyer	44	41	31	29	33	30	108
Impellitteri	30	48	12	19	21	33	63
Wagner	32	37	23	27	31	36	86

[a] Party club officer or member.   [b] No club activity.

SOURCE: Lowi, Theodore J., *At the Pleasure of the Mayor*. Doctoral dissertation, Yale University, 1960, unpublished.

But the zealous and systematic interest of party leaders in influencing the choices of appointing officers does not make the party invariably the most influential participants in the appointing process. In fact, their competitors have steadily narrowed the areas in which the party leaders have the strongest voice. Civil service rules and procedures have made the appointments of more than three fourths of the city's employees (as distinct from its officials) relatively immune to the influence of party leaders, and a comparable evolution has taken place in similar state and federal positions in which the city's party leaders once had an ascendant appointing role. In addition, the party leaders have gradually been forced to yield ground to other participants in particular appointment areas: to the organized bureaucracies, for example, in the Police, Fire, Sanitation, and Education departments; to professional associations in the Health, Welfare, and Traffic departments; and to labor leaders in some other agencies. Symptomatic of these trends has been the increasing disinclination of Mayors to permit party leaders to nominate themselves for high appointive office, a trend given sharp emphasis by Mayor Wagner's declaration following his election in 1953 that District and County Leaders were not eligible for appointment as heads of departments or agencies.

There are some areas, however, in which party leaders have preferred access in influencing appointments. First in importance in this respect are the appointments made by the judges and the courts. For these positions, described fully in a later chapter, the party leaders have not only the most effective opportunities for "nomination" of eligible appointees, but it is to

TABLE 38. MAYORAL APPOINTMENTS TO SALARIED CABINET POSTS, 1898–1957, SHOWING PARTY ACTIVITY OF SALARIED APPOINTEES

Mayor	Salaried appointees						
	Party activity[a]		No party activity[b]		Not ascertained		Total
	Number	Per cent	Number	Per cent	Number	Per cent	number
Van Wyck	45	88	..	..	6	12	51
Low	22	65	5	15	7	20	34
McClellan	56	67	14	16.5	14	16.5	84
Gaynor	24	60	9	23	7	17	40
Mitchel	19	41	12	25	15	34	46
Hylan	61	72	7	8	17	20	85
Walker	55	82	7	10	5	8	67
O'Brien	36	77	2	4	9	19	47
La Guardia	29	27	42	39	37	34	108
O'Dwyer	40	50	17	21	23	29	80
Impellitteri	25	53	8	17	14	30	47
Wagner	26	42	16	26	18	32	62

[a] Party club officer or member.   [b] No club activity.

SOURCE: Lowi, Theodore J., *At the Pleasure of the Mayor.* Doctoral dissertation, Yale University, 1960, unpublished.

these positions that party leaders are most successful in securing appointments for themselves. Some of these positions in the courts (especially in the Surrogates' Courts) are highly prized by the party leaders, whether held by themselves or by their nominees. A second favorable area for party leaders comprises certain appointments made by the Mayor, especially to the positions of deputy commissioner, departmental secretary, and city Magistrate, but the success of party leaders in influencing these appointments varies from administration to administration and, in the case of the first two categories, from department to department. Another area of favorable opportunity for party leaders is the staff appointments made by the five District Attorneys in the city (although for twenty years Dewey and Hogan in the New York County office have turned to bar associations, law firms, and law schools more often than to party leaders for staff suggestions). Borough Presidents and Comptrollers are also generally favorably disposed, as is the Council, to party leaders' nominations.

Among department heads, boards and commissions, and special authorities, the party leaders find greatly varying reactions to their nominees for appointment to subordinate posts, reactions ranging from cold hostility through aloofness to cordiality. But in almost all these appointments, the party leaders can usually count upon strong competition from other participants in the appointing process. When city party leaders turn to gubernatorial and other state government appointments, they encounter comparable obstacles and trends, similar areas of advantage, and similar growth of competition.

The influence of party leaders depends on whether the officials upon whom they exert their leverage are of their own party or at least of an allied party. Within each party, party leaders are also competitive with each other. The County Leaders within the city contend with each other to influence all those appointing officers who have more than a countywide jurisdiction, and, within the county organizations, Assembly District Leaders vie with each other for both quality and quantity in appointive positions "allocated" to them. This intraparty rivalry tends to increase the chances for other participants in the appointing process to exercise influence on the choice of officials and employees.

In the sixty years of the Greater City, the influence of party leaders in the appointing process has slowly, but for the most part steadily, declined. Many forces have contributed to this, but not least has been the rise of other competitors in the appointing process, transforming it from its earliest characteristics of close bargaining between appointing officers and party leaders to more extensive competition among many participants, a competition varying from appointment to appointment.

Nongovernmental Interest Groups. These numerous groups play a varied but influential role in appointments. If it tends to be either sporadic or specialized in contrast to the systematic and comprehensive role of the party leaders, it is nevertheless a significant factor in the decisions of appointing officers. And if nongovernmental groups tend to give other goals than appointments a higher emphasis in their formal and publicized group objectives, they nevertheless do not fail to give persistent and frequently effective attention to the particular positions they regard as important to their interests. Quite often the nongovernmental interest groups will assert that they do not nominate or endorse specified individuals for appointment, but that they stress instead the kind of qualifications and the kinds of policies which should be represented in the appointees. This posture, however, will not ordinarily deter the group from presenting to an appointing officer, especially if requested to do so, a list of prototypes or eligibles for his guidance.

This point of protocol enables the interest groups to maintain their claim to being nonpolitical, but does not noticeably reduce their influence in the appointing process.

Most nongovernmental groups, it was noted in Chapter III, limit their participation in politics to special sectors of the government. Their interest in appointments specifically is similarly restricted. Thus, for example, the Citizens Committee for Children will focus its attention upon those appointments in the several agencies which are charged with carrying out programs affecting children; the Citizens Housing and Planning Council upon appointments to positions in housing and planning agencies; the county medical societies upon appointments in the health and hospital agencies; the bar associations upon appointments to the Corporation Counsel's staff, to the courts, and to District Attorney's staffs; the labor unions upon appointments to agencies dealing prominently with labor questions; the religious organizations upon appointments in the welfare and educational systems; tax-conscious groups upon appointments to managerial and fiscal positions; and real estate groups upon appointments in building inspection, licensing, and enforcement agencies. No group will necessarily confine its participation in the appointment process exclusively to such specialized areas, but the attention of most groups will be most heavily concentrated upon appointments in selected agencies or functions.

A smaller number of groups seek broader participation in the appointment process. Some civic organizations (for example, the Citizens Union, or the League of Women Voters) are concerned with the "improvement" of the appointment process in general. These groups frequently urge appointing officers to use procedures which would make their choices among alternative candidates more visible and open, by announcing tentative choices in advance of appointment and allowing time for "public" comment on their qualifications before formal appointment, or by holding public hearings on the qualifications of proposed appointees. These are in essence proposals to broaden the number of participants in the appointing process and are seemingly designed to reduce the influence of "insiders" in the process by making it more open and competitive, serving also—and not just incidentally —to enhance the influence of the civic groups themselves. Still other groups, particularly ethnic and racial associations, concentrate more upon general claims for "recognition" and "balanced representation" in appointments than in influencing appointments to particular positions, although once such recognition is obtained in a particular office the ethnic or racial group is likely to regard it as a permanent acquisition of the group. These ethnic and racial groups also seem more inclined than most other nongovernmental groups to use the party leaders as intermediaries in seeking to influence appointing officers, although some other groups (for example, labor unions, real estate groups, religious groups) also find the party-leader channel at times useful and appropriate.

No single category of nongovernmental interest groups (professional, business, labor, ethnic, racial, religious, or civic) can realistically regard itself as having greater influence upon appointments than the party leaders as a group, except in the interest group's own area of special concentration. But the exception is of great significance, for cumulatively the interest groups span the whole range of appointing officers and thus some of them compete with the party leaders almost everywhere on approximately equal terms, and often on quite favorable terms. If they often refrain from naming a specific appointee, they at least draw the profile of qualifications in such specific terms that the appointing officer's range of choice is quite narrow and in effect confined to the list of prototypes or eligibles presented by the interest group or groups.

The Organized Bureaucracies. The organized bureaucracies are even more specialized in their participation in the appointment process than are the nongovernmental groups, but they are nonetheless potent participants. Most of the organized bureaucracies confine their attention to the appointments made in the agency in which their membership is concentrated. Their basic aspiration in the appointment process is, it would seem, to confine all such appointments to their own members, invoking for that purpose the values of "career service," "promotion from within," "nonpolitical appointments," and other doctrinal formulae for controlling the discretion of appointing officers and limiting the intervention of other competing participants in the appointment process. To these appeals is frequently added an emphasis upon the risks and costs of appointing an outsider whom the staffs will allegedly resist.

Like nongovernmental groups, bureaucratic groups characteristically refrain from urging the appointment of a particular person but emphasize instead the source from which the appointee should be chosen (that is, from the eligible membership of the permanent staff of the agency). The Police bureaucracy has been among the most successful participants in the appointment process, its accomplishments being demonstrated by the steady trend, almost uninterrupted over more than a generation, toward the appointment of Police Commissioners and deputy commissioners "from the ranks." The Fire Department bureaucracy, the Corrections bureaucracy, the Sanitation bureaucracy, the Welfare bureaucracy, and the teachers' bureaucracies have not been much less successful as participants in the appointment process in their several agencies. The Transit bureaucracy has had less time and less success, but it has not been denied an increasingly influential role. In departments and agencies where professional staffs predominate, the influence of these bureaucracies upon appointing officers is likely to be substantial, as is also the role of other cohesive bureaucracies in other departments, agencies, and bureaus. If they cannot always be influential in the appointment of department and agency heads, these groups can usually play a significant part in appointments to such subordinate positions as deputy commissioner, division director, or bureau chief.

The city bureaucracies find their optimum opportunities for influence on appointing officers in the departments and agencies under the Mayor. They have fewer opportunities and lesser influence on judges and courts as appointing officers, and on District Attorneys, Borough Presidents, or legislators. The state government and federal government bureaucracies also exercise influence mainly on the appointing officers in the executive branch agencies, playing no consistently significant part in the choices made by other state and federal appointing officers.

The Press and Other Communication Media. The communication media have a distinctive function in the appointing process. The newspapers especially, by their reports on the negotiations and bargaining surrounding appointments as well as on the qualifications of the appointees, serve to make the appointing process more visible than it would otherwise be. This visibility tends both to increase the number of participants in the appointment process and to aid some participants while inhibiting others. In its reports and comments upon the appointment process, the press also assists— often deliberately, occasionally inadvertently—one participant or candidate as against others, and so becomes itself a participant in the process. The communication media thus may enter the appointment process as reporters, commentators, monitors, censors, or as participants.

The attention of the media of mass communication, as far as appointments are concerned, is ordinarily centered primarily upon the most prominent city offices—members of the Mayor's staff, department heads, Magistrates— and upon major appointments in and from the city by the Governor and the President. But no category of appointments entirely escapes attention. A scandal or irregularity in an agency may engender close scrutiny for a time of even minor appointments. A newspaper may itself conduct an "investigation" which will lead to its subsequent active participation in the appointment process. This participation takes varied forms, ranging from especially full reporting of the roles played by the several participants, through expressions of approval or disapproval of some of these participants, to the explicit endorsement of a type of candidate or even a particular candidate. In their usual participation in the appointment process, the communication media tend to reveal several consistent attitudes: implicit hostility (often made explicit) toward party leaders as participants; friendliness toward civic, professional, and business groups as participants; aloofness toward labor union, ethnic, racial, and religious groups as participants; and susceptibility to the claims of the bureaucracies for "career" appointments.

Methods of Influencing Appointing Officers

The strategies of the participants in the appointing process consist of narrowing the discretion of appointing officers, in most cases to a restricted category of eligibles, less frequently to specific individuals.

Restricting the Size of the Field of Choice. One extensively employed and effective method for controlling the choices to be made by appointing officers, reducing the influence of some participants while increasing the influence of others, is to establish the rules under which the appointment is to be made. The participant in the appointing process who can write these rules, or who can adapt them to his purposes, is at a great advantage. Such rules, which are numerous in the city's appointment processes, are of two major types: some of the rules specify the *qualifications* which the appointee must have; other rules prescribe the *procedure* by which the appointment must be made.

The most familiar and comprehensive of these requirements are to be found in the civil service laws and rules, regulating the appointments to the great bulk of city, state, and federal positions. These laws and rules prescribe the examinations, the construction of lists of eligibles, the certification of eligibles to appointing officers, and the ways in which appointing officers may make appointments from among the certified eligibles. These rules have their earliest origins in the efforts of certain participants (the civil service reform groups and their allies, including the communication media) to reduce—and preferably, from the reformers' perspective, to eliminate—the influence of party leaders on appointing officers. The extension and elaboration of these rules in recent decades may be attributed in large degree to the bureaucracies. The effects of these rules upon the appointing process have been several: the influence of party leaders upon many appointments has been sharply, but gradually, reduced; the officials charged with administration of the rules (the Civil Service Commissions and personnel officers) have acquired great influence over appointing officers; the bureaucracies have been able to limit the influence of other participants while increasing their own; and the nongovernmental groups, while generally benefiting, have also been compelled to divide their attention among those who make the rules, those who administer them, and those who make appointments under them.

But civil service laws and rules are not the only type of requirement which affects the appointment process. Qualifications and other requirements are frequently used to limit the discretion of appointing officers and to provide advantages or disadvantages to particular participants. Thus, for example, the charter prescribes that the Mayor may appoint as Health Commissioner only a person who is "a doctor of medicine or the holder of a degree in public health received from a college or university after at least two years of graduate study, and [who] shall have had at least eight years' experience either in public health administration or in college or university public health teaching or in both"; and that the Commissioner of Investigation must be "a member of the bar of the state of New York in good standing." Similar prescriptions specify the qualifications for a number of deputy commissioners. Other types of requirements prescribe city residence or borough residence for appointees, while still others require the appointing officer to make bipartisan appointments to certain boards and commissions. The effect of these several types of requirements is to narrow the field of choice from which appointing officers may recruit, and to confer advantage upon those participants who are most influential in that narrower field. In general, party leaders are limited beneficiaries under these rules, while nongovernmental interest groups secure somewhat greater advantage.

These formal rules of charter and other statutory requirements are supplemented by informal rules and traditions which have substantial effects upon the appointment process. Such rules and traditions—more precisely, the expectations on the part of claimant groups and the anticipation of such claims on the part of appointing officers—usually rest on the capacity of the claimants to embarrass or hinder unresponsive appointing officers by withholding cooperation, generating unfavorable publicity, punishing the officers involved or their superiors at the polls, or similar weapons. At any rate, whatever the sources of the practices, they have developed vigorously and are scrupulously observed.

The creation of a "job image," for instance, is one of the familiar strategies of those participants in the appointment process who wish to limit the field of choice as a way of increasing their influence over an appointing officer. This partially explains the traditions or presumptions that the Police Commissioner should be a "career man," the Public Works Commissioner an engineer, the Personnel Director "a professional personnelist," the Hospitals Commissioner a doctor of medicine, the Welfare Commissioner a social worker, the Treasurer a banker or businessman, and so on. Each of these informal requirements or traditions increases the opportunities of some participants to influence the appointment process for the specific job, while it also decreases the opportunities of other participants.

Another such important restriction on the range of choice of appointing officers is the "allocation" of particular positions to a special sphere of influence. By this strategy appointing officers are persuaded that certain positions "belong" to one or another group, and the choice by the appointing officer is thus confined to appointees nominated by, or acceptable to, the

"owner" of the positions. A classic illustration of this technique is the established tradition that the Mayor, in appointing the nine members of the
Board of Education, shall allocate three members to each of the three main
religious groups: three Catholics, three Jews, three Protestants. Another
illustration is provided by the informal allocation, in effect for almost four
decades, of one of the three positions on the municipal Civil Service Commission to a Negro. Other informal allocations are represented by habitual
claims made by Borough Presidents and borough party leaders that particular positions "belong" to Queens, or Brooklyn, or The Bronx. These
geographical allocations may in fact be claimed within counties and boroughs
even by an Assembly District party leader, inclined to regard a triumph
in one appointment as a permanent "grant" of the position to his district.
Still other "allocations" are claimed by ethnic groups, by labor groups
(as, for example, positions in the city Department of Labor), by professional
groups (as, for example, the medical societies view the professional positions
on the Board of Health and the Board of Hospitals), and by bureaucratic
groups.

Yet another way of restricting the field is to acquire informal "veto rights,"
that is, the power to prevent the selection of a particular candidate for an
appointment. The exercise of a veto by a group does more than block a
particular individual; it also serves to indicate concretely the tolerances of
the interested group, to establish criteria of acceptability, and thus to de-
lineate the boundaries of the reservoir of eligibles. Reinforced by a kind of
"courtesy" toward participants by appointing officers that makes the veto
power ordinarily conclusive, it is one of the most effective and economical
weapons possessed by the various participants in the appointment process.
Attempts at such vetoes may, of course, range from the mild to the uncom-
promising, and even a vigorous effort by a marginal participant may not
prevail over the will of strong supporters or a determined appointing officer.
But in the main, an explicit veto by a participant of recognized status will
turn the appointing officer toward another choice.

All participants find some occasions to use their veto rights in the appointment process. Party leaders use it to limit the growth of faction and insurgency; labor unions find it useful as a substitute for nominations of their
own; bar associations use it in their role as monitors over appointments to
the courts; and other interest groups, as well as the bureaucracies and the
communication media, find the veto a sharp weapon for preventing what
they regard in a particular instance as an intolerable or undesirable solution
to a contest in which they have failed to achieve their own preferred goal.

Lacking sufficient power to exercise veto rights in particular cases, certain
participants aspire less to exert direct measurable influence upon the choice
made by the appointing officer than merely to be consulted or informed.

These participants see their requirements or obligations as being substantially met if they are "in the know" in advance of the formal appointment, so that they may, if they choose, themselves inform their constituencies, their unsuccessful nominees, or even their competitors. Party leaders, for example, often urge this procedure for appointments to positions over which they recognize they have no control, thus conserving at least the appearance of omniscience. Other disadvantaged participants in particular appointment contests seek a similar preservation of their claims to influence, or at least their continued status as practitioners in good standing. The appointing officers often oblige.

All these modes of influencing appointments tend to limit appointing authorities to classes of possible appointees. The claimants do not actually name the appointees; the appointing officials still have some freedom of choice within each category. Occasionally, however, some participants feel strong enough to specify particular names; they "nominate" the candidate for elevation to public office or appointment.

Nominating Candidates for Appointment. Of all the groups engaged in efforts to influence appointments, party leaders and public officials are the ones that characteristically urge the appointment of a specific individual, only now and then suggesting more than one name. Other participants are more inclined to assume a posture of interest in "job performance" rather than in "candidates," and therefore to emphasize the *type* of appointee, the desired qualifications and other characteristics, the source of recruitment, and to present the names of prototypes or of a number of "prospects." By these means, however, such groups frequently arrange to elicit from the appointing officers "requests" for firm and specific nominations and to fulfill these requests. Sometimes the situation is sufficiently open to permit "self-nomination"; this is not typical, however, and a "self-nominator," after taking the initiative, normally seeks group support. Still more rarely, an appointee is "drafted"—but usually not without sponsorship by some influential participant or by an appointing officer determined to break a stalemate among other competing participants or to avoid an unattractive alternative appointment. Appointing officers are not infrequently confronted with the task of choosing from among a number of specific candidates, each nominated by some group he may not casually ignore, with any choice bearing costs as well as benefits.

When one of the participants in the appointment process has nominated a candidate for a position, the nominator then usually proceeds to secure endorsements from as many other participants as the nominator regards as necessary or useful; the candidate will often join actively in this search for endorsements. Some participants find it desirable to be "endorsers" more often than nominators, regarding the risks of endorsement as less than those of nomination and the benefits as equivalent. Others, especially party leaders, ordinarily prefer the role of nomination.

Trading and Bargaining. The contestants for the stakes of politics have not been slow to seize the opportunities to use the appointing process for bargaining purposes. Influence over this process has been added to the other media of political exchange, so that public policies, governmental decisions, campaign contributions, nominations to elective positions, and other forms of recognition or advantage are affected by hopes and expectations of appointment, and appointments are governed in part by concessions in these other areas. All the experienced, major participants acquire skills and aspirations for the accomplishment of simple or complex "parlays" in which risk and speculation add zest to the process. Thus officials, party leaders, interest groups, and bureaucracies sometimes work out intricate accommodations and exchanges with each other, involving perhaps a series of appointive jobs, elective positions, innovations in policies, specific governmental decisions, and other considerations. One fascination of this practice is that all the participants emerge with the feelings of winners, although no one can calculate the exact net gains.

The appointment process, then, is not a simple one. To the great variety of appointments to be made by a great number of appointing officers there must be added the interplay of numerous competitive participants using a complex set of strategies and techniques of influence. There are at least two main consequences: first, most participants in the appointment process must seek alliances and accommodations with other participants; second, most appointing officers must make their ultimate choices of appointees after weighing the claims of the competing participants as well as considering what the appointing officer perceives to be the "objective" merits of each of the candidates.

SELECTED ILLUSTRATIONS OF THE APPOINTMENT PROCESS

The formal power of appointment rests in the hands of the appointing officer. It is his action which the other participants must seek to influence, directly or indirectly. Although the other participants in many instances succeed (by statutory or other rule, by custom or pressure) in restricting the appointing officer's initiative and discretion, he nevertheless always performs the final act of appointment. This is the appointing officer's basic claim to his own continued status in the appointment process.

The initiative and discretion of appointing officers vary from office to office, from time to time, and with other circumstances. Some of these variations may be seen when the appointment process is examined from the perspectives of several major types of appointing officers in their appointments to specific types of positions.

How Mayors Appoint Department Heads

When Mayors appoint department heads, they engage in an appointment process which has "high visibility." The communication media give these appointments prominent attention, engaging in much advance speculation about the Mayor's intentions, the rival prospects and their sponsors, and the strategies of influence being directed at the Mayor. The party leaders of the Mayor's party are alert to the impending appointments, sensitive to the fact that department heads are themselves both appointing officers and decision-makers whose future appointments and decisions the party leaders will wish to influence. Among the nongovernmental interest groups and the bureaucracies, each appointment of a department head attracts its own distinctive cluster of groups and pressures. And each such appointment is a magnet for candidates who see in the office a desirable form of public, political, or professional recognition, an opportunity for the higher exercise of personal skills or the realization of policy goals, or an upward step in a public or private career. Some offices draw more attention and competition than others, but no department head appointment is left to the wholly unassisted initiative and discretion of the Mayor himself. Invariably, there are some participants looking over his shoulder, and usually there are several attempting to direct his eyes toward a favored candidate.

A Mayor arrives at his choice for most department head positions conscious that his act is under wide observation, that many seek to influence it, and that he will be fortunate if his selection evokes more applause than criticism. The support he loses in one choice he must somehow seek to recover in another. When he completes the roster of appointments of department heads, he must hope that other officials, party leaders, interest groups, bureaucracies, and the communication media will each find sufficient satisfaction in the whole range of his department head appointments so that effective praise will exceed effective blame. He may, of course, make further concessions to disappointed participants when other types of appointments are made, as when he appoints Magistrates or when department heads appoint their deputies, but the skill and judgment with which he resolves the competition for the department head positions will be decisive for the course of his administration.

Mayors have developed several standard methods for limiting their recognized hazards in choosing department heads. The Mayor may move quickly, making the appointment before the pressures have had an opportunity to form. He may delay, hoping that undesirable nominees will lose support. He may test the strength of candidates and their sponsors by encouraging rumors that this or that prospect is being considered. He may resort to "high prestige" candidates, selected on his own initiative, to avoid appointing candidates of lesser public standing urged upon him by influential

participants. Or he may change the traditional qualifications for a particular post, specifying new standards of selection which throw the customary
participants off balance, forcing them to seek new types of candidates more
to the Mayor's liking.

There is a discernible pattern in the appointment of department heads
by New York City Mayors, a pattern in which is found a mixture of mayoral
initiative and of accommodation to the claims of other participants. The
pattern is blurred in some degree by the fact that many appointees owe
their appointments to more than one factor or influence. Some choices may
be described as "personal" appointments by the Mayor (for example,
Corporation Counsels Windels by La Guardia and Burke by Wagner;
Police Commissioner Warren by Walker; Investigations Commissioner
Tenney by Wagner). Others are appointments reflecting the influence of
professional associations and societies as participants in the appointing
process (the Health, Hospitals, and Welfare Commissioners in the La
Guardia, O'Dwyer, Impellitteri, and Wagner administrations). Some represent concessions to the bureaucracies as sources of recruitment (Police, Fire,
and Sanitation Commissioners in recent decades). Still others reveal the
personal capacity of incumbents to retain office (Park Commissioner Moses
since 1934; Public Works Commissioner Zurmuhlen since 1947). The department head who receives his appointment primarily through sponsorship by
party leaders has become increasingly difficult to identify during the past
twenty-five years.

The considerations which influence Mayors in their choice of department
heads stand in interesting contrast to the conditions which surround several
other categories of "low-visibility" appointments made by the Mayor. In
two of these categories the Mayor has more freedom of action than he has
in choosing department heads; in two other categories he has less freedom
of action. In choosing his own staff (the Deputy Mayor, the City Administrator, the several "assistants to the Mayor"), he has few insistent claimants
outside his own circle of intimates. Thus he may more fully recognize here
the claims of his own preferences, his own past commitments, his present
need of help, and his future aspirations for himself and for his protegés.
Similarly, in his virtually unlimited power to appoint citizen committees
for the purpose of advice, study, or "problem-solving," the Mayor may act
primarily upon his own initiative and discretion. He may be guided by
strategic considerations in his selections (seeking support in some instances,
delay or protection in another, delegating substantial power in others), but
the strategy is mainly of his own choosing and, the selections being numerous,
he may indulge his own judgment freely.

Very different are the influences affecting his choices when he appoints
the members of multimembered boards and commissions. Here the claims
of borough representation, of ethnic, racial, and religious group "recog-

nition" and "balance," of party obligation, of interest group and bureau-cratic demands, move in upon him in varying patterns but with insistent force. And when he turns to still another category, the appointment of Magistrates and other judges, he is beset by the urgent and persistent pressures of the party leaders with their traditional prerogatives for these positions. A Fusion Mayor may profit from the factional competition within his coali-tion, and thus use these appointments to suit other purposes, but a Demo-cratic Mayor will regard himself as fortunate if he can find opportunities here to bargain with party leaders at all—usually by conceding to them on judgeships in return for his own greater freedom in making other types of appointments.

In the textbooks on municipal government, New York City's Mayor is identified as "strong" partly because of his broad appointing power un-hindered by any formal requirements of advice and confirmation by other governmental organs. There is no doubt that this power has substantially improved his bargaining position in relation to other contestants for the stakes of politics. Yet it would clearly be a gross error to conclude that his appointing authority is in all respects unfettered. Because it is broad, it must be employed cautiously, for the Mayor cannot plead constitutional mandates or inability as an excuse for rejecting demands and recommenda-tions. In some respects, the Mayor is hardly able to preserve any more freedom to name his own department heads than those officials enjoy in choosing their subordinates. The system imposes its constraints on all appointing officers from the highest to the lowest.

How Department Heads Appoint Their Deputies

The charter provides that "any head of a department may appoint and at pleasure remove as many deputies as may be provided for by law." When a department head looks further to discover what is "provided for by law" he finds that the charter specifies the number of deputies he may appoint (the Police Commissioner may appoint seven, the Fire Commissioner three, most other commissioners two or fewer), and that the charter or some state statute often prescribes qualifications for the appointee. One of the two deputies in Finance must be a certified public accountant, one of the two deputies in Housing and Buildings must have "at least ten years' experience as an architect or as a builder or as a professional engineer employed in structural work"; one of the two deputies in Traffic must be "a licensed professional engineer and shall have had at least five years' practical experience in traffic engineering." The department head finds also that the position of deputy commissioner is in the classified civil service and therefore, unless by petition to the city's personnel agency it has been placed in the "exempt" class, subject to additional qualification and procedural requirements.

Beyond these formal limitations, the department head will find that other forces also seek to guide his choices in appointing his deputies. He will ordinarily be under instructions from the Mayor to discuss such appointments with him in advance of any commitment. In these consultations, the Mayor may merely seek advance information and an opportunity to veto certain choices; or he may intervene on behalf of other officials, party leaders, interest groups, or an interested bureaucracy; or he may have a choice of his own. The Commissioner may discover that a member of the Mayor's staff to whom such matters are delegated is seeking to guide the Mayor toward a choice the staff member prefers. In addition, the department head will be under direct pressures from the elements in his own personal or departmental "constituency"—from other officials or party leaders to whom he is obligated for past or hoped-for assistance in his own career; from the interest groups with a stake in the policies and decisions of his agency; from borough organizations, or ethnic, racial, and religious groups, seeking recognition; from the organized bureaucracies in his agency. Beyond these forces, the department head will be conscious of the monitoring role of the civic groups and the communication media, with their capacity to create a favorable or unfavorable public image of his decision in choosing a deputy. In short, as an appointing officer, he feels more hedged in than autonomous.

Department heads respond in several ways to these conditions. Some move with ingenuity, energy, and determination to widen the area of their own initiative and discretion. Others accept the established equilibrium of forces, following the precedents of former heads of the department. Still others yield to the most forceful of the present claimants to the pending appointment. Police and Sanitation Commissioners, for example, have long yielded to their agency bureaucracies as the most influential participants in the appointment of their deputies. The Health, Hospitals, and Welfare Commissioners listen most attentively to the professional associations in their interest group constituencies. Corporation Counsels and Investigation Commissioners usually heed the Mayor and the party leaders. The Parks Commissioner avoids the dilemmas of his fellow department heads by having no deputies. Generally, in the choice of deputies by most commissioners, the claims of traditional patterns in each department are powerful; the risks and values of the established equilibrium in each agency appear to the Commissioner to be known and measurable, those of innovation comparatively unpredictable.

How Department Heads Appoint Bureau Chiefs

When a department head turns from the appointing process which governs his choice of a deputy or other principal assistant to the choice of a bureau chief, he enters a different environment. Here the rules governing the appointing process are more formal and more elaborate, and the department head finds that, except through the exercise of special ingenuity, he has little opportunity to discover candidates upon his own initiative or to avoid a narrow choice among the few eligibles presented to him by an inexorable procedure.

Bureau chiefs, although they are to be found under many other titles (director, assistant commissioner, superintendent, administrator), have some clear distinguishing characteristics. In a departmental hierarchy, the bureau chief usually ranks next below the deputy commissioners. In charge of an organizational unit of considerable importance in the department, he is a participant with influence in the department's decision-making, not infrequently a decision maker in his own right, and invariably an official charged with supervising others in carrying out departmental or bureau policies. The appointment of a bureau chief is accordingly a matter of much concern to the department head as the appointing officer, as it is to all other participants who have a stake in such positions or in the bureau's field of operations. The rules and procedures under which the department head must act serve not only to limit his choice, but to place all save a few participants at a disadvantage in their opportunities to influence the department head. The Civil Service Law and rules place most of the bureau chief positions (perhaps three fourths of them) in the "competitive" class and, narrowing the field still further, require that the appointment usually be made from a ranked list of eligibles resulting from a competitive promotion examination limited to competitors from among the higher ranking permanent staff of the bureau itself. By closely guarded rule and tradition, the methods of competition give advantage to seniority and experience in the bureau. These several rules and customs represent the success of the civil service reform and allied groups in reducing the power of the party leaders to intervene in the appointment of bureau chiefs. They represent also, and perhaps now more significantly, the triumph of the bureaucratic groups in confining the choice of the appointing officer to candidates from within a small designated segment of the bureaucracy itself.

Not all department heads are so closely restricted. Some bureau chief positions are "exempt" and some others are "noncompetitive." The Corporation Counsel, the Commissioner of Investigations, and the Hospitals Commissioner, among others, have the opportunities presented by these classifications in appointing some of their bureau chiefs. Their freedom of choice is widened, but the number of participants who may try to influence their decision is also increased. Even so, the department head ordinarily has a greater autonomy than he does when the post is competitive. In the Police Department, the chief inspector and other grades of inspectors are appointed at the discretion of the Police Commissioner from among those holding the rank of captain in the uniformed force. In making these appointments the Police Commissioner, himself ordinarily a graduate from the police bureaucracy, is subjected primarily to the rival pulls of police factions and his own personal ties, but other participants (party leaders, other officials, ethnic and religious groups, other interest groups) make some efforts to influence his choice from among the captains, who are themselves not invariably passive candidates but seek what help they can bring to bear as influence upon the Commissioner. Yet he is one of the Commissioners with fewer formal limitations than is customary.

The department head who wishes to expand his field of choice when he appoints a bureau chief must thus be inventive, patient, and persistent. One method to which he may resort is to reorganize his department, creating new bureaus or redefining the functions of existing bureaus. He may thus argue that new qualifications are required for bureau chiefs, enlarging the number and types of competitors who may take the examination. Another method sometimes used by a department head is to propose the transfer of an eligible civil servant from another bureau or department, appointing him as bureau chief with the consent of the city's Personnel Department. Still another method is to persuade the Personnel Department that a simultaneous "open competitive" and "promotion" examination should be held, hoping that higher standards of examining and wider competition will enlarge his field of choice; or the department head may petition successfully for an open competitive examination only, arguing that there is not sufficient competition within the ranks to justify a closed promotion examination. All these efforts tend to yield narrow gains in freedom of choice by the department head. He is more fortunate if he has an opportunity to appoint a "provisional" bureau chief as his own choice while the examination process is under way. There is some chance that the provisional appointee may be allowed to compete and thus become eligible for regular appointment, and the department head will at least have had his choice in office for a time.

Normally in the typical appointment of a bureau chief, the department head is conscious of the narrow choice with which the highly formalized rules and procedures, the effective instrument of the bureaucracies, confront him. The city's personnel agency officials and staff are quite influential participants in the appointment of bureau chiefs, deriving their influence from their opportunities to enforce rigidly or flexibly the rules for the selection of bureau chiefs. In making his choice, the department head may also feel pressure from other officials (elective or appointive, colleagues or superiors), party leaders, and professional or ethnic or religious or other groups. If the appointment is a provisional one, he may find one or more of these advisers especially difficult to resist. Nevertheless, it is safe to say that, as a general rule, the appointment of bureau chiefs is largely the domain of the bureaucracies as the most powerful participants, achieving their dominance through rules and practices that they have helped to establish in their interest and that they continue to refine and guard. The department head may make the formal choice, but his signature merely affirms the appointment of that bureaucrat whose selection was preordained.

How the Board of Education Chooses Its Top Staff

Appointments are made under somewhat different circumstances when boards, commissions, and special authorities act as the appointing officers. In some degree, the practices of the Board of Education are illustrative of this process.

The Board (nine nonsalaried members serving seven-year terms and removable by the Mayor only on charges and after a hearing) is the appointing authority for the large organization over which it presides. It "elects" a Superintendent of Schools and formally appoints a deputy superintendent, 8 associate superintendents, approximately 40 assistant superintendents, almost 900 school principals, and more than 20 bureau and office directors, as well as ratifying the selection of all other employees of the agency. Some of these appointments are for fixed terms, but the great majority are for "indefinite" or "permanent" tenure. In a few cases the Board appoints without formal advice, but most are made upon nomination by the Superintendent of Schools. The Board and the Superintendent exercise most of their respective appointing powers under comprehensive rules and procedures set down in the state Education Law and the state Civil Service Law, or issued by the state Commissioner of Education, or established by the Board itself. The appointing process thus tends to be highly formalized, predictable, and restricted as to participants.

The crucial act of appointment by the Board is the selection of the Superintendent, since once he is appointed the *de facto* appointing power lodges mainly in his hands, the Board usually merely ratifying his choices for deputy, associate, and assistant superintendents, and for school principals (the last, however, taken in practice from lists of successful competitors in examinations). The Board does not have many opportunities to select a Superintendent, for, although he is formally "elected" for a six-year term, "reelection" is taken for granted until he reaches the compulsory retirement age of seventy. In the six decades of the Greater City, the Board of Education has appointed only seven Superintendents of Schools, the most recent appointee taking office in September, 1958. In making these choices, the Board is confronted with deep-seated determination and powerfully organized endeavors on the part of the teachers' and the superintendents' bureaucracies to confine the Board's choice to candidates who are high-ranking officials within the school system itself. Other participants make strenuous efforts to break into this closed circle, some of them by urging the Board, for example, to appoint a "citizens advisory committee" which would assist in a nation-wide search for outstanding candidates. In 1957 this method was urged by the Public Education Association and other civic and professional groups, supported generally by the press, in an attempt to widen the Board's area of choice for the vacancy occurring in 1958. The Board did conduct a search, but it did not heed the advice to set up an advisory committee of citizens.

The Mayor, the party leaders, and most of the interest groups have become accustomed to their roles as marginal participants in the choice of a Super-intendent. Only the religious interest groups appear to have a more direct access, relying upon their status as established by the equal tripartite divi-sion of the members of the Board among the three major religious faiths. In consequence of this posture and power of the several participants in selecting a Superintendent, with the Board's own bureaucracies so predomi-nant in the process, the Board has six times chosen a Superintendent from within the ranks of the associate and assistant superintendents in its own school system. The single exception, in 1958, was a selection from the top staff of a sister agency (the city's Board of Higher Education), the appointee being the son of a former assistant superintendent in the city's schools.

The Board appoints a deputy superintendent, the associate and assistant superintendents, and the school principals upon the nomination of the Superintendent. The deputy and the associates serve six-year terms and are almost invariably reappointed; if one of them fails of reappointment, he must be immediately appointed as an assistant superintendent. The assistant superintendents and the school principals acquire permanent tenure after a probationary period of three years. In these appointments, such initiative as exists for the appointing officer resides mainly with the Superintendent. The Board may bargain with him within narrow limits, but the major exercise of discretion and choice is absorbed by the bargaining which takes place between the Superintendent and the bureaucratic groups that attempt to influence his nominations to the Board. Both stages of the appointing process are characterized by low visibility to outsiders. Bureaucrats and bureaucratic groups, abetted occasionally by other participants brought in as allies of the moment, compete with each other in a comparatively closed world, in which the Superintendent himself is hedged in by rules of pro-cedure, formal devices of selection, strong emphasis upon seniority, and close bargains. The Board presides over a process it cannot penetrate. The Superintendent may bargain with those above and those below him, but the rules of the game give him no special advantage. The typical appointment is a triumph for the bureaucratic participants.

When the Board appoints directors of bureaus and offices whose functions are outside the ordinary range of pedagogy (for example, Board Secretary,

Office of Business Affairs, Bureau of Supplies, Bureau of Construction, Bureau of Plant Operations and Maintenance), the scene changes and new participants enter the process. Each of these appointments has its own distinctive cluster of claimants, but in general the Board has more initiative and discretion of its own—and the Mayor, other officials, party leaders, a wide range of interest groups, and a different set of bureaucratic groups have greater opportunities for access to the Board while it is weighing each choice. In these instances, the Board deals with competitive constellations of groups, not with a tight-knit monopolistic influence such as confronts the Board when it makes its appointments to educational posts.

How District Attorneys Appoint Assistant District Attorneys

The five elected District Attorneys, one in each of the five counties within the city, appoint their respective staffs within a quite dissimilar field of forces from those with which the Mayor, the department heads, or the Board of Education must deal as appointing officers. Each District Attorney is an elected official. His powers and duties are defined in state statutes. The personnel system for his staff is supervised by the State Civil Service Department and, while his budget is provided by the city government, he enjoys some important budget safeguards, including the statutory right of veto over decreases in his budget. The District Attorney thus tends to regard his office as autonomous.

The most important appointments made by District Attorneys are to the positions of Assistant District Attorney. These are "exempt" positions (that is, by provision of state civil service rules, they are not subject to the examining or certifying procedures of the State Personnel Department, but are appointments made by the District Attorney free of such formal controls). In making his selections for appointment to these assistantships, the District Attorney confronts the party leaders of his county party organization as the most insistent claimants. He is reminded, if need be, that his nomination was their gift to him and that his election depended, at least in considerable part, upon their efforts. He understands, too, that his future career as an elected or appointed official (a judge, perhaps) is not unrelated to the good will of these party leaders. He soon learns, also, that he is dealing with a more cohesive party organization than is the Mayor as appointing officer. The Mayor deals with five competing county organizations, while the District Attorney must bargain with a single County Leader flanked by Assembly District Leaders (who have usually composed in caucus their own competitive hopes before they present their claims to the District Attorney).

But the District Attorney is not without some opportunities for bargaining. He may insist upon standards of competence and integrity and upon the right to veto particular nominees of the party leaders while inviting them to submit additional proposals. He may ask the county bar associations, or leaders of the bar, to assist him in the appraisal of candidates, using their reports for veto and other bargaining purposes with the party leaders. He may welcome the entry of other participants (judges, legislators, appointed officials) with their own candidates. Or he may risk the hazards of factionalism by bargaining with some district party leaders against others as a way of increasing his own field of choice. All these methods he must use cautiously; when he completes the appointment of his corps of assistants, the results must be accepted as a reasonable bargain by the party leaders. If they are actively displeased, the costs for the District Attorney are likely to be high.

A different and unusual appointing process has prevailed for almost twenty years in the District Attorney's office in New York County. In 1941, following the aggressive investigative record of Thomas E. Dewey in that office (1938–1941), Frank S. Hogan was nominated by both the Democratic and Republican parties and elected District Attorney. He has been similarly nominated and elected in four succeeding elections, his present term expiring in 1961. In terms of the traditional relation of his office to the party system, District Attorney Hogan would thus be expected to deal, as an appointing officer, with the party leaders of both parties. In practice, he seems to find it unnecessary to bargain with any of them. The political settlement which placed him in office and keeps him there, and from which neither party seems able to escape, presents him with a novel freedom of staff choice. The party leaders have found no effective way to bargain with him in bipartisan harness. He can consequently turn to sources of his own choosing for the recruitment of his Assistant District Attorneys. Party leaders must compete, seemingly on disadvantageous terms, with law schools, law firms, and bar associations as sources of supply for these positions. The party leaders, for their part, seem to possess only two choices: they can refrain from nominating, or endorsing the appointment of, the District Attorney for any higher office—the mayoralty, the governorship, a United States senatorship, or a judgeship; or they can elevate him to higher office as a way of attempting to restore normality in his office. But the District Attorney is secure in his present office, it would seem, as long as he chooses to hold it.

Variations on a Common Theme

Obviously, because each appointing officer has personal, organizational, political, and legal assets and liabilities of his own, as well as the special opportunities or limitations of his situation at the moment vacancies must be filled, there is no single pattern for all appointments to office. But the differences are comparable to the variations on a common theme; there is a basic form that comes through no matter how *ad hoc* the individual cases seem. That form is one of give and take, in which appointing power is with extremely rare exceptions not carte blanche to the official on whom it is conferred. Few indeed are the appointing officers whose formal authority makes them masters of the appointing process; far more often, the formal authority is simply a ticket to enter the fray, and may serve as a bargaining counter to a canny possessor.

THE REMOVAL PROCESS

The removal process is a subsidiary phase of the appointing process. The power to remove is usually, although not invariably, vested in the official who has the power to appoint. Accordingly, like the power to appoint, it is distributed among many different officials. In further similarity, the power to remove is surrounded by many formal rules and procedures, supplemented by traditions and customs which also bind the usual exercise of the power. These rules tend to affect not only the removing officer's behavior, but also to confer advantages upon some groups that aspire to influence the removal process while other groups are placed at a disadvantage. The groups seeking to influence the decision of a removing officer do not differ markedly from those participating in the appointing process.

The Formal Rules

The statutes and other formal rules governing the removal process are in general intended to make the exercise of the power difficult, and the long prevailing tendency has been to make it more so. The charter provides that, in the case of most department heads, the Mayor may "at pleasure remove" them, and this power is also granted by the charter or statute to other elected officials and to most department heads with respect to those of their principal assistants who are in the exempt class under the Civil Service Law and rules. For all practical purposes, the generous grant of removal power stops there. Various restraints then become the rule. Terms of office may be fixed, creating at least a presumption of tenure protected against simple removal. For members of most boards and commissions, for appointed judges, and for various other officials, the fixed or "indefinite" term is accompanied by the requirement that removal shall be "for cause," sometimes after "notice," and often after a "hearing" before the removing officer or his delegate.

For employees, as distinct from officials, and particularly for those employees who are in the "competitive" class (the great majority of all employees, city, state, and federal), the statutes and rules provide ordinarily that removal must be for cause, the charges given to the employee in writing, and an opportunity for answer allowed. These rules are increasingly supplemented by provisions for a formal hearing, for representation, and for appeal to and review by another authority. Most such proceedings may also be reviewed by the courts. Some employee groups are protected against removal by additional rules: veterans, teachers, policemen, and firemen by special statutes; other groups by "labor-management" agreements secured by employee unions through negotiations with officials, such as the Transit, Sanitation, Parks, Hospitals, and other employee groups have obtained.

For most officials, the use of the removal power is hedged about with restrictions even more formidable than those which surround the appointing power. In consequence, the removing officers seek substitute methods which are less frustrating, less hazardous, less costly in time and energy. The search for substitutes is not marked by easy success, but a set of informal devices has been developed which have largely replaced the formal removal process.

The Substitutes for Removal

The removal power is employed by removing officers primarily as a bargaining weapon in solving problems requiring the replacement of an incumbent. The removing officer in effect negotiates with the incumbent, proposing, cajoling, or issuing flat terms of settlement, as the particular situation allows or requires. The terms which may thus be negotiated with, or imposed by ultimatum upon, the incumbent extend over a wide range: transfer to another post, a reassignment to lesser or ambiguous duties, a simple demotion, an induced retirement, a suspension from duties for a fixed or an indefinite period, or a "voluntary" resignation. These devices represent on some occasions the ways by which justice may be tempered with mercy. In other instances they reflect concessions to one or more influential participants who have discovered ways to persuade the removing officer to soften the use of his formal powers. In still other, and perhaps the most numerous, cases the use of these substitutes for removal is an acknowledgment by the removing officer that the formal rules make the removal power itself too costly to use except as a lever for securing a negotiated solution. Without such a lever the removing officer would be powerless; in that sense, the removal power, though seldom used as such, is indispensable.

The Participants in the Removal Process

The removing officer does not exercise his removal powers under only the restraints of impersonal rules and procedures; he is also ordinarily beset by some groups which press him toward compromise or no action at all. Each proposed removal, like each pending appointment, attracts pressures and influences upon the official who has the power to remove. Other officials, party leaders, interest groups, and bureaucratic groups come forward, in various manifestations and combinations, to "advise" the removing official upon his course of action. If the proposed action involves an incumbent charged with malfeasance, the civic groups and the communication media will usually raise a public hue and cry for his removal, while other groups may more quietly counsel less drastic action. If the problem centers upon nonfeasance, a different formation of pressures will develop. If the difficulty be insubordination, the incumbent may often count not merely upon his usual sources of support against removal, but also upon those groups in whose interest his insurgency was taken and those who generally endorse independence.

The most influential participants in the removal process are the organized bureaucracies and the veterans' interest groups. They benefit primarily from the rules and procedures surrounding the process which are largely their own handiwork as well as effectively designed to restrict the removing officer's freedom of action. For certain positions, other interest groups may sometimes have a strategic influence either in supporting or opposing the use of the removal power. Against selected targets, the communication media have potent influence.

SUMMARY

In the nominating process, as we have seen in an earlier chapter, the party leaders have a firm grasp on the levers of decision; all other participants must try to influence the party leaders. In the elections, the electorate holds the ultimate power of choice; all the other contestants must try to influence them. In the appointment and removal processes, the officials who appoint or remove stand at the center of the processes, holding the formal power to appoint or not, to remove or not. But these officials enjoy less autonomy, less initiative and choice, than do the party leaders in the nominating process or the electorate on Election Day. Appointing and removing officials are compelled to exercise their powers under more restrictive rules. They are also more vulnerable to the intervention of other participants, some of whom are given special opportunities for influence under the rules and procedures they have succeeded in establishing.

It has long been customary to assume that, outside the career civil service, the party leaders were the most influential in determining who would be appointed or removed. This would seem to be true only in quite limited areas and to be frequently exaggerated even there. The party leaders are confronted by strong competition from other participants in almost every appointment or removal, and in the majority of cases the party leaders are not the most influential. The appointing and removing officials themselves find some opportunities for relative autonomy in their choices. Some interest group constellations have found it possible to be dominant in particular appointment and removal environments. The longer-term gains would seem to belong most clearly to the organized bureaucracies, whose influence in appointments and removals has steadily expanded beyond the boundaries of the traditional career positions into the top ranks of the executive agencies. If appointments and removals at the beginning of the century may be accurately described as being aspects of party leader politics, they may now be more accurately called aspects of interest group politics and bureaucratic politics.

FROM PERSONNEL TO PROGRAM AND POLICY

Contestants do not give up their quest for the prizes of politics when their preferred choices are denied nomination for elective office. They do not quit the struggle when their favorite nominee fails to win elective office. Nor do they resignedly withdraw from the contest when other participants win out in the competition to name appointees to office. On the contrary, defeats of this kind may induce them to redouble their efforts but in still another arena—that of policy and program rather than personnel. The strife to influence the content of governmental decisions goes on constantly regardless of who occupies office. While the distribution of public office and employment is one of the major stakes of political action and also determines the effectiveness of demands made on officials and employees, maneuvering to secure office is only a fraction of the broader political process. The remainder—the strategies of influencing governmental decisions—is described in the next part of this volume.

BIBLIOGRAPHY

The appointing and removal powers of the Mayor, the Board of Estimate, the Council, the Comptroller, the Borough Presidents, the Commissioners and the Boards, the District Attorneys and the judges are contained in the following sources: the charter, the Administrative Code, the Education Law, the Judiciary Law, and the several special courts reported in Clevenger's *Annual Practice of New York*.

NEW YORK'S MAYORS AND THEIR APPOINTMENTS
(arranged by mayoralties)

Alexander, De Alva Stanwood, *Four Famous New Yorkers*, vol. 4 of *A Political History of New York State, 1882–1905*. 4 vols. Henry Holt and Co., New York, 1923, p. 358. The appointments made by Mayor Van Wyck.

Van Wyck, Frederick, *Recollections of an Old New Yorker*. Liveright Publishing Corp., New York, 1932, pp. 272–274. The quality of Mayor Van Wyck's appointments.

Low, Benjamin R. C., *Seth Low*. G. P. Putnam's Sons, New York, 1925, p. 70. A favorable view of Mayor Low's appointments.

Fosdick, Raymond B., *Chronicle of a Generation*. Harper and Bros., New York, 1958, pp. 85–86. Some observations about Mayor McClellan's appointments.

Syrett, Harold C., editor, *The Gentleman and the Tiger: The Autobiography of George B. McClellan, Jr.* J. B. Lippincott Co., Philadelphia, 1956, pp. 182–186, 190–191, 218–219, 230–243. Mayor McClellan's appointments after his election in 1903 and following his election in 1905.

Carmer, Carl, "From Van Wyck to O'Dwyer," in Allan Nevins and John A. Krout, *The Greater City: New York, 1898–1948.* Columbia University Press, New York, 1948, pp. 76, 78. Appointments made by Mayors McClellan and Gaynor.

Hochman, William Russell, *William J. Gaynor: The Years of Fruition.* University Microfilms, Publication no. 12,309, Ann Arbor, Mich., 1955. Doctoral dissertation, Columbia University, 1955. Mayor Gaynor's appointments.

Pink, Louis A., *Gaynor: The Tammany Mayor Who Swallowed the Tiger.* International Press, New York, 1931, pp. 143–149. Mayor Gaynor's appointments and their political consequences.

Smith, Mortimer, *William Jay Gaynor: Mayor of New York.* Henry Regnery, Chicago, 1951, pp. 80–85. How Mayor Gaynor failed to support the Tammany and Brooklyn Democratic machines with patronage.

Hazelton, Henry I., *The Borough of Brooklyn and Queens, Counties of Nassau and Suffolk, Long Island, New York, 1609–1924.* 3 vols. Lewis Historical Publishing Co., New York, 1925, vol. 3, p. 1549. A succinct characterization of the kinds of appointments Mayor Gaynor made.

Amberg, Edward, and William H. Allen, *Civic Lessons from Mayor Mitchel's Defeat.* Institute for Public Service, New York, 1921, pp. 42, 44. Mayor Mitchel's appointments and civil service.

Citizens Union, "Epidemics for Patronage," *The Searchlight,* vol. 14, June, 1924. The Citizens Union evaluates the work of Mayor Hylan in the area of patronage and appointments.

Whalen, Grover A., *Mr. New York: The Autobiography of Grover A. Whalen.* G. P. Putnam's Sons, New York, 1955, pp. 28–33. How some of Mayor Hylan's appointments were made.

Crowell, Paul, and A. H. Raskin, "New York: 'Greatest City in the World,'" in Robert S. Allen, editor, *Our Fair City.* Vanguard Press, New York, 1947, pp. 37–58. Mayor O'Brien's appointments (p. 49).

Allen, William H., *Why Tammanies Revive: La Guardia's Mis-Guard.* Institute for Public Service, New York, 1937, pp. 20–33. An unfavorable view of Mayor La Guardia's appointments during his first term in office.

Chamberlain, John, "Mayor La Guardia," *Yale Review,* vol. 29, September, 1934, pp. 11–27. The quality of Mayor La Guardia's appointments during his first and second terms.

Childs, Richard S., "New York City Elections as a Problem in Political Science," *National Municipal Review,* vol. 24, January, 1935, pp. 23–26. The dilemmas of a reform Mayor in the use of patronage.

Belous, Charles, *Faith in Fusion.* Vantage Press, New York, 1951, pp. 30–34. Fusion administration appointments.

Chadbourne, Ellis, *New York Blazes the Way.* Municipal Affairs Pamphlets, no. 1, The Citizens' Movement, New York, 1934, pp. 4–7. A favorable view of the major appointments made by Mayor La Guardia during his first administration.

Connery, Robert H., "New York City Cleans House," *National Municipal Review,* vol. 23, February, 1934, pp. 100–103. Mayor La Guardia's earliest appointments in his first administration.

La Guardia, Fiorello, "New York City Blazes the Trail," a radio broadcast in *You and Your Government Series.* National Municipal League, New York, 1934. Mayor La Guardia describes his appointments during his first administration.

"Principles and Policies of Administration," Rebecca B. Rankin, editor, *New York Advancing: World's Fair Edition.* Publishers Printing Co., New York, 1939, pp. xv–xxvi. Mayor La Guardia sets forth the principles which guided his appointments and the appointments made by his commissioners during the first five years of his administrations.

Limpus, Lowell M., and Burr Leyson, *This Man La Guardia.* E. P. Dutton and Co., New York, 1938, pp. 377–379. The quality of Mayor La Guardia's original appointments in 1934.

Moscow, Warren, *Politics in the Empire State*. Alfred A. Knopf, New York, 1948, p. 24. Mayor La Guardia and the appointment of "political favorites."

Moses, Robert, *La Guardia: A Salute and a Memoir*. Simon and Schuster, New York, 1957. The kind of men Mayor La Guardia appointed.

Crowell, Paul, and A. H. Raskin, "Greatest City in the World," in Robert S. Allen, *Our Fair City*. Vanguard Press, New York, 1947, pp. 37–58. Mayor O'Dwyer's appointments in 1946, his first year in office (pp. 41–44).

Mockridge, Norton, and Robert H. Prall, *The Big Fix*. Henry Holt and Co., New York, 1954, pp. 84–86. Mayor O'Dwyer's appointments in 1946.

Bergerman, Milton, "An Appraisal of the Impellitteri Record," *The Searchlight*, vol. 42, May, 1952. The Chairman of Citizens Union evaluates the appointments made by Mayor Impellitteri during the first half of his administration.

Hamburger, Philip, "The Mayor: Profile of Robert F. Wagner," *The New Yorker*, vol. 32, February 2, 1957, pp. 54–55, 59–60. How political figures make bids for office and the kind of appointments Wagner made.

Lowi, Theodore J., *At the Pleasure of the Mayor*. Doctoral dissertation, Yale University, 1960, unpublished. A study of Mayors' cabinets in New York from Van Wyck to Wagner.

SOME APPRAISALS OF APPOINTING POWERS

Bryce, James, "The Mayoralty Election in New York," *Contemporary Review*, vol. 72, November, 1897, pp. 751–752. Why the appointing powers of the first Mayor made control of the city administration so important.

Low, Seth, "Brooklyn's Charter," an address delivered in City Hall, Rochester, New York, February 19, 1885; reprinted in *Addresses and Papers on Municipal Government by Seth Low*. New York, 1891, pp. 9–24. The future Mayor of New York explains the importance of centering the power of appointment and removal in the Mayor under Brooklyn's "Strong Mayor" plan (pp. 11–16).

Mitchel, John Purroy, "The Office of Mayor," *Proceedings* of the Academy of Political Science in the City of New York, vol. 5, April, 1915, pp. 479–494. Mayor Mitchel describes the appointing power as the most important of all the Mayor's duties—and tells why (pp. 479–482).

New York City Charter Revision Commission 1907, *Report of Revision Commission of 1907 to the Governor of the State of New York Pursuant to the Provisions of Chapter 600 of the Laws of 1907*. Evening Post, New York, 1907, pp. 21–25. A strong recommendation that the appointing powers of the Mayor be enhanced.

Shaw, Frederick, *History of the New York City Legislature*. Columbia University Press, New York, 1954, pp. 80–84, 244. Appointments made by the Board of Aldermen and by the City Council.

Syrett, Harold C., *The City of Brooklyn, 1865–1898: A Political History*. Columbia University Press, New York, 1944, pp. 90–94. How the Mayor's power to make appointments without confirmation was established in Brooklyn, a system taken over later by the Greater New York Charter.

Tanzer, Lawrence A., *The New York City Charter*. Clark Boardman Co., New York, 1937, pp. 23, 480. The Mayor's appointing power as described by the counsel of the 1936 Charter Commission and by the Commission itself.

Wheeler, Everett P., *Sixty Years of American Life*. E. P. Dutton and Co., New York, 1917. Origin of the appointing power of the Mayor of New York City (pp. 362 and 363.) The merit system following consolidation of the city (pp. 306–309) and appointments of Mayor Seth Low (pp. 397–398).

APPOINTMENTS AND POLITICS

Breen, Matthew P., *Thirty Years of New York Politics Up-to-Date*. The Author, New York, 1899, pp. 43–44. Patronage deals between the two major parties in the city.

Civil Service Reform Association, *Report of the Executive Committee of the Civil Service Reform Association, 1881–1917; Report of the Executive Committee of the Civil Service Reform Association and Treasurer's Report, 1918–1943; The New York Civil Service, Annual Reports for 1944–1950;* and *Annual Reports to the Public on the New York Civil Service.* The Association, New York, 1951 to date. These annual reports of the Civil Service Reform Association indicate the trends in appointments, civil service, and patronage in New York since 1881.

Finegan, James E., *Tammany at Bay.* Dodd, Mead and Co., New York, 1933, pp. 49–54, 66, 78, 183–195, 225–226. The role of patronage in New York City politics.

Flynn, Edward J., *You're the Boss.* Viking Press, New York, 1947, pp. 62–63, 115–116. The Bronx County Leader's views on political appointments.

Gosnell, Harold F., *Boss Platt and His New York Machine.* University of Chicago Press, Chicago, 1924, pp. 229–231, 246–248. How patronage was dispensed in New York City at the turn of the century.

Ivins, William M., *Machine Politics and Money in Elections in New York City.* Harper and Bros., New York, 1887, pp. 13–14. Patronage and the "cement of office."

Lavine, Emanuel H., *"Gimme": Or How Politicians Get Rich.* Vanguard Press, New York, 1931, pp. 19–26, 75–79. The influence of politics on appointments.

Luthin, Reinhard H., *American Demagogues: Twentieth Century.* Beacon Press, Boston, 1954, pp. 229–230. How Vito Marcantonio, as American Labor party Leader, distributed patronage in his district.

Riordan, William L., *Plunkitt of Tammany Hall.* Alfred A. Knopf, New York, 1948, pp. 15–21. A professional politician explains why the spoils system is preferable to the civil service system.

Thomas, Norman, and Paul Blanshard, *What's the Matter with New York?* Macmillan Co., New York, 1932, pp. 30–43. How the power of appointment helps weld the political machine together.

DISCUSSIONS OF REMOVALS AND REMOVAL POWER

Bingham, Theodore A., "Why I Was Removed," *Van Norden Magazine,* vol. 5, September, 1909, pp. 591–596. The Police Commissioner removed by Mayor McClellan sets forth his story.

Fosdick, Raymond B., *Chronicle of a Generation.* Harper and Bros., New York, 1958. Gaynor's Commissioner of Accounts tells the story of the removals of Borough President Louis F. Haffen of The Bronx and John F. Ahearn of Manhattan (pp. 83–84) as well as Lawrence Gresser of Queens (pp. 95–97).

Leonard, John W., *History of the City of New York, 1609–1909.* Journal of Commerce and Commercial Bulletin, New York, 1910, p. 414. Removal of the municipal Civil Service Commission by Mayor McClellan.

Northrop, W. B., editor, *Some of Mayor Gaynor's Letters and Speeches.* Greaves Publishing Co., New York, 1913, pp. 145–146. Mayor Gaynor's views on the removal of officials.

Rosenberg, Bernard, *Removal Standards for the Classified Civil Service as Determined by New York State Courts.* Master's thesis, New York University, 1940, unpublished.

Syrett, Harold C., editor, *The Gentleman and the Tiger: The Autobiography of George B. McClellan, Jr.* J. B. Lippincott Co., Philadelphia, 1956. The removal of Borough Presidents Haffen of the Bronx and Ahearn of Manhattan (pp. 290–292); how Mayor McClellan removed his Civil Service Commission (p. 210).

Whalen, Grover A., *Mr. New York: The Autobiography of Grover A. Whalen.* G. P. Putnam's Sons, New York, 1955, pp. 35–38, 59. Some of Mayor Hylan's removals and how they were accomplished.

Wolford, Irene B., *A Study of the Removal of Civil Service Employees in New York State.* Master's thesis, New York University, 1940, unpublished.

PART THREE

STRATEGIES OF THE CONTESTANTS: SHAPING GOVERNMENTAL DECISIONS

CHAPTER VIII

Administrators of the Line Agencies

LINE ADMINISTRATORS, GOVERNMENTAL DECISIONS, AND THE PRIZES OF POLITICS

MANY PRIZES OF POLITICS, it was noted earlier, are commonly contained and distributed in governmental decisions affecting public services, financial benefits, and costs to the people of the city. For this reason, many groups organize to participate in the governmental process, seeking by their strategies to determine the nature of the governmental decisions relevant to their own situations.

These participants are most often concerned with the official behavior of the line agencies—that is, the administrative agencies in direct contact with all or part of the populace that perform the regulatory, enforcement, and service functions of government. The immediate targets of the participants' efforts may be laws, executive orders, rules and regulations, or judicial judgments. The concrete objective usually is to influence the actions of tax collectors, policemen, or inspectors; to affect the location of schools, firehouses, health centers, libraries, traffic signals, or playgrounds; or perhaps to increase the size of salary checks or welfare payments. Statutes and other high-level decisions are means to concrete ends; it is the ends that seem to count most heavily in the contest for the stakes of politics. In the last analysis, the day-to-day actions of specific public officers and employees in the line bureaus and departments are the vehicles in which the stakes are carried.

The high commands of the line agencies—the Commissioners, their deputies and assistants, and their bureau chiefs—are key figures in the governmental process. They possess the formal legal powers of their agencies—the power to promulgate rules and regulations having the force of law; to fix the levels and quality of service; to set conditions for, or withhold, licenses and permits, and to suspend or revoke them; to deploy work forces and set project priorities; and to intervene in individual cases handled by their agencies. In addition to their formal authority, they are often treated as experts in their particular areas of public policy. But perhaps most important of all is that many agency leaders have, or develop, powerful incentives to function actively and aggressively in the performance of their tasks and in

249

defense of their agencies. For some, the motive is apparently simply pride in a job well done. For others, it is a desire to acquire reputations that will enable them to advance to higher positions, appointive or elective, in government, or to call their talents to the attention of others. In some cases it may be nothing more than a desire to avoid the discredit that is the lot of an administrator who fails to furnish leadership, and whose agency consequently falls into a state of disorganization and incompetence. A few seem simply to enjoy the exercise of power. Some have leadership thrust upon them by the pressures of their subordinates, their clientele, their political superiors, or by crisis. In any event, whatever the motivation, many agency chiefs are drawn into the center of the political arena.

Because they are legal repositories of authority and responsibility, widely regarded as experts in their fields, and often self-conscious and energetic leaders, line agency heads are foci of many efforts to influence governmental decision-making. It is to them that a great deal of legislative, executive, and court action is addressed. It is to them that other administrators, employees, and interest groups turn with demands of various kinds. While all claims and mandates and requests do not have the same standing or success, the attention paid the line officers by all kinds of participants in politics enhances their importance still further.

To be important, however, is not the same as to be a free agent. The very circumstances that draw the attention of the various participants, by subjecting the line administrators to batteries of pressures and legal requirements and suggestions and advice, in the end limit the administrators' discretion. Almost every move they make affects somebody, either favorably or adversely; almost every failure to move pleases some people and provokes others. Moreover, the administrators are vulnerable; the jurisdiction of their agencies is not immutably fixed, their appropriations are not guaranteed, their job tenure is generally far from secure. Scarcely a year goes by without the birth of a new municipal agency, the elimination or absorption of an old one, a major modification of an existing one. A line agency head is not in a risk-free situation. He cannot make decisions as he pleases, without reference to the field of forces in which he operates, if he does not wish to jeopardize the position of his agency, his own career, or the programs and projects to which he is personally, professionally, and organizationally committed. He cannot disregard decisions made elsewhere in the governmental system for the same reasons. To impress his own preferences on the decision-making process, or even merely to prevent policies unacceptable to him from being adopted, he must learn to deal with the world in which he lives. In other words, he must learn to use his considerable resources to produce the kinds of decisions he wants and needs. He must formulate strategies that make the most of his opportunities and minimize his hazards. He must be a manipulator, or he will become an instrument in the hands of others and possibly pay high costs as a consequence.

THE STRATEGIES OF LINE ADMINISTRATORS

Getting Internal Control

The *sine qua non* for the exercise of influence upon governmental decisions by line agency heads is to gain control of the subordinates in their departments and bureaus. To be sure, an administrator can live at peace with his subordinates by routinely ratifying their proposals for running the agency and managing its program. But their perceptions of the policies to be followed are, because they see things from a different vantage point, ordinarily narrower than the perceptions of their chiefs. The latter will be subject to ranges of pressures and sources of information and advice largely unknown to the men in the lower ranks or in exceedingly specialized occupations. Agency heads will be aware of opportunities and dangers, of complications and repercussions, that subordinates often do not realize exist. Frequently, the heads will be freer of the habits, traditions, and vested interests in the *status quo* that stifle not only innovation and inventiveness but even adaptiveness to changing conditions on the part of those at lower levels of the hierarchies. In the short run it may be more convenient to surrender to the hierarchies than to assume the taxing role of leader. In the long run, however, this may simply be courting disaster.

Gaining control of subordinates in city departments and bureaus is not a simple task. It is true that just being commissioner or bureau chief is a major aid in this respect, for the title and position invest the incumbent with the symbols of legitimacy, the formal signs that he has the "right" to demand and receive the allegiance and obedience of his staff. But this is seldom enough by itself.

In the first place, as noted in the preceding chapter, a commissioner usually finds he does not have a free hand in selecting his subordinates. Even his own deputies, assistants, and bureau chiefs, whose influence on his own actions every commissioner knows will be considerable, are not often selected for their loyalty to him. The Mayor and the leaders of the Mayor's party often have candidates of their own for these positions, and other officials, the bureaucracies, the press, and nongovernmental groups also generally offer counsel backed by the implied threat of sanctions if they are disregarded. Over other personnel in his department, the commissioner usually has still less choice; most are career civil servants who come from within the ranks of their own services. So a commissioner cannot easily surround himself with aides he knows will do his bidding and who will see that others in the agency do so also. On the contrary, he must often exert his leadership through subordinates who are at best neutral, at worst openly hostile, and who are always well aware of the limitations of his power. If he is clever and fortunate, he can make sufficient personnel changes to establish a fairly high degree of control. Commissioners of Police and Fire, in particular, attempt periodically to accomplish this by reassigning officers (at all levels down to the middle ranks) in what the newspapers customarily describe as "shake-ups." But this is not a managerial implement to be used frequently and in sweeping proportions, nor is its efficacy at all certain.

In the second place, commissioners normally cannot count on their own personal and professional reputations to produce enthusiastic receptivity to their proposals. Although they may be widely recognized as excellent administrators and experts in the subject matter of their agencies, they are apt to be regarded as novices and "laymen" by those who have spent their lives in the agencies—indeed, in a single bureau or division. If a commissioner comes from within the career ranks, as increasing numbers in recent years have done, he may enjoy the confidence of his staff only so long as he continues to behave like a career executive. If he is not from the ranks, he is likely to be considered a temporary outsider. Even Health Commissioners brought in from outside because of their outstanding professional reputations have on occasion been treated as virtual amateurs by the strongly entrenched permanent personnel of the bureaus under them.

Commissioners are also hampered, in the third place, by their comparatively rapid turnover. Under them, career civil servants continue indefinitely, and many of the permanent staff look on their formal chiefs (the commissioners and their deputies) as birds of passage. *Bureau* chiefs who have risen to their positions of command by promotion from within often enjoy the deference of their subordinates because they are viewed as true members of their units and because they know and control the details of large budgets. Their personnel identify with them and respect them. *Commissioners* who stay in office for a brief number of years, to be supplanted by other strangers to the bureaucracies under them, rarely know the advantages of these strong social and personal ties as wellsprings of zealous rank and file support.

In the fourth place, commissioners sometimes discover that bureaus in their departments develop independent sources of outside support—often, among the interest groups they regulate. To the outside observer, such groups appear to be part of the broad clientele of the department, but the department heads find that they furnish support to the particular bureau with which they are associated rather than to the department as a whole. Frequently this is reinforced by common professional identifications between the personnel of the bureau and the interests with which they are linked. Sanitarians and restaurant operators, for example, or health inspectors and commercial exterminators often have had similar training and experience, and a substantial part of the bureaus' staffs is either recruited from the regulated industry or has hopes of returning to it eventually.

Some commissioners try to ingratiate themselves with their bureaucracies by fighting to get for them the things they want—higher classifications, better pay scales, more liberal fringe benefits, and similar advantages. A commissioner who comes to be regarded as a champion of his staff can often count on more willing compliance with his innovations in substantive program. He achieves at least an approximation of the support an individual moved up from the ranks would receive for the same efforts. The commissioner who resorts to this strategy, however, runs the risk of being "captured" by his subordinates, and becoming a defender of the state of affairs to which they, by habit, are wedded. A few have avoided this pitfall and, after winning acceptance, have used this source of authority to work many changes of organization, procedure, and program. Others have been entrapped by their efforts to earn the confidence of the career personnel, and have become followers of the "insiders" rather than leaders and innovators.

This does not mean commissioners are often confronted with open defiance of their directives if they assert their formal powers. It does mean they can be thwarted by reluctance, persistence of old habits and customs, neglect, and resistance on the part of their subordinates. Commissioners therefore have their strongest impact on the decisions and behavior of their staffs only when they follow up instructions with personal inspection to make sure commands are executed as intended. Personal attention, backed by the legitimate authority of office and the possibility of official sanctions, is most likely to elicit the kind of action desired by a department head. That is why many department heads concentrate on only a restricted segment of the whole range of activities of their agencies when they want to introduce new emphases or new functions. And that is why they often leave the rest of the duties of their organizations to career people who perform them in the customary way.

Manipulation of the External Environment

If an agency head in the city government is not at least as energetic in protecting the jurisdiction and income of his organization as he is in winning control of its internal affairs, he may soon be left with little worth controlling. Manipulation of the external environment presumes a certain degree of internal control, but there is more to it than that. Agency survival also requires expertness in "external relations."

External relations on behalf of each agency has become the unique (but not the sole) function of its department head and bureau chiefs. They have evolved four basic techniques for performing it: (1) creation of a favorable climate of public opinion; (2) cultivation of active constituencies; (3) concessions to, or understandings with, actual or potential wielders of punitive sanctions against them; and (4) truces with other governmental agencies.

Creating a Favorable Climate of Opinion. Like executives of all large organizations, commissioners of the city's line agencies conduct public relations programs beamed at the entire population with which they are concerned— in this case, usually all the people of the city. The methods are those traditionally employed in the public relations profession: news releases sent to newspapers and other mass media of communication when items of more or less routine interest are involved; newsletters and similar publications mailed to public opinion leaders; press conferences and conducted tours of physical installations for unusual achievements; and public relations officers, or their equivalent under other titles, who manage these matters, to whom reporters seeking information can turn for quick help when they need it, and who can ensure that the reporters understand the agencies' side of every question. The opening of a new facility, the inauguration of a new service, and even the expansion or improvement or intensification of an old one, generally get fairly conspicuous display in the local press, presumably because these things are of general community interest. They are welcomed by city reporters and editors. The newsworthiness of such items is enhanced by the appearance of prominent elected officials, from assemblymen up to the Governor, who wish to be identified with a new enterprise. Coverage by the mass media thus satisfies the needs and desires of many, among whom are the heads of departments and their subordinates.

And so it happens that there is a ceremony when ground is broken for any kind of city construction, and when the cornerstone is laid, and when the facility is opened. Some years ago there was a ribbon-cutting ceremony opening a new highway before the highway was completely paved since the paving could not be completed before Election Day. This also explains why the signs in front of big construction projects while they are going up normally bear the names of half a dozen or more officials. It indicates why a great deal of attention was given in the press to the Fire Commissioner's campaign against careless demolition practices and unsafe storage of inflammables following the spectacular fire in the old John Wanamaker building; to the project of the Department of Buildings to compel all landlords to maintain their properties at the level required by law after housing groups in the city and a number of tenement house fires focused the public spotlight on the rapid spread of the slums; to the Department of Traffic's figures on time saved by the introduction of one-way avenues; to the Transit Authority's experiments with air-conditioned subway cars and buses; to the punishment of officers in the Fire and Police Departments convicted in departmental trials of accepting gifts and tips; and to many other similar developments treated saliently in the city's newspapers. It accounts for the play in the press for new schools, housing projects, bridges, reservoirs, sewage disposal units, and the like. By calling notice publicly to efforts to compensate for past shortcomings, and by playing up self-initiated accomplishments, department heads build their own reputations and followings as individuals; simultaneously, they strengthen the strategic positions of their departments.

As in merchandising, the product is often its own best advertisement. City and other government line agencies building and managing great public works are thus more fortunate than many. The reputations enjoyed by members of the Port of New York Authority and by Commissioner Robert Moses rest in considerable part upon the fact that people use, see, enjoy, and benefit from the facilities to which their names are attached. The tunnels and bridges, highways and parks, and playgrounds and beaches testify to millions of citizens that these are men who get things done. For the agencies, the use of their facilities thus serves a triple service—solidifying community support for them, maximizing their earnings, as well as providing New York City and the surrounding areas with needed services. In less dramatic fashion, and on a much smaller scale but with similar results, some other city agencies have adopted comparable tactics. The Transit Authority has expanded off-hour service on the subways in efforts to win back riders who turned to other means of transportation rather than wait twenty minutes to half an hour for trains, and it posts car-cards and distributes free baseball schedules to point up the number of places served by its lines. Museums and botanical gardens and zoological parks also post notices in public places and run special shows to attract clientele. The Public Library makes special vacation arrangements for the loan of books and thus maintains a brisk level of business during the summer, when its patronage ordinarily falls off. The Board of Education throws its facilities open to parents each year during Open School Week. It would be cynical to argue that these actions are taken for no other purpose than to benefit the administrative organizations or their leaders; in many cases, the measures doubtless spring from motivations to perform a social service. Whatever the motivations, however, one of the consequences is establishment of a friendly attitude on the part of the general public, of special constituencies, and of the organs that make the laws and control the budget.

Service functions lend themselves much more readily to "advertising" than regulatory or enforcement functions. New services and facilities are visible and usable; they speak for themselves of the proficiency of the agencies operating them, and they can ordinarily be instituted or constructed without need of widespread public cooperation. Regulation or enforcement, on the other hand, is generally out of sight of all but those affected, is likely to be taken for granted by the general population, and is sure to arouse some opposition and complaint from those regulated. Furthermore, regulatory agencies must secure compliance; their work does not depend on them alone but on the behavior of others. Now and then, an agency head promotes his cause with a spectacular regulatory campaign. Most of the time, he steers a course calculated to produce enough compliance with requirements to avoid scandalous or numerous violations without provoking storms of opposition from the regulated interests. A quiet state of affairs is often the most successful kind of public relations for regulatory and enforcement activities.

Another kind of public relations is the managed demonstration. One of the most spectacular of these was a recent intensive undertaking by the Police Commissioner to "saturate" high crime-rate areas with foot patrolmen. With policemen on every corner all through the day and night, and with roving patrols covering the areas between, he reported, all types of offenses dropped. He inferred from this that budget increases enabling him to expand the size of the police force would reduce crime throughout the city. With the news of the experiment prominently reported in all the major daily newspapers, the demonstration doubtless helped him obtain what he sought. A generation earlier, the Department of Health constructed health centers and stationed district health officers in neighborhoods with the highest disease and death rates in the city. The concentration and coordination of these health "shock troops" was declared to have brought down sharply both the incidence of disease and fatalities and was a prelude to the construction of additional health centers and the engagement of additional personnel to man them in other areas. More recently, the Fire Commissioner has received attention for his fire prevention campaign, which he reported to have cut sharply the number of fires and the amount of damage. In this way, line agency heads endeavor, and often succeed, in mobilizing public opinion behind them.

The impending crisis is also employed as a public relations method. One such instance in 1957 was a blistering condemnation of conditions in Bellevue Hospital by eight division heads of that institution; these officers, who numbered among them two Nobel Prize winners, released to the press expressions of alarm and approaching disaster and called for complete renovation and substantial new construction to bring the most famous of the city's hospitals up to satisfactory standards. In like fashion, Police Department crime statistics often give rise to newspaper headlines about crime waves. Toxic substances in the atmosphere were reported by the Department of Air Pollution Control to have reached deadly proportions in some areas. The Department of Buildings complains of the continued spread of urban blight despite its best efforts. The Board of Education itself points up local shortages of classroom space, unfavorable teacher-pupil ratios, and school overcrowding with the likelihood of even worse conditions if drastic remedial measures are not adopted. This is not to say these problems are not real or that the crises are deliberately invented or manufactured. In every case the facts tend to bear out the anxieties of the agencies. Nevertheless, the agency heads or their subordinates employ these situations to arouse public opinion. By well-timed self-exposure they proclaim their competence, their zeal, and their devotion to the public interest and, at the same time, indicate they are hampered by lack of funds and manpower in the performance of their jobs. No city department head has apparently ever gone quite so far as United States Postmaster General Summerfield, who slashed postal service and threatened not to restore it unless his budget requests were fulfilled. The difference, however, is one of degree rather than kind.

Finally, purely educational activities by line agencies often serve public relations purposes. Health Department posters on poison control, for example, not only alert the public to a real safety hazard, but also call attention to the department, its leaders, and its program. Similarly, widespread distribution of Fire Department leaflets on the dangers of kerosene heaters and training programs on methods of fire prevention offered in the public schools perform a valuable public service while also presenting the agency to the populace in a benevolent light.

Whatever the specific tactics of these public relations efforts by city commissioners, the results are not easily assessed. It cannot be proved that efforts put into public relations definitely protect the jurisdiction and income of line departments and bureaus. On the other hand, the evidence strongly suggests that the Mayor, the Board of Estimate, the City Council, the Bureau of the Budget, and other important legislative, executive, and financial institutions of the city government hesitate to refuse requests for appropriations and power by agencies in high popular favor. The political liabilities of such action, particularly in the case of an agency whose head would not hesitate to denounce his official superiors, are far too great. It could hurt the party in power badly at the following election. Moreover, on the reverse side of the coin is the fact that the achievements of the line agencies reflect credit on the elective as well as the administrative officers of government. Not only do the other officials fear to curtail the jurisdiction and expenditures of the better known and respected departments, but they are apt to want to aid them as far as possible in order to reap the benefits of their achievements. Unquestionably, the agencies with the greatest public relations attainments and programs have also been the ones to enjoy the greatest support from the general public, the press, and from the money-providing organs of the city government.

Cultivating Active Constituencies. Public opinion is amorphous, ambiguous, and apparently capricious a good deal of the time. Hence, while it is a valuable implement for most agency heads, it is not entirely reliable. That is why most commissioners and bureau chiefs foster continuing and helpful relations with nongovernmental groups, and often call upon these allies to aid them in

their battles against contractions of jurisdiction and curtailment of appropriations, and to back their struggles to expand their powers or expenditures.
Nongovernmental groups have many means of influencing the decisions and
actions of government officials and employees; consequently, those agency
heads who wish to influence other public officers seek to invoke the assistance
of nongovernmental allies. The groups, in turn, seek to exercise influence over
the agency heads. The groups that help and the groups that oppose the commissioner may be thought of as his "constituency."

By and large, nongovernmental groups are not created by city agencies for
strategic purposes, nor are governmental decisions and actions the sole, or
even the chief, concerns of such groups. They ordinarily have more than one
purpose and more than a single origin. A few, to be sure, are encouraged by
the departments with which they are associated; Parent-Teachers Associations, for example, owe much of their vigor to Board of Education support
and help. But this is the exception rather than the rule as far as the allies of
line agencies are concerned; agency heads make use of groups they are not
instrumental in forming or leading (and are in turn used by the groups).

Although they will accept assistance from every quarter, agency heads
depend most heavily on permanent and persistent sources, for these are the
ones with the resources, the skills, the reputations, and the lines of access to
make their weight felt in the topmost levels of government. Generally, these
tend to be clientele groups (associations of people served or regulated by a
given agency), professional groups (from whose ranks the agency's dominant
professional work force is selected), and functional groups (whose social or
economic activities parallel those of the agency), but others are also often
involved. Some agency heads have constituencies composed of groups of all
three kinds; no agency head is without at least one. Connected with the
Board of Education, for instance, are the United Parents Association (a
clientele group), the local affiliates of the National Education Association (a
professional group), the Public Education Association and the Citizens Committee for Children (functional groups). At times, the Board is also buttressed
by teachers' trade unions and teachers colleges. In the cases of the Department of Health and the Department of Hospitals, there are many health and
welfare organizations and their "peak association," the Community Council
of Greater New York; the American Public Health Association; the medical
societies in the city; the New York Academy of Medicine; and the American
Nurses Association. The Department of Traffic is inevitably in close contact
with bus companies, retail trade associations, labor unions, and the local
units of the American Automobile Association. Welfare organizations and
associations of welfare workers, as well as recipients of welfare benefits, constitute important segments of the constituencies of the Department of Welfare. Neighborhood groups and the Park Association of New York City keep

in touch with the work of the Department of Parks. The businesses and trades licensed by the Department of Licenses follow its fortunes. Owners and drivers of taxis are linked to the Hack Bureau of the Police Department. No matter what the line agency, it is sure to have at least one, and usually several, nongovernmental groups whose interests are intertwined with its own in some way and thus constitute the agency's constituency.

Many times these nongovernmental groups need no prompting from the agency head to apply their own modes of influence in defense of the agency's powers, appropriations, and position. On their own initiative, and in pursuit of their own interests, they can be counted upon to take forceful action. At other times, agency heads let it be known that a struggle is impending and informally call their allies to the fore when they are needed. To be able to call them requires lines of communication, so the lines of communication are carefully kept open. Contacts are established and maintained; group leaders are assured of ready access to the department or bureau head; informal meetings and briefing sessions are arranged; the groups are consulted, given opportunities to appear at both closed and open hearings, and notified in advance of pending moves by their respective agencies. In every possible way, their "natural" attachment to the well-being of particular agencies is intensified by deliberately cultivated bonds, for the groups are often influential and invaluable friends to the agencies.

Concessions. They are also demanding ones. Although they may frequently come to the defense of a city agency, they do not invariably endorse whatever the agency does. On the contrary, they generally have notions of their own about what the contents of decisions ought to be and what courses of action should be followed. The lines of access kept open by agency heads for their own strategic purposes also serve the strategic purposes of the groups; they employ the channels of communication to let their own demands upon the agencies be known. Indeed, administrators dare not close these lines even if they want to, for every group that is a powerful ally could also be a formidable enemy. The department heads and bureau chiefs therefore listen; that is the minimum price of coalition.

Commissioners must make concessions, too. It is not just a matter of hearing the groups out in cathartic sessions but of keeping them sufficiently satisfied to retain their support. Sometimes commissioners will not make an appointment to a particular post without first clearing the choice with a group deeply interested in it. Rarely will a group be able to exercise a veto on more than a few positions, and rarely will its own direct representatives be appointed even to those. Power over choice of staff, where it exists at all, is more often negative and restricted. Sometimes commissioners will discuss forthcoming policy and program changes with various groups and adjust their ideas in the light of the groups' criticisms and recommendations. Sometimes an agency head will accept the advice of a "satellite" group with respect to an individual order or action. Occasionally, a group is virtually coopted into a department as an influential advisory body. Thus the decisions and actions of line agencies are commonly influenced strongly by the constellation of nongovernmental groups in which the agencies are placed. The influence of these groups is often salutary. Departmental and bureau programs are often improved because of nongovernmental group participation in their formulation. It is also clear that agency heads yield lukewarmly to these groups on many issues of substance in order to assure the survival and growth of the agencies they command.

Chiefs of regulatory and enforcement agencies are under special compulsions to work out adjustments with their constituencies, especially with their clientele groups. If administration is exceedingly severe and literal, the interests the agencies are charged with controlling and inspecting may resist by political action, or, even more drastically, by wholesale noncompliance. The collapse of administrative effectiveness may lead to the transfer of responsibility to other agencies, the abandonment of a program, and to the disgrace of the agency leader and his associates. By the same token, however, lax enforcement designed to placate clientele may give rise to conditions that threaten the safety or welfare of the public, to scandals, or to attacks from groups favoring enforcement. Deliberate ineffectiveness can often be as damaging as impotence. Agency heads in this position normally come to informal, often tacit, understandings with the people they regulate, conceding to them by displays of tolerance and "reasonableness," trying by this technique to secure enough compliance to satisfy also the interests insisting on regulation.

In addition, agency heads frequently make concessions to nongovernmental groups not closely identified with their particular agencies, groups that do not often intervene on behalf of those agencies, but that occasionally make claims and are in position to constitute powerful opposition if they are not somehow conciliated. The demands of the religious and ethnic groups fall into this classification. There is normally a balance among the Superintendent and Associate Superintendents of the Department of Education, with Catholic, Protestant, and Jewish segments of the population equally represented, and with the demands of Negro New Yorkers beginning to receive increasing attention here. When the Board of Education recently acceded to Catholic wishes for a policy statement encouraging the inculcation of spiritual values in pupils in the public schools, it was compelled to moderate the original version to make it acceptable to protesting Jewish and Protestant groups, who contended that the initial formulation threatened to permit sectarian religious training in the public school system.

Protestant and Jewish groups again joined to resist acquiescence by the Commission of Hospitals in Catholic objections to the dispensing of contraceptive devices in municipal hospitals. The insistence of some religious groups is also largely responsible for the Department of Welfare policy of assigning children's welfare cases to social workers of the same religion as the children. Negro criticisms of the boundary lines of areas served by public elementary and high schools stimulated a Department of Education survey to find ways of reducing virtual segregation created by the concentration of white and Negro populations in different neighborhoods. None of these groups rush to the aid of these departments when the departments press their pleas for funds and struggle to protect their jurisdiction, but they can make so much difficulty for agency heads that the administrators try to accommodate them whenever possible.

For the same reasons, agency heads often try to conciliate party leaders. Party hierarchies can be redoubtable foes of an administrator and his agency. Usually the influence they attempt to exert on administrative decisions and actions relates to the selection or advancement of personnel, or to individual concessions—such as exemptions from formal regulations, dropping prosecutions, hastening the processing of applications—for party followers, members, supporters, and workers. But they may sometimes intervene in broader policy matters as well.

Finally, concessions are made to the Mayor, the Board of Estimate, and the City Council. Jointly, and individually in varying degrees, as later discussion will show, these top city officials have extensive formal powers over budgets, jurisdiction, and personnel of all city departments and agencies. Consequently, the expected reactions of the citywide organs of government are taken into consideration in the formulation of decisions and courses of action by agency heads, at least to avoid instigation of punitive measures, and, positively, to win sympathy and friendship. Top-level intervention in the operations and internal affairs of the line agencies is far from continuous, and it often takes the form of informal requests like those of party functionaries. It is not unheard of for an administrator to refuse outright to comply with such unofficial demands, and it is fairly common for administrators to dilute or neutralize instructions from above by delay and inaction. For all that, though, no agency leader can afford persistently to ignore the wishes of the major political officers, whether these wishes are tacit or explicit, official or unofficial, general or specific. These desires therefore become important factors in what agency heads decide to do.

Cultivating constituencies is primarily a way of winning friends. Concessions are made for the purpose of avoiding antagonisms. Both are accomplished partly by submission to the will of individuals and groups outside the boundaries of the agencies *per se*.

Truces with Other Agencies. The fourth strategy of city agency heads is to stabilize their situations by reaching understandings with other line departments and bureaus. The lines of jurisdiction separating one agency from another are often blurred, and a good deal of administrative rivalry is generated by endeavors on the part of administrators to carve out areas of power in which their own organizations are indisputably in control.

There are many places in the government and politics of the city in which rivalries have occurred. The Board of Standards and Appeals, for instance, recently fought off an attempt by the City Planning Commission to acquire some of the Board's power over allowance of variations from zoning regulations. The Department of Traffic defeated the bid of a specially created New York City Parking Authority for control of parking meters and parking-meter revenues and off-street parking facilities. The Department of Marine and Aviation lost its fight to retain control of Idlewild and La Guardia Airports but has thus far fended off proposals to transfer municipally owned piers to the Port of New York Authority, to which the air terminals were leased. A more recent clash of opinion developed over whether to lodge authority to regulate and supervise private refuse collectors in the Department of Licenses or the Department of Sanitation. Agencies vie with each other for jurisdiction and appropriations. Sometimes they even compete to avoid program assignments that are especially difficult and controversial. The Commissioner of Hospitals and the Commissioner of Correction have both tried to prevent lodging responsibility for treatment of narcotics addicts in their departments, and the Department of Health has been restive under burdens of building inspection the Commissioner and the Board of Health would generally prefer to have placed entirely on the Department of Buildings.

However, there are many places in the city government in which rivalries might be expected but which have been stabilized by agreement. School physicians and nurses could be under the Department of Health or the Department of Education; by agreement, they are now under the former, although there is still some vestigial controversy over custody of pupils' health records. Social work services of the Department of Education and the New York City Youth Board overlap. Some aspects of housing are inspected by the Bureau of Sanitary Inspections of the Health Department, some by the Department of Buildings, some by the Division of Interior Electrical Inspections of the Department of Water Supply, Gas, and Electricity, and some by the Fire Department. The Department of Markets as well as the Department of Health has a hand in regulating some food-handling establishments. There are a number of parallels between the out-patient services of the Department of Hospitals and some of the clinics run by the Department of Health. The Department of Traffic relies on the Police Department to enforce its regulations (and does not have a force of inspectors of its own, as the Department of Sanitation does). The city Transit Authority, however, has its own police force. Many line departments besides the Department of Licenses issue licenses of different kinds. There are endless ambiguities of jurisdiction that could precipitate bitter battles. But most line administrators much prefer to work out understandings by negotiation and agreement. They have difficulty enough without being distracted by jurisdictional fights with their colleagues.

Similarly, they work out understandings with their state and federal counterparts. Many municipal agencies are bound closely to the administrative machinery of other levels of government. These sometimes provoke unrestrained hostilities, such as developed between the City Construction Coordinator and the Administrator of the Federal Housing and Home Finance Agency with respect to federal aid for the projected cultural center in Lincoln Square, but are more frequently adjusted quietly and amicably.

The Counterpoise of Forces

With so many factors to keep in mind and so many different kinds of demands to contend with, the life of a line agency chief in the city is not an easy one. Virtually every decision, every action, is a compromise, or reflects a past compromise, or is a compromise with anticipated alignments of forces. The factor preventing most line executives from completely losing control of the policies and programs of their agencies is the very pluralism of the forces with which they must deal. They play one off against the other, which permits them to follow their own preferences part of the time.

The configuration of claimants on each side of every controversy is often composed of quite disparate groups. On birth control questions, for example, Protestant and Jewish religious groups may be joined with medical associations and welfare groups, as well as with planned parenthood organizations. On the handling of child welfare cases, a professional society of social workers was at odds with Catholic groups. Increase of governmental medical services for the public may be backed by the American Public Health Association, yet opposed by medical societies. Traffic and parking regulations may set bus companies and truckers and taxicab operators and garage owners and the American Automobile Association against each other, and may possibly arouse businessmen in the areas affected. Neighborhood groups threatened with displacement by new roadways or civic improvements may battle with all their strength against planning and motorist and cultural groups. The divisions are not always neat and symmetrical. Any combination of elements, including parts of the bureaucracies involved, may form to support or oppose an agency on any question.

Agency heads usually become adept at calculating the gains and costs of various courses of action, and the opportunities for the satisfaction of their personal values, or they do not stay in office long. All kinds of things must be considered: the effect on public relations generally; the probabilities that a given contender feels strongly enough about an issue, and has enough staying power and skill, to be a useful ally or an opponent worth watching in subsequent agency tribulations; the other connections and modes of influence of the combatants; the reactions of other political officers of government; the chance that quiescent groups, assuming the decisions will go the way they prefer, may spring into action if their expectations are not realized; and many others. In the end, of course, a great deal depends on each administrator's intuition and experience, for there is no mathematical calculus to answer these questions. A good deal of the time, they yield to the forces they think will give them the strongest support in the long run—or at least provide the weakest resistance to other phases of the agency program. Frequently, they try to work out compromises. Sometimes they take refuge in inaction, and let the contending interests fight on until one or the other seems clearly to have the upper hand. Sometimes they act and then manage to convince the objectors that they had no other choice. Occasionally, they do exactly what they want and hope the antagonists will stalemate each other.

At bottom, what the governmental line agencies in the city do is a compound of customary routine, strategies for survival, and a small increment of periodic innovation. The first of these is sure to continue as long as the second is successfully accomplished. Accomplishment of the second hinges, in turn, on the third, for a static organization in the dynamic world of New York City politics is marked for eventual extinction. It is the second and third elements of the compound that fall within the personal province of the agency heads: hence their strategies directed at getting internal control of their agencies, winning external support and avoiding external attacks, and balancing the forces around them so that they can introduce innovations. These are some of the factors at work shaping the pattern of governmental services, regulation, and enforcement activities in New York.

SELECTED EXAMPLES OF LINE ADMINISTRATORS IN ACTION

Fire Department

The Fire Commissioner heads a line agency of size and importance. In 1958 its total staff numbered close to 13,000, its uniformed force being approximately 12,000, organized in companies, battalions, and divisions. The agency has two main assignments: first, to extinguish fires (in 1957 it fought 53,072 fires, of which 22,415 were fires inside buildings); second, to prevent fires (inspections and licenses being the agency's main reliance, with occasional bursts of emphasis on public education concerning fire hazards). The Fire Commissioner's persistent dilemmas as head of the agency are imbedded in these two assignments. In the extinguishment of fires, how can he keep his agency—its organization structure, its personnel, its methods, and its equipment—abreast of the advances in fire-fighting technology and the changes in the city's fire hazards? How can he secure an optimum balance of agency emphasis between fire fighting and fire prevention?

The formal powers of the Fire Commissioner seem at first glance quite adequate for his leadership and initiative in meeting these questions. "The commissioner," says the charter, "shall have sole and exclusive power and

TABLE 39. NEW YORK CITY FIRE COMMISSIONERS, CAREER AND NON-CAREER INCUMBENTS[a], 1898–1959

Commissioner	Tenure as commissioner	Prior experience: highest career (C) position in dept. or principal noncareer (NC) position		
		Position	C	NC
John J. Scannell	Jan., 1898–Dec., 1901	Promoter, gambler; Fire Commissioner, 1893–96		x
Thomas Sturgis	Jan., 1902–Dec., 1903	Banker, realtor; Fire Commissioner, 1896–98		x
Nicholas J. Hayes	Jan., 1904–Dec., 1905	Clerk, State Supreme Court		x
John H. O'Brien	Jan., 1906–Sept., 1906	Political reporter, New York Sun; Secretary to Mayor McClellan, 1904–06		x
Francis J. Lantry	Oct., 1906–Jan., 1908	Wholesale meat business; alderman, 1892–96; Commissioner of Correction, 1898–01, 1904–06		x
Hugh Bonner	Feb., 1908–Mar., 1908	Fire Chief	x[b]	
Nicholas J. Hayes	Apr., 1908–Dec., 1909	See above; Sheriff, 1906–07		x
Rhinelander Waldo	Jan., 1910–May, 1911	Army officer; First Deputy Police Commissioner, 1906–08		x
Joseph Johnson	June, 1911–Dec., 1913	Reporter, New York World; Deputy Fire Commissioner, 1910–12		x
Robert Adamson	Jan., 1914–Dec., 1917	Editor, New York World; Secretary to Mayor Gaynor		x
Thomas J. Drennan	Jan., 1918–Apr., 1926	Deputy Kings County Clerk and other offices		x
John J. Dorman	May, 1926–Dec., 1933	Court Clerk (Kings County) and other offices		x
John J. McElligott	Jan., 1934–Apr., 1941	Fire Chief	x	
Patrick J. Walsh	May, 1941–Dec., 1945	Acting Fire Chief	x	
Frank J. Quayle	Jan., 1946–Nov., 1950	Business executive; Brooklyn Postmaster, 1940–46		x
George P. Monaghan	Jan., 1951–July, 1951	Asst. District Attorney (New York County)		x
Jacob Grumet	Aug., 1951–Jan., 1954	Asst. District Attorney (New York County); private practice		x
Edward F. Cavanagh	Feb., 1954 to date	Lawyer and executive; Commissioner of Marine and Aviation and other offices, 1947–54		x

[a] *Career:* service in the ranks of the Fire Department filled on a competitive basis. *Noncareer:* service outside the Department or in Deputy Commissioner positions.

[b] Died in office.

Source: Lowi, Theodore J., *At the Pleasure of the Mayor.* Doctoral dissertation, Yale University, 1960, unpublished.

perform all duties for the government, discipline, management, maintenance and direction of the fire department and the premises and property in the custody thereof." In additional specific terms, the Commissioner and his agency are given exclusive power to extinguish fires; to approve all containers for combustibles and other fire hazards; to control the fire alarm system; to make and enforce regulations concerning the manufacture, storage, sale, transportation, and use of hazardous materials; to inspect any and all places

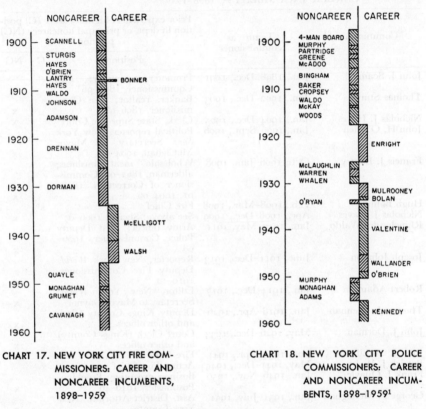

CHART 17. NEW YORK CITY FIRE COM-
MISSIONERS: CAREER AND
NONCAREER INCUMBENTS,
1898–1959

CHART 18. NEW YORK CITY POLICE
COMMISSIONERS: CAREER
AND NONCAREER INCUM-
BENTS, 1898–1959[1]

for fire hazards. In exercising his regulatory powers, the Commissioner is subject to the controls of the state Labor Law, the Multiple Dwelling Law, the city's Building Code and other parts of the Administrative Code, the Sanitary Code and other regulations of the Board of Health, and to the rules and decisions of the Board of Standards and Appeals. But these are not highly restrictive upon his leadership and discretion.

The Commissioner's first and major difficulty in exercising initiative is the problem of securing sufficient internal control of his organization. He is him-

[1] See p. 286.

self appointed by the Mayor and serves at the Mayor's pleasure; unless he is a career commissioner, he is therefore ordinarily closely allied to the Mayor. The charter permits him to appoint three deputy commissioners, but he must usually bargain with the Mayor and the party leaders on these appointments and yield one or more of the posts to them. These are the standard requirements imposed on most commissioners; the Fire Commissioner's troubles merely begin with them. The central barriers to the Commissioner's opportunities for initiative and innovation are three: first, operational control of the Department's fire-fighting and fire-prevention forces is vested in the Fire Chief, a career official; second, the personnel system of the Department deprives the Commissioner of any important chance to recruit or promote personnel who might share or support his ideas; third, the Uniformed Firemen's Association, and the allied officer groups, have the power, if not to make the Commissioner do what they want, to prevent his doing what they strongly disapprove. Career Fire Commissioners tend to accept these circumstances as a way of life. Products of the system, themselves, they find its traditions and habits familiar and natural. "Civilian" Commissioners chafe under the restraints, but do not often succeed with proposals for change in policy, organization, or methods.

Fire Commissioners aspiring to exercise leadership in carrying out the assignments of the Department have tried to break through the monolithic structure of power headed by the Fire Chief, but the Commissioner lacks leverage for the effort. Neither he nor his three deputies (if they each agreed to join him) can pierce the chain-of-command running down from Fire Chief to Deputy Chief to Battalion Chief to Captain to Lieutenant to Fireman, a system which characterizes both the fire-fighting and the fire-prevention organization. No Commissioner has been so bold as to propose staffing the fire prevention activities with civilian engineers and other specialists, recruited under a more flexible personnel system, a plan which might enable him to increase his leadership opportunities. And few Commissioners have questioned the closed promotion system which restricts the judgment of the Fire Commissioner even more than that of the Police Commissioner in an analogous situation. The Fire Department's organized bureaucracies have sufficient power to inhibit any such change.

At least three major consequences flow from the Fire Commissioner's inability to lead his agency. First, the Department gives secondary attention to fire prevention. Fire fighting, the Citizens Budget Commission was told when it studied the Department in 1948, "can be depended upon," and while fire prevention "does some good, it is resented by many people and it costs money." In 1952 the Mayor's Committee on Management Survey found a comparable attitude. These premises are a natural product of an organization all of whose members are recruited, trained, honored, and promoted as fire fighters rather than as fire preventers. Fire prevention administration calls for specialized knowledge and skills which are not systematically provided or rewarded by the system. The Fire Commissioner cannot persuade his existing organization to give first or equal emphasis to fire prevention, nor does he have the actual power to change the organization to achieve that purpose.

Second, the Fire Commissioner cannot lead his organization toward innovation and progress in fire-fighting technology. The uniformed staff follows its own pace in such matters. The Fire Commissioner is inhibited in his leadership not only by the power structure headed by the Fire Chief, but he also lacks the necessary specialists in engineering, chemistry, and other relevant fields of technology because the personnel system of the agency cannot produce them. Even if he were to import into the Department some new fire-fighting ideas of outside specialists (from fire underwriters' laboratories or from the Navy, Army, or Air Force, for example), the Commissioner would have difficulty in securing for such innovations a genuine acceptance and application by his uniformed forces, isolated as they are from new discoveries in their closed, tradition-oriented bureaucratic society. They have moved reluctantly, stage by stage, from hand-drawn to horse-drawn to motor-driven equipment. They will not be hurried from water to chemistry or into the use of other technological discoveries at an unsettling speed.

Finally, the Fire Commissioner must accept a static organization and a static system of procedures in the management of his department. He cannot create a Commissioner's staff of sufficient numbers and status to help him lead the agency. He cannot abolish a special Brooklyn office, although successive studies have shown its irrelevancy to the fire-fighting and fire-prevention functions. He cannot organize, redistrict, or reduce in any significant degree the number of fire districts, fire station houses, and fire companies, although studies may have convinced him that present arrangements are obsolete and inefficient. He cannot secure the data for a critical analysis of the Department's present performance, nor can he establish systems of statistical and other analyses for the forward planning of fire-fighting and fire-prevention programs. He cannot do these things because he cannot persuade his organization to agree to, and support, his proposals. He encounters instead a variety of opposition, ranging from the doubts and delays of high officers, through the increasing resistance of line officers, to the often strident and public hostility of the organized fire bureaucracies. Innovations in policy, technology, organization, or procedures are rare for Fire Commissioners.

The Fire Commissioner has no helpful constituency to assist him in any aspirations he may have for leadership and initiative. The groups representing those businesses and activities subject to inspection and licensing by the Fire Department have no enthusiasm for changes which would enlarge the

Commissioner's discretion. The National Board of Fire Underwriters maintains a cautious attitude. It does not assign a rating to the New York City Fire Department, but it did endorse the Mayor's Committee on Management Survey's recommendations for reduction, relocation, and realignment of fire-fighting companies. The economy groups are cautious, too, in their support of the Fire Commissioner. The communication media are most interested in the drama of fire fighting; they pay much less attention to fire prevention, to modernizing the Department, or to the Commissioner's need for support. The party leaders exhibit marked deference to the Department's organized bureaucracies.

The Commissioner can turn to the Mayor for help. The Mayor will often, but not always, respond. It is the Board of Estimate, however, whose consent and help is necessary for most innovations, and the Board is more inclined to listen to the views and sentiments of the uniformed force than to the Mayor and Commissioner combined.

Department of Buildings

The Commissioner of Buildings heads a line agency of intermediate size (approximately 1,500 employees), but he faces a task of immense difficulty and his choices of strategy as an administrator are characterized by persistent dilemmas. The job of the Department of Buildings is to ensure by a system of inspections and certificates the safety for use and occupancy of every building and structure in the city, and by inspection and sanctions to secure safe and sanitary housing for all dwellers in tenements and other multiple dwellings. The agency thus has a regulatory assignment, a governmental role invariably surrounded by frustrations and risks for the officials involved.

The troubled evolution of the Department as an organization is itself testimony to the uncertainties of purpose and method which have accompanied the functions of the agency. When the charter of 1901 was adopted, the regulation of buildings was left with the five Borough Presidents, in recognition of the many "local" forces which demanded accommodation in the application of the Building Code (a part of the Administrative Code) and other regulatory controls. However, when the social reformers of a half century ago won a victory in their battle against "the tenements," they preferred to entrust the enforcement of the Multiple Dwelling Law not to the Borough Presidents, but to a new city department—the Tenement House Department. Thus matters stood until 1938, when the new charter established a Department of Housing and Buildings, transferring the functions of the Borough Presidents in this field, as well as the functions of regulating multiple dwellings, to the new department (renamed the Department of Buildings in 1957).

The Commissioner of Buildings and his two deputies accordingly administer an agency which has two quite distinctive assignments: first, the issuance of permits and certificates for all buildings and structures in the city under the terms of the city's Building Code, the state Labor Law, the rules and regulations of the city's Board of Standards and Appeals, and other related statutes and rules; second, the enforcement of safety and sanitary standards in multiple dwellings under the terms of the state Multiple Dwelling Law, the more stringent city Multiple Dwelling Code (a part of the Administrative Code), and other related statutes and rules. These two main tasks of the Department have some common elements, but they also bring to the Commissioner the difficulties of working under two quite different sets of rules, dealing with two sets of constituencies, and competing or cooperating with two groups of other governmental agencies. One assignment does not strengthen his hand in performing the other. Further, the laws and rules under which his agency exercises its powers are highly complex and detailed. They are less the product of his predecessors' recommendations than they are of the ceaseless efforts of his constituencies to win points in statute or rule. And both the courts and the Board of Standards and Appeals show a decided tendency to review his agency's actions in detail. The Commissioner's instructions thus come less from the Mayor than they do from state and local law and rules written for him by others, and under which his exercise of discretion is subject to close and frequent review by the Board and the courts.

Moreover, the Commissioner does not find it easy to establish his leadership or control over the internal organization of his department. Until 1957 the charter required that there be "in each borough a branch office and a borough superintendent." The Borough Superintendent was made, for all practical purposes, an autonomous official, his actions being subject to review only by the Board of Standards and Appeals—not by the Commissioner. This concession to borough autonomy, and to the interest groups accustomed to that arrangement, was also accompanied by a requirement that there should be a Division of Housing within the Department, its head to be one of the deputy commissioners. The Commissioner was able, in 1957, to gain greater control over his agency by reorganization, which placed Borough Superintendents under his supervision and permitted him to consolidate the functions and staff of the Housing Division with other functions of his agency. But the difficulties of internal control by the Commissioner persist. The attitudes and habits of the staff are set deep in the past arrangements, and the tenure and status of its members are protected by civil service law and rules enforced by the city's Personnel Department.

The Commissioner has no great assets when he deals with the other agencies of the city government. The organized groups in his constituency are in such matters more often hostile than helpful to him. His leverage with the Bureau of the Budget is accordingly slight, as it is also with the Personnel Department. He cannot often command high priority with the Law Department, upon whose staff he depends for assistance in the prosecution of housing violations. The Department of Investigation is not infrequently an inquisitor of his staff, as are also the District Attorneys, for the head of a regulatory agency soon learns that staff irregularities are an endemic phenomenon. Both the Fire Department and the Department of Air Pollution Control have inspectional and licensing powers that compete with their own. Inspections are also conducted by the Department of Health, partly under regulations of the Board of Health and partly under more general housing legislation; both the Department and the Board are said to be resentful of having to perform services they regard as more appropriate for the Department of Buildings, and they tend to be critical of every Buildings Commissioner. The State Department of Labor, too, is a critical observer of many of his actions. But most of all, the Commissioner of Buildings feels the supervisory weight of the Board of Standards and Appeals and of the courts: the Board not only makes rules for him to enforce, but it also has sweeping powers of review over the specific actions of his agency. The courts have equally extensive control over the sanctions (fines or imprisonment) which are his main reliance in the enforcement of safety and sanitary standards in multiple dwellings. In short, the Commissioner is not a favorably situated bargainer when he deals with the other agencies of the city government.

The Commissioner's difficulties arise in considerable part out of the nature of his interest group constituency. There are several elements in this constituency: the building and construction industry, the real estate owners and managers, the labor unions of the building and construction trades, the architectural and engineering professions, and the citizen and professional associations concerned with the housing conditions of the low-income population. Only the last-named—the housing groups—can be counted upon consistently by the Commissioner as defenders of his powers. All the others feel the pinch of his regulations and so are more inclined to limit than to expand his initiative and discretion. To the builders (for example, the Building Congress, the Building Trade Employers Association, the Metropolitan Builders Association), the permits and certificates of the Buildings Department are restraints which they prefer to minimize while acknowledging their necessity. The owners and managers of real estate (organized, for example, in the Real Estate Board of New York, the Commerce and Industry Association, and others) share these attitudes, as do the organizations of architects and engineers. To the interested labor unions (for example, the carpenters, bricklayers, electricians, plumbers, building employees), the Department of Buildings is a guardian of the gains which they have won in labor laws and building codes; they do not expect initiative and leadership from its leaders and staff.

The Commissioner of Buildings has few opportunities to cultivate active and helpful constituencies or to create a favorable climate of public opinion that would provide him with support and bargaining power. In this respect, he shares a common condition with most regulatory agencies: created often through the efforts of an aroused public opinion, they are gradually left to deal primarily with those whom they regulate. The Commissioner can expect occasional assistance from the civic groups (for example, the Citizens Union, the Citizens Housing and Planning Council), the charitable, religious, and social welfare groups (for example, the Community Council of New York), and from various tenant organizations (usually temporary in character). But these groups are more likely to be critical of his concessions to others than to give him consistent support. The press will take its main cues from these criticisms and from periodic investigations of alleged irregularities in the agency. No Commissioner of Buildings has ever been a hero to the city press.

The relations between the party leaders and the Department of Buildings have low visibility. Historically, these accommodations were arranged mainly in the semiautonomous borough offices and (except perhaps for multiple dwelling enforcement matters) seem still to be centered there despite the recent reorganization of the agency. In their dealings with the Department, the party leaders tend to share the views of the regulated groups that the Commissioner should be sympathetic and flexible in his use of the regulatory power. The party leaders have no disposition to encourage him in aggressive use or expansion of his jurisdiction. Only the Mayor has consistent tendencies to assist him in the vigorous exercise of his powers and duties, but the Mayor is isolated from the Department by the barriers of highly detailed statutes and rules, by the buffer of the autonomous Board of Standards and Appeals, and by the borough-centered traditions and loyalties of the staff.

Without other allies of weight and influence, without opportunities to form a broadly supporting public opinion, each Commissioner of Buildings is brought back, whatever his initial aspirations, to the necessity of a settlement with the groups whose activities he regulates. It is with them that he must make his peace.

Department of Health

The Commissioner of Health directs a line agency that has 5,000 employees and is engaged in wide-ranging assignments, including health research and services and the enforcement of sanitary regulations. The scope of these activities is suggested by the fact that in a typical recent year about 3,000,000 clinical examinations and 430,000 home visits were made by health service units, while 6,000,000 pounds of meat and 1,500,000 quarts of milk were checked for quality by the regulatory units. The regulatory assignment is the oldest function of the Department, research the second oldest, and health services the latest. Each of these three assignments presents a separate set of opportunities and difficulties to the Commissioner, and the relations of each to the other two are an additional problem.

The regulatory assignments of the Department are found primarily in the city's Sanitary Code, a set of regulations, having the force and effect of law, enacted by the city's Board of Health under authority granted by the state Public Health Law and the city charter; the Public Health Law and the charter make the Board in effect a special local legislature with power to add to or amend the existing regulations in all matters affecting health in the city. The Board is composed of five members: the Commissioner of Health is chairman; the remaining four members are appointed by the Mayor for eight-year, staggered terms. Two of the four members must be physicians who have had at least ten years' experience in clinical medicine or in public health to qualify for appointment; the Commissioner must be a physician with at least eight years of such experience. Members of the Board, other than the Commissioner, may be removed by the Mayor only on written charges and after a hearing before the Mayor. This powerful and unusual legislative institution (an appointed legislature with broad law-making powers, subject to no veto) is an important factor in the life of the Health Commissioner, its aura of power and influence including not only the regulatory powers of the Department (since the Board sits as a court of appeals from denials and revocations of licenses and from other acts of the Commissioner), but affecting its research and service programs as well.

The research assignments flow in part from the Sanitary Code and in part from the Department's own initiative, while the health services are hinged to state financial grants-in-aid (and, indirectly and less extensively, to federal grants) as well as to departmental initiative. Each of the three major assignments of the Department is interlaced with the assignments and jurisdictions of other city agencies: the regulatory assignment with the Departments of Air Pollution Control, Buildings, Public Works, Sanitation, Water Supply, and others; the research assignment with the Department of Hospitals and others; the health services with Education, Welfare, and many others. State and federal agencies (for example, the State Health Department, the United States Labor Department, the United States Public Health Service) also have their joint concerns with the city's Health Department. The Health Commissioner is required to exercise his leadership in an unusually complex environment.

The Health Commissioner's aspirations to secure internal control of the Department encounter the separatist and autonomous tendencies of the Department's three different bureaucratic groups, each clustered around one specialized assignment. The regulatory bureaus look more to the Sanitary Code for authority and guidance than to the Commissioner, partly, it would seem, because they feel their function does not rank first with the Commis-

sioner. The research groups are anchored in the Department's central bureaus and laboratories, proud of their history and of their contributions to
public health science, but frequently feeling, too, that their once-highest
priority on the Commissioner's agenda has been lost. The service groups are
clustered around the District Health Centers and the related central bureaus,
confident of their high priority, but long frustrated in their efforts to become
the Department's center of gravity. For more than forty years, Health Commissioners have sought to decentralize the major activities of the agency to
the District Health Centers as a method of giving greater emphasis to the
services of the Department and of "bringing the Department to the people."
The regulatory and the research bureaus have resisted, since 1915, and successive Commissioners have found it impossible or impractical to break the
stalemate.

The Commissioner is also confronted with the related stresses prevailing
between staff groups of different values and orientation; for example, inspectional groups, sanitary engineering groups, research scientists, clinical practitioners, nurses, health educators, and others. The Commissioner, in addition,
is dependent for a substantial amount of departmental work upon a medical
staff which is part time, its members being also engaged in private practice,
research, or teaching. These staff members have strong autonomous tendencies. Despite these several problems, the Health Commissioner does frequently succeed in introducing innovations in the policy, organization, and
methods of the Department, his opportunities to do so being greatest in the
service assignment, much less in the domains of the regulatory and the
research bureaus. Securing internal control is, for him, an arduous but not
impossible task.

The interest group constituency of the Health Department presents the
Commissioner with a more difficult set of forces if he wishes to be himself a
source of initiative and innovation. The Mayor is most likely to have appointed the Commissioner upon the nomination of some of the important
health and medical groups. The Commissioner is required by the charter to
be a member of the health and medical profession; and it is not unknown for
the Commissioner to choose a deputy commissioner for the Department after
consultation with the appropriate constituency groups. These factors make
for a considerable dependency by the Commissioner upon the health and
medical groups. These groups—the county medical societies, the State
Medical Society, the American Medical Association, the New York Academy
of Medicine, the American Public Health Association, the medical schools
and the schools of public health, and the various associations of laymen
interested in health and medicine—have the most privileged access to the
Department. Their assistance is requested or offered on many matters. The
professional staff of the Department are members and often leaders in these

groups, the most influential of which are informally represented on the Board of Health. The Commissioner's innovations must fall within their range of tolerance if he is to escape frustration. If he needs constituency support, as he almost always does, his ideas must closely conform to theirs before positive help is granted.

The constituency groups whose members' activities or properties are inspected, licensed, or regulated by the Health Department have a different attitude toward the Commissioner. The groups representing the food industry (processors and vendors of meat, milk, and other foods), the restaurants and hotels, the drug industry, the landlords and managers of multiple dwellings— all these feel the regulatory weight of the Department and attempt to modify its rules and its enforcement activities toward convenient accommodations with their practices. They address their attention to the Board of Health when they feel the Commissioner is too aggressive in policy or inspection. If the Board does not listen, they seek to inhibit any expansion of regulatory budgets or staffs. The constituency groups in the regulatory field of the Commissioner's work do not object to the Department's role as a "better business bureau" for the regulated industries, imposing governmental sanctions against those who violate the industry's own code, but they lack enthusiasm for any regulatory policy which moves beyond that level of minimum regulation, and they will usually resist such innovations forcefully. The Health Commissioner cannot often count upon these constituency groups for help in the exercise of initiative and leadership in health administration.

The Board of Health and the Health Commissioner together represent an impressive concentration of self-contained power and influence but are relatively isolated from the representative organs of the city government. When the Board and the Commissioner proposed in 1954 that the city's water supply be treated with fluoride as a preventive against tooth decay, they had no difficulty in securing the strong support of their health and medical constituency groups. But the Board and the Commissioner could not themselves carry out this program, as they can many other programs. A budget appropriation (to the Department of Water Supply, Gas, and Electricity) by the Board of Estimate was necessary, and the actual fluoridation was an assignment for the chemists, engineers, and other staff of the Water Supply Department. The support of the Mayor was not too difficult to enlist, but the Board and the Commissioner could not get much further in four years of effort. The Water Supply staff and Commissioner resisted the proposal, seeing its performance as a risk and burden for them while all credit for success would go to the Health Department. The climactic public hearings of the Board of Estimate in 1957 saw a great demonstration of unity and strength by the Board of Health, the Commissioner of Health and the Health staff, the health and medical constituency groups and their allies—all performing their appropriate tasks in a highly articulate and coherent presentation of the case for fluoridation. The opposition was heterogeneous, emotional, often incoherent. But the Health Board, the Commissioner, the leaders of the health and medical groups spoke as comparative strangers to the members of the Board of Estimate. They had not often been before that Board, relying usually upon their own self-sufficient legislative and administrative powers and resources. Confronted by a choice between the proposal of one group of comparative strangers and the intense opposition of another, the members of the Board of Estimate took the course of prudence and least immediate risk. In an act characteristic of the Board as an institution, they postponed action. The Health Commissioner and his allies continued their efforts, but at the end of 1959 the Board of Estimate still held the proposal under consideration. Isolation from the city's general political institutions had revealed one of its costs for the Health Commissioner.

Department of Hospitals

The Commissioner of Hospitals heads one of the city's largest line agencies. In 1957 his staff numbered almost 36,000, operated 15 general and 13 specialized hospitals (in which more than 260,000 patients spent over six million patient-days); in addition, it provided almost 800,000 patient-days of home care and handled two and a half million clinic visits. Established as a Department in 1929 to take over the activities of the Board of Trustees of Bellevue and Allied Hospitals, the Board of Ambulance Service, the hospital services of the Health Department, and other hospital units and activities, the Department of Hospitals is still a loose-knit confederation of separate institutions and activities. The Department has two main formal assignments: to provide hospital care "primarily for . . . the indigent poor" of the city; and to regulate the private proprietary hospitals and other private proprietary institutions for medical or nursing care, unless these are otherwise supervised. The Department also engages in extensive programs of medical and nursing education and research, especially in collaboration with the six medical schools in the city that are affiliated with the Department.

The Commissioner of Hospitals shares his powers with a Board of Hospitals, an Advisory Council, and (in each hospital) a Medical Board. His opportunities for leadership and initiative by securing internal control over the Department are accordingly severely limited. He is more nearly a presiding officer, a spokesman, an ambassador of the Department than he is its directing head.

The Board of Hospitals consists of the Commissioner as chairman and ten members, "five of whom shall be doctors of medicine possessed of broad medical, public health and hospital background and experience, and five of whom shall be laymen distinguished in community or business affairs."

The ten members are appointed by the Mayor for five-year terms, the terms of one physician and one layman expiring each year. They serve without compensation and may be removed only on charges by, and after a hearing before, the Mayor. The Board has extensive powers over the Department: the development and maintenance of long-range programs of hospital service; the development and enforcement of standards and methods of efficiency in the Department; the approval of the capital and expense budget estimates of the Department before the Commissioner submits them to the City Planning Commission, the Budget Director, or the Mayor; the review of any action of the Commissioner with respect to the revocation of a license. The Board is also empowered to promulgate a Hospital Code, and to add to or amend it; a violation of the Code is a misdemeanor. The Board's promulgation or amendment of the Code does not require any further approval; it takes effect after filing with the City Clerk and publication in the *City Record* for three days. The Commissioner is thus made, in effect, the agent of the Board in the general management of the Department.

The Advisory Council consists of one representative selected from and by the Medical Board of each hospital in the Department (28 in 1958) and seven members, who need not be physicians, appointed by the Mayor. The members of the Council serve without compensation and their terms are indefinite. The Council has a broad and ambiguous assignment: In the words of the charter, it is to "advise the commissioner in respect to all matters submitted by him" and "on its own initiative [to] recommend to the commissioner such changes of administration in the department or in any hospital or institution or service under the jurisdiction as may seem to it advisable." It is to have access to "all records and other documents" of the Department. The Council is in essence a device for protecting the autonomy of the 28 separate hospitals, and the Medical Board in each of them, against any inclination on the part of the Commissioner to integrate or centralize the management of the Department. In view of this, no Commissioner has tried very vigorously to move in such a direction, and the Council has consequently been quite inactive.

The Medical Board in each hospital—the attending and consulting physicians and surgeons—is appointed by the medical staff, subject to such general rules as the Commissioner may prescribe. While the Commissioner appoints the initial medical staff for each new hospital, every subsequent medical staff vacancy is filled by the Commissioner only after consultation with the Medical Board, and medical staff appointments may be terminated by him only after such consultation. The Medical Board also nominates the medical house officers for appointment by the Commissioner. Consequently, except for his initial staff appointments, the Commissioner has little voice in the composition of Board or staff. The Medical Board in each hospital is also empowered to establish regulations to govern the medical procedures in the hospital and, after approval by the Commissioner, these procedures must be enforced by the superintendent or other head of the hospital.

The 28 separate Medical Boards are the centers of gravity in the management of the Department. Their members are not employees of the Commissioner or his agents, the hospital superintendents. They are physicians in private practice, contributing their part-time services to the Department as attending and consulting physicians. (Together with their colleagues on the medical staffs, they constitute 7,500 of the Department's staff of 9,500 physicians.) The Commissioner, the hospital superintendents, and the deputy superintendents are dependent upon the Medical Boards and the medical staffs; the latter have no comparable dependence upon him or his superintendents.

The Commissioner has other difficulties in securing internal control over the Department he is presumed to lead. One of these is presented by the unusual personnel system under which he is required to operate. Of his 36,000 employees, only five positions are in the "exempt" class—that is, available to him (subject to bargaining with party leaders and the Mayor) for his use as positions for the general management of the Department. To add to his difficulties, only about 8,400 jobs are in the "competitive" class; of the remainder, 26,200 are "noncompetitive" and 1,400 are in the "labor" class. Many of the noncompetitive and labor positions are difficult to recruit for, or have high turnover rates, or are low-paid and otherwise unattractive. Party leaders sometimes make patronage demands for these posts on behalf of constituents with few other job opportunities, and Commissioners cannot easily reject such demands even when the persons recommended are liabilities rather than assets. In more recent years, the State, County and Municipal Employees union of the American Federation of Labor and Congress of Industrial Organizations (AFL-CIO) has made rapid progress in organizing the noncompetitive and labor employees. None of these circumstances assists the Commissioner in his efforts to lead the Department.

Nor does the Hospitals Commissioner derive many opportunities for leadership from his relations to the interest groups in the Department's constituency. The most powerful of these—the medical societies, the medical schools, the voluntary and proprietary hospitals and other comparable institutions in the city, the nursing schools and organizations, the lay groups in the health field, the social workers and related groups—do not need his help. They have superior access in their relations with the Hospital Board and the Medical Boards. On the rare occasions when they disagree among themselves, the Commissioner assumes great risks of future difficulties if he does not remain neutral. Other interest groups, such as the religious groups in the birth control controversy of 1957–1958, find the Commissioner vulnerable to their intervention, while the communication media urge him to exercise a leadership he does not have the resources to assume.

Board of Education

The school system of the city constitutes the largest of the city's line agencies. In 1957 its staff numbered almost 50,000; its annual operating budget reached $470 million; its annual capital budget amounted to an additional $113 million. Almost one million students attended the 828 schools in the system.

The direction of this complex enterprise was long shared by the Board of Education, its formal head, with the Board of Superintendents, which was

TABLE 40. SUPERINTENDENTS OF NEW YORK CITY SCHOOLS: PREVIOUS POSITIONS AND TENURE IN OFFICE

Superintendent	Position at time of appointment	Tenure as superintendent
William H. Maxwell	Superintendent of Schools, City of Brooklyn, 1887–1898	1898–1918
William L. Ettinger	Associate Superintendent, New York City schools, 1913–1918	1918–1924
William J. O'Shea	Associate Superintendent, New York City schools, 1918–1924	1924–1934
Harold G. Campbell	Associate Superintendent, New York City schools, 1924–1934	1934–1942
John E. Wade	Associate Superintendent, New York City schools, 1927–1942	1942–1947
William Jansen	Assistant Superintendent, New York City schools, 1935–1947	1947–1958
John J. Theobald	President of Queens College, 1949–1958; on leave as Deputy Mayor, 1956–1958; first "outsider" selected for Superintendent in six decades.	1958–

SOURCE: Compiled from the records of the New York City Board of Education, 1898–1959.

more nearly the agency's actual center of gravity. The Board of Education is composed of nine nonsalaried members, each serving a seven-year term, the expiration dates being staggered. The members are appointed by the Mayor but may be removed by him only on formal charges and after a hearing. Two members must be appointed from each borough except Richmond, which has one member. The Board of Education, in turn, appoints the Superintendent of Schools and, upon his nomination, a Deputy Superintendent and eight Associate Superintendents; these ten officials constitute the Board of Superintendents. Although these ten school officials are formally appointed for six-year terms, they invariably serve in their posts until retirement. They may be removed by the Board of Education during term only on formal charges and after a hearing. These 19 officials (the 9 members of the Board of

Education and the 10 members of the Board of Superintendents) are, once appointed, secure in their offices. For many years they presided together over a separate principality of the city government, dependent upon the Mayor and the Board of Estimate for their budgets, subject to detailed provisions of the state Education Law and to the supervision of the State Department of Education, but more nearly autonomous in relation to the central institutions of the city government than any other agency (save perhaps the Triborough Bridge and Tunnel Authority). Changes in the Education Law and in the by-laws of the Board of Education in recent years have formally strengthened the hand of the Superintendent, and reduced the power of the Board of Superintendents to override his wishes. The new Superintendent appointed in 1958 seems aware of his broadened prerogatives and prepared to exercise them, but it remains to be seen whether even a better armed and unusually determined man can succeed in escaping from the traditional restraints upon his discretion.

The Superintendent of Schools is the visible, full-time, permanent head of the school system, comparable in some degree to the commissioner who heads the more typical line agency. He exercises his powers, however, in a more complex environment; his difficulties and frustrations are correspondingly greater. These begin with the barriers which stand between him and the achievement of sufficient internal control over his department to assure some opportunity for leadership and initiative of his own. There are at least four of these barriers. First, the Education Law and the by-laws of the Board of Education require a great multitude of exceedingly detailed proposals from the Superintendent to come before it for reference to its committees prior to formal Board action. Second, the Board of Superintendents guards the precedents and traditions of the system against any innovations proposed by the Superintendent, delaying its support until the momentum is lost, or withholding its approval altogether. Third, the state Education Law in its details (themselves most often the product of past staff strategies), and the State Education Department as the statute's guardian, inhibit the Superintendent's aspirations for leadership. Fourth, the organized bureaucracies of the school system resist any of the Superintendent's inclinations toward changes which do not appeal to them. Against these barriers the Superintendent has insufficient leverage to accomplish much in terms of his own leadership. He must wait patiently for the rare opportunities which come his way to influence the internal organization of his agency, or its staffing practices, or its educational policies.

The Superintendent of Schools is enclosed by the Board of Education on the one hand and (unless the present incumbent is able to depart from heretofore standard practice) by the Board of Superintendents on the other, much as the Mayor is absorbed into the Board of Estimate. The two school Boards each operate in an environment of low visibility approaching complete privacy. The Superintendent must, in effect, exercise his leadership within two separate caucuses, and he cannot ordinarily first address his proposals, or appeal from Board decisions, to a larger public forum. Instead, he is under compelling pressure to preserve the outward appearances of agreement and unanimity.

The Board of Education conducts most of its business through its five standing committees: Finance and Budget, Buildings and Sites, Law, Instructional Affairs, Retirement. These committees are not only the main engines of Board influence upon the Superintendent and the school system; they are also the main gateways for the entry of other participants: the Budget Director and the City Planning Commission seeking to influence operating or capital budget decisions, a Borough President seeking to influence the location of a new school, a religious group seeking to influence instructional policy or a personnel action, another interest group seeking to influence school construction decisions, a party leader sponsoring a promotion for a constituent, a teachers' organization opposing a Superintendent's proposal. The Board's committees are bargaining stations in the school system's political process, but the committees are themselves participants in the bargaining. Their main target of influence is the Superintendent. Their methods are to delay, to modify, to veto his proposals, as ways of securing concessions from him which will contribute to their own goals or will satisfy some of the demands upon them by other participants.

The Superintendent of Schools nominates the Deputy Superintendent and the eight Associate Superintendents for appointment by the Board of Education, but this does not mean that his leadership and initiative are enthusiastically accepted by the members of the Board of Superintendents. He nominates them from a limited field of eligibles. Despite their limited (six-year) terms, reappointment in office is normally almost assured, so that their position comes close to permanent tenure. At least until very recently, the Superintendent has to them been simply the chairman of a committee (the Board of Superintendents) with one vote in ten—one of their number, elevated by chance or influence, expected to conform to their settled traditions and values, and especially so in dealing with the fields of their specialized assignments. For more than forty years successive Boards of Superintendents have patiently instructed Superintendents in the limits of power, the risks of innovation, and the necessities of unanimity if the Superintendent is to bargain successfully with the Board of Education. In the closed world in which these ten school officials operate, each familiar with the values and aspirations of the others and accustomed to mutual accommodations, the strongest inclinations run toward minimal changes in institutional habits. Even bold and energetic Superintendents quickly learn how inelastic is their organizational environment. The Board of Superintendents has other assets in its task of keeping the Superintendent within its orbit of influence. The state Education Law limits the initiative and discretion of the Superintendent; the State Department of Education limits him further; the organized teachers' groups are a potent source of restraints. Even more specific restraints upon his discretion are enforced by the Board of Examiners, a statutory board of members holding permanent tenure, which examines all applicants for entrance as teachers and members of the system for promotion to higher ranks, and thus control the eligibles from among whom the Superintendent must choose in nominating persons for appointment to all key posts up to the rank of assistant superintendent. He cannot break out of the closed world of his organization and recruit "new blood" to assist him with innovative ideas and strategic support. He cannot even choose freely from within the organization itself. (Superintendent Jansen spent three years, from 1955 to 1958, attempting to secure his own inside choice as science director, succeeding only in August, 1958, on the eve of his retirement. Superintendents cannot fight many such battles.)

In sum, the Superintendent of Schools presides over but cannot lead the school system. His opportunities for initiative are squeezed within narrow confines by a triangle of forces—those embodied in the Board of Education, in the Board of Superintendents, and in the organized teachers' groups—and this triangle is reinforced by the statutory details which the three groups, separately and together, have over the years succeeded in having placed in the state Education Law and guarded by the watchful eye of the State Department of Education. The isolation of the Superintendent from the Mayor does not add to the Superintendent's autonomy and leadership; instead, it helps to explain his subordination to the triangle of forces which surrounds him.

When the school officials (in their corporate unity) cross the East River from their Brooklyn headquarters to deal with the Mayor and the Board of Estimate at City Hall, they come mainly to talk about money and budgets, although they will come to the Mayor also when harassed by investigations into juvenile delinquency or other forms of trouble which they hope the Mayor will shoulder as more his problem than theirs. In the budget processes, whether for operating expenses or capital expenditures, the school officials are the largest single claimants for the scarce resources of city moneys. They are privileged claimants, too, with more numerous and articulate supporters than opponents. If they get less than they ask for, in the sharp competition with other claimants, they are also treated with deference. Nevertheless, in these sessions they are often required to bargain: to accept a different location for a school, under the combined or separate pressures of a parents' group, a real estate group, the Budget Director, the Comptroller, or a Borough President; to acknowledge barbs of criticism from a member of the Board of Estimate for alleged arrogance or aloofness toward a past request by the member and to promise future sympathetic consideration; to defend some educational or fiscal policy, often conceding error and assuring remedy before the next budget request. For the moment, the isolation and autonomy of the school system is pierced and its officials are held accountable for some of their actions to someone other than themselves. But the moment is brief and the scrutiny is inescapably limited in scope. The self-governing status of the school officialdom and its allied bureaucracy is only mildly impaired.

The school officials must deal also with a complex and many-sided constituency of interest groups. Some of these have privileged access and decided influence, some are aggressive although lacking easy access, some are quiet and persistent in the pursuit of specialized goals, some are dependent upon the officials and follow their lead, and others are temporary and concentrate upon an immediate issue. The net impact of all is reduced by their competition with each other and by the sophistication of the school officials in dealing with them.

The religious groups have the most intimate access. A long tradition of having each of the three major religious faiths in the city represented on the Board of Education was institutionalized in 1948 by expanding the Board membership from seven to nine, making it possible to allocate three seats to each faith. Ethnic and racial accommodations are also made within this religious distribution. There are also strong pressures to extend "balanced representation" of these ethnic, racial, and religious groups downward into the membership of the Board of Superintendents and the holders of other key director positions. The architects of these arrangements, including the school officials and the religious group leaders, presumably anticipate peace and equilibrium as a consequence of this controlled competition. Its effects upon the doctrines of secular education are not discussed by the framers of the settlement. The observable consequence is that the leaders of religious groups, and the leaders of associated ethnic and racial groups, are given a special access to the administrators of the school system, and that the Board of Education exercises virtually no control over any school sponsored by a religious body.

A more localized and more amorphous constituency element is institutionalized in the 54 local boards, each consisting of 5 unsalaried members, appointed by the Borough Presidents (14 boards in Manhattan, 10 in The Bronx, 20 in Brooklyn, 8 in Queens, and 2 in Richmond). Through these local boards, whose formal responsibilities are ambiguous, the Borough Presidents, the Assembly District party leaders, assemblymen and councilmen, parent groups, local religious and patriotic groups, and other local interests find opportunities to influence assistant superintendents (one for each board's district) and school principals in some of the minutiae of local school administration. The local boards and their activities are not looked upon with favor by the Board of Education, the Board of Superintendents, or the organized teachers' groups. Their formal assignment is therefore unlikely to be either clarified or expanded, although there have been some attempts at this recently.

The number, location, and construction of new schools is an issue which tends to break out of the ordinary pattern of school officials' decision-making. The Board of Education's Committee on Buildings and Sites is one of the Board's most influential groups. Its course tends to be somewhat autonomous in relation both to the Board of Education and to the Board of Superintendents. The Committee tries to anticipate the forces it will encounter in the long road it must travel from its first proposal to a finished school building: its own hearings on plans and proposals from the Superintendent's special staffs, the Board's hearings, the City Planning Commission's hearings on the capital budget, the Board of Estimate's hearings on the same, the acquisition of the site, the approval of building plans, the appropriation of the funds for construction, the letting and approval of contracts for construction and equipment. At each of these stages there are opportunities for intervention and influence by other officials, other agencies, parents' groups, economy groups, ethnic and racial and religious groups, real estate groups, party leaders, architectural firms, builders, suppliers, and others. The interest group constituency of the Board of Estimate (reflected especially in the offices of Borough Presidents) tends to dominate this process more than does the constituency of the Board of Education.

Other interest groups seek to influence other types of decisions in the conduct of the public schools. For example, the Public Education Association, an elite organization of limited membership and rather general educational goals, depending largely upon the communication media for its exercise of influence, sought unsuccessfully in 1957 to persuade the Board of Education to appoint a citizens' committee to assist the Board in its recruitment of a new Superintendent of Schools. The Citizens Committee for Children, a comparable organization, seeks mainly to introduce into the school system the values and methods of social workers, child psychologists, and psychiatrists. The city units of the National Association for the Advancement of Colored People and the Urban League, by contrast, have in recent years led determined and dramatic assaults upon the Board in the interests of more complete racial integration, recruiting many allies in their drive and compelling the Board of Education to yield ground. The Board of Superintendents and the teachers' organizations, however, have been less influenced by the demands that they alter settled practices in school zoning and teacher assignments.

The parents' groups are the least influential of the nongovernmental associations with which the school officials deal. These groups, including their central organizations—the citywide United Parents Association, for example, and Federations of Mothers Clubs in the boroughs—are dependent upon the school officials for their agenda, their information, their methods. They move within the orbit of officialdom, assistants to and allies of the officials, especially in their local units. Minor triumphs are occasionally theirs when they influence the location of a school, a local safety arrangement for the children, a personnel change in a particular school, or the physical rehabilitation of a school building. Upon the central policies and practices of officialdom and bureaucracy, the parent organizations have a peripheral impact only. They almost always follow the lead of the school officials.

The city's school officials, as the heads of a separate governmental principality, find it necessary to yield their autonomy at important points to only four groups: the three religious groups who have established their claim to equal representation in the top command positions; the Board of Estimate and its constituency groups in the capital budget process; the State Department of Education as the guardian of the state Education Law; and the organized teachers on the staff of the school system. The Superintendent of Schools does not enjoy sole and full command of the system. Leadership has instead been syndicated in the two Boards, the Superintendent being, at least until recently, *primus inter pares*. The 19 school officials in whom leadership is syndicated have an intimate relationship with the leaders of three of the groups with whom they must share power: the leaders of the religious groups, the leaders of the State Department of Education, the leaders of the teachers' organizations. The Board of Estimate and its allies are the only outsiders able to intervene. On balance, the school officials enjoy an unusual capacity for self government.

Police Department[1]

The Police Commissioner heads the most visible, the most publicized, the most dramatic and controversial of the city's line agencies. His Department is also one of the city's largest, its staff numbering over 26,000 at the end of 1957, of which more than 25,000 were members of the uniformed force. Representing one of the oldest of the city government's functions, but confronted with constantly changing problems and pressures in its assignments, the Department presents to the Police Commissioner and his deputies complexities and dilemmas not often matched in difficulty in the city's other line agencies.

The Police Department has the broadest regulatory assignment among all the regulatory activities of the city government. From the charter alone, the Department derives a sweeping obligation and power to "preserve the public peace, prevent crime, detect and arrest offenders, . . . preserve order . . . , enforce and prevent the violation of all laws and ordinances . . . ," accom-

[1] See Chart 18, p. 266.

TABLE 41. NEW YORK CITY POLICE COMMISSIONERS, CAREER AND NONCAREER INCUMBENTS,[a] 1898–1959

Commissioner	Tenure as commissioner	Prior experience: highest career (C) position in dept. or principal noncareer (NC) position		
		Position	C	NC
Bernard J. York, Pres.[b]	Jan., 1898–Feb., 1901	Clerk of Court Special Sessions—Kings		x
John B. Sexton	Jan., 1898–Feb., 1901	Under-sheriff, N. Y. County		x
Theodore L. Hamilton	Jan., 1898–May, 1898	Contractor and builder, N. Y. County		x
William E. Philips	Jan., 1898–May, 1898	Produce business, Kings		x
Jacob Hess	May, 1898–Feb., 1901	Member, Board of Electrical Control		x
Henry E. Abell	Jan., 1899–Feb., 1901	Member, N. Y. S. Assembly		x
Michael C. Murphy	Feb., 1901–Dec., 1901	Member, N. Y. S. Senate		x
John N. Partridge	Jan., 1902–Dec., 1902	State Supt. of Public Works		x
Francis J. Greene	Jan., 1903–Dec., 1903	Maj. Gen., U.S. Army Retired; Corporate Director		x
William McAdoo	Jan., 1904–Dec., 1905	U.S. Congress, Asst. Sec'y, Navy		x
Theodore A. Bingham	Jan., 1906–July, 1909	Brig. Gen., U.S. Army Retired		x
William F. Baker	July, 1909–Oct., 1910	Member, City Civil Service Commission		x
James C. Cropsey	Oct., 1910–May, 1911	Private practice of law		x
Rhinelander Waldo	May, 1911–Dec., 1913	Deputy Police Commissioner[c]		x
Douglas I. McKay	Jan., 1914–Apr., 1914	1st Deputy Police Commissioner[c]		x
Arthur Woods	Apr., 1914–Dec., 1917	4th Deputy Police Commissioner[c] and cotton broker		x
Frederick H. Bugher	Jan., 1918–Jan., 1918	1st Deputy Police Commissioner[c]		x
Richard E. Enright	Jan., 1918–Dec., 1925	Police Captain	x	
George V. McLaughlin	Jan., 1926–Apr., 1927	Deputy State Bank Supt.		x
Joseph A. Warren	Apr., 1927–Dec., 1928	Atty. for State Health Department; Commissioner of Accounts		x
Grover A. Whalen	Dec., 1928–May, 1930	Business Manager; Commissioner of Public Works		x
Edward P. Mulrooney	May, 1930–Apr., 1933	Asst. Chief Inspector	x	
James S. Bolan	Apr., 1933–Dec., 1933	Deputy Inspector	x	
John F. O'Ryan	Jan., 1934–Sept., 1934	Maj. Gen., U.S. Army Retired; State Transit Comm.		x
Lewis J. Valentine	Sept., 1934–Sept., 1945	Chief Inspector	x	
Arthur W. Wallander	Sept., 1945–Mar., 1949	Deputy Chief Inspector	x	
William P. O'Brien	Mar., 1949–Sept., 1950	3rd Deputy Commissioner	x	
Thomas F. Murphy	Sept., 1950–July, 1951	Asst. U.S. Attorney, Southern N.Y. District		x
George P. Monaghan	July, 1951–Dec., 1953	Fire Commissioner		x
Francis W. H. Adams	Jan., 1954–July, 1955	Asst. U.S. Attorney General; lawyer		x
Stephen P. Kennedy	Aug., 1955 to date	Chief Inspector	x	

[a] *Career:* service in the ranks of the police force filled on a competitive basis. *Noncareer:* service outside the Department or in Deputy Commissioner positions.

[b] 1898–1900, a Board of Police Commissioners: 4 members, bipartisan.

[c] Served more than two years in Department, but not careerists.

SOURCE: Lowi, Theodore J., *At the Pleasure of the Mayor.* Doctoral dissertation, Yale University, 1960, unpublished.

panied by a series of more specific assignments. But the greater body of the Department's assignments comes from state laws and local ordinances and codes containing extensive regulatory and law enforcement provisions which the Department is expected to apply to all violators. Still other provisions of charter and statute make the Police Commissioner the licensing, inspecting, or supervising authority over certain trades (for example, public dance halls, cabarets, taxicabs and taxi drivers, pawnbrokers, cartmen, and others). To all these regulatory assignments of the Department there must also be added the traditional and widespread expectations that the police force is a service agency, obliged to attend to the countless necessities and conveniences of an urban population for whom the police are a visible and available resource. The Commissioner can find few boundaries to his responsibilities; he has less difficulty in discovering the limits of his opportunities and resources.

The Police Commissioner's hopes for the exercise of personal leadership and initiative as the responsible head of his Department revolve around his capacity to secure internal control over his agency, his relations with the Mayor, with other city officials and the party leaders, and with the Department's complex constituency. These basic conditions of his leadership and initiative are rarely fully mastered by the Police Commissioner. Resolute outsiders and insiders, in their turn as Commissioners, have each expended great energies and varied strategies upon this dilemma without triumphant results. Other Commissioners have accepted the prevailing arrangements, expressing satisfaction in quite marginal increments of change; still others have moved quickly on to more responsible or less taxing environments.

Securing internal control of the Department is the insurmountable barrier to leadership, initiative, and innovation by Police Commissioners. The Commissioner is not lacking in formal power for this purpose. The charter declares that he "shall have cognizance and control of the government, administration, disposition and discipline of the department, and control of the police force of the department" and, further, that he "shall be the chief executive officer of the police force." But these formal powers must in reality be exercised in the context of a personnel system which blunts their use, in the face of the close-knit organized police bureaucracies determined to limit the Commissioner's initiative and discretion, and through an organization structure designed to preserve the traditions of the force and its settled patterns of operation. The Commissioner has few "civilian" helpers; they are mainly clerical and custodial. The personnel system dictates that every member of the uniformed police force must be first recruited and inducted as a patrolman, a "rookie" without special skills or knowledge who enters upon a long apprenticeship in the tradition-centered doctrines and practices of the force, rising slowly rank by rank through examinations which also emphasize seniority and mastery of the Department's established codes of police practice.

The police captains who emerge from this process of advancement by apprenticeship, indoctrination, and seniority constitute the pool of talent from which the Commissioner must select his officers for the command posts and the managerial tasks of the Department—the deputy inspectors, the inspectors, the deputy chief inspectors, the assistant chief inspectors, and the Chief Inspector who is the head of the uniformed force. In recent decades, Police Commissioners have increasingly chosen, or have been persuaded, to select their deputy commissioners from this group also. Thus the Commissioner is enclosed within (or ostracized by, if he does not conform) a personnel system which limits his choices of key personnel and provides him but rarely with fellow champions of innovation, or with experts and specialists in fields of knowledge (technological and sociological) which might transform police administration under his leadership, or even with that modicum of competition in ideas among different segments of his staff which might give him limited opportunities for catalytic action as Commissioner.

If the personnel system confronts the Commissioner with a tradition-centered top command—"the top brass," composed of approximately 100 inspectors at various grades and of not quite 200 captains—the organized police bureaucracies (lieutenants, sergeants, patrolmen) bring additional restrictive pressures to bear upon him. Mayor McClellan observed long ago that the Police Department was "run by the inspectors," not by the Commissioner; for the past several decades, he would have needed to add "and by the police bureaucracies." They have power inside the Department to mold the behavior of their members in such ways as will reduce the impact of any change in policy or procedure sponsored by the Commissioner. They have secured special protections for their members in both state statutes and city rules, which preserve their capacity to resist without much risk of reprisal or severe discipline. They have power in the more general political arena, where officials and party leaders have learned to listen to them and to act sympathetically. Police Commissioners may bristle at bureaucratic boldness and evoke the symbols of command and discipline, but the organized police groups are confident and persistent; they are on familiar ground and have often waited out these storms before. Their goal is self-direction in their accustomed ways, not an eager responsiveness to either the "top brass" or the current Commissioner.

The twin forces of the Department's closed personnel system and the organized police bureaucracies help to preserve a third barrier to leadership by the Commissioner—an organization structure awkwardly suited to the Commissioner's purposes of leadership and innovation. The basic structure is traditional and does not yield much to the requirements of changes in policies and in assignments, or of advances in police technology developed elsewhere. Organizationally, the Department is wedded to performing its work through

geographical units—precincts, districts and divisions, borough commands—
at the expense of greater specialization and mobility of its resources. The
major concessions to specialization which have been made (the detective,
traffic, and emergency service patrol groups) are themselves each organized
geographically. In this and other ways specialized personnel is almost invariably squeezed into the geographical chains-of-command. Methods and procedures must also conform to the mold of geography, affecting adversely the
attraction and feasibility of almost every proposed change in technology or
policy. Police Commissioners are only occasionally aware of this tyranny of
geography as an organizational vise; they have no managerial staff to develop
for them the alternatives in police organization and procedures which might
give them unsuspected opportunities for breaking the crust of custom and
habits in police administration. For example, the Police Commissioner was
forced in 1949 to yield the traffic planning assignment to a new city agency
because his personnel system and his organizational arrangements could produce neither the specialized personnel (the traffic planners, traffic engineers,
and statistical analysts) nor the specialized methods necessary to handle the
traffic problem at a high level of experiment and innovation.

The closed personnel system, the power of the police bureaucracies, and
the inflexible organization structure of the Department have an additional
by-product for the Commissioner: he must expend a great part of his energies
in attempts at "policing the police." His problems are concentrated in two
phenomena: police corruption and police violence. However aggressively the
Commissioner pursues the goal of police integrity by the use of special squads
to investigate the force, by shake-ups and transfers of command, by swift
suspensions and other forms of discipline, he accepts ultimately that police
corruption is endemic to his organization, and that he is fortunate if he can
prevent its reaching epidemic proportions. He lacks the resources to do more.
On the score of police violence, he is compelled to yield in a different fashion:
he must almost invariably take a tough line in justification of the use of force
by the police, whether it be rationalizing the promiscuous use of the club,
the gun, or the "third degree." His organization (and his own training,
if he is a career Commissioner) does not permit him to depart from this
doctrine.

Police Commissioners thus exercise formal but essentially peripheral control over the Police Department. They can dramatize the role of the Department in the life of the city; they can urge forcefully and often successfully the
expansion of the Department in numbers and budget and thus win some
internal support; they can lead crusades against selected targets ("round-ups"
of alleged vagrants; raids on gamblers, narcotic "rings," houses of prostitution; arrests of alleged subversives); and they can be stern disciplinarians in
dealing with individual members of the force who violate overtly the regula-

tions of the Department. But these are the outer boundaries of their control. The more positive measures of leadership are beyond their reach.

Police Commissioners in New York City have long sought an autonomous status for their Department with freedom from supervision by the Mayor, from interventions by party leaders, and from jurisdictional invasions by other governmental agencies. "No outside interference" has been their uniform motto for several decades, and all external influences have usually been condemned as "politics." In seeking to maximize the self-directing capacity of the Department, Commissioners have presumably sought also to maximize their own opportunities for leadership and direction of the police agency. But autonomy for the Department has also meant isolation for the Commissioner from sources which might help him in his difficult task of securing internal control. The police bureaucracy seems to be the main beneficiary of the autonomy which the Police Commissioners have secured.

Freedom from supervision by the Mayor has been a special target of the drive for police autonomy. Mayoral interest in police policy and police administration has been consistently rebuffed by equating it with the interests of party leaders or, more ambiguously, with politics. In their acceptance of this formula for ostracizing Mayors from any opportunities to assume general responsibility for leadership in law enforcement, the Police Commissioners have had the support of the police bureaucracy, the civic groups, the communication media, and others. There is a general consensus that Mayors merit only the blame for police failures. The assistance which Mayors might give Police Commissioners in their efforts to acquire leadership within the Department has been forfeited in preference for the ambiguous formula of autonomy.

Removal of the influence of party leaders from police administration has also been a goal of most Police Commissioners, supported by the police bureaucracy and by almost all the articulate voices in the city. Several Commissioners have given this problem high priority, and the long-term trend in the Department has been to reduce steadily the opportunities of party leaders to intervene overtly either in the personnel system or in police policy. The most striking example is the neutralization of the police role in election administration. The upper limits of the trend are to be found, however, in the disposition of individual members of the force to build mutually useful relationships with party leaders. If party leaders have been largely excluded at headquarters, they are not yet ignored in the precincts or other local commands. One consequence of this development may be that the Commissoner is isolated from the party leaders in a way in which his lieutenants, detectives, captains, and inspectors are not.

Other governmental agencies give Police Commissioners less difficulty. The Police Commissioners are especially able to escape some of the tight controls of the overhead agencies—Budget, Personnel, Law, Investigation, and others—which so often burden the discretion of other department heads. With other line agencies, the relations are often more complex and sometimes characterized by jurisdictional friction, for example, with District Attorneys, and the Departments of Education, Fire, Health, Sanitation, Traffic, Welfare, the Youth Board, and the special authorities. In the main, however, the Police Department tends more often to have its own way, the other agencies yielding to its power, its autonomy, and its cohesiveness. The other side of the medal is the Police Commissioner's limited opportunities to offer firm cooperation with other agencies even when he wishes to do so. His control over his own Department is not sufficient for him to pledge its affirmative participation in programs involving important innovations in police attitudes or methods.

The Police Department has one of the most complex constituencies among the city's line agencies. It is the object of relatively constant attention from a wider range of nongovernmental groups than any other single agency. With such extensive attention directed at them, Police Commissioners have great difficulty in deciding to which voices they must listen most receptively, and on what subjects. The most relevant constituency elements are difficult to identify. Fragmentation in organization and ambivalence in attitudes toward the Department are their most distinctive characteristics. Police Commissioners never quite succeed in identifying the hard core either of their supporting groups or of the opposition groups with whom they must come to terms. The formations and their attitudes tend to be fluid and unpredictable.

There are a few certainties upon which the Police Commissioner can reasonably depend in his dealings with the Department's constituency, but the sum total of these several certainties is likely to confront him with as many inconsistencies as clarifications. He can usually expect more support than opposition for proposals to expand the size of the police force; the economy groups have a traditional tolerance for police budgets, and most other groups are regularly demanding more police services. He can count upon the groups licensed or inspected by the Department to attempt to capture the licensing and inspection units of his organization, thus threatening his control over policy and exposing him to the risks of unfavorable exposés. He can reasonably anticipate that the communication media, especially the press, will be ambivalent in their attitudes toward him and his agency, publicizing with equal zeal and emphasis the dramatic accomplishments of the police and the sordid chapters of police corruption and violence. He will note, too, that the merchant and automobile associations urging more effective traffic control are also inclined to condemn "arbitrary" or "rigid" enforcement techniques. Each religious group presses for its doctrines of law enforcement. Employer groups urge strict supervision of picketing; labor unions emphasize their hard-won standards of strict neutrality by the police in labor disputes. Some groups demand a hard line by police toward juvenile delinquents; others insist upon a subordinate role for the police in such matters. Some voices advocate wide use of the nightstick and the dragnet against gangsters, punks, and gamblers; others, such as bar associations, civil liberties groups, and some communication media, remind the Police Commissioner of the due process of law. There are no "peak associations" tying these groups together, either as support or opposition. The prime difficulty for the Police Commissioner is that, while his highly fragmented constituency can cause him much trouble, he cannot expect much help from it; he cannot, in fact, find even a stable and significant center of opposition with which he might reach long-term accommodations. Nor does his constituency furnish him with a lever which he might use to move the police bureaucracy toward greater responsiveness to his leadership.

The Police Commissioner—isolated from the Mayor and other elected officials, from the party leaders, and from other agencies, and confronted by an unstructured, fragmented constituency—is thus cut off from effective external alliances and thrust back upon his own limited resources in attempting to lead and direct the police bureaucracy. Autonomy for the Department spells isolation for the Commissioner. With energy and resolution, and some public relations skill, he may create a favorable public image of himself as an omnipresent, incorruptible, and determined administrator. He may exploit the competitive relation between the 300 members of "the brass" and the 24,000 members of the rank and file, in ways that may increase somewhat his influence with both; he may emphatically invoke the semimilitary command structure and vocabulary of the Department to make his purposes unambiguous. He may find tangible and intangible rewards to bestow as incentives for innovation and for responsiveness to his leadership, and he may exhort his officers and men to aspire to the status of a profession, to embrace the trends toward modernization, to take the lead among police systems. All these efforts will help him in his leadership, but their combined long-range increment is not strikingly large. In the end, whatever the dash and determination at the beginning, the Commissioners yield to the necessity of being more the spokesman and the advocate than the leader and the innovator.

District Attorneys

The District Attorney in each of the five counties within the city heads a line agency whose function is to investigate, and, when warranted, to secure indictments and to institute and conduct prosecutions (in the courts of the county) of persons alleged to have committed crimes. As an elected official, chosen every four years by the voters of his county, he has some opportunities and privileges not available to the appointed heads of other line agencies, for he stands outside the ordinary hierarchy of supervision by the Mayor, the city's overhead agencies, and the Board of Estimate. His office, too, is sufficiently often an avenue to higher position in the political world to give the District Attorney special prestige among other officials and groups with whom he must deal. Dewey and Whitman, for example, advanced from the office to the governorship, De Luca to the lieutenant-governorship, O'Dwyer to the mayoralty, McDonald and others to judgeships. The District Attorney is thus a privileged line agency head. But he does not escape several difficulties if he aspires to initiative and autonomy for himself.

Whether a District Attorney secures internal control over his own organization depends largely upon his accommodations with the party leaders of his county. His nomination and renomination, his advancement to higher elected political posts, are decisions largely determined by the party leaders. Their demands for recognition when the District Attorney makes his staff appointments are difficult for him to ignore. He can use his own status and prestige as an elected official to bargain with the party leaders, but (except in rare instances, as, for example, Frank S. Hogan of New York County) he must yield to a substantial portion of their requests. Having done so, he has usually surrendered part of his control over his own office, and he may be compelled to yield still more of his control if he listens and concedes, as is true of most District Attorneys, to the argument that his assistants should be permitted to continue their outside practice of the law.

When the District Attorney deals with other city agencies and officials, he ordinarily has substantial advantages. His assignments and methods are not under city control; they are spelled out by state law, chiefly in the County Law, the Penal Law, and the Code of Criminal Procedure. His staff is employed under rules administered by the State Personnel Department, and his budget, though borne by the city, may not be decreased without his consent. He has a strategic relationship to the Police Department, which is dependent upon him for the prosecution of those whom the police arrest. He determines in large part the agenda of the grand juries and of the criminal courts. With state executive and administrative agencies and officials, however, he has fewer advantages. The Governor can remove him from office or supersede him with a special prosecutor. The Attorney General can intervene with criticism or with a competitive program of investigation and prosecution. The State Crime Commission can also exhibit competitive tendencies. Nor is he always untroubled by federal agencies; the Department of Justice, the United States Attorney in the appropriate district, or the FBI may separately or together enter areas of investigation and prosecution which the District Attorney regards as his own. To these there must also be added, from time to time, state legislative inquiries or congressional investigations which move into the District Attorney's domain, occasionally even investigating the conduct of his own office.

The District Attorney has superior opportunities to create a favorable climate of opinion, for he deals with dramatic, even sensational, materials capable of effective presentation to, and by, the communication media in ways which will cast him as a hero. But to use these opportunities (as, for example, did Whitman, Dewey, O'Dwyer, McDonald), he must decide that he is as much an investigator as he is prosecutor. This decision will be regarded as competitive by the Police Commissioner and his staff, who regard investigation as their own assignment, and it will be viewed anxiously by the party leaders, who fear the District Attorney's zeal may damage their accommodations or hurt the reputation of the party. The District Attorney will thus be caught between those forces that urge him toward crusading investigations (the press, the Grand Jurors' Association, the civic groups, and others) and those that counsel moderation and the role of formal prosecutor rather than investigator (as will ordinarily the party leaders, the bar associations and others concerned with due process of law, and those who are being investigated). Most District Attorneys choose the role of prosecutor, seeking indictments and convictions among those alleged law violators whose actions have been investigated initially by others—for example, the Police Department or the Department of Investigation. Their own investigational role is made supplementary rather than dominant.

A second dilemma also confronts a District Attorney. Shall he exert every effort to secure conviction for the crime as charged in the indictment, or shall he agree to a plea of guilty to a lesser offense? Many complexities and subtleties of law enforcement are involved in the decision, but a common policy has clearly emerged: prosecutors and judges encourage the lesser plea, and it is accepted in disposing of more than three fourths (perhaps as many as nine tenths) of the indictments obtained in the city. This policy has a number of advantages for both prosecutors and judges: it tempers justice with mercy; it reduces the burden of work and costs for both, making the process manageable; it gives the prosecutor a high record of successful dispositions of cases; it allows room for bargaining by the defendant and his friends; and the District Attorney can claim an effective performance as prosecutor, while arousing a minimum of criticism and opposition.

Civic reform groups have on occasion proposed that the five District Attorney offices in the city be consolidated into one office. Against this idea, various objections have been advanced, two of which are the connection of the office with the county court systems and the county grand juries, and the risks of entrusting the prosecuting power to Tammany. But the importance of the office to each set of county party leaders appears to be the main barrier to consolidation. The office is itself an important one to the party leaders as a place where candidates for other offices can be groomed and tested, the staff positions in the office are useful places for young lawyers starting up the party or official career ladders, and the kinds of decisions the office makes (to investigate or not, to prosecute or not, to ask for severe or moderate penalties) are each of great importance to the party leaders. In a consolidated office, the five sets of party leaders in the counties would be compelled to compete with one another, and still other participants might enter the bargaining process with power and influence. The costs and risks of such a change are clear to most party leaders; they are also clear to incumbent District Attorneys.

Department of Traffic

The Traffic Commissioner heads one of the newer line agencies of the city, his agency having reached departmental status in June, 1950. The establishment of the Department of Traffic was preceded by a half-century of Police Department responsibility for the traffic-control function, a task which had grown in complexity and difficulty for the police agency but which that agency was reluctant to surrender. The years 1946–1949 brought a crisis of congestion to the city's streets as the number of motor vehicles sharply increased and the traditional police traffic methods failed to ameliorate conditions. A series of civic groups began to study the traffic problem and to urge upon Mayor O'Dwyer the creation of new governmental machinery which would enable the city to formulate and carry out new traffic control programs.

The first response of the O'Dwyer administration, in early 1949, revealed basic uncertainties about the kind of agency needed as well as an appreciation of the complexities of the assignment. The initial "solution" was the establishment of a seven-member Traffic Commission, authorized to formulate and recommend policies, plans, and regulations for the control of traffic. Six members served *ex officio:* the Commissioner of Public Works, the chairman of the Triborough Bridge and Tunnel Authority, the chairman of the City Planning Commission, the chairman of the Board of Transportation, the Police Commissioner, and the Chief Engineer of the Board of Estimate, who served as chairman. The seventh member was the executive director of Traffic Engineering, a newly established staff unit for the commission. Each of the six agencies represented had important stakes and responsibilities in the traffic policies and programs of the city government, but the *ex officio* participation of the six agency heads in the new Traffic Commission produced more in debate about jurisdictional boundaries than it did in traffic control plans or performance. After eighteen months this experiment in collaboration was abandoned; the Traffic Commission was abolished and a Department of Traffic was established. The uncertainties of 1949 were thus considerably reduced in 1950, but some of them still persist.

The Traffic Commissioner is given an impressive series of formal powers and responsibilities by the charter: the power to make rules and regulations for the conduct of vehicular and pedestrian traffic in the city, enforceable by fine and imprisonment; to determine the design of, and to install and maintain, all traffic signs and signals; to establish parking meter zones, install and maintain meters, and with the consent of the Board of Estimate use the revenues for operation of the meter system or other traffic improvements; to develop and manage off-street parking facilities; to prepare and submit to the Mayor a proposed comprehensive city traffic plan, and to make other recommendations, studies and reports on traffic improvement. The Commissioner's difficultes do not lie in these formal grants of the charter but in the limitations and inhibitions he finds elsewhere. Nor does he encounter any important difficulty in securing internal command over his agency; his staff is, to a considerable extent, newly recruited into the city's civil service, is largely of the incumbent Commissioner's own selection, shares his values and attitudes toward the agency's assignment, and being small in size (under 500) permits an intimacy of leadership and direction by the Commissioner.

The Commissioner's difficulties begin when he moves toward the energetic use of his formal powers and the implementation of the plans developed by his staff. These difficulties center in his dependence upon several other agencies and in his competitive relationship with still others. He can, for example, modernize the rules and regulations for traffic control, but he must depend upon the Police Department and the traffic courts, presided over by city magistrates, to enforce the new rules and regulations. These two groups have marked tendencies toward autonomous policy-making on their own, and they share with each other a much longer tradition of mutual accommodation than does either with the new traffic agency. The result is a selective enforcement of his rules which the Traffic Commissioner cannot prevent. The Commissioner finds, too, that his writ does not run on those city streets, highways, parkways, approaches and exits under the jurisdiction of the Triborough Bridge and Tunnel Authority, the Parks Department, and the Port of New York Authority. These facilities pour vehicular traffic in great volume into the streets where his traffic rules and signals must absorb the shock, but he cannot control the volume, the timing, or the direction of the blow. The Commissioner also discovers that Borough Presidents and the Commissioner of Public Works have independent capacities to affect his traffic control plans. The widening of streets, the timing and location of street repairs, the building or repair of bridges, all produce special problems for the traffic control agency, over which its influence tends to be marginal. The Traffic Commissioner has, further, been periodically confronted with the efforts of the City Construction Coordinator to establish a city Parking Authority which would take over the operation and the revenues of the parking meters, the regulation of parking, and the construction and operation of off-street parking facilities, especially garages. Although this proposed splintering of his agency has so far been averted, progress toward adequate off-street facilities has been slowed by the City Planning Commission, the Budget Director, and in the Board of Estimate and elsewhere due, in some part at least, to the vigorous advocacy of the alternative proposal.

The difficulties of the Traffic Commissioner in his relationship to other agencies help explain additional handicaps. He has had limited success in securing budget appropriations from the Budget Director and the Board of Estimate and in securing the salary levels for his professional staff he has requested from the Personnel Director and the Board of Estimate. Nor has he their approval for recruiting staff members outside the residence requirements of local law. His efforts to secure high priority assistance from the City Planning Commission in the development of a comprehensive plan for parking facilities in the city are a further disappointment.

The instability of the Traffic Department's relations to other agencies led Mayor Wagner in 1955 to establish an Interdepartmental Traffic Council, its seven members being the Traffic Commissioner, the Police Commissioner, the Sanitation Commissioner, the City Administrator, an assistant to the Mayor, and two members of the City Council. Its history has not demonstrated that it can solve the Traffic Commissioner's major dilemmas. For example, one of its conclusions in 1957 was that alleviation of traffic congestion in the garment district should be regarded as part of a comprehensive plan for the whole area, embracing land use, zoning, building rehabilitation, new construction, as well as traffic flow, methods of loading and unloading, and parking, a long-range task assigned prayerfully by the Traffic Council to the City Planning Commission. Meanwhile, the Traffic Commissioner must wait.

The uncertainties of the Traffic Commissioner in his bargaining position with other city agencies are matched by uncertainties in his dealings with his interest-group constituency. The civic groups can usually be counted upon for timely and consistent support. In 1957 the Citizens Union presented a certificate of meritorious performance to the Commissioner, signed also by fifteen other groups, and the organizations representing automobile owners, especially the Automobile Club of New York, are active in championship of the traffic agency and its programs. The communication media, too, incline toward general endorsement and favorable attention. But other groups tend to make conflicting demands upon the Traffic Commissioner. The merchants want the traffic rules to serve the convenience of shoppers; the trucking industry wants the rules to give priority to loading, unloading, and hauling goods; the bus companies want the rules to maximize bus patronage (thus resisting one-way avenues); while other transit interests view traffic control as an opportunity to create more favorable competitive terms for themselves against the passenger automobile. Some labor unions (especially the Teamsters and the Transport Workers Union) see traffic control plans as direct threats to their economic interests and protest vigorously against such proposals, while still other unions, as do the garment workers, regard drastic traffic changes as indirectly threatening their employment. The Traffic Commissioner thus confronts a constituency which is united in its demands for traffic improvement but divides sharply in its reaction to each specific traffic rule. On few issues can the Traffic Commissioner rally support from a dominant proportion of his constituency. Some elements will support him, others will vigorously oppose him, while still others will be indifferent. The Traffic Commissioner seems unlikely to become the captive of any powerful segment of his constituency; neither does he appear able to organize and lead a constituency formation which would give him the power to bargain on favorable terms with the other agencies which now sharply limit his leadership opportunities.

The Traffic Commissioner derives both advantages and disadvantages from the intractable nature of the traffic problem itself. The steady and highly visible growth of traffic congestion aids him in securing approval of some of his proposals, since his critics concede the necessity for some action and yet disagree among themselves as to alternative remedies. This advantage has enabled the Commissioner to embark upon such dramatic programs as the one-way avenues (over the objections of merchants, bus companies, and bus unions), to extend the parking meter system to exceed 50,000 meters, to modernize much of the traffic signal system, to experiment widely with street markings and with pedestrian traffic. Yet disadvantages also flow from the inherent stubbornness of the traffic problem. The growth of congestion keeps pace with, if indeed it does not outrun, the Commissioner's solutions. This declining yield from each specific solution adopted strengthens the hand of the critics and makes more difficult the acceptance of comprehensive traffic improvement plans. Time seems to run against the Traffic Commissioner's leadership.

The difficult environment in which Traffic Commissioners find themselves affords Mayors few opportunities to assist. Mayors cannot, on behalf of the traffic agency, imprudently challenge the combined or separate political power of the Police Commissioner, the special authorities, the City Construction Coordinator, the City Planning Commission, the Borough Presidents, and the various constituency elements which from time to time oppose the plans of the Traffic Commissioner. Instead, both Mayor and Traffic Commissioner are required to cultivate patience, awaiting the opportunity to combine their efforts to secure more freedom of action for the traffic agency.

Sanitation Department

The Commissioner of Sanitation has formal responsibility for one of the largest of the city's line agencies, his staff numbering almost 15,000. The functions of his agency are comparatively noncontroversial, attract only occasional widespread public attention, and rarely provide the Commissioner with opportunities for dramatic forms of leadership or for advancement up a political, professional, or business career ladder. One consequence of these factors is that the Commissioner and his deputies are increasingly recruited from the higher ranks of the Department's permanent staff.

The Department of Sanitation has the tasks of cleaning the city's streets and collecting, removing, and disposing of the city's wastes. For these purposes, it maintains and operates a large fleet of several thousand trucks and other motorized equipment, a dozen large incinerator plants, a varying number of land fills, and more than forty scows and barges working out of seven water-front disposal stations. The Commissioner thus heads an organization in which leadership involves both the managerial skills required in organizing and directing the work of a large staff and the engineering technology associated with a large pool of complex equipment and plant. The Commissioner's leadership aspirations and dilemmas revolve around these dual aspects of his assignment: organizing and directing the manpower of his department; continuously modernizing his plant and equipment while maximizing its present utility.

The Commissioner's efforts to secure internal control of his agency encounter two major difficulties. The first represents the continuing effects of the Department's former attachment to the Borough Presidents, the present Department being largely the product of a consolidation effected in 1929. The Commissioner is still required by the charter to maintain a branch office in each borough, a fact which both limits his discretion in organizing the Department's work and increases the opportunities of borough officials and other borough groups to intervene in the management of the Department. While successive Commissioners during the past three decades have gradually reduced these centrifugal tendencies, they are still strong and persistent.

The second, and the more important, of the Commissioner's difficulties in securing internal control of his Department is to be found in the self-directing inclinations and capacities of his staff, especially the large union-organized segment of the sanitation bureaucracy. The large staff of the Department, strategically deployed in its work over the whole geographical spread of the city, was once an important asset to the party leaders, who found it not only a patronage resource but useful also in the performance of routine party tasks (for example, in collecting signatures for petitions). This relationship was fruitful to party leaders for almost four decades, but it began to decline in 1939–1940 when the La Guardia Civil Service Commission transferred most of the staff from the labor to the competitive class under the Civil Service Law, a change which isolated party leaders from direct influence upon both the appointment and the tenure of the sanitation staff. This step was followed, in the next decade, by the gradual but eventually almost complete unionization of the rank and file of sanitation workers. Sanitation Commissioners now confront within the Department a labor union which has determined leadership and a set of goals to which the Commissioner is compelled to accommodate his managerial and technological objectives, the two sets of goals being only occasionally and fortuitously consistent.

Commissioners of Sanitation since 1929 have thus seen a dramatic change in the nature of the competition to their aspirations for leadership and control of the department. Until 1940 the competition was provided mainly by the party leaders in alliance with several party-oriented employee organizations. In the 1950's the competition is furnished by the leadership of Teamsters Local 831, to which the Department's rank-and-file staff belongs. Commissioners have adjusted to these changing circumstances in a logical fashion: most of the earlier Commissioners were immersed in the party system, the transition Commissioners were ambivalent as between identifications with party or bureaucracy, and the later Commissioners have turned steadily toward the necessary bargaining with and concessions to the leaders of the staff labor union.

Sanitation Commissioners, in their aspirations to control their department, derive little important help from Mayors or the Board of Estimate. The agency provides few opportunities for Mayors to develop public policy. Higher priorities tend to crowd it off the Mayor's agenda, even if he were convinced that his assistance to the Commissioner would be decisive. In the Board of Estimate, the Department's bureaucracy can ordinarily exercise more influence than the Commissioner. Nor does the Commissioner find opportunities for effective alliances with the heads of other agencies; although the Health, Police, and Traffic Commissioners are frequently cooperative, they cannot contribute directly to the Commissioner's efforts to achieve internal control of his own department.

When the Commissioner turns to his constituency, he encounters a wide range of groups who urge that the services of his agency be improved or expanded: more frequent cleaning of streets, more rapid removal of snow and ice from the streets, more frequent removal of wastes, more efficient and unobtrusive incinerators, fewer open dumps and land fills. These groups demanding service are balanced by others demanding economies in the operations of the Department, stressing opportunities for mechanization and other technological advances, and opposing increases in the Commissioner's budget for manpower or capital plant. He can frequently amass strong constituency support, including extensive help from the communication media, in campaigns to promote a "Clean City" through citizen cooperation. Such support and campaigns give him some help in getting his agency's job performed more satisfactorily, and often adds to his personal prestige, but it assists him only indirectly in his leadership of his Department.

The Sanitation Commissioner exercises his main opportunities for leadership in close bargaining with the leaders of the largely autonomous union organization of his own employees. This tendency is being steadily confirmed by the custom of selecting Commissioners from the "career" ranks of the agency and by the increasing recognition of the sanitation union as the exclusive bargaining representative of the rank-and-file staff of the Department, the influence and independence of the union leaders being enhanced by its affiliation with a large outside labor union. The Commissioner organizes his agency's work, allocates and directs the agency's manpower, supervises performance, and introduces managerial and technological innovations within the limited range of discretion which his bargaining resources and skills can win from the leaders of the sanitation bureaucracy. When he is a "career" product himself, the adjustment to a modest leadership role is presumably made less difficult by an already acquired commitment on his part to the traditions of the Department.

Department of Correction

The Commissioner of Correction directs a line agency which is responsible for the care and custody of prisoners in the city's 9 prisons, 29 court detention pens, and 2 hospital prison wards. With a staff of almost 2,400 employees, the Commissioner during 1957 had custody of 120,334 persons (representing an average daily prisoner population of about 7,000), of whom during the whole year 24,872 were prisoners under sentence and 95,462 were being held for trial. This is an assignment of magnitude and complexity to which the Department of Correction can bring only limited assets and allies. And the assignment brings to the Commissioner an enduring and frustrating dilemma of policy: whether to emphasize custody and punishment, or to stress care and rehabilitation.

This unresolved question of policy is reflected in most of the stresses and strains which confront the Commissioner in his efforts to create and lead a viable agency: in the problems of overcrowded and obsolescent prisons, in the difficulties of agency organization and staffing, in the relations of the Department to other city agencies, and in the divisions within the agency's constituency of interest groups. The Commissioner is usually caught between the forces emphasizing custody and the forces urging rehabilitation as the prime goal of the Department. To choose overtly between them is to invite strong resistance from the groups favoring the opposite course; to attempt a middle way involves the risks of pleasing neither side. No Commissioner has found it easy to discover the optimum course of action.

The Commissioner of Correction and his deputies are, from the first, faced with difficulties in securing sufficient internal control of the agency to give them an opportunity for leadership and initiative. Their choices in the organizational structure of the Department are sharply limited through the necessities imposed by the existence of 40 separate physical facilities. These institutions must be manned and managed as separate organizational units, for many of them (the prisons) represent large capital investments, and others exist as parts of other agencies' facilities (as do the court pens and the hospital wards). Their limitations as physical facilities must be ordinarily accepted by the Commissioner as one of the facts of life. Second, the Commissioner and his deputies must deal with a uniformed force of correction officers who are strongly entrenched within the city's personnel system, who have long been organized as officer groups for the purposes of bargaining and self-protection, who have long maintained a closed promotion ladder up through the rank of warden, who are more custody-minded than rehabilitation-minded, and who look with skepticism if not hostility upon the entry into the Department of rehabilitation-oriented staff (such as social workers, psychologists, psychiatrists, educators). The Commissioner who chooses to emphasize prisoner rehabilitation ordinarily has only four methods of ameliorating these staff resistances, none of them as yet notably successful: strengthening the top command of the Department above the rank of warden with "new blood"; periodic mass reassignment of personnel (the "shake-up" technique imitating the Police and Fire Department examples); indoctrinating custodial personnel in training courses emphasizing rehabilitation values; and increasing the noncustodial staff of social workers and others. Even the most energetic Commissioner makes but slow headway toward leadership over the custodial staff unless he accepts their traditions and aspirations toward autonomy.

The Commissioner of Correction brings few strong bargaining assets to the Department's dealings with other city agencies. The Department's most direct clientele (the prisoners and their families) are with few exceptions a group without political power; they must depend upon surrogate groups for representation of their interests. The State Correction Commission and the City Parole Commission may ordinarily be counted upon to assist the Commissioner, but their opportunities to do so are restricted. The party leaders intervene sporadically in the Department's affairs; when they do, the Commissioner is ordinarily vulnerable to their demands. In the main, the Commissioner has limited influence with the Budget Director and the Personnel Director; the Commissioner of Investigation is an inquisitor rather than an ally; the Police Commissioner, the District Attorneys, the grand juries, and the courts are more often critics than supporters. If the Commissioner of Correction is to find an official ally and supporter, he must turn to the Mayor and the City Administrator; but they cannot help the Commissioner much or often unless he can bring some other support to his side.

When the Commissioner turns to his constituency in search of this support, he is confronted again with the conflict between those groups who stress custody and those who stress prisoner rehabilitation as opposing goals for the Department. In general, the constituencies associated with the Police Department, the District Attorneys, and the grand juries tend to urge custodial values upon the Commissioner. The religious groups, the charitable and welfare groups, the social workers, the schools of social work, some medical groups, and some civic groups incline strongly toward rehabilitation values. The press tends to divide its sentiments, responding alternately to the conflicting goals as one group or the other finds opportunities to dramatize its views. The Commissioner is thus again faced with the Department's enduring dilemma. In 1957 the Commissioner made a choice which may become a binding precedent: with the assistance of the Mayor and the City Administrator, he chose to institutionalize the rehabilitation goal for the Department through the establishment of a Board of Correction. This nine-member, unsalaried board, its members serving six-year staggered terms, seems designed to give to the Commissioner an intimate and informed constituency which will strengthen the bargaining power of the Department in its emphasis upon prisoner rehabilitation. Its initial composition includes members drawn from prominent leadership positions in the Community Council of Greater New York, the Urban League, the Catholic Big Brothers, the Protestant Council, the New York Foundation, the Fordham School of Social Service, the Riverside Church, the Hillcrest Center for Children, and the Citizens Union. The Board's formal assignment is to inspect the Department's institutions, to propose long-range plans to the Mayor and the Commissioner, and to ensure penological advances in the Department's correctional programs. Its more important informal assignment will no doubt be to assist the Commissioner who chooses rehabilitation goals and to deter the Commissioner who does not.

The Commissioner has been historically weakest in the capital budget process. Obsolete and overcrowded prisons have been the insurmountable problem for Commissioners for more than a half century. No sufficiently influential array of groups support the Department's capital budget requests against the more powerful competitive demands of other departments and agencies.

THE ORDEALS AND TRIUMPHS OF LINE AGENCY LEADERS

Faced by awesome combinations of forces with vested interests in the existing situation, few commissioners are willing to invest the energy and take the risks required to make extensive changes in policy, organization, or procedure. They can easily create a general impression of vigor and drive by working assiduously to intensify prevailing activities—to add new policemen or firemen or teachers or other personnel, to increase the number of police stations or firehouses or schools or hospitals or parks or other installations, to augment services—in short, to do more and more of what has traditionally been done, and to do it in the customary way. In such efforts, they can normally count on the enthusiastic support of their career bureaucracies, partly because the bureaucrats, as specialists, believe ardently in the importance and desirability of the programs they administer, and partly because expansion of this kind opens additional opportunities for advancement without disturbing the settled arrangements and long-standing accommodations worked out in the past. They can depend on the backing of the clientele they serve or regulate, who hope for better service on the one hand and, on the other, suppression of violators of regulations whose violations give them competitive advantages over more conscientious business rivals, and on the approval of the party organizations who hope at least for benefits on Election Day, and perhaps for more immediate returns in the form of enlarged patronage opportunities. Economy-oriented tax-paying groups and the financial officers of the city may battle proposals for intensified activity, but they are less effective than their adversaries because the service-demanders are more numerous, and because each coalition of line administrators, bureaucrats, and associated nongovernmental groups concentrates on a narrow range of the spectrum of public functions while their opponents spread their resources over the entire field. The Mayor and the Board of Estimate, it will later be seen, tend to ratify the agreements reached by the contending factions. So line administrators are not idle, nor are they paralyzed by the powerful field of forces in which they find themselves. But the *courses* of action open to them are the traditional ones; they find it easiest to be active and dynamic, and to achieve successes, when they strengthen the ongoing system. The strategies available to them discourage departures from routine, introduction of extensive alterations, experiments in program or method, for the strategies are most effective within the established framework. The path of innovation is rocky, twisting, and full of pitfalls.

Another opportunity for dynamism is offered by dramatic "clean-ups" and managerial "improvements." Again, these rarely work profound transformations of policy, organization, or procedure; but they frequently add to the luster of the existing state of affairs by robbing complaints of corruption and inefficiency of their force. And they win the plaudits of reform and civic groups, professional organizations, and exponents of economy. Nothing really changes, but the familiar things are done better, more honestly, and perhaps more cheaply. Line agency chiefs are often able to accomplish a great deal of this nature by following their standard strategies.

Yet innovations do occur; the system is not static. The impetus may come from a scandal, an alarming deterioration of service, a higher level of government (especially through financial grants), a reform administration, or a singularly energetic administrator undaunted by the magnitude of the task he sets for himself. The innovations, however, are usually limited in scope; they strike at selected parts of a program or agency, not at everything simultaneously. They are incremental, not total.

Indeed, the scale of innovation, even under the pressures of crisis, can hardly be much greater than this. For the strategies of the line administrator—winning internal control of his agencies, and manipulating his environment—require, as we have seen, accommodations with all the participants in the contest for the stakes of politics who are concerned with the agency decisions. To render himself less vulnerable to all the conflicting and contradictory demands and instructions, and to all the forms of resistance and opposition to his will, the agency head has to muster the support of all the friends he can find and strike bargains with everyone around him. To preserve his discretion in some areas of his jurisdiction, he must surrender in others. He has to placate his allies to keep them on his side and pacify those who are rarely active in his aid lest they use their influence to injure him and his agency. He has to balance a welter of factors to survive, let alone to progress, for virtually everyone he deals with has an independent source of power.

In working out their adjustments, line agency chiefs often become so proficient in negotiating with other contestants that they achieve a high degree of immunity from the leadership of the central organs of government. Together with their friends and allies, and their professional and bureaucratic counterparts in other levels of government, they emerge as central— but not necessarily dominant—figures in functional islands of decision-making power. Their impress on the substance of governmental decisions is therefore considerable. Nevertheless, their freedom of action is sharply restricted. That is why the exceptional line agency chief who is so skilled at setting the pressures upon him against one another that he has numerous occasions to satisfy his creativity and his cravings for leadership towers over his fellows on the governmental scene.

BIBLIOGRAPHY

GENERAL

Caldwell, Lynton K., *The Government and Administration of New York*. Thomas Y. Crowell Co., New York, 1954. An authoritative book on New York State which devotes considerable space to New York City and city-state relations.

Simon, H. A., D. W. Smithburg, and V. A. Thompson, *Public Administration*. Alfred A. Knopf, New York, 1950. This unusual text in public administration explores the tactics and strategies of the executives of public agencies.

DEPARTMENT OF AIR POLLUTION CONTROL

Official Sources and Issuances

New York City Charter, chap. 47 (as added by Local Law 114, 1952), secs. 1071–1075.

New York City Administrative Code, chap. 47, secs. 1072–1074.

Annual Reports, 1954, 1955, 1956, and 1957 (in monthly newsletters).

Rules and Regulations Including Fee Schedule for the Issuance of Permits and Certificates in Conformance with Chapter 47 of the Administrative Code of the City of New York. The Department, New York, 1954.

Newsletter, February, 1955 to date (issued monthly).

Surveys and Discussions

Maxwell, William S., "Air Pollution Control in the City of New York," *East Side Chamber News*, August–September, 1953, pp. 4, 6–7. Problems confronting the newly created Department of Air Pollution Control.

Morrison, Donal M., *You Can Do Something About Smoke*. Citizens Union Research Foundation, New York, 1952. A plea for better smoke control just prior to the creation of the Department of Air Pollution Control.

New York City, Bureau of the Budget, Division of Analysis, *The City of New York: Air Pollution Control.* The Bureau, New York, 1953. Analyzes the organization, structure, policies, and operating procedures of the Department of Air Pollution Control.

DEPARTMENT OF BUILDINGS

Official Sources and Issuances

New York City Charter, chap. 26, secs. 641–652 (as amended by Local Law 112, 1955).

New York City Administrative Code, chap. 26, secs. 641–645.

Department of Buildings, *Annual Reports*, 1938, 1939, 1940 (published annually); 1941–1944 (1 vol.); 1945–1949 (1 vol.); 1938–1953 (published annually); 1954–1955 (1 vol.), 1956 to date (published annually).

> *Building Laws of the City of New York.* City Record, New York, 1955. (Kept up to date with new matter inserted in binder at Municipal Reference Library.) Laws, rules, and regulations relating to the erection, construction, maintenance, and alterations of buildings in New York City.

McKinney's Consolidated Laws of New York, Annotated, *Multiple Dwelling Law*, Book 35A. Edward Thompson, Brooklyn, 1946. Kept up to date with annual supplements.

Surveys and Discussions

Birnbaum, Herbert, "Enacting the City's Building Laws," *Real Estate News*, May, 1958, pp. 169–170. How the New York City Building Code is drafted.

Chait, Frieda, *Indexes to the Building Laws of the City of New York*. Record Press, New York, 1955. Provides easy access to the Building Code, to relevant sections of the Administrative Code, and a Department and statute index.

Christian, Joseph J., "A Summary of Multiple Dwelling Regulations," *Real Estate News*, February, 1959, pp. 46–49. An outline of the New York City dwelling regulations.

City Club of New York, *Report on Charter Revision*. The Club, New York, 1921, pp. 28–29. A critical review of the work of the Tenement House Department, the predecessor of the Division of Housing in the present Department of Buildings.

Comer, John P., *New York City Building Control: 1800–1941*. Columbia University Press, New York, 1942. Traces the organization and functions of the precursors to the Department of Buildings and the evolution of the present Department.

Levy, Beryl, and Shirley A. Siegel, *Toward City Conservation: A Memorandum for New Yorkers on Aspects of Urban Renewal.* League of West Side Organizations, New York, 1959. Considers the work of the Building Department in the context of conservation and rehabilitation of housing, as described in the Federal Housing Act of 1954.

McGoldrick, Joseph D., Seymour Graubard, and R. J. Horowitz, *Building Regulations in New York City: A Study in Administration, Law and Procedure.* Commonwealth Fund, New York, 1944. A study of the Building Code and enforcement of building regulations in New York City.

Morris, Richard B., "The Metropolis of the State," chap. 6 in vol. 10 of Alexander C. Flick, editor, *History of the State of New York*. 10 vols. Columbia University Press, New York, 1937, pp. 181–184. The early history of building regulations in New York City.

Murphy, John J., "The Tenement House Department," *Proceedings* of the Academy of Political Science in the City of New York, vol. 5, April, 1915, pp. 522–524. The work of the Department in 1915.

New York City, Commissioners of Accounts and New York Bureau of Municipal Research, *Government of the City of New York: A Survey of Its Organization and Functions.* J. J. Little and Ives Co., New York, 1915, pp. 618, 842–873. A survey of the functioning of the Board of Building Examiners and the Tenement House Department in 1915.

Mayor's Committee on Management Survey, *Modern Management for the City of New York.* 2 vols. The Committee, New York, 1953, vol. 2, pp. 326–327. A brief presentation of the problems and operation of the Department of Housing and Building.

Municipal Reference Library, "Looking Ahead," *Municipal Reference Library Notes,* vol. 33, January, 1956. The state Multiple Dwelling Law and the city's Multiple Dwelling Code—a commentary.

DEPARTMENT OF CORRECTION

Official Sources and Issuances

New York City Charter, chap. 25, secs. 621–666, as amended by chap. 644, Laws of 1946, Local Law No. 25, 1957, and a referendum approved by the voters of New York City at a general election held in 1941.

New York City Administrative Code, chap. 25, secs. 623–625.

Department of Correction, *Annual Reports,* 1902–1931 (published annually); 1934–1941 (1 vol.); 1941–1942 (1 vol.); 1945–1948 (1 vol.); 1949–1951 (1 vol.); 1952 to date (published annually).

Surveys and Discussions

Citizens Budget Commission of New York, *A Better Government for a Better City: A Study of Five Departments of the City of New York at the Request of Honorable William O'Dwyer, Mayor.* The Commission, New York, 1948, pp. 264–283. An analysis of the methods and procedures of the Department of Correction.

Davis, Katharine Bement, "The Department of Correction," *Proceedings* of the Academy of Political Science in the City of New York, vol. 5, April, 1915, pp. 564–575. Mitchel's Commissioner of Correction discusses the Department's history, organization, and future plans.

Kross, Anna M., "An Army Raised Against Our System," New York County Lawyers Association, *Bar Bulletin,* May, 1955, pp. 19–24. What happens to those imprisoned behind bars, as seen by the Commissioner of Correction.

New York City Commissioner of Accounts and New York Bureau of Municipal Research, *Government of the City of New York: A Survey of Its Organization and Function.* J. J. Little and Ives Co., New York, 1915, pp. 992–1022. The work of the Department of Correction in 1915.

New York City Mayor's Committee on the Department of Correction, *Organization and Management of the Department of Correction.* Office of the Mayor, Division of Administration, New York, 1956. An analysis of the recommendations of the New York County Grand Jury and of Commissioner Anna M. Kross for improving conditions in the Department of Correction.

DISTRICT ATTORNEYS

Official Sources and Issuances

New York State Constitution. The provision for electing District Attorneys in the five counties of New York City are set forth in the following provisions of the state constitution: Art. 9, secs. 5 and 6, as renumbered by the Constitutional Convention of 1938 and approved by vote of the people, November 8, 1938.

McKinney's Consolidated Laws of New York Annotated, Book 10-B, *Correction Law.* Edward Thompson Co., Brooklyn, N. Y., 1944. Kept up to date with annual supplements. The state law regulating jails and parole procedures. Many of the regulations name New York City specifically. Supplemented by judicial decisions relating to these laws.

Book 11, *County Law*. Edward Thompson Co., Brooklyn, N. Y., 1950. Article 24, secs. 926–936 set forth the rules governing the elections, terms, records, duties, and salaries of the District Attorneys and Assistant District Attorneys in New York City. Also contain relevant judicial decisions.

Commentaries

Botein, Bernard, *The Prosecutor*. Simon and Schuster, New York, 1956. A fictionalized portrait of a District Attorney, which manages to ask some searching questions.

Cohen, Julius Henry, *They Builded Better Than They Knew*. Julian Messner, New York, 1946. pp. 64–69. A portrait of William Travers Jerome, one of New York County's great District Attorneys, 1902–1909.

Danforth, Harold R., and James D. Horan, *The D.A.'s Man*. Crown Publishers, New York, 1957. The New York County District Attorney's office under Thomas E. Dewey and Frank S. Hogan.

DeLuca, George B., "A District Attorney Reports," *New York State Bar Bulletin*, July, 1954, pp. 209–219. Crime and criminals in Bronx County as seen by a District Attorney.

Finegan, James E., *Tammany at Bay*. Dodd, Mead and Co., New York, 1933, pp. 270–272. The "breakdown" of county prosecution in 1934.

Lavine, Emanuel H., *Secrets of the Metropolitan Police*. Garden City Publishing Co., Garden City, N. Y., 1937, pp. 161–176. District Attorneys and their political relationships.

MacKaye, Milton, "St. George of Manhattan: Profile of William Travers Jerome," *The New Yorker*, vol. 7, January 30, 1932, pp. 19–23. The story of a reform District Attorney of New York County.

Men of Affairs in New York: An Historical Work. L. R. Hamersley and Co., New York, 1906, pp. 91–92. The life and career of William Travers Jerome.

Mockridge, Norton, and Robert H. Prall, *The Big Fix*. Henry Holt and Co., New York, 1954. A gambling syndicate with wide connections in the city government exposed by a District Attorney in Kings County.

Northrop, William B., and John B. Northrop, *The Insolence of Office: The Story of the Seabury Investigations*. G. P. Putnam's Sons, New York, 1932, pp. 115–122. The investigation of the office of District Attorney of New York County.

O'Neill, John J., *The Office of District Attorney in New York State*. Master's thesis, The City College, 1958, unpublished.

Seabury, Samuel, *Report and Opinion of Samuel Seabury, Commissioner, in the Matter of the Investigation, Under Commission Issued by the Governor of the State of New York, of Charges Made Against the Honorable Thomas C. T. Crain, District Attorney of New York*. New York, August 31, 1931. An inquiry into the District Attorney's office, during a period of exposure and scandal.

Train, Arthur, *From the District Attorney's Office*. Charles Scribner's Sons, New York, 1939. A popular writer gives his impressions of the District Attorney's office and other aspects of city government when he was assigned to that office.

Williams, Edward A., "The Crain Removal Case and Statistical Charts," *National Municipal Review*, vol. 21, April, 1932, pp. 232–241. Certain aspects of the investigation into the office of District Attorney of New York County.

EDUCATION

Legislative and Charter Provisions for Education

New York City Charter, chap. 20, secs. 521–526.

New York City Administrative Code, chap. 20, secs. 521–526.

McKinney's Consolidated Laws of New York Annotated, Book 16, *Education Law*. 3 vols. Edward Thompson Co., Brooklyn, N. Y., 1953. Kept up to date with annual supplements. The text of the basic law which regulates education in New York City, with judicial decisions relating to the law.

The City Club of New York, *Report on Charter Revision*. The Club, New York, 1921, pp. 35–36. Recommendations specifically applying to the charter and what it had to say about the Department of Education.

Willington, Matilda M., *New York State and City Charter Provisions for Board of Education: A Study of the Organization and Enumerated Powers*. Doctoral dissertation, Fordham University, 1939.

Periodic Reports on Public Education

New York City, Board of Education, *Journal of the Board of Education of the City of New York* 1898–to date. The official record of the proceedings of the Board of Education, from the time of the consolidation of Greater New York to the present. A complete set of these proceedings may be found in the Reference Section of the Bureau of Educational Program Research and Statistics, Board of Education headquarters, 110 Livingston Street, Brooklyn 1, New York.

Board of Education, *Annual Reports*, 1898, 1899, 1900 (published annually). May be consulted in the Professional Library of the Board of Education, 110 Livingston Street, Brooklyn 1, N. Y.

Board of Education, *Minutes of the Board of Superintendents*, 1902–1944 (printed) and *Minutes of the Board of Superintendents*, 1947 to date (mimeographed). (No minutes issued for the years 1945 and 1946.) Volumes containing the proceedings of the Board of Superintendents. Copies in the library of the Bureau of Educational Program Research and Statistics at Board of Education headquarters.

Board of Education, Bureau of Reference, Research and Statistics, *Reports to the New York State Education Department*, 1917–1918 through 1951–1952; and Bureau of Administrative and Budgetary Research, *Reports to the New York State Education Department*, 1952–1953 through 1955–1956. Future reports will be made by the Bureau of Educational Program Research and Statistics.

Superintendent of Schools, *Annual Reports, 1899–1935*. The *Nineteenth Annual Report* drops the word "City," and the 33d, 34th, and 35th *Annual Reports* end the school year on June 30. The 36th *Annual Report* is divided into two volumes, one being the Statistical Section. (See next citation for Statistical Section reports.) The 37th *Annual Report* (1934–1935) through the 48th *Annual Report* (1944–1945) are called "All the Children." Since 1945, the *Annual Reports*, except for the Statistical Section, have been paperbound volumes, devoted to special activities of the Board of Education. The most complete set may be found in the Bureau of Educational Program Research, Board of Education headquarters, 110 Livingston Street, Brooklyn 1, N. Y.

Superintendent of Schools, *Statistical Section, Annual Reports, 1935–1957*. Since 1933–1934 the *Annual Reports* of the Superintendent of Schools have each had one volume devoted to a Statistical Section. For 1952–1956, Bureau of Administrative and Budgetary Research. For 1956–1957, Bureau of Educational Program Research and Statistics.

Administration and Management of Schools

Churchill, Thomas W., "The Board of Education," *Proceedings* of the Academy of Political Science in the City of New York, vol. 5, April, 1915, pp. 583–612. The President of the Board of Education in 1915 discusses the problems relating to the management of the school system.

Citizens Budget Commission, *Should New York City Adopt Fiscal Independence for Education?* The Commission, New York, 1950. A discussion of the pros and cons.

Cohen, Rose M., *The Financial Control of Education in the Consolidated City of New York*. Teachers College, Columbia University, New York, 1948. Emphasizes the interrelationship between the school system, the municipal government, and the state. Covers the period 1900–1944.

Crane, Ella E., *The Board of Education of the City of New York*. Master's thesis, Columbia University, 1919, unpublished.

Dworkis, Martin B., *The Impact of Puerto Rican Migration on Governmental Services in New York City*. New York University Press, New York, 1957, pp. 31–44. Explains how the flow of large numbers of newly arrived islanders has affected the Board of Education and its schools.

Maller, Julius B., editor, Mayor's Committee on Management Survey, *Taking Stock of School Management*. Proceedings of the New York City Education Conference, held January 16, 1952, at Board of Education headquarters.

Marshall, James, *New York City's Public Schools: A Report on Their Improvement*. Herald Tribune, New York, 1952. A former member of the Board of Education makes some revealing statements about the top governing body of the city's school system.

Moore, Ernest C., *How New York City Administers Its Schools: A Constructive Study*. World Book Co., Yonkers-on-Hudson, N. Y., 1913. An early "management survey" of the structure and functioning of the New York City school system.

New York City, Board of Education, *Community in Action: A Report on a Social Integration Project in School Districts 12, 13 and 14, Manhattan, 1951–1958*. The Board, New York, 1959. How school authorities worked with civic and community organizations to promote interracial understanding in a problem area.

Board of Education, *Report of Survey of Public School System, City of New York 1924*. The Board, New York, 1929. A self-appraisal of many facets of the work of the school system of the city.

City Administrator of New York, *Board of Education: Organization and Management of School Planning and Construction*. The Administrator, New York, 1959. A searching examination of school planning, construction, and financing.

Commissioners of Accounts and New York Bureau of Municipal Research, *Government of the City of New York: A Survey of Its Organization and Functions*. J. J. Little and Ives Co., New York, 1915, pp. 336–437. Evaluates the functioning of the Department of Education in 1915.

Mayor's Executive Committee on Administration, *Department of Education: A Survey of the Organization and Clerical Operations of the Board of Examiners*. Bureau of the Budget, New York, 1949.

Mayor's Committee on Management Survey, *Modern Management for the City of New York*. 2 vols. The Committee, New York, 1953, vol. 1, pp. 244–245; vol. 2, pp. 30–33, 84–85, 451–506, 858–859, 866–871. A summary of the findings and conclusions of the detailed studies made by the Mayor's Committee.

New York State, Commission on School Buildings, Strayer, George D., *Final Report of the New York City Subcommittee*. Legislative Document no. 60, Commission on School Buildings, Albany, 1944. Examines the administration and financing of public education in New York City.

State Commissioner's Committee on Inquiry into Charges of Waste and Extravagance in the Construction of School Buildings in New York City, *School Construction in New York City*. State Education Department, Albany, 1959. An examination of charges made by the city Comptroller.

Temporary State Commission on Coordination of State Activities, *Report to the Governor and to the Legislature*. Legislative Document no. 77, Williams Press, Albany, 1951. Touches on state aid to education at a number of points, such as special aid for reducing class size and state aid for adult education.

Temporary State Commission on Coordination of State Activities, *Third Interim Report*. Legislative Document no. 64, Williams Press, Albany, 1949. How the state supervises the schools of New York City.

Perry, Cyrus C., *Review of Determinations by the Board of Examiners of the New York City Board of Education*. Master's thesis, Columbia University, 1941, unpublished.

Public Education Association, *A Citizen's Guide to the New York City Public Schools*. The Association, New York, 1958. A brief explanation of the structure and functioning of the New York City school system and its relationships with municipal officials and public municipal bodies.

Rivelson, Lena T., *Historical Development and Organization of the Board of Education of the City of New York*. Master's thesis, Columbia University, 1919, unpublished.

Strayer, George D., and Louis E. Yavner, *Administrative Management of the School System of New York City: A View in Perspective and a Summary of Recommendations*. Mayor's Committee on Management Survey, New York, 1951. A summary volume which digests the work of the larger report by the same authors and highlights their recommendations.

Administrative Management of the School System: Report of Survey of the Board of Education and the Board of Higher Education, Mayor's Committee on Management Survey, New York, 1951. 2 vols.

Interim Report on the Administrative Management of the School System of the City of New York: Some Aspects of the Division of Housing and Related Administrative Problems. Mayor's Committee on Management Survey, New York, 1951.

Personalities in the School System

Abelow, Samuel P., Dr. *William H. Maxwell: The First Superintendent of Schools of the City of New York.* Scheba Publishing Co., Brooklyn, 1934. A biography of the city's first Superintendent of Schools, which also reveals a great deal about the public schools of his day.

Maxwell, William H., *A Quarter Century of Public School Development.* American Book Co., New York, 1912. The Superintendent of Brooklyn in the last years of that municipality and the first Superintendent of Schools of Greater New York in the early years of consolidation presents his views on education in New York City.

Patri, Angelo, *A Schoolmaster of the Great City.* Macmillan Co., New York, 1917. This frank autobiography reveals much about the New York City schools of his day.

Public Higher Education in New York City

Coulton, Thomas E., *A City College in Action: Struggle and Achievement at Brooklyn College, 1930–1955.* Harper and Bros., New York, 1955. The story of a municipally supported college.

Rudy, S. Willis, *The College of the City of New York: A History, 1847–1947.* City College Press, New York, 1949. A history of an experiment in free higher education.

White, Samuel P., *Hunter College: Eighty-Five Years of Service.* Lantern Press, New York, 1955. A history of a municipal college.

DEPARTMENT OF FINANCE

Official Sources and Issuances

New York City Charter, chap. 17, secs. 411–421.

New York City Administrative Code, chap. 17.

Department of Finance, *Annual Reports* of the Treasurer, fiscal years 1938–1953 (published annually); *Annual Report to the Mayor, 1958.*

Surveys and Discussions

Bruère, Henry, *New York City's Administrative Program, 1914–1916.* M. B. Brown and Co., New York, 1916, pp. 60–61. The city's Department of Finance during the Mitchel administration.

Nelson, Robert E., *An Administrative Study of the New York City Department of Finance.* Master's thesis, Columbia University, 1942, unpublished.

New York City, Mayor's Committee on Management Survey, *Department of Finance: Office of the City Collector.* Bureau of the Budget, New York, 1953.

New York State, Temporary State Commission to Study the Organizational Structure of the Government of the City of New York, *Four Steps to Better Government of New York City: A Plan for Action.* 2 vols. The Commission, New York, 1953, vol. 2, pp. 25–26. Proposals for a unified Department of Taxation and Finance.

Tanzer, Lawrence A., *The New York City Charter.* Clark Boardman Co., New York, 1937, pp. 136–138, 219. What the Thacher Commission's charter said about the Department of Finance.

FIRE DEPARTMENT

Official Sources and Issuances

New York City Charter, chap. 19, secs. 481–494, as amended by Local Law 8, 1947.

New York City Administrative Code, chap. 19, secs. 487a–491a.

Fire Department, *Annual Reports,* 1898; 1899–1900 (1 vol.); 1901–1952 (published annually); 1953–1954 (1 vol.); 1955 to date (published annually).

Surveys and Discussions

Adamson, Robert, "Fire Administration," *Proceedings* of the Academy of Political Science in the City of New York, vol. 5, April, 1915, pp. 544–556. The Fire Department in a transitional stage, with the motor replacing the horse, the high-pressure water system, the fire engine, and the gasoline and steam engines.

Citizens Budget Commission of New York, *A Better Government for a Better City: A Study of Five Departments of the City of New York at the Request of Honorable William O'Dwyer, Mayor.* The Commission, New York, 1948, pp. 285–376. The administration and functioning of the Fire Department.

Driscoll, Clement J., "Discussion of Fire Administration," *Proceedings* of the Academy of Political Science in the City of New York, vol. 5, April, 1915, pp. 557–563. A member of the Bureau of Municipal Research discusses administrative problems relating to fire fighting.

Dunshee, Kenneth H., *As You Pass By.* Hastings House, New York, 1952. Fire-fighting operations in the historic past.

Katsaros, James, "New York City Fire Department: Development of Its Organization and Functions, 1865–1949," 1949. Typewritten copy in Municipal Reference Library.

Limpus, Lowell M., *History of the New York Fire Department.* E. P. Dutton and Co., New York, 1940. Relates the story of the Fire Department, how it grew, and how it functioned in 1940.

New York City Commissioners of Accounts and New York Bureau of Municipal Research, *Government of the City of New York: A Survey of Its Organization and Functions.* J. J. Little and Ives Co., New York, 1915, pp. 574–615. Appraises the work of the Fire Department, just before the Constitutional Convention of 1915.

Mayor's Committee on Management Survey, *Modern Management for the City of New York.* 2 vols. The Committee, New York, 1953, vol. 2, pp. 42–45, 321–322, 709–817, 860. A survey of the special Fire Department studies, conducted by the Mayor's Committee.

Mayor's Commission on Management Survey, *Documents on Fire Department Studies.* The Committee, New York, 1952. Summaries, findings, and recommendations on five reports.

Mayor's Executive Committee on Administration, *Fire Department: Supplementary Report— Reorganization of the Fire Department.* Bureau of the Budget, New York, 1949.

DEPARTMENT OF HEALTH

Official Sources and Issuances

New York City Charter, chap. 22, secs. 561–568.

New York City Administrative Code, chap. 22, secs. 552–567.

Board of Health, *The Sanitary Code of the City of New York.* City Record, New York, 1957. The rules and regulations of the Department of Health, known as the Sanitary Code, under sec. 558 of the city charter.

New York City Health Code, effective October 1, 1959. Revision and replacement of the Sanitary Code.

Department of Health, *Annual Reports,* 1898–1909 (published annually); 1910–1911 (1 vol.); 1912–1929 (published annually); 1930–1931 (1 vol.); 1932–1937 (summaries, 1934 and 1935, typewritten); 1938–1940 (published annually); 1941–1944 (summaries); 1941–1945 (1 vol., vital statistics); 1946 and 1947 (summaries); 1941–1948 (1 vol.); 1950–1954 (published annually); 1955–1956 (biennial report); 1957 (annual review); 1958 (annual report).

Legislative Drafting Research Fund, New York City Health Code, Preliminary Drafts. Columbia University, Legislative Drafting Research Fund, Sanitary Code Revision Project, mimeographed, 1956. Preliminary drafts of the revision of the Sanitary Code prepared for the Board of Health by the Legislative Drafting Research Fund.

Surveys and Discussions

American Public Health Association, *Study of the Department of Health, City of New York.* Mayor's Committee on Management Survey, New York, 1952. A technical analysis.

Barrington Associations, Inc., *Survey of Business Management and Procedures in the Department of Health, City of New York.* Mayor's Committee on Management Survey, New York, 1951. An efficiency analysis.

Baumgartner, Leona, "Fifty Years of Child Health Services in New York City," *Municipal Reference Library Notes,* vol. 34, May, 1959, pp. 137–138. The Health Commissioner presents the highlights in the development of the Division of Child Hygiene since its inception.

Blake, John, *Historical Study of the Development of the New York City Department of Health.* Mayor's Committee on Management Survey, New York, 1951. The evolution of a city agency.

City Club of New York, *Report on Charter Revision.* The Club, New York, 1921, pp. 25–28. Observations on the Department of Health in 1921.

Dworkis, Martin B., *The Impact of Puerto Rican Migration on Governmental Services in New York City.* New York University Press, New York, 1957, pp. 45–52. The Department of Health and the Puerto Rican in-migrants.

Goldwater, S. S., "Public Health and Sanitation," *Proceedings* of the Academy of Political Science in the City of New York, vol. 5, April, 1915, pp. 495–521. An examination of the structure and functioning of the Department of Health in 1915.

Kaufman, Herbert, *The New York City Health Centers.* Inter-University Case Program, University of Alabama Press, University, Ala., 1959. Problems of organization and re-organization in the New York City Health Department.

Levine, Eugene, *Modern Federalism in Public Health: An Analysis of New York City's Relations with Other Governments in the Field of Public Health.* Master's thesis, New York University, 1950, unpublished.

New York City, Commissioners of Accounts and New York Bureau of Municipal Research, *Government of the City of New York: A Survey of Its Organizations and Functions .*J. J. Little and Ives Co., New York, 1915, pp. 620–743. A survey of the work of the Department of Health.

Mayor's Committee on Management Survey, *Modern Management for the City of New York.* 2 vols. The Committee, New York, 1953. Vol. 1, pp. 242–243, an excellent introduction, to the subject of municipal health administration, and vol. 2, pp. 38–40, 626–677, a *précis* of the reports of the specialized studies of the Mayor's Committee.

Mayor's Executive Committee on Administration, *Department of Health: Proposed Re-organization of the Department of Health.* Bureau of the Budget, New York, 1948. A critical appraisal.

Roueché, Berton, *Eleven Blue Men and Other Narratives of Medical Detection.* Little, Brown and Co., Boston, 1953.

DEPARTMENT OF HOSPITALS

Official Sources and Issuances

New York City Charter, chap. 23, secs. 581–588.

New York City Administrative Code, chap. 23, secs. 581–587.

Board of Hospitals, *Hospital Code of New York City.*

Department of Hospitals, *Annual Reports:* 1929, 1930, 1935, 1936, 1937–1943, 1946 to date (published annually).

Surveys and Discussions

City Club of New York, *Report on Charter Revision.* The Club, New York, 1921, pp. 25–28. The Department of Bellevue and Allied Hospitals in 1921 examined critically.

Cutolo, Salvatore R., *Bellevue Is My Home.* Doubleday and Co., New York, 1956. An account of the work of the largest city hospital by a doctor long associated with Bellevue Hospital.

Dworkis, Martin B., *The Impact of Puerto Rican Migration on Governmental Services in New York City*. New York University Press, New York, 1957, pp. 52–53. How the influx of islanders has affected the work of the Department of Hospitals.

Ginzberg, Eli, *A Pattern for Hospital Care: Final Report of the New York State Hospital Study*. Columbia University Press, New York, 1949, pp. 149–169. A comprehensive study of hospital care in the state, including an analysis of the municipal hospital system of New York.

Maynard, Lorraine, and Lawrence Miscall, *Bellevue*. Julian Messner, Inc., New York, 1940. A sympathetic picture.

New York City, Commissioners of Accounts and New York Bureau of Municipal Research, *Government of the City of New York: A Survey of Its Organization and Functions*. J. J. Little and Ives Co., New York, 1915, pp. 792–840. A description of the functioning of the Department of Bellevue and Allied Hospitals.

    Mayor's Executive Committee on Administration, *Department of Hospitals: A Study of the Executive Administration of the Department of Hospitals of the City of New York*. Bureau of the Budget, New York, 1948. A management survey.

    Mayor's Committee on Management Survey, *Modern Management for the City of New York*. 2 vols. The Committee, New York, 1953, vol. 1, pp. 36–38, 311–314, 595–625, 859. A digest of the findings of studies on municipal hospitals and their problems.

    Mayor's Committee on Management Survey, *New York City Department of Hospitals*. 4 vols. Booz, Allen, and Hamilton, Management Consultants, New York, 1951. A detailed survey of the organization and administration of the Department of Hospitals.

O'Hanlon, George, "The Hospitals of the City of New York," *Proceedings* of the Academy of Political Science in the City of New York, vol. 5, April, 1915, pp. 525–527. The medical superintendent of Bellevue and Allied Hospitals in 1915 describes the administration of these institutions.

Starr, John, *Hospital City*. Crown Publishers, New York, 1957.

POLICE DEPARTMENT

Official Sources and Issuances

New York City Charter, chap. 18, secs. 431–439 (as amended by Local Law 6, 1946, Local Law 43, 1954, Local Law 2, 1949, Local Law 27, 1954, and Local Law 39, 1947).

New York City Administrative Code, chap. 18, secs. 434a–436.

Police Department, *Annual Reports*, 1898–1905 (published annually); 1906–1907 (1 vol.); 1908–1942 (published annually); 1943–1944 (1 vol.); 1945–1946 (1 vol.); 1947 to date (published annually).

Organization and Administration of the Police Department

Berger, Meyer, "The Finest," in Alexander Klein, editor, *The Empire City*. Rinehart and Co., New York, 1955, pp. 348–354. A great reporter describes the work of the Police Department from Police Commissioner to the street patrolman.

Caputo, Rudolph R., "The New York City Transit Police Department," *Law and Order*, April, 1959, pp. 6–8, 10–12, 67.

Citizens Budget Commission of New York, *A Better Government for a Better City: A Study of Five Departments of the City at the Request of Honorable William O'Dwyer, Mayor*. The Commission, New York, 1948, pp. 216–263. The organization and operation of the Police Department.

Citizens Union, "Police Reconstruction," *The Searchlight*, vol. 3, March 10, 1913. This special police number offers a summary of a variety of plans for reform of the police force of the day.

City Club of New York, *Report on Charter Revision*. The Club, New York, 1921, pp. 29–30. An evaluation of the charter provisions relating to the Police Department of the day.

Crump, Irving, and John W. Newton, *Our Police*. Dodd Mead and Co., New York, 1935. A graphic presentation of the work of the New York City police.

Driscoll, Clement J., "Discussion of Police Administration," *Proceedings* of the Academy of Political Science in the City of New York, vol. 5, April, 1915, pp. 540–543. A Deputy Police Commissioner outlines some of the difficulties in police administration in New York City.

Dworkis, Martin B., *The Impact of Puerto Rican Migration on Governmental Services in New York City*. New York University Press, New York, 1957, pp. 54–62. Police problems created by mass migration of islanders.

Hang, Ching Hui, *Police Administration in New York, Chicago, and Philadelphia*. Doctoral dissertation, University of Illinois, 1921.

Institute of Public Administration, *The New York Police Survey: Summary Volume*. Mayor's Committee on Management Survey, New York, 1952.

Katsaros, James, "Development of Its [the Police Department] Organization and Functions, 1643–1948," Municipal Archives, 1949. Gives highlights of work of Department.

Newman, George Sheridan, *Description and Analysis of the Organization of the Police Department of the City of New York*. Master's thesis, Columbia University, 1940, unpublished.

New York City, Commissioners of Accounts and New York Bureau of Municipal Research, *Goverment of the City of New York: A Survey of Its Organization and Functions*. J. J. Little and Ives Co., New York, 1915, pp. 542–572. The operation of the Police Department in 1915.

Mayor's Committee on Management Survey, *Modern Management for the City of New York*. 2 vols. The Committee, New York, 1953, vol. 2, pp. 45–48, 322–324, 818–852, 860. A brief exposition of the studies made by the Mayor's Committee on Police Administration.

Schachne, Carolyn F., *Some Aspects in the History of the Police Department of the City of New York, 1870–1901*. Master's thesis, Columbia University, 1940, unpublished.

Smith, Bruce, *Police Systems in the United States*. Harper and Bros., New York, 1949, pp. 240–242. An incisive presentation of the structure and organization of the Police Department of New York City.

Smith, Bruce, and others, *The New York Police Survey*. Mayor's Committee on Management Survey, New York, 1952. A study prepared by the Institute of Public Administration.

Syrett, Harold C., editor, *The Gentleman and the Tiger: The Autobiography of George B. McClellan, Jr.* J. B. Lippincott Co., Philadelphia, 1956, pp. 199–206, 234–237, 295–299. An account of the police force under the Mayor of New York, 1904–1909.

Wheeler, Everett P., *Sixty Years of American Life*. E. P. Dutton and Co., New York, 1917, pp. 373–379. From Police Board to Police Commissioner as head of the Department: how the change was made.

Woo, Young Fan, *A Study of Municipal Police Personnel, with Special Reference to the City of New York*. Master's thesis, Columbia University, 1940, unpublished.

Woods, Arthur, "Police Administration," *Proceedings* of the Academy of Political Science in the City of New York, vol. 5, April, 1915, pp. 532–539. The Commissioner of Police describes the work of that agency in 1915 and his plans for the future.

Police Investigations and Why They Started

Arm, Walter, *Pay-Off! The Inside Story of Big City Corruption*. Appleton-Century-Crofts, New York, 1951. How a large segment of the police force cooperated with a gambling ring and how the relationship was revealed.

Katsaros, James, "List of Investigations into Police Conditions in New York City Made by State and City Authorities and Private Organizations, 1831–1949" (1949). Typewritten copy in Municipal Reference Library.

Lavine, Emanuel H., *Secrets of the Metropolitan Police*. Garden City Publishing Co., Garden City, N. Y., 1937. Some of the less savory aspects of police operations in an age of exposure.

Mockridge, Norton, and Robert H. Prall, *The Big Fix*. Henry Holt and Co., New York, 1954. How a gambling syndicate won over certain portions of the police and how that relationship was exposed.

New York City Board of Aldermen, *Report of the Special Committee of the Board of Aldermen to the City of New York Appointed August 5, 1912 to Investigate the Police Department.* M. B. Brown and Co., New York, 1913. An investigation that led to a "shake-up" and reform of the Police Department, and which helped elect a City Fusion administration.

New York State Legislature, *Report and Proceedings of the Senate Committee to Investigate the Police Department of the City of New York.* 5 vols. J. B. Lyon, Albany, 1895. The investigation by the Lexow Committee.

Northrop, William B., and John B. Northrop, *The Insolence of Office: The Story of the Seabury Investigation.* G. P. Putnam's Sons, New York, 1932, pp. 25–40. A picture of the vice squad in 1930–1932.

Reid, Edward, *The Shame of New York.* Random House, New York, 1953. An exposure of the relationship between criminals and certain elements of the police force in New York.

Thomas, Norman, and Paul Blanshard, *What's the Matter with New York?* Macmillan Co., New York, 1932, pp. 144–149. What the investigations of the thirties revealed about the vice squad.

Personalities and Personal Recollections

Alexander, Jack, "Independent Cop: Profile of Lewis J. Valentine," *The New Yorker*, vol. 12, October 3, 1936, pp. 21–27; October 10, 1936, pp. 26–30; and October 17, 1936, pp. 30–40. The biography of a Police Commissioner which reveals much about the Police Department and the men who operate it.

Limpus, Lowell M., *Honest Cop: Lewis J. Valentine; Being a Chronicle of the Commissioner's Thirty-Six Years in the New York Police Department.* E. P. Dutton and Co., New York, 1939. Written with the assistance of Commissioner Valentine, who opened the files of the Police Department to the author's inspection.

McAdoo, William, *Guarding a Great City.* Harper and Bros., New York, 1906. New York's Police Commissioner from 1904–1906 discusses the problems of the Police Department and its Commissioners.

McAllister, Robert, and Floyd Miller, *The Kind of Guy I Am.* McGraw-Hill Book Co., New York, 1957. The story of a man who started as a patrolman in 1921 and rose to a Deputy Inspector in 1953 offers a view of the organization and activities of the city's Police Department over three decades.

Reynolds, Quentin, *Headquarters.* Harper and Bros., New York, 1955. Ostensibly the story of Frank Phillips, Commanding Officer of the Detective Bureau, the volume also gives an overview of the Police Department.

Roosevelt, Theodore, *An Autobiography.* Macmillan Co., New York, 1914. Theodore Roosevelt's impressions as Police Commissioner, just before the consolidation of the city (pp. 172–208). Excerpted in Hermann Hagedorn, editor, *The Theodore Roosevelt Treasury: A Self-Portrait from His Writings.* G. P. Putnam's Sons, New York, 1957, pp. 93–104.

Steffens, Lincoln, *Autobiography.* Literary Guild, New York, 1931, pp. 197–230. Recollections of a police reporter in New York.

Ulmann, Albert, *New Yorkers from Stuyvesant to Roosevelt.* Chaucer Head Book Shop, New York, 1928, pp. 236–238. A brief glimpse of the New York City Police Department on the eve of consolidation may be found in this biography of Theodore Roosevelt, who served as President of the Police Board from 1895–1897.

Valentine, Lewis J., *Police Night Stick: The Autobiography of Lewis J. Valentine.* Dial Press, New York, 1947. Memoirs of a police chief.

Wallander, Arthur W., "Reminiscences." Columbia University Oral History Collection, Special Collections, Butler Library. A Police Commissioner tells of his work on the city's police force (1914–1949).

Walling, George W., *Recollections of a New York Chief of Police.* Caxton Book Co., New York, 1887. A graphic description of police work in New York before the consolidation of the city.

Whalen, Grover A., *Mr. New York: Autobiography of Grover A. Whalen*. G. P. Putnam's Sons, New York, 1955, pp. 135–165. Recollections as Police Commissioner.
Scrapbooks. In Municipal Archives, 231 vols.

Willemse, Cornelius W., *A Cop Remembers*. E. P. Dutton and Co., New York, 1933. Recollections of a police officer who saw much of police methods and organization.

DEPARTMENT OF SANITATION

Official Sources and Issuances

New York City Charter, chap. 31, secs. 751–759 (as amended by Local Law 36, 1957).

New York City Administrative Code, chap. 31, secs. 751–759.

Board of Health, *The Sanitary Code of the City of New York, Including Regulations as Amended to December 21, 1956*. City Record, New York, 1957. More recent regulations may be found in the Municipal Reference Library, bound with recent regulations of other city departments.

Citizens Committee to Keep New York City Clean, *Digest of New York City Sanitary Code*. The Committee, New York, 1916. A brief summary of the salient points in the Sanitary Code.

Department of Street Cleaning, *Annual Reports*, 1898–1901 (published annually); 1902–1911 (1 vol.); 1912–1918 (published annually); 1919–1920 (1 vol.); and 1921–1929 (published annually).

Department of Sanitation, *Annual Reports*, 1930, 1931, 1934–1940, 1946 to date (published annually).

Surveys and Discussions

Citizens Budget Commission of New York, *A Better Government for a Better City: A Study of Five Departments of the City of New York at the Request of Honorable William O'Dwyer, Mayor*. The Commission, New York, 1948. The functioning of the Sanitation Department with specific recommendations for streamlining its procedures.

City Club of New York, *Report on Charter Revision*. The Club, New York, 1921, pp. 18–19. An appraisal of the work of the Street Cleaning Department of 1921.

Morrison, Donal M., *Gotham Cleans Its Doorstep*. Citizens Union Research Foundation, New York, 1950. The problem of disposing of the city's wastes.

New York City, Commissioners of Accounts and New York Bureau of Municipal Research, *Government of the City of New York: A Survey of Its Organization and Functions*. J. J. Little and Ives Co., New York, 1915, pp. 966–990. A critical appraisal of the functioning of the Department of Street Cleaning.

Mayor's Committee on Management Survey, *Modern Management for the City of New York*. 2 vols. The Committee, New York, 1953, vol. 2. pp. 40–42, 678–708, 859. The work of the Department of Sanitation as viewed by the Mayor's Committee.

Mayor's Executive Committee on Administration. *Department of Sanitation: Study of the Organization Structure*. Bureau of the Budget, New York, 1948. A management survey.

Municipal Reference Library, "Looking Ahead," *Municipal Reference Library Notes*, vol. 33, January, 1956. Some observations on the city's Sanitary Code.

Rogus, Casimir A., "What New York Has Learned About Street Cleaning," *The American City*, July, 1951.

Trundle Engineering Company, *Department of Sanitation of the City of New York*. Mayor's Committee on Management Survey, New York, 1951. A technical analysis.

TRAFFIC DEPARTMENT

Official Sources and Issuances

New York City Charter, chap. 46, secs. 1061–1064 (as added by Local Law 2, 1949, and amended by Local Law 102, 1949, and Local Law 27, 1950).

Department of Traffic, *Traffic Regulations Established by the Commissioner of Traffic Under Authority of Chapter 46 of the New York City Charter.* The Department, New York, July 1, 1958.

Annual Reports, 1950–1951 (1 vol.), 1953, 1954, 1956.

Bulletin, published monthly, September, 1953, to date.

Traffic Engineering Newsletter, March, 1959, to date. A monthly publication of the Department of Traffic.

McKinney's Consolidated Laws of New York, Annotated, Book 62-A. *Vehicle and Traffic Law.* Edward Thompson Co., Brooklyn, N. Y. Kept up to date with annual supplements. State laws that regulate vehicles and traffic in New York City, including court interpretations.

Surveys and Discussions

Citizens Budget Commission, *City Traffic Control.* The Commission, New York, 1948. An analysis of the city's traffic problems, as a result of which a Traffic Commission was proposed.

Citizens Union, "A Citizen Union Program to Relieve Traffic Congestion," *The Searchlight* vol. 38, December, 1948. A call for a separate over-all traffic agency, which preceded the creation of the present Department of Traffic.

"Crisis in Traffic," *The Searchlight,* vol. 42, March, 1952. An outline of the city's traffic problems and the role of the newly organized Department of Traffic.

McInerney, Timothy J., "The Pedestrian Safety Campaign in New York City," *Traffic Quarterly,* April, 1959, pp. 283–293.

New York City Municipal Reference Library, *Municipal Reference Library Notes,* vol. 31, no 2, February, 1949. A description of the newly established 1949 Traffic Commission.

"Looking Ahead," *Municipal Reference Library Notes,* vol. 33, January, 1956. A brief discussion of the Traffic Code.

Ross, Victor, "Traffic Control in New York City," *Law and Order,* June, 1957, pp. 5, 46–48. Problems of traffic regulations in the city's streets.

Wiley, T. T., *A Safe Journey.* Citizens Union Research Foundation, New York, 1948. The Commissioner of Traffic discusses the problems of his department and efforts being made to solve them.

DEPARTMENT OF WELFARE

Official Sources and Issuances

New York City Charter, chap. 24, secs. 601–604.

New York City Administrative Code, chap. 24, secs. 603 and 604.

Department of Public Welfare, *Annual Reports,* 1920–1926 (published annually); 1930, 1931, 1932 (on film at New York Public Library); 1934–1937 (published annually).

Department of Welfare, *Annual Reports,* 1938–1939, 1939–1940, 1948, 1949, 1951, and 1955 to date (published annually).

McKinney's Consolidated Laws of New York, Annotated, Book 52-A, *Social Welfare Law.* Edward Thompson Co., Brooklyn, N. Y., 1941. Kept up to date with annual supplements. Known as the State Charities Law until 1929. Has been of great importance since the depression of 1929. This volume contains a historical introduction by the Honorable Nathaniel Fensterstock, Assistant Attorney General of New York. These are the rules that govern official welfare agencies in New York City. Relevant judicial decisions are included.

Surveys and Discussions

Blair, Paxton, "Reminiscences." Columbia University Oral History Collection, Special Collections, Butler Library. An account of the New York City Welfare Department.

City Club of New York, *Report on Charter Revision.* The Club, New York, 1921, pp. 25–28. Recommendations relating to the Board of Child Welfare and the Department of Public Welfare.

Dworkis, Martin B., *The Impact of Puerto Rican Migration on Governmental Services in New York City*. New York University Press, New York, 1957, pp. 27–30. How the arrival of hundreds of thousands of Puerto Ricans has affected the work of the Department of Welfare.

Institute of Public Administration, *Intergovernmental Relations in Welfare Administration*. Mayor's Committee on Management Survey, New York, 1952.

Kingsbury, John A., "The Department of Charities," *Proceedings* of the Academy of Political Science in the City of New York, vol. 5, April, 1915, pp. 576–580. The Commissioner of the Department outlines its history and its operations in 1915.

New York City, Commissioners of Accounts and New York Bureau of Municipal Research, *Government of the City of New York: A Survey of Its Organization and Functions*. J. J. Little and Ives Co., New York, 1915, pp. 744–791. An analysis of the work of the Department of Public Charities.

Mayor's Committee on Management Survey, *Modern Management for the City of New York*. 2 vols. The Committee, New York, 1953. Vol. 1, pp. 243–244, a general overview of municipal welfare administration; vol. 2, pp. 34–36, 327–330, 507–594, 859, an outline of the findings and conclusions of the studies on welfare administration in New York City made by the Mayor's Committee on Management Survey.

New York State Department of Social Welfare, "Report of the Inquiry into the Administration of Public Welfare in New York City," pp. 25–47 of the 1947 *Annual Report* of the Department, 1948.

Public Administration Service, *Administrative Decentralization in the Department of Welfare*. Mayor's Committee on Management Survey, New York, 1951. A study of the Department's structure and organization.

Welfare and Health Council of New York City, *Statistical and Research Activities of Municipal Welfare, Health and Education Agencies in New York City*. The Council, New York, 1955, pp. 24–25. Research activities carried on by the Department of Welfare.

CHAPTER IX

Officials of Special Authorities

THE STATUS OF SPECIAL AUTHORITIES

Their Position in Government

UNTIL 1921 when one spoke of a state or local public agency in New York State it was fairly clear that the reference was either to a line or overhead agency of the state government or to one of its political subdivisions (including school districts). Then a new governmental form appeared on the scene— new, that is, to New York State, although the government corporation device, to which public authorities are related, had been used earlier by the federal government and by some foreign governments. But the prototype of the authorities in New York State was the Port of London Authority organized in 1909; it was the model for the state's first public authority venture, the Port of New York Authority (established jointly by New York and New Jersey in 1921), and, with modifications, for almost all of the later ones. In the ensuing years, up to 1955, 52 additional authorities were created in New York State (of which 33 were active at the start of 1956), as well as 67 housing authorities (of which 45 were active), and three additional ones were set up in 1956.

As governmental instruments, they have thus had a meteoric rise, and if they were to be created and to survive in the future at the same rate as in the past, the state would be teeming with them in a few generations, a prospect alarming to some observers of the political scene. The alarm stems not merely from hostility to the growth of governmental activity; it comes also from the inability to fit this newcomer into the existing governmental framework. "The degree of autonomy granted such authorities," declared the Temporary State Commission on the Coordination of State Activities, "and their relationships to the traditional operations and the regular departments of the state government pose problems which may affect the efficient, responsive and responsible conduct of administration." And the Commission staff reported, "The public authority in New York State operates in a legal context which is the result of change and experimentation. . . . Its status in the framework of government has not yet been definitely fixed, and the legal framework for authority operation is far from final."

Six of these strange new creatures are currently at work within the borders of New York City—five exclusively within the municipality, one in the whole port area, which includes the harbor areas of New Jersey. They are all that remain of a total of 13 created to function in this territory, their number having been thinned by consolidation, and, in a few cases, by failure to get started. No two are exactly alike in structure or function, but they all exist in the interstices between governmental and private organizations, and between the city and the state.

Their Functions

Functionally, they are line agencies. They serve the public directly through the construction and operation of various kinds of facilities used by the people of the city and the metropolitan area, and they make regulations governing the public in the use of those services and facilities.

The Port of New York Authority. This agency, the first of the long parade of public authorities in New York State, is charged with developing the "terminal, transportation, and other facilities" within the port district, a territory extending roughly 20 miles in every direction from the Statue of Liberty. Established in 1921 by a compact between the states of New York and New Jersey, which was approved by Congress, it was originally intended to obtain cooperation among the railroads serving the area so as to reduce switching, lighter, and barge costs, and to free many of the region's piers used by the railroads for world shipping. However, its efforts to introduce joint use of yards, stations, engines, and rights of way; to construct a union beltline railroad in Manhattan; and to secure reciprocal switching, shared carfloats, and other cooperative practices—all came to naught. There are only a few important instances of joint use of equipment or installations of this kind, and many piers throughout the harbor are still devoted exclusively to railroad operations.

When the Authority embarked on a program of acquiring, constructing, and operating facilities on its own, however, its advances were remarkable. It moved in directions not originally contemplated as its central program, but it made rapid progress in those directions. In 1928, it opened two bridges between Staten Island and New Jersey. In 1931, it opened a third such bridge, acquired the Holland Tunnel (which had been built earlier by a different interstate body), and finished the George Washington Bridge. In 1932, it opened a Union Inland Freight Terminal in Manhattan, for handling less-than-carload freight and transferring much trucking congestion away from the crowded waterfront. In 1938, the first tube of the Lincoln Tunnel commenced operations. In 1944, the Authority took over a grain terminal and piers in Brooklyn from New York State. In 1945, the second tube, and in 1957, the third tube, of the Lincoln Tunnel were completed. In 1947, the Port body leased La Guardia and Idlewild Airports from New York City to complete, expand, improve, and manage them. Newark Airport was similarly added to its airport terminal network shortly afterward and it bought Teterboro Airport (in New Jersey) for air freight traffic. It built a truck terminal in Manhattan in 1949, one in Newark in 1950, and put up a union bus terminal in Manhattan in 1951. Port Newark and Hoboken's piers are leased to it for development and administration. In less than forty years the Port Authority has grown from a plan on paper to a multifunctional operation with an investment approaching a billion dollars.

The Triborough Bridge and Tunnel Authority. Created by the State of New York in 1946, this agency is a consolidation of a number of previous authorities. Originally, the Triborough Bridge Authority was set up in 1933 to construct the Triborough Bridge linking Manhattan, The Bronx, and Queens, a project first conceived as early as 1916 but not completed until federal depression assistance for municipal public works was extended. The bridge was opened to traffic in 1936, the first intracity toll bridge in New York City. In the same period, the Marine Parkway Authority was established to construct a toll bridge and roadway connecting Brooklyn with the Rockaway beaches in Queens; the Henry Hudson Parkway Authority was founded to put up a toll bridge between the northern tip of Manhattan and The Bronx; and the Queens-Midtown Tunnel Authority was added to the roster to build a vehicular toll link between Queens and central Manhattan. In 1936, the Queens-Midtown Tunnel Authority was superseded by the New York City Tunnel Authority, with power to complete the Queens tunnel and to construct another between the Battery (at the southern tip of Manhattan) and Brooklyn. In 1938, the Henry Hudson and the Marine Parkway Authorities were fused to form the New York City Parkway Authority, which soon added the Cross Bay toll bridge between central Queens and the beach areas to its other facilities. In 1940, the Parkway Authority was absorbed by the Triborough Bridge Authority, which meanwhile built a new bridge between The Bronx and the Whitestone section of Queens. In 1946, the New York City Tunnel Authority was also absorbed by the Triborough Authority, which was then designated the Triborough Bridge and Tunnel Authority, and given exclusive power to construct bridges and tunnels connecting the boroughs of the city. In the next decade, strengthened by the combined toll-charging structures of no fewer than five other authorities now placed under its jurisdiction, it completed the Brooklyn-Battery Tunnel, the Battery Parking Garage, an airlines terminal building, and built the New York Coliseum in Columbus Circle. The depression-born child of adversity reached opulent maturity in less than a quarter of a century.

The New York City Housing Authority. The Housing Authority was also sired by the depression, having been established by the city in 1934 under state legislation enacted the same year in order to permit municipalities in New York to take advantage of the federal aid for housing then available. Its purpose was (and still is) the construction and management of low-rent housing projects for low-income families, and, more recently, some "middle-income" housing. Altogether it has built over 80 public housing projects containing more than 88,000 dwelling units in the last twenty-five years, and there are more in progress and in the planning stage; its properties are worth about $2 billion.

The New York City Transit Authority. The Transit Authority was established in 1953 over the objections of the Mayor and other city officials when the Governor and the state legislature insisted that this was a preferable alternative to granting the city new taxing authority to meet the deficits of transit operation. It took over and now operates 327 route miles of subways and elevated transit railways and 580 route miles of bus routes, all owned by the city and previously managed for it by the Board of Transportation. The original pattern of transit operation in the city was private, though under public supervision, but the private operators were unable to make the system pay, despite the fact that the city financed construction of the subways and leased the rights of way to the private operators. The Board of Transportation tried to follow the original pattern when, with federal depression help, it completed new lines in 1932, but it was unable to find anyone to operate them on a leasehold or contract basis and thus found itself in the business of running subways. In 1940 it bought from the receivers the properties of the older lines and undertook to unify the entire system. Meanwhile, it undertook to provide bus service where private capital refused to venture. Deficits mounted after World War II, especially in the rapid transit system, and increases in fares failed to stem the tide. It was at this point that the city approached the state, as it had recurrently, for new tax sources to meet transit deficits. The state responded by creating the Transit Authority to take over the transit functions and directed it to pay operating expenses from operating revenues. The Transit Authority was directed by its enabling statute to dispose of its surface lines to private companies, but it was unable to do so because the companies refused to bid on any but the most profitable routes. Improved management and maintenance practices have since eliminated over-all bus line deficits, so the Authority has held on to these operations. Since its inception, the Authority has expanded its subway services, improved service and purchased new equipment, and renovated its rights of way.

The Planetarium Authority. This agency was established in 1933 for the sole purpose of erecting a planetarium as part of the Museum of Natural History. By selling bonds to the Reconstruction Finance Corporation, accepting a private donation to purchase the planetarium projection instrument, and accepting the city's donation of the land on which the institution stands, it was able to construct the planetarium. By 1939, however, it was in default on its bonds. In 1949 the RFC, taking a loss on its $650,000 investment, sold the bonds to the Museum of Natural History, which is now the sole creditor of the Authority. The board of the Authority is identical with the Board of Trustees of the museum, so the Authority, though legally in existence, is nothing more than a bookkeeping item today. Its objective achieved, it is defunct for all practical purposes.

The Brooklyn Sports Center Authority. Established in 1956 by state legislation enacted at the request of the city, this Authority was to build a sports arena to house the Brooklyn Dodgers. Before the members of the Authority could decide on a course of action, however, the Dodgers and the Giants both moved to the West Coast, and the sense of urgency driving the agency (since this was the event it was designed to prevent) declined. Although rumors persist that it may yet build a stadium for some other National League baseball team, it is, for the time being, dormant.

Reasons for the Appearance and Growth of the Authorities

Authorities come into existence and thrive for financial, political, and jurisdictional reasons. The financial imperatives are perhaps the most compelling: since the state constitution places a ceiling on the amount of indebtedness the city may incur, and since the city is constantly pressing on that ceiling, the city simply cannot borrow enough to finance many needed improvements. The compulsion has been ameliorated by an amendment to the constitution permitting exclusion of self-liquidating projects (or of that proportion of the indebtedness for the project that is covered by project revenues) from the debt limit. Nevertheless, many authorities got their start before the amendment, and they are convenient instruments to employ when new facilities are needed and problems of financing present themselves. Moreover, the constitution contains a limit on the capacity of the city to finance its activities by property taxation. With the city at this limit all the time and virtually every other source of tax revenue exploited as fully as possible, it cannot afford to take on new responsibilities that might add to its regular expenses even temporarily. Thus confined, the city turns to the authorities, which, as will shortly be seen, with one partial exception, have their own sources of capital and operating funds.

Jurisdictional reasons are behind the creation of the Port Authority. The functions it was called upon to perform cut across the boundaries of two states and many local units of government in the metropolitan region. No other governmental institution was legally equipped to do the needed work. Once it got started, it was aided by the fiscal problems of New York City as the city sought to escape from its fiscal limitations by calling upon the Port Authority to assume some of its functions.

The political reasons are demonstrated by the story of the Transit Authority. It was no accident that the Authority was created in a mayoral election year, when the prospect of a fare rise (which it was clear the Authority would have to put into effect in order to fulfill its statutory obligation to incur no operating losses) would presumably hurt the Democratic administration of the city. The legislature, after all, was controlled by the Republicans and though the city administration fought the measure, and later instituted an unsuccessful suit to prevent it, the law carried. (The Democrats managed to write in a provision that changes in transit fares by the Authority could be effected only within the first six months of any year; the Authority was thus prevented from introducing a rise potentially injurious to the Democrats in the 1953 election year, for, under this provision, it was created too late to make any change at once.)

In addition, terms of statutory reference of authorities are sometimes alleged to "take them out of politics," an argument convincing to some political decision-makers. It might perhaps be more accurate, for reasons suggested later in this chapter, to say laws on public authorities change the arena in which political contest over their decisions takes place; also, serious questions have been raised about trying to withdraw public agencies from the normal competitive processes of democratic politics. Nevertheless, the slogan is often advanced, and apparently often accepted at face value.

Financial, political, and jurisdictional factors underlie the birth of the authorities, and help sustain them once they appear. But the rapid, vigorous growth of these bodies is the product of aggressive and skillful leadership. Their managers have developed strategies and tactics under which the organizations thrive. They need all their skills, too, for the authorities, being large distributors of the stakes of politics, are foci of pressures from many parts of the community.

Pressures on the Authorities

While scarcely a resident of the city has been unaffected in one way or another by the activities of the authorities, only some half a dozen categories of groups have been actively engaged in trying to influence their policies and programs. Conspicuously missing from this list are the party hierarchies, whose principal sources of influence are their services in the election of officials and who are unable to make much of an impact on the authorities because these are removed from the parties' immediate zone of power.

The Users. Without exception, the users of the authorities' facilities are interested in keeping charges down to a minimum. Motorists demand the lowest possible tolls. Airlines, truckers, and bus operators insist on the lowest fees and rents. Passengers resist every increase in fares. Tenants oppose increases in rent.

Simultaneously, users call for more service. Drivers seek more roads, bridges, and tunnels to alleviate traffic jams, speed travel, and make driving more pleasant. Airlines want counter space, hangar space, aprons that minimize the distances their planes have to taxi, improved runways, and safety devices. Truck and bus companies want ample loading space. Passengers want better lighting, more trains, cleaner and safer stations. Tenants want faster repairs, more frequent painting, special police protection, more and larger dwelling units.

Bondholders. People who invest in the securities of authorities want their investments made as secure as possible. They favor use charges that ensure sufficient income to pay interest and protect principal. They prefer large reserves as cushions against disaster. They distrust additional capital investments unless these promise to bring in high returns swiftly. They object to the construction of rival facilities that might reduce the returns from existing ones.

The Inconvenienced. Much of the time, building anything new in New York means something old must be torn down first. The people who have to make way do not usually do so happily. Homeowners displaced to make way for a road or a bridge approach fight to have the route changed, and they are often joined by local merchants whose market is reduced by the displacement of residents and by the bisection of their neighborhoods by highways. Businessmen complain not only of the difficulties of relocation, but of the loss of local contacts and good will. Even slum tenants compelled to move to make way for slum clearance projects and low-rental housing resist, for they must find new quarters at slum-rent levels in a city in which housing is still tight. Uprooting large numbers of people, most of whom do not return when the new facilities are completed, disrupts party organizations and local voting patterns. It is difficult to take the long view when one suffers intensely in the immediate present; wherever these discommoded groups find a channel of influence to defend themselves, they make use of it.

Competitors. Each of the four major authorities has at least one rival. For the Port and Triborough Authorities, these tend to be municipal line agencies. The Department of Marine and Aviation, for example, fought bitterly, but unsuccessfully, to keep the municipal airports under its jurisdiction, and with equal vehemence successfully opposed an offer of the Port Authority to assume jurisdiction over the city's piers. Similarly, the bridges within the city were once built by the Department of Public Works rather than by a separate authority.

For the Transit Authority, the competitors are private bus companies, which would like to take over the profitable lines run by the Authority, and reduce competition from its other lines. The Consolidated Edison Company has made successful bids to acquire the Authority's powerhouses, and to supply commercial power for the subway system. Furthermore, the Port and Triborough Authorities are in a sense rivals of the Transit Authority, for all their facilities encourage automobile traffic rather than the use of the subways.

Landlords of residential dwellings—particularly of slum dwellings, which generally produce high rates of return on investment—tend to regard the Housing Authority as a kind of foe. In the first place, the construction of large numbers of public, low-rent buildings tends to reduce the economic pressure that keeps rents high, although the rate of construction has thus far barely kept pace with the razing of residential accommodations. In the second place, the Housing Authority concentrates on replacement of the worst slums with decent housing and thus decreases the opportunities for this kind of investment. In the third place, some private landlords object to public housing on the more general grounds that it competes with all private housing.

Derivative Beneficiaries. On the other side, generally aligned with the users, are the interests that benefit incidentally from the services of the authorities. In particular, merchants in the center of the city depend on the transit system to bring them their customers; corporation headquarters and manufacturers and businessmen depend on it to carry their personnel; real estate owners everywhere know their properties appreciate greatly in value when served by rapid transit lines. Similarly, roads and bridges push up real property values in areas previously inaccessible and stimulate car ownership and all its attendant businesses. Tall apartment buildings put up by the Housing Authority are a boon to nearby merchants who are not displaced by them.

In addition, thousands of people are employed by the authorities. By and large, they tend to side with users in favoring expansions of service and facilities, for these mean more jobs and opportunities for advancement. On the other hand, they are often at odds with the users in that their demands for wage increases and other benefits tend to drive charges up. This is especially significant in the case of the Transit Authority, which employs some 42,000 people, well over one third of them tightly organized in the Transport Workers Union and led by the militant Michael Quill. Though they resist cuts in service, they also resist heavier workloads, which, along with their wage demands, help keep fare increases constantly in the offing.

Civic Groups, Functional Groups, and the Press. Generally speaking, civic groups line up behind the authorities because they like the authorities' allegedly nonpolitical, businesslike management. The authorities are also supported by planning and housing groups, who see them doing much for transportation, transit, housing, and slum clearance that might otherwise not be done. The major newspapers and other media of communication, for similar reasons, tend to treat the authorities favorably in their news coverage and to back them editorially.

Goals of the Leaders. In short, in the hands of authorities lie offices, money, services, and intangible satisfactions—the moving forces in the governmental process. Inevitably, the authorities are targets of influence exerted by all the groups interested in their actions and decisions—interested, in other words, in the distribution of the rewards of politics.

The leaders of the authorities thus face many of the same problems as their colleagues in regular bureaus and departments. The survival and growth of their organizations are their responsibilities. For reasons of their own, they have program objectives they would like to see attained. In the face of all the pressures confronting them, they find these duties are not easy to discharge; the task requires great ingenuity. Every advantage must be seized, every weakness guarded. They must know their opportunities, and recognize their hazards.

Relative Immunity to Outside Influence

Authority leaders enjoy some advantages over the heads of ordinary line agencies in their planning to promote the security and growth of their organizations and in registering their personal ideas on the policies of the organizations. They are not so vulnerable to onslaughts from contestants for the rewards of politics who are displeased with their policies, and they are not so easily reached by external influences, for there are provisions of law that insulate them against many forms of attack and pressure.

Security of Tenure. In the first place, the heads of the authorities and all their top aides enjoy much greater security of tenure than most of their line agency counterparts. The members of the boards and their chairmen (except for the Housing Authority) all have longer terms than the men who appoint them, and, in turn, have a relatively free hand in the selection of their own permanent staffs. The governing board of the Port Authority consists of 12 members, 6 (including 4 voting residents of New York City) appointed by the Governor of New York, and 6 by the Governor of New Jersey, all with the consent of the Senates of their respective states. They have overlapping six-year terms. The three members of the Triborough Bridge and Tunnel Authority are appointed by the Mayor for overlapping six-year terms. Two of the three members of the Housing Authority appointed by the Mayor have overlapping five-year terms; the chairman, however, serves at the Mayor's pleasure. One member of the three-man board of the Transit Authority is appointed by the Mayor, one by the Governor, and a chairman by the other two; their terms are six years, arranged to produce the standard overlapping pattern. Even the Sports Center Authority members, of whom there are three, have overlapping six-year tenures, while the Planetarium Authority, consisting of the trustees of the Museum of Natural History, is self-perpetuating. Thus all the authorities are run by bodies composed of men with longer terms than those of the officers who appoint them (except for the chairman of the Housing Authority), and staggering the periods of service precludes expiration of the terms of office of all members of any body during any one term of office of the chief executives who name them. In addition, the chairmen of two of the authorities—the Port Authority and the Transit Authority—are selected by the other members rather than by elected executives, and not more than two members of the Housing Authority may be members of the same political party. Insofar as the mode of accession to office and the uncertainty of tenure of public officials are significant elements in the vulnerability of these officials to influence wielded by electorates, parties, nongovernmental groups, and other officials (particularly the appointing officials), the authorities' chiefs are obviously well shielded from many kinds of direct pressure.

They are further shielded by the statutory provisions on the removal of authority members. Unlike most ordinary department heads, who serve at the pleasure of the chief executives over them, authority members in every case may be dismissed only on statements of charges by their appointing officers, and after a hearing. This is not so substantial a protection as it might seem, for removal is such an extreme penalty, and so thick with possibilities of stirring storms of controversy, that it is not imposed casually or frequently even when there are no restrictions on it. Still, the awareness on the part of ordinary line administrators that the instrument is available to their superiors is apparently sobering and conducive to greater docility than the department leaders might otherwise be inclined to display. Threat of removal can often extract a resignation from a reluctant department head; in any case, it is like a loaded gun, which need not be fired to secure obedience from the persons at whom it is leveled. When restraints are imposed on the use of the weapon, as they have been with respect to the removal of authority heads, its effectiveness is somewhat reduced. No member of any authority has been removed from office, nor have any resigned under threat of removal. Their principal aides and assistants are almost invariably men of long tenure, whether or not they are protected by formal merit system provisions, and all personnel of all the authorities below the very highest grades are protected by strictly observed merit systems. From top to bottom, authority personnel enjoy a large measure of job security.

Fiscal Powers. In the second place, while ordinary line departments may not spend money for any purpose unless authorized by appropriation legislation, every authority conducts a revenue-producing operation (or series of operations) and has what amounts to full discretion in the use of its income. The Port Authority, for example, collects tolls and fees from users of its bridges and tunnels and airports; rents from concessionaires, who find its facilities profitable places to open businesses; and from users who need space to handle their activities (such as airlines, with their ticket and baggage counters, their hangars for airplane repairs and maintenance); and charges for the use of its other facilities (such as its grain terminal and truck terminals). The Triborough Authority derives its revenues from similar sources. The Transit Authority depends almost completely on fares, although there are supplementary sources, such as billboard and car-card advertising in its trains, buses, and stations, and concession rents for stores, vending machines, and other businesses in subway passages. The Housing Authority receives

TABLE 42. FINANCES OF THE MAJOR SPECIAL AUTHORITIES IN NEW YORK CITY
In millions of dollars

Authority	Assets	Debt outstanding	Debt service	Operating expenses	Operating revenues
N.Y.C. Housing	$1,200	$1,150	$33	$ 49	$ 65
N.Y.C. Transit	2,000[a]	1,525[b]	. .[c]	270	259
Triborough Bridge & Tunnel	491	244	4	7[d]	40[d]
Port of New York	900	508	40	43	93
Total	$4,591	$3,427	$77	$369	$457

[a] Transit Authority estimate of actual historical cost of transit facilities administered by the Authority. Reproduction cost at 1958 price levels estimated by the Authority at $6 billion. The facilities belong to the city, not the Authority.

[b] Transit debt is an obligation of the city, not the Authority.

[c] City pays transit debt service charges.

[d] Figures include sums for Coliseum project.

SOURCES: *Annual Reports* of the Authorities; *Annual Report* of the Comptroller of New York City, 1958; New York City Transit Authority.

rents from its tenants, plus operating subsidies from the federal, state, and city governments. The Planetarium charges admission to its displays. The Sports Center Authority was to receive rent from the baseball club that used its stadium, from other groups that hired the arena when the club was away, and from food and drink concessions. All the authorities thus have independent incomes.

The significance of this is fourfold. First, the authorities do not have to undergo the public budget hearings before the Board of Estimate, at which so many of the pressures on ordinary line agencies are brought to bear. Second, the authorities do not have to defend their plans and projected expenditures to budget and fiscal officers of the city or any other government. They have to explain their behavior after spending, when they are audited, as is the case with all private corporations, but they are not compelled to do so in advance or to modify their programs and policies to win the approval of the overhead agencies, as do many line agencies. Third, they are not exposed to deprivations of income through appropriations delays or slashes, a common means of subduing line agencies. Fourth, they are not limited by the detailed appropriation items of the regular expense budget of the city. In sum, their operating policy decisions, as these are reflected in their budgets, are made internally rather than in dealings with outside agencies and officials, in private rather than in public, and the authorities are the undisputed masters of their own operating resources.

They also control the rates of their tolls, charges, and rents. The Housing Authority is somewhat limited in this respect because its rent schedules are supervised by housing officials of the state or federal governments, or financial officers of the city, depending on where its subsidies for any project come from. And the Transit Authority must hold a hearing on fare changes if the Board of Estimate requests it, although the Board of Estimate cannot veto the Authority's final decision. The Port Authority and the Triborough Authority are guided wholly by their own assessments of their financial situations and their obligations to their bondholders. The latter two, as a matter of fact, have been able to build up large reserve funds that improve their general financial standings and at the same time provide them with large sums of money to finance new projects. The Port Authority, for example, was able to dip into its reserves to commence work on Idlewild Airport even before it floated bonds to raise money for completing the job, and the Triborough Authority paid for the Coliseum entirely out of reserves from earnings. Control of earnings, together with large reserves in the case of the Port and Triborough Authorities, and with freedom to spend as they see fit, has given the authorities a latitude of discretion that no line agencies enjoy.

All the authorities but the Transit Authority enjoy similar independence in raising funds for capital improvements. Regular line agencies depend on appropriations for these purposes. The general government borrows on its own credit to provide the wherewithal to build long-lived structures and facilities, then appropriates for them project by project, so that line-agency capital budget requests run the same gantlet as do their expense budgets, with the added scrutiny and public hearings of the City Planning Commission. By contrast, the authorities, although they must secure approval of their projects as described below, are empowered to issue bonds of their own. They depend on their own credit rather than the credit of any general government, although the Housing Authority's standing has been greatly helped by city guarantees of its securities. Ordinary department heads doubtless view with envy the comparative autonomy of the authorities as regular departmental capital budgets move slowly along the procedural paths of the city government.

The Transit Authority, however, must go through the same procedures the line departments and bureaus do, for it has no borrowing power and gets its money for capital improvements in the ordinary fashion. Yet even the Transit Authority has been in a strong position, for it came into existence shortly after $500 million of indebtedness for subway construction was exempted from the constitutional debt limit, and the city could take advantage of this new borrowing capacity only by financing the Authority, with its exclusive jurisdiction over the subways.

Practical and legal considerations serve as restraints on the fiscal powers of the authorities. If they are not prudent, their credit standing (and hence their capacity to grow) suffers. They cannot sustain losing propositions, because they depend on revenues for income. The lack of taxing power is a check. They have obligations to their bondholders and dare not embark on dubious ventures that would prevent them from fulfilling these responsibilities. The bondholders, after all, are creditors. The enabling acts of authorities often contain provisions dealing with rates of interest, debt maxima, and similar fiscal matters. So the authorities are not altogether unfettered financially. Just the same, compared to regular line agencies, they are exceptionally free.

Administrative Elbowroom. They are also freer in a number of less important ways. They make their own arrangements for purchasing instead of going through and abiding by the regulations of an external purchasing unit. They control their own internal structure and procedures. They have their own legal staffs and handle their own legal affairs. They employ consultants in their own discretion. They are authorized to make rules and regulations governing the use of their facilities. Of the four major authorities, all but the Transit Authority are possessed of some powers of eminent domain. In addition, the Housing Authority has powers of investigation, including the power to enter private premises and to compel attendance of witnesses and production of papers. Although all but the Port Authority are under the New York City Department of Personnel for most matters of personnel management, they all enjoy great discretion in personnel management because they do not depend on appropriations to meet their payrolls. The Port Authority has established a separate merit system of its own which is administered entirely by its own officials. Thus, for many of their day-to-day administrative problems, the authorities are able to work out their own solutions; they do not have to obtain permission or cooperation from agencies and officers outside their own ranks, nor do outsiders intervene in their internal management.

The Importance of Insulation. Since ordinary line agencies' leaders are susceptible to many kinds of pressures from which authorities are spared, they must be more cautious about giving offense. Their decisions must be made with a view to avoiding profound provocations of the executives who appointed them, lest they be replaced by persons more amenable to the desires of the executives. Policies and programs must be formulated with the prejudices and preferences of overhead agencies and appropriating bodies in mind, lest these organs block, or at least delay, some vital component of projected courses of action and thereby hold them up or diminish their force or scope. Authorities, because of the insulation shielding them, are less vulnerable and therefore less inclined to appease the other governmental officials who exert pressure on them.

Line agency vulnerability to other public officers and agencies has a "multiplier" effect. Each external wielder of influence is himself subject to pressure, so people trying to influence a line department can get at their target indirectly even when they cannot reach it directly. The aggregate of lines of access and pressure is thus multiplied many times; each agency is influenced not only by other officials with power over it, but by all the participants in politics who can influence *them*, too. Therefore, when a public organization is exempted from many kinds of control and intervention by other officials and agencies, it is also excepted from a host of secondary influences to which it would otherwise be exposed. The insulation of the authorities thus reduces many times the influences on the decisions and actions of their leaders and renders them relatively immune compared to regular departments. It encourages them to do what they want rather than what others demand.

Susceptibilities to Outside Influence

But they are by no means totally invulnerable to influences originating outside themselves. Areas of vulnerability, though fewer and smaller than those of regular departments, exist. Casual participants in the contest to influence governmental decisions and actions, weakly motivated contestants, temporary or *ad hoc* groups, and political amateurs and dilettantes are often hard put to find the proper levers, or, having found them, to apply pressure to them. Determined, experienced, professional contestants, however, know where to look and what to do. The authorities are not outside the political arena.

Vetoes and Deprivations. Land use in the City of New York is under the control of the Board of Estimate. The City Planning Commission plays a large part in zoning and land-use regulation, and Borough Presidents individually have important roles also. But the ultimate decisions, the "last say," rest with the Board as an entity.

All the authorities are engaged in construction affected by land-use regulations—particularly the Port and Triborough Authorities, whose bridges and tunnels require elaborate networks of approaches as well as the erection of the central facilities themselves. The Board of Estimate is in a position to obstruct their proposed projects. On at least one occasion it exercised this power and delayed the start of work on the third tube of the Lincoln Tunnel until the Port Authority and Commissioner Robert Moses came to terms on the connections between the tunnel and a projected crosstown expressway. The Board of Estimate, a body composed entirely of elected officials, thus possesses a stout stick for its dealings with all the authorities; it can bargain if it chooses—for itself in the collective sense, for any of its members, or for other officials or groups to whom it may be responsible for one reason or another.

Over and above this general instrument of control, there are special ones connected with each authority. The Governor of New York or of New Jersey may veto resolutions of the Port Authority by disapproving the minutes of the Authority board meetings at which they were adopted. Any of its proposed projects may thus be blocked. Rules and regulations for the improvement of navigation and commerce promulgated by the Port Authority require concurrence or prior authorization by legislation in both states. The Authority customarily acquires an unambiguous basis for new projects by obtaining authorizing statutes from both states. Although it might conceivably proceed under the terms of its general authorization, it usually does not do so, and refusal by either state to enact requested legislation would presumably constitute a death blow to proposed undertakings.

The Housing Authority is economically dependent on city guarantees of the principal and interest of its indebtedness. Were it not for this, its borrowing would be so expensive that it would have great difficulty operating its projects at rents within the reach of its clientele. (A special constitutional amendment permits the city to lend its credit to the Housing Authority; as a general rule, it may not lend its credit to anybody.) The Authority's economic position is further reinforced by federal, state, and city loans for construction and by cash subsidies from all three governments for operation of specific low-rent projects. Although its properties are not subject to taxation, the Authority is required to make payments to the city in lieu of taxes. Under no circumstances may it pay more than specified maxima, but, below these ceilings, the amounts of the payments are set by negotiation with the city.

The Transit Authority gets all its money for capital improvements from the city, having no long-term borrowing authorization.

The Board of Estimate must approve the acquisition (as well as the use) of property in connection with a large-scale arterial highway program planned jointly by the Triborough and Port Authorities, and it is empowered by state legislation to require redemption of Triborough bonds for this project prior to maturity. (The Board promptly used this power to force

Triborough reconsideration of some of the approach routes to the contemplated Narrows Bridge.)

Finally, the Corps of Engineers of the United States Army has jurisdiction over navigable waters. All structures, including bridges and tunnels, that encroach on such waters must have this agency's approval. Many projects of the Port and Triborough Authorities (as well as of some regular line agencies) could therefore be constructed only with the assent of the Corps.

Federal, state, or city officials, or any combination of these, both elective and appointive, are thus armed with implements with which to influence the behavior of the authorities. They can veto authority projects, or they can withhold legal and financial support the authorities need to proceed. In return for doing neither of these things, they can procure policy concessions from the authorities. These powers are employed much more sparingly than one might expect. However, there are suggestions that overt use is infrequent because of behind-the-scenes negotiations, and because authority leaders formulate their decisions in the light of what they anticipate other officials might do in response. At any rate, the levers are there for the other officials to pull, and they do pull them from time to time, usually with telling effect. These, then, are some of the chinks in the armor of the authorities.

The Mutability of Legislation. Although there is a chapter in the consolidated laws of New York State called the Public Authorities Law, it is not a general statute applicable to all the authorities in the state, but a compilation of their individual enabling acts. The enabling acts, which define the structure and powers of the organizations to which they pertain, vary a good deal. As ordinary legislation, they may be individually amended to extend or contract the authorizations granted the authorities, or even repealed. Moreover, since each organization is controlled by a separate section, it is relatively easy to pass legislation affecting any one without becoming involved in complicated repercussions on all the others. While the legislature may be under some restraints because it is bound by the Constitution of the United States not to violate the obligations of contract (and bonds are contracts), the authorities are quite vulnerable through their legislation. And legislators, as elected officials, are responsive to the insistent demands of their constituents.

The legislature (the legislatures of New York and New Jersey, in the case of the Port Authority) can exercise statutory influence on the authorities in three ways. One is to refuse to enact laws conferring on an authority the powers it requests in order to embark on a new project. The second is to write very detailed specifications and limitations into the statutes. The third is to threaten to amend or repeal statutes under which an authority functions. The contents of the statutes are crucial to the welfare of the authorities, for the laws not only determine what they may do but also set conditions enabling them to get favorable rates of interest on their loans, or even to sell their bonds at all. Here are found the immunities from suit, the exclusive jurisdiction (assuring bondholders that rival facilities, cutting into the revenues on which interest and principal payments depend, will not be constructed), exemptions from local taxation, debt ceilings, rights to set charges and rents and tolls, power of eminent domain, the purposes for which money may be borrowed and spent, and all the other powers that permit the authorities to operate the way they do. Here, in short, are found the conditions of their very existence.

Seldom, if ever, have punitive amendments been adopted, and no legislation establishing an authority has ever been repealed while the authority was functioning (except for mergers). Yet there have now and then been rumblings of a menacing character as groups unable to influence authorities directly turned their attention to legislative techniques. The Port Authority, for instance, had to rush to Washington to block a proposed repealer of congressional approval of the New York-New Jersey Port Compact. Certainly, authority leaders are not unaware of these dangers and adopt strategies and tactics that take them into account.

Investigations. An unfriendly official investigation can be a burden to its subject. The subject may not be guilty of any wrongdoing or incompetence or even of any errors of judgment. A hostile investigator, if he is so inclined, can put him in a bad light just the same, and this may lead to attacks on other vulnerable points. At best, an investigation conducted with hostility or malice can be inconvenient; at worst, it can be embarrassing or injurious.

None of the authorities is immune to official investigations. The thrust could come through the office of the Governor (of either Governor where the Port Authority is concerned), from the state Comptroller, from the Attorney General, or from the legislature (either legislature, for the Port Authority) or one of its committees. The state Housing Commissioner could look into the Housing Authority. Where federal aid is involved, federal officials might elect to conduct an examination. The city, through its Comptroller, Commissioner of Investigation, or Council, might make inquiries (even into those facilities of the Port Authority leased from the city, despite the bi-state nature of the agency). All of these could doubtless find sufficient legal power to justify such probes, and they are amply equipped to make them searching once they get them in motion.

It would be misleading to give the impression that the authorities live in terror of investigations. But they would certainly rather avoid the bother, the controversy, and the risks of unpredictable consequences that investigations entail. (The Housing Authority, for example, was reorganized at its top level as a result of a city investigation. And the Port Authority's reduction of tolls for commuters happened to occur when talk of a legislative investigation of its rate structure was in the air.) The threat of investigation is thus not a highly potent mode of influence on the authorities, but it is not one to be ignored either.

The Need to Maneuver

To sum up, the leaders of the authorities are major figures in the decisions and actions that distribute the prizes of politics. Consequently, many contestants for those prizes are deeply concerned about what the authorities do and employ every means at their command of influencing their behavior. The authorities are relatively well shielded against outside influences by their security of tenure, their fiscal independence, and their administrative freedom. At the same time, they are vulnerable to vetoes and deprivations, to changes in their enabling legislation, and to investigations. These are the circumstances in which the leaders attempt to promote the growth and prosperity of their organizations and press forward to attain their program goals.

STRATEGIES AND TACTICS OF AUTHORITY LEADERS

Building Reputations

The Importance of Reputations. All public officers depend ultimately on public support for their security and influence—even authority leaders, despite their sources of autonomy. For there are many people who dislike the authority device—that is, who are unfriendly to the institution rather than merely desirous of influencing it. The chief officials of the city oppose the assignment of public functions to organizations over which their control is not so great as their control of ordinary line departments. The heads of some line departments see the growth of the authorities as encroachments on their jurisdiction. Students of government have expressed alarm over the proliferation of relatively self-governing agencies, the dismemberment of general units of government, the diffusion of leadership and responsibility, and the alleged "distortion" of the total public investment by diverting more and more capital expenditure from vital facilities that do not produce revenues (schools, public hospitals, parks, playgrounds) to those that do generate income and are therefore easier to finance. The authorities are not so universally acclaimed that they can afford to let the public grow hostile, or even indifferent; they need the support of public opinion.

In addition, although the market for authority bonds is based on hard-headed calculations of assets, income, and liabilities, reputation for sound management has a great effect on such judgments. Whether loans can be floated at reasonable rates of interest—indeed, whether bonds can be sold at all—hinges on the name the authorities make for themselves.

Finally, when the authorities seek to expand—to enter into new functions, to take over the work of other agencies, or even to intensify the kinds of services they traditionally perform—their ability to stand off attacks on their vulnerable points is directly related to the esteem in which they are held. Generally, they contend they can do jobs the city itself cannot do so well, or cannot do at all. The respect in which they are held determines how persuasive this contention will be.

Consequently, all the authorities pay a great deal of attention to public relations. The Port and Triborough Authorities are particularly cognizant of the significance of public favor, for their multifunctional operations bring them into competition with a larger number of agencies than the Transit and Housing Authorities. Yet the latter, too, utilize this strategy extensively.

Techniques. Their techniques of public relations are not very different from those of regular line agencies. In part, they rely on their facilities to "sell themselves": towering bridges and spectacular vehicular tunnels are impressive feats of engineering that speak for themselves. Neat and clean, if architecturally undistinguished, buildings and housing projects are good advertising, and some of them, such as the Port Authority's international terminal at Idlewild Airport, are landmarks in design. Modern, well-lighted subway cars and buses, faster service, and brightly illuminated stations bespeak the competence and zeal of those who provide them. But authority heads also publicize their works, especially in the daily press. Every facility is opened with a flourish, with ceremonies attended by prominent officials and private citizens, and prior briefings, behind-the-scenes tours, and prepared packets and pictures for reporters. News releases flow regularly to the communication media. Editorial and feature writers are courted, and every effort made to see that they appreciate the authorities' objectives and points of view. In the Port Authority, the Director of Public Relations sits in on policy conferences as an equal of engineering, legal, and financial personnel; public relations premises are treated as no less important than the purely technical ones.

By these measures, the authorities have succeeded in enhancing the impression made by their accomplishments. The public relations techniques, however, have done far more than this; they have also created a strong public image of the authorities as efficient, free of politics, dynamic, and public-welfare conscious. The image, to be sure, is as strategically useful as it is an accurate reflection of their behavior; it is one of their greatest assets in their battles to endure and to grow. They protect the image by avoiding any breath of scandal, any suggestion of ineptitude, and foster it by wooing the working press assiduously.

The methods have succeeded, by and large. The authorities—especially the Port of New York Authority and the Triborough Bridge and Tunnel

Authority—have enjoyed the support of the press in most of the controversies in which they have become involved. They have generally been portrayed sympathetically, and their virtues widely extolled.

Managing Constituencies

Although the authorities, being more independent than ordinary line departments, need constituency support less often, there are times when they are grateful for active backing. The Port Authority, for example, might not have been able to lease the municipal airports from the city had it not been assisted by a committee representing all the major airlines in the area when it applied for special enabling legislation in Albany and Trenton, and by representatives of a number of investment bankers when it was trying to convince the Board of Estimate that its bonds could be more easily sold than those of a competing organization seeking jurisdiction over the two air terminals. The Transit Authority's rejection of proposals that it sell its bus lines has been strengthened by the support of the Transport Workers Union. Some Housing Authority projects might well have been blocked by neighborhood opposition had the agency not been backed by influential civic and planning and housing groups. Opposition to the new Coliseum was not a serious problem to the Triborough Authority because businessmen in need of convention and exhibition space were vociferously insisting on a large hall and did not care a great deal about the fine points of location. All the authorities have invoked the influence of other elements in the community at one time or another.

Like all public agencies, the sensitivity of the authorities to their own vulnerability often induces them to make concessions to rising tides of protest before these gather sufficient force to reach destructive proportions. The Port Authority balanced opposition to jet planes on the part of residents in the vicinity of its airports, who were already bitterly resentful of the noise of piston engines, against pressure from the airlines (plus claims of effective noise suppression), and at first let the planes in only on an extremely limited basis. It closed down Newark Airport for a year after three airliners crashed in streets in the area, and the outraged local population, led by local officials, was vehement and menacing. It reduced its tolls for commuters on its Hudson River crossings at least partly in response to insistent demands by the commuters and some of their elected representatives. Similarly, the Transit Authority, after a series of assaults and robberies in deserted subway stations late at night produced demands for countermeasures, organized a special transit police force, and for a time published schedules of night service so people would not have long waits on the lonely platforms. It also built a new entrance to the Times Square subway station when complaints arose (particularly in *The New York Times*) about the closing of an old stairway. The Housing Authority increased its protective forces when tenants began to raise a hue and cry about incidents of violence and vandalism in some projects, and reorganized its guard system entirely when newspapers took up the issue. When storms of disapproval gather, a common strategy for turning them aside before they break is to move "voluntarily" in the direction they are tending; sometimes, this even transforms rancor into approval and gratitude.

The authorities also coopt representatives of the most powerful elements in their constituencies to sit on the authority boards. This tends to make it awkward for those elements to attack authority actions, and more or less commits them to support the authorities by giving them a voice in the formulation of authority decisions prior to promulgation. Thus, for example, shipping, transportation, commercial, and financial leaders are prominent on the board of the Port Authority; railroad and labor relations experts sit on the Transit Authority; management and housing specialists are on the Housing Authority; men of repute in finance and engineering are colleagues of Commissioner Moses on the Triborough Authority. Of course, the authorities do not formally appoint their own board members. But, as was noted in the chapter on the process of appointment to office, official appointing officers do not generally exercise a free hand when they select people. They look for advice and they respond to demands. As far as the authorities are concerned, when vacancies are to be filled the appointers frequently follow the suggestions of sitting board members and the general managers (or, as they are called in some cases, the executive directors). The suggestions from these sources, in turn, are often offered with a view to strengthening the positions of the authorities the new appointees will join, which means the appointees are recommended at least in part because of their connections with the interests with which the authorities must get along in order to survive. So it is accurate to say the authorities coopt members who will do them the most good. In a sense, they thus appease their public at the same time they disarm their loudest and strongest claimants.

Aggressiveness

The authorities have generally pursued a policy of continuous expansion. In a sense, this is a strategy that safeguards their continued existence. Were it not for this they would be reduced to mere caretaker operations as soon as their bonds were paid off, and the pressure for them to reduce their charges accordingly would cut their revenues, eventually make their bonds unattractive to investors, and thus prevent them from embarking on new ventures. The process is circular. As long as they keep borrowing to expand, their commitments to their bondholders justify their existing tolls and rents; and as long as they maintain their present tolls and rents, their capacity to borrow for expansion remains unimpaired. Since they are independent enough to chart their own courses of action, and since the reputations they have established and their manipulation of their constituencies have reduced their vulnerability, they are able to push ahead with few anxieties. That is why they have records of rapid growth, and why they seek new outlets for their energies. The Port Authority has repeatedly indicated its interest in taking over the city's piers. The Housing Authority constantly has new projects in the design stage. The Triborough Authority has already gone to the limit of its authorized borrowing capacity. The Transit Authority, although it is not quite in the same position as the others because it has no borrowing authorization of its own, has nevertheless added new lines and interconnections as well as new equipment and improvements on its old ones.

As a matter of fact, the Port and Triborough bodies recently joined hands in a vast program for arterial highway development that neither of them could accomplish alone. Together they worked out plans and secured necessary legislative permission for construction of a new bridge from The Bronx to Queens, another across The Narrows from Brooklyn to Staten Island, a second deck for the George Washington Bridge, and a network of highways and approaches linking these facilities. The state legislature showed some concern for the autonomy they would gain through this union by emphasizing the Board of Estimate power to disapprove the acquisition of property for the projected facilities, and by authorizing the city to require redemption of the bonds for this project prior to maturity. But the legislature permitted the joint undertaking, allowing two authorities to engage in an undertaking far more extensive than the simple sum of their individual efforts would be.

Perhaps the most extraordinary example of aggressive leadership is that provided by the chairman of the Triborough Bridge and Tunnel Authority since its inception, Commissioner Robert Moses. His force derives in part from the many positions he holds in addition to the chairmanship of the Authority, for his many jobs clothe him with great influence in City Hall and Albany: he is Commissioner of the Department of Parks of New York City, City Construction Coordinator, a member of the City Planning Commission, chairman of the Mayor's Committee on Slum Clearance, head of the Office of Planning and Construction of the City Office of Civil Defense, a member of the New York City Youth Board, president of the Long Island State Park Commission, chairman of the State Council of Parks, president of the Jones Beach State Parkway Authority and of the Bethpage (Long Island) Park Authority, and chairman of the New York State Power Authority. (The first and the last are the only paid posts.) His many positions are as much a result of his effectiveness as a cause of it; work gravitates to him because of his unique combination of talents. He is not only brilliant, articulate, imaginative, energetic, honest, and confident, but he is completely unawed by the stature of those he deals with. He cows his critics and opponents by his personal dynamism, mordant wit, and slashing mode of attack: "Mr. Moses," commented a feature writer in *The New York Times*, "uses a head-on collision approach in dealing with his critics. Sometimes he plasters them with facts. Sometimes he resorts to ridicule. One cardinal rule he seems to follow: when replying to a critic, never actually answer him. Instead, make a new attack." He does not hesitate to engage in acrimonious disputes with anyone; he made obliquely sarcastic comments about the President when the nation's Chief Executive appeared at the opening of the Triborough Bridge, battled repeatedly and furiously with Mayor La Guardia, exchanged public contumelies with a City Comptroller, and fought openly with the Administrator of the Housing and Home Finance Agency in Washington. The newspapers and other mass media treat him with admiration and even affection; he is always good copy. Everywhere, he is respected and perhaps a little feared. Under his leadership, the Triborough Authority has forged ahead in size and scope.

Not all the authorities can boast a chief as aggressive as Robert Moses. But the difference is one of degree rather than kind. The authorities employ aggressiveness as one of the strategies of survival and goal achievement. They have done more than make the most of the opportunities presented them in their enabling statutes; they have gone beyond this to create their own opportunities.

STRATEGIC VICTORIES AND THEIR HAZARDS

It is a truism that participants in the political process never get everything they want and are constrained by the process to acquiesce in many things of which they do not fully approve or with which they are not in full sympathy. This generalization applies to the leaders of the authorities no less than their fellow contestants for the stakes of political action. The authority chiefs, however, are distinguished by their singular successes in effectuating policies and programs they prefer personally. Their insulation has stood them in good stead, and their strategies have made the most of the advantages insulation affords them. They have so directed their activities that outside influences on their behavior probably play a far smaller role in their decisions than in the decisions of most other public agencies and institutions.

The very triumphs of the authorities have given rise to searching, increasingly skeptical second-looks at this administrative device. It has been questioned on the grounds that public functions should not be several steps removed from constant control by the elected executives of the city, and that decisions about the quality, quantity, and kinds of public service, and the charges for it, should not be shielded from public pressures any more than decisions about taxation are. It has been challenged on managerial grounds for diffusing leadership at a time when the need for governmental coordination steadily becomes more urgent. Doubts have been raised on economic grounds about the efficacy of resorting to borrowing on the basis of revenue bonds not backed by tax powers. These are invariably more costly than the interest rates charged the city because the city has its capacity to tax behind its funded debt. The irony of the greatest city in the world being unable to support services that special authorities, lacking powers of taxation and police powers, are capable of financing has begun to generate puzzlement and dubiety. The skewing of governmental resources, particularly public investment, away from service functions that do not pay their way and toward enterprises that make money has also engendered anxiety. And the more rapidly the authorities grow, and the more self-directing they appear, the more profound are the uncertainties and anxieties about their position.

It is improbable that extensive changes in the situation will occur in the immediate future. The factors underlying the appearance and expansion of authorities are still operative, and the leaders of the authorities are still excellent strategists. In the long run, however, the scattered and wavering disquiet may consolidate and crystallize. The constitutional amendment excluding self-liquidating projects (or the self-liquidating portion of the indebtedness for any project) from the constitutional debt limit is a straw in the wind, and it has already enabled the city's Department of Marine and Aviation to renovate some of the municipal piers without financial embarrassment to the city and without relinquishing control of the operation. Eventually, movements to broaden the city's power to introduce new forms of taxation without the requirement of state legislative approval may gain ground. Ultimately, the limitations on property taxes and on municipal debt may come under direct fire. Efforts to free the city from financial restrictions will always face determined opposition from groups with a stake in the *status quo*, and from interests in Albany eager to retain influence on city decisions. The relaxation of restraints is therefore not imminent, and the special authorities consequently remain secure in the knowledge that the forces that bred them will continue to sustain them. All the same, the relative self-direction of the authorities and their dominance over decisions embodying many stakes of politics are likely to arouse more and more apprehension. The strategies of the authority leaders in the future may well shift from being aggressive and confidently aloof from partisan politics to being defensive and increasingly conciliatory.

BIBLIOGRAPHY

GENERAL

McLean, Joseph E., "Use and Abuse of Authorities," *National Municipal Review*, vol. 42, October, 1953, pp. 438–444. An appraisal of authorities, with a look at the Port of New York Authority.

New York State Constitutional Convention Committee, *New York City Government: Functions and Problems*, vol. 5 of *Reports and Studies*. Burland Printing Co., New York, 1938, pp.96–107. A general review of the authorities in New York City in 1938.

State and Local Government in New York. J. B. Lyon Co., Albany, 1938, pp. 189–193. Contains a brief discussion of "quasi-governmental agencies known as authorities," as they existed in New York State in 1938.

Problems Relating to Home Rule and Local Goverment, vol. 11 of *Reports and Studies*. J. B. Lyon Co., Albany, 1938, chap. 9, pp. 238–245. "Constitutional Aspects of Public Authorities" indicates the nature of public authorities and the constitutional problems related to such authorities.

New York State, Temporary State Commission on Coordination of State Authorities, *First Interim Staff Report on Public Authorities in New York State*. Legislative Document no. 55, 1954, Williams Press, Albany, 1954. A treatise on public authorities.

Staff Report on Public Authorities Under New York State. Legislative Document no. 46, 1956, Williams Press, Albany, 1956. An inventory of public authorities. A survey of the experience of every public authority in New York State.

Preliminary Staff Report on a Proposal for the Regionalization of Existing Highways and Bridge Authorities. Legislative Document no. 24, 1955, Williams Press, Albany, 1955. Traces the development and organization of public authorities in New York City and State.

BROOKLYN SPORTS CENTER AUTHORITY
(Created by Chap. 951, Laws of 1956)

NEW YORK CITY HOUSING AUTHORITY
(Created by Chap. 311, Laws of 1935)

New York City Housing Authority, *Annual Reports*, 1934; 1935–1936; 1938–1941 (published annually); 1943; 1946–1947 (1 vol.); 1947 to date (published annually); 1954, *Foundations for Better Government;* 1955, *Building Better Government;* 1956, *Better Government, A Year of Progress;* 1957, *Better Government, The City and The Challenge;* 1958, *Better Government, The Continuing Effort*. Describe the efforts of the New York City Housing Authority to provide adequate housing for all income groups.

Management Department, *Annual Reports*, 1947–1952 (published annually).

Personnel Department, *Annual Reports*, 1950 to date (published annually).

Division of Administration, "Police Protection in the New York City Housing Authority." The Division, New York, 1957, mimeographed.

New York City, Mayor's Committee on Management Survey, *Modern Management for the City of New York*. 2 vols. The Committee, New York, 1953, vol. 1, pp. 230–232, 250. Some of the problems confronting the Housing Authority.

New York Chapter of the American Institute of Architects, *The Significance of the Work of the New York City Housing Authority*. The Institute, New York, 1949. An evaluation of the large-scale housing work of the Authority.

Pink, Louis H., "Reminiscences." Columbia University Oral History Collection, Special Collections, Butler Library. One of the men instrumental in creating the Housing Authority tells the story.

Rodgers, Cleveland, and Rebecca B. Rankin, *New York: The World's Capital City*. Harper and Bros., New York, 1948, pp. 290–296. The work of the city's Housing Authority.

PLANETARIUM AUTHORITY
(Created by Chap. 214, Laws of 1933)

PORT OF NEW YORK AUTHORITY

New York State Constitution and New Jersey Constitution, *Compact Between the States of New York and New Jersey, 1921, for the Creation of the "Port of New York District" and the Establishment of the "Port of New York Authority" for the Comprehensive Development of the Port of New York, Entered into Pursuant to Chap. 154, Laws of New York, 1921; Chap. 151, Laws of New Jersey, 1921* (Approved by Public Resolution 17 of the 67th Congress). The Authority, New York.

The Port of New York Authority: Treatises and Statutes, vol. 1, 1921–1948, vol. 2, 1949–1951. *Temporary Supplements: 1952–1954; 1955–1958* typewritten. These supplements may be found in the Port of New York Authority library. They indicate the treaties, laws of Congress, and state laws which have authorized the activities of the Port of New York Authority.

Port of New York Authority, *Annual Reports, Report with Plan for the Comprehensive Development of the Port of New York,* December 21, 1921; *Progress Report,* Port of New York Authority, February 21, 1923; and *Annual Reports,* Port of New York Authority, 1923 to date.

Annual Financial Reports, 1951 to date, published annually.

A Monograph. The Authority, New York, 1936. A review of the early history, organization, and operations of the Authority.

Twenty-Fifth Anniversary: The Port of New York Authority. The Authority, New York, 1946. The Authority describes its own activities.

Bard, Erwin Wilkie, *The Port of New York Authority.* Columbia University Press, New York, 1939. A study of the Authority in its formative years.

Bird, Frederick L., *A Study of the Port of New York Authority.* Dun and Bradstreet, New York, 1949. Stresses the financial aspects of the Authority's operations.

Bollens, John C., *Special District Governments in the United States.* University of California Press, Berkeley, 1957, pp. 68–71. The Port of New York Authority compared with other outstanding single-purpose districts.

Cohen, Julius Henry, *They Builded Better Than They Knew.* Julian Messner, New York, 1946, pp. 257–306. The founding and early years of the Port of New York Authority, as one intimately associated with the Authority viewed it.

Fair, Marvin L., *Port Administration in the United States.* Cornell Maritime Press, Cambridge, Md., 1954, pp. 41–79. The Port of New York Authority considered in the context of port authorities in the entire United States.

Kaufman, Herbert, "Gotham in the Air Age," in Harold Stein, editor, *Public Administration and Policy Development: A Case Book,* prepared by the Inter-University Case Program, Harcourt, Brace and Co., New York, 1952, pp. 143–197. How the Port of New York Authority took over the task of handling air traffic for the New York metropolitan region.

SUBWAY UNIFICATION

New York City Transit Commission, *Proposed Plan and Agreement of Unification and Adjustment for the Acquisition and Unification, under Public Ownership and Control, of Rapid Transit Railroads and Related Properties in the City of New York of the Interborough and Manhattan Transit Systems.* The Commission, New York, 1939.

Plan and Agreement of Unification and Adjustment for the Acquisition and Unification, under Public Ownership and Control, of Rapid Transit Railroads and Related Properties in the City of New York of the Interborough and Manhattan Transit Systems. The Commission, New York, 1939.

Plan and Agreement of Unification and Adjustment for the Acquisition and Unification, under Public Ownership and Control, of Rapid Transit and Related Power Properties and Omnibus Lines of the Brooklyn-Manhattan Transit System in the City of New York. The Commission, New York, 1939. These documents outline the agreements made by municipal authorities and holders of securities of private transit corporations when the city took over and unified the transit systems.

Report of the Special Counsel to the Transit Commission Metropolitan Division, Department of Public Service of the State of New York on the Proposed Plan and Agreement of Unification and Readjustment for the Acquisition and Unification under Public Ownership and Control of Rapid Transit and Surface Railroads and Related Power Properties and Omnibus Lines of the Brooklyn-Manhattan Transit System in the City of New York. June 23, 1939.

Report of the Special Counsel to the Transit Commission, Metropolitan Division, Department of Public Service of the State of New York on the Proposed Plan and Agreement of Unification and Readjustment for the Acquisition and Unification Under Public Ownership and Control of Rapid Transit Railroads and Related Properties in the City of New York of the Interborough and Manhattan Transit Systems. August 25, 1939. These "Cuthell Reports," named after the state Transit Commissions special counsel, review the problem of unification and disclose the plan of unification to which the city and holders of securities of private transport companies agreed.

"Gotham Transit Goal," *Business Week*, August 12, 1939, pp. 25, 26. Describes the efforts of the city to purchase and unify subway properties.

"Subway Merger," *Newsweek*, vol. 15, June 24, 1940, p. 60. A brief resumé of the terms under which transit unification was accomplished and the effects of these terms on the city's transportation system.

Morris, Newbold, and Dana Lee Thomas, *Let the Chips Fall: My Battle Against Corruption.* Appleton-Century-Crofts, New York, 1955, pp. 132–133. One of the representatives of the Board of Estimate in the negotiations between the city and the holders of securities of the private transportation systems during transit unification gives his impressions of the proceedings.

BOARD OF TRANSPORTATION

New York City, Board of Transportation, *Report to John F. Hylan, Mayor, City of New York, Chairman, Board of Estimate and Apportionment.* M. B. Brown, New York, 1925, July 1–December 31, 1924.

Second, Third, Fourth, and Fifth "Anniversary Reports." Press releases (mimeographed) issued first week of July, 1926, 1927, 1928, and 1929.

"Annual Reports," 1929, 1930, and 1931. Press releases (mimeographed) issued December 30, 1929, January 1, 1931, and "Sunday" (otherwise undated).

"Independent City Subway First Anniversary." A press release (mimeographed), dated September 11, 1933.

"Report to the Board of Estimate and Apportionment," May 3, 1935. A typewritten report of the financial results of operations, early 1932 to December 31, 1934.

"Annual Report of Secretary, 1935." A typewritten report of construction and operation of Independent Lines.

"Annual Reports of Secretary," 1936–1940. Mimeographed reports of construction and operation of Independent Systems.

Report Including Analysis of Operations of the New York City Transit System for Five Years Ended June 30, 1945. The Board, New York, 1945. A printed report on operations and finances.

A Report to the Mayor and the People of the Activities and Services Rendered During the Past Three-and-a-Half Years by the Employees of the Board of Transportation of New York City. Pacific Printing Co., New York, 1949. A printed brochure on the work of the Board from January 1, 1946, to June 30, 1949.

New York City, Board of Transportation, *Contracts, Construction, and Equipment* (monthly), vol. 24, January–December, 1947; vol. 25, January–December, 1948; vol. 26, January-December, 1949; vol. 27 (January, 1950, only). Progress on construction and equipment contracts for municipal transit lines.

Transit Record (a continuation of *Transit Record Supplement* cited below), vol. 5, December, 1924–November, 1925 (12 issues); vol. 6, December, 1925–December, 1926 (12 issues); vol. 7, January–December, 1927 (12 issues); succeeding volumes up to and including vol. 32 issued monthly until the end of 1952. In 1953 only six issues were published (vol. 33).

Proceedings, vol. 1, January 1, 1924–December 31, 1924 through vol. 73, January 1, 1953–June 12, 1953. Calendar and minutes of official business of the Board of Transportation.

Opinions of Counsel Relative to Interpretation of Laws Affecting Rapid Transit Matters Particularly as Applicable to Questions Submitted by the Successive Authorities Having Jurisdiction Thereof, Namely, Public Service Commission for the First District (from July 1, 1907 to May 28, 1919), Transit Construction Commissioner (from May 29, 1919 to April 25, 1921), Transit Commission (from April 26, 1921 to June 30, 1924) and Board of Transportation (from July 1, 1924 to December 31, 1932). The Board, New York, 1932. A brief historical review of the several boards and commissions that regulated public transportation in New York City, 1891–1932, together with court decisions relating to their powers.

New York City Transit System Operating Budget for the Fiscal Years Ending June 30, 1943–June 30, 1953.

New York State Public Service Commission, First District, *Public Service Record*, vol. 1, June–December, 1914 (7 issues); vol. 2, January–December, 1915 (12 issues); vol. 3, January–December, 1916 (12 issues); vol. 4, January–December, 1917 (12 issues); vol. 5, January–December, 1918 (10 issues); vol. 6, January–November, 1919 (9 issues).

New York State Transit Construction Commissioner. *Transit Construction Record* (a continuation of *Public Service Record* cited above), vol. 7, January–December, 1920 (12 issues); vol. 8, January–June, 1921 (6 issues).

New York State Transit Commission, *Transit Record Supplement* (a monthly), vol. 1, July, 1921–June, 1922; vol. 2, July, 1922–June, 1923; vol. 3, July, 1923–June, 1924; vol. 4, July, 1924, only.

TRANSIT AUTHORITY

(Created by Chap. 200, Laws of 1953)

New York City, Transit Authority, *Transit Record* (a continuation of the *Transit Record* issued by the Board of Transportation), vol. 33, last six months of 1953; vol. 34, 1954; vol. 35, 1955. Volumes have been issued annually since 1955. Describes results of operation of municipal transit lines.

Operating Budget for the Fiscal Year Ending June 30, 1954, to date. The official budget which has governed the expenditures of the Transit Authority.

Annual Reports, fiscal years, 1954, 1955, 1956, 1957, 1958. Official reports of the work of the Transit Authority.

Minutes and Proceedings, 1952 to date. The official record of the business of the Transit Authority.

Caputo, Rudolph R., "The New York City Transit Police Department," *Law and Order*, April, 1959, pp. 6–8, 10–12, 67.

Day and Zimmerman, Inc., and Coverdale and Colpitts, "Joint Report of Engineers on the Organization, Methods and Procedures of the Board of Transportation and Its Various Operations to the Board of Transportation of the City of New York." New York, 1951. A report prepared for the Board of Transportation at the request of the Mayor's Committee on Management Survey.

Klein, Harris J., *Report to the People by Transit Authority Member Harris J. Klein, June 27, 1955.* The Author, New York, 1955. The personal views of a former Transit Authority member on how the city's transportation system should be run.

New York City, Mayor's Committee on Management Survey, *Modern Management for the City of New York.* 2 vols. The Committee, New York, 1953, vol. 1, pp. 135–175, 227–230, 249–250, 278–293; vol. 2, pp. 25–28, 72–74, 91, 363–425, and 857–858. An analysis of transit conditions which led to the creation of the Transit Authority.

Mayor's Special Transit Committee, *The Coordination of Public Transportation.* The Committee, New York, July 31, 1951. A special citizen's report that helped crystallize public opinion in favor of a Transit Authority.

New York State Constitutional Convention Committee, *New York City Government: Functions and Problems*, vol. 5 of *Reports and Studies*. Burland Printing Co., New York, 1938, pp. 108–142. A sketch of the history of rapid transit in New York City and a presentation of the problems that led to the creation of the Transit Authority.

Reid, William, *Papers*. Correspondence and selected papers of William Reid, Commissioner of Board of Transportation and Deputy Mayor, 1944–1951. In Municipal Archives.

Rukeyser, Louis R., "New York Formed Transit Authority to End Gigantic Losses under Municipal Operation" (April 1, 1957); "Railroader, Moneyman, Peacemaker Run Giant New York Transit System" (April 2, 1957); "Committee Probing New York Transit amid Echoes of 'Twenties' " (April 3, 1957); "Wildcat Strike Severed New York's Arteries, Spotlighted Its Transit Labor Troubles" (April 4, 1957); and "Transit Unit Works No Miracles, Just Seeks Goals" (April 5, 1957), *Baltimore Evening Sun*. A series of articles that covered some of the salient problems of the city's transit system.

"Some Observations of the New York City Transit Authority," *St. John's Law Review*, December, 1953, pp. 174–190.

Transit Improvement Association, *Facts About Modern Transit*. The Association, New York, 1950. A publication that puts the facts about New York City subways in perspective.

Vickery, William S., *The Revision of the Rapid Transit Fare Structure of the City of New York*. Mayor's Committee on Management Survey, New York, 1952. A review of some of the conditions which led to the creation of the Transit Authority.

Waterman, Arthur J., *Integration of Rapid Transit Facilities of the City of New York*. Doctoral dissertation, New York University, 1940. Background of the work of the Transit Authority.

White, J. G., Engineering Company, *Report on Power Supply of New York City Transit System*. New York, 1951. A report to the Board of Transportation prepared at the request of the Mayor's Committee on Management Survey.

TRIBOROUGH BRIDGE AUTHORITY
(Created by Chap. 145, Laws of 1933)

Moses, Robert, *Working for the People: Promise and Performance in Public Service*. Harper and Bros., New York, 1956. The author's views are presented through these excerpts from his writings and speeches.

Profiles from the New Yorker. Alfred A. Knopf, New York, 1938. Contains an essay on Robert Moses.

Rodgers, Cleveland, *New York Plans for the Future*. Harper and Bros., New York, 1943. A member of the City Planning Commission describes the achievements of the Triborough Bridge Authority.

Robert Moses: Builder for Democracy. Henry Holt and Co., New York, 1952. A laudatory exposition.

Triborough Bridge Authority, *Annual Reports*, 1937–1945, published annually.

Triborough Bridge and Tunnel Authority, *Annual Reports*, 1946 to date, published annually.

CHAPTER X

Leaders of the Overhead Agencies

THE LEADERS OF THE OVERHEAD AGENCIES of the city government are important participants in the political process. The prizes they distribute flow from their assignment to exercise close supervision and influence over many types of decisions by the line agency administrators, their capacity to influence the decisions of the Mayor and the Board of Estimate on many matters, and the fact that they direct a significant number of line operations in their own agencies. In doing all these things, the overhead agencies exert influence not only on each other and on the constituencies which each acquires but also on the constituencies of the line agencies (as well as on the party leaders, and the organized bureaucracies). In turn, the overhead agencies are themselves targets for all participants affected by their decisions.

The overhead agency leaders are thus fully involved in the political process, not isolated from it. They shape not only many of the "internal" and "bureaucratic" procedures of the city government; they also have a substantial impact upon all the programs and policies of the city government. It is true (and sharply revealing of the values that guide them) that the leaders and staffs of most overhead agencies appear to make decisions without conscious consideration of their program implications, but the impact upon broad public policy and upon governmental performance is nonetheless considerable. Their influence and decisions are stakes and prizes in the city's political contest.

" 'Overhead' agencies" is not a category that can be precisely defined. For the purposes of this study it will be regarded as including the following ten city agencies: the Law Department, the Investigation Department, the Bureau of the Budget, the City Planning Department, the City Construction Coordinator, the Personnel Department, the Department of Labor, the Department of Purchase, the Art Commission, and the City Record. The offices of the Comptroller and of the City Administrator, each of which has some overhead characteristics, will be discussed in the chapters on the Board of Estimate and the Mayor, respectively.

349

THE TASKS OF OVERHEAD AGENCIES AS STAKES
IN THE CITY'S POLITICS

Making Decisions Affecting Other Agencies

Some overhead agencies have assignments that cut across the work of most, or at least many, of the other administrative agencies of the city government. Thus, for example, the overhead agency entrusted with the budget process —the Bureau of the Budget—has jurisdiction over all but a few of the other city agencies. The Personnel Department has a similar jurisdictional reach, as do a number of other overhead agencies. Some, on the other hand, have a more restricted role in making decisions that affect other agencies. The work of the Art Commission has significant impact upon only those agencies concerned with works of art, while the City Record is more a provider of service than a supervisor. But while the range and intensity of the role varies among the overhead agencies, each is importantly engaged, and some of them primarily engaged, in making decisions governing the behavior and the decisions of other agencies, decisions which are important stakes in the political contest for all the major participants.

The consequences are substantial. The line agency administrators especially are compelled to share their decision-making with each overhead agency, making them important centers of power and influence in the city's politics.

Conducting Line Operations of Their Own

The power and influence of overhead agencies is also enhanced by the fact that most of them, in addition to making decisions affecting other agencies, also carry out one or more "line" operations of their own—that is, they deal directly with the public in the performance of particular governmental functions for the city. These line responsibilities of overhead agencies are usually related closely to the internal overhead function of each agency. For example, the function of examining applicants for city jobs by the personnel agency is related to its assignment to provide eligibles for appointment. The conciliation and mediation functions of the city labor agency are a corollary of its assignment to handle the city's own labor relations with its employees. These line responsibilities vary greatly in their importance among the overhead agencies: for some, it is a minor and incidental function; for others, its significance is equal to, or even greater than, the agency's overhead assignment. Some overhead agencies have no line responsibilities at all.

The presence or absence of line functions in its assignment has an important effect upon the prizes it distributes and upon its political behavior. The effect is primarily upon the nature of the overhead agency's constituency and, consequently, upon the values emphasized in the decisions the overhead agency leader makes affecting other agencies, as well as upon the political orientation and direction of the advice the overhead agency will give the Mayor or the Board of Estimate. The constituency of an overhead agency with no line operation (or only a minor one) will be shaped quite differently from that of an overhead agency involved with an "outside" constituency.

Advising the Mayor and the Board of Estimate

The heads of overhead agencies have both broader responsibilities and greater opportunities for advice to the Mayor and to the Board of Estimate than do the heads of line agencies. These greater responsibilities and opportunities flow from a number of sources. They are often stated in the formal assignments of the overhead agencies found in the charter or other statutes. They are a natural by-product of the fact that overhead agencies deal with decisions and problems which cut across all, or much of, the range of governmental activities, giving them a broad contact with, or knowledge of, the dilemmas which confront the Mayor and the Board of Estimate. Furthermore, overhead agency leaders can profit, if they wish, from the tradition that it is their business to serve as "staff" to the Mayor or the Board.

Not all overhead agencies have prominent roles in advising the Mayor and the Board of Estimate on a wide range of decisions, but several have crucial assignments that give them a central position in providing influential advice on the most important matters. Some have sanctions of law, or sources of independent power, which add great weight to their advice; others must depend upon the personal relationships between their chief officers and the Mayor or the members of the Board of Estimate, or upon the inherent quality of their advice. The content, frequency, and impact of overhead agency advice accordingly varies greatly among them.

Few overhead agency leaders have the same conditions and opportunities of access to both the Mayor and the Board of Estimate. Tradition, law, and the nature of the overhead agency's constituency tie some more closely to the Mayor, others to the Board of Estimate, and still others have a somewhat autonomous role. The heads of some overhead agencies see the Mayor quite frequently, others but rarely. Some are frequently and importantly involved directly in Board of Estimate deliberations; others have only infrequent and indirect involvement. Nor do these characteristics provide a safe guide for determining the orientation of the overhead agency's advice: for example, the heads of four overhead agencies sit in the Mayor's weekly "cabinet" sessions, but it would be hazardous to conclude that these four agencies are concerned primarily with advising the Mayor rather than the Board of Estimate. This ambivalence and ambiguity in the advisory role of each overhead agency is a persistent dilemma for its chief: it is difficult for him to determine which is the more influential route, it is risky for him and for his agency to choose overtly between them, but to attempt to serve both with fine impartiality is to ignore the deep institutional rivalry between the Mayor and the Board.

THE STRATEGIES OF OVERHEAD AGENCY LEADERS

The main tasks of overhead agencies—making decisions affecting the work of other agencies, the performance of line functions by the overhead agencies themselves, and advising the Mayor and the Board of Estimate on a wide range of decisions which either or both must make—lend to the agencies' leaders great importance as participants in the determination of how the shares in the stakes of city politics will be apportioned among the contestants. Their capacity to influence the decisions of the Mayor or the Board of Estimate, or both; their power to approve, modify, or nullify the decisions of other agencies; and their direct control over the performance of certain city functions, their own line responsibilities—all these make the overhead agencies important magnets for contestants in the political process of the city, and make their leadership and control a significant political stake. These characteristics shape the political life of each overhead agency leader. Each becomes a contestant in the political process and also becomes an object of pressure, a prize to be captured or an ally to be gained by one or another of the many competing contestants.

Carrying out his formal assignments involves a series of accommodations to the political contest; he must himself have a program of strategy and tactics. Although there are variations from one overhead agency to another, the general pattern as seen by a leader of the overhead agency takes on four important forms: (1) resolving the dilemmas of his relationships to the Mayor and the Board of Estimate; (2) identifying and building a constituency for his agency; (3) balancing the support and demands from that constituency and reconciling this balance with other pressures; and (4) developing alliances as well as managing rivalries with other agencies. Each of these problems of accommodation is interlocked with the others.

Choosing Between Mayor and Board of Estimate

The Mayor and the members of the Board of Estimate are major participants in the political contest. They are also rivals. As individuals with broad experience and strong career aspirations, and as the leaders of important rival governmental institutions, they are sharply aware of the importance of the overhead agencies in the distribution of the stakes of the city's politics. Each accordingly makes purposeful and persistent efforts to tie the assets of the overhead agencies to his own personal and institutional objectives. The overhead agency leader is consequently confronted almost daily with the necessity of accommodating the advice and decisions of his agency to this tug of pressures—sometimes implicit, sometimes quite explicit, in its reflection of the great institutional rivalry which prevails between the Mayor as the elected chief executive, on the one hand, and the Board of Estimate as the city government's center of gravity on the other.

The language of the charter and other statutory statements of his formal assignment sometimes affect a leader's choice as to whether he and his agency will identify themselves primarily with the Mayor or with the Board of Estimate. Thus the Corporation Counsel and the Commissioner of Investigation are nudged toward the Mayor, while the City Planning Commission is more formally identified with the Board of Estimate. But for some of the overhead agencies, the formal assignments are sufficiently ambiguous to leave the choice open.

Even where the formal language seems reasonably clear as to the locus of responsibility and identification, other factors may blur or determine the choice for the leaders of the overhead agencies. For example, if the decisions made by an overhead agency affecting other agencies must be approved by the Mayor or the Board of Estimate or both before the decisions have binding validity, then the overhead agency is to some extent drawn into the orbit of the approving or vetoing authority. Thus the Mayor is given by statute the power to approve or reject any proposed changes in the personnel rules of the city. The Board of Estimate, on the other hand, retains authority to approve or disapprove most changes in the budget during the budget year. The leaders of most overhead agencies discover, however, that not all their decisions are subject to such review, that not all those subject to review are reviewed by the same authority. The personnel director, for example, must take some decisions to the Board of Estimate; the budget director must take some of his to the Mayor. The Mayor and the Board each often have the power to interpose in matters formally assigned for review to the other. Further, the power of review is sometimes assigned to both the Mayor and the Board of Estimate. In short, the power to review his decisions, whether vested in the Mayor, the Board of Estimate, or both is likely to complicate the overhead agency leader's choice of his identification and loyalty.

Usage and tradition will have resolved some of this dilemma for the incoming leader of an overhead agency, for some agencies have long since settled into a pattern of strong identification either with the Mayor or with the Board of Estimate, others into a pattern of studied ambiguity on the question, and others into a pattern of semiautonomous relationships with both institutions, leaving themselves relatively free to work out their own accommodations with their constituencies. But there is always the possibility that some new wind of doctrine or a forceful Mayor, an aggressive Board of Estimate, or some new or old interest group with ideas for change will intervene to upset the settled pattern of behavior for the overhead agency leader. Consequently, no overhead agency leader can ever view his relationships to the Mayor and the

Board of Estimate with complete equanimity. For him, the choice is always either a chronic, an episodic, or a potential source of trouble.

Identifying and Building a Constituency

The fact that an overhead agency is in a position to offer influential advice to the Mayor or the Board of Estimate (or to both), the fact that the overhead agency makes some decisions in its own right (or subject to only limited review) which greatly affect the decisions of other agencies, and the fact that most overhead agencies carry out line functions of their own—all these powers of the overhead agency leader attract the attention of other participants in the city's political process. Not only do the Mayor and the members of the Board of Estimate reach out competitively to exercise such control as they can manage over these agencies, but so also do the organized bureaucracies, the nongovernmental interest groups, and the party leaders. The bureaucracies and the other interest groups which aim at influencing a particular overhead agency are those that have a stake in the kinds of advice which the agency gives to the Mayor and the Board of Estimate, as well as in the kinds of decisions that lie within the overhead agency's jurisdiction. The party leaders tend to concentrate their attention upon those overhead agency leaders whose functions (like those of personnel and investigation) touch most intimately upon the stakes close to party organization concerns.

These bureaucracies, interest groups, and party leaders are, so to speak, the self-identifying elements of an overhead agency's constituency. They come into the agency's constituency whether they are invited by the agency or not, and they usually assume self-defined roles. They constitute, from the agency leader's point of view, a stubborn "fact of life" with which he must make what accommodations he can. He can either yield to this self-identified constituency, passively accepting an established pattern in which the groups have defined their own roles and objectives, or he can attempt to lead them, or to bargain and negotiate with them, capitalizing upon any competition among them and attempting to work out slowly a new equilibrium of support and demands from them. The second course may give his agency some degree of initiative; the first will make it a closely guarded prisoner of its constituency.

Some leaders of overhead agencies attempt a third course. They seek to broaden the constituency of the agency and to give it a competitive rather than a monolithic structure by inviting the attention and encouraging the participation of other groups in the decision-making activities of the agency. In so doing, the agency leaders seek essentially to gain or preserve initiative and autonomy for themselves, either to determine the content of their advice and their decisions, or to identify themselves more freely with the Mayor, or with the Board of Estimate, or with a preferred element in the agency constituency.

If an overhead agency leadership seeks to broaden or reconstruct an agency constituency, the press and the other communication media will ordinarily be used as important instruments. Public attention seems to attract group attention which has previously been latent, and the agency leadership can use the factors of emphasis, timing, and even open invitation in an effort to recruit new and desired elements into the agency constituency. The civic interest groups are another potential source for new constituency elements, since their range of interest is wide. But to these prospects, the agency leadership must usually seek to add new constituency elements which have an enduring economic stake in the agency's work.

The freedom of the leader of an overhead agency to build a broader constituency and to deal with it on terms favorable to himself depends upon several factors: the degree to which the agency is already committed by its tradition to a constituency able to protect its status, the cohesiveness of the established constituency, and the capacity of the agency to attract new constituency elements or revise the goals of some of the present elements. The size, the cohesiveness, the intensity of interest, and the stability of an agency's constituency all influence its role with the agency. In these respects, as we shall soon see, the constituencies of overhead agencies vary greatly. Some are quite small in number of members but have elite status, cohesiveness, and stability. Some are quite large but possess an almost monolithic structure with regard to the decisions with which the overhead agency deals; others are large but contain highly competitive internal elements. Some overhead agencies have constituencies which are quite stable, while others are fluctuating and erratic. Some agencies have to seek out their constituencies, while others are overwhelmed by aggressive, self-nominated ones.

Despite this great variety in the nature and roles of overhead agency constituencies, two general types can be identified. First, some overhead agencies have constituencies which are predominantly intragovernmental (as, for example, the personnel and budget agencies). Second, some overhead agencies have constituencies which are primarily nongovernmental (as, for example, the planning agency). Most overhead agencies, however, confront a constituency which is composed of changing combinations of intragovernmental and nongovernmental elements.

Balancing Constituency Support and Demands

The constituency of an overhead agency ordinarily makes its demands at the three crucial points of the agency's work previously noted: (1) It seeks to influence the kinds of advice the agency will give to the Mayor or the Board of Estimate; (2) it seeks to shape the decisions the overhead agency makes affecting the decisions of other agencies; and (3) it seeks to guide the agency in setting the goals and methods of the "line" functions the overhead agency performs.

In these efforts to influence, if not to control, the goals and decisions of an overhead agency, the constituency elements, singly or collectively, cooperatively or competitively with each other, use all the modes of influence available to experienced and inventive participants. They attempt to participate in the selection of those who hold the top positions of leadership in the agency and to influence the kind, size, and organization of staff for the agency. They participate in the formal public proceedings of the agency, demanding, condemning, or suggesting. They seek opportunities and agreements which will maximize informal consultation with the leaders and the staff of the agency. They work at developing personal ties of friendship between leaders of the agency and leaders of the constituency. They use the weapons of publicity to coerce or support agency decisions. This imposing list of techniques does not exhaust their arsenal of methods. They may attempt to influence the agency by appeals to higher or equivalent levels of the governmental hierarchy—to other overhead agencies, to line agencies, to the Mayor, to the Board of Estimate, the courts, the Council, the state legislature, or others.

The leader of an overhead agency who wishes to lead rather than be led by his constituency does not ordinarily face a comforting prospect of success. Yet he is not without resources for the risk-taking involved. As a public official he has a legitimacy of status through which he can usually invoke claims of the public interest more persuasively than can most constituency leaders. He also usually has at his disposal, if not a monopoly, at least a greater amount of information about a question than do his constituency critics. And he frequently has the advantage of position: it is he who promulgates the decision. The constituency can speak only of the costs of controversy and delay, its capacity to reverse the decision elsewhere, or to punish the agency or its leader on another occasion or in another place.

The relationship between the overhead agency leader and his constituency customarily calls for bargaining and negotiation. The leader of an overhead agency thus learns to search for those demands from the constituency which are most nearly consistent with his goals, which can be accepted at least cost to his other sources of support, and which leave him least impaired for the next bargaining encounter. The agency leader also learns to be alert for competitive claims represented by separate elements of the constituency, to make these differences visible and emphatic, and to use these conflicts to enlarge his own initiative and autonomy in relationship to his constituency. The agency leader can also seek constantly to broaden the constituency, to increase its internal competitive structure, and to develop a broader base of latent and potential group support in the general public.

But in the overhead agencies of the New York City government, few agency leaders find opportunities and incentives to engage in systematic hard bargaining with their constituencies. On balance, and over the long haul, the constituency leaders drive the harder bargain.

Developing Alliances and Managing Rivalries with Other Agencies

The nature of an overhead agency's assignment in the city government will largely determine with which other agencies its chief will have competitive relationships and with which he will need to work out mutual concessions and alliances. The fact that an overhead agency leader advises the Mayor or the Board of Estimate in a specialized functional field affecting the fortunes of many agencies, and that his agency makes rules limiting the discretion of other agency leaders, means that each overhead agency leader confronts a tendency toward hostility from most other agencies. Tension between an overhead agency and the line agencies affected by its rules tends to be endemic. The need for accommodation to some and alliance with others is therefore great, as a way of strengthening the overhead agency leader for his almost inescapable rivalry with some of the remaining agencies.

The overhead agency leader may reduce the risks for himself by softening the rules when they apply to the most powerful, as do the Budget Director and the Personnel Director with the Borough Presidents, the Comptroller, the Park Commissioner, and the Police Commissioner, for example. Tension and competition between one overhead agency leader and another is less universal, but when their separate rule-making activities affect the same general decision-making areas in the line agencies (as when the rules of the budget agency and those of the personnel agency conflict and collide with respect to some line agencies) then the rivalry between the leaders is usually both strong and persistent.

As a consequence of these forces, the leader of an overhead agency seeks an equilibrium in the relationships of his agency to other agency leaders. The difficulty of this task varies widely among the overhead agencies. Some leaders are fortunate because their rules evoke little or infrequently expressed resistance. Some are rarely competitive with other overhead agencies. Some are protected by a close identification with the Mayor, or with the Board of Estimate. Some are shielded from other agencies by a powerful constituency organization. But even the most favorably situated must ordinarily make some lasting accommodations, form some alliances, and attempt to manage skillfully some troublesome rivalries with other agency leaders. And these matters must always be handled in relationship to other and changing factors in the environment of the overhead agency leader: his relationship with the Mayor, the Board of Estimate, the agency's constituency, the communication media, and the unanticipated or underestimated issue which may quickly upset the whole calculated equilibrium.

STRATEGIES OF PARTICULAR OVERHEAD AGENCIES

The opportunities, dilemmas, and risks which confront the leaders of over-head agencies as they carry out their assignments in the midst of a complex political environment are best illustrated by a discussion of the tasks and strategies of individual agencies.

The Law Department

The Corporation Counsel holds an office of high prestige in the city government, a prize of high status in the political contest. Several factors account for this significance. The incumbents of the office have traditionally enjoyed a close intimacy with the Mayor. The office has attracted talent of comparatively high order and has led usually to desirable promotions up the political or the legal career ladders (to a judgeship, for example, or to membership in a leading law firm). The Corporation Counsel heads a large staff of lawyers, perhaps justifiably described as "the largest legal firm in the city," thus holding at his disposal several hundred (almost a hundred being "exempt") choice assignments for members of a profession that has a unique intimacy with, and special skills in, the political process. These staff members themselves tend to have strong career aspirations in politics, and they often bring to the Corporation Counsel and his key assistants considerable political influence of their own. The Law Department accordingly represents a concentration of both legal talent and political power.

The assignments given to the Law Department by Chapter 16 of the charter, by other laws, and by usage amount in effect to a monopoly over the legal business of the city government. "Except as otherwise provided by law," the charter declares, "the corporation counsel shall be attorney and counsel for the city and every agency thereof and shall have charge and conduct of all the law business of the city and its agencies and in which the city is interested." Few city officials possess so sweeping and unequivocal a statement of jurisdiction, and few are so free of formal compulsions to share their power with others.

The Corporation Counsel is also comparatively free from the dilemma that besets several other overhead agencies: both his formal position and the nature of his work make him primarily an adviser to the Mayor, with only minimal formal requirements to work with the Board of Estimate. But he does not entirely escape the problem. His powers to conduct legal proceedings concerning streets, acquiring real estate for the city, and preparing all legal papers for the city (including contracts, leases, deeds, and bonds) bring him directly into the realm of the Board, and this is sharply recognized by the charter provision that the Board may direct changes to be made in the form of contracts and specifications. He is further involved with the Board and with one of its most powerful members by the charter provision that he may not settle any claim for or against the city "without the previous written approval of the comptroller."

The powers and opportunities of the Corporation Counsel to make decisions affecting the policies and practices of other agencies (both overhead and line) are extensive and relatively untrammeled. He may decide whether any agency has, or lacks, the legal power to do something it wishes to do; or whether it has, or does not have, a legal obligation to do something it does not wish to do. He may determine the procedure of an agency by defining the legal requirements for such a procedure. He may decide whether to sue or not to sue, or to defend a suit or yield the point, in situations of great importance to the agencies concerned. The discretion to make these choices (within the range of judgment permitted by the clarity or ambiguity of the statutes and their interpretation by the courts) is preserved for the Corporation Counsel by the charter provision that "the corporation counsel may assign an assistant or assistants to any agency, and no officer or agency, unless it be herein otherwise especially provided, shall have or employ any attorney or counsel" except where a judgment might affect the officer individually, in which instance the officer may at his own expense have his own attorney. The Corporation Counsel, unless the Mayor yields to an agency appeal and directs otherwise, accordingly has the power and the method to compel the agency to accept his advice. His influence in this respect is enhanced by the manner in which legal guidance and supervision is exercised by the Corporation Counsel. He does not issue a manual of legal rules to guide the agencies' decisions. Instead, he reserves the right to inspect each decision in its legal aspects as it arises, and on its own legal merits as he or his staff see the merits. His discretion is not institutionalized and thus is not made easier for others to anticipate and limit; rather, he retains the maximum of flexibility and initiative in the exercise of his judgments.

Three factors limit the Corporation Counsel. First, he cannot ordinarily take the initiative, but must wait for others (the agencies or private litigants) to bring matters to him for legal opinion or action. Second, he performs no important line function, from which he might derive opportunities for initiative. (He can, however, frequently anticipate the course of action agencies are likely to take; and if he wishes he can, especially through his prerogatives as legal adviser to the Mayor, intervene with his opinion before it is formally requested.) Third, he cannot regard casually the power of the agencies to reject his advice and appeal to the Mayor. The Mayor will most often uphold him, but he cannot draw too often or too heavily upon his credit.

The Corporation Counsel deals with two important constituency elements. He and his staff, and the work they do, are deeply immersed in the legal profession and are the objects of sustained attention from the several bar associations of the city. The bar associations, especially through their committees, often assume the roles of monitors and critics of the quality of the staff and work of the Law Department and on some occasions have assisted in recruiting or screening applicants for its staff. The law firms of the city, particularly those whose practice tends toward litigation or negotiation with the city government, or whose members have important roles in the political process, are a continuing source of influence upon the Department—the more so since many of the staff members have expectations of a future career in such firms or anticipate the need for their help in the political career arena. Further, some specialized groups of lawyers—tax attorneys, real estate attorneys, civil service lawyers, and others—have important stakes in the maintenance of friendly access to the appropriate members of the Corporation Counsel's staff. In short, the Corporation Counsel carries out his functions within a climate profoundly affected by his status, and that of his staff, in the legal profession. In this relationship, the organized elements of the profession have great power to confer or withhold the award of high status, which some Corporation Counsels have bid for with merit and vigor.

The second major constituency element with which the Corporation Counsel must deal is composed of the political party organizations, especially those party leaders most important in the Mayor's nomination and election. Several score of the professional positions in the Department, and virtually all the important ones, are "exempt" from the formal rules of competitive selection and advancement. The appointments are consequently at the discretion of the Corporation Counsel. This special arrangement of the personnel rules (a tradition also for most legal staffs in other governmental jurisdictions) makes the Corporation Counsel vulnerable to the claims made by the five party leaders of the county organizations in the city for staff appointments, and to the recommendations they make concerning assignments and promotions within the Department.

The vulnerability of Corporation Counsels to party organizations in making staff appointments, assignments, and promotions varies in degree and kind. Those who serve "Fusion" Mayors (whose debt to any single party group is often unclear) feel it least, but perhaps are the more open to bar association and other legal profession pressures. Those who serve Mayors representing a continuation of the same party in office are under more pressure to retain the staff than to displace it. In preserving some discretion for himself in staffing his agency, the Corporation Counsel has ordinarily three main resources in strategy and tactics: he can attempt to encourage the sponsors to present more qualified applicants than he has positions to award, and then arrive at strategic choices among the competing applicants and sponsors; he can encourage competition between the party organizations as claimants and the organized groups in the legal profession as monitors and claimants; he can also seek to become, as several Corporation Counsels have been, one of the main patronage advisers to the Mayor, successfully resisting in this general capacity the demands upon him for appointments to his own staff which he regards as unmeritorious or, if necessary, deflecting them to other places. The Corporation Counsel who can command and use skillfully all three of these resources has an opportunity to be master in his own house.

The Corporation Counsel, being close to the Mayor as a general rule and having a virtually monopolistic role as attorney and counsel for the city and its agencies, is under few compulsions to make concessions to, or form alliances with, other agencies, and his position is so advantageous as to discourage most jurisdictional rivalries. His main concern is how to live with the courts; how to deal with those agencies that can, or can attempt to, ignore or set aside his legal advice is a secondary problem. The courts are the ultimate arbiters of his most important decisions. His record in the courts largely determines his prestige with the Mayor and with the agencies and fosters their willingness or reluctance to accept his predictions as to what decisions and procedures will be upheld or disapproved when tested by litigation. His status with the legal profession is at stake also. The Corporation Counsel and his staff must approach the courts (especially the higher courts) with deference, not only because this is the code and tradition of the legal profession but also because the judges with whom he is most concerned are themselves elected officials, jealous of their independent status and conscious of their power. Some of the Corporation Counsel's most painful dilemmas revolve around his efforts to reconcile his anticipations of what the judges will say, the wishes of the Mayor or of a forceful agency head, and his own personal judgment as to what ought to be done. In most instances, where litigation is at all likely, he must confine his own preferences, as well as those of the Mayor and the agencies, within the limits of his best guess as to what the courts will decree.

The agencies present a more manageable problem to the Corporation Counsel. The agencies are not clients in the usual sense. They cannot take their legal business elsewhere, nor can they tell their counsel the limits of his discretion. They are, in effect, "captive" clients. They can attempt to persuade the Corporation Counsel to their view, but, if they cannot do so, they must yield to him unless they can successfully appeal to the Mayor or to someone else to whom the Corporation Counsel will listen sympathetically. Few agencies can accomplish this feat. It requires unusual political power on the part of the agency, or it must be a case with particular appeal to the Mayor, to a member of the Board of Estimate, or to the public. There are some agencies, of course, which are allowed to have their own counsel; and there are others which have sufficient legal autonomy of other kinds to cause the Corporation Counsel to give way. In general, though, the Corporation

Counsel is in an exceptionally strong position. Yet despite his advantages in his relationships with the agencies as clients, the Corporation Counsel must always weigh the possibility that an agency will appeal to the Mayor or elsewhere and must calculate the risks to himself and the Law Department, in status and prestige, if he is overruled.

The Law Department thus has an enviable position among overhead agencies. It is closely attached to the Mayor, and comparatively free of the stresses between the Mayor and the Board of Estimate. It has an unambiguous assignment and a virtual monopoly over the performance of its central function. It is not distracted, or its life complicated, by a line assignment. It has a constituency which contains competing claimants, and its relationships to other institutions of government are carried out under rules and standards which, with respect to the courts, are predictable and, with respect to the agencies as clients, are advantageous to the Law Department. No other overhead agency has both a status so important and a political life so comparatively uncomplicated.

The Department of Investigation

The Commissioner of Investigation holds an office of unpredictable consequences for its incumbents. The opportunities for prominence have been somewhat overbalanced, in the history of the Department, by the chances for obscurity. John Purroy Mitchel made the office an escalator for himself which led first to the presidency of the Board of Aldermen and then to the mayoralty. Raymond Fosdick found in it opportunities to lay the foundations of a national reputation and a distinguished career. William H. Herlands found the office an important rung in his career ladder leading eventually to a federal judgeship. John M. Murtagh rose from the office to be Chief City Magistrate. But these, and few others, are exceptions in the history of an office of uncertain prestige.

The uncertainties of the office arise out of the anomalies and the ambiguities of its assignment in the city government. The formal assignment in Chapter 34 of the charter is quite sweeping. The Commissioner is empowered to "make any investigation directed by the mayor or the council"; he is also "authorized and empowered to make any study or investigation which in his opinion may be in the best interests of the city." In making any such studies or investigations, he or his deputies are empowered to compel the attendance of witnesses, administer oaths to and examine any persons he may deem necessary. He is required to maintain "a complaint bureau in the department which shall receive complaints from the public." The charter also gives the Commissioner (as well as others) the sanction of dismissal over any official or employee refusing to testify.

These powers and duties seem straightforward enough, but difficulties lie just beneath the surface. Is the Commissioner of Investigation an investigator for the Mayor, taking his leads from, and limiting his energies to, the necessities seen by the Mayor, or is he the institutionalized public conscience, sending his investigators energetically into every situation where complaints or his considered judgment take him, accompanying his efforts with calculated publicity, presenting the Mayor in effect with *faits accomplis?* To choose the first is ordinarily to accept comparative obscurity and to expose himself to pressures and criticism from the press, the interest groups, and perhaps the more general public for failures to investigate on his own initiative and to make his findings public. To choose the role of the autonomous public conscience is to invite the sanctions of the Mayor (who may remove him at pleasure) and the hostility of all those powerfully placed who are, or may be, hurt by his inquiries. Moreover, no matter how he resolves this dilemma, he is still confronted with others. Is he to investigate governmental agencies primarily (these are the duties stressed specifically by the charter) or is he to include private persons or groups as important objects of his scrutiny? In the investigation of governmental agencies, is he to be no respecter of persons, examining the affairs of members of the Board of Estimate, of the Council, the more powerful heads of departments, even members of the Mayor's own official household, with the same initiative and energy as he inquires into the official and private lives of rank-and-file bureaucrats? Is he to seek mainly the more overt forms of malfeasance (those subject to punishment as violations of law or providing a basis for administrative sanctions—dismissal, forced resignation, suspension), or is he to emphasize misfeasance and non-feasance in office, thus becoming a management adviser to the Mayor and the agencies?

The Commissioner of Investigation is compelled to make these choices and to reconsider his course almost every day. He usually attempts to avoid making his choices overt and rigid. In a climate of uncertainty, blurred choices are the mark of prudence. In the main, of course, the Commissioner must do what the Mayor permits, and a Mayor's permission will range from a tight curb through aloof toleration to enthusiastic support. Fusion Mayors, or other Mayors disenchanted with the *status quo* (as McClellan or Gaynor), will ordinarily give their Commissioner of Investigation a broad freedom to scourge all suspected malfeasants, misfeasants, or nonfeasants. For them, the Commissioner is an instrument of control or discipline over intractable forces. Mayors who hold office under other terms and conditions will keep a tighter rein over the Commissioner.

The Commissioner of Investigation's usual desire and his compelling necessity to identify himself, his policies, and his practices with the Mayor are made difficult by the nature of the Commissioner's constituency. The elements of this constituency push him in several different directions. The party leaders, aware of the explosive potential for damage to their interests in the investigatory power, attempt to establish a rule of reason and tolerance in the Commissioner's behavior. They have several opportunities to emphasize their views. The party leaders have an advisory role to the Mayor in the selection of the Commissioner. They seek in all their subsequent contacts with the Commissioner to stress their common interests with him. They usually have an important part in staffing the agency, since many investigators in the department (like the attorneys in the Law Department) are "exempt" appointees. In this latter opportunity, the party leaders attempt to insure themselves against an unpredictable Commissioner by providing him with a predictable staff. The Commissioner, in turn, finds his discretion as to his staff determined largely by the Mayor's attitude toward the party leaders. He may be permitted, as were Mitchel under McClellan and Blanshard under La Guardia, to choose his staff upon austere standards, or he may find he must choose from among lists of names approved by the party leaders. He has no other constituency element which will give him much help in this matter.

The organized groups in the city bureaucracy present the Commissioner with a different kind of problem. Employee unions and other employee groups seek mainly to protect their members against what they regard as the punitive attacks of investigators upon the established mores of the bureaucracy and upon the individual rights and dignities of their members—or as the efforts of investigators to place the sins and errors of officialdom upon the backs of the employees. But the attitudes and strategies of the bureaucracies toward the Commissioner are not always homogeneous or consistent. Some groups or unions may seek his help against competitive organizations, or they may charge him with partiality among them, or they may collaborate or compete with the party organizations or other interest groups to limit or guide the Commissioner's course. The net effect of their influence, however, like that of the party organizations, is to inhibit rather than to enhance the Commissioner's discretion, whether or not in doing so they find themselves in agreement with the Mayor.

The nongovernmental interest groups (especially those of the reform variety) and the communication media play a different part in the Commissioner's constituency. They work to enhance his initiative, to urge upon him the role of the public conscience. They propose as models the performance of Mitchel and Blanshard in the office. Publicity is their main device for pressure upon the Commissioner, as it is also their main reward to him when he conforms to their model of behavior. He should investigate, they assert, the situations they and others bring to his attention, whether the Mayor agrees or not; and he should report to the public as well as to the Mayor, so that the public may judge both his findings and the Mayor's actions. This is their sustained drumbeat upon the Commissioner's ears throughout his term. Not even a Mitchel or a Blanshard can yield to them fully. Every Commissioner yields some or persuades the Mayor to do so.

He cannot yield completely because of the Mayor's obligation to set limits to the exposure of weakness in his own administration, but there are other inhibitions also. The Commissioner is not the only investigator; he does not have the kind of monopoly of function given to the Corporation Counsel. The five District Attorneys in the city not only have broad powers of investigation in their own right, but the Commissioner of Investigation must also depend upon each of them to prosecute any violations of law the Commissioner discovers. Moreover, the District Attorneys are elected officials, mindful of their own jurisdictional claims, their own official obligations and career aspirations. The Commissioner therefore cannot ignore their demands for consultation, for some agreement on jurisdiction, and for public acknowledgment of their participation. The Police Department, too, has a wide and overlapping assignment in investigation; its capacity to enforce a protocol of relationships with the Department of Investigation is not much less than that of the District Attorneys. The Corporation Counsel is not an investigator, but he is attorney and counsel to the Commissioner of Investigation, and his judgments are a part of the Commissioner's controlling environment. The City Council, too, has the power to direct the Commissioner to make an investigation and on occasion does so, but it also has independent investigatory powers of its own which it may use to anticipate, compete with, or complicate and confuse the Commissioner's investigations—a phenomenon familiar to the Gaynor and La Guardia commissioners. (In this particular Council relationship, irony has more recently been provided by the extensive 1957 investigations which the Commissioner has made of members of the Council, some at the Council's request and some on his own or the Mayor's initiative.)

The state government also has investigatory institutions capable of competition with the Commissioner. A state Attorney General may move in or threaten to do so. The Governor has at his disposal a Crime Commission (until 1958 called a Department of Investigation) which seemed to some to hang like Damocles' sword over the Impellitteri administration. The state legislature has its powers of investigation, too—with its committees not infrequently disposed to use them, even in areas where the Commissioner is already at work or where he prefers to have no one enter. As he surveys the competitive world of investigations—District Attorneys, Police Department, state agencies, and state legislatures, even an occasional federal inquiry by United States attorneys, the FBI, or a congressional committee—the Commissioner not infrequently must contemplate the possibility of the ultimate Pandora's box for him: all the investigators simultaneously competing with or even investigating each other!

The Department of Investigation has an unenviable position among the city's overhead agencies. It is closely attached to the Mayor, but most Mayors tend to restrict its scope. It has an ambiguous assignment, is beset by competition over jurisdiction, and has only a minor line function (the receiving of public complaints) which gives it no major strength. Its constituency contains powerful elements, some of which seek to restrict its role, and some of which counsel action that would expose it to conflicts with the Mayor.

The Bureau of the Budget

The Director of the Bureau of the Budget holds an office with great power but without fame. In its thirty-year history as an overhead agency in the city government, most of its Directors have wielded extensive influence during their incumbency, but only one has risen to higher office. The function of the office is one of austerity without drama, of influence gained through an infinite attention to detail rather than to broad policy, of power exercised to preserve the *status quo* rather than in behalf of innovation, of maintaining the precarious balance of the city's revenues and expenditures by disappointing the expectations of both the service-demanding and the money-providing forces in the city's political process. These are prescriptions for unpopularity, although they may from time to time evoke some grudging admiration for the tactical and technical skills displayed by the Budget Director, and for a saving obscurity.

Budget Directors have ordinarily brought with them into office no important political status of their own. What they have in the way of power they acquire mainly from the office and its function. This power, substantial as it is, has few public dimensions. It is, so to speak, "inside" power, accumulated through an endless series of discrete, anonymous decisions made throughout the budget year, and bringing the Budget Director into the foreground of public attention on only a few occasions: when he issues the call for departmental estimates, when the departments appear before him to defend their requests, when he joins the Mayor in the annual budget "retreat," when he journeys with the Mayor to Albany for state financial assistance, and on a few other less regularly scheduled events. In all, or at least most, of these situations, the Budget Director speaks from a protected position. He cannot be outmatched in his manipulation of financial statistics and he is sheltered by the Mayor's presence or by his confidence that the Mayor must support him. But most of all, he is protected by the budget process itself, its complexities of detail and intricacies of interpretation being fashioned ideally for such defensive purposes.

The charter confers upon the Budget Director the power to prepare the annual "executive" budget, that is, the budget for annual operating expenses which the Mayor submits to the Board of Estimate on or before April 1 each year. In this preparation he is empowered to require estimates from the agencies, to acquire data from them, to survey the agencies (if he wishes) to determine their requirements, and to hold hearings at which agency heads justify their estimates. The charter also gives him the further power to participate in the preparation of the capital budget at two stages—at the beginning, by reporting through the Mayor to the City Planning Commission his recommendations as to the maximum amount of the capital budget and, at the midpoint of the capital budget process, by submitting to the Board of Estimate his comments and recommendations on the proposed capital budget. Custom, not unaided by Budget Directors, has given him additional and

TABLE 43. BUDGET DIRECTORS OF NEW YORK CITY: PREVIOUS POSITIONS AND TENURE IN OFFICE

Director	Previous position	Tenure as director	Mayors served
Edward Buckley	Commissioner of Purchase	June, 1924–Dec., 1925	Hylan
Charles L. Koehler	Secretary, Health Department	Feb., 1926–Apr., 1933	Walker, O'Brien
Maurice Stephenson	Deputy State Tax Commissioner	Apr., 1933–Dec., 1933	O'Brien
Rufus E. McGahen	Secretary and Legislative Representative, Citizens Union	Jan., 1934–Aug., 1936	La Guardia
Leo J. McDermott	Staff of Citizens Union; Assistant Budget Director	Aug., 1936–Dec., 1937	La Guardia
Kenneth Dayton	Deputy Commissioner of Accounts, Assistant Budget Director	Dec., 1937–Dec., 1942	La Guardia
Thomas J. Patterson	Assistant Budget Director	Mar., 1943–Mar., 1952	La Guardia, O'Dwyer, Impellitteri
Abraham Beame	Assistant Budget Director	Mar., 1952 to date	Impellitteri, Wagner

SOURCE: Lowi, Theodore J., *At the Pleasure of the Mayor*. Doctoral dissertation, Yale University, 1960, unpublished.

equally important powers in the administration of the budget during the year, after its formal adoption. These powers find their most important expression in the "terms and conditions" which the Board of Estimate is empowered to set forth and under which all appropriations are administered. These terms and conditions, largely the product of recommendations by successive Budget Directors, give to the Budget Director close continuing control over the individual budget decisions of almost all department and agency heads during the year.

The most crucial choice in the historical development of the Bureau of the Budget turned on the question as to whether the Director was to be an agent of the Mayor or whether he was to be instead the *de facto* agent of the Board of Estimate. The agency began its history as a Board of Estimate institution.

Then, for approximately a decade under La Guardia, it was more a mayoralty agency than a Board agency (although never free of deep involvement with the Board). This phase has been followed by a slow but steady journey back to close identification with the Board. There are signs that the future may confer an almost autonomous status upon the Director, his influences over the Board already showing evidence of steady increase.

The present status, confirmed by almost two decades of tendencies, seems to be: the Budget Director must, in all matters formal and ritualistic, appear to be the Mayor's instrument, but he must make his peace with the Board of Estimate by being in fact and in fealty its agent. This choice, adhered to by more than one Budget Director, is in part the product of the kind of budget process used by the city, in part the result of the agency's judgment of its greater opportunities for influence, in part the consequence of Budget Directors' desires to become "career" officials by attaching themselves to the Board as the center of power which has the greatest continuity in the city government. The risks of mayoral anger or resentment are always latent and sometimes explode in force, but the Budget Director's defenses are not inconsiderable. To his claims of innocence he can bring the support of the ambiguous language of the charter, he can cite the necessities (which all Mayors must recognize) of deference to the Board, and he can usually yield the particular point to the Mayor in the confidence that the Board will understand the matter. The basic pattern of his close identification and collaboration with the Board in the budget process he cannot greatly change. Their partnership is deeply satisfying and rewarding both to the Board and to the Director. There are no foreseeable incentives for either party to want to lessen its intimacy, let alone to dissolve it.

The central explanation for this phenomenon is to be found in the role which the charter gives to the Board of Estimate in the expenditure process and in the budget tools which the Board and the Budget Director have found at hand, or have developed, to consolidate their collaborative positions in the expenditure system. In essence, the budget process is one in which the Mayor formally proposes to the Board of Estimate an almost incredibly detailed "line item" budget which the Budget Director has in fact prepared and of which only he and his staff are masters. Thereafter, budget decisions and administration are a virtual monopoly of the Board and the Director. Further helping the partnership of the Board and the Director is the fact that the tax and the debt limits imposed upon the city by the state constitution, and the restricted taxing powers granted by the state legislature, produce a constant pressure of city expenditures and borrowings against the city's revenue and debt ceilings. Some of the most important choices in the city's political process therefore take the form of discretion exercised by manipulating in minute and complex detail the scarce resources of the city to meet its tight expense and capital budgets. This is the field of discretion which the Board and the Director have claimed as their own. The calendars of the Board carry eloquent evidence of the quantity, the detail, the intimacy, and the fruits of their close partnership.

This close collaboration between the Board of Estimate and the Budget Director shelters him from hostile constituencies and relieves him of the need for friendly ones. He can and does make himself comparatively inaccessible to his critics and holds himself aloof from those who court him. In this practice, he is aided considerably by the close-knit character of his small staff, hand-picked by transfer from other agencies or hand-raised within the Bureau by advancement from clerical ranks. New kinds of budget doctrine do not seep in through the recruitment of "new blood" for the staff; no "open competitive" examinations are held for its professional ranks.

Nevertheless, the Director is not left wholly unexposed to a constituency. Some of the city's most articulate interest groups have within the last decade found a weapon of some potency, by seizing upon a demand (widely supported by new budget doctrine in national, state, and local governments elsewhere) for a change from the "line item" budget to a "program" or "performance" budget. This change would open up the budget process to more critical public scrutiny, increase the discretion of the Mayor and agency heads to make budget decisions, and restrict the opportunities of the Board of Estimate and the Budget Director to make their traditional detailed expenditure decisions. The Citizens Budget Commission and its allies, representing the money-providing constituencies, and the Citizens Union along with other service-demanding groups have joined in an extensive campaign to compel the change. They have had the support of the influential reports of the Mayor's Management Survey (1952) and the Temporary State Commission to Study the Organizational Structure of New York City (the Josephs Commission, 1953–1954), and of a substantial portion of the press. The Budget Director, finding himself on the defensive, at least ideologically, has yielded ground slowly and mainly in formal terms. "Program" budgets have been prepared as illustrative and explanatory annexes, but the "line-item" budget remains as the formal appropriation statute while the "terms and conditions" are still unimpaired instruments of Budget Director and Board control. The Board of Estimate meanwhile has, for its part, been spared the arrows of the critics who share the widespread general deference toward the Board. It has thus been able to ignore the issue with customary imperturbability.

The organized bureaucracies attack upon a different flank. They move upon the Board of Estimate and upon the Mayor, seeking thus to influence the Budget Director. Their demands are mainly aimed at higher wages and salaries, at increased numbers and rate of promotion, and at additional fringe benefits (more favorable retirement age, higher pension contributions by the city, and so on). To these demands the Budget Director is more sympathetic than he is to proposals that he change the budget process. His response to the bureaucracies is geared to the prevailing strategic tendencies of the members of the Board of Estimate.

The party leaders do not loom so large in the Budget Director's constituency as do the nongovernmental groups and the organized bureaucracies. The Board of Estimate, itself an institution close to the party organization, sets the metes and bounds of this relationship, its members transmitting to the Budget Director more of the party organization expectations than are transmitted directly by party leaders to him, except perhaps from the party leaders in the Director's "home" borough. But there are occasions when the party leaders seek direct access to the Budget Director: a desired promotion for a party constituent, a salary increase, support for a department head who seeks a certificate to fill a vacancy, or a favored site location for a city project. This is the small change of a Budget Director's currency, but each item represents a stake of some importance to a party leader trying to work out a complex combination of agreements or attempting to demonstrate that he has influence in the needed places.

His close alliance with the Board of Estimate gives the Budget Director great strength in dealing with the rivalries of the Bureau with other agencies, and it reduces his need for making concessions or forming alliances. For example, the Bureau has moved steadily into the areas of decision in which the Department of Personnel has formal claims to initiative and leadership. The Budget Director has now so consolidated his position in city personnel administration that he is in effect the senior partner of the Personnel Director in the development of personnel policies and in making many individual personnel decisions, a partnership in which the Personnel Director proposes and the Budget Director disposes. A main device through which this predominance has been established is the use of the "terms and conditions" of the expense budget as an instrument of personnel control, channeling an increasing number of personnel decisions to the Board of Estimate, to which the Budget Director is primary adviser and agent.

In his relationships with the City Planning Commission, to which the charter gives formal responsibility for the preparation of the capital budget, the Budget Director has been largely successful in extending his influence beyond the charter boundaries of his role as adviser and commentator on the capital budget. The history of this relationship is instructive. When the capital budget was inaugurated by the new charter in 1938, the Planning Commission lacked staff to prepare a capital budget, and so for a decade the Budget Director's staff performed the task. In 1949, as the Planning Commission began to take over the task of preparation, the charter was amended to give the Budget Director the specific powers of comment and recommendation, his second report to go directly to the Board of Estimate. Furthermore, the Budget Director's influence over the capital budget is enhanced by the additional and greater opportunities that arise when the capital budget reaches the stage of action by the Board of Estimate upon individual capital items. The capital budget and program as adopted each year is not an appropriation; it is at most simply a formal statement of intentions. Capital projects are thereafter individually acted upon by the Board of Estimate. It is in this process that the Budget Director's voice is more frequently and more influentially heard than is the voice of the Planning Commission.

To the Borough Presidents, to the Comptroller, and to certain department heads the Budget Director must make some special concessions. The Borough Presidents and the Comptroller are explicitly exempted from some of the onerous "terms and conditions" of the expense budget. (It is at least mildly ironic, and somewhat revealing, that the President of the Council and the Mayor are not exempt.) The Comptroller, because of his extensive fiscal powers, is an object of special concern to the Budget Director. The fact that each recognizes the risks of competition and the fruits of cooperation with each other has led to an implicit and mutually respected alliance. The Borough Presidents and the Comptroller represent the core of the Board of Estimate as an institution; with them, the Budget Director has his most enduring ties.

Concessions to influential department heads are guided by the Budget Director's calculus of their strength at a particular time or on a particular demand. Commissioner Moses (most of whose operations are, as public authorities or as state agencies, outside the Budget Director's reach) has long been able to secure for the Parks Department a special status at the Budget Bureau. Most Police Commissioners have been treated with deference. Other Commissioners from time to time are able to secure special consideration, capitalizing upon public support, or upon a special relationship with the Mayor, or upon the prospects of the Budget Director's future career, but these tend to be episodic. The Budget Director manages these matters with minimal concession and maximal skill.

The Budget Director and his Bureau occupy a position of high status among overhead agencies. The budget function is crucial to the life of almost every agency, the special authorities alone escaping its controls. The Budget Director has a near-monopoly of the budget function, sharing only the capital budget process and that upon terms favorable to himself. The expense budget system is highly centralized and is firmly in his hands. His close intimacy with the Board of Estimate is purchased at low cost to his power and influence. The budget is too large and too complex for the Board to manage in detail, so most decisions devolve upon him as the Board's trusted agent. The Board is his shield, while he is the Board's most valued asset. The cloud on his horizon is still a distant one: the possibility that an aggressive and determined Mayor might join with the forces demanding a budget system which would be genuinely executive in character and in administration and cast in "performance" or "program" appropriation form. If that cloud grows, the Budget Director will be compelled to consider painful choices: to stand openly with the Board of Estimate or to transfer his resources and loyalties to the Mayor. Meanwhile, in terms of power and influence, he has no cause to envy any other overhead agency.

The City Planning Department and Commission

The City Planning Commission, an agency founded upon great expectations, has lived through two decades of frustrations and disappointments to itself and to its supporters. Its assignments are of great moment to the government and politics of the city, but its grasp on its functions is uncertain, and its political and jurisdictional footing is insecure. Charged with the adventurous responsibility for introducing innovation and rationality into the political process of a city long accustomed to opportunistic bargaining among vested political and economic interests of great strength, the Commission has, after blunting its lance in several sorties, been compelled to spend its main energies in studious preparation for the eventual exercise of its powers and in protective preservation of its formal charter assignments.

The first dilemma of the Commission flows from the premises of its organizational status. Chapter 8 of the 1938 charter was in effect a *coup d'état* by the "planners" and their allies. This victory established a city planning agency with great formal powers and gave it a position of political independence, apparently intended to be an autonomous "fourth power" in the government of the city. To accomplish this objective of political autonomy, the Commission was made a body of seven members, six of them to serve eight-year terms (the terms overlapping so that the majority of the members would be immune to the appointing power of any Mayor's single four-year term), the seventh the Chief Engineer of the Board of Estimate, a career civil servant, holding his position indefinitely. The six appointed members were placed beyond the Mayor's power of removal for any differences in policy. Removal was restricted to "proof of official misconduct or of negligence in official duties or of conduct in any manner connected with his official duties which tends to discredit his office, or of mental or physical inability to perform his duties," and "before removal he shall receive a copy of the charges and shall be entitled to a hearing before the mayor and to the assistance of counsel at such hearing." The initial *coup d'état* was carried over into the appointment of an original commission the majority of whose members were committed to the premise that the agency should be an institution of experts with an authoritative voice in the decisions of the city government, yet be itself aloof and protected without the necessities of bargaining with and making concessions to "the politicians" and other "special interests."

But organizational and political autonomy and independence, unsupported by a powerful constituency, usually lead only to isolation and impotence or to stalemate and frustration. All these have been the portion of the Planning Commission, although it has had an important impact upon the city's political and governmental processes and its occasional moments of triumph. Its aspirations for "fourth power" status have been slowly moderated, with the

TABLE 44. MEMBERS OF THE NEW YORK CITY PLANNING COMMISSION, 1938–1959

Commissioner	Tenure in office	Appointing mayor
Adolph Berle[a]	Jan., 1938–Mar., 1938	La Guardia
Arthur V. Sheridan	Jan., 1938–June, 1942	La Guardia
Edwin A. Salmon[a]	Jan., 1938–Sept., 1941; Sept., 1941–Nov., 1947	La Guardia
Cleveland Rodgers	Jan., 1938–Dec., 1951	La Guardia
Lawrence M. Orton	Jan., 1938–Dec., 1940; Jan., 1941–Dec., 1948; Jan., 1949–Dec., 1956; Jan., 1957 to date	La Guardia, O'Dwyer, Wagner
Rexford Tugwell[a]	Apr., 1938–Aug., 1941	La Guardia
Robert Moses[b]	Sept., 1941–Dec., 1945; Jan., 1946–Dec., 1953; Jan., 1954 to date	La Guardia, O'Dwyer, Wagner
Irving V. A. Huie[b]	June, 1942–Dec., 1945	La Guardia
Goodhue Livingston, Jr.	Sept., 1945–Dec., 1952; Jan., 1953 to date	La Guardia, Impellitteri
Newbold Morris	Dec., 1945–Feb., 1948	La Guardia
Robert F. Wagner, Jr.[a]	Nov., 1947–Dec., 1949	O'Dwyer
Francis J. Bloustein	Feb., 1948–Dec., 1955; Jan., 1956 to date	O'Dwyer, Wagner
Jerry Finklestein[a]	Jan., 1950–Dec., 1950	O'Dwyer
John J. Bennett[a]	Jan., 1951–Dec., 1955	Impellitteri
Charles J. Sturba	Jan., 1952 to date	Impellitteri
James Felt[a]	Jan., 1956 to date	Wagner

[a] Chairman. (Salmon was chairman 1941–1947 only.)

[b] Served without compensation.

SOURCE: Lowi, Theodore J., *At the Pleasure of the Mayor*. Doctoral dissertation, Yale University, 1960, unpublished.

mutations in its membership, the several rebuffs in its attempted exercise of autonomous power, and the changes in the doctrine of the planning movement. It now increasingly seeks identification with the Mayor, hoping to borrow for its plans the help of his political power, but the formal charter barriers remain between the Commission and the chief executive and make collaboration awkward, especially for the Mayor.

The second dilemma of the Commission centers around its formal charter assignments. The Commission has three major tasks: to prepare and maintain "a master plan of the city"; to prepare proposed zoning regulations for submission to the Board of Estimate; to prepare annually the proposed annual capital budget and an accompanying five-year capital program for submission to the Board of Estimate. Despite the assumptions imbedded in the charter provisions, these powers and duties are highly "political." The austere and esthetic forms of planning proposed by the planning "experts" are regularly submerged by the more experienced, more vigorous and strident spokesmen for the goals of officialdom, of competing administrative agencies, of the political parties, of real estate and construction and public utilities and other interest groups. Against these forces, the Commission's claims of "fourth branch of government" status, and the aspirations of planners for rationality and symmetry in the city's growth, provide a thin shield for the Commission's powers of initiative and for its influence in each of the succeeding stages of its proposals.

The preparation, adoption, and modification of "a master plan of the city" is the most distinctive and impressive of the Commission's formal powers. The inclusiveness of the charter prescription of the master plan is unusual: it "shall show desirable streets, roads, highways and the grades thereof, public places, bridges and tunnels and the approaches thereto, viaducts, parks, public reservations, parkways, squares, playgrounds, roadways in parks, sites for public buildings and structures, building zone districts, pierhead and bulkhead lines, docks and wharves, waterways, routes of railroads, omnibuses and ferries, locations of drainage systems, sewers, sewage treatment plants, incinerators, water conduits and other public utilities privately or publicly owned, and such other features, changes and additions as will provide for the improvement of the city and its future growth and development and afford adequate facilities for the housing, transportation, distribution, comfort, convenience, health and welfare of its population." This assignment is cast in almost ideal language for the planner's concept of the planning function, but its accomplishment has demanded a greater share of omniscience and omnipotence than has been granted the Commission or its staff. Two decades have yielded no formally adopted comprehensive master plan as envisaged in the charter. Instead, the city map as it existed in 1938 has been taken over by the Commission (as the charter provides), and the Commission has, after one great preliminary effort at the inauguration of a full-blown master plan, worked patiently at changing this map (a kind of primitive master plan). But it has been compelled to record on it the plans and decisions of others more often than its own.

The power to prepare zoning regulations, adding to or amending the regulations in existence at the time the Commission came into being, has given it difficulties similar to those encountered in preparing the master plan. The Commission has been ambitious to prepare and secure adoption of a comprehensive new zoning code, modernizing a code which has grown by bits and pieces since the adoption of the famous code of 1916, but has not yet been able to do so. One such effort in 1951 withered before the heat of criticism generated in the Commission's own public hearings; the proposed code was not submitted to the Board of Estimate. Another effort is under way in 1959. The Commission's political isolation is most sharply evident in these attempts to introduce the planners' innovations and rationality into a domain where other political forces have been deeply entrenched. As in the master plan assignment, the Commission has so far had to rely mainly upon piece-by-piece modifications in the code, surrendering the initiative to others more often than seizing it.

The preparation of the capital budget and program has also been a controversial task for the Commission. The assignment was intended to give the Commission a strategic opportunity to guide the city government's own public works activities into agreeable conformity with the Commission's master plan for the city. This was to be accomplished by the Commission's annual preparation of a capital budget containing all projects recommended for the ensuing capital budget year and a capital program for the five succeeding years. But the lack of a master plan has left the Commission without an impressive criterion for judgment among competing projects with powerful sponsors, and the entry of the Commission into the capital budget process has earned for it, from time to time, the hostility of the Mayor, the Comptroller, the Budget Director, the Construction Coordinator, and the Board of Estimate. These competitors each have differing objectives and differing points of access to the capital budget process, but each tends to agree with all the others in reducing Commission initiative and discretion, and each of them has greater opportunities to influence the action stages of the capital budget process than does the Commission.

The Planning Commission has ordinarily had few opportunities to serve as a principal adviser to the Mayor. On the contrary, the fate of all its major efforts lie mainly in the hands of the Board of Estimate. The nature of the Mayor's appointing and removal power over the members of the Commission, the eight-year term of six members and the permanent tenure of the seventh, the fact that the chairman, though designated by the Mayor, serves as such for his full term, and the aura of doctrine that the Commission should be "independent"—all these serve to attenuate the relationship with the Mayor and make it awkward, even risky, for Mayors to count upon the Commission for advice. The multiple membership of the Commission adds to the difficulties of advice to the Mayor; he cannot be sure when the chairman speaks for himself and when he speaks for the Commission. Mayor Wagner in 1956 began an experiment of closer relationships with the new chairman, James Felt, by making him a member of the Mayor's own "cabinet," and their felicitous relationship has given the Commission higher status and some

TABLE 45. NEW YORK CITY'S CAPITAL BUDGET, 1957–1958

Current and cumulative authorizations and expenditures by nature of improvements

Object classification number	Nature of improvement	Authorizations and expenditures July 1, 1957 to June 30, 1958		Cumulative authorizations and expenditures to June 30, 1958		Balance of authorizations June 30, 1958
		Authorizations (Net)	Expenditures	Authorizations (Net)	Expenditures	
	Buildings:					
1	Administrative buildings	$216,164.63	$411,464.18	$2,802,589.72	$2,618,773.58	$183,816.14
2	Asphalt plants	27,748.00	123,524.73	294,131.82	212,343.09	81,788.73
3	Armories	1,000,000.00	1,000,000.00	1,000,000.00	1,000,000.00	..
5	Colleges	12,287,596.00	4,658,897.48	52,227,720.54	37,150,242.19	15,077,478.35
7	Courts	31,491,905.97	8,711,756.86	60,801,906.35	27,945,260.58	32,856,645.77
11	Firehouses	1,564,066.86	360,236.14	3,404,175.29	1,419,719.11	1,984,456.18
13	Garages	1,134.88	7,499.99	811,126.23	788,697.45	22,428.78
14	Off-street parking facilities	4,795,414.96	1,567,281.08	7,615,037.69	3,489,623.42	4,125,414.27
15	Hospitals and allied buildings	2,221,597.42	9,291,380.51	215,296,484.74	203,075,848.04	12,220,636.70
18	Health and teaching centers	1,149,508.10	496,214.83	8,476,077.11	6,852,173.15	1,623,903.96
20	Libraries	1,604,338.78	1,926,153.55	21,158,870.69	18,759,010.19	2,408,860.50
22	Laboratory buildings	3,900,000.00	54,259.63	4,097,441.78	199,525.56	3,897,916.22
24	Markets	108,630.60	192,712.37	3,009,350.47	2,812,206.01	197,144.46
27	Museums	2,335,605.09	1,270,432.52	21,791,759.21	18,796,562.53	2,995,196.68
29	Police stations	1,128,168.93	127,062.51	2,223,730.13	1,078,119.67	1,145,610.46
30	Prisons	577,430.00	482,192.18	11,719,434.05	10,703,773.11	1,015,660.94
32	Reformatories	.20	..	53,312.38	53,312.38	..
33	Repair shops	522,630.79	57,693.04	2,686,824.14	2,184,082.85	502,741.29
	Schools:					
35	Elementary	35,418,462.56	45,636,022.36	372,841,353.20	328,861,548.53	43,979,804.67
38	Elementary and junior high	35,811,309.32	51,078,381.48	240,903,365.89	189,536,679.06	51,366,686.83
41	High, academic, and vocational	22,313,567.74	24,344,578.17	112,090,043.42	76,345,251.45	35,744,791.97
43	Storehouses	36,160.00	217.06	3,034,044.65	2,962,564.72	71,479.93
46	Training schools (Police, Fire, etc.)	517,601.24	541,926.53	3,321,459.97	2,952,652.34	368,807.63
48	Welfare centers	727,417.49	1,400,962.29	13,792,126.38	13,326,105.43	466,020.95
49	Buildings not otherwise classified	1,039,332.93	2,586,358.67	17,737,309.39	15,896,233.12	1,841,076.27
	Other than Buildings:					
50	Civilian Defense requirements	273,809.00	193,689.62	4,282,692.00	3,138,464.77	1,144,227.23
51	Airports	*371,507.43*	1,525.00	12,564,496.54	12,561,511.09	2,985.45

54	Beaches, public	1,012,208.44	3,954,512.44	17,129,049.61	14,956,454.40	2,172,595.21
56	Bridges	3,493,350.14	5,449,759.67	55,568,374.29	50,431,110.29	5,137,264.00
58	Commemorative structures	120,720.00	72,037.94	245,720.00	185,153.68	60,566.32
59	Communication systems	853,744.45	744,816.07	7,782,625.81	6,469,721.42	1,312,904.39
62	Docks, piers, wharves, marginal streets, etc.	14,014,188.80	6,608,178.94	55,202,150.79	43,088,502.96	12,113,647.83
64	Dikes, boat channels, sea walls, jetties, etc.	*213.98*	2,735.34	183,036.02	145,135.61	37,900.41
66	Fire, police, ferryboats, and ferry terminals	1,298,671.93	3,013,322.52	13,951,427.88	12,007,424.08	1,944,003.80
69	Machinery and equipment, not part of original installation	3,688,100.00	5,317,865.13	36,529,214.50	32,384,301.31	4,144,913.19
71	Parks	6,516,958.63	6,335,517.15	39,164,044.67	33,331,933.00	5,832,111.67
74	Playgrounds and recreational areas (not in parks)	2,646,855.71	3,938,732.91	26,744,363.41	20,994,670.10	5,749,693.31
76	Waste purification and sewage disposal plants	7,059,779.74	6,761,571.64	139,575,890.60	121,921,926.19	17,653,964.41
78	Roads, streets, highways, and parkways	3,348,361.50	1,318,629.37	26,956,600.85	22,192,559.73	4,764,041.12
82	Transit	44,051,173.62	105,806,651.29	1,061,154,143.00	939,695,937.59	121,458,205.41
85	Revolving funds and suspense accounts	100,000.00	142,005.59	1,665,000.00	1,360,119.43	304,880.57
86	Incinerators, unloading plants, and disposal stations	10,387,915.19	8,945,574.26	71,491,863.26	54,848,912.06	16,642,951.20
87	Sewers, trunk lines, and connecting lines	185,000.00	172,014.82	2,412,300.00	2,226,490.09	185,809.91
89	Traffic signals	1,910,500.00	1,618,441.23	13,778,712.64	10,561,201.34	3,217,511.30
90	Viaducts, tunnels, over and underpasses, and culverts	131,900.55	196,916.88	1,791,090.40	1,418,001.86	373,088.54
	Water supply:					
93	Sources and structures	15,391,818.00	45,986,566.13	612,767,843.24	523,486,511.24	89,281,332.00
95	Distribution system	1,000,000.00	..	675,000.00	533,494.97	141,505.03
96	Administration		484,098.19	1,000,000.00	484,098.19	515,901.81
99	Not otherwise classified	4,517,913.94	5,193,116.04	75,390,928.64	67,666,573.83	7,724,354.81
600	Slum clearance	16,051,257.7	5,356,301.11	103,527,438.73	103,529,742.83	2,304.10[a]
	Grand total	$299,069,358.05	$373,941,727.44	$3,564,723,682.12[b]	$3,048,631,259.62[b]	$516,092,422.50

[a] Deficit represents part of balance due from federal government.

[b] Closed accounts amounting to $100,873,051.20 eliminated from cumulative totals.

SOURCE: *Annual Report* of the Comptroller of New York City, 1959, p. 213.

satisfying achievements. But most Mayors have been cautious, using their powers to limit rather than to expand the Commission's realm.

The Board of Estimate suffers from fewer inhibitions. It has recognized the role of the Commission as competitive to itself and has moved steadily to reduce the threat—not by absorbing the Commission into the Board's own family (as in the case of the Budget Director) nor by friendly alliance, but by a policy of containment, using its extensive powers to halt Commission plans, to adulterate Commission proposals, and to manipulate these proposals in terms of the Board's own institutional objectives. The Board has many resources for this purpose. Its Chief Engineer is the only permanent member of the Commission; the Board can change the city map or master plan against the Commission's advice by a three-fourths vote. The Board can veto a zoning proposal by a three-fourths vote. The Board may transfer any capital project from the capital program to the capital budget, or it may include a new capital project against the advice of the Commission by a three-fourths vote; and, since the capital budget is not an appropriation, the Board remains in charge of the schedule at all subsequent stages, usually transforming the capital budget during the year in important and extensive ways. Nor is this all: each Borough President has the power to appoint an advisory planning board to advise the Commission and himself, and Borough Presidents must approve for transmission to the Commission the maps showing the subdivision of land into streets, avenues, public places, and blocks. The Comptroller has extensive responsibilities with respect to the public debt and city borrowings, together with specific opportunities under the charter to intervene in the capital budget process. The Board has also the resources of its intimate partnership with the Director of the Budget. The sum of these powers and opportunities, possessed by the Board or by its individual members, puts the Board in a position of predominance over the Commission.

The Planning Commission has some unusual features as an overhead agency: each of its major activities represents an inextricable mixture of overhead and line functions. The master plan—or, rather, its pale substitute, the city map—involves both the regulation of the behavior of other agencies (those engaged in public works, for example) and the behavior of private groups and individuals (providing utilities, transportation, real estate, construction, and other goods and services). The zoning regulations involve both public and private uses of the land in the city in many and significant ways. The preparation of the capital budget, while primarily controlling the discretion of other agencies, has its direct impact upon many nongovernmental groups (the choice between schools and hospitals, or bridges and tunnels, the taking or not taking of their land, the location of a service or a nuisance near them, and so on). This intermixing of line and overhead functions gives the Commission one of the most active and most heterogeneous constituencies in the city government, a constituency which is unstable, largely unstructured, and containing at any one moment many more voices of criticism and dissent than dependable sources of support.

The Commission has great difficulty in identifying and coming to terms with a stable constituency. As the agent of innovation and rationality, the Commission can count upon consistent support from but a few elements, and these only in general rather than in particular terms. The civic groups, including especially those concerned with planning and housing, regularly endorse the general objectives of the Commission and ordinarily support its particular objectives, but tend just as consistently to urge the Commission to adopt a pace that adds to the risks of its always precarious relationships with the Board of Estimate and other sections of officialdom. The press, too, is in general benevolently inclined toward the Commission as an institution, but it will often respond critically when the Commission is in trouble with the business elements of its constituency.

Elsewhere in its constituency, the Commission encounters pressures to reduce its passion for innovation, for rational planning, for symmetry in the city's growth. In general, the real estate interests, the building and construction industries, the transportation and utility groups, and many other related or similar formations argue for minimum change in the settled patterns of bargaining and mutual concessions, for a public policy which leaves planning to the decisions of the market and to the ingenuity of its participants. The political party organizations hold aloof from the planning institution, relying mainly upon the Board of Estimate. The labor groups do not ordinarily feel involved in the planning process, intervening in *ad hoc* fashion but relying also mainly on the Board. In sum, then, the Planning Commission draws little strength and comfort from its constituency.

Because the Commission thus confronts its rivalries with other agencies as an institution lacking the powerful protection of either the Mayor or the Board of Estimate, and without a strong supporting constituency, its vulnerability is great. One consequence has been the disinclination of the Mayor and Board of Estimate to give the Commission an adequate budget and staff. Another result has been Commission inability to maintain unity within its own membership. The 1938 charter began the process of fragmentation by the inclusion of the Board of Estimate's Chief Engineer. The tendency was greatly accelerated by the adoption of subsequent legislation to permit Robert Moses to serve as a member while continuing to hold his position as Parks Commissioner, Construction Coordinator, and several other offices, thus bringing into membership on the Commission one of the major claimants in the capital budget process and an articulate critic of comprehensive planning. Still another consequence of the Commission's orphan status in the political process has been the pronounced capacity of the Comptroller, the

Budget Director, the Construction Coordinator, and several powerful agencies (notably the Parks Department, the special authorities, the Board of Education, and others at times) to present the Commission with manifestoes, *faits accomplis*, or other demonstrations of strength to which the Commission has had to yield.

The City Planning Commission occupies an almost unique position among the overhead agencies of the city government. It has the most ambitious and far-reaching formal assignment among them all: the mission to transform the city's growth from pluralistic politics and private ingenuities into an ordered symmetry of rational plans, controlled decisions, and even-paced progress along the whole front of the city's life. Given this task, fit for the philosopher-kings among the planners, and "protected" from "politics" by the carefully designed safeguards of the charter, the Commission has found itself inescapably and inevitably involved in the city's political process, a milieu to which the planner is a stranger, for which he has not been trained, and in which he is subjected to recurrent shock. The enduring enigma about the City Planning Commission is not its failure to realize the aspirations of its creators but rather how it has survived at all. This survival includes a recurrently renewed determination to perform its high and idealistic assignment, a striking demonstration of the capacity of widespread latent (even though vague) aspirations shared by many relatively unorganized groups to sustain an agency without being able to provide it with sufficient thrust to perform its mission. Survival, and the satisfactions of some increase in planned innovations, but not in large comprehensive plans, is the past and present position of the Commission. To increase its influence on city governmental decisions, the Commission needs a powerful ally whose interests are broadly consistent with its basic objectives.

The City Construction Coordinator

This office has been one of steady growth in power and influence since its establishment in January, 1946. In its origins, it appeared to most participants and observers (perhaps to all except its author) to be a temporary agency, created to coordinate and expedite the reentry of the city government into public works activities at the end of the war, a reentry complicated by scarcities of construction materials, rising costs, uncertainties in labor agreements and construction contracts, and by the large but as yet comparatively unexplored possibilities of state and national government financial assistance to the city in postwar construction of public works, housing, and other facilities. The local law establishing the office was the first legislative act of the new O'Dwyer administration (Local Law No. 1, February 25, 1946). This local law, in addition to creating the office of Coordinator, also authorized the Mayor and the Comptroller to enter into contracts with federal or state agencies, in accordance with federal or state legislation providing funds for public works to be carried out by any city agency.

Under the Local Law of 1946, the Coordinator was empowered "to schedule . . . and expedite the work of all agencies of the City . . . represent the City in its relations with cooperating state and federal agencies . . . investigate the prices of basic building materials, and labor and contract conditions in the local market with a view to bringing about agreements on reasonable terms . . ."; he has the further "duty and function of accelerating said programs . . . , and shall currently present to the mayor, the board of estimate, the city council, and other proper city officials, and also to the agencies of the state and federal government concerned, reports on the progress of all plans and projects. . . ." The Mayor was also authorized to confer other duties and powers upon the Coordinator. The office acquired new powers in 1949 when another local law (Local Law No. 104, December 1949) extended the contractual powers of the Mayor and the Comptroller to include contracts for funds made available under the Federal Housing Act of 1949 and any supplemental legislation for urban redevelopment, urban renewal, and slum clearance. As a corollary action, the Mayor designated the Coordinator as chairman of the newly created Mayor's Committee on Slum Clearance. The Coordinator had thus become by 1950 not only the expediter and coordinator of the public works programs of all the city's agencies; he was now also the key initiator and supervisor of its far-flung renewal, redevelopment, and slum clearance programs; and he was, in addition, the chief representative of the city in dealing with the state government and the federal government in all these matters.

The office of City Construction Coordinator thus has evolved from a temporary postwar agency to a firmly established and influential overhead agency, possessing the power to modify, postpone, or override the decisions of the line agencies of the city government. In this evolution it has been aided greatly by the fact that it is one of the important institutionalized expressions of the unusual power exercised in the city's political process by one man: Robert Moses, who has been the Coordinator since the establishment of the office. With his powers and talents, he is able to sit astride the planning and the execution of the capital budget much as the Budget Director does for the expense budget; the procedural system differs, but the substance of supervision is comparable. A greater difference is that the Coordinator does not need to defer to the Board of Estimate; when he wishes to do so, he can usually prevail over the Board.

A Coordinator whom the Mayor appoints and may remove at pleasure would seem at first glance to be an instrument and resource of the Mayor's leadership. But the Coordinator is not an ordinary incumbent. He holds an array of other offices, most of them beyond the Mayor's reach. He has a powerful constituency, built around the totality of these offices, which is responsive to him and which he manipulates with great skill. He has great prestige with the communication media, for which he regularly provides the drama of his personality engaged in many battles, some of them of his own staging and direction. He is, in short, irremovable—and Mayors yield to his leadership and influence, knowing that the fact or the myth of his untouchability contains greater risks than prudent men will knowingly assume. The office of Construction Coordinator is thus an overhead agency of unusual autonomy, neither needing nor heeding very much the preference of either the Mayor or the Board of Estimate. Possessing constituencies of great potency, with which the Coordinator has long since (and in varied capacities) come to terms favorable to his leadership, the office also needs few allies among other agencies, since the Coordinator alone can supply a solid phalanx of allies he himself leads.

The Personnel Department and the Civil Service Commission

The Personnel Department and the city Civil Service Commission together comprise an overhead agency with extensive powers over the decisions of other city agencies. The agency finds its major assignments in the New York State Civil Service Law; Chapter 35 of the charter is simply a duplication of a section of the state legislation. These assignments include most of the familiar functions of personnel management: to classify and grade positions; to recruit applicants for such positions, to conduct examinations for these applicants, to establish eligible lists and to certify eligibles to appointing officers, to investigate the character and qualifications of eligibles; to certify the payrolls of city agencies; to develop salary and wage plans, standards of working conditions, vacation and leave plans for submission to the Board of Estimate; to administer the safety, incentive, and related personnel programs; to conduct investigations concerning any matter affecting the Civil Service Law; to institute in-service training programs; to hear appeals concerning grievances, discrimination, discipline; to aid in the development of departmental personnel offices; and the somewhat unusual power to conduct examinations of applicants for certain city licenses and permits.

In the exercise of most of these powers, the personnel agency is constrained by an unusually detailed state law, by numerous court decisions interpreting that law during the more than seventy years of its history, by the rules of the state Civil Service Commission and its extensive powers of supervision over the city personnel agency, and by its own rules which the city Commission can change only with the separate approval of the Mayor and the state Civil Service Commission. Of all the city's overhead agencies, the Personnel Department operates within the tightest frame of law and rules, under the fullest state administrative supervision, and within the severest restraints of tradition-sanctioned or court-imposed procedural requirements.

The restrictions upon the initiative and the discretion of his agency are among the Personnel Director's chief difficulties when he attempts to respond to the new pressures upon him to become one of the Mayor's principal advisers and managerial agents. These pressures are now considerable, having been a matter of agitation for almost a decade. They are nurtured by the new doctrines of the chief executive's responsibility for personnel management (a doctrinal trend widely reflected in the attempted reorientation of central personnel agencies in the federal government, the states, and other cities, and in the current popularity of decentralized personnel systems in business organizations); they are increasingly emphasized by city department and agency heads and were supported by the proposals of the Mayor's Committee on Management Survey (1952) and of the Josephs Commission on the Government of New York City (1954). The 1954 amendments to the state Civil Service Law and to the charter gave a formal basis to this trend. The Personnel Director was made the head of a new Personnel Department and chairman of the three-member Civil Service Commission. He holds office at the pleasure of the Mayor, unlike his two colleagues on the Commission who serve six-year terms and may be removed only on charges and after a hearing. (Prior to 1954, the Municipal Civil Service Commission, composed of three members serving six-year staggered terms, was the head of the city's personnel agency. The new Director is thus much closer to the Mayor than his predecessors.) In addition to these formal statutory changes in his relations to the Mayor, the Personnel Director has also been made a member of Mayor Wagner's "cabinet."

But the Personnel Director has limited capacity to commit his agency and its resources to the Mayor's needs. The Director shares his more crucial powers with his two colleagues and cannot outvote them; so he must return to consult them while the Mayor waits. The Director is shackled by statutory and procedural restraints. He is aware of the competing pressures upon him from the Board of Estimate and its *de facto* agent, the Budget Director; and he feels upon his back the weight of a constituency which has the power to punish him if his exercise of discretion displeases them. As a result, the Personnel Director must be a cautious participant in the Mayor's cabinet. He must counsel delay, or argue against most innovation, or leave active participation to others. These are not traits which lead to positive influence or close collaboration with the Mayor.

The Personnel Director must work often with the Board of Estimate. The Board has powers which he must respect: it has the ultimate authority over his plans for the classification of positions, his salary and wage plan proposals, his plans for standardizing and regulating working conditions, vacation and leave regulations. In addition, the Board is less inclined toward innovation than are Mayors and department heads, and (even more importantly) the Board is more consistently sympathetic with the demands of the Personnel

Director's dominant constituency elements than with him if he opposes his constituency. In short, the Personnel Director goes before the Board with the knowledge that if he has correctly anticipated the Board's preferences he will also usually be supported by his major constituency elements. In contrast, when he meets with the Mayor, who responds largely to the demands of his department heads or to his own aspirations for chief executive leadership, the Personnel Director knows he usually is caught between these pressures and his constituency. He can ordinarily come to terms with the Board at less cost and risk to himself than if he yields to the Mayor.

The Personnel Department is an agency now cautiously seeking a new equilibrium among a complex galaxy of pressures: the persistent demands of its constituency, the new consciousness of Mayors concerning the Department's uses and liabilities, the new and pressing clamor of departments and agencies for decentralized personnel management enlarging their managerial discretion, the awakening appetite of the Board of Estimate to add the personnel function to its system of controls, the sharpened rivalry of the Budget Director, and the emergence of the city Department of Labor as a potential opponent or ally. The path toward this new equilibrium is shrouded in fog and slippery under foot. The agency leadership is aware of its risks but uncertain as to which are the greater and which are avoidable. The agency staff is oriented toward its past status, inclined to measure risks in terms of degree of change from that status.

The discovery of a new equilibrium for the Personnel Department is mainly a problem in the constituency relationships of the Department. The agency exercises powers that impinge directly upon the managerial decisions of all other agencies. With but a few exceptions (the educational staffs, county offices, and certain courts being the main ones), the appointment, promotion, and most other significant changes in status, as well as the compensation and working conditions, of all personnel in the public service of the city come under the close scrutiny of the central personnel agency. These powers constitute restraints upon the managerial discretion of agency heads matched only by the powers of the Budget Director, and even he has no jurisdiction over the "authorities" (see Chapter IX) where the Personnel Department's control does reach. In addition to these overhead functions, the Personnel Department has an important line function: it deals with and examines a large population of applicants for city jobs and for some city licenses and permits. These overhead and line functions of the Personnel Department together represent a series of important stakes in the political process; as such, they attract a large, multidimensional, quite vigorous constituency for the Personnel Department.

For several decades of its earlier history, the city's personnel agency had, so to speak, a two-party constituency. On the one side were the civil service reform groups and their various interest group allies, usually including most of the communication media. On the other side were the party organizations and the larger portion of officialdom. The civil service reform pressures sought to use the Civil Service Commission (which then headed the personnel agency) to exclude the party organizations from any influence upon the appointment, promotion, or tenure of city employees. The party leaders, in turn, sought to limit the jurisdiction of the Commission, to manipulate its procedures, and thus to remain influential in the personnel system. The victory went slowly but steadily to the reformers as the Commission brought a higher and higher proportion of personnel into the competitive class or into other categories of selection and tenure to which the party organizations found access only with difficulty and with sharply reduced influence.

Victory for the reformers, however, brought a different constituency to the Commission. The reformers fell away, their mission seemingly accomplished. The party organizations accepted the *status quo*, seeking practical accommodations with the new system rather than a return to naked patronage. The new constituency element which then moved in, from a base of earlier beginnings, was composed of the emerging, self-conscious, self-confident, and increasingly organized bureaucracies. Their tenure protected by the new rules of the game, their numbers growing steadily, their own discretionary powers expanding as higher posts were brought under the competitive and tenure-protected system, these bureaucratic groups soon became the dominant element in the Commission's constituency and remain so in the constituency of the Personnel Department. They have attracted formidable allies: first, the "civil service" press, composed of two weekly newspapers of wide circulation among civil servants and officialdom which alert the rank-and-file bureaucrats to pending decisions affecting their interests, and monitor the Commission's agenda with critical eyes, and a half-dozen or more special columnists in the daily newspapers, with similar functions; second, the labor unions, whose leaders seek to enlist, or have recruited, bureaucratic groups into membership or affiliation; third, the "civil service" lawyers, an articulate and skillful group whose practice is based upon litigation in the personnel field; and, finally, some of the ethnic interest groups whose members and leaders find the prevailing personnel system either an advantage or disadvantage to their aspirations.

The bureaucracies and their allies are the primary participants in the Personnel Department's decision-making. They outrank the party leaders, who now deal more often with bureaucratic leaders than with the leaders of the Personnel Department. They have isolated the Personnel Director from other potential constituencies (for example, the educational institutions, the mass communication media). They usually outbid the Mayor and the Board of Estimate in the competition for influence over the Personnel Director and his staff. In their relationships with the Personnel Department the organized bureaucracies have at least three important advantages: they seek mainly to preserve the statutory and procedural *status quo* in personnel policy and practice; they find the tight frame of state law and supervision to their strategic and tactical advantage; and they deal less directly with the Personnel Director than with his permanent staff, itself a part of the bureaucracy sharing with the leaders of the organized bureaucracies a common regard for bureaucratic comfort and convenience. The Personnel Department has worked out a stable relationship with its constituency. It has done so by becoming the constituency's instrument, not its leader.

Hemmed in by detailed statutes and procedures on the one hand and by a hard-bargaining constituency on the other, the Personnel Department is vulnerable to its rivals and competitors among the other agencies of the city government—in all those areas where the statutes do not fully protect it or where its bureaucratic constituency cannot provide a shield or does not care to do so. Thus, the Budget Director, armed with the strength of the Board of Estimate and comparatively impervious to direct constituency pressures himself, can roam almost at will in the Personnel Director's jurisdiction. He controls the schedules of examinations and sometimes decides whether the proposed examination shall be open-competitive or for promotion. He delays the promotion of eligibles if he regards the salary increase too great for the top-ranking candidates. He withholds certificates to agencies to fill vacancies or replace provisionals, to the embarrassment of the personnel agency which must deal with impatient eligibles or explain to critics why provisionals remain. He makes himself senior partner in the classification and compensation decisions of the personnel agency. To all these indignities the Personnel Director must submit because he lacks the power to resist them.

The Commission on Intergroup Relations hears appeals from city employees in claims of racial, nationality, or religious discrimination. The Department of Investigation can supplant the Personnel Department's investigatory powers, as it has in recent years in the loyalty and security field. To strong line departments, the Personnel Director must yield wherever his constituency is slow or reluctant to help him. To the Police Department, he must allow a free hand in the selection, promotion, and tenure of detectives; to the Health and Hospital Departments, broad discretion in the personnel system for part-time medical staffs; to Commissioner Moses, a generous freedom in the transfer of personnel and in the use of architectural and engineering consultants; and to the Comptroller and Borough Presidents, that measure of discretion appropriate to their elective status. Most of all, perhaps, he must be sensitive to the special needs of the courts, weighing their powers to review a wide range of his decisions in the extensive litigation which characterizes personnel management in a state where the constitution contains a mandate to maintain a merit system and the statutes elaborate rather than delegate to the personnel agency the detailed requirements of that system. And, more recently, he must also give attention to a newly emerging overhead agency—the Department of Labor, a potential ally or rival to the Personnel Department.

The Personnel Director heads an overhead agency of great but unrealized potential. The office is held motionless between the wall of statutory-procedural detail and the unrelenting pressures of a cohesive and determined constituency. The Mayor lacks the power and the opportunities to break the stalemate; the Board of Estimate has no incentive or inclination to do so. The civil service reformers and their allies aim their lances at the periphery of the Personnel Director's problem: at the dwindling residue of patronage, not at his subjugation to his bureaucratic constituency. The Personnel Director and his colleagues on the Commission do not bring to the personnel agency any high status of their own among overhead agency leaders, and they are beset by rivals and critics in both line and overhead agencies. The office of Director is new; in the past, the Civil Service Commission also was not a strategic rung in the career ladder of officialdom. Anonymity has been the usual fate of its members; punishing controversy has been an alternative; rarely has there been an opportunity for career enhancement. The agency is so hedged in by all these forces that its opportunities for initiative and for discretionary exercise of judgment are few.

The Department of Labor

The Department of Labor is the fledgling among the overhead agencies of the city government. Established as a department in 1954 but going back in its development to La Guardia's appointment of a "labor secretary" on his own mayoralty staff in the 1930's, the Labor Department has not yet discovered its permanent place and role in the competitive world of the city's line and overhead agencies. That place and role is still a matter for speculation and conjecture, both for the Labor Commissioner and for the other agencies.

The Department began its governmental and political life as a protégé of Mayor Wagner, who saw in its creation and in its function an application to the city scene of principles embodied in national labor legislation by his father as United States Senator. The agency has remained close to the Mayor, has moved with caution and much consultation, and has remained prudently anonymous on most occasions. When it has taken the stage prominently, there has been careful emphasis on its representation of the Mayor.

The analogy between the Department's role and the role of the National Labor Relations Board is more symbolic than substantive. The formal charter assignments to the Labor Department are much more limited than, and quite different from, those of the NLRB. The assignments are of two kinds: first, the Commissioner has "the power . . . and duty in an existing, imminent or threatened labor dispute within the city which, in his opinion, may endanger or threaten the health, safety or welfare of the people of the city, to take such steps as he may deem expedient to effect a voluntary, amicable and expeditious adjustment and settlement of the differences and issues between employers and employees . . . "; second, the Commissioner has "the power to hear and consider grievances of city employees or groups of city employees, to make findings and recommendations with reference to such grievances and to certify the same to the Mayor. . . ." In carrying out these functions, the Commissioner also has the power to hold private or public hearings, administer oaths, take testimony and receive evidence, issue rules governing proceedings before him, make investigations, collect data, and report to the Mayor "upon the conditions of labor and matters affecting employment both public and private within the city."

The first assignment is a line function. It involves the Commissioner, his deputies, and his staff in direct relations with the private employers and employer groups in the city and with employees and their labor unions. In these relationships, the Commissioner may, so far as the formal language of the charter goes, act upon his own initiative as a mediator, a conciliator, a voluntary arbitrator. His formal relationship to the Mayor in these matters is often no more or less direct than that of the typical line department head.

The second assignment is an overhead function. It involves the Commissioner in a scrutiny and supervision of labor relations of the other agencies of the city government with their own employees. Here he acts as a formal agent of inquiry and advice for the Mayor, but it may be expected that out of these activities will emerge rules and standards issued by the Mayor (or perhaps local or state statutes) which will entrust regulatory power to the Labor Department over the labor relations of city agencies. Even now such beginnings are apparent; and even now, also, the posture of the Labor Department in its inquiries, hearings, findings, and recommendations have substantial, if still largely informal, impact upon the labor relations policies of city agencies. The Mayor's Executive Order of 1958, establishing a code of labor relations for city agencies in dealing with their employees, seems clearly to forecast the Department's main function: to encourage and systematize the unionization of the city's employees. The power to grant to one organized group a certificate of exclusive bargaining representation while denying it to another group is a power of great significance to the leaders of the organized bureaucracies. These leaders will be supporters or critics of the Labor Commissioner, depending upon their fortunes in securing or losing the valued certificate. The train of events set in motion by the granting of the first exclusive certificate to the Uniformed Sanitationmen's Association (an affiliate of the Teamsters' union) in August, 1958, may establish, as additional certificates are issued, the firm outlines of the Labor Commissioner's constituency. The question which is now implicit will then become explicit: Is the Commissioner to lead his constituency of organized bureaucratic groups, or is he to be led by them?

The Labor Commissioner and his agency began as, and still remain, instruments of the Mayor. The Board of Estimate has shown no strong inclinations to raid the Mayor's personal creation, perhaps because the prize is not yet important enough to excite temptation. The snares and pitfalls of labor disputes are risks which prudent members of the Board are willing, at least in the pioneer and experimental years, to leave to the Mayor. The headaches of employee grievances are viewed similarly by the Board. But success or the building of substantive power by the Labor Department in either of its assignments may arouse the interest of the Board.

It is in constituency relationships, however, that the greatest uncertainties surround the Labor Department and its status with, and responsiveness to, the Mayor. The Department's constituency is still forming, but its outlines are already largely evident. The labor unions, and the organized bureaucracies with labor union aims or affiliations, are its emerging major components. This is, in the main, a constituency similar to the one that confronts and dominates the Personnel Department, but there is an important difference in the center of gravity in the two formations: the Personnel Department's constituency is heavily weighted toward the "internal" bureaucratic groups, and, among them, toward the older, less labor-union-inclined groups; the Labor Department's constituency is heavily weighted toward the "external" nongovernmental labor unions (due, in part, to the Department's first assignment), while among the bureaucratic groups, the Department leans toward the newer, more labor-union-inclined or directly affiliated groups. This overlap of their constituencies presents to the Labor Department and the Personnel Department possibilities of either future competition or collaboration.

The formation of this labor union and union-inclined-or-affiliated bureaucratic group constituency for the Labor Department might conceivably stimulate a competitive constituency element composed of private employer organizations allied with those segments of the bureaucracy which are resistant to the forms and aims of labor unions as appropriate associations for themselves (the professions, the agency managers and supervisors, the party-oriented civil servants). But this would appear to be an unlikely and unstable combination. The more predictable shape of the Labor Department's emerging constituency seems to be one which has strong labor-union orientation, led by the officers of the organized bureaucracies.

As the Labor Department develops its programs of action, and as its constituency takes firmer shape around the stakes of politics which the Department

then represents, the now latent stresses of its relationships will become important and visible to the relevant participants. The Mayor will conceivably be
confronted with the questions: Is the Labor Commissioner a representative of
his own "labor" and organized bureaucratic constituency, or is he an objective adviser whose main loyalty is to the Mayor? Is the Labor Commissioner
sensitive to the managerial necessities of the Mayor's department heads, or
is he an instrument of the organized bureaucracies seeking to maximize
employee protections by reducing managerial discretion? The Board of Estimate, in its turn, will appraise the Labor Department's influence upon the
Board's own pattern of accommodations with the organized bureaucracies.
The department and agency heads will probably view a new set of overhead
rules issued and enforced by the Labor Department as an added and un-
wanted burden and limitation upon them and will seek to persuade the
Mayor to modify his endorsement and soften the rules, or else will strive for
their own individual special arrangements with the Labor Department, using
such resources as they possess for such purposes. The Police Commissioner
reacted vigorously to Labor Department proposals in 1958, seeing in them a
threat of labor union status or affiliation for patrolmen. The Budget Director,
the Comptroller, the Personnel Director, the Commissioner of Investigation,
and perhaps others must each reappraise their interests to calculate the adjustments (whether rivalry or alliance) they need to make to preserve or
enhance their own roles. Nor will the Labor Department be exempt from
similar necessities to make its choices. These are the uncertainties and the
dynamics, the opportunities and the risks, a new overhead agency brings with
it into the city's political contest.

Other Overhead Agencies

There are three other overhead agencies to which briefer attention will be
given. They are the Department of Purchase, the Art Commission, and the
City Record.

The Commissioner of Purchase is empowered "to purchase, store and
distribute all supplies, materials or equipment required by any department,
office, board, body or commission of the city," or by any office of any county
within the city if payment is from the city treasury. The Commissioner is also
chairman of the seven-member Board of Standardization (three members
from Purchase, two from the Comptroller's staff, one from the Budget
Bureau, one from the staff of the Board of Estimate) which has the power
and duty "to classify all supplies, material and equipment; to adopt . . .
standards . . . ; to prepare and submit to the board of estimate for adoption,
and after such adoption to promulgate and enforce, written specifications"
for all standard commodities. The Commissioner is also empowered to take
possession of and to sell all surplus or waste materials of city agencies. The

Department thus has supervisory powers over all city agencies (except the Boards of Education and Higher Education, which are specifically exempted) in their purchases of materials, and over all vendors of such supplies.

The Commissioner moves more in the orbit of the Comptroller, the Board of Estimate, and the Budget Director than in that of the Mayor. The Comptroller's inspection staff has the power to inspect all purchased materials for compliance with the written specifications and standards; the Board of Estimate adopts the specifications, the Commissioner simply presiding over the board that prepares them. The Budget Director controls the flow of funds into the agency budgets upon which purchase requisitions are based. The Commissioner has no powerful constituency to support him; the vendors as a group are his critics, or his master if he seeks their support.

The Art Commission has eleven members. Four of these are the Mayor, the president of the Metropolitan Museum of Art, the president of the New York Public Library, the president of the Brooklyn Institute of Arts and Sciences. The remaining seven (a painter, a sculptor, an architect, a landscape architect, and three "laymen") are appointed by the Mayor for three-year terms from a list of names submitted by the Fine Arts Federation of New York. They serve without compensation.

The Commission has an extensive jurisdiction over all works of art acquired by gift or purchase, or constructed by the city, or placed as private property upon land belonging to the city ("work of art" is defined inclusively by the charter, as ranging from monuments to lamps, benches, and traffic signals); over the design of buildings, bridges, docks, and other structures on public lands; and over the maintenance of monuments, sculpture, and paintings belonging to the city. Its approval in writing is required in all such situations, except that in the case of buildings or structures costing less than $250,000 the Mayor or the Council may request it not to act, and except that the Park Commissioner may also refuse to consent to the erection or acceptance of any structure on lands under his jurisdiction. But the Commission must act within sixty days after submission or its consent is not necessary.

The Art Commission, as can be seen from the method of its membership selection, is an institutionalized expression of the power of a small but elite and articulate constituency: the Fine Arts Federation. Its extensive powers as an overhead agency are kept within the limits desired by officialdom by a simple budgetary stratagem: the sixty-day limit on its actions over the great number of submissions is squeezed against the spare time resources of Commission members and the full time of its staff of two employees. What the Commission cannot inspect, it cannot disapprove; one major battle over a disapproval will consume its resources for weeks.

The City Record is under the direction of a Supervisor appointed by the Mayor. The Supervisor publishes a daily paper, *The City Record,* in which appear all notices and advertisements required by law to be published in municipal corporation papers. They may appear nowhere else at public expense, except as required by law and with the specific authorization of the Supervisor and the approval of the Mayor and the Comptroller. The Supervisor also publishes the lists of registered voters, the annual record of assessed valuation of real estate, and the annual *Official Directory* of the City of New York. His office has a long-established and stable function, a quiescent constituency, and few rivals or critics among the other agencies.

CONCLUSIONS

The ten overhead agencies of the city government, it will be remembered, have three main functions: to make and enforce decisions affecting the work and discretion of other agencies; to perform certain "line" work of their own; and to form a part of the structure of information and advice to the Mayor and the Board of Estimate. The discussion of the role of the leaders of each of these agencies in this chapter has revealed how unevenly the generalizations fit each overhead agency when it is viewed separately as a living institution. It has revealed, too, how deeply these agency leaders are immersed in the city's political process because of the stakes and prizes they influence or themselves distribute.

The System of Control

The formal justification for the existence of overhead agencies is frequently cast in three main arguments. Overhead agencies, it is said, ensure uniformity of policies and procedures in the performance of certain governmental activities which cut across the work of all agencies (such as budgeting, personnel management, legal advice and litigation, land use and public works planning, purchasing, investigation). Such uniformity of policy and procedure is alleged to promote efficiency and economy, prevent favoritism, and ensure high standards. Centralization of control over these activities presumably provides a focus of responsibility for uniformity and consistency and for standards of performance.

The overhead agencies of the New York City government owe their origins in large part to these justifications, and their present functions are most frequently explained in these terms or in some variation of them. Each overhead agency is inclined to question or to set limits to the justification of any other overhead agency, but rarely to its own; the line agency administrators characteristically regard all the claims for overhead agencies as grossly exaggerated. Partisanship and the rivalry between agencies is reflected in these attitudes. They obscure a more important point: the imposition of uniform policies and procedures upon other agencies by the overhead agencies is a form of political power, involving some of the stakes of city politics. The overhead agency leaders are participants in the city's political contest. Their exercise of power and influence thus raises other questions. If they are the guardians of uniformity and efficiency, who is to be guardian over them: the Mayor, the Board of Estimate, or some other participant in the political process?

The Structure of Information and Advice

When the overhead agencies are viewed as comprising a part of the structure of information and advice to the central decision-makers of the city government (the Mayor and the Board of Estimate), the most striking feature of the relationship is how sparsely the Mayor is served. At best, he can count only three of these ten overhead agencies as presenting to him information and advice which is meant primarily to assist him. These are the Law Department, the Investigation Department, and the Labor Department. The information and advice from the others he must recognize as intended primarily to influence him, to bring him into agreement with the Board of Estimate or with a particular overhead agency's constituency. If the Mayor is to have information and advice on issues and decisions from the perspective of the Mayor's responsibilities and aspirations, he must have other resources than the help these ten overhead agencies provide him.

The Board of Estimate is better served by the overhead agencies. For one thing, its need for information and advice is of a different order. The burdens of innovation in policy, of broad programs and consistency in performance, rest most heavily upon the Mayor; the Board is the guardian of continuity, accustomed to bargaining and negotiating its way from decision to decision, engaged in tactical adjustments rather than in grand strategy. It looks to some overhead agencies for assistance in this process, while it seeks also and more importantly to curb any tendencies on the part of any of them toward innovation or broad programming. In this purpose, the Board has been more successful than not. Those overhead agencies it cannot coopt into its own processes it has curbed. A majority of them are either Board agents or Board hostages, or cannot give the Board much trouble.

Some overhead agencies seek autonomous roles in their relationships to the Mayor and Board of Estimate. They wish to represent their constituencies free from any but the most formal subordination to either the Mayor or the Board of Estimate. Every overhead agency has this tendency; some are in a position to indulge it.

The structure of information and advice provided to the Mayor and the Board of Estimate by the overhead agencies in the city government is thus fragmented: some of the overhead agency leaders have an orientation toward the Mayor's needs, some serve the rival purposes of the Board of Estimate, some speak for their own agency constituencies. Both information and advice

are competitive, as the literature of public administration frequently prescribes, but they are not presented in the focus of debate before a chief executive considering alternatives of policy and decision: it flows instead along
separate streams of the city's political process. The main beneficiaries among
the participants in the city's political process are the Board of Estimate and
the organized bureaucracies.

BIBLIOGRAPHY

ART COMMISSION

Official Sources and Issuances
New York City Charter, chap. 37, secs. 851–856.

Art Commission, *Annual Reports*, 1902–1927 (published annually); 1928–1929 (1 vol.);
    1930–1937 (single condensed report); and 1940–1941 (single typed report).

"Rules and Procedure," filed with the City Clerk, March 22, 1939. Republished in *City
    Record*, April 10, 1939, p. 2460. Amendment to this publication, filed with City Clerk,
    November 25, 1941. Republished in *City Record*, December 11, 1941, p. 6921.

"Watchdog of the City's Art," *This Week*, *New York Herald Tribune*, April 6, 1947,
    pp. 8–9, 32.

BUREAU OF THE BUDGET

Official Sources and Issuances
New York City Charter, chap. 6, secs. 111–132, as amended by Local Law 21, 1955; Local
    Law 90, 1955; Local Law 9, 1942; Local Law 66, 1955; chap. 710, Laws of 1943;
    chap. 338, Laws of 1945; chap. 9, secs. 211–224, as amended by Local Law 19, 1949.

New York City Administrative Code, chap. 6, secs. 112 and 113.

New York City, Bureau of the Budget, *Budget*. The Mayor's annual recommendations for
    current expenses and revenues. Accompanied by the Mayor's annual Budget Message.

Annual Reports on the Administrative Management Program, 1948 and 1948–1950 (summary).

Surveys and Discussion
Bernstein, Betty, Natalie Davison, and Katherine Strauss, *What Are They Doing with Our
    Money? A Study of the New York City Budget*. Citizens Committee on Children of New
    York City and Women's City Club of New York, New York, 1954. How the Bureau
    of the Budget operates and the kind of budget it prepares.

Bernstein, Julius, *Effective Administration Through Performance Budgeting*. Master's thesis, City
    College, 1957, unpublished.

Buck, A. E., *Budgeting and Financial Management of the City of New York*. Mayor's Committee
    on Management Survey, New York, 1951. A study of the city's fiscal administration.

Citizens Budget Commission of New York, *A Better Government for a Better City: A Study of
    Five Departments of the City of New York at the Request of Hon. William O'Dwyer, Mayor*.
    The Commission, New York, 1948, pp. 152–164. An analysis of budget making and
    the work of the Bureau of the Budget.

Annual Report, 1955. The Commission, New York. Shows how the line budget might be
    improved by a performance budget.

Citizens Union, *The City Gets a Check-Up*. Citizens Union Research Foundation, New York,
    1954, pp. 5–8, 10, 13. Recommendations of the Mayor's Committee on Management
    Survey and the Temporary State Commission to Study the Organizational Structure
    of the City of New York relating to budget administration and procedures.

Cohen, Leonard N., *Administrative Analysis of the New York City Bureau of the Budget*. City College Library, New York, 1942. An unpublished survey of the history, organization, and administration of the Budget Bureau, by a municipal research associate.

Lahee, Arnold W., *The New York City Budget*. Bureau of Municipal Research, New York, 1917. Traces an expense budget procedure.

Lehman, Herbert H., *The Finances and Financial Administration of New York City: Recommendations and Report of the Sub-Committee on Budget, Finance, and Revenue, of the City Committee on Plan and Survey*. Columbia University Press, New York, 1928. A report which preceded and helped create the Bureau of the Budget.

New York City, Board of Management Improvement, *Summary Report of New York City's Management Improvement Program, 1948–1952*. The Board, New York, 1953. Summarizes efforts to evaluate and assess the functioning of municipal administrative agencies during the O'Dwyer and Impellitteri administrations.

Board of Management Improvement Program, *A Summary Report of New York City's Management Improvement Program, 1948–1950*. Bureau of the Budget, New York, 1951. Studies of the work of city agencies conducted by the Bureau of the Budget.

Mayor's Committee on Management Survey, *Modern Management for the City of New York*. 2 vols. The Committee, New York, 1953, vol. 1, pp. 7–8, 17–18, 41, 87–134, 257–258, 264–265; vol. 2. pp. 80–83. Observations and recommendations on the municipal budget system.

New York State, Temporary State Commission to Study the Organizational Structure of the Government of the City of New York, *Four Steps to Better Government of New York City: A Plan for Action*. 2 vols. The Commission, New York, 1953, vol. 1, pp. 11, 12, 19–23, 58–70, 107–114; vol. 2, pp. 8–9, 11, 17–18. Recommendations for improving budget administration under the Director of the Budget.

Ross, Lillian, "$1,031,961,754.63," *The New Yorker*, vol. 23, July 12, 1947, pp. 27–40. A detailed and graphic account of the operations of the Bureau of the Budget.

CITY CONSTRUCTION COORDINATOR

Official Sources and Issuances

New York City Charter, Local Law No. 1, 1946. Establishes the office of City Construction Coordinator.

City Construction Coordinator, *Arterial Progress*, a quarterly report, commencing January 1959.

Surveys and Discussions

Mackaye, Milton, "Public Servant: Robert Moses," *Profiles from the New Yorker*. Alfred A. Knopf, New York, 1938, pp. 287–296. Reprinted from *The New Yorker*, vol. 10, March 10, 1934, pp. 26–29.

Moses, Robert, *Theory and Practice in Politics*. Harvard University Press, Cambridge, Mass., 1939. The city's Construction Coordinator expresses his views.

Working for the People: Promise and Performance in Public Service. Harper and Bros., New York, 1956.

Rodgers, Cleveland, *New York Plans for the Future*. Harper and Bros., New York, 1943. A member of the City Planning Commission pays tribute to the Construction Coordinator.

Robert Moses: Builder for Democracy. Henry Holt and Co., New York, 1952. A favorable biography of the city's Construction Coordinator.

DEPARTMENT OF CITY PLANNING

Official Sources and Issuances

New York City Charter, chap. 8, secs. 191–202 (as amended by chap. 339, Laws of 1952, chap. 56, Laws of 1953, chap. 195, Laws of 1957, chap. 127, Laws of 1957, Local Law 8, 1951, and Local Law 11, 1956).

New York City Administrative Code, chap. 8, secs. 191–202.

New York City, City Planning Commission, *Annual Reports*, 1938–1940 (published annually); 1941–1950 (1 vol.); 1951, 1952–1953 (1 vol.); 1954–1955 (1 vol.).

Bulletin, November 22, 1954, to date (issued irregularly).

Newsletter, April, 1956, to date. A monthly publication devoted to a variety of subjects within the purview of the Department.

Proposed Capital Budget [for each year] and the Capital Program for the Next Succeeding Five Calendar Years. The Commission's recommended capital improvement outlays.

McKinney's Consolidated Laws of New York, Annotated, Book 20, *General City Law*. Edward Thompson Co., Brooklyn, N. Y., 1951. Sections 26–39 deal with the forms, powers, and functions of planning boards in the cities of New York State. This volume includes judicial interpretation of the law.

Citizens Union, Sub-Committee on Zoning, "Rezoning the City of New York," *The Searchlight*, vol. 41, November, 1951. One of the major areas of the work of the City Planning Commission.

Surveys and Discussions

McAneny, George, "Reminiscences." Columbia University Oral History Collection, Special Collections, Butler Library. Describes the origins of the City Planning Commission.

Millett, John D., *The Administrative Role of the City Planning Commission in the Top Management Structure of New York City*. Mayor's Committee on Management Survey, New York, 1952. An appraisal of the agency.

New York City, Mayor's Committee on Management Survey, *Modern Management for the City of New York*. 2 vols. The Committee, New York, 1953, vol. 1, pp. 24, 235–236; vol. 2, pp. 12–14, 92–115. An analysis of the work of the City Planning Commission and recommendations for giving it greater vitality.

New York City Planning Commission, "Zoning: New York Tries Again," *Architectural Forum*, April, 1959, pp. 123, 206, 210. One of the most important proposals put forth by the Commission since its inception.

New York State, Temporary State Commission to Study the Organizational Structure of the Government of the City of New York, *Four Steps to Better Government of New York City: A Plan for Action*. 2 vols. The Commission, New York, 1953, vol. 2, pp. 26–27. The Commission's recommendations relating to city planning organization.

Rodgers, Cleveland, *New York Plans for the Future*. Harper and Bros., New York, 1943, pp. 147–200. A member of the City Planning Commission explains the problems of planning and the role of the agency.

"Reminiscences." Columbia University Oral History Collection, Special Collections, Butler Library. A member of the Planning Commission tells of some aspects of its work, 1938–1950.

Rodgers, Cleveland, and Rebecca Rankin, *New York: The World's Capital City*. Harper and Bros., New York, 1948, pp. 303–308, 357–365. Outlines some phases of the work of the City Planning Commission and some of its major problems.

Tanzer, Lawrence A., *The New York City Charter*. Clark Boardman Co., New York, 1937, pp. 75–82, 84–85, 102, 210–211. The provisions for the City Planning Commission in the city charter of 1938.

Tugwell, Rexford G., "Implementing the General Interest," *Public Administration Review*, vol. 1, Autumn, 1940, pp. 32–49. The early history and problems of the City Planning Commission.

"New York in Perspective," in William A. Robson, *Great Cities of the World*. Macmillan Co., New York, 1955, pp. 411–448. The former head of the Department of City Planning explains the structure, functions, and handicaps of the Department and Planning Commission (pp. 422, 423–425).

Welfare and Health Council of New York, *City Statistical and Research Activities of Municipal Welfare, Health, and Education Agencies in New York City*. The Council, New York, 1955, pp. 10–13. How the Department of City Planning is organized for research.

CITY RECORD

Official Sources and Issuances

New York City Charter, chap. 38, secs. 871–873 (as amended by Local Law 169, 1939, and Local Law 26, 1954).

New York City Administrative Code, chap. 38, secs. 971–972.

City Record, June 24, 1873, to date. This is the official journal of the City of New York. Published daily except Sundays and legal holidays, this publication contains advertising required to be done for the city and notices required to be published by law. It also prints such official matters as minutes of meetings of the Art Commission and City Planning Commission and the Journal of Proceedings of meetings of the Council and Board of Estimate.

Annual Reports of the Supervisor, 1910–1911 (1 vol.); 1912–1918 (published annually); 1919–1920 (1 vol.); 1922–1924 (1 vol.); 1925–1933 (published annually); published in the *City Record*: 1934–1936 (March 3, 1938); 1937–1938 (June 5, 1939); 1939–1940 (November 28, 1940); 1941–1942 (November 28, 1942); 1944–1945 (November 16, 1945); 1945–1946 (January 20, 1947); 1946–1948 (September 10, 1948); 1948–1949 (August 11, 1949); 1949–1950 (September 7, 1950); 1950–1951 (August 16, 1951); 1951–1952 (September 11, 1952); 1952–1953 (August 13, 1953); 1953–1954 (October 14, 1954); 1954–1955 (September 22, 1955); 1955–1956 (September 18, 1956); 1956–1957 (September 25, 1957); and 1957–1958 (November 14, 1958).

Surveys and Discussions

Bruère, Henry, *New York City's Administrative Progress, 1914–1916.* M. B. Brown Co., New York, 1916, pp. 204–210. Improvement in the *City Record* during 1914–1916.

New York City Commissioners of Accounts and New York Bureau of Municipal Research, *Government of the City of New York.* J. J. Little and Ives Co., New York, 1915, pp. 1136–1141. Describes the *City Record* as it was operated in 1915.

Tanzer, Lawrence A., *The New York City Charter.* Clark Boardman Co., New York, 1937, pp. 197–199, 227. The associate counsel of the Thacher Charter Commission describes the work of the *City Record*.

DEPARTMENT OF INVESTIGATION

Official Sources and Issuances

New York City Charter, chap. 34, secs. 801–805.

New York City Administrative Code, chap. 34, sec. 803.

Department of Investigation, *Annual Report*, 1938 (no report since).

Surveys and Discussions

Allen, William H., *Why Tammanies Revive: La Guardia's Mis-Guard.* Institute for Public Service, New York, 1937. The activities of the Commissioner of Accounts during the first La Guardia administration.

Blanshard, Paul, *Investigating City Government in the La Guardia Administration.* Department of Investigation and Accounts, New York, 1937. Four years of work of the predecessor of the present Department of Investigation.

"New York City's Business Activities," radio broadcast in *You and Your Government Series.* National Municipal League, New York, 1934. The Commissioner of Accounts (predecessor of the Commissioner of Investigation) describes the work of his office in the first La Guardia administration.

Citizens Union, *Scrapbooks.* 206 vols. In reference section of New York Public Library, Astor Branch. Vols. 113–116 cover the office of Commissioner of Accounts, 1922–1935.

City Affairs Committee, "The Eyes and Ears of the Administration," *Bulletin*, April, 1937. An evaluation of the work of the Department of Investigation and Accounts.

Fosdick, Raymond B., *Chronicle of a Generation.* Harper and Bros., New York, 1958, pp. 78–121. The office of Commissioner of Accounts under Mayors McClellan and Gaynor.

Nelson, F. L., "Raymond B. Fosdick, New York's Commissioner of Accounts," *World Today*, vol. 21, August, 1911, pp. 941–945. Mayor Gaynor's Commissioner of Accounts.

Olmsted, Sophia A., "The Municipal Power of Investigation," *National Municipal Review*, vol. 25, November, 1936, pp. 649–653. A comparison with corresponding departments in other cities shows that the New York City Department of Investigation has powers that are almost unique.

Seidman, Harold, *Investigating Municipal Administration*. Institute of Public Administration, New York, 1941. Doctoral dissertation, Yale University. A scholarly treatise that traces the origins of the Department of Investigation and evaluates its functioning.

Tanzer, Lawrence A., *The New York City Charter*. Clark Boardman Co., New York, 1937, pp. 189–191, 226. The work of the Department of Investigation, as described by the Associate Counsel of the Thacher Charter Commission.

Waldron, W., "City Watchdog: Commissioner of Investigation," *Survey Graphic*, vol. 28, March, 1939, pp. 210–211. Reprinted in condensed form in *Reader's Digest*, vol. 34, March, 1939, pp. 105–108.

Wallstein, Leonard M., "Reminiscences." Columbia University Oral History Collection, Special Collections, Butler Library. Public investigations by a Commissioner of Accounts.

LABOR DEPARTMENT
(See Bibliography for Chapter XI.)

LAW DEPARTMENT

Official Sources and Issuances

New York City Charter, chap. 16, secs. 391–397, as amended by chap. 710, part 3, sec. 569, Laws of 1943 and chap. 338, Laws of 1945. Establish the Law Department and define its powers.

New York City Administrative Code, chap. 16, secs. 391–397.

Law Department, *Annual Reports*, 1898–1932 (published annually); 1934–1940 (published annually); 1952–1953, 1954–1955, 1956–1957.

Surveys and Discussions

Blair, Paxton, "Reminiscences." Columbia University Oral History Collection, Special Collections, Butler Library. A former Assistant Corporation Counsel recalls the Law Department under the La Guardia administration.

Bruère, Henry, *New York City's Administrative Progress, 1914–1916*. M. B. Brown and Co., New York, 1916, pp. 231–237. Progress in the city's Law Department.

Fosdick, Raymond B., *Chronicle of a Generation*. Harper and Bros., New York, 1958, pp. 87–88. An Assistant Corporation Counsel relates his experiences in the Law Department.

Greener, John H., *A History of the Office of the Corporation Counsel and the Law Department of the City of New York*. Privately printed, New York City Law Department, New York, 1925. A brief account of the development and organization of New York City's Law Department.

Hurley, Denis M., "Administrative and Procedural Problems of New York City's Law Department," *Law Review Digest*, July-August, 1954, pp. 62–70. Some phases of the work of the Law Department.

Isaacs, Julius, *Oath of Devotion*. E. P. Dutton and Co., New York, 1949, pp. 126–147. The work of the city's Law Department, during a critical period of its history.

"Reminiscences." Columbia University Oral History Collection, Special Collections, Butler Library. Recollections of the Law Department by an Assistant Corporation Counsel (1934–1935).

Morris, Newbold, and Dana Lee Thomas, *Let the Chips Fall*. Appleton-Century-Crofts, New York, 1955, pp. 95–97. Recollections of life in the Law Department by an Assistant Corporation Counsel who later attained greater prominence in municipal affairs.

Polk, Frank L., *Papers*. Yale University. The collected papers of the Corporation Counsel during the Mitchel administration.

Saxe, Martin, "Reminiscences." Columbia University Oral History Collection, Special Collections, Butler Library. The work of an Assistant Corporation Counsel in the early years of the century.

Windels, Paul, "Reminiscences." Columbia University Oral History Collection, Special Collections, Butler Library. Describes his experiences in the Law Department as Corporation Counsel.

DEPARTMENT OF PERSONNEL

Official Sources and Issuances

New York City Charter, chap. 35, secs. 811–819 (as amended by chap. 354, Laws of 1954).

New York City Administrative Code, chap. 35.

New York State Constitution, Art. V, sec. 9.

McKinney's Consolidated Laws of New York, Annotated, Book 9, *Civil Service Law*. Edward Thompson Co., Brooklyn, N. Y., 1946. Kept up to date with annual supplements. Contains the text of civil service provisions of the state constitution, as well as the Civil Service Law, with all its amendments, that governs the work of the city's Personnel Department and the Civil Service Commission. Includes judicial interpretations.

Civil Service Commission, "Rules of the City Civil Service Commission of New York," 1955 to date. A mimeographed folder, kept up to date.

Annual Reports: 1898–1932 (published annually); 1933–1934 (1 vol.); 1935–1938 (published annually); 1939–1940 (1 vol.); 1940–1942 (1 vol.); 1942–1943 (1 vol.); 1943–1945 (1 vol); 1945–1946 (1 vol.); and 1947–1953 (published annually).

Department of Personnel, *Annual Reports:* 1954–1955 (1 vol.); and 1955 to date (published annually).

Surveys and Discussions

Allen, William H., *Why Tammanies Revive: La Guardia's Mis-Guard*. Institute for Public Service, New York, 1937, pp. 117–122. Civil service during Mayor La Guardia's first administration.

Baikie, Edith, *Civil Service in the City of New York*. Citizens Budget Commission, New York, 1938. A comprehensive study of the operation of civil service in the city.

Blume, Rita, *Exempt Positions in the Municipal Civil Service*. Master's thesis, Columbia University, 1941, unpublished.

Bruère, Henry, *New York City's Administrative Progress, 1914–1916*. M. B. Brown and Co., 1916, pp. 211–230. Efforts to improve the city's civil service during a reform administration.

Chang, Yu-Tsai, *An Analysis of the Recruitment and Placement Policies of the Municipal Civil Service Commission of the City of New York*. Master's thesis, New York University, 1949, unpublished.

City Club of New York, *The New York City Charter*. The Club, New York, 1921, pp. 33–35. Some recommendations relating to the Civil Service Commission.

Griffenhagen and Associates, *Classification and Compensation of the Service of the City of New York*. 4 vols. Mayor's Committee on Management Survey, New York, 1951. A technical survey.

Klein, Michael, *Service Rating in the New York City Civil Service*. Master's thesis, Columbia University, 1941, unpublished.

Lang, Theodore H., *An Evaluation of the Personnel Function as Administered in Operating Agencies of the Municipal Government of New York*. Doctoral dissertation, New York University, 1951. The Deputy Personnel Director of the Department of Personnel writes on practices in city agencies.

New York City, Bureau of the Budget, *The City of New York Civil Service Commission: A Study of the Functions and Organizational Structure of the Civil Service Agency of the City of New York.* The Bureau, New York, 1951. An analysis of structure and operations.

Mayor's Committee on Management Survey, *Modern Management for the City of New York.* 2 vols. The Committee, New York, 1953, vol. 1, pp. 5–6, 18–20, 59–86; vol. 2, pp. 14–17, 116–222, 856. The major findings of the Mayor's Committee.

Department of Personnel, *Seventy-Fifth Anniversary: Civil Service.* Foreword by Mayor Robert F. Wagner. Grant Advertising Co., New York, 1959. A popular presentation of the development of civil service, the kinds of work performed by civil servants, the merit system, the training and study programs, and opportunities for promotion and advancement.

New York State, Temporary State Commission on Coordination of State Activities, *Staff Report on the Department of Civil Service.* Legislative Document no. 42, 1953, Williams Press, Albany, 1953. A study which influenced the reorganization of the New York City Civil Service Commission.

Temporary State Commission to Study the Organizational Structure of the Government of the City of New York, *Four Steps to Better Government of New York City: A Plan for Action.* 2 vols. The Commission, New York, 1953, vol. 1, pp. 11, 23–25, 71–82, 115–121; vol. 2, pp. 9, 11–12, 18. The Commission's proposals for modernizing the city's personnel administration.

O'Reilly, J. J., and Lachausee, Charles, *The Chief Handbook on Civil Service.* The Chief, New York, 1908. Describes the types of positions open to civil service in New York City in 1908.

Sayre, Wallace S., and Herbert Kaufman, *Personnel Administration in the Government of New York City.* Mayor's Committee on Management Survey, New York, 1952. A survey of personnel management in the city government, with recommendations for improvement.

Sayre, Wallace S., and Milton Mandell, *Education and the Civil Service in New York City.* Office of Education, U.S. Department of the Interior, Bulletin 1937, no. 20, Government Printing Office, Washington, 1938. The role of education in recruitment policies, examinations, and in-service training in the city's civil service.

Sayre, Wallace S., and Warner Moss, "A Civil Service Program for New York," *National Municipal Review,* vol. 24, April, 1935, pp. 208–211, 223. Areas in which a reform administration had an opportunity to revitalize civil service in the city.

Schechter, Joseph, "Personnel Management in the City of New York," *Public Personnel Review,* October, 1957, pp. 203–213. The Personnel Director describes the new personnel program and the personnel structure which went into effect in New York City in 1954.

Shen, Kwan C., *The Civil Service Examination in the City of New York.* Master's thesis, Columbia University, 1925, unpublished.

Small, Goldie M., *The Civil Service in New York City, with Special Reference to the Problems of 1926–1937.* Master's thesis, Columbia University, 1938, unpublished.

Stahl, Oscar Glenn, *Training Public Career Servants for the City of New York.* Doctoral dissertation, New York University, 1936.

Tanzer, Lawrence A., *The New York City Charter.* Clark Boardman Co., New York, 1937, pp. 191–193, 226. The Associate Counsel of the Thacher Charter Commission describes the work of the Civil Service Commission.

Wagner, Robert F., "Modernizing New York City's Personnel System," *Good Government,* November–December, 1957, pp. 50–53. Recent developments in the city's Department of Personnel.

Weissberg, Morris, *Civil Service Rights: New York City and State.* Able Publishing Co., New York, 1950. A reference source for the guiding principles, statutes, and case law relating to civil service.

Wheeler, Everett P., *Sixty Years of American Life.* E. P. Dutton and Co., New York, 1917, pp. 281–294, 300–309, 343–344. The origins of civil service in New York City.

Yavner, Louis E., and Edith Baikie, *For Better Personnel Administration in the City of New York*. Citizens Budget Commission, New York, 1946. Recommendations for improved, integrated personnel administration.

DEPARTMENT OF PURCHASE

Official Sources and Issuances

New York City Charter, chap. 33, secs. 781–785 (as amended by Local Law 4, 1957).

New York City Administrative Code, chap. 32, secs. 773a and 773b.

Department of Purchase, *Annual Reports*, 1934–1938 (published annually); 1939–1940, 1940–1941, 1942–1945, 1948–1949, 1949–1950, 1954, 1955–1957.

New York State *Laws* of 1919, chap. 321; 1920, chap. 783; 1923, chap. 890. These statutes are the legal base for the Department of Purchase.

Surveys and Discussions

City Club of New York, *The New York City Charter*. The Club, New York, 1921, pp. 24–25. Describes the origins of the present Department of Purchase.

New York City, Mayor's Committee on Management Survey, *Modern Management for the City of New York*. 2 vols. The Committee, New York, 1953, vol. 1, p. 25; vol. 2, pp. 316–318. A brief review of the principal recommendations of the Mayor's Committee; an overview of the work of the department.

Saybold, Geneva, B., " 'Gyp' Vendor & Company," *National Municipal Review*, vol. 24, June, 1935, pp. 314–317. The work of the New York City Department of Purchase.

Whalen, Grover A., *Mr. New York: The Autobiography of Grover A. Whalen*. G. P. Putnam's Sons, New York, 1955, pp. 61–64. The early days of the Board of Purchase.

CHAPTER XI

Leaders of the Organized City
Bureaucracies

THE BUREAUCRATS IN THE CITY GOVERNMENT are important participants in the city's politics. Like the other participants—the party leaders, the elected and appointed officials, the leaders of nongovernmental groups—they seek to influence a wide range of governmental decisions which have special relevance to their interests. Some they can influence as individual members of the city's numerous administrative agencies. Opportunities for individual influence vary from agency to agency and are greatly affected by the rank and status of the bureaucrat. For the most part, the bureaucrats influence the decisions of the city government through their efforts as organized groups: as associations, societies, and unions. It is the leaders of these organized bureaucracies who participate systematically and continuously in the city's political process, dealing with party leaders, city and state officials, and leaders of nongovernmental groups.

The leaders of the organized bureaucracies represent their members in ways not unlike those used by party leaders, elected and appointed officials, and leaders of nongovernmental groups. In doing so, they respond to the special assets which their followers possess and take into account their followers' special liabilities. The bureaucratic leaders recognize and make use of the fact that their followers are both numerous and insiders, a part of the city government. Some have full-time, intimate contact with many of the decision-makers their leaders are trying to influence. Some have a firsthand acquaintance with, sometimes almost a monopoly of, the information essential to a decision. They often have an additional resource for influence: the bureaucrats themselves frequently carry out the decisions, and thus can control their interpretation and modification in practice—in short, play a decisive role in the success or failure of a decision. Few other leaders in city politics have more strategically placed and experienced followers. These assets help to make the leaders of the organized bureaucracies important participants; the goals they seek they are likely to attain.

These leaders are not a monolithic group. The groups they lead are numerous and separate, often competitive with each other, each group tending to pursue its own separate goals.[1] The leaders of each group must seek allies not merely among other bureaucratic groups but also among the other participants. But there is room and need for collaboration among all the bureaucratic groups on some goals, and their separatist aims and methods have had some common tendencies since their emergence several decades ago as important participants in the city's political life.

MAJOR STRATEGIES OF THE ORGANIZED BUREAUCRACIES

Building Prestige and Legitimacy by Organization and Neutrality

The strategies of the leaders of the organized bureaucracies in the city's political process flow from the image of their followers as bureaucrats, the specific opportunities they perceive for the exercise of influence, and their need for alliances with other participants. Seeing their members as bureaucrats requires special attention to demands for status, recognition, and prestige both in the community and among the other participants. Despite their increasing influence, the bureaucrats are sensitive and defensive about status, a result of assumptions which they and others make concerning the climate of public opinion toward public employees. They are the butt of unflattering comments about their industriousness, their ambitions, their integrity, their worth to the community. These are ancient burdens of the American public servant, and they are shared by almost all other occupations and professions, who also feel the stings of a society which regards few groups with deference. The civil servant has been trained to feel that he is the object of more than his allotted share of disapproval.

The bureaucrats are also sensitive to the restricted status that formal governmental doctrine assigns them in decision-making. In formal theory and tradition, they are "employees," deprived of initiative and decision in policy matters. They are reminded, with unflattering emphasis and frequency, that they are neither elected officials nor in any other sense the "representatives" of sovereign citizens, but are paid servants of others having legitimate powers of initiation and decision in public policy. No other major participant in the city's politics is vexed with such elaborate questioning of its legitimacy as a contestant, although the party leaders and some interest group leaders may feel on occasion that they have a similar cross to bear.

The bureaucracies seek to raise their status and to assert the legitimacy of their role by a number of accommodations and strategies. One is to organize. The organized group has the strength of numbers and of continuity; it can secure a hearing where the lone bureaucrat cannot, and it reduces the risks of reprisal. The organized group can provide a "society" within itself, having its own prizes of prestige, leadership, and legitimacy to dis-

[1] See Tables A, B, and C in Appendix C.

tribute. The rise and proliferation of group life among the city's bureaucracies in this century have been striking in numbers and in survival.

Organization brings other opportunities and satisfactions. The bureaucratic group can become a part of the general labor movement by affiliation with a labor union of regional or national importance. If its members regard themselves as part of a profession, the group can seek affiliation with a larger professional society. These affiliations have strong attractions both in influence and prestige and have been made by most of the city's bureaucracies.

Another accommodation by the city's bureaucracies in their search for prestige and status has been to adopt and modify the civil service reformers' doctrine of the "impartial" or "neutral" career civil servant. For the reformers this concept was intended to promote the acceptability of the merit system up to the highest posts below the elected executive. For the city's bureaucracies it has additional connotations: it is used to obscure and thus to justify initiative and decision by the bureaucracies, to increase the amount of discretion delegated to them, and to validate the role of the "expert" or "experienced" civil servant in his contests with other participants in the city's political struggle.

Each of these accommodations has its risks. Affiliation with a labor union may mean subordination to an organization more interested in its nongovernmental membership than in the expectations of its bureaucratic members, or more interested in manipulation of the political assets of the bureaucratic membership than in solving their problems. Affiliation with a professional society may mean a similar subordination. Acceptance of the doctrine of "impartiality" represents a gain for the city's bureaucracies in their efforts to improve their status and prestige and to strengthen their claims to legitimacy in the political contest, but it also often imposes inhibitions upon the exercise of their political and party strengths.

Control Over Personnel Systems

The strategy most continuously used by the leaders of the city's bureaucracies is their effort to control the city government's policies and practices of employment. The bureaucracies have an obvious and special interest in the personnel management policies which determine their own pay, their rate and opportunity of advancement, their hours of work, the kind and amount of work they do, the settlement of their grievances, their tenure protections, their vacation and other leave privileges, their eligibility for retirement, their contribution to the retirement systems, and the amount of their pensions after retirement. These matters are so important to the bureaucracies that their leaders seek not merely to participate in the decisions but to be the dominant participants. This dominant or controlling role in the determination of personnel policies can rarely be achieved in the formal sphere of decision-making, but it can often be accomplished in the informal relationships—that is, in the bargaining processes of the city's political contest.

The ceaseless search of the bureaucracies for a controlling position in developing the personnel policies and practices of the city government leads them into many facets of the political process. Some concentrate on the state legislature to spell out personnel policies in state statutes (for example, by the teachers in the city's schools and colleges); it leads others to focus attention on elected city officials (by the police and fire groups, for example); others give increasing attention to the city's Personnel Department, and still others to the newly established Labor Department. All bureaucratic groups use the courts to protect their gains.

Leaders of the city's bureaucracies have the greatest difficulty when they seek to determine salaries and wages. They have the power and position to resist efforts to reduce their compensation rates in a period of downward movement in prices, but they are less successful in their efforts to raise them in an inflationary period. Here they suffer from two important disabilities: they compete with each other in their assault upon the resources of a tight budget (for example, teachers versus patrolmen versus firemen versus sanitationmen); they encounter, too, the resistance of the tax-conscious, money-providing interest groups that do not strongly oppose many other personnel aims of the bureaucracies.

This group of city leaders nevertheless has an impressive record in shaping the city's personnel systems. The statutes of the state government, the Administrative Code of the city, the rules and regulations of the Personnel Department and of the Labor Department, the traditions and practices of the heads of departments and agencies—all these bear testimony to the steady march of the city's bureaucracies toward personnel systems reflecting policies and practices which are largely the product of their own influence.

Maximizing Bureaucratic Autonomy

Control over the city's personnel systems serves as an even more significant goal. Bureaucratic groups, especially as they mature in their organization and in their self-awareness as cohesive groups, share with all other groups the aspiration to be self-directing, self-sufficient, and autonomous. In fact, bureaucracies appear to represent one of the strongest expressions of this general tendency. In the city, where several of the large organized bureaucracies are notably mature and self-conscious, they give evidence of desiring to live a life of their own, to create a self-contained world of their own, to make their own choices of direction and emphasis, to decide for themselves the methods and procedures they will use. Bargaining, alliances, and opposition are recognized necessities, but the consistently held goal is an aspiration for the nearest approach to autonomy that can be negotiated.

The first aim of the leaders of the city's bureaucracies, in seeking autonomy, is to minimize the burden of supervision they receive from other participants. Their accepted techniques are numerous: appointing and removal powers can be limited or neutralized; powers of discipline can be softened by statute, rule, or contract; supervisors and managers can be required to be products of the bureaucratic system itself. But the most important strategic method is to secure wide acceptance of an inviolate status, a taboo against "political interference" or the intervention of "special interests." Once armed with this status, the organized bureaucracy can assert boldly, or can depend upon the press or some other participant to assert for it, a claim to freedom from supervision. Few bureaucracies achieve the full flower of this inviolable status, but most of them strive for it. The teachers, the police, the medical and health groups, the social workers, and others have frequently found it either a shield or a weapon. "No political interference" or "no special interests" in this or that field of administration is quite often a slogan for autonomy not merely from the interventions of party leaders but also for autonomy from the exercise of supervision by a Mayor, the line agency administrators, the Board of Estimate, or any other "outsider," official or unofficial.

The second strategic aim of the leaders of the city's bureaucracies in their search for autonomy is to achieve a maximum and assured role in formulating the policies that become the workload of the bureaucracy. For example, the leaders of the police organizations seek a law enforcement policy that suits the traditions and aspirations of the police bureaucracy—not a code that represents the intrusions of social workers, traffic experts, lawyers and judges, and the communication media into the traditions of the police. The leaders of the fire bureaucracy have similar attitudes, as do the leaders of the teachers, the transit workers, the welfare workers, and others. The city's bureaucracies regard policies determining the amount, kind, direction, and emphasis of their work as matters in which they have important and legitimate concern. They are conscious of their experience and knowledge in their specialized fields, and they are aware that they will probably bear the brunt of error while others claim the credit for success. Their leaders regard as necessary the protection of their group values and their settled traditions against the enthusiasm and whims of "amateurs" or "innovators." As a consequence, the leaders of the city's bureaucracies use every avenue they possess to influence the formation of public policy in ways that will increase, or least disturb, their opportunities to live their lives autonomously.

They seek even more confidently and successfully a third goal of autonomy—control of the procedures under which their members work. Here they have most of the strategic and tactical advantages. Other participants have limited information and criteria upon which to intervene and still less capacity to ensure that formal concessions are, in fact, carried out. Some opportunities for "outside" intervention do arise, as when the courts invalidate an existing procedure and prescribe a new one, or when technological progress compels an important change in procedure (the shift from water to chemicals in fire fighting, or the adoption of motor patrols in the police, for example). But these are limited in scope. The bureaucracies tend to absorb them reluctantly and slowly, modifying them if possible to fit into going procedures with the least change in settled habits.

In the main, the city's bureaucracies have achieved autonomy not only in their procedural life. Their leaders have also an influential role in shaping public policies that constitute their workload, a marked success in coopting or absorbing many posts of formal supervision into their own membership, and a considerable capacity to limit interventions by other participants. If their autonomy does not yet match their aspirations, the leaders can draw comfort from the trends in their favor.

The leaders of the city's bureaucracies are a conservative force in the political contest. The stakes they seek are primarily those that minimize innovation and change. Their drive for autonomy is largely an effort to reduce the influence of the outside "movers and shakers" upon settled routines. Their rhetoric often has an imperialistic sound, their tactics are sometimes aggressive and turbulent, but their concrete goals remain conservative. The policy and procedural *status quo* of today, or perhaps yesterday's in some matters, is their accepted milieu. Their proposals for change and even their demands for higher salaries and wages (where their greatest discomfort appears) are incremental rather than radical. In the city's political process the leaders of the organized bureaucracies are an anchor, not a force driving forward.

THE TACTICS OF LEADERS OF ORGANIZED BUREAUCRACIES

Forming Alliances

The leaders of the city's bureaucracies need allies, as do all other participants in the city's political contest. Their problem is to find alliances that are the most durable, the most productive, the least costly. In their search for allies, leaders find occasions to unite with each other, to join with organized bureaucracies outside the city government (in the state and in other local governments), to affiliate with the labor movement, to develop links with the organized professions, to seek the help of the communication media, and occasionally to risk the hazards of an alliance with party leaders or a heavy commitment to a politically ambitious bureaucrat (with an Enright or a Prial, for example, as we shall soon see).

General City Associations. Unity with each other is apparently difficult despite the extent to which they share general goals and aims. Their particularistic drives tend to overshadow their common interests. The most enduring alliance has been between the police and fire associations, but even their unity is not without its interruptions and frictions. Most teachers' organizations (there are at least a hundred of them) have since 1924 worked together on many matters through the Joint Committee of Teachers' Organizations, their unity limited by differences between high-school teachers, junior high staffs, and elementary-school staffs, and by important defections. But there has been no successful and enduring general union of city employees. True, there have been some efforts to create a general "peak association" of all the organized bureaucratic groups in the city government. Frank Prial saw this as an early goal for the Civil Service Forum, and at the height of his effort in 1917 could claim twenty affiliated organizations (including the Patrolmen's Benevolent Association and some state and federal groups) with a total membership claim of 150,000. In the 1917 mayoralty election, Prial used an additional instrument to unify most bureaucratic groups to defeat Mitchel and elect Hylan—the Conference Committee of Allied Civil Service Employees, with Prial as chairman. Fifteen years later the 1932–1933 salary and wage reduction efforts of the Walker and McKee administrations were fought by a Joint Committee of civil service employee groups, the Teachers' Union supplying the chairman, Abraham Lefkowitz. In late 1933 the successor to this group—the Allied Civil Service Conference, Lefkowitz remaining as chairman—endorsed O'Brien for Mayor (against La Guardia) and Prial for Comptroller.

The record would seem to indicate that organizational unity of all the city's bureaucratic groups can be achieved only in a time of crisis and only on limited issues.

Functional Associations. Association of organizations of city employees in particular departments and functional specialities with counterparts in other governmental jurisdictions has furnished leverage against state governmental leaders. The (New York City) Joint Committee of Teachers' Organizations, for example, has worked closely since 1924 with the New York State Teachers' Association, but the two groups have not attempted a formal merger. The firemen's associations have since 1932 participated in the six-member New York State Firemen's Legislative Committee, an arrangement which had even earlier beginnings. Similarly, the city's police associations have since 1924 been active members of the New York State Police Conference, an organization of all police associations in the state. Its legislative committee of four members includes two from New York City's Patrolmen's Benevolent Association. These coalitions of teachers, firemen, and policemen with their statewide bureaucratic allies are intended primarily to strengthen their relationships with the state legislature, the Governor, the Comptroller, the Attorney General, and frequently with a state administrative agency (for example, the teachers with the Department of Education).

Labor Union Affiliations. Affiliation with labor unions is a growing method of alliance for many parts of the bureaucracy. At least one of the teachers' organizations has had an AFL affiliation since 1916, but neither the Teachers' Union nor the Teachers' Guild has ever been able to win a majority of the teachers away from their preferences for professional associations rather than labor unions. The city's firemen's organization, on the other hand, has been fully affiliated with the AFL International Association of Firefighters since 1918. The skilled tradesmen among the city's employees have for several decades belonged as individuals, or as separate locals, to the appropriate craft unions, thus enjoying the benefits of the "prevailing rate" provisions of Section 220 of the state Labor Law. But the more important labor union affiliations by the city's bureaucratic groups are of later origins. In the 1930's the major attempts to "unionize" the city employees were made by two CIO affiliates—the State, County, and Municipal Workers (SCMWA), and the Transport Workers Union (TWU). The TWU has survived in strength; the SCMWA first dwindled, then became the United Public Workers, and, after its expulsion from the CIO as a Communist-dominated union, disappeared. In the postwar years since 1946 the most vigorous efforts at unionization have centered in the State, County, and Municipal Employees (SCME)—first an AFL, now an AFL-CIO affiliate—and in the Teamsters' Union. The SCME aims at general civil service memberships but has been most successful in the Hospitals, Welfare, and Parks Departments. The Teamsters have had their greatest success in the Sanitation Department.

The trends in labor union affiliation by the organized bureaucracies are upward, as are the tendencies of individual city employees to join labor-affiliated organizations. These trends and tendencies point toward new forms and new practices in the dominant alliances of the city's organized bureaucracies.

Affiliation with Professional Associations. The development of links with professional associations is a tendency on the part of most bureaucratic groups that have such opportunities. Aside from the teachers, with their great numbers and strong professional orientation, these ties with outside professional groups are a main source of strength for many smaller bureaucratic groups: the social workers, the health groups, the engineers and architects, and the public administration and related groups. The most common pattern is individual membership held by the city employee in a professional society, but sometimes a local chapter composed of city employees is established. Such affiliation serves many purposes. One of them is the possibility of allies for the bureaucratic group whenever help is needed. Knowledge of, participation in, and especially a leadership role in professional standard-setting and enforcement are also a source of strength in the political contest in which bureaucrats are engaged. Aid in the protection of guild standards in recruitment and promotion, compensation, methods of work, the policy content of decisions by administrators—all these, and more, the professional members of the city's bureaucracy may expect and frequently receive from their ties with professional societies.

Other Alliances. The newspapers and the other nongovernmental groups represent more difficult forms of alliance for the leaders of the city's bureaucracies. These leaders have a long-nurtured conviction that most interest groups in the city either represent the forces of "economy" seeking to reduce their wages and numbers or represent forces seeking innovation and reorganization in the settled policies and practices to which the bureaucracies are accustomed. They tend, too, to regard the newspapers and other media as agents or partners of the interest groups in a program to limit the autonomy, privileges, and conveniences of the bureaucracy. Newspaper predilection for exposés makes them suspect as allies of the leaders of most organized bureaucracies. Alliances with the press and with most interest groups are accordingly a temporary and cautious commitment to cooperation. There are some exceptions: the weekly civil service press, some friendly columnists of proved reliability, the lawyers in civil service and labor relations practice, and an occasional interest group. But these are alliances which frequently depend upon transient ties of personal contact between the leaders of the bureaucratic group and the outsiders. Each bureaucratic organization as a whole tends to view them with the caution born of a sense of city history.

Party Alliances. A growing sense of caution also characterizes the relationships of the leaders of the organized bureaucracies with party leaders and with the politically ambitious bureaucrat. Most leaders of the organized bureaucracies would prefer to deal with party leaders from an independent position of strength, not within the confines of a close alliance; they would prefer, too, to avoid commitment to the political star of a bureaucrat who aspires to leave the bureaucracy behind him. For both the union-oriented and the profession-oriented bureaucracies, the trend in dealing with party leaders is toward detachment and aloofness, an impersonal bargaining process in which the leader of the bureaucratic organization tries to control the agenda and avoid entangling alliances.

Influencing Who Gets Office

The participation of the city's bureaucracies in the nomination and election of officials is surrounded by myth, uncertainty, and rumor. The myth is rooted in the plausible assumptions of the "patronage" era that the "civil service" vote was then a vote which could be manipulated and delivered by the party leaders. The myth persists in the premises of commentators but evidently not in the behavior of party leaders. Party leaders are sensitive to the attitudes of large blocs of civil servants; they do not, however, offer nominations to bureaucratic leaders who bring no other claims, nor do they consult them very often or systematically about the nomination of others.

The uncertainty and rumor flow from the occasional demonstrations of bureaucratic participation in nominations and elections, suggesting to some that these infrequent outcroppings indicate more regular and influential participation than is ordinarily apparent. There is, for example, the substantial political career which Frank J. Prial, in the period between 1915 and 1940, built upon a bureaucratic base (mainly the Civil Service Forum and *The Chief*, a weekly civil service newspaper owned by Prial), culminating in his 1932 insurgent primary nomination as Comptroller on the Democratic ticket. There is, too, the overt participation by the police and fire groups in the election campaign for O'Dwyer in 1949. And there is also the councilmanic career of Transport Workers' president Michael Quill (1938–1949), built upon the assistance of the Transport Workers Union and others in his election. But even if these instances are generously multiplied on the assumption that the influence of bureaucracies is a private rather than a public matter, and that for lesser offices the influence may be more often exerted, there is little evidence that party leaders defer to bureaucratic groups in nominations, or that elections are significantly influenced by them. In the nominating and electoral process, the bureaucrats are seemingly minor participants.

Choosing Agency Administrators

The influence of the leaders of the bureaucracies in the appointment of agency officials, however, is much more substantial. Their major asset in the appointment process is their capacity to exploit the general public affection (especially among the civic groups and the communication media) for the appointment of "career" commissioners, "career" deputies, and "career" bureau chiefs. Through emphasis upon this policy the leaders of the bureaucracies try to confine the appointing officer's choice to the ranks of the bureaucracy. The leaders may not name the particular appointee to be chosen, but they can make certain that he comes from among their own ranks. The appointment process in some departments and agencies has, in this sense, been "ceded" by Mayors and other participants largely to the bureaucratic groups that dominate the membership of the agencies (Education, Police, Fire, Sanitation, for example); in others, a bargain has been struck between the leaders of the bureaucratic groups inside and the leaders of the constituency interest groups outside the agency (Health, Hospitals, Welfare, for example), limiting the appointing discretion of other participants, including the Mayor. In still other agencies, the influence of the leaders of the bureaucratic groups is restricted to certain posts, or to a veto over nominees, or to an occasional tactical triumph. The influence of bureaucratic groups

over appointments is also evidently a function of time: it appears to increase
as the Mayor's occupancy of his office continues.

In some agencies, leaders' claims to appointive positions are buttressed by
law or civil service rule. Thus the position of bureau chief is normally included within the "competitive" class, and by rule or tradition competition
for these posts is almost invariably confined to the ranks of each unit's
bureaucracy. In some instances, posts higher than bureau chiefs are included
in the area of "competitive" selection: the second-ranking position in the
Fire Department (the post of Fire Chief) is a specific example. To these
formal concessions of a dominant role to the bureaucracies in the appointment process must be added the equally important informal concessions
that are a product of the capacity of the leaders of the bureaucracies to
bargain effectively in the city's political contest. The Police Department
provides a striking illustration. Here the police bureaucracy holds a complete
monopoly over the source of appointments to all the chief bureau posts (the
various grades of Inspectors) and over the general manager's post (the
Chief Inspector), a near monopoly over the deputy commissioner posts, and
is approaching a monopoly over the commissionership itself. The Board of
Education is another major illustration of the ability of the leaders of the
bureaucracies to control the source of eligibles for appointment of the
officials who are to be their supervisors. Only rarely are executive appointments in the school system made from outside the ranks of the Board's own
bureaucracy. The Fire Department and the Sanitation Department provide
similar examples. These four departments provide the most visible evidence
of the trend. There are others in which the tendencies are less pronounced
or have more recently begun, but the general direction is clear in them also:
the leaders of the bureaucracies are increasing their claims and their gains
as major participants in the appointment of the city's agency heads and
administrators.

Control Over Career Opportunities

The leaders of the city's bureaucracies have had great success in their
efforts to maximize and protect the career opportunities of their members.
To this end, they employ four main tactics: excluding "outsiders" (that is,
any nonbureaucrat) from eligibility to posts above the entrance level; limiting
eligibility for competition among bureaucrats to narrow departmental,
bureau, or occupational groups; making seniority the main, or at least an
important, test for advancement to higher posts; and, through these three
controls, making certain that not only agency heads and deputies, when
that can be managed, but that even more uniformly the supervisors and other
managers will come from within the bureaucracies and will thus be the
products of bureaucratic indoctrination. The primary doctrinal rationaliza-

tion for this system of advancement and promotion is condensed into the phrase "promotion from within." For the civil service reformers who developed the general doctrine, promotion from within was a method for limiting the intervention of party organization leaders. For the city's bureaucracies who have applied the doctrine to their own strategic goals, it is an unexcelled method for limiting the discretion of all outsiders—including Mayors, departmental commissioners and administrators, and other managers and supervisors.

In their pursuit of this goal of a series of "closed" bureaucracies, the leaders of the city's bureaucratic groups have been able to avoid competition among themselves. They have aroused little sustained and consistent opposition from other participants in the political contest, and they have had the support of the civil service reform tradition, a doctrine that has disarmed or given an awkward posture to such potential critics as department heads, civic groups, and the press. The consequence has been an impressive strategic victory for the organized bureaucracies of the city government. New York City has a closed bureaucratic system matched by few governmental jurisdictions. All police officers must begin as patrolmen, all fire officers as firemen, all sanitation foremen and superintendents as sanitationmen, all general administrators as clerks, and so on throughout most of the city service.

The amount of "new blood" that the city bureaucracies must absorb is minimal, and practically all of it is at the lowest ranks. The Mayor, his commissioners, and their deputies are confronted by a series of closed bureaucratic formations to which they have access only through bureau chiefs and other supervisors who are the seasoned products of the bureaucracies themselves.

Building Membership

In the last analysis, the effectiveness of all the strategies and tactics of the leaders of the organized bureaucracies depends on the organizations' capacities to attract and hold a substantial body of members. The bureaucratic leader has three major choices. He may organize the group around an agency, including all ranks and functional types of personnel, or almost all of them (which is the case, for example, with the police and fire associations). Such a leader may also use a federation of associations to recognize the hierarchical rank of the members (as fire lieutenants or police captains, for example). He may organize the group around a functional group—a profession, a specialized part of a profession, or a subprofessional field of work, or around a skill or craft—as social workers, or engineers and architects, or electricians. Or he may aspire to organize an inclusive citywide membership, inviting all members of the bureaucracies to join, regardless of agency, function, or occupation.

These choices bring varying dilemmas. All choices are beset by intra-bureaucratic rivalries within the agency staffs (differences of rank, of function, of status under the personnel rules) and are often caught up in intralabor-movement jurisdictional competition. Each choice must also be made in the absence of a firm and unambiguous labor or employee relations policy on the part of the city government. The more striking historical successes have belonged to the organizations that have concentrated on a single agency, but the rise of labor-affiliated organizations in recent years may point to increasing advantages for the more inclusive membership type of organization. Meanwhile the leaders of organized bureaucracies make their choices in an environment of uncertainty.

Since New York City bureaucrats, like most Americans, engage in a rich associational life, they characteristically belong to other types of organizations related in other ways to their place and kind of work in the bureaucracy. Some are fraternal organizations that are primarily social, others are religious groups, and still others are ethnic societies, reinforcing and preserving the sense of nationality. But these groups are not the primary instruments for participation by the bureaucracies in the city's political contest, although they do sometimes engage in it. It is chiefly the occupational groups previously described that provide the most persistent and effective associations for bureaucratic purposes *per se.*

Participating in Formal Proceedings

The city's bureaucracies, in their organized manifestations, do not conform to the stereotype of the anonymous, voiceless civil servant. Their representatives and spokesmen are among the most constant, sometimes among the most strident, participants in the formal public proceedings of the city government and, somewhat less often, in comparable proceedings of the state government. On these formal occasions the bureaucracies attempt openly to assert their general political power, to impress officialdom with the strength of their numbers, to appeal to their latent public support, and to assemble their allies in the political contest for a show of unity and determination. These are also opportunities for the leaders of employee groups to demonstrate to their members the worth of organization, to recruit new members in competition with other organized groups, and to compensate with public access to officialdom for whatever they may lack in informal access.

The formal proceedings in which the leaders participate are both general and specialized. Some concentrate on particular governmental institutions. The leaders of organized teachers' groups focus their formal appearances upon the Board of Education, the state legislature, and the Board of Estimate. Leaders of the police and fire bureaucracies center their attention upon the

Board of Estimate, the state legislature, and, less frequently, upon such proceedings as take place before the Civil Service Commission and the Budget Director. The leaders of organized bureaucracies affiliated with labor unions tend to concentrate upon proceedings before the Board of Estimate, the Comptroller, the Budget Director, the Labor Department. Others are regular participants in the hearings of the Civil Service Commission, while all use the opportunities afforded by departmental hearings on grievances or disciplinary cases. And each holds in reserve, and occasionally uses, the formal proceedings of the courts to gain or protect some right of the organization or its individual members.

The stakes most frequently sought in these formal proceedings are related to the personnel systems. Salaries and wages, pensions and retirement, hours and conditions of work, promotion and advancement opportunities—these are the hardy perennials of their presentations and demands. They seek status and prestige also, but the drive for autonomy is mainly through other channels.

In their use of formal proceedings, the leaders resort to a variety of techniques. They may appear in mass and offer a long list of rank-and-file speakers. They may borrow the methods of labor unions, and picket the hearings before, during, and after their formal presentation, seeking to dramatize or intimidate. They may speak in impassioned tones or calmly, spontaneously or systematically, through their own leaders or through their lawyers. The choice of tactics will depend upon the nature of the forum, the personalities of the leaders, or the emotional involvement of the membership in the issue. The minimum objective is to influence the pending decision.

Using Informal Bargaining

Formal proceedings are supplemented by informal contacts with members of the officialdom, with political party leaders, with interest group leaders, or with other strategically placed bureaucratic leaders. The smaller organized bureaucracies depend largely upon such contacts, the groups organized as professional associations have a predisposition toward these less visible forms of influence in preference to the more formal and overt "labor union" methods, and the party-oriented organizations (for example, the Civil Service Forum) have a tradition of seeking their goals informally. But the leaders of all organized bureaucracies, and of some relatively unorganized groupings, use whatever informal contacts they have and work toward increasing their number and effectiveness.

The informal bargaining process has some important attractions. It is flexible and tentative. The participants can probe the contingencies, minimize their risks, modify the terms of their mutual commitments—in short, deal comfortably with each other.

Publicity

The city's bureaucracies, in common with all other participants in the political contest, wield influence through publicity. They are not dependent alone upon publicity in the daily newspapers which they can generate by appearing in the formal proceedings of the city and state governments, although this publicity is of considerable importance to them. They have at least three additional resources: their own press (which is addressed primarily to their own members but is read also by others), the "civil service" weeklies, and the "civil service" columns in the city's daily newspapers. In addition, several organized bureaucracies have their own public relations officers whose function is to secure favorable publicity in other ways.

The majority of the city's organized bureaucracies publish a newspaper, newsletter, or magazine for circulation among their membership. The primary purpose is to retain membership, keep members informed, build their morale, alert them to issues and opportunities for organization action. But they are intended to serve other purposes as well: to recruit additional members and to influence the readers among the officialdom and other interest group leaders (especially among the relevant constituency interest groups). In general, the leaders of the organized bureaucracies provide a greater quantity of information for their members than do the party leaders or the other interest group leaders for their memberships.

The civil service weeklies are another publicity resource for the leaders of the city's bureaucracies. For more than fifty years *The Chief* has had a wide audience among the bureaucracies and officialdom. For several decades it was linked closely to the political career of its publisher, Frank J. Prial, and to the Civil Service Forum. More recently it has also been affiliated informally with the State, County, and Municipal Employees, an AFL-CIO organization. But its influence has been broader than these ties would at first suggest. From 1914 to 1939 it was the most important single factor in the whole climate of the city bureaucracy, whose aspirations, expectations, and tactics were largely set by *The Chief*. Especially from 1918 to 1934, this weekly closely monitored the decisions and practices of the Civil Service Commission, enjoyed almost exclusive access to the Commission's newsworthy actions, praising its performance or thundering disapproval when the Commission departed from the preferences of the Forum. For the two decades since 1937, *The Civil Service Leader* has shared this role and competed for dominance in its exercise. Established with the encouragement of the La Guardia-appointed members of the Commission, *The Leader* has been associated with the political career of Jerry Finkelstein (who was prominent in the O'Dwyer administration), has been linked most consistently with the associations of state government employees, but has also been an important factor in the life of the organized bureaucracies of the city. These two weeklies are important forces in shaping bureaucratic sentiments and attitudes, in marshaling pressure before the Civil Service Commission and the Personnel Department in favor of or against proposals, and in influencing the attitudes of those members of officialdom who depend upon *The Chief* and *The Leader* to reflect the preferences of the city's bureaucracies. While some organizations appear to have preferred access to their pages, the weeklies are sufficiently competitive with each other, and their columns adequately open, to give the majority of the organized bureaucracies a medium of useful, and in some instances indispensable, publicity.

The leaders of the city's bureaucracies cannot match either officialdom or the nongovernmental interest groups in their publicity resources. Nevertheless, they possess impressive capacities to make their voices heard—more clearly by officialdom than by the general public, it is true, but it is the ear of officialdom which they most desire.

Representation and Bargaining

A relatively new strategy for the city's bureaucracies is provided by the recent establishment of representation and bargaining arrangements to determine many city government personnel policies and practices. This device, borrowed from the general labor movement and amounting to an adaptation of collective bargaining, is of increasing importance to the large bureaucratic formations in the city government, especially to those formally affiliated with labor unions. It provides a new instrument for participation by the leaders of the bureaucracies in personnel decision-making; it adds greatly to their claims to legitimacy as participants in the decision-making process; and, increasingly, it puts in the terms of a formal agreement the concessions and gains which were previously subject to the uncertainties of informal understandings and pledges.

The formal recognition of employee organizations, especially any proposal for exclusive recognition as bargaining representation and the signing of formal agreements with such employee organizations, was long resisted by city officialdom and by most other participants as illegal, improper, or impractical. The resistance gradually gave way before the persistent drive of employee organizations aided by the general labor movement, first in the administration of the "prevailing rate" wage provisions for skilled workers in the state Labor Law, and then in negotiations with the city's transit employees. But the Wagner administration, beginning in 1954, has accelerated this trend by establishing a broad new policy to encourage the organization of employees, to give formal and exclusive recognition to groups representing a majority of employees in a designated bargaining unit, and to require that each agency under the Mayor's jurisdiction establish a system and procedure for conducting labor-management relations between the agency and its employee organizations. This policy was first introduced as an "interim order" issued by Mayor Wagner in 1954. After more than three years of experience, the policy was made a permanent one by the Mayor's issuance of an executive order in March, 1958. The interim order of 1954 was given greater substance and impetus by Board of Estimate approval in 1956 of a dues "check off" system for certain employee organizations, an arrangement under which the city government deducts the dues from the employees' pay checks and transfers them to the organization.

The city Labor Department is the main formal source of these new policies (although the Mayor's personal interest and support are indicated in the phrase "Little Wagner Act," frequently applied to the 1958 executive order). The Department is also the agency which issues the certificate of exclusive bargaining representation, giving to the recognized organization a monopoly of representation for a year and being subject to renewal. The Department is, in addition, the author of the main outlines of the labor-management system and procedures in the agencies. The emphasis of the Department is upon the hearing and disposition of "grievances," an elastic term which the leaders of the organized bureaucracies are just beginning to explore.

Recognition of exclusive bargaining representation leads into the more difficult question: How shall the bargain be formalized between the city government and the employee organization? Both city officials and leaders of organized bureaucracies approach with caution the idea of a formal contract comparable to those signed by labor and management in the private realm. Legal complexities and uncertainties inhibit the officials. Leaders of the employee organizations are not certain they want to put all their eggs into the contract basket. Their many assets in other directions (especially their capacity to deal with the state legislature, the Board of Estimate, and the Mayor, for example) might be forfeited in part or altogether. The result is usually a formal memorandum of understanding issued by city officials; if it requires employee consent, then each employee may sign it as an individual.

These new policies present differential strategic opportunities to the leaders of different types of organized bureaucracies. They are most attractive to groups like the transport workers or the sanitation employees. It was not an accident that the first certificate of exclusive recognition was issued by the Labor Department to the uniformed Sanitationmen's Association, a Teamsters' affiliate (the Transit Authority, being a public authority with great autonomy, had earlier given the Transport Workers Union such recognition). The new opportunities are less congenial to leaders of groups whose members have strong professional aspirations (as do the teachers and the social workers) and to leaders of groups who have long relied upon bargaining with party leaders, legislators, and other officials (as has the Civil Service Forum). The new policies, however, may be modified to suit the sensitivities of the professional groups. Teachers, for example, have had since 1952 a formal "staff relations" understanding with the Board of Education, an understanding embodying some of the elements of formal labor-management agreements. The new arrangements under the city's Department of Labor will be most enthusiastically embraced by those labor-oriented groups commanding a clear majority in a designated bargaining unit.

These new opportunities will not supplant the more traditional modes of influence used by leaders of the organized bureaucracies. For them, the new forms of recognition and bargaining will be an important additional weapon but not a full substitute for their present advantages. All of them will no doubt seek to increase, to conserve, and to use fully their other resources as participants in the city's political process: their present statutory advantages, their access to city officials, their roles as influential constituencies of the Department of Personnel and the Department of Labor, and their alliances with other participants. These more political modes of their influence will continue to be important.

Influencing Public Policy

The leaders of the organized bureaucracies concentrate their attention and efforts primarily upon the city's personnel system in all its many ramifications, giving only occasional attention to other aspects of public policy. The Transport Workers Union, however, expressed its strong views against the proposed sale of city-owned power plants, on questions of the subway fare, and on the extent of city-owned and city-operated bus systems. The leaders of associations of welfare employees hold and often publicly express explicit policy positions concerning the levels of public assistance to families on relief. The organization of Correction Department officers is concerned about the public policy which defines the nature of prisoner custody. The teachers' organizations are interested in public policies determining, for example, the kinds and functions of the high schools in the city's school system. But these are usually secondary preoccupations of the leaders of the organized bureaucracies.

The impact of the organized bureaucracies and their leaders upon public policy is largely indirect. It is achieved often through the separate actions of the individual bureaucrats as members of the departments and agencies of the city government. But the nexus between the leaders of the organized bureaucracies and the actions of the bureaucrats in the formal governmental hierarchy is a strong and important one: it is the leaders who have largely created the climate of autonomy and the values of the closed bureaucracies within which the individual bureaucrats express their preferences and exercise their influence in public policy.

Providing Information and Alternatives

The decisions of the city government are promulgated by the elected and the higher appointed officials, but these decisions are usually based upon information and alternative recommendations provided in large part by the city's bureaucrats. These resources and opportunities of bureaucrats within the official city hierarchy supplement the influence of the leaders of the organized bureaucracies. The amount and kind of information, the method of presentation, the manner in which alternatives are identified and appraised, and the making of, or abstention from, recommendations—all provide opportunities for the bureaucracies to impress their own discretion and preferences on the decisions as promulgated. The members of the city's bureaucracies, especially those who have won their way to the higher posts, are aware of this fact and are sophisticated practitioners in the use of information and of alternatives to guide decision-making by officialdom. In their exercise of such influence they are usually relieved of any sense of usurpation by a conviction that, as "experts" with more knowledge and experience in the situation than most officials, the bureaucrats are the best judges of what is desirable and feasible.

The bureaucracies do not have an undisputed monopoly over the information and the alternative lines of action which the officials have before them when they consider a problem and make their formal decisions. The interest groups, the newspapers, and other communication media provide a frequently competitive stream of information and advice. The Mayor or a commissioner may augment this resource by appointing an *ad hoc* committee to bring him a systematic report of findings or recommendations, a committee on which bureaucratic members may be balanced by others, or outnumbered by outsiders, or from which bureaucratic members may be excluded. Public hearings may serve a similar purpose for officials by exposing the information and advice from the bureaucracy to the test of outside appraisal. But these are methods which the Mayor or other officials lack energy, time, and resources to apply to most decisions. For the great majority the officials are heavily dependent upon information and advice from the bureaucracies.

The bureaucracies frequently compete with each other in the information and advice they give officials. Thus the social worker (or welfare) bureaucrats will stress one set of information and alternatives of action, the police bureaucrats another, when dealing, for example, with the causes and remedies for juvenile delinquency. This competition gives the officials some greater freedom of choice on occasion, but the result is quite often a stalemate unless the Mayor, commissioner, or other official as the case may be has an additional source of information and advice. Such a source, especially a source which will appraise the situation from the perspective of the official, is frequently lacking.

On the other hand, the bureaucracies do not compete on a great number of decisions. Within a particular department, a single bureaucratic group may have an effective monopoly of information and advice over decisions in its category of work. Issues which rise to the Mayor or the Board of Estimate are more likely to invite competitive advice, but even most of these will be presented in terms of information and recommendation provided mainly by the bureaucracies most concerned.

The city's bureaucrats are skilled practitioners in the art of presenting information which controls the range of choice open to officials. The useful techniques are many. The information may be incomplete, omitting data which point away from the preferred decision. It may be overdetailed, confusing the official until he is led to clear ground by the recommendation preferred by the reporter. The report may omit alternative solutions, driving exclusively at the bureaucracy's recommendation, or it may subject an alternative proposal to devastating criticism, while leaving the preferred solution unexamined. There are a hundred variations and combinations. The objective is constant: to guide the official's decision into the channels which the bureaucrats regard as wise and prudent. Nor is this a consciously Machiavellian game or a mere expression of agency bias. Instead, it is for most of them a proved technique for guarding the public interest as they perceive it.

Translating Decision Into Performance

The resources of the leaders of the organized bureaucracies are supplemented in still another way. The city's bureaucracies are the instruments through which the formal policy decisions of the city officials are transformed into concrete acts of performance, the day-to-day work of the city's governmental agencies. In formal theory, this role is frequently described as being purely ministerial, devoid of discretion and choice. The bureaucrat is thought of as the arms and legs, not the directing brain but the automaton, guided by the official decision. In reality, it is in execution that the bureaucrats have their most nearly complete monopoly and their greatest autonomy in affecting policy. They give shape and meaning to the official decisions, and they do so under conditions favorable to them. Here the initiative and discretion lie in their hands; others must influence them.

Three major sources of influence must be contended with by the bureaucrats if they are to maximize their autonomous role in translating decisions into performance: executive and legislative officials, constituency interest groups, and the courts.

Executive and legislative officials frequently attempt to make each decision or policy an unambiguous instruction. But this is always difficult, often impossible, and the passage of time almost always works on the side of the bureaucrats by soon turning a clear instruction into an ambiguous one. In many instances, too, the officials find an ambiguous decision more prudent for them than an unequivocal one. And, in their participation in the decision-making process, the bureaucrats find frequent opportunities to encourage delegation of power and discretion to themselves and to discourage issuance of binding instructions. Finally, flexibility and discretion in administration have many supporters among all the participants in the city's political process. Thus bureaucratic influence is preserved. Even when executive and legislative officials accompany their policy instructions with procedural requirements, intended to restrain the autonomy of the bureaucracies, the situation may remain unchanged, for although these have their limited effectiveness, they too are subject to obsolescence and to unanticipated consequences. The bureaucracies are skilled at absorbing these procedures into their own autonomous systems of behavior.

The officials have a second method of controlling the discretion of bureaucrats. This is the machinery of supervision. Here the main burden falls upon the executive officials, although legislators may use the appropriating and investigating powers to make their sanctions felt. In their search for autonomy the city bureaucracies profit considerably from the rivalry between executive and legislative institutions (for example, between the Mayor and the Board of Estimate) in their competitive supervisory aims and efforts. Advantage flows to the bureaucracies also from the limited reach of super-vision over the majority of their actions (the supervisor cannot monitor every decision, or often even a majority of them). But the city's bureaucracies profit even more from their gradual absorption of the supervisory posts by members of the bureaucracy itself. A supervisor (at the bureau chief level, for example) who has long been and still remains a member of a close-knit bureaucracy takes an affirmative view of the autonomous role of himself and his colleagues in carrying out the decisions of higher officialdom.

The leaders of the city's bureaucracies must also find a level of accommodation with the constituency interest groups that each of them confronts and upon whose support many of them heavily depend. This accommodation will vary from major concessions to quite minor ones. The interest groups use many of the same devices as officialdom in their efforts to control the discretion of the bureaucracies with which they are most concerned. They strive frequently for tight policy guides in law or in executive instructions, they urge procedural controls, and they alert executives and legislators to the need for closer supervision. But they do more: they use all the sanctions at their disposal, including the weapon of publicity, the threat of the withdrawal of their support, and the persuasiveness of their personal contacts. Their main limitation is the specialization of their interest and their actions; many, and in some situations most, of the actions of bureaucrats are outside the supervision of potent interest groups. Nevertheless, the leaders of the city's bureaucracies probably concede more of their autonomy to their interest group constituencies than to officialdom.

The courts are another source of control over bureaucratic discretion in carrying out policy decisions. The judges have opportunities to give their own precise interpretation to ambiguous policy instructions, to hold the bureaucrats to the procedural requirements of laws and executive orders, to modify these requirements in terms of due process or statutory interpretation, to add procedural restraints of their own, and on occasion to admonish or punish bureaucrats for actions they deem an abuse of discretion. These are important controls, but in most instances their quantitative coverage of the discretionary acts of the bureaucracies is highly limited. Some bureaucrats are for all practical purposes immune to such supervision, others have little difficulty in anticipating it, while a few are made continuously conscious of its presence.

The city's bureaucrats enjoy their most autonomous role in translating the decisions of officialdom into performance. Their central position in this process makes them the leading arbiters of what abstract policy will mean in concrete action. As arbiters, they are agents of their own values and goals, not merely the hired instruments of others.

STRATEGIES AND TACTICS OF PARTICULAR ORGANIZED BUREAUCRACIES

The Teachers' Organizations

For more than forty years the teachers in the public schools of New York City have stood poised in some uncertainty between reliance upon professional societies or affiliation with the organized labor movement. Their decisions about association have continued to favor professional groups, but many teachers have chosen to belong to both a professional society and a labor union affiliate. This choice has been open to them since 1916, when the Teachers' Union of New York City became Local 5 of the American Federation of Teachers, AFL. In 1935 the Teachers' Guild was organized by an insurgent group in protest against the left-wing ties of the Teachers' Union, and in 1941, upon the expulsion of the latter from the AFT, the Guild became the AFL affiliate. Neither the Union nor the Guild, nor the two together, ever commanded a majority membership among the teachers, although they have provided much of the militancy and the strategy to the whole array of teachers' groups.

The most characteristic attribute of the teachers' organizations is their division into specialized and fragmented associations: into associations of elementary-school teachers, junior-high teachers, high-school teachers; borough groups (for example, the Brooklyn Teachers' Association); associations of principals, of superintendents, and so on; subject-matter associations (teachers of mathematics, history, and so on); and into even more specialized groups. The total evidently exceeds one hundred. Multiple group membership is widespread. Professional specialization, and the enhancement or protection of the status of each specialized group, are the mainsprings of diversity and fragmentation.

Certain of these teacher groups are large and cohesive; some are large and uncohesive; some are small and cohesive. For twenty years (1916–1935) the Teachers' Union attempted to weld the diverse groups into "a single union," and for more than twenty years (1935–1959) the Teachers' Guild has tried for the same goal of unity. A consequence of this and related forces has been an approach to centralization in the form of the Joint Committee of Teachers' Organizations, an arrangement established in 1924, representing 65 teacher associations with a claimed combined membership of 28,000. But the Teachers' Guild is not a member of the Joint Committee, nor is the High School Teachers' Association, and these two organizations claim to represent 15,000 and 8,000 teachers respectively. Competition, independence in action, and separatist goals on many issues are thus more normal than cooperation among the teachers. Their conflicts, however, are more dramatic and noticeable than are the steady lines of consistency which run through the majority of their separately asserted demands. The full consequences of their diverse organizational activities make the teachers an extraordinarily successful bureaucratic constellation. As participants in the political contest they have many assets, are never without strength, and their leaders often are the dominant partners in educational decision-making.

In their participation in the political contest the leaders of the teachers' organizations look first to Albany. The Joint Committee finds allies there by collaborating with teachers of other school jurisdictions in the state, while the Guild gets assistance from the labor unions. Both find a Republican legislature tolerant, and sometimes generous, toward the teachers' aspirations for decisions which will limit the discretion, or direct the action, of the New York City officials, who are usually Democrats. The concentration upon the state legislature by the teachers' organizations takes, first, the form of placing in the state Education Law the detailed personnel provisions all bureaucracies find desirable—spelling out the methods and standards of selection, of compensation, of tenure and retirement, of conditions of work, and so on. Second, the legislature has been, and continues to be, encouraged and influenced by the teachers' groups to make the State Department of Education an additional and independent channel of access and appeal for the review of decisions by the New York City Board of Education or its officials, decisions which the teachers' organizations sometimes find unpalatable. Third, the leaders of the teachers' groups are interested and often influential in the legislature's decisions on grants of funds to the city for educational purposes. In Albany, too, the leaders of the teachers' organizations must make certain that the Governor will not veto, or perhaps can be enlisted to support, the actions they seek from the legislature. They must also maintain their contacts with the Commissioner of Education and his assistants, but here they can count on the fellowship of the whole educational bureaucracy, state and city. In all these relationships, the leaders of the Joint Committee appear to have access superior to that of the Guild. In short, the teachers' organizations return annually from Albany with more assets than liabilities. The content of the Education Law, the usual benevolence of the Governor, the fraternal attitudes of the State Department of Education, are all testimony to the rewarding status of the leaders of the teachers' organizations as experienced participants in the political process.

At home, the leaders of the teachers' organizations focus their attention upon the Board of Education, the Board of Superintendents, the Board of Examiners, and the Teachers' Retirement Board. Here, too, their influence is strong and their capacity for controlling their environment considerable. The Board of Education, an unsalaried body whose members are appointed by the Mayor for seven-year staggered terms and are removable by him only on formal charges, is given by the Education Law and by prevailing educational doctrine a marked degree of autonomy in relationship to the Mayor and other city officials. This autonomy generally shields the Board from city officialdom (indeed, tends to isolate it from both help and hindrance), but it does not shield the Board from the leaders of the teachers' organizations or from the outside interest groups in the Board's constituency. The leaders of the organized teachers have not been able to secure membership on the Board for their own members (Johanna M. Lindhof, president of the Kindergarten-6B Teachers' Association, a member of the Board from 1936 to 1943, being the sole exception), but in most matters they have a powerful, frequently a dominant, voice in the Board's decisions. The Board itself has limited discretion in curriculum questions; what the state Education Law and the state Education Commissioner leave for local choice, the leaders of the teachers' groups can strongly influence. The Board has even less discretion in personnel matters. The controls issued from Albany in state law and rules developed largely under the influence of the leaders of the teachers' organizations themselves bind the discretion of the Board to procedures and policies the leaders of the teachers prefer. If they cannot move the Board to take all the action the teachers want, they can achieve their alternative goal: the Board is immobilized in any effort to move in directions the leaders of the teachers strongly resist.

The Board of Superintendents (composed of the Superintendent of Schools, the Deputy Superintendent, and eight Associate Superintendents) is the full-time policy and managerial head of the city's school system. With it, the leaders of the teachers' organizations, especially the Joint Committee, have even more satisfactory terms of access and influence. The superintendents are themselves products of the New York City educational bureaucracy; no "new blood" from other systems has troubled them for more than a generation. Graduates from, and still at least nominal members of, the teachers' organizations with whom they deal, the superintendents may not please the bureaucracies in their every decision, but they are committed to the same traditions and practices, and the leaders of the teachers' organizations have infrequent cause to fear them as a source of innovation and change. There is, too, the additional insurance of the detailed controls of the state Education Law and the state Education Commissioner.

The Board of Examiners, a unique institution in American education, is at once a civil service reformer's dream, a bureaucrat's delight, and an official's nightmare. Composed of nine members (eight with permanent tenure, the ninth being the Superintendent or an Associate representing the Superintendent), this Board has by statute a semiautonomous status in relation to the Board of Education and the Board of Superintendents. It administers competitive and qualifying examinations to all teacher applicants and to all candidates for promotion up through the rank of principal. The application by the Board of Examiners of the "promotion from within" doctrine, so affectionately regarded by all bureaucratic groups, is zealously pursued, with the consequence that the New York City educational bureaucracy is apparently more tightly closed than any other in the United States. The membership of the Board of Examiners itself is recruited from within the bureaucracy it serves. When this cherished practice was broken in the one instance on record (in 1937), the appointment of the outsider (who had earlier been a member of the system) was contested in litigation carried to the Court of Appeals.

The Teachers' Retirement Board is designed to preserve the separate character of the educational retirement system, to protect it from adulteration of its benefits and traditions by contact with other retirement systems, and to provide it with an administration in which the teachers have an effective voice. A seven-member body, it has three teacher members elected by members of the Teachers' Retirement Association for three-year terms. The President of the Board of Education and the Comptroller are *ex officio* members; the other two, one of whom must be a member of the Board of Education, are appointed and removable at pleasure by the Mayor.

The leaders of the organized teachers have at 110 Livingston Street in Brooklyn (the headquarters of the Boards of Education, Superintendents, and Examiners), as they have in Albany, the status of effective, even pre-ferred, participants in the political process. It is only when they move toward City Hall that they meet strong competition, although still as powerful participants.

It is the "expense" budget (not the "capital" budget, for the teachers' organizations do not much concern themselves with how many schools will be built, nor with the kind and location) that brings the teachers' organiza-tions to City Hall, seeking to increase the numbers of teachers, their salaries, or otherwise improve their status. They bring with them both their gains made at Albany (salary schedules in the Education Law, the grants-in-aid or expectations thereof) and almost invariably the support of the Boards of Education and Superintendents. But they are nevertheless vulnerable. In the first place, they are frequently divided among themselves; they usually cannot agree upon a unified salary policy. The high-school teachers want more than elementary teachers are to get, while the Guild and the elementary groups want a single salary schedule for all teachers. The principals want a wider margin of salary than the teachers approve, and other groups have their own divisive demands. In the second place, the leaders of the teachers' organizations confront a Mayor, a Budget Director, and a Board of Estimate all harassed by a tight budget. A host of other bureaucracies, joined by the officials of their respective agencies and their supporting constituency interest groups, are also present, demanding their full share of scarce budget dollars, and the teachers are also met by the resisting voices of the tax-paying interest groups, asserting the merits of economy and the risks of taxation. Third, the teachers' organizations are comparative strangers to the official-dom and the other participants at City Hall. The costs of their flirtations at Albany and of their aloofness most of the year in their isolated fiefdom at 110 Livingston Street are now levied against the leaders of the teachers' organizations. Conscious of their vulnerability, these leaders often drop their professional etiquette and resort to massed demonstrations of numerical strength, to picketing, to boycotts of extracurricular duties, and to other displays of frustration and intransigence. In this way they sometimes lose the support of their own friendly interest groups (the parents' associations and others) and stiffen City Hall resistance. The leaders of the teachers' organizations leave City Hall with some gains but often badly bruised in status and further divided among themselves. It is at City Hall that the leaders of the teachers' organizations are most regularly reminded of the pluralistic character of New York City's politics, of the costs and limitations of their isolation from the general political contest, and of the curbs which democratic politics place upon the aspirations for autonomy held by any bureaucracy, even the one which has developed the most systematic ration-alization of its immunity from supervision.

When the record of the city's teachers' organizations as participants in the political contest at Albany, at 110 Livingston Street, and at City Hall is balanced, the result is testimony to their comparative success in achieving bureaucratic goals. Despite fragmentation, divisiveness, and internal competition, conflicts which are costly to their combined potential power, they have enhanced their status and prestige (compensating for their wounds at City Hall with triumphs elsewhere), they have a satisfying control over their own personnel system and their career opportunities, and they have established for themselves an autonomy in the determination of educational policy and procedure which the leaders and members of most other bureaucracies must envy.

The Police and Fire Organizations

The organizations of policemen and firemen in New York City began in the early 1890's as "benevolent" associations, and their formative years extend down to 1914. They have never possessed the self-conscious "professional" aspirations so strong with the teachers, but they too have confronted the dilemma of "unionization." For the firemen, this question was answered affirmatively in 1918 by affiliation with the AFL. The police have been inhibited in such inclination by law and tradition, and their associations have continued to be divorced from the labor movement.

Police and fire personnel have avoided the pronounced fragmentation of the teachers in their organizational development. Each rank has its separate association in each department. These, however, are not only less numerous than the teachers' subdivisions, but there has been a further tendency toward unification provided by the tradition that the two largest associations (the Patrolmen's Benevolent Association for the police and the Uniformed Firemen's Association for the firemen) should take the lead for the others in the political contest. The Joint Council for all city police and fire organizations has also served to bridge the separate aims of the different organizations more effectively than has the Joint Committee for the teachers. But there are nonetheless some major separatist tendencies. The officer associations (inspectors, captains, lieutenants, battalion chiefs) frequently diverge from the rank-and-file groups in each department, especially in terms of immediate goals. Each association prefers to live so far as possible a separate group life, and this leads to some constant differentiation of role for the leaders of each. There is the further fact that the fire organizations may look toward the labor movement for allies, while the police must find theirs elsewhere.

The leaders of the city's police and fire associations are experienced and strategically placed participants in the political contest. The police forces were, so to speak, born in politics, served a long apprenticeship as the indentured servants of the party organizations, and continue to exercise powers of the most intimate concern to party leaders. The fire forces, growing out of volunteer fire groups, were also initially intimately bound to the party organizations. Considering these origins, the leaders of the police and fire associations have placed a surprising distance between themselves and the party leaders. The party leaders continue to court them because of the sanctions which the police can impose and the privileges they can bestow in their discretion, and because of the strength in numbers, strategically distributed over the city, which both the police and the fire forces represent. Firemen, too, have their important acts of discretion (in inspection, for example), and they have leisure hours which, long ago at least, could be devoted to the party. But the main drive of the police and fire groups, as with almost all bureaucratic groups, is toward an autonomous, not a subordinate or even a committed, relationship to the party organizations.

The leaders of the police and fire organizations as participants in the city's political process look first, as do the teachers, to Albany, where they enjoy some basic advantages. This tradition was firmly established before the "home rule" acts gave the city government power to do many things the associations wished, and their leaders have never been persuaded of the logic of abandoning Albany. To the state legislature they have gone for a variety of gains and protections: hours of work, pension rights, rates of pay, promotion procedures, relief from liability, and other elements of their personnel system. If they have not succeeded in securing a parallel to the Education Law, neither have they returned annually from Albany emptyhanded. What they have gained gives them leverage; and the existence of the Albany channel of access is always an additional, alternative line.

The leaders of the police and fire associations focus their attention most continuously upon their own agencies—the top command of the Police and Fire Departments. Here their first aim has been to reduce, as drastically as they can, the access of outsiders to the decision-making process and to absorb the supervisory and executive ranks of the two departments into their own bureaucratic system. With the aid of the state legislature, the approval of civil service reformers and the newspapers and other communication media, the indulgence of the Civil Service Commission, and the gradual concessions of hard-pressed Mayors, they have succeeded, perhaps even beyond their own expectations. The two departments are now closed in the most exact sense. The police and fire bureaucracies are supervised and directed by officers and officials whom they recognize and regard as "their own," whose values and capacities they understand and whose decisions they feel confident they can anticipate, contain, or manipulate if the temptations of departmental top leadership should lead to idiosyncrasy and disregard of accepted routines of policy or practice. The virus of "new

blood," that carrier of new doctrines and new technology, is now limited to
the newest recruits, at the lowest rank, where its contagion can be slowed
by the low temperatures of long indoctrination before freedom of movement
is allowed. In the Police Department, the closed system now extends by
accepted custom up to and including the Commissioner, with only one or
two secondary posts of limited assignment open to outsiders. In the Fire
Department, the custom does not yet so regularly include the Commissioner,
but he is isolated from the uniformed staff and the trend is evidently toward
the absorption of his post into the bureaucracy.

Police and Fire Commissioners and their "high brass" associates have
their occasional respective differences with the leaders of the police and fire
associations, but the associations have nevertheless steadily cemented their
command over the terms and conditions of their personnel system. In
pursuit of this goal, the leaders of the associations have profited from the
state constitutional guarantees of a competitive merit system, the general
provisions of the state Civil Service Law, plus some special statutory provisions for the police and fire forces, and they have exercised some of their
most persuasive influence on the city's Personnel Department and Civil
Service Commission. Promotion to all ranks in the Fire Department (including the position of Fire Chief, second in command under the Commissioner)
is by competitive examination limited to members of the next lower rank,
the examination being conducted by the city's Personnel Department, and
seniority being usually decisive in the rating. In the Police Department,
competitive examinations of like character control all promotions through
the rank of Captain (except for detectives) and all higher positions in the
force must be filled from the ranks of Captains. Dismissals in each force are
inhibited by special statutory safeguards. Each force has a special and
separate pension fund, each with a board on which the respective associations
are represented.

As with the teachers' organizations, it is when they move toward City
Hall as participants in the city's political contest that the leaders of the
police and fire bureaucracies encounter most resistance. And it is also
primarily budget questions which bring them to the Mayor and the Board
of Estimate: higher salaries, hours of work, pension contributions, retirement
rights; whether the city should have more policemen and firemen, or higher
paid men on shorter tours of duty. The leaders of the police and fire associations are usually better united on such issues than the teachers are, and
they usually have the support of their Commissioners (although these
officials will tend to urge additions to their manpower quotas more consistently than higher wages or shorter work weeks), but they encounter other
competing agencies, bureaucracies, and interest groups pleading before a

Mayor and a Board with limited budget resources. The "economy" interest groups are more tolerant with police and fire groups than they are with the teachers, but they tend also to prefer greater manpower over higher wages or fewer hours. The result is frequent frustration for the members of the associations, belligerent tactics by their leaders, delay and avoidance by officialdom. (A favored strategy of the 1920's and 1930's was to refer the issue to popular referendum by the voters of the city, the associations winning while the officials not only saved money by the delay but transferred the onus of the costs to "the people.")

The leaders of the police and fire associations have other business to transact at City Hall. Police graft and irregularities are an endemic and perennial phenomenon, and the fire forces, in their inspection and licensing duties, are periodically susceptible. The Commissioner of Investigation and his staff (not without some competition from the District Attorneys) are normally the instruments of exposure and sanctions. The leaders of the police and fire associations (themselves sometimes the subject of investigation) seek usually to avoid involvement; but they will often speak in defense of their members, referring eloquently to "a few rotten apples," or, if the net of investigation spreads wide, they are likely to charge that the inquiries are "vindictive," "fishing expeditions," or "lynching parties." Even Mayors are not always immune from such attacks by the leaders of the associations.

Police and fire association leaders are decreasingly tempted to form overt alliances with party leaders. Old associations and traditions are not easily dissolved, but the association members tend to view major commitments or concessions to party leaders as hazardous for their own association leaders and unfruitful for the rank-and-file members. Newer channels and modes of influence are more stable and more rewarding. Close alliance with party leaders is an adventure which most bureaucrats would prefer to confine to the lone wolf bureaucrat, or to the tactical necessities of the day, excluding such alliance from the agenda of their major associational strategy.

The leaders of the police and fire associations live a more beleaguered life as political contestants than do the leaders of the teachers' groups, but they do not need to envy many other city bureaucracies. They have influential access at Albany; they are usually viewed with tolerance by the newspapers (for which their members provide more drama and color than do other bureaucracies); the "economy" groups are more indulgent toward them; they have largely achieved their goals in their closed personnel systems; and they are more than ordinarily secure in their own "citadels," their own departments into which fewer and fewer outsiders (whether Mayors, other officials, party leaders, or interest groups) are allowed to intrude except on terms of deference and a willingness to subscribe to the established mores.

The Civil Service Forum

The Civil Service Forum provides a contrast in many respects with the teachers' organizations and the police and fire associations. For one thing, it has been throughout its history a party-oriented organization in the city's bureaucracies. Furthermore, its leaders have not concentrated attention upon the employees in any one agency or in any one occupational group; instead, they have sought to have Forum "councils" (or local units) in as many agencies and in as many occupational groups as possible. Nor have they tried energetically for great numbers of members, seeming to prefer the existence of a manageable nucleus of leaders and members in an agency or an occupational group who could assert representation of the whole. And, in further contrast, the Forum would appear to be on the decline, while the teachers' and the police and fire associations retain and increase their earlier vigor.

In formal arrangement, the Forum is a federation of "councils," usually one for each agency or for each occupational group. Some of these councils are composed of state or county government employees, and even a few composed of federal employees working in the city. But the preponderant number of councils are city employee groups. As a whole, the Forum claims to have 350 councils representing 15,000 employees. The councils pay nominal dues to the Forum; the individual members pay nominal dues to the councils. In this latter respect, the Forum is not unlike the teachers' associations and their Joint Committee. The result, for the Forum, is a tight leadership structure and a weak membership position.

The modes of influence relied upon by the leaders of the Forum have been primarily four: alliance with ("subordination to" is perhaps the more accurate phrase) a party-oriented leader, Frank J. Prial, and his close associates; privileged access to the city's Civil Service Commission; preparing or endorsing, and lobbying for the enactment of, personnel legislation at Albany; litigation in the courts for gains or protections to its membership. The Mayor, the Board of Estimate, and the Council have been lesser objects of attention, but not unimportant to the Forum leaders.

The rise and decline of the Civil Service Forum is, to a large degree, the story of the career of Frank J. Prial. That career had its formal beginnings in 1903 when Prial entered the city service as a competitive class employee (examiner of sewer claims, at $1,050; by 1909, he was earning $5,000). In 1910 he became President of the New York Civil Service Society, an organization of employees and, in the 1913 mayoralty elections, campaigned energetically for the Democratic ticket and against the Mitchel ticket. The Comptroller dismissed Prial as a consequence in 1914, whereupon he became a Deputy Commissioner of Labor in the state government. The administrative reforms of the new Mitchel regime aroused widespread uncertainties and fears among the city employees, providing Prial with an opportunity to launch a broader organization. In late 1914, Prial established the Civil Service Forum with the aid of Joseph J. O'Reilly, then owner and editor of *The Chief*, and Richard E. Enright, president of the Police Lieutenants Association. Prial became the Forum's president, holding the post until the late 1930's. The Forum became the prime weapon of the city employees against the Mitchel reforms, and, in 1917, Prial and Enright used it as a force for Hylan's successful candidacy for Mayor.

With Hylan's inauguration in 1918, Prial, the Forum, and Enright became insiders—Prial as a Deputy Comptroller (a post he held until 1934), Enright as Police Commissioner (the Forum being by this time primarily Prial's domain). Two years later, Prial bought *The Chief* from O'Reilly. Thus by 1920 Prial had constructed the base of his influence and power: he was a Deputy Comptroller with strategic access to the Board of Estimate, he was president of the Forum, he owned the civil service weekly, *The Chief*, and soon he added a fourth element, an alliance with the Delehanty Institute, the city's largest civil service "cram school." With these assets, Prial moved toward an influential role in the city's Democratic party. The Forum thereafter consistently endorsed that party's nominees for city office, and Prial regarded himself as one of its leaders. There were limits to his party role, however (he was not in the regular party hierarchy, but led a functional constituency in competition with the District Leaders), and in 1932 he could secure the nomination for Comptroller only through an insurgent candidacy in the primary. Thereafter, his star slowly declined, his political assets essentially reduced to *The Chief*, the Forum, and his alliance with Delehanty. For the Civil Service Forum, as an employee organization, the Prial career had meant that it had secured his official and party influence and the help of his newspaper (*The Chief*) at the price of becoming his agent—indeed, almost his personal possession—his career aims taking precedence over the Forum's own goals.

Concentration upon the city's Civil Service Commission has been the Forum's second preoccupation. From 1918 to 1935, Prial and *The Chief* could assure privileged access for the Forum to the Commission; after 1935, when the first La Guardia Civil Service Commissioners began to restrict and standardize this access, and especially after 1938, when the *Civil Service Leader* and the daily civil service newspaper columnists made their first appearance, Prial and *The Chief* could aid the Forum only with zealous criticism of the Commission, while the Forum was forced to share its once almost exclusive access with other employee organizations. After 1945 there was some restoration of the pre-1935 status, but in form more than substance. Nevertheless, the Forum continues to be a not unimportant influence in the decisions of the Personnel Department and the Civil Service Commission. From them, the Forum seeks decisions which will shape the city's personnel system in the direction of general bureaucratic goals: "promotion from within," emphasis on seniority as a criterion of advancement, restriction of managerial and supervisory discretion in assignments and supervision, protection of tenure—and, perhaps most importantly, decisions which will introduce the least amount of innovation in the personnel system.

To the membership, the leaders of the Forum have always emphasized the values of its legislative and litigation activities. It prepares an annual legislative program of bills to be introduced in the state legislature at Albany (and a few for action by the City Council and Board of Estimate). Its representatives are active at the legislative sessions, but they do not have the status of either the teachers' or the fire and police spokesmen. They must depend upon their personal contacts and upon chance alliances with other bureaucratic groups. The results of the Forum's legislative work are of uncertain dimensions, but it claims credit for much of the amending of the state Civil Service Law since 1920, a large amount of which restricts official discretion in personnel management. One of the Forum's most ambitious projects (the Wicks bill of 1935) would have subjected every act of the state and municipal Civil Service Commissions to judicial review. After objections had been filed by the state and city Civil Service Commissions, and by Mayor La Guardia, Governor Lehman vetoed the bill. This bill reflects the Forum's tendency to rely on the courts as much as on statutes, a strategy that fits the needs of an organization aspiring to deal with many agencies without having large membership in any, to make as many bargains as it can through party channels. Such an organization can use statutory efforts and litigation with more success than it can use bargaining techniques or systematic agreements with department heads. The courts and the legislature are, for the Forum, arenas in which much symbolic effort can be demonstrated, where failure can be variously explained, and where success, however formal, can be dramatically publicized.

The Civil Service Forum as a bureaucratic organization has demonstrated the risks for such organizations in attempting to achieve their goals through an alliance with a party leader. The leaders of the Forum have stood apart from the labor movement and from the professional associations; they have not concentrated their efforts upon the officials of one or a few departments, but rather upon legislators, courts, and a single overhead agency. As a consequence, when the party leader with whom it was allied lost his bid for citywide elective office in 1932, and when its special access to the Civil Service Commission was broken in 1935, the Forum was greatly disadvantaged. As Prial's party role declined during the late 1930's, the Forum was badly disoriented. It could be belligerent in its attacks upon resisting officialdom and it could draw some blood in battle, but its hitting and staying powers were limited. When it was simultaneously challenged within the bureaucracies by the entry of new organizations allied with the AFL and CIO, the leaders of the Forum could retain only the smaller remnants of its greater days in the Hylan-Walker-O'Brien years. During the last decade, the leaders of the Forum have seemingly been absorbed in a holding action, their hopes for a return to high prominence restrained by awareness of powerful competition on all sides.

The Transport Workers Union

The Transport Workers Union is a result of the wave of unionization produced by Section 7A of the National Industrial Recovery Act and the National Labor Relations Act of the early New Deal, but its roots go back into the bitter struggles in the labor relations of the IRT and BMT subways as privately operated transit systems. The first efforts at unionization leading directly to the organization of TWU were directed in 1933 at the employees of these then privately operated lines. The organizers had initial difficulties in finding an official link to the general labor movement. Rejected in 1935 by the Amalgamated Association of Street, Electric Railway, and Motor Coach Employees (AFL), and by the New York Lodge of Machinists (AFL), the TWU in 1936 finally obtained a charter from the international office of the Machinists and in 1937 the permission of New York City's Central Trades and Labor Council (AFL) to organize transit workers in the city's three rapid transit systems (thus including the city-owned Independent line). But this charter and permission were regarded as ambiguous, and in 1937 the leaders of TWU moved to the newly formed CIO, the arrangements being completed on October 5, 1937, with the formal establishment, in a constitutional convention, of the Transport Workers Union of America, CIO.

TWU thus arrived on the scene three years before the city purchased the two private systems and unified them into a single city-owned and city-operated system. The main initial energies of the union leaders were centered upon the private systems. Before unification, TWU had "closed shop" collective bargaining contracts with both private companies, and these contracts were not due to terminate until a date more than a year beyond the legal take-over by the city. On the city's own Independent System, TWU was unable to win comparable status by contract, but it moved quickly into a dominant position in its relationships with competing employee organizations. One of its competitors was the Civil Service Forum; another was the AFL's Amalgamated. In January, 1937, the Board of Transportation reluctantly yielded to pressures for election of representative committees of employees by classification groups. Of the 79 delegates elected, TWU and Amalgamated together won 51, the Forum 28; TWU then won a majority of the 11-member central committee chosen by the 79 delegates, but the Board decided to deal with classification groups separately. TWU had

nonetheless demonstrated its position of dominance among the employees—
and unification solidified this status in 1940 when TWU's massive membership in the two private systems were added to the transit system's employee
population. This position it has maintained, though not without some
difficulty, in the two subsequent decades.

As a participant in the city's political contest, the leaders of the TWU
have relied upon at least five modes of influence and points of access: (1)
emphasis upon a labor-management contract, with TWU as sole bargaining
agent, as the only satisfactory answer to labor relations in the city's transit
system; (2) use of TWU's affiliation with the labor movement, exploiting
especially the good offices of the CIO national presidents and of the local
CIO central council (a resource somewhat diminished since the AFL-CIO
merger); (3) concentration of attention and pressure upon the Board of
Transportation and its successor, the New York City Transit Authority;
(4) direct and indirect pressure upon the Mayor, as a useful leverage against
the Board and the Authority; and (5) a decade (1936–1946) of close ties
with a minority political party (the ALP), followed by increasing aloofness
from involvement with political parties or party leaders. These strategies
and tactics provide significant contrasts and similarities with those of the
teachers' organizations, the police and fire associations, and the Civil Service
Forum. TWU leaders have no major preoccupation with the state legislature
at Albany, no marked tendency to rely upon the courts. For their political
party adventuring they chose a minority party, not the majority party as
did the Forum. Their identification with the labor movement is stronger
than that of the firemen, and their commitment to formal collective bargaining is much greater than that of any other group. TWU shares with leaders of
the teachers, firemen, and policemen an opportunity not afforded to the
Forum—a concentration of influence upon one agency of the city government.

The TWU drive for a formal collective bargaining contract with the
Board of Transportation began before unification, produced more than a
decade of wrangling before TWU leaders secured what they regarded as a
reasonable facsimile of their goal, and even yet reflects strains and stresses
between TWU and the Transit Authority. TWU leaders at first demanded
the full reproduction, in TWU's labor relations with the Board, of the status
TWU had with the private lines. Only slowly did the union leaders learn
what they could and must yield in the new civil service setting. The Board,
for its part, stood just as stiffly on its doctrine that collective bargaining
and exclusive recognition were inappropriate, illegal, and impossible. TWU
leaders annually threatened to strike, making all the noisy and symbolic,
and some of the real, preparations—but never actually went on strike. The
Board as regularly cited the strike possibility as conclusive proof that there
could be no collective bargaining in the public service (collective bargaining

being, the Board argued, meaningless without the right to strike, and the strike being intolerable in the public service). Matters stood thus at stalemate, interim arrangements punctuated at intervals with explosive disputes, until, under the Wagner administration, TWU ultimately received from the Transit Authority recognition as the exclusive bargaining agent for most transit employees.

The TWU achieved its goal of contractual armistice with the Board of Transportation and its successor, the Transit Authority, in large part by drawing upon its resources in the general labor movement. The international president, Michael J. Quill, did not delegate TWU's dealing with the Board to the officers of Local 100, the unit which included the city's transit employees. Instead, he took the lead himself and used all his top officials, international and local, to assemble an unrelenting pressure upon the Board at its every formal hearing and through every medium at his disposal. The other New York City CIO officials were enlisted collectively in their council (Quill was for several years president of the New York City CIO council) and as individual officials. And, as a carefully conserved ace, Quill produced on frequent and strategic occasions the strongest CIO voice, its successive national presidents: John L. Lewis and Philip A. Murray. These interventions were usually directed at the Mayor, but the Board of Transportation was never left unaware of their weight, and occasionally the Board was addressed or visited directly. It took more than a decade of these combined and selective barrages, but the TWU leaders ultimately "tamed" the Board, in the sense that TWU yielded only in semantics while first the Board and then the Authority yielded in substance.

TWU leaders gave attention to the Mayors primarily for the purpose of flanking the Board. The members of the Board had a semiautonomous status under the Mayor; he appointed them, but for fixed terms, and they could be removed only on formal charges and after a hearing. Too, they operated under state laws which gave them additional autonomous power. Nevertheless, the Mayors could not escape involvement; their position as the city's elected chief executive and the impact of TWU's strategy combined to pull them into the contest. Quill's communications and manifestoes were often addressed to the Mayor, but the main influence upon the Mayors was that of Lewis or Murray. The Mayors worked for adjustment (La Guardia threatening, cajoling, delaying, yielding a little; O'Dwyer delaying, then yielding more); they "softened" the Board by interim agreement which gave more to TWU than the Board had offered, by urging and forcing labor relations improvements, and (especially under O'Dwyer) by appointing to the Board members who took a more flexible view of the problem.

The responsiveness of the Mayors to TWU leaders was affected by TWU's role in the political party system. The union was not yet a year old before

TWU leaders were active in the newly formed American Labor party, while in 1937 Quill was elected to the City Council in the first proportional representation election. His role in the ALP and subsequently was like his behavior in the union: he was aggressive, impetuous, articulate, and perennially active—as councilman until 1950 and as a party "spokesman." But he was mainly concerned with making his ALP affiliation yield advantages for TWU. The forum was political, but the goal was the TWU's. La Guardia was not pleased with TWU's demands but made some concessions; O'Dwyer, supported by Quill, TWU, and ALP in the 1945 election, was more conciliatory. The yield to TWU from its ALP affiliation was on net profitable for almost a decade. Thereafter the leftist tendencies of the party, its alienation from other parties, and its losses to the Liberal party led TWU leaders and members (long restive under the leftist label attached to the union itself) to reassess its commitment to the ALP and to a gradual disassociation. Few evidences have since appeared to indicate any inclination by TWU leaders toward close affiliation with any party organization, although it is frequently emphatic in its endorsements.

The TWU leaders after more than two decades are confirmed in their commitment to labor movement affiliation and to the collective bargaining goal. These are their primary assets as participants in the city's political contest. TWU has a commanding position in its own agency, but it does not have the assets which the teachers' organizations and the police and fire associations enjoy. It has not been able, nor is it likely, to absorb the machinery of supervision into its own membership or its own graduates. The members of the Authority board remain comparatively aloof and autonomous, the managers and specialists of the system are outside the reach of TWU's "promotion from within" controls, and the Civil Service Law was shaped in large measure before TWU became a participant. There are other employee organizations asserting their claims to recognition and charging that TWU's membership is no longer a majority in some areas. But within these limits, TWU leaders have learned how to use the collective bargaining mode to accomplish a tight control over a large part of the Transit Authority's personnel system, to assert a powerful influence in the wage and salary decisions, and to establish a closed bureaucracy up to the middle management levels. And they can be reasonably confident that TWU's future will not be so rough as its past.

State, County, and Municipal Employees, AFL-CIO, New York City District Council 37

The SCME is a general union of government employees at the state and local levels, aspiring in New York City to organize employees in all agencies and all occupations except where it may agree to cede jurisdiction to another union. In these characteristics it resembles the Civil Service Forum; it differs from the Forum in its affiliation with the labor movement and in many of its strategies and tactics. SCME shares with the TWU a preoccupation with the collective bargaining instrument but is compelled by its traditions and its strategic position to be more moderate in its demands for recognition and exclusive status. As a consequence, SCME leaders have a greater interest in legislation, in litigation, in the city's overhead agencies, and in seeking allies than do TWU leaders.

Nationally and locally, SCME has led a beleaguered life within the labor movement, and its troubles are not yet over. Chartered by the AFL in October, 1936, after some reluctance because it was not a craft union and thus threatened the jurisdiction of such AFL unions, the SCME quickly lost its more aggressive membership to the CIO (the State, County, and Municipal Workers, chartered in July, 1937) and even more quickly learned from an AFL convention in June, 1937, that it would not be allowed to organize government employees in any craft where an AFL union claimed jurisdiction—for example, highway workers, metal trades, teamsters, building service employees, inspectors. In addition, CIO's SCMWA and its successor (UPWA) gave the AFL's SCME aggressive opposition for a decade; the Teamsters, the Building Service Employees, and other craft unions still continue to plague SCME's jurisdictional hopes.

SCME first prominently entered New York City in 1941 in an effort to organize the employees of the Sanitation Department. After a decade and a half of organizing work, SCME leaders now claim membership in 33 city departments and agencies, with a total claimed membership of 25,000. SCME's greatest membership strength is claimed in the Departments of Parks, Hospitals, Public Works, and Welfare. SCME's competition is with the other organizations having general membership aims—the Forum, Teamsters' Local 237, the Building Service Employees Union, the United Mine Workers District 50, and with the AFL craft unions and Teamsters' Local 831 (Sanitationmen) whose voices are strong in the Central Trades and Labor Council. This is SCME's greatest organizational dilemma: it is a labor union, but it cannot fully work out its peace with, and secure high protected status in, the general labor movement. It can compete on favorable terms with the Forum, but its labor union competitors present a much higher hurdle.

The modes of influence and the points of access upon which the leaders of SCME's District Council 37 depend in the city's political contest are: its labor movement affiliation; a drive toward the collective bargaining contract; concentration of attention upon the Departments of Labor and Personnel, upon department and agency heads, and to a lesser extent upon the state legislature and the courts; some efforts to reach the Mayor, the Board of

Estimate, and the Council; a tenuous alliance with *The Chief;* and some tentative entries into endorsement of candidates in primaries and elections. These widely dispersed strategies and tactics are the necessities of the leaders of an organization which aspires to do what no other employee organization in the city has yet been able to accomplish: that is, to be a general, citywide employee association, to be a labor union espousing collective bargaining in every department, to come to satisfactory terms with powerful competing labor unions having strength in both public and private employment, to count upon overhead agencies to which it does not yet have privileged access, to forego the temptation of concentrating upon one or two citadel departments in which it might be dominant, and to avoid entangling alliances with the party leaders. Attempting to accomplish so much, yet moderate by tradition and in leadership, SCME is compelled to try all modes and all avenues in the political contest. Its leaders are not yet a dominant participant at any point, although their comparative rationality and reasonableness often make them, for city officials, a welcome alternative to the leaders of less stable and more strident groups.

The SCME leaders use the demand for the collective bargaining contract more as evocative symbol than as rigid doctrine. They accept the symbol, if signed and sealed as a memorandum of understanding, as a substitute for the usual fine print and precise words of the contract. Recognition and assured access is their first aim; the full panoply of conventional collective bargaining is a goal deferred.

In their use of labor movement affiliation, the SCME leaders are also compelled to realize that their labor ties are more symbolic than powerful. The national SCME organization was always viewed skeptically by the AFL top leadership (never more than lukewarm toward unions composed primarily of government employees, and hostile toward SCME tendencies to encroach upon the craft unions), while the newly merged AFL-CIO top command has had higher priorities than the problems of the comparatively small SCME. In New York City the problems of SCME's leaders have been even more severe. The AFL-CIO local merger being delayed, SCME's District Council 37 has been left to deal with AFL's inhospitable Central Trades and Labor Council, in which the traditional craft union attitudes have been strengthened by the long-established ties of that Council to the local Democratic party leaders and officialdom. Nor is national SCME headquarters able to provide the kind of help that TWU has been able to command from its national leadership and from the CIO's top officials before the merger. The result of all these factors in SCME's relationship to the labor movement is that SCME's New York City leaders can assert the significance of its labor affiliation and evoke the symbols of power in that affiliation, but they cannot demonstrate its potency in ways which convince the other participants. Officials, interest group leaders, party leaders, and even prospective members of SCME assess the strength of SCME as a participant in the contest not in terms of its affiliation with the labor movement but in terms of SCME's local demonstrations of influence.

SCME leaders have free and hospitable access to the city's Labor Department and Personnel Department, but without the highest priority and with no evident special privilege. With department and agency heads, SCME leaders have varying degrees of access and status, ranging from mild preference over competing employee groups, through indifference, to cold hostility. In no single department or agency do they approach the position of dominant insider enjoyed by leaders of TWU and the Teamsters, nor by leaders of the teachers' organizations and the police and fire associations, in their respective citadel agencies. Instead, the SCME leaders must sometimes seek the help of the Labor Department when they want an audience with a department or agency head. In the state legislature, the SCME pursues energetically an annual legislative program, maintaining a representative in Albany during the annual sessions. It has secured sponsorship of its bills without too much difficulty (relying principally upon two legislators it has endorsed and aided in campaigns), but its statutory product is difficult to measure. SCME leaders cannot yet match the Forum's leaders much longer application to the legislative goal nor are they yet close to commanding the influence exerted by the leaders of the teachers, the firemen, and the policemen.

In all these efforts—representation and bargaining; labor movement affiliation; concentration upon the Labor Department, the Personnel Department, department heads, the state legislature—SCME leaders pursue conventional bureaucratic goals. They are moderate in most demands and have learned the strategy and tactics of concession as a means to shield their vulnerability as bargaining participants, but they have not been inventive in fashioning new goals or novel strategies. SCME is an imitator, not an innovator. Proceduralization of the personnel system, promotion from within, further proceduralizing in the terms of bargaining agreements, absorption of the supervisory personnel into the bureaucratic subculture—these are the familiar aims of the SCME leaders. In the concrete realities which surround them in the city's political contest, the SCME leaders cannot hope for early attainment of these goals in the gratifying measure granted the leaders of the teachers' organizations, the police and fire associations, the TWU, and even to the Forum in its days of pride and power. Especially does the absorption of the higher levels of supervision and managerial direction in the departments and the agencies remain beyond SCME's foreseeable reach.

SCME leaders have great logical potential as participants in the city's political contest. In a little more than a decade, SCME has achieved a role of some considerable importance. Its growth in numbers and status has been steady, if unspectacular. In the years of the Wagner administration it has particularly improved the terms of its access to the city's governmental decision-makers, finding in the Labor Department a new and valuable asset. SCME's basic future dilemmas would seem to be three: Can its leaders come to viable and advantageous terms with their labor movement competitors? Can they secure high status in a sufficient number of city departments and agencies to provide a solid base for SCME's distinctive and ambitious hopes to be a general union of city employees? Can they develop the required levels of innovation, inventiveness, and adaptability in goals and strategies to fit the unusual role they aspire to play among the employee groups? Prudent forecasters, taking into account the strength of SCME's labor movement rivals, the difficulties surrounding SCME's expectations as a general citywide employee association, and the record of SCME as imitator rather than innovator, will hesitate to make affirmative predictions about the resolution of any one of SCME's three dilemmas. Meanwhile, SCME leaders as influential participants in the city's political contest add their not inconsiderable weight to the efforts of the city's organized bureaucracies to play an autonomous role in the decisions affecting the policies and procedures of the city government.

Sanitationmen (Local 831, International Brotherhood of Teamsters)

The "drivers" and "sweepers" of the Department of Sanitation began their organizational life in 1914, responding to the same anti-Mitchel-reform stimulus that energized the police and fire associations, and the teachers' organizations, and that led to the founding of the Civil Service Forum. By the 1920's, the drivers were organized in two different groups: the Drivers of Manhattan, Bronx, Brooklyn, and Richmond, under Abe Kasoff's leadership, and the Queensboro Protective Association, with Mike Morro as leader, an organization which combined driver and sweeper membership. The sweepers were also in two separate groups: the Brooklyn Sweepers, under Anthony Grego; the Manhattan, Bronx, and Richmond Sweepers, under Elias Shapiro. This unusual pattern was largely a result of the way the sanitation function was organized before a single department was established in 1929. In an effort toward unity, Kasoff, Morro, Grego, and Shapiro formed their four separate organizations into a Joint Council of Drivers and Sweepers, with some formal ties to the Civil Service Forum.

The Joint Council of Drivers and Sweepers was from the first a party-oriented federation. In considerable part, it followed the lead of Prial and *The Chief*, but its four leaders made their separate individual bargains with the party leaders in the boroughs. The great bulk of the employees in the four associations were in the "labor class" under the civil service rules, and thus outside the protections of the "competitive class" status. This fact, and the usefulness of their numbers in petition circulation, voter canvassing, and other party activities, made the associations a special object of attention from the party leaders. Other characteristics of these associations—the centralized nature of their internal government, the personalized objectives of their leaders, the lack of information accessible to the membership, and the divided management of the sanitation function—combined with their party orientation to make these groups somewhat ineffective instruments for their membership although perhaps reasonably satisfying to their leadership. When the La Guardia Civil Service Commission in 1939 moved to reclassify the workers from the "labor class" to the "competitive class" as "sanitation-men" and thus give them new status and added protections (especially from the demands of party leaders), the leaders of the associations were alarmed and resistant. As Kasoff put it, "Leave us the same as we stood for twenty-five years. We are satisfied."

The leaders of the Joint Council were without serious competition in the organization of sanitation employees for almost thirty years. The limited goals and party alliances of the leaders produced a kind of stable partnership in the agency: the agency's management and the association leadership found it possible to deal with each other, only the membership being restive. In 1941 CIO's SCMWA began a determined drive to organize the sanitationmen, but the leaders of the four associations (with official assistance) welcomed AFL's SCME as an alternative that would offer fewer threats to their continued leadership. This proved to be an unstable arrangement. The postwar years found the SCME, the Building Service Union, the United Mine Workers District 50, and the Teamsters all competing for a dominant position in the Department. Within less than a decade, the Teamsters had triumphed over all the others.

The leaders of Teamsters' Local 831 bring to their role in the Sanitation Department not only the kinds of assets and strategies the TWU has in the city's transit system but also some of those held and used by the police and fire associations and the teachers' organizations. The leaders of Local 831, like the leaders of TWU, emphasize exclusive recognition and bargaining as a means of assuring their access and participation in the decision-making process, and as the device for recording in the binding words of an understanding some of the more important of the decisions in which they are most interested. Like the TWU leaders also, they exploit their affiliation with the labor movement. Further, like TWU, the police and fire associations, and the teachers' organizations, the Teamsters' leaders have their citadel agency—the Department of Sanitation. In these three respects they are comparatively free of the liabilities which plague SCME. But the Teamsters' leaders have an additional strategy and asset of great importance, one not enjoyed by TWU or SCME: they can realistically aspire, as can the police, fire, and teacher organizations, to absorb the whole machinery of supervision and management into their own membership climate.

The Teamsters' leaders thus depend primarily upon these four modes of influence: exclusive recognition and bargaining; affiliation with the labor movement; concentration upon the Department of Sanitation; and absorption of the supervisory, managerial, and executive leadership of that large department into their own active or alumni membership. In seeking their goals, the Teamsters' leaders give primary attention to the Commissioner of Sanitation and his deputies, the Budget Director, the Labor Commissioner, the Comptroller, and the Board of Estimate. Neither the Teamsters nor their predecessor (the Joint Council) has given much attention to the state legislature, although they use Section 220 of the Labor Law in their bargaining. Their relationship with party leaders is less intimate than was that of the Joint Council, but is not a neglected asset.

The leaders of Local 831 enter the bargaining process assured of the consent and support of the Department's top command. The friendly, almost cozy, relationships between the leaders of sanitation employee groups and the Commissioner and his deputies have a long history, going far back into the years of the Joint Council. When Commissioner Mulrain in 1956 responded to charges that Teamster leaders were devoting all their time to union work while on the city payroll, he explained that the practice was "thirty-five or forty years" old, helped "keep his boys happy" and maintained a "high level of employee morale." The leadership of the Department is, in fact, as much a product of the agency's own bureaucracy as is that of the Police or Fire Departments or the Board of Education. For more than a decade, the Commissioner and his deputies have been recruited from the departmental bureaucracy, and the Teamsters' leaders are not without influence in their selection and retention in office. The top command of the Department responds more often to the leaders of Local 831 than to the Mayor or the Board of Estimate.

One result of this striking relationship is that the actual collective bargaining (even including the resolution of many grievances) for the Department is conducted between the Teamsters' leaders and the Director of the Budget. In these negotiations, invariably affecting wages directly or indirectly, the union leaders use the strategic and tactical opportunities provided, on the one hand, by their contention that sanitationmen come under the "prevailing rate" provisions of Section 220 of the state Labor Law (a Comptroller's determination) and, on the other hand, that they are entitled to all their compensation rights under the state Civil Service Law (a Personnel Director's determination). The rights under one or both rules are typically reserved for possible future litigation in the individual contracts signed by each sanitationman. Budget Director resistance to their demands is frequently met by the union leaders with appeals to the Labor Commissioner, to the Mayor, or to the Board of Estimate—sometimes with mass demonstrations before the latter. They need all this additional help in their wage negotiations because in these negotiations (like the teachers and policemen and firemen) they leave the citadel of their department and enter the city's broader political contest, and their stature as participant in the larger arena is less imposing.

Next to their power and influence within the Sanitation Department, the greatest asset of the leaders of Local 831 is their affiliation with the labor movement. In the Teamsters' International, in the local Teamsters' Council, and in the Central Trades and Labor Council, Local 831 leaders have a status at least equal to TWU's in its affiliations and more potent than SCME's. They benefited considerably in recent years from the fact that a Teamster official was president of the Central Trades and Labor Council, was sympathetic with their competition against SCME, and guided the Council in the exercise of its strength to assist Local 831.

Teamsters' Local 831 has seemingly achieved a secure position in its own house and in the house of labor. It was the first group to receive the certificate of exclusive recognition from the city's Labor Department under the Mayor's executive order of 1958. Its status in the Sanitation Department is a dominant one, whether the test be promotion from within, the introduction of technological improvements into the Department's work methods or equipment, or the absorption of the Department's supervisory authority. Its relationships with the labor movement are useful and satisfying to Local 831's leadership. Some stresses have been produced by the "time of troubles" which the Teamsters' International has recently encountered with the AFL, with its own internal leadership divisions, and with the investigations of the United States Senate. But these have not yet involved Local 831 leaders directly. In their secure position, the leaders of Local 831 contribute their important share to the general drive for bureaucratic autonomy and self-direction and do so as increasingly confident participants in the city's political contest.

CONCLUSIONS

Several major trends and tendencies characterize the role of the leaders of the city's bureaucracies as participants in the city's political process: (1) Control over the personnel system (especially securing a closed system) remains the most concrete goal. (2) There is a trend toward unionization, or toward its facsimile when the term "union" is unattractive to members or is a liability to them. (3) There is a tendency toward the formation of large groups although jurisdictional battles still flourish. (4) There is a movement away from alliances with party leaders and party organizations, although campaign contributions and campaign endorsements by some organized bureaucracies are still significant. (5) There is an increasing reliance upon the formal institutions and procedures of labor-management relations. (6) There is continued concentration upon "citadel" agencies by the most influential of the organized bureaucracies, despite the efforts of SCME to modify or reverse this trend. (7) There is an impressive growth in the capacities of the bureaucracies to achieve comparative autonomy and self-direction in their relations with officialdom.

The major consequences of the participation in the city's political process by the leaders of the organized bureaucracies may be summed up in their habit of strong resistance to change. Their influence is most often exercised against innovations in public policy, in technology, in jurisdictional arrangements, in the organizational structure of departments and agencies, and in the administrative procedures of the city government. Their strongest drives are toward higher salaries and wages and toward the other elements of the personnel systems which enhance tenure protections, limit competition for advancement, and resist the interventions of other participants. Accordingly, when Mayors and department heads attempt to lead and direct the bureaucrats of the city government, they do so with few realistic expectations that the response will be prompt and affirmative. What the city government does, for whom, how quickly, by what methods, and at what costs—all these reflect in no small part the participation and influence of the leaders and members of the city's bureaucracies in the political process.

BIBLIOGRAPHY

GENERAL

The Chief. A weekly newspaper, published since 1897. Calling itself the "Civil Employees' Weekly," this publication presents news articles and editorials that reflect the interests and views of civil service workers in New York City.

Civil Service Leader. Published weekly, 1924–1958. Published 48 times a year, 1948 to date (biweekly in July and August). "America's largest weekly for public employees," as this newspaper calls itself, offers news of interest to municipal employees and editorials that reflect their viewpoints.

Finegan, James E., *Tammany at Bay*. Dodd, Mead and Co., New York, 1933, pp. 36–37, 106–108, 207–208. The influence of municipal employees, particularly those led by Frank J. Prial, on politics in the early 1930's.

Kippel, Philip, *The Rise and History of the Organization Movement in New York Municipal Civil Service*. Master's thesis, Columbia University, 1939, unpublished.

Mackaye, Milton, *The Tin Box Parade: A Handbook for Larceny*. Robert M. McBride and Co., New York, 1934. Includes discussion of Frank J. Prial, editor of *The Chief*, in his bid for the comptrollership in the elections of 1932.

Moscow, Warren, *Politics in the Empire State*. Alfred A. Knopf, New York, 1948, pp. 201–202. Lobbying by civil service employees at Albany.

Schweppe, Emma, *The Firemen's and Patrolmen's Unions in the City of New York: A Case Study in Public Employees Unions.* King's Crown Press, New York, 1948. A study in the history of municipal employee unions.

Spero, Sterlin D., *Government as Employer.* Remsen Press, New York, 1948, pp. 205–212. A brief history of the Civil Service Forum in New York City and Part II, generally, for organized bureaucracies.

Spring 3100. A monthly magazine "of-by-for New York's finest." A house organ published by the city's Police Department since March, 1930.

Zeller, Belle, *Pressure Politics in New York.* Prentice-Hall, New York, 1937, pp. 167–180, 195–204. How representatives of teachers' organizations and civil service employees lobby at Albany.

THE DEPARTMENT OF LABOR AND NEW YORK CITY'S PROGRAMS OF LABOR RELATIONS FOR MUNICIPAL EMPLOYEES

New York City Charter, chap. 49, sec. 1112 (as added by Local Law 1954, no. 1).

New York City, Board of Estimate. Authorization for payroll checkoff of union dues and rules and regulations governing its administration: (1) Board of Estimate, *Journal of Proceedings,* 1956, pp. 9822–9824 (August 30, 1956). (Board of Estimate Cal. No. 61); (2) *Ibid.,* 1957, pp. 13, 596–598 (December 5, 1957). (Board of Estimate Cal. No. 258).

Department of Labor, *Annual Reports:* 1954, 1955, 1956, 1957, 1958. All these reports were published during the year following the period covered. They outline Mayor Wagner's labor policies for municipal employees.

Department of Labor, *Bulletin,* July 21, 1958. A notice to participating employee organizations, relating to administering payroll checkoff of dues.

Department of Labor, *Preliminary Report on Labor Relations in the Municipal Service.* The Department, New York, 1954. A study of labor relations in public service which helped Mayor Wagner formulate his program of labor relations with municipal employees.

Department of Labor, *Labor Relations Series.* The Department, New York, 1955.
 1. Klaus, Ida, *The Right of Public Employees to Organize—In Theory and In Practice.*
 2. Klaus, Ida, *Recognition of Organized Groups of Public Employees.*
 3. Salsburg, Sidney W., *Extent of Recognition and the Bargaining Unit in Public Employment.*
 4. Karpf, Estelle M., *The Ascertainment of Representative Status for Organizations of Public Employees.*
 5. *Organization and Recognition of Supervisors in Public Employment.*
 6. *The Collective Bargaining Process in Public Employment.*
 7. *Government as Employer-Participant in the Collective Dealing Process.*
 8. *The Collective Agreement in Public Employment.*
 9. *Unresolved Disputes in Public Employment.*
These nine monographs published by the city Department of Labor serve as guides for the several municipal departments in their relations with their employees.

Department of Labor, *Report on Program of Labor Relations for New York City Employees.* The Department, New York, 1957. Summary of efforts to give employees the right to organize, to have their policy recommendations heard, and to present grievances.

Office of the Mayor, "Interim Order on the Conduct of Relations between the City of New York and Its Employees," July 21, 1954. This executive order gave municipal employees the right to join associations of fellow employees and authorized grievance procedures for resolving complaints.

Office of the Mayor, "Amendment to Section 6 of the Interim Order," March 14, 1955. This executive order stated that in departments in which the membership of all qualified labor organizations was not representative of a substantial number of employees, the establishment of joint labor relations committees was not mandatory.

Office of the Mayor, "Executive Order No. 38," May 16, 1957. Sets forth general principles for giving municipal employees time during working hours for presenting grievances and performing specified types of work for employees' associations.

Office of the Mayor, "Executive Order No. 49," March 31, 1958. Replaced the "Interim Order" of July 21, 1954, and established the right of municipal employees to join labor organizations and seek adjustment of their grievances.

"An Analysis by Local 94 of New York's 'Little Wagner Act'," *International Fire Fighter*, April, 1959, pp. 17–19.

Salsburg, Sidney W., *The Checkoff of Union Dues in Municipal Government*. Department of Labor, New York, 1956. A survey of practices in this area in the United States, which also specifically examines the procedures of the New York City Transit Authority.

PROFESSIONAL STAFF AND CIVIL SERVICE EMPLOYEES UNDER THE BOARD OF EDUCATION

American Federation of Teachers, Commission on Educational Reconstruction, *Organizing the Teaching Profession*. Free Press, Glencoe, Ill., 1955, *passim*. The story of Local 2 and Local 5, New York City teacher unions, is considered as part of the general history of teacher unionism in the United States.

Antell, Henry, "Levels of Participation in School Administration," *Strengthening Democracy*, vol. 5, October, 1952, pp. 1, 6. A generalized discussion of teacher participation in school policy-making.

The Brooklyn Teacher, 1873 to date. This organ of the Brooklyn Teachers Association is one of the oldest publications of New York City employees that is still published.

Greenberg, Jacob, "Report on Staff Relations (Administrative Staff)," April 15, 1955. A report prepared for the Board of Education on the operation of grievance and policy consultation procedures established in 1952 for civil service employees of the Board of Education.

Report on Staff Relations (Pedagogic), April 13, 1955, mimeographed. An evaluation of the original teachers' staff relations plan, prepared by the Deputy Superintendent of Schools for the Board of Education. It includes specific recommendations for improvement.

Guild Bulletin, December 17, 1940, to present. Issued irregularly. Organ of the New York Teachers Guild, Local 2, American Federation of Teachers. Vol. 1, published during the school year 1941–1942, was mimeographed. Vol. 2, published during the school year 1942–1943, and all successive volumes have been printed.

High School Teacher, 1956 to date. Monthly newspaper, the official organ of the High School Teachers Association of New York City.

New York City, Department of Education, *Report of the Committee to Study Staff Relations in the New York City Schools*, February 21, 1952. Written in the form of a committee report, this document served as the original charter for the teachers' staff relations plan.

Report of the Committee to Study Staff Relations for Civil Service Employees. Board of Education of the City of New York, New York, 1952. This is actually a constitution, giving civil service employees of the Board of Education the right to present grievances and to have their recommendations on policy matters considered.

Staff Relations Plan for the Professional Staff. Board of Education of the City of New York, New York, 1956. This document outlines the revised staff relations plan for teachers which has been in effect since it was ratified by a referendum of the pedagogical staff in 1957.

"Documents of the Committee to Evaluate the Staff Relations Plan, January, 1956–April, 1956." 3 vols. Contains minutes of meetings, reports of subcommittees, press notices, results of referenda, and other documentary materials relating to the work of the committee that revised the teachers' staff relations plan in 1956. Available in the Bureau of Educational Program Research and Statistics, Board of Education of the City of New York, 110 Livingston Street, Brooklyn 1, New York.

"Documents of the Superintendent's Committee, for Revising the Plan of the Policy Consultation Committee, March, 1959–May 1959." 1 vol. Documentary material relating to the work of a committee that revised the teachers' staff relations plan, incorporating in it certain elements of the constitution of the Teachers' Council. Available in the Bureau of Educational Program Research and Statistics.

"The Teachers' Council of the Department of Education of the City of New York: Its History, Purpose, Organization, Work." July, 1916, mimeographed. Pamphlet in Reference Library of Bureau of Educational Program Research and Statistics, Board of Education of the City of New York. Early history of an effort to give teachers a voice in policy-making in the Department of Education.

Teachers' Council:

Annual Report of President and of Recording Secretary for the Year 1917, printed.

Annual Report of the Teachers' Council for the Year Ending December 31, 1919, mimeographed.

Annual Report of President and of Recording Secretary, for the Years 1920–1930. The story of an experiment in offering teachers a voice in top-level policy-making. (May be consulted in the Reference Library of the Bureau of Educational Program Research and Statistics of the Board of Education.)

Teachers' Council, 1930. A printed yearbook and manual of the Teachers' Council, set up to give the teachers a voice in top-level policy-making.

Constitution and By-Laws of the Teachers' Council of the City of New York. Board of Education, New York, 1957. A plan in effect from 1913 to 1959, which attempted to give teachers a voice in the deliberations of the Board of Education.

Reiner, William B., and Frederick Shaw, *An Evaluation of the Pedagogic Staff Relations Plan—1955.* Bureau of Administrative and Budgetary Research, Board of Education, New York, 1956. An official appraisal of the functioning of the teachers' staff relations plan during its third year of operation.

Schweitzer, Samuel I., "Dare We Try More Democratic School Administration?" *Strengthening Democracy*, vol. 9, November–December, 1956, pp. 1–2, 6–7. The values of policy consultation under the teachers' staff relations plan.

Shaw, Frederick, "School Administration and Better Human Relations," *Journal of Educational Sociology*, vol. 30, May, 1957, pp. 414–422. Describes the industrial origins and rationale of the teachers' staff relations plan, as well as evaluating its functioning. Reprinted in *High Points*, vol. 40, January, 1958, pp. 34–44.

An Evaluation of the Staff Relations Program for the Educational Staff. Bureau of Administrative and Budgetary Research, New York, 1955. An appraisal of the functioning of the teachers' staff relations program, in terms of its aims and objectives, during the first year of operation.

Wrightstone, J. Wayne, and Frederick Shaw, "Proposed Revisions in the Staff Relations Plan," *Strengthening Democracy*, vol. 9, October, 1956, pp. 2, 6. Indicates the areas in the original teachers' staff relations plan where revisions were needed and what revisions were made. The authors served as chairman and secretary, respectively, of the Committee to Evaluate the Professional Staff Relations Plan.

EMPLOYEES OF THE TRANSIT AUTHORITY

American Arbitration Association. "Report on the Conduct of the Election for Employees of the Transit Authority," July 13, 1954.

"Report on the Findings and Certification of Election Held Among Hourly Paid Employees of the Transit Authority Held December 16, 1957," December 17, 1957. Filed in the Office of the Secretary of the Transit Authority.

Booz, Allen, and Hamilton, Management Consultants, "Report on Recommended Plan for Distribution of Wage Inequity Fund," May 7, 1958. Filed in Office of Secretary of Transit Commission.

Comerford, James J., *Adjustment of Labor Unions to Civil Service Status: The Transport Workers' Union and the New York City Government.* Master's thesis, Columbia University, 1941, unpublished.

Freund, Peter, Bruno Stein, and Lois MacDonald, *The Grievance Process in New York City Transit.* Graduate School of Public Administration and Social Service, New York University, New York, 1956. A part of a plan for employees and how it functions.

McGinley, James J., *Labor Relations in the New York Rapid Transit Systems, 1904–1949.* King's Crown Press, New York, 1944. A thorough and scholarly work.

Morris, Newbold, and Dana Lee Thomas, *Let the Chips Fall.* Appleton-Century-Crofts, New York, 1955, pp. 194–195. How the La Guardia administration successfully handled a subway strike.

Raskin, A. H., "Presenting the Phenomenon Called Quill," *The New York Times Magazine*, March 5, 1950. A portrait of the Transport Workers Union leader.

New York City, Board of Transportation, "Memorandum of Understanding," June 27, 1950. Agreements between the Board of Transportation and various labor unions representing its employees. Filed in the Office of the Secretary, New York City Transit Authority.

Board of Transportation, *Proceedings*, 1940, vol. 36, April 3, 1940. Relates to labor contract with employees.

Board of Transportation, "Rules and Regulations Governing Employees Engaged in the Operation of the New York City Transit System," June 1, 1952, and supplements. Filed in the Office of the Secretary of the Transit Authority.

Board of Transportation, "Schedule of Working Conditions," plus supplements, for: Car and Bus Maintenance Departments, Conductors, Maintenance of Way Department, Motormen, Employees in Power Departments, Employees in the Station Department, Towermen, all July 1, 1950; Employees in the Title of Railroad Watchmen, September 18, 1951. These eight documents are filed in the Office of the Secretary of the Transit Authority.

Board of Transportation, *Three and One-Half Year Report*, June 30, 1949. The Board, New York, 1949. Contains numerous references to problems relating to employees and their organizations.

Mayor's Committee on Management Survey, *Modern Management for the City of New York*. 2 vols. The Committee, New York, 1953, vol. 2, pp. 379–380. Problems relating to employees of the city's transit system.

Mayor's Committee Appointed to Study Labor Relations on the City Transit System, *Report of the Committee dated April 28, 1943*. The Committee, New York, 1943. A discussion of the problems of workers on private transportation lines who became employees of city-owned lines.

Mayor's Transit Committee, *Report to Hon. William O'Dwyer, Mayor of the City of New York*. The Committee, New York, 1946. A survey of many facets of labor relations in the city's transit system.

Mayor's Transit Fact-Finding Committee, *Report to Hon. Robert F. Wagner*. The Committee, New York, May 17, 1954. An inquiry into a labor dispute between the New York City Transit Authority and its employees and the various labor unions representing them.

Transit Authority, *Annual Reports*, fiscal years, 1954, pp. 4–7; 1956, pp. 11–14; 1957, pp. 11–12; 1958, pp. 15–18. These volumes summarize the problems of the Transit Authority in the field of labor relations, recounting how they dealt with union organizations, strikes, grievance procedures, and other issues relating to labor problems.

Transit Authority:
"Agreement Made as of the 1st Day of July, 1954" between New York City Transit Authority and various unions representing hourly paid employees.
"Agreements Made as of the 1st Day of January, 1958" between New York City Transit Authority and duly elected unions representing hourly rated employees. Filed in Office of Secretary, New York City Transit Authority.

Transit Authority, "Agreement made as of the 1st Day of January, 1958, by and between New York City Transit Authority . . . and Transport Workers Union of America, AFL-CIO and Transport Workers Union of America, Local 100, AFL-CIO." An agreement that recognized the unions as bargaining agents, set up conditions for wage votes, working conditions and sick care, and authorized grievance procedures.

Transit Fact-Finding Board, *Report of the Board to Hon. William O'Dwyer, May 31, 1950*. The Board, New York, 1950. A special report which highlighted labor relations.

Special Transit Committee, *Report of the Committee to Hon. Vincent R. Impellitteri on Transition to a 40-Hour Week, June 27, 1951*. The Committee, New York, 1951. A special report that preceded the permanent introduction of the 5-day 40-hour week in the city's transit system.

Transit Fact-Finding Committee, *Report to New York City Transit Authority*. The Committee, New York, November 30, 1957. Report of findings on labor disputes between the Authority and the various labor unions representing its employees.

New York State, Senate Committee on the Affairs of the City of New York, *First Interim Report on the Inquiry into the Public Transit System of New York, Including Minority Report.* New York State Legislative Document, May 15, 1957. Considers a variety of labor problems among employees and employee associations of the Transit Authority.

Smith, Thelma, "New York City Labor Problems in Transit System: List of References, 1941–1949." 1950, typewritten. Copy at Municipal Reference Library.

Transport Workers Union of America, *Union Security Means a Good Job.* The Union, New York, 1946. A pamphlet written in a time of crisis in the city's transit system.

Transport Workers Union of America, *And Then Came TWU.* The Union, New York, 1950. A pamphlet that gives details on the progress of labor relations in the city's transit system.

STATE, COUNTY, AND MUNCIPAL EMPLOYEES (SCME)

State, County, and Municipal Employees (SCME)—District Council 37:
 The Union Spotlight. Published July–August, 1947.
 AFL Union Spotlight. Published monthly, September, 1947–October, 1948.
 AFL Spotlight. Published monthly, November, 1948–December, 1949. Resumed publication for one issue—August, 1952.
 Spotlight. Published monthly, September, 1952–February, 1953. Published twice a month, March, 1953–June, 1953. Published July–August, 1953, and once or twice a month thereafter.
 Public Employee Press. Published every two weeks—June, 1959, to date (26 copies a year).

CHAPTER XII

Party Leaders and
Governmental Decisions

NARROW SCOPE OF PARTY INTEREST

The Need for Selectivity

PARTY LEADERS give most of their energy and attention to the decisions governing nominations, elections, and appointments—that is, to the decisions determining who shall hold office. But they are not indifferent to other types of governmental decisions, especially any that affect their influence over the nominating, electing, and appointing processes. The interest of party leaders in public policy seems to vary directly with its possible effect upon their role in choosing officials. In fact, this perception of their relation to public policy impels party leaders to be most concerned with discrete aspects of policy and its application rather than its range and content.

In the government and politics of New York City, it is the County Leaders and the Assembly District Leaders, among the leaders in each party, who have most to do with governmental decisions. The Election District Captains are not significant participants in influencing decisions of officials, although they do provide much of the agenda for such efforts. Thus the number of party leaders actively and continually attempting to influence official decisions does not greatly exceed four hundred in both major parties, counting in both major parties all the Assembly District Leaders, their women coleaders, and the County Leaders in the city's five counties. These four hundred party leaders obviously cannot intervene in more than a small fraction of the many thousands of decisions made daily in all three branches, and at all three levels, of government by the thousands of officials and the several hundred thousand public employees. The party leaders must be highly selective in their interventions if they are to conserve their time and energy for their primary task—influencing the nomination and election, or the appointment, of public officials. Accordingly, the party leaders count heavily upon the officials, when arriving at governmental decisions, to take the party interest into account without prompting. The party leaders themselves intervene chiefly when other participants—the party leaders' own constituencies, non-

452

governmental groups, organized bureaucracies, or some public officials—persuade the leaders that they must participate directly, or when the leaders' own positions and sources of influence in their respective parties are involved.

Areas of Persistent Influence

Party leaders are most easily persuaded to intervene in four classes of governmental decisions: those affecting political parties and elections, appointments to office, the voter appeal of their party, and those concerning petitioners among their constituents. Unless an official decision affects one or more of these interests, the party leader is likely to be indifferent toward it.

Election Laws and Administration. Party leaders have responsibilities to their party organizations. As corporation executives are loyal to "the company," and as bureaucrats are loyal to "the agency," so party leaders are dedicated to "the party." The official decisions that most immediately affect their organizational interests are those embodied in the provisions of the statutes governing the structure, composition, and functions of parties and other political bodies; the procedures for effecting nominations and conducting elections; and the behavior of everyone charged with the administration of such statutes. These statutes and administrative actions frequently determine whether party functionaries possess unqualified control of party machinery and all phases of the electoral process (as they apparently did in New York City in the latter part of the last century and the early part of this one), or whether they will have to negotiate with other groups, continually face contests and battles with insurgent groups furnished with a firm enough legal base seriously to challenge incumbent party leaders, and whether third parties will in practice be suppressed instead of having real opportunities to compete with the major parties. Drawing district boundaries for the constituencies from which elective officials are chosen makes a big difference to party functionaries because the probabilities that they will carry their districts generally depend on how the lines are drawn.

On the whole, where election laws are concerned, party leaders tend to be conservative, for their authority is rooted in the existing system. The thrust for change normally comes from insurgents seeking to dislodge the prevailing leaders, from reform groups outside the parties trying to give themselves a greater voice in nominations, and from political associations who ascribe their inability to win a place on election ballots to the stringencies of the procedures set forth in the law. The regular party organizations in the city—especially the normally dominant Democratic organizations—fought, for example, against the introduction of primaries, and managed to secure a return to the convention system at the level of statewide office. They resisted the institution of proportional representation in the City Council, and succeeded (in large part by repeatedly stressing the presence of two Communists in that body) in

1947 in obtaining its repeal. The Democratic regulars ridiculed proposals for permanent personal registration (the ascendancy of the inner core in the nominating process and of the party in elections, after all, depends partly on low turnouts in both) until it became apparent that the costs of continued opposition were far higher than the costs of acquiescence. They have also delayed the use of voting machines in party primaries in the city, although this was authorized by state law.

The major parties can also be sources of suggestions for change, when change is to their advantage. In 1953 Republican County Leader John R. Crews of Brooklyn sponsored a revision of Congressional District boundaries in that borough so as to assure his organization of winning at least one seat in a strangely shaped and somewhat lightly populated, but strongly Republican, district. In 1957, as described earlier, the Republicans attempted to modify the Election Law to make joint Democratic-Liberal nominations more difficult to consummate than had been the case up to then. In 1959 the Republicans sponsored a measure in Albany providing for a late primary in New York City at a time when Democratic intraparty conflict was rife, and Republican party leaders apparently hoped to prolong it as long as possible, and at the same time to reduce to the minimum the time for healing the wounds after the primaries and before the election. Sometimes the parties join hands in formulating election legislation, as they did in 1947, when the Election Law was amended to prevent candidates with strong personal followings from capturing the nominations of both parties against the will of the leaders.

Whether party leaders take positions as defenders of the *status quo* or proponents of change, election laws and administration are decisions in which they invariably display intense interest and in which they can be expected to intervene with all the modes of influence at their command. There are many governmental decisions, including policy questions that generate great storms of controversy in the press and in the community, from which party leaders stand resolutely aloof, perhaps because their own followers are divided and any stand is worse than no stand at all, perhaps because their own organizational welfare is not directly involved. But even if only details of election legislation or procedure are at stake, the party leaders can be expected to be on the scene, and at work with all their energy, at once.

Opportunities for Appointments. Another type of governmental decision regarding which party leaders are often active is the creation or abolition of appointive posts and the establishment of qualifications for appointees. As a general rule, they tend to favor the establishment of additional jobs and to resist the reduction in the number of jobs they might be influential in filling. They also tend to oppose the requirement of qualifications and procedures that reduce their part in the selection of officials and employees. Thus, for instance, Harrison Tweed, who had been chairman of the Temporary Commission on the Courts, in 1958 attributed the defeat of the Commission's recommendations for court reform in large part to opposition from "politicians" to reorganizations and improvements that might reduce party leaders' capacity to reward supporters with judgeships and other court jobs. Leo Egan, of *The New York Times,* also reported that, "Many court clerkships and other nonjudicial jobs are now regarded as sinecures for politicians whose main efforts are devoted to their organizations. Many leaders fear these jobs might be abolished or the pay cut substantially if the present system were altered." And Samuel Smoleff, the counsel of the Citizens Union, declared the Surrogates' Courts had been exempted from court reorganization proposals because such reforms would have diminished large sources of patronage by removing many positions from control of county "bosses." Similarly, Democratic party leaders were for many years successful in preventing centralization of a number of city functions originally located in county and borough offices. Not until the administration of Fiorello La Guardia was it possible to establish one city Department of Parks, a single city Sheriff (under the merit system), an integrated Department of Public Works, and a single City Register, for the division of these operations among the five subdivisions of the city provided the county party organizations with generous numbers of jobs and other rewards. Indeed, despite the centralizing achievements of the La Guardia period, the borough offices remain, a *New York Post* survey recently revealed, centers of patronage and preserves of the parties able, because of party leader interest in them, to stand off all attempts at official investigation, reorganization, and reform. At the same time, it will be seen later, leaders of both parties often cooperate in the creation of new judicial posts—in 1958 overriding the objections of Mayor Wagner, who protested against the additional expense to the city.

Office is one of the political rewards party leaders seek for their organizations, and it is a medium of exchange they use to hold their organization together. Whenever a statute or administrative regulation touches this political currency in some way, they characteristically do all in their power to secure a decision that strengthens their organizations and their own positions in those organizations.

Maximizing Votes. Party leaders are widely regarded as responsible, and regard themselves as responsible, for carrying the districts of which they are in charge for the candidates of their respective parties. As "organization men" they work at this for the good of the party. At the same time, they try to do a good job in order to strengthen their own personal and organizational claims on political rewards.

These organizational interests induce party leaders to encourage the public officials identified with their respective parties to adopt policies believed to be popular with the voters. Many times the party leaders who urge these decisions do not themselves appear to be particularly concerned with the contents of the policies they support. If it appears that the policy will help them accomplish their own mission of getting votes, they may well back it even if they opposed it with equal vigor a short time before when the tide of public opinion appeared to be running in the other direction. For the same reason, party leaders urge officials who are members of their party to promulgate decisions of little substantive significance (since these are more easily adopted than major substantive changes) but of great propaganda value for vote-getting. In the year of a mayoral election, for example, there is almost always at least a token reduction in property taxes in the city, but, of necessity, the city being in a hard-pressed financial situation, the reduction is miniscule and symbolic despite the great outpourings of rhetoric it provokes on the part of the party in power. Likewise, the hierarchy of the party in power can usually be counted upon to point with pride to purely hortatory resolutions and declarations of policy (such as some of those of the City Council advising, commending, or criticizing the President for his handling of international relations) even though these actions have no practical consequences. Party leaders sometimes regard a loud blank as being just as effective as a live bullet in attracting votes. Party leaders are not necessarily neutral with respect to policy, but, where their own interests and the interests of their organizations are not immediately and directly involved, they may take any side on any question, or no side at all if there is no electoral advantage in it.

This, for example, was one of the reasons Thomas J. Curran, former New York County Republican Leader, came out strongly against a relaxation of rent control laws in the state in 1955, although the policy had been adopted by Republican legislators in Albany. He warned that passage of the measure would cut the Republican vote in the city "tremendously," and blamed a Republican-sponsored 1953 law permitting 15 per cent rent increases for alienating low-income tenants while at the same time engendering "apathy" among Republican apartment-dwellers on Park Avenue. On the Democratic side, Carmine De Sapio, Democratic Leader of New York County, appeared personally before the Board of Estimate to testify against proposals to widen a roadway through Washington Square Park, a project that had aroused storms of protest among residents in this Greenwich Village Assembly District. Similarly, Brooklyn Democratic Leader Joseph Sharkey and Borough President John Cashmore waged vehement, vociferous, and highly visible warfare against an approach to the projected Narrows Bridge that required razing large numbers of Brooklyn homes. Along with Assembly District Leaders from the area affected, they appeared at public hearings everywhere to voice their opposition and the opposition of their constituents. On the other hand, the party leaders temporized and delayed and maintained long silences during a 1957 controversy over a City Council bill to prohibit racial and religious discrimination in private housing. Caught between pressures from minority groups on the one hand, and many conservative, two-family home-owners and realty groups on the other, they could not decide which way to move. It is by no means clear what the personal preferences of any of these party leaders were on any of the issues involved. There is, however, reason to suspect that at least some took stands personally uncongenial to them because this is what they thought they had to do to win votes for their organizations.

Help for Individual Petitioners. In addition to promoting decisions and actions calculated to appeal to large numbers of voters, party leaders are required by the expectations of their constituents to intervene in decisions when they are petitioned for aid. In a city the size of New York, it is obviously impossible for party leaders to accommodate more than a very small percentage of the electorate. However, helping even a relatively small number of people is presumed to build a reputation and a reservoir of good will that has a "pay off" in primary and general elections. Each beneficiary, it is surmised, becomes an ambassador among his friends and neighbors, an emissary whose grateful enthusiasm about his benefactor makes him a more persuasive evangelist among those with whom he comes in personal contact than professional party workers, candidates themselves, or even their paid advertising agencies could ever hope to be. Moreover, recipients of party favors may sometimes be drawn upon for voluntary labor in primary or election campaigns. Third, those who have enjoyed party largesse may show their gratitude by donating to party campaign funds. So, along with large-scale appeals to masses of voters, party leaders apply the personal touch in the form of assistance for individual petitioners.

In a minority of cases, petitioners seek to change governmental policies and programs in some respect. The party leaders are for the most part neutral toward the policy questions involved and try to get what is asked simply to satisfy the petitioners and to render them beholden. Most of the time, the petitioners are not seeking to make or change policy; rather, they want exemptions from the policies and procedures in force. Some of these are so familiar they need no rehearsal here—evasion of penalties for traffic violations, a son helped out of trouble with the law, the tolerated violation of the Building Code, the immunity of a bookmaker from arrest and prosecution, and similar dispensations. But there are less heralded types of benefactions, too, many of which have nothing to do with violations of the law. Applications for licenses, for example, are sometimes speeded on their way through administrative channels at the behest of a party functionary ingratiating himself with a constituent. A tax assessment may be modified. The terms of a franchise may be eased or reinterpreted. Specifications in a construction contract may reduce the contractor's cost. A federal agency or a United States attorney may settle for the cessation of a federally proscribed business practice instead of prosecuting the offender. A private bill may be put through Congress to confer citizenship or admit to the country a person otherwise unqualified for these privileges. An individual entitled morally, but not legally, to compensation from the state may be aided by special legislation. A tenant unable to make a landlord fulfill his obligations under rent control laws, and too unfamiliar with administrative processes to press his claim through the appropriate public offices, may find an informed and sympathetic spokesman and champion in a party leader.

The federal, state, and city governments touch the people of the city in a thousand different ways daily. Many, trying to hasten or mitigate action in their individual cases, turn to the only persons in politics with whom they may have had personal contact: an Election District Captain or an Assembly District Leader. Trying to satisfy these supplicants takes much of the time and energy of members of the party hierarchies at the lower levels, and most of them are conscientious in the performance of these tasks (even to the point of paying out-of-pocket expenses themselves) because this is considered the most effective way of establishing a party following in an area. Some of the favors sought are trifling; others may mean large sums of money to the petitioners. To the party leaders, all are important, for they present opportunities to win new friends, hold old ones, and influence voters.

Taking stock of the range of individual interests and organizational responsibilities and commitments of party leaders, it is clear they can be expected to wield whatever influence they possess in connection with a wide variety of governmental decisions. From most of the governmental officials and employees with whom they get in touch, they get a hearing at least, generally a respectful one, often a friendly one, and sometimes a highly fruitful one.

SOURCES OF PARTY LEADERS' INFLUENCE

Services Rendered by Party Leaders

Elected officials depend heavily on party leaders for nomination and election. In view of the almost unshakeable grasp of party leaders on the nominating process, the debt of elected officials to the leaders of their respective parties requires little explanation. Even Mayor Vincent Impellitteri, who broke away from the regular Democratic organization and defeated the regular Democratic candidate in the special election of 1950, gave jobs and granted other favors to leaders of the faction he had vanquished in an obvious effort to win renomination for himself in 1953. Almost without exception, elected officeholders are desirous of reelection or election to higher office; consequently, they do all they can to maintain cordial relations with the party hierarchies that control nominations.

It is not self-evident, however, that the work of party hierarchies is crucial for the success of election campaigns. If officeholders could achieve electoral victories without the aid of regular party workers, they would be less inclined to heed the requests of the leaders. Most candidates apparently do believe the field forces of their parties are indispensable. Their belief is not without foundation. As mentioned in the discussion of elections, each time there has been a split in one of the major parties in the recent political history of the city, those parts of the organization that broke away succeeded in carrying with them substantial numbers of voters in their respective areas, indicating the probability that their field units (which the regular party organizations could not replace on short notice) were able to exercise considerable influence upon voters. The ability of the ALP and then the Liberal party to command substantial support that other independent bodies, although longer in politics, could never muster might also be partially ascribed to the manpower the ALP and Liberals could draw from the labor unions to work for their candidates. Conversely, nominees who enjoyed something less than the enthusiastic favor of the leaders of their party in the city have been badly cut at the polls. The coldness between Franklin D. Roosevelt, Jr., and Carmine G. De Sapio, when Roosevelt ran for Attorney General of the state in 1954, was an open secret, and Roosevelt's defeat in spite of the strong showing he made upstate may be explained at least in part by the relative indifference to his fate on the part of the Democratic field organization in the city, for Roosevelt did much worse here than had been expected. In 1956 when the leaders of the Democratic party seemed to show far more interest in the senatorial candidacy of Mayor Wagner and in the welfare of some local candidates than they did in Adlai Stevenson, Wagner ran well ahead of Stevenson throughout the city. The evidence is far from conclusive, for a great many other factors in addition to party effort in the field entered into the final outcomes; but the evidence, though not entirely probative, is strongly indicative.

So most officeholders, always somewhat uncertain about their prospects for renomination, reelection, or advancement, are disposed to cooperate with the party leaders on whose labors they believe they depend.

Many appointed officials and employees also owe their positions, in part at east, to the intermediation of party leaders. To show their gratitude, they may employ their official powers to satisfy the requests of their sponsors. Even if appointees are not directly indebted to any party leaders, they often cannot be unaware that the top strata of the government—the elected officials and the politically appointed executives—do have debts to the party hierarchies. Subordinate offices and employees thus frequently take their cues from the behavior of their superiors. Since party leaders have access to, influence with, and friendly reception by the top officials, the other levels commonly display the same cordiality.

TABLE 46. PARTY POSTS, PUBLIC OFFICES, AND OCCUPATIONS OF MAJOR-PARTY COUNTY LEADERS IN POWER JULY, 1959

County and party	Leader and occupation	Party posts held during career[a]	Public offices held during career
BRONX Democratic	Charles A. Buckley, government service; construction business	Chairman of County Executive Committee, Aug. 27, 1953 to date; Leader, 8th Assembly District; state committeeman; national convention delegate, 1948, 1952, 1956	Congressman, 1935 to date; Chairman of the House Public Works Committee, 1950 to date; City Chamberlain, 1929–1933; state tax appraiser, 1923–28; New York City Board of Aldermen, 1918–23
Republican	Herman Winner, government service	Chairman of the County Committee, March 23, 1957 to date; Secretary of the County Committee, 1934–57; Leader, 1st Assembly District; state committeeman	Chief Clerk, Bronx Office, Board of Elections, 1945 to date
KINGS Democratic	Joseph T. Sharkey, government service; insurance	Member of State Executive Committee; national convention delegate, 1948, 1952, 1956; Chairman of the County Executive Committee, Aug. 9, 1954 to date; Leader, 4th Assembly District; state committeeman	Vice-Chairman and majority leader of the City Council, March 13, 1940 to date; city councilman, 1938–40; New York City Board of Aldermen, 1933–37
Republican	John R. Crews, government service	Chairman of the County Executive Committee, 1934 to date; Chairman of the County Committee, 1943 to date; Leader, 10th Assembly District; state committeeman; national convention delegate, 1948, 1952, 1956	Commissioner, Board of Elections, Jan. 1, 1943 to date; Board of Taxes and Assessments, 1929–33; Chief Clerk, 2d District Municipal Court, 1925–29; assemblyman, 1920–21
NEW YORK Democratic	Carmine G. DeSapio, government service; insurance	County Leader, July, 1949 to date; Chairman of the County Committee, Dec. 15, 1954 to date; national committeeman, Feb. 13, 1954 to date; member Democratic State Executive Committee, 1954 to date; Leader, 1st Assembly District, 1939 to date; national convention delegate, 1948, 1952, 1956	New York Secretary of State, 1955–58; Commissioner, Board of Elections, Jan. 1, 1947–Jan. 1, 1955; secretary to Supreme Court Justice Louis A. Valente, 1938–39; secretary to City Court Justice Vincent S. Lippe, 1935–38

Republican	Bernard Newman, government service; law	Chairman of County Committee, Sept. 9, 1958 to date; Chairman of the Law Committee of the County Committee; Leader, 6th Assembly District South, 1955 to date; state committeeman; national convention delegate, 1956	Official Referee, Appellate Division, First Department, 1948 to date; secretary to Supreme Court Justice Samuel H. Hofstadter, 1942–48; Assistant Corporation Counsel, 1936–42
QUEENS Democratic	Robert R. Battipaglia, retail liquor business	Chairman of the County Executive Committee, Sept. 9, 1958–July 3, 1959 (Battipaglia is presently contesting his ouster); Leader, 1st Assembly District; state committeeman	Queens Superintendent of Highways, Jan. 1958–Jan. 23, 1959; Queens Deputy Sheriff, 1928–36
Republican	Frank Kenna, government service	Chairman of County Executive Committee, Jan. 11, 1947 to date; Chairman of the County Committee, Jan. 11, 1947 to date; Leader, 1st Assembly District, 1926 to date; member of the State Executive Committee; county campaign manager, 1941–47; national convention delegate, 1948, 1952, 1956	Clerk to Supreme Court Justice Henry G. Wenzel, Jr., Appellate Division, Second Department, 1933 to date
RICHMOND Democratic	Joseph A. McKinney, government service	Chairman of County Committee, Jan. 11, 1957 to date	Clerk to Supreme Court Justice Edward G. Baker, 2d Judicial District, 1957 to date; City Court Justice, Richmond County Branch, Dec. 6, 1955–Dec. 31, 1956; Municipal Court Justice, Borough of Richmond, 1st District, 1945–Dec. 6, 1955; Chief Clerk of Richmond County District Attorney, 1933–41
Republican	James A. Flood, law	Chairman of the County Committee, Sept. 1957 to date; Vice-Chairman, 1955–57	None

a National convention delegate membership from 1948 only.

The Sanctions of Party Leaders

If government officials and employees were in no way dependent upon, or obligated to, party leaders, they would still be likely to heed some of the requests of party leaders because the party organizations often possess some power to impose sanctions, over and above those connected with nomination, election, and appointment. This power is most often exercised through legislative bodies, for much of the authority of government in American society is invested in legislatures, and, at the same time, the individual legislators usually have their roots deep in the local areas controlled by party leaders. This combination of legislative power and legislative responsiveness to party organizations makes legislators especially suitable instruments for the purposes of party leaders. This suitability is enhanced by legislative procedures and practices that enable adroit legislators, as individuals, to have a profound impact on the collective actions of the bodies of which they are members. Moreover, some congressmen, state assemblymen and senators, and city councilmen are themselves party leaders and so are in a position to take direct action against recalcitrant public officers and employees. Party leaders do sometimes turn to executives and administrators when they want to punish an uncooperative public servant, but legislatures are more frequently the avenues of retaliation.

The most common type of retaliatory tactic is blocking legislation favored by the uncooperative official. Sometimes, this includes appropriations. The legislative process is such that legislation is more easily stopped than passed. An assemblyman or congressman, for example, from the territory of a District Leader who has been rebuffed in his efforts to secure favorable action, can sometimes single-handedly delay or prevent the passage of bills, particularly if he is a member or chairman of the committee through which the bills pass, and if he can muster even a little support from other legislators. Legislators also occasionally succeed in attaching crippling amendments to legislation originated by uncooperative officials, and they manage from time to time to append riders to appropriation acts that hobble the officials who refuse to cooperate. This is not so easily done as blocking legislation, for the proponents of the bills are often in a position to block the hostile provisions. Nevertheless, many bills run such a hazardous course that their proponents prefer to avoid any unnecessary fights, so that party leaders, through their legislative representatives, are often able in this way to extract concessions from other legislators, executive and administrative leaders, and even from the judicial branch under certain circumstances. Finally, District Leaders whose requests of officials are denied may persuade their friends in the legislature to launch investigations of the programs favored and supported by the hostile individuals. The legislative friends of District Leaders can also use their legislative immunity from suit to publicize accusations and criticisms damaging to agencies and programs desired by their unfriendly colleagues.

Dependence on party services, moral obligations and gratitude, and fear of retaliation thus combine to assure party leaders that the world of officialdom will usually be one in which they can make themselves heard and make their influence felt. But it is not a world in which all officials are powerless to resist the dictates of the party leaders. Many officials exhibit a high degree of autonomy.

The Multiple Roles of Party Leaders

The participation by party leaders in governmental decisions is strengthened (and also obscured) by the several overlapping roles which most party leaders play in the politics and government of the city. They are frequently

TABLE 47. DEMOCRATIC AND REPUBLICAN DISTRICT LEADERS IN GOVERNMENT POSITIONS (FEDERAL, STATE, COUNTY, OR CITY) AS OF JANUARY 1, 1952

County	Total leaders	In government, 1952		In government, 1952 or previously	
		Number	Per cent	Number	Per cent
DEMOCRATIC LEADERS					
New York	35	28	80	32	91
Bronx	14	10	71	14	100
Kings	23	19	83	21	91
Queens	25	16	64	24	96
Richmond	5	5	100	5	100
Total Democrats	102	78	77	96	94
REPUBLICAN LEADERS					
New York	31	15	48	28	91
Bronx	13	13	100	13	100
Kings	24	20	83	22	92
Queens	24	16	67	17	71
Richmond	5	3	60	4	80
Total Republicans	97	67	71	84	87
Total for both parties	199	145	73	180	90

SOURCE: New York State Crime (Proskauer) Commission, Public Hearing No. 4, 1952, vol. 6, p. 53, mimeographed.

officials in a county, the city, the state, or in the federal government. Most of them are also engaged more or less regularly in a private occupation, profession, or business. In addition, they are leaders in, or are strongly identified with, one or more nongovernmental associations. All of them as party leaders are leaders of and perceive themselves as representing the interests of a local electoral constituency—an Assembly District, or a part of one, or a county. And each of them is a member of a party executive committee for his county, frequently of a state party committee, and occasionally of a national party committee. Since they encounter governmental decisions in each of these five major roles, it is often difficult for the party leaders themselves to know in which role they are acting when they become involved in making a particular governmental decision.

For example, some party leaders in New York City are also congressmen; some are state legislators; others are city councilmen. Still others hold city, state, or federal executive office. Some are county or borough officials. A considerable number occupy positions in the courts (although not as judges). The party leader who is also an official has a dual set of obligations; some of his decisions as an official will reflect his perceptions and necessities as a party leader. In addition, and perhaps more importantly, the party leader who intervenes in a governmental decision is often dealing with a fellow official. The access of official to official, between whom there are often many *official* accommodations and common interests, usually strengthens the party leader when intervening for a party interest.

The nongovernmental careers or occupations of New York City party leaders vary. Most of them are lawyers, but many are in real estate, insurance, the building or construction industry, labor unions, or some other phase of commerce and industry. Such party leaders often specialize in attempting to influence those governmental decisions which are of greatest interest to themselves or to their business and professional colleagues. The party leader who is also an insurance broker may give special attention to governmental decisions affecting insurance, both as they may affect himself as a broker (the party leader's own financial or professional success may often turn upon such alertness) and as they may affect other party leaders or his constituents who come to rely upon him in this field of governmental decisions. Reciprocity with other party leaders may permit him to call upon them in their fields of specialization. Thus the party leader who is also an official and is engaged in a private occupation has resources for intervention in governmental decisions which extend beyond his assets as a party leader.

Most party leaders in New York City, active and prominent in one or more nongovernmental associations, acquire both obligations and resources from their leadership in such associations. The groups look to the party leader for help in influencing governmental decisions; the leader can, in turn, often deal with officials from his base as an ethnic group leader, a leader in a professional society, a labor union, or some other nongovernmental association. Such ties occasionally provide the party leader with an influential link to an official who is also a leader or member of the association for which the party leader speaks or whose influence he invokes.

The most numerous interventions by New York City party leaders in governmental decisions flow from the demands made upon them as the representatives of local electoral constituencies. Some constituents deal directly with their members of Congress, the state legislature, or the City Council;

some with the President, Governor, Mayor, or with executive agencies. But a large number seek advice and help from the party leaders; these make up the bulk of the numerous "contracts" which every party leader undertakes to carry out for his constituents. These contracts are the small currency of the party organization's system of incentives for many of its followers. Insurgency is invited by their neglect, so most party leaders are industrious and inventive in discharging the contracts expeditiously, or at least in making a convincing demonstration of effort. Carrying out a contract usually involves influencing a governmental decision, although often a quite routine one. This is the most burdensome role of the party leader, and he calls upon all his resources in attempting to meet its time-consuming requirements. If he is a majority party leader, he impresses into his service not merely his Captains but also the congressman, the state senator, the assemblyman, and the city councilmen to the extent he can command their help; he reaches out, too, for assistance from all those others he has directly helped to become officials in other branches of government. If he is a minority party leader, he has less help, but he will invariably find some access at some level, national, state, or local.

The party leader takes some of his most difficult problems of access and influence to his county executive committee or, in the case of County Leaders, to the state committee. These committees of party leaders also have some special problems of their own: it is they who must ordinarily undertake to exercise party influence over legislative delegations and over chief executives. While these committees, like the individual party leaders who are their members, are concerned mainly with nominations, elections, and appointments, they must also give frequent attention to the business of influencing other types of governmental decisions (city legislation against discrimination in private housing, state legislation on rent control, or gubernatorial tax-reduction proposals) in order to maximize, or at least to preserve, party organization control of nominations and influence upon elections. The party leaders in such situations derive their policy positions largely from their estimates of the probable effects of particular policies upon electorates in approaching elections.

In his efforts to influence governmental decisions, then, each party leader in the city is himself influenced by the five major roles he plays—as an official, a business or professional or working man, a nongovernmental group leader, a local constituency leader, and a party executive. His capacity to exercise influence is rarely measured wholly by his status as a party leader alone. Nor is his intervention in a governmental decision ordinarily perceived by the official making the decision as being merely the intervention of a party leader representing a purely party interest. Instead, to the decision-maker, the intervention usually carries with it also the connotations of the request of a fellow official, perhaps of a fellow professional in law or some other occupation, possibly of a colleague in a nongovernmental association, and sometimes of a fellow member of the party executive. The experienced party leader exploits all those connotations which will add weight to his intervention.

POINTS OF INTERVENTION BY PARTY LEADERS

Legislative Decisions

Assembly District Leaders in the Democratic party have direct and satisfying access to some of the decisions of state assemblymen elected from their Assembly Districts. Access to state senators and city councilmen is complicated by the fact that these officials are elected from several Assembly Districts and so must respond to the interventions of more than one party leader. Republican District Leaders in the city do not ordinarily succeed in electing state senators or assemblymen or city councilmen; accordingly, they must usually work out indirect lines of access to the state legislature, depending upon the cooperation of their few successful colleagues or upon the state committee of their party.

But the nature of most legislative decisions, requiring the action of a delegation rather than that of an individual legislator, compels the party leaders in both parties to work largely through their County Leaders, who in turn must rely upon the majority or minority leaders in each house of the legislature. Thus the District Leader in either party is several steps removed from direct impact upon most state and city legislative decisions and certainly from the most important ones. Even the five County Leaders must adjust their differences with each other, as well as allow some measure of discretion to the majority and minority legislative leaders. Only the District or County Leader who is himself a legislator escapes some of these frustrations, and even he is inhibited by the necessities of party unity when the roll call arrives.

Congressmen elected from the city escape close attention from party leaders in part because of the size of their constituencies but even more because most of their legislative decisions are of marginal concern to party leaders. As an intervenor in executive-branch decisions of the national government, however, the congressman frequently acts as an emissary of the party leader. And, of course, some District and County Leaders in the city are themselves congressmen. The United States Senator is even more removed from effective access by individual party leaders; his statewide electoral constituency and long term make it possible for him to confine his deference to the most important county and state leaders and to bargain effectively with them.

Party leaders thus have greatly varying capacity to influence legislative decisions. The five Democratic County Leaders can by agreement among themselves successfully control the decisions of the Democratic city councilmen, provided the Mayor or the communication media do not aggressively challenge the party leaders, in which event the results are not easily predicted. The same County Leaders, if they can agree with each other and if a Democratic Governor does not aggressively oppose them, can usually determine the legislative behavior of the Democratic state senators and assemblymen from the city. The Republican County Leaders have no similar opportunities in the City Council, and they have less capacity to direct the decisions of Republican state legislators from the city, who must usually be permitted to calculate for themselves what decisions will allow them to survive in the next election. In all these matters, the Assembly District Leaders must ordinarily yield to the judgment of the County Leaders of their party as to what is desirable for the party. The District Leaders' own influence is confined to those actions of individual legislators about which the County Leaders are indifferent. Even those assemblymen, senators, and councilmen who are also party leaders must work within this context.

Judicial Decisions

The opportunities and capacities of party leaders to influence decisions in the judiciary also vary widely. City Magistrates, appointed by the Mayor for ten-year terms, usually are indebted to one or more District Leaders for help in their original appointments; reappointment or promotion to a higher post depends upon similar help. Municipal Court justices, elected from local districts for ten-year terms, have a comparable indebtedness to District Leaders. In the middle ranges of the judicial hierarchy, as the terms become longer, the convention of renomination stronger, and the constituency larger, the access and influence of County Leaders become more important in efforts to influence decisions, but even their opportunities are limited. At the upper ranges of the judicial system—the state appellate courts and the federal courts, the judges of the latter having life tenure—the party leaders have a more remote status and sharply limited access. Democratic party leaders have superior access most of the time to the lower courts in the city; Republican leaders share opportunities more equally in the higher courts.

Party leaders are helped considerably in their efforts to influence judicial decisions by the presence of a large number of party leaders in positions in the courts' administrative systems. District Leaders and County Leaders thus are usually not required to deal directly with judges but may instead deal with a fellow party leader who is also an officer of the court. Since the party leader is most often seeking less to influence directly the judge's decision than to acquire information about probabilities, this access to an officer of the court is frequently sufficient. Certain courts, notably the Surrogates' Courts in each county, which collectively, according to the counsel of the Citizens Union, appoint several thousand special guardians, executors, and administrators of estates, with total fees running to several millions of dollars each year, have a special importance to party leaders, and the leaders' efforts to establish effective access to them is therefore pursued more systematically than in other courts.

Party leaders in the city do not appear able to influence very many judicial decisions. Their interventions must be selective and largely for information about procedures, timing, and the probable range of the pending decision. With this intelligence in hand, the party leader can either regard his obligation to his constituent as discharged or he can devise new strategies for additional efforts to make the decision more palatable. In the main, the party leaders attempt to make omniscience serve as an acceptable substitute for omnipotence in the field of judicial decisions.

County Decisions

In the five counties within the city, the party leaders, besides their concern with court decisions, are profoundly interested in the decisions of the District Attorneys. Here they are greatly aided by the dependence of the District Attorneys upon the party leaders for nomination and renomination, for advancement to higher posts, and in the selection of staff. Except in New York County during the past twenty years, almost every District Leader, and each County Leader, can count upon the presence in their county's District Attorney's office of one or more staff members directly indebted to the party leader for appointment and tenure. This provides a kind of access for party leaders matched only by the access to the state legislature supplied by the assemblyman from each district. Party leaders apparently use this arrangement, as they use their access to the courts, largely to provide needed and timely information, but there are also evidently some opportunities to influence the substance of decisions made by the District Attorney's offices, particularly with respect to what to investigate, what to prosecute, and what charges to make.

Party leaders nevertheless occasionally have their difficulties with District Attorneys. In addition to the independence displayed by Dewey and Hogan in New York County since 1938, there have been the episodes of insurgency by O'Dwyer and McDonald in Kings County. In these instances, intimacy between party leaders and District Attorneys may have yielded some advance intimations of impending party difficulties, but it provided no effective leverage with which party leaders might halt or avoid punishing investigations.

City Executive Decisions

In the wide range of the multitudinous decisions made daily by the city's executives, administrators, and civil servants, the party leaders are concerned with exercising influence over those decisions which are included in the contracts the leaders have acquired from their constituents, over those which affect the nomination, election, or appointment processes, and over those which affect the public or private career or aspirations of the party leader himself. The extensive decentralization of decision-making among the numerous executive agencies requires party leaders to maintain several different points of access to the executive branch, for there are many places in which the party leaders have relatively little influence over decisions.

The members of the Board of Estimate are frequently objects of attention from party leaders concerning decisions of the Board. County Leaders are more directly involved in such efforts than are most District Leaders. Of the members of the Board, Borough Presidents tend to be most responsive to party leaders (a tendency reinforced by the fact that Borough Presidents are themselves occasionally District Leaders or County Leaders), while the President of the Council and the Mayor tend to be less responsive, and the Comptroller to occupy a middle position. In the Board's executive sessions, the views of party leaders are sometimes reported to the Board and may have a visible impact upon its decisions. But the Board's own institutional preferences and the views of other participants in the city's political process usually carry a greater weight in Board decisions than do the party leaders standing alone. Party leaders, understanding this fact, do not attempt directly to influence very many Board actions.

Party leaders stand in varying relationship to department heads. The nature of the appointment process (described in Chapter VII) being what it is, some commissioners owe their appointments to, and depend for their future careers upon, party leaders; a larger number have no strong obligations or expectations of this kind, owing their appointments to other forces and basing their career plans upon other foundations. To deal with the agencies headed by commissioners who stand apart from the party organizations, the party leaders need other points of entry. Most of these are provided by the presence, in each department, of one or more deputy commissioners, departmental secretaries, or other appointees who are past and present beneficiaries of the party leaders and whose career expectations are tied to continued assistance from party leaders. The party leaders also depend to a considerable extent upon access to certain members of the permanent staffs of the departments—to bureau chiefs, inspectors, commanding officers in the uniformed forces, investigators, chief clerks, and to others able to provide information, exercise discretion, and exercise influence within the agency. These arrangements will differ markedly from agency to agency, from party leader to party leader, and from time to time. Their net value to party leaders interested in influencing agency decisions depends quite heavily upon a complex system of reciprocity among party leaders in which the access of each leader is shared with other party leaders. Since party leaders compete with each other, the system of reciprocity is always imperfect.

Democratic party leaders have an advantage over Republican party leaders in access to the city's executive agencies, except when Fusion administrations occupy City Hall. But Republican leaders nevertheless usually manage to have some point of friendly contact in each agency, relying most often upon some member of the agency's permanent staff who finds the relationship useful to himself.

State and Federal Executive Decisions

Party leaders in the city attempt to intervene in the executive branch decisions of the state and federal governments in much the same manner and for much the same reasons as they do in city executive decisions. Their most frequent interventions are with the field offices of the state and federal governments located in the city, but they will reach out to Albany or to Washington when circumstances require. Access to elected officials at the state and federal levels is supplemented, as is the case with city executives, by the development of contacts with appointed officials at the heads of departments and agencies, their deputies, and members of the permanent staffs. For access to executive officials at Albany, party leaders in the city often also use assemblymen or state senators as agents, while for similar purposes in Washington, congressmen (or even United States Senators) are drafted into service as intermediaries.

When a Republican Governor sits at Albany or a Republican President in Washington, the Republican party leaders in the city have some important advantages of access to the executive agencies of those governments over the Democratic party leaders. Conversely, in the 1930's (with a Democratic President and Governor, and La Guardia as Mayor), the Republican party leaders in the city had severely limited access to the decision-makers. Ordinarily, each set of party leaders in the city is able to count upon preferred access to the executive branch in at least one level of government.

WHY OFFICIALS RESIST

Yet public officials are not merely cat's paws of party leaders. They have policy preferences of their own. They have their own careers to think of. They cannot be totally unresponsive to the requirements of their jobs. Official responsibility often stimulates the private conscience of even the most cynical opportunist. Public officers and employees are subject to a great many pressures over and above those of party leaders; they unconsciously adopt the perspectives and values of the organizations of which they are part, or which they lead. They discover the bargaining power that comes with official position; shortly after the 1958 elections, for example, when the Republicans won striking statewide victories, Mayor Wagner declared (in a statement more sweeping than his subsequent actions, it must be admitted) that elected officials, in order to prevent such defeats in the future, should and would take a more active part in party affairs than they had in the past. Officials, in short, have strong incentives to seek escape from the claims and advice of party leaders, as well as inducements to comply. Party leaders find that the official opportunities to resist party importunity are rather broad.

Competing Demands by Party Leaders

Diversity, the cachet of New York City, manifests itself in competing and conflicting demands upon government officials and employees by party leaders. Their interests as individuals often clash, and dissimilarities in the composition of the populations of their respective areas impel them to make claims on public servants that are competitive or irreconcilable. Furthermore, the resources and services dispensed by governmental agencies are not unlimited, and all the requests for special consideration of applications for apartments in public housing, for stalls in public markets, for priority in the issuance of licenses to operate taxis, for example, simply cannot be granted. While minority groups press for local laws against discrimination in private housing, homeowners oppose the increase in governmental controls restricting their use of their property, and both groups find party spokesmen to urge the policy they prefer. A landlord appeals to a party leader to induce an inspector to modify a decision necessitating extensive and expensive repairs, while a tenant asks another party leader to see if the landlord cannot be compelled to render the services required by law. One District Leader tries to have a juvenile delinquent let off lightly, while another leader from a neighboring district reports that his constituents want better protection in the form of more vigorous action against juvenile gangs. During the early construction phases of New York International Airport (when the advantages of massive investments, newly created jobs, and prospects of increased business obscured later problems of noise from low-flying planes), party leaders in The Bronx argued that the new field belonged in their borough rather than in Queens. Government officials and employees quickly learn to point out these inconsistencies to party leaders, who can hardly blame the public servants for not satisfying everybody. Adept use of clashes of this kind allows public officials and employees to neutralize the competing claims and often to follow the policies they themselves prefer. It also permits them to persuade the party leaders that the adoption of objective, nonpartisan, professional standards in deciding questions of the kind at issue is the easiest way out for everybody concerned. The strategy is not totally effective; officeholders at all levels are not so insensitive as to please nobody. Yet many a party leader, championing the cause of a supporter, merely goes through the motions to demonstrate that he is not indifferent. A shrewd public official, aware of the semiritualistic nature of the operation, will often play along with it to the extent of talking sympathetically with the functionary's "client," thus confirming for the client the conscientiousness and influence of the functionary, but in most cases granting nothing that would not have been granted anyway. The official thus retains control of the decision and without provoking the party leader. Conflicts in demands and expectations of competing party leaders generate an atmosphere in which the official can choose his own occasions to accede to their wishes.

Freedom from Dependence or Obligation

Many public officials, both elected and appointed, as well as public employees are relatively free from dependence on, or commitments to, party leaders. For some, this freedom derives from their extraordinary personal popularity and vote-getting ability. Alfred E. Smith, Franklin D. Roosevelt, Herbert Lehman, Thomas E. Dewey, and Irving M. Ives, for example, consistently attracted so many votes on their own that the party leaders could not convincingly argue they owed their victories to the party leaders. As a matter of fact, it would have been just as reasonable for these high officeholders to contend that their victories put the party leaders more in their debt than they in the debt of the leaders. While all these officials did maintain good relations with most of the leaders of their parties, they dealt with the leaders as equals.

In a few instances, officials achieve such stature and reputation as to afford them immunity from the ordinary crosscurrents of partisan politics. A prime illustration is Robert Moses, who has been appointed to high office by municipal and state chief executives of both parties despite the fact that he is an avowed Republican and once ran for governor on the Republican ticket. His prestige is so great and his contributions to the welfare of the city so valued, that none of his nominal superiors has dared to remove him. Although Moses openly supported William O'Dwyer's opponent in the mayoralty election of 1945, O'Dwyer announced during the campaign that, if elected, he would retain Moses. Not only was Moses kept on as Park Commissioner but he was also made City Construction Coordinator with perhaps more power than any other appointive officer then in the municipal government. Being so secure, Moses has rarely found it necessary to bargain on matters of policy. He can pursue a self-directing course, not hesitating to engage in battles publicly with local, state, and national officials in defense of his programs and projects. The capacity of party leaders alone to influence his decisions is decidedly small. Only the officials of the Port of New York Authority can equal this degree of autonomy from party pressures, although two recent Police Commissioners—Francis W. H. Adams and Stephen P. Kennedy—have perhaps approached it.

The officials and staff of some of the more technical governmental agencies have been able to rely on the highly specialized nature of their work to mini-

mize the influence of party leaders. As requirements for specialized training
are raised and as the new requirements are imbedded in law, their independence is braced, for they would not be easily replaced at the salaries
generally offered in government service and their successors would probably
have the same professional background that made the original incumbents
unamenable to party influence. In addition, their professional associations
and their clienteles, in addition to the newspapers and civic groups, give them
such strong support that they can often afford to reject the demands of party
leaders. The city departments in the strongest position in this respect are
Health, Hospitals, Air Pollution Control, and Traffic, although they are not
the only ones. On the other hand, their leaders often reach understandings
with party leaders, and one city Health Commissioner was so skillful that he
eventually became a United States Senator.

Finally, the development of civil service—New York State and New York
City followed close behind the federal government in the enactment of the
Civil Service Law, and their systems are among the oldest and most inclusive
in the country—has eliminated one of the principal forms of leverage by party
leaders upon the decisions and behavior of public officers and employees:
the control of jobs. Public servants protected by merit system procedures are
not ordinarily indebted to any party for their appointments or promotions,
and they have tenure that safeguards them from political removal. Although
party influence has not been entirely excluded from public personnel administration in spite of merit system protection, the merit system has sharply
diminished the ability of party leaders to determine the content of many
governmental decisions. This weakening of party influence has had, as one of
its consequences, an increase in the role of the bureaucracy in formulating
and executing public policy. As the relative political power of the bureaucracy
has grown, its disposition to do what party leaders want has declined.

The Limitations of Sanctions

In addition to the autonomy stemming both from conflicts in the demands
of party leaders and from the freedom of officials from dependence on party
services, a measure of liberty also comes to officials and employees out of the
knowledge that the punitive devices of party leaders are not always swift or
certain. If the mode of party punishment is to withhold a nomination or
election campaign services, several years may elapse before the penalty can
be put into effect. Over an interval of this length, specific irritations subside
or are forgotten, or conditions change and palliate them. The element of
compromise is so fundamental and pervasive a component of politics in New
York City that grudges developed in the heat of the moment often abate and
give way to negotiation rather quickly. For instance, even after Vincent

Impellitteri ran independently and defeated the regular Democratic candidate for Mayor, and after he had waged a bitter fight against Robert F. Wagner for the Democratic nomination in the 1953 election, the regular Democratic organization was responsible for his appointment to a judgeship. Officeholders may consequently be disposed to take some risks when party leaders press them on specific decisions and choose instead to follow their own inclinations or to reach accommodations with claimants other than the party leaders.

Nor can any particular party leader be sure of preventing or obtaining from any branch of government at any level the kind of action that chastises or injures uncooperative officeholders and their agencies. Many sorts of influences are at work in the formation of any official decision, and the desires of an individual party leader, or even of a group of them, do not always prevail over the competing factors. The uncertainty is increased when officeholders are backed in their independence by strong coalitions of newspapers, civic groups, bureaucratic interests, and clientele groups. Consequently, many officials decline to comply with the demands of party leaders in matters relating to their official decisions.

Party leaders can and do register their preferences and their claims on many governmental actions. But federal, state, and city officeholders in and from the city are not often mere pawns manipulated arbitrarily by the party leaders. Officials are frequently quite independent of them, and almost always a good deal more than mere passive instruments.

PARTY LEADERS AND PUBLIC POLICY

With respect to many governmental decisions, party leaders are not very different in their objectives and strategies from other contestants in the city's political process. Some are interested in one program or policy area, some in another. The things they urge are often inconsistent. They have access to public officeholders, and they have some of the means to induce officeholders to comply with their requests. But their power over officeholders is limited in many ways, and they must bargain and negotiate with them, not always successfully, in quest of the things they want. They can rarely issue orders that will be obeyed like military commands. This, of course, is the story for most of the participants in the political process in New York City.

The most distinctive characteristic of the party leaders as participants in the city's political process is their relative neutrality toward the content of public policy. In the main, they are interested most often in exceptions to policy or program rather than in its broad alteration. They seek procedural exceptions—a higher priority for their petitioner, an amelioration of the rules in behalf of their client, an individual advantage in a complex system, a dispensation of mercy rather than impersonal justice—more often than they seek a change in basic public policy or program. They are agents of accommodation between the austere rationality of policy and the unique characteristics of the individual case. Officials, bureaucrats, and interest groups acquire commitments to policy objectives and their logical forms of administration; the party leaders, by contrast, remain uncommitted. Their commitment is to the party, to its viability, to electoral victory, and to office as the symbol and substance of party vitality. The party leader who is overtly committed to policy or program is acting out of his role as party leader, perhaps submerging his mission as party leader under a greater commitment to his role as a public official, as a representative of a constituency, a profession, or some other nongovernmental group.

In only one major policy area do the party leaders tower over the other contestants: in the field of election legislation and its administration. Even here, their control is not absolute, as the adoption of a system of direct primaries in the state and permanent personal registration in the city demonstrate. These procedures originated with, and were advocated by, groups other than the party hierarchies, and they were eventually instituted even though the attitudes of the party leaders ranged from outright opposition to an utter lack of enthusiasm. Nonetheless, no other contestants exert so much influence on governmental decisions affecting the conduct of party leaders and public elections as do the party leaders of the major parties.

In New York City, the Democrats, since they win a higher number of electoral victories, tend to have somewhat more influence on governmental decisions. More officeholders in and from the city are tied to the Democrats in one way or another. But both the Republicans and the Liberals are able to sway some official decisions, too. The Republicans have direct claim on officeholders in elective and appointive positions (chiefly in the state and federal governments) who are obligated to them, and they have their stable grip on the state legislature as well as their intermittent control of the governorship, the presidency, and Congress. For influencing governmental decisions, these are extremely effective levers. The Liberals, in their turn, have their claimed balance of power in state and city elections. Republican and Liberal party leaders sometimes apply their influence by getting in touch with their Democratic counterparts, who may recognize Democratic vulnerability and cooperate. Sometimes Republican and Liberal party leaders go directly to the officials and employees. On the whole, the Republicans are more influential outside the city than in it, and the Liberals are only as influential as the Democrats care to let them be. The minority party leaders are generally no more influential in shaping governmental actions and decisions than nongovernmental groups, and much less influential than many of these.

All party leaders like to give the impression that they can get any government to do anything they request; to the extent this impression gains currency, their own power is apt to be enhanced. In practice, while their impact on public decisions—particularly decisions applicable to individuals rather than to broad categories of policy—is not to be ignored, it is certainly not so great as they claim. In many areas of governmental activity, other contestants have far deeper and broader effects. Except for the Election Law, party leaders do not stand out among the multitude of groups taking part in the city's process of public policy formation.

BIBLIOGRAPHY

GENERAL

See the references to general texts following Chapter VI. Note especially Key, V. O., Jr., *Politics, Parties, and Pressure Groups*. 4th ed. Thomas Y. Crowell Co., New York, 1958, chap. 13; and Penniman, Howard K., *Sait's American Parties and Elections*. 5th ed. Appleton-Century-Crofts, New York, 1952, chap. 9.

PARTIES IN NEW YORK, 1898-1958
(See also references for Chapters I, VI, XVIII; also Appendix A.)

Bennett, William S., "Reminiscences." Columbia University Oral History Collection, Special Collections, Butler Library. New York City politics under Mayors Van Wyck, McClellan, Gaynor, and La Guardia.

Crowell, Paul, and A. H. Raskin, "New York: Greatest City in the World" in *Our Fair City* by Robert S. Allen, editor, Vanguard Press, New York, 1949, chap. 2, pp. 51–54. Sketches the rise and decline of major and minor political parties, from the mid-thirties to the mid-forties.

Curran, Henry H., *Pillar to Post*. Charles Scribner's Sons, New York, 1941. The Republican candidate for Mayor in 1921 reviews his career.

Dickstein, Samuel, "Reminiscences." Columbia University Oral History Collection, Special Collections, Butler Library. New York politics, 1923–1945.

Hartman, William J., *Politics and Patronage: The New York Custom House, 1852–1902*. Doctoral dissertation, Columbia University, 1952.

Klein, Henry H., *My Last Fifty Years*. The Author, New York, 1935. The autobiography of a New Yorker prominent in city politics.

McGoldrick, Joseph D., "A Scrapbook of Politics." The Author, New York, 1929. Comments, excerpts from journals, and summaries of articles on a great variety of topics relating to the politics and political life of New York City. In New York Public Library.

Stillman, John S., "Reminiscences." Columbia University Oral History Collection, Special Collections, Butler Library. An intimate view of New York politics, 1948–1950.

REPUBLICAN PARTY

Chapman, Alger B., "Reminiscences." Columbia University Oral History Collection, Special Collections, Butler Library. Discusses New York Republican politics, 1930–1949.

Davenport, Frederick M., "Reminiscences." Columbia University Oral History Collection, Special Collections, Butler Library. New York Republican politics.

Howe, Wirt, *New York at the Turn of the Century: 1899–1916.* The Author, Toronto, 1946. Republican district politics and political organization.

Morris, Newbold, and Dana Lee Thomas, *Let the Chips Fall.* Appleton-Century-Crofts, New York, 1955, pp. 63–72, 104–109, 202–211, 241–243, 284–294. Recollections of Republican party politics in New York City from the 1920's to the 1950's. Also American Labor party politics, pp. 141, 198.

Prendergast, William A., "Reminiscences." Columbia University Oral History Collection, Special Collections, Butler Library. Republican politics in New York City, 1880–1930.

Robinson, Beverly, "Reminiscences." Columbia University Oral History Collection, Special Collections, Butler Library. A district worker gives an insight into Republican party politics, 1904–1916.

Saxe, Martin, *Newspaper Clippings and Letters,* 1905–1909. Columbia University Oral History Collection, Special Collections, Butler Library. Republican political activities in Manhattan.

Zinn, Howard, *Fiorello La Guardia in Congress.* University Microfilms, Ann Arbor, Mich., 1958. Doctoral dissertation, Columbia University, 1958. La Guardia's experiences in the Republican party prior to his election to the mayoralty.

THIRD PARTIES

Barker, Charles A., *Henry George.* Oxford University Press, New York, 1955, pp. 611–619. Some aspects of the municipal campaign of 1897, in which Henry George was a candidate.

Belous, Charles, *Faith in Fusion.* Vantage Press, New York, 1951, pp. 67–72, 78–91. The structure of party machinery in New York City, written from the Fusion viewpoint and some observations on minority parties.

De Mille, Anna G., *Henry George: Citizen of the World.* University of North Carolina Press, Chapel Hill, 1950, pp. 224–237. This biography covers George's campaign for the mayoralty in 1897.

Flournoy, Houston I., *The Liberal Party in New York State.* University Microfilms, Publication no. 70,115, Ann Arbor, Mich., 1957. Doctoral dissertation, Princeton, 1956. An analysis of an important minor party in New York City.

George, Henry, Jr., *The Life of Henry George.* Doubleday, Doran and Co., New York, 1930, pp. 593–609. The municipal campaign of 1897 and the part Henry George played in it.

Josephson, Matthew, *Sidney Hillman: Statesman of American Labor.* Doubleday and Co., Garden City, N. Y., 1954, pp. 400, 600–606. The formation of the American Labor party in New York; right wing and left wing of the American Labor party and the formation of the Liberal party.

Luthin, Reinhard H., *American Demagogues: Twentieth Century.* Beacon Press, Boston, 1954, pp. 208–235. The career of Vito Marcantonio sheds light on the rise and fall of the American Labor party.

Moscow, Warren, *Politics in the Empire State.* Alfred A. Knopf, New York, 1948, pp. 102–119. An account of the "splinter" parties.

Thomas, Norman, "Reminiscences." Columbia University Oral History Collection, Special Collections, Butler Library.

TAMMANY (AND OTHER) BOSSES

Allen, William H., *Al Smith's Tammany Hall: Champion Political Vampire.* Institute for Public Service, New York, 1928. An attack on Tammany Hall, written during the presidential campaign of 1928.

Breen, Matthew P., *Thirty Years of New York Politics Up-to-Date.* The Author, New York, 1899. Glimpses of the times, work, and influence of John Kelly and Richard Croker of Tammany Hall and Hugh McLaughlin of Brooklyn.

Busch, Niven, "The Emerald Boss: Profile of John H. McCooey," *The New Yorker*, vol. 4, March 12, 1927, pp. 25–28. How the undisputed boss of Brooklyn attained and maintained his power.

Busch, Noel F., "Boss Without Cigar: Profile of Kenneth Simpson," *The New Yorker*, vol. 15, October 28, 1939, pp. 21–27. The leader of Manhattan's Republicans.

Creel, George, "The Tammany Take," *Collier's*, vol. 151, February 8, 1932, pp. 7–8, 30–32. The material rewards of politics.

Finegan, James E., *Tammany at Bay*. Dodd, Mead and Co., New York, 1933. Parties and party strategies in New York City in the early 1930's.

Flynn, Edward J., *You're the Boss: My Story of a Life in Practical Politics*. The Viking Press, New York, 1947. Autobiography of the Bronx Leader.

"Bosses and Machines," *Atlantic Monthly*, vol. 189, May, 1947, pp. 34–40. A spirited defense of the role played by bosses in city government.

"Reminiscences." Columbia University Oral History Collection, Special Collections, Butler Library. A County Leader relates his experiences in Democratic party politics.

Ford, James L., *Hot Corn Ike*. E. P. Dutton and Co., New York, 1923. A fictionalized account of the maneuvering of political bosses in New York City in the closing years of the nineteenth century.

Franklin, Allan, *The Trail of the Tiger*. The Author, New York, 1928. Written during the presidential campaign of 1928, this volume is an attack on the methods and tactics of Richard Croker and Charles F. Murphy of Tammany Hall.

Friedman, Jacob A., *The Impeachment of Governor William Sulzer*. Columbia University Press, New York, 1939, pp. 38–116, 117–126, 148–180, 241–259. The removal of the Governor as an illustration of the power of Charles F. Murphy.

Garrett, Oliver H. P., "Profile of Samuel S. Koenig," *The New Yorker*, vol. 2, March 6, 1926, pp. 15–16. The long-time Republican leader of Manhattan.

Gosnell, Harold F., *Boss Platt and His New York Machine*. University of Chicago Press, Chicago, 1924. A study of the boss of New York State.

Graham, Frank, *Al Smith, American*. G. P. Putnam's Sons, New York, 1945. The career and political influence of the governor and of other leaders of the Democratic party in New York.

Handlin, Oscar, *Al Smith and His America*. Little, Brown and Co., Boston, 1958. A popular biography of the New York Governor.

Harlow, Alvin F., *Old Bowery Days: The Chronicles of a Famous Street*. D. Appleton and Co., New York, 1931, pp. 487–529. District politics and its ramifications in one section of the city during the reign of "Big Tim" Sullivan.

Hazelton, Henry I., *The Boroughs of Brooklyn and Queens, Counties of Nassau and Suffolk, Long Island, New York, 1609–1924*. 3 vols. Lewis Historical Publishing Co., New York, 1925, vol. 3, pp. 1541–1546. The life, political history, and influence of Patrick Henry McCarren. This is one of the most complete accounts of his life. An account of Charles F. Murphy's leadership, vol. 3, pp. 1552–1557.

Heilbroner, Robert L., "Carmine G. De Sapio: The Smile on the Face of the Tiger," *Harper's Magazine*, vol. 209, July, 1954, pp. 23–33.

Hettrick, John T., "Reminiscences." Columbia University Oral History Project, Special Collections, Butler Library. A graphic portrait of the character and influence of Charles F. Murphy.

Johnston, Alva, "No More Lawyers: Profile of George W. Olvany," *The New Yorker*, vol. 7, January 9, 1932, pp. 22–25. Portrait of a Tammany boss.

Key, V. O., Jr., *The Techniques of Political Graft in the United States*. Doctoral dissertation, University of Chicago Libraries, Chicago, 1936. Practices in New York City as well as other cities are considered.

Kilroe, Edwin P., Abraham Kaplan, and Joseph Johnson. *The Story of Tammany*. Democratic Organization County Committee, New York, 1924. An official Tammany history.

Kilroe Collection in Special Collections Department, Butler Library, Columbia University. A collection of volumes, manuscripts, letters, and scrapbooks relating to the political and social history of Tammany Hall.

Koenig, Samuel S., "Reminiscences." Columbia University Oral History Collection, Special Collections, Butler Library. The story of a former Republican county leader of Manhattan.

La Guardia, Fiorello H., "Bosses Are Bunk: A Reply to Ed Flynn," *Atlantic Monthly*, vol. 180, July, 1947, pp. 21–24. An attack on the influence of party leaders in city government.

Lavine, Emanuel H., *"Gimme": Or How Politicians Get Rich*. Vanguard Press, New York, 1931. A journalistic exposé.

Secrets of the Metropolitan Police. Garden City Publishing Co., Garden City, N. Y., 1937, pp. 67–104. A journalistic version of how political bosses operate.

Leonard, Ira, *The New York City Mayoralty Election of 1909: A Study in the Realities of Reform Politics*. Master's thesis, City College, New York, 1959, unpublished. A picture of Charles F. Murphy and his influence.

Lewis, Alfred Henry, *The Boss, and How He Came to Rule New York*. Sully and Kleintreich, New York, 1904. A fictional autobiography of Richard Croker.

Loth, David, *Public Plunder: A History of Graft in America*. Garrick and Evans, New York, 1938, pp. 215–225. Describes New York under the party leadership of Richard Croker.

Lynch, Denis T., *"Boss" Tweed: The Story of a Grim Generation*. Boni and Liveright, New York, 1927. The life of a political boss.

McGoldrick, Joseph D., "The New Tammany," *The American Mercury*, vol. 15, September, 1928, pp. 1–12. Democratic party organization in the twenties.

McGurrin, James, *Bourke Cockran: A Free Lance in American Politics*. Charles Scribner's Sons, New York, 1948, pp. 179–186. Richard Croker's influence in the years immediately following the consolidation of the city.

Mackaye, Milton A., *The Tin Box Parade: A Handbook for Larceny*. Robert M. McBride Co., New York, 1934. A journalistic series of portraits of political figures at the time of the Seabury investigations.

Morris, Richard, "Charles Francis Murphy," *Dictionary of American Biography*. Charles Scribner's Sons, New York, 1934, vol. 13, pp. 346–347. A brief but penetrating study of the man and his methods of control.

Moscow, Warren, "Exit the Boss, Enter the Leader," *The New York Times Magazine*, June 22, 1947. How the old style boss has given way to the modern leader.

Politics in the Empire State. Alfred A. Knopf, New York, 1948, pp. 127–136. Some observations on the leadership of certain county leaders: John F. Curry, James J. Dowling, Christopher D. Sullivan, Michael J. Kennedy, Edward V. Loughlin and Frank J. Sampson, of Tammany Hall; Samuel Koenig, Kenneth F. Simpson, and Thomas J. Curran, Republican leaders in Manhattan; John Y. McKane, John H. McCooey, Frank V. Kelly, and John Cashmore, Democratic leaders of Brooklyn; Frederick J. H. Kracke and John R. Crews, Republican leaders of Brooklyn; Edward J. Flynn, Democratic leader of the Bronx and John J. Knewitz, Republican leader of the Bronx.

Moskowitz, Henry, *Alfred E. Smith: An American Career*. Thomas Selzer, New York, 1924. A sympathetic biography of the Governor from New York City.

Munro, William B., *Personality in Politics: Reformers, Bosses, and Leaders—What They Do and How They Do It*. Macmillan Co., New York, 1924, pp. 58–60. Contrasts the methods and influence of Tweed, Croker, and Murphy.

Myers, Gustavus, *The History of Tammany Hall*. Boni and Liveright, New York, 1917.

"The New Tammany," *Century Magazine*, vol. 112, August, 1926, pp. 385–394. A description of the city's Democratic machine at a time when it had reached the height of its prestige.

Peel, Roy V., "The Political Machine of New York City," *American Political Science Review*, vol. 27, August, 1933, pp. 611–618.

Peterson, Isabel, "Murphy," *American Mercury*, vol. 14, July, 1928, pp. 347–354. An essay on the Tammany leader.

Prendergast, William A., "Reminiscences." Columbia University Oral History Collection, Special Collections, Butler Library. Recollections of Samuel S. Koenig, County Leader of Manhattan.

Pringle, Henry F., "Local Boy Makes Good: Profile of John Francis Curry," *The New Yorker*, vol. 5, August 13, 1929, pp. 21–24. Portrait of a Tammany leader and his work with the county machine.

Riordan, William L., *Plunkitt of Tammany Hall*. Alfred A. Knopf, New York, 1948. The views of a Tammany district leader at the turn of the century.

Ross, Irwin, "Big City Machines and Liberal Voters," *Commentary*, vol. 10, October, 1950, pp. 301–308. De Sapio and Murphy contrasted.

Rovere, Richard H., "Nothing Much to It: Profile of Edward Joseph Flynn," *The New Yorker*, vol. 21, September 8, 1945, pp. 28–41. A portrait of the Bronx Democratic leader.

Shaw, William B., "Richard Croker," *Dictionary of American Biography*. Charles Scribner's Sons, New York, 1930, vol. 4, pp. 550–559.

Smith, Alfred E., *The Citizen and His Government*. Harper and Bros., New York, 1935. Observations on the responsibilities and tasks of political leaders.

——— *Up to Now: An Autobiography*. Viking Press, New York, 1929. Al Smith's own story of his life and of Democratic politics in the city, the state, and the nation.

Stebbins, Charles M., *Tammany Hall: Its History, Organization and Methods*. Stebbins and Co. Brooklyn, N. Y., 1921. An unfriendly view of Tammany leaders John Kelly, Richard Croker, and Charles F. Murphy.

Steffens, Lincoln, *Autobiography*. Literary Guild, New York, 1931, pp. 231–238. Recollections of Richard Croker and his "bossship."

Stoddard, Northrup, *Master of Manhattan: The Life of Richard Croker*. Longmans Green and Co., New York, 1931. A biography of the Tammany leader.

Syrett, Harold C., *The City of Brooklyn, 1865–1898: A Political History*. Columbia University Press, New York, 1944, pp. 70–86. Chapter entitled "Orders from Willoughby Street" is reprinted in Mary E. Murphy, Mark Murphy, and Ralph F. Weld, *A Treasury of Brooklyn*. William Sloane Associates, New York, 1949, pp. 152–166. Hugh McLaughlin, Democratic boss of Brooklyn, 1873–1903.

Tanner, Edwin P., "State Politics from Cleveland to Sulzer," vol. 7, pp. 169–198 in Alexander C. Flick, editor, *History of the State of New York*. 10 vols. Columbia University Press, New York, 1935. The story of "Honest John" Kelly, pp. 172–177, Richard Croker, pp. 177–184, and Charles F. Murphy, pp. 184–198.

Thomas, Norman, and Paul Blanshard, *What's the Matter with New York: A National Problem*. Macmillan Co., New York, 1932.

Thomas, Samuel Bell, *The Boss or The Governor*. The Truth Publishing Co., New York, 1914. Written shortly after Governor Sulzer was impeached and removed, this volume attacks Charles F. Murphy, leader of Tammany Hall.

Van Devander, Charles W., *The Big Bosses*. Harwell Soskin, New York, 1944. Reflections on the operations of Tammany leaders over two decades.

Warner, Emily Smith, and Daniel Hawthorne, *The Happy Warrior*. Doubleday and Co., Garden City, N. Y., 1956.

Werner, M. R., *Tammany Hall*. Doubleday, Doran and Co., New York, 1928. A graphic history of the New York Democratic organization.

Whalen, Grover A., *Mr. New York: The Autobiography of Grover A. Whalen*. G. P. Putnam's Sons, New York, 1955. A prominent Democrat tells his own story.

Zink, Harold, *City Bosses in the United States: A Study of Twenty Municipal Bosses*. Duke University Press, Durham, N. C., 1930. Describes the public careers of the following leaders in New York politics: "Big Tim" Sullivan of the Bowery, William M. Tweed, "Honest John" Kelly, Richard Croker, Charles F. Murphy, and George W. Olvany, all of Tammany Hall; Hugh McLaughlin of Brooklyn.

CHAPTER XIII

Nongovernmental Groups
and Governmental Action

PEOPLE TURN TO THEIR GOVERNMENTS to obtain protection and services not conveniently obtainable in the market place or elsewhere. Consequently, what governments—public officers and employees—do is important to them. Naturally they try to influence the decisions of officeholders in all levels and all branches of government, organizing themselves into groups for this purpose, or employing groups established with other ends in view. Nongovernmental groups have thus become major elements in government and politics in New York City.

All groups are not equally concerned with all aspects of government or with all governmental decisions. Those with a broad range of political interests and a record of frequent intervention in governmental decision-making (the civic groups in the first quadrant of Chart 7 described in Chapter III) tend to be process-oriented, to concentrate on governmental methods and on the rules of the game. Those characterized by a relatively narrower scope of interest and a high rate of participation (the second quadrant) in governmental decisions are often program-oriented (or agency-oriented); they follow everything a particular agency or cluster of agencies do and are relatively indifferent to events outside this central concern. Groups with a narrow range of interest and low or intermittent participation in governmental decision-making (those in the third quadrant) tend to be issue-oriented, each addressing itself chiefly to a single question affecting it at a particular moment. Groups marked by broad interests and low participation (those in the sparsely populated fourth quadrant) are often structure-oriented and thus tend to focus their attention especially on decisions about governmental organization. Decisions of all four kinds overlap, but those that are primarily of one kind—primarily about processes, or agencies and programs, or specific substantive issues, or structure—commonly evoke responses from different arrays of nongovernmental groups.

Although different kinds and combinations of groups are moved to action by various decisions, all groups resemble each other in two important respects. First, like the parties, they are run by relatively small inner cores of activists (including professional staffs, in the case of the larger, better financed, and better organized groups), whose leadership commonly spans long periods. The inner cores of the nongovernmental groups must take care that their policies and strategies do not alienate members and other supporters. But the breadth of discretion left to the leaders is substantial, and the supervision by the rank and file of the membership is at best intermittent and nominal.

Second, in all groups the modes of influencing public officers and employees are essentially alike. Some make more frequent use of one strategy and some more consistently employ another. The selection of instruments of influence at their disposal, though, is circumscribed, so the methods of all groups are broadly similar.

WHAT NONGOVERNMENTAL GROUPS DO IN THE CITY'S POLITICAL SYSTEM

Influencing Officeholders Directly

Express Views at Public Hearings. No matter who is in office, nongovernmental groups concerned about governmental decisions of any kind customarily take advantage of opportunities to present their views directly to public officials and members of the bureaucracies at public hearings. This mode of influence is probably the most common and is employed even by groups without much political experience or sophistication. Not every group is in a position to use the other strategies, but practically any of them can resort to this one.

The major targets for public testimony by groups in the city are the Board of Estimate, the City Planning Commission, and some committees of the City Council. More than twenty-five times in the course of each year the Board of Estimate assembles in public session to take action on items of city business ranging from matters of minor administrative detail to major policy choices. While the Board meets in executive session before each public session and apparently arrives at decisions in these private meetings which are later formalized in the open meetings, interested members of the general public and representatives of organizations are encouraged to appear and present their views on matters on the agenda. Individuals and groups of every kind descend, often in great numbers, upon these hearings to try to force favorable action on measures they support or to block or delay action on proposals they oppose. From time to time they succeed in their efforts, even compelling the Board to reverse or defer a decision previously reached in executive session. The agenda for virtually every Board meeting contain at least one or a few items that provoke respresentatives of some sector of the city or some group to come out to press their claims. Crowds of witnesses demanding an opportunity to speak invariably turn up when the expense budget and the capital budget are under consideration. A wider variety of groups appear and testify and submit written statements of their positions at the Board of Estimate than at any other formally institutionalized proceedings anywhere in the city government, making this one of the more widely used techniques in trying to influence governmental decisions.

By way of illustration, a survey of groups represented before the Board in five selected years (1927, 1937, 1947, 1951, and 1955) revealed some 1,900 appearances and communications on items ranging from observance of Memorial Day through protests against public incinerators to problems of teachers' salaries, the executive budget, and the capital budget. Ten subjects accounted for two thirds of all the appearances and communications: specific items in the executive budget (24 per cent); amendments to zoning regulations (8 per cent); acquisition by the city of title to land, general comments on the executive budget, and bus routes, franchises, and fares (6 per cent each); subway fares, items in the capital budget, low-rent housing, and public parks (4 per cent each). More recently (in 1957) the question of fluoridation of the city's water supply drew such crowds of group representatives and self-appointed witnesses seeking to testify that the hearing room was jammed to capacity and the hearing continued for many hours. In general, issues in education and health attracted the largest numbers of organizations during the five years studied. One civic organization, the Citizens Union, appeared more frequently than any other group. The United Real Estate Owners' Association, the Queens Chamber of Commerce, the League of Women Voters, the Bronx Board of Trade, the Fifth Avenue Association, and the Civil Service Forum were not far behind. The Citizens Budget Commission, the New York Real Estate Board, and the Commerce and Industry Association were somewhat less frequent visitors but appeared often enough to stand out. On the other hand, a number of groups active in other ways are conspicuously rare witnesses: the bar associations and medical societies in the city seldom come, official representatives of the Catholic Church and other religious groups do not turn up many times; and several associations of businessmen on important streets such as the Broadway Association, the Twenty-Third Street Association, the Thirty-Fourth Street Association, and the Sixth Avenue Association do not match the zeal of their Fifth Avenue colleagues. All these apparently rely on other modes of influence. Except for the civic groups, most of those represented at Board of Estimate hearings appear only in connection with decisions affecting the particular programs and agencies with which they are concerned, and sometimes only in connection with specific items within those programs. They do not speak on other aspects of city government when these come up on the Board's agenda.

The parade of witnesses before the City Planning Commission generally consists of many of the same groups, although the lists are not identical. The

Planning Commission is required by the charter to hold hearings on the capital budget (for construction projects of all kinds), on the adoption or amendment of zoning regulations, and on proposed variances from existing zoning regulations before these are submitted to the Board of Estimate for review and final disposition. Many groups take advantage of these opportunities to register their views. Planning Commission hearings are thus attended by individuals and groups almost equal in numbers and variety to those drawn to the Board of Estimate.

The City Council and the state legislature are less frequently employed by nongovernmental groups in the city as forums for public appearances. The Council is not a powerful body in most decisions of the city government, and its committees hold fewer hearings than do the Board of Estimate and the Planning Commission. Occasionally, a controversial proposal for local legislation will bring out many groups from all over the city, but, as a rule, they do not concentrate so heavily on the Council as on the Board and the Commission. Since much of the legislation considered by the state legislature affects the city and its residents, local nongovernmental groups testify at committee hearings in Albany, but not so often or in such large numbers as before the local bodies. They appear only infrequently at congressional hearings, partly because the legislative questions that touch their interests more often arise at the state and city levels, and partly because some of them (such as business, labor, housing, automobile, health, welfare, and other groups) delegate this work to the national associations with which they are associated.

Likewise, formal administrative proceedings are not commonly attended by city groups. At the city level there are not many parallels to the hearings of the great federal regulatory agencies (such as the Interstate Commerce Commission, the Federal Communications Commission, the Federal Trade Commission, the National Labor Relations Board, and others). In the city government, administrative agencies make more use of informal consultation than of formal hearings, and many of the functions of the federal agencies, insofar as they have any local counterparts, are performed by the Board of Estimate. Nor are a great many such hearings held by agencies at the state government level. When a pending decision impinges on the activities of a local group, the group does not hesitate to air its position at whatever formal administrative hearings are held, whether city, state, or federal. Generally speaking, though, this is not the main governmental preoccupation of such groups and not their main way of influencing administrative decisions.

In short, nongovernmental groups in New York seem to be moved to action by decisions of a relatively specific nature rather than by questions of general public policy. That is why the second and third quadrants of Chart 7 in Chapter III are the most heavily populated. Such questions as whether a school will be built in their neighborhood, or an apartment house allowed in an area of small homes, or bus fares increased, or fluorine added to water are particularly likely to arouse nongovernmental groups, at least as far as appearances at formal hearings go. Once they are aroused, they express themselves forcefully to the responsible officials to get what they want or prevent what they oppose. Then, wherever they can find a forum— at City Hall, Albany, or Washington; in legislatures, executive bodies, or administrative agencies—they tell the deciding officers what they think, what they hope for, and what they demand.

Consult Informally. Public officials invite nongovernmental groups and private citizens to participate in open forums, but they also consult with them in private and informal meetings to sound them out on pending or proposed steps or to seek their support. Perhaps even more often, the leaders of nongovernmental groups themselves seek out the public officials to present their views informally. It is thus quite natural and usual for public officers to talk over their plans and projects with their several constituencies. The Mayor, for example, or other members of the Board of Estimate, or city councilmen, or department and agency heads, uncertain about what to do with respect to specific measures, may call in the leaders of various groups for their opinions and advice. Just as often the nongovernmental leaders anticipate the call and appear at the officials' doors. They may be spokesmen for the county medical societies or the Public Health Association if a health measure is pending, or for the Citizens Housing and Planning Council if housing projects are involved, or for voluntary welfare associations if welfare policy is being considered. Informal liaison is maintained between the officials of the Fire Department and associations of fire insurance companies, organizations representing the several businesses regulated by the Department, and suppliers of fire-fighting equipment; between the Department of Hospitals and the medical schools in the city; between the Department and the Board of Health and the cosmetics and foods processing industries; between the City Planning Commission and planning groups like the Regional Plan Association on the one hand and economic groups like the Real Estate Board of New York on the other; between the Bureau of the Budget and the Citizens Budget Commission; between the Board of Education and the United Parents Association, the Public Education Association, and similar groups. Utility companies, traction companies, owners of large real estate properties, universities, and others (each frequently of a size and importance to constitute a nongovernmental group in itself) often send their "delegates" to City Hall and to appropriate city administrative agencies to protect and promote their interests. The contacts for most groups are largely with city agencies, but are not confined to them. Federal and state administrators also confer with their clientele regarding decisions under consideration, and their clientele usually include local individuals and organizations.

At informal conferences, as at formal hearings, officeholders tend to act in their official capacities. But they are private citizens, too, and in their ordinary personal, professional, and social relationships they often come into contact with the leaders of various organizations. These contacts afford the nongovernmental leaders additional opportunities to make their views, their needs, their hopes, and their expectations known in high governmental circles. Indeed, some groups apparently cultivate links with officials; the Citizens Budget Commission, for example, holds several "Meet the Government" luncheons each year for New York City officials and its own members. A personal friend of Mayor Wagner induced the Mayor to promise access to the files of the New York Police Department so that the records could be dramatized for television programs (a concession bitterly—and successfully— opposed by the Police Commissioner when it became known). The extent to which city policy is shaped by such relationships cannot be easily or accurately assessed on the basis of the available evidence, but the evidence is sufficient to suggest that unofficial contacts, though mostly *ad hoc* and unplanned rather than systematically calculated, do play a part.

These practices contribute significantly to the vitality of democratic processes. Informal consultation often counteracts the danger that government officials will act arbitrarily, in disregard of the legitimate needs and desires of those they serve and regulate. It also helps provide officeholders with information and informed judgments permitting them to avoid unsound policy moves. Finally, it constitutes a source of innovations and improvements in policy and practice. It has, in short, become an important method of keeping government responsive to widely representative groups by enabling such groups to impress their points of view on governmental decisions.

Yet it cannot be denied that there are informal relationships that transgress the bounds of propriety. The limits of acceptability are often blurred; legitimate pressure and illicit methods shade off into each other. Nevertheless, there is evidence that clearly improper, and often illegal, practices— chiefly the payment of personal, private compensation to public officers and employees for official decisions advantageous to the payers—play a part in the formulation and execution of public policy. For obvious reasons, the evidence is fragmentary, and the extent of such illegitimacy is not easily determined; that it exists, however, seems beyond question. It seems to occur mainly in connection with the enforcement of the law and represents endeavors to evade established policy. This would appear to be the import of "protection" arrangements for underworld gambling, prostitution, and narcotics syndicates, which are periodically exposed by investigations and prosecutions; of a ring of traffic policemen revealed to have sold motorists cards granting immunity to traffic tickets; of the concession by a Commissioner of Buildings that contractors frequently "tip" building inspectors. These methods also reach into the shaping of policy, as was revealed by the exposures of the Walker administration scandals, and the more recent resignation of several city councilmen under fire for having promoted legislation especially beneficial to firms in which they had interests or which they represented. Illicit modes of persuasion must therefore be included among the informal kinds of influence. They are doubtless not the general rule, but they are not unknown.

Provide Advice and Service. Some groups are given opportunities to register their preferences when their representatives are coopted into, or persuasively offer themselves for, government service on advisory bodies. Such service almost always consumes considerable time and energy but the representatives of groups agree—and even seek—to take part in it because they see possibilities of helping shape the pattern of governmental activity, of applying greater leverage to governmental decisions than they could otherwise develop. The leverage is restricted, for the officers who appoint such committees generally retain formal discretion to accept or reject the committees' recommendations, or to modify them before putting them into operation. Nevertheless, some committees have had a profound impact on some aspects of government, as did, for example, the Mayor's Committee on Management Survey (which conducted a "Little Hoover Commission" type of study of city agencies from 1950 to 1952) and the Mayor's Advisory Council (established by Mayor Wagner in 1954). One or two advisory bodies (the Mayor's Committee on Unity, for instance, which advised on race relations and was eventually succeeded by a regular agency of government, the Commission on Intergroup Relations) have even been incorporated into the government as official planning and line units, partly at the urging of the leaders of relevant nongovernmental groups who compose the most likely recruits for staffing the new agencies and thus get a chance to serve their cause from inside the government. For the nongovernmental groups concerned with the area of jurisdiction of a particular committee, representation on such a committee is an important opportunity.

From the point of view of the appointing officers, such committees serve other purposes. They may promote among the interests represented a consensus on projected controversial policies. They may furnish support to justify actions for which an official does not want to take sole responsibility. They may provide a convenient excuse to delay action. They may generate new ideas for governmental programs, structures, and procedures. They may constitute channels of information alternative to the official bureaucracies. They may win opinion leaders to the side of the officials. The composition of committees usually depends on the ends the appointing officers have in mind; some are carefully constructed to comprise all relevant groups and interests, while others are designed to give special weight to a particular set of groups and opinions (as was the Board of Education's Commission on Integration, 1955–1958). The committee members thus use the bodies to further their own objectives, but they are simultaneously used by the officials who establish them. Even when the groups are more used than served, however, representation on committees of this kind gives them at least the appearance of access and influence they might otherwise lack.

Now and then nongovernmental groups are asked by public officials to conduct studies or make reports that serve as bases for governmental actions. This is done when there is insufficient money in the budget for public agencies to do the work, or when an organization is unusually well equipped to conduct the project, or when an organization makes a timely bid to perform the service as part of its general strategy, or when an official wants the perspective of observers outside the government. Only the larger, well-financed groups are in a position to initiate or comply with such requests. Thus, the executive secretary of the Citizens Union has prepared financial reports for the Director of the Budget, and the Citizens Budget Commission carried out a management survey of five city departments for the Mayor. Specialized groups assemble data utilized by public agencies—statistics on health or welfare or recreation or land use, for example. Occasionally, groups also make themselves helpful to officials by substantiating and championing agency requests for funds, jurisdiction, and personnel. The advantages for officials in all such cases are obvious. At the same time the groups are able to exert influence on the contents of decisions by furnishing some of the premises on which the decisions are made. Furthermore, by aiding officials, they strengthen the bonds that link the officials to the groups, improve group access to public decision-makers, create obligations on the part of public servants that give the groups leverage in other situations, and foster agency predispositions to comply with their suggestions about the conduct of public business. This mode of influence is not the most common one, for the number of groups with the resources to employ it is not large, and even they can employ it only intermittently. Since it places those who are able to avail themselves of it in a favorable position at times, it must not be overlooked.

To sum up, getting their share of the stakes of political action in the city means, to the nongovernmental groups, that they must influence governmental decisions. They attempt to do so by approaching the officials and the bureaucrats of the city, the state, and the federal government at public hearings, at informal conferences, in unofficial surroundings, and (for city officers chiefly) by providing manpower and services. Simultaneously, they often apply pressure indirectly, pressure that may be harder to resist than frontal approaches.

Indirect Modes of Influence

The "indirect" modes of influence have one feature in common: the influence of each nongovernmental group using them is exerted not upon the officers or employees whose decisions and actions are the ultimate target, but upon other people—some inside government, some outside—whose ability to elicit favorable responses from the appropriate officers and employees is greater than that of the group itself. Sometimes the intermediary is diffuse—the climate of opinion. Sometimes it is a relevant segment of the public—the clientele of the officials and employees involved. Sometimes it is a party or another governmental organ or agency. Sometimes it is another nongovernmental group or coalition of groups.

Influencing the Selection of Officeholders. One way for a group to be fairly sure the governmental decisions in which it is interested will coincide with its own preferences is to help pick the men who make them. Under ideal circumstances, from the group's point of view, the officers and employees would then need no prompting; they would do what the group wants without being told because they were properly picked. Even in a less-than-perfect situation (from the group's point of view), the group instrumental in installing a man in office may then have a claim upon him that makes him responsive to its wishes. Such a claim is especially forceful when backed by the ability to effect an officeholder's removal. Hence, many groups in the city exert all the pressure they can muster to influence nominations by the party leaders, electoral choices by the electorate, appointment decisions by appointing officials, and to secure the ousters of officeholders they oppose.

Since the party leaders are in control of nominations, most nongovernmental groups have only tenuous influence on the selection of candidates. Newspapers, for example, have managed to make their voices heard in the inner cores of the parties, at least with respect to ticket leaders, party leaders apparently responding to the effects of editorials, endorsements, reporting, polls, and predictions of the press, and sometimes deferring to the newspapers in order to win their support. William Randolph Hearst, for instance, was reportedly invited by Charles F. Murphy, then head of Tammany Hall, to pick the Democratic mayoral candidate in 1917 so that Tammany could be sure of having the Hearst papers on its side. Hearst had earlier utilized his newspapers to secure his own nomination and election to Congress, and then his nomination for mayor, and finally his nomination for Governor. Joseph Pulitzer and Roy Howard were also "kingmakers" in city politics; though not so spectacular in this respect as Hearst, they did occasionally wield vetoes of some candidates for nomination and successfully urged others. More recently, the *Daily News* played a significant role in the victory of Mayor Impellitteri in the special election of 1950.

Fusion nominations for city offices long offered special opportunities for influence by nongovernmental leaders. Party chiefs sometimes consult with prominent prospective donors of campaign contributions before nominating candidates for the mayoralty and other high offices, thus assuring the flow of funds to finance the campaigns. The preferences of racial, religious, and nationality groups are usually anticipated and often accommodated. Persons of prestige are asked for advice now and then so as to obtain their backing. But, generally speaking, the influence of nongovernmental groups on nominations has been limited in scope and erratic; they constitute a secondary challenge to the domination of this phase of politics by the inner cores of the parties.

Nongovernmental groups are far more prominent in efforts to influence voters. How decisive their activities are is uncertain, for so many factors are at play on the behavior of the electorate of the city that they may cancel each other out. At any rate, the electorate seems quite self-willed. All kinds of groups are active in political campaigns, and if campaign efforts mean anything at all in terms of election outcomes, then the nongovernmental groups must be considered among the major determinants of the results. Some give money to the parties and to the "independent committees" for the candidates they prefer. Some purchase advertisements for the men they favor and send their own and party literature to their members. Some stage rallies and invite speakers. The most eminent members of other groups lend their names and reputations to the campaign managers. Some publicly rate or endorse (or denounce) candidates. The press runs news items, feature stories, editorial comments, endorsements. Unions sometimes supply labor for campaign chores. Few nongovernmental groups devote themselves as completely to election campaigns as do the parties, but the groups parallel the parties in many ways. After Election Day many of them take pains to remind the party hierarchies and elected officeholders of their contributions to the struggle.

Regardless of who is elected, nongovernmental groups often propose names for appointment to the offices in which the groups are interested. At the very least, they usually try to prevent the appointment of officers and employees they consider inimical to their own interests. Some have even achieved institutional recognition of their claims in the form of legal or customary requirements that eligibility for appointment to particular posts be confined to members of the groups in question. Appointments to the Board of Health and the Board of Hospitals, for example, are dominated by medical and health groups, while the three major religious faiths are equally represented on the Board of Education. A number of commissionerships are under differing but comparable restrictions. Such arrangements represent the cession of substantial power to the favored groups. Even groups not similarly favored exert claims on the staffing of agencies. Some press their demands upon appointing officers personally. They transmit them through party functionaries. They stress their campaign services. They point to their special technical competence to evaluate the qualifications of prospective officeholders. They secure legislative provisions spelling out minimum qualifications. They raise a public clamor to embarrass officials into complying with their demands. They may even institute suit in courts.

Only the groups that are consistently active in the governmental decision-making process, whether on a broad or a narrow front (that is to say, in the first or second quadrant), and the press are sufficiently financed, organized, informed, staffed, and equipped to pursue these tactics systematically. But there are enough of them, and they are watchful and industrious enough, to make their collective impact of considerable importance. They direct their energies at all three levels of government (but especially at the city, and at those federal and state officers and employees stationed in the city), and at all three branches of government. They are not equally successful in all of these, but they are not totally ineffectual in any of them.

Arousing Public Opinion. From the point of view of a particular nongovernmental group, the men nominated by the parties may be the wrong men; the men elected may be the least friendly of the nominees; and the men appointed may be just as hostile to the group as the elected officials. Yet this is by no means interpreted as a signal to the group to retire from the field, submitting meekly to every decision made by these antagonistic officeholders. On the contrary, such a situation often spurs the group to intensified use of other forms of indirect influence. The group takes measures to arouse public opinion; to influence the general public to pressure public officers and employees into making the decisions and adopting the programs and policies urged by the group. This technique comes close to being universal.

A campaign to arouse public opinion with respect to a pending issue may be aimed at the whole population of the city or at only that sector of it likely to be influential (and within reach of the group) in the specific case; the latter course of action is usually the choice when the general public cannot be stirred. Drawing the attention and stimulating the interest of a large audience in the city lie within the power only of the mass media of communication—in practice, of the major English-language dailies. A series of articles on any aspect of government by any one of them, if treated prominently or spectacularly, is likely to cause a good deal of comment and generate a good many questions in official circles and among the general citizenry. (The afternoon dailies, and the *Daily News* in the morning, are especially inclined to initiate "crusades" of their own, supported by a series of stories.) A sensational exposure, a revelation of scandal, can set off a wave of popular indignation strong enough to compel remedial or symbolic action by officials lest the criticisms be felt at the polls later on. A story that appears on the front pages of all the newspapers, even for a day, may have the same effect. By constant reiteration, by implication, by editorial comment, by feature items, as well as by straight news coverage, the press is sometimes able to instigate public outrage or to summon up popular enthusiasm. Even the major newspapers cannot do this at will; if there is no basis in fact for reports, or if minor occurrences are blown up out of all proportion by a reporter or his editor, the stories are apt to collapse fairly quickly or even to be laughed off. And if attempts to provoke the public are made too often, they lose their effectiveness. This is not something to be done every day. But, whenever it is done at all, it is almost always through the medium of the principal dailies in the city.

The origins of newspaper efforts are manifold. There are the highly subjective and variable canons of journalistic "newsworthiness." There is the journalistic sense of civic virtue. There are the reporters' desires to build their own reputations. There is the hope of providing entertaining news and of building circulation. There is the political motivation of publishers to help the parties or the officials they identify with, to hurt those they oppose. There is the information function. Above all, there is the vulnerability of public officials and bureaucrats to newspaper coverage. Their sensitivity, the tradition that all public affairs are open to public scrutiny, and the inability of most officeholders to strike back make them exceptionally attractive to coverage by newspapermen.

Elected officials worry about newspaper treatment because it may have electoral repercussions, while appointed officers and employees fear it may affect their jurisdiction. Sympathetic, or even neutral coverage, may help them get ahead in their careers or achieve programs dear to them; negative treatment may do just the opposite. It may alienate their supporters or gain new ones for them. Governmental decisions of all kinds in the city are often profoundly influenced by anticipated or actual press reactions.

Nongovernmental groups therefore toil to get the city's English-language dailies to publicize the groups' attitudes toward pending decisions and to induce them to back their positions as forcefully as possible. News releases are the most common means, although a few groups succeed in attracting reporters to press conferences, and a still smaller number utilize their personal contacts with publishers and newspaper staffs to obtain the coverage they want. Letters to the editors, particularly of *The New York Times*, are sent in for publication. Picket lines around City Hall, though rarely used by long-established nongovernmental groups, usually can be counted upon to draw attention to a group's cause. Sensational or dramatic statements at public hearings may also win places on the front pages, and testimony is often prepared with this end in view. Only a small percentage of this material gets more than routine treatment, but enough of it does to make many officials sensitive to the groups that produce it, for anything might conceivably explode into an issue of major proportions.

Short of reaching the general population of the city, nongovernmental groups may aim their campaigns at influential parts of it. The foreign-language press, the Negro newspapers, trade journals, union house organs, and even scores of intermittent newssheets each serving a neighborhood are not without influence. The larger groups maintain mailing lists and send their materials to their own members and as many other people as they can; they also hand out leaflets in the streets on occasion. Some hold open meetings and invite all who are interested. Some circulate petitions and send them to responsible officials and organize "write-in" campaigns by their supporters. Generally, these methods are applied to administrative decisions—the location of a school or library or health center, the installation of an escalator in a subway station, the erection of a traffic signal at an intersection—but they have also been exploited in connection with broader policy matters, such as the rate of the city sales tax.

The newspapers themselves, and the nongovernmental groups with professional staffs, are probably the most consistently successful in arousing public opinion and creating an atmosphere that persuades officeholders to heed their views. Program-oriented groups (those in the second quadrant) do not individually employ this quite so frequently or effectively although, taken collectively, their impact is doubtless considerable. Issue-oriented groups only occasionally excite the whole city with their plaints, and structure-oriented groups hardly ever. The fact that there are so many groups urging so many different or contradictory things, and that officeholders, too, can reach the public through the press and other media, makes it impossible for any group to manipulate public attitudes and reactions at will, or to get everything it asks for. Yet the use of publicity, or the mere threat of its use, does often persuade officeholders to accommodate various groups at various times.

Invoking Party Intervention. Government officials and employees in New York City respond to public opinion, but public opinion seldom gives a clear mandate with regard to particular decisions even when groups have succeeded in arousing it. For this reason, nongovernmental groups in the city regularly solicit the aid of other sources of influence on officeholders. Party leaders wield much influence of this kind.

In their capacities as party managers, however, party leaders are not enthusiastically receptive to the approaches of nongovernmental groups. The groups can theoretically help party election campaign efforts, but their chief method of helping is the uncertain and imponderable one of using their weight with their own members and their prestige with others to bring votes to the candidates of the party they favor. Ethnic, racial, and religious groups appear to be most successful in evoking party leader assistance. Financial contributions would be tangible and important, but they seem more often to come from individual donors than from the groups that are engaged in influencing governmental decisions. Some labor unions mobilize teams to do the party chore work, but only in campaigns of special interest to the union leaders. Moreover, groups that intervene frequently in the making of governmental decisions—those in the first and second quadrants, the process- and program-oriented organizations—are generally careful to avoid complete identification with one party or another because they hope to maintain their influence regardless of who is in power. For some this means aiding both major parties, but for most it means donning the mantle of nonpartisanship and disengagement from party affiliations. On the other hand, groups that intervene rarely in governmental decision-making commonly lack the resources and the continuity to make much of a difference in elections. Many groups, as *organizations*, therefore have no direct claim on the parties, and the party leaders do not jump every time nongovernmental groups crack their whips.

The leaders of many groups, however, as *individuals*, maintain personal contacts with party leaders. Just as some people contribute to both major parties so as to have access to the ascendant leaders no matter which one is victorious in any election, so a few groups build their leadership corps with some men having contacts in one party and some having contacts in the others; they employ a "two-platoon" system for negotiation with party leaders. Whether or not a group has the resources or the interest to employ such sophisticated tactics, it is sure to take advantage of whatever personal ties with either party organization have been established by any of its leaders. This is often the main channel of communication with the parties and the chief way in which the assistance of the parties can be invoked by a group.

Thus the parties do act to aid some of the programs and policies advocated by nongovernmental groups, but the reasons are not generally evident. Because few groups have strong claims on, or sanctions against, the party hierarchies, however, the parties have not become their chief instruments of influence, or their principal allies.

Invoking Official Assistance. Another manner of influencing the decisions and actions of a particular officeholder or set of officeholders is to summon the aid of another officeholder or set of officeholders more sympathetic to the petitioner's cause and in a position to compel (or at least induce) the first official (or set of officials) to do what is desired by the petitioning group. It is more frequently employed by groups to block action than to initiate it, but it may be used for both.

Most of the time, this procedure is to appeal to a higher official. In the case of city officers and employees, this usually means the Mayor, or someone close to him (including members of his staff and his department heads), the Board of Estimate (or one of its members), the Board of Health or Hospitals or Education, or, more rarely, the City Council or a councilman. Sometimes an overhead agency is approached. Where a group goes depends on the authority of the various higher officials to obtain the decision denied at a lower level, and how much leverage the appellant can apply to the various authorities to whom it might appeal. Besides asking for the usual actions to correct the lower official—mandates to do what is asked, adjustments of appropriation legislation, or a veto of some kind—appellants often seek a reorganization or change of jurisdiction that will put the kind of decision involved in the hands of a friendlier agency. If the appeal is from an act of a state or federal officeholder, the appeal process is roughly the same, but at the appropriate governmental level. In general, elective officers and their retinues exhibit a greater responsiveness than appointive officers, but not always.

If satisfaction is not secured from some city official, determined groups then turn to the state government for help. Local organization leaders often make the three-hour trip to Albany to see whether they can get state executives, administrators, bureaucrats, or legislators to persuade or require a city official to do what they want him to, or to get the state government to take the desired action itself.

Federal officials are occasionally in a position to influence the behavior of local officers and employees. Once in a while, therefore, city groups may turn to the federal government to compel or modify or prevent local actions. More often, however, when city groups appear in Washington or a federal regional administrative office in matters of this kind, they are operating in concert with, not in opposition to, city officeholders.

Appeal to the courts—now and then to federal courts, but to state courts in the overwhelming majority of such proceedings—is the final method of getting official actions. The ordinary legal bases for suit against a government have been expanded to permit so-called taxpayers' suits (discussed further in Chapter XV) against the city on relatively general grounds. This device has been used by a variety of groups for quite different purposes. In one case, a group vehemently opposed to views of Bertrand Russell instituted such a proceeding in 1939 to enjoin the Board of Higher Education from employing Lord Russell to teach philosophy at City College. The group won its point without the case ever coming to trial, for the invitation to the famous philosopher was quashed by the Mayor when the affair precipitated a great deal of adverse publicity. More recently, a civic group (the Citizens Union) instituted a taxpayer's suit to test a local law designed to restore to the President of the Borough of The Bronx all the back salary he would have received had his salary not been reduced during the stringent years of the depression two decades earlier. The same organization also brought suit to compel the removal of a city Director of Purchase on the grounds that he did not have the qualifications specified in the charter. Courts, in short, offer nongovernmental groups in the city a chance to influence officials in the other branches indirectly when they cannot do so directly.

Thus the diversity of the systems of government in New York enrich the collection of implements of influence in the storehouse of nongovernmental groups. For these groups have learned to use one segment of government to apply pressure to others. At all levels, in all branches, they find means of applying pressure.

Coalescing. Sometimes nongovernmental groups, unable to achieve their ends by all other means combined, join to make a concerted effort. There is much less of this than one might suppose; on the whole, they tend to act autonomously with respect to one another even when their positions on particular issues coincide. Nevertheless, coordinative machinery of a limited kind does exist. The staff directors of the major civic groups have formed a Civic Executives' Conference. The Industrial Council of New York City is an association of CIO unions in the city; the Central Trades and Labor Council is a league of AFL unions in the city. (The two have recently been fused by the amalgamation of the parent organizations.) Health and welfare bodies, both religious and nonsectarian, have banded together to support the Community Council of Greater New York. The Joint Conference for Better Government in New York City is a federation claiming representation of 130 civic and taxpayer groups. Diocesan and archdiocesan officers of the Catholic Church coordinate the policy positions of the hierarchy and of the numerous Catholic lay organizations in matters in which church doctrine is involved. The Protestant Council of the City of New York performs a similar function for Protestant groups, and the Rabbinical Board of Greater New York speaks for many Jewish groups. Parent-Teacher Associations are joined in the United Parents' Association, settlement houses in the United Neighborhood Houses. Working together through common organizations like these, aggregates of groups can sometimes affect governmental decisions more extensively than any of them working alone. Despite this, perhaps because joint action presents its own problem, there is a good deal of working alone.

To recapitulate, private citizens and nongovernmental groups not only approach officials directly in order to influence their decisions and actions; they also approach other people to accomplish this. They operate on party hierarchies, electorates, and appointing officers to place the personnel they want in office. They try to manipulate public opinion. They seek aid from party functionaries in connection with specified decisions as well as with personnel. They invoke the support of some officials against others. They resort to the courts. They even use each other. They leave no stone unturned. The pressure on holders of public office is continuous.

SOME NONGOVERNMENTAL GROUPS AT WORK

Citizens Union of New York

The Citizens Union, probably the most widely known and influential civic organization among the city's multitude of nongovernmental groups, was established in 1897, the year which also saw the first election of officials for the government of the Greater City. The roots of the Union, however, went back at least fifteen years earlier—to 1882, when the City Reform Club was organized and led by a group of young reformers—patricians all, including such later distinguished names as John Jay Chapman, his cousin William Jay Schieffelin, Richard Welling, and Theodore Roosevelt. A decade later, in 1892, the City Club replaced the Reform Club. Under the leadership of Edmond Kelly (an intimate associate of Welling), R. Fulton Cutting, and others it began the organization of the Good Government Clubs (dubbed "Goo Goos" by the regular party leaders) which played a considerable role in the 1894 election of reform Mayor William L. Strong.

The founding of the Citizens Union in 1897 was primarily an act of the City Club's leaders (Cutting, Welling, Schieffelin, Kelly, Elihu Root, and others) who wished to see the forces of civic reform participate directly and effectively in the elections for the first Mayor and other officials of the newly created Greater City. Other notable names among the founders were Carl Schurz, Nicholas Murray Butler, Jacob Schiff, and J. Pierpont Morgan. The Union thus began its life as a municipal political party, establishing for that purpose district clubs in most of the city's Assembly and Aldermanic Districts (building upon the example and the resources of the earlier Good Government Clubs) and nominating candidates for office. Its first candidate for Mayor, Seth Low in 1897, was defeated because the Republicans refused to join a Fusion movement, but in 1901 Low was elected with joint Citizens Union and Republican support. Thereafter the Union's role as a municipal political party began to decline and its functions as a civic group began to receive greater emphasis. When the vestigial district organizations were finally liquidated in 1918, the transformation of the Citizens Union from local party to civic group was formally completed.

The decade of R. Fulton Cutting's chairmanship of the Union (1897–1909) marks the period of its major efforts to establish itself as a municipal political party which would effectively separate the politics of the city from the politics of New York State and the nation. In addition to the more orthodox reform planks of the period (the merit system, economy, efficiency, expertise, and official integrity), the Union showed such strong inclinations toward municipal ownership of public utilities that *The New York Times* in 1900 chided Cutting for proposing that the city become "an experiment station for socialism." Throughout its more than sixty years, the Union has tended to maintain this early blend of conservative leadership with moderate liberalism in program. After Cutting became chairman of the newly established Bureau of Municipal Research (a pioneer unit for expert research into municipal governmental problems, and an outgrowth of one of the Union's central branches, the Bureau for Civic Betterment), Schieffelin became chairman of the Union, an office he held for thirty-two years. Under Schieffelin's leadership, the Union gradually developed its organization and program as a civic group. The essential elements of this development have been: a leadership core and a small full-time staff, both of great continuity; a group of carefully organized committees which carry out much of the Union's work; a modest budget; a concentration of the Union's attention upon elections, the state legislature, and the major officials at City Hall; and a broad range of interest in almost all matters that affect the government and politics of the city.

The Citizens Union now has approximately 3,000 members. Of these, about 250 are quite active in the leadership and affairs of the Union—as officers and members of its Executive Committee, its Committee on Legislation, its Committee on Local Candidates, and its more specialized committees on City Planning, on Fiscal Affairs and Management, on Traffic, and on other problems for which committees are established from time to time. The members of these committees are broadly representative of the general membership of the Union. The majority are engaged in the professions, lawyers being the most numerous. Leadership in the Union is quite centralized; the Executive Committee is essentially a self-perpetuating group and decides all major Union policy. The Union's chairman selects the chairmen of all other committees—except for the City Committee, the nominal governing body of the Union (but actually a large group of sponsors and advisers) which is elected by the general membership present at the annual business meeting of the Union. In practice, the officers and the Executive Committee determine the course the Union will take on all important matters.

As an experienced participant in the city's political contest, the Citizens Union has three main foci of activity: the evaluation of candidates for public office, the appraisal of state legislation affecting the city, and the scrutiny of the performance of officials at City Hall.

In the appraisal of candidates for office, the work of the Union rarely involves the nominating process but is primarily concerned with evaluating the qualifications of candidates for election. The process of evaluation begins annually when the Union's Committee on Local Candidates, assisted by the Union's executive secretary and its counsel, sends questionnaires to the candidates and interviews them, analyzes their responses and their previous official performance and other qualifications, and then recommends to the Union's Executive Committee that it either "endorse" the candidate (the strongest form of Union support), or indicate that the candidate is "preferred" over opposing candidates, or note that the candidate is "qualified," or give no rating if the evidence of qualifications does not persuade the committee. All candidates for city offices, all candidates for the state legislature from districts within the city, all candidates for county office in the city, and all candidates for elected judgeships in the city are included in this evaluation process. After review and approval by the Executive Committee, these ratings of candidates by the Union are released to the press and other media of communication. All the ratings of candidates (together with biographical data on every candidate to be voted on) are then printed in a booklet—the Union's *Voters Directory*, of which 75,000 to 100,000 copies are distributed during October. The newspapers, as well as other civic groups, depend heavily upon the Union's evaluations as guides to their own endorsements of, or opposition to, candidates.

The Union's participation in state legislation is carried out by the Union's executive secretary and its Committee on Legislation. The executive secretary and the Chairman of the Union's Committee on Legislation prepare in December of each year the "Citizens Union Program of State Legislation" for special emphasis by the Union during the session beginning in January. With this program, approved by the Executive Committee, the executive secretary spends the first part of each week in Albany during the legislative session, working with legislative committees and individual legislators to move forward the Union's program. Quite often, he drafts specific legislation for introduction by friendly legislators, sometimes receiving assistance in the drafting from one of the Union's special committees. Each Friday evening during the legislative session (January to April), the executive secretary meets with the Union's Committee on Legislation, reporting on his work at Albany and assisting the Committee in its painstaking analysis of each of the more important pending bills which affect the city, usually about three hundred in all. Each bill is classified as "approved" or "opposed," the degree of approval or opposition is indicated, and amendments are often proposed. As these judgments of the Union are arrived at, they are circulated to most legislators during the following week both in writing and orally by the executive secretary. As bills are passed by the legislature, the Governor is informed of the Union's attitude toward each bill it has acted on and is urged to approve or to veto the bill in accordance with the Union's judgment of its merits. At the conclusion of each session, the executive secretary prepares a report on the session's performance (particularly in terms of the Union's legislative program). For the benefit of the Union's Committee on Local Candidates, he also appraises and rates the record of each legislator from the city.

Officialdom at City Hall is made to feel the influence of the Citizens Union in a variety of ways. In the first place, the Union is often one of the architects of Fusion tickets for the mayoralty and other city offices; in every city election it supports or disapproves the several candidates for Mayor, Comptroller, Council President, Borough President, and councilman. The Union is also represented at every public session of the Board of Estimate and frequently is among the groups urging the Board to take or to refrain from some proposed action. The Council, too, is regularly reminded of the Union's observations of its activities, especially through the presence of the Union's representative at its committee meetings and general sessions and by the regular publication of the Union's *Council Digest*. Specialized agencies of the city government—the Planning Commission, the Budget Bureau, the Traffic Department, and others—are the object of attention from the Union's special committees. In addition, and perhaps most important, the executive secretary, the counsel, and the Executive Committee of the Union sit together in weekly judgment on the performance and plans of the city administration, frequently announcing the Union's approval or condemnation of the acts of city officialdom. The Union relies most heavily on the press to give wide and prominent circulation to the Union's views, but it also depends importantly upon the capacity of its executive secretary to negotiate with city officials and upon the skill of its counsel to litigate the Union's position in the courts when both publicity and negotiation fail to produce the desired results.

The nature of the Union's main concerns is illustrated by some of its major recent accomplishments. It took a leading part in the 1936 revision of the charter, especially in the establishment of proportional representation. It was a leader in the 1941 reorganization of the five county governments within the city, an action accomplished by initiative and referendum. It shared with the League of Women Voters the leadership of the twenty-year drive to secure permanent personal registration of voters. It took a major part in establishing the city Department of Air Pollution Control. It was at the head of the movement securing the 1958 county Home Rule Amendment to the state constitution. Its staff drafted, and the Union successfully supported, the 1957 statute permitting initiative petitions for charter amendments or revision under easier requirements for voters' signatures.

No other nongovernmental group in the city surpasses the Citizens Union in the wide range of its interests in governmental matters and in the frequency of its interventions in the city's political process. These characteristics of the Union are the product of several factors: (1) the origins of the Union as a municipal political party with a broad platform for the governance of the city; (2) the stability and long experience of its leadership core;[1] (3) the Union's choice of the "rules of the contest" as its domain of major interest, an incentive to scrutinize the whole range of the city's government and politics; and (4) the nature of the Union's active membership, especially the influence of members who are lawyers and educators with their inclinations to perceive the role of a civic organization in broad and inclusive terms.

The Citizens Union finds its most constant and valuable ally in the city newspapers. It is the Union's capacity to secure wide dissemination of its views, and frequently to get these views influentially endorsed by the communication media, that gives greatest potency to the work of its officers, committees, and staff. Candidates and officeholders can seldom be indifferent to the proposals or the indictments of a group which can speak forcefully, under favorable auspices, to so many of their constituents. The news release is, consequently, the most familiar and most frequently used weapon in the arsenal of the Union. The Union's demonstrated capacity to use this weapon, established by more than a half-century of experience, is a factor in the Union's ability to negotiate, to bargain with, and to secure concessions from officialdom at City Hall and at Albany, thus aiding substantially the Union's claims for the inherent merit and expertise of its proposals. The city's press, in turn, has long found the Union to be a regular and reliable source of news, a useful guide for many of its editorial positions, and a valued source of information for its staffs. This mutually agreeable collaboration has had a long and rarely interrupted history. Since 1954, the Union has also expanded its efforts to include weekly programs on television and radio, the Union's officers on these occasions interviewing public officials (as high as the Mayor and the Governor) and candidates for public office.

The Union finds frequent opportunities to join with certain other nongovernmental groups in combined efforts to exert influence in governmental affairs. The Men's and the Women's City Clubs, the League of Women Voters, the Citizens Committee on Children, and the Citizens Housing and Planning Council are among the most frequent allies. The Public Education Association, the United Parents Association, the United Neighborhood Houses, the Citizens Budget Commission, the Civil Service Reform Association, the Commerce and Industry Association, and the Chamber of Commerce are often joined. In the main, however, the Citizens Union,

---

[1] Several members of the Executive Committee have served as such for thirty or forty years, others for twenty-five years, a majority for more than a decade. The chairmen of other committees characteristically serve many years in their posts, while the executive secretary and the counsel have each held their posts twenty-five years.

conscious of its premier position as a civic group in the city, prefers to take its own individual stand.

Commerce and Industry Association

The Merchants Association, predecessor of the Commerce and Industry Association, was established in 1897. It began its organizational life in the year when the Greater City was being established. In 1941 it was reorganized as the Commerce and Industry Association, its membership and activities being broadened. The Association is now a general association of mercantile, manufacturing, insurance, utilities, real estate, building construction, banking, shipping, and other business organizations in the city.

As was true of its predecessor organization, the Commerce and Industry Association is a multipurpose organization. It performs many services for its members, providing information and advice on a wide range of matters: on social security regulations, benefits, and taxes; on export and import opportunities, regulations, procedures, and related problems; on domestic transportation services, facilities, and regulations; on unemployment insurance problems; on industrial relations problems and practices, on salary and wage standards; and other personnel management problems. As a participant in the city's political and governmental process, the Association conducts most of its activities through a staff division, the Governmental Affairs Department.

The leadership group of the Commerce and Industry Association is found in its Board of Directors, the chairmen and members of its 36 standing committees, and the senior members of its full-time staff. Altogether these amount to about 400 active leaders in a total membership of 4,000 corporations and individuals. The Board of Directors, which may be regarded as the inner core of the Association's formal leadership, consists mainly of the presidents, executive vice presidents, and vice presidents of the city's large corporations. Some of the city's leading law firms, accounting firms, advertising agencies, and engineering offices also serve on the Board, which was composed of 34 members in 1959. The Executive Vice President of the Association (a full-time officer) and the senior staff members provide a main point of continuity in Association policies and activities, but in practice, the leadership of the Association is even more highly centralized. The President of the Association is empowered under its by-laws to appoint an Executive Committee, consisting of the officers of the Association and "not less than three nor more than seven Directors," three members of the Committee being a quorum. The Committee may exercise the full authority of the Board, reporting its actions to the Board for information rather than for ratification.

The Association does not confine its governmental and political activities to the city and its government. Throughout its history it has also been much interested in the national and state governments. At present, the Association, in its participation in the political and governmental process, gives three quarters of its attention to matters governmental and political at Albany, in the state government generally, and to City Hall and its affairs, with the national government receiving the remaining quarter.

The founders and early organizers of the Merchants Association included William F. King, a drygoods merchant and wholesaler, the Association's first president and the prime mover in its establishment; William L. Strong, also a merchant and the reform Mayor of New York from 1894 to 1898; Frederick Wurster, a manufacturer and the reform Mayor of Brooklyn, 1894–1898; and John Starin, owner and operator of a Hudson River steamboat fleet. From the beginning, business objectives and political objectives were intermingled in the activities of the Association. Regulation of railroad and utility rates and services, improved rapid transit for the city, municipal ownership of electric power, deepening and widening of New York harbor, modernization of the city government's accounting methods, investigation and exposure of irregularities in the "Ramapo water scheme" were among the issues which dominated the activities of the Association's first decade. These matters took Association representatives to Washington and to Albany as well as to City Hall. As the economic complexion of the city changed, the relative strength of merchants among the Association members declined; increasingly the center of gravity shifted, over the decades, to banking, real estate, insurance, utilities, construction, and manufacturing members. By 1930 the most numerous class of members were in banking and finance. Changes in membership and leadership have brought new types of activities by the Association. Concern with salary and wage standards in the city's labor market and labor-management relations; revision of the state unemployment insurance law, of the city's Building Code, and of the state workmen's compensation system; opposition to the proposed city purchase of a Staten Island power plant in 1943; and interest in urban renewal legislation are illustrations of its more recent targets of attention.

As these activities indicate, the Commerce and Industry Association does not focus its major interests upon the city's budget processes (as does the Citizens Budget Commission, discussed below). Its greater interest is in the regulations and the services of the city government having special significance for the members of the business community whom the Association represents. While it has a major interest in taxes on business transactions, it is also active in connection with the real property tax and so it actively supports the Citizens Budget Commission's efforts to prevent an increase in that tax, provided taxes more distasteful to the Association are not the alternative. The Association gives constant attention to local laws and administrative codes which control the discretion of its members in their ways of doing business. Accordingly, the Association deals frequently with the Comptroller, the Health Commissioner, the Buildings Commissioner, the Traffic Commissioner, and the heads of similar agencies.

Association spokesmen make frequent appearances before the public sessions of the Board of Estimate and the committees of the Council. But the press release and the public statement are much less relied upon by the Association than is private negotiation by Association officers, committee chairmen, or other specially chosen Association representatives with the city official or officials (elected or appointed) having jurisdiction over the issues with which the Association is concerned.

The Association maintains an office at Albany, headed by the Association's associate counsel. His functions include providing members of the Association information they request concerning the operations of the state government, and participating in the drafting, securing the enactment, and guiding state officials and the bureaucracies in the application of state regulations and statutes. When the legislature is in session, and on other special occasions, the Association's officers, staff, and committees assist the Albany office in the representation of the Association's interests in the policies and activities of the state government. As in its relations with City Hall, the Association at Albany relies importantly upon private negotiations with officialdom.

The Association finds its most consistent allies among the other associations of the business community. Association Board members frequently serve also on the boards or committees of these other business groups. The New York Chamber of Commerce, the Empire State Chamber of Commerce, the Board of Trade, the Real Estate Board, the Citizens Budget Commission, and varying combinations of the several hundred borough, local, and "street" or "avenue" associations in the city often join with the Commerce and Industry Association in efforts to influence city and state officials and agencies. On such occasions the Association will often assume the leadership role among the allies, but it will yield this position to one of the allied groups if that strategy seems superior. Leadership ordinarily goes to the organization which first seizes the initiative on an issue of common concern.

The Association is less often, but not infrequently, allied with the civic groups of the city. These alliances are usually confined to issues in which economy, efficiency, or integrity is being emphasized. On rarer occasions, as in the mayoralty elections of 1933, the Association's predecessor participated in the support of Fusion candidates, but the more typical affiliation of the Association with nonbusiness groups is illustrated by the active support of charter revision in 1936.

The Commerce and Industry Association and the Citizens Budget Commission are the two most active organizations in the business community as participants in the city's political process. They are not directly competitive with each other, the Citizens Budget Commission concentrating upon the budget systems of the city while the Association gives its attention to a wider range of governmental issues important to businessmen. Nor does the Association have any obvious rivalry or other difficulty in its relations with the city's other major business associations, each of which has its own specialized assignment as an instrument of influence for the city's varied business groups.

Citizens Budget Commission

The Citizens Budget Commission, established in June, 1932, had its origin in the city's financial crisis of that year—a depression crisis common to all the cities and states in the nation and to the nation itself. The immediate purpose of the CBC in 1932 was to participate in decisions concerning the city's financial rescue. Its long-range goal was to emphasize "economy and efficiency" in the city's government. In announcing CBC's formation in 1932, its sponsors said the organization would "work with the director of the budget in preparing the annual appropriations of the City" and would thus "focus citizen activities on the point where spending originates."

The Commission's founders included representatives of the city's largest corporate taxpayers—especially large Manhattan real estate interests, merchants, and bankers—and its leadership and membership have not greatly changed during the more than twenty-five years of its history. The Commission's first Board of Trustees in 1932 included Peter Grimm (president of the Real Estate Board of New York, 1927–1931, as well as long-time president of William A. White and Sons, one of the city's largest real estate firms), Henry Bruère (president of the Bowery Savings Bank), Lewis E. Pierson (Irving Trust Company), William Church Osborn (a leading attorney), Raymond B. Fosdick (like Bruère, a former commissioner in the Mitchel administration), J. Barstow Smull (president of the New York Chamber of Commerce), Thomas J. Watson (president of the Merchants Association). The Commission's 1959 Board of Trustees includes a comparable roster of the city's business leaders.

The Commission's membership now represents about six hundred corporations, associated with the CBC through the individual membership of one or more officers of each corporation. The CBC is financed by contributions from these members, ranging in amounts from $10 to $2,500, providing an annual budget of about $100,000 a year. Within its membership, the leadership of the Citizens Budget Commission is highly centralized. The Board of Trustees contains a broad representation of the city's business life, but the center of gravity for CBC policy and action is to be found in the Board's executive committee.

The Commission does not depend upon working committees of its members; the work of the organization is done by a full-time professional staff under the leadership of an executive director. During its twenty-five year history, the leadership of the CBC has been largely centered in three major personalities: Peter Grimm, mentioned above; Robert W. Dowling, president of CBC since 1947, and a prominent figure in the Democratic party in the city; Harold Riegelman, first secretary and subsequently the long-term chief counsel to the CBC, a leading attorney and a leader in the Republican party in the city.

The Citizens Budget Commission participates in the city's political process as a leading spokesman for the large revenue-providing groups in the city. It is, accordingly, a frequent and skillful participant on a specialized range of issues. The CBC's primary assignment is the guardianship of the limitations on the taxing and borrowing powers of the city government which were reaffirmed in or newly written into the New York State Constitution of 1894. This assignment leads the CBC to concentrate its attention upon the two major expenditure processes of the city government: the expense budget and the capital budget. Thus the main targets of influence for the CBC in the city government are the Budget Director, the City Planning Commission, the Mayor, and the other members of the Board of Estimate. Its access to the Budget Director is one of CBC's most jealously guarded and carefully nurtured assets.

In its methods of operation as a participant in the city's financial decisions, the Citizens Budget Commission emphasizes systematic factual analyses of city expenditures, city revenues, and the managerial efficiency of the city government's service activities. It is a severe critic of all inefficiency and an eloquent advocate of changes that it believes would promote financial savings. The stress of its findings is usually less upon the reduction of services than upon the opportunities for the improvement of management, but it rarely recommends the expansion of existing city services. Since its greatest concern is with the tax on real property, the CBC bases most of its proposals upon the immediate and long-range consequences it believes the proposals will have on the costs of doing business in the city—particularly on the real property tax rate.

Much of the Citizens Budget Commission's influence as a participant in the city's political system is exercised through close and intimate bargaining by the leaders of the CBC with the Budget Director, the City Planning Commissioners, the Mayor, the Comptroller, and other members of the Board of Estimate. This effort is also extended on occasion to officials of the state and national governments when they are involved in city financial questions. In these off-the-record relationships, the prestige of the Citizens Budget Commission leaders in the business community, as well as the roles of Dowling and Riegelman in the Democratic and Republican parties, are assets of great importance to the CBC, both in securing an audience and in the attention paid to its views. One related technique used effectively by the Citizens Budget Commission several times each year is the holding of "Meet the Government" luncheons at which city officials are present as guests of honor. "These friendly, sociable gatherings are one of the Citizens Budget Commission's 'best bets'," the Commission's 1955 annual report recorded.

The Citizens Budget Commission does not confine its activities to these types of negotiation. Its counsel and its executive director are among the most frequent speakers at the public sessions of the Board of Estimate, usually stressing the expenditure and revenue aspects of whatever issues the Board may then be considering. CBC appearances at the City Planning Commission's capital budget sessions are no less regular. In relevant proceedings at Albany it is a consistent advocate of economy for the city government. The Commission's status with city officialdom is illustrated by its capacity to perform semiofficial tasks for the city government. For example, in 1933 Mayor O'Brien requested CBC to draft an executive budget bill and a capital outlay bill. Both bills became law. In 1947 Mayor O'Dwyer asked the Commission to survey five city departments, an assignment which produced in 1948 a CBC report entitled *A Better Government for a Better City*. At least eight trustees and officers of the Commission served as members of the Mayor's Committee on Management Survey in 1950–1952, and several have also served on Mayor Wagner's Advisory Council since 1953.

Press releases, too, are an important part of the Citizens Budget Commission's methods of exercising influence. CBC staff studies, themselves the most systematic continuing analyses of the city's fiscal management available to the public, are regularly made the subject of carefully prepared press releases; the statements of its officers before public bodies and in other forums are invariably given to the press in advance, and CBC spokesmen engage often in presenting its views in letters-to-the-editors of the leading newspapers. The congenial relations between the press and the CBC are symbolized in the awards the Citizens Budget Commission makes to several city newspapers and to newspaper staff members each year at a special awards dinner, the citations being given by the CBC for what it regards as outstanding coverage of city news, especially its financial aspects.

The Citizens Budget Commission works in close alliance with the Commerce and Industry Association, the New York Real Estate Board, the New York Chamber of Commerce, and the numerous mercantile and real estate associations in the city. Harold Riegelman, as the Citizens Budget Commission counsel, is often the spokesman before the Board of Estimate and elsewhere for a group of associations allied on a particular issue with the CBC.

With the civic groups (the Citizens Union, the League of Women Voters, the Men's and Women's City Clubs, and others), the Citizens Budget Commission has less consistent alliances. The CBC takes great care to emphasize its own civic image, underscoring its research activities and its devotion to "the facts" and strategically minimizing its preoccupation with economy and the tax rates. It often collaborates with the civic groups, but it may part company with them if they are sharply critical of the Budget Director, or if they espouse new city government programs or the expansion of existing city services, either of which represents substantial additional expenditures. The CBC in such instances is reluctant to jeopardize its needed access to the Budget Bureau, nor can it endorse policies which might lead to increased taxes, especially if the real property tax rate is to be affected. On most substantive issues in which civic groups become involved, the Commission attempts to remain neutral, usually confining the emphasis of its views to the financial costs of the proposals. On a few issues, however, it will support increased expenditures when a particular city service has a special relevance to its membership; for example, the CBC will usually support an increase in the size of the police force or in expenditures for traffic improvement.

The Citizens Budget Commission is the most active, the most specialized, and one of the most effective representatives of the business community in the city's political process. Its primary function is to guard the most important taxpaying groups in the city against all avoidable increases in their tax bills, a function the CBC has performed with energy and skill for a quarter century.

Central Trades and Labor Council

The Central Trades and Labor Council has been an influential participant in the city's political process since the establishment of the Greater City. As an organization, the Council has several purposes: to adjust jurisdictional and other differences among its member unions, to combine the resources and strategy of the city's labor unions in certain disputes with employers, and to exercise labor union influence in the city's government and politics. Only rarely has its political purpose received primary emphasis in the Council.

The Council is a body of delegates representing each of the AFL unions in the city, their membership being variously estimated at 750,000 to 850,000. When the pending merger of the AFL Council with the city's CIO Council is completed, the combined membership will approach 1,500,000. The Council is thus, and will seemingly continue to be, the largest membership association among the nongovernmental groups in the city. It is accordingly a group toward which party leaders and city officials ordinarily exhibit deference. When the Council is able to achieve unity on, and to give priority to, its political goals, it can wield great influence. But the Council is rarely able to muster its strength in such fashion, with the result that its influence has tended to be specialized and limited, not unlike that achieved by non-governmental groups of small membership.

In its participation in the politics and the government of the city, the Council has typically given its attention to nominations and elections; to local laws and codes affecting the licensing of trades, building standards, and the regulation of strikes and picketing—as well as to the agencies administering these activities; to the Comptroller's, the Budget Director's, and the Board of Estimate's powers in determining the prevailing rates of wages; and to the Mayor's appointing powers.

The Council has had an almost unbroken history of endorsing the major candidates of the Democratic party for city office. Under the leadership of Joseph P. Ryan, long the president of the Council, it endorsed Walker for Mayor in 1925 and 1929, O'Brien in 1932 and 1933, Mahoney in 1937 (after first endorsing La Guardia, and then reversing its position in October), while under the presidency of Martin T. Lacey it endorsed O'Dwyer in 1941, 1944, and 1945, bolted to Impellitteri in 1950, but endorsed Wagner in 1953 and 1957. These endorsements are not invariably accompanied by support for the entire ticket. In 1957 the Council endorsed the Republican candidate for Queens Borough President, James A. Lundy, as well as a Republican candidate for the City Council, Stanley Isaacs. With most of the Mayors thus endorsed, especially with Mayor O'Dwyer, the Council president has had a special status, possessing considerable influence in the appointment process and in decisions of public policy.

The Council, responding to the interests of its building trades members, has also had a long interest in influencing the content of the city's Building Code and in its administration by the Buildings Department and the Board of Standards and Appeals. The Council has had a related interest in the issuance and regulation of licenses which affect the members of some of its affiliated unions. Of equal (or perhaps even greater) earlier importance to the Council as a participant in the city's political process was its long drive to neutralize the police force in its attitudes toward strikes and picketing, a goal finally accomplished in the first term of the La Guardia administration. No less important to the Council, although it was not prominent in its creation, was the establishment in 1954 of the city Labor Department, an agency providing additional access for all labor groups to the Mayor and other city officials.

The Council has always had only a limited capacity to speak for the whole labor movement in the city and considerable difficulty in speaking authoritatively even for the leaders and members of those unions which belong to the Council. The member unions are each jealous of their own autonomy, in labor-management matters as well as in matters governmental and political. Groups of these member unions are often joined in other councils of their own, as in the Building and Construction Trades Council and the Teamsters' Joint Council. These special councils, as well as the individual unions, often have separate goals in the city's political process. The garment trades unions, for example, have seldom felt fully committed to the political goals of the Council, which they have regarded, with general accuracy, as being dominated by the building trades, the longshoremen, and teamsters. The labor unions thus have often spoken to City Hall with numerous and competitive voices.

The Council's influence in the city's political process has been diminished by the rise of the CIO unions in the city and by their organization into their own separate council. The AFL council did not join in the creation of the American Labor party in 1936 nor follow its lead in support of La Guardia in 1937 and 1941. And the Council has played no important part in the leadership of the Liberal party established in 1944, although some of the Council's member unions joined with some CIO unions in launching that party. The Council has preferred instead to rely upon its traditional pattern of close affiliation with the leaders of the city's majority party. Whether this tradition will be modified as one of the consequences of the pending merger with CIO unions into a new AFL-CIO Council is uncertain, but the persistence of the long-established pattern is suggested by the 1957 choice of a building trades union leader—Harry Van Arsdale, of the Electrical Workers —to succeed Lacey as Council president and presumably to head the merged organization when it is formally established in 1959.[1]

The Council finds its allies primarily in the labor movement, although not without some of the difficulties suggested above. It rarely joins with the civic groups (in contrast with a greater inclination of the CIO Council to do so), and it is even rarer for it to join with groups representing the business community, although this combination occurs at times on building code matters and infrequently on tax questions. In the main, the Council pursues its own separate way, relying upon its own weight in campaign endorsements and in off-the-record bargaining with party leaders and city officials for limited goals.

PATTERNS OF GROUP INFLUENCE

Restricted Scope

Possibly the most striking characteristic of the behavior of the city's nongovernmental groups is that even those groups with the widest range of interests, and with records of almost constant participation in the governmental decision-making process, are quite specialized, while those that

---

[1] The merger of the AFL and CIO Councils was completed in late 1959, with Van Arsdale as president of the combined organization. The description of labor's participation in the city's political process presented here will thus slowly change, probably in the direction of greater and more unified influence.

concentrate on particular areas of governmental activity are for the most part indifferent to what goes on in other areas. The civic groups center their attention on the rules of the contest—seeing that they are observed and enforced, trying to improve them, cutting across all functions with a heavier emphasis on process than on substance. Functional groups, on the other hand, deal with process, structure, and substance, but primarily in the one chosen arena, such as taxes and expenditures, education, health, welfare, housing, recreation, or hospitals, in which each is deeply involved. Whether constantly active (in quadrant two) or concerned only about one decision on an *ad hoc* basis (in quadrant three), functional groups pay attention to restricted portions of the governmental spectrum. All groups use all available modes of influence, although in different degrees, but each group applies them to its own program in order to obtain its share of the stakes of city politics.

As a consequence, the inner core of each group develops close relationships with one, or at most, a few agencies. In some particular segment of officialdom, leaders of each group are usually received whenever they request an audience, their advice considered seriously when offered and often incorporated in official decisions, their views canvassed when not volunteered. In a manner of speaking, many group leaders become intimate parts of the city's machinery of governmental decision in certain spheres. They are nongovernmental in the sense that they cannot *promulgate* binding orders and rules the way officeholders clothed with public authority can, but they often have as much to say about what officeholders promulgate as the officeholders themselves, let alone the parties and other contestants for political prizes. Officeholders feel compelled to cooperate with them because they have so much influence, knowledge, and interest. Out of this official acceptance grows an integration of portions of government with relevant nongovernmental groups.

Civic groups tend to work most closely with overhead agencies and the Mayor's staff. Program groups are identified chiefly with their appropriate line agencies—health and medical groups with the Departments of Health and Hospitals, charitable organizations with the Department of Welfare, educational associations with the Board of Education, contractors with the Department of Public Works, builders and landlords and building managers with the Department of Buildings, and so on. Planning groups concentrate on the City Planning Commission and the Housing Authority, as well as on other special authorities. Churches and associations of churches focus on education, welfare, and, with respect to certain issues (for example, the distribution of contraceptive devices and instruction in their use), on health and hospitals. Ethnic groups address themselves to the Commission on Intergroup Relations, among other agencies. Taxpayer associations are concerned largely with the financial agencies of the city. Geographical and veterans' organizations, as well as individuals acting on their own behalf, are linked for the most part with line agencies, although not always with a particular one; they move from one to another depending on what they want at any given moment, what issues have come to a head, and what decisions are pending. The kind of group makes no difference; the leaders of all of them seek out official allies. Those that intervene only intermittently in governmental affairs are not able to build up strong ties; that is why they are forced to make appearances before the Board of Estimate the keystone of their program of action. But even they try to find officeholders in various agencies who will pay special attention to their plaints and pleas.

Of course, like parties and governmental agencies, nongovernmental groups are not monolithic. They encompass many interests and many points of view, and their leaders must pay heed to these divergent attitudes and objectives in order to prevent their organizations from dissolving. In the execution of the strategies of the organizations, however, it is the small managerial cores that decide which goals will be emphasized and which modes of influence will be employed. These inner circles operate under fewer membership restraints, in many respects, than party leaders and governmental officials subject to the formal requirements of primary and general elections. Consequently, they often speak with a single voice, and negotiate with unity and authority, in pursuit of the ends they consider important. For many purposes, the active leaders of nongovernmental groups *are* the groups in relations with officials and with other groups.

It may therefore be said that governmental decisions affecting the people of the City of New York emerge from many decision centers, each center a cluster of officials and employees and associated nongovernmental group leaders. While some group leaders rove over a number of centers, their impact on any single one is (except, perhaps, for the press and the civic groups) smaller than the impact of the groups that concentrate on that center exclusively. And what comes out of any one center is not ordinarily carefully integrated with what comes out of the others.

For a group to converge on one center the firepower of all modes of influence at its command is an obvious technique for making the most of its resources. Yet this calculation does not seem to be the origin of the pattern of relationships between nongovernmental groups and public servants. Rather, it has arisen because each group has a circumscribed area of interest. Governmental functions and official decisions that fall outside a group's interest simply do not bring the group into play. But every decision falls within someone's expertise and concern, and the affected organizations bring all their methods of influence to bear on relevant decisions. Many small islands of decision-making develop, and they are self-reinforcing because nongovernmental groups then discover that partial monopolies are advantageous tactical arrangements for them. The pattern, having evolved, persists.

Uncertainty

No group, regardless of how many channels of influence are available to it, can be certain that its efforts will result in the official decisions it wants. There are almost always other groups demanding something else. Whichever side prevails can be sure the other will promptly employ alternative channels of influence to have the decision reversed. Defeated in one agency, claimants turn to another; repulsed in one branch of government, they appeal to another; vanquished at the local level, they may carry the fight to Albany or even to Washington. That is why negotiation and compromise are the normal procedures; every group gets less than it sought, but more than it might have obtained had it been inactive.

Moreover, party leaders, public officials, and bureaucrats are not completely submissive, nor are their decisions, policies, and programs mere resultants of the external forces exerted on them. They have their own ideas and interests and their own commitments to the objectives of their jobs. Formal authority being lodged in their hands, they are particularly well situated to make their views the official ones. None of them, it is true, can ignore the other participants in the political process; all possess some sanctions, and even the most powerful and popular governmental officers need at least the tolerance, if not the active cooperation, of those around them. Other participants grow restive with officials cool to the wants and preferences of the people they represent. Most party leaders and officeholders are adept at manipulating levers, too; they have their own sources of influence, and they are often able to stand off the assaults of nongovernmental groups ready to tell them what to do. Indeed, in most instances, the relationship of nongovernmental groups to party leaders and officialdom in the many centers of decision in the city's governmental process is mutually advantageous; it gives the groups access to the officials, but it also permits officials to marshall their constituencies for their own purposes.

Clearly, no group as a claimant on public officers and employees can be sure in advance that things will go the way it would prefer. It may get all it asks for; it may get only a part; it may get none; it may even precipitate a controversy that sets it back. Uncertainty is built into the system.

Two Camps

Because there is a great deal of fluidity in the system, nongovernmental groups, party leaders, and officeholders constantly realign themselves on different questions. They do not necessarily move out of their respective centers of special interest and expertise, but they constantly form and reform their alliances within them. In this respect, things shift all the time.

Nevertheless, one fairly persistent division cuts across the whole governmental scene: the line separating service-demanding from money-providing forces. The line is particularly evident in the appearances before the Board of Estimate. Functional groups and neighborhood (and other geographical) associations of all kinds appear to press for additional services, or expansion or improvement of existing ones, or to fight against curtailment of services. In this they are generally aligned with agency heads, hoping to better their programs through increased appropriations for capital projects and current expenditures, and with members of the bureaucracy pressing for pay raises. At the same time, taxpayer groups insist that expenditures be trimmed to permit the city to operate without increases in taxes, even if this requires holding down the variety or quality of services offered. The chief financial officers of the city—especially the Comptroller and the Director of the Budget—tend to side with them.

The line is not hard and fast. At one time or another, everybody is on the service-demanding side. Property-owning groups that object vociferously to rises in property tax rates favor subway extensions in their areas (for these increase the value of their holdings), and merchant groups that protest against increases in sales taxes are in the forefront of the campaigns for more public parking facilities (to make it easier for customers to patronize their stores). Many groups who insist on more schools and teachers, or more police protection, or additional parks will also fight against a city income tax. The division between the camps is blurred.

Nevertheless, it can be predicted confidently that the two camps will form every year. The insistence that service be rendered on an ever-increasing scale is unfailing, and the resistance of those who pay a large part of the bill is equally enduring. Lower income groups tend to make up the core of the service-demanders, who therefore count among their numbers the most depressed and deprived segments of the population, Negroes and Puerto Ricans especially. More advantaged groups, economically and socially, compose the money-providers. Observers unfamiliar with the New York City system of government might logically infer that the money-providers would have greater influence by far, since their access to the highest level of officialdom and their resources are presumably better. In fact, the quantity of services has steadily grown over the years; in the long run, despite temporary setbacks, the secular trend is unmistakable. The call for services has steadily won out.

Wide Access to Government

This suggests the fourth and final attribute of the patterns of group influence: the system functions in such a way that anyone who feels strongly enough about any governmental decision need not feel, or be, entirely helpless to do something about it. No one is entirely alienated; the statement, "You can't fight City Hall!" does not describe the governmental process that now obtains in New York. For any group can fight City Hall, almost every group does, and many are remarkably effective. Governmental decisions by all public officeholders in the city are affected by nongovernmental groups.

This process is not without its costs. The main cost is the comparative ease with which proposed actions by government can be blocked or emasculated. Every positive policy, every new idea, must run a gantlet fatal to many. Originality and innovation always face a hostile reception; the odds at the start favor the obstructors.

Opinions about the costs and benefits of these arrangements are far from unanimous. The balance between the need for community leadership and the desire for group influence on governmental decisions is always delicate. However the New York City adjustment may be evaluated, one feature of it will probably gain widespread agreement: this is indeed an open political system.

BIBLIOGRAPHY

GENERAL

Key, V. O., Jr., *Politics, Parties, and Pressure Groups.* 4th ed. Thomas Y. Crowell Co., New York, 1948, Part 3.

Lasswell, Harold D., *Politics: Who Gets What, When, How.* Whittlesey House, New York, 1936, Parts 2 and 3.

Lasswell, Harold D., and Abraham Kaplan, *Power and Society.* Yale University Press, New Haven, 1950, Part 2.

Truman, David B., *The Governmental Process.* Alfred A. Knopf, New York, 1955, Part 3.

WITH SPECIFIC REFERENCE TO NEW YORK CITY

Allen, William H., "Reminiscences" and correspondence. Columbia University Oral History Collection, Special Collections, Butler Library. Describes the work of the New York City Bureau of Municipal Research and other civic organizations.

Why Tammanies Revive: La Guardia's Mis-Guard. Institute for Public Service, New York, 1937, pp. 34–42. The role of civic associations in municipal affairs during Mayor La Guardia's first administration.

Almond, Gabriel A., *Plutocracy and Politics in New York City.* Microfilmed doctoral dissertation, University of Chicago, 1939.

Amberg, Eda, and William H. Allen, *Civic Lessons from Mayor Mitchel's Defeat.* Institute for Public Service, New York, 1921, pp. 59–68. The role of civic agencies during the Mitchel administration.

Amy, Henry J., *Tax Limitation in New York City.* Citizens Budget Commission, New York, 1937. A spirited defense of a provision of the state constitution written at the behest of taxpayer groups.

Binkerd, Robert S., "Reminiscences." Columbia University Oral History Collection, Special Collections, Butler Library. The work of the Citizens Union as recalled by a member.

Bishop, Joseph B., *The Chronicle of One Hundred and Fifty Years: The Chamber of Commerce of the State of New York, 1768–1918*. Charles Scribner's Sons, New York, 1918. One of the oldest nongovernmental bodies located in the city—its history and influence on public affairs.

Breen, William H., *Thirty Years of New York Politics Up-to-Date*. The Author, New York, 1899, pp. 98–106. Owners of transportation lines and their efforts to influence the city government.

Bruère, Henry, "Bureau of Municipal Research and Better Government in New York City," *World's Work*, vol. 23, April, 1912, pp. 683–686.

"Reminiscences." Columbia University Oral History Collection, Special Collections, Butler Library. Describes the work and influence of the Bureau of Municipal Research, a pioneer civic organization.

Bunzl, Mrs. Walter, "Reminiscences." Columbia University Oral History Collection, Special Collections, Butler Library. The work of the Citizens Union described by an officer.

Bureau of Municipal Research, *Six Years of Municipal Research for Greater New York: Record for 1906–1911*. The Bureau, New York, 1912.

Municipal Research, 1913–1921. Official organ of the Bureau of Municipal Research. In the eight years it was published there were 95 numbers. Indicates the interest and scope of activities of this civic group.

Ten Years of Municipal Research. The Bureau, New York, 1915. A summary of the work of the Bureau and its impact on New York City government during its first decade.

Central Labor Council, *Labor Chronicle*, 1928 to date. A newspaper published 11 times a year, i.e., an issue for each month except July and August; a separate issue covers both of these months. This newspaper registers activities of importance in the Central Labor Council, including those involving the city government.

Chamber of Commerce of the Borough of Queens, *Queensborough*. The Municipal Reference Library contains numbers from vol. 1, May, 1914, through vol. 33, December, 1957. The issues of this journal indicate the interests and activities of the members of the group.

Childs, Richard S., *Civic Victories: The Story of an Unfinished Revolution*. Harper and Bros., New York, 1952. A general treatment of reform movements which touches on New York City frequently.

"Reminiscences." Columbia University Oral History Collection, Special Collections, Butler Library. The Citizens Union described by one of its leaders.

Citizens Budget Commission, *Annual Reports*, 1932 to date. These publications of a tax-payers' group interested in promoting economy picture the activities and interests of the organization.

"Releases," October, 1938–December, 1941 (bound volume); January, 1942–December, 1944 (bound volume); January, 1945–November, 1946 (packet); January, 1947–November, 1954 (packet), mimeographed. In main reading room, Astor Branch, New York Public Library. These releases, which deal with a wide variety of topics, illustrate the organization's range of interest and variety of activities.

News, 1937–1946. Four-page journal, 10 vols., 1937–1946. All volumes have two numbers, except vol. 1 (1937), 7 numbers; vol. 5 (1941), 4; and vol. 9 (1945), 1. The news and views of the Citizens Budget Commission. On file in the New York Public Library (Astor Branch).

"Report on . . . Executive Budget," annually, to date. A series of mimeographed press releases, offering the view of this taxpayers group on the current expense budget each year. In the New York Public Library (Astor Branch).

Transit Primer: The Facts of Rapid Transit Unification. The Commission, New York, 1934.

Transit Handbook: Analysis of the Rapid Transit Problem in New York City. The Commission, New York, 1934.

The Story of Pensions in New York City. The Commission, New York, 1934.

Economy and the New York City Budget. The Commission, New York, 1953.

Management Fundamentals and City Government. The Commission, New York, 1952. A plea for economy in budgeting made before the Board of Estimate by the Citizens Budget Commission and allied taxpayer groups.

The P.F.B.'s [Planning, Financing, Budgeting] of Capital Budgeting. The Commission, New York, 1952. A brief, presented to the City Planning Commission, on the proposed capital budget for the calendar year 1953.

Save New York City. The Commission, New York, 1940. A summary of briefs presented to the Board of Estimate in 1940, indicating possible savings in the executive budget and a long-range program for economy.

Citizens Union, *Annual Reports*, 1915, 1916, 1923, 1897–1926 (1 vol.), 1897–1927 (1 vol.), 1897–1929 (1 vol.), 1897–1930 (1 vol.), 1931, 1897–1932 (1 vol.), 1897–1933 (1 vol.), 1897–1934 (1 vol.), 1934–1958 (published annually). These annual reports and forecasts illustrate the purpose, methods, scope, and accomplishments of the work of the Citizens Union.

Reports of the Committee on Legislation of the Citizens Union for the Sessions of 1905–1940 (36 annual reports). A record of regular and special sessions of the state legislature which presented annual reports on the work of the legislature, its actions on important bills, and the voting records of individual legislators elected in New York City.

Voters Directory. Published annually as a special issue of *The Searchlight*, 1915–1951 (called the "Voters Guide," 1915–1917). Published separately, 1952 to date. An annual publication that offers citizens a "guide to informed voting" by appraising the candidates for local offices on the basis of their education, ability, and past records and by offering recommendations on referenda presented to the electorate.

Across from City Hall, 1949 to date. A monthly newsletter that presents a summary of the activities of the Citizens Union.

City Council Record. Citizens Union, New York, 1938 to date. A complete record of bills and resolutions introduced into the City Council, indicating what happened to each. Also a record of bills and resolutions introduced by each councilman.

"A Quarter Century of the Citizens Union: A Chapter in the Political History of New York City," *The Searchlight*, vol. 12, December 14, 1922. An official history of the first 25 years of the Citizens Union, which recounts its origin, aims, methods of operation, and accomplishments.

"1897–1947: A Half Century of the Citizens Union," *The Searchlight*, vol. 37, November, 1947. A "doggerel history" which reviews the highlights of the work of the Citizens Union in humorous verse.

Citizens Union Collection. A collection of pamphlets, scrapbooks, and office files of Citizens Union, housed by the City College Library. At City College, Bernard M. Baruch School of Business and Public Administration, 17 Lexington Avenue, New York 10, New York.

A collection of pamphlets, scrapbooks, and office files, donated by the Citizens Union. At Columbia University, Special Collections, Butler Library.

Citizens Union Research Foundation, New York:

Smoleff, Samuel D., *Compacts for Clean Waters*. 1949. A study of intergovernmental cooperation to combat water pollution.

Morrison, Donal M., *Gotham Cleans Its Doorstep*. 1950. An analysis of the city's sewage disposal program.

You Can Do Something about Smoke. 1952. Suggestions for air pollution abatement.

Keat, James S., *Some Answers to New York City Problems*. A summary of reports submitted to the Mayor's Committee on Management Survey.

Childs, Richard S., *Appointive Municipal Administrators under Mayors*. 1953. A review of the experience of other cities.

The City Gets a Check-Up. 1954. A summary of the reports of the Mayor's Committee on Management Survey and the Temporary State Commission to Study the Organizational Structure of the City of New York.

Smoleff, Samuel D., *Tomorrow in and Around New York*. 1954. The facts and needs of the metropolitan region.

Oravetz, Kalman A., *New York Courts on Trial*. 1955. A report on a plan for simplification of New York's court system.

Operation "Colossus." 1956. Progress of regional planning in the metropolitan area.

Bard, Albert S., *Aesthetics and City Planning*. 1957. Exterior appearance and municipal planning.

Wiley, T. T., *A Safe Journey*. 1958. The city's Commissioner of Traffic outlines some problems of traffic engineering.

City Club of New York, "Executive Committee Minutes, 1908–1910." In New York Historical Society.

Civil Service Reform Association:
Report of the Executive Committee of the Civil Service Reform Association, 1881–1917.

Report of the Executive Committee of the Civil Service Reform Association and Treasurer's Report, 1918–1943.

The New York Civil Service. Annual reports for 1944–1950.

Annual Reports to the Public on the New York Civil Service, 1951 to date. Indicate the activities of the Civil Service Reform Associations.

Cohen, Julius Henry, *They Builded Better Than They Knew*. Julian Messner, New York, 1946, pp. 21–31. A portrait of a worker in civic associations—Horace Deming.

Commerce and Industry Association of New York, *Annual Reports*, 1942 to date. Published as separate pamphlets. Indicate the activities of the largest Chamber of Commerce in the Eastern United States.

Commerce and Industry Bulletin, published by the Merchants' Association of New York, April 30, 1941 to July 30, 1941. This organization later became the Commerce and Industry Association.

Commerce and Industry Bulletin, August 27, 1941–November 15, 1957.

Voice of New York Business, November 22, 1957, to date (a weekly newsletter). News and views on national, state, municipal, and metropolitan problems.

In the Legislative Hopper, 1954 to date. A newsletter containing news of federal and city activities with emphasis on state legislative action, published weekly while the state legislature is in session. Successor to the following publications: *Legislative News Letter*, 1947; *Albany News Letter*, 1948; and *Albany News Bulletin*, 1949, 1950.

Know Your Legislators (1954, 1955, 1957, 1958, and 1959). A pamphlet that urges the members of the Association to "tell their legislators what they think" and that helps to identify national, state, and city legislators.

Tax Bulletin, January 4, 1957, to date. Published irregularly, this bulletin indicates its members' interest in taxes, federal, state, and local.

C.I.O. Council of New York City, *New York City Trade Union Handbook*. Annual. A trade union directory and manual.

Curran, Henry H., *John Citizen's Job*. Charles Scribner's Sons, New York, 1924. A veteran of politics in New York City offers his observations on many phases of the game.

The City Club of New York. The City Club, New York, 1935. Reprinted from an article in the *New York Herald Tribune*, January 29, 1928. A brief outline of the history and accomplishments of the organization.

Pillar to Post. Charles Scribner's Sons, New York, 1941, pp. 312–320. The counsel to the City Club tells how his organization influenced the municipal government.

Dodds, Harold W., "New York Citizens Budget Commission," *National Municipal Review*, vol. 25, March, 1936, pp. 192–193, 196. A review of the work of the Commission in its early years.

Earle, Genevieve, "Reminiscences." Columbia University Oral History Collection, Special Collections, Butler Library. Exposition of the tactics of the officials of the Brooklyn Bureau of Social Service and the Women's City Club.

Hirsch, Mark D., *William C. Whitney: Modern Warwick*. Dodd, Mead and Co., New York, 1948, pp. 511–540. Street railways and politics at the turn of the century.

Klein, Henry H., *Politics, Government, and the Public Utilities in New York City*. The Author, New York, 1953. An exposé of the influence exerted by public utilities on the city government.

League of Women Voters of New York. *They Represent You.* Annually. Instructions to voters on when, how, and to whom they may express their views on public affairs.

Levy, Beryl H., and Shirley A. Siegel, *Toward City Conservation: A Memorandum for New Yorkers on Aspects of Urban Renewal.* West Side Organizations, New York, 1959. The Housing Act of 1954 called for citizen backing of urban renewal. This pamphlet demonstrates citizen participation in the city.

Lundberg, Ferdinand, *Imperial Hearst: A Social Biography.* Equinox Cooperative Press, New York, 1936. The life and work of an influential newspaper publisher.

MacDonald, Dwight, "Profile of George Harvey Hallett, Jr.," *The New Yorker*, vol. 29, August 22, 1953, pp. 31–49.

Manzinos, Alex, *Pressure Groups and the New York City Mayor's Management Survey.* Master's thesis, City College of New York, 1953, unpublished.

Mayor's Committee on Management Survey, *Modern Management for the City of New York.* 2 vols. The Committee, New York, 1953, vol. 1, pp. 256–258. Proposals for integrating the work of citizen groups with the functioning of the city government.

McAneny, George, "Reminiscences." Columbia University Oral History Collection, Special Collections, Butler Library. Observations about the Civil Service Reform League, the Citizens Union, and the City Club by a man who served as president of the City Club.

McGoldrick, Joseph, "A Scrapbook of Politics." The Author, New York, 1929. Contains descriptions of civic organizations and citizens' groups, such as voters' leagues, the City Club, and the Citizens Union and Bureau of Municipal Research. See especially Papers nos. 8456, 8734, 8735, 8747, 8748, 8952, and 9400. In New York Public Library.

Merchants' Association of New York, *Annual Reports*, published in pamphlet form 1899, 1900, 1901, 1904; in *Yearbook*, 1905–1931; in *Greater New York*, 1932–1940; in pamphlet form, 1941. Indicate the association's operations and the scope of its work.
Greater New York, 1912–1915 (weekly bulletin); *Greater New York*, 1928–1941, published irregularly about eight or nine times per year. The organ of the Merchants' Association, now the Commerce and Industry Association.

Moscow, Warren, *Politics in the Empire State.* Alfred A. Knopf, New York, 1948, pp. 42–51. How politics in New York City reflects the ethnic and nationality groups that comprise its population.

New York Educational Conference Board, *Review of Fiscal Policy for Public Education in New York State*, 1947 to date. This association of organizations interested in public education publishes this annual review of state and local finances as they relate to the needs of public education in New York, the focus being on the adequacy of state support.

New York State, Department of Labor, *Directory of Labor Organizations in New York State, 1955.* The Department, New York, 1956.

New York, Woman Suffrage Collection, 1869–1919, *Minutes of Woman Suffrage Association of New York State, 1869–1917; Minutes of Woman Suffrage Party of New York City, 1910–1919;* also miscellaneous papers. Special Collections, Columbia University, Butler Library.

Pink, Louis H., "Reminiscences." Columbia University Oral History Collection, Special Collections, Butler Library. Briefly describes the work of welfare organizations, such as the University Settlement and Neighborhood Guild, in which the author was involved before going into public life.

Prendergast, William A., "Reminiscences." Columbia University Oral History Collection, Special Collections, Butler Library. Observations on civic organizations such as the Bureau of Municipal Research, the Citizens Union, and the City Club.

Pringle, Henry F., "Wet Hope: Profile of Henry Hastings Curran," *The New Yorker*, vol. 6, June 14, 1930, pp. 22–25. The duties of a counsel to the City Club of New York.

Public Education Association, *Annual Reports*, published irregularly since the inception of the organization in 1895.

The Public and the Schools, 1918 to date. A printed newsletter or bulletin, reflecting the views of the Public Education Association, which has been published irregularly since its inception.

School Volunteer News, 1958 to date (published about three times a year). The organ of the School Volunteers, an auxiliary of the Public Education Association.

Special Reports:

Leggett, Stanton F., and William S. Vincent, *A Program for Meeting the Needs of New York City Public Schools, 1947.* Published jointly with the New York State Educational Conference Board.

"Let's Close the Schools," 1948. A plea for more city and state funds to raise the educational standards of the city's public schools.

The Status of Public School Education of Negro and Puerto Rican Children in New York City, 1955. Prepared jointly with the New York University Research Center for Human Relations and financed by the Fund for the Republic.

Popper, Hermine I., How Difficult Are the Difficult Schools? 1959. A survey of conditions in the public schools which draw their population from underprivileged neighborhoods.

"Rejected Youth or Rejected Schools?" 1959, mimeographed. A report on the past, present, and future of the city's continuation schools.

These reports indicate the scope and breadth of the Association's interests.

Fiscal Policy for Public Education in the State of New York, 1947; A Review of Fiscal Policy for Public Education in New York State, 1948; and *1953 Review of Fiscal Policy for Public Education in New York State, 1952.* Present the views and reactions of the Public Education Association to then current programs of state aid for education.

PEA Looks at Teacher Training: The Public and the Schools, 1951; and *Toward Improving Teacher Selection for New York City Schools,* 1950. Prepared by the Special Committee on Teaching Training, these pamphlets present the findings of that body.

Released Time for Religious Education in New York City's Schools, 1943, 1945, 1949. Separate publications for each of these years. These pamphlets state the views of the Committee on Released Time of the Public Education Association.

The Possibility of Economics in School Construction, 1951; Teachers' Recommendations for Elementary School Buildings, 1951; Size of Elementary School Units, 1951; and *How the School Building Can Be Planned to Serve Other Community Heads,* 1951. These publications offer the views of the Committee on Modern School Building Needs of the Public Education Association.

Look at Your School, 1951, and *The Good Elementary School,* 1953. Publications prepared by the Childhood Education Committee of the Public Education Association.

A Citizen's Guide to the New York City Public Schools. The Association, New York, 1958. Explains how the Association carries out its aim of "proposing . . . such changes in their [the public schools'] organization, management, or educational methods as may seem necessary or desirable" and how it tries to gain acceptance of these proposals.

Purdy, Lawson, "Reminiscences." Columbia University Oral History Collection, Special Collections, Butler Library. A social worker who was affiliated with such organizations as the Tax Reform Association (1896–1906) and the Charity Organization Society (1918–1923) tells how civic organizations attempt to influence city officials.

Ranschburg, Herbert J., *The Role of a Civic Agency.* Doctoral dissertation, New York University, 1957, unpublished. A study of the Citizens Budget Commission by a staff member.

Regional Plan Association, *Annual Reports,* 1929 to date. The annual reports of a citizen metropolitan organization.

Ross, Lillian, "$1,031,961,754.63," *The New Yorker,* vol. 23, July 12, 1947, pp. 27–40. Pleas by nongovernmental groups at budget hearings.

Schieffelin, William J., "Reminiscences." Columbia University Oral History Collection, Special Collections, Butler Library. The long-time chairman of the Citizens Union explains how it influenced city affairs.

Shaw, Frederick, *History of the New York City Legislature*. Columbia University Press, New York, 1954. Some comparisons between the showing of citizen groups before the Board of Estimate and the old Board of Aldermen and City Council, pp. 74–75, 79–80, 227; the Merchants' Association and the Building Code, pp. 77–78; members of citizens' groups help draft the city charter, pp. 168, 169.

Stewart, Frank M., *A Half Century of Municipal Reform*. University of California Press, Berkeley, 1950. Primarily a history of the National Municipal League, this volume refers often to the work of New York City reform groups, such as the Citizens Union and the New York Bureau of Municipal Research.

Syrett, Harold C., editor, *The Gentleman and the Tiger: The Autobiography of George B. McClellan, Jr.* J. B. Lippincott Co., Philadelphia, 1956, pp. 292–295. How Mayor McClellan viewed civic associations.

Tanzer, Lawrence A., "Reminiscences." Columbia University Oral History Collection, Special Collections, Butler Library. A detailed exposition of the work of the Citizens Union—its origins, operations, accomplishments, and methods of obtaining results.

Tebbel, John, *The Life and Good Times of William Randolph Hearst*. E. P. Dutton and Co., New York, 1952. Appraises the career and influence of a prominent newspaper owner.

Ware, Caroline F., *Greenwich Village, 1920–1930*. Houghton Mifflin Co., Boston, 1935, pp. 161–166. This neighborhood study indicates how Italian residents of that day were striving for political power.

Welling, Richard. *Richard Welling Papers*. New York Public Library, Manuscript Division. Papers of a life-long reformer who served in many civic organizations.

As the Twig Is Bent. G. P. Putnam's Sons, New York, 1942. The autobiography of a municipal reformer.

Wheeler, Everett P., *Sixty Years of American Life*. E. P. Dutton and Co., New York, 1917. Beginnings of reform associations: "Good Government" Clubs, p. 337; The City Club of New York, pp. 338–339; and The Citizens Union, pp. 358–367.

Winkler, John K., *William Randolph Hearst*. Hastings House, Publishers Inc., New York, 1955. The impact of an ambitious newspaper publisher on public affairs in New York City.

Winton, Harry, *Parents Can Influence Legislation*. United Parents Association, New York, 1951. A legislative guide or handbook, written for the use of local parent associations.

Wise, Stephen, *Challenging Years*. G. P. Putnam's Sons, New York, 1949, pp. 15–20. This autobiography relates the part the author played in the City Affairs Committee in the early 1930's.

Zeller, Belle, *Pressure Politics in New York*. Prentice-Hall, New York, 1937, pp. 133–155, 211–222. Group activities and pressures in Albany.

CHAPTER XIV

Courts and Politics

THE PLACE OF THE COURTS IN THE POLITICAL CONTEST

Their Dual Role

LIKE ALL OTHER GOVERNMENTAL officials and employees engaged in the quest for the stakes of political contest, judges and their staffs are both claimants and distributors. The special character of the judicial process sets them apart from those whose primary functions are the formulation and management of government programs, so they are most conveniently treated separately. Nevertheless, they are participants in the political contest, involved as fully as all the others who take part in it. Many individuals and groups expend a great deal of energy trying to influence court personnel (from judges down); judges and other court personnel, in turn, exert all the influence they can bring to bear upon some other contestants when certain questions are to be decided. Judges and their staffs are not without their modes of exercising influence, nor are they invulnerable to the pressures of others.

No Courts Are "Local"

In a strict sense, there is no such thing as a wholly local court in New York State. As regards federal courts, this point requires no elaboration. As regards all other courts, even the lowest ones in the state judicial hierarchy are governed by state legislation covering jurisdiction, procedure, and method of selection and removal and tenure of judges; moreover, all courts are at least mentioned, and many of the higher ones are treated quite specifically, in the state constitution itself. Even most nonjudicial court personnel lie beyond the powers of the city; some are provided for in statutes, some are placed loosely under the jurisdiction of the state Civil Service Department, and many are entirely under the discretion of the judges they serve. Most court expenses are mandated upon the city, with judicial salaries usually set by state law and nonjudicial salaries often fixed by the judges themselves. While the city pays, it does not itself decide what the size of its bill will be. Currently, the court system costs the city over $30 million a year.

To be sure, the city has some discretion. State law permits it to fix the number and the boundaries of the districts of Magistrates' Courts, for example, and to set the salaries of these judges and administrative staffs. And the city is permitted to and does increase the salaries of many judges over and above the figures set in state law. The power of the state over the court system, however, is so extensive, and the measure of freedom allowed the city is so restricted, that all courts other than federal are generally regarded, and most realistically considered, as organs of the state.

The Court System in New York City

Jurisdictions. Although it is something of an oversimplification, it may be said that there are in New York City eight courts of original jurisdiction, three of which are criminal courts, three of which are civil, and two special.

TABLE 48. FEDERAL COURTS OF IMPORTANCE TO NEW YORK CITY, JANUARY 1, 1959

Court (Jurisdiction national unless otherwise noted)	Total number of judges	Number of judges from New York City[a]
U.S. Supreme Court	9	..
U.S. Court of Claims	5	..
U.S. Court of Customs and Patent Appeals	5	..
U.S. Customs Court	9	..
U.S. Court of Appeals, Second Circuit[b]	6	4
U.S. District Court, Southern District[c]	18	19
U.S. District Court, Eastern District[d]	6	5
Tax Court of the United States	16	1
Total	74	29

[a] Estimated [b] Connecticut, New York, Vermont.

[c] Counties of Bronx, New York, Columbia, Dutchess, Greene, Orange, Putnam, Rockland, Sullivan, Ulster, and Westchester.

[d] Counties of Kings, Queens, Nassau, Richmond, and Suffolk.

The criminal courts, listed in ascending order according to the severity of the maximum penalties they may impose, are the Magistrates' Courts, the Court of Special Sessions, and the County Courts.[1] The civil courts, arranged in ascending order according to the authorized maximum dollar amount of claimed damages they may handle, are the Municipal Court, the City Court, and the Trial and Special "Terms" (divisions) of the Supreme Court, which also possesses, but rarely exercises, jurisdiction in criminal cases. The special courts are the Surrogates' Courts, for wills, estates, adoptions, and guardianships, and the Domestic Relations Court of the City of New York.

Appeals lie from these tribunals to either the Appellate Term of the Supreme Court, the Appellate Division of the Supreme Court, or the Court of Appeals. The Appellate Term hears appeals from the judgments of the Municipal Court and the City Court, and litigants may appeal further to the

[1] Called the Court of General Sessions in New York County.

TABLE 49. STATE COURTS AND JUDGESHIPS OF IMPORTANCE TO NEW YORK CITY, JANUARY 1, 1959
Arranged in Ascending Order by Size of Territorial Jurisdiction

Territory	Civil	Criminal	Other
Less than county	Municipal Court: 28 districts, plus special "parts" — 118	Magistrates' Courts: 32 district and special courts, plus special units — 50	
County	29	County Courts (in New York County—i.e., Manhattan—called Court of General Sessions) — 23	Surrogates' Courts — 6
More than county, less than city	Trial, Appellate, and Special Terms of the Supreme Court. First (New York and Bronx Counties), Second (Kings and Richmond Counties), and part of Tenth (Queens County) Judicial Districts are in New York City — 63ª	63ª	
	Appellate Division of the Supreme Court. First Department and part of the Second Department are in New York City. Must be sitting Supreme Court Justices.		
City	City Court — 69	Court of Special Sessions — 24	Domestic Relations Court — 23
State	15	Court of Appeals — 7	Court of Claims — 8
Total	294ª		

ª Does not include vacancies or justices from Nassau and Suffolk Counties (that are in the Tenth Judicial District), which together total 12 seats.

Appellate Division and ultimately to the Court of Appeals, the highest court in the state. With but two exceptions, appeals from all other courts lie to the Appellate Division, and hence to the Court of Appeals. The exceptions are appeals from decisions of magistrates, which lie to the Court of Special Sessions (making this a court of appellate as well as original jurisdiction) and

TABLE 50. STATE COURT SYSTEM: LINES OF APPEAL FROM COURTS IN NEW YORK CITY

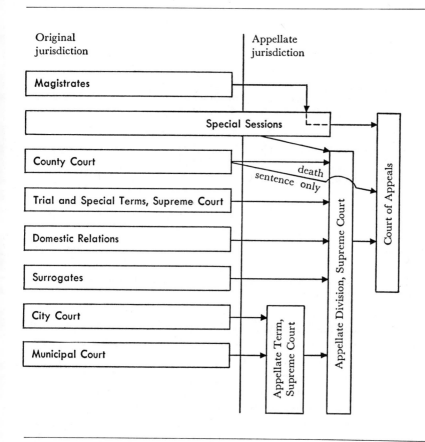

thence directly to the Court of Appeals; and first-degree murder cases, which are appealed directly from the County Courts (the Court of General Sessions in New York County) to the Court of Appeals.

The vast bulk of the litigation in, or affecting, the city takes place within this hierarchy. In addition, however, there is a state Court of Claims that handles suits against the state, and the federal courts[1] that hear cases in which city residents and officers are frequently involved. By volume, the preponderance of litigation originating in or affecting the city that is handled in these special state courts and in the federal tribunals is substantially less than that disposed of in the courts discussed earlier, but they are in no sense less important, whether evaluated by the social and political consequences of their decisions or by their prominence in the government and politics of New York City.

TABLE 51. MODE OF SELECTION OF JUDGES[a]

From wholly within city		From a territory in which the city or a part of the city is contained		Total
Appointed: By Mayor:		By Governor:		
Magistrates	50	Court of Claims	8	
Special Sessions	24	By President:		
Domestic Relations	23	Federal Courts	74	
Total	97	Total	82	179
Elected: Municipal Court	68	New York Supreme Court	20[b]	
City Court	22	New York Court of Appeals	7	
County Court (and General Sessions)	23			
Surrogates'	6			
New York Supreme Court	55			
Total	174	Total	27	201
Grand Total	271		109	380

[a] Figures as of January 1, 1959.

[b] Although all 20 are elected from the Tenth Judicial District (Queens, Nassau, Suffolk Counties), 8 are regularly from Queens.

The Manpower of the Judiciary. As of the beginning of 1959 there were 380 seats on the benches of all these courts of immediate relevance to the government and politics of New York City. A total of 271 of them are in districts wholly within the boundaries of the city and are therefore filled by city residents. The remaining 109 (including the 74 federal judgeships) have districts of which the whole city or sections of the city are part; of these, at least 44 places are occupied by city residents. There are thus 315 places currently held by New Yorkers. In the course of time, this figure varies somewhat because of the 109 seats from jurisdictions not wholly within the city. It rises as additional city residents are appointed to vacancies in this category, falls

[1] The United States District Courts for the Southern District, in which New York and Bronx Counties lie, and for the Eastern District, in which the remaining three counties are located; the United States Court of Appeals for the Second Circuit; and the federal courts of nationwide jurisdiction, including the Court of Claims, the Court of Customs and Patent Appeals, the Customs Court, the Tax Court, and the Supreme Court itself.

as city residents die or depart and are replaced by personnel from other parts of these areas. By and large, however, the total does not deviate extensively from the present one.

A great deal of maneuvering and bargaining attends the filling of any of the 380 places as New Yorkers of all factions of all parties compete with each other and with party organizations outside the city to obtain as many as they can of the 109 places on courts with jurisdiction extending beyond the city, and with each other alone for the 271 places inside the city. Not counting interim appointments to vacancies on elective courts, the Mayor appoints 97 of the 380 judges, the Governor, 8, the President, 74, for a total of 179. Of the 201 elected judges, 174 are elected from constituencies entirely within the city, 27 from constituencies extending beyond the city. Localism and popular election thus predominate in the composition of the judiciary in the courts discussed here.

TABLE 52. CONSTITUENCIES OF ELECTIVE COURTS

Constituency	Court	Number of judges[a]	
Smaller-than-county districts	Municipal Court	..	68
Counties	County Courts	23	
	Surrogates Court	6	
	City Court	22	
			51
Larger than counties, smaller than city (Judicial Districts)	Supreme Court[b]		
	First District	36	
	Second District	19	
	Tenth District	20	
			75
Entire city		..	..
Entire state	Court of Appeals		7
Total			201

[a] As of January 1, 1959.

[b] First District: New York and Bronx Counties; Second District: Kings and Richmond Counties; Tenth District: Queens, Nassau (L.I.), and Suffolk (L.I.) Counties. Only eight of the justices from this District currently come from Queens.

The Governmental Importance of the Courts

Collectively, the decisions of all these courts and of all these judges mean a great deal to the community as a whole. The freedom, the security, the welfare, the health, the fortunes of people are greatly affected by what the judiciary does; the impact of 380 judges is considerable. Moreover, there are so many of them that they are of enormous significance to the parties, to the institutions of the legal profession, and to the careers of lawyers. Finally, when they act in concert in pursuit of their common interests, the judges often have major effects on particular segments of public policy. In all these respects, they are part of the political and governmental processes.

JUDGES AS DISTRIBUTORS OF PRIZES

As Umpires Between Other Contestants

In particular, judges settle disputes—disputes involving money, services, office, reputations, and even life and liberty, disputes between litigants invoking governmental powers to implement their claims upon each other, upon the parties, and upon governmental officials and employees. Judicial decisions thus determine, in part, who gets what. Private citizens and nongovernmental groups may be contending with one another, or they may contest the action, or inaction, of officials or employees at any level of government.

TABLE 53. JUDICIAL SALARIES, JANUARY 1, 1959
In thousands of dollars

Court	Associate judge's salary	Presiding judge's salary
Magistrates'	$16	$19
Municipal	17	19
Special Sessions	19.5	21
Domestic Relations	19.5	21
Claims (New York State)	22	..
U.S. District	22.5	..
U.S. Tax	22.5	..
U.S. Customs	22.5	..
U.S. Claims	25.5	..
U.S. Circuit	25.5	..
U.S. Customs and Patents Appeals	25.5	..
County (and General Sessions)	34.5	..
Surrogates'	34.5[a]	..
Supreme Court (state)	34.5[b]	..
U.S. Supreme Court	35	35.5
Appellate Division	36.5[c]	38[d]
Court of Appeals	37.5[e]	40[e]

[a] $33,000 in Richmond.

[b] $21,000 by the state, the balance by the city or appropriate county.

[c] $23,000 by the state, the balance by the city or appropriate county.

[d] $23,500 by the state, the balance by the city or appropriate county.

[e] Includes $5,000 for expenses.

Government officials often bring suit against one another, or, when this is precluded by existing law (the city, for example, is unable to sue the state), may achieve the same effect by staging taxpayer suits. Law enforcement officers of all kinds represent the state in litigation with alleged law violators. Public officials and employees sometimes bring actions against their employers; the city, being a corporation rather than a "sovereign" power, is especially vulnerable to attacks of this kind. Voters, candidates, and party members frequently challenge party leaders—sometimes within their own parties, sometimes in other parties—in the courts. At one time or another, virtually every possible combination of those identified as contestants for the rewards of governmental action appears in the courts. And the judges, in deciding the questions at issue, in effect employ governmental authority in such a way as to allocate some of the prizes. Most of the time, judges are umpires rather than players. But, after all, how a contest comes out depends in large measure on what the umpires do.

As Interpreters of the Rules

Judicial decisions often do much more than settle the immediate question in litigation. They often determine the content and scope of the constitutional and statutory provisions earlier characterized as "the rules of the game," and they may sometimes upset state legislation, local legislation (far more frequently), or administrative rules and regulations, instead of merely invalidating a specific governmental act under a particular rule. The way in which judges dispose of election cases has far-reaching effects on the relationships among the parties and especially among the factions within parties. Judicial attitudes and actions of both kinds generally strengthen the positions of some contestants seeking to influence governmental policy and reduce the leverage of others—rarely does an interpretation of the rules of the game affect equally all who are concerned with them—sometimes regardless of what the judges intend or prefer, but effectively just the same. Thus, for example, when the courts construe narrowly the meaning of the phrase "government, property, and affairs of the city" in the Home Rule Act, the Home Rule Law, and the home rule provisions of the constitution (discussed at length in the next chapter), they permit state officers to intervene more extensively in the governance of the city than a different construction of the language would allow. When they ruled that the principle of separation of powers does not apply to governments of cities,[1] they denied to the Mayor powers and immunities associated with the chief executives in Albany and Washington, particularly in his relations with the City Council. When they refused to invalidate inequalities of representation growing out of failure to reapportion the lines of the old aldermanic districts,[2] they buttressed the Democratic majority that benefited from the prevailing situation; when, on the other hand, they refused to hold proportional representation unconstitutional,[3] they strengthened the hands of the minority parties in the city. When they upheld the power of the city, under permissive state legislation, to enact rent control laws,[4] they won the plaudits of the tenants and the condemnation of the landlords, and the net result was to increase the popularity of the Democratic officers who were responsible for the measure. When they declared municipal

[1] *Matter of La Guardia v. Smith*, 288 N.Y. 1 (1942).
[2] *People on Relation of Boyle v. Cruise*, 189 N.Y. Supp. 338 (1921).
[3] *Matter of Mooney v. Cohen*, 272 N.Y. 33 (1936).
[4] *Molnar v. Curtin*, 273 App. Div. 322 (1948).

employees were subject to the federal income tax, the result from the point of view of these persons was a reduction in salary. It has been said the law is what the judges say it is; while this assertion, without qualification, is unquestionably an exaggeration, it reflects the fundamental truth of the proposition that the distribution of rewards among the contestants striving to influence governmental decisions is shaped to a large extent by what judges say the rules are.

As Appointing Officers

The 315 judges in or from the city are the formal appointing officers for several thousand employees constituting the nonjudicial staffs of the court system. The exact number of such appointees outside the competitive civil service is difficult to ascertain, but it apparently amounts to some four or five hundred. A relatively small number of appointees, in turn, are themselves appointing officers who formally name staffs of their own.

From the standpoint of salary, prestige, responsibility, and prominence, the most important of the judicial appointees are the County Clerks and the Public Administrators. The County Clerks, appointed and removable by the Appellate Division of the Supreme Court, receive $15,000 a year, except in Richmond, where the County Clerk gets $10,500; as custodians of all the books, records, and papers of their respective counties, and as clerks of their respective County Courts and of the Supreme Court when it sits in their counties, they have substantial staffs of their own. The Public Administrators are appointed by the Surrogates; they administer estates for which, for one reason or another, no other executor is available, and they have employees to assist them. The Public Administrator in New York County is paid $15,000; in Kings, $10,750; in Queens, $8,750; in Bronx, $4,000 and fees; in Richmond, $5,925.

Even the less visible positions, however, are frequently highly remunerative. The Chief Clerks of some of the courts receive as much as $20,000, while many fall in the range from $9,500 to $11,500, and their deputies normally are not far behind. Individual judges frequently have clerks who earn as much as $10,500, and some have confidential attendants in addition who get from $5,000 to $7,000. Three courts have Commissioners of Records in the same salary bracket as the clerks, and the Commissioners' deputies are proportionately well paid. There are also secretaries and law assistants who may be paid from $5,000 to $15,000. At the lower levels stand the clerks to the Justices of the Municipal Court, whose salaries are about $3,800 a year for each, and some courtroom personnel. Many of these salaries are set by the judges themselves, and are mandated upon the city by state legislation. Furthermore, there are numerous appointments as commissioners in mortgage foreclosure which yield substantial fees, as administrators of the estates of persons who die intestate, as guardians, and as referees, all of these quite apart from the appointments to positions on the public payrolls. The judges are thus formal dispensers of jobs and benefits, many of them highly rewarding.

Not all the appointments to public positions are wholly at the discretion of the judges. Most are under the jurisdiction of the city or state personnel agencies, and the appointments must be made from lists of the names of people who have passed a competitive, or at least a qualifying, examination. Party considerations play significant parts in the selection of personnel for some posts. And the necessity of having competent personnel to perform many of the duties incidental to the judicial process is an imperative which cannot be ignored; hence, as a matter of common practice, law clerks in the federal courts, the Court of Appeals, the Appellate Division, and many parts of the State Supreme Court are selected by the judges from the top law school graduates without reference to political recommendations. So the judges are not without restrictions, both legal and practical, on their range of choice. But they are the formal appointing officers in all these instances, and their discretion, if not unlimited, is still quite broad. Their appointing authority places them squarely and prominently in the political struggle.

JUDGES AS CONTESTANTS: THE REWARDS OF JUDICIAL OFFICE

Honorific Rewards

Judges do not merely distribute the rewards of politics, however; they also share in them. They occupy places of great prestige; both in the courtroom and outside, they are deferred to by their legal colleagues, by the social groups in which they move, and by the rest of officialdom. Attorneys engaged in trial work constantly feel the weight of the authority of the jurists who sit on the bench above them, ruling on their efforts, controlling the procedure, and occasionally subjecting them to criticism and caustic comments to which they are in no position to reply. Even the most prominent lawyers appearing before the most obscure judges cannot escape the fact that the latter are their superiors in the courtroom. And the habits—indeed, the obligations—of deference accorded by tradition to those who sit in the highest positions in an old and esteemed profession carry over; in court and out, judges are automatically part of the legal élite, and it is not surprising that so many lawyers yearn to sit on the bench. The sense of the majesty of the law and of the judges who represent it is even more impressive to laymen involved in judicial proceedings, even for nothing more important than traffic violations; the robes, the formalities, the authority of these men elevate them to something apart from ordinary human beings. Judges, like physicians, are surrounded by an honorific aura that to many is both awesome and wonderful.

TABLE 54. JUDICIAL SALARIES, JANUARY 1, 1959, BY SALARY RANGE

Salary range	State judges		Federal judges		Total
$16,000–$19,999	All Magistrates	50			
	All Municipal Court justices	68			
	Associate Special Sessions justices	23			
	Associate Domestic Relations justices	22			
	Total	163			163
$20,000–$24,999	Chief Justice, Special Sessions	1	Judges of District Courts	24	
	Presiding justice, Domestic Relations	1	Judges of Tax Court	16	
	All judges, Court of Claims	8	Judges of Customs Court	9	
	Total	10	Total	49	59
$25,000–$29,999	Justices of City Court	22	Judges of Customs and Patent Appeals	5	
			Judges of Court of Claims	5	
			Judges of Circuit Courts	6	
	Total	22	Total	16	38
$30,000–$34,999	Judges of County Courts (and General Sessions)	23	..		
	Surrogates	6			
	Supreme Court Justices	62			
	Total	91			91
$35,000 or over	Justices of Appellate Division	13[a]	Justices of U.S. Supreme Court	9	
	Justices of Court of Appeals	7			
	Total	20	Total	9	29

[a] Plus one from the Ninth Judicial District.

Salary and Working Conditions

So, too, are the material rewards. Of the 380 judgeships treated in this analysis, none brings a salary of less than $16,000 a year, and one—the Chief Judge of the State Court of Appeals—earns (including a $5,000 allowance for expenses) $40,000. More specifically, 163 are paid $16,000 or over, but less than $20,000; 59 receive $20,000 or more, but less than $25,000; 38 have salaries of $25,000 or more, but less than $30,000; 91 get $30,000 or over, but less than $35,000; 29 are paid over $35,000. This puts virtually all of them in the highest income brackets in American officialdom, and many of them well above federal cabinet officers, Representatives, and Senators. Moreover, constitutional provisions forbid reductions in the salaries of judges while they are completing a term of office (not at all, therefore, for lifetime appointees while they continue to serve). Finally, many of them are covered by rather liberal pension plans.

Working conditions are relatively pleasant. The work is taxing, it is true, for the strain of intense concentration and heavy responsibility in the courtroom is wearing. Moreover, work in the courtroom is only part of the job; many additional hours are spent poring over briefs, perusing legal literature, and trying to achieve agreement between litigants in informal sessions in judges' chambers. Still, judges have greater freedom in allocating their time than many other officials. Court sessions do not normally begin until ten o'clock, and are commonly recessed by four in the afternoon. During the

TABLE 55. JUDICIAL TERMS OF OFFICE

Term in years	Court	Number of judges	Per cent of total number
9	Claims (State)	8	2.1
10	Magistrates', Special Sessions, Domestic Relations, Municipal, City	187	49.2
12	U.S. Tax Court	16	4.2
14	County, General Sessions, Surrogates, Supreme (State), Court of Appeals	111[a]	29.2
Life	U.S. District, U.S. Customs, U.S. Circuit, U.S. Customs and Patent Appeals, U.S. Claims, U.S. Supreme	58	15.3
	Total	380	100.0

[a] Includes those Supreme Court justices serving five-year terms in the Appellate Division.

summer months, some courts virtually suspend operations, and some have only abbreviated sessions presided over by a small percentage of the full judicial staffs. Vacation periods are generous. Most judges have comfortable offices, adequate professional assistance, and ample secretarial help.

Finally, to a larger extent than most other public officials, judges may be said to be their own bosses. To be sure, there are administrative and procedural requirements they must observe. And they may be assigned by their chief judge to categories of adjudication they find not especially attractive. Most important of all, the opinions of virtually every judge are subject to review by higher courts, and no judge likes to be reversed. Nevertheless, each judge is in full command of his own courtroom, sets his own pace, and is insulated from many of the external pressures and imperatives that sometimes come to control the public lives of other public officials. In an increasingly frenetic, bureaucratized world, this feature of judicial positions is probably sometimes even more alluring than the unusually favorable salaries, hours, and working conditions.

Tenure and Advancement

Judges have exceptionally long terms of office compared with other public officials. Just under 50 per cent of the 380 treated here have ten-year terms; over 29 per cent have fourteen-year terms; more than 15 per cent have life tenure. Four per cent have twelve-year terms. Only 2 per cent have terms of less than ten years; the eight judges of the State Court of Claims are appointed for nine years. Thus many judges span several administrations, enjoying a degree of security unmatched by few other elective or appointive officials of comparable salary and stature. Not even the so-called permanent civil servants, few of whom ever attain to salaries even approaching judicial compensation, are, in practice, more secure in their jobs.

TABLE 56. DEMOCRATIC AND REPUBLICAN DISTRICT LEADERS IN NON-JUDICIAL STATE COURT POSITIONS AS OF JANUARY 1, 1952

County	Total leaders	In court posts, 1952		In court posts, 1952 or previously	
		Number	Per cent	Number	Per cent
DEMOCRATIC LEADERS					
New York	35	16	46	18	51
Bronx	14	2	14	4	29
Kings	23	10	43	13	57
Queens	25	4	16	7	28
Richmond	5	2	40	3	60
Total Democrats	102	34	33	45	44
REPUBLICAN LEADERS					
New York	31	2	6	7	23
Bronx	13	6	46	6	46
Kings	24	9	38	9	38
Queens	24	6	25	9	38
Richmond	5	0	–	0	..
Total Republicans	97	23	24	31	32
Total for both parties	199	57	29	76	38

SOURCE: New York State Crime (Proskauer) Commission, Public Hearing No. 4, 1952, vol. 6, p. 54, mimeographed.

A number of informal practices tend to lengthen the already impressive duration of judges' formal terms. The Mayor and the Governor frequently reappoint judges who have satisfactorily completed their terms of service; and both major parties customarily endorse sitting judges running for reelection without regard to party, except in the most unusual circumstances. Consequently, anyone who enters the judicial hierarchy knows there is a very high probability that he can remain as long as he wants. Furthermore, the ranks

of the higher courts are to a substantial extent filled by advancement of the
incumbents of lower judicial posts; this is true of the patterns of both appointments and nominations. Thus, although the number of vacancies filled each
year exceeds what would be expected if every judge served out his full term,
this does not mean the position of the judges is fraught with uncertainties.
Many vacancies are created by the resignations of judges moving up to
higher courts, the retirement of judges who have reached the (state) mandatory retirement age after long years on the bench, and by the illness and death
of men who have grown old in the judicial branch. In practice, men and
women who enter the judiciary frequently remain there as long as they are
able to function and would like to stay. There are, of course, exceptions to
this generalization, but it applies to a large number of the judges considered
in this chapter.

For some, judicial office is the capstone of a political career. Among the
judges sitting in 1958, not only were there individuals who once occupied
comparatively minor posts in one or another of the branches and levels of
government, but there are also former congressmen, an ex-Mayor, former
District Attorneys, a former Borough President, a former Deputy Mayor, and
at least two former city department heads. For others, the courts have been
primarily safe way-stations on the road to other political offices. In recent
years two judges have left the bench to run for Mayor, and others have
resigned to accept other appointive offices, or to seek other elective offices.
Six of the fourteen men who have been Mayor or Acting Mayor of the
Greater City since its formation in 1898 were judges at some point in their
prior careers, and several moved directly from the bench to City Hall.
Judicial office thus functions as both a fitting climax to a life in politics and
as a snug niche in which to bide one's time.

Bargaining Position

A further reward of judicial office is the bargaining leverage it affords its
incumbents. As referees between other contestants, as interpreters of the rules,
and as appointing officers—in short, as distributors of prizes—judges are
often in a position to give other people what they want, and they can presumably employ this opportunity to obtain in exchange what they, the
judges, want for themselves. Actually, there is little probative evidence that
judicial prerogatives and privileges are used for this purpose, although the
Seabury Investigation of the Magistrates' Courts in New York City in 1932,
as well as the exposure of some individual judges in other courts in the past,
demonstrate that this was not always the case. Today, however, although
surveillance of the courts by professional associations of lawyers and by civic
groups has grown more thorough and more stringent than ever before, one
only occasionally hears the charge that a judge conducted a trial or decided

a case on the basis of a favor done him by one of the litigants or because of a request denied him by one of the parties at suit. There is reason to suspect that practices of this kind occur, but the supposition is unproved.

In the matter of nonjudicial court appointments, things are quite different. There can be little question that (excepting the federal courts and the higher state courts, as noted above) most of the jobs over which judges have broad discretion are filled not so much on the basis of the competence of the candidates as for the value of particular appointments in paying political debts to the party leaders responsible for the judges' election or appointment and in position to affect their future careers. The same is true of the appointment of referees in foreclosures, special guardians, commissioners in incompetency proceedings, and referees to hold hearings. Indeed, it appears likely that many more nonjudicial positions in the court system have been created than are necessary to perform the work of the courts, that many of those who occupy these positions have little idea of their responsibilities, and that some of them never actually report to their duty stations except on payday. Naturally, some of these discretionary appointees are highly competent and hard working, or the judicial system would break down; this is perhaps especially true of merit system appointees under the supervision of the state or city personnel departments. (In the federal courts, where there is a well-developed centralized institution for judicial administration, the standards are particularly high.)

Prominent among the rewards of judicial office, then, stand the opportunities for bargaining that accompany elevation to the bench. Although the powers of judicial decision are not often employed for this purpose, the powers of appointment are, and it will become apparent in later discussion that the use of this bargaining implement is one of the factors accounting for the high rewards in the judicial branch.

DIFFERENCES BETWEEN JUDGES AND OTHER CONTESTANTS

While judges, since they share in the distribution of the stakes of politics and can use their control over the distribution of other prizes to buttress their own claims and those of their allies, may thus be treated in much the same fashion as other governmental participants in the contest for these stakes, the distinguishing features of the judicial process and judicial institutions must not be overlooked. On the whole, the distinctions between the courts and other governmental institutions and practices are differences in degree rather than in kind. But the differences are sufficiently pronounced to warrant particular attention.

Take, for instance, the Anglo-Saxon juridical principle of judicial independence. This tradition is reflected in the deliberate insulation of judges from many types of control exercised by legislatures and chief executives over other public officers and employees; hence, the security of tenure, the unusually strong safeguards against suspension or removal, the constitutional and statutory bans on reductions in the salaries of sitting judges, and the weakness of overhead agency controls upon the courts. The procedures that keep the other agencies of government responsive and "accountable" to elected legislators and executives have purposely been rendered inapplicable to the courts; they contravene the principle of judicial independence. Some administrative agencies, it is true, achieve substantial autonomy, sometimes by the way they are structured (as, for example, in the case of regulatory commissions, public corporations, and public authorities), sometimes by accident, and sometimes by virtue of the personalities and strategic skills of their leaders. But no other agencies are shielded as are the courts by so many built-in protections, by such strong constitutional and statutory and traditional bulwarks. Even judges are not totally immune to pressure and retaliation, but successful assaults on their redoubt are less frequent. Figuratively speaking, they can follow the dictates of conscience almost to the extent of thumbing their noses with impunity at those outside the judicial hierarchy. Other things discussed in this chapter make it most improbable that they will feel so inclined, but the fact that they could conceivably do so sets them apart from most of their governmental colleagues.

In addition, the formality of judicial procedure, the weight of legal traditions, the ethical norms instilled through professional training and policed in a general way by professional organizations, and supervision of lower courts by higher ones appointed by other chief executives or elected from other constituencies, all combine to restrict the avenues of access to judges and to limit both their opportunities and their willingness to use their decision-making powers for bargaining purposes. Again, this is only a relative proposition; it is not impossible to negotiate with, or bring pressure to bear upon, a judge, but it is rather more difficult to reach a judge this way than to reach other public officials who are regarded, and who regard themselves, as having a primarily "representative" function in contrast with the emphasis on judicial independence.

Taking account of these qualifications (which apply primarily only to the processes of judicial decision and less to appointments by judges), it may be said that the factors identified in the foregoing paragraphs tend to reduce the vulnerability of judges to the pressures of other claimants on the prizes of politics, and to limit (but by no means to eliminate, particularly in the lower courts) the responsiveness of judges to some influences from outside the courts and the legal profession.

The distinctions between judges and other participants in the contest for the rewards of politics can easily be overdrawn. All the participants have much in common, and judges are participants. But it is important to bear in mind that the independence of the judiciary is one of the central values around which our court system is organized, and that judicial procedure is less flexible, less hidden from scrutiny, more circumscribed by expectations of neutrality and impartiality and by the traditions of the legal profession, than most of the other institutions involved in the governmental process.

COURTS AND THE PARTIES

The Importance of the Court System to the Parties

Incentives to Party Workers. The court system provides much of the fuel for party engines. It is true, as noted in an earlier chapter, that many party workers are satisfied with relatively nominal material rewards. But almost invariably, predominant among the ranks of those who give unstintingly of their time and energy and money to their party are lawyers striving for positions on the bench, and both lawyers and nonlawyers endeavoring to establish claims on other court posts. On the one hand, this enables the parties to recruit, hold, and motivate a large body of willing, industrious, and often able workers in their cause. On the other hand, it helps the parties maintain a measure of discipline in their ranks and among officeholders who owe their positions to their respective parties.

Positions in the court system are not the only ones furnishing motivations for party workers, of course. But one must climb to the highest echelons of the executive branch in any level of government before the scale of remuneration begins to approach that which obtains for even minor judgeships. In the legislative branch, with the exception of Congress, salaries do not compare at all (although the pay of city councilmen, relative to the time and effort their jobs require, are exceedingly generous though less than half in absolute figures of the pay of a city magistrate). At the same time, judges need not be concerned, except at long intervals, about the ordinary vicissitudes of politics or the recurrent financial crises and economy drives that sometimes sweep other public officials and employees from office or result in cuts in pay. Furthermore, as noted earlier, even many nonjudicial employees of the court system—County Clerks, court clerks, judges' clerks, and Public Administrators, for example—commonly receive salaries rivaling those of bureau chiefs and Deputy Commissioners and far exceeding the pay of local and state legislators. For jobs of this kind, people are willing to work and wait, to accept the onerous chores of party activity, to fill for a time less prized posts and less rewarding ones, and to follow their leaders. The unusual attractiveness of court system emoluments thus plays a large part in the maintenance of party organizations.

Not only does the judicial system provide strong incentives, and in relative abundance, but it does so on a continuing basis. In the first place, 322 of the entire 380 judgeships (and 286 of the 315 occupied by New York City residents) have fixed terms, and the terms are staggered so that part of the membership of each such court comes up for reappointment or reelection annually; each year, therefore, some vacancies are sure to occur. In the second place, despite efforts to keep the number of expirations roughly equal each year, retirements, deaths, resignations, and the intermittent addition of new posts disrupt the regularity of the cycle and increase the actual number of vacancies to more than the expected number. (Retirement at the end of the year in which a judge turns seventy is mandatory under the state constitution. Furthermore, elevation to the bench often comes relatively late in life. Still further, since judgeships are, as observed earlier, convenient positions from which to wait for still greater opportunities, there are voluntary resignations.) Thus, from 1947 to 1957, a total of 500 vacancies—a figure far in excess of mathematical prediction—were filled in the 380 places. With as many as 40 to almost 50 openings a year, it is not difficult to advance many judges to higher courts and simultaneously to introduce perhaps 15 or more deserving and qualified party workers into the judiciary. In any four-year period, this source of high-level jobs is likely to prove richer than any other; the legislative and executive branches help keep the parties going with many lesser rewards, but they provide fewer big prizes. The plenitude of choice jobs in the courts increases enormously the ability of party leaders to reinvigorate the loyalties of the congeries of Assembly District and clubhouse organizations of which the parties are composed. District Leaders play key parts in the accession to office of both appointed and elected judges, and they work hard for their parties in order to justify their claims to as many of these positions for their followers as they can. One factor holding the parties together despite powerful centrifugal tendencies is the number of judicial offices available, which helps the County Leaders placate every area and every unit of their parties in the long run.[1]

The profusion of court positions also facilitates the satisfaction of many demands by religious, ethnic, and national elements in every party in the city. Dealings of this kind are neither clandestine nor unconscious. Party officers have testified to seeking out Irish or Italian or Jewish candidates for appointment or election to judicial office, and, more recently, Negroes and Puerto Ricans have begun to take their place in the judiciary. The demands are overt; ethnic groups have high regard for the prestige of the courts, and

---

[1] Two factors limit the freedom of party leaders in their efforts to fill all the demands upon them. One is the residence requirements for elective judgeships, and for some appointive judgeships. The other is the unusual concentration of judges in Manhattan, a concentration far out of proportion to this borough's population. This imbalance may be explained in part by the accidents of history, the clustering of business and governmental activities in the downtown area, and the customary failure of governmental districting to keep pace with population shifts.

for the opportunities for professional and social advancement offered by judicial offices. The efforts to satisfy these demands are candid. This does not mean there is any formula for the automatic partitioning of the prizes, or that there is any mathematical balance among the claimant groups. On the contrary, the calculus of adjustment is intricate, so that one or two high judicial offices allocated to one group may offset the nomination of a member of another group for executive or legislative office, or the appointment of a member of another group to an administrative position. The number of judgeships thus permits the parties to diversify the basis of their electoral strength.

It also enables the parties to reconcile individuals politically eligible for high office, who, denied a top spot on a ticket, might decide to run independently or negotiate with the opposition. And it gives party leaders a chance to repay the loyal party workers who cannot easily be given more prominent positions. (Thus, for example, two former Mayors—Hylan and Impellitteri—accepted judicial posts after being denied renomination for the mayoralty.) Moreover, a judgeship is sometimes a convenient way of neutralizing a District Attorney or other law enforcement officer whose zeal in his enforcement practices offends important party supporters.

The attraction and the number of judicial offices is probably one reason for the abundance of lawyers in politics. Even without the stimulus of positions on the court, politics would probably become the vocation of many lawyers. Their skills equip them to perform the legal services of which the political clubs and their members seem always to stand in need, their profession often allows them to allocate their time as they see fit, and their training tends to encourage the versatility needed for negotiations among contending and competing individuals. If they are partners in large law firms, they may continue to share in the profits of the firm although they direct the major part of their energies to their political pursuits (partly because these often work to the financial benefit of the firm). When to all of this is added the allurement of numerous, highly valued judgeships for which only lawyers are eligible, the magnetism apparently becomes almost irresistible. So lawyers come eagerly to politics. Except for the general requirement that every judge be an attorney admitted (from three to ten years earlier, depending on the judgeship) to the bar of the state, the statutes are virtually silent on the professional qualifications of judges. Nevertheless, professional legal standing is always requisite, thereby removing nonlawyers from competition for many of the best positions the political system can offer, and putting on this occupation a premium that brings its practitioners to the parties.

Added to the judgeships themselves are the remunerative appointments as referees, guardians, administrators, and executors of estates mentioned above. There are enough rewards of this kind—particularly in the hands of the

Surrogates—to make working for the parties worthwhile.[1] Even lawyers with small hopes of becoming judges themselves are thus drawn to the parties. But, it must be added, the hope of becoming a judge does not die easily in those who once set their sights that high.

While the incentives of judicial office appeal particularly to lawyers, they are important also to nonlawyers in the parties. As noted earlier, the courts employ, in addition to judges, several thousand individuals to perform the work of the judicial system. All but several hundred of these are in the competitive civil service. These hundreds add substantially to the reservoir of rewards party leaders can use to attract and motivate followers, and it is not unlikely that at least a portion of the classified positions are filled by the party faithful through manipulation of the provisions of the Civil Service Law. Some of this patronage is used by some judges to provide employment for relatives and personal friends. By and large, however, the judges accept the recommendations of District Leaders in filling the choicer posts. Indeed, many District Leaders and County Chairmen themselves have found well-paid judicial clerkships a convenient source of income to sustain them while they perform their demanding party services. The New York State Crime Commission reported that in 1952, 29 per cent of the 199 District Leaders of both major parties in the city were employed in the court system, and that 38 per cent of them were either serving at that time or had served there in the past. Although most of the jobs entailed legal work, almost three quarters of the District Leaders holding them were not lawyers. A more recent study by the Citizens Union of the clerks to the resident Justices of the Supreme Court alone revealed that more than one third are District Leaders or County Chairmen, with both parties being well represented. District Leaders are not the only party functionaries to find sources of personal income in the court system; Captains and other organization workers are also frequently employed here. However, the fact that so many District Leaders are employed by the judiciary is a rough indication of the importance to the parties of nonjudicial posts in the court system, and the District Leaders constitute only the visible segments of the iceberg, no studies having yet been made that penetrate much below this level. But there is little doubt that the grip of the parties on judicial patronage is quite firm. Indeed, there are instances on record of judges submitting to demands by some party leaders that they

[1] Indeed, it has been said that control of the Surrogates in New York County sustained the Democratic party in the county during the lean years of the thirties. The long terms of the Democratic Surrogates elected prior to the accession of Mayor La Guardia saved these positions for Tammany Hall in the defeats it suffered at the polls in that period. With the rewards thus available to its supporters, it was able to hold itself together despite the fact that it was displaced in City Hall, cut off from federal support by President Roosevelt (whose nomination Tammany fought in the 1932 Democratic National Convention), who favored Edward J. Flynn's Bronx organization, and was treated coldly by Governor Lehman (who identified with the Roosevelt-Flynn alliance).

discharge the secretaries in their employ and replace them with appointees suggested by the faction in ascendancy. So it is not just the judiciary per se that makes the court system important to the parties; rather, it is all that goes with the judgeships as well as the judgeships themselves that helps the parties build and maintain their organizations.

The Judicial System as a Source of Party Revenue. A man who wants to be a judge must normally be a party insider, and, in addition, must be prepared in many cases to donate substantial sums of money to the organization of the appropriate party leader whose influence will be the chief factor in his nomination for appointment or election. This practice obtains even when the aspirant has worked long and hard for his party and is well qualified for the post. And he is expected, once in office, to contribute generously to his party in its fund-raising campaigns.

Some District Leaders can apparently extract as much as a year's salary plus an additional "campaign fund" of several thousand dollars.[1] For *elective* office, the amount is frequently set on the basis of a fixed sum (from $50 to $100) for each Election District in the judicial area. The smallest of these territories, Municipal Court Districts, normally encompass between 145 and 180 Election Districts, and the prospective candidate is therefore expected to furnish up to $20,000 over all. The charges are higher for judgeships on higher courts having larger constituencies. Practically no reliable evidence is available on the finances underlying judicial *appointments*, but since it is demonstrable that the appointing chief executives tend to rely very heavily upon their party functionaries to supply them with the names of men to be appointed to fill judicial vacancies, it is possible, if not probable, that similar practices prevail.

Not much is known, either, about what happens to payments of this kind. By and large, it would appear that the District Leaders take a substantial part of it themselves for their own and party uses, and divide the remainder among their workers in the Election Districts. This is apparently regarded in party circles as an ordinary part of the revenues of the District Leader and of the party workers in the field; presumably, for shouldering the burdens of party work, and for their services to their parties and to their candidates, the members of the party hierarchies are widely regarded as entitled to this form of party resource and personal compensation. Most candidates for elective office, and even for appointive office, outside the judiciary as well as in it, give money to their respective party units for putting forth their names and assisting them in their quests; in addition, some of the money donated by the general public for election campaigns ends up in the hands of local party personnel. In this fashion, the party organizations manage to "pay" their

[1] It is rumored among lawyers that there is a "going rate" for judgeships, currently the equivalent of two years' salary for that office.

regular "staffs." A substantial part of this recompense comes from those who would like to be judges.

Moreover, since those who attain the bench or nonjudicial court posts generally seek to strengthen their chances for advancement and to ensure that, if they are not promoted, they will at least be renominated or reappointed at the expiration of their term, they can almost always be counted upon to contribute generously to all fund-raising efforts and to heed the advice of their party mentors in matters of appointment and perhaps even of decision.

Like all organizations of the modern world, parties need money to operate. Clearly, one of the primary reasons the court system is of such profound concern to the parties is that this is where a part of their money comes from.

Protection of Party Interests. In one additional and final respect, the court system is important to the parties. In the Supreme Court, where many decisions about electoral conduct and procedure are in practice decided (though subject to appeal which infrequently materializes), judges who are beholden to party organizations will probably be less sympathetic to challengers to party discipline and authority than would critics of "machine politics." The method of selecting judges greatly reduces (if it does not preclude altogether) the likelihood that party organizations will often be confronted with hostile judges. The pattern of judicial rulings interpreting Election Law provisions governing designating and nominating procedures and the use of party names by insurgent groups in any of the parties seem to bear out this inference. So, too, do other more isolated decisions in other courts—as, for example, a magistrate's dismissal of the charges against members of a Democratic club who were arrested for gambling and for using loud and boisterous language. The magistrate ruled that "political organizations are to be allowed to meet without interference." Admittedly, the evidence that the party obligations of the judges are controlling in these cases is far from conclusive, and there are certainly important judgments one would not anticipate on the basis of party loyalty. Many other elements, which the judges themselves do not control (such as the working of statutes), are operative here. Nevertheless, one reason the parties display such deep interest in the judiciary is that their own organizational security rests to a significant extent in the hands of the judges.

The Importance of the Parties to the Judiciary

Parties and Judicial Selection. Except perhaps for the highly skilled court jobs, such as court stenographer, nobody gets one of the better judicial or nonjudicial positions in the court system without going through party channels.

When a judicial appointment, whether for a full term, the remainder of a term, or until the next election, is to be made by a chief executive, the usual procedure is for the County Leader in whose territory the court sits (or who is acknowledged by other County Leaders as a result of some earlier bargain to have first claim on the filling of the next vacancy) to determine which of his District Leaders is entitled to nominate the appointee for this post. An able County Leader generally succeeds in balancing the distribution of these prizes among his constituent units so that his decisions are accepted by his party subordinates. While most County Leaders manage well enough in this regard, even the best of them may run into strong objections from clubs that feel they have been victims of discrimination or neglect. When this happens the County Leader may relieve the tension by promising future openings to the offended groups, or by reallocating the existing vacancy to the plaintiffs and mollifying the deprived groups with a lesser prize, or with the promise of a better one in the future. Occasionally a group of District Leaders may get together and agree among themselves on the distribution of nominations and appointments; in such cases, their County Leader commonly endorses their decision. Once agreement is reached in one fashion or another, the name of the candidate is put before the appointing executive, who, in most cases, promptly appoints the organization choice. The procedure is roughly the same in each of the major parties, whenever it has captured the office of the chief executive at City Hall, in Albany, or in Washington, while the third parties can hope at best to be granted one or two places (for which their own party hierarchies, like those of the major parties, select the candidates) in return for their support in the elections—particularly in close elections. (Only the highest federal positions seem to be more or less exempt from these practices.)

The hold of the inner cores of the parties on nominations for elective judgeships is, as was noted in the discussion of the nominating process, equally strong, if not stronger. Almost all the nominations made by the rank and file of the parties in direct primaries are dominated by the Assembly District Leaders in each jurisdiction; the primaries are little more than ratifications of the individuals the Leaders select. For Municipal Court nominations it is primarily the Leaders whose Assembly Districts fall within each Municipal Court District who bargain with each other and arrive at decisions on their slate of nominees. For the County Courts (including the Court of General Sessions in New York County), the City Court, and the Surrogates, it is the County Executive Committees, made up of all the Assembly District Leaders in each county, negotiating with each other and with their County Leaders (who are occasionally overruled by coalitions of their District Leaders), who are chiefly responsible for the choices. The county committeemen routinely go along with the Leaders, and the voters in the parties are seldom offered alternatives in the primaries, although the contests are usually energetically fought when they do occur.

Similarly, the nomination of candidates for the Supreme Court by party conventions in each of the Judicial Districts of the state is controlled by the County Leaders in those areas; the convention delegates almost invariably accept the names presented by them. Even the nominees for the Court of Appeals, selected by the state conventions of the several parties, are chosen largely by bargaining among County Leaders from all parts of the state. (As a result, at least three or four of the justices are virtually certain to come from New York City, the remainder from upstate and suburban sections.) In short, no part of the judiciary, however high, is divorced from the parties.

The parties are important, too, to those who seek to or do occupy non-judicial offices in the court system as well as to judges. Most judges maintain amicable relations with their party sponsors (past, present, and future) by employing their discretion in making appointments to install in office people recommended by District Leaders, which, as noted above, frequently means appointing the District Leaders and County Chairmen themselves, among others. Indeed, one judge is reported to have been so assiduous in satisfying claims made upon him by a District Leader that he accepted the Leader's recommendation for every appointment without regard to the qualifications of the candidates, and then found himself compelled to engage competent assistants at his own expense. Appointed court officers with appointive powers of their own adopt in the same manner and for the same reasons their party organizations' suggestions as to whom to select. It may therefore be said that nearly everybody in a more important position in the court system owes his position in good part to the support of some party functionary, and that even some holding lesser posts (probably including a number of posts nominally protected by Civil Service Law and regulations) are similarly indebted.

Few are the aspects of government in which the influence of the parties is never felt at all. Nowhere in government, however, is that influence more pervasive and profound than in the court system.

Judicial Election Campaigns. Candidates for elective judgeships find the parties especially important to them because of the character of judicial electoral campaigns. For one thing, campaigning has somehow come to be considered inconsistent with the dignity and the duties of judicial office—a rather strange myth in the light of the way judicial candidates are chosen, but one that helps obscure the realities of judicial politics from the eyes of many voters and that is therefore scrupulously observed. Candidates for judicial office do not ordinarily make "political" speeches, do not appear regularly at campaign rallies and demonstrations, or engage in the usual campaign practices designed to bring candidates into personal contact with as much of the electorate as possible; indeed, the statements of campaign expenditures by judicial candidates generally (and, in a technical sense, no doubt accurately) show no personal outlays. Barred from the opportunity of applying their own energies and talents and personalities to their own election, the candidates for judgeships are forced, even more than colleagues running for places in the other branches of government, to rely on the established party machinery for vote-getting. The "citizens' committees" that spring up to promote the election of a particular candidate are occasionally made up of persons who for professional or personal reasons are willing to work for his victory. Far more frequently, these are merely the parties in other guises, establishing these auxiliary associations to avoid legal limitations on campaign expenses, to obtain donations from people reluctant to give money to political parties themselves, and to exploit the myth that their judicial candidates have independent rather than merely partisan support. Organizing in this fashion is not by itself sufficient to guarantee election, but lack of it is enough to make defeat virtually certain in a close contest.

In the second place, nominees for judicial office commonly enjoy the endorsements of both major parties; this is one of the reasons for their security of tenure. Originally, the custom of joint nomination apparently applied only to judges who had completed a full term on the bench. Judges appointed to fill vacancies in an elective court until the next election, and candidates running for judicial office without any prior service in the positions at stake, ordinarily encountered an opposing candidate from the other major party. Over the years, however, the parties began to make bargains with each other involving temporarily appointed incumbents and even nonincumbents, so that many more candidates for judicial office make their runs uncontested than the "sitting-judge" tradition would lead one to anticipate. For example, twice since the end of World War II, more than 80 per cent of the judicial seats to be filled by election were won by candidates having both Republican and Democratic nominations. On the other hand, there is nothing fixed about this ratio, the number of joint endorsements by the major parties having fallen as low as 2 out of 14 elective judgeships in 1952. Indeed, in one case in 1955, another in 1956, and two in 1957, one or the other of the major parties refused to endorse an elected sitting judge renominated by the other party and instead put up a candidate of its own. The number of dual nominations clearly depends on a great many delicate adjustments. This point is underscored by the bipartisan deals behind the creation of new judicial posts. In 1931, 12 new court positions were created in the Second Judicial District. None of them, however, was contested in the election. Democratic leaders agreed to endorse Republican candidates for 5 of the 12 new seats in return for Republican support in getting the Republican-dominated state legislature to establish the positions, and the Republicans in the Judicial District completed the bargain by endorsing seven Democrats for the remaining seven vacancies. A similar understanding underlay the passage of bills in 1956 creating new seats on the Supreme Court in the First, Second, and Tenth Judicial Districts. This measure was opposed by Mayor Wagner (allegedly on the grounds that the city would be unable to finance its share of the additional costs) and Governor Harriman vetoed it, but a new agreement between the parties dividing the seats (by joint endorsement) resulted in the establishment of seven additional seats in the Tenth District in 1958. Since bipartisan endorsement makes election a certainty, and since it also depends upon agreements reached by the County and District Leaders of the regular party organizations, every judicial candidate doubtless awaits tensely the outcome of negotiations regarding his own situation. He cannot help being aware that the decision is his party's and not his to make. Candidates from districts that are strongholds of their own party need not, of course, worry about this phase of the electoral process. In doubtful districts, and in districts where the opposition party is in firm control, what the party functionaries do is of deep concern to the candidates.

In sum, aspirants to elective judicial posts, after having surmounted the obstacles to nomination, are not freed from dependence on the parties for the attainment of their objectives.

The Emoluments of Office. Since World War II, judicial salaries have risen rapidly. In large measure, this must be ascribed to inflation and to the widespread consensus that levels of judicial compensation should keep pace with the rest of the economy. To a lesser extent, it must be attributed to the skill of the judges themselves. Although the traditions and public expectations of dignity and reserve have somewhat hampered their quest for higher pay, they have managed to press their claims quietly and discreetly through their own groupings (such as Magistrates' Associations, the County Judges' Association, and others). They have had some assistance from professional associations of lawyers and civic groups, but the initiative has not come from this quarter. The real thrust, the driving force, and the strategies behind increases in the compensation of judges have originated to a large degree in the party hierarchies, which have strong incentives to elevate salary levels, and which (as was noted earlier) have the influence in the legislature and the Executive Mansion to attain their objectives.

The interest of the parties in judicial salaries is clear. The better the pay, the more attractive the office; the easier it is to get willing workers, to get generous contributions from office seekers and officeholders. So bills providing increases for the judges of now one court, now another, are introduced virtually every year. This is not to say, on the one hand, that judges do not welcome these raises, or, on the other, that they do not deserve them. But they get many of them because party leaders, for reasons of their own, fight for them. In a sense, the benefits to sitting judges are more or less incidental. Just the same, their debt to party leaders is real.

Similarly, judges on the bench enjoy the advantages accruing from increases in the number of seats in the higher courts. For them, it means additional possibilities of advancement. But this is not the principal benefit to party leaders; for party leaders, new judgeships mean more rewards to distribute to party workers and, therefore, more compliant party units. To be sure, most courts of civil jurisdiction have been swamped by litigation, and some cases take several years to come to trial; under these conditions, there are reasons other than pure partisanship and sources other than party leaders behind proposals for additional judgeships. The main drive, however, seems to originate with County and District Leaders; the incidental benefits are more or less accidental. To judges, these incidental benefits are often important, and so, consequently, are the party organizations responsible for them.

Mutual Accommodation

The relationship between courts and parties—as, indeed, between the parties and all elected or politically appointed government officials and employees—is thus one of mutual benefit and accommodation. The court system is important to the parties; the parties are important to the judiciary. As things are now constituted, this is an inevitable and an indissoluble bond.

COURTS AND CHIEF EXECUTIVES

The power of appointment is useful to the appointing officer in two ways. He may employ it to install in office individuals of his own choosing. He may also use it to install in office someone favored by somebody else in return for a favor or a series of favors by that "somebody else."

The appointment of judges by chief executives is more widely used for the second purpose—bargaining—than for the first. For chief executives are generally not in a position to *direct* their legislative bodies to do what they, the executives, want. Nor can they easily *compel* party organizations to do their bidding. Nor, for that matter, are they always able to *command* all administrative agencies; many of these are quite autonomous. So the executives, lacking adequate sticks, must employ carrots whenever they can. Hence, they make appointments recommended by legislators or party leaders in return for support for their programs or candidacies, and they move administrators into choice jobs if the administrators are faithful to the chief executives. But the programs of chief executives are more dependent on the actions of administrative officers than of judges (although there are important exceptions). Executives, as a result, seem more inclined to try to induct the persons they individually prefer into many high administrative positions and to use judicial office to bargain with legislatures, parties, and with administrators hoping for seats on the bench eventually. The two purposes often merge, but they are distinguishable.

The President, the Governor, and the Mayor are equipped to bargain with varying degree of effectiveness in the political contest in New York City. From this special point of view, the Mayor may well be in the strongest formal position of the three. The President appoints to vacancies in all of the federal judgeships whose respective jurisdictions include New York City, but the names he proposes must win the consent of the Senate. Because of the practice of senatorial courtesy, he is obliged to come to terms with the Senators of the states affected when he appoints men to United States District Courts, and he must reach agreement with the Senate committee on the judiciary and other senatorial leaders when filling vacancies on higher courts. As for the Governor, the only court appointed by him is the State Court of Claims, and he, like the President, must obtain the consent of the upper house of his legislature before his appointments to vacancies take effect. The Governor is also empowered to make interim appointments—that is, appointments effective only until judges elected at the next general election can take their seats—to fill vacancies on the City Court, the County Courts (including General Sessions in New York County), the Surrogates' Courts, the Supreme Court, and the Court of Appeals. (If the state Senate is in session when he makes the appointments, the consent of that body must be obtained.) In addition, from among the sitting Supreme Court Justices, the Governor names seven to the Appellate Division in each of the two Judicial Departments that include the city (and five in each of the other two Judicial Departments into which the state is divided). But the Mayor fills all unoccupied seats in a total of 97 appointive judgeships, and he makes interim appointments to vacancies in the ranks of the 68 Municipal Court Justices, all without the necessity of concurrence or approval by any other governmental institution. (Although the "sitting-judge rule" did not originally cover interim appointees, some of these judges receive bipartisan endorsement at election time. Power to elevate men to the bench for short periods is thus more useful to chief executives than the brief duration of the initial interval suggests.)

The chief executives freely use their powers of judicial appointment as currency in political negotiations. This enables them to do many of the things they were presumably elected to do. It also enables party leaders to exert great influence over the choice of appointed judges. The executives thus gain some control over policy; the parties thus get jobs for their people.

COURTS AND OTHER CONTESTANTS

Besides the party leaders and chief executives, only professional associations of lawyers, the Citizens Union, and the press exert any significant, visible influence on the composition of the court system. Insofar as the claims of ethnic, national, and religious groups and of neighborhood consciousness affect the courts, they make themselves felt through the party hierarchies, or, in a general way, through the voting behavior of the electorates, both discussed earlier. The impacts of the lawyers, the press, and the Citizens Union are more direct and distinct.

There are many professional associations of lawyers in New York City. Especially prominent is the Association of the Bar of the City of New York, which is a citywide organization. In addition, there is a bar association in each of the five counties (the New York County Lawyers' Association being the largest in the metropolitan region and second in size in the country only to the American Bar Association). Each year the Association of the Bar rates all the candidates for judicial office, after their nomination, as "outstandingly qualified," "qualified" or "unqualified." Each of the county bar associations does the same most of the time for all judicial nominees within their respective areas. These findings are printed in moderate quantities and distributed to the membership of the organizations and to the press, ordinarily receiving something more than routine attention but less than front-page coverage from the latter. There is also a Metropolitan Trial Lawyers' Association, but it is generally more concerned with court organization and procedure than with the choice of judges.

The actions of the bar associations have had little, if any, effect on the choice of nominees for judicial office. Indeed, until 1956 the parties made only sporadic efforts to solicit the opinions of the bar associations regarding prospective nominees; the bar associations were thus in no position to bring any weight to bear on the selection of candidates. In that year, in response to the persistent urging of the Association of the Bar and of *The New York Times*, the New York County Leaders of both major parties pledged themselves to seek systematically the opinions of the bar associations about all prospective candidates prior to nomination. Whether this will have any discernible effect, and whether the party organizations in the other counties will follow suit, remains to be seen; the complaints that led to the adoption of this policy constitute convincing evidence that the professional legal associations have heretofore been largely ineffective in their efforts to influence the nominating process.

Their impact on elections also appears to be limited. Were this not the case, they would not feel compelled to try to intervene at an earlier stage; they would be content, if they could assure the defeat of a candidate by withholding their approval, to punish the parties in this fashion if the parties put forth unqualified candidates. But their ratings apparently do not sway electorates (perhaps because almost all the candidates are called "qualified"). Consequently, if they are to influence the composition and caliber of the judiciary to a larger extent than they have managed to affect in the past, the bar associations must somehow manage to intervene in the selection of nominees. Otherwise, they become little more than helpless bystanders.

If their role in nominations should become more prominent, the lawyers in the parties would probably move in to take over the leadership of the bar associations. The charge has already been leveled that the Bronx and Kings (Brooklyn) County Bar Associations are dominated by Democrats, and that the New York County (Manhattan) Lawyers' Association is controlled by Republicans, with the alleged result that the endorsements more closely reflect political preferences than professional judgments. If party domination is not the case now, it is likely to develop should the bar associations become more influential. Thus the prevailing situation is unlikely to change significantly in the immediate future.

The Citizens Union operates in much the same way as the bar associations, except that it uses a four-category rating scale ranging from "unqualified" through "qualified," "qualified and preferred" to "endorsed." Its influence on the nomination and election of judges, however, is no greater than that of the bar associations, particularly since it tends to follow the lead of the Association of the Bar.

Some of the daily newspapers grumble editorially about the process of judicial selection, and all of them express editorial preferences for judicial along with other candidates, but their recommendations sometimes cancel each other out. Anyway, it is doubtful that they control the voting behavior of their readers. Consequently there are no indications that the parties vie for their support when choosing nominees for judicial office.

Thus the dominance of the party hierarchies over the selection of elected judges is virtually uncontested by the only respectable nongovernmental groups in the community that consistently pay any attention to this phase of politics. The ascendancy of the inner cores of the parties over the selection of appointed judges is even more complete, for there is customarily no evaluation by nongovernmental groups at any stage of the appointive process, and only the most egregious incompetence or dishonesty is likely to attract any significant attention from them at all.

In the organization and procedure of the courts, as contrasted with the actual naming of judges, groups other than the parties have had greater (though not necessarily decisive) influence. The two issues are not completely separable, of course; while emphasis on *how* the courts are structured and *how* they operate may be distinguished from *what* they decide and *who* makes the decisions, these are related to each other. Nevertheless, it is on the *how* that groups other than the parties ordinarily concentrate, placing their greatest stress on increased speed, lower costs, and more symmetrical patterns of organization.

Agitation among lawyers' associations and civic groups and the press for modernizing the whole court system of the state resulted in the creation by the state legislature in 1953 of a Temporary Commission on the Courts (the "Tweed Commission"), appointed by the Governor. When the Commission brought in its report in 1956, proposing sweeping revisions of the system in order to achieve greater standardization and order, it provoked a storm of controversy. In general, civic groups and the press backed the recommendations, several of the lawyers' societies cautiously supported large parts of them but took exception to others, Mayor Wagner appointed a Citizens Commission on the Courts in New York City and subsequently endorsed this body's approval of most (but not all) of the provisions of the Tweed Commission plan. On the other hand, social welfare agencies tended to oppose the proposed abolition of special Youth Courts they had been instrumental in establishing, the State Association of Towns (and other such associations of public agencies and officials) attacked the revamping of inferior courts of local jurisdiction, associations of Magistrates and of County Judges, among other judicial officers, criticized the portions of the report affecting them, and the Chief Judge of the Court of Appeals urged caution. The Commission modified its plan to satisfy many of the critics, but in the end the opposition of many Republicans throughout the state, speaking through their representatives in the legislature, coupled with a lack of enthusiasm on the part of Democratic leaders, led to the defeat of the recommended reorganization, and the Commission went out of existence. It would appear from this that the parties play a large part even in matters of court organization and procedure, although no other aspects of the court system result in the active participation of so many groups. Organization and procedure and discussions of efficiency bring the nonparty groups out; they do not always prevail, but more is heard from them on these questions than on the selection of individual judges.

Efficiency is also a primary target of the Judicial Conference of the state, which consists of the Chief Judge of the Court of Appeals, the presiding Justices of the Appellate Division of the Supreme Court in each of the four Judicial Departments in the state, and, for terms of two years, one Supreme Court Justice (not in an Appellate Division) chosen by their associates in each Judicial Department. The Conference compiles and publishes judicial statistics, surveys "jurisdiction, procedure, practice, rules, and administration of all of the courts of the state," reporting its findings annually to the legislature and recommending legislation to improve the administration of justice. In addition, it studies the operation of the courts and tries to win the cooperation of judges throughout the state in improving court performance, speeding justice, and reducing waste and inefficiency. In New York City, the Association of the Bar and the Citizens Union have made studies of possible economies in judicial administration in recent years, and the City Administrator has advanced suggestions for consolidating Municipal Courts to save personnel, equipment, and space, and to effect other improvements.

The control of the party leaders over judicial *machinery* is thus shared with a great many other contestants in the political arena. It is in the naming of court *personnel* that their ascendancy is all but unchallenged in practice.

Clandestinely, however, one element of the population outside the parties in New York City plays a role in the selection of some judges: the underworld. The extent of underworld influence is difficult to assess and is probably limited, but it is unquestionably present and probably extends to both elective and appointive posts. Both the New York State Crime Commission (the Proskauer Commission) and the Special United States Senate Committee to Investigate Organized Crime in Interstate Commerce (the Kefauver Committee) elicited testimony from witnesses about the connections between known gangsters and racketeers on the one hand and some judges on the other. The leaders of large-scale unlawful enterprises—gambling, prostitution, narcotics handling, and extortion through counterfeit labor unions and spurious trade and industrial associations—generally have a good deal of cash on hand, and, since some of it finds its way into units of each party, it occasionally influences some choices of nominees and finances parts of some campaigns.

Yet the underworld, like the other nongovernmental and nonparty groups interested in the judiciary, stands on the periphery of the arena. At the center are the party hierarchies and the judges and other court personnel. The roles of all the others in the staffing of the court system are secondary by comparison.

CONCLUSION: THE COURTS AND PUBLIC POLICY

Judicial decisions, like the decisions of other governmental institutions, are vehicles of public policy. Inevitably, therefore, judges are targets of influence exerted by other contestants in the struggle for the stakes of politics. The strategies of the contestants are the same as they are with respect to other policy-forming institutions: (1) efforts to determine the choice of policy-making personnel, and (2) attempts to sway the decisions of the personnel who actually come to occupy office.

The methods of influencing policy decisions made by judges are somewhat different from those applied to other organs of government. Tenure, tradition, procedure, and myth render them less susceptible than other officials to many of the standard techniques of political pressure. They are, to be sure, not impervious to pressure, but they are in especially favored positions to resist if they choose, and find fewer imperatives to bargain or cultivate support than the members of the other governmental branches. Policy decisions of judges are thus made in a field of forces in which many contestants are of limited effectiveness at best, and from which many are excluded for all practical purposes. This probably tends to skew their decisions in a different direction from the decisions of officials who face competitive elections far more frequently, or who depend on alliances with a functional constituency for strength. At any rate, the influences on judicial decisions are not obvious.

One natural channel of influence of this kind would be the parties. The bonds between courts and the parties are numerous and strong. The willingness of party leaders to transmit to the courts the requests of constituents is widely recognized; except when the interests of the parties themselves are at stake, party leaders tend to be more concerned with the jobs, the revenues, and the loyalty supplied by the men they put in office than by the substance of court decisions and, as far as policy goes, are apparently as happy to press one way as another as a favor to a supporter. To what extent party hierarchies actually employ their dominance over selection of court personnel for such purposes is not known, but the opportunities certainly exist, and the temptations must be very strong.

Thus, whereas much of the maneuvering and negotiation elsewhere in government are overtly and explicitly oriented toward shaping the substance of decisions, the visible foci of judicial politics are selection of personnel and design of organization and procedures. The forces concerned with the substantive aspects of political questions are hampered; the forces with the greatest influence are commonly neutral with respect to content. Professional associations of lawyers and civic organizations must be content to direct their attention to raising the general professional standards of appointment and to improving judicial machinery. Public policy is often affected or formed by judicial decisions, but the policy questions are rarely highly perceptible or widely discussed. In appearance, at least, judicial politics is a politics of personnel and procedure rather than of program. Although policy flows out of it, the policy seems often to be an unwitting by-product of other considerations, and sometimes to be the work of contestants who see in the special processes of the judicial world opportunities to escape from the competition in the other branches of government. The full significance of the courts in the formulation of public policy still remains to be explored.

BIBLIOGRAPHY

OFFICIAL SOURCES AND REPORTS

New York City, Board of City Magistrates, *Annual Reports*, 1st Division: 1899–1914 (published annually); 1915 (consolidated with 2d Division); 2d Division: 1898–1901 (published annually); 1908–1914 (published annually); 1915 (consolidated with 1st Division). Single *Reports:* 1915–1932 (published annually); 1933, *City Record* (May 11, 1934); 1934–1955 (published annually); 1956, *City Record*, May 16, 1957; 1957, *City Record*, May 15, 1958; 1958, *City Record*, June 4, 1959.

Board of City Magistrates, *Annual Report of the Adolescents' Court, Brooklyn.* Published annually.

Board of City Magistrates, *Rules and Regulations,* January 1, 1924; *Rules and Regulations,* September 19, 1940; *Rules and Regulations,* March 20, 1941; *Rules and Regulations,* May 12, 1948.

Court of Special Sessions, *Annual Reports*: 1911–1932, 1933 to date.

Court of Special Sessions, *Annual Reports of the Chief Justice,* 1953–1956.

Domestic Relations Court, *Annual Reports,* published 1933–1940 annually; 1941–1943 (1 vol.); 1943–1944 (1 vol.); 1953–1954 (1 vol.), and 1955 to date (published annually).

Municipal Court, *Annual Reports,* 1927–1933 (published annually); 1934–1938 (1 vol.); 1939–1941 (1 vol.); 1942 to date (published annually).

New York State Constitution. Provisions relating to the courts of New York City may be found in the following sections of the state constitution: Art. V, sec. 11; Art. VI, secs. 13–19.

New York State Crime Commission, *Second Report to the Attorney General and the Legislature of the State of New York.* Legislative Document no. 40, March 9, 1953, pp. 13–18, 23–24. Presents the highlights of hearings which showed how the selection of judges, judicial candidates, and court personnel were influenced by political leaders.

New York State Joint Legislative Committee to Investigate the Affairs of the City of New York, *Report to the Legislature,* December 28, 1932, pp. 36–38. Recommendations of the Hofstadter Committee, whose counsel was Samuel Seabury, which suggested changes in the Surrogates' Court of New York County and among the Commissioners of Juries.

New York State, Temporary Commission on the Courts, *Report to the Governor and the Legislature of the State of New York* (1956). Legislative Document no. 18, Williams Press, Albany, 1956. Part of a series of comprehensive studies of our judicial system, this publication analyzes calendar congestion, court delays, and the cost of administering justice and offers constructive proposals relating to children and families in courts.

Report to the Governor and the Legislature of the State of New York (1957). Legislative Document no. 6, Williams Press, Albany, 1956–1957. 4 vols. Vol. 1, Recommendations for a Simplified State-Wide Court System; vol. 2, Recommendations for Amendments to the Youth Court Act (chap. 838 of the Laws of 1956); vol. 3, First Preliminary Report of the Advisory Committee on Practice and Procedure; vol. 4, Recommendations Respecting Calendar Congestion and Delay.

New York State, Judicial Conference of the State of New York, *Annual Reports*: First, Legislative Document no. 74, 1956; Second, Legislative Document no. 88, 1957; Third, Legislative Document no. 91, 1958; Fourth, Legislative Document no. 94, 1959.

U.S. Senate, Special Committee to Investigate Organized Crime in Interstate Commerce. United States Senate, *Hearings,* 1950–1951. 19 parts. Part 7, pp. 1433–1434, 1518–1521, 1530–1531, 1550–1552, and 1586–1600. These are the verbatim proceedings of the so-called Kefauver Committee. Part 7, dealing with New York and New Jersey, indicates how the underworld was able to influence judicial conventions and political choices of judges during the 1940's, a period of Tammany weakness.

APPRAISALS AND SUGGESTIONS FOR CHANGE IN NEW YORK CITY'S COURTS

Association of the Bar of the City of New York, *Bad Housekeeping: The Administration of the New York Courts.* The Association, New York, 1955. A critical survey of the administration of New York courts.

Botein, Bernard, *Trial Judge: The Candid, Behind-the-Bench Story of Justice Bernard Botein.* Simon and Schuster, New York, 1952.

Citizens Budget Commission, *The Cost of the Administration of the Courts in the City of New York: A Factual Study.* The Commission, New York, 1933. An indictment of judicial administration in the city.

Citizens Union, "Judges and Politics," *The Searchlight,* vol. 20, February, 1930. An analysis by the Citizens Union of the weaknesses of the courts in New York City on the eve of the Seabury probe of the Magistrates' Courts.

"Who Picks Our Judges?" *The Searchlight*, vol. 43, December, 1953. An argument against the elective system of selecting New York judges.

Civil Service Reform Association, *Report of the Executive Committee, 1932*. The Association, New York, 1932. Includes a list of political district leaders and their relatives, who held jobs exempt from civil service examinations.

Commissioners of Accounts and New York Bureau of Municipal Research, *Government of the City of New York*. J. J. Little and Ives Co., New York, 1915, pp. 1074–1135. An analysis of the city courts in 1914.

Curran, Henry H., *John Citizen's Job*. Charles Scribner's Sons, 1924, pp. 199–205, 208–214. An experienced politician tells how district political workers attempt to influence the courts.

Diamond, Theodore, *Politics and the Judiciary in New York City*. Master's thesis, Columbia University, 1959, unpublished.

Finegan, James E., *Tammany at Bay*. Dodd, Mead, and Co., New York, 1933, pp. 20–23, 87–88, 108–116, 133–136, 164–166. The judiciary and politics.

Gallantz, George C., "Judicial Selection—A Metropolitan Proposal," *New York State Bar Bulletin*, April, 1953, pp. 101–106. An indictment of the system of electing judges in New York City and a plea for the Missouri plan.

Moley, Raymond, "When Politics Seasons Justice," *Yale Review*, vol. 21, Spring, 1932, pp. 448–465. Political influences in the city's courts.

Moscow, Warren, *Politics in the Empire State*. Alfred A. Knopf, New York, 1948, pp. 148–165. An appraisal of the New York judiciary.

New York City, Chamber of Commerce, Special Committee on Law Reform, "Political Patronage in the Courts," *Monthly Bulletin of the Chamber of Commerce of the State of New York*, vol. 29, June, 1937, pp. 59–106. A critical review of the system of foreclosure of mortgages in the courts of New York City.

New York State Constitutional Convention Committee, *New York City Government: Functions and Problems*. Vol. 5 of *Reports and Studies*. Burland Printing Co., New York, 1938, pp. 221–225. Chapter 13, The Cost of Courts in New York City, indicates who paid how much for judicial service within the city at the time this survey was made.

Problems Relating to Judicial Administration and Organization. Vol. 9 of *Reports and Studies*. J. B. Lyon Co., Albany, 1938, pp. 1087–1157. Sets forth the framework of the state court system as of 1938 in detail, and suggests ways of reorganizing the judicial structure in New York City.

New York State Temporary Commission on the Courts of the State of New York, *A Proposed Simplified State-Wide Court System*. Report of the Subcommittee on Modernization and Simplification of the Court Structure. The Commission, New York, 1955. This comprehensive series of proposals for the entire state includes the courts of New York City within its purview.

Recommendation for a Simplified State-Wide Court System, 1957 Report to the Governor and the Legislature of the State of New York. The Commission, New York, 1956. A series of recommendations for improving the judicial system of the state and of the city.

Northrop, William B., and John B. Northrop, *The Insolence of Office: The Story of the Seabury Investigations*. George Putnam's Sons, New York, 1932, pp. 12–114. Describes the investigations and exposures of the courts of New York City during the administration of Mayor Walker.

Oravetz, Kalman, *New York Courts on Trial*. Citizens Union Research Foundation, New York, 1955. A plea for simplification of the court system in New York City.

Ransom, William L., "Discussion of the Administrative Organization of the Courts," *Proceedings* of the Academy of Political Science in the City of New York, vol. 5, April, 1915, pp. 687–694. A critical evaluation by a judge of the City Court.

Thomas, Norman, and Paul Blanshard, *What's the Matter with New York?* Macmillan Co., New York, 1932, pp. 92–129. The judicial scandals of the 1920's and 1930's in New York City.

MAGISTRATES' COURTS

Branson, Bernard, "New York Experiments with Traffic Court School for Traffic Violators," *Police*, March–April, 1959, pp. 62–66. An experiment in the Magistrates' Courts.

Citizens Union, *Scrapbooks*. 206 vols. Reference section of the New York Public Library, Astor Branch. Volume 203 covers the investigation of the Magistrates' Courts by Samuel Seabury.

City Club of New York, *The Magistrates' Court*. The Club, New York, 1932.

Curran, Henry H., *Magistrates' Courts*. Charles Scribner's Sons, New York, 1942. An account that stresses the human element.

Isaacs, Julius, *Oath of Devotion*. E. P. Dutton and Co., New York, 1949, pp. 169–302. A thoughtful and searching examination of the work of the Magistrates' Courts.

"Reminiscences." Columbia University Oral History Collection, Special Collections, Butler Library. Some acute observations on the Magistrates' Courts of New York City by a man who served on the bench.

Moley, Raymond, *Tribunes of the People: The Past and Future of the New York Magistrates' Courts*. Yale University Press, New Haven, 1932. Reports the results of a study for the Joint Legislative Committee whose counsel was Samuel Seabury, and of a survey for the Commission on the Administration of Justice in New York State.

Murphy, Raphael R., "Proceedings in a Magistrate's Court under the Laws of New York," *Fordham Law Review*, Spring, 1955, pp. 53–70.

Murtagh, John M., "Functions of Magistrates' Courts," *Bar Bulletin*, March, 1953, pp. 173–178. New York City's Chief Magistrate decries the policy of "millions for punishment, pennies for prevention."

New York City, Bureau of the Budget, *Magistrates' Courts: A Survey of the Current Practices in Processing of Summons for Traffic Violations*. The Bureau, New York, 1948.

Seabury, Samuel S., *Final Report of Samuel Seabury, Referee in the Matter of the Investigation of the Magistrates' Courts in the First Judicial Department and the Magistrates Thereof, and of the Attorneys-at-Law Practicing in Said Courts*. Lawyers Press, New York, 1932. A report which revealed scandalous political influence in the courts.

THE COURTS AND NEW YORK CITY YOUTH

Brill, Jeanette G., and E. George Payne, *The Adolescent Court and Crime Prevention*, Pitman Publishing Corp., New York, 1938. The story of an experiment with adolescent offenders in the courts of Kings County.

Cooper, Irving Ben, "The Drama of Youth in our Criminal Courts," *Federal Probation*, March, 1955, pp. 36–42. Observations concerning the juvenile courts of New York City.

"Youthful Offenders and the Community," *Focus*, July, 1954, pp. 115–120, 127. The Chief Justice of the Court of Special Sessions reports on the juvenile courts.

Cooper, Irving Ben, and Harry W. Lindeman, "Juvenile Court Judges Plead for More Adequate Facilities," *Journal of the American Judicature Society*, April, 1958, pp. 172–178. A description of conditions in the New York City juvenile courts.

Gellhorn, Walter, Jacob D. Hyman, and Sidney H. Asch, *Children and Families in the Courts of New York City*. Dodd, Mead and Co., New York, 1954. A study of the administration of laws relating to families in the courts of the city, made by a special committee of the Association of the Bar of the City of New York.

Goldstein, Jonah J., *The Family in Court*. Clark Boardman, New York, 1934. A city magistrate discusses the "laws' mishandling of domestic relations."

Kahn, Alfred J., *A Court for Children*. Columbia University Press, New York, 1923. A study of the New York Children's Courts.

New York State Citizens' Committee of One Hundred for Children and Youths, *The Four Million*. The Committee, Albany, 1951, pp. 137–169. Outlines the court facilities for wayward youths in New York City.

CHAPTER XV

Officials of Other Governments in the City's Political Process

INTERGOVERNMENTAL RELATIONSHIPS

THE OFFICIALS of the governments of New York State, the United States, and of neighboring states and localities are deeply involved in the government and politics of New York City. This is due to the dependence of all the major components of a modern industrial society upon each other, an interdependence engendered by the economic, transportation, and communication systems. A more specific reason, however, is the division and sharing of powers, functions, and responsibilities among the city, the higher levels of government, and adjacent units of government. For both these reasons, officials and employees of other governments are constantly drawn, or inject themselves, into the contest for the stakes of politics in the city. By the same token, officials and employees of the city are constantly engaged in efforts to influence their counterparts in other governments.

The City Is an Agent

All three levels of government operate within the City of New York, serving, regulating, and taxing the inhabitants. But there is an important difference between federal and state officials and employees as against city officials and employees. The personnel of the federal agencies (the largest in the area being the Post Office Department, the Department of Defense, the Treasury Department, and the State Department, but with many others also represented) are engaged exclusively in executing the provisions of federal law. Similarly, the personnel of the state agencies in the city (all 20 departments of the state government are represented here) are concerned primarily with the execution of state law. Most city officials and employees, however, are in both theory and practice agents of the state government (or, in a few instances, such as some phases of welfare, arterial highways, and urban renewal and slum clearance, also agents of the federal government). That is to say, the laws they administer are almost entirely laws enacted by the state government (or, in the cases noted, by the federal government),

558

and their activities are supervised in varying measure by state (and/or federal) personnel.

This aspect of the situation of New York City is by no means unique to New York. In American constitutional theory, municipal corporations are traditionally regarded as creatures of the state governments. There is no inherent right of local self-government, and their existence and powers, as well as the designation and powers of their officials, are subject to state control except as the state constitution provides otherwise. They are held to function in a dual capacity, namely, as agents of the state and as organizations for the provision of local service. The attitude engendered by this tradition is particularly evident in the detail and specificity of the state laws administered by the New York City Board of Education, Department of Welfare, Department of Personnel, Board of Elections, finance agencies, as well as the Police, Fire, Buildings, and Correction Departments. (The first three of these are also tightly supervised by state administrative officers.) The Housing, Transit, and Triborough Bridge and Tunnel Authorities, creatures of the state like the city itself, are similarly circumscribed by state law. Indeed, while most of the remaining agencies and officers of the city carry out local law essentially, their programs planned and directed primarily at the municipal level, they, too, derive their authority from broad state legislative authorizations and are limited by a variety of broad statutory restrictions.

The influence of the federal government upon the city government springs not from constitutional theory but from fiscal preeminence. Federal financial assistance, it is true, has not only been warmly welcomed but actively sought by city officials. Nevertheless, the purposes for which federal money has been made available have been federal purposes, and the federal government has quite naturally exercised the prerogative of every donor to set conditions for every grant and to check up to make sure that the conditions are fulfilled.

Thus, constitutional theory and financial realities have combined to cast city officials and employees in the role of agents of the higher levels of government. The relationship is firmly established and widely accepted; many federal and state officials deem it their right and duty to influence decisions and actions of city officials and employees, and the latter have had little choice but to accept this as their lot.

The City Is a Claimant

Federal and state officials are furnished with incentives to influence decisions and actions of city officials not only by the general view that the city is an agent of the higher units of government but also by the requests and demands of the city officials themselves. City officials exert these claims upon the other governmental levels for several reasons. First, they are not indifferent to the decisions and actions of federal and state personnel directly serving, regulating, and taxing the people of the city. Second, they are continually in need of financial assistance to maintain (let alone to expand) their own operations. Third, their powers are limited, and they are compelled constantly to seek new authority to meet new conditions.

Thus, for example, city leaders (as well as congressmen from the city and the United States Senators from New York) tend to seek increases in the New York harbor work of the United States Army Corps of Engineers. They labor to get for New York City a substantial share of the contracts for defense and other federal functions and to demand adequate federal services (which bring with them both jobs and payrolls) for this area. Mayor La Guardia used all the influence he could muster to try to persuade the Post Office Department to designate Floyd Bennett Field in Brooklyn instead of Newark Airport as the airmail terminus for the metropolitan region. Mayor Wagner urged the federal government to adjust its tax program so as to aid commuter railroad services. In much the same fashion, but on a smaller scale, city officials bring pressure to bear on the state government. If their demands are met, city leaders may regard as solved, at least temporarily, problems with which they would otherwise have to deal. If their requests are rejected, they may find themselves compelled to allocate their own time and energy and some of the fiscal resources of the city to solving or alleviating these problems. If the Corps of Engineers, for instance, were to reduce drastically its dredging of the harbor, it is not unlikely that the city government would have to assume all or part of this burden in order to protect the flow of commerce so important to the economy of the region. Curtailed defense contracts and federal expenditures in the city usually mean a heavier welfare load and perhaps a significant decline in tax revenues. One factor leading to the construction of La Guardia Airport was La Guardia's inability to persuade the Post Office Department to name Floyd Bennett Field as the regional airmail terminal; New York became the terminal when the new field was completed. It seems unlikely that federal and state tax policies will—or, for that matter, can—relieve fully the acute commuter railroad crisis in the metropolitan area, and this will continue to occupy the attention of city officials for a long time to come and probably to claim an increasing share of the finances of the municipality. In short, what state and federal officials do or fail to do in the way of direct service in the New York area will play an important part in the behavior and policies of city leaders. In this sense, then, the federal and state governments often influence the contest for the stakes of politics within the city, and the influence is frequently a response to a request of the city officials themselves.

City leaders also generate federal and state influence by their success in securing financial aid from those levels of government. State constitutional tax and debt limits circumscribe the ability of the city to raise and borrow money. Even if these were entirely removed, the city would still be restricted by economic considerations—specifically, the danger of driving business and residents out of New York, and of injuring the city government's credit standing in the bond market. Furthermore, many of the most productive forms of taxation—excise, liquor and tobacco and gasoline sales, and income—have been so extensively employed by the state and federal governments that any but the most modest additional city levies would make the totals prohibitive. This confines the city in effect to a relatively inelastic tax base (real property) supplemented by a variety of "nuisance" taxes and a general retail sales tax. To render even its traditional services, let alone the new ones for which a dynamic city constantly creates a demand, such as public health and social welfare, traffic management, air pollution control, and slum clearance, the city has been forced to seek fiscal help from the state legislature and Congress. Whenever such help is forthcoming, it usually brings with it some policy stipulations, some form of supervision and control, and occasionally some inquiry or investigation to assess the urgency of the alleged need. Indeed, Governor Dewey responded in 1953 to one of the city's repeated requests for funds by securing legislation creating a Temporary State Commission to study the government of the city to determine whether the needs could be met by increasing the efficiency of the city's governmental machinery. Governor Rockefeller in 1959 similarly obtained legislation establishing a temporary state-city commission (a "Little Hoover Commission") to examine the city government and propose improvements in its structure and functioning. The search for money often brings the city a measure of relief, but it also results in increased federal and state influence in the municipal governmental decision-making process.

The same is true of the city's quest for additional authority. Despite a home-rule amendment to the state constitution, and amplifying home-rule legislation, city leaders are not free to regulate or tax citizens within the city's borders in any way they like nor can they provide at will any services they want to. They must always find a constitutional or statutory base for the activities of the city government. In general, new enterprises, new programs and policies, and new forms of taxation cannot be fitted into existing provisions. The city is obliged to apply for grants of additional power. For some purposes—for example, to construct bridges over navigable waters—it needs the approval of federal officials. Consequently, city leaders themselves constantly involve state and federal officers in the local decision-making process. That is not to suggest that city officials are pleased with this state of affairs nor does it imply necessarily that the higher levels of government are displeased with it. On the contrary, it will shortly be seen that the state government in particular insists on preserving it. Nevertheless, things being as they are, the immediate cause of much of the participation of state and federal officials and employees in the government and politics of the city is the initiative taken by city leaders in quest of added powers.

In sum, not necessarily because city officials prefer it but because they often cannot help it, their role as claimants upon the higher levels of government for direct service, financial assistance, and additional authority has provided impetus and justification for the exercise of continual influence upon city decisions by the higher units of government.

The Effects of Partisan Differences

State incentives to maintain controls over city decisions and actions (and city determination to break away if possible) are furnished also by the differences between the constituencies of the two governments. In the state legislature the nonurban components of the population, both rural and suburban, and a number of upstate cities, are extremely influential, and they distrust the city. Prejudices and fears have grown out of real dissimilarities—between the cosmopolitanism, ethnic diversity, tolerance of unorthodox belief and behavior, crowding, speed, and noise of the city, and the comparative stability, quiet, and homogeneity of behavior and thought in the countryside and the suburbs. By the same token, many city dwellers have formed images of "rubes" from the backwoods, of rustic, isolated, provincial, parochial "hayseeds." Nonurban elements refuse to relinquish the weapons with which they are able to keep the metropolitan giant in their midst from overwhelming them, and, incidentally, from what they consider self-destruction and immorality, while the people and the politicians of the city strive to break free of what is regarded as a rural yoke upon their necks.

Still more significantly, the state legislature is normally dominated by Republicans, while the Democrats enjoy the advantage in the city most of the time. Each party camp uses its institutional base as a means of harrying the opposition for electoral purposes and extracting concessions for policy purposes. To assist Republican candidates in the city, the Republican legislators rarely miss an opportunity, especially in the period just before elections, to embarrass or harass their opponents. At the same time, Democrats seldom pass up a chance to parade before the public what they describe as state discrimination against the city and to blame the state for all the city's problems and shortcomings, charges designed to injure the Republican electoral efforts in the city. The fact that each party enjoys its greatest strength at a level of government different from its opposition's stronghold impels both of them to make forays into the other's territory for strategic ends; partisan advantage thus lies behind many attempts at intergovernmental influence and many efforts to shift burdens and responsibilities.

The City Is a Neighbor

As the core city of a metropolitan region comprising some fifteen million people spread over three states and served by dozens of units of government, New York City's programs and policies affect many other communities, and the programs and policies of the other communities often play a part in the success or failure of the city's own endeavors. For example, if New York and its neighbors do not jointly plan for sewage disposal, they may (and, indeed, once did) pollute each other's bathing beaches and perhaps their water supplies. Only by joint action can they hope to keep motor traffic moving freely—or even at all—throughout the region. Maintenance of rapid transit and commutation facilities can be achieved only on a cooperative basis. Public health problems are singularly indifferent to political boundaries. The Port of New York does not consist solely of New York City but comprises a large number of New Jersey communities. Residents of the entire metropolitan area cross jurisdictional lines to make use of recreational facilities in adjoining localities. New York's water supply, brought from sources as far as 120 miles upstate, passes through scores of communities on the way. For all these and many similar reasons, the officials of nearby governments are moved to try to influence the governmental leaders in New York City, and New York City leaders are likewise brought into contact with their neighbors. Thus, governmental decisions in New York City are affected by actions taken outside the city and at the same time are often shaped by consideration of the effects they might have on the whole metropolitan region.

Strategies of Nongovernmental Groups, Bureaucratic Groups, and Party Leaders

As was noted in the discussions of the strategies of the various contestants for the stakes of politics in New York City, these contestants do not confine their activities exclusively to the New York City arena. Rebuffed at one level of government or party organization, they bring their influence to bear on others as they pursue their objectives. Appreciating the power of the instruments of influence upon the city available to the officials of higher governments (described below), nongovernmental groups, the organized bureaucracies, and local party leaders take advantage of whatever lines of access to the higher levels are open to them and try to persuade their contacts at those levels to encourage, compel, or block specified city actions. Indeed, as previously noted, city leaders sometimes send contestants to the higher levels to build up support for measures the city leaders themselves favor, or to deflect annoying pressures by persistent claimants, or because the city truly lacks the authority or the resources to meet the demands made upon it.

In any case, all these strategies add to the involvements of other governments in governmental and political decisions in the city.

The Pattern of Relationships

Other governments are thus important participants in the government and politics of New York City. For them, as for all the other participants, the interests and values shared by all—the overriding commitment to the preservation of the system—produce workable arrangements despite the complexities and seeming delicacy of the decision-making mechanisms. In a broad sense, everybody is determined to prevent the system from breaking down. Nevertheless, bargaining pervades the relationships among the officials of the governments involved. There is competition and conflict, negotiation and compromise, maneuver and strategy, as the officials of governments outside the city employ all the instruments of influence at their command to control city decisions and as city officials reply to these endeavors with countermeasures of their own.

THE CITY, THE STATE, AND THE FEDERAL GOVERNMENT

Instruments of Influence Available to the Officials of the Higher Governments

It is not easy to discuss in an orderly, comprehensive, and concise fashion the methods by which officials and employees of the federal and state governments exercise influence upon personnel of the city government. In the first place, the techniques are so numerous that even when they are more or less loosely grouped at least half a dozen categories are required to encompass them all. In the second place, their effects are difficult to trace because city officials anticipate possible federal and state actions and formulate their own decisions accordingly; overt applications of the modes of influence are but crude indices of their consequences. In the third place, there are many forms of action—constitutional, executive, legislative, administrative, and judicial —and each mode or category of influence may take a number of these forms. In the fourth place, the modes and forms of federal and state influence are not the same for every governmental function. All intricacies must be borne in mind in the course of the somewhat simplified discussion that follows.

Restrictions of Power. The principal methods by which the higher levels of government influence the decisions of city officials and employees are: (1) imposition of general restrictions on the scope of their legal authority, and (2) explicit restrictions on the exercise of the limited authority they are permitted to wield.

As a creation of the state, the city enjoys no powers other than those specifically granted to it, virtually all of which take the form of state legislation. Only one provision of the state constitution—the so-called Home Rule Amendment, discussed later in this chapter, conferring on cities power "to enact local laws relating to its property, affairs or government"—serves as an important source of authority for the city government, but even it depends for its operation on implementing state statutes. Moreover, the meaning of "home rule" has consistently been construed narrowly by the courts. Consequently, it is to the laws of the state, and to the city charter adopted by the people of the city under the terms of state law, that one must turn to find the basis for the city's jurisdiction.

The legal status of the city's charter is roughly equivalent to that of a legislative statute; indeed, until the state enacted legislation establishing a procedure by which the people of a city might locally formulate and locally adopt their own charter, all charters were simply ordinary state statutes. The present New York City Charter was prepared by a locally appointed Charter Commission and adopted by the voters of the city at a general election held in 1938. (It has been amended many times since then by state acts passed at the request of the city and by local action.) But the Charter Commission could not give the city government any powers it (the Commission) wanted; it could only organize and provide for the exercise of such powers as the enabling state legislation authorized it to deal with. The state carefully reserved to itself a great many powers, perhaps the most important of them being powers of taxation, and the city must return to the legislature for specific authorization to take action on these subjects each time the need arises. Moreover, since the provisions of the charter describe what city officers are empowered to do, they implicitly prohibit these officers from doing anything that is not expressly stated or clearly implied. The charter, then, by specifying the extent of the powers of city officials, at the same time establishes the limits of their powers.

In addition to the charter, general statutes applying alike to all cities confer authority on local officials and, by the wording of the grant, limit them to the performance, in their discretion, of only the actions authorized. Thus, for example, city officers will look not only to the charter but to the state Public Health Law, Public Welfare Law, Education Law, Civil Service Law, and so on, as the case may be, to find out what they may do (and, by the same token, what they may not do). There are also statutes of the same nature applicable to only designated classes of cities, New York being a class by itself.

All these legislative enactments, taken together, define a sphere of action for the city. But, because they are both limited and limiting in scope, they assure state officials of the opportunity—indeed, they compel the Governor and state legislators—to take part in the governmental decision-making processes of the city. Much of the time, when the city leaders seek to expand their jurisdiction or to embark on new programs, they must request new statutory authority. Many such requests are occasions for intense bargaining.

The obverse of limited grants of jurisdiction as a way of restricting power is specific prohibitions and restrictions on the use of such discretion as has been conferred. The Constitution of the United States, the constitution of New York State, and the legislation and treaties or compacts of these units of government all contain provisions that restrict the powers of municipal officials. Most of these, however, concern the rights of citizens in general with respect to public officers, describe the division of powers in the federal system, or apply broadly to the ethics of all public servants. They are extremely important, for they establish the character of the governmental process. But there is no need to rehearse them here, for, while they constitute the backdrop against which the action here under consideration takes place, they are only occasionally employed as instruments of influence by higher levels of government upon the city. Perhaps the only constitutional provisions of which note need be made here are those dealing with local finances, which impose a large number of limitations on the fiscal discretion of municipal corporations. The most important of these for the immediate purposes of this discussion are the ceilings on New York City's debt-incurring power (two sections deal exclusively with New York City and hold its borrowing to 10 per cent of a five-year average of full valuation of taxable real estate) and on the amounts the city may raise by real estate taxes for local purposes (2.5 per cent of a five-year average of full valuation of taxable real estate). There are even fewer relevant specific *statutory* prohibitions and restrictions upon the city; since the terms of the grants of authority to the city are already sufficiently limiting, added explicit injunctions tend to be superfluous. It is seldom necessary for the state to tell the city what it must not do; instead, permission may be withheld by mere silence. In the relations between the city and the state, the way power is granted tends to be more significant than the formal barriers to its use.

Occasionally the state limits the power of the general city government by assigning the jurisdiction over particular functions to comparatively independent bodies. This it has done in the cases of the Board and Department of Health and the Board and Department of Hospitals. They are governed by many state laws, but they are also exempt from most of the state laws that control the health and hospital functions of other communities and from the provisions of the state Sanitary Code (a body of state administrative regulations). Nor do they carry out local laws of the municipal corporation (save for a few minor exceptions) although their operations are financed by the city and their personnel are city officers and employees. Instead, the legislature has delegated to the two Boards a large proportion of the powers which the legislature itself exercises with respect to these functions for the rest of the state, or which it has directed state administrative officers to exercise. The two city Departments, respectively, carry out the rulings of the Boards. To be sure, their top officers are appointed by the Mayor and controlled by city budgeting, personnel, purchasing, and other requirements. But with respect to public health and public hospitals, the Boards are in important respects little legislative bodies with their own administrative arms.

In all these ways, the higher levels of government—particularly the state, through legislative action—control governmental decisions in the City of New York, and, indeed, influence the very nature of the political contest. The capacity to restrict the power of municipal officials is an effective instrument for this end.

Mandates. The second major category of modes of influence comprises mandates to city officers and employees—that is, commands regarding what they must do rather than instructions about what they may or may not do. A number of important mandates appear in the form of state constitutional provisions, but the vast majority are legislative or administrative actions supplemented by judicial decisions.

The article on suffrage in the state constitution, for example, prescribes the qualifications of voters (for local as well as for statewide elections), methods of identifying voters, manner of voting, bipartisan registration and election boards, permanent registration, and other aspects of the conduct of elections. The article on officers and civil departments declares that "appointments and promotions in the civil service of the state and of all the civil divisions thereof, including cities and villages, shall be made according to merit and fitness to be ascertained, as far as practicable, by examination which, as far as practicable, shall be competitive"; provides for veterans' preference and credits; and makes public service pension and retirement plans contractual obligations of the government involved and forbids diminution or impairment of benefits. The article on the judiciary deals extensively with the structure of courts and the tenure of judges, and covers New York City both by general provisions and by detailed special provisions. A section of the article on local governments directs that the election of city officers and certain county officers be held in odd-numbered years. It must be remembered that provisions of the state constitution operate as limitations upon state officers as well as upon city leaders; the former as well as the latter lose some freedom of action. Yet, although both are aware of this situation, it still sometimes appears, from the point of view of the city, that constitutional directives are just another way in which the state exerts influence upon governmental decisions and actions in the city.

This feeling is much stronger with respect to legislative mandates than constitutional mandates. For legislative mandates, although they vary a good deal from function to function, are on the whole more numerous and specific and usually more rigidly controlling. Election procedure is the best example of this. The composition of the Board of Elections, the salaries of the members, the number and general location of branch offices, the Board's duties and powers, and similar specifications for Election District Boards of Registry and Election, as well as the details of every aspect of the electoral process right down to the provision of flags and pencils, are fully spelled out in the state Election Law, and the expenses of these operations are made a charge upon the city. The organization and powers of the New York City Board of Education are in similar fashion itemized in the state Education Law as are many particulars of the employment and payment of teachers, minimum length of school sessions, rules of student attendance, subjects of instruction, rental liability, and the like. Moreover, New York City is required to appropriate each year for the school system an amount equal to 0.62 per cent of the assessed valuation of the taxable property in the city, an amount far below what the city ordinarily does spend, but which in any event constitutes a floor below which city expenditures on education may not drop. The state Welfare Law, conforming to the terms of federal grants-in-aid (discussed below) for the four programs supported by the federal government and independently in the case of other welfare activities, also particularizes many aspects of welfare organization and procedure in the city, setting up such specific criteria for the distribution of welfare assistance (and broadly authorizing the state Board of Social Welfare to add to the detailed specifications) that the city Welfare Department is left with little more than the ministerial function of identifying the people eligible for its aid. The Civil Service Law, implementing the civil service provisions of the constitution, requires the establishment of a municipal personnel agency to execute the intent of the law and spells out the intent in detailed sections covering such topics as classification, promotion, transfer, reinstatement, reduction in grade, exceptions from competitive examination, and so forth. Sections of half a dozen laws or more describe in full particulars the methods to be practiced by city officials in assessing, taxing, borrowing, debt management, and other fiscal operations of the city. The composition, powers, duties, and procedures of the Board of Water Supply are set forth with great specificity in a statute. The procedures for enacting local laws, as well as for adopting or amending a charter, are detailed at length in the Home Rule Law.

Similarly, the Departments of Police, Fire, Buildings, and Correction, and the Chief Medical Examiner are engaged in most respects in the enforcement of state law as elaborated by local additions to the statutes. The Penal Law, the Tenement House Law, the Labor Law, the Prison Law, and the Public Health Law all contain many provisions governing these agencies, and many other provisions affecting them are scattered throughout the other laws of the state. True, the means of enforcement and the rigor of administration are left to a considerable extent in local hands. But the contents of the laws are formal state responsibilities, and the local officers merely carry them out. Moreover, in carrying them out, they must observe the requirements of other state statutes regarding investigation, apprehension, arrest, and so on. There are statutory directives that policemen and firemen be included in the competitive class of civil service, that set their maximum tours of duty, that specify two-week annual vacations for them (since 1911), that establish a forty-hour work week and rotation of shifts for them, and even one that orders that they be issued identification cards to permit them to use public transportation without charge. The police and fire forces have been active in Albany in their own behalf. The result of all this, of course, is to make these city officers agents of the state at least to the same degree that they are agents of the city government.

Not all city departments are subjected to such tight control through legislative mandates. But not a single one is entirely free from legislative directives. As a means by which the state influences the behavior of city officers, this technique is powerful, and its power is all the more impressive because of the selectivity and accuracy with which it may be employed.

In several areas, mandates take the form of administrative rules and regulations. The state Education Law, for example, delegates broad rule-making power over state and local educational activities to the Board of Regents. The rules of the Board fill 57 pages, and elaborate on the provisions of statutes dealing with the issuance of teaching certificates, examinations for teachers, compulsory education, certificates of literacy for voting, licensing for motion pictures, subversive activities of teachers, and many other subjects. The Education Law also confers extensive rule-making powers on the state Commissioner of Education, to whom the Board has further subdelegated authority to implement in a specific fashion the more general policies enunciated by the Regents.

In the field of city finance, the state Comptroller (who is head of the Department of Audit and Control) has authority to prescribe regulations concerning minimum requirements for notices of sales of bonds, the cancellation or destruction of obligations, and the procedure for the issuance of new registered obligations. Moreover, on application from a municipality, he may exclude from the debt-contracting limitations of the municipal corporation designated types of indebtedness.

Welfare officials in the city are governed not only by state administrative regulations but by the regulations of federal officials as well. The Bureau of Public Assistance of the Social Security Administration, which is in turn a component of the federal Department of Health, Education, and Welfare, furnishes an outline to state Welfare Departments applying for welfare grants-in-aid from the federal government. These outlines set the format for state plans for each of the assistance programs supported by federal funds, and the plans, once approved by the federal agency, become the basic controlling documents for the administration of these programs. They are supplemented by a *Handbook of Public Assistance Administration* put out by the Bureau of Public Assistance, which sets forth in great detail administrative standards and the ways and means of carrying out public assistance programs. Observing federal regulations wherever they apply, and formulating comparable regulations of its own for those programs that do not receive any federal money, the state Board of Social Welfare issues rules and orders binding upon city welfare officers, the city constituting one of the state's welfare districts. The Board of Social Welfare acts through the Department of Social Welfare to see that its intent is translated into practice. Furthermore, the state Social Welfare Department regularly publishes Welfare Bulletins, a series of regulatory and informational issuances to county and city welfare agencies, and approves a Local Administrative Plan describing local welfare policy, procedure, and administrative organization in detail.

The state Civil Service Commission, alone among the agencies closely supervising city officials within its purview, does not oversee its charges largely by means of its own regulations, although it is empowered to issue them. This does not mean that the intensity of superintendence is not high; on the contrary, the surveillance is stringent. But other methods are employed in this instance, as described below, to the same ends and with the same effects.

Aside from these programs, supervision of city officials by state administrative officers is the exception rather than the rule. Most city agencies need not consult an extensive body of state administrative issuances to determine the scope and limits of their authority. Where, however, devices of this nature have been established, they have vested in the responsible higher administrative officials vast power to influence city policies, and their impact upon the pattern of city activities has been considerable.

Judges have opportunities to issue mandates to city officers and employees when these officers or employees apply to the courts for sanctions against the violators of administrative decisions, and when the city or its officers are defendants in suits brought against them. They are in many ways far more vulnerable to suit than their federal and state counterparts, for citizens may invoke against the city not only all the protections and guarantees they may call upon to defend their rights against invasion by the federal and state governments, but others as well. In particular, the city's liability in tort—damage and negligence cases—is broader than those of the higher levels of government. Furthermore, other bases for suit were created by the state legislature in the so-called Taxpayers' Act, which permits taxpayers in the municipalities of the state to sue municipal officials "to prevent any illegal official act on the part of any such officers, agents, commissioners or other persons, or to prevent waste or injury to, or to restore or make good, any property, funds or estate of such . . . municipal corporation. . . ." The same Act also permits the holders of bonds of subdivisions of the state to bring suit for damages against public officers whose "misfeasance, malfeasance or negligence" in issuing bonds or coupons causes the damage to the bondholder. Still another section of the same Act authorizes any municipal corporation "which has been or shall be compelled to pay any negotiable bond, or any coupon originally attached to such bond, by the judgment of a court of competent jurisdiction, because of the misfeasance, malfeasance or negligence of any public officer or agent of such municipal corporation . . ." to begin an action in court against such officer and to recover the amount paid, with interest from the time of payment. Moreover, a companion statute to the Taxpayers' Act authorizes the state to "sue for money, funds, credits and property held by public corporations, boards, officers or agents for public purposes which had been wrongfully converted or disposed of. . . ." Although judicial mandates technically concern only the individual cases at issue before the courts, the judicial practice of observing precedent invests many cases with a significance reaching far beyond the particular parties in controversy. Federal and state judges are thus important participants in the city's governmental processes.

It should not be inferred that every mandate upon the city government by the higher levels of government is resented or opposed. On the contrary, some of them are welcomed because they direct the city with a voice of higher authority to do things the city leaders wish to do anyway, but for which they do not want to bear the onus. On the whole, however, mandates— particularly those of the state legislature or state administrative agencies —tend to breed considerable local irritation because they limit the discretion of the local authorities. Mandates are effective modes of influence, and those who are influenced do not always respond to their exercise with enthusiasm.

Grants-in-Aid. The third of the general categories of higher level governmental influences on the officials and employees of the city is grants-in-aid. Over one fifth of the city's annual expense budget is financed in this fashion (the other four fifths coming from local taxes and other local sources of revenue). Almost 17 per cent of this money comes from the state, the remainder (almost 5 per cent) from the federal government (most of it, however, coming through state channels rather than directly).

Of the state aid, four fifths is allocated to specific functions. Over 43 per cent is for education; almost 25 per cent is for welfare, more than 10 per cent is for health and hospitals. A little over 20 per cent is not earmarked for any function, but is for general city purposes. The remaining state aid, a little over 1 per cent of the total, is designated for two specific programs. Most federal aid is earmarked for welfare, which makes up almost 95 per cent of the total of federal grants for current expenses; the bulk of the remainder goes for hospitals and education.

Both the state and the federal governments contribute to some city capital improvement expenses. The largest single item is slum clearance, with the federal government already committed to a contribution of almost $85 million over the years, of which nearly $34 million has already been received by the city. Hospital construction, civil defense, and other functions have also received more modest aid from the higher governments in connection with capital improvements at various times.

TABLE 57. STATE GRANTS TO THE CITY FOR CURRENT EXPENSES, 1957–1958

Function		Amount	Per cent of total state grants for each function[a]
Education		$145,946,827.94	43.3
Health		17,517,803.53	5.2
Hospitals		16,902,217.29	5.0
Social welfare		83,916,077.37	24.9
Youth Board		2,146,416.30	.6
Public libraries		1,740,260.24	.4
General purpose[b]			
Per capita assistance[c]	$53,176,560.72		15.8
Motor vehicle registration fees	9,057,746.01		2.7
Unallocated	914,710.29		.2
Shared taxes[d]	5,777,512.16		1.7
Total, general purpose		68,926,529.18	20.4
Total, state grants		$337,096,131.85	100.0

[a] Figures do not add to 100 because of rounding.

[b] May be divided among the various functions in the city's discretion; not earmarked.

[c] Includes $500,000.00 for Police Pension Fund.

[d] City's share of state-imposed taxes.

SOURCE: *Annual Report* of the Comptroller of New York City, 1957–1958.

One can only speculate on what has been the precise impact of these grants-in-aid upon the pattern of city services. It seems logical, although it has not been demonstrated, that city leaders would place heavy stress on those activities for which aid is available, for as a general rule the amount of aid is conditional upon the amount of local effort. Whether or not this is the case, it is certainly clear that the sudden withdrawal of all aid funds would compel the city to divert funds from other services to sustain the currently aided functions even if these functions were drastically curtailed. Similarly, if general-purpose funds were to be cut off, the city would either have to reduce its services or increase its taxes or both. That is to say, although it is impossible to state exactly in what respects and with what results grants-in-aid influence governmental decisions within the city, there can be no doubt that the effects *in toto* have been substantial.

Grants-in-aid often carry conditions relating not only to the ends to which the financial aid may be put, but the methods by which the aided programs are to be administered. The city Department of Welfare, for instance, must observe the provisions of the federal Social Security Act and the regulations of the Social Security Administration that no one receiving benefits financed in part by federal funds be denied the right to apply for assistance, nor refused a formal hearing if he is dissatisfied with the way he is treated. Furthermore, the personnel of the state agency and local Welfare Departments must operate under a merit system. The state Board and Department of Social Welfare exercise tight control over the city Welfare Department's organization, administrative procedures, and facilities as well as over the substantive aspects of its program. Library grants are conditioned upon the requirement that all residents of the city be allowed to use the

TABLE 58. FEDERAL GRANTS TO THE CITY FOR CURRENT EXPENSES, 1957–1958

Function	Amount	Per cent of total federal grants for each function
Civil defense	$20,000.00	0.02
Correction	43,025.26	0.05
Education	1,073,806.14	1.14
Health	146,631.72	0.16
Hospitals	3,659,130.03	3.87
Social welfare	89,531,349.08	94.76
Total	$94,473,942.23	100.00

SOURCE: *Annual Report* of the Comptroller of New York City, 1957–1958.

libraries free, that librarians meet the training specifications set by the state Commissioner of Education, and that library standards be at or above a stated minimum. State funds for tuberculosis control may be withheld if the city constructs a tuberculosis hospital having more than 500 beds, if it has space but refuses to accept a patient recommended by the state Commissioner of Health, if an approved patient is requested or required to pay for treatment, or if the hospital fails to comply with the rules prescribed by the state Commissioner of Health. In the case of education, administrative practices as well as substantive educational policy are so tightly regulated by the provisions of state legislation and the rules of the Board of Regents and the Department of Education that additional qualifications are rarely necessary in connection with grants-in-aid; nevertheless, administrative refinement and interpretation of the definitions of the activities eligible for state assistance sometimes add to the stringency of the requirements.

TABLE 59. PROPORTION OF CITY EXPENDITURES FINANCED BY FEDERAL AND STATE GRANTS, BY FUNCTIONS, 1957–1958 (CURRENT EXPENSES ONLY)

Function	Total expenditure by the city	Federal grant for function	Federal grant as per cent of expenditure for function	State grant for function	State grant as per cent of expenditure for function	Total federal and state grants for function	State and federal grants as per cent of expenditure for function
Education and libraries	$ 416,407,522.94	$ 1,073,806.14	0.2	$147,687,088.18	35.5	$148,760,894.32	35.7
Debt service	348,915,379.86	..	..	..	..	..	..
Social welfare	279,950,938.07	89,531,349.08	31.9	83,916,077.37	29.9	173,447,426.45	61.8
Public safety	239,695,895.33	..	..	..	..	..	..
Pension funds[a]	194,314,897.48	..	..	..	..	..	..
Hospitals	132,805,059.39	3,659,130.03	2.8	16,902,217.29	12.7	20,561,347.32	15.5
Sanitation and health	122,598,369.92	146,631.72	0.1	17,517,803.53	14.3	17,664,435.25	14.4
General government	92,695,284.38	..	..	..	..	..	..
Public enterprises	49,872,570.05	..	..	..	..	..	..
Parks, cultural, recreational	34,109,211.12	..	..	..	..	..	..
Correction and judicial	29,440,984.06	43,025.36	0.1	..	..	43,025.36	0.1
County expense	22,069,445.34	..	..	..	..	..	..
General Fund Reserve	9,859,437.00	..	..	..	..	..	..
Tax deficiency	7,298,680.00	..	..	..	..	..	..
Other	22,466,516.47	20,000.00[d]	0.1	2,146,416.30[e]	9.5	2,166,416.30	9.6
All functions	$2,002,500,191.41	$94,473,942.33	4.7	268,169,602.67	13.4	362,643,545.00	18.1
General Purpose							
(Per capita assistance)[b]				(53,176,560.72)			
(Motor vehicle reg. fees)				(9,057,746.01			
(Unallocated)				914,710.29)			
(Shared taxes)[c]				(5,777,512.16)			
Total general purpose				68,926,529.18	3.4		
Grand totals	$2,002,500,191.41	$94,473,942.33	4.7	$337,096,131.85	16.8	$421,570,074.18	21.5

[a] Does not include $500,000 from state for Police Pension Fund. This figure is in per capita assistance.
[b] See Note a. [c] City share of state-imposed taxes. [d] Civil Defense. [e] Youth Board.
SOURCE: *Annual Report* of the Comptroller of New York City, 1957–1958.

TABLE 60. FEDERAL AID TO NEW YORK CITY FOR SLUM CLEARANCE

Approved project cost and city and federal participation

| Project | | Approved project cost | Land sold to sponsor | City's participation | | Federal participation | | |
No.	Name			Land retained	City's contribution	Federal grant	Cash received	Balance due
	Sponsored Projects:							
604	Corlears Hook	$5,627,408.00	$1,049,240.00	$76,953.00	$1,500,405.00	$3,000,810.00	$2,089,689.00	$911,121.00
605	Harlem	6,823,948.00	1,174,911.00	..	1,883,013.00	3,766,024.00	2,308,478.00	1,457,546.00
606	North Harlem	5,205,137.00	1,111,250.00	..	1,364,629.00	2,729,258.00	1,655,158.00	1,074,100.00
608	West Park (Manhattantown)	20,006,541.00	3,106,711.00	845,202.00	5,351,544.00	10,703,084.00	7,372,543.00	3,330,541.00
609	Morningside	5,842,448.00	1,302,046.00	..	1,513,467.00	3,026,935.00	2,179,393.00	847,542.00
610	Fort Greene	6,111,904.00	1,862,245.50	107,250.00	1,380,802.50	2,761,606.00	2,065,952.00	695,654.00
611	Columbus Circle	12,003,075.00	3,421,222.00	..	2,860,618.00	5,721,235.00	4,439,642.00	1,281,593.00
612	New York University—Bellevue	8,973,444.00	2,898,078.75	..	2,025,122.25	4,050,243.00	2,825,044.00	1,225,199.00
613	Pratt Institute	10,825,189.00	1,997,860.00	221,679.00	2,868,550.00	5,737,100.00	3,313,175.00	2,423,925.00
614	Washington Square Southeast	19,042,263.00	6,666,954.00	..	4,125,103.00	8,250,206.00	5,687,655.00	2,562,551.00
617	Seward Park	9,777,156.00	1,455,597.00	..	2,773,853.00	5,547,706.00	..	5,547,706.00
618	Park Row	4,449,244.00	574,000.00	..	1,288,748.00	2,577,496.00	..	2,577,496.00
619	Lincoln square	52,217,982.00	13,071,051.56	361,033.00	13,169,321.15	26,338,642.29	..	26,338,642.29
	Total sponsored projects	$166,896,739.00	$39,691,166.81	$1,612,117.00	$42,105,175.90	$84,210,345.29	$33,936,729.00	$50,273,616.29

Source: *Annual Report* of the Comptroller of New York City, 1957–1958.

Additional controls are also attached to federal aid to the city for capital outlays; to obtain these moneys, the city has had to meet specifications laid down by the federal administrative agencies handling the various programs. In short, many of the modes of influence employed by administrative officers of the higher levels of government derive their force at least in part from the existence of grants-in-aid programs. To be sure, unaided functions are also subject to the careful supervision and influence of state administrative officers. But it is no accident that the aided programs are among the most stringently controlled. The theoretical possibility that funds will be withheld for noncompliance with directives adds to the authority with which federal and state administrators of these activities may speak.

Despite the prominence of grants-in-aid in the pattern of governmental decisions in New York City, it would be misleading to suggest that the sole, or even the chief, purpose of the grant system is to enable federal and state officials to inject themselves into local affairs. On the contrary, a variety of objectives lie back of the practice. Equalization is one of the outstanding ones, the idea being that the quantity and quality of service rendered by the governments of poorer communities should not be permitted to drop below a minimum level even if this means that wealthier communities in effect contribute to their support. Equalization also means that the financial burden of supplying at least the minimum level of public services will not be permitted to grow oppressively heavy in less fortunate areas as contrasted with those that are better situated. The underlying principle is that all the people of the state have a common interest in the prevention of glaring disparities in these regards, and that the state government has an obligation to use its statewide taxing powers to this end. In fact, more than half of the state budget consists of assistance to local governments. Some communities receive more from the state treasury than they pay into it in revenue collections, while others (New York City included) pay in more than they receive. Differences of opinion over the wisdom of this policy have engendered many heated arguments between city leaders on the one hand and state officers and their upstate constituencies on the other. Nevertheless, it is apparent that the policy is the result in part of a genuine state concern with a more equitable distribution of public services and burdens rather than simply a calculated strategy by which the state government can achieve a large measure of influence in local political processes.

Another goal of grants-in-aid by the state has been to add a stable source of income to the revenues of local governments. Property taxes, the traditional mainstay of local public finance, are increasingly incapable of sustaining the broadening spectrum of governmental activities, and such other sources of revenue as most localities are in a position to tap are generally profoundly affected by local economic conditions and therefore tend to be rather volatile. The diversified economy of the state as a whole furnishes a much more dependable revenue base. Grants-in-aid permit the state government to level out some of the extreme oscillations in the financial positions of local governments.

Decentralization is a third purpose of the grants-in-aid system. Were this not a widely held value, higher levels of government might well undertake to provide services directly instead of encouraging the subdivisions of the states to furnish them locally. But "keeping government close to the people" is a slogan—a matter of principle for some people, a cynical matter of expediency for others—that still has great vitality. (It must also be observed, however, that state and local political organizations defensive of their own interests can sometimes be won over to a new program if they are assured that they will have a part in its administration.)

Even though there are many reasons for resort to grants-in-aid by higher levels of government, one of the end-products is the influence of the benefactor upon the decisions and actions of the beneficiary. Intentional or not, the result is there.

As a matter of fact, the attainment of influence is often a conscious motive. The offer of money is unquestionably made deliberately to induce the recipients to fulfill the conditions of the grant. In the relations between New York City and New York State the assistance earmarked for particular functions has certainly had as one of its consequences an increase in federal and state legislative and administrative influence upon the city.

Clearance. The fourth broad category of federal and state influence upon city decisions is the requirement of approval of city actions as a condition of their taking effect. Almost invariably this authority is wielded by administrative officers of the federal and state governments, chiefly—but not exclusively—in connection with financially assisted programs.

The federal Bureau of Public Assistance, for instance, requires the filing of state welfare plans before federal aid is made available for that function, and the state Department of Social Welfare likewise requires the submission of such plans by local welfare agencies. In both cases, the higher level may refuse to accept a plan, or to accept particular features of it, and may thus compel the lower level to conform to its wishes. Once the plans are agreed upon they may not be amended without higher approval. The plans embody a great deal of detail about organizational structure, substantive policy, and administrative procedure.

In like fashion, the federal Bureau of Public Roads, the State Highway Department, and the City Planning Commission, not to mention the City Construction Coordinator, work closely together in drafting arterial highway projects and the municipal officials must arrive at an understanding with their counterparts in the other governments before they can proceed with construction assured that the financial assistance requested will be forthcoming. Similarly, decisions by the Housing and Home Finance Administrator in Washington determining which housing projects and slum clearance projects are eligible for federal contributions, and setting the size of federal contributions (agreements usually arrived at by negotiations between the Chairman of the Mayor's Committee on Slum Clearance, who is also the City Construction Coordinator, and the Federal Administrator) affect the size, number, and character of urban renewal measures. Even in the field of public health, where the New York City Board and Department of Health enjoy an unusual degree of freedom, prior approval by the state Commissioner of Health of expansions of going programs or embarkations upon new ones must be obtained before the new activities are assisted under the system of general public health grants now furnished by the state.

This method of administrative supervision has reached its highest degree of refinement in the way it is utilized by the state Civil Service Commission. Although the Commission is authorized to make rules and regulations (within the framework of the Civil Service Law) having, when approved by the Governor, the effect of law on the state public service and on the employees and officers of all subdivisions of the state, it has not chosen to employ this mode of control over local governments. Instead, it requires that the New York City Civil Service Commission, like other local personnel agencies, obtain the approval of the state body for every rule and regulation proposed by the city agency before such rule or regulation takes effect. Furthermore, by unanimous vote the state Commissioners may at any time rescind any rule, classification, examination, or eligible list of the city Commission, and may nullify all appointments made from a list rescinded in this fashion; while the state agency must explain its action in writing, and must give the city time to explain its own action in person, the state Commission's decision, unless disapproved by the Governor, is final.

Prior administrative approval is thus applied only to a limited segment of the entire spectrum of city activities, but wherever it is employed it proves itself a highly selective and powerful instrument of influence.

Review of City Actions. The fifth category of means of influence comprises three procedures for keeping federal and state officials informed about what the city is doing: reporting, hearing appeals, and conducting investigations. In a strict sense, these procedures in and of themselves are not controls on the behavior of municipal officers and employees. However, since they furnish the data which may lead to applications of the other modes of influence, or even to the imposition of sanctions (including withholding anticipated grants-in-aid), they are essential parts of the control system. Moreover, exposure is itself a sanction because it is humiliating and because of its potential consequence on the personal careers and political fortunes of those who are exposed.

Reports are the most routine of the review devices. A number of municipal agencies report regularly to the appropriate state officers. The city Welfare Department, for example, submits detailed annual reports to the state Commissioner of Social Welfare and monthly reports to the state Department of Audit and Control; in addition, the accounts of federally aided programs are audited by federal officers. The New York City Board of Education each year submits to the state Commissioner of Education a full statistical and financial report and such special reports on any aspect of its activities and properties as he requests. The New York City Civil Service Commission renders to the Governor for transmission to the legislature a report covering its important activities each year and suggesting methods of improving and extending the merit system. The city Health Department must support its requests for state financial aid by furnishing to the state Commissioner of Health such data as he may require. In the field of finance, every city must file with the state Comptroller within sixty days after the close of its fiscal year a statement of its debt-contracting power as of the close of that year, and must file a debt statement as well between three and fifteen days before the sale of bonds which are required to be sold at public sale. Cities and villages must also file with the Comptroller of the state, before they adopt their budgets, statements indicating how much they may raise by real estate taxes within the constitutional limits and the estimated yield of proposed taxes on real estate. A copy of the budget as adopted must later be filed with the Comptroller, accompanied by a statement of the actual amount of the taxes levied on real estate. In all these areas of activity the state officers are supplied with a substantial and often detailed record of the policies and performance of their municipal colleagues.

As regards the second method of review, formal lines of administrative appeal from the decisions and actions of three municipal departments lead directly to the heads of their corresponding state agencies rather than to any city officer. These are the Departments of Education, Welfare, and Personnel.

The most sweeping procedures of this kind are set up in the state Education Law which provides, "any person conceiving himself aggrieved may appeal or petition to the Commissioner of Education who is hereby authorized and required to examine and decide the same. . . ." The list of acts, or failures to act, by school officers and employees which constitute grievances within the meaning of this provision are correspondingly sweeping, as are the powers of the Commissioner of Education to dispose of such appeals. The law permits aggrieved parties to appeal not only because a school officer or employee did what he was forbidden to do, or failed to do what he was commanded to do, but even on the grounds that he, in his discretion, did not do what he was authorized to do.

An applicant for assistance under one of the public welfare programs may appeal to the state Commissioner of Welfare because he objects to a ruling of city Welfare officials, because his application has not been acted upon within thirty days, or because he feels that the denial of his application is improper or the amount allowed him is inadequate. The state Commissioner of Welfare may, in his discretion, hold hearings and is invested with broad powers to dispose of such cases as he sees fit.

City employees in the classified service who are suspended, demoted, or removed by their department heads may appeal this action either to the city Civil Service Commission, to the Supreme Court, or to the state Civil Service Commission. If the employee elects to appeal to either administrative agency rather than to the court, the findings of that agency are final. If the appellant bases his proceedings on a charge of discrimination on account of race, he may appeal first to the city Civil Service Commission, and, failing to receive satisfaction there, may carry his action to the state body.

Administrative appeal is not the only, or even the principal, method by which an aggrieved person may seek redress. But when a procedure is established opening channels from municipal agencies to the state level, as in the cases of education and welfare and civil service, this adds significantly to the oversight and control of some kinds of city decisions.

State officers do not have to wait for formal reports or appeals to apprise themselves of what goes on in the city government. Through the third method of review, the power of investigation, they may take the initiative themselves. The initiative may come from state administrative officers. The state Board of Social Welfare, and the Department, for example, are empowered to institute investigations of every phase of public assistance. The Commissioner of Education may conduct examinations and inspections of all schools and school systems in the state, both public and private. All the records of the municipal personnel agency are "at all times subject to the inspections of the state Civil Service Commission," which may administer oaths, subpoena individuals and documents, and investigate any person in the public service. The state Health Commissioner and his representatives are authorized to examine and inspect all local health practices and facilities, and the law makes it a duty of local health officers to assist him in the discharge of this responsibility. In the field of law enforcement and administration of justice, the Attorney General, "whenever in his judgment the public interest requires it . . . may, with the approval of the Governor, . . . inquire into matters concerning the public peace, public safety and public justice. For such purpose he may . . . appoint and employ, and at pleasure remove . . ." the staff required.

Investigations may also be conducted under judicial auspices. The city charter provides that "a summary inquiry into any alleged violation or neglect of duty in relation to the property, government or affairs of the city may be conducted under an order to be made by any justice of the supreme court in the first or second judicial district on application of the mayor, the comptroller, the president of the council, any five councilmen, the commissioner of investigation or any five citizens who are taxpayers. . . . Such inquiry shall be conducted before and shall be controlled by the justice making the order or any other justice of the supreme court in the same district." The heads of all departments and bureaus except Police and Law must furnish copies of their records to any taxpayer who pays a fee specified in the charter; the records must be kept open to inspection without charge.

Historically, however, the most important investigations have been those instituted by the state legislature or the Governor. In 1894, the Lexow Committee of the state Senate revealed corruption in the Police Department and irregularities in elections. In 1899, the Mazet Committee of the state Assembly disclosed that Tammany officials and party leaders were using their influence on the city government to enrich themselves. In 1909, and again in 1916, reports by joint committees of both houses of the legislature aired details about the finances of New York City. In 1922, the Myer Committee, another joint body, brought forth additional evidence of mismanagement and graft. In 1931 and 1932 an examination of the government of the city was conducted by a joint legislative committee, for which Judge Samuel Seabury, who had previously brought to light wrongdoing in the Magistrates' Courts and examined the office of the District Attorney of New York County, served as counsel. In the election year of 1957 one Republican state senator from the city proposed a legislative investigation into the city's transit system, and a special joint committee established to serve as a "watchdog" (to keep an eye, it would seem, on the Democratic Governor of the state) indicated it might turn its attention to newspaper charges of graft in the city's Department of Buildings. Extensive reforms followed the Lexow and Mazet and Seabury investigations. The others had no direct, immediate, perceptible effects, other perhaps than to remind city officials of the potentialities of legislative investigative power and to inspire them to correct defects or to agree to bargaining whenever serious investigations seemed to be in the offing.

The Governor, too, has the power to launch investigations through specially appointed investigative officers or bodies, or through his regular staff. Thus, the second of the Seabury investigations (which contributed to the eventual resignation of Mayor Walker, a major split within the ranks of the Democratic party in New York City, and thereby to the subsequent victory of Fiorello H. La Guardia) was conducted by Judge Seabury at the request of Governor Roosevelt, who appointed him a Commissioner to report on charges against the District Attorney of New York County. And between 1951 and 1953 the State Crime Commission (often called the Proskauer Commission, after its chairman, Joseph M. Proskauer), appointed by the

Attorney General in response to an executive order of Governor Dewey issued under the provisions of a law of long standing, exposed connections between criminals and politics in New York and Richmond Counties (and in two upstate counties) and disclosed abuses and corruption on the New York City waterfront. In 1953, at the behest of the Governor, the legislature authorized a Commission to Study the Organizational Structure of the Government of the City of New York, with five members appointed by the Chief Executive and two each by the President of the Senate and the Speaker of the Assembly. Sober rather than sensational, its report was one of the factors leading to the creation of the office of City Administrator, to the revamping of the city's personnel setup, and to other changes. In fact, all these commissions of investigation left a wake of structural and procedural reform. More recently (1956) the power of the Governor was demonstrated again, although in towns other than the city, when Governor Harriman's Commissioner of Investigation revealed practices by some local officers that ended in many resignations.

By and large, legislative and executive investigations have been the most inclusive, the most searching, and the most publicized of all, and they, therefore, have had the most far-reaching effects. But the less spectacular review procedures have a collective and continuous impact that in the long run is probably as great, if not greater. Comparatively unobtrusively, they serve the purposes of state officers laboring to influence the decisions and behavior of municipal officers and employees. In any event, all the instruments of review taken together constitute an imposing array of influences upon the government of the city.

Removal from Office and Other Sanctions. Every mode of influence discussed thus far may be used punitively by state and federal officials (or, more rarely, may be employed as rewards). The various types of restrictions on city power, for instance, may be tightened or made less stringent. During the nineteenth century, for short periods, the health and police functions of the municipal corporation were taken from it and assigned to special agencies created by the state. In recent years, the transfer of jurisdiction over the city-owned subway and bus lines to the Transit Authority was accomplished by state legislation enacted over the protest of many city leaders. Mandates may also be used to restrict the discretion of city officers. The legislation establishing the Transit Authority, for example, makes it mandatory for the operating expenses of the subway system to be met by revenues from the subway system and represents in part an expression of state irritation with city requests for additional financial aid and new taxing power while holding fares at a level inadequate to cover operating costs. The possibility that grants-in-aid or other forms of fiscal assistance or relief may be denied or withheld is another potential sanction that induces city officials to respond receptively (though sometimes reluctantly) to the advice, recommendations, and directives of state legislative, executive, and administrative officials. Investigations, and even some appeals cases, take on a penal aspect for the investigated municipal leaders, who at best are stung by the implied rebuke and at worst may be sorely embarrassed by the glare of unfavorable publicity. In general, of course, all these modes of influence are not ordinarily exercised in a punitive or vindictive way; on the contrary, such a use of them is distinctly the exception. On the other hand they can be and have been used as sanctions, and the officers and employees of the city are not unmindful of this potentiality.

A more drastic punitive power—the power to remove local officials—is lodged in the state government by the state constitution, legislation, and the New York City Charter. Under the constitution, District Attorneys in the city are subject to removal by the Governor. The state Education Law confers on the Commissioner of Education authority to remove any trustee, member of the Board of Education, Superintendent, or other school officer. The charter empowers the Governor to remove the Mayor, the Comptroller, the President of the City Council, the Borough Presidents, and the Police Commissioners. In each case, the accused official is entitled to copies of the charges against him and an opportunity to be heard in his defense; the top city leaders, however, may be summarily suspended for thirty days pending their hearings.

Penalties of such severity are rarely imposed, but they are not unknown. As a result of the Seabury investigations, the Sheriff of New York County (an office later abolished along with all other county sheriffs' offices within the city and replaced by a single city sheriff appointed under civil service procedures) was removed by Governor Franklin D. Roosevelt. The resignation of Mayor Walker was also generally attributed to the imminence of his removal by Governor Roosevelt. Only offenses of the greatest seriousness are likely to provoke the exercise of removal powers, but the powers are available and consequently reinforce other methods of persuasion.

An Appraisal of State Modes of Influence. This overview of the ways in which the state exerts influence upon the decisions and actions of city officials and employees makes it clear that state legislation is by far the most pervasive. In eleven functional areas (education, welfare, personnel management, fiscal administration, election administration, police, fire, buildings, correction, housing, and transit), officials and employees identified essentially with the city government are actually engaged in carrying out the provisions of state statutes rather than locally adopted legislation. (These functions absorb by far the greater part of the administrative expenses of the city and comprise well over half of the total expense budget even including debt service, judicial, legislative, and other nonadministrative costs; the proportions are even greater when health and hospitals, whose special status was described above, are taken into account.) Local direction plays a much more prominent part in the performance of other local services, but even they derive their existence from general state legislation and are conducted within a framework of statutory provisions. Administrative supervision, while quite stringent where it is applied, is confined chiefly to the fields of education, welfare, and health. Constitutional, executive, and judicial influences are important, but less sweeping and continuous than the other forms. Thus the city has by no means been totally deprived of discretion.

The atmosphere of state-city relations is not one of unremitting hostility. Much of the influence of the state is brought to bear not by coercion but by cooperation and agreement among officials of two units of government intent upon doing the best jobs they can and working in harmony with one another, both formally and informally, more often than in conflict.

Nevertheless, the constraints under which they must operate are often irritating to the officials of the greatest city in the world. The power of rural elements in the state legislature, and the long periods of control of the legislature (and of the governorship) by the Republican party, aggravate the tensions. As a result, the officers of the city have not submitted passively to their colleagues in the higher levels of government.

Counterinfluences Employed by City Officials

Raising the Banner of Home Rule. By the second half of the nineteenth century, the increasing urbanization of the state lent sufficient strength to the cities to rebel against both the continuous intervention of the state legislature in local affairs and the necessity of going to the state capitol for approval of every minor change or innovation. New York and other municipalities were able to press with intermittent success for a greater measure of local self-government, or "home rule."

One of their strategies was negative in approach—that is, to introduce into the state constitution restrictions on the authority of the state government to enact special legislation with respect to individual cities. Thus the constitution of 1846 contained a section confining private or local bills in the legislature to one subject each, that subject to be expressed in the title, and also provided for election or appointment of local officers by electors or authorities they served (thereby barring selection of local officials by the state executive or legislature). An amendment adopted in 1874 prohibited private or local bills on a specified list of subjects and permitted only general laws on those topics. The greatest single limitation came in the constitution of 1894, which included a provision requiring the legislature to "act in relation to the property, affairs or government of any city only by general laws which shall in terms and in effect apply alike to all cities" except with the approval of the Mayor, or, if he objected, upon repassage of the legislation. This restriction was further tightened in the Home Rule Amendment of 1923, which permitted special legislation to take effect only if it were supported by a message from the Governor declaring that an emergency made the enactment of the law imperative and if it were then passed by a two-thirds vote of both houses; moreover, cities were authorized to "repeal, supersede or modify" by their own action special state laws already on the books dealing with their own property, affairs, or government. The limitation was made still stricter in the constitution of 1938, which permits the enactment by the state legislature of special legislation (still by a two-thirds vote of both houses) relating to individual cities only when the Mayor and the Council, or the Council alone by a two-thirds vote, request it in writing.

A second strategy was positive—a quest for a broader grant of municipal authority. In 1913 the state enacted a Home Rule Act, providing that "every city is granted power to regulate and control its property and local affairs and is granted all the rights, privileges and jurisdiction necessary and proper for carrying such power into execution," and empowering every city, "subject to the Constitution and the general laws of this State," to conduct 23 specified kinds of programs that seemed to run the entire gamut of municipal functions. The Home Rule Amendment of 1923 declared that "Every city shall have the power to adopt and amend local laws not inconsistent with the Constitution and laws of the State relating to its property, affairs or government." This principle was reiterated in the Home Rule Law of 1924, which implemented the Home Rule Amendment and spelled out the procedure by which charters were to be locally framed and adopted and local laws were to be enacted.

These grants of authority proved to be less comprehensive than some of their advocates apparently anticipated. In the first place, laws applicable to classes of cities rather than to all the cities in the state have been held not to violate the ban on special legislation, and the allocation of New York City to a class by itself has been upheld. In the second place, the meaning of the phrase "property, affairs or government" of cities has been narrowly construed by the courts. They have ruled that the phrase does not include any matters of substantial state concern or permeated with state interest; consequently on such matters the state legislature is not debarred from enacting special legislation nor is any city authorized to act by constitutional or legislative home rule provisions. Thus, a state law designed to make the Multiple Dwelling Law applicable to cities of more than 800,000 inhabitants (that is, New York City alone) was judged not to invade municipal property, affairs, or government. In another case, the sewers of a city were held not to be an aspect of its property, affairs, or government. The same logic was applied to a local law regulating plumbers, and New York City's transit system has also been treated as a matter of state concern. Local taxing power has been held to be a matter of state interest. Rulings of this kind have preserved for the state government considerable freedom to pass laws relating to individual municipalities regardless of local preferences, and city governments, reluctant to rely on their uncertain home-rule powers, frequently request special legislation to remove any doubts as to their authority to take particular actions. Nevertheless, the volume of special legislation concerning New York City has declined appreciably in the last sixty-five years, and the range of city activities has expanded greatly. Home rule has not meant unfettered local self-government, but it has given the city a little more freedom from state influence than the city might otherwise enjoy.

Claims on Elected Officials with Statewide Constituencies. No elected officer whose constituency comprises the entire state can afford to ignore the claims of New York City leaders—party leaders and officials, both. To win, the Democrats must roll up substantial majorities in the city in order to overcome their deficits in upstate areas; the Republicans, conversely, must hold down the size of Democratic majorities in the city to assure victory for themselves. Candidates from both sides must therefore ingratiate themselves with the voters of the city, and they cannot afford to be identified as indifferent or hostile to the pleas of the voters or their representatives.

It is not always important whether the statewide officials (including the presidential and vice-presidential electors; the United States Senators; the Governor, Lieutenant Governor, Attorney General, and Comptroller; and the Justices of the Court of Appeals) are of the same party as the local officials and party leaders. Generally, of course, there is greater rapport if they are of the same political persuasion. But they may accommodate each other even when they are in opposing organizations, while sometimes there are battles within a single party. Tammany Hall, for example, could not prevent the Seabury investigations under Governor Franklin D. Roosevelt (and retaliated by fighting bitterly against his nomination for President in 1932, going even to the length of refusing to make the nomination unanimous after it was clear that Roosevelt had won it). Governor Thomas E. Dewey consented reluctantly in 1953 to a redrawing of Congressional District boundaries in Brooklyn proposed by the Republican Leader of Kings County (who wanted to create a peculiarly shaped district in which his party could be sure of winning a congressional seat), although it was apparent at the time that the Governor had no appetite for this stratagem and was even doubtful that the courts would sanction it. On the other hand, Democratic Governor Lehman often worked amicably with Mayor La Guardia, who had Republican backing, and Governor Dewey was reported to have reached informal understandings with Mayor Impellitteri, who had been a Democrat and eventually returned to the Democratic fold. Across party lines and within them, local officials and party functionaries possess the means of inducing men in higher levels of government to listen to them. Through their contacts with their party hierarchies in Albany, in Washington, through their control of the nominating process, and through their influence with electorates, they can apply a great deal of leverage. And they do.

The City's Legislative Delegations. Additional levers of counterinfluence that may be applied by the city's leaders are the city's legislative delegations in Congress and, more importantly, in the state legislature. New York City is apportioned 22 of the state's 45 United States Representatives. One of the state's United States Senators ordinarily comes from the city. In the state Senate, 25 of the 58 seats are allocated to the city, and 65 of the 150 state assemblymen come from districts in New York City. Mathematically, the city is somewhat underrepresented, the percentage of the total population of the state being a bit larger than its assigned percentage of legislative seats. The disparity has been shrinking rapidly, however, because of the rapid growth of suburban areas. In any event, whether laboring under a handicap or not, the city's representatives have long been in a strong position to modify the influence of the higher levels of government upon New York.

The strength of their position grows out of the standard procedures of legislative bodies; even an individual legislator, by the force of his own personality and intellect and the bargaining effectiveness of his votes in committee and on the floor, can have a profound impact on the content of those legislative decisions in which he has a particular interest and responsibility, and large blocs of legislators like those from New York can, if they are disciplined, have a collective impact far greater than the sum of their individual effectiveness. Some of the potential benefits of maneuvering as a bloc are lost to New York City delegations because they are not always unified; they frequently split along party lines on issues that clearly divide the parties generally. But a number of factors reduce this disadvantage. First, Democrats and Republicans from the city tend to join with each other on matters of purely local interest, the informal codes of both parties allowing for deviations from the respective party lines on matters of this kind. (Governor Rockefeller actually convened the entire New York State delegations to both houses of Congress to encourage them to serve as an *ad hoc* committee for obtaining a greater number of federal contracts for the Empire State.) Second, in both Albany and Washington, legislative delegations from other urban communities can sometimes be counted upon, regardless of their political affiliations, to make common cause with those from New York City on matters of joint interest. Third, Republicans constitute only a small part of the city's delegations, so that the Democrats alone make up a city bloc of votes of substantial weight as long as they hang together, as they generally do. Fourth, Democrats from other parts of the state (when there are any) and from other parts of the country often support their colleagues from the city in the state legislature and in Congress, respectively, in order to preserve the unity of the party. Finally, since the Republicans generally control the state legislature, the onus for failure to heed city requests tends to fall on their party; consequently, Republican party functionaries from the city often urge them to protect the party's position in the city by acquiescing to some degree in city pleas and proposals.

From their long experience as a continuing minority, the city's legislative delegations have learned to use their bargaining power effectively. Consequently, they have been able to prevent the higher levels of government from completely dominating the local decision-making process.

"Lobbying" by City Officials. When city officials want federal or state legislation enacted, or modifications of existing statutes or pending bills, or to block bills in the legislative pipe line, or to promote or block or change administrative actions, they behave as do private citizens or interest groups concerned with legislative actions; they lobby. They go to Washington or to Albany to testify at hearings, to present their views privately to legislators and administrators, to plead, to cajole, to bargain, to threaten. If it will help their cause, they visit party leaders and the chief executives if possible.

Because the contacts between the city and the federal government are neither so numerous nor so close as those with the state, lobbying of this kind by city officials is far more commonplace in Albany than in Washington, although it is by no means unknown in the nation's capital. In the state capital, an assistant to the Mayor serves as legislative representative of the city and is on hand all the time the legislature is in session and a good deal of the time during the rest of the year. Like his private counterparts, his job is to keep his clients—the leaders of the city—informed of proposed action, both legislative and administrative, impinging on the interests of the city and of its people, to provide ammunition for assemblymen and senators from the city in connection with measures affecting the city, to enlist the aid of allies in all branches of government and outside the government, to testify formally when necessary, and to make the city's voice heard in all the corners that the city's legislative delegations, burdened with legislative responsibilities, have no time to reach. Occasionally, in cases of extreme urgency, the Mayor or the Comptroller of the city may go to Albany personally to boost or to block a particular action, and department heads appear routinely whenever measures affecting their functions are under consideration.

Like all lobbyists, city officials enlist the support of allies. Often, the allies are nongovernmental groups—civic, neighborhood, and central business groups supporting passage of a proposed amendment authorizing the city to borrow half a billion dollars outside the debt limit in order to improve and extend rapid transit; parents' associations and other groups interested in education backing state aid to the city schools; the Automobile Club of New

York urging a share of vehicle registration fees for the city (to permit it to lift an automobile-use tax); and many others. Sometimes the allies are city bureaucrats, who have their own lines of access through the legislature and through fellow bureaucrats in state administrative agencies. Teachers, for instance, joined the city in its quest for greater state aid for city education (at the suggestion of the Board of Education and the Mayor, who pointed out that the city could not afford pay increases for them unless the state financial assistance was forthcoming). Sometimes the allies are the mayors of other large cities working together in the United States Conference of Mayors, or the chief executives of the municipalities of the state joined in a state Conference of Mayors and Other Municipal Officers. Sometimes the allies are private individuals of high repute and personal influence. When, for example, an urban redevelopment project ardently favored by the City Construction Coordinator threatened to bog down because the Housing and Home Finance Administrator in Washington could not see his way clear to furnishing all the money requested, Nelson A. Rockefeller, then a private citizen interested in the improvement of the part of the city affected, visited the White House and the Capitol, and an understanding was reached shortly. Sometimes, party leaders help them. Occasionally, city leaders are able to mobilize all the different kinds of allies. In any case, they invoke the assistance of all the friends they can find whenever they need it.

Sometimes city officers who refer the various claimants to higher governments seek primarily to deflect from themselves pressures which they cannot satisfy and to which they can therefore respond in no other way. More generally, however, the effect of these excursions by nongovernmental groups to the state and national capitols is to educate officials at those levels to the plight of the city, to take some of the curse of suspected chicanery off city leaders by furnishing proof that their pleas for assistance are genuine, and to demonstrate by displays of solidarity between the officers of the city and those they govern that the city has indeed achieved a consensus on the questions at issue. In coalition with nongovernmental groups, city leaders often accomplish what they could not achieve alone.

The success of these tactics is not fully indicated by the frequency with which lobbying city officers obtain all or even part of the specific results they seek with each individual effort. For even when they fail in a particular instance, they inject into the premises of action of officials on higher levels a greater awareness of the problems and dilemmas of managing a great city. It seems reasonable to infer that these repeated contacts produce a cumulative effect ultimately reflected in an increasingly judicious and sympathetic use by the higher levels of government of their modes of influence upon the city. Seen from this point of view, lobbying by city officials is an important counter-influence.

Litigation by the City. Although the city, as a creature of the state government, may not sue the state to challenge its actions with respect to the city, there is another procedure by which the city may secure a judicial test of such state actions. Since the Taxpayers' Act facilitates taxpayer suits against the city, city officers sometimes arrange to have a cooperative private citizen institute proceedings against the city to enjoin it from complying with some state requirement. Ordinarily, the state will be represented in such proceedings in order to defend its action. The litigation then takes the form of a contest between the city and the state. As previously noted, the courts have taken a narrow view of municipal powers and a correspondingly broad view of state authority over municipalities, so this instrument of counterinfluence has not availed the city. But it is employed repeatedly, if intermittently, and now and then produces changes in judicial attitude, in constitutional requirements, or in statutory provisions that may amplify its importance many times. For this reason, it intensifies the caution of state officers who deal with the city, and is even now of some value to city officials despite the rarity of their victories in court.

Getting Direct Federal Aid. State governments throughout the nation regard with cold, unfriendly eyes all direct contact between their local subdivisions and the federal government, except perhaps for run-of-the-mill cooperation among administrative field officers in specialized services. During the emergency days of the depression in the thirties, the Public Works Administration channeled federal funds directly to local governments to help them put through capital construction projects they had been forced to defer because of the economic crisis. After World War II, the Federal Airport Act and Title I (the section dealing with urban redevelopment and slum clearance) of the Housing Act of 1949 (later broadened by Title IV of the Housing Act of 1954) gave more or less permanent footing to a system of grants to localities for these operations. For the rest, federal aid is formally channeled through the state. The state has been by-passed, but not on a very large scale.

Yet the problems of metropolitan regions have slowly been moving from obscure corners of the political stage to the center, and it is not unlikely that they will soon receive as much attention from the federal government as agriculture, natural resources, rural electrification, health and welfare, and other domestic programs. More than half the population of the country lives in 175 metropolitan areas, and it is clear that their weaknesses and difficulties threaten not just their own well-being, but the future of the whole United States. They are no longer local; they are national. The federal government may want to stay clear of direct responsibility for these problems. The states may want the federal government to keep out. But the federal government will probably be drawn into closer and more extensive direct relations with municipalities.

The states may respond by tightening their controls over cities and blocking direct federal aid; in the end, however, such a policy must drive the cities to Washington and hasten the development of legislative and administrative bypasses. On the other hand, if the states want to deal more sympathetically and understandingly with cities in order to delay or forestall such a development, they will have to make many concessions to their urban subdivisions. Tactically, therefore, it seems inevitable that cities will call for more direct federal aid in the hope that they can thus extract compromises from their increasingly anxious states, or perhaps get help from Washington, or both.

As yet, this urban strategy is in its infancy. But it may be anticipated that the pressure of events combined with the determination of cities to use to the fullest every technique of counterinfluence at their command will see it through a robust childhood to an early maturity. Federal aid will become a defensive weapon.

Counterinfluences in Perspective. The counterinfluences collectively enable city leaders to bargain with officials and employees of higher levels of government when the representatives of the higher levels employ their own instruments of influence to control decisions and behavior of the city government. In the bargaining process, the most frequently used and the most effective counterinfluences are (1) the claims made upon elected officials with state-wide constituencies and (2) the strategies of the city's legislative delegations. The city's position in the political system of the state and of the nation lends great force to these, and the nature of the instruments themselves permits them to be applied to particular issues with a degree of selectivity. These two methods have been the most successful ones from the city's point of view. By contrast, although lobbying by municipal officers is extremely helpful in the long run, it is comparatively seldom effective in any individual controversy; even its long-run effectiveness probably derives at least in part from the potential power of the other two devices. Invocation of the symbol "home rule" has proved to be of only slight strategic value to the city, chiefly because the courts have construed it in restricted and restrictive terms. For the same reason, the utility of litigation by the city has been limited, and its service has been minor harassment and dramatic expression of protest. Direct federal aid to cities is still too experimental to allow a considered assessment of its effectiveness, but it is probably safe to predict, in the light of the federal structure of our system of government, that it will be a long time before it becomes a common phenomenon.

Nevertheless, from the two main modes of counterinfluence, the city gains the ability to exert considerable pressure upon the decisions of the state and federal governments. This, in turn, enables the city to negotiate from strength with the higher levels, to moderate their influences upon city decisions, and to extract desired concessions from them.

If the officers of the state and federal governments did not possess the media of influence at their disposal, their roles in the contest for the stakes of politics in New York City would unquestionably be much smaller, and perhaps insignificant. If the city were deprived of the means with which it defends such independence as it enjoys, on the other hand, chances are that few decisions of significance would be made at the municipal level. The city is still in a subordinate position, but its sources of strength are sufficient to make the representatives of higher governments simply participants in the city's decision-making process rather than undisputed masters of it.

Interlevel Cooperation

Our three-level system of government probably would not work at all were there not a considerable reservoir of good will among the officers and employees of all the units of government involved. To be sure, there are rivalries, efforts to gain partisan advantage, hostilities, and attempts at domination. But the underlying tone of the relationships is set by what is evidently a desire to serve the people well. It is permeated with a willingness to negotiate, to search for and abide by mutually agreeable understandings, to reach reasonable compromises among reasonable men whose commitment to the system as a whole ultimately outweighs their personal or organizational aspirations. Potentially destructive tensions are held in check by the context of cooperation.

The evidences of cooperation are not so easily identified as the manifestations of tension because the outcroppings of conflict tend to receive more attention than the far more common phenomenon of men routinely working together in harmony to conduct the day-to-day operations that in the aggregate compose much of what is called public policy. But there are a few indications of the fundamental accord underlying the relations among levels of government. One of these is the growing concern over the rapidly developing unity of technicians engaged in the administration of the same specialties at the several levels of government. So cordial have the relations among the technicians become that some students of government have expressed disquiet over the possibilities of excessive professionalization of the public service. Indeed, the Advisory Committee on Local Government of the United States Commission on Intergovernmental Relations noted uneasily the appearance of "vertical functional autocracies, composed of functional specialists at two or more governmental levels," and concluded these "have had, in some cases, an injurious influence on federal-aid programs." The bonds among the specialists, the means by which they achieve an impressive harmony of purpose and practice, are cemented by professional societies and associations that transcend the jurisdictional lines of units of government. Some of them, such as the American Public Health Association, the American Association of

School Administrators, the American Hospital Association, the American Public Welfare Association, the American Society for Public Administration, the Society for Personnel Administration, the Public Personnel Association, the Municipal Finance Officers Association, the American Public Works Association, the National Association of Housing and Redevelopment Officers, and many others, are national in scope. Many local specialists also meet with each other in statewide organizations, their conferences held under state auspices and attended by state officials, and they are often represented on state committees studying problems falling within their spheres of interest. Whether or not the professional solidarity achieved in this fashion is cause for alarm, it is certainly a demonstration that there is a good deal of agreement among officers and employees at different levels of government.

Another sign of the general desire for cooperation is the establishment of formal machinery designed to discover means of resolving outstanding conflicts. For example, President Eisenhower appointed a Commission on Intergovernmental Relations which explored the whole area of federal-state relations, federal-local relations, and the impact of the federal government on state-local relations; the Commission rendered its report, accompanied by 14 special studies, in 1955. At the state level, a Temporary Commission on the Fiscal Affairs of State Government submitted a report on, and a series of staff studies of, fiscal management that gave close attention to intergovernmental problems. In 1956 New York State and New York City set up a joint committee to concentrate exclusively on the fiscal relations between these two jurisdictions. The "Little Hoover Commission" created by the state in 1959 to study and recommend ways of improving the government of the city includes members appointed by the Mayor (but the cooperative aspects are somewhat minimized by the fact that seven of the nine members represent the state government). Although the reports and studies completed to date have not resulted in extensive readjustments of current practice, they have helped to dissipate some of the sources of friction and may be taken as indicative of the rapport among the city, the state, and the federal government.

The political parties also surmount the barriers between levels of government. Higher party ranks are filled by men who also fill party posts at lower levels, and party leadership in the state legislature and in Congress includes representatives whose perspectives reflect the conditions in their localities as well as those of the higher governments of which they are parts. This overlapping of personnel compels a reconciliation of the aspirations of the three levels of government, providing a thrust toward mutual accommodation that ameliorates the impetus toward division and separation implicit in our governmental structure.

Thus, while tensions of long standing persist, the forces for unity have up to now proved themselves stronger.

THE CITY AND ITS NEIGHBORS

Since New York City is the core of a vast metropolitan area encompassing a concentration of some fifteen million people governed by scores of units of government, it can neither solve its own problems without the cooperation of its neighbors, nor can its neighbors function satisfactorily without the cooperation of the city. Consequently, neighboring governments use whatever modes of influence they can to influence governmental decisions in the city, and the city often reciprocates. In this sense, the officials of nearby communities must be regarded as participants in the city's decision-making processes, and city officers often take an indirect part in determining the actions of other communities in the metropolitan region.

Perhaps the outstanding feature of these interrelationships is their *ad hoc*, unsystematic quality—at least until recent years. Most of the cooperative mutual influences have been handled chiefly on an informal basis by administrative agencies—primarily in the course of performing their daily tasks, but partly through their statewide associations. To be sure, many of their understandings take effect only upon ratification by the highest authorities of their respective jurisdictions. But the substantive agreements have been worked out by negotiations among technical personnel on a piecemeal basis as the needs have arisen.

Thus, for example, the parkways built by the city join at the borders of the municipality with the parkways of Westchester to the North, Nassau to the East, and New Jersey to the West. The city's water supply, drawn in part from the headwaters of the Delaware River some 120 miles distant, and from reservoirs closer by but still outside the city, floods lands under the jurisdiction of other governments and flows through scores of local governmental jurisdictions. Backed by constitutional and statutory powers, the city's Board of Water Supply arranges for purchase of necessary land, for payment of rentals in some places, for diversion of water for use by some of the communities through which the city's water supply passes, and for the policing of property acquired for this purpose by the city. Similarly, public health officers, sanitation officers, and police officers often work hand in hand on their common problems.

More systematic and formal arrangements profoundly affecting activities of the city government, arrangements in which the city plays a conspicuous part despite the fact that the primary responsibility for them has been assumed by the state government, are five interstate agencies established by compacts between New York State and one or more adjacent states. The oldest of these is the Port of New York Authority, which was described in an earlier chapter. Later (in 1936) came the Interstate Sanitation Commission, a New York-New Jersey-Connecticut body charged with the reduction of water pollution in an area reaching from the Sandy Hook section of the Jersey Coast through New York harbor and the lower part of the Hudson River to Long Island Sound and the south shore of Long Island. The Interstate Commission on the Delaware River Basin (known as INCODEL) was created in 1939 by agreement among New York, New Jersey, Pennsylvania, and Delaware for systematic development and division of the natural resources—primarily the water resources—of the Delaware watershed. In 1953 New York and New Jersey set up the Waterfront Commission of New York Harbor, a bistate instrumentality, for the purpose of registering longshoremen and licensing pier superintendents, hiring agents, port watchmen, and stevedores, in order to eliminate criminal and corrupt practices in the handling of water-borne freight within the port and to regularize the employment of waterfront workers. New York and New Jersey joined hands again in 1954 to create the Metropolitan Rapid Transit Commission to study the rapid transit needs of the bistate metropolitan area and to propose measures to meet those needs. (This Commission went out of existence two years later, when it submitted its final report. No action was taken on its specific recommendations, but the report did dramatize many features of the regional transit problem.) The governing boards of these interstate agencies are appointed by the Governors of the participating states, and New York City as a governmental unit is not formally represented. But city residents are in practice prominent in the leadership of the agencies, and the city has therefore been able to exert some influence upon their decisions, all of which touch areas of vital importance in the political process of the municipality.

In 1956 a new development of great significance occurred when Mayor Wagner called a conference of elected representatives of more than 40 major units of government in a 21-county area embracing the city and the surrounding region. The metropolitan region had grown so large and so rapidly, he explained, that the problems of its communities could no longer be solved on a purely local plane. The participants in the conference discussed transportation, traffic, highways, recreation, water supply, air pollution, and other common problems and established a temporary steering committee to put the organization on a permanent footing. In 1957 a permanent structure was adopted, took the name "Metropolitan Regional Council," heard reports from its committees, and adopted a resolution opposing bills in Congress to contract federal regulatory powers over the prices of natural gas in interstate commerce. In 1958 the Council joined with the Regional Plan Association, a private planning organization, to conduct a study of park, recreational, and open space in the metropolitan region, financing the research with a grant from a foundation. By this time, Mayor Wagner, as chairman of the Council, was expressing hopes that the progress of the organization would lead to its elevation from a voluntary association of public officials having no legal stand-

ing of its own and no independent source of funds to official status with
financial support from the member governments and perhaps eventual
authority to supervise any future unifunctional interstate agencies created in
the New York area. Early in 1959 a special committee of experts appointed
by the Regional Plan Association, while not going quite so far as the Mayor,
did urge official recognition and support of the new unit. The Council may
well be an augury of the pattern of the future, for it is the first machinery
established in the metropolitan area for regional coordination and cooperation in more than one governmental function. Too young at this stage to have
yet exerted much influence on governmental decisions, the Metropolitan
Regional Council has had such a vigorous start and such a warm response
that its influence appears likely to increase gradually but steadily in the years
ahead.

Like the cooperative ones, the competitive and coercive modes of influence
in the relations between the city and its neighbors tend to be sporadic and
ad hoc rather than continuous and calculated. For example, Newark and New
York competed aggressively for airline business during the thirties (their rivalry not being fully resolved until both cities leased their airports to the Port
of New York Authority for operation according to a regional plan). The State
of Pennsylvania rejected an agreement proposed by INCODEL, and the
division of water from the headwaters of the Delaware is still regulated by a
Special Master appointed by the United States Supreme Court as a result of
an earlier suit between Pennsylvania and New York City. The decision of
Westchester County to restrict the use of its parks to its own residents aroused
indignation among city officials and some threats of retaliation. The city and
Westchester County have also had some controversies over the location of
collection booths on some toll roads. New Jersey and Connecticut were irri-
tated with New York City when Mayor Wagner accepted the advice of a
panel of experts and refused to take action to raise the city's minimum legal
age for the purchase of liquor to that of the neighboring states (a city policy
that allegedly weakened the effectiveness of Connecticut and New Jersey
legislation designed to keep liquor from minors, and a policy that also attracted to the city a great deal of teen-age business). Tax and land-use
policies have also been determined at times by competition between the city
and its neighboring governments as champions of the interests of their respective business constituencies. Rivalry, no less than collaboration, has been
spotty and unpredictable.

The haphazard character of the relationships between New York City and
its neighbors has resulted from their relative independence of each other in
the past with respect to all but a few governmental functions. Only occasionally did problems reach a stage sufficiently acute to force them to pay close
attention to each other and to try to influence each other's actions. For this

reason, the officers and employees of neighboring governments have played only a small and intermittent part in the contest for the stakes of politics within the city. But shifts of population, of business, and of industry and differential rates of population growth are changing all that swiftly. The interdependence of all the communities in the region is so pronounced that it can no longer be ignored or approached in a piecemeal fashion. A new set of close interrelationships is in the making. Inevitably, what nearby localities do will have an ever greater impact on what the city does, and vice versa. The size of the political and governmental arena is expanding.

SUMMARY

The student of the New York City political contest must recognize that the officials of other governments, both higher and coordinate, are also participants. The distribution of the stakes, the sharing of the rewards, the content of decisions in the city government are not determined exclusively within the city boundaries; they are influenced by the action of other governments.

Sometimes those who exert this influence seem unaware of their impact. For a long time, this was true of the relations between the city and its neighbors. All these governments made decisions without much reference to one another save for isolated problems demanding joint action and for piecemeal cooperation by functional specialists. Each decision doubtless had repercussions throughout the region, forcing action by the individual governments, but there were few signs that they recognized their interdependence. Social and economic changes of the last generation, however, have made such interdependence impossible to overlook. Consequently, the efforts of each government to influence the others have gained in intensity and are likely to go on doing so. Officials of neighboring communities seem likely to become deliberate and conscious participants in each other's political processes. It remains to be seen what instruments of influence they will develop, and with what success these will be employed.

The officials of the "higher" governments—the federal government and the state, but particularly the latter—have long been engaged in strategies to influence the city. In the case of the federal government, the intervention has been rather limited by the American pattern of federation, in which the states are necessarily the custodians of local government. In the case of the state government, the traditional powers over local government, exercised primarily through legislative power but also through grants-in-aid and administrative supervision in selected functions, have played a major role in the city government's decisions.

The city has not been a docile subject. Its capacity to influence Albany is in many ways less impressive than Albany's capacity to influence it, but it has used its available means with great resourcefulness. Its leaders have therefore been able to bargain for favorable consideration, and to block or at least blunt some of the state influences, and thereby to preserve the vitality of the contest in the city. The contest in the city is not just an extension of another contest going on at higher levels, despite the importance of the higher levels in what happens at the local level; the city is an arena in itself. Nevertheless, because the city is part of a federal system and a metropolitan community, actors who are not "on stage" in a technical sense are cast in important roles just the same.

BIBLIOGRAPHY

STATE RELATIONSHIPS IN GENERAL

Caldwell, Lynton K., *The Government and Administration of New York.* Thomas Y. Crowell Co., New York, 1954. An authoritative book on New York State which devotes considerable space to New York City-State relations.

Macmahon, Arthur W., *The Statutory Sources of New York City Government.* M. B. Brown Co., New York, 1923. An analysis of state statutes serving as sources of city authority.

McKinney's Consolidated Laws of New York, Annotated, Book 23, *General Municipal Law.* Edward Thompson Co., Brooklyn, N. Y., 1954. Kept up to date with annual supplements. The general municipal law defines the powers, privileges, limitations, and liabilities of counties, towns, cities, and villages as municipal corporations. Some of the provisions of the general municipal law relate specifically to New York City. This volume is introduced by a history of general municipal law, written by Charles W. Potter, chief municipal consultant of the State Department of Audit and Control. Judicial decisions are included.

Book 20, *General City Law.* Edward Thompson Co., Brooklyn, N. Y., 1951. Kept up to date with annual supplements. General statutory provisions regarding judicial decisions are included.

Moscow, Warren, *Politics in the Empire State.* Alfred A. Knopf, New York, 1948, pp. 216–224. Intergovernmental relations are discussed.

New York State Constitutional Convention Committee, *New York City Government: Functions and Problems.* Vol. 5 of *Reports and Studies.* Burland Printing Co., New York, 1938, pp. 226–246. New York State constitutional provisions affecting New York City.

State and Local Government in New York, J. B. Lyon Co., Albany, 1938. Describes the relationship between the state and municipalities in the areas of public health, social welfare, and education at the time it was written.

Department of Audit and Control, Division of Municipal Affairs, *Municipal Affairs Review,* November, 1957, to date. Issued twice a month, except during July and August. A bulletin devoted to municipal affairs, particularly state-city fiscal relations.

Special Legislative Committee on the Revision and Simplification of the Constitution. Inter-Law School Committee, *Report on the Problem of Simplification of the Constitution.* Legislative Document no. 57, May, 1958.

SOME SPECIFIC AREAS OF STATE CONTROL

McKinney's Consolidated Laws of New York, Annotated, Book 9, *Civil Service Law.* Edward Thompson Co., Brooklyn, N. Y., 1946. Kept up to date with annual supplements. The laws that govern and regulate the work of New York City's Department of Personnel and Civil Service Commission. Contains relevant judicial interpretations.

Book 16, *Education Law.* 3 vols. (called "Parts 1, 2 and 3"). Edward Thompson Co., Brooklyn, N. Y., 1953. Kept up to date with annual supplements. The basic text of this law was drawn up by the Joint Legislative Committee on the State Education System in 1947 and enacted by the state legislature the same year. Numerous sections apply specifically to the Board of Education and the City of New York. Contains pertinent judicial decisions.

Book 35A, *Multiple Dwelling Law.* Edward Thompson Co., Brooklyn, N. Y., 1946. Kept up to date with annual supplements. The courts have held that the state may regulate multiple dwellings within New York City. This act presents the complete state law on this subject. Introduced by an essay on the historical development of the multiple dwelling law, by the Hon. MacNail Mitchell, member of the Assembly and chairman of the Joint Legislative Committee on Housing and Public Dwellings. Includes appropriate judicial decisions.

New York State, Constitutional Convention Committee, *Problems Relating to Executive Administration and Powers.* Vol. 8 of *Reports and Studies.* J. B. Lyon Co., Albany, 1938, pp. 302–310. Outlines the framework of state control of education under the Department of Education and the Board of Regents.

Problems Relating to Bill of Rights and General Welfare. Vol. 6 of *Reports and Studies.* J. B. Lyon Co., Albany, 1938, pp. 482–511. Treats state control and regulation of social welfare including state-local relations in this area.

Problems Relating to Bill of Rights and General Welfare. Vol. 6 of *Reports and Studies.* J. B. Lyon Co., Albany, 1938, pp. 511–513. Considers state control of public health.

New York State, Temporary State Commission on Coordination of State Activities, *Staff Report on the Department of Civil Service.* Legislative Document no. 42, 1953, Williams Press, Albany, 1953. A study which had a direct impact on the State Department of Civil Service and on the reorganization of the New York City Civil Service Commission.

Third Interim Report. Legislative Document no. 64, 1949, Williams Press, Albany, 1949. Analyzes a number of educational functions in which the state supervises the schools of New York City.

Institute of Public Administration, *Intergovernmental Relations in Welfare Administration.* Mayor's Committee on Management Survey, New York, 1952. A study of the Department's external relations.

Piskor, Frank P., *State-City Relations in Civil Service Administration in New York State: 1938–1942.* Doctoral dissertation, Syracuse University, 1950.

HOME RULE

Desmond, Thomas C., "State Control of Cities," in Herbert L. Marx, *Community Planning.* The H. W. Wilson Co., New York, 1956, pp. 167–174. ("The Reference Shelf," vol. 28, no. 4). A reprint of an article by a New York State senator, originally published in *The New York Times Magazine,* which speaks with authority on the relationships between New York State and its bigger cities. Senator Desmond was the long-time chairman of the Senate Committee on Affairs of Cities.

Hallett, George H., "Redefining Home Rule for New York Cities," *National Municipal Review,* vol. 28, June, 1939, pp. 456–474. An account of the new constitutional provisions relating to home rule adopted by the Convention of 1938.

McBain, Howard Lee, "The New York Proposal for Home Rule," *Political Science Quarterly,* vol. 37, December, 1922, pp. 655–680. An analysis of the Home Rule Amendment in New York State.

McGoldrick, Joseph D., "Home Rule in New York State," *American Political Science Review,* vol. 19, November, 1925, pp. 693–706. A discussion of home rule in New York not long after it went into effect.

The Law and Practice of Home Rule: 1916–1930. Columbia University Press, New York, 1933, pp. 263–289. City-state relations just before and during the early period of home rule. Deals with home rule in New York not long after its adoption.

"What Municipal Home Rule Means Today, New York," *National Municipal Review,* vol. 21, December, 1932, pp. 671–678. Home rule in its early years in New York.

McKinney's Consolidated Laws of New York, Annotated, Book 7A, *City Home Rule Law*. Edward
   Thompson Co., Brooklyn, N. Y., 1952. Kept up to date with annual supplements.
   A comprehensive presentation of the New York State constitutional provisions for city
   home rule and the city home rule law. Many of the sections were drafted specifically
   for New York City. Includes judicial decisions relevant to the subject.

New York State Constitution Home Rule Provisions. "Home rule" is authorized in the
   following sections of the state constitution: Art. IX, Sec. 11, prohibits passage of special
   city laws by the legislature, except under specified conditions (as renumbered and
   amended by Constitutional Convention of 1938 and approved by vote of the
   people, November 8, 1938); Art. IX, Sec. 12, grants cities power to enact local laws
   relating to property, affairs or government (as renumbered and amended by Constitutional Convention of 1938 and approved by vote of people November 8, 1938).

Constitutional Convention Committee, *Problems Relating to Home Rule and Local Government*. Vol. 11 of *Reports and Studies*. J. B. Lyon Co., Albany, 1938. Chap. 1, city and
   county home rule: summary of salient problems, pp. 1–16; chap. 2, a survey of city
   home rule in New York State, pp. 17–78; chap. 3, county home rule in New York
   State, pp. 79–100; chap. 4, extension of home rule to villages of first class, pp. 101–105;
   chap. 5, constitutional restrictions on the selection of local officers, pp. 106–123.
   Appendix A, City and County Home Rule Provisions of New York State Constitution,
   pp. 255–259; Appendix B, Local Laws and Emergency Legislation under City Home
   Rule, pp. 260–271. Presents a comprehensive review of the home rule provisions of the
   state constitution as they existed in 1938.

Prendergast, William A., "Reminiscences." Columbia University Oral History Collection,
   Special Collections, Butler Library. The movement for home rule, before adoption of
   the Home Rule Amendment, reported by a former Comptroller of the City of New
   York.

Richland, W. Bernard, "Constitutional City Home Rule in New York, I," *Columbia Law
   Review*, vol. 54, 1954, p. 311.
   "Constitutional City Home Rule in New York, II," *Columbia Law Review*, vol. 55, 1955,
   p. 598.
   "Statutory and Practical Limitations upon New York City's Legislation Powers,"
   Fordham Law Review, vol. 24, 1955, p. 326.

Shaw, Frederick, *The History of the New York City Legislature*. Columbia University Press,
   New York, 1954, pp. 42–55, 180–182. Indicates the extent to which the Home Rule
   Act transferred power to govern New York City from the state legislature to the local
   legislature.

Tanzer, Lawrence A., "Home Rule: A Proposal for a Revision of the Municipal Article of
   the Constitution," *Proceedings* of the Academy of Political Science, vol. 5, no. 2,
   January, 1915, pp. 301–341. An expert on home rule for cities presents his views.

   "Municipal Home Rule in New York," *National Municipal Review*, vol. 14, April, 1925,
   pp. 246–253. A survey of the home rule law shortly after its enactment.

   "Political Strategy Nullifies Home Rule in New York," *National Municipal Review*, vol. 22,
   January, 1933, pp. 16–19, 23. Some of the reasons why home rule proved ineffective.

   "Reminiscences." Columbia University Oral History Collection, Special Collections,
   Butler Library. An active supporter of home rule and an expert on home rule law
   traces the progress of the home rule movement.

Weiner, Joseph L., "Municipal Home Rule in New York," *Columbia Law Review*, vol. 37,
   April, 1937, pp. 557–581. Evaluates the effectiveness of home rule.

CITY-STATE FISCAL RELATIONSHIPS

Blank, David M., *Reform of State-Local Fiscal Relations in New York State*. University Micro-
   films, Publication no. 2101, Ann Arbor, Mich., 1951. Doctoral dissertation, Columbia
   University, 1950. An analysis of the revision of the state-local tax and grant system in
   New York in 1946.

"Reform of State-Local Fiscal Relations in New York," *National Tax Journal*, December, 1950, pp. 326–347, and March, 1951, pp. 77–91. A summary of the Moore Plan, enacted in New York State in 1946 and some judgments relating to its effects on federal, state, and local finance.

Chamber of Commerce of the State of New York, Committee on City Affairs, "The Final Report of the New York State-New York City Fiscal Relations Committee," *Monthly Bulletin of the Chamber of Commerce of the State of New York*, February, 1957, pp. 367–380.

Citizens Budget Commission, *The Constitutional Tax Limit*. The Commission, New York, 1950. A summary of the problem as viewed by a staunch defender of such limitations.

Governmental Affairs Institute, *A Survey Report on the Impact of Federal Grants-in-Aid on the Structure and Functions of State and Local Governments*. Government Printing Office, Washington, 1955, An ancillary report to that of the Federal Commission on Intergovernmental Relations, prepared by a private group.

Haig, Robert M., and Carl S. Shoup, *The Revenue Problem of the City of New York and a Proposed Program*. Mayor's Committee on Management Survey, New York, 1951. A discussion of state and federal grants as a source of municipal revenue.

Haig, Robert M., Carl S. Shoup, and Lyle C. Fitch, *The Financial Problem of the City of New York*. Mayor's Committee on Management Survey, New York, 1952. A comprehensive analysis of New York City finances which includes recommendations regarding state and federal aid.

McKinney's Consolidated Laws of New York, Annotated, Book 33, *Local Finance Law*. Edward Thompson Co., Brooklyn, N. Y., 1945. Kept up to date with annual supplements. The basic law in this volume was drafted by the Temporary State Commission for Codification and Revision of the Laws Relating to Municipal Finance, known as the "Municipal Finance Commission," and enacted by the state legislature in 1945. Some of its provisions apply directly to New York City. Relevant court decisions are analyzed.

New York City, Mayor's Committee to Study Finances, *Report of Subcommittee on State-City Fiscal Relations*. The Committee, New York, January 9, 1943. An intensive study of the special problems involved.

Bureau of the Budget, *The Case for New York City: Its Financial Relationships with the State*. The Bureau, New York, 1954. The budget director of New York City states the official city view of city-state relationships.

New York State, Constitutional Convention Committee, *New York City Government: Functions and Problems*. Vol. 5 of *Reports and Studies*. Burland Printing Co., New York, 1938. Chapter 3, Constitutional Provisions Affecting New York City, pp. 21–49, indicates how the state constitution affected such areas as home rule, tax limitations and debt limitations, county government, the merit system, the courts, possibility of removal of local officials by the Governor and reapportionment at the time this survey was made; chap. 4, Home Rule, pp. 50–65, discusses the subject of the chapter; chap. 5, Constitutional Limitations on New York City's Debt, pp. 91–95; chap. 6, Constitutional Tax Limitation, pp. 164–181; chap. 10, State's Financial Aid to New York City, pp. 164–181; and chap. 11, Mandatory Expenditures, pp. 182–210.

Constitutional Convention Committee, *Problems Relating to Taxation and Finance*. Vol. 10 of *Reports and Studies*. J. B. Lyon Co., Albany, 1938, pp. 403–444. Considers state and municipal aid to housing. Part 2 considers problems of local taxation and expenditures, pp. 147–238, and Part 3 goes into problems of local indebtedness, pp. 287–388.

Department of Audit and Control, *New York City Finances*. The Department, Albany, 1954. A special report prepared for Governor Dewey by a group of state officials reviewing the New York City financial picture as it then existed.

Department of Audit and Control, *State Aid to Local Government*. The Department, Albany, 1958. Explains how the state renders financial assistance to its municipalities.

New York State Legislature, Joint Legislative Committee on the State Education System, *Interim Report of the New York City Sub-Committee Concerning Administration and Financing of That Part of the Public Education System of the City of New York under the Control of That City's Board of Education*. Legislative Document no. 55, 1943. A report on administration and finances.

New York State—New York City Fiscal Relations Committee, *A Report to the Governor of the State of New York and the Mayor of the City of New York.* The Committee, Albany, 1956. Stresses the need for state responsibility for sound governmental and fiscal relations and city responsibility for fiscal planning.

New York State, Temporary Commission on the Fiscal Affairs of State Government, *A Program for Continued Progress in Fiscal Management.* The Commission, New York, 1955. 2 vols. The sections dealing with state-local relationships contain specific references to New York City.

Temporary State Commission on Coordination of State Activities, *Report to the Governor and to the Legislature.* Legislative Document no. 77, 1951. Williams Press, Albany, 1951. Touches on matters relating to state aid, such as state aid for adult education, special aid to the New York City schools for reducing class size, and general apportionment of aid to education.

Phillips, Jackson R. E., *Intergovernmental Fiscal Relations and the City of New York.* University Microfilms, Ann Arbor, Mich., 1957. Doctoral dissertation, Columbia University, 1956.

U. S. Committee on Intergovernmental Relations, *Federal, State and Local Government Fiscal Relations.* Government Printing Office, Washington, 1943. An inquiry into intergovernmental fiscal relations by the Treasury Department.

STATE INVESTIGATIONS OF CITY AFFAIRS

State Investigations of the City—Official Reports, arranged chronologically

New York State, Senate Committee on Cities, *Testimony Taken Pursuant to Resolution Adopted January 20, 1890.* J. B. Lyon Co., Albany, 1891. 5 vols. The work of the Fassett Committee.

Senate Committee to Investigate the Police Department of the City of New York, *Report and Proceedings.* J. B. Lyon Co., Albany, 1895. 5 vols., The work of the famous Lexow Committee.

Index to the Testimony and Proceedings before the Lexow Committee Investigating the New York Police Department. Wynkoop Hallenback Crawford, Albany, 1899.

Assembly, Investigation of the Offices and Departments of the City of New York by a Special Committee, *Report of Counsel,* December 22, 1899. J. B. Lyon Co., Albany, 1899. A report by the counsel to the Mazet Committee.

Special Committee of the Assembly Appointed to Investigate the Public Officers and Departments of the City of New York and of the Counties Therein Included, *Final Report.* 5 vols. J. B. Lyon Co., Albany, 1900. The report of the Mazet Committee.

Joint Committee of the Senate and Assembly of the State of New York. Appointed to Investigate the Finances of New York City, *Proceedings.* J. B. Lyon Co., Albany, 1909. The verbatim proceedings of this legislative inquiry, which met in New York City, 1908–1909.

Joint Committee of the Senate and Assembly of the State of New York Appointed to Investigate the Finances of the City of New York, *Report.* The Committee, Albany, 1909. The report of a committee which sought to find evidences of wrongdoing in New York City.

Joint Legislative Committee for the Investigation of the Finances of the City of New York, *Report.* The Committee, Albany, 1916. Report of a joint committee of the state legislature.

Joint Legislative Committee to Investigate the Affairs of the City of New York, *Proceedings.* Marshall and Munson, New York, 1921. The verbatim testimony taken by the Meyer Committee.

Joint Legislative Committee to Investigate the Affairs of the City of New York, *First Report.* Fremont Payne, New York, 1921. Initial report of the Meyer Committee which investigated affairs of the city.

Joint Legislative Committee to Investigate the Affairs of the City of New York, *Report and Summary of the Evidence.* J. B. Lyon Co., Albany, 1922. Report of the Meyer Committee.

Joint Legislative Committee to Investigate the Affairs of the City of New York, *Transcript of Hearings, 1931–1932.* Marshall and Munson, New York, 1932. 71 vols. mimeographed. Transcript of proceedings of the Joint Legislative Committee, Samuel Seabury, Counsel.

Joint Committee to Investigate the Departments of the City of New York, "Minutes of Executive Sessions," April 20, 1931–April 29, 1932. Conference of the joint legislative committee, Samuel Seabury, counsel, typewritten copy in Kent Hall, Columbia University.

Seabury, Samuel, Commissioner, in the Matter of Investigation under Commission Issued by the Governor of the State of New York of Charges Made against the Hon. Thomas C. T. Crain, District Attorney of New York, *Report and Opinion.* New York, August 31, 1931. The second Seabury inquiry, which preceded his general investigation of the city's government.

Referee in the Matter of the Investigation of the Magistrates' Courts in the First Judicial Department and the Magistrates Thereof, and of the Attorneys-at-Law Practicing in Said Courts, First Report. Lawyers Press, New York, 1932. The first of three Seabury investigations.

In the Matter of the Investigation of the Departments of the Government of the City of New York: Intermediate Report, January 25, 1932. First of Samuel Seabury's reports as counsel to a joint legislative committee.

In the Matter of the Investigation of the Departments of the Government of the City of New York: Second Intermediate Report. December 19, 1932. Second report made by Samuel Seabury.

In the Matter of the Investigation of the Departments of the Government of the City of New York: Final Report to the Members of the Joint Legislative Committee to Investigate the Administration of the Various Departments of the City of New York. December 27, 1932. The final report of Samuel Seabury.

New York State, Joint Legislative Committee to Investigate the Affairs of the City of New York: *Report to the Legislature.* December 28, 1932. The report of the Committee for which Seabury served as counsel.

Amen, John Harlan, "Report of Kings County Investigation 1938–1942." New York State Attorney General, n.d. (Mr. Amen's letter of transmittal is dated November 30, 1942.) The official report of a state investigation of law enforcement activities in Kings County.

New York State Crime Commission, *Public Hearings* (No. 4) Conducted by the New York State Crime Commission Pursuant to the Governor's Executive Order of March 29, 1951 (November 13, 1952–November 19, 1952). 4 vols. mimeographed. Verbatim testimony of the hearings of the "Proskauer Commission" in New York City.

Public Hearings (No. 5, Port of New York Waterfront). 6 vols., mimeographed. Stenographic transcription of hearings of the "Proskauer Commission" held in New York County Court House, December 3, 1952–March 17, 1953.

Papers relating to the Commission's Investigation of Waterfront Crime, 1952–1953. Special Collections, Butler Library, Columbia University.

First Report to the Governor, the Attorney General and the Legislature of the State of New York, Legislative Document no. 23 (1951); *Second Report to the Governor, the Attorney General and the Legislature of the State of New York,* Legislative Document no. 40 (1953); *Third Report to the Governor, the Attorney General and the Legislature of the State of New York,* Legislative Document no. 68 (1953); *Fourth Report to the Governor, the Attorney General and the Legislature of the State of New York,* Legislative Document no. 70 (1953); *Fifth and Final Report to the Governor, the Attorney General and the Legislature of the State of New York,* Legislative Document no. 52 (1954). Williams Press, Albany, First to Fourth, 1953; Fifth, 1954. The reports of the "Proskauer Commission," which investigated the relationship between organized crime and local government.

New York State, *Record of the Public Hearings Held by Gov. Thomas E. Dewey on the Recommendations of the New York State Crime Commission for Remedying Conditions on the Waterfront of the Port of New York,* June 8 and 9, 1953. Publishers Printing Co., New York, 1953.

COMMENTS ON INVESTIGATIONS

Bellush, Bernard, *Franklin D. Roosevelt as Governor of New York*. Columbia University Press, New York, 1955, pp. 269–281. The legislative investigation of New York City and the resignation of Mayor Walker.

Boyer, Richard O., "Inquisitor: Profile of Samuel Seabury," *The New Yorker*, vol. 7, June 27, 1931, pp. 20–23. The man who held the stage in a dramatic legislative investigation of the affairs of the city.

Chambers, Walter, *Samuel Seabury: A Challenge*. Century Co., New York, 1932. A eulogistic life of Seabury, written while the investigation of New York City government was in progress.

Citizens Union, *Facts versus Flourishes and Ruffles: What Four Years of Hylan, Hearst and Murphy Have Done to New York*. The Union, New York, 1921. A digest and interpretation of the findings of the Meyer Committee.

Dewey, John, editor, *New York and the Seabury Investigation*. City Affairs Committee, New York, 1933. Reflections on the Seabury investigations.

Fine, Nathan, *The Collapse of the Seabury Investigation*. Rand School Press, New York, 1932. Presents the Socialist views of the Seabury probe.

Gribetz, Louis J., and Joseph Kaye, *Jimmie Walker: The Story of a Personality*. Dial Press, New York, 1932, pp. 259–353. A detailed description of the Seabury investigation and Mayor Walker, favorable to Walker.

Missall, J. Ellsworth, *The Moreland Act: Executive Inquiry in the State of New York*. King's Crown Press, New York, 1946. An inquiry into the origins, procedures, and accomplishments of this form of executive inquiry.

New York State Constitutional Convention Committee, *Problems Relating to Executive Administration and Powers*, vol. 8 of *Reports and Studies*. J. B. Lyon Co., Albany, 1938, pp. 231–260. Sets forth some of the conditions under which local officers may be removed by state executive action.

Northrop, William B., and John B. Northrop, *The Insolence of Office: The Story of the Seabury Investigations*. G. P. Putnam's Sons, New York, 1932. Three state investigations of the city: the inquiry into the Magistrates' Courts, the District Attorney's office in New York County, and the affairs of New York City.

Parkhurst, C. H., *My Forty Years in New York*. Macmillan Co., New York, 1923, pp. 106–145. Memoirs of a minister whose crusade led to the overthrow of Tammany in 1894 and to the Lexow Committee.

Thomas, Norman, and Paul Blanshard, *What's the Matter with New York?* Macmillan Co., New York, 1932, pp. 177–195. Governor Franklin D. Roosevelt and Mayor Walker.

Werner, M. R., *It Happened In New York*. Coward-McCann, New York, 1957, pp. 36–116. The Lexow Committee and Dr. Parkhurst's crusade.

Williams, Edward A., "The Crain Removal Case and Statistical Charts," *National Municipal Review*, vol. 21, April, 1932, pp. 232–241. Some observations on the second Seabury Investigation.

THE NEW YORK METROPOLITAN AREA

Adams, Thomas, "Regional Planning in New York," *National Municipal Review*, October, 1925, p. 621. Problems facing governmental agencies in the New York area.

Armstrong, Robert H., and Homer Hoyt, *Decentralization in New York City*. The Urban Land Institute, Chicago, 1941. Some of the basic factors of population redistribution which create the need for new relationships with neighboring communities.

Duffus, Robert L., *Mastering a Metropolis: Planning the Future of the New York Region.* Harper and Bros., New York, 1930. An early volume that probed the need for and problems of New York metropolitan integration.

Gulick, Luther, "Broad Regional Planning for New York Metropolitan Area," *Better Roads,* January, 1955, pp. 23, 24. Expounds the view that the New York Metropolitan Region needs a new layer of local government to deal with unmet needs.

Kaufman, Herbert, "Gotham in the Air Age," in Harold Stein, editor, *Public Administration and Policy Development: A Case Book.* Inter-University Case Program, Harcourt, Brace and Co., New York, 1952, pp. 143–197. The need for metropolitan integration in one area, and how this need was met.

Levine, Eugene, *Modern Federalism in Public Health: An Analysis of New York City's Relations with Other Governments in the Field of Public Health.* Master's thesis, New York University, 1950, unpublished.

New York–New Jersey Metropolitan Rapid Transit Commission, *Interim Report on the Activities of the Commission.* The Commission, New York, 1955. Describes joint efforts to cooperate on mass transportation problems.

Joint Report on the Problem of Providing Improved Mass Transportation between the City of New York and New Jersey, Westchester, and Long Island. The Commission, New York, 1954. Intergovernmental efforts to solve the problem of street congestion in mid-Manhattan and neighboring communities.

Oravetz, Kalman A., *Operation "Colossus."* Citizens Union Research Foundation, New York, 1956. Describes progress in regional planning in the metropolitan area.

Regional Plan Association, *The Economic Status of the New York Metropolitan Region in 1944.* The Association, New York, 1944.

Metropolis in the Making: The Next Twenty-five Years in the New York Metropolitan Region. The Association, New York, 1955. The Proceedings of the 25th Anniversary celebration of the Association.

Shaw, Frederick, "The World's Best Bombing Run: Metropolitan Regions in the Middle States," *Annual Proceedings of the Middle States Council for the Social Studies,* vol. 52, 1955, pp. 12–20. Outlines the basic problems of metropolitan areas in the Middle Atlantic region, with particular reference to New York City, and indicates possible forms of metropolitan integration.

Smoleff, Samuel D., *Compacts for Clean Waters.* Citizens Union Research Foundation, New York, 1949. Intergovernmental cooperation to combat water pollution.

Tomorrow in and around New York City. Citizens Union Research Foundation, New York, 1954. A plea for closer meshing of the governments in the metropolitan area of Greater New York.

Studenski, Paul, "New York Area Still Stymied," *National Municipal Review,* May, 1954, pp. 235–239, 242. Slow progress of joint planning in the New York City metropolitan area.

The Government of Metropolitan Areas in the United States. National Municipal League, New York, 1930. The first comprehensive study, this volume is useful for its references to the New York metropolitan area.

Tableman, Betty, *Governmental Organization in Metropolitan Areas.* University of Michigan Press, Ann Arbor, 1951. Contains many references to the New York area.

Wagner, Robert F., "Metropolitan Regional Cooperation," *Mayor and Manager,* February 1958, pp. 6–7, 21. Advances in political integration of the New York City metropolitan area.

Windels, Paul, "The Metropolitan Region at the Crossroads," *Bulletin* of the Regional Plan Association, no. 70, June, 1958, pp. 3–7. The need for metropolitan integration in the New York area.

Zimmerman, Frederick L., and Mitchell Wendell, "The New York Metropolitan Area," *State Government,* November, 1956, pp. 222–225. The background for political integration of the various units in the New York City metropolitan region.

The New York Metropolitan Region Study

Chinitz, Benjamin, *Freight and the Metropolis.* Harvard University Press, Cambridge, Mass., 1960. An analysis of the impact of changing methods of freight transportation upon the economic development of the New York region.

Handlin, Oscar, *The Newcomers.* Harvard University Press, Cambridge, Mass., 1959. A new approach to the Negro and Puerto Rican problem is found in analogies drawn from the experience of earlier, white immigrants to the area.

Helfgott, Roy B., Eric Gustafson, and James M. Hund. Max Hall, editor, *Made in New York.* Harvard University Press, Cambridge, Mass., 1959. The editor's introduction elucidates case studies of the factors affecting the location of three urban industries: women's apparel, printing and publishing, and electronics.

Hoover, Edgar M., and Raymond Vernon, *Anatomy of a Metropolis.* Harvard University Press, Cambridge, Mass., 1959. An area study of unprecedented analytical scope, dealing with the changing interrelationship between the region's old cities and the growing communities about them.

Lichtenberg, Robert M., Edgar M. Hoover, and Louise P. Lerdau, *One Tenth of a Nation.* Harvard University Press, Cambridge, Mass., 1960. A study of the New York area's development in competition with the rest of the nation, drawing upon a fund of observations from patterns developed in other large metropolitan areas.

Robbins, Sidney M., Ira O. Scott, and Nestor E. Terleckyj, *Money Metropolis.* Harvard University Press, Cambridge, Mass., 1960. Factors influencing the area's concentration of financial institutions and its future as the nation's money capital.

Segal, Martin, *Wages in the Metropolis.* Harvard University Press, Cambridge, Mass., 1960. An investigation of the New York region's wage structure and its affect on the location of industries.

Vernon, Raymond, *Metropolis 1985.* Harvard University Press, Cambridge, Mass., 1960. A synthesis and elaboration of the entire New York Metropolitan Region Study, formulating projections for the region's economic and population development to 1985.

Wood, Robert C., *1400 Governments.* Harvard University Press, Cambridge, Mass, 1960. The response of local governments to economic and population changes within the region and the corresponding results of their actions.

CHAPTER XVI

The Council

A LEGISLATURE IN FORM

Structure

"The council," provides the city charter, "shall be vested with the legislative power of the city, and shall be the local legislative body of the city, with the sole power to adopt local laws. . . ." It consists of 25 councilmen, each elected from Councilmanic Districts coterminous with state Senatorial Districts in the city, plus the President of the City Council, who is elected on a citywide basis. Nine councilmen are from Brooklyn, six from Manhattan, five from The Bronx, four from Queens, and one from Richmond, all elected at the same time as the Mayor for four-year terms. Their basic salary is $7,000 a year, but contingent expense allowances and other additions bring the total received by each ordinary councilman to $10,000, by the Chairman of the Finance Committee and the Chairman of the General Welfare Committee to $12,500, by the Minority Leader to $13,500 and by the Vice-Chairman (a post usually held by the Majority Leader) to $16,500.

Ordinarily, the Council meets one afternoon a week for ten months of the year; it omits meetings in July and August, and therefore assembles about thirty-five times in an average year. The President of the Council is presiding officer and is permitted to participate in its deliberations, but he casts no votes except to break ties; the Vice-Chairman (who is chosen by the members of the Council) acts as President when the regular President is absent.

As is the case with all American legislative bodies, work is divided among committees. There are a dozen of them (Buildings; City Affairs; City Employees and Veterans; Finance; General Welfare; Health and Education; Housing; Labor and Industry; Parks and Thoroughfares; Rules, Privileges and Elections; State Legislation; Codification), 10 composed of 11 members each, 2 with 8 members each.

Powers and Functions

The powers and functions of the Council fall into four categories: substantive legislation, appropriation, investigation, and public discussion. It is not empowered to confirm any appointments (although it does appoint a Clerk of the Council, who is also the City Clerk, with certain ministerial and record-keeping duties), nor to impeach or try officers of the other branches of government; however, it is the judge of the qualifications of its own members.

TABLE 61. PRESENT STRUCTURE AND OFFICERS OF THE NEW YORK CITY COUNCIL

PRINCIPAL OFFICERS

President
Vice-Chairman and Majority Leader
Minority Leader
Chairman of Finance Committee
Chairman of General Welfare Committee

COMMITTEES	Number of members
Buildings	11
City Affairs	11
City Employees and Veterans	11
Finance	11
General Welfare	11
Health and Education	8
Housing	11
Labor and Industry	11
Parks and Thoroughfares	11
Rules, Privileges, and Elections	11
State Legislation	11
Codification	8

BOROUGH DISTRIBUTION OF SEATS

Brooklyn	9
Manhattan	6
Queens	5
The Bronx	4
Richmond	1
Total	25

All official enactments affecting the structure of the city government, the powers and duties of its officers, or terms of office or compensation, take the form of local laws and must be passed by the Council. So, too, must all local legislation regulating the behavior and relationships of all persons within the jurisdiction of the city. Charter amendments must also be approved by the Council, unless initiated and ratified by the voters directly by means of the initiative and referendum. Most of the Administrative Code—embodying the bulk of the municipal legislation governing the people of the city, the grants to local administrative agencies of authority not already conferred by state legislation or the city charter, and municipal governmental procedure—consists of enactments of the Council. Most local laws, however, as described below, require the approval of the Board of Estimate; many require the approval of the voters in a referendum; and all are subject to veto by the Mayor. The Mayor may not approve local laws without holding a public hearing, and his veto may be overridden by a two-thirds vote of the Council.

Both the current and capital budgets must be passed by the Council. The actions it may take on these documents are tightly circumscribed by provisions noted more fully later on; nevertheless, Council reductions in either budget may be enforced even over the objections of the Mayor and the Board of Estimate by three quarters of all the councilmen.

The charter authorizes the Council to appoint special committees to investigate anything having to do with the property, affairs, or government of the city or any of the counties within it. Any such committee may compel attendance and production of records, examine witnesses, and take testimony under oath.

State legislation applicable to New York City alone may not be enacted by the legislature unless requested by the city through a resolution passed by the Council and signed by the Mayor. Moreover, the Council can make such a request by a two-thirds vote even if the Mayor opposes it. It thus plays a part in city-state relations, which were discussed at greater length in the preceding chapter.

Finally, every councilman may air his views from the floor of the Council. It is a forum that obtains for them fuller and more prominent press coverage than they would enjoy if they spoke only as private citizens, and it is especially important for minority members whose parties hold no other local office with such almost automatic access to the front pages. Council debate is a means of publicizing more than one side of controversial measures and furnishes opportunities for the ventilation of broad social principles that the burden of daily routines and the narrow scope of responsibility keep from open discussion elsewhere in the city government.

The list of Council powers is not so extensive as that of the state legislature or of Congress. Just the same, it is an impressive array of powers in form. Yet the Council is more shadow than substance.

THE FORM IS EMPTY

Legal Limitations of the Council

Other Lawmakers. In the first place, despite the sweeping language of the city charter, a great deal of the law affecting the people and the governing of New York is embodied in bodies of law formulated and adopted by other organs. In the preceding chapter on relations between the city and other governments, it was shown that the Constitution and statutes of the United States and interpretations of them by federal courts, the state constitution and statutes and judicial constructions of these laws by state judges, and executive and administrative actions by federal and state officials, all circumscribe the discretion of the Council. State institutions are especially important in this regard. The constitution of New York State contains structural, procedural, and substantive requirements and restrictions. Many city agencies are engaged in the administration and enforcement of state legislation rather than of local enactments, and many city officers, employees, and residents are more immediately controlled by the laws and administrative regulations of the state than by the City Council. These lie beyond the authority of the Council; it cannot prevent or modify these forms of legislation nor can it repeal them or substitute its own local laws for them. Many decisions of concern to the people of New York City are not made or significantly influenced by the City Council.

Particularly noteworthy is the power vested in the New York City Board of Health. Although appointed by the Mayor and paid by the city, the Board is really an arm of the state, granted authority to issue regulations as binding as those of the state legislature. Into the Board's area of competence—the Sanitary Code—the Council may not enter at all. To all intents and purposes, the Board is a unifunctional legislative body, and its lawmaking function is one that would presumably have been entrusted to the City Council along with its powers over other public functions and services if special historical circumstances had not led to these unusual arrangements.

Assigned to the Board of Estimate are a number of responsibilities ordinarily associated with the functions of a legislative body and most of which, indeed, were the province of the Council's predecessor (under the charter in force until the present one replaced it in 1938), the Board of Aldermen. The most important of these are control of franchises for public utilities, including transportation, within city limits; control of city finances; control of city personnel; control of city property; and control over city planning and zoning. The Board of Estimate can also approve modifications of the enacted budget without reference to the Council. Furthermore, the "residual" power of the city—the power not specifically allocated to any organ—falls to the Board of Estimate. In practically all other governments, this belongs to the legislative body, but in New York City it has been taken away from the legislature along with the other functions noted.

The charter itself contains many provisions about the organization, powers, and procedures of administrative agencies, elsewhere often found in ordinary legislation rather than fundamental law. Most city departments are established and governed by the charter. While it is true that the Council ordinarily has a hand in amending the charter, and that these agencies are consequently not entirely beyond reach of this body, the Board of Estimate has an absolute veto over amendments voted by the Council. Moreover, the charter may be amended without a vote of either the Council or the Board of Estimate; the charter permits initiation of amendments by petition and ratification by the voters in a referendum. Thus, the ability to organize and reorganize administrative structure, one of the foundation stones of legislative influence, is not truly lodged in the local legislature.

In point of fact, no legislative body at any level is the exclusive source of law in its jurisdiction. But they are usually the primary source, with immense power over many others; they are clearly first. It can hardly be said that the Council is even *primus inter pares;* at best, it is simply one among many.

Special Restrictions. In the second place, even such legislative power as it has is tightly hemmed in. Although it is endowed with "the sole power to adopt local laws," many of the bills it is called upon to pass are, in the same manner as proposed amendments to the charter, subject to absolute veto by the Board of Estimate; it cannot override the Board as it can the Mayor. All bills on a list of 18 subjects must be submitted to the voters in a referendum and take effect only with the approval of the electorate. It may only reduce the expense budget; it may not add or increase items or alter their terms and conditions. Furthermore, it has only twenty[1] days to consider the budget—a document as large as the Manhattan telephone directory, and exceedingly complicated. If it fails to act in this period, the document as certified to the Council by the Mayor after Board of Estimate approval is automatically declared adopted, so the Council cannot even hold it up. And if the Mayor vetoes Council budget slashes, it takes three quarters of the full membership (rather than the ordinary two thirds) to sustain its actions. Similarly, the Council must act on the capital budget in twenty[2] days, may only strike out authorizations of capital projects, and can override a veto by the Mayor only with 75 per cent (or more) of all the councilmen. It has virtually nothing at all to do with city borrowing and management of the city debt, which are responsibilities of the Comptroller. "Sole power" of legislation does not mean great power under these conditions.

The Record: Modest Achievement

An Abundance of Trifles. In the period from 1938 to 1956 approximately 2,100 local laws were passed by the City Council with an average of 105 a year, the low being 25 (in 1944), the high 202 (in 1951). Roughly 30 per cent of these dealt with naming streets, parks, and playgrounds; 25 per cent were detailed alterations of the Building Code (changes in specifications for valves of certain kinds, for example); another 12 per cent transferred property from the jurisdiction of one city agency to another or to a borough office. These minor or fundamentally administrative acts thus made up two thirds of all local laws. The remaining one third included legislation in connection with all the other functions and programs of the city, amendments to

[1] From the time the Board of Estimate has acted. However, the Board rarely makes extensive changes, so the budget is available to the Council, in approximately the form the Council must act on, for a total of 50 days. The Mayor submits the budget on April 1; the Board of Estimate must act on it by May 1; the Council must act on it by April 21.

[2] From the time the Board of Estimate acts; it has 57 days after initial submission by the City Planning Commission, however.

the charter, taxation, city employees, and a scattering of enactments on other subjects, including authorizations of cemeteries. What is more, most of the 2,100 laws required concurrence of the Board of Estimate as well as approval by the Mayor.

In addition, the Council passed a large number of resolutions that did not become part of the Administrative Code, the standing corpus of legislation governing the officials and the people of the city. Included among these resolutions were many pertaining to the internal organization and procedure of the Council; suggestions (without the force of law) to city officials and agencies on how to handle some specific issue or problem; greetings or good wishes to dignitaries; expressions of approval of federal, state, or city actions (such as an endorsement of public action to make driving safe and sane); and even advice to federal officers (to President Truman, for example, on how to solve a meat shortage and on how to instruct American delegates to the United Nations).

TABLE 62. SUBJECTS AND NUMBER OF LOCAL LAWS PASSED BY THE COUNCIL, 1938–1956

Subject of law	Number, 1938–1956	Per cent of total
City Council	3	0.1
Borough offices	13	0.7
Comptroller	7	0.3
Taxation	128	6.4
Assessable improvements	10	0.5
Changing names	569	28.0
Transferring and assigning city realty	297	14.6
Police Department	74	3.6
Fire Department	62	3.1
Department of Parks	5	0.2
Department of Health	12	0.6
Department of Correction	3	0.1
Department of Buildings	493	24.1
Department of Water Supply, Gas, and Electricity	15	0.8
Department of Sanitation	9	0.4
Department of Licenses	57	2.8
Property of city	5	0.2
Department of Markets	9	0.4
City Register	4	0.1
Authorization of land for cemeteries	16	0.8
Amending the charter	44	2.2
Department of Finance	12	0.6
Employees of the city	53	2.6
Officers and employees	18	0.9
Emergency defense	43	2.2
Obligations of the city	3	0.1
Amendment of Inferior Criminal Courts Act	5	0.2
Others	71	3.5
Total	2,040	100.0

SOURCES: "The New York City Council—Its Authorization, Operations, and Limitations," *St. John's Law Review*, vol. 29, May, 1955, pp. 266, 279–289; *Index to Local Laws*, Municipal Reference Library.

Interlarded among the trivialities were a number of important acts: laws on rent control, garage and parking regulations, fire safety for multiple dwellings, traffic control, smoke control, the office of City Administrator, discrimination in private housing, and others. Some resolutions were significant. The Council approval of the budget is handled this way and so are requests to the state legislature to enact special legislation for the city. All these must be approved by the Board of Estimate and/or the Mayor, so Council passage is not the end of the story. But they are all accomplishments in which the Council plays a significant formal part.

TABLE 63. NUMBER OF LOCAL LAWS PASSED AN-
NUALLY BY THE COUNCIL, 1938–1956

Year	Number of local laws
1938	74
1939	181
1940	147
1941	120
1942	52
1943	49
1944	25
1945	52
1946	44
1947	81
1948	92
1949	111
1950	119
1951	202
1952	166
1953	193
1954	129
1955	118
1956	85
Total	2,040
Average	107.4

SOURCES: "The New York City Council—Its Authorization, Operations and Limitations," *St. John's Law Review*, vol. 29, May, 1955, pp. 266, 278–279; and *Index to Local Laws*, Municipal Reference Library.

There can be no question that the great majority of Council actions either relate to its internal operations, minutiae, or trivia. Though the comment of one wag that the chief activity of the Council is naming streets is certainly unnecessarily ungenerous, there is just enough truth in this hyperbole to give it some sting. The legislative record of the City Council has certainly not been distinguished. Nor is its record as a guardian of the public purse.

The Council and the Purse Strings. The appropriation powers of legislatures have historically been their principal weapon in their relations with executives and bureaucracies; indeed, they are the source of modern legislative institutions, and a bulwark of American legislatures under the system of separation of powers. Yet the City Council, in spite of its formal power to delete or reduce budgetary items, has in practice each year simply passed a resolution adding an enacting clause to the budget document; the budgets come out of the Council almost exactly as they go into it. For example, from 1938 to 1956, inclusive, 19 expense budgets totaling about $22 billion were submitted to it. It attempted to effect cuts in only four of them, was met with a veto in three of the four cases, and managed to override the veto of part of its reductions in only one of the three. The combined reductions of all four actions came to a little over $3 million, or a bit more than 0.01 per cent of the budget totals.

Investigations. Legislative investigations have been used for many purposes —to gather information on which to base legislation, to expose wrongdoing in office, to harry the political opposition, to further the political careers of the investigators. In both Congress and the state legislature, there have been many illustrations of all these; many have served several purposes at once. The function has thus often been abused, but it has never been seriously curtailed because the solid achievements have made the costs worth paying, the risks worth taking. There are monumental landmarks left by some legislative inquiries.

Virtually the only use of investigative authority made by the New York City Council was the harassment of Mayor La Guardia by the Democratic majority during the late 1930's and early 1940's. In the years just following World War II, it is true, Councilman Walter R. Hart conducted a significant and effective inquiry into discrimination against minorities by medical schools in the city; this was one factor in the modification of these practices. And in 1957 the Council did investigate charges that some of its members, in violation of the express prohibitions in the charter, had direct interests in some of the business transactions of the city, or accepted remuneration for the use of their influence; several councilmen resigned under threat of removal as a result. But even this investigation came about because of exposures by the Commissioner of Investigation. In Council hands, except as an occasional annoyance for Mayors of a party opposing the Council majority, the investigative instrument has fallen into disuse. It has not been greatly abused, perhaps, but only because it has not been employed.

This state of affairs cannot be blamed on a lack of Council power. Of all the functions assigned to the Council, none is so broad as this. Investigations may be undertaken without the approval of the Board of Estimate or the Mayor. Anything related to any aspect of city government may be examined. No office, not even that of Mayor, is immune from Council probing. The Commissioner of Investigation may be utilized by the Council to assist it, or if it prefers, it may engage its own counsel and staff. The failure to carry on investigations is not a matter of legal inability to do so; rather, it is a lack of willingness to do so.

The Council as a Forum. For the minority party, the Council has served as a valuable platform from which to assail the majority and to focus attention on manipulations that might otherwise go undetected by the press and the public. With the minority now reduced to one Republican, or two at most, the majority has had no trouble adopting the measures it favors over minority objections. But the vigor and determination and brilliant tactics of the Minority Leader, Stanley M. Isaacs, an experienced, informed, persistent politician, keeps a spotlight of publicity on Democratic policies and maneuvers. Though he cannot block them on the floor, his success in raising the hue and cry has probably deterred or altered many measures that might well have passed routinely and in obscurity.

As a forum for the public, on the other hand, the Council has not been nearly so prominent as the Board of Estimate, the City Planning Commission, or the committees of Congress and the state legislature. The Council committees do not meet often. The most active one, the General Welfare Committee, in which most of the important bills are handled, held only 17 meetings in 1955; the Finance Committee met twelve times; the Committee on State Legislation, nine times; the City Affairs Committee, eight times; the remaining ones met five times or less, and three did not assemble at all. Furthermore, only a dozen of the meetings involved public hearings (11 conducted by the General Welfare Committee), and hearings were sparsely attended to say the least. The public does not display much interest in the Council (which is natural, considering its position and its record), and they have few opportunities to present their view formally in any case.

Inertia and Docility

Lack of Drive. By and large, the Council has been content to follow the lead of the administration. The Mayor, the Board of Estimate, and the administrative agencies propose; the Council routinely ratifies. To be sure, some important measures originated with councilmen—notably, the rent control law and the ban on racial and religious discrimination in housing, noted above—but most of its actions are virtually automatic adoptions of measures drafted in the executive branch.

Most American legislative bodies have slipped into a reviewing role; the Council is not unusual in this. Legislative leaders in Washington and Albany have tried persistently to seize control of policy from the President and the Governor, respectively, even when these offices have been occupied by men of their own party; a brisk rivalry is characteristic of legislative-executive relations at those levels. Nonetheless, the chief executives and their administrative agencies developed into the driving forces of government, supplying initiative, formulating programs, proposing policies. Creative drive comes mostly from the executive branch today; legislators screen, check, and revise far more frequently than they generate policy.

The Council is distinct, however, in the degree to which it has accepted a relatively passive role. In Congress and the state legislature, important administration measures rarely go through without scrutiny and some revision; in the Council, they are generally approved automatically precisely as submitted. In Congress and the state legislature, committee consideration of bills is often searching; in the Council, it is usually perfunctory. In Congress and the state legislature, reports of inadequate governmental service or performance, or of wrongdoing by public officers or private citizens, may touch off legislative examination and criticism; in the Council, they produce no response.

Occasionally, it is true, the Council does delay passage of measures sought by a Mayor and his staff, particularly when a majority of the councilmen and the Mayor are of different parties, as they were during most of Mayor La Guardia's administration. This happens also when they are of the same party, as Mayor Wagner discovered when he proposed amendments to the multiple dwelling provisions of the Administrative Code, for example, and when he requested resolutions suspending the Lyons Law (which requires that appointees to city offices be residents of the city unless specific exemption is granted) in certain cases. The purpose of such delay, however, is very rarely related to questions of policy. During the La Guardia administration, it was apparently primarily to harass the chief executive. Under Democratic Mayors, it is usually to extract from the executive an agreement to appoint favored individuals to office, generally to judgeships. This is an illustration of councilmen functioning in their roles as representatives of the party leaders in their respective areas. A Mayor may resist pressures of this kind if the measure at issue does not strike him as worth the price asked, or if he is confident of his ability to subdue the Council with weapons of his own. Mayors often accede, however, in order to achieve a larger policy objective or perhaps a personal objective. The Council thus does possess significant bargaining *potential*, but it characteristically employs this to very limited ends unrelated to substantive policy. Most of the time, it merely ratifies proposals placed before it by the executive branch. Often, it does so routinely; when it can, it extracts a price for its approval. In either case, as far as the content of policy decisions is concerned, the executive leads and the Council follows.

Reasons for Passivity. The dispersion among many law-making bodies of the functions commonly vested in legislatures, and the restrictions on the powers that were granted to it, doubtless contribute to draining away the vitality of the Council. It is a victim of its own predecessor. Before the charter of 1936—

the one currently in force—took effect in 1938, the legislative power of the city was in the Board of Aldermen, a body of 65 members. Its functions were far more inclusive than those of the Council, but they were so abused that the epithets "Boodle Board" and "Forty Thieves," coined in the days before the formation of the Greater City by consolidation in 1898, would not be washed away. When the new charter was drawn, the distrust of the city legislature was manifested in the reduced authority of the Council, a diminution so striking that one observer called it the "virtual disappearance of the legislative branch." This diminution owed its adoption also to the doctrine that policy and administration are separate and distinct and should not be lodged in the same organ. The Council was to be freed of concern with administrative detail in order to concentrate on broad policy. (It soon became apparent that broad policy emerges from a series of narrow decisions. That is why the Board of Estimate, confined in theory to administrative matters, evolved into the main instrument of the municipal government.) This combination of factors produced a Council with little to do. Councilmen could hardly help recognizing their own futility; this may well have engendered their submissiveness.

Because the Council is a relatively quiescent body, it does not attract many men of leadership caliber; because it does not attract leaders, it remains quiescent. From 1938 to 1957, 78 men held Council seats. Not one progressed to citywide office (the mayoralty, the comptrollership, the presidency of the Council). Not one advanced to statewide elective office. Only one became a Borough President (in Richmond, in 1955). More than 30, it is true, moved subsequently into other legislative positions (but seldom to Congress) and into administrative positions, and 10 became judges. But councilmanic office has not been a springboard to prominence. For a few, it is a career in itself. For a larger number (particularly those nonprofessional politicians drawn temporarily into politics during La Guardia's administration), it is a minor digression in nonpolitical and nongovernmental careers. For most, it is apparently a vestibule in which to wait quietly for better, though not more visible, posts. There are some unusually able and devoted men in the Council, but it is more a gathering of party wheelhorses than a breeding ground of leaders.

One-party dominance may intensify its weaknesses. Prior to the operation of the original version of the present charter in 1938, the Democrats consistently won from 85 to 98 per cent of the seats on the Board of Aldermen, although their popular vote was not nearly so one-sided. This added to the persuasiveness of those who advocated election of councilmen by the Hare system of proportional representation, designed to produce Councils whose composition comes closer to the actual division of the popular votes among the parties, and this plan was incorporated in the new charter. (The councilmen

TABLE 64. COMPOSITION OF NEW YORK CITY COUNCIL AND ITS PREDECESSOR, THE BOARD OF ALDERMEN

Year elected	Total seats	Composition by parties		
		Parties represented	Number of seats	Per cent of total seats[a]
1901	73	Democratic	36	49
		Republican	37	51
1903	73	Democratic	51	70
		Republican	22	30
1905	73	Democratic	26	36
		Republican	41	56
		Not known	6	8
1907	73	Democratic	48	66
		Republican	24	33
		Not known	1	1
1909	73	Democratic	40	55
		Republican	33	45
1911	73	Democratic	35	48
		Republican	38	52
1913	73	Democratic	32	44
		Republican	40	55
		Not known	1	1
1915	73	Democratic	53	73
		Republican	20	27
1917	67	Democratic	45	67
		Republican	15	23
		Not known	7	10
1919	67	Democratic	35	52
		Republican	25	37
		Socialist	4	6
		Fusion	3	5
1921	65	Democratic	48	74
		Republican	12	18
		Republican-Democratic	5	8
1923	65	Democratic	57	88
		Republican	8	12
1925	65	Democratic	62	95
		Republican	3	5
1927	65	Democratic	58	89
		Republican	7	11
1929	65	Democratic	61	94
		Republican	4	6
1931	65	Democratic	64	98
		Republican	1	2
1933	65	Democratic	18	28
		Republican	2	3
		Democratic-Recovery	29	44
		Republican-City Fusion	14	21
		Democratic-Jefferson	1	2
		Democratic-Law Preservation-Recovery	1	2

TABLE 64. COMPOSITION OF NEW YORK CITY COUNCIL AND ITS
PREDECESSOR, THE BOARD OF ALDERMEN (Continued)

Year elected	Total seats	Composition by parties		
		Parties represented	Number of seats	Per cent total seats[a]
1935	65	Democratic	60	92
		Republican	2	3
		Democratic-Jefferson	2	3
		Republican-Fusion	1	2
1937	26	Democratic	14	54
		Republican	3	12
		American Labor	5	19
		Fusion	3	12
		Independent	1	4
1939	21	Democratic	14	67
		Republican	2	9
		American Labor	2	9
		City Fusion-Citizens Nonpartisan	2	9
		Independent	1	5
1941	26	Democratic	17	65
		Republican	2	8
		American Labor	2	8
		City Fusion-Citizens Nonpartisan	2	8
		Communist	1	4
		Independent	1	4
		American Labor-City Fusion	1	4
1943	17	Democratic	11	65
		Republican	3	17
		Communist	2	12
		American Labor	1	6
1945	23	Democratic	14	61
		Republican	3	13
		Liberal	2	9
		Communist	2	9
		American Labor	1	4
		Democratic-American Labor	1	4
1949	25	Democratic	20	80
		Democratic-Liberal	3	12
		Democratic-Republican-Liberal	1	4
		Republican-Liberal	1	4
1953	25	Democratic	20	80
		Republican	2	8
		Democratic-Liberal	2	8
		Democratic-Republican	1	4
1957	25	Democratic	19	76
		Democratic-Liberal	2	8
		Democratic-City Fusion	2	8
		Democratic-Liberal-City Fusion	1	4
		Republican-Liberal	1	4

[a] Figures may not total 100 per cent because of rounding.

SOURCES: *Annual Reports*, New York City Board of Elections; *Official Directory of the City of New York; The City Record.*

then had two-year terms, and their number depended on the number of votes cast in the election.) In the first PR election, the Democrats captured only 13 out of 26 places, and were opposed by a coalition of 5 American Laborites, 3 Republicans, 3 Fusionists, and 2 insurgent Democrats. But the two insurgents soon returned to the fold, and the Democrats were never again to have less than a majority. The councilmanic term of office was doubled in 1945, and then, in 1947, proportional representation was abandoned in favor of the present method of election of councilmen from state Senatorial Districts. The Democrats, of course, had never been enthusiastic about PR, and played on the presence in the Council of left-wing American Labor party representatives and two Communists to secure its defeat. The Republicans did not fight the Democrats on this. Overwhelming Democratic majorities promptly returned; they won 24 of the 25 seats in the next citywide election (1949), 23 in 1953, and 24 again in 1957.

Under a lesser Mayor than Fiorello La Guardia, the Democratic majority might have been able to assume a larger role in making governmental decisions; as it was, the Democrats did succeed in badgering him. La Guardia, however, was so agile, so politically astute, so energetic, and so immensely popular, that they were no match for him. With his unexpected and continually shifting alliances (including some with influential Democrats), explosive temperament, talent for invective, genius for ridicule, and with a press that loved his outbursts because they made such colorful copy, he beat the Council majority into submission, when he was not circumventing the city legislature altogether.

When La Guardia departed from City Hall, the Democrats regained it; all three Mayors since then have been Democrats (although Impellitteri came in over the opposition of the regular organization). Whereas they had previously been cowed by the chief executive, the councilmen now found themselves bound by the obligations and demands of party discipline and the possibilities of party sanctions. Thus, since the Council was established in 1938, its members have had no chance to seize the initiative.

At the federal level, and to a lesser extent at the state level, both branches change hands from time to time. In the city, the Democrats are in virtually continuous, overwhelming control of the legislature. The swings in Albany and Washington help keep legislative leaders in fighting trim. The situation in New York City apparently produces tactical paralysis and erosion of the will.

Unexercised Powers. The City Council is in a weaker position than other legislative bodies—indeed, it is not at all a legislative body in the usual sense. Yet it has demonstrated by its occasional upsurges that it can do more than it has done. Councilmen can and have authored significant local laws and maneuvered them through. They can threaten to withhold action in order to gain bargaining power; indeed, when Mayor Wagner urged a change in the city charter to facilitate charter revision, councilmen of both parties joined in refusing to pass the proposal unless the Mayor publicly guaranteed that the Council itself would not be eliminated by any contemplated changes in the organic law of the municipality. And they do enjoy broad powers of investigation. They simply do not use the equipment at their disposal. When proposals to increase its authority were advanced in 1940, the minority leader observed "that the Council had yet to demonstrate it deserved broader powers, for it had never adequately exercised those it possessed." The observation is as valid today as it was then.

Increasingly, the Council is on the defensive. In 1957 the Citizens Budget Commission recommended strongly that it be abolished and its functions, such as they are, be transferred to other organs of government. Conceivably, the challenge to institutional pride could galvanize the Council to action. Meanwhile, the Council's influence on governmental decisions, never very great, is ebbing, and the weakening of its strength has made it still more hesitant (for fear of provoking drastic action by its critics) to use those powers it possesses.

THE COUNCIL AND GOVERNMENT DECISIONS

As individuals, the councilmen enjoy some of the rewards of politics simply by being elected. The salary, relative to the duties, is reasonably high. The demands of the job are rather small for most of them. Members of the Council have access to top city officials and high party functionaries, and they command some deference in administrative agencies. Minor perquisites —little privileges and services—come with the post. Some lawyers and other independent professionals get business that might otherwise not flow to them. The fruits of this office are not spectacular, but they are modestly satisfying, particularly to party workers who are simply waiting for better opportunities.

As individuals, councilmen are also in a position to use their access to aid other participants in the political process. In particular, they can do favors for members of party clubs in the Assembly District they represent, thus ingratiate themselves with the District Leaders, and develop claims on future nominations and appointments. Whether or not their generosity is self-serving, it is displayed in the distribution of small benefits; councilmen are minor distributors of the stakes of political participation.

As a collectivity, on the other hand, their impact on the governmental decisions by which most stakes are distributed is negligible. They seldom originate action and seldom prevent or modify actions instituted by others. As an entity, the Council has not exerted as much influence on the pattern of governmental activity—on public policies and programs—as many nongovernmental groups whose formal leverage is not so great. Its weakness is self-reinforcing; other contestants for the prizes of politics, inside government and outside, do not approach it, and the bargaining position that can be built up by selective assistance and the threat of deprivations of assistance is denied it. It is ignored and by-passed by nongovernmental groups, by bureaucrats, and by governmental leaders of the city and other jurisdictions.

In Congress and the state legislatures many social conflicts and functions come to a head. These bodies are internally disunited; localism and lack of party discipline make the behavior of some of them highly unpredictable, and present them with great difficulties in resolving the problems confronting them. But they do usually serve as arenas in which issues are sharpened and at least the general outlines of policy are shaped. The major questions of the day are filtered through these bodies, and the treatment of questions at these central points furnishes a modicum of integration to the governments of which they are part.

The Council does not. The population of the city works out its adjustments, its distributions of the rewards of political action, in many ways and many places, but the Council is hardly ever one of them. It is certainly no counterpoise to the autonomous functioning of the many decision centers in the political life of the city. On the contrary, though it is one of the only three citywide governmental institutions in New York (the mayoralty and the Board of Estimate are the others), it probably adds, in its own small way, to the fragmentation.

BIBLIOGRAPHY

OFFICIAL SOURCES AND ISSUANCES

New York City Charter, chap. 2, secs. 21–45; chap. 6, secs. 118, 124; chap. 7, sec. 169; chap. 9, sec. 222; chap. 12, sec. 293; chap. 34, sec. 803; chap. 40, secs. 890, 896, 903.

New York City Administrative Code, chap. 2.

New York City, Board of Aldermen, *Proceedings, 1898–1901*. Official journal of the lower house of the city's legislative body from consolidation to the charter of 1901.

Proceedings, 1902–1923. The official record of the Board of Aldermen under the 1902 charter to 1923.

General Index and Progressive Register in Detail of All the Proceedings of the Board of Aldermen of the City of New York during the Years 1914 and 1915. J. J. Little and Ives Co., New York, 1916. A complete record of the work of one of the most active Boards of Aldermen.

Record of the Work of the Board of Aldermen, January 1, 1914 to July 6, 1915. M. B. Brown Co., New York, 1915. Published by a Board of Aldermen which was proud of its accomplishments.

Special Committee Appointed August 5, 1912, to Investigate the Police Department, *Report*. M. B. Brown Co., New York, 1913. The most famous investigation undertaken by the Board of Aldermen.

New York City, Board of Aldermen and Municipal Assembly, *Proceedings, 1924–1937*. The official record of the Board of Aldermen from "home rule" to the 1936 charter.

New York City, Council, *Proceedings, 1938* to date. The official record of the Council under the 1936 charter.

New York City, Municipal Assembly, *Proceedings, 1898–1901*. Official journal of the city legislative body from consolidation to the charter of 1901.

COMMENTARIES

Belous, Charles, *Faith in Fusion.* Vantage Press, New York, 1951, pp. 41–66. Contrasts between the Board of Aldermen and the first Council elected by proportional representation, written by a member of the first Council.

Chamber of Commerce of the State of New York, *Proportional Representation: What It is and How It Works in New York City.* The Chamber, New York, 1947. Arguments for and against proportional representation, based on its operation in the City Council.

Citizens Union, *City Council Record,* annually 1938 to date. A record of all bills and resolutions introduced in the Council, with notes on what happened to each; a record of bills and resolutions introduced by individual councilmen.

"Evidence for P.R. in the 1948 Elections," *The Searchlight,* vol. 38, December, 1948. A plea for the return of proportional representation to the City Council.

Scrapbooks. 206 vols. Vols. 77–79 cover the Board of Aldermen and city clerk, 1922–1931. In reference section of New York Public Library, Astor Branch.

"The First P.R. Council," *The Searchlight,* vol. 29, October, 1939. A review of the record of the first New York City Council elected under proportional representation.

Reports for the 1910–1917 Terms. Citizens Union, New York, 1911–1917. The city legislature as seen by a civic group.

Committee on Legislation, *Municipal Assembly Record, 1924–1937.* A summary of all legislation, proposed and passed, in the Aldermanic Branch of the Municipal Assembly.

City Affairs Committee, *Those Aldermen.* The Committee, New York, January, 1933. A not too complimentary analysis of the Board of Aldermen a few years before its demise.

Clark, Evans, and Charles Solomon, *The Socialists in the New York City Board of Aldermen: A Record of Six Months.* Rand School, New York, 1918. The Socialists evaluate their own record in the Board of Aldermen.

Conkling, Alfred R., *City Government in the United States.* D. Appleton and Co., New York, 1899. A former member of the Board of Aldermen discusses political control of that body just prior to consolidation of the city.

Curran, Henry H., "Fifty Years of Public Service," *The New York Times Magazine,* December 7, 1947. A former majority leader of the Board of Aldermen recalls past scenes in the city legislature.

Pillar to Post. Charles Scribner's Sons, New York, 1941, pp. 125–187. The reminiscences of a former majority leader and minority leader in the Board of Aldermen.

Van Tassel and Big Bill. Charles Scribner's Sons, New York, 1923. The fictionalized account of an alderman, closely following the author's career in the Board of Aldermen.

Earle, Genevieve, *Personal Papers.* Special Collections, Columbia University, Butler Library. The papers of the City Council's minority leader. Typewritten and mimeographed.

"Reminiscences." Columbia University Oral History Collection, Special Collections, Butler Library. The minority leader of the City Council relates how the minority operated.

Forbes, Russell, "The Municipal Assembly—New York's Home Rule Legislature," *National Municipal Review,* vol. 18, October, 1929, pp. 632–634. The Board of Aldermen as the lower branch of the municipal home rule legislature.

Garrett, Oliver H. P., "One of the Boys: Profile of Ruth Pratt," *The New Yorker,* vol. 2, April 24, 1926, pp. 21–22. Portrait of a minority member of the Board of Aldermen.

Gustaferro, Margaret, *The Personnel of the Board of Aldermen of New York, 1918–1928.* Master's thesis, Columbia University, 1929, unpublished. The type of men elected to seats in the city's legislature.

Hallett, George, *Real Majority Rule.* Brooklyn Eagle Press, Brooklyn, 1935. A pamphlet presenting a strong plea for proportional representation for the city legislature.

Proportional Representation—The Key to Democracy. National Municipal League, New York, 1940. A general treatment of the subject which relies heavily on examples taken from the Board of Aldermen and City Council in New York City.

Hallett, George H., and William R. Radin, "New York City Reconsidering P.R.," *National Municipal Review*, May, 1958, pp. 239–241. An assessment of the chances for a return of proportional representation.

Hellman, Geoffrey T., "The Festive Touch: Profile of Joseph Clark Baldwin III," *The New Yorker*, vol. 19, February 27, 1943, pp. 22–32; March 6, 1943. Portrait of a minority leader of the Board of Aldermen.

Hermens, F. A., *Democracy or Anarchy? A Study of Proportional Representation.* University of Notre Dame Press, Notre Dame, Ind., 1941. A treatise on proportional representation that draws heavily on the experience of New York's City Council.

Isaacs, Stanley, "Reminiscences." Columbia University Oral History Collection, Special Collections, Butler Library. The minority leader of the City Council tells his story.

Jonas, Harold J., "An Alderman in New York City, 1887–1888, as Seen in His Journal," *New York History*, vol. 29, 1948, pp. 187–202.

Lazarus, Reuben, "The Council: Origin, History, Evolution," address delivered at College of City of New York, November 18, 1941. The head of the Board of Statutory Consolidation traces the development of the Council from colonial days. Typewritten. In Municipal Reference Library.

League of Women Voters of New York, *How Our City Laws Are Made.* The League, New York, 1948. A brief explanation of the operation of the City Council.

McAneny, George, *Papers.* The collected papers of the President of the Board of Aldermen during the Mitchel Administration. At Princeton University.

McGoldrick, Joseph D., "Our City Councils: New York—The Eclipse of the Aldermen," *National Municipal Review*, vol. 14, June, 1925, pp. 360–368. Why the Board of Aldermen was a "fifth wheel" in the municipal government.

McKenzie, Catherine, "A Portrait of the New York Alderman," *The New York Times Magazine*, January 28, 1934.

Morris, Newbold, and Dana Lee Thomas, *Let the Chips Fall.* Appleton-Century-Crofts, New York, 1955, pp. 97–109, 121–131. Reminiscences about life in the old Board of Aldermen and the City Council by a man who started as alderman and later became President of the City Council.

Moses, Robert, *Theory and Practice in Politics.* Harvard University Press, Cambridge, Mass., 1939, pp. 39–40. Robert Moses expresses his disapproval of P.R.

National Municipal League, "New York Elects Democratic Council by District System," *National Municipal Review*, vol. 28, December, 1949, pp. 566–567. The first election for Council after the abolition of P.R., and how that change affected the results.

New York City Council, *Report of the Special Investigating Committee of the Council of the City of New York, Adopted December 23, 1946.* A report, submitted under the chairmanship of Councilman Walter R. Hart, which found evidence of discrimination in graduate and professional education, directed against graduates of the New York City secondary schools.

"The New York City Council—Its Authorization, Operations and Limitations," *St. John's Law Review*, vol. 29, May, 1955, p. 266.

New York Commerce and Industry Association, "Report Concerning Election of the New York City Council by P.R.," 1947. A mimeographed study of five P.R. elections for the City Council, prepared when a referendum on P.R. was before the voting public.

Owen, Russell, " 'S.R.O.' Sign out at City Hall," *The New York Times Magazine*, January 30, 1938. How the City Council proved the "best show in town" during its first years of operation.

Pratt, Ruth, "Men Are Bad Housekeepers," *Harpers Magazine*, vol. 154, May 1927, pp. 682–688. The first woman alderman describes her experiences (and disillusionment) in the city legislature.

Prince, Helen H., *The New York City Council.* Master's thesis, Columbia University, 1940, unpublished.

Pringle, Henry F., "Wet Hope: Profile of Henry Hastings Curran," *The New Yorker*, vol. 6, June 14, 1930, pp. 22–25. Career of a majority leader of the Board of Aldermen.

Raskin, A. H., "Presenting the Phenomenon Called Quill," *The New York Times Magazine*, March 5, 1950. Profile of a labor leader who served as city councilman.

Raskin, Marvin, *New York City Tries P. R.* Master's thesis, New York University, 1938, unpublished. Reflections on the adoption of proportional representation for the City Council.

Robinson, Beverly, "Reminiscences." Columbia University Oral History Collection, Special Collections, Butler Library. Recollections of the Board of Aldermen by a man who served in 1903 and 1904.

Roher, Miriam, "Mrs. Minority," *National Municipal Review*, vol. 29, September, 1940, pp. 585–589, 631. A portrait of Mrs. Genevieve Earle, Minority Leader of the Council.

Ross, Lillian, "$1,031,961,754.63," *The New Yorker*, vol. 22, July 12, 1947, pp. 27–40. An account of the expense budget in the Council.

Rovere, Richard H., "Good Citizen: Profile of Newbold Morris," *The New Yorker*, vol. 20, October 28, 1944, pp. 26–36; November 4, 1944, pp. 28–38. Profile of an alderman who later became President of the first Council.

"The Big Hello: Profile of Peter J. McGuinness," *The New Yorker*, vol. 22, January 12, 1946, pp. 29–38; January 19, 1946, pp. 26–38. One of the colorful characters in the Board of Aldermen.

Schieffelin, William J., "P.R. and New Yorkers," *The Survey*, vol. 26, no. 12, December, 1937, pp. 567–571. Condensed as "P.R. Thwarts Machine Politicians," *Reader's Digest*, vol. 31, September, 1937, pp. 43–46. A favorable view of P.R. in New York City, by a prominent civic figure.

"Reminiscences." Columbia University Oral History Collection, Special Collections, Butler Library. Impressions of how proportional representation worked by a prominent candidate for the City Council.

Schwartz, Asher William, "A Study of the New York City Council," 1940. An analysis of legislation in the Council, prepared for Minority Leader Genevieve Earle. Typewritten copy in Municipal Reference Library.

Shaw, Frederick, "Democrats Poll 51.7% of New York Votes; Seat 92% of Candidates," *National Municipal Review*, vol. 43, March, 1954, pp. 146–147, 155. An analysis of the councilmanic elections of 1949 and 1953 and their results.

History of the New York City Legislature. Columbia University Press, New York, 1954. A study of the Board of Aldermen and City Council.

Sherman, Philemon T., *Inside the Machine: Two Years in the Board of Aldermen, 1898–1899.* Cooke and Fry, New York, 1901. A graphic account of the first Municipal Assembly of the consolidated city.

Stiehl, Laura, *Consideration of the Budget in the New York City Board of Aldermen.* Master's thesis, Columbia University, 1927, unpublished.

Thacher, Thomas D., "Reminiscences." Columbia University Oral History Collection, Special Collections, Butler Library. The Chairman of the Charter Commission which submitted proportional representation to the voters comments on how the proposal found its way to referendum and how it worked out in the City Council.

Woolf, S. J., "Lone Republican Among Our Aldermen," *The New York Times Magazine*, June 25, 1933. The position of the minority leader of the Board of Aldermen, when he was outnumbered 64 to 1.

Zeller, Belle, and Hugh A. Bone, "The Repeal of P.R. in New York City—Ten Years in Retrospect," *American Political Science Review*, vol. 42, December, 1948, pp. 1127–1148. Review of the operation of proportional representation in New York City and reasons for its repeal.

CHAPTER XVII

The Board of Estimate

THE BOARD OF ESTIMATE occupies the center of gravity in the city's political process. Almost all other participants ultimately converge upon the Board because of the inclusiveness of its powers. The other participants may begin their efforts elsewhere—with the party leaders, or the Mayor, or department heads—but because the Board's consent is so often necessary before an action can be taken, most participants eventually must come to the Board. Some contestants prefer to begin with the Board.

The Board also provides, in its biweekly public meetings, the central stage for the city's political contest. On no other occasion can most of the participants be assured of an equally favorable opportunity to speak directly to so important a group of the city's decision-makers: the eight members of the Board (the Mayor, the President of the Council, the Comptroller, the five Borough Presidents) on the dais; the Deputy Mayor, the City Administrator, the Director of the Budget, and usually several department and agency heads in attendance near the dais; numerous interest group leaders on the list of speakers or in the audience; representatives of the press and other communication media present to report the proceedings to a larger public. All these together act as a powerful magnet to bring most of the participants before the Board, to speak directly to its members, to recruit allies, to refute competitors, to demonstrate their alertness and influence, to reach the ears of the general public.

The Board is, however, more than a center of gravity and the provider of a central stage for the city's political contest. The Board of Estimate as an institution is itself also a contestant, perhaps the most powerful single participant, in the city's political process. This power is the result of a number of extraordinary characteristics combining to make the Board a unique political and governmental institution. It has the most generous grant of formal powers of all the city's governmental institutions; its eight members are the most influential elected officials in the city government; it has developed a mode of operation which maximizes both its formal and informal powers; the relationships of its members with the party leaders are close and usually stable; it has high prestige with the other participants, particularly with those to whom it provides a public forum; and its institutional life, especially its informal processes, is surrounded by a helpful amount of mystery.

The story of the Board of Estimate is the history of an institution steadily acquiring more formal power, regularly enhancing its informal powers, increasingly fulfilling its own expectations as an institution. This institutional success has been achieved most clearly at the expense of the Board of Aldermen and its successor, the Council—but also at the cost of the Mayor.

THE BOARD'S ASSETS: FORMAL AND INFORMAL

The Board's Formal Powers

The Board of Estimate is endowed by the charter with broad powers, crucial to the city's political contest. These powers are in four categories: (1) those shared with the Council; (2) those exercised without Council participation; (3) the Board's "residual" powers; (4) Board powers subject to the Mayor's veto and those not subject to veto.

Powers Shared with the Council. The Council has "the sole power to adopt local laws . . . without requiring the concurrence of any other body or officer" except that the Mayor's veto requires a two-thirds vote of all councilmen to override, certain local laws must be submitted to referendum, and the Board of Estimate must concur in specified instances. These instances are described by the charter as follows: "A local law amending and repealing any provision of this charter, or transferring or changing the powers and duties of, or conferring powers or duties upon, or prescribing the qualifications, number, mode of selection or removal, terms of office or compensation of officers or employees of the city or of any agency, or reducing or repealing taxes, fees or charges receivable by the city or interest or penalties thereon, shall not become effective unless approved by the board of estimate." It has been difficult for the Council to discover local laws which do not come within this requirement. The Council consequently has no important power in adopting local laws which the Board does not share on equal terms; the Board is, in effect, the upper chamber in a bicameral city legislature.

The Board also shares with the Council its powers in the enactment of the expense budget, but on terms advantageous to the Board. For, while the Board may make any changes it wishes in the Mayor's executive budget, the Council in considering the budget as adopted by the Board of Estimate may only "reduce or omit any item in the budget . . . but it may not add or increase any item or vary the titles, description, terms or conditions of administration specified therein." Since the Mayor may veto any Council change in the budget, and a three-fourths vote of all councilmen is necessary to override the veto, the Board of Estimate may accurately regard the Council's share in the expense budget process as merely formal and symbolic, subtracting nothing of importance from the Board's monopolistic position.

In the enactment of the capital budget, the Board also must share formal power with the Council which may, in considering the capital budget adopted by the Board, "strike out in its entirety any authorization . . . but may not add to or increase or vary the terms or conditions of any authorization. . . ." If during the year the Board adds projects to, or increases the authorization for a project in, the capital budget, the Council's consent is required. The Council has found no way to use either of these powers as a device for sharing with the Board in the capital budget process.

In these three fields of formal powers—the enactment of local laws, the expense budget, the capital budget—the Board of Estimate has the dominant role. In the adoption of local laws the Board has an equal voice with the Council in all legislation of any importance; and the Board's greater institutional and political powers mean that, while the Board may usually influence the Council, the Council can rarely influence the Board. In both the expense budget and capital budget processes, the Board has the dominating role, the Council a minimal one.

Nor does the Board share these powers with the other participants in the city's political contest. The Mayor, the department and agency heads, and the City Planning Commission (in the capital budget process only) have their various roles, but it is the Board of Estimate which has the central role in each of these three processes.

Board Powers Not Shared with the Council. The Board of Estimate would be a powerful political and governmental institution if it had only the three preceding sets of powers which it shares with the Council on terms so favorable to itself. But the Board has many other powers which it does not share with the Council at all; it is these additional, unshared powers of the Board which make it the paramount city institution.

The additional powers may be discussed in the following five subcategories: (a) financial controls, (b) control of city property, (c) control of franchises, (d) control of city personnel, and (e) control of city planning and zoning. Many of these powers once belonged to, or were shared by, the Council's predecessor institution, the Board of Aldermen, but each of them has now belonged to the Board of Estimate for more than twenty years.

Financial Controls. The Board's preeminent position in the two budget processes and in local laws dealing with finance is supplemented by other powers in financial matters over which the Board has exclusive power, or has power shared only with the Comptroller, or, more rarely, with the Mayor. (The Comptroller and the Mayor always have their four votes each as members of the 22-vote Board; the reference here is to their separate powers in their own respective offices.) The most extensive and important of these financial powers is the authority of the Board to alter the expense budget during the fiscal year by transferring moneys from one major appropriation to another, and to authorize the Director of the Budget, subject to the Board's approval and upon an agency head's request, to transfer funds from one budget line to another. These powers are so frequently and extensively exercised that the Board substantially remakes the budget during the year. The Mayor introduces the budget and the Council ratifies it after the Board is finished with its initial transformation of the Mayor's budget, but thereafter the Board (aided by its trusted agent, the Budget Director) is undisputed master of the expense budget's many changes during the fiscal year.

The Board has other significant financial powers: it has the power and duty "to fix the salary of every officer or person whose compensation is paid from the city treasury" except as otherwise provided by law; to approve the rates to be charged for water, wharfage, parking, lease of city property; to regulate the letting of contracts, to set standard specifications for city purchases, and to regulate the disposal of surplus property and materials. Nor are these all: the Board of Estimate supervises the "assessable improvements" system of the city, the Board's Chief Engineer approving those costing less than $10,000, the Board itself acting upon all other proposals of Local Improvement Boards in each Borough or taking the initiative itself.

The cumulative fiscal controls of the Board of Estimate are so inclusive and so central that the Board in this field of the political contest overshadows both the Council and the Mayor; only the Comptroller could give the Board significant competition in financial matters, and he is usually a member of the Board's "inner circle."

Control of City Property. "No real property and no interest thereon may be acquired by the city," declares the charter, "and no real property of the city may be sold, leased, exchanged or otherwise disposed of except with the approval of the board of estimate and as may be provided by law unless such power is expressly vested by law in another agency." In addition to this control over the acquisition and disposal of city property, the Board has control over the use of city property, having the power with the Mayor's approval "to assign to use for any public purposes any city property, for whatsoever purpose originally acquired, which it may find to be no longer required for such purpose and may assign space in any city building to any agency."

Control of Franchises. The power to grant franchises once belonged to the Board of Aldermen, but in 1905 it was transferred to the then existing Board of Estimate and Apportionment. The charter now provides that: "The board of estimate shall have the control of the streets of the city, except as in this charter otherwise provided, and shall have the exclusive power in behalf of the city to grant franchises or rights or make contracts providing for or involving the occupation or use of any of the streets of the city, whether on, under or over the surface thereof, for railroads, pipe or other conduits or ways or otherwise for the transportation of persons or property or the transmission of gas, electricity, steam, light, heat or power, or the installation of transformer vaults, and to give the consent of the city to any franchise or right of any kind or nature whatsoever for or relating to the occupation or use of the streets of the city under the provisions of the constitution or of any statute."

To this control over franchises by the Board is added its control over "revocable consents." The charter provides that: "Consent to construct and use for private use pipes, conduits and tunnels under, railroad tracks upon, and connecting bridges over any of the streets of the city shall be by resolution of the board of estimate . . . revocable at any time by resolution of the board of estimate. . . ."

The resolutions of the Board with respect both to franchises and to revocable consents require "the separate and additional approval" of the Mayor, a provision which gives the Mayor one of his rare veto opportunities in dealing with the Board—and this particular veto is of course an absolute veto.

Control of City Personnel. The Board of Estimate, in addition to the control over compensation noted above under the Board's financial controls, has other personnel controls. "The board of estimate may at any time," says the charter, "subject to the provisions of this charter and of the civil service law and except as otherwise provided by statute, create, abolish or modify positions and grades of persons paid from the city treasury." In 1954 a new and ambiguous provision was added to the charter, giving to the newly established Director of Personnel the power "to develop salary and wage plans and standard rules governing working conditions, vacations and leaves in agencies of the city for submission to the mayor, the board of estimate, the civil service commission, the city administrator and the budget director." The Personnel Director and the Budget Director have since acted upon the assumption that this new section, when read in the context of other Board powers, requires the approval of the Board of Estimate for all such plans and rules. The Board also has another personnel power of great importance; it is "the head of the New York City employees' retirement system" and in this capacity, subject to other provisions of law, has the power to "establish rules and regulations for the administration and transaction of the business of the system and for the control of its funds."

These personnel powers of the Board are not so inclusive as the powers it wields in finance, in property, or in franchises—largely because the state Civil Service Law controls so much of personnel management—but the Board's personnel powers nevertheless exceed those of the Mayor, and, of course, greatly overshadow those of the Council.

Control Over City Planning and Zoning. From 1916 to 1938, the Board of Estimate and Apportionment exercised the powers of zoning and other planning functions, still earlier a prerogative of the Board of Aldermen. The establishment of the City Planning Commission in 1938 reduced the powers of the Board of Estimate in zoning and planning by requiring the Board to act by a three-fourths vote in setting aside any provision of the master plan or of the zoning regulations adopted by the Planning Commission. The Board has not lost its commanding position, however, the Planning Commission having as yet failed to develop either a comprehensive master plan or a comprehensive new zoning ordinance.

These five types of powers exercised by the Board of Estimate without participation by the Council—financial, property, franchise, personnel, planning—make the Board the central institution in the city's political contest, especially when they are combined with the powers which the Board shares with the Council, on the favorable terms which the Board enjoys through its influence over the Council. But the Board has still other powers and advantages in its relationship to other participants in the political contest.

The Board's "Residual" Powers. The charter declares: "The board of estimate, subject to this charter, shall exercise all the powers vested in the city except as otherwise provided by law." The Board is thus heir to all the powers vested generally in the city unless the power is clearly lodged by law in some other agency. In all cases of ambiguity, the Board has the strongest claim to jurisdiction, a claim which before 1938 could be asserted by the Board of Aldermen. The clause has not seen much formal use, but its psychological uses are considerable and its very ambiguity serves to expand the Board's strategic opportunities.

The Board and the Mayor's Veto. Most of the powers exercised by the Board of Estimate are beyond the reach of the Mayor's veto powers. He may veto local laws after their passage by the Council and by the Board. If he does veto such a local law, only the Council, by a two-thirds vote of all councilmen, may override it (the Board having no further part in the proceedings). The Mayor also has an absolute veto over two types of resolutions by the Board: those dealing with franchises and revocable consents and those assigning city property to a new use.

In all its other powers, the Board is confronted by no threat of a veto. The Mayor may cast his four votes on a resolution, but he may not exercise the usual prerogative of a chief executive by entering a veto. The Board having acted, the Mayor's signature is not needed. Considering the range of these Board powers exempt from chief executive veto, the advantage to the Board is substantial.

The formal powers of the Board of Estimate—those shared with the Council plus those exercised independently of the Council, plus the Board's residual powers, plus its freedom in most areas from the Mayor's veto—make the Board a formidable institution. In the distribution of the stakes of the city's politics, the Board has only one close competitor for preeminence—the mayoralty—and in this competition the Board has important resources in addition to its great array of formal powers.

The Board's Membership

One of the Board's greatest assets is the nature of its membership. Its eight members, the most prominent elected officials in the city, are each elected to, and held primarily responsible for their performance in, another office. That is, all membership in the Board of Estimate is *ex officio;* no one is elected directly to the Board. Each member thus brings to the Board not merely his allotted number of votes (four each for the Mayor, the Comptroller, the President of the Council; two each for the five Borough Presidents), but also the power, the facilities, and the prestige of his own separate office.

The member's role in his own office is the one he emphasizes to his electoral constituency; his role in the Board is largely reserved for the low-visibility bargaining which the Board's procedures enhance. The Board as a formal institution is highly visible, especially in its biweekly public meetings, but its decision-making process is one of quite low visibility. Its members thus enjoy the exercise of power in its proceedings without the penalties of individual responsibility; for all the members except the Mayor, who cannot ordinarily obscure the nature of his role in the Board, this opportunity to exercise power without the costs of direct responsibility is a cherished asset.

The Mayor. As chairman of the Board (when he personally attends) and as the official upon whom the widest public expectations are focused, the Mayor is the most visible and prominent member of the Board, but he is rarely its master. The great political and governmental powers of the mayoralty (to be discussed in the following chapter) represent the major institutional rival of the Board in the city's political contest, but as a member of the Board the Mayor is operating on his rival's home ground, mainly under rules and customs devised by the Board itself. The Mayor, by his very membership and by his participation in the Board's executive session deliberations, is inhibited in his other strategies, for he is thus ordinarily shorn of his capacity as elected chief executive to appeal from the Board to his own broader constituency. The Mayor's membership on the Board is an asset to the Board, a liability to the Mayor.

The President of the Council. This office, like that of Vice-President of the United States and of Lieutenant Governor in the state, is one of ambiguity and inhibited anticipation. In itself, the office is the purely formal one of presiding officer over an institution of secondary importance; it acquires its major importance from its incumbent's four votes on the Board of Estimate, but this role has its dilemmas; the real importance of the office lies in the chance that the President of the Council may become the Mayor by succession or election. This chance became reality for Mitchel and Impellitteri; McClellan, La Guardia, Morris, and Halley all held the office before their nominations for Mayor.

As a member of the Board, the President of the Council brings to its bargaining processes the fewest assets of any of the members. His staff is small, far from matching the staffs which bring to other members the information and advice that equip them with bargaining power; his opportunities to appeal to a broad and distinctive constituency of his own are limited; his efforts to carve out a function for himself invariably tread upon the jurisdictional toes of powerful rivals. To exercise influence beyond the weight of his four votes—indeed to give them any significance—the President of the Council is faced with a perennial dilemma: whether to join his fortunes with the Mayor, or to move toward the orbit of the Comptroller and the Borough Presidents. Each alliance has its risks for an official who has few resources for defense against others.

The Comptroller. This official is the potential giant of the Board. His formal powers in his own office do not match the Mayor's, but they are solid powers of great importance and they fit comfortably into the powers of the Board as an institution. As a member of the Board, the Comptroller's substantial official powers serve as a magnet to draw around him the rivalries toward the Mayor felt by the other members, and thus to make the Comptroller the focus and the guardian of the Board as an institutional rival to the Mayor. In the degree to which the Board of Estimate is comparable to the United States Senate as a "citadel" or "club," the Comptroller is the central member of the "club."

The Comptroller, not the Mayor, is the city's chief financial officer. He combines in his fiscal powers most of those exercised at the national level by the Secretary of the Treasury, the Comptroller General, the Council of Economic Advisers, and some others. His advice is directed, not to the Mayor, toward whom he has no charter responsibilities, but to the Board of Estimate primarily, to other agencies in some instances, and often to the Comptroller's own public constituency. A brief recital of his powers demonstrates their substance and their scope.

The Comptroller is authorized by the charter to "advise the board of estimate on the financial conditions of the city or any phase thereof and make such recommendations, comments and criticisms in regard to the operations, fiscal policies and financial transactions of the city as he may deem advisable in the public interest"; "to investigate all matters relating to or affecting the finances of the city" with the power of subpoena and taking testimony under oath; the "power and . . . duty to audit all vouchers before payment and prepare warrants, to audit all official accounts and to audit annually the accrual and collection of all revenues and receipts and to prescribe methods of recording, reporting and accounting in the several agencies"; "to settle and adjust all claims in favor of or against the city"; "administer and manage the several sinking funds of the city and all other trust funds held by the city";

TABLE 65. PERSONNEL OF THE NEW YORK C

Year	Mayor	Comptroller	President, Board of Aldermen after 1937, City Council
1902	Seth Low	E.M. Grout	C.V. Fornes
1903	"	*	"
1904	G.B. McClellan	"	"
1905	"	"	"
1906	*	Herman Metz	Patrick McGowan
1907	"	"	"
1908	"	"	"
1909	"	"	"
1910	W.J. Gaynor	W.A. Prendergast	J.P. Mitchel
1911	"	"	"
1912	"	"	"
1913	"	"	"
1914	J.P. Mitchel	*	George McAneny
1915	"	"	"
1916	"	"	F.L. Dowling
1917	"	"	A.E. Smith
1918	J.F. Hylan	C.L. Craig	R.L. Moran
1919	"	"	F.H. LaGuardia
1920	"	"	"
1921	"	"	Murray Hulbert
1922	*	*	"
1923	"	"	"
1924	"	"	W.T. Collins
1925	"	"	J.V. McKee
1926	J.J. Walker	C.W. Berry	"
1927	"	"	"
1928	"	"	"
1929	*	*	*
1930	"	"	"
1931	"	"	"
1932	"	"	"
1933	J.P. O'Brien	George McAneny	
1934	F.H. LaGuardia	Arthur Cunningham	B.S. Deutsch
1935	"	J.D. McGoldrick	"
1936	"	F.J. Taylor	T.J. Sullivan
1937	"	"	W.F. Brunner
1938	*	J.D. McGoldrick	Newbold Morris
1939	"	"	"
1940	"	"	"
1941	*	*	*
1942	"	"	"
1943	"	"	"
1944	"	"	"
1945	"	"	"
1946	William O'Dwyer	Lazarus Joseph	V.R. Impellitteri
1947	"	"	"
1948	*	*	*
1949	"	"	J.T. Sharkey
1950	V.R. Impellitteri	"	Rudolph Halley
1951	"	"	"
1952	"	"	"
1953	"	"	Abe Stark
1954	R.F. Wagner	L.E. Gerosa	"
1955	"	"	"
1956	"	"	"
1957	*	*	*
1958	"	"	"
1959			

* Reelected.

Manhattan	Brooklyn	Bronx	Queens	Richmond	Year
		Borough Presidents			
A. Cantor	J.E. Swanstrom	L.F. Haffen	Frank Bowley	George Cromwell	1902
"	"	"	"	"	1903
F. Ahearn	M.W. Littleton	*	Joseph Cassidy	*	1904
"	"	"	"	"	1905
"	B.S. Coler	*	Joseph Bermel	*	1906
"	"	"	"	"	1907
"	"	"	"	"	1908
George McAneny	Alfred Steers	C.E. Miller	Lawrence Gresser	"	1909
"	"	"	"	*	1910
"	"	"	"	"	1911
"	"	"	M.E. Connolly	"	1912
"	"	"	"	"	1913
Marcus Marks	Lewis Pounds	Douglas Mathewson	*	Calvin VanName	1914
"	"	"	"	C.L. McCormack	1915
"	"	"	"	"	1916
L. Dowling	Edward Riegelman	Henry Bruckner	*	*	1917
"	"	"	"	"	1918
H. Curran	"	"	"	"	1919
"	"	"	"	"	1920
Julius Miller	*	*	*	"	1921
"	"	"	"	M.J. Cahill	1922
"	"	"	"	J.A. Lynch	1923
"	Joseph Guider	"	"	"	1924
*	*	*	*	"	1925
"	J.J. Byrne	"	"	*	1926
"	"	"	"	"	1927
*	"	"	B.M. Patten	"	1928
	Henry Hesterberg	*	G.U. Harvey	"	1929
Samuel Levy	*	"	*	*	1930
*	"	"	"	"	1931
"	"	"	"	"	1932
*	Peter Corey	James J. Lyons	*	J.A. Palma	1933
	Raymond Ingersoll				1934
"	"	"	"	"	1935
"	"	"	"	"	1936
Stanley Isaacs	*	*	*	*	1937
"	"	"	"	"	1938
"	John Cashmore	"	"	"	1939
"	"	"	"	"	1940
J Nathan	*	*	J.A. Burke	*	1941
"	"	"	"	"	1942
"	"	"	"	"	1943
"	"	"	"	"	1944
E. Rogers	*	*	*	C.A. Hall	1945
"	"	"	"	"	1946
"	"	"	"	"	1947
"	"	"	"	"	1948
F. Wagner	*	*	M.H. Fitzgerald	*	1949
"	"	"	"	"	1950
"	"	"	J.A. Lundy	"	1951
"	"	"	"	"	1952
Alan Jack	*	*	*	E.G. Baker	1953
"	"	"	"	A.V. Maniscalco	1954
"	"	"	"	"	1955
"	"	"	"	"	1956
*	*	*	F.J. Crisona	*	1957
"	"	"	J.T. Clancy	"	1958
					1959

SOURCES: McGoldrick, J. D.; "The Board of Estimate and Apportionment of New York City," *National Municipal Review*, Supplement, vol. 18, no. 2 (reprinted and revised May, 1932), p. 5; *Official Directory of the City of New York*, 1933–1959.

"keep the accounts of the city"; publish annually "a full and detailed statement of the receipts and expenditures of the city and the cash balance or surplus at the end of the year, the different sources of city revenue and the amount received from each, the several appropriations made, the objects for which they were made and the amounts of moneys expended under each, the money borrowed on the credit of the city, the amount of each loan, the authority under which it was made and the terms on which it was obtained." These are substantial powers of financial administration in any government, but the Comptroller's powers do not end here.

Four times during each year the Comptroller has an opportunity to issue formal statements of great public and political importance—one designed to influence the size and nature of the expense budget, one to influence the tax rate on real property, one to influence the city's debt policy, and a fourth to influence the size and content of the capital budget. These messages are issued, with ceremony and emphasis, from the Comptroller's office on the fifth floor of the Municipal Building, after careful attention not only to the requirements of the charter and the city's finances but also to the political role of the Comptroller in the city government. These reports of the Comptroller provide varying strategic and tactical opportunities—sometimes to lecture the Mayor, often to woo the banking and real estate constituencies of the Comptroller, usually to pose before the communication media as financial statesman.

The first of these messages flows from the charter requirement that "not later than the fifteenth day of February in each year, the comptroller shall submit to the board of estimate . . . a certified statement . . . which shall contain," among other things, an estimate of receipts for the coming fiscal year from all sources except real estate taxes, a statement of tax collections and the tax deficiency account, the condition of the several city funds and the requirements of debt service. This statement sets the stage for the Budget Director and the Mayor in their preparation of the executive budget. The Comptroller may be pessimistic or optimistic, according to his mood, or strategy, or judgment; his predictions control the range of discretion for all the decision-makers in the budget process.

The second message comes from the charter provision that "the comptroller shall prepare and submit to the council, between the fifteenth and twentieth days of June, a statement setting forth the amount of the budget as fixed for the ensuing fiscal year and also an estimate of the probable amount of receipts into the city treasury . . . from all the sources of revenue of the general fund." These two figures (and the Comptroller has great discretion in estimating the second) control the Council, when the total assessment of real property is reported by the President of the Tax Commission, in fixing the real estate tax rate. The Comptroller may, when he wishes, anticipate the

June date of the charter by issuing his first estimates as early as mid-April, as he did in 1957 with the good news of a tax reduction which the Mayor no doubt would himself have enjoyed announcing.

The Comptroller's third opportunity arises out of the charter's injunction that "not later than the fifteenth day of August in each year, the comptroller shall submit . . . a report . . . setting forth the amount and nature of all obligations authorized on account of each pending capital project, the liabilities incurred for each project outstanding on the first day of July and setting forth and commenting in detail upon the city's financial condition and advising as to the maximum amount and nature of debt which in his opinion the city may soundly incur for capital projects. . . ." The Comptroller usually chooses to play a jeremiad role on this occasion, lecturing all upon the virtues of economy, reassuring the banking, lending, and tax-paying constituencies with his doctrines of economy and stability. The size of the capital budget is largely determined by the Comptroller's optimistic or pessimistic mood in this message.

The fourth message rests upon the charter requirement that "not later than the fifteenth day of November, the comptroller shall submit to the board of estimate . . . a report . . . containing such comments and recommendations with respect to the proposed capital budget and program as he may deem advisable." The Comptroller usually deems it advisable to urge economy, to select priorities suited to his own preferences, and to emphasize his alertness and that of his office to the austere requirements of sound city finances. The Board of Estimate's choices among capital projects is greatly influenced by the Comptroller's mood and preferences in this message.

No other city official has such timely and carefully staged opportunities to influence fiscal policy as these four messages provide to the Comptroller. But the Comptroller has still other assets as a participant in the Board of Estimate.

He may authorize the expenditure of moneys from the capital accrual and the real property funds, has custody of the securities in the four sinking funds of the city and determines the investment of their moneys, approves payments to Borough Presidents for their expenses in assessable improvements, settles claims for assessments, inspects and accepts or rejects all deliveries of supplies, materials, or equipment for the city, with the Mayor and Treasurer (by majority vote) selects the banks or trust companies in which all moneys of the city are to be deposited and fixes the rate of interest these institutions must agree to pay in order to qualify as depositaries, and supervises the collection of the excise taxes of the city.

The Comptroller brings to the Board the power and prestige of the city's chief financial officer and of an official elected by a citywide electoral constituency. He can also, and usually does, draw to his support the real estate and banking groups of the city. All these assets make him an object of constant public attention, exceeded only by the attention-drawing capacities of the Mayor and matched only by those of Commissioner Moses and the Police Commissioner. His formal powers and his public status combine to make him the pivot of the Board of Estimate, especially in that institution's rivalry with the Mayor. The upper limits of his opportunities are also clear. No comptroller has ever been nominated for the mayoralty nor has any ever held a higher elective office afterward.

The Borough Presidents. These offices were once, a half century or less ago, important administrative establishments. Successive charter amendments and revisions have transferred one after another of their former functions to centralized city departments under the Mayor. The Borough Presidents now are primarily significant as members of the Board of Estimate rather than as heads of administrative activities at the five Borough Halls.

The Borough Presidents retain some important administrative functions, primarily relating to the building and maintenance of the boroughs' local streets, roads, bridges, and tunnels, regulating certain uses of the streets, and control of borough sewers and drainage systems. That is, each Borough President heads his borough's public works activities; but these are steadily reduced in significance as borough streets become arterial highways, as the bridges and tunnels are made parts of larger systems, and other agencies (for example, the public authorities) build parkways and expressways across their boroughs. The Borough Presidents would be minor officials if they were no more than the heads of their respective administrative domains.

It is in the Board of Estimate as representatives of the boroughs (coterminous with the counties, around which the political parties shape their organizations), that the Borough Presidents achieve their importance as officials. Each speaks for his borough, and behind him perceptive observers (other members of the Board, especially) can usually see the strength of his County Leader, or at least a group of Assembly District Leaders, as well as a borough constituency of uncertain but tangible dimensions.

The Borough Presidents bring to the Board neither the impressive formal powers of the Mayor or of the Comptroller, nor the ambiguous potential of the President of the Council; instead, each Borough President brings to the Board a consciousness that he represents a county party organization with which (unless he is a Fusion official) he ordinarily has close ties, and that he has the formal capacity to claim that he speaks, as no other member of the Board can, for the special interests of his borough. These are claims difficult to dispute, risky to ignore. Moreover, the Borough Presidents sense their common cause as a group in the Board, maintain together a practice of "borough courtesy" which they often succeed in persuading the citywide members to observe, while in addition they seek to join with the Comptroller in a bargaining alliance which can guide the Board in the majority of its decisions. These tendencies are less pronounced, less regular in pattern, but present neverthe-less, in a Fusion administration because the relationship between Borough Presidents and County Leaders is then less stable or even nonexistent.

Six of the eight members of the Board add important assets to the Board as a political and governmental institution. The Comptroller and the Bor-ough Presidents find that strengthening the Board is also a way of strengthen-ing their own offices. The Mayor, on the other hand, contributes to the Board's strength mainly by subtracting or surrendering some of the separate assets of the mayoralty. The President of the Council, with four votes as his only lever, is most often neither an asset nor a liability to the Board.

The Board thus adds to its impressive formal powers the great strength of its members individually and collectively, and to these two assets it also adds a third: the aptness of its procedures to the conservation and enhancement of its influence as a participant in the city's political contest.

The Board's Procedures

The charter imposes only a few simple procedural restrictions upon the Board of Estimate. There are several requirements for a two-thirds or three-fourths majority and a few requiring unanimous action, but most acts may be "by resolution adopted by a majority of the whole number of votes authorized to be cast by all the members of the board"; that is, by 12 votes out of 22. The charter further provides that "no resolution or amendment of any resolution shall be passed at the same meeting at which it is originally pre-sented unless by a three-fourths vote or shall be finally passed except at a meeting open to the public." A quorum of the Board is defined by the charter as "a sufficient number of members thereof to cast 12 votes, includ-ing at least two of the members authorized to cast four votes each." The first meeting of the Board each year is called by notice from the Mayor; thereafter, the Board itself determines its own schedule. The Mayor, or in his absence the President of the Council, presides at all meetings. The Board must keep a journal of each meeting, which is a public record, and a full stenographic record of all public meetings must be kept on file also as a public record, a transcript being available to "any taxpayer" on payment of "reasonable fees." Except for these charter requirements, the Board "may adopt rules for the conduct of its proceedings not inconsistent with the pro-visions of law, and such rules shall not be suspended at any meeting except by affirmative vote of two-thirds of the votes which all members present are entitled to cast."

Committees of the Board. The Board of Estimate chooses not to make much use of committees. In its earlier history, the Board had almost a score of standing committees and many special committees in addition, but these were gradually abandoned in the 1920's. Today only two standing committees remain: the Committee of the Whole, and the Committee on the Acquisition and Disposition of City Property (composed of the Mayor, the Comptroller, and the President of the Council). The use of special committees has almost disappeared.

Although any such small body would find limited use for committees, the Board also finds little use for committees because it wishes to avoid any public revelation of division within its membership. Committee action, with its prospects of majority and minority reports, and the further possibilities of Board rejection or division, would cut across the strong institutional drive of the Board to achieve unanimity in all its public proceedings.

Bureaus of the Board. The Board of Estimate has found a substitute for committees in its staff bureaus. Of these there are four: the Bureau of the Secretary, the Bureau of Franchises, the Bureau of Engineering, and the Bureau of Retirement and Pensions. The Board also tends to regard the Bureau of the Budget, the City Planning Commission, and, to a growing extent, the Department of Personnel, as staff agencies of the Board. To these seven bureaus (especially to its own four and to the Bureau of the Budget) the Board refers the great bulk of those matters which it once referred to committees of its own members.

This use of well-staffed bureaus has many advantages for the Board as an institution. It provides the Board with expert information and advice; it helps to make the workload of the Board manageable; it gives the members of the Board the time, and perhaps even the alternatives, for the bargaining which is the Board's essential *modus vivendi*. Even more important to the Board is the fact that the bureaus in their work and their reports do not threaten the collective unity of the Board in its public decisions. The members need not commit themselves prematurely; when the bureaus do report, the Board still has time, if more time be needed, to bargain out a formula for unanimity.

No Public Debate. The Board of Estimate is further aided in its search for a public show of unanimity by its tradition of listening to others in its public meetings but avoiding debate among its own membership. In its biweekly public meetings the eight members of the Board sit *en bloc* on a raised dais, facing their audience and the speakers who wish to address them. The Board's public proceedings thus resemble in part the public hearing of a legislative committee—but without some of the substantial characteristics of such a hearing (for example, the purposeful interrogation of witnesses, the analytical development of issues and alternatives). The members of the Board may listen without comment, they may encourage or heckle the speakers, they may twit or praise each other, or they may make relevant or irrelevant declarations from time to time.

Whatever the variations in member behavior, no systematic presentation, defense, or criticism of proposed public policy emerges from participation in the discussion by the members of the Board themselves. The accepted fine art of Board behavior is to listen, to question, to display knowledge and alertness—but to avoid commitment either in sustained debate or in explicit declaration of policy.

This protocol of Board behavior is not infrequently breached by intransigent members only partially committed to the Board's values and traditions of sacrificing public debate to private bargaining, but these occasions produce bickering rather than a structured discussion of the issues. The procedures of the Board are not designed, and in fact make it almost impossible, for the members to oppose each other in the form of legislative debate: the calendar is long, the speakers' list is often extensive, the expectations of the audience are for a public hearing, not a Board debate—and the Board would not wish any of these arrangements to be otherwise.

Uses of Postponement. If the Board of Estimate is not a publicly deliberative body, it is nevertheless a deliberate one. It does not engage in a final public vote until all the avenues to unanimity have been patiently explored. On most matters its rules ensure against precipitate tests of Board unity; an item on first appearance is typically referred to a bureau of the Board or to the Budget Director. (It is a matter of some significance that the greatest number of referrals from, and reports to, the Board involve the Budget Director.) If an item returns to the calendar before agreement has been worked out within the Board, or if unanticipated public opposition appears, the offending item may be laid over until a later meeting, and this process may be repeated, if necessary, until the effort to find a formula, or an occasion, for unanimity has been successful.

Postponement does not often embarrass the Board. Its calendar contains so many items that to "lay over" or "refer" one fourth to one half of the items is a practice taken for granted by all participants and observers. Subterfuge is not involved; the postponed item must eventually come back to the public calendar or die in the files. No habit of the Board is so deeply imbedded, and so rarely challenged, as is its practice of delay.

Ad Hoc Decisions; Minimum Delegation. The Board of Estimate uses legislation sparingly; in fact, it ordinarily succumbs to the enactment of general rules, under which others may exercise discretion, only when local laws are before it. In the exercise of all its own powers, the Board makes no general rules, delegates no final authority, but instead requires each successive instance to come before it for Board action. When it does vary from this code of behavior, an infrequent aberration, it is more likely to do so for the Comptroller or the Budget Director than for the Mayor or any of his agencies.

The Board thus conserves its powers as an institution, and as a participant in the city's political contest, by requiring that every separate decision within the reach of its broad jurisdiction shall come before it for final action. This practice confronts the Board at each meeting with a calendar of from 200 to 600 separate items, totaling during the year as many as 15,000 calendar items, of which perhaps half are nonduplicating. Nor is this a new phenomenon; in 1928, the Board disposed of 12,000 items.

The Board reveals no disposition to change this practice of avoiding delegation to others under legislation or general rules enacted by the Board. To modify this pattern would reduce the political and governmental powers of the Board, while increasing those of the Mayor and of the agencies more responsive to his direction. If it is to hold and enhance its role as a participant in the city's political contest, the Board as an institution must retain its detailed, specific decision-making opportunities even though these practices carry the Board deep into the territory usually regarded as the prerogative of the chief executive and the administrative agencies under his supervision.

Executive Sessions of the Board. The key to the Board's procedural system are its "executive sessions," formally the meeting of its committee of the whole, to which a day or more is devoted by the Board shortly preceding the day of its public meeting. The sparse use of committees, the use of bureaus as substitutes for committees, the tactics of postponement, and the avoidance of general legislation—all these depend for their effectiveness upon their culmination in the executive session, where the Board finds the optimum conditions for its special role in the city's political contest.

The executive session of the Board meets to consider a calendar of items virtually identical with those which will concern it a day or two later in its public session. But now the Board meets behind closed doors, in the presence of its own members, their selected assistants, and such other public officials as may have been invited by the Board. There is no record of proceedings; all is informal and confidential. The Board's bureau chiefs and the ubiquitous Budget Director do most of the briefing of Board members on particular items. The members of the Board then disclose their initial sentiments. On many familiar items there is a quick establishment of unanimity, frequently aided by the bureaus' capacity to anticipate the formula which will unify the Board. When agreement proves difficult, the Board will usually clear the room of all nonmembers and then proceed to a bargained adjustment of their differences or to an agreement to delay. When the day's executive session is concluded, the Board knows which items will be on its public calendar for action that week and which will be held back for further negotiation; it knows which items will be unanimously enacted, or the extent and nature of any unavoidable dissent by members in public; it knows which items on the public calendar will be "laid over" for a future public meeting, and which items will be referred to whom for "further study."

The blueprint of Board behavior at the next public meeting is thus laid out in detail, and it is understood that each Board member is by his participation in the executive session now fully committed to its agreements. Only the rare event of a strong, unanticipated public reaction at the public meeting, or in the communication media, will upset the Board's predetermined course of action—and for that eventuality, the Board also has a settled formula: the item will be laid over. Another executive session of the Board will subsequently dispose of it in terms suited to the Board's carefully considered reappraisal of the bargain earlier arrived at.

It is in its executive sessions that the Board reaches the peak of its strength and genius as a political and governmental institution. It is here that the Board's influence as a participant in the city's political contest is at its highest. For it is in these executive sessions of the Board that the Mayor, with his great separate powers and high public status, is disarmed and humbled and made a prisoner of the Board's cult of unanimity. It is in these executive sessions, too, that the Budget Director is most fully absorbed into the Board's orbit of influence, the City Planning Commission brought to terms preferred by the Board, and other overhead and line agencies made to feel the benefits of alliance with the Board or the penalties of divergence.

The executive session of the Board is in essence a caucus. Those who attend are committed to its private bargaining processes. They are committed also to abide by its decisions except where the members as a matter of grace concede to a particular member his special necessities to record a public dissent, but such a privilege must not be too often claimed, nor can it be exercised in a way to disclose the secrets of the caucus. Those who would like to stay away, and thus remain uncommitted, are faced with the price of being uninformed, of being outside the bargaining process, of being subject in many ways to the sanctions and displeasure of the Board. The consequence has been that, with rare exceptions, all members attend the caucus, accept its rules with only infrequent displays of insurgency, and subscribe increasingly to the caucus objective of private bargaining followed by public unanimity. While the caucus system has its difficulties and variations under a Fusion Board, the net result is less than drastic in its difference.

The Cult of Unanimity. The Board of Estimate as an institution of power and influence in the city's political contest would be most vulnerable in its public meetings if those who guide its destinies had not long been at special pains to maintain the unity of the Board when it meets in public. Its standing and special committees were long ago absorbed into its caucus system, its bureaus have been developed as an aid to unanimity, public debate has been avoided, and the executive session has been refined into an institutional guarantee of public unity. The public meeting of the Board now convenes to confirm, and to give legitimate effect to, the decisions earlier made in full detail in the executive session.

The outcome is an institutional miracle. Some public meetings of the Board, with more than 300 separate items (often with more than 500), will record not a single dissenting or abstaining vote. Others will reveal a single item on which a dissent is registered, while dissent on as many as five items is extraordinary. In 12 meetings selected at random during 1955, with calendar items for the 12 meetings amounting to 4,958, only 11 "split votes" were recorded—3,141 being unanimous, the remainder "laid over," referred, or filed. Even when the "routine" nature of many items (themselves an index of detailed Board control) and the disposition of small, intimate bodies to be unanimous in public votes are both taken into account, the Board's unanimity is impressive and unusual. The temptations of the members to use the powers and opportunities of their separate offices, to appeal to their own public constituencies, have obviously been curbed. Even the Mayor must usually sit mute, committed to the bargains of the executive session, bargains purchased most often at the price of mayoral concessions to other members of the Board.

The procedural system and traditions of the Board of Estimate reflect an institutional genius for adapting the Board's formal powers and its membership to a pattern of operations which conserves and maximizes the Board's influence as a major participant in the city's political contest. The Board has been successful in absorbing rather than surrendering power, in curbing the powers of the Mayor, its most influential rival in the political contest, and in doing these things so unobtrusively that other participants have found few opportunities to complain.

THE BOARD AND OTHER MAJOR PARTICIPANTS

The Board of Estimate has such extensive powers that it attracts the constant attention of the other important participants in the political contest. We have seen how several of the line agencies are drawn into the Board's orbit, how some of the overhead agencies are absorbed into alliance with the Board, and how several of the organized bureaucracies focus their efforts at influence upon the Board. We have seen also how the Council operates in the Board's shadow, and we shall see in the next chapter that the Mayor is deeply involved with the Board in a rivalry in which the Board has at least a net advantage of position. But two other major participants—the party leaders, and the nongovernmental groups—will be discussed here.

The Party Leaders and the Board

The members of the Board of Estimate hold the eight most important elective offices in the city government. Nominations to these offices lie more completely within the influence of the party leaders than that of any other participant in the political contest. Election to these offices involves the efforts of additional participants, but the role of the party leaders is still ordinarily a dominant one. Further, the eight members of the Board usually aspire to renomination and reelection, or else they hope for other and higher posts on the party or governmental career ladder—aspirations which, in either event, are subject to the important if not conclusive influence of party leaders. The ties between the members of the Board and the party leaders (especially the five County Leaders) in most instances are consequently direct, frequent, and of importance both to the officials and to the party leaders.

The links of a member of the Board with his party organization are almost always closest with the County Leader of the borough in which the member resides. Of these relationships, those between the County Leader and the Borough President are the easiest to work out and to maintain. These two have the same jurisdictional boundaries; their working relationships can be relatively uncomplicated. The three members with citywide constituencies (the Mayor, Comptroller, and President of the Council) have a more difficult pattern to work out. The Comptroller and the President of the Council are usually most closely linked to the County Leader in their respective home boroughs, but they each must also work out some relationship with the other four County Leaders as a way of recognizing the contribution which those leaders made to the official's nomination and election, and the role the leaders will play in future nominating and electing situations. The Mayor has an even more difficult problem; he must seek to deal with all five County Leaders on a plane of equality among them.

Where collective Board of Estimate action is concerned, each County Leader relies most frequently and regularly upon his Borough President. The Borough President is the official spokesman for the borough and county; he is usually more indebted to and dependent upon the County Leader than are the citywide officials; and his lighter official duties make him more accessible to the party leader. The County Leaders also court the Comptroller, both for his own separate powers in finance and for his influence in the Board; his 4 votes, when added to the Borough Presidents' 10, constitute a comfortable majority of the Board's 22. The Comptroller's tendency and capacity to polarize around himself the balance of bargaining power in the Board is an additional attraction to the party leaders, especially on issues where the Mayor is giving them difficulties. The President of the Council is less often an object of attention from the party leaders.

For the Borough Presidents and the Comptroller, the main significance of their relationship to the County Leaders is that it strengthens the hand of the Board against the Mayor. The working alliance has a similar attraction for the party leaders; the Board helps them often to restrain the impetuous tendencies of Mayors who are more responsive to their broad constituencies than to party organization advice. The Board's procedural system makes the working relationships between the party leaders and the Board members an unobtrusive and easy process. Access to the executive session is restricted, the party leaders cannot be present, but they have favored, indirect entry. The

Board's methods give time, too, for full communication, provide a time and place for bargaining in the Board's executive sessions, and the secrecy of the caucus surrounds the party leaders' intervention through the Borough Presidents or other members. For all the official and party participants except the Mayor (and perhaps on occasion the President of the Council), the pattern is one of optimum arrangements: maximum exercise of influence with minimum risk of accountability.

Nongovernmental Groups and the Board

The public meetings of the Board of Estimate are the great gathering place of the nongovernmental participants in the city's political contest. They come by the hundreds, perhaps even thousands, during the year—by scores to a major budget session, in considerable number to other meetings, and the Board is rarely confronted by an audience with no representative present, able and anxious to speak. Their leaders come to support or object to an item, to lecture or cajole, to threaten or to plead, to praise or to criticize. Often their fire is aimed as much at each other as at the noncommittal members of the Board. They come mainly because no other forum in the city matches, for their purposes, the forum provided by the Board in its regular schedule of meetings, the presence of high officialdom, the focus of the communication media, the attendance of allies and competitors.

Some nongovernmental groups give specialized attention to particular parts of the Board's agenda; others watch over the whole calendar of the Board. Some appear infrequently; others are in almost constant attendance. The budget sessions bring out almost all of them. Some address the Board as strangers, some on the basis of long and close acquaintance. Toward some the Board is friendly, tolerant, even indulgent; towards others it is aloof, occasionally biting. On the whole, the Board enjoys its role in the sun of public attention, treating its speakers and its audience as valued assets. Seldom is such prominence for all the participants (Board members and speakers alike) purchased at similar bargain rates.

The consequences of these repeated appearances of many groups before the most prominent and the central public forum of the city government are not easy to assess, or even to identify. The most pervasive result is a widespread sense of participation; no group is alienated from the city's political process when its leaders can speak directly to the city's most prominent officials, in the presence of the representatives of other groups of the highest prestige. For the leaders and members of these groups, there is a valued opportunity to be informed by others, to become a part of an informed electorate, however briefly on however narrow an issue. For the leaders of the nongovernmental groups, there is also the more tangible reward of demonstrating to the group's own membership the worth of the association and the alertness of the leaders of the group to the issues which concern the membership. There is a related chance to recruit new members and new contributors for the group by a show of wisdom, information, or eloquence. For some there is the added satisfaction of a fight for the public interest. All this takes place before the eyes of an attentive corps of newspaper reporters who will give prominence to the events.

The more experienced among the nongovernmental representatives appearing before the Board know the odds against a substantial exercise of influence over the Board's immediate actions. They know that the Board's executive session has probably already arrived at a decision, and they understand how unlikely a reversal or modification is. But they know, too, that the opportunities for influence are not altogether absent. An unanticipated common front among the speakers, or the unexpected touching of a sensitive political nerve, may cause the Board to defer action, and action deferred is a new opportunity for influence. Then, too, the experienced representative may be using a present occasion to influence a future item (knowing the Board has sensitive ears for such nuances), or to provide the grounds for influence sooner or later in another place (before the Mayor, in an administrative agency, in the state legislature, in the courts, or in the press).

The Board's public forum is one of its own great assets as an institution and as a participant in the city's political contest. At minimal cost to its procedural system (especially to its private bargaining in its executive session caucus), the Board enlists on its side the affection and support of all the nongovernmental groups who need the stage the Board provides for the performance of their role and who cannot find its equivalent elsewhere in the city government (the Council, even if so disposed, lacks the power to make its public sessions equally significant). For many groups, this stage is deemed to be so essential to their functioning, and it is so difficult for them to imagine a substitute, that they do not examine the price they pay for their periodic appearances. They prize and support the Board as an institution, encourage the expansion of its powers, overlook the realities of the Board's caucus, counting their minutes on the Board's stage as measures of their influence. A few groups understand that the forum is symbolic; they look to other avenues of influence, using the Board's stage for more limited purposes. But so universal is the gratitude of the leaders of the nongovernmental groups to the Board for the use of the Board's public stage, that the Board as an institution is more nearly immune from criticism than is any other participant in the city's political contest.

VARIATIONS UNDER FUSION

When all the members of the Board, or a majority of them, at a given time have been elected on a Fusion ticket (that is, a combination of Republicans and others in the joint endorsement of a list of negotiated nominations), the Board may undergo some important transformations in its behavior. The executive session caucus may decline somewhat in its importance, the Mayor may gain in leadership opportunities, the Comptroller may be inhibited in his independent role, and the Borough Presidents may have less stable ties to the party leaders. All these possibilities are related to the differences between a majority party (Democratic) city administration and a coalition administration.

First, the recruitment of the Fusion members of the Board is conducted under quite different circumstances and their relationships to each other are different. Fusion nominees for Borough President, Comptroller, President of the Council and Mayor are more likely to have had careers as insurgent, independent, or nonparty leaders. They are likely to have varied and divergent aspirations for their future careers. They are not likely to have known each other long or intimately. They are inclined to be program- or policy-oriented rather than party-oriented. And they tend to be individualistic, resistant to group unity or discipline, and relatively unpredictable in their responses to new issues. They are as likely to be openly competitive with each other as they are to be cohesive in action. The executive session caucus seems to some of them to be an unattractive institution.

Second, the Fusion Board members and the party leaders are not often comfortable collaborators. The Fusion Borough President, for example, must deal not only with the Republican County Leader but also with the leaders who organized his remaining electoral support (often not less than half of his total vote). For the Fusion Comptroller, President of the Council, or Mayor, this problem is multiplied by its ramifications in five counties. The result is that Fusion members of the Board usually maintain a detachment from party leaders not feasible for majority party members of the Board. The Board's caucus is thus often reduced in its effectiveness as a source of public unanimity for the Board, the Comptroller is deprived of some of his opportunities to form and lead a Board majority, and the Mayor may be able either to stand apart from the Board or lead it from within.

Third, Fusion Boards have revealed varying attitudes toward Mayors. In the Low administration (1902–1903) the Board was a new institution, its members just entering upon the search for the boundaries of the Board's power and influence, and so not prepared to test its opportunities fully. In the Gaynor administration (1910–1913) the Fusion Board confronted a majority party Mayor and demonstrated, under the leadership of Mitchel, then President of the Board of Aldermen, that the Board could often control an aggressive and self-willed chief executive. In the Mitchel administration (1914–1917) the Fusion Board and the Fusion Mayor were more compatible, but Mitchel frequently chafed under Board controls. In the three La Guardia administrations (1934–1945) the Fusion Board majorities and the Fusion Mayor often clashed; the Mayor, by boycotting most of the executive sessions, by appealing to the public against the Board, and by occasionally directing his attacks at a Democratic or a Republican Borough President, managed to lead the Board more often than he was led by it—but in his third term his leadership over the Board was precarious.

All these variations, while having some important consequences for the Board, do not alter the essential characteristics of the Board as the institution at the center of the city's political contest. The Fusion Board is less united in its rivalry with the Mayor, the Mayor is less curbed by the Board, the party leaders have less direct access, but these differences are in degree rather than in kind. The Board survives Fusion administrations unimpaired in its primacy.

DILEMMAS AND CONSEQUENCES

The Board of Estimate is a complex and subtle institution. It is powerful as a Board, wielding great influence over almost all city officials and employees, over most official decisions and actions. As such a center of power, it is an object of pressure and influence from all other participants in the political process, and it is more successfully influenced by some (by the Budget Bureau, its own bureaus, the organized bureaucracies, the party leaders) than by others. As an institution, it is itself a conscious participant in the city's political process, seeking to preserve and enhance its own power as against the rival institutions of the mayoralty and the separate administrative agencies.

But it is also a Board composed of individual members, each of whom is a participant in the city's political process as an individual official. The Board, as an institution, is primarily an instrument for each of them in the pursuit of his own separate goals. The actions of the Board are largely a product of the accommodations each can make with the others in pursuit of these separate goals. As an institution it is thus more an agency of accommodation than of leadership or unity. The consequences of its behavior are significant, but they are not a great contribution to coherence, integration, or innovation in the city's political process.

Four major consequences flow from the nature and strength of Board of Estimate participation in the city's political process. Taken together these four consequences make the Board the single most powerful participant in the distribution of the stakes of city politics.

First, the Board of Estimate has swallowed up the Council's functions. The charter-makers of 1936 described the Council as holding "the legislative power of the city" in one paragraph, but took the substance of that power away in later paragraphs which make the Board of Estimate preeminent.

The result is that the city government has no genuine legislative process, for while the Board exercises many of the powers of a legislature, it does not function like one. A legislature in formal theory has several distinctive characteristics: it is composed of members of formally equal status and equal vote; its salient proceedings are public; it engages in structured public debate between its members, who are either sponsors or critics of proposed actions or current governmental performance; it has substantial powers which are exercised primarily through statutes of general application. With the swallowing up of the Council by the Board, New York City has no such legislative institution. It has, instead, a caucus of officials, acting *ex officio* as members of the Board of Estimate.

Second, the Board of Estimate has a commanding position within the city government over the city's financial and personnel policies and management. This role the Board has achieved by combining in practice its own formal charter powers with the extensive separate powers of the Comptroller, by using these combined powers to coopt the Budget Director and the Personnel Director into the Board's sphere of operations, and by dealing warily with the City Construction Coordinator (a semiautonomous center of power, of no great comfort to any other official participant). It is the Board of Estimate, not the Mayor, which manages the finances and the personnel of the city government. While the state constitution and state laws sharply limit the discretion of the city government in both finance and personnel, the Board is the master of such discretion as the city enjoys. The Mayor and his administrative agencies, and the service-demanding nongovernmental groups, may propose new programs or suggest modifications of existing ones; the Board centers its interest upon the minutiae of the city's finances and upon the ways in which proposed changes affect the fortunes of the city's bureaucracies. The preoccupation of the Board with finances recruits for the Board some cautious support from the revenue-providing interest groups, especially when the latter are alarmed by the Mayor's sympathetic responses to his service-demanding (and thus money-spending) constituencies. The Board also benefits by the gravitation of the city's organized bureaucracies toward the change-resisting Board and away from the innovating tendencies of the Mayor and some of his commissioners.

Third, the Board of Estimate is a major conservative force in the city's political contest. The Board, like the party leaders and the bureaucracies, has an affinity for the *status quo*. Its dominant characteristic is its capacity to absorb, as if it were a great sponge, the constant stream of proposals for change which flow in upon the Board from the Mayor, from the commissioners of departments and agencies, from the nongovernmental groups and the communication media, from all those who would like to be Mayor, and from all the other sources of dynamism in the city. The Board's powers and its procedural system are shaped to resist the unsettling effects of these proposals upon the equilibrium of forces which the Board as an institution represents: the Board can refer, postpone, or bargain among the many proposals; while others talk about goals and programs, the Board (especially through the Comptroller and the Budget Director) can turn the vocabulary to one of scarce money or to disputed alternatives of jurisdiction for proposed programs. Proposers of change are thus transformed from pressures upon the Board to competitors with each other, while the Board pursues quietly its own inscrutable course, shielded by its caucus, its financial and personnel powers, its tradition of public unanimity, and the symbolic uses of its public forum.

Finally, the Board of Estimate seeks with substantial success to contain the Mayor, holding him to the rules of bargaining and to the commitments of the caucus in the Board's own executive sessions. This development is contrary to the hopes of the charter-makers at the turn of the century and of their successors in 1936. Their assumption was that the Board would be led by the votes of the "big three" (the Mayor, the Comptroller, and the President of the Council), that these three citywide officials would act together, and that the Mayor would lead them—thus blanketing the votes of the five Borough Presidents. This was wishful thinking in 1901, discounting as it did the nature of the city's party system, the relationships of County Leaders to Borough Presidents, and the evident tendencies of the Comptroller toward competition with the Mayor. In 1936, the theory had been so clearly refuted by a generation of Board history that the Charter Commission action can be explained only as a higher form of innocence or as a subtle vote of confidence in continued Board supremacy over the Mayor.

The reality is that the Board is not often led by the Mayor; instead, it unites against him if necessary, absorbs him into the Board as a member without special status if it can. Only twice in six decades can the Mayor be said to have called the tune for the Board: for a while under Mitchel, for a little longer under La Guardia—but for neither did the role of Board leadership span the Mayor's full tenure in office. The Mayor, even a Mitchel or a La Guardia, cannot lead the Board for long because he has no effective sanctions against the Board. He has no general veto over its actions; only La Guardia found it possible to stay away from the Board's caucus. Once he enters it he is not only shorn of his greatest strength (his capacity to invoke in broad public appeals the symbol and reality of his office as representing all the people of the city), but he is also committed to endure silently the agreements reached in the caucus whose rules of the game bind him as much as any other member. The Mayor ordinarily cannot even single out for special sanctions his rivals in the Board; these rivals are protected not only by the anonymity of the caucus and by the unanimity of the Board in public but also by the necessities of party unity emphasized by all the power of the County Leaders in the party.

The Board of Estimate may be said to be composed of the Mayor and of seven other members who would have liked to be Mayor, or who hope soon to be Mayor, or who had preferences for Mayor other than the incumbent. These feelings are usually held most strongly by the Comptroller and the President of the Council. The Borough Presidents share them too, however, and have additional imperatives for regarding the Mayor as a rival. When to these sentiments, aspirations, and necessities are added the special powers of the Comptroller as chief financial officer, with their built-in rivalry to the Mayor, the most natural and logical (indeed the almost inescapable) majority alliance within the Board is not one among the "big three" but between the Comptroller and the five Borough Presidents. Their combined 14 votes are the core of the Board as an institution—the President of the Council may move back and forth across the line, pulled by the Mayor in one instance and by a County Leader in another (or even striking out on his own), and a Borough President may be lost now and then from the caucus majority; but the prevailing bargains are most often struck by the Comptroller and his five Borough President associates.

Of the three most important central institutions of the city government (the Council, the Board of Estimate, the mayoralty), it is the Board of Estimate which has most fully realized its own expectations as a participant in the city's political contest. The Council has disappointed even its least hopeful members. And the Mayor, as the city's elected chief executive and the most prominent participant in its political contest, would have been more fortunate if he could have exchanged his membership and his four votes on the Board for a separate existence as elected chief executive. As a member of the Board and a reluctant guest in its caucus he is less the elected chief executive of the city than the Board's hostage. On the chessboard of the city's politics, the Mayor may be king, but the Board of Estimate is queen.

BIBLIOGRAPHY

OFFICIAL SOURCES AND ISSUANCES

New York City Charter: chap. 1, sec. 10; chap. 2, sec. 23; chap. 3, secs. 61–71; chap. 4, secs. 81–83; chap. 5, secs. 91–94; chap. 6, secs. 118–126, chap. 7, secs. 168–169; chap. 9, secs. 212–224; chap. 10, secs. 253, 255; chap. 11, secs. 275–278.

New York City Administrative Code, chaps. 3–6, 9–15.

New York City Board of Estimate, "Rules of Procedure for the Conduct of the Business of the Board," *City Record*, May 3, 1946, p. 2031.
  and Apportionment, *Minutes*, 1871–1873 (2 vols.), 1873–1888 (15 vols.), 1906–1934 (222 vols.).
  Proceedings, 1889–1897 (9 vols.), 1898–1906 (51 vols.).
  Journal of Proceedings, 1934–1957 (195 vols.).
  Most of the important business done by the city—budgets, franchises, important local laws, and so forth—are recorded in these pages.

Annual Reports of the Bureau of Engineering, 1934–1938. Résumé.

Annual Reports of the Bureau of Real Estate, 1951–1956.

Annual Reports of the Chief Engineer, 1902–1919 (published annually); 1933–1934, summary published in *City Record*, March 1, 1935, pp. 1502–1503.

Annual Reports of the Comptroller, 1907–1938 (23 vols.); 1939 (1 vol.); 1940–1941, 1941–1942, 1943 (published annually); 1943–1957 (14 vols.). Detailed statements of the receipts and expenditures of the city during the fiscal year, the different sources of revenue and the amount received from each, the appropriations made, and the amounts expended under each.

DISCUSSIONS AND COMMENTARIES

Allen, William H., *Al Smith's Tammany Hall: Champion Political Vampire.* Institute for Public Service, New York, 1928, pp. 132–142; 316–318. Some observations on the policies of the Board of Estimate during Governor Smith's period of service and during the 1920's.

Arent, Lenora, *Electric Franchises in New York City.* Doctoral dissertation, Columbia University, 1919.

Caldwell, Lynton K., *The Government and Administration of New York.* Thomas Y. Crowell Co., New York, 1954, pp. 149–157. The administrative, legislative, and financial authority of the Board of Estimate.

Carman, Harry J., *The Street Surface Railway Franchises of New York City.* Columbia University Press, New York, 1919.

Citizens Union, Committee on Legislation, *Municipal Assembly Record,* 1924–1937. A summary of all legislation, proposed and enacted, by the Board of Estimate Branch of the Municipal Assembly from the time home rule went into effect until the new charter became a reality.

Scrapbooks. 206 vols. Vols. 61–76 cover the Board of Estimate and its financial work, 1922–1935. In reference section of New York Public Library, Astor Branch.

City Club of New York, *Report on Charter Revision.* The Club, New York, 1921, pp. 7–12; 15–18. A critical evaluation of the role of the Board of Estimate and Apportionment in 1921 as well as the offices of the Borough Presidents.

Deutsch, Bernard S., "Charter Revision—The Board of Estimate and the Board of Aldermen," *Real Estate News,* May, 1935, pp. 160–161, 174–177. The President of the Board of Aldermen explains his views on reforms in the Board of Estimate.

Forbes, Russell, "The Municipal Assembly—New York's Home Rule Legislature," *National Municipal Review,* vol. 18, October, 1929, pp. 632–634. How the Board of Estimate operated as the upper branch of the city's home rule legislature.

"Government of the City of New York in the Board of Estimate and Apportionment," Municipal Reference Library, New York, 1932. Typewritten copy in Municipal Reference Library.

Jaboolian, Arax, "Evolution and History of the New York City Board of Estimate and Apportionment from 1853 to 1938," February 27, 1940. Typewritten copy in Municipal Reference Library.

La Guardia, Fiorello, "New York City Blazes the Trail," radio broadcast in *You and Your Government Series.* National Municipal League, New York, 1934. Emphasizes the dominant role of the Board of Estimate in governing New York City.

League of Women Voters of New York, "Board of Estimate of the City of New York." The League, New York, 1949, mimeographed.

Mathewson, Douglas, "Highways, Street Cleaning, and Public Works," *Proceedings of the Academy of Political Science in the City of New York,* vol. 5, April, 1915, pp. 653–664. The President of the Borough of The Bronx discusses some of the administrative functions of his office.

McGoldrick, Joseph D., "The Board of Estimate and Apportionment of the City of New York," supplement to the *National Municipal Review,* vol. 18, February, 1929, revised and reprinted May, 1932, pp. 3–29. A comprehensive portrait of the work of the Board.

Mills, Quincy Sharpe, "What New York City Is Doing Under a Commission Form of Government," a reprint from *Outlook*, August 25, 1915. The Board of Estimate and Apportionment is compared with the commission type of municipal government. On the shelves of the Municipal Reference Library.

Mitchel, John Purroy, "The Office of Mayor," *Proceedings* of the Academy of Political Science in the City of New York, vol. 5, April, 1915, pp. 479–494. Mayor Mitchel indicates why the actions of the Board of Estimate and Apportionment are among the most important of all municipal operations in New York City.

New York City, Division of Administration, *Organization, Procedures, and Practices: Bureau of Real Estate*. The Division, New York, 1958. An analysis of a Board of Estimate Bureau preceding its 1959 transformation into a city department.

Mayor's Committee on Management Survey, *Modern Management for the City of New York*. 2 vols. The Committee, New York, 1953, vol. 1, pp. 24–25, 30–31; vol. 2, pp. 318–321, 324–325. Recommendations for strengthening the Board of Estimate and its several officials.

New York State Charter Revision Commission of 1907, *Report to the Governor of the State of New York Pursuant to the Provisions of Chapter 600 of the Laws of 1907*. Evening Post, New York, 1907, pp. 36–39. A strong recommendation that the powers of the then existing Board of Estimate and Apportionment be enlarged.

New York State, Temporary State Commission to Study the Organizational Structure of the Government of the City of New York, *Four Steps to Better Government of New York City: A Plan for Action*. 2 vols. The Commission, New York, 1953, vol. 2, pp. 23–25. The Commission's recommendations relating to the procedures of the Board of Estimate and the borough presidents.

Pounds, Lewis H., "Discussion of Highways and Public Works," *Proceedings* of the Academy of Political Science in the City of New York, vol. 5, April, 1915, pp. 670–675. The administrative operations of the Borough President discussed by the incumbent in Brooklyn.

Rankin, Rebecca B., *Guide to the Municipal Government of the City of New York*. 7th ed. Record Press, New York, 1952, pp. 24–39. A summary view of the work of the members of the Board of Estimate, collectively and individually.

"History of New York City's Board of Estimate and Apportionment," December, 1949. Typewritten copy in Municipal Reference Library.

Rankin, Rebecca B., editor, *New York Advancing: World's Fair Edition*. Municipal Reference Library, New York, 1939, pp. 1–5. A summary of the work of the Board of Estimate shortly after the 1936 charter went into effect.

Shaw, Frederick, *History of the New York City Legislature*. Columbia University Press, New York, 1954. Primarily devoted to the Board of Aldermen and the City Council, this work touches on the operation of the Board of Estimate at frequent points.

Smith, Herman A., "The Work of the Chief Engineer's Office," *Real Estate News*, January, 1932, pp. 12–13, 24.

Tanzer, Lawrence A., *The New York City Charter*. Clark Boardman Co., New York, 1937, pp. 43–44, 46–64, 115–118, 206–209, 211–212. The work of the Board of Estimate as described by the 1936 Charter Commission's Associate Counsel.

Wheeler, Everett P., *Sixty Years of American Life*. E. P. Dutton and Co., New York, 1917, pp. 364–365. The importance of the Board in the original municipal government of the consolidated city.

FINANCIAL WORK OF THE BOARD OF ESTIMATE

Finegan, James E., *Tammany at Bay*. Dodd, Mead and Co., New York, 1933, pp. 267–274. The importance of the Comptroller in the city government.

Haig, Robert M., and Carl S. Shoup, *Fiscal Independence for Public Education in the City of New York*. Mayor's Committee on Management Survey, New York, 1951. A critical evaluation of the pros and cons on the subject, which touches on the financial authority of the Board of Estimate.

The Financial Problems of the City of New York. Mayor's Committee on Management Survey, New York, 1952. A comprehensive summary of the finance project of the Mayor's Committee on Management Survey. Contains a description and analysis of the city's finances, together with a series of suggestions and recommendations.

Lahee, Arnold W., *The New York City Budget.* Bureau of Municipal Research, New York, 1917. Indicates the role the Board of Estimate played in budget making before 1917.

Ma, Yin Ch'u, *The Finances of the City of New York.* Columbia University Press, New York, 1914, pp. 91–99. Doctoral dissertation, Columbia University. Action of the Board of Estimate and Apportionment on the annual city budget.

McKee, Joseph V., "Billion Dollar Bills," *Saturday Evening Post,* March 26, 1932, pp. 34–41. The President of the Board of Aldermen discusses the "how" and "what" of the budget that body considers.

Prendergast, William A., "Financial Administration, Budget and Tax Rate," *Proceedings* of the Academy of Political Science in the City of New York, vol. 5, no. 3, 1915, pp. 633–647. The Comptroller discusses some phases of the work of his department.

Rankin, Rebecca B., "The Treasurer, Chamberlain, and Comptroller of the City of New York: History of Its Financial Offices, 1653–1949." 1949. Typewritten copy in Municipal Reference Library.

Ross, Lillian, "$1,031,961,754.63," *The New Yorker,* vol. 23, July 12, 1947, pp. 27–40. A picture of the Board of Estimate acting on the annual expense budget.

MEN WHO SERVED ON THE BOARD OF ESTIMATE

Curran, Henry H., *Pillar to Post.* Charles Scribner's Sons, New York, 1941, pp. 256–257. Recollections of a Borough President of Manhattan.

Hapgood, Norman, and Henry Moskowitz, *Up from the City Streets: Alfred E. Smith.* Grosset and Dunlap, New York, 1927, pp. 143–148. Smith's experiences as President of the Board of Aldermen.

Hazelton, Henry I., *The Boroughs of Brooklyn and Queens, Counties of Nassau and Suffolk, Long Island, New York, 1609–1924.* 3 vols. Lewis Historical Publishing Co., New York, 1925, vol. 3, pp. 1557–1574. The lives of the Borough Presidents of Brooklyn, 1898–1924, and their work.

Isaacs, Stanley, "Reminiscences." Columbia University Oral History Collection, Special Collections, Butler Library. Mr. Isaacs relates his work as Borough President of Manhattan.

Mackaye, Milton, "Professor in Politics: Profile of Joseph D. McGoldrick," *The New Yorker,* vol. 10, August 11, 1934, pp. 19–22. Portrait of an unusual Comptroller.

McAneny, George, "Reminiscences." Columbia University Oral History Collection, Special Collections, Butler Library. Recollections of a member of the Board of Estimate who served as President of the Borough of Manhattan and as President of the Board of Aldermen.

Morris, Charles, *Men of Affairs in New York: An Historical Work.* L. R. Hamersley and Co., New York, 1906, pp. 133–134, the career of Herman A. Metz, Comptroller of the City; the life and career of Bird S. Coler, Borough President of Brooklyn, pp. 223–224.

Morris, Newbold, and Dana Lee Thomas, *Let the Chips Fall.* Appleton-Century-Crofts, New York, 1955, pp. 131–136, 144–187, 246–247, 282–284. Recollections of Morris' activities in the Board of Estimate as President of the Council.

Morris, Richard B., "John Purroy Mitchel," *Dictionary of American Biography.* Charles Scribner's Sons, New York, vol. 17, 1934. Offers the salient facts about Mitchel's career in the Board of Estimate.

Prendergast, William A., *Papers.* Columbia University Oral History Collection, Special Collections, Butler Library. Papers of the city's Comptroller, 1912–1921.

"Reminiscences." Columbia University Oral History Collection, Special Collections, Butler Library. Recollections of Prendergast's work as Comptroller under the Gaynor and Mitchel administrations (1910–1917).

Pringle, Henry F., "Bringing Up the City Fathers: Profile of Joseph V. McKee," *The New Yorker*, vol. 3, September 10, 1927, pp. 19–22. The life and work of a President of the Board of Aldermen.

"Jimmy Walker," *The American Mercury*, vol. 9, November, 1926, pp. 272–279. How the Broadway influence was felt in the Board of Estimate during the Walker administration.

"Wet Hope: Profile of Henry Hastings Curran," *The New Yorker*, vol. 6, June 14, 1930, pp. 22–25. Career of Curran as Borough President of Manhattan on the Board of Estimate.

Rovere, Richard H., "Good Citizen: Profile of Newbold Morris," *The New Yorker*, vol. 20, October 28, 1944, pp. 26–36; November 4, 1944, pp. 28–38. The personality and career of the first President of the City Council.

Schriftgiesser, Karl, "Portrait of a Mayor: Fiorello La Guardia," *Atlantic Monthly*, vol. 161, January, 1938, pp. 55–63. Mayor La Guardia's career on the Board of Estimate as President of Board of Aldermen.

Smith, Mortimer, *William Jay Gaynor: Mayor of New York*. Henry Regnery, Chicago, 1951, pp. 85–86. Mayor Gaynor and his Board of Estimate.

Syrett, Harold C., editor, *The Gentleman and the Tiger: The Autobiography of George B. McClellan, Jr.* J. B. Lippincott Co., Philadelphia, 1956, pp. 206–208, 214–215, 253–254. Mayor McClellan's impression of his Board of Estimate.

Thomas, Norman, and Paul Blanshard, *What's the Matter with New York?* Macmillan Co., New York, 1932, pp. 196–209, the story of George U. Harvey, Borough President of Queens; the story of certain franchises and the Board of Estimate, pp. 210–228.

Warner, Richard, "On the Up: Profile of George Upton Harvey," *The New Yorker*, vol. 6, May 31, 1930, pp. 24–27. A portrait of a Borough President and his work.

Wells, James L., Louis F. Haffen, and Josia A. Briggs, editors, *The Bronx and Its People, A History: 1609–1927*. Lewis Historical Publishing Co., New York, 1927, vol. 3, pp. 18–19. The career of Louis F. Haffen, Borough President of the Bronx.

CHAPTER XVIII

The Mayor

THE OFFICE OF MAYOR, like the presidency and the governorship, is an institution of many purposes, the object of many expectations from the city's citizens, officials, party leaders, bureaucrats, and interest groups, and the source of both rewards and frustrations for its incumbent. But above all these variations and inconsistencies, the office of Mayor is first and fundamentally a symbol of unity for the city. The Mayor and his office are the visible expression of the city, its personification as an organized community, its leading ceremonial figure on occasions of state.

Yet the Mayor has a still more important role in the life of the city. He is the central focus of responsibility and accountability for all that occurs in the city: he is the problem-solver, the crisis-handler, the man-to-blame for all the defects of the governing process in the city. Out of diversity and fragmentation, widespread autonomy and competition, separate islands of power, and numerous restrictions, he is called upon to bring unity and action. The expectations of the electorate, of the organized groups of all types, and especially of the communication media, center sharply upon the Mayor. His office is the most perceptible, the most impressive; it is taken for granted that he has the most power and thus the capacity to act vigorously in the solution of the city's problems great and small. Failure to meet these high expectations is taken to mean not lack of vigor in the office but in the man.

Most of the city's Mayors have responded affirmatively to these demands. Their initial conceptions of the office have frequently led them at first to accept as feasible the high expectations that are so widely held. Even after they themselves have learned the limitations of the office, they discover no compensating reduction in the expectations of others: the Mayor is still held fully responsible and accountable. As a consequence, the Mayor is thus required, by the nature of the office he holds, to seek ways and means through which he may lead and unify the political and governmental forces of the city. He finds through his own experience and that of his predecessors in office that he has three main strategies (in descending order of emphasis upon his own personal leadership): acting vigorously and quickly as an initiator and innovator himself in discovering and sponsoring solutions to the city's problems; acting as an arbitrator by choosing among the solutions offered by others, and then pressing hard for the adoption of his chosen solution; or acting as a simple mediator between the competing forces, each with its different solution, by moderating the points of conflict and seeking consensus in a compromise. He may, of course, use these methods alternately or in combination. But he cannot often escape direct personal involvement either as initiator and innovator or as arbitrator or mediator. Most Mayors find themselves compelled by the nature of the office, their political posture, and their personalities to be mediators more often than arbitrators, and to be arbitrators more often than innovators.

THE MAYOR HAS FOUR JOBS

The Mayor of New York City occupies an office of many facets. It is an office of ceremony and ritual, but it is not merely an honorific office like the mayoralty of a British city. It is an office of extensive executive powers, but it is not austerely managerial after the style of the city manager's position. It is an office with significant legislative responsibilities, but it deals with several very different kinds of legislative institutions. It is an office important to the party system, but the Mayor must carry out his party leadership in a party environment quite different from that in which Presidents and Governors function as party leaders. Each of these major facets of the office of Mayor imposes a separate role. He must, so to speak, wear from time to time (and often simultaneously) four different "hats": one as "chief of state" for the city, one as "chief executive," one as "chief legislator," and still another as "chief of party."

Chief of State for the City

The office of Mayor in New York was an office of ceremony long before it was an office of power. Tradition and custom, the city as the main port of entry for foreign notables coming to the United States, the long history of the city as the nation's largest—all these and other forces have combined to make the Mayor the city's first citizen, its chief spokesman and its chief host, and the most prominent among all the Mayors of the United States. The role is arduous and inescapable; it consumes the Mayor's time, but it also confers power upon him. He must issue formal proclamations launching community drives or awarding the city's recognition to deserving groups or persons; he must welcome distinguished visitors; he must appear as principal speaker or guest of honor at scores of meetings, breakfasts, luncheons, and dinners each month; he must see an unending stream of citizens great and small, listen to their petitions or demands, and respond to many other intercessions that come to him by letter or telephone. In short, he must make himself visible, accessible, communicative, and responsive to the city and its people. This is one of the most important ways by which the Mayor establishes the popular image of himself and his office. This image is, in turn, an indispensable source of power to the Mayor when he attempts to act as innovator, arbitrator, or mediator in his roles as chief executive, chief legislator, or chief of party.

Chief Executive

"The mayor shall be the chief executive officer of the city," the charter declares. This ambiguous clause of the charter is not, however, the main foundation of the Mayor's role as chief executive. He is chief executive also because charter provisions confer on him powers as an appointing officer and powers to supervise most of the administrative agencies. But most importantly, the chief executive role is the product of demands by the electorate, the interest groups, and the communication media for a focus of responsibility and accountability in the complex, much-divided city government.

Does the Traffic Commissioner disagree with the Police Commissioner? The Mayor must intervene and resolve the difference. Does the Hospitals Commissioner disagree with the medical societies? Does the Transit Authority face a strike by the subway employees? Does the Board of Education falter under the juvenile delinquency problem? Has a bureau chief of the Board of Estimate been exposed in irregularities? Has a District Attorney charged collusion between police and the underworld? Does a citizen group allege a crisis in tenant relocation, or in low-cost housing, or in the pending destruction of a park? Or do limited revenues prevent the expansion or inauguration of strongly desired services? In all such conflicts—and there will be a score like them each week—the Mayor is assumed to be responsible for finding a solution and to be accountable for any failure, no matter what the limitations upon his formal powers. It is enough for most participants in the city's political process that the Mayor is the chief executive, the highest ranking city official, the most visible and accessible of all the city officials, the symbol of "the administration" in power. If he lacks the power to do what they consider necessary, they nevertheless demand that he find a way to a solution.

The Mayor as chief executive is held hostage not only for the conduct of all officials and all employees of the city, for their personal integrity, their wisdom in policy, and their efficiency in performance. He must also, if he is to escape censure, meet with dispatch and vigor all the emergencies, short-range and long-range, that the city and its people encounter while he is in office, whether it be preserving the economy of the port against far-flung competition, the rescue of city merchants from the inroads of suburban shopping centers, the settlement of a strike, or maintaining the stature of the city in the world of baseball. The Mayor may demur at some of these responsibilities, pointing to the Council, the Board of Estimate, the state government, or to the laws that restrict him; if he does so, the Council retreats into its fortress of anonymity, the Board of Estimate becomes invisible in its executive session, the state government remains at a safe distance. But the Mayor remains visible and vulnerable: he is still held to the sharp demands of his role as chief executive.

Chief Legislator

The necessities of his role as chief executive provide the main impulse for the Mayor's role as chief legislator. If the Mayor must find solutions for all major emergencies, if he must exercise surveillance over all administrative agencies to control both their integrity and their performance, then he must turn often to the remedies of legislation. For it is the constitutional and statutory rules that often inhibit the most rational or the most direct solution; not infrequently these rules are themselves the cause of the current shape of the problem.

But when the Mayor transfers his dilemmas as chief executive to his role as chief legislator, he discovers that, while in a few instances he may direct his leadership efforts at the Council and in a considerably greater number at the Board of Estimate, he must more frequently be an ambassador to the Governor and state legislature at Albany, and on occasion to the President and Congress in Washington. In fact, the Mayor is expected by most participants in the city's political process to have a more formal and comprehensive annual "program" for presentation at Albany than he need have for local legislative action at City Hall. Even if the Mayor did not choose to meet these expectations (a hazardous choice from which most Mayors refrain), he would be compelled nevertheless to devote major attention, as the city's chief legislator, to Albany activities by the simple fact that almost all other participants try to use the route of state legislation to achieve their favored solutions and advantages, and the Mayor cannot avoid judging and supporting or opposing their proposals. Faced by these expectations and requirements, the Mayor ordinarily recognizes that his opportunities as chief legislator center mainly on Albany, and it is to the Governor and state legislature that he presents both his most important and his most numerous legislative proposals.

The Mayor's role as chief legislator at City Hall, however, is not a minor one. He is held by most participants to the same strict level of responsibility and accountability for Council and Board of Estimate behavior as he is held, in his chief executive role, for the conduct of administrative agencies and employees. If individual councilmen are charged with a lack of integrity, the Mayor is expected to investigate them and, if the discovered facts indicate guilt, to urge their removal (an extraordinary relationship between executive and legislature). A similar obligation seemingly involves the Mayor in a responsibility for the conduct of members of the Board of Estimate, although its exercise has been marked by caution since the dramatic removal of several Borough Presidents in the days of Mayor McClellan and his Commissioner of Accounts, John P. Mitchel. Beyond these unusual responsibilities for legislative morality, the Mayor is chief legislator at City Hall not simply because of his formal charter powers in legislation, but, more significantly, because he cannot avoid the role. He is held responsible and accountable for more than the behavior of the local legislators; he is charged with their legislative product as well. His limitations of power and office are not accepted as excuses by most participants. As chief of state for the city and as its chief executive he is required by prevailing sentiment to be chief legislator as well. If he cannot manage the role, he will be judged to have failed not merely as chief legislator but as Mayor.

Chief of Party

The demands of his other three roles impel the Mayor toward his role as chief of party. If he is to meet the great expectations directed at his office as chief of state, chief executive, and chief legislator, he must have the assistance of his party and its influential institutions. An additional consideration also drives the Mayor toward the role of party chief. He is held responsible and accountable for the behavior and performance of his party's leaders. The reputation of his party becomes in large part his reputation. Even Fusion or insurgent Mayors, while capitalizing upon their real or feigned hostility to party organizations, cannot escape from the necessity to deal with the organized groups that support them, or from some responsibility and accountability for the conduct of such groups. Each Mayor has found that he needs to be chief of party to protect his own prestige and the prestige of his office against the hazards of unsupervised party behavior.

The Mayor's electoral constituency, including not only those who voted for him but all those others who accept his victory, expects him to be the leader of his party. This broad constituency, surpassing in scope and numbers the constituency of any other city official, looks to the Mayor as its chief spokesman in general party matters. Even more explicitly, the Mayor's popular constituency expects him to command the resources of the party organization in carrying out his duties as chief executive and as chief legislator. If he permits party leaders to obstruct him, the Mayor's constituency may show hostility toward party leaders, but it is not likely to excuse the Mayor for his failure. In the constituency's view, the Mayor who cannot be chief of his party is a "weak" Mayor.

A Handicapped Leader

The Mayor of New York—as chief of state for the city, as chief executive, as chief legislator, and as chief of party—is compelled increasingly to assume leadership responsibilities similar to those of Presidents and Governors. But the Mayors must do so under less favorable circumstances than those faced by these chief executives. The Mayor's public status, his constitutional and statutory powers, and his managerial assistance are all much more modest than those of his fellow executives.

THE OFFICE: RESOURCES AND LIMITATIONS

The history of the office of Mayor in New York City is not a story of aggrandizement; rather it is a history of slow and arduous development, and it is not yet an office richly endowed with the powers and the supporting institutions usually associated with chief executive offices.

The Mayor's Staff

The Mayor's staff is primarily a product of the period beginning in 1934. The landmarks in its growth are, first, the slow addition of professional level assistants to the earlier secretarial, stenographic, and clerical staff; second, the borrowing of professional staff from the city agencies and departments; third, the establishment of the office of Deputy Mayor in 1938; fourth, the establishment of the Division of Administration, headed by a City Administrator, in 1954.

The Assistants to the Mayor. The Mayor's staff began with the gradual addition to his office of assistants as successive Mayors discovered need for help. In 1959 these assistants numbered 12: the assistant to the Mayor, an executive secretary (who serves as press secretary), an assistant executive secretary, three assistants to the Mayor (without formal portfolio), a legislative representative (primarily assigned to legislative matters at Albany), two legal aides, an office manager, an educational assistant, and a secretary to the Mayor. These 12 assistants are supported by a staff which in 1959 numbered about 45.

The pattern for this staff is the product of precedent and tradition. Each Mayor has tended to add to what he inherited from his immediate predecessor, changing incumbents freely although not completely, but rarely taking time or initiative to reorganize duties or assignments in any systematic manner. Few Mayors have had a high interest in staff organization or have brought to the office any direct experience with the question. Most Mayors have accepted the arrangements they found in existence, simply adding another assistant whenever a particular burden of office became oppressive. Assignments and rank among these positions tend to be fluid and unpredictable, varying with the personalities and interests of Mayors, the personalities and sponsors of the incumbents, and the high and low tides of problems pressing in upon the Mayor. But one or two persons usually provide a base of continuity, serving through several administrations.

Mayors have rarely been happy with their staff arrangements, an experience common to most chief executives. They have not, however, known what to do about the problem, and they have not been persuaded by their occasional expert advisers that the permanent benefits of staff reorganization would clearly exceed the immediate political and other costs the Mayors could perceive. The prevailing tendency has been to let the traditional staff pattern continue, evolving step by step, while turning also to new and separate units.

The Deputy Mayor. Ambiguity of purpose and duties has surrounded this office since its creation by the charter-makers of 1936. Some of the framers of the charter regarded the office as a response to the Mayor's need for assistance and would have made it an office of powers; La Guardia, the Mayor at the time, had no wish to delegate such powers and saw risks in specific grants of authority. The resulting compromise in the charter provided that "the mayor may appoint a deputy mayor who shall possess such of the powers of the mayor and for such times and subject to such conditions as shall be expressed in written authority to be signed by the mayor," except the power to appoint or remove, to approve or veto local laws or resolutions, to act as a magistrate, or to hold hearings which the Mayor is required by law to hold personally. The office is thus whatever the Mayor chooses to make it, and Mayors have followed an erratic pattern in their use of it. Under some Mayors, the Deputy Mayor has been a shadowy official, holding an honorific title but with no explicit duties; under other Mayors he has been given duties primarily managerial; still other Mayors have found the office useful in party affairs. The most consistent use of the office has been as the Mayor's agent and representative in Board of Estimate matters, and as "trouble shooter" for the Mayor in the preliminary handling or full mediation of problems which the Mayor lacks time for or wishes to avoid.

The office of Deputy Mayor is an asset of great potential for any Mayor who wishes to use it with purpose and consistency. None has fully done so. The liabilities of the office arise largely out of its erratic history since its creation, the brief tenure of its many incumbents, and the fact that no coherent pattern of duties has become sufficiently stabilized to fix the office at a high level of prestige and influence which can be transferred from one incumbent to the next. The persistent dilemmas of the office of Deputy Mayor are three: What is to be its main core of duties (assisting the Mayor in Board of Estimate liaison, or serving as the Mayor's trouble shooter, or organizing and assisting in the ceremonial duties of the Mayor)? What is to be the hierarchical relationship of the Deputy Mayor to the Mayor's other assistants? What are to be the jurisdictional boundaries between the Deputy Mayor and the City Administrator? These uncertainties diminish the office and reduce its usefulness to the Mayor.

The City Administrator. Fewer ambiguities and uncertainties beset the City Administrator and the Division of Administration which he heads. The charter amendment of 1953 is quite explicit in the assignment of duties to the

Deputy Mayor	Highest previous public office	Tenure as Deputy Mayor	Subsequent public office
Henry H. Curran	Borough President; Magistrate	Jan., 1938–June, 1939	Chief Magistrate (1939–1945); Justice, Court of Special Sessions (1945–1947)
Rufus E. McGahen[a]	Budget Director; Board of Water Supply	July, 1939–Dec., 1945	Board of Water Supply (1936–1953)
George E. Spargo[a]	General Manager, Triborough Bridge and Tunnel Authority	Jan., 1946–Apr., 1946	General Manager, Triborough Bridge and Tunnel Authority
Thomas J. Corcoran	Chief Counsel, Governor Lehman	Apr., 1946–Jan., 1947	Justice, State Supreme Court
John J. Bennett	State Attorney General; Corporation Counsel	Jan., 1947–Dec., 1949	Chairman, City Planning Commission (1950–1955)
William Reid	Member and Chairman, Board of Transportation (N.Y.C.)	Jan., 1950–Sept., 1950	Chairman, City Housing Authority
Charles Horowitz	Assistant Corporation Counsel	Oct., 1950–Dec., 1953	Justice, Domestic Relations Court
Henry Epstein	State Solicitor General	Jan., 1954–Dec., 1955	Justice, State Supreme Court
John J. Theobald	President, Queens College	Jan., 1956–Dec., 1958	Superintendent of Schools
Paul T. O'Keefe	None	Jan., 1959 to date	

[a] Served without compensation while holding permanent position noted.

SOURCE: Lowi, Theodore J., *At the Pleasure of the Mayor*. Doctoral dissertation, Yale University, 1960, unpublished.

City Administrator. He is to be the Mayor's chief managerial assistant, supervising and coordinating the work of agencies under the jurisdiction of the Mayor, establishing management standards, and reporting to the Mayor on "impending policy decisions affecting the management of the city and its agencies." To carry out these responsibilities, he may appoint three Deputy City Administrators and the necessary staff for the Division of Administration. This staff in 1959 numbered about 60.

The debate that accompanied the establishment of the City Administrator's office in December, 1953, centered not upon the need for the office, but upon the scope of its powers. The Josephs Commission (the Temporary State Commission to Study the Organizational Structure of New York City, appointed by Governor Dewey in 1953) recommended, and the civic groups generally urged, that the City Administrator have the power to appoint and remove the heads of departments with the approval of the Mayor and, perhaps more importantly, that he have direct supervision over the budget and personnel agencies. Mayor-elect Wagner and his advisers chose not to give these powers to the City Administrator in the statutes that were prepared and enacted. As a result, the City Administrators have confronted, in a continuing jurisdictional struggle, a competitive budget office and an aloof personnel agency, both inclined more toward the Board of Estimate than toward the Mayor. The departments and agencies, too, have powers of bargaining and of resistance to the City Administrator's "supervision" and "coordination" which they would not possess if the City Administrator had the initiative in appointing and removing department heads.

The explicit assignment of duties to the City Administrator is accompanied by some equally explicit exceptions: his supervision of agencies "under the jurisdiction of the mayor" is qualified by a provision which reads "except the law department, the department of investigation, the bureau of the budget, the city construction coordinator, the boards, commissions and authorities." These exceptions remove a substantial part of the city government from the supervisory and coordinating powers of the City Administrator (although he may, at least in theory, enter these jurisdictions armed with one of his other powers, to study and report to the Mayor). He is also precluded by these exceptions from direct participation in the capital and expense budget processes, the domains of the Budget Director, the Construction Coordinator, the City Planning Commission, and the Board of Estimate. The powers and duties of the City Administrator are, especially in contrast to those of the Deputy Mayor, quite specific; but they are "soft" powers (to supervise, to coordinate, to establish standards, to analyze and report), and they are clearly limited in their jurisdictional reach.

The City Administrator and the Division of Administration have nevertheless become the most fully realized assets of the Mayor's office. They have become the Mayor's most active problem-solvers, especially in matters requiring interdepartmental agreements or departmental reorganizations. They have yet to weather a change of administration, but Mayor Wagner's successor will have strong incentives to retain an important instrument of leadership if he wishes to be Mayor rather than merely the presiding officer of the Board of Estimate.

The Mayor's "Cabinet." Mayor Wagner established in 1954, under the stimulus of City Administrator Luther Gulick, a "cabinet" composed not of the heads of the line departments and agencies, but of officials of overhead agencies. This group, meeting under the Mayor's chairmanship and with the City Administrator responsible for the formal agenda, has had a somewhat fluctuating schedule of meetings and membership, but its "regular" members include the following: the City Administrator and his deputies, the Deputy Mayor, the Corporation Counsel, the Budget Director, the Personnel Director, the Chairman of the City Planning Commission, and several of the assistants to the Mayor—a total of 15 members or more. The City Administrator's original concept of the group was that it would be a committee meeting of the Mayor's "controllers," those who plan and administer the allocation of the resources of manpower and money to the line agencies in charge of the city government's operations. The main purpose of the cabinet was to inform and advise the Mayor each week concerning the problems, in both policy and managerial terms, which the members of the group individually and collectively identified as having priority claims upon his attention.

The Mayor's cabinet has not escaped the familiar difficulties of similar efforts to aid Presidents and Governors, and its particular composition and methods of operation have added others of its own. Some members protect their own separate jurisdictions by withholding items from the agenda, hoping to present them to the Mayor on a more private occasion or reserving them for unilateral action. Others listen and perhaps comment, but withhold commitment. At least one potent controller—the Construction Coordinator— is not a member. The consequence of these and other frailties is that the cabinet has not grown in stature and effectiveness; its agenda have declined in quality, its meetings in frequency, and its product in usefulness to the Mayor. Its survival as a viable institution is doubtful.

Overhead Agency Officials. In the formal terms of the charter, the Mayor may also regard the heads of certain overhead agencies as members of his staff and look to them as a resource of advice and information. Several of these—the Corporation Counsel, the Budget Director, the Personnel Director, the Planning Commission Chairman—are regular members of the Mayor's cabinet, while others—the Commissioner of Investigation, the Construction Coordinator, and the Purchase Commissioner—are not. But the formal terms of the charter are modified sharply in the political process. Of these several officials, only the Corporation Counsel and the Investigation Commissioner stand in practice in a "staff" relationship to the Mayor.

Department Heads. A few Mayors have aspired to use their department heads as part of their staff. No Mayor has found it feasible. There are too many department heads to sit as an effective committee. When seen separately, each one has his own agenda of concerns special to his department, and has little time, inclination, or capacity to offer the Mayor general advice or information. Mayors learn to accept this as one of the hard facts of mayoral life.

The Mayor's Committees. Pressed for help, Mayors supplement their staff by the appointment of a great number and variety of committees to explore problems and suggest solutions, to mediate disputes, to give the Mayor time to assess situations, to delay the inevitable a little while, or to reduce the political risks and costs of change. There are perhaps, at any one time, a hundred such committees in motion or, more often, in innocuous desuetude. These include committees of officials to bridge the interests of several agencies or departments, mixed committees of officials and citizens, and citizens' committees. Some have broad, some narrow, assignments; some have a brief life, others a long one. Some are provided with a staff; others must do without. Some are successful; some disappear from sight; others are noisy and unproductive. Mayors learn the varied benefits and failures of committees but find few ways by which to avoid the risks. On balance, committees seem more useful than harmful, and Mayors have steadily increased their number and broadened their assignments. But Mayors have no adequate machinery for planning the effective use of committees, for defining their assignments, for selecting chairmen and members, for assisting them, for terminating them when their work is done or their performance unsatisfactory. A classic illustration of these circumstances is provided in the slow decline into mere ritualistic existence of the Mayor's Advisory Council with its extensive committee structure, after an elaborate establishment and installation in 1954 as an announced high instrument of citizen participation in the formation and execution of public policy.

The City Administrator is charged by the charter with part of the responsibility for the use of committees but apparently has not yet found a method for assuming the task. Meanwhile the Mayor must use committees somewhat indiscriminatingly, frequently on the initiative of others, and sometimes when he would rather not have a committee at all, or would prefer a different chairman and membership from those he is persuaded to accept.

The Limitations of the Mayor's Staff. The several elements of the Mayor's staff do not yet form a coherent whole. In organization and strength the Mayor's staff cannot yet match, in terms of the relative demands upon the two offices, the pattern and quality of the President's White House staff and the Executive Office of the President. The Mayor's staff more nearly approaches but does not yet equal, for his needs and purposes, the staff elements now available to the Governor of New York.

What the Mayor in person has always needed throughout the history of the office since 1898, is assistance in securing personal perspective on, and personal command over, the issues that ought to be decided by the Mayor and by nobody else. Most of his present help is provided by officials and agencies serving their own purposes, and the purposes of other participants in the political contest, as assiduously as they serve the Mayor in strictly mayoral terms. Few Mayors have clearly understood this need, and fewer still have known how to find and use such scarce talent. This help most needed by Mayors is in its essence political help and advice, supplied by persons sensitive to and sensible about the Mayor's full dimensional role in the city's political contest, aware of the subleties of strategy in the timing and the boldness, the caution, or the finality with which the Mayor uses, for his purposes of leadership, the resources of his office. It is this political help (in the broadest sense of the word "political") rather than managerial assistance that the Mayor most needs.

But it is upon present staff resources, whatever their limitations, that the Mayor must still heavily depend for assistance in his roles as chief of state, chief executive, chief legislator, and chief of party.

The Chief-of-State Function

A Mayor must depend primarily upon himself in his role as chief of state. The institutionalization of the role is still quite rudimentary and the forms of assistance are specialized rather than comprehensive. The press secretary apparently occupies the central staff position for this role, but his interests tend to focus upon the Mayor's relationships with the communication media —upon press releases, press conferences, radio and television appearances by the Mayor. The stage which the press secretary has constantly in mind is thus an important but restricted aspect of the Mayor's responsibilities as chief of state. The Deputy Mayor in some administrations has also assisted the Mayor in the chief-of-state role, sometimes in planning the Mayor's use of the role and at other times acting as the Mayor's delegate on ceremonial and other occasions of state. The Commissioner of Commerce and Public Events has an even more specialized task: he stages for the Mayor the receptions, parades, luncheons, dinners, and other occasions of honor to the city's distinguished visitors and guests, sometimes with such personal flair (as was long the case, even before the creation of the special office, with Grover Whalen as the city's "official greeter") that the Mayor becomes a background figure.

These three officials—the press secretary, the Deputy Mayor, the Commerce Commissioner—are the Mayor's main resources as chief of state. The office of City Administrator supplies some secondary but significant help; it prepares the Mayor's annual report to the public and assists in the preparation of some of the Mayor's more significant public statements. Some other agencies provide sporadic help on request. All these resources are without unifying and coordinating direction except as the Mayor may himself provide it. As chief of state, the Mayor's main resource is found not in the scope and quality of his assistance but in the traditions and customs of his office.

The major limitations of the chief-of-state function for the Mayors of New York arise out of their failure to perceive the full potential of the role. Most Mayors have regarded the role as more burden than asset and have sought staff assistants who would restrict the role rather than reshape and expand it. No Mayor (except La Guardia on occasion) has conceived the opportunities of the chief-of-state function as Theodore Roosevelt and Woodrow Wilson grasped those of the press and the presidency, or as Al Smith used the public forum during his governorship, Franklin D. Roosevelt the press and radio, and Thomas E. Dewey the press, radio, and television. The Mayors have mistaken the difficulties of the role for its essence, its minutiae for its purpose.

Being poorly conceived of by Mayors, the chief-of-state function has quite naturally been poorly staffed and poorly managed. Thus, for example, the Mayor's press conferences (if they may be called such) have evolved in forms more convenient to the press than to serve the purposes of the Mayor. They are frequent, unscheduled, unplanned, episodic, the initiative as to time and content belonging more often to the press corps than to the Mayor. The morning's news stories and editorials more often set the day's agenda for the Mayor and his associates than do the Mayor and his staff. In most of their relations with the press, most Mayors are "off balance" and on the defensive much of the time. In other instances the chief-of-state role is often expended carelessly and cheaply, the Mayor's appearance and participation being allowed to serve solely the purposes of others when it might quite easily be planned to serve the Mayor's needs also. In general, the time and energy that the Mayor can invest in his role as chief of state is most often rationed out in fragments to meet the pressures that pour in upon the office. Much less often is it used dramatically and purposefully to create power and influence for the Mayor to use as chief executive, chief legislator, or chief of party.

The Chief-Executive Function

Most of the formal charter and other statutory powers of the Mayor relate to his role as chief executive. He is "the chief executive officer of the city"; he appoints "the heads of departments, all commissioners and all other officers not elected by the people, except as otherwise provided by law"; he may "whenever in his judgment the public interest shall so require . . . remove from office any public officer holding office by appointment from a mayor of the city, except officers for whose removal other provision is made by law"; he has the duty "to keep himself informed of the doings of the several agencies of the city and to see to the proper administration of its affairs and the efficient conduct of its business"; and "to be vigilant and active in causing all provisions of law to be executed and enforced." He also has the power to supervise the preparation of the executive budget and to submit it to the Board of Estimate, to participate in the preparation of the capital budget; and to require from department heads "reports of their operations and action."

These formal grants of executive power are not unimpressive when taken at their face value and on first reading. But they require closer examination. The provision that the Mayor is "the chief executive officer" is a designation of office, not a clear grant of power in itself. The appointing power is granted in forthright terms and is the Mayor's most important single executive power. In his freedom from any need for confirmation of his appointees by the Council or Board of Estimate, the Mayor benefits from a long tradition, dating back to Assemblyman Theodore Roosevelt's amendments to the New York City Charter and to the "Seth Low Charter" for Brooklyn, both of the early 1880's. Yet the clause "except as otherwise provided by law" is a significant limitation of the Mayor's power; many such provisions of law do, in fact, restrict him in appointments. The removal power is granted in terms parallel to the Mayor's appointing power, and the two powers together provide the main justification for the familiar description of the New York City Mayor as a "strong mayor" among the various types of city governments in the United States. But the Mayor's removal power is also limited by the clause, "except officers for whose removal other provision is made by law," and there are more such restrictive provisions concerning removal than appointment. The "duty" to supervise agencies and "to see to the proper administration" and "the efficient conduct" of the city's affairs is not a direct grant of power but rather an obligation, as is also the injunction to "be vigilant and active" in the execution of the laws. Mayors have found few opportunities to draw power from these provisions; they are instead mainly the source of expectations and demands from others.

Some of the usual chief-executive powers are omitted from the grants of authority to the Mayor. The Mayor is not the chief fiscal officer of the city; the Comptroller has greater financial powers than does the Mayor. Nor does the Mayor have budget powers comparable to those of the President or the Governor; he has the formal power to direct the preparation of "the executive budget" step in the expense budget process, together with a minor role in the preparation of the capital budget, but the modification, and thus the larger elements of the administration of both budgets, belong to the Board of Estimate. In another managerial field, the management of personnel, the

TABLE 67. MAYORAL APPOINTMENTS

Agencies and Departments whose heads are appointed by Mayor	Boards and Commissions to which Mayor appoints some or all members or serves as member himself
1. Air Pollution Control Department 2. Bureau of the Budget 3. Buildings Department 4. City Construction Coordinator 5. City marshals (83) 6. City Planning Department 7. City Record 8. City Register 9. City Sheriff 10. Civil Defense Office 11. Commerce and Public Events Dept. 12. Correction Department 13. Division of Administration 14. Finance Department 15. Fire Department 16. Health Department 17. Hospitals Department 18. Investigation Department 19. Labor Department 20. Law Department 21. Licenses Department 22. Marine and Aviation Department 23. Markets Department 24. Medical Examiner 25. Municipal Broadcasting System 26. Parks Department 27. Personnel Department 28. Police Department 29. Public Works Department 30. Purchase Department 31. Real Estate Department 32. Sanitation Department 33. Tax Department 34. Traffic Department 35. Veterans Affairs Division 36. Water Supply, Gas, and Electricity Department 37. Welfare Department	1. Alcoholic Beverage Control Board, New York City 2. Art Commission 3. Banking Commission 4. Board of Assessors 5. Board of Correction 6. Board of Education 7. Board of Health 8. Board of Higher Education 9. Board of Hospitals 10. Board of Standards and Appeals 11. Board of Statutory Consolidation 12. Board of Water Supply 13. Career and Salary Board of Appeals 14. City Civil Service Commission 15. City Planning Commission 16. Commission on Foster Care of Children 17. Commission on Inter-Group Relations 18. Council on Port Development 19. Fire Department Pension and Life Insurance Fund 20. Health Insurance Board 21. Mental Health Board 22. Parole Commission 23. Police Pension Fund 24. Slum Clearance Committee 25. Tax Commission 26. Teachers' Retirement Board 27. Transit Authority Commission 28. Uniformed Forces Salary Appeals Board 29. Urban Renewal Board 30. Youth Board *Boards of Special Authorities* 31. Housing Authority 32. Transit Authority 33. Triborough Bridge and Tunnel Authority

SOURCE: *Official Directory of the City of New York*, 1959.

Mayor has limitations and frustrations exceeding those of most chief executives. In the power to reorganize agencies and departments, the Mayor has no formal power or actual leverage to compare even faintly with the initiative that Presidents have possessed for almost three decades. Another main limitation upon the Mayor as chief executive lies in the autonomous tendencies of agencies and departments, especially those headed by boards and commissions, or organized as public authorities. These tendencies toward autonomy are usually favored by provisions of law that limit the Mayor's power to appoint or remove the heads of agencies or in some other fashion restrict his power to supervise their performance. It is to the Board of Estimate, not to the Mayor, that these agencies and departments must defer most often.

As chief executive, the Mayor has limited resources in staff assistance as well as in formal powers. The City Administrator and the Deputy Mayor are his main assets. Others provide occasional and specialized help: the Corporation Counsel, the Investigations Commissioner, some of the assistants to the Mayor. In addition, he may make cautious use of the Budget Director and the Personnel Director, keeping alert to their intimate connections with the Board of Estimate. The cabinet, some heads of departments, the official and citizens committees—all these have their frequent but specialized values to the Mayor as chief executive. If Mayors realize that they have more help as chief executive than as chief of state, they can rarely feel they have enough.

The Mayor has a trinity of responsibilities as chief executive: he stands as hostage for the virtue and efficiency of all officials and employees; he is viewed as the principal solver of problems and handler of crises for the city; and he bears the main burden of decisions regarding priorities in the allocation of the city's scarce resources among the many competing claimants for services, each claimant usually being an apostle of economy against all other claimants. To meet these three demanding sets of responsibilities, the Mayor's powers and resources are not so imposing as the popular image of his office suggests. Beset by the high expectations of his constituency, the Mayor must call upon all the resources of his office, using as chief executive what he can borrow from his roles as chief of state, chief of party, and chief legislator. Even so, he needs more.

The Mayor's Legislative Function

The formal powers that support the Mayor in his role as chief legislator are few and familiar. It is his "duty" as Mayor "to communicate to the council, at least once in each year, a general statement of the finances, government and affairs of the city, with a summary statement of the activities of the agencies of the city"; it is also his "duty" to "recommend to the council all such measures as he shall deem expedient." These duties are accompanied by the grant of a veto power over local laws or resolutions passed by the Council which he must exercise within thirty days; if the Mayor disapproves, his action may be overridden by "the votes of two-thirds of all the councilmen." (The Mayor may also disapprove a local law which has been approved by the Board of Estimate as well as the Council; in such event, the Council alone is required to act on a proposal to override the veto and may do so by the same two-thirds vote.) The Mayor has an additional legislative role as chairman of the Board of Estimate, and as a member of that body has four votes, but he has no veto power over Board of Estimate resolutions, which is that Board's characteristic mode of action. In the budget process, the Mayor may veto any reduction or omission of items by the Council in the expense budget as adopted by the Board of Estimate; if he does so, the Council may override the veto by the votes of "three-fourths of all the councilmen." The Mayor has no veto in the capital budget process, nor does he have any formal part in the legislative activities of the Board of Health, a significant and virtually autonomous legislative body. Almost wholly unexplored and unexploited as a legislative resource for the Mayor are his uncertain but substantial powers to issue executive orders. Finally, among his legislative powers, the Mayor may request (with the concurrence of the Council) the state legislature to enact special legislation for the city.

It is one of the astonishments of Mayors to discover that their most formidable legislative powers are directed at the legislative body—the Council—which can be of least help to them as Mayor. The Mayor can master the Council if he chooses (although a Fusion Mayor will have some difficulties, lacking majority party support there), but such mastery is of limited use. The Council can drag its feet, or exact its price for consent, but it can do nothing else of real importance on its own. The Board of Estimate and the state legislature hold the keys to all significant legislation. In relation to these two legislative institutions, the Mayor as chief legislator has only the power to request and to try to persuade.

The knowledge that the Council is the mere shadow of a legislative body has led Mayors to make limited use of their formal powers to send messages to the Council and to propose a program of legislative action by that body. The annual message is sent regularly with due ceremony, but it is more a report of accomplishments to the public than a presentation of city problems, and it makes only the most general proposals for councilmanic action. Nor is it followed by supplementary messages outlining a comprehensive legislative program for the Council. The single annual message to the Council is perceived by Mayors as a convenient public relations opportunity for a report that can be addressed to the Council but actually aimed at the general public. To do more than that is apparently regarded as uneconomical use of the Mayor's energies as chief legislator. The main transactions of Council legislative business are left to direct negotiation by the departments and agencies with the Council. Should the Council display any rare and unexpected tendencies toward initiative against the Mayor's wishes, his veto power is sufficient to check it; Mayors are not often troubled by a runaway Council. If the Council delays or withholds its approval from legislation desired by the Mayor (as it stalled the 1957 Sharkey-Brown-Isaacs bill against racial or religious discrimination in housing and the Mayor's proposal for a Charter Revision Commission in 1958–1959, for example), the Mayor relies mainly upon his influence with the County Leaders of his party, upon the agitation of nongovernmental groups, some bargains with Council leaders, and upon the communication media to compel Council agreement.

The Mayor has few opportunities to present a comprehensive legislative program to the Board of Estimate or even to address it by message on a major item of legislation. The Board does not encourage such formal behavior on the part of one of its members, even though he be the chairman and the Mayor, and few Mayors have used their power to do so. Instead, the Mayor is ordinarily required by the custom and sanctions of the Board to present his proposals as items on the Board calendar in the same manner as any other member. His presentation of the executive budget to the Board and the Council is the main exception to this rule. If the Mayor is to be chief legislator, he cannot rely upon formal messages to the Board of Estimate for that purpose. Lacking a veto over its resolutions also, he must persuade the Board by other means than by message or formal disapproval.

Faced by this series of difficulties in legislative leadership at City Hall, Mayors turn perforce to Albany. To the Governor and to the state legislature, the Mayor annually presents a program of legislative hopes and demands from the city, financial proposals usually being predominant, but with other legislative items included. The Mayor has several strategic advantages when he thus turns to the state government: he can ordinarily expect a Democratic Governor to be sympathetic to the claims of the largest element in the Governor's constituency, or he can bring significant pressure upon a Republican Governor who must avoid the appearance of hostility to the city's electorate. The Mayor can also usually count upon the help of the minority leaders in the legislature, who are almost invariably legislators from the city. He can, and frequently does, himself journey to Albany to present his proposals, hoping to dramatize their urgency and to strengthen his hand. In later stages of the legislative process, both Democratic and Republican Governors will usually listen attentively to the Mayor's objections to bills before them and will often veto them on the Mayor's request.

But the legislative terrain at Albany is nevertheless a difficult one for the Mayor. The Governor and the legislature have separate problems of their own, often being preoccupied by their struggles with each other (the Governor looking toward his own reelection or toward the White House, the legislature divided between those who would help him and those who would stop him). The leaders of the Republican majority in the legislature have no strong inclination to help a New York City Mayor, even if he be a Fusionist; they often have powerful incentives to limit the aspirations of any Mayor. Interest groups can often exercise more influence with legislators, or Governors, than can the Mayor. Against these several hazards, a Mayor has no choice but to try; if he falters at Albany, he can hardly expect to recoup his legislative losses at City Hall.

The Mayor's role as chief legislator is his most arduous one. Not only are his formal powers for its performance essentially irrelevant, being oriented to the Council rather than aimed at the legislative bodies more important for the city, but the staff assistance available to him in his capacity as chief legislator is also scattered and largely uncoordinated. The Corporation Counsel and his staff provide extensive and continuing technical assistance and advice to the Mayor in the field of legislation, but the Corporation Counsel does not often have clear leadership responsibilities for shaping the Mayor's legislative program. The Deputy Mayor has a varying assignment in Board of Estimate legislation, but his role is more one of day-to-day agency for the Mayor than one of programming and long-range strategy. The Mayor's legislative representative at Albany is usually a legislative technician and tactician for the Mayor, skillful in legislative mechanics and familiar with legislative personalities, but not a man of policy, program, or broad legislative strategy. These three officials are the Mayor's mainstays as chief legislator. Other assistants and agencies play more specialized parts: the City Administrator and the Budget Director in financial legislation, the legal aides to the Mayor in routine local legislation, the department and agency heads in their particular fields of interest or specialization. The whole pattern of staff assistance to the Mayor as chief legislator is one of divided responsibilities performed in considerable isolation from each other. Such unity and coherence as obtains depends mainly upon the Mayor's own unaided instincts and efforts.

Mayors have more clearly grasped the day-to-day necessities of the chief-legislator role than its larger opportunities. The splintering of the role between attention to the Council, the Board of Estimate, and the state legislature has baffled Mayors for decades and promises to continue as a major perplexity. Each of these legislative arenas presents its own set of difficulties for the Mayor as chief legislator. Discovery and development of a unified strategy that would effectively serve the Mayor as leader in all three is an act of imagination and determination for which Mayors have had little time to spare and little help from advisers. Fragmented strategy has been accompanied and augmented by a fragmented staff. Tactics for meeting today's difficulties have long taken precedence over the planning of tomorrow's strategy. Even the Mayor's state legislative program, his only approach to a comprehensive planning effort as chief legislator, is most often developed in an atmosphere of haste and crisis. In Council and Board of Estimate legislation, all the Mayor's plans and programs are specialized, and only rarely is the pressure of events anticipated in ways that give the Mayor opportunity for initiative on a broad front of legislation. At Albany and at City Hall tactics of improvisation and survival are the usual portion served up to him by a fragmented and harassed legislative staff.

The great uses of the communication media to which Presidents and Governors may turn in presenting their legislative programs are lost to the Mayor by default. The Mayor has little opportunity to summon up the full resources of his roles as chief of state and chief executive to support his role as chief legislator; he is compelled to turn more often to his resources as chief of party. Party leaders can help Mayors to influence legislation.

As Chief of Party

No formal powers explicitly support the Mayor in his role as chief of party. His power to appoint and remove department heads and other commissioners, together with his opportunity to guide or control the appointments and removals made by these officials, is the most directly relevant and essential to his party role, and some other powers have their occasional usefulness to him. But it is from other sources that the Mayor derives his major claims to be recognized by the party leaders as their chief. As the successful candidate of his party for the city's highest office, he can remind the five County Leaders that he is their most important asset, representing in his office and person the broadest and largest electoral constituency in the city. If the party leaders claim that their organizations "delivered" this constituency to the Mayor, he may not only respond with persuasive skepticism but may also suggest that taking the constituency away from him is now a costly and hazardous venture.

As chief of state and as chief executive, the Mayor has sanctions against the party leaders which are sharp and punishing. The electorate delights in Mayors who mount crusades against "machines" and "bosses," while the mass communication media applaud and dramatize the crusader as hero. Aspirants to, and incumbents in, office can be made to feel the punitive lash of the appointing and removing powers exercised by a Mayor at war with the party leaders. But the Mayor knows that the party leaders have formidable countersanctions. Both Mayor and party leaders share the knowledge that they can greatly hurt or greatly help each other. Each tends to bargain for a point of optimum accommodation of interests. The Mayor must aim at that level of party leadership for himself that will enable him to meet the high expectations of his constituency.

The Mayor is both helped and hindered by the absence of a citywide party organization. Wagner could assert in 1958 that he was "the titular head of the Democratic party in the city," but this role remains more a potentiality than an accepted fact. Since there is no stable hierarchy among the five County Leaders, and no settled machinery for the collective reconciliation of their separate demands upon the Mayor, the Mayor may often profit from their competition with each other. On the other hand, if there were a city committee whose chairman was the Mayor's designee (as Presidents and Governors manage in parallel circumstances), the Mayor might reasonably expect to benefit from a more stable and more predictable structure for bargaining with party leaders. The uncertainties of the existing arrangement are great; the New York County Leader asserts a traditional claim of leadership in each party, but the Mayor discovers that this does not shield him from the direct and competitive pressures of the other County Leaders and of many District Leaders who break through the formal channels to bargain with the Mayor for their districts. The Mayor also learns quickly the risks that attend the satisfaction of one claimant at the expense of several others.

The Mayor is at a disadvantage in the nominating process. He may ordinarily secure his own renomination (although McClellan and Hylan were each denied a third nomination and Impellitteri a second), but he has little apparent influence in the nomination of his successor. He has indirect rather than direct opportunities to influence other city and county nominations. The Mayor also plays only a secondary role in state and national nominating conventions. There is often no cohesive "city delegation"; when there is, there is no certainty that the Mayor will head it. To these disabilities must be added, too, the history of the mayoralty as the last powerful position to be occupied by its incumbents; no Mayor has gone on to high elective executive or legislative office, and to the future influence such an office would confer. Mayors are therefore deprived of the present leverage that might be afforded by party leader anticipation of their future power. Consequently, in the nominating process, the Mayor has few opportunities to be chief of party.

More useful currency for bargaining with party leaders is found by Mayors in their appointing power. Magistracies, deputy commissionerships, and lesser "exempt," "provisional," or "noncompetitive" positions are the main denominations; the other and higher posts the Mayor must largely reserve for nonparty purposes. The measure of a Mayor's success in these patronage bargains is the amount of party leader support he gets in return, particularly the help he gets from party leaders in his role as chief executive (for which the Mayor needs the loyalty and energies of his executive appointees) and in his role as chief legislator (in which the Mayor needs the party leaders' considerable influence over the legislators in their party). Fortunate is the Mayor who can feel he is fully repaid.

Fusion Mayors have an anomalous party role. Low, Mitchel, and La Guardia were each elected after joint nomination by the Republican party and other Fusion groups. Their campaigns for election were strongly "anti-party" in spirit and vocabulary. After election, each of these Mayors was under strong pressure and considerable obligation to bargain with two separate party structures (one a fully organized but minority party, its orientation toward Albany and Washington rather than City Hall; the other more a loose-jointed committee than a party organization), while continuing simultaneously a posture of unrelenting boycott against all party organization. The resulting dilemmas and contradictions were numerous and confusing to the Fusion Mayors as well as to party leaders, officials, interest groups, the communication media, and to the general public. The ultimate governmental product of these unconventional relationships was on the whole a superior one, but its explanation remains elusive.

Mayors need help in their party role as in their other functions. They lack the time to give this duty all the attention it requires. However, the assistance they receive in this capacity (whether they are Democrats or Fusionists) is not highly visible. A taint of illegitimacy attends the function whether it be rendered to Presidents, Governors, or the Mayors of New York, and the Mayors are the least favored with public tolerance for their party leadership role. The civic groups, the communication media, the bureaucracies, and others all share and express a cultivated distaste for any formal arrangements that bring to the party leaders any accreditation as full and open participants in the governing process. Nor are the County Leaders of the parties favorably disposed toward the institutionalization of aides to help Mayors handle their party function; they prefer to deal directly with the Mayor rather than with intermediaries. But Mayors must respond to their own necessities. They resort to various expediencies: La Guardia and Wagner initially used their respective Corporation Counsels, Windels and Burke; O'Dwyer and Impellitteri, "patronage" assistants on their immediate staff; some Deputy Mayors have been a main reliance; on some occasions, outsiders, largely or fleetingly anonymous, have served a Mayor as party advisers and assistants; and in other instances, the Mayors (for example, Van Wyck, Hylan, and O'Brien) abdicated their potential role as chief of party to the leading party functionaries.

The prevailing characteristics of all these arrangements seem to be impermanence, instability, uncertainties of jurisdiction, and absence of responsibility for developing a comprehensive bargaining strategy. The Mayors of New York have found no office so useful to them for such purpose as the recent Governors of New York (F. D. Roosevelt, Lehman, Dewey, and Harriman) have found in the state office of Secretary of State (successively occupied as party leadership posts by Edward J. Flynn, Democratic Leader in The Bronx; Thomas J. Curran, Republican Leader in Manhattan; and Carmine De Sapio, Democratic Leader in Manhattan). Nor have any of the Mayors been able to secure the kinds of party assistance that Presidents have had—as did Theodore Roosevelt, for example, from Cortelyou and Payne; Wilson from Tumulty and Burleson; Franklin Roosevelt from Farley and Flynn; Eisenhower from Adams and Hall.

The Mayor's role as chief of party is not only strenuous; it is also used defensively more often than aggressively. The opportunities for its use are largely unstandardized and unpredictable, making its use for long-range purposes difficult. For these reasons Mayors have not been able to maximize the role, and it is not clear that any Mayor has grasped the full potential that the role would possess for a chief executive who could surmount the initial barriers. No Mayor seems to have given so systematic and determined attention to the development of his role as chief of party as did, for example, Smith and Dewey in the governorship and the two Roosevelts in the presidency.

The Opportunities and Limitations of the Office

In sum, the four separate roles of the Mayor—as chief of state, as chief executive, as chief legislator, and as chief of party—have several common characteristics. Each role is a response to great and compelling expectations from the city's general public and from the major participants in the city's political process. They are genuine roles that the Mayor must in some fashion perform; the Mayor cannot without peril choose one and ignore the others. Each role is also an opportunity, not merely a duty. It can be seized boldly and imaginatively, or reluctantly and passively. Within fairly broad limits, each role is flexible, made large or small by the Mayor's own conception of the dimensions of his office and of each of his roles in the office. In the main, Mayors have inclined toward lesser exercise of the potentialities of the office, and of each of its roles, than has been shown to be feasible by its most imaginative and energetic occupants. The limited perception of the office and its separate roles on the part of most Mayors has been accompanied by inadequate assistance for the Mayor in each role. The chief-executive role is the best supported (a consequence of the Mayors' superior grasp of this role), but it, too, is understaffed, and its awkward organization is hardly a model for imitation. Poor perception of each role and poor staffing for its performance are joined intimately with an additional limitation: the reciprocal uses of the separate roles to support each other are quite often overlooked and are rarely exploited fully.

The fundamental limitation upon the Mayor's performance in his several roles, however, is to be found in the inadequacies of his formal powers. His appointing and removal powers are circumscribed in scope and hedged about with restrictions, his fiscal and personnel powers are few, and his power to supervise is blunted by numerous built-in forms of autonomy for agencies and departments. His legislative powers are largely confined to the irrelevant councilmanic arena. These are formidable obstacles even to a Mayor who has a high conception of the office and a great determination to bring to each of his roles all his energy and imagination.

THE OFFICE AND THE MAN

The aspirations a Mayor brings to the office and the leadership he displays there are in large part determined by the stature and quality of the men who are recruited for the office by the nominating and electing processes of the city. What kinds of men want to be Mayor? What kinds can be persuaded to seek nomination for the office? Which kinds can achieve nomination? And what types are elected to the office?

The Nominees for Mayor: Eligibility Characteristics

The office of Mayor has an uncertain status among the higher political positions. It is not sought by the Governors or ex-Governors of the state, or by its United States Senators (save by Senator Copeland in 1937, who failed to win it). Members of the President's cabinet who come from the city do not offer themselves as prospects while in office, and only one ex-cabinet member (Benjamin F. Tracy in 1897) has been a candidate. Members of the Governor's cabinet are rarely among the aspirants, Edward Corsi in 1950 and Robert Christenberry in 1957 being the only examples. The most outstanding figures in the city's civic, cultural, and business communities have seldom been led to seek the office. And military heroes have not been among the nominees.

But if the office of Mayor is not a magnet for these political and public leaders, it is a goal for almost all others. No single office serves as a channel to a mayoralty nomination, as, for example, the governorship of a pivotal state is a channel to presidential nomination. The field of prospects for mayoral nominations is consequently larger and less predictable than that for the governorship or the presidency.

There have been 19 elections for Mayor in the sixty-year history of the Greater City (a switch from a four-year term to a two-year term in 1902 and then back to a four-year term in 1906, plus special elections in 1932 and 1950, accounting for this total). In almost every one of these elections, there have been more than two competing tickets, each having a candidate for Mayor. In the 19 elections, at least 66 separate mayoral nominations can be identified, involving 36 different nominees. Of these 36 nominees for Mayor, beginning with the election of 1897 and including the election of 1957, the Democrats have presented a total of 12 candidates—10 without any other significant endorsement, 2 with joint endorsement (O'Dwyer, 1945, with an American Labor party nomination; Pecora, 1950, with a Liberal party nomination), while Wagner had a Liberal party nomination in 1957 but not in 1953. The Republicans have presented a total of 15 nominees—9 (excluding La Guardia, who was first nominated in 1929 without other endorsement) with no other major endorsement, 6 with joint endorsement (Low, Bannard, Mitchel, La Guardia, having had Fusion nominations, while La Guardia in 1937 and 1941 also had ALP nominations, and Goldstein and Morris, in 1945 and 1949, respectively, had Liberal party designations). In addition, third parties or other political groups have supplied 9 other candidates:

Hearst in 1905 and 1909; Hillquit in 1917 and 1932; Thomas in 1929; McKee in 1933; Marcantonio in 1949; Impellitteri and Ross in 1950; Halley and McAvoy ·in 1953. These 36 do not constitute a complete list of all nominees for Mayor since 1897 (a number of splinter groups or poorly supported nominees are omitted), but from them we may discover the major characteristics which make aspirants eligible for a nomination.

Borough of Residence. When national party conventions nominate candidates for the presidency, they do not often ignore the importance of the state in which the candidate resides. A similar geographical consideration, although not so easily measured, guides the state party conventions when they nominate candidates for the governorship of New York. Party leaders and the leaders of other political groups, when they come to nominate candidates for the mayoralty, exhibit a similar sensitivity to the actual or mythical relationship between a candidate's residence and his strength as nominee.

Of the 36 nominees from 1897 to 1957, 24 were, at the time of nomination, residents of the Borough of Manhattan, 11 were residents of Brooklyn, and 1 was a resident of The Bronx. The Boroughs of Queens and Richmond have been unrepresented among these mayoral nominees. This two-to-one preference for Manhattan as the borough of residence for the nominees of all parties and groups is explained in part by Manhattan's earlier population and electoral predominance. This predominance was lost by 1920, but the tradition of Manhattan's priority has persisted. When Brooklyn reached the top position in population and votes, its preeminence was somewhat blurred by the accompanying rise of The Bronx and Queens as populous boroughs.

The different parties react to borough of residence for nominees in about the same pattern. Of the 12 Democratic nominees, 8 have been Manhattanites, 4 came from Brooklyn. Of the 15 Republican candidates, 10 have resided in Manhattan, 5 in Brooklyn. Of the 9 third-party nominees, 6 have lived in Manhattan, 2 in Brooklyn, and 1 in The Bronx.

Occupation. Most of the 36 nominees for Mayor have been lawyers: this was the case for 28, or three fourths of all the nominees. Eight have not been lawyers: Low, Hearst, Waterman, Thomas, Pounds, Corsi, McAvoy, and Christenberry. Of the eight nonlawyers, five have been Republican nominees, three have been the candidates of third parties. The Democrats have invariably nominated lawyers. This preference for lawyers as nominees for Mayor is not unusual in American politics. The choice of nominees for President, Senators, Governors, congressmen, and other offices shows a similar, if less emphatic, tendency.

Preceding Political Career. Nomination for the office of Mayor in New York comes almost without exception to men with some prior participation in politics. The Democratic party emphasizes prior elective office as a qualification, having yielded on the point only once—in the 1901 nomination of

Edward M. Shepard. The Republicans are required by their minority status to be somewhat less exacting; of their 15 nominees, 4 held no elective office before nomination, although 3 of these had extensive political activity to their credit. The 9 third-party nominees include 5 who had held prior elective office; the remaining 4 had extensive experience in appointive office, as prior candidates, or in party organization affairs. Thus, of the 36 nominees, 27 had held prior elective office; and only 2 (Bannard in 1909, Waterman in 1925) lacked any kind of extensive exposure to the political process. The profession of politics is clearly the main gateway to the mayoral nomination in New York and is treated as such even by those nominating groups professing "nonpartisanship."

The particular political ladders by which aspirants climb to a mayoral nomination are not easily described. There are many different kinds of ladders; in a precise sense, no two nominees have followed an identical one. But some patterns do exist. If we look at the positions held by nominees immediately preceding, or at the time of, their first nomination to the mayoralty, we discover that five were then incumbents in a citywide elective office—the presidency of the Board of Aldermen or, after 1937, of the Council (Mitchel, McKee, Morris, Impellitteri, Halley); five others held an elective judgeship (Van Wyck, Gaynor, Hylan, O'Brien, Pecora); three were congressmen (McClellan, La Guardia, Marcantonio); two were Borough Presidents of Manhattan (Curran, Wagner); one was a state senator (Walker); one was a Brooklyn District Attorney (O'Dwyer); one held an appointive post in the Governor's cabinet (Corsi). The remaining 17 were not in public office at the time of nomination, but 9 of these had earlier held elective posts and 3 others earlier appointive positions. Two others were active in "civic politics" (Edward M. Shepard, William M. Ivins), two were active third-party leaders (Hillquit, Thomas), while only Bannard and Waterman were essentially "amateurs" in politics.

Renomination. A prior nomination for Mayor is an asset in securing an additional nomination. Of the 36 nominees, 12 have been nominated for the office of Mayor more than once. La Guardia holds the record with four nominations: 1929, 1933, 1937, 1941. Low (1897, 1901, 1903) and O'Dwyer (1941, 1945, 1949) stand second with their three nominations each. Nine others were twice nominated: McClellan (1903, 1905), Mitchel (1913, 1917), Hylan (1917, 1921), Hillquit (1917, 1932), Walker (1925, 1929), O'Brien (1932, 1933), Morris (1945, 1949), and Wagner (1953, 1957). Counting the nine additional endorsements that were received by six of these nominees as the result of joint nominations (Low in 1901, 1903; Mitchel in 1913, La Guardia in 1933, 1937, 1941; O'Dwyer in 1945; Morris in 1949; Wagner in 1957), these 12 nominees received 37 separate nominations, more than half the total of 66 nominations between 1897 and 1957.

Renomination is an important factor in the nominating process for the Democratic party (6 of their 12 nominees received renomination), less important for Republicans (only 4 of their 15 nominees), and a little less for the third parties (2 of their 9).

Religious Affiliations. The "balanced ticket" for city campaigns begins with the nominations for the office of Mayor. Religious affiliations thus become one of the criteria of eligibility for nominees. Of the 36 nominees for Mayor, 18 have been Protestant, 13 Catholic, and 5 Jewish. Some indication of the trends in these characteristics of nominees is provided by the fact that, of the 19 nominees since 1928 (the midway point since 1897), 7 were Protestant, 8 Catholic, 4 Jewish.

Of the 12 Democratic nominees, 7 have been Catholic, 5 Protestant; since 1928, 4 Catholic, 1 Protestant. The 15 Republican nominees have been: 10 Protestant, 3 Catholic, 2 Jewish; since 1928, 4 Protestant, 1 Catholic, 2 Jewish. The third parties have divided their 9 nominations among 3 Catholics, 3 Protestants, 3 Jews; since 1928, among 3 Catholics, 2 Protestants, 2 Jews. The parties thus seem to respond quite differently to religious affiliation in selecting their nominees.

Ethnic Characteristics. The balanced ticket also involves the ethnic and national characteristics of nominees, but these factors are less easily defined and measured by party leaders and the electorate. Taking the broad and vague definitions of ethnic groups used by party leaders and nominees themselves in deciding on such matters, the 36 nominees for the Mayoralty may be described as follows: 14 would seem to belong to the Irish group (including Robert F. Wagner, who as the son of a German Methodist father and an Irish Catholic mother, himself a Catholic married to a Protestant, and his children Catholic, is a delight to both ticket-balancers and electorates); 12 to "old stock" ethnic groups (British and Dutch primarily); 5 to the Jewish group (which by the logic of politics is both a religious and an ethnic group); and 5 to the Italian group (including Fiorello H. La Guardia, who as an Italian Protestant with Jewish ancestors plus multilingual capacities was also almost a "balanced ticket" in himself). Since 1928 the 19 nominees have been distributed: 6 to the Irish group, 4 to the Jewish group, 5 to the Italian group (4 of these in the 1950 election alone).

The parties respond to the ethnic factors in somewhat differing fashions. Of the 12 Democratic nominees, 8 have been Irish, 3 "old stock," 1 Italian; since 1928, the 5 Democratic nominees have been: 4 Irish, 1 Italian. Of the 15 Republican nominees, 7 have been "old stock," 4 Irish, 2 Jewish, 2 Italian; since 1928, the 7 Republican nominees have been: 3 "old stock," 2 Jewish, 2 Italian. Of the 9 nominees presented by third parties, 2 have been Irish, 2 "old stock," 3 Jewish, 2 Italian; since 1928, 2 Irish, 1 "old stock," 2 Jewish, 2 Italian.

The first Irish candidate for Mayor was nominated by the Republicans in 1897 (Tracy, a Protestant); the Democrats' first Irish nominee was Gaynor, also a Protestant, in 1909. The first Jewish nominee was Hillquit, presented by the Socialists in 1917; the Republicans' first Jewish candidate was Goldstein, in 1945. The first Italian nominee was La Guardia (a Protestant), the 1929 choice of the Republicans; the Democratic first was Pecora (also a Protestant) in 1950. The first Catholic nominees were presented in the election of 1913: McCall by the Democrats, Mitchel by the Republicans and Fusionists.

The Eligibles: A Summary. The party leaders, the leaders of other nominating groups, and the electorates in several primary contests have selected from among many aspirants 36 nominees, in 19 separate elections for Mayor over a sixty-year period. Among these 36 nominees, the most typical has been a resident of Manhattan (24 nominees), a lawyer (28 nominees), and has previously held an elective office (27 nominees). Other traits of eligibility are less widely shared among nominees but each has its considerable importance. Prior election to a citywide office, to a judgeship, or to Congress is a significant asset. Ethnic and religious characteristics are less decisive.

Choosing Nominees for Mayor

The Process of Selection. The political party leaders, especially the five County Leaders of each party, are the central participants in the nomination of candidates for Mayor by both the Democratic and Republican parties. Yet other participants are frequently able to exert decisive influence upon the choice of party leaders, profiting in part from the fact that the County Leaders are often in competition with each other. State or federal officials may enter into the process; Governor Smith in 1925 intervened with his veto of Hylan for renomination, and in 1945 Governor Dewey was active in the Republican nomination of Jonah Goldstein. Similarly, newspaper publishers may influence the choice of the party leaders, as did Hearst in the 1917 nomination of Hylan and Roy Howard in La Guardia's 1933 nomination. Republican party leaders are also vulnerable to the demands of other political groups whose help they need for the construction of a Fusion or joint ticket, yielding in 1901 to the supporters of Low (whom they had rejected in 1897), to the partisans of Mitchel in 1913 (when the party leaders clearly preferred Charles S. Whitman), to La Guardia in 1933 (when they wanted John F. O'Ryan), and, in 1949, to the advocates of Newbold Morris (who had been passed over in 1945) as a way of securing the Liberal party endorsement.

Third-party nominations are the product of a somewhat different structure and process. The nominating group may be quite centralized, as in the Citizens Union nomination of Low in 1897, the Municipal Ownership League nomination of Hearst in 1905 and his Civic Alliance nomination of 1909, the Socialist nominations of Hillquit in 1917 and 1932 and of Thomas in 1929, the American Labor party nominations of Marcantonio in 1949, Ross in 1950, and McAvoy in 1953, and the Liberal party nomination of Halley in 1953. In other instances, the nomination may be the decision of a faction of defecting regular party leaders, as in the 1933 nomination of McKee and the 1950 nomination of Impellitteri. In still other cases, the nomination is arrived at after bargaining among the third-party leaders, or the leaders of other political groups, on the one hand and Democratic or Republican party leaders on the other. This is the process in all Fusion nominations, and in all the joint nominations of more recent years (La Guardia by the Republicans and the ALP in 1937 and 1941, O'Dwyer by the Democrats and the ALP in 1945, Goldstein by the Republicans and Liberals in 1945, Morris by the Republicans and Liberals in 1949, Pecora by the Democrats and Liberals in 1950, Wagner by the Democrats and Liberals in 1957).

Aspirants for the nomination are themselves not always passive. They often seek to influence individual County Leaders, or all five of them, by the enlistment of outside support from ethnic and religious groups, the press, or state and federal officials. Even more directly, they may challenge, or threaten to challenge, the choice of party leaders in the party primary as did William M. Bennett, in his successful bid against Mitchel in the 1917 Republican primary, and La Guardia in his unsuccessful effort in the 1921 Republican primary and in his effective ultimatum to the Republican leaders preceding their 1929 choice.

The Gains and Costs of Nominations. Nominees emerge from the nominating process with profits or losses, aside from the nomination itself. These gains or costs affect the candidate's fortunes in the election; and, if he is elected, his assets and liabilities in office. Whether the gains exceed the losses depends in part upon the skills which the nominee and his supporters bring to the nominating process.

Low's nomination by Republicans and Fusionists in 1901, for example, was managed in a manner which secured the almost unanimous support of the press for his election as Mayor. Hylan's nomination in 1917 with the assistance of Hearst brought him not only important support in the election campaign but gave him leverage with which to resist the claims of Murphy and other Democratic County Leaders when, as Mayor, he appointed department heads and other officials. La Guardia in 1933 successfully bargained with the nominating leaders for a Board of Estimate ticket reflecting his own preferences for the majority of those nominations, thus securing both a widely approved ticket as an asset in the election campaign and Board of Estimate colleagues who would accept his leadership. O'Dwyer insisted upon and received similar concessions in 1945. And Wagner was needed so badly by the Democratic county leaders to prevent Impellitteri's nomination in 1953 that he could, during the campaign and later, assert a greater independence in his use of the appointing power.

But the costs of nomination are the more frequent phenomena. Van Wyck's indebtedness to Croker was so complete that he was almost powerless in office. Gaynor secured his nomination from the Democratic leaders in 1909 under such awkward circumstances that he was embarrassed throughout the election campaign and lost the Board of Estimate to the Fusion opposition. Bennett won the 1917 Republican nomination in a primary race disapproved by the party leaders and so had little strength in the election. Hylan, while profiting from Hearst's support in 1917, acquired not only an obligation to Hearst, but earned also the determined hostility of Al Smith, who ultimately helped unseat him. La Guardia in 1933 could not avoid an implicit commitment to appoint his principal rival for nomination, O'Ryan, to an important post in his administration. Corsi and Pecora each received his nomination in 1950 as a part of the grand strategy of his party organization in state politics— the Republicans to hold the governorship, the Democrats to capture it; each candidate found his fortunes in the municipal election adversely affected by his lower priority in the state party struggle.

Nominees Who Become Mayor

The nominators (Democratic and Republican party leaders, leaders of third parties, the leaders of other political groups, and various other types of intervenors) establish the criteria of eligibility and select the nominees for Mayor. In doing so, they try to anticipate the ultimate decision of the electorate. As far as direct participation is concerned, however, the electorate is confined to choosing from among those who have survived the bargaining and screening processes used by the nominators and who have emerged as nominees. (Only rarely do the rank-and-file members of a party have an opportunity to choose the nominee in a primary: the only instances have been Bennett against Mitchel in 1917, Curran against La Guardia in 1921, Bennett against La Guardia in 1929, Copeland against La Guardia in 1937, Davis against La Guardia in 1941—all in the Republican party; Hylan against Walker in 1925, Copeland against Mahoney in 1937, Impellitteri against Wagner in 1953—all in the Democratic party. The majority group of party leaders lost only one of these eight primary contests: Bennett's victory over Mitchel in 1917.)

The electorates confirm some of the criteria of selection used by the nominators and modify others. Twelve Mayors have been elected to the office since 1897. Nine of these have been residents of Manhattan, a slightly higher ratio than among the 36 nominees, but this is offset somewhat by the fact that Mayor Low had twice been Mayor of Brooklyn in the 1880's before

TABLE 68. MAYORS OF NEW YORK SINCE 1898: AGE AT INAUGURATION, TENURE, OTHER PUBLIC OFFICES[a]

Mayor	Age at inauguration	Preceding office	Tenure as Mayor	Subsequent public offices
Robert A. Van Wyck	48	Judge of City Court, 1889–1897	1898–1901	Defeated as candidate for Supreme Court, 1901
Seth Low	52	President, Columbia University, 1889–1901	1902–1903	Member, New York State Constitutional Convention, 1915
George B. McClellan	38	Congressman, 1894–1903	1904–1909	None
William J. Gaynor	62	Justice, Supreme Court, Second District, 1893–1909	1910–1913	Died while Mayor
John P. Mitchel	34	President, Board of Aldermen, 1910–1913	1914–1917	Died July, 1918
John F. Hylan	50	County Judge, Kings County, 1914–1917	1918–1925	Justice, Children's Court, 1930–1936
James J. Walker	45	State senator, 1914–1925	1926–1932	Assistant Counsel, State Transit Commission, 1937
John P. O'Brien	60	Surrogate, New York County, 1923–1932	1933	Official Referee, Supreme Court, 1934–1943
Fiorello H. La Guardia	52	Congressman, 1923–1933	1934–1945	Director, UNRRA, 1946
William O'Dwyer	55	District Attorney, Kings County, 1940–1945	1946–1950	Ambassador to Mexico, 1950–1952
Vincent R. Impellitteri	50	President, City Council, 1946–1950	1950–1953	Justice, Special Sessions, 1954 to date
Robert F. Wagner	43	Borough President, Manhattan, 1950–1953	1954 to date	Nominated for U.S. Senate, 1956; defeated

[a] Ardolph L. Kline served as Acting Mayor, September–December, 1913; Joseph V. McKee, September–December, 1932; Vincent R. Impellitteri, September–October, 1950.

moving to Manhattan and becoming president of Columbia University. Eleven Mayors have been lawyers, Low being the exception.[1]

Every Mayor had been previously elected to another office. Three of the 12 had won election to the citywide office of President of the Board of Aldermen (Mitchel, La Guardia) or its successor, President of the Council (Impellitteri), thus acquiring the acquaintance of the citywide constituency. In addition, McClellan had been elected President of the Board of Aldermen in 1893, before the creation of the Greater City. Six had previously been elected

[1] All Mayors except Gaynor have been college or law school graduates. Van Wyck, Columbia Law School; Low, Columbia College; McClellan, Princeton (plus study at Columbia and New York Law Schools); Mitchel, Columbia College and New York Law School; Hylan, New York Law School; Walker, New York Law School; O'Brien, Holy Cross and Georgetown Law School; La Guardia, New York University Law School; O'Dwyer and Impellitteri, Fordham Law School; Wagner, Yale and Yale Law School (with a year at the Harvard Business School).

to a countywide office: Van Wyck, Gaynor, Hylan, and O'Brien to judge-ships, O'Dwyer as a District Attorney, Wagner as a Borough President. Low had been twice elected Mayor of Brooklyn, and Walker had been several times elected to the state legislature (five times from a Senatorial District), and had served as his party leader in the state Senate for six years. Most Mayors had also held additional elective or appointive offices: Low as member of the 1896 Charter Commission for the Greater City; McClellan as congressman; Mitchel as Gaynor's Commissioner of Accounts; Hylan as Magistrate (appointed by McClellan); O'Brien as Hylan's Corporation Counsel (after twenty years as Assistant Corporation Counsel); La Guardia as congressman; O'Dwyer as Magistrate (appointed by Acting Mayor McKee in 1932) and as a County Judge elected in 1938; Impellitteri as secretary to a Supreme Court Justice; Wagner as assemblyman and succes-sively as O'Dwyer's Commissioner of Taxes, Commissioner of Housing and Buildings, and Chairman of the City Planning Commission. When offered a choice, the electorate has chosen as Mayor those nominees who were the most devoted to the profession of politics; no amateurs have been selected. "Professionals only" is a criterion even more strictly enforced by the elec-torate than by the nominators.

Six Mayors have been reelected, La Guardia winning three terms. McClel-lan, Hylan, Walker, O'Dwyer, and Wagner (all Democratic nominees) were twice elected. Low and Mitchel, although renominated, failed of reelection.

The city's electorates have chosen seven Catholics and five Protestants as Mayors. The first four Mayors (Van Wyck, Low, McClellan, Gaynor) were Protestants. The first Catholic Mayor was Mitchel, a Republican and Fusion nominee; La Guardia was the only subsequent Protestant Mayor. The first three Mayors were of old stock descent; of the subsequent nine, seven have been of Irish descent (Wagner, as one of the seven, being of German descent also), and two have been of Italian descent.

"Tammany" and the Mayoralty

The widespread and persistent myth that the New York mayoralty belongs most of the time to Tammany does not stand up under close examination. If Tammany is taken in its precise meaning as a pejorative synonym for the New York County Democratic party organization, then it can be said to have exercised dominant supervision over the city's Mayors for less than a fourth of the sixty-year period since 1897. The four years of Van Wyck, the two years of McClellan's first term, the seven years of Walker, the one year of O'Brien—fourteen years in total—may be described as Tammany years. This span of years is exceeded by the eighteen years of Fusion Mayors: Low, two years; Mitchel, four years; La Guardia, twelve years. The "Tammany" years are also exceeded by the almost seventeen years during which the mayoralty was occupied by "Brooklyn" Mayors, who responded more directly and fully to the Kings County Leaders than to those in the Wigwam: Gaynor's four years, Hylan's eight, and O'Dwyer's four years and eight months. Nor can the Tammany years be stretched to include the seven years when Democratic "insurgents," although from New York County, occupied the Mayor's office: the four years of McClellan's second term were dramatized by frontal warfare with Murphy, the three years of Impellitteri's administration by factional skirmishes with De Sapio. And Wagner's six years have been characterized much less by Tammany dominance than by Wagner's independence. For forty-eight of the sixty-two years since 1897, then, Tammany has had limited, difficult, or nonexistent access to the Mayor's office.

If Tammany is more broadly defined as the working coalition of the five Democratic County Leaders and their Assembly District Leaders, then the years of its dominance over the mayoralty may be somewhat extended. Yet the Gaynor, Hylan, O'Dwyer, and Impellitteri years—twenty years in all—cannot be added without important qualifications. The Leaders were never comfortable in their dealings with Gaynor, they competed against Hearst in negotiating with Hylan, they could neither easily persuade O'Dwyer nor predict his behavior in matters important to them, and Impellitteri frustrated them with his alternating moods of concession and hostility; in the end, the dominant factions were driven to liquidate Hylan and Impellitteri politically in strenuous and potentially hazardous primary battles. And Wagner does not fit the mold of party leader domination; he bargains more as first among equals than from the foot of the table. Even by a broader definition of Tammany and a softer definition of dominance, then, the mayoralty can hardly be said to have belonged to Tammany much more than half the time since 1897. The mayoralty is more accurately described as Tammany's Achilles' heel.

The Performance of Mayors in Office

The performance of Mayors in office depends upon several factors: What is their conception of the office? Do they perceive it as having great or small dimensions? Are they impressed with its opportunities or with its limitations? What personal style and skills do they bring to the office? In what ways do they try to create an image of themselves which would add to the strength of the office? What is their degree of skill in the strategies and tactics of politics? What other political assets do they bring to the office or acquire while in office? Do these assets exceed their liabilities, and do they increase or decrease during the term in office? What kinds of problems, governmental and political, do they confront while in office? How sharply do they perceive these problems? How do they define the Mayor's role in handling these problems? Finally, and in summary, to what extent are they innovators and initiators? to what extent arbitrators between the proposals of others? to what extent merely mediators and presiding officers?

The Top Rank: La Guardia and Mitchel. By all these criteria of performance, *Fiorello La Guardia* clearly ranks first among the eleven Mayors who have completed their terms in the office (Wagner, still in office, being excluded from this appraisal). La Guardia's view of the office was large; he was not dismayed by any obstacles; his personal style was inimitable; his energy in office limitless; his strategic and tactical skills numerous, varied, and bold; his other political assets substantial; his perception of his problems and of his role sharp and aggressive. In all his actions, he had great zest for innovation, a strong pride in his own initiative, forcefulness in arbitration, and a marked distaste for passive mediation.

When La Guardia became Mayor (at age fifty-two), he had looked at the office as a goal for fifteen years. Impatient waiting and striving had simply whetted his appetite for the leadership opportunities he saw in the office; deference to party leaders, to the Board of Estimate, or to other institutions of influence had no place in his view of the mayoralty—his twenty-year role as an autonomous insurgent prior to his elevation to this office had become his established political style. His intention from the first was to make himself as Mayor a highly visible chief executive, a symbol of energy and motion, accepting responsibility in all things as a weapon against his opponents, seeking to be omnipresent and omniscient and invincible rather than simply dignified. He thus created an image aptly suited to the times, his own personality, and the lessons of his own embattled career. His political assets were both a product of his experienced skills and a gift of the times. A lifetime of politics had made him wise and ruthless as a participant in the strategy and tactics of party leaders, officials, bureaucrats, interest groups, and other forces in the political process. This knowledge, coupled with his determination to lead rather than follow, made him the manager in ticket-making for Board of Estimate membership, in his appointment of others to office, and in the selection of governmental objectives.

The times were propitious, too; he could not have arrived in the office at a better time for the exercise of his skills in the office as he conceived it. He was a man of action, and the depression crisis in the city demanded action in the mayoralty as it did in the presidency. His major opposition—the Democratic party—had been shattered by the Seabury exposures and by its stubborn hostility to Roosevelt; the President gave La Guardia his indispensable if sometimes cautious support, and the Governor was at least a friendly neutral. The Republican leaders had no great strength with which to oppose La Guardia; they were out of power in Washington and Albany, much more heavily dependent upon the Mayor than he upon them. The Fusionist leaders, and later the leaders of the American Labor party, were poorly organized and relatively unskilled in bargaining with so experienced a strategist and tactician as La Guardia; he intimidated and outwitted them from the beginning.

As chief of state, La Guardia played his part to the hilt. His presence and energy filled the city; he personified its depression-era and wartime moods as no other Mayor has succeeded in doing—not even Walker in his sparkling era—and La Guardia more fully understood the political uses of the role than any other Mayor. If he was at first hesitant to use the potentiality of Gracie Mansion as a new dimension of the office, he seized upon its opportunities as soon as he was convinced.

As chief executive, he made the fewest concessions to administrative autonomy, viewed his department heads with a skepticism bordering on suspicion, breathed down their necks with his close supervision, and was ferociously impatient with default. All problems were his to solve, the administrative agencies were his mere instruments, and failures were described as the triumphs of his enemies over his own strenuous efforts.

As chief legislator, he ignored the Democrat-dominated Board of Aldermen and its successor, the Council, or bludgeoned it with charges of subservience to "the machine"; his concentration was upon the Board of Estimate and the state legislature. With the Board, he minimized his involvement in both its executive and public sessions, choosing to stand as much apart from its bargaining processes as he could manage, reserving the leverage of his office for more public pressures upon the Board. His deference to the Board was confined to formal occasions; when it stood in his way, he rarely hesitated to hit hard at its more recalcitrant or more vulnerable members. With the state legislature, he ceaselessly exploited the benevolent tendencies of Governor Lehman and used fully his advantages over the Republicans during their lean decade. To assist with both Board of Estimate and the state government, La Guardia turned often to Washington, where a cooperative President and La Guardia's long experience in Congress gave him help in many ways.

As chief of party, La Guardia had a complex and contradictory role. His public posture was one of hostility to party, party leaders, and party organization; offstage, he was compelled, as is any Mayor, to lead his party or be the prisoner of its leaders. La Guardia, choosing to be party chief, had to lead a difficult combination: the city Republican party organization, concerned more with recapturing the governorship and the presidency than with keeping an insurgent in City Hall; the "Fusionists," preoccupied with separating City Hall from state and national politics; and, after 1936, the American Labor party, in its first eight years much more interested in keeping Roosevelt in the presidency than La Guardia in the mayoralty. The role as chief of party was, under these circumstances, virtually impossible, but La Guardia obscured this fact from others if not from himself. He cajoled and denounced the leaders in sufficient measure to be twice renominated and twice reelected, and to secure their often reluctant help in other matters.

In sum, La Guardia played all his roles together with an effectiveness not matched by any other Mayor; he met each role with determination and force. There is no evidence that he did not relish each minute of each role for most of his twelve years in office.

The main shortcomings of the La Guardia administration were that it could not sustain its high level through its third term and that it left few permanent institutional assets to the office of Mayor. The two difficulties flow from a common source: the La Guardia mayoralty was all energy and improvisation; there was little attention to the building of an office, as the two Roosevelts did for the presidency. When La Guardia's zest and energies flagged in his third term, when the President turned his attention to war and a Republican Governor took over in Albany, and when the people of the city became absorbed in the war effort, the mayoralty was isolated and overshadowed. La Guardia could not adjust his style and methods to the new environment. The administration continued to operate at a level above average; the momentum of eight years carried it forward, and the Mayor could still summon up all his old capacities for emergencies. But the public image of the Mayor and the mayoralty were slowly diminishing, and a fourth term was seen by all as quite unlikely—although he could probably have had it if he had wanted it strongly.

John Purroy Mitchel was elected Mayor when he was thirty-four years of age. He had observed two Mayors at close range. McClellan had made him Commissioner of Accounts in 1907 when he was twenty-eight, and, as the Mayor's chief investigator, he had forced the ouster of two Borough Presidents. As President of the Board of Aldermen, to which he was elected as a Fusionist in 1909, Mitchel had for four years watched Gaynor in the mayoralty and had been acting Mayor several times during Gaynor's absences or illness.

Mitchel, like La Guardia, saw the mayoralty in large dimensions, and he was ambitious to test his capacities for leadership in the office. In personality he had force and style ("chivalrous," his opponent Hillquit repeatedly called him), conveying an image of dedication and competence, controlled energy and straightforward strategy, a sharp intelligence and a gift for seizing the initiative and holding firmly to his objectives. In the handsome young Mayor, the public was inclined to see the young aristocrat as hero, not the seasoned and resourceful field commander they were to see in La Guardia a generation later.

As chief of state, Mitchel was an effective model of dignity and restraint; he was highly visible, a symbol of integrity and energy but without passion for his cause or against his opponents. He was cool and dispassionate, lucid and convincing, impersonal and logical. The press respected him; the electorate admired but did not embrace him as one of their own. The essence of the role as chief of state escaped him; he found it a burden rather than an exciting opportunity, but he did not shirk or cheapen it. It was as chief executive that Mitchel excelled. This was the role he best understood, and he welcomed its exactions. Here he was all competence and rationality, expending his appointing power shrewdly in the recruitment of the ablest talent the city's administration had ever had, perhaps the ablest group of department heads in all the city's history. For example, his police administration set an unmatched record for the city before or after. His theme was the modernization and integrity of administration, and to these goals he devoted his greatest energies—not by intervention and close supervision, but by a generous encouragement of his appointees and strong support for them against any attack. He accepted responsibility for all the city's problems but did not make their solution his personal task; they were delegated to his commissioners, an act of political self-denial which La Guardia knew how to resist.

As chief legislator, Mitchel was less perceptive than as chief executive, but he had the good fortune of his own majority on the Board of Estimate and, for his first two years, on the Board of Aldermen as well. He discharged the role with efficiency, although at a lower level of aspiration and demand than did La Guardia. Administration, not legislation, held Mitchel's strongest attention.

As chief of party, Mitchel's tasks were even more difficult than La Guardia's, and he lacked both La Guardia's zest for the strategy and tactics of party politics and his long experience with its subtleties. Mitchel was a Democrat, but as Mayor he was the nominee of the Republicans and the Fusionists, a status he had held also for the four preceding years as President of the Board of Aldermen. The Fusionists he could deal with comfortably, but the Republican leaders (especially after they recaptured the governorship in 1914) were inclined to be intransigent. It was his future career aspirations that pulled Mitchel toward the Democratic party and added to his difficulties with the Republican leaders, for Mitchel had close ties with United States Senator O'Gorman, Assistant Secretary of the Navy Franklin D. Roosevelt, and President Wilson. In this tangled web of party relationships, Mitchel could find no sure footing. His difficulties are sharply illustrated by his loss of the Republican nomination in the 1917 primary contest to the obscure William M. Bennett although Mitchel had the formal support of the Republican County Leaders. La Guardia, faced by similar threats in 1937 and 1941, took nothing for granted, but instead used his intimate knowledge of such hazards to safeguard his candidacy. In his chief-of-party role, Mitchel was adroit and determined, avoiding domination by the party leaders but achieving only a limited leadership over them; he had neither La Guardia's relish nor experience for the role.

The Mitchel mayoralty ranks second only to La Guardia's by all the criteria of performance. Under Mitchel the office of Mayor was a source of initiative, a center of energy, a symbol of dignity and integrity. Its major shortcoming was that it was more managerial than political; it earned the admiration of the professionals in administration and in social reform, but it could not convey the spirit or the passion of these accomplishments to the electorate. Even so, the Mitchel record would apparently have earned his reelection if he had not (like La Guardia after his third election) run afoul of the crosscurrents of war. It was Hillquit, with his crusade for "peace," not the Republican insurgent Bennett or the resurgent Democrats under Hylan, who defeated Mitchel in November, 1917 (Hillquit's 145,322 votes almost reached Mitchel's 155,497). It is also a tribute to Mitchel that his four years in the mayoralty could earn second place to La Guardia's twelve years in the office.

The Middle Rank: Gaynor, Low, McClellan, O'Dwyer. These four Mayors each brought a considerable measure of distinction and force to the office. Their conception of the office was, in each instance, an affirmative one, but of smaller dimensions than the vision of La Guardia and Mitchel. Each had an instinct for the initiative, but the grasp was not firm and obstacles produced frustration or retreat into the mediator role. Their governmental goals were limited. In political skills and related assets, O'Dwyer was the most generously endowed; Gaynor, Low, and McClellan found their party roles difficult, their relationships with party leaders awkward and strained.

William J. Gaynor's long experience as a judge (1897–1909) contributed little of direct value to him as Mayor. Entering the office at age sixty-two, he chose to play his role as chief of state with the air of a wit and scholar—the wit being sharp and frequently irascible, the scholarship somewhat pretentious and ponderous; the resulting image was eccentric. As chief executive, he used his relative freedom from the Democratic party leaders (all other members of the Board of Estimate being Fusionist) to appoint department heads of his own preference, but his choices were erratic (the Police Department, for example, never being brought effectively under command and eventually damaging his reputation seriously with the Becker-Rosenthal scandals). He was unable to lead the Board of Estimate, losing to its members in his efforts to guide the Board on the subway contracts and in his attempts to revise the charter through action of the state legislature. Only in his bold and furious attacks upon Hearst did he win the status of popular hero. Gaynor reached often for the initiative but could not break through the stalemate of forces surrounding him. His concept of his roles was not of sufficient scope, his efforts not sufficiently consistent, to give him that portion of leadership which La Guardia and Mitchel would have secured for themselves in a comparable environment.

Seth Low brought high public stature to the office of Mayor when he was inaugurated in 1902, at the age of fifty-two. A merchant prince of the nineteenth century (he liquidated his father's firm, A. A. Low & Co., in 1887 for $12 million), twice a distinguished Mayor of Brooklyn while in his early thirties, president of Columbia University for over a decade (1890–1901), member of the 1896 Charter Commission and of the 1899 Rapid Transit Board established to plan the city's first subway, a strong independent candidate for Mayor in 1897, he began his term in the office with prestige and status unmatched by any other Mayor. But he brought to the office no broad governmental or political objectives. He saw his assignment in the limited frame of reform: to clean the Augean stables of the Van Wyck-Croker era, to restore honesty and integrity to the city administration, not to expand its functions nor set new goals for it. Efficiency was a sufficient aspiration. Nor did his visible and articulate constituency demand much more of him. To Platt and the other Republican leaders, he was a necessary price for victory over the Croker organization; they had no plans for advancing him to a higher post. To the Fusionists, he was a trusted instrument of reform; his concept of the Mayor's office was theirs, too. Low met these requirements with austere competence, but his political sophistication was not sufficient to give him control of several agencies (the police, for example, bringing him troubles throughout his term). In his two years in office (he held the first of the two-year terms provided under the charter of 1901), Low "cleaned house," but he had little time, and few inclinations, to do more.

George B. McClellan brought his father's famous, if controversial, name to the mayoralty when he was inaugurated in 1904 at the age of thirty-eight. But he also brought much in personal capacities and political experience. President of the Board of Aldermen by grace of Croker's necessities in the election of 1892, he had served for two years, on several occasions being Acting Mayor ("the Boy Mayor," at age twenty-seven); foreseeing defeat at City Hall in 1894, he had cajoled Croker into a nomination for Congress where for five terms, remote from Croker's interests and supervision, he had served with distinction (building up seniority, reputation, and influence on the Ways and Means Committee). In 1903 Murphy (now in Croker's seat) had pressed him into the candidacy for Mayor as the type who could, and did, defeat Low. McClellan would have preferred to stay in Washington, but in his view the mayoralty might also lead upward, and he was both young and ambitious. In his first term he was energetic and determined to hold the initiative, bargaining with Murphy and other Democratic leaders for a reasonable level of talent in his department heads (bringing in his Police Commissioner from outside the city, for example). As chief of state, he was smooth and accomplished, speaking fluently in French, German, or Italian if the occasion demanded and earning an early reputation as the best qualified Democratic

Mayor since Abram S. Hewitt in 1887–1888. But it was in his second term (1906–1910, the 1901 charter having been amended in the interim to establish a four-year term in place of the original two-year term), after his narrow and disputed victory over Hearst in 1905, that McClellan showed his best mettle as Mayor. Breaking sharply and completely with Murphy over appointments to key department head positions, McClellan set out to challenge Murphy's party leadership by opposing his 1906 choice for the gubernatorial nomination and, in 1907, by supporting insurgent candidates for Assembly District Leaders against Murphy's designees, both efforts failing. Greater success flowed from another step: the unleashing of his Commissioner of Accounts, John P. Mitchel, against the Borough Presidents of Manhattan and The Bronx, both of whom were in Murphy's personal domain and were removed from office after Mitchel's exposures. McClellan thus made the strongest effort of any Democratic Mayor to assert his dominance over the party leaders. The result was stalemate: he could hurt Murphy, but he could not unseat him; he could hold the initiative in department head appointments, but he had forfeited renomination or promotion to a higher post. McClellan reached, somewhat belatedly, for a conception of the mayoralty comparable to that of Mitchel and La Guardia, but the odds were heavily against him and his base was unprepared. His effort relied too much upon the chief-of-party role alone.

William O'Dwyer brought to the office of Mayor a commanding presence, the halo of a gang-busting District Attorney, and more than a decade of political experience. When inaugurated in 1946 at age fifty-five, he had risen from Irish immigrant boy to patrolman, graduate of Fordham Law School, lawyer, magistrate for five years, County Court judge for two years, Kings County District Attorney for six years, three years' war service in the Army Air Force (reaching the temporary rank of brigadier general), and twice Democratic candidate for Mayor. His greatest single asset was his demonstrated popularity with the electorate. He had won his elective judgeship by a wide margin; he was victorious in his first District Attorney contest by an equally impressive show of electoral strength, and in his second such contest (as absentee candidate in a colonel's uniform) by the unanimous endorsement of the Democratic, Republican, and American Labor parties. His first mayoralty candidacy against La Guardia in 1941 had brought him a surprising 47 per cent of the total vote, and he had won the mayoralty in 1945 with a record 57 per cent. His electoral strength gave support to the impression of independence and initiative he had created as judge and District Attorney.

His conception of the mayoralty, however, failed to exploit his obvious assets. From the first, he was seized by a habit of Hamlet-like introspection and indecision, oppressed by the dilemmas and complexities of his tasks. This pattern was varied by irregular bursts of vigor and decision, but, on the whole, he was more awed than energized by the office. He wrestled industriously with the postwar difficulties of schools, hospitals, transportation, and traffic; he fought dramatically for assistance at Albany (where Governor Dewey was preoccupied with priorities that did not often include helping a Democratic Mayor); and he drew upon his military experience to improve the machinery and practices of his city administration. He conducted, with sporadic interest and results, a symbolic warfare against Tammany, but it was a faction, not the institution, he sought to change. In his key appointments, his behavior was typically ambivalent: for some departments he chose executives of high competence and integrity, in others he yielded to forces that eventually damaged both himself and the city. His instinct was not to seek reelection, but he could not resist the insistence of his followers, especially since he had no attractive alternatives. Within the first year of his second term he was overwhelmed by the sudden explosion of his cumulative defaults and concessions into scandals approaching the Seabury exposés of two decades earlier. Resignation to become Ambassador to Mexico was no less a grim necessity than a welcome opportunity. O'Dwyer, beginning with the most promising assets of any Democratic Mayor since McClellan, could not firmly grasp, because he did not clearly comprehend, the full potential of the office.

The Others: Hylan, Impellitteri, O'Brien, Van Wyck, Walker. None of these five Mayors added luster or dimension to the office. Van Wyck could not break the Croker vise, retreating into voiceless abdication. Hylan spoke haltingly in the vocabulary of Hearst and let his office drift. Walker exploited the mood of his times, ignoring the tasks of his office. O'Brien was lost in the rubble of the Walker administration, his personal integrity and ineptitude obscured by the loud factional quarrels of his party and his efforts drowned by the onrush of depression-born emergencies. Impellitteri, elected by chance, retreated into his self-described role as presiding officer of the Board of Estimate, sharing initiative and responsibility generously with any who would ease his burdens of accountability. These five Mayors brought few aspirations to the office; they acquired no affirmative objectives from their acquaintance with the opportunities of the office. Each of them diminished the office.

And Afterward

The office of Mayor is the end of a career, not an office which leads to higher posts. The office uses up the man. Wagner's 1956 nomination for the United States Senate was the first break in a sixty-year tradition which has inexorably consigned Mayors to comparative obscurity after departure from the office, and it is yet to be demonstrated that nomination to higher office can be followed by election.[1]

SUMMARY

The office of Mayor is potentially an office of great strength. As the highly visible personification of the city's government and its people, as spokesman for the city's largest constituencies, the Mayor can be a force of great importance in the governing of the city. The office has attracted more than an ordinary share of strong personalities, some of them ambitious to lead and to accomplish, welcoming responsibilities as opportunities and persisting against difficulty. Such men find the appointing power of the office a potent lever for their purposes. They use this and other resources of the office to recruit allies for the construction of a successful coalition which can prevail over opposition and inertia. But even these "strong Mayors" find the office a strenuous experience.

The greater powers of the office are available only to those Mayors who understand its full political dimensions. They must possess, as did La Guardia, a high sophistication about the nature and uses of political power, and a strong appetite for exercising such power themselves. Their instincts and

[1] Van Wyck left the office at the end of 1901, when he was 52 years of age. Denied renomination by the provisions of the charter of that time (although he probably could not have secured it in any event), he had been consoled with a nomination for the state Supreme Court, but was defeated in the 1901 election. After five obscure but allegedly profitable years in law and business, he married and removed to Paris where he died in 1918 at age 68.

Low retired from the office (a defeated candidate for reelection in 1903) at age 54. He moved to Bedford, in Westchester County, where he became a farmer and a leader in farm cooperatives; his interest in labor-management relations led to the presidency of the National Civic Federation in 1907 and to appointment by President Wilson to the Colorado Coal Commission in 1914; he was president of the New York Chamber of Commerce in 1914, and a prominent member of the New York State Constitutional Convention in 1915. He died in Bedford in 1916 at age 66.

McClellan left the office at age 44. After one year in law, he joined the Princeton faculty in 1911, serving for 20 years; afterward, he lived in Washington until his death in 1940 at age 75.

Gaynor died in office at age 65.

Mitchel, leaving the office at age 38 and almost immediately becoming a major in the Air Corps, was killed in a training accident six months later.

Hylan was retired from the office at age 58, after his primary defeat in 1925. He practiced law for four years, and was then appointed by Walker to the Children's Court in 1930; reappointed by La Guardia, he served until his death in 1936 at age 68.

Walker resigned from the mayoralty in 1932 at age 51. After three years in Europe and England, and five obscure years in New York, he was designated by La Guardia in 1940 as a "czar" in the clothing industry; he died in 1946 at age 65.

O'Brien was 61 when he left the office at the end of 1933. He practiced law and served as a court referee for several years; in retirement, he lived until 1951, dying at age 78.

La Guardia was 63 when he retired at the close of 1945. He was first a special ambassador to Brazil in early 1946, then for a year the Director General of UNRRA (1946–1947), dying in September, 1947, a few months before his 65th birthday.

O'Dwyer resigned in September, 1950 (at age 60) to become Ambassador to Mexico, resigning from that office in late 1952. He has since practiced law in Mexico City.

Impellitteri left office at the end of 1953 at age 54. Appointed to the Court of Special Sessions by Wagner in January, 1954, he still serves in that office.

aspirations must lead them to use their formal powers primarily as strategic resources in the political arena and to broaden their public constituency by the dramatic use of all their formal and informal opportunities. Sophistication about managerial opportunities will help also, but only if combined with energy and more than ordinary political sense and skill, as it was in Mitchel.

For lesser men the office of Mayor is an office of weakness. Average men as President are more fortunate; the office reinforces the man. But the mayoralty is the highly vulnerable symbol of all defects in the city and its government. It is within close reach of its critics. And against these demands, an ordinary Mayor can bring only limited resources to bear. His fiscal powers are few; his managerial reach is curtailed by insufficient staff inadequately organized for his own needs; his powers to supervise are reduced by the numerous islands of autonomy among the administrative agencies; his inclinations toward initiative and innovation are resisted by the inertial weight of the bureaucracies and their constituencies. His legislative powers are scattered, many of them vanishing into the caucus of the Board of Estimate, where he is outbargained and outvoted. As party chief he must extemporize, moving on awkward ground. Confronted by all these liabilities, the lesser Mayors are overwhelmed.

As an institution of unity and coherence in the governing of the city, the mayoralty is superior in function and performance to the Council. Its strong rival is the Board of Estimate. The most significant characteristic of all three central institutions in the city's political contest is their vulnerability to the forces and institutions of fragmentation and autonomy. Numerous, separate centers of power are the dominant phenomena of the city's politics and government. The forces and institutions of integration and central direction are secondary and subordinate in power, although ironically they rank highest in the expectations and demands of all the major participants in the city's politics—demands made forcefully upon all three central institutions, but most especially upon the Mayor.

BIBLIOGRAPHY

OFFICIAL SOURCES AND ISSUANCES

Charter and Administrative Code Provisions

New York City Charter, chaps. 1, 2, 3, 6–9, and *passim* for appointing and removing power.

New York City Administrative Code, chap. 1.

Annual Messages of the Mayors of the City of New York, arranged chronologically

Messages of Robert A. Van Wyck, Mayor, to the Municipal Assembly, 1898–1901. M. B. Brown Co., New York, 1898–1901. Bound in one volume by Municipal Reference Library, call no. M45.01.

Mayor's Messages, New York City, 1902–1916. Annual messages of Mayors Low, McClellan, Gaynor, and Mitchel. Bound in one volume by Municipal Reference Library, call no. M45.01.

Second Inaugural Address of Mayor John F. Hylan of the City of New York at the City Hall, Monday, January Second, Nineteen Twenty-Two. M. B. Brown and Co., New York, 1922.

Mayors' Annual Messages, 1947–1953. Annual messages of Mayors O'Dwyer and Impellitteri. Bound in one volume by Municipal Reference Library, call no. M45.01.

Mayors' Annual Messages to the Council: 1940, 1941, 1944, 1948, 1954. Mimeographed or printed copies of the annual addresses to the City Council made by Mayors La Guardia, O'Dwyer, and Wagner. Bound separately by the Municipal Reference Library, call no. M45.01.

Other annual messages may be found in the printed *Proceedings* of the city legislature. The following official volumes contain these messages:
Proceedings of the Board of Aldermen of the City of New York, 1902–1923;
Proceedings of the Board of Aldermen and Municipal Assembly, Aldermanic Branch, 1924–1937;
and *Proceedings of the Council of the City of New York, 1938* to date.

Mayor Wagner's *Annual Reports: Foundations for Better Government: First Annual Report, 1954; Building Better Government: Second Annual Report, 1955; Better Government: A Year of Progress: Third Annual Report, 1956; Better Government: The City and the Challenge, 1957;* and *Better Government: The Continuing Effort, the Year 1958.* Each of these reports was published in the year following the period covered. These annual reports to the public have been issued by Mayor Wagner in addition to his annual message to the City Council.

Mayoralty papers. Official papers of all Mayors and Acting Mayors of Greater New York (Van Wyck, Low, McClellan, Gaynor, Kline, Mitchel, Hylan, Walker, McKee, O'Brien, La Guardia, O'Dwyer, Impellitteri, and Wagner) arranged chronologically by administration. Municipal Archives, New York City.

Annual Financial Messages of the Mayor, Delivered on Submission of the Annual Budget, arranged chronologically

Financial Message of the Mayor of the City of New York to the Board of Aldermen, May 29, 1906. M. B. Brown and Co., New York, 1906. Budget message of Mayor McClellan. Bound by Municipal Reference Library.

Message by the Honorable James J. Walker, Mayor of the City of New York, to the Board of Estimate and Apportionment, Submitting the Tentative Budget for 1930, October 10, 1929. Bound by Municipal Reference Library.

Message by the Honorable James J. Walker to the Board of Estimate and Apportionment in Transmitting the Tentative Budget for 1931 (October 10, 1930). Bound by Municipal Reference Library.

Message by the Honorable John P. O'Brien to the Board of Estimate and Apportionment of the City of New York in Submitting the Executive Budget for 1934 (October 2, 1933). Bound by Municipal Reference Library.

Budget Messages of Mayor F. H. La Guardia, 1934–1945. Bound in one volume by Municipal Reference Library.

Budget Messages of Mayors O'Dwyer and Impellitteri, 1946–1952. Bound in one volume by Municipal Reference Library.

Message of the Mayor of the City of New York to the Board of Estimate and the City Council, Submitting the Executive Budget for the Fiscal Year 1957–1958, April 1, 1957; *Fiscal Year 1958–1959,* April 1, 1958. On file in Municipal Reference Library.

Other financial messages, delivered on submission of the annual budget, may be found in the same sources as indicated for the Mayors' annual messages.

THE MAYORALTY AND MANAGERIAL LEADERSHIP

Academy of Political Science in the City of New York, "The Government of the City of New York," *Proceedings,* vol. 5, April, 1915, pp. 1–15. Some observations and reflections on the office of Mayor in 1915.

Bernstein, David, "New York City Installs a City Administrator," *GRA Reporter,* Second Quarter, 1954, pp. 21–22.

Childs, Richard S., *Appointive Administrators Under Mayors: A Review of the Precedents.* Citizens Union Research Foundation, New York, 1953. A plea for an appointed administrator by the man who "invented" the city manager plan.

Curran, Henry H., *Pillar to Post.* Charles Scribner's Sons, New York, 1941, pp. 344–376. New York's former Deputy Mayor recalls his experiences in that position.

Gulick, Luther, "Reminiscences." Columbia University Oral History Collection, Special Collections, Butler Library. Describes the reorganization of the government of New York City in 1954–1956 to place the City Administrator as "second-in-command" to the Mayor and Dr. Gulick's work as City Administrator.

Kong, Chew-Kawn, *The Role of the City Administrator in New York City.* Management Services Associates, New York, 1958. A study of the evolution and functioning of the City Administrator's office in New York City.

Lowi, Theodore J., *At the Pleasure of the Mayor.* Doctoral dissertation, Yale University, 1960, unpublished. A study of Mayors' cabinets in New York from Van Wyck to Wagner.

New York City, Mayor's Committee on Management Survey, *Modern Management for the City of New York.* 2 vols. The Committee, New York, 1953, vol. 1, pp. 20–24, 26, 30–31, 41, 55–57. Recommendations for strengthening the office of the Mayor.

McGoldrick, Joseph D., "Is the City Manager Plan Suitable for New York?" *National Municipal Review,* vol. 21, May, 1932, pp. 289–292.

Citizens Union, "New York Needs an Administrator," *The Searchlight,* vol. 43, January, 1953. The report of a special committee of the Citizens Union which recommended an appointive trained administrator.

Schieffelin, William J., "The City Manager Plan Is Suitable for New York," *National Municipal Review,* vol. 21, May, 1932, pp. 293–295. A plea for change in the city's top management.

Smith, Frank, *Office of the Deputy Mayor.* Master's thesis, City College of New York, 1957, unpublished.

Tanzer, Lawrence A., *The New York City Charter.* Clark Boardman Co., New York, 1937, pp. 22–26. The Associate Counsel to the Thacher Charter Commission explains how it provided for the mayoralty.

New York State, Temporary State Commission to Study the Organizational Structure of the Government of the City of New York, *Four Steps to Better Government of New York City: A Plan for Action.* 2 vols. The Commission, New York, 1953, vol. 1, pp. 6–19, 31–57, 85–96; vol. 2, pp. 8–17, 21–23. Discusses the need for strengthening the managerial structure of New York City's government and makes specific recommendations relating to the Mayor's office. The Division of Administration was established partly on the basis of this report.

Tugwell, Rexford G., "New York in Perspective," in William A. Robson, *Great Cities of the World.* Macmillan Co., New York, 1955, pp. 421, 422, 425–429. The erstwhile head of the City Planning Commission describes the work of the Mayor and the administrators who served under him.

Zucker, William H., *The Role of the Mayor in the New York City Expense Budget Process.* Doctoral dissertation, Harvard University, 1954, unpublished.

REMINISCENCES BY AND ABOUT MAYORS SINCE CONSOLIDATION
(arranged by mayoral administrations)

Van Wyck

Van Wyck, Frederick, *Recollections of an Old New Yorker.* Boni and Liveright, New York, 1932. Mayor Van Wyck's cousin recalls some phases of his administration.

Low

Bogard, Milo T., editor, *The Redemption of New York.* P. F. McBreen and Sons, New York, 1902. A review of the election of 1901 by New Yorkers who contributed to the victory of Seth Low.

Low, Benjamin R. C., *Seth Low*. G. P. Putnam's Sons, New York, 1925. Life and career of Seth Low, Mayor of New York.

Seth Low *Papers*. Seth Low Collection, Low Library, Columbia University. Letters and manuscript material.

McAneny, George, "Reminiscences." Columbia University Oral History Collection, Special Collections, Butler Library. Recollections of Mayors Low and Gaynor and their administrations.

Morris, Charles, *Men of Affairs in New York: An Historical Work*. L. R. Hamersley and Co., New York, 1906, pp. 75–76. The life and career of Mayor Seth Low.

Steffens, Lincoln, *The Shame of the Cities*. Sagamore Press, New York, 1957, pp. 195–214. Originally published as the Low administration drew to its close; a famous reporter appraises the Mayor and his administration.

Autobiography. The Literary Guild, New York, 1931, pp. 430–435. A great reporter views the administration of Mayor Seth Low.

McClellan

George B. McClellan, Jr., *Papers*. Library of Congress, Washington. The collected papers of the city's Mayor, 1904–1909.

Diary, Letter Books, and Newspaper Scrapbooks. New York Historical Society. Documents relating to the third Mayor of the consolidated city.

Mackaye, Milton, "Out of the Past: Profile of George Brinton McClellan," *The New Yorker*, vol. 8, May 28, 1932, pp. 21–25. Portrait of a Mayor, many years after.

Morris, Charles, *Men of Affairs in New York: An Historical Work*. L. R. Hamersley and Co., New York, 1906, pp. 257–258. The career of George B. McClellan, Mayor of the city at the time this was written.

Syrett, Harold C., editor, *The Gentleman and the Tiger: The Autobiography of George B. McClellan, Jr.* J. B. Lippincott Co., Philadelphia, 1956. The memoirs of the third Mayor.

Gaynor

Hochman, William Russell, *William J. Gaynor: The Years of Fruition*. University Microfilms, Publication no. 12,309, Ann Arbor, Mich., 1955. Doctoral dissertation, Columbia University, 1955. The life and career of a colorful Mayor.

Ingersoll, Raymond V., "An Estimate of Mayor Gaynor," *National Municipal Review*, vol. 3, January, 1914, pp. 78–83.

New York City Municipal Reference Library, "Selected List of Materials by and about William J. Gaynor." Compiled by the Municipal Reference Library, May 14, 1933. In the vertical files. References to magazine articles, newspaper items, and cartoon collections by and about Mayor Gaynor.

Northrop, W. B., editor, *Some of Mayor Gaynor's Letters and Speeches*. Greaves Publishing Co., New York, 1913. A selected group of letters and speeches. Indexed.

Pink, Louis Heaton, *Gaynor: The Man Who Swallowed the Tiger*. International Press, New York, 1931. A sympathetic and favorable biography.

"Reminiscences." Columbia University Oral History Collection, Special Collections, Butler Library. Recollections of the life and administration of Mayor Gaynor.

Smith, Mortimer, "Mayor Gaynor—A Political Maverick," *American Mercury*, vol. 69, October, 1949, pp. 469–476. Story of an "incorrigible individualist."

William Jay Gaynor: Mayor of New York. Henry Regnery, Chicago, 1951. A biography of Mayor Gaynor.

Syrett, Harold C., *The City of Brooklyn, 1865–1898*. Columbia University Press, New York, 1944, pp. 198–214. The early career of Mayor Gaynor.

Mitchel

Amberg, Eda, and William H. Allen, *Civic Lessons from Mayor Mitchel's Defeat.* Institute for Public Service, New York, 1921.

Bruère, Henry, *New York City's Administrative Progress, 1914–1916.* M. B. Brown and Co., New York, 1916. A reform administration's portrayal of the changes it introduced.

Cruger, Bertram D., "Reminiscences." Columbia University Oral History Collection, Special Collections, Butler Library. Mayor John Purroy Mitchel's secretary tells about some phases of his work on the job.

Citizens Union, "Fusion Vindicated," *The Searchlight*, vol. 5, May 4, 1915. The Citizens Union's favorable appraisal of the first 15 months of Mayor Mitchel's administration.

McBain, Howard Lee, "John Purroy Mitchel," *National Municipal Review*, vol. 7, September, 1918, pp. 504–506. A political scientist evaluates the Mayor's career.

Mitchel, John Purroy, *Papers.* Library of Congress, Washington. Letters, speeches, memoranda, newspaper clippings, and other original source material relating to the sixth Mayor.

"The Office of Mayor," *Proceedings* of the Academy of Political Science in the City of New York, vol. 5, April, 1915, pp. 479–494. The powers and duties of the office and their importance, described by the incumbent Mayor.

Various speeches: 1914–1916. Speeches of Mayor Mitchel, bound by Municipal Reference Library, call no. M45.59. Typewritten and printed.

Street, Julian, "New York's Fighting Mayor," *Collier's Weekly*, vol. 59, August 25, 1917, pp. 6–7, 38. A favorable view of Mayor Mitchel's administration.

Hylan

Bullock, William, "Hylan," *American Mercury*, vol. 1, April, 1924, pp. 444–450. Tells why "the Hylans rise over brains and personality."

Hapgood, Norman, and Henry Moskowitz, *Up from the City Streets: A Life of Alfred E. Smith.* Harcourt, Brace and Co., New York, 1928, pp. 144–147, 162, 174, 207–210. Some phases of Mayor Hylan's career and personality.

Hylan, John F., *Seven Years of Progress: Important Public Improvements and Achievements by the Municipal and Borough Governments of the City of New York.* M. B. Brown and Co., New York, 1925. A report submitted by the Mayor to the Board of Aldermen, which summarizes his "record of service" during the years 1918 to 1925.

"Hylan's Hold on New York," *The Literary Digest*, vol. 71, November 19, 1921, p. 12. An unfavorable view of Hylan's first administration.

New York City Municipal Reference Library, *Mayor's Speeches: Hylan, 1918–1924.* Printed speeches of Mayor John F. Hylan, 1 vol., Municipal Reference Library, call no. M45.59.

Pringle, Henry F., "Wet Hope: Profile of Henry Hastings Curran," *The New Yorker*, vol. 6, June 14, 1930, pp. 22–25. Some phases of Mayor Hylan's mayoralty.

Walker

Citizens Union, "Two Years of Walker," *The Searchlight*, vol. 18, February, 1928. An appraisal of the initial period of the Walker administration by the Citizens Union.

"Walker Regime Reviewed," *The Searchlight*, vol. 19, June, 1929. The Citizens Union evaluates the strengths and weaknesses of Mayor Walker's first administration.

Donner, Donald D., *The Political Eclipse of James J. Walker.* Master's thesis, Columbia University, 1954, unpublished.

Fowler, Gene, *Beau James: The Life and Times of Jimmy Walker.* Viking Press, New York, 1949. A favorable biography.

Fuller, Hector, *Abroad with Mayor Walker.* Shields Publishing Co., New York, 1958. A eulogistic account of one phase of Mayor Walker's career.

Gribetz, Louis J., and Joseph Kaye, *Jimmie Walker: The Story of a Personality.* Dial Press, New York, 1932. A favorable biography.

McGoldrick, Joseph D., "Our American Mayors: 'Jimmy' Walker," *National Municipal Review*, vol. 17, October, 1928, pp. 567–577. An appraisal of Mayor Walker during his first administration.

Pringle, Henry F., "Jimmy Walker," *American Mercury*, vol. 9, November, 1926, pp. 272–279. A review of Walker's career as Mayor when it was "still too early to pass judgment."

Thomas, Norman, and Paul Blanshard, *What's the Matter with New York?* Macmillan Co., New York, 1932, pp. 155–176. A review of the less savory phases of Mayor Walker's administration.

McKee

Blanshard, Paul, "La Guardia vs. McKee," *The Nation*, vol. 137, October 25, 1933, pp. 474–477. Some observations on the political career of Acting Mayor McKee.

Flynn, Edward J., *You're the Boss*. Viking Press, New York, 1947, pp. 52, 102–103, 127–129, 133–138. McKee's sponsor discusses his career.

"New York Amazed by Its New Mayor," *Literary Digest*, vol. 114, September 24, 1932, p. 9. A favorable view of McKee as Acting Mayor.

"Will-o'-the-Wisp McKee," *The New Republic*, vol. 73, November 30, 1932, p. 60. An unfavorable view of the Acting Mayor.

O'Brien

Crowell, Paul, and A. H. Raskin, "New York: 'Greatest City in the World'," in Robert S. Allen, editor, *Our Fair City*. Vanguard Press, New York, 1947, pp. 37–58. A newspaperman's view of Mayor O'Brien, p. 49.

Flynn, Edward J., *You're the Boss*. Viking Press, New York, 1947, pp. 129–130, 132–134, 139–140. Some observations on O'Brien, the man and the Mayor.

Johnston, Alva, "The Scholar in Politics: Profile of Mayor John P. O'Brien," *The New Yorker*, vol. 9, July 1, 1933, pp. 18–21; July 8, 1933. Portrait of O'Brien as "one of the choicest flowers of Tammany Hall."

Rodgers, Cleveland, *Robert Moses: Builder for Democracy*. Henry Holt and Co., New York, 1952, pp. 73–75, 78–79, 97–98, 328. Some aspects of Mayor O'Brien's personality and his administration.

La Guardia

Allen, William H., *Why Tammanies Revive: La Guardia's Mis-Guard*. Institute for Public Service, New York, 1937. A slashing attack on the first La Guardia administration.

Bunzl, Mrs. Walter, "Reminiscences." Columbia University Oral History Collection, Special Collections, Butler Library. Recollections of Mayor La Guardia.

Chamberlain, John, "Mayor La Guardia," *Yale Review*, vol. 29, September, 1939, pp. 11–27. The political personality of the Mayor.

Cuneo, Ernest, *Life with Fiorello*. Macmillan Co., New York, 1955. An intimate portrait by a man who was closely associated with the Mayor.

Franklin, Jay, *La Guardia: A Biography*, Modern Age, New York, 1937.

Gavit, John P., "La Guardia—Portrait of a Mayor," *Survey Graphic*, vol. 25, January, 1936, pp. 7–12, 55–58.

Isaacs, Julius, *Oath of Devotion*. E. P. Dutton and Co., New York, 1949, pp. 105–125. Recollections of La Guardia, the man and the Mayor.

"Reminiscences." Columbia University Oral History Collection, Special Collections, Butler Library. Recollections of La Guardia and his administrations.

Isaacs, Stanley, "Reminiscences." Columbia University Oral History Collection, Special Collections, Butler Library. The former Borough President of Manhattan and co-worker with La Guardia in the Republican party tells of his relations with and impressions of the Mayor.

La Guardia, Fiorello H., *The Making of an Insurgent: Autobiography: 1882–1919.* J. B. Lippincott Co., Philadelphia, 1948. His early career.

Fusion party campaign scrapbook of foreign-language newspaper comments, 1934–1938. Municipal Archives, New York City.

Personal papers. 123 file drawers of material relating to La Guardia's personal and public life, arranged alphabetically by subject. Municipal Archives, New York City.

La Guardia, Mrs. Marie, "Reminiscences." Columbia University Oral History Collection, Special Collections, Butler Library. Personal recollections of Mayor La Guardia, related by his wife.

Limpus, Lowell M., and Burr Leyson, *This Man La Guardia.* E. P. Dutton and Co., New York, 1938. A full-scale biography of La Guardia through his second election to the mayoralty.

Mann, Arthur, *La Guardia: A Fighter Against His Times, 1882–1933.* J. B. Lippincott Co., Philadelphia, 1959. First volume of the definitive biography of La Guardia.

Moscow, Warren, *Politics in the Empire State.* Alfred A. Knopf, New York, 1948, pp. 23–24. A pungent account of La Guardia's administrations as Mayor.

Moses, Robert, *La Guardia: A Salute and a Memoir.* Simon and Schuster, New York, 1957. The "most troublesome member of the late Mayor's official family" writes about La Guardia.

Rankin, Rebecca B., editor, *New York Advancing: A Scientific Approach to Municipal Government.* Municipal Reference Library, New York, 1936. Describes the functioning of municipal government of New York City in 1934 and 1935, the first two years of the La Guardia administration.

Salter, J. T., editor, *The American Politician.* University of North Carolina Press, Chapel Hill, 1938, pp. 3–46. Paul J. Kern's essay on La Guardia.

Schriftgiesser, Karl, "Portrait of a Mayor: Fiorello La Guardia," *Atlantic Monthly,* vol. 161, January, 1938, pp. 55–63. A study of La Guardia at the end of his first term in office.

Tugwell, Rexford G., *The Art of Politics as Practiced by Three Great Americans: Franklin Delano Roosevelt, Luis Muñoz Marín, and Fiorello H. La Guardia.* Doubleday and Co., New York, 1958. The former City Planning Commissioner, associated with La Guardia from 1938–1941, reflects on the qualities that made him a political leader.

Windels, Paul, "Reminiscences." Columbia University Oral History Collection, Special Collections, Butler Library. A memoir of the La Guardia administration by a member of the Mayor's cabinet.

O'Dwyer

Crowell, Paul, and A. H. Raskin, "New York: 'Greatest City in the World'," in Robert S. Allen, editor, *Our Fair City.* Vanguard Press, New York, 1947, pp. 40–58.

Mockridge, Norton, and Robert H. Prall, *The Big Fix.* Henry Holt and Co., New York, 1954. Ostensibly the story of the smashing of a gambling syndicate, this volume is a full-scale outline of O'Dwyer's career as well.

Municipal Reference Library, *The Public Career of William O'Dwyer,* 1950. Bound by Municipal Reference Library, mimeographed. Favorable articles, editorials and feature write-ups, culled from newspapers and periodicals, covering O'Dwyer's career from 1932–1949, gathered together for the use of speakers and campaign workers in the municipal election of 1949.

O'Dwyer, William, Personal papers. Correspondence, speeches, press releases, photographs, clippings, phonograph records, and other material relating to the career of O'Dwyer as District Attorney, Army officer, Mayor, and Ambassador to Mexico, 1932–1957. Municipal Archives, New York City.

Scrapbooks, 1946–1950. 79 vols. Municipal Archives, New York City.

Royer, Fanchon, "Our Ambassador in Mexico," *The Catholic World,* vol. 176, November, 1952, pp. 110–115. Some phases of O'Dwyer's postmayoral career.

Impellitteri

Citizens Union, "An Appraisal of the Impellitteri Record," *The Searchlight*, vol. 42, May, 1952. The President of the Citizens Union emphasizes the shortcomings of Impellitteri's administration.

Impellitteri, Vincent R., *Scrapbooks*. 2 vols. Newspaper clippings relating chiefly to the period when Impellitteri was Acting Mayor, January–February, 1950, August–September, 1950. Municipal Archives, New York City.

Scrapbooks. 61 vols. Newspaper clippings relating to Impellitteri's mayoralty, August 16, 1950–January 2, 1954. Municipal Archives, New York City.

Wagner

Hamburger, Philip, "The Mayor: Profile of Robert F. Wagner," *The New Yorker*, vol. 32, January 26, 1957, pp. 39–67; February 2, 1957, pp. 39–69. Wagner's life and political career.

Kenworthy, E. W., "The Emergence of Mayor Wagner," *The New York Times Magazine*, August 14, 1955.

Additional Reminiscences and Commentaries

Citizens Union, *Scrapbooks*, 206 vols. Vols. 47–55 cover the Mayors of the City, 1922–1935. In Reference Section of New York Public Library, Astor Branch.

Earle, Genevieve, "Reminiscences." Columbia University Oral History Collection, Special Collections, Butler Library. A civic leader gives her impressions of the La Guardia and O'Dwyer administrations.

Fein, Albert, *New York City Politics from 1897–1903: A Study in Political Party Leadership*. Master's thesis, Columbia University, 1954, unpublished. The administrations of Mayors Van Wyck, Low, and McClellan.

Gibbons, Edward R., *Mayoralty Nominations in New York*. Master's thesis, Columbia University, 1930, unpublished. A historical survey.

Hamburger, Philip, *Mayor Watching and Other Pleasures*. Rinehart and Co., New York, 1958. Personal observations of Mayors La Guardia, O'Dwyer, Impellitteri, and Wagner.

Morris, Newbold, and Dana Lee Thomas, *Let the Chips Fall*. Appleton-Century-Crofts, New York, 1955. Recollections of Mayor La Guardia by two of his most prominent admirers and followers, pp. 71–95, 101–102, 104–105, and 110–121, 131–143, 187–214, 282–284. Some recollections of Mayor Walker (pp. 145–148) and of Mayor O'Dwyer (pp. 215–245).

Prendergast, William A., "Reminiscences." Columbia University Oral History Collection, Special Collections, Butler Library. Recollections of the administrations of Mayors Gaynor and Mitchel by their Comptroller.

Rodgers, Cleveland, and Rebecca Rankin, *New York: The World's Capital City*. Harper and Bros., New York, 1948, pp. 93–130. A brief review of the highlights in the administration of all mayors since the consolidation of the city, from Van Wyck to O'Dwyer.

Tanzer, Lawrence A., "Reminiscences." Columbia University Oral History Collection, Special Collections, Butler Library. Personal reactions of a lawyer and civic worker to Mayors Hylan, Walker, McKee, and La Guardia.

Whalen, Grover A., *Mr. New York: Autobiography of Grover A. Whalen*. G. P. Putnam's Sons, New York, 1955. Recollections of Grover Whalen as Mayor Hylan's Secretary (pp. 24–80), Mayor Walker's Police Commissioner (pp. 132–165), and as long-time chairman of the Mayor's Committee for the reception of distinguished guests (pp. 81–104 and 116–131).

PART FOUR
CONCLUSIONS

CHAPTER XIX

Risks, Rewards, and Remedies

A FULL VIEW AND A FAIR JUDGMENT of New York City's many-faceted political and governmental system has been a matter of national as well as local debate for at least a century and a half. Historians and journalists, statesmen and politicians, social scientists and other analysts, writers in verse and prose have all been fascinated by the power, the variety, the size, and the significance of the city, its politics, and its government. But they have not achieved consensus. The city in the nation, the city in the state, the city in its metropolitan region, the city as a city, the quality of its political and governmental life—all these remain, and will continue, as matters of debate and discussion, of interest and concern—for the nation as well as for the city.

The most striking characteristic of the city's politics and government is one of scale. No other American city approaches the magnitude, scope, variety, and complexity of the city's governmental tasks and accomplishments. Nor does any other city represent so important a political prize, in its electorate and its government, in the national party contest. Nor can any other city match the drama, the color, and the special style of the city's own politics. In all these respects the city is imperial, if not unique, among American cities.

The city's politics and government have been more widely known for their defects than for their claims to excellence. This notoriety rather than fame for the city has been the product of many causes. There has been the city's high visibility as the nation's largest urban center. There have been the effective processes of exposure built into the city's political system. There have been the highly articulate voices of dissent and criticism always present in the city. There have been, too, the scale and theatrical qualities of the defects in the city's political system. And the citizens of the city have themselves been more given to eloquence in their indignation at "failures" than in their pride over "successes." Notoriety is, in this sense, perhaps itself a valid claim to fame for the city: the city's political and governmental system has never produced contentment, acquiescence, or a sense of lasting defeat among its critics. The voice of the critic has often had the most attentive audience.

The city's political system is, in fact, vigorously and incessantly competitive. The stakes of the city's politics are large, the contestants are numerous and determined, the rules of the competition are known to and enforced against each other by the competitors themselves, and the city's electorate is so uncommitted to any particular contestant as to heighten the competition for the electorate's support or consent. No single ruling élite dominates the political and governmental system of New York City.

CHARACTERISTICS OF THE CITY'S SYSTEM

A Multiplicity of Decision Centers

The decisions that distribute the prizes of politics in New York City issue from a large number of sources.

Each source consists of two parts: a "core group" at the center, invested by the rules with the formal authority to legitimize decisions (that is, to promulgate them in the prescribed forms and according to the specified procedures that make them binding under the rules) and a constellation of "satellite groups," seeking to influence the authoritative issuances of the core group. The five large categories of participants in the city's political contest whose roles have been described in this volume—the party leaders, the elected and appointed public officials, the organized bureaucracies, the numerous nongovernmental associations (including the mass media of communication), the officials and agencies of other governments—play their parts upon the many stages the city provides. The most visible of these stages are those provided by the formal decision centers in each of which a core group and its satellite groups occupy the middle of the stage. Every center (every core group and its satellite groups), whatever its stage, must also continuously acknowledge the supervising presence of the city's electorate, possessing the propensity and the capacity to intervene decisively in the contest on the side of one contestant or the other.

Party leaders are core groups for nominations. They function as satellites, however, in many decisions about appointments, and in connection with substantive program and policy decisions in their role as brokers for other claimants. The city's electorate is the core group for electoral decisions, where it has a virtual monopoly. Other participants in the contest for the stakes of politics may exert considerable influence on the electorate, but only in the same fashion as satellite groups in other special areas influence each appropriate core group.

In all other decision centers the core groups are composed of officials. Most prominent among these core groups are the officials presiding over the decision centers of the general organs of government—the Mayor, the Board of Estimate, the Council, and the legislators and executives at the higher levels of government. Their decisions spread across the entire spectrum of the city's governmental functions and activities; consequently, all the other participants in the political process are, at one time or another and in varying combinations, satellite groups to these central core groups, trying to influence their actions. Each of their decisions, it is true, evokes active responses only from those participants particularly interested in the affected sphere of governmental activity, but most of their decisions prove to be of interest to some participants in all the five major categories (though rarely to all participants in all categories). In the course of time, most groups taking part in the city's politics apply leverage to the core groups in the general governmental institutions in efforts to secure favorable decisions. The courts are also general organs, and therefore the judges as the core group in that arena are of interest to most contestants at one time or another, but the modes of influence exerted on them are somewhat more restricted and institutionalized than those exerted on the core groups of other general organs.

Functionally specialized officials constitute the core groups for decisions in particular functional areas of governmental action, whether these are in line agencies (such as the Board of Education, the Department of Welfare, the Police Department, the Fire Department, the Department of Health), in special authorities (Transit, Housing, Triborough Bridge and Tunnel, or the Port of New York Authority), or in overhead agencies (the Budget Bureau, the Personnel Department, the Law Department, the City Planning Department, for example). Each of these decision centers is surrounded by satellite groups especially concerned with its decisions—the leaders of the interests served, the interests regulated, professional societies and associations, organized bureaucracies, labor unions, suppliers of revenues and materials, and others. Usually, the groups concerned chiefly with particular functions are uninterested in decisions in other, unrelated functional areas, so that most of the decisions (about appointments as well as programs and policies) in each decision center are worked out by an interplay among the specialized core and its satellite groups.

Most officials have a dual role. They appear not merely in core groups but also as satellites of other officials. From the point of view of the general organs, for instance, the agency heads are claimants endeavoring to influence decisions in the city's central governmental institutions. From the point of view of a department head, the general organs are satellites making demands. Although the general organs' influence on agency leaders is especially strong, it is not by any measure complete domination; the agency leaders commonly preserve a region of autonomy free from invasion by the central organs as well as from other groups and institutions. Department heads also often see their own official colleagues (particularly the heads of overhead agencies), as well as the leaders of the organized bureaucracies, acting as satellite groups, as wielders of influence, and as competitors. Their counterparts in other governments tend to appear in the same light. Other officials (themselves core groups in their own respective areas) are thus likely to appear among the satellites of any particular official core group.

The leaders of the city's organized bureaucracies are, strictly speaking, never members of a core group but always a satellite group seeking to exert influence over one or more core groups. Their role is not without ambiguity in this respect, however, for many bureaucrats also occupy significant decision-making posts in the city government. As members or leaders in their organized bureaucratic groups, these bureaucrats thus occasionally play a dual part; as leaders or members of satellite groups they engage in efforts to influence the actions of a core group in which they are also members. But these are not yet typical situations. In most instances, the leaders of the organized bureaucracies are satellite groups.

The leaders of the city's nongovernmental groups never formally constitute core groups, but appear instead as satellites. Functionally specialized groups, being close to the agency officials whose decisions affect them, are not far from the center of the particular arena in which they operate. But, except when they are coopted into what amounts to a part of officialdom, they cannot do what the core groups do: issue authoritative, official, binding decisions. As satellites, some of the civic groups, and the communication media, are active and frequently highly influential in a broad range of functional spheres. In any specific functional area of governmental activity, however, it is the specialized, well-organized, persistent, professionally staffed nongovernmental organizations that continuously affect the pattern of decisions. Core groups of officials tend to estimate the reactions of other nongovernmental groups that might be galvanized to action by specific decisions, and the officials respond to the representations of such groups when these groups are sufficiently provoked to exert pressure. But the impact of these organizations is more intermittent and uncertain than that of those with sustained and specialized programs of influence. Yet even the specialized are compelled by the nature of the rules to accept roles as satellites.

Decisions as Accommodations

No single group of participants in the city's political contest is self-sufficient in its power to make decisions or require decisions of others. Every decision of importance is consequently the product of mutual accommodation. Building temporary or lasting alliances, working out immediate or enduring settlements between allies or competitors, and bargaining for an improved position in the decision centers are the continuing preoccupations of all leaders— whether party leaders, public officials, leaders of organized bureaucracies, or leaders of nongovernmental groups.

Each core group is constantly bargaining and reaching understandings of varying comprehensiveness and stability with some of its satellite groups, seeking a coalition of forces which will enable it to issue decisions that will stand against the opposition of those outside the coalition. The satellite groups, in turn, are just as constantly bargaining with each other for alliances on specific decisions or more permanent agreements. These accommodations between core and satellite group and among satellite groups represent an infinite variety of bargains, some leaving the core group with considerable freedom of movement, others tying it into close partnership with other members of an alliance, and still others imprisoning it within a powerful coalition of satellite groups. Since almost all core groups confront a competing and often numerous field of satellite groups, bargaining is perpetual.

Bargaining and accommodation are equally characteristic of the relations between one core group plus its satellites and other core groups with their satellites. These accommodations are necessary since some core groups have supervisory authority over others, some have competing jurisdictional claims, and almost all are competitors for the scarce dollars available through the budget.

Indeed, core groups themselves do not exhibit solid internal unity; each is in many respects a microcosm of the entire system. The central organs of government, for example, are in reality mosaics: The Board of Estimate with its powerful borough representatives, the office of Mayor with its many commissioners and assistants chosen by expediency rather than preference, the Council composed of councilmen representing small districts and operating through many committees—all three are assemblages of many parts. The state legislature, the Governor, and the other elected and appointed state executives are similarly divided when they become involved in the city's government and politics. Even more so are the central institutions of the federal government dealing with the city.

In much the same way, the city's administrative agencies are not monoliths but aggregates of components enjoying varying degrees of autonomy. Each department head must learn to deal with his deputies and assistants, his bureau chiefs, sometimes his organized bureaucracies. The organized bureaucracies are likewise splintered along functional, religious, professional, trade union, rank, and other lines. Party leaders may be described as a class but, in fact, they constitute a large number of rather independent participants in city government, rivaling each other, bargaining with each other, working out more or less unstable agreements with each other. The electorate itself, the sometimes remote and nebulous presence that shapes and colors the entire contest for the stakes of politics, is composed of a multitude of subdivisions —the various geographical constituencies, the regular voters and those who appear only for spectacular electoral battles, the party-line voters and the selective nonvoters, the ticket-splitters, the ethnic and religious voters, the ideological voters of all persuasions, as well as the social and economic class voters.

The process of bargaining, in short, reaches into the core of each decision center and is not confined to relations between core groups, or between core groups and their satellites, or between satellites. If there is any single feature of the system of government and politics in New York City that may be called ubiquitous and invariant, it would seem to be the prevalence of mutual accommodation. Every program and policy represents a compromise among the interested participants.

Partial Self-Containment of Decision Centers

The decisions that flow from each constellation of groups active in each of the city's decision centers are ordinarily formulated and carried out without much calculated consideration of the decisions emanating from the other centers. They are usually made in terms of the special perspectives and values of the groups with particular interests in the governmental functions or activities affecting them. Only occasionally are they formulated in a broader frame of reference.

This fragmentation of governmental decision-making in the city is partially offset by features of the system tending to introduce more or less common premises of decision into the centers. A major "balance wheel" has been noted by David B. Truman: the overlapping memberships of many groups in society. The same individuals turn up in many contexts and in many guises, carrying to each the viewpoints and information acquired in the others. A second balance wheel is the frequency with which the core groups of one center operate as satellite groups in other centers; no center is completely isolated from the others. Overhead agencies serve as a third unifying element, for they cut across the whole range of governmental functions and activities, introducing, within the limits of their own specialties, a common set of assumptions and goals into many of the decisions of other centers. A fourth unifying factor is represented by the civic groups and the press, which exert their influence on a wide variety of decision centers without regard to the subject-matter specialties of the centers. They are not equally effective everywhere, and they are seldom so effective in any given center as the more specialized participants in it, but they help to relate what happens in every center to what goes on in others. Finally, the central institutions of government (including the courts) operate under relatively few functional restrictions and therefore make decisions with respect to all phases of the city's government and politics. Collectively, their perspectives are broad, their interests are inclusive, their desire to rationalize and balance the actions in all decision centers are strong, and their formal authority to impose a common basis for decisions is superior to that of other groups. These five factors help to keep the system from flying apart.

Yet the autonomous nature of the core group and its satellite groups in each decision center is striking. Although the leaders may belong to many groups, they behave, when particular decisions are at issue, with a remarkable lack of ambivalence. The interests immediately at stake provide the criteria of action, and they often seem unambiguous; at any given moment, group leaders and members act as though they had only one interest, one membership, at that moment. Most participants are galvanized to action by only a relatively narrow range of issues and ignore most others no matter where they occur; as a result, most of the actors in any center share very special interests in the problems at hand, and the casual outsider or the intermittent satellite group has much less effect on the decisions made there than do the strongly motivated "regulars." As modes of integrating the decisions of the city's whole governmental system, the balance wheels have therefore not been spectacularly successful.

What is perhaps most surprising is the failure of the central organs of government to provide a high level of integration for the city's system. The Council has been weak, the Board of Estimate inert, the Mayor handicapped. The government at Albany cannot do the job of pulling the decision centers of the city together, even if it were so inclined. This would mean running the city, a task the state is unable and unwilling to assume, a task that would not win it the thanks of the city's residents or of other residents of the state. Moreover, the state government has not been inclined to strengthen the central institutions of the city, but has enacted legislation and created agencies that intensify the independence of many local officials. State administrative supervision of city agencies has encouraged many city officers and employees to develop close links with their functional counterparts in the state capital, and to rely on these to buttress their resistance to leadership from the city's central institutions. The nature of the judicial process renders the courts incapable of performing an integrative function. Thus, despite the opportunities for integration presented by the formal powers of the city's central institutions, they have generally either officially ratified the agreements reached by the active participants in each decision center, which are offered to them as the consensus of experts and interested groups, or, on an *ad hoc* basis, have chosen one or another alternative suggested when the experts and interested groups have been divided on an issue. It is in the latter role that the city's central institutions have had their greatest significance. Seldom have they imposed, on their own initiative, a common set of objectives on all the centers of decision. The central institutions are important participants in all the decision-making in the contest for the stakes of politics in the city, but they are rarely the prime movers or the overriding forces.

As a result, most individual decisions are shaped by a small percentage of the city's population—indeed, by a small percentage of those who engage actively in its politics—because only the participants directly concerned have the time, energy, skill, and motivation to do much about them. The city government is most accurately visualized as a series of semiautonomous little worlds, each of which brings forth official programs and policies through the interaction of its own inhabitants. There are commentators who assert that Tammany, or Wall Street, or the Cathedral, or the labor czars, or the bureaucracy, or even the underworld rules New York. Some of these, it is true, are especially influential in shaping some decisions in some specialized areas. Taking the system over-all, however, none, nor all combined, can be said to be in command; large segments of the city's government do not attract their attention at all. New York's huge and diverse system of government and politics is a loose-knit and multicentered network in which decisions are reached by ceaseless bargaining and fluctuating alliances among the major categories of participants in each center, and in which the centers are partially but strikingly isolated from one another.

THE PERILS OF A MULTICENTERED SYSTEM

Tendencies Toward Stasis

One consequence of this ordering of the city's political relationships is that every proposal for change must run a gantlet that is often fatal. The system is more favorable to defenders of the *status quo* than to innovators. It is inherently conservative. The reasons for this are threefold.

No Change Without Cost. In the first place, every modification of the existing state of affairs—of the rules, of personnel, of governmental or administrative structure or procedure, or of public policies and programs—entails the fear of cost for some participants as well as hope of gain for the proponents. Any proposed increase in dollar costs, for example, stirs up the revenue-providing nongovernmental groups and their allies among the core groups. Proposals to change regulatory policies arouse quick opposition from the regulated groups and their core group allies if the proposal is to tighten regulation; from the protected groups and their official allies if the proposal is to relax regulation. Curtailed service angers those served and alarms the core groups of officials, as well as the bureaucracies, whose status, jurisdiction, and jobs are threatened, while expanded service alerts those who must pay the dollar costs as well as those who are competing for dollars to be expended for other purposes. Proposals for public works represent threats of displacement for some groups, risks in property values and neighborhood amenities for others. Proposals to reorganize agencies or other governmental and political institutions change adversely the lines of access to decision centers for some groups, affect adversely the career ladders of others, reduce the status and prestige of some others. In most instances, the costs of change are more intensely perceived by participants close to the center of decisions than are the benefits of innovation.

Those who perceive the costs of change in the city's going system have strategies and weapons with which to resist. They ordinarily have prizes to withhold, inducements to offer, sanctions to impose. The core groups of party leaders, for example, have nominations to confer or deny; they have, in addition, experience and skill in the exercise of influence in campaigns, elections, and appointments to office. The core groups of officials have their formal authority of decision with which to bargain with other groups. The organized bureaucracies can resist change by dragging their feet, the issuance of threats to strike or to "demonstrate," or appeals to allies or to the general public. Nongovernmental groups can use their special knowledge and skills, mobilize their members, resort to publicity in criticism of a proposed change. Almost all the participants have allies at other levels of government to whom they may turn for help in their opposition to a proposal. And most participants can threaten to withdraw from existing alliances as a sanction against change. The prospects for any advocate of change are intense opposition: lengthy, costly, wearing maneuvering and negotiation, and uncertainty about results until the last battle is won. If the *anticipation* of such a struggle, with all its costs in money, time, energy, and the possible disruption of longstanding friendships and alliances, is not enough to discourage campaigns in support of many proposed innovations, the strain and the drain of the *actual* fight may well exhaust the supporters and induce them to abandon their causes before they have come near their goals.

Official Hesitancy. In the second place, public officers and employees, whose action is required to make official the decisions reached by the participants in the specialized centers in which they operate, are ordinarily reluctant to move vigorously when there is extensive opposition within the constellation of interested individuals and groups. For they, as the formal authors of changes, are most likely to bear the brunt of enmities and retaliations provoked by adverse consequences of departure from established practice. They are the visible and vulnerable targets of blame for failures, though they must often share with others any credit for achievements. If they yield to demands of economy groups to curtail services or expenditures, the groups that are hurt direct their retribution against the officials in the decision centers and not against the originators of the reductions (who may have virtually compelled the decisions) or the less salient officials in other decision centers who may have cooperated with the economy groups (the Comptroller, for example, or the Director of the Budget). On the other hand, if officials yield to service-demanding groups or other groups (such as the bureaucracies) urging increased service and expenditures that are followed by fiscal crisis and rises in taxation, they may feel the wrath of those affected. If fluorine is added to the city's drinking water at the behest of health and dental groups and their allies in the Health Department, and if there should be later charges of fluorine poisoning attributed to engineering difficulties connected with keeping the fluorine content of the water within safe tolerances, it is the elected members of the Board of Estimate and the water supply engineers who will pay the penalty; hence their unwillingness to go ahead with this program despite the impressive array of advocates behind it. Indeed, officials are understandably wary even when there is a general consensus on the desirability of a particular novelty, for they must try to take into account consequences unanticipated by the assenters. They are doubly cautious when an important and highly vocal segment of their constituency stresses the dangers and costs. So the world of officialdom is often prudent when confronted by recommendations for innovation.

Incentives to Delay. When the specialists and other groups immediately interested in decisions disagree sharply among themselves about the wisdom or soundness of a proposed measure, or when the participants in one decision center line up in opposition to an action taken or projected in another decision center, the controversy is likely to find its way to the general organs of government, usually to the Mayor and the Board of Estimate, but frequently to the Governor and the state legislature. These governmental leaders then find they must choose between courses of action on which the experts and other informed interests are themselves divided. They must weigh the possible consequences of the choices they face—the possibilities of serious errors of judgment, of alienation of substantial blocs of voters, or repercussions on contributions to their parties and their campaigns. The course of prudence for them, therefore, is to temporize in the hope that the disagreements will work themselves out, or that they will have time enough to inform themselves more fully about the situations, or that the circumstances giving rise to the clashes will pass and obviate the need for their action, or that one side or the other will lose heart and abandon its fight. Sometimes they simply defer decision; this is the characteristic strategy of the Board of Estimate. Sometimes they set up study commissions to investigate and bring in recommendations. Rarely do they leap eagerly into the fray.

If some of the participants resort to litigation as part of their strategy, they may find the judges less hesitant to decide (because of the insulation of the courts, designed to encourage judicial independence). They also discover that legal proceedings are often protracted, costly, and time-consuming. This lends to litigation a special attraction and utility for the opponents of change.

The Tortuous Path. Changes of any magnitude thus encounter a long, rocky, twisting path from conception to realization. They are likely to be blocked almost at the start unless their authors revise and modify them to appease strong opponents, and to win the active and enthusiastic support of their allies. At the outset, the authors are likely to be the only zealous advocates in any decision center, and their proposals will face a group of equally zealous critics and a large number of relatively indifferent (that is, unaffected) observers. To overcome the objections and to stimulate the indifferent, plans must be adjusted—altered here, modified there, strengthened in another place. After all the bargaining and concessions, a plan may well have lost much of its substance, much of its novelty. If plans are radical, they seldom survive; if they survive, they seldom work major changes in the going system.

There is nothing intrinsically desirable about change. But it becomes a problem of major importance to the well-being of the city if the governmental system has such a built-in resistance to change, such a tendency to suppress innovation, that it cannot keep up with the problems that confront it in a constantly and rapidly changing world. A city in stasis faces the potential fate of many of the great urban centers of the past, whose glories are all in archives and museums, whose significance is solely historical.

Neglect of Communitywide Perspectives

Another risk inherent in the multicentered system of New York City's government and politics is the subordination of widely shared community values to the special interests of the separate and numerous "islands of power" within it. The tendencies of each core group and its attendant satellite groups to arrive at decisions maximizing their own special interests, including the comfort and convenience of officials and bureaucrats, are sometimes described as characteristic products of the system.

The fact is clear that only a few central institutions in the city produce decisions made on the basis of premises relevant to the entire community. Moreover, these central institutions often actually possess no more than the role of satellite groups with respect to the core groups in each decision center; although they may have theoretical, formal superiority over all the other groups, the central institutions often function, in fact, merely as additional participants in the decision-making processes rather than as masters of the system. They most often appear vulnerable to, and anxious about, the capacity of "lesser" contestants to extract concessions from them. If communitywide perspectives are introduced into the governmental decision-making system, this is usually an incidental by-product of the interaction of special interests.

Weakening of Popular Control

Since each decision center in the city's government and politics has attained a high degree of self-containment, the problem of exerting popular control over them has been complicated. For one thing, it is difficult to assign responsibility for unpopular policies. For another, and more importantly, the capacity of these many separate centers to maintain their essential autonomy, to outwait efforts to supervise them from outside each center itself, or to adulterate the effects of such efforts, sometimes seems so great that popular control over these "free-wheeling" islands takes on a largely ritualistic character. In many ways, the electoral mechanisms of popular control are predicated on the assumption that the officials voted into office are in full command of policy and program, and that the other components of governmental machinery are little more than executors of their collective will. The preferences of the general populace, registered through the medium of elections, thus have an opportunity to impress themselves on what the government—all the public officers and employees—actually do. To the extent that what these public officials and bureaucrats do is actually decided in a host of relatively independent centers of decision, much of the force of the assumptions about the electoral mandate is dissipated. In New York City elected officials have not achieved full command of policy and program.

Frustration of Leadership

Leadership is a difficult concept to define, but any definition would surely include among its elements, first, the coordination of the system (that is, relating the activities of the various parts so that the operations of the whole are beset by a minimum of confusion, conflict, and contradiction, and contribute significantly to the end-product) and, second, the main responsibility for innovation (so that the system does not become obsolete or lose its efficiency and appropriateness for its time and circumstances). Neither of these elements appears to be promoted by the multicentered system of politics and government in New York, and they may, in fact, be positively discouraged.

With little effective attention being paid to the over-all structure and functioning of the system, its design and its output often appear to have an almost chance quality. In its entirety, it often displays a lack of rational ordering, of a sustained sense of direction. Someone once defined a camel as a horse designed by a committee. One might apply similar contumely to the appearance of the New York City governmental system, and add that the same complaint is in many ways appropriate to its behavior as well as its organization.

ACHIEVEMENTS OF THE SYSTEM

Openness, Responsiveness, and Tolerance

Because the city's system is multicentered, then, it harbors traits that may be serious risks to its own continued existence. But it also has qualities richly rewarding to all the inhabitants of the city and particularly to the active participants in the contest for the stakes of politics.

One of these qualities is its openness. No part of the city's large and varied population is alienated from participation in the system. The channels of access to the points of decision are numerous, and most of them are open to any group alert to the opportunities offered and persistent in pursuit of its objectives. All the diverse elements in the city, in competition with each other, can and do partake of the stakes of politics; if none gets all it wants, neither is any excluded.

Consequently, no group is helpless to defend itself, powerless to prevent others from riding roughshod over it, or unable to assert its claims and protect its rights. The great number of *de facto* vetoes built into the system intensifies the tendencies toward immobilization that constitute one of the hazards of the system, but these vetoes also enable every group to obstruct governmental decisions that fail to take its interests into account, to restrain governmental actions that ignore its rights or its aspirations, and to employ its possession of veto power as a basis from which to bargain for recognition and concessions. Furthermore, the abundance of decision centers enables each group to concentrate on selected arenas of special importance to it instead of being cast into a broader environment in which it might have far more difficulty making its voice heard. Some inhabitants of the city have been slower than others to make use of the weapons the political system places within their grasp, but most—even immigrants from lands with altogether different traditions—have learned quickly, and there are not many who accept passively whatever the system deals out. They have learned that governmental decisions of every kind in the city are responsive to the demands upon the decision centers.

The city's system is, at the very least, tolerant of differences of every kind, and usually is even more than that: it engenders official respect for differences. That is not to say the forces working everywhere for orthodoxy and conformity are not at work in New York, or that the city is free from racial, religious, and ethnic prejudices. It does not mean that dissenters and minorities of all kinds are welcomed, or that their claims are immediately and warmly acknowledged and fulfilled. It does mean, however, that they are not suppressed, and that in official and party circles they will generally receive respectful attention. It does mean that personal antagonisms to groups or creeds will generally be stifled by officials. It does mean that candidates and party leaders will not only recognize, but will court the favor of, groups of every kind. And it does mean that third parties and insurgent factions in the major parties cannot be prevented (in spite of the roadblocks often thrown in their paths) from challenging the dominant political parties and factions. There are too many points of entry, too many opportunities for retaliation, too many methods of self-protection and self-assertion, for bigotry or intolerance or fear of heterodoxy to become major elements of official decisions or behavior.

If these attributes are measures of the democratic qualities of a governmental system, then New York City's system must be rated highly democratic. It may run the serious risks noted above, and it may pay a cost in terms of engineering concepts of efficiency, but the system can justly claim to possess openness, responsiveness, and tolerance as essential characteristics of its democracy.

Growth, Progress, and Flexibility

The city's system may also claim to have functioned remarkably well in other ways and to have been unexpectedly creative and adaptive in its six decades.

The quantity and quality of governmental services are high. The difficulties of providing these services to eight million people are immense, but the city government, almost as a matter of routine, has mastered most problems of size and complexity that confront it, and performs without fanfare tasks that would overwhelm the leaders and institutions of communities less accustomed to dealing with the dilemmas of policy and the difficulties of administration presented by the magnitude and intricacy of the city's operations. Every day, the government of the city competently discharges a staggering burden of responsibility.

To be able to do so has required considerable governmental inventiveness and daring. Some of the innovations to which New Yorkers may point with pride as examples of the adaptiveness of their institutions include, among others, the "consolidation" or creation of the Greater City in 1898; the invention of that unique and controversial institution, the Board of Estimate; the early establishment of a Tenement House Department; the beginning of a subway system in 1905 and its expansion, eventual unification, and city operation; the pioneer zoning code of 1916; the steady expansion and maintenance of an unexcelled water supply system; the Health Department's pioneering district health plan in 1915 and its subsequent growth; the establishment of a Department of Hospitals in 1929; the first City Housing Authority in 1934; the transformation of the city's park system since 1934; the charter of 1938, with its creation of a City Planning Commission, the office of Deputy Mayor, and the experiment with proportional representation in the election of councilmen; the creation of a Traffic Department in 1949, an Air Pollution Control Department in 1953, and the office of City Administrator in 1954. The city government, in short, has not been static over the years.

One reason for these innovations is that many forces outside the system impose changes in its operation. The increase in the city's population—especially during the period of mass immigration—and its shifting distribution among the boroughs, for instance, has forced constant adjustments in the pattern of public services and has continually altered the political strength and complexion of various sections. The changing composition of the population—in ethnic, national, and religious characteristics, in income distribution, in occupational categories, in age—has had similar effects. Changes in the city's economy, with some activities rising (such as corporate management) and others declining (such as heavy manufacturing), lead to differing demands upon the system. Economic cycles of inflation and depression generate fiscal pressures, leading often to new coalitions, new types of decisions, new organizations and structures (of which the special authorities are perhaps a prime illustration). Science and technology also have great impacts on the system, introducing new tasks and problems (as in the case of the automobile and the airplane), providing new goals and methods (as in public health), offering new challenges (as does the St. Lawrence Seaway), and creating new demands for change from nongovernmental groups. Obsolescence or deterioration of the city's physical plant (the spread of slums, the growth of depressed business districts, the aging of the port facilities, for example) constitute problems crying for solution, and move previously quiescent groups to political action that brings new pressures, new centers of influence. Financial assistance and inducements offered by the state and by the federal government are often additional incentives to strike out in new directions.

So, too, are the changing aspirations and expectations of the city's general public, reflected especially in the mass media of communication and in the rise of new nongovernmental groups. This is particularly true of those participants in the system whose interests and expectations are not sufficiently satisfied by their roles in it. Leaders of minority ethnic and racial groups, for example, demand changes that will more nearly meet the expectations of their constituents for representation in party and public office and for governmental solutions to some of their social and economic problems. Leaders in the professions often advocate changes that will in their view represent progress toward higher professional standards. Leaders of "civic" and "reform" groups are almost by definition cast in the role of dissenters, critics, and advocates of change in the system, although their energies are usually centered upon limited aspects of the system. As agents of change, they are mainly effective in changing the formal rules of the system (particularly in efforts to make the actions of the participants more ethical and more visible, and the actors more responsible and accountable for their methods and decisions) and in enforcing these rules by exposure and criticism of violation. A great variety of groups—some long-lived, some quite transitory—from time to time succeed in breaking into the system at some point, carrying demands for change which are regarded by the established participants in a particular decision center as "visionary" or "ideological" or "impractical," but these "crusades" are now and then successful. The communication media are not only valued allies of almost all of these groups demanding change, but the press itself is both a reporter and a critic of the system. As a participant-critic in the city's multicentered system, the press is one of the most constant advocates of change, although in no sense does it speak with a single or consistent voice.

Another source of change within the system is those highly visible and usually dramatic public figures who build their careers as apostles of innovation. These leaders perceive the opportunities and the rewards (personal and impersonal) in being skilled and persistent "mavericks" within the system—as rule-changers, as builders of new centers of decisions and of new coalitions of participants, and as creators of new sets of incentives. And the system has also exhibited an unusual capacity to produce outstanding elected and appointed officials as effective leaders in the city's politics and government. The list of the twelve mayors of the city—a list that includes such names as Low, McClellan, Gaynor, Mitchel, La Guardia, Wagner—cannot be matched in quality, it has been asserted, by any other city. Other outstanding leaders cited as products of the city's political system include Theodore Roosevelt, Al Smith, Robert F. Wagner, Sr., each having begun his political and governmental career as a state legislator elected from the city. The administrators of the city's departments and agencies, it is also claimed, compare favorably and are usually superior in quality, capacity, and performance to those of other cities and of the state governments.

As still another source of change within the system itself, there is the fact that every change tends to produce further change in a kind of slow-motion chain-reaction. Recognition of one set of claimants to nomination, for instance, encourages other claimants to increase their efforts. A subway system rearranges the distribution of population, requiring adjustments in many public policies and in many agency decisions. An expanded highway system generates new traffic; traffic congestion requires the establishment of a new city department; and increased reliance upon automobiles brings crises in subway transit and commuter railways. These kinds of changes, springing from many separate and only loosely coordinated decision centers, are more numerous than they might be if they were directed from a single center; thus the existence of a multicentered system often is in itself a contributor to the process of change.

The exposé or highly publicized scandal is also a cause of change. In these situations, leaders of one of the core groups (or an ally, or the two together) are discovered to have violated the formal rules, or at least some of the informal rules. The discovery of the violation is usually made by one of the participants in the system—sometimes by officials of another level of government, at other times by a satellite group, on other occasions by a supervising or a competitive core group, often by the press, not infrequently by a nongovernmental group with a general interest in the whole system (rather than in a single area of decision). The scandal often leads to change, especially if it produces a new coalition of participants advocating specific reforms. The rules may thus be changed, new agencies established or old ones reorganized, new core groups (with their accompanying satellite groups) created.

These exposés have happened often enough to give wide circulation to the notion that the government and politics of New York City hold high rank, if not the highest place, among American cities in the art and practice of official corruption. Actually, this impression is largely the result of the tendency of the city's system to ferret out and give great and dramatic publicity to violations of the rules. The system might properly claim first rank among American cities in the art and practice of exposing corruption. The very fragmentation of the city's system places such high obstacles in the way of the conspiracy and secrecy essential to exploitation, and there are so many participants whose specialization is exposure (the press, insurgent and dissenting participants of many kinds, and the civic groups that often assume the mantle of surrogate for the public conscience) that corruption is difficult to perpetrate, let alone to conceal. Nevertheless the myth of wholesale public corruption continues, in part because it has a perennial usefulness to some of those who participate in the political process (the minority groups, civic groups, economy groups, the press, and, on a short-term basis, the insurgent party groups); in part because New Yorkers, like Texans, take a perverse pride in, and often add to, the exaggerations that award a kind of ironic distinction to themselves and their city; and in part because the myth has become a familiar part of the city's political process itself. Its disappearance would compel alterations in the premises and bargaining vocabulary of the participants that they are unlikely to welcome. The myth gives added impetus to the search for corruption and gains in acceptance whenever the search is successful.

THE QUEST FOR IMPROVEMENT OF THE SYSTEM

Thus, in spite of the perils of the multicentered system of government and politics in New York, the system has proved highly democratic and vigorously adaptive and flexible. Yet the perils cannot be lightly dismissed. The trends and tendencies are what count, and it is by no means certain that as the city and its social and economic life become more intensively specialized, and as the number of decision centers increases correspondingly, the dangers will not grow greater and the democratic features and flexibility of the system decline. So efforts to improve the system are likely to continue to be unremitting.

What constitutes "improvement" of the city's politics and government is almost always a matter for debate. Moreover, the motivations behind each proposal are usually mixed. While every participant is, or professes to be, in favor of those recommendations that will magnify the achievements of the system without adding to its risks, it is difficult to avoid the conclusion that the maintenance or increase of his own role and influence in the system ranks high on the hierarchy of values of each participant. This is seldom made explicit in public debate, but it helps to explain the behavior of many who engage in the public discourse. The proponents of any change emphasize only the benefits of the change, simplify the goals of the proposal, and ignore the adverse consequences for some participants. The opponents stress the costs of the proposal, impute complex, partisan, or obscure goals to the proponents, and ignore the advantages the plan might have. A detached observer of these debates would often conclude that many a proposal would accomplish much that is claimed for it, but that it would also have some of the consequences claimed by the opponents, and the observer might wonder why the net balance of the two sets of consequences is so rarely made the point of the debate. He might perceive also that neither proponents nor opponents seem highly skilled in predicting the wider range of consequences the proposal is likely to have on the city's system.

Proposals for changing or improving the system are numerous and constantly appearing; the more important and more enduring may be thought of as constituting several large "packages" of reform ideas. These have provided many of the major premises of the continuing debate between the participants in the city's politics. Some of these packages have been firmly established as part of the system, and the debate concerning them is either quiescent or centers around their maintenance or their minor modification. Other packages contain items that have been tried and abandoned but continue to find advocates. Still others represent ideas that have been the object of recurrent agitation but have not achieved acceptance.

"Limit the Powers of the City Government"

In the last quarter of the nineteenth century, the pivotal idea of reform in the city's political and governmental system was to limit the powers of the city government by restrictions on its powers written into the state constitution. The most specific and enduring of these restrictions set upper limits on the amount the city may levy in taxes on real property and on the amount the city may borrow through the issuance of bonds of indebtedness. First appearing in 1876, and confirmed in the state constitutions of 1894 and 1938, these restrictions are jealously guarded as parts of the city's system by the revenue-providing constituencies in the city and by the officials of the state government whose power in the city is enhanced by the provisions. The provisions were so successfully defended, and were for many decades so infrequently debated, that the restrictions amounted to a kind of "settlement" between the competing participants. More recently, breaches have been made in the settlement by those participants who have successfully fought for increased financial grants-in-aid to the city, for successive constitutional amendments that have raised the percentage limits on taxes, and for other amendments that have exempted from the debt limit city bond issues for designated purposes (such as subways, hospitals, water supply) and for the self-liquidating portions of revenue-producing investments. But a broad and effective ceiling on city taxing and borrowing powers remains.

Other important and hardy limitations are embodied in many state statutes—the Education Law, for one example; the Election Law, for another. These limitations represent the victories of one set of participants, the defeats of another. The passage of time often affects the consequences of these limitations for different participants, making some advantages obsolete, transforming others into liabilities. The attitudes of the participants tend to reflect these changes; their current posture concerning state-limitations will ordinarily reflect their current strategic necessities.

The reformers who sponsor and support these and similar restrictions on the powers of the city government are mainly those participants in the system who believe they wield more influence at Albany than at City Hall. They include prominently the party leaders and officials of the Republican party, the leaders of the interest groups representing the main revenue-providing constituencies and their allies, other participants whose leaders fear their interests and opportunities may suffer at the hands of city officials unless these officials are curbed, and still others who prefer to have two opportunities for bargaining—one at City Hall and one at Albany. The attitudes of the various participants in the system are often affected by the composition and policies of the party leaders and the officials who occupy, for the moment, the dominant position at Albany or at City Hall; that is, considerations of group strategy, as well as constitutional principle, are importantly involved.

"Grant Home Rule to the City"

A reform package with a seemingly directly opposed major premise, home rule for the city rather than state limitations on the city, has been offered for more than a half-century as a way to improve the operation of the system. As a slogan, a strategic weapon in debates within the system, the general proposal has had great vogue; as a set of concrete objectives, home rule has escaped successful definition. The most explicit expression of the plan has been the goal of home rule with respect to the structure of the city government, but even in this few supporters find it possible or desirable to be consistent; and when they encounter the question of home rule with respect to the substantive powers of the city government, all is confusion, uncertainty, and inconsistency.

The dilemma that the concept of home rule presents to each major participant in the city's political process is embraced in the question: Is the city government the most favorable arena for the exercise of *our* influence? Most groups—party leaders, officials, organized bureaucracies, and nongovernmental groups—discover that the answer to this question varies with time and issue. They discover, too, that they often derive some advantage from being able to pursue their goals simultaneously at Albany and at City Hall, and from having these two centers in competition with each other. Home rule has also been employed by state officials desirous of escaping involvement in some of the city's problems (or pleased, for partisan reasons, to let these problems grow worse). As an abstraction, it is widely endorsed. As an instrument of strategy, it may be invoked as a justification for (or in opposition to) a proposal, or it may be ignored.

"Separate the Politics of the City"

Another reform effort of long duration is the attempt to isolate the politics of the city from the politics of the state and the nation. Proponents of this effort argue that the governing of the city is a problem separate from that of governing the higher jurisdictions, that state and national issues dividing the political parties have no application to the government of the city, and that their presence in city elections is distracting and confusing to the city electorate.

The most substantial victory of the proponents of this reform has been the "settlement," antedating the creation of the Greater City in 1898 and still in effect, providing that elections for city offices shall be held in an off-year—that is, neither a presidential nor a gubernatorial election year. The main purpose of this arrangement is to reduce the influence of the party leaders, the officials of the state and national governments, and the hard-core partisans in the city electorate, while enhancing the influence of other participants in the city's nominating and electing processes. Whether these results are, in fact, consistently obtained is not easily determined. It is apparent that party leaders and state and national officials are not indifferent to, and usually participate actively in the effort to influence, the outcome of city elections because they recognize that more than City Hall offices and opportunities are at stake. The strength of the competing parties in city elections importantly affects their prospects in coming state and national elections. It is apparent also that the proponents of a separate politics for the city do not always find the formula the most useful one available for their own objectives. Thus when the Charter Commission appointed by La Guardia, and composed mainly of advocates of a separate politics, submitted its proposed new charter to referendum, it chose the presidential election of 1936, not a special city election, as the most appropriate occasion for an electoral judgment, since a presidential election brings out the largest number of independent voters and these were assumed to be favorably disposed toward the new charter.

Another manifestation of the effort to establish a separate politics for the city is found in the attempts to establish political parties which will confine themselves primarily to city contests and city issues. The Citizens Union in the election of 1897, the Fusion Committee of the Mitchel elections, and the City Fusion party of 1933 are examples of these efforts. Their survival capacity has been unimpressive. The decade of proportional representation as a method for electing members of the Council represents a related effort toward a separate politics, for it was expected to encourage the nomination and election of councilmen through channels other than the established political parties.

The major participants in the city's political system react to the proposal of a separate city politics in terms of its perceived effects upon their individual fortunes. The Democratic party leaders and public officials have accepted the tradition of separate elections but resist any further extension of the doctrine; the Republican party leaders and public officials share this attitude, but also find their own occasional uses for the doctrine as a base upon which to establish a Fusion alliance. For most other participants the doctrine has merely temporary and strategic significance; they are indifferent to it most of the time. Only a few "civic" nongovernmental groups find the idea consistently attractive as a formula for increasing their influence.

"Improve the Existing Party System"

Some participants in the city's political system emphasize reforms in the organization and operations of the party system: the improvement of election administration, the "democratization" of the party organizations and of the nominating process, the encouragement of two-party or multiparty competition, the use of the initiative and referendum. Most of these proposals have a history that spans the life of the Greater City, several of them have been largely achieved, while others continue as items of debate and aspiration.

Proposals for the reform of election administration have had the most substantial and lasting acceptance: steady improvement in the integrity and efficiency of the processes for registering voters, the use of voting machines, tighter supervision over the casting and the counting of the votes, and higher visibility and accountability in other aspects of election administration. These changes in the rules of the game, largely originated by the nongovernmental groups, are no longer the object of frequent or significant debate. Practically all the participants now regard these aspects of existing election administration, including even the recently adopted changes, as satisfactory rules for the system.

By contrast, the selection, tenure, and powers of party leaders are a perennial subject for debate by many of the participants. Insurgent leaders and groups within the parties (especially within the majority party), some nongovernmental groups (for example, civic, ethnic, racial, trade union), and the communication media are the most articulate protagonists of "democratization" in the party organizations. They commonly seek changes in the Election

Law and the party rules which would facilitate insurgency against established leaders, a goal to be achieved by maximizing rank-and-file participation in the decision-making processes of the party organizations: for example, electing District Leaders in party primaries, expanding membership in party clubs beyond the circle of party "activists" to include all party members, transforming these clubs into "town meetings" for party members at which party decisions would be openly debated and decided by vote. Party leaders and public officials recognize these proposals as designed to reduce their power and increase the powers of other participants in the system; they yield only as much as they find they must concede in the bargaining which these proposals require. The party leaders and the public officials in the majority party are also generally aware that these proposals are aimed most sharply at them, rather than at the other political parties, and that one of the risks represented by the democratization program is the probability that the resulting intraparty competition might weaken the whole structure of their organization.

Democratization of the nominating process presents a similar array of protagonists and opponents. Insurgents and their allies allege that the rules now confer many advantages upon the party leaders and impose many disadvantages upon the other aspiring participants in decisions concerning party nominations. Party leaders defend the reasonableness of the existing rules and argue that the proposed changes would expose the parties to the risks of factionalism and disintegration, substituting intraparty for interparty competition. Fortunately for the party leaders, the fact that most of the proposed changes would have to be applied throughout the state produces opposition to democratization by both Republican and Democratic party leaders and public officials (since each party is the majority party in an important part of the state, and thus each would face comparable risks from the change).

The efforts to create a "two-party" or "multiparty" city politics encounters the effective opposition of the two major parties, determined to protect their stakes in national, state, and local governments. Democratic party leaders and public officials at all levels of government perceive their voting strength in the city as linked closely to all their fortunes, including the possession of the governorship and the presidency; they cannot exchange their majority in the city for the abstract goal of two-party competition. Their Republican counterparts cannot embrace the two-party goal either, except in rhetoric, without hazard to their own predominance outside the city. Their brief experiment with proportional representation in the Council convinced most of them that a multiparty politics in the city costs them more than they gain. Two-party and multiparty politics for the city do not represent attractive alternatives for party leaders and public officials in the two major parties. The proposals do present favorable incentives to other participants: leaders of minority parties and their allies; insurgent or impatient ethnic, religious, and racial groups; civic groups, the communication media, and others interested in wielding influence across party lines.

Expanded use of the initiative and the referendum in the city are proposals intended to shift certain categories of decisions from one core group to another: usually from a core group of officials to the electorate. Some proponents have a sufficiently consistent position on this proposal to make their commitment an ideological one (as do, for example, a few of the civic groups), but most participants see the initiative and referendum simply as strategic opportunities or liabilities. Thus the fire and police bureaucracies have on occasion favored a referendum on pay increases they could not secure from officialdom; the opponents of fluoridation of drinking water have recommended a referendum on the question, believing the electorate to represent a more favorable arena for their argument, while the proponents of fluoridation reject this suggestion as inappropriate for electoral judgment; and officialdom sometimes sees the initiative and referendum as devices for transferring the risks and responsibilities of a troublesome decision to other hands.

Proposals to improve the existing party system, then, are primarily the strategies of particular participants to improve their bargaining position in the city's multicentered system of power. The main thrust of the suggested reforms is aimed at reducing the presumed advantages held by party leaders and public officials and at increasing the influence of other participants. The full consequences of the proposals are rarely explored in the public debates of the participants.

"Provide Nonpartisan Government for the City"

One of the oldest and most frequently articulated goals of reform in the city is the ambiguous proposal that the city government should "be taken out of politics." The methods for achieving this end (for example, the "nonpartisan" ballot, the city manager plan, the extension of the merit system and the career services, the delegation of power to "experts" or other trusted groups) on inspection turn out to be devices for transferring power from party leaders and elected officials, not to the electorate or "the people" as is often claimed by the protagonists, but to particular nongovernmental groups and to the bureaucracies.

The proposal for a nonpartisan ballot—that is, an election ballot devoid of all clues as to the party affiliation or endorsement of the candidates—has had limited acceptance in the city. The idea has had proponents, but they have failed to recruit sufficiently powerful allies to launch a formal application in any city election. The party leaders of all parties have recognized its main purpose and its most probable consequence: the subordination of their influence, the fragmentation and factionalization of the parties, and the increased power of nongovernmental groups and the bureaucracies.

Similarly the city manager plan, while not lacking in powerful and articulate advocates at several points in the city's history, has failed to attract an alliance of support having the power to secure its establishment. The plan, in essence, would most probably transfer influence in the city's political system from party leaders, elected executives, and their usual allies, to a quite different alliance: to those nongovernmental groups capable of competing with the party leaders in a nonpartisan proportional representation election of councilmen, to the permanent bureaucracies in the city departments and agencies, and to the "professional" (that is, bureaucracy-oriented) city manager in the role of mediator between the council and the bureaucracies. The viability of such an alliance for the governing of the city is doubtful, but the most likely consequence would seem to be even greater autonomy for all those numerous islands of power which are now based primarily upon an alliance of a cluster of nongovernmental groups and/or an organized bureaucracy.

Extending the merit system of employment for city employees has had, in contrast to the unsuccessful proposals for nonpartisan elections and for a council-manager form of city government, a history of steady and eventually almost complete acceptance in the city's government. The competitive examination as a method of selection and promotion is now applied to most city positions; the noncompetitive examination is used for most others, and only a very small proportion remain in the "exempt" class. Other personnel rules and practices also serve to establish and maintain career services in the bureaus and departments of the city government. Thus the reformers—in this instance, a long-sustained alliance among civic groups, several other interest groups, the communication media, and the emerging bureaucracies themselves—have accomplished their purposes with unusual success: the merit system and the career system have become firmly established in the rules of the game, while the party leaders and elected officials have been reduced to the exercise of marginal influence upon most city employment. The consequences have included not merely the anticipated increase in competence and conventional rationality in the conduct of the city government, but also, and equally significant, the rise of a new form of political power in the city: the career bureaucracies, and especially the organized bureaucracies. Once closely allied to, and greatly dependent upon, the party leaders, the bureaucracies now have the status and the capacity of autonomous participants in the city's political process—a political life of their own and an important share in the stakes of the city's politics.

A closely related formula for taking parts of the city government "out of politics" is represented by the efforts to create "nonpolitical" agencies, insulated by rule or practice from intervention by party leaders or supervision by elected officials. The special authorities (for example, the transit, housing, bridge-tunnel-parkway authorities), the Board of Health, the Board of Education (and especially the proposal to give to education "fiscal independence" through a grant of separate taxing and borrowing authority) are important examples of this reform, as are also the assertions that the Mayor and other "politicians" (even though they are elected officials) should not "interfere" in police administration, hospital administration, park administration, or other domains of the city government marked out for rule by the experts. The premises of this reform movement have secured wide acceptance among many of the participants in the city's political process and the application of the premises has been extensive. The consequences of this trend have been a strengthening of the tendencies toward a multicentered system of power in the city and a weakening of the influence of party leaders and of elected officials, especially the Mayor. The direct beneficiaries of the movement have been the nongovernmental interest groups that constitute the intimate "constituencies" of the nonpolitical agencies, the career bureaucracies of these agencies, and in fewer instances the appointed officials who are the formal heads of these agencies. Taking a governmental function or an agency out of politics is thus most realistically viewed in New York City as transferring it from the "politics" of elected officials (particularly the elected chief executive) to the "politics" of strategically located interest groups, or organized bureaucracies, or autonomy-minded appointed executives, or some alliance of these three types.

"Improve the City's Administrative Machinery and Processes"

Most participants in the city's multicentered politics have from time to time found it useful to subscribe to the doctrines of efficiency, economy, and rationality in administration which were so effectively concentrated in the "scientific management" movement early in the century and have been the essence of subsequent programs for administrative reorganization in local, state, and national governments. In New York City the impact of this movement came early and has been sustained by its continued appeal to many of the participants in the city's politics. Proposals and actions to centralize and integrate the city government's administrative agencies, to modernize their methods of work, and to impose standards of economy and efficiency upon the agencies, were a leading preoccupation of the Low administration (1902–1904). The Bureau of Municipal Research, a nongovernmental civic agency dedicated to rationality and efficiency in administration, supplied much of the agenda of reform for the Mitchel administration (1914–1918). The Charter Commission of 1934–1936 wrote many proposals of this kind into the new charter adopted in 1938. Mayor O'Dwyer commissioned the Citizens Budget Commission in 1947 to apply these criteria to five major city agencies.

Mayor O'Dwyer also, in early 1950, instituted the comprehensive study of the Mayor's Committee on Management Survey, which was to be followed by the work of the Temporary State Commission on New York City Government (1953–1954), the New York State-New York City Fiscal Relations Committee (1956–1957), and the state-city "Little Hoover Commission," which began its work in 1959. Each of these efforts produced changes in the structure and the procedures of the city's administrative agencies, the changes being aimed primarily at reducing the sins of waste, duplication, and other identified inefficiencies.

The civic groups have found most of these recommendations and actions both congenial to their ideological commitments and strategically advantageous to them as participants. The interest groups representing revenue-providing constituencies have been similarly favorable to most of the reorganization programs. The communication media have tended to give consistent support. At the other end of the scale among the participants, the party leaders and the organized bureaucracies have shown the least enthusiasm. Other participants, including most officials and the interest group constituencies of most agencies, have revealed a less consistent pattern. They have usually endorsed the goals of economy, efficiency, and rationality, but they have also appraised each specific proposal more particularly by the criteria of their own strategic necessities in the city's political system.

The net consequence of these opposed views has usually been a compromise among the participants most directly involved in each change: the values of efficiency, economy, and rationality are endorsed by all, while the gains and losses in power by the participants are held within the limits established by the vigorous bargaining among them. The gaps between the proposals and the changes actually made provide much of the grist for the next administrative survey and its new package of recommendations. Administrative reorganization and management improvement efforts thus tend to become a continuous activity within the city's governmental and political system, as the four major surveys of the 1950's, and the recent institutionalization of the function in the work of the City Administrator's office, all eloquently testify.

"Strengthen the Mayor"

Among American cities the idea of a "strong" mayor has long had its most favorable reception in New York City. When the Greater City was established in 1898, the two great cities from which it was formed (Brooklyn and New York) each had long had a strong-mayor tradition. The office was continued in that pattern: a four-year term, generous power to appoint heads of agencies and departments without confirmation requirements, and other important formal grants of authority. Most subsequent charter proposals and revisions have paid deference to this tradition, and many of the changes have clarified the powers of the Mayor or in some instances added directly or indirectly to his powers. In its formal powers the office has for more than sixty years been protected against direct loss and has usually acquired some additional formal powers in each decade: for example, new powers under the charter of 1938, and by the charter amendments of 1953 establishing the City Administrator and the Personnel Director. "Strengthening" the Mayor has had wide popularity as a doctrine among the participants in the city's political system, but the doctrine has had sufficient ambiguity to permit rival centers of power to hold the Mayor's actual power constant while theirs was increased.

The greatest of these rival power centers had its unobtrusive beginnings when the charter of 1901 established the Board of Estimate in approximately its present title and form. Power and influence have since gravitated steadily to this unique political and governmental institution, so aptly suited to the city's boroughs and their politics. Most participants in the city's political system have found the Board to be, for their several purposes, the superior institution for the struggle, the bargaining, and the accommodation of interests upon which they each depend. As a consequence, the Mayor must seek to use the Board for these purposes also. The Board, not the Mayor, thus becomes the institution to which the most important unresolved issues of the city's politics are brought for ultimate settlement. The utility of the Board for most participants is underscored by its immunity from any major efforts since 1901 to alter its composition, its powers, or its place in the system.

The vulnerability of the Mayor is also the product of the capacity of the many centers of power in the city's political system to maintain their autonomy against any but his strongest disposition to intervene in their affairs, as well as their preference for dealing directly with the Board of Estimate. The values of autonomy in the city's multicentered system of power are so important to the participants in each of these subsystems that few of them find any long-range advantages in increasing the actual power of the Mayor, lest he use that increased power to reduce their self-containment.

An additional major difficulty confronts those who propose strengthening the office of Mayor. This difficulty lies in the awkward relationship of the Mayor to the party leaders. The absence of a citywide party institution deprives the Mayor of needed opportunities to lead his party in his rivalry to the Board of Estimate; the borough (or county) party system which now prevails favors the Board rather than the Mayor. Fusion Mayors gain some advantage in this respect from their capacity to impose their leadership upon the unstable coalition which nominated and elected them; Democratic Mayors, however, are sharply limited by the close alliance that usually then exists between the Board and the borough (county) party organizations. In both types of situations, the party leadership opportunities of the Mayor are severely restricted.

Most of the participants in the city's political contest are wedded to the existing multicentered system of power. To strengthen the Mayor in any substantial degree would require them to risk the loss of some of their present power on the chance that their influence would be as great or greater in the new center of power built up around a stronger Mayor. Few contestants see this as a promising risk.

Criteria of Judgment

There are no panaceas for the grand transformation of the city's present governmental and political system into a system which all or most participants would regard as ideal, or even as demonstrably superior to the existing arrangements. Those who present comprehensive blueprints for such sweeping purposes seek, perhaps somewhat unwittingly, to install themselves or their allies in the seats of power and to override all their "unenlightened" opponents. Similarly, those who oppose any change at all in the system are expressing a preference for the existing distribution of power. And those who propose or oppose specific suggestions for reform, without passing judgment upon the total system, are also usually responding to the supposed effects of the change upon their own role in the system.

Appraisal of proposed changes in the city's system, then, requires not simply a consideration of the abstract merits or defects of the proposal, but even more importantly an analysis of its probable effects upon the city's political contest and upon the several contestants, since every change strengthens the relative influence of some participants and weakens others. The crucial questions for the analyst—whether voter, official, bureaucrat, civic leader, businessman or labor leader, editorial writer, or party leader— are: Whose hand is strengthened, whose weakened, by the proposal? Whose hand do I want to strengthen? Whose hand do I want to weaken?

Some reformers tend to place their hopes on the city's career bureaucracies. Some prefer the insurgent groups within the parties. Others place their faith in the civic, or professional, or business, or labor leaders, heading the nongovernmental associations that participate in the city's political system. Still others would strengthen the Mayor as the elected chief executive and as party leader. Still others are more certain about whose hand they want to weaken—for example, the hand of the party leaders or the Albany officials— than they are about whose is to be strengthened. The solution advocated depends usually on who has been chosen for a champion and who has been identified as an antagonist.

Among all the programs of reform offered recurrently for the improvement of the city's political and governmental system, the authors of this study would at this time endorse as the most promising those that would increase the powers and the opportunities for leadership by the Mayor. An immediate and minimal program for adding to the influence of the Mayor is provided by those proposals of the Josephs Commission of 1953–1954 which have still not been put into practice, particularly those relating to expanding the functions and powers of the City Administrator while keeping that official "the Mayor's man." A long-range goal might be revision of state statutes, the city charter, the Administrative Code, and the other "rules" of the political contest, that now confer authority directly on department heads and bureau chiefs, redrafting them in such a way as to transfer to the Mayor the administrative powers of the city government now possessed and exercised independently by many officials theoretically subordinate to him. The Mayor's hand would be considerably fortified if he could delegate and rescind or modify delegations of power to those who serve under him; the blunderbuss of removal is too crude an instrument for many purposes of government and administration. But the most extensive expansion of mayoral power can be achieved only by changes in the powers and functions of the Board of Estimate, and in the relationships of the Board to the Mayor. The Board's control of financial and administrative detail has in general been one important cause of the limitations of the office of Mayor; the Mayor has been deprived of some of the most valued and effective managerial tools an executive can wield. Shifting control of such detail to the Mayor would equip the mayoralty with means of influence on program and policy that he cannot hope to attain under present conditions, and would establish a more rational and satisfactory balance between the Board of Estimate as a legislative body and the Mayor as chief executive of the city. Indeed, it may one day prove advantageous to the Mayor to be separated from the Board, for the price he pays for his voice in its deliberations often seems quite high compared to the influence his presence in its meetings affords him. If such a separation of powers should ever come to pass, it would then be appropriate to assess the possibilities of reducing the ambiguities and rivalries generated by the existence of two independently elected officials (the Comptroller and the President of the City Council) whose constituencies, like the Mayor's, are citywide.

The specifics of the measures to strengthen the position of the Mayor, however, may be less important than their purpose; present shortcomings, problems, and needs make the mayoralty the logical focus for remedial action. His constituencies are the broadest and most inclusive, his exercise of power the most visible and responsible, and his leadership the most responsive to the innovations and integration needed by a system which tends toward stalemate and fragmentation. As a center for the settlement of conflicts among the more specialized centers of power, as a central check upon their drive toward extreme autonomy, and as a potential source of affirmative, innovating leadership to moderate their parochialism, the office of Mayor is a much more promising institution in action, visibility, and responsibility than is the Board of Estimate with its commitments to a secret caucus, its delays, and its compromises reached in low visibility.

The most lasting impressions created by a systematic analysis of New York City's political and governmental system as a whole are of its democratic virtues: its qualities of openness, its commitments to bargaining and accommodation among participants, its receptivity to new participants, its opportunities for the exercise of leadership by an unmatched variety and number of the city's residents new and old. Defects accompany these virtues, and in some situations overshadow them, but the City of New York can confidently ask: What other large American city is as democratically and as well governed?

APPENDICES

APPENDIX A

Memoirs, Biographies, and Autobiographies
Of Prominent New Yorkers

Abelow, Samuel P., *Dr. William H. Maxwell: The First Superintendent of Schools of New York City*. Scheba Publishing Co., Brooklyn, 1934. A biography of the city's first Superintendent of Schools.

Arm, Walter, *Pay-Off!* Appleton-Century-Crofts, New York, 1951. How a courageous District Attorney smashed a gambling syndicate.

Baldwin, Joseph Clark, III, *Flowers for the Judge*. Coward-McCann, New York, 1950. Autobiography of a New Yorker who served as Minority Leader of the Board of Aldermen, as councilman, as state senator, and as congressman. He also held Republican party offices.

Barker, Charles A., *Henry George*. Oxford University Press, New York, 1955. A reformer who was twice nominated for Mayor.

Carlson, Oliver, and Ernest S. Bates, *Hearst: Lord of San Simeon*. Viking Press, New York, 1936. The career of a publisher who exerted a great influence over New York politics.

Chambers, Walter, *Samuel Seabury: A Challenge*. Century Co., New York, 1932. A portrait of the counsel to an important state investigation committee.

Cohen, Julius Henry, *They Builded Better Than They Knew*. Julian Messner, New York, 1946. Portraits of civic figures.

Cohen, Naomi W., *The Public Career of Oscar S. Straus*. Doctoral dissertation, Columbia University, 1955.

Cuneo, Ernest, *Life with Fiorello*. Macmillan Co., New York, 1955. A close look at the Mayor, by a man who was intimately associated with him.

Curran, Henry H., *Pillar to Post*. Charles Scribner's Sons, New York, 1941. The autobiography of a former Borough President of Manhattan, Majority Leader of the Board of Aldermen, Deputy Mayor, and Chief Magistrate.

Cutolo, Salvatore R., *Bellevue Is My Home*. Doubleday and Co., Garden City, N. Y., 1956. An account by a doctor long associated with Bellevue Hospital.

Danforth, Harold R., and James D. Horan, *The D.A.'s Man.* Crown Publishers, New York, 1957. An Assistant District Attorney under Thomas E. Dewey and Frank S. Hogan.

Farley, James A., *Behind the Ballots.* Harcourt, Brace and Co., New York, 1938. An important figure in state and national affairs whose political activities frequently affected politics in New York City.

Foord, John, *The Life and Public Services of Andrew Haswell Green.* Doubleday, Page and Co., Garden City, N. Y., 1913. A biography of one of the chief architects of consolidation.

Fowler, Gene, *Beau James: The Life and Times of Jimmy Walker.* Viking Press, New York, 1949. A biography notable for its wealth of anecdotes.

Franklin, Jay, *La Guardia: A Biography.* Modern Age, New York, 1937. Information about politics during La Guardia's first administration.

Fosdick, Raymond B., *Chronicle of a Generation.* Harper and Bros., New York, 1958. The autobiography of Mayor Gaynor's Commissioner of Accounts.

Gosnell, Harold F., *Boss Platt and His New York Machine.* University of Chicago Press, Chicago, 1924. A turn-of-the-century Republican state leader who exerted great influence on the city's Republican party.

Graham, Frank, *Al Smith, American.* G. P. Putnam's Sons, New York, 1945.

Gribetz, Louis J., and Joseph Kaye, *Jimmie Walker: Story of a Personality.* Dial Press, New York, 1932. A favorable view of the Mayor.

Hall, Edward H., *A Short Biography of Andrew Haswell Green.* New York, 1904. Reprinted from *Ninth Annual Report of American Scenic and Historic Preservation Society*, of which it forms Appendix A.

Handlin, Oscar, *Al Smith and His America.* Little, Brown and Co., Boston, 1958.

Hapgood, Norman, and Henry Moskowitz, *Up from the City Streets.* Grosset & Dunlap, New York, 1928. A sympathetic story of Al Smith, told with insight into the city's political life.

Hillquit, Morris, *Loose Leaves from a Busy Life.* Macmillan Co., New York, 1934. The autobiography of the Socialist candidate for Mayor in 1917.

Hirsch, Mark D., *William C. Whitney: Modern Warwick.* Dodd, Mead and Co., New York, 1948. The biography of a New Yorker prominent in municipal affairs in the nineteenth century.

Hochman, William Russell, *William J. Gaynor: The Years of Fruition.* Publication no. 12,309, University Microfilms, Ann Arbor, Mich., 1955. A detailed biography of the Mayor based on a careful study of original sources.

Hylan, John F., *Autobiography*. Rotary Press, New York, 1922.

Isaacs, Julius, *Oath of Devotion*. E. P. Dutton and Co., New York, 1949. A public official relates his story.

Josephson, Matthew, *Sidney Hillman: Statesman of American Labor*. Doubleday and Co., Garden City, N. Y., 1952. The life of a man closely identified with the "splinter" parties.

Klein, Henry H., *My Last Fifty Years*. The Author, New York, 1935. The autobiography of a New Yorker prominent in city politics.

La Guardia, Fiorello H., *The Making of an Insurgent*. J. B. Lippincott Co., Philadelphia, 1948. The Mayor's autobiography to the year 1919.

Limpus, Lowell M., and Burr Leyson, *This Man La Guardia*. E. P. Dutton and Co., New York, 1938. A full scale biography of the Mayor.
Honest Cop: Lewis J. Valentine. E. P. Dutton and Co., New York, 1939. The story of a notable Police Commissioner.

Low, Benjamin R. C., *Seth Low*. G. P. Putnam's Sons, New York, 1955. The career of the city's second Mayor.

Luthin, Richard H., *American Demagogues: Twentieth Century*. The Beacon Press, Boston, 1954. A detailed portrait of Vito Marcantonio.

MacKaye, Milton A., *The Tin Box Parade: A Handbook for Larceny*. Robert M. McBride and Co., New York, 1934. Journalistic sketches of public figures and political personalities.

Mann, Arthur, *La Guardia: A Fighter Against His Times, 1882–1933*. J. B. Lippincott Co., Philadelphia, 1959. First volume of the definitive biography of La Guardia.

McAdoo, William, *Guarding a Great City*. Harper and Bros., New York, 1906. Recollections of a Police Commissioner.

McAllister, Robert, and Floyd Miller, *The Kind of Guy I Am*. McGraw-Hill Book Co., New York, 1957. Story of a famous policeman.

McGurrin, James, *Bourke Cochran: A Freelance in American Politics*. Charles Scribner's Sons, New York, 1948. Biography of a Tammany leader.

Mockridge, Norton, and Robert H. Prall, *The Big Fix*. Henry Holt and Co., New York, 1954. The story of District Attorney Miles McDonald and Mayor O'Dwyer.

Morris, Charles, *Men of Affairs in New York: An Historical Work*. L. R. Hamersley and Co., New York, 1906. The life and careers of important men in public affairs of the day.

Morris, Newbold, and Dana Lee Thomas, *Let the Chips Fall*. Appleton-Century-Crofts, New York, 1955. Recollections of a former alderman and President of the Council.

Moskowitz, Henry, *Alfred E. Smith: An American Career*. Thomas Seltzer, New York, 1924. A favorable account.

Moses, Robert, *La Guardia: A Salute and a Memoir*. Simon and Schuster, New York, 1957.

Northrop, W. B., editor, *Some of Mayor Gaynor's Letters and Speeches*. Greaves Publishing Co., New York, 1913. Mayor Gaynor's views on a variety of subjects.

Parkhurst, C. H., *My Forty Years in New York*. Macmillan Co., New York, 1923. The life story of a reformer.

Patri, Angelo, *A Schoolmaster of the Great City*. Macmillan Co., New York, 1917. The autobiography of a teacher and administrator in the city's public schools.

Perkins, Frances, *The Roosevelt I Knew*. Viking Press, New York, 1946.

Pink, Louis H., *Gaynor: The Man Who Swallowed the Tiger*. International Press, New York, 1931. A sympathetic biography.

Pringle, Henry F., *Alfred E. Smith: A Critical Study*. Macy-Macius, New York, 1927.

Reynolds, Quentin, *Headquarters*. Harper and Bros., New York, 1955. Many aspects of the Police Department are explored in this biography of Frank Phillips.

Roosevelt, Theodore, *An Autobiography*. Macmillan Co., New York, 1914. Impressions of New York City public life before the city's consolidation.

Salter, J. T., editor, *The American Politician*. University of North Carolina Press, Chapel Hill, 1938. Contains an essay on Mayor La Guardia by Paul J. Kern.

Smith, Alfred E., *Up to Now*. Viking Press, New York, 1929. Autobiography.

Smith, Mortimer, *William Jay Gaynor: Mayor of New York*. Henry Regnery Co., Chicago, 1951.

Syrett, Harold C., *The Gentleman and the Tiger: The Autobiography of George B. McClellan, Jr.* J. B. Lippincott Co., Philadelphia, 1956. The edited journal of the city's third Mayor.

Train, Arthur, *From the District Attorney's Office*. Charles Scribner's Sons, New York, 1939.

Tugwell, Rexford G., *The Art of Politics As Practiced by Three Great Americans: Franklin Delano Roosevelt, Louis Muñoz Marín, and Fiorello H. La Guardia*. Doubleday and Co., New York, 1958.

Valentine, Lewis J., *Police Night Stick*. Dial Press, New York, 1947. The autobiography of a Police Commissioner.

Van Wyck, Frederick, *Recollections of an Old New Yorker*. Boni and Liveright, New York, 1932. Reminiscences of a cousin of Mayor Van Wyck.

Waldman, Louis, *Labor Lawyer*. E. P. Dutton and Co., New York, 1944. Autobiography of a political figure closely connected with minor parties in the city.

Walling, George W., *Recollections of a New York Chief of Police*. Caxton Book Co., New York, 1887. Memoirs of the head of New York's Police Department before consolidation of the city.

Warner, Emily Smith, with Daniel Hawthorne, *The Happy Warrior: A Biography of My Father*. Doubleday and Co., Garden City, N. Y., 1956. Reminiscences of one of Al Smith's daughters.

Warner, Richard F., "On the Way Up: Profile of George Upton Harvey," *The New Yorker*, vol. 6, May 31, 1930, pp. 24–27. Portrait of the Borough President of Queens.

Welling, Richard, *As the Twig Is Bent*. G. P. Putnam's Sons, New York, 1942. The autobiography of a notable civic figure.

Whalen, Grover, *Mr. New York: The Autobiography of Grover Whalen*. G. P. Putnam's Sons, New York, 1955.

Wheeler, Everett P., *Sixty Years of American Life*. E. P. Dutton and Co., New York, 1917. The autobiography of a former member of the Civil Service Commission who was deeply involved in public affairs in the city.

Willemse, Cornelius, *A Cop Remembers*. E. P. Dutton and Co., New York, 1933. A famous policeman whose story covers several decades on the force.

Wise, Stephen B., *Challenging Years*. G. P. Putnam's Sons, New York, 1949. Autobiography.

Zinn, Howard, *Fiorello La Guardia in Congress*. University Microfilms, Ann Arbor, Mich., 1958. Doctoral dissertation, Columbia University, 1958.

APPENDIX B

Sources of Information About New York City

LIBRARIES, DEPOSITORIES, AND OTHER SOURCES
OF COLLECTED INFORMATION IN THE NEW YORK AREA

Board of Elections, 400 Broome Street, New York 13, New York. Contains official records of all general elections and maps of various types of political districts, many of great historical interest.

Brooklyn College, Bedford Avenue at Avenue H, Brooklyn 10, New York. Contains a special collection of books on Brooklyn and by Brooklyn authors.

Citizens' Housing and Planning Council of New York, 20 West 40th Street, New York 18, New York. Specializes in the areas of housing and city planning.

Citizens Union of the City of New York, 5 Beekman Street, New York 38, New York. This small library emphasizes city-state relations, the New York City Council and Board of Estimate, and other subjects of interest to students of New York City government.

The City College, Bernard M. Baruch School of Business and Public Administration, 17 Lexington Avenue, New York 10, New York, and The City College, Convent Avenue and 139th Street, New York 31, New York. Contains large collections of books, pamphlets, and government publications on New York City government.

Columbia University Libraries: Special Collections Department, 654 Butler Library. Contains a variety of collections on New York City government, such as the Kilroe Collection of Tammaniana, the Oral History Project (consisting of a collection of typescripts of reminiscences and memoirs of men and women who were prominent in New York City politics), the New York Woman Suffrage Collection, and the Citizens Union Collection.

Columbia University Law Library, Kent Hall, 116th Street and Amsterdam Avenue, New York. Items of special interest to students of New York City government, such as the original documents of the Charter Revision Commission of 1936, the minutes of the executive sessions of the committee which investigated New York City affairs in 1931, etc.

746

Journalism Library, 303 Journalism Building, New York 27, New York. Has valuable files of newspaper clippings, from 1890 to date.

Burgess-Carpenter Libraries, Butler Library. Established primarily to serve faculty and students of the Graduate Faculty of Political Science, these libraries are valuable for researchers in the field of local government, administration, and history.

New York School of Social Work, 2 East 91st Street, New York 28, New York. Particularly valuable in the area of government and social welfare.

Avery Library. Has a noteworthy collection of material on city planning.

Commerce and Industry Association of New York, 99 Church Street, New York 7, New York. A valuable collection of books, pamphlets, and periodicals relating to city-state relations, city finances, taxation, and city planning.

Institute of Public Administration Library, 684 Park Avenue, New York 21, New York. Originally the Bureau of Municipal Research, a pioneer agency in studying municipal administration, this private collection includes the files of the Bureau, which contain sole copies of research studies on early New York City administration.

James T. White and Co., 101 Fifth Avenue, New York 3, New York. Created primarily to serve the staff of the *National Cyclopedia of American Biography*, this library is particularly valuable for researchers in local biography.

Library of Congress, Washington, D.C. The presence of all copyright material in the United States makes this library a valuable and unique source of information. Also contains manuscript collections in relation to New York City, such as the papers of George B. McClellan, Jr., John Purroy Mitchel, and Theodore Roosevelt.

Long Island Historical Society, 130 Pierrepont Street, Brooklyn 1, New York. Specializes in Brooklyn and Long Island. Contains books, scrapbooks, and manuscript collections. (A charge for inspecting manuscripts.)

Municipal Archives and Records Center (a branch of the New York Public Library), 283 William Street, New York 38, New York. Established by the Mayor's Municipal Archives Committee, this Center contains the public papers of the Mayors of the city from 1849 to the present, the personal papers of Mayor F. H. La Guardia, scrapbooks of leading personalities in municipal life in the twentieth century, metropolitan newspapers, coroners' records, a map collection, and a large group of photographs relating to the city's physical growth.

Municipal Reference Library, 2230 Municipal Building, New York 7, New York. Specializing in city affairs, the Municipal Reference Library has a most important collection of material for the study of New York City's government and administration. Virtually all printed material relating to these subjects in recent years may be found here. Every city department is required to deposit copies of their reports. The library has over 100,000 volumes on municipal administration.

Public Health Division, 125 Worth Street, New York 13, New York. This library contains more than a collection of volumes on medicine and public health. It is the official depository of the city's Department of Health and has many New York City documents on the administration of hospitals and public health administration.

Museum of the City of New York, 1220 Fifth Avenue, New York 29, New York. Possesses a large collection of books, pamphlets, newspapers, and periodicals relating to New York City.

National Civil Service League, 315 Fifth Avenue, New York 16, New York. This library is particularly rich in pamphlet material relating to the city's civil service and personnel administration.

National Municipal League, 47 East 68th Street, New York 21, New York. This library, established to serve editors and contributors to the *National Municipal Review*, students of municipal government, and civic groups, emphasizes city and state government, civil service, elections, legislative bodies, and citizen actions. Students of New York City government will find its archives rich in materials on proportional representation and home rule.

New York Chamber of Commerce, 65 Liberty Street, New York 5, New York. This library is particularly strong on New York City government and history and on New York State legislation relating to the city.

New York City Board of Education Libraries, Professional Library, Second Floor; Library of Bureau of Educational Program Research and Statistics, Seventh Floor; both at 110 Livingston Street, Brooklyn 1, New York. Open to Board of Education employees and other qualified users, these libraries contain the most complete collections of *Journals* of the Board of Education and the Board of Superintendents, as well as printed and documentary materials relating to the New York City schools.

New York City Department of Labor Library, 93 Worth Street, New York 13, New York. Open to qualified persons, this library contains a collection of books, pamphlets, and manuscript material relating to labor relations among municipal employees in New York City, the United States, and Canada.

New York Historical Society, 170 Central Park West, New York 24, New York. Specializes in New York City history.

New York Public Library, Fifth Avenue and 42d Street, New York 18, New York. Economics Division (Room 228): contains valuable printed sources relating to such subjects as public administration and city planning; Local History and Genealogy Division (Room 315G): one of the best collections of printed volumes on New York City government; and American History Division (Room 315A): strong on New York State and city-state relations.

New York State Division of Housing, 270 Broadway, New York 7, New York. Contains material relating to such subjects as building codes, housing developments, community surveys, and city planning and zoning.

The New York Times, 229 West 43rd Street, New York 36, New York. The clipping reference files (morgue) contain about 1,600,000 different biographical headings and 60,000 different subject headings.

Port of New York Authority Library, 111 Eighth Avenue, New York 11, New York. The shelf and vertical file collections are devoted largely to matters that relate to the work of the Port Authority.

Regional Plan Association, 205 East 42d Street, New York 17, New York. The principal resources of this library are devoted to regional planning, particularly in the New York metropolitan region.

Union Club, 701 Park Avenue, New York 21, New York. Has a special collection on New York City history.

BIBLIOGRAPHIES ON NEW YORK CITY

Brooklyn Public Library, *List of Books on Greater New York in the Brooklyn Public Library*. 3d ed. The Library, Brooklyn, 1909.

Dunn, James T., "Masters' Theses and Doctoral Dissertations in New York History (1897–1951)," *New York History*, vol. 33, April, 1952, pp. 232–236; July, 1952, pp. 356–358; October, 1952, pp. 461–466. Primarily devoted to work on historical research, this compilation includes relevant studies in the area of New York City government.

Eiberson, Harold, and Sidney Ditzion, "Sources for the Study of the New York Area: A Bibliographic Essay." The New York Area Research Council, City College, New York, 1957. This mimeographed publication is a valuable guide to source materials and secondary sources relating to the government and administration of New York City.

Government Affairs Foundation, *Metropolitan Communities: A Bibliography*. Public Administration Service, Chicago, 1956. Includes numerous references to New York City and the New York metropolitan region.

Institute of Public Administration, *Selected Recent References on Materials Relating to the Operation of the Government of the City of New York*. The Institute, New York, 1959.

Municipal Reference Library Notes, 1914 to date (indexed). Lists the city's own publications.

New York Historical Society, "Books about New York City, Primarily History, Published from 1898–1947." The Society, New York, 1948, typewritten. May be consulted in the New York Historical Society.

New York Public Library, "Selected List of Works Relating to City Planning and Allied Subjects," *New York Public Library Bulletin*, vol. 17, 1913, pp. 930–960; "Selected List of References Bearing on the City Plan of New York," *New York Public Library Bulletin*, vol. 17, 1913, pp. 396–408.

New York (State) Library, *A Checklist of Official Publications of the State of New York*. Published by the Government and Exchange Office of the Library, 1947 to date. Issued monthly, this publication contains references to reports and documents of all state agencies.

Port of New York Authority, *A Selected Bibliography of the Port of New York Authority, 1921–56*. The Authority, New York, 1956. A useful bibliography about publications on the Authority.

Reynolds, James B., editor, *Civic Bibliography for Greater New York*. Charities Publication Committee, New York, 1911. This Russell Sage Foundation publication is an important source on municipal affairs in New York City up to 1911.

Selected Bibliography on Revision of the New York City Charter. School of Public Affairs, Princeton, N. J., 1933. A comprehensive bibliography of the city government from the time of consolidation.

"Selected List of Material by and about William J. Gaynor, compiled by the Municipal Reference Library, May 15, 1933." References to magazine articles, newspaper items, and cartoon collections by and about Mayor Gaynor. In their vertical files.

Shaw, Frederick, *The History of the New York City Legislature*. Columbia University Press, New York, 1954, pp. 265–284. Bibliographic appendix includes political, administrative, and biographical references to New York City.

Shaw, Thomas S., *Index to Profile Sketches in* The New Yorker *Magazine*. F. W. Faxon Co., Boston, 1946. A listing of profile sketches of personalities, including New York municipal officials and politicians, which appeared in *The New Yorker* from February 21, 1925 to February 17, 1940.

Smith, Thelma, "New York City Labor Problems in Transit Systems: List of References, 1941–49," 1950. Typewritten copy in Municipal Reference Library.

Spielvogel, Samuel, *A Selected Bibliography on City and Regional Planning*. The Scarecrow Press, Washington, 1951.

Stokes, Isaac Newton Phelps, *The Iconography of Manhattan Island, 1498–1909; Compiled from Original Sources and Illustrated by Photo-Intaglio Reproductions.* 6 vols. R. H. Dodd, New York, 1925–1928. A unique guide to literature and to archives on New York City.

GUIDES TO LIBRARY RESOURCES

American Library Directory. R. R. Bowker Co., New York, 1954. Arranged by state and city, this guide offers help on use of library collections in the city.

Brown, Karl, *A Guide to the Reference Collections of the New York Public Library.* The Library, New York, 1941.

Downs, Robert B., *Resources of New York City Libraries.* American Library Association, Chicago, 1942. A thoroughgoing survey of libraries in New York City and the materials for study and research they contain.

Johnston, W. D., "Library Resources of New York City," *Columbia University Quarterly*, vol. 13, 1911, pp. 163–172.

New York Historical Society, *Survey of the Manuscript Collections in the New York Historical Society.* The Society, New York, 1941.

New York Law Institute, *The New York Law Institute Library.* The Institute, New York, 1935. Describes the history and resources of the library.

New York Library Club, *Manual.* The Club, New York, 1922. A valuable library directory and list of special collections in New York City.

New York Public Library, *Bulletin*, 1897 to date. Many numbers include bibliographies or checklists, especially for materials in the New York Public Library. In 1937 it published an Index to vols. 1–40, which had a complete record of all items in the publication from 1897 to date.

"Checklist of General Municipal Documents of New York City, and of New York State Documents and Other Papers, Relating to the City in the New York Public Library," *New York Public Library Bulletin*, vol. 5, 1901, pp. 5–19.

"Checklist of General Serial Municipal Documents of Brooklyn in the New York Public Library," *New York Public Library Bulletin*, vol. 6, 1902, pp. 12–19.

"Checklist of Works in the New York Public Library Relating to the History of Brooklyn, and of Other Places on Long Island Now Included in the City of New York," *New York Public Library Bulletin*, vol. 6, 1902, pp. 77–83.

"Checklist of Works Relating to the History (General, Political, etc.) of the City of New York in the New York Public Library," *New York Public Library Bulletin*, vol. 5, 1901, pp. 97–127.

"Checklist of Works Relating to the Schools and to the Educational History of the City of New York in the New York Public Library," *New York Public Library Bulletin*, vol. 5, 1901, pp. 233–260.

"List of City Charters, Ordinances, and Collected Documents in the New York Public Library," *New York Public Library Bulletin*, vol. 16, 1912, pp. 631–719, 799–871, 885–947; vol. 17, 1913, pp. 7–78, 255–296, 315–359.

"Manuscript Collection in New York Public Library," *New York Public Library Bulletin*, vol. 5, 1901, pp. 306–336; vol. 19, 1915, pp. 149–165.

Special Libraries Associations, New York Chapter, *Special Libraries Directory of Greater New York*. The Association, New York, 1956. A useful and convenient guide to specialized collections and the circumstances under which they may be consulted.

United States Works Progress Administration, Division of Professional and Service Projects, *Guide to Manuscript Depositories in New York City*. Historical Records Survey, New York, 1941.

Historical Records Survey, *Inventories of the County and Borough Archives of New York City: Richmond County and Borough (Staten Island)*. Historical Records Survey, New York, 1939.

Inventory of County Archives of New York City. Historical Records Survey, New York, 1940, vol. 1, Bronx County; vol. 2, Richmond County and Borough; and vol. 3, Kings County.

Vormalker, Rose L., *Special Library Resources*. Special Libraries Association, New York, 1941. Provides a guide to the holdings of about seventy-five libraries in New York City.

APPENDIX C

Governmental Organization Within the
City of New York

by Robert H. Connery

This Appendix with its accompanying charts constitutes the Sixth Edition (1960) of GOVERNMENTAL ORGANIZATION WITHIN THE CITY OF NEW YORK, *a publication of the Institute of Public Administration. The document may be obtained separately from the Institute, 684 Park Avenue, New York 21, New York.*

With the permission of Luther Gulick, president of the Institute, the document is included here because it provides a valuable base of information for the discussion of the political and governmental process in New York City. Readers of GOVERNING NEW YORK CITY *will find useful the comprehensive description of the organization of the city government through which the process operates.*

The text and charts for the pamphlet were prepared by Robert H. Connery, a senior member of the Institute staff, with the assistance of Pearl H. Hack and Edward Mueller.

The City of New York

THE MOST STRIKING ASPECT of governmental organization in New York City is the fact that "metropolitan New York" extends far beyond the boundaries of the City of New York. We are here concerned, however, almost exclusively with that part of the metropolitan area included within the *City of New York*. Created in 1898, the present city was brought about by the consolidation of the cities of New York and Brooklyn with neighboring portions of lower Westchester, Long Island, together with Staten Island. The boundaries fixed in 1898 have not changed, although the city charter has been amended from time to time and the governmental structure has been changed greatly over the past sixty years.

Included within the city are five counties and five boroughs with coterminous boundaries. These are the county of New York, which is also the borough of Manhattan; Kings County, which is also the borough of Brooklyn; and the three counties and boroughs that have the same names, The Bronx, Queens, and Richmond (Staten Island). In the past half-century there has been a gradual "withering away" of the separate county and borough governments and a transfer of functions to the City of New York. Today these units are so integrated with the city government that they may be considered parts of the city rather than independent political units. The only exceptions are found, at the county level, in the court system, the office of district attorney, and the county clerks and, at the borough level, in the borough public works office which handles the building and maintenance of streets and local sewers.

The City of New York is a municipal corporation—that is, a public corporation with broad but specified governmental powers within fixed geographical boundaries. The general plan of the government is set forth in the city charter. The last complete revision of the charter occurred in 1936 when a new charter was approved by the legislature and accepted by the voters in the November election. It went into effect in 1938, but there have been many amendments since that time.

The charter now provides for (1) a single, elected executive, the Mayor, (2) a small Board of Estimate made up of persons elected to fill other posts in the city government—the Mayor, the Comptroller, the President of the City Council, and the five Borough Presidents, and (3) a larger City Council elected from 25 single member districts and exercising no other functions besides the legislative one. This is the formal organization of the city government. Extensive as are the legal powers of the Mayor, his informal political power is even more impressive. Elected by the people of the entire city rather than a single district or borough, and with media of mass communication at his command, he is in a unique position to exercise wide leadership in all aspects of the city's government.

The charter is intended to provide only the structural framework and major powers of the city and its officials. The details of laws relating to the city are left to the New York City Administrative Code, which derived from a variety of legal sources. The code was enacted in 1938 after an exhaustive two-and-a-half-years study of all the laws relating to the government of the City of New York, including previous charters, state laws, and municipal ordinances as interpreted by the courts. Since that date, the code has been amended frequently. Not included in either the charter or the code are the rules and regulations of the various city agencies incidental to the performance of their respective functions, as well as many state laws affecting local administration. The charter, the code, and the departmental regulations have all been subjected over the years to numerous court tests. The most recent (1957) annotated edition of the charter and the code fills six substantial volumes, of which the four relating to the code alone average over 800 pages apiece.

A description of the organization of the present governmental organization within New York City in chart form will be found on page 756. It should be noted that Chart I presents in summary form the whole governmental structure and the remaining three charts describe in greater detail the organization of particular parts of the government. Chart II outlines the organization of the Mayor's administrative staff, Chart III presents the administrative organization of the City of New York, and Chart IV shows the judicial structure.

State and federal activities within the City of New York have increased rapidly, particularly since 1932, and today play an important part in the life of the city. Moreover, public authorities such as the Transit Authority, the Triborough Bridge and Tunnel Authority, and the Housing Authority— as well as the older Port of New York Authority—have had an impressive development during the decade 1949–1959. These public authorities are semiautonomous bodies. Indeed the expansion of governmental activities within the boundaries of, but not operated by, the City of New York has been one of the most remarkable aspects of the past decade. This development seems to have been brought about by several factors. Some of the most difficult city problems, such as transportation and traffic, involve much more than the city itself. Consequently a governmental agency with wider powers, like the Port of New York Authority, which could operate in the New Jersey-New York portion of the metropolitan area, seemed necessary. But, in addition, the fact that the city's powers to incur debts and to levy taxes are limited by the state, and that urban residents are demanding more and better

CHART I. THE GOVERNMENT OF NEW YORK CITY

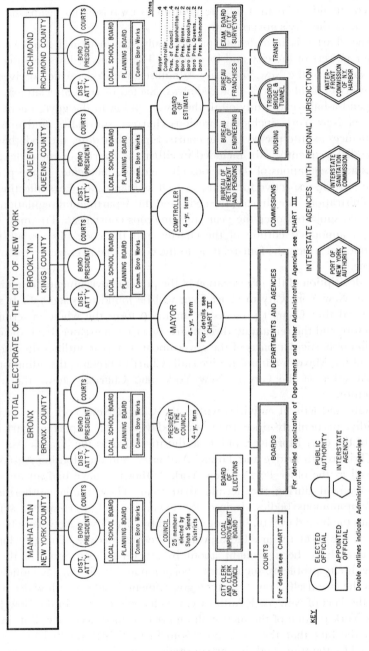

756

governmental services, led to the creation of public authorities that could operate outside these limitations. Thus the decade of 1949–1959 has been marked not only by a steady increase in the amount of city services, the size of city budgets, and the number of city personnel, but also by a tremendous expansion in governmental activities within the city which are not part of the city government of New York.

Probably the best single measure of this growth of city services is found in these figures: In 1900 the city hired 1 employee for every 100 inhabitants; in 1949, there were 1.9 city employees for every 100 inhabitants; and in 1959 there are 2.5 employees for every 100 inhabitants. In this growth of city activities, one development has been spectacular and indicative. It was the transfer of the major burden of welfare functions from churches, private charities, and the family to the city, with the vast extension of the social security, welfare, housing, health, and hospital programs under city adminis- tration with much of the financing coming from the state and the federal governments. As the result of these developments, the city now has greatly expanded its human welfare functions. These developments may be traced in the changing structure of the government.

LEGISLATIVE AGENCIES

The charter vests "the legislative power of the city" in the *Council*, but it should be remembered that this power is subject to the veto of the Mayor and the approval by the Board of Estimate of all local laws amending the charter or affecting the administration or finances of the city. In addition, local improvement boards exercise a limited legislative power as regards local assessable improvements and many city departments may establish codes and regulations which have the effect of law. Although the Commission that framed the 1936 charter no doubt intended the Council to be the principal legislative body in the city government, this is not what, in fact, has happened.

The *Mayor* is not only the chief executive but also plays an important part in the legislative process. As political leader of the city he frequently proposes legislation and guides its progress through legislative channels. He not only makes an annual report to the Council, but can send it special messages recommending legislation he considers necessary. All local laws and resolu- tions must come to him for approval. He is required to hold a public hearing, after five days' notice, before approving or vetoing a law. He does not have a pocket veto. Legally the Council may override a veto within thirty days by a two-thirds majority vote, but has not done so in twenty years. The Mayor has an item veto on the expense budget which can be overridden only by a three-fourths vote of the Council.

In the referendum held in 1947, the proportional representation system of electing councilmen was abolished and a new system adopted whereby councilmen are elected from state senate districts, one councilman from each district. Under the new system, which took effect in 1949, there are six councilmen from Manhattan, five from The Bronx, nine from Brooklyn, four from Queens, and one from Richmond. Councilmen are elected for four-year terms.

The *President of the Council* is elected at large for a four-year term. He presides at meetings of the Council and votes only when there is a tie. He also serves on the Board of Estimate where he has four votes. In the event of the death or resignation of the Mayor, the President of the Council serves as Acting Mayor until the next regular election. With some restrictions he also acts as Mayor when the chief executive is absent from the city.

The Council is authorized by the charter to appoint a clerk who is also the *City Clerk* as well as Clerk of the Council. He not only keeps a record of the proceedings of the Council but also is custodian of all city records not by law confided to other officials. He keeps a public record of all local laws, ordinances, and franchises passed by the Council and the Board of Estimate. His term is six years.

The *Board of Elections* enforces the state Election Law and administers all public elections held in the city. The four members of the Board represent the parties that cast the highest and the next highest vote for Governor in the preceding election. The members are appointed for four-year terms by the council and are subject to removal by the Governor.

The *Board of Estimate* is both a legislative and an administrative agency. It is authorized to exercise, subject to the charter, "all power vested in the city except as otherwise provided by law." Composed of the Mayor, with four votes, the Comptroller, four votes, the President of the Council, four votes, the Presidents of each of the five boroughs with two votes apiece, the Board frequently plays a decisive role in determining and carrying out administrative policy as well as legislation.

The Board of Estimate serves as a second legislative chamber on a wide variety of local laws. These include laws amending or repealing charter provisions; conferring, transferring, or changing the powers and duties, or prescribing the qualification, number, mode of selection or removal, term of office, or compensation of any officer, employee, or agency of the city; and laws reducing or repealing any taxes, fees, or charges receivable by the city. Since there are very few local laws that do not concern either personnel or taxes, the Board participates in most major legislation.

Another important aspect of the Board of Estimate's work concerns the city budget, which is prepared by the Bureau of the Budget under the direction of the Mayor and submitted by him to the Board of Estimate for approval or modification. Once passed by the Board, after extensive public hearings, it is then submitted to the City Council, which may reduce or omit but not increase or add items. The Mayor has veto power over the Council's action which may be overridden only by a two-thirds majority. Under these restrictions the Council rarely changes the budget. Changes in the budget once it has been passed that involve either reducing or increasing salaries or transferring funds between items must have the approval of the Board of Estimate as well as the Mayor. The Board's calendar during the year is filled with proposals concerning such budgetary transfers. Thus the Board is heavily involved in day-to-day administrative decisions. Usually these decisions are made in executive session where the Mayor is simply first among equals. A great deal, consequently, depends upon a Mayor's skill in using his recognized position as chief executive to carry a majority of the Board's votes along with him in support of his program.

Although the former Bureau of Real Estate was made an executive department responsible to the Mayor in 1959, five other administrative agencies continue to operate directly under the control of the Board of Estimate.

The *Bureau of Engineering* reports to the Board on local improvements and on proposals for new parks and sewage disposal plants. The Chief Engineer of the Bureau of Engineering is a member of the City Planning Commission and serves as consultant on engineering problems of other commissions and agencies. The *Examining Board of City Surveyors* conducts oral and written examinations for surveyors who wish to have the title and status of "City Surveyor." The Board of Estimate has the power to grant franchises and revocable consents for the use of public streets and property; the *Bureau of Franchises* is the agent for this power and reports to the Board of Estimate.

The Board of Estimate is trustee for the funds of the New York City Employees Retirement System. The system is administered by the *Bureau of Retirement and Pensions.* It provides for retirement allowances, loans, and death benefits for about half of the city employees. Teachers, other employees of the Board of Education, policemen, and firemen have separate retirement systems. All systems now open for membership are on an actuarial basis.

The *Health Insurance Board* was established under the Board of Estimate in 1946 to act as agent and to set up rules and procedures for all city employees who wish to participate in the Health Insurance Plan. The plan is a nonprofit organization operating throughout the metropolitan area.

EXECUTIVE AND ADMINISTRATIVE AGENCIES

The *Mayor* is the chief executive of the city. The bare language of the charter gives an incomplete picture of the extent of his authority. In actual practice he is responsible for the administration and the proper conduct of the business of the city departments and commissions. He has powers to appoint and remove commissioners, heads of departments, and numerous other officers. As a matter of long-standing tradition, the Mayor is vested with the powers of a magistrate. As presiding officer of the Board of Estimate with four votes and as Mayor, he has extensive budgetary and legislative powers. The breadth of his powers as executive, legislative, and administrative chief executive are indicated repeatedly throughout these pages. Whether or not all incumbents exercise the full potentialities of their position is, of course, a matter of personality, ability, and desire.

The Mayor is elected at large by the voters of the city for a four-year term. He may be suspended from office by the Governor for thirty days or removed from office by the Governor for cause after charges have been preferred and an opportunity given for a hearing with due advance notice.

The Mayor's administrative cabinet, used for the first time in 1954, brings together the Mayor, the Deputy Mayor, the City Administrator and his deputies, the Corporation Counsel, the Director of the Budget, the Director of Personnel, the Chairman of the City Planning Commission, and the executive assistants to the Mayor for the discussion of administrative problems. Meeting with prepared agenda, the cabinet has proved to be a useful tool for the Mayor and his chief policy planning and coordinating officers. These meetings have afforded an opportunity for the exchange of information concerning the city's business and in many instances have laid the groundwork for major policy decisions.

The Mayor's Principal Administrative Assistants

One of the major recommendations of the Mayor's Committee on Management Survey of the City of New York in 1953 was that the Mayor be provided with the management tools and the personnel needed to make the office of the chief executive function properly. In implementing this recommendation the posts of City Administrator and Director of Personnel were established and the personal staff of the Mayor somewhat enlarged.

Unfortunately some confusion has crept into the nomenclature of the city's administration, particularly concerning the term "Office of the Mayor." Apparently without much reason some agencies are designated in some official documents, but not necessarily in others, as part of the Office of the Mayor. The city charter, the city budget, and the Administrative Code are not in agreement in the use of this designation. Some important top administrative units are not part of the Office of the Mayor, while others performing ordinary line functions are. For this reason no attempt is made here to describe the Office of the Mayor but rather to set forth the work of the principal administrative assistants to the Mayor.

The *Deputy Mayor* is appointed and is subject to removal by the Mayor. The purpose of this office is to relieve the Mayor of time-consuming tasks and of some of his administrative and ceremonial responsibilities. Upon written authorization of the Mayor, the Deputy Mayor may act for the Mayor except

CHART II. THE MAYOR'S STAFF AND ADMINISTRATIVE CABINET

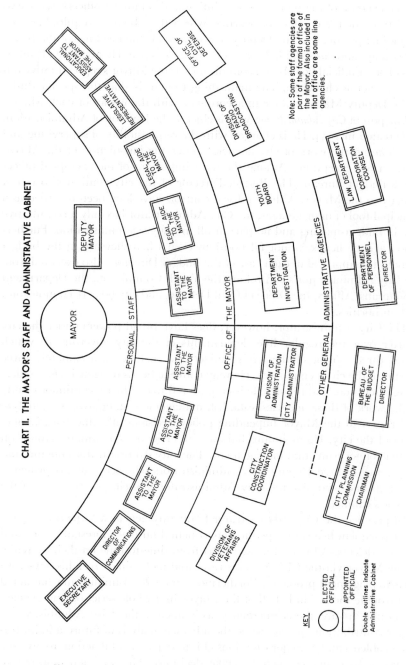

Note: Some staff agencies are part of the formal office of the Mayor. Also included in that office are some line agencies.

MAYOR

PERSONAL STAFF

DEPUTY MAYOR

EDUCATIONAL ASSISTANT TO THE MAYOR

LEGISLATIVE REPRESENTATIVE

LEGAL AIDE TO THE MAYOR

LEGAL AIDE TO THE MAYOR

ASSISTANT TO THE MAYOR

ASSISTANT TO THE MAYOR

ASSISTANT TO THE MAYOR

ASSISTANT TO THE MAYOR

DIRECTOR OF COMMUNICATIONS

EXECUTIVE SECRETARY

OFFICE OF THE MAYOR

OFFICE OF CIVILSE DEFENSE

DIVISION OF RADIO BROADCASTING

YOUTH BOARD

DEPARTMENT OF INVESTIGATION

DIVISION OF ADMINISTRATION
CITY ADMINISTRATOR

CITY CONSTRUCTION COORDINATOR

DIVISION OF VETERANS AFFAIRS

ADMINISTRATIVE AGENCIES

LAW DEPARTMENT
CORPORATION COUNSEL

DEPARTMENT OF PERSONNEL
DIRECTOR

OTHER GENERAL

BUREAU OF THE BUDGET
DIRECTOR

CITY PLANNING COMMISSION
CHAIRMAN

KEY

○ ELECTED OFFICIAL

□ APPOINTED OFFICIAL

Double outlines indicate Administrative Cabinet

761

for the exercise of the powers of appointing and removing officers, service as magistrate, or the conduct of hearings which the Mayor is required by law to conduct personally. The Deputy Mayor attends the meetings of the Board of Estimate and casts the Mayor's vote in his absence. He also attends meetings of other official boards and commissions as the Mayor's representative but may not act as chairman. The main thing to note is that the specific duties of the Deputy Mayor change in accordance with the wishes of each Mayor.

The post of *City Administrator*, who is chief of the Division of Administration, was created in 1954. He is charged with the responsibility of supervising and coordinating the work of city agencies under the jurisdiction of the Mayor with certain exceptions. Among the most important of the exempted offices is the Budget Bureau. The Budget Director of the city continues to report directly to the Mayor. Although fiscal controls have long been regarded as a principal tool of management, the City Administrator has only a consultative role in budget-making and no part at all in budget administration. Furthermore, agency heads cannot fill positions even when they are in the budget without the approval in each case of the Budget Director. Also excepted from the City Administrator's control are the Youth Commission, the Department of Veterans' Affairs, the Office of Civil Defense, and city boards, commissions, and authorities.

The City Administrator, however, does have broad powers under the city charter over the regular line departments of the city government, which spend three fourths of the city's budget and include approximately three fourths of the city's employees. He may convene heads of agencies for conference, discussion, and report. He is empowered to conduct a continuous study of the work of these agencies, establish management standards, and analyze and report to the Mayor impending policy decisions affecting the management of the city. He maintains liaison with civic and community groups on matters of governmental management. The City Administrator appoints and may remove three Deputy City Administrators who serve as his principal assistants and who, like the City Administrator himself, are members of the Mayor's cabinet.

In practice the City Administrator frequently acts as a "friend at court" for department heads to expedite departmental business, forestall errors, and remedy defects. All departments report from time to time on their activities to the Mayor via the City Administrator and increasingly seek his advice on their management problems. Furthermore, the City Administrator has acted as a trouble shooter in behalf of the Mayor in a whole series of emergencies. Important as are these emergency assignments, the City Administrator's major contribution appears to be the advance analysis of future administrative problems and of major questions of interdepartmental action, to give the Mayor a basis upon which to make decisions. This function of program operations, research, and program development resembles the similar function recently emphasized in large private corporations.

Each year the Mayor is required by the city charter to report to the Council upon "the state of the City" in somewhat the same way that the President of the United States reports to the Congress upon "the state of the Union." Since 1954 the Mayor's annual report has been compiled by the City Administrator's office. The report is largely factual and is accompanied by a message from the Mayor dealing with major policies of the administration. The annual report has become a useful management device through comparison of statistical data from year to year and through the inclusion of a list of management goals for the coming year in each report. These data offer a standard of measurement not only to city officials but also to the general public in determining the progress being made in the city's government.

The *Bureau of the Budget* annually prepares the executive budget for the Mayor, which provides for the current running expenses of the city. Equally important is the Bureau's work in carrying the budget into effect after the budget has been passed by the Board of Estimate and the City Council. The Budget Director's jurisdiction in overseeing expenditures includes both the expense and the capital budgets. Once the budgets have been passed by the Board of Estimate and the City Council and signed by the Mayor they are binding on all city agencies. Transfers of funds are permitted between items only upon recommendation of the Director of the Budget and approval by the Mayor and the Board of Estimate. As customary in normal budget practices, lump sum appropriations are provided for new activities and these too are administered by the Budget Bureau in conjunction with the city agency responsible until sufficient time has elapsed to develop accurate cost data.

The *City Planning Commission* is composed of the Chief Engineer of the Board of Estimate and six members appointed by the Mayor for eight-year overlapping terms. The Chairman of the Commission is the Director of the Department of City Planning, which is the administrative agent for the Commission. After hearings, the Commission is responsible for the development and adoption and continuous modification of a "master plan" of the city. The master plan is a forward-looking map of desirable streets, parks, water and sewer developments, traffic and harbor improvements, building zones, public and private utilities, and school and other buildings designed to provide for the growth and welfare of the city. The Commission is also custodian of the "city map" which establishes streets and grades, and must register all changes authorized by law. Changes in the city map or in the zoning regulations, or the filing of a map or plot for the subdivision of land, in general may be effected by the approval of the Commission and a majority vote of the Board of Estimate or by a three-fourths vote of the Board of Estimate without the approval of the Commission.

The City Planning Commission annually prepares the capital budget for capital projects to be undertaken during the following six years. This is done on the basis of departmental recommendations and reports from the Comptroller, the Director of the Budget, and the Mayor. The capital budget is submitted to the Board of Estimate and to the Council. The Council may not increase the amount of any authorization but either approve or strike out an item. The capital budget is not subject to the Mayor's veto. There are citizen Advisory Planning Boards in each borough, appointed by the Borough Presidents for six-year overlapping terms on a nonsalaried basis to advise the Planning Commission.

The *Department of Personnel* and *the City Civil Service Commission*, reorganized in 1954, are composed of a Personnel Director (also Chairman of the Civil Service Commission) and two other members, not more than one of whom may be of the same political party as the Chairman. They are appointed by the Mayor: the Chairman for a term coterminous with that of the Mayor, the others for six-year terms. Members of the Commission, except for the Chairman, may not be removed without cause and a hearing. Members may also be removed by the state Civil Service Commission on charges after a hearing. The Department recruits personnel and schedules and conducts examinations for civil service positions and for the issuance of city licenses; establishes, promulgates, and certifies lists of eligible candidates; determines which eligible lists are appropriate to fill positions; regulates appointments and promotions; investigates applicants for positions; certifies payrolls for 230,000 employees in 1,100 job titles; administers incentive, safety, training, and other personnel programs; makes studies and recommends changes in grade or classification of 187,000 civil service positions. The number of personnel and the agencies they serve are shown in Tables A, B, and C and the number of persons examined by the Department of Personnel in 1958 in Table D. Salaries of the principal political and administrative officers of the city are shown in Table E.

The *Career and Salary Board of Appeals* was established by the Board of Estimate in 1954 to hear protests and appeals on salary allocations and salary reallocations with respect to classes of positions under the Career and Salary Plan. It is composed of five unpaid members appointed by the Mayor, including at least two members representing employees. After hearings, the Board makes recommendations to the Board of Estimate for salary changes.

The *Career and Salary Plan Classification Appeals Board* was established by the city Civil Service Commission in 1954 to hear protests and appeals on position classification and reclassification with respect to classes of positions under the Career and Salary Plan. The membership is the same as the Board mentioned above.

TABLE A. NUMBER OF CITY EMPLOYEES UNDER THE JURISDICTION OF THE DEPARTMENT OF PERSONNEL AS OF DECEMBER 31, 1959

Agency	Un-classified[a]	Exempt[b]	Com-petitive[c]	Labor[d]	Noncom-petitive[e]	On military leave[f]	Total
Air Pollution Control, Dept. of	3	3	94	—	—	—	100
Art Commission	—	1	1	—	—	—	2
Assessors, Board of	3	—	23	—	—	—	26
Borough President:							
Bronx	1	12	832	—	1	2	846
Brooklyn	1	9	1,189	—	—	6	1,199
Manhattan	1	12	1,133	—	—	5	1,146
Queens	1	12	1,707	—	—	3	1,720
Richmond	1	11	469	—	1	—	481
Bronx Community College	—	—	17	5	1	—	23
Budget, Bureau of	—	2	151	—	—	—	153
Buildings, Dept. of	1	4	1,227	2	—	—	1,234
Chief Medical Examiner, Office of	—	—	80	—	4	—	84
City Clerk and Council	59	2	33	—	—	1	94
City Planning Commission	5	2	169	—	6	—	182
City Record	—	1	9	—	—	—	10
Colleges:							
City	—	—	383	124	10	—	517
Brooklyn	—	—	218	103	6	—	327
Hunter	—	—	236	118	6	—	360
Queens	—	—	123	44	6	—	173
Commerce and Public Events, Dept. of	—	3	42	—	13	—	58
Commission on Intergroup Relations	—	1	43	—	—	—	44
Comptroller	1	12	1,728	1	3	4	1,745
Correction, Dept. of	1	3	2,222	—	84	—	2,310
Courts:							
City	24	26	212	—	7	—	269
Domestic Relations	23	3	539	—	2	1	567
Magistrates'	54	2	723	—	—	1	779
Municipal	67	68	376	—	2	1	513
Special Sessions	24	2	228	—	—	—	254
Education, Board of: (Nonteaching)	—	9	3,683	13	5,949	4	9,652
Elections, Board of	254	—	2	—	—	—	256

Agency	Un-classified[a]	Exempt[b]	Com-petitive[c]	Labor[d]	Noncom-petitive[e]	On military leave[f]	Total
Estimate, Board of:							
Employees' Retirement	—	—	192	—	—	2	192
Engineering	—	—	31	—	—	—	31
Franchise	—	1	16	—	—	—	17
Secretary	—	1	32	—	—	—	33
Finance, Dept. of	2	4	1,205	—	—	2	1,211
Fire, Dept. of	1	8	11,849	1	—	25	11,863
Health, Dept. of	1	3	3,717	275	1,226	20	5,222
Higher Education, Board of: (Nonteaching)	—	1	165	7	2	—	175
Hospitals, Dept. of	1	5	8,551	1,181	27,759	126	37,497
Investigation, Dept. of	1	41	41	—	—	—	83
Labor, Dept. of	1	4	26	—	5	—	36
Law, Dept. of	1	99	535	—	3	2	638
Licenses, Dept. of	1	5	106	—	—	—	112
Marine and Aviation, Dept. of	1	5	1,313	43	4	3	1,366
Markets, Dept. of	1	8	318	—	2	—	329
Mayor's Office	1	12	45	—	—	—	58
Civil Defense	1	—	167	—	—	3	168
Division of Administration	—	6	55	—	6	—	67
Division of Veterans' Affairs	—	—	20	—	4	—	24
Mayor's Advisory Council	—	—	—	—	—	—	—
Municipal Broadcasting	1	—	72	—	—	—	73
Youth Board	1	1	267	—	24	1	293
Mental Health Board	—	1	27	—	2	1	30
New York City Community College	—	—	62	17	25	1	104
Parks, Dept. of	1	—	5,562	44	322	1	5,930
Parole Commission	3	—	42	—	—	—	45
Personnel, Dept. of	3	1	332	—	4	—	340
Police, Dept. of	1	10	24,501	291	1,303	101	26,106
Public Works, Dept. of	1	3	3,900	1,024	—	7	4,928
Purchase, Dept. of	1	6	615	3	2	1	627
Queens Community College	—	—	3	—	1	—	4
Real Estate, Dept. of	1	3	251	—	33	—	288
Register	—	1	234	—	2	—	236

Sanitation, Dept. of	1	5	13,422	–	14	20	13,442
Sheriff	–	1	113	3	3	–	120
Standards and Appeals, Board of	5	1	30	3	1	–	37
Staten Island Community College	–	–	11	–	1	–	15
Tax Department	7	5	431	–	–	–	443
Teachers' Retirement	–	1	123	–	–	–	124
Traffic, Dept. of	1	4	435	–	2	3	442
Water Supply, Board of	3	10	606	1	48	7	668
Water Supply, Gas and Electricity, Dept. of	1	4	2,625	–	13	7	2,643
Welfare, Dept. of	1	5	7,367	180	764	35	8,317
Total	568	465	107,288	3,488	37,693	385[e]	149,501

[a] Unclassified service: The unclassified service includes elective officers, judges, heads of departments or commissions, legislative personnel and teaching personnel. Classified service: The classified service comprises four classes: exempt, noncompetitive, competitive and labor.

[b] Exempt class: Appointments in the exempt class are made by heads of departments without regard to civil service procedures or qualifications. Typical exempt class positions are: deputy commissioners, secretary to a department, and clerks to judicial officers.

[c] Competitive class: The competitive class includes all positions for which it is practicable to recruit through competitive examinations.

[d] Labor Class: Labor Class positions encompass laboring jobs where the Civil Service Commission prescribes experience and age requirements and may hold certain rudimentary tests.

[e] Noncompetitive Class: Appointments in the noncompetitive class are made by department heads without competition, but the appointee must meet minimum qualifications established by the Civil Service Commission.

[f] Employees on military leave are not included in total figures.

Source: *Annual Report* of the Mayor of New York City, 1959.

TABLE B. NUMBER OF EMPLOYEES OF PUBLIC AUTHORITIES AS OF DECEMBER 31, 1959

Agency	Un-classified	Exempt	Com-petitive	Labor	Non-competitive	On military leave[a]	Total
New York City Transit Authority	3	22	35,586	1	48	39	35,660
Triborough Bridge and Tunnel Authority	–	2	782	20	1	–	805
New York City Housing Authority	3	5	7,372	2	397	17	7,779
Total	6	29	43,740	23	446	56	44,244

[a] Employees on military leave are not included in total figures.

Source: *Annual Report* of the Mayor of New York City, 1959.

TABLE C. ADDITIONAL EMPLOYEES PAID BY CITY BUT NOT UNDER JURISDICTION OF DEPARTMENT OF PERSONNEL

Museums	888	County Courts' offices	642
Libraries	3,706	District Attorneys' offices	574
Zoos	176	Public Administrators' offices	34
College teachers	2,568	Surrogates' Courts	325
Primary and secondary teachers	42,883	Supreme Court	912
County clerks' offices	358		
		Total	53,066

SOURCE: *Annual Report* of the Mayor of New York City, 1959.

TABLE D. NUMBER OF PERSONS APPLYING, EXAMINED, AND CERTIFIED BY THE DEPARTMENT OF PERSONNEL DURING 1959

Number of applications filed	94,008	Number of persons certified[a]	71,826
Number of examinations held	297	Number of persons appointed	15,394
Number of candidates examined	60,661		

[a] Includes persons certified from lists established prior to 1959.
SOURCE: *Annual Report* of the Mayor of New York City, 1959.

The *Department of Investigation* acts as additional eyes and ears for the Mayor. It is headed by a Commissioner who holds office at the pleasure of the Mayor. The Commissioner is required to be a member in good standing of the New York State bar. He has broad powers under the charter to make any investigation directed by the Mayor or the Council, or any study or investigation "which in his opinion may be in the best interests of the city, including but not limited to investigations of the affairs, function, accounts, methods, personnel, or efficiency of any agency."

The office of *City Construction Coordinator* was established by law in 1946 to expedite the construction of city public works projects which were being delayed because of shortages of labor and materials. Continued ever since, the duties of the Coordinator are to "schedule and, upon approval of the projects by the Mayor and the governing bodies of the city, to expedite the work of all agencies of the city and to represent the city in its relations with cooperating state and federal agencies engaged in the postwar public works program." The Coordinator is appointed for an indefinite term by the Mayor and uses the staff of other city agencies.

OPERATING AGENCIES

The administrative departments and agencies within the government of New York City are briefly described in the pages that follow. For the convenience of the reader the agencies are somewhat arbitrarily grouped under the functional headings of city finances, service agencies, safety, general welfare, information and recording, health, education, and recreation, public works, utilities, and transportation. Some attention is given to public authori-

TABLE E. SALARIES OF PRINCIPAL POLITICAL AND ADMINISTRATIVE OFFICERS, CITY OF NEW YORK, 1959–1960 BUDGET

	Salary
Mayor	$40,000
Deputy Mayor	25,000
Executive Secretary	20,000
Assistant to the Mayor	17,500
Principal Attorney	17,500
Assistant to the Mayor	15,000
Assistant to the Mayor	13,000
Comptroller	30,000
First Deputy Comptroller	25,000
Second Deputy Comptroller	22,500
City Council	
President of the City Council	25,000
Majority Leader	16,500
Minority Leader	12,500
Council Member	7,000
City Administrator	30,000
First Deputy City Administrator	25,000
Second Deputy City Administrator	20,000
Third Deputy City Administrator	20,000
Director of the Budget	25,000
Assistant Director of the Budget	20,000
Corporation Counsel	25,000
First Assistant Corporation Counsel	20,000
Personnel Director	25,000
Deputy Director of Personnel	16,000
Five Borough Presidents, each	25,000
4 Commissioners of Borough Works, each	15,000
1 Commissioner of Borough Works (Richmond)	10,500
Treasurer (Finance Department)	20,000
President of the Tax Commission	20,000
Commissioner of Licenses	20,000
Commissioner of Purchase	20,000
City Register	16,000
Chairman of the City Planning Commission	22,500
Commissioner of Labor	20,000
Commissioner of Investigation	20,000
Commissioner of Public Works	25,000
Director of Radio Communication	10,500
Commissioner of Commerce and Public Events	1
First Deputy Commissioner	20,000
Superintendent of Schools	37,500
Deputy Superintendent	25,000
8 Associate Superintendents, each	18,750
39 Assistant Superintendents, each	16,000
Commissioner of Parks	25,000
Commissioner of Welfare	22,500
Police Commissioner	25,000
Fire Commissioner	25,000
Commissioner of Traffic	22,500
Commissioner of Health	22,500
Commissioner of Hospitals	25,000
Commissioner of Sanitation	25,000
Commissioner of Correction	20,000
Commissioner of Marine and Aviation	20,000
Commissioner of Water Supply, Gas, and Electricity	20,000
Commissioner of Markets	20,000
Commissioner of Buildings	22,500
Chairman, Board of Standards and Appeals	17,500
Director of Civil Defense	17,500
Commissioner of Air Pollution	20,000
Director of Community Mental Health	22,500
Board of Water Supply	
1 Commissioner	20,000
2 Commissioners, each	15,000

CHART III. ADMINISTRATIVE ORGANIZATION OF NEW YORK CITY

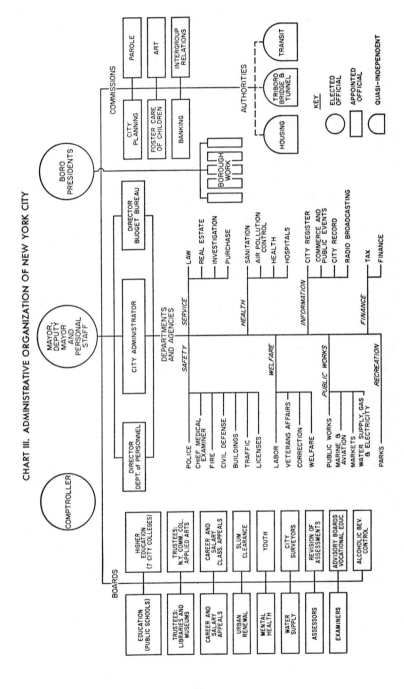

ties, the court system, borough offices, state and interstate agencies with local jurisdiction, and federal activities. It should be noted that four new line departments were created by charter amendment since 1949—Labor, Air Pollution Control, Traffic, and Commerce and Public Events. Furthermore, the Bureau of Real Estate, formerly directly responsible to the Board of Estimate, was made a regular city department under the Mayor.

City Finances

Major responsibility for initiating the fiscal and budget policy of the city rests with the Mayor, working through the Bureau of the Budget and the Planning Commission, as explained above.

A number of highly important financial responsibilities are, however, assigned to the *Comptroller*. He is elected by the people at large and serves for a four-year term. He has four votes as a member of the Board of Estimate. It is his duty to advise the Board of Estimate on the financial condition and policies of the city, to settle and adjust claims, to manage trust funds, to prescribe accounting methods, to audit the accounts of the city, to approve the disbursement of funds, and to manage the sale and retirement of the city's financial obligations. He is a member of the Board of Revision of Assessments and the Banking Commission, as well as of a number of city retirement and pension agencies. The following bureaus are in his office: Accounting, Audit, Engineering, Law and Adjustment, Municipal Investigation and Statistics, and Excise Taxes.

The *Banking Commission* determines in which banks the city money shall be deposited and under what conditions. The Mayor is chairman of this Commission; other members are the Treasurer and the Comptroller.

The *Department of Finance* collects all taxes and assessments and pays all money on warrants drawn by the Comptroller. It provides for the safekeeping of all money paid into the city including trust funds and sinking funds. The Department is headed by the *Treasurer* who is appointed by the Mayor. The Department includes two bureaus, the Bureau of City Collections, headed by the City Collector, and the Bureau of Receipts and Disbursement.

The *Tax Department* is headed by the President of the Tax Commission. The Department has a staff of assessors who appraise the value of real property and prepare the annual assessment rolls. The Tax Commission is appointed by the Mayor and consists of the President and six Commissioners among whom there must be at least one resident of each borough. The Commission has the duty of reviewing and correcting all assessments of real property for taxation. Its action is subject to review only by the courts.

The *Board of Assessors* advises the Board of Estimate on assessments for public improvements and makes all assessments for such improvements except those required by law to be confirmed by a court of record. The three members of this Board are appointed by the Mayor for indefinite terms. The Board settles claims for damages caused by public improvements.

The *Board of Revision of Assessments* consists of the Comptroller, the Corporation Counsel, and the President of the Tax Commission. It reviews appeals from the decisions of the Board of Assessors.

Agencies Serving the City Government

In addition to the agencies concerned with finance, there are other agencies whose major function is to keep the wheels of government rolling. These agencies serve the public indirectly.

The *Law Department* is headed by the *Corporation Counsel*. It conducts the legal business of the city, has charge of litigation in which the city is interested, prepares bonds, leases, bids, other documents, assists with preparation of legislation, and is the legal adviser to the Mayor and other city officials. The Corporation Counsel is appointed by the Mayor and is a member of his cabinet. Associated with this Department is the *Board of Statutory Consolidation* consisting of the Mayor, the Comptroller, the Corporation Counsel, and the President of the Council *ex officiis*. The Board supervised the codification of all the laws of the city into one administrative code. The work of keeping the code up to date is now carried on by the Law Department.

The *Department of Purchase* serves all agencies of the government with the exception of the educational system. It purchases stores and distributes all supplies, materials, or equipment needed by the city agencies. Within the Department of Purchase is the *Board of Standardization*, which prepares specifications and classifies equipment and materials subject to the action of the Board of Estimate. The Board of Standardization consists of the Commissioner of Purchase or a representative, as chairman, an engineer from the Board of Estimate, an engineer and another subordinate of the Comptroller's office, a representative of the Budget Director, an engineer and another subordinate of the Department of Purchase. All serve *ex officiis* without additional pay.

The *Department of Real Estate* was created in 1959. It took over the responsibilities of the Bureau of Real Estate which were to manage affairs concerning the use, lease, sale, or purchase of city real property. The Department is headed by a Commissioner appointed by the Mayor. Among its other duties it supervises the relocation of persons who have to find new living quarters because of urban renewal projects.

Safety

The *Police Department* has the duty of preserving the public peace and of law enforcement. Among its functions are patrolling streets, regulating traffic, preventing, investigating, and detecting crime, criminal identification, the issuance of certain licenses, the recovery of lost property, and the location of missing persons. The Commissioner of Police is appointed by the Mayor for a five-year term. He is removable in the public interest before that time either by the Governor or the Mayor, and if so removed, is ineligible for reappointment to the same position. The Police Pension Fund, with a separate Board of Trustees, provides pensions for members of the police force.

The *Chief Medical Examiner* performs the duties historically discharged by coroners. He investigates sudden, suspicious, and violent deaths and reports to the District Attorney, a county officer. He is required by the charter to be a doctor of medicine, and a skilled pathologist and microscopist. He is appointed by the Mayor from the classified civil service.

The *Fire Department* has the task of extinguishing fires within the city. In addition, it investigates the origin of fires, enforces laws concerning fire precautions, maintains a training school for members of the force, and conducts an extensive program of fire prevention. The Fire Department Pension Fund and Life Insurance Fund with a separate Board of Trustees administers pensions, funds, and life insurance plans for members of the Fire Department.

The *Department of Buildings* has jurisdiction over approximately 786,000 buildings. Its responsibility is to protect the lives and safety of the city's residents in their homes and their places of work. The Department administers the state Multiple Dwelling Code, the Building Code, the zoning regulations, certain sections of the state Labor Law affecting factory buildings, and numerous city ordinances pertaining to buildings. This Department has the right of inspection and issues building permits and certificates of occupancy.

The *Board of Standards and Appeals* consists of five Commissioners appointed by the Mayor for six-year terms; two of these must be experienced and qualified architects, one an experienced and qualified structural engineer, one a mechanical engineer, and one a layman. As part of the city's management improvement program a full-time professional director was provided for the Board in 1957. The new Director, who must be a qualified architect or engineer, is appointed by and removable at the pleasure of the Board. The Board has the sole right to permit deviations in the zoning laws and building codes. It enacts rules concerning building construction and alterations, plumbing and drainage, elevators and fire precautions. It hears appeals from the administrative decisions made by the borough superintendents of the Department of Buildings and by officials of the Fire Department or any other agency.

There are two city committees concerned with better housing whose work deserves notice. The *Mayor's Committee on Slum Clearance*, as its title indicates, is an agency whose purpose is to advance slum clearance and promote redevelopment under the provisions of Title 1 of the National Housing Act. It is composed of six members appointed and removable by the Mayor. The

Urban Renewal Board, created by the Mayor in 1958, tries to preserve basically sound existing structures through a combination of conservation and rehabilitation and thus prevent the growth of slums. The Board is composed of the Chairman of the City Planning Commission, the Budget Director, the Chief Engineer, the Corporation Counsel, the heads of the Real Estate and Buildings Departments, and the Chairman of the City Housing Authority.

The *Department of Licenses* is the principal agency through which the city acts to protect consumers against illegal or unfair merchandising practices or conditions. The Department licenses 77 different occupations or activities, including many types of business dealing with the general public—holding sales, practicing specified trades and professions, operating bowling alleys, and so on. In recent years the Department has emphasized control over illegal business and advertising practices. Other city departments also have jurisdiction in granting certain licenses, but generally of a specialized nature closely connected with their work. The Department of Health, for example, issues licenses for various food handling establishments; the Department of Buildings for the construction and alteration of buildings; the Fire Department for the storage and use of dangerous chemicals; and the Department of Marine and Aviation for use of waterfront property.

The *New York City Office of Civil Defense* is part of the Mayor's office. It is headed by a Director who holds office at the Mayor's pleasure. Its duty is to cooperate with federal and state civil defense agencies in coordinating the city's planning for this function.

The *Department of Traffic*, headed by a single Commissioner appointed by the Mayor, supplanted the multihead Traffic Commission in 1950. The Commissioner appoints two deputies who assist him in his duties of making rules and regulations for the conduct of vehicular traffic and pedestrian traffic; establishing the design, type, size, and location of traffic signals and signs; making recommendations regarding parking meters, the location of highway lights and the intensity of street illumination; and making over-all plans for the amelioration of traffic conditions. The municipally owned off-street parking facilities are managed through this Department.

General Welfare

All agencies of the city government have direct or indirect concern for the general welfare of the citizens, but those whose principal duties are in the broad field of social work are described in this section.

The *Department of Welfare* is a huge organization with many responsibilities. It gives financial assistance to people in need, provides shelter for homeless men and women, and has the care, custody, and disposition of the feeble-minded, the sick, infirm, and the blind. It provides medical, nursing, and visiting housekeeper service for those unable to afford private care. In 1941 the Board of Child Welfare was discontinued and its duties in the administration of federal Aid to Dependent Children under the Social Security Act were transferred to the Department of Welfare. The Department has an extensive program for the care of neglected, dependent, and delinquent children, in their own homes, in foster homes, and in city and subsidized private institutions.

The *Department of Labor*, created in 1954, is headed by a Commissioner appointed by the Mayor. It was originally established as a division in the Mayor's office by executive order in 1946. It studies labor relations in the public service, develops negotiation procedures in the municipal civil service, and provides collective bargaining for private industry. Recently, it has entered the area of employee organizing activity involving voluntary hospitals, private educational institutions, and the city's cultural and charitable agencies.

The *New York City Commission for the Foster Care of Children* was established by law in 1946. It consists of the Commissioner of Welfare as chairman, the Commissioner of Health, the Presiding Justice of the Domestic Relations Court, and 12 public members appointed by the Mayor for six-year terms. Its purpose is to study and make recommendations to the Mayor on needs for temporary facilities for the care of dependent, neglected, and delinquent children, and as to standards and policies in the administration and operation of children's shelters.

The purpose of the *New York City Youth Board* is to promote the welfare of children and youths under twenty-one years by subsidizing the expansion of the recreational programs and guidance services of both public and private agencies. It aims at the prevention of juvenile delinquency. Fifty per cent of the cost of the program is paid by the city and 50 per cent by the State of New York. Presently the Board is composed of 28 members, 18 of whom are laymen appointed by the Mayor; the remainder serve because of other offices they hold and include, among others, the Presiding Justice of the Domestic Relations Court, the Superintendent of Schools, the Commissioner of Health, the Commissioner of Parks, the Commissioner of Welfare, the Police Commissioner, the Chairman of the Housing Authority. A Commissioner of Youth Services conducts its work. The Board was established by law in 1947 as part of the Mayor's office.

The *Commission on Intergroup Relations* replaced the Mayor's Committee on Unity. The Commission is charged with promoting mutual understanding among racial and religious groups. The new enlarged agency is devoted to eliminating discrimination and segregation in every aspect of city life. It has the special responsibility of administering the Fair Housing Practices Law of 1958. The Commission is composed of 15 nonsalaried members appointed by the Mayor.

New York City Division of Veterans' Affairs was organized in the Mayor's office in 1945 to give information and assistance to returning servicemen. Its purpose is to provide veterans with counseling and vocational guidance. This includes information on veterans' rights under federal, state, and local programs, especially with regard to home loans, educational benefits, and employment opportunities.

The *Department of Correction* has both a safety and a welfare function. It has charge of institutions for the care and custody of felons, misdemeanants, violators of ordinances and local laws, and for the detention of witnesses. In cooperation with the Department of Welfare, it has charge of interments in Potter's Field on Hart's Island. *The Parole Commission* works in conjunction with the Department of Correction. The Parole Commission makes investigations of applicants who are eligible for parole and has supervision of parolees. The Commission consists of the Commissioner of Correction, the Police Commissioner, and three others appointed by the Mayor for ten-year terms, one of whom is designated as Chairman by the Mayor.

Information and Recording

The *Division of Radio Broadcasting* (Municipal Broadcasting System) is a city-owned and -operated radio station. Its purposes include "the instruction, recreation, and welfare of the inhabitants of the city."

The *Supervisor of the City Record* has charge of printing the official journal of the government, the *City Record*. In addition, this agency prints departmental reports, pamphlets, and the Official Directory or "Green Book."

The heads of both agencies are appointed by the Mayor.

In 1955 the *Department of Commerce and Public Events* was reorganized and its work expanded. Today it has the duty of promoting programs designed to encourage and stimulate the well-being, development, and expansion of business, industry, and commerce in the city. This Department is headed by a nonsalaried Commissioner.

An important part of the Department's work is to arrange for the entertainment of distinguished visitors to the city. Heads of foreign states, foreign ministers, and other distinguished statesmen as well as national conventions of fraternal and business groups all have a claim on the services of this agency to make their visit to the city more enjoyable and thus to promote good will and cooperation.

In 1942 the first *City Register* took office. He replaced the five county registers whose offices were abolished by law. The City Register is appointed by the Mayor from a list of those who qualify under a competitive civil service examination. He is removable only for cause. The functions of the office are to record deeds, mortgages, contracts of sale, leases, and other instruments affecting title to realty. The office files conditional sales, makes searches, and furnishes certified copies of documents.

Health

The *Department of Health* has jurisdiction over all matters affecting the general health of the city's inhabitants although there are a number of other city agencies concerned with special aspects of health as indicated below. Through its many bureaus and, in particular, through the 27 health centers and 78 child health stations located in all parts of the city, it brings its services to the people. Within the Department is the Board of Health, which has powers to enforce, amend, or repeal any part of the Health Code, issue emergency health orders, grant permits for conducting activities that affect the public health, and record vital statistics. The Board of Health is composed of the Commissioner of Health as chairman and four others. Professional qualifications are prescribed in the charter for all Board members. They are appointed by the Mayor for eight-year overlapping terms and receive no salary.

The *New York City Community Mental Health Board*, created as a charter agency in 1954, is composed of the Commissioners of Health and Welfare, two physicians, and five other members all appointed by the Mayor. The Chairman is designated by the Mayor and all members are nonsalaried. The work of the Board is conducted by a Director, whose chief responsibility is to review and evaluate community mental health services and facilities in the city and to submit to the Mayor and Council a program of community mental health services. He also exercises general supervision over the treatment of patients in services which are maintained by the Community Mental Health Board. The Board was created in accordance with the provisions of the New York State Community Mental Health Services Act of 1954, which provides for state funds to match expenditures by local governments for mental health services.

The *Department of Hospitals* has charge of the 28 city hospitals and numerous other institutions for the care of the sick and infirm. These institutions are for people who cannot pay for private care as well as for the protection of public health. The Department issues licenses for private hospitals and convalescent homes unless otherwise provided by law. The Commissioner of Hospitals, who is head of the Department, is aided by an Advisory Council. This Council consists of one representative of the Medical Board of each hospital and seven members appointed by the Mayor. There is a Medical Board in each hospital elected by the staff of the hospital. The Medical Boards consult with the Commissioner on staff appointments and removals and, with the approval of the head of each institution, make proposals for new regulations for hospital medical practice and procedure.

The *Department of Sanitation* cleans over 10,000 curb miles of streets, removes waste and refuse, clears away snow and ice, and operates incinerators. In cooperation with the Department of Parks, it fills waste land for use as parks and playgrounds. It carries on an educational program for a clean city.

Since 1952 air pollution control, formerly the responsibility of the Bureau of Smoke Control in the Department of Buildings, has been administered by the separate *Department of Air Pollution Control*. It is charged to prevent the emission into the open air of harmful or objectionable substances including, but not limited to, smoke, soot, ashes, dust, fumes, gas, vapors, odors, and any products of combustion or incomplete combustion resulting from the use of fuel-burning equipment or the burning of refuse.

Education and Recreation

The *Board of Education* has general control of the public school system. It is composed of 9 nonsalaried members appointed by the Mayor for seven-year overlapping terms. The Board of Education elects the *Superintendent of Schools*, who is responsible for the administration of the school system. The Deputy, 8 Associate, and 39 Assistant Superintendents are nominated by the Superintendent and appointed by the Board of Education. The Board of Superintendents directs the work of a number of bureaus and programs with specialized functions in carrying out the administration of the public school system.

There are other boards that supplement the work of these two principal Boards in the educational system. Each of the 54 school districts in the city has its own advisory *Local School Board* for the purpose of considering local school needs. The five members of each Local School Board are appointed by the President of the borough in which the Board is located; members serve without salary for five-year terms. There is also an *Advisory Board for Vocational and Extension Education*, composed of seven members who are representatives of local trades, industries, and occupations.

The *Board of Examiners* conducts examinations of teachers for placement on eligible lists. All appointments of teachers are made from these lists. The Board of Examiners consists of nine members appointed by the Board of Education, including the Superintendent of Schools. The examiners have permanent tenure after successfully completing a six-month probation period.

There are two retirement systems for employees of the Board of Education. The *Teachers' Retirement Board* administers the Teachers' Retirement System. Of the seven members of the Board, two are appointed by the Mayor for an indefinite term, one of whom must be a member of the Board of Education. Three are teachers elected by the Teachers' Retirement Association for three-year terms. The President of the Board of Education and the Comptroller are also members. The Administrative Employees' Retirement System is under the direction of the Board of Education.

Among the many educational institutions of the city are the seven public colleges maintained by New York City for its residents. They are: the College of the City of New York, Brooklyn College, Hunter College, Queens College, and Queens Borough, Staten Island, and Bronx Community Colleges. These colleges are administered by the *Board of Higher Education*. This Board has 21 nonsalaried members appointed by the Mayor, plus the President of the Board of Education (which operates the city's primary and secondary schools). Each of the colleges has its own president as its chief executive.

Among the newer educational institutions is the New York City Community College of Applied Arts and Science. It operates under the direction of a separate Board of nine trustees—five appointed by the Mayor and four city residents appointed by the Governor.

New York's many cultural institutions provide education and recreation to the people of the city and to visitors from all over the world. Among these are the Metropolitan Museum of Art, the Museum of the City of New York, the American Museum of Natural History, the Planetarium Authority of the American Museum of Natural History, the New York Botanical Garden, the New York Zoological Society, the Staten Island Zoological Society, the Brooklyn Institute of Arts and Sciences, the Staten Island Institute of Arts and Sciences, the New York Public Library, the Brooklyn Public Library, and the Queens Borough Public Library. The libraries are city institutions and the Mayor appoints the Boards of the Brooklyn and Queens Borough Libraries with the exception of *ex officio* members. The museums, institutes, and zoological societies all have governing boards on which municipal officials serve as *ex officio* members. Some of these institutions are wholly financed by the city; others have private funds and are partially subsidized by the city. These cultural institutions serve not only residents of the city but also suburbanites.

The *Department of Parks* has jurisdiction over the parks and parkways of the city. It selects sites, maintains and beautifies parks, and provides recreational programs. In addition, the Department has the authority to plan and establish a unified parkway system which combines playground space with highways. The Department's program is administered within each borough by a Borough Director. The Commissioner of Parks, appointed by the Mayor, is a member *ex officio* of the governing boards of many civic agencies and institutions including the City Planning Commission.

Public Works, Utilities, Transportation

The *Department of Public Works* is responsible for the development of plans and the construction, alteration, repair, and maintenance of many city buildings, bridges, intercepting sewers, sewage disposal plants, and other structures. It does not maintain buildings of the Departments of Correction and Hospitals, the Board of Education, and some other departmental and borough buildings. Street construction and maintenance is the responsibility of the five borough public works offices and not of the Department. However, it acts in an advisory capacity for these departments. The Commissioner, who is head of the Department, is appointed and subject to removal by the Mayor.

The *Art Commission* has supervision of the design of works of art and buildings to be erected in public places. Works of art, buildings, and other structures must be approved by the Commission before being purchased or accepted as a gift. Existing works of art cannot be moved or altered without its permission. The Commission consists of the Mayor, three members *ex officiis*, and seven other members appointed by the Mayor. The appointed members must include a painter, a sculptor, an architect, a landscape architect, and three members not actively engaged in the fine arts. They are selected from a list of nominees submitted to the Mayor by the Fine Arts Federation of New York.

The *Department of Markets* is concerned with the distribution of food. It enforces the state Agriculture and Markets Law and laws on standard weights and measures. It operates the city's terminal markets and supervises open-air markets and issues licenses to pushcart and other peddlers.

The *Department of Marine and Aviation*, formerly the Department of Docks, has control of wharf property, ferries, helicopter landing ports, and seaplane bases owned by the city. The municipal airports were leased for fifty years to the Port of New York Authority in 1947.

The *Department of Water Supply, Gas, and Electricity* has charge of water supply, purification, and distribution. Water rates are fixed by the Department subject to the approval of the Board of Estimate. In addition, it is responsible for the lighting of streets, parks, and public buildings; it supervises and regulates the distribution of gas, electricity, and steam, inspects electrical wiring and appliances, and carries on such other activities as are necessary to its major purposes. Attached to the Department is an Electrical License Board of seven members appointed by the Commissioner to issue licenses to electricians and motion-picture operators.

The *Board of Water Supply*, composed of three Commissioners appointed by the Mayor for life, is responsible for the development of future sources of water supply. It studies future needs and constructs systems when authorized by the Mayor and the Board of Estimate. Once a facility has been completed it is turned over to the Department of Water Supply, Gas, and Electricity.

ADVISORY COMMITTEES

There has been a phenomenal growth in the use of the nonstatutory advisory committees in the past few years. The effect has been widespread and of great significance. The Mayor's Committee on Management Survey advised in one of its general recommendations that the huge reservoir of men and women of ability and civic responsibility who reside in New York City should be tapped to aid the city government. To be sure, various committees, boards, and commissions, with memberships partly drawn from the public, have long been a part of the formal machinery of government. These are established, however, by law and should be distinguished from the committees that operate without specific legislative authorization or mandate.

A survey of committees in city activities undertaken by the City Administrator's office reveals that there are at least a hundred citywide committees operating within the framework of the city government. Committee functions are as wide as the city government itself. For example, to name only a few, the Mayor has advisory committees covering such subjects as pedestrian safety, commuter services, living music, the aged, athletic activities, the World's Fair, pensions, probation, television policy, and welfare and relief. There also are many specialized committees attached to various city agencies such as Corrections, Police, Hospitals, Education, Labor, and the various staff agencies; and finally, a number of interdepartmental committees such as Interdepartmental Rodent Control Committee, Interdepartmental Traffic Council, Interdepartmental Board of Sanitary Protection of the Public Water Supply, and Interdepartmental Committee for a Clean City. All in all, advisory committees are coming to play an increasingly vital role in government in the City of New York.

PUBLIC AUTHORITIES

The *New York City Housing Authority* is concerned with the clearance of slum areas and the erection and maintenance of adequate housing for families of low and middle income. Its work is directed by a Board of five Commissioners appointed by the Mayor. Four Commissioners serve without salary for five years with overlapping terms; the Chairman receives a salary and serves for an indefinite term.

The *New York City Transit Authority* operates the City Transit System which consists of all the subways and elevated lines in the city and city-owned bus lines. The Authority is also responsible for the planning and construction of all new transit lines. One member is appointed by the Governor and one by the Mayor. These two select the third member who is the Chairman. Terms are for six years.

The *Triborough Bridge and Tunnel Authority* composed of three members appointed by the Mayor has jurisdiction over six bridges, the Queens Midtown Tunnel, the Brooklyn-Battery Tunnel, and the New York Coliseum. The former New York City Parkway Authority and the Tunnel Authority are now merged with the Triborough Bridge and Tunnel Authority.

THE COURT SYSTEM

Like all its government the city's court system is a maze of federal, state, county, and municipal jurisdictions. Moreover, the nomenclature is confusing for the layman. Consequently, no attempt is made here to present a full account of the court system within New York City and particularly of the route appeals may take. Chart IV shows the various kinds of courts, indicating whether they are city, county, or state, and the number of their judges and the manner of their selection. Note should be made that some judges are elected and others appointed either by the Mayor or the Governor, and that terms are uniformly long compared to most city or state officials. Furthermore, vacancies are filled either until the next election or for the remainder of the term in some instances by the Mayor and in others by the Governor. There is considerable difference in this regard between courts, but much of this information can be found on Chart IV showing the judicial organization within the City of New York.

The principal law enforcement officer, apart from the Police Department, in each of the five counties within the City of New York is the *District Attorney*. There are five District Attorneys, each elected by the voters of their respective counties for a four-year term. District Attorneys are removable by the Governor after a hearing. Vacancies are filled by the Governor for the remainder of the year in which they occur. Each District Attorney appoints such Assistant District Attorneys as the needs of his county dictate. Usually the actual trial of cases is in the hands of these Assistant District Attorneys.

The Mayor appoints 83 *City Marshals* each for a term of six years who are attached to the courts for the purpose of serving orders and processes. They are not paid a regular salary but allowed fees for each action.

Local Courts in New York City

The *City Magistrates' Courts* are the first courts to hear criminal complaints. They try persons accused of minor offenses and lesser misdemeanors and provide a hearing for persons accused of more serious crimes. In the event that they determine that sufficient evidence exists to warrant holding persons accused of more serious offenses for trial in the higher courts, they admit to bail and fix the amount of the bail bond in accordance with the statutes.

There are 50 magistrates appointed by the Mayor for a ten-year term. One of their number is named Chief Magistrate and exercises considerable administrative authority over the assignment of judges to various courts. Magistrates hold court in various parts of the city and there are also a number of special Magistrates' Courts, such as the Adolescent, Gamblers, Traffic, Weekend, Night, and Narcotics, among others.

CHART IV. JUDICIAL ORGANIZATION IN NEW YORK CITY

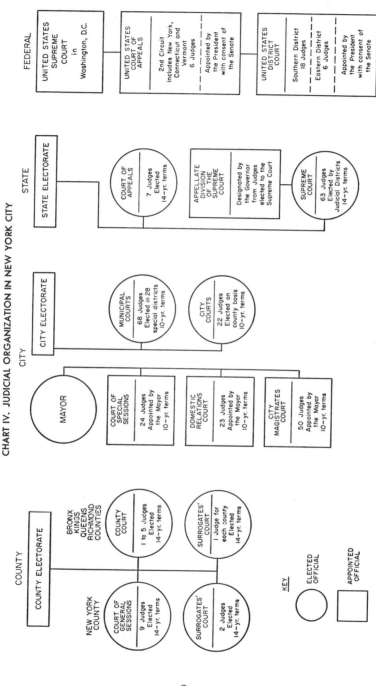

FEDERAL

UNITED STATES SUPREME COURT in Washington, D.C.

UNITED STATES COURT OF APPEALS
2nd Circuit includes New York, Connecticut and Vermont
6 Judges
Appointed by the President with consent of the Senate

UNITED STATES DISTRICT COURT
Southern District 18 Judges
Eastern District 6 Judges
Appointed by the President with consent of the Senate

STATE

STATE ELECTORATE

COURT OF APPEALS
7 Judges Elected 14-yr. terms

APPELLATE DIVISION OF THE SUPREME COURT
Designated by the Governor from Judges elected to the Supreme Court

SUPREME COURT
63 Judges Elected by Judicial Districts 14-yr. terms

CITY

CITY ELECTORATE

MUNICIPAL COURTS
68 Judges Elected in 28 special districts 10-yr. terms

CITY COURTS
22 Judges Elected on county basis 10-yr. terms

MAYOR

COURT OF SPECIAL SESSIONS
24 Judges Appointed by the Mayor 10-yr. terms

DOMESTIC RELATIONS COURT
23 Judges Appointed by the Mayor 10-yr. terms

CITY MAGISTRATES COURT
50 Judges Appointed by the Mayor 10-yr. terms

COUNTY

COUNTY ELECTORATE

BRONX KINGS QUEENS RICHMOND COUNTIES

COUNTY COURT
1 to 5 Judges Elected 14-yr. terms

SURROGATES' COURT
1 Judge for each county Elected 14-yr. terms

NEW YORK COUNTY

COURT OF GENERAL SESSIONS
9 Judges Elected 14-yr. terms

SURROGATES' COURT
2 Judges Elected 14-yr. terms

KEY
ELECTED OFFICIAL
APPOINTED OFFICIAL

The *Court of Special Sessions* has general jurisdiction of all misdemeanors. It is made up of 24 justices each appointed by the Mayor for a ten-year term. Three justices sit as a bench of judges in each court without a jury.

The *Municipal Courts* have jurisdiction over civil actions involving not more than $3,000. The Small Claims part, where a simplified procedure is used, covers actions involving $100 or less. There are 68 judges elected from 28 special judicial districts for a ten-year term. When vacancies occur the Mayor is required to fill them for the remainder of the year within twenty days after they occur. At the next general election vacancies are filled for full terms.

Civil actions involving not more than $6,000 fall within the jurisdiction of the *City Courts*. These courts are staffed by 22 judges. They are elected on a county basis for ten-year terms. Vacancies are filled by the Governor until the next general election.

The *Domestic Relations Court* has two divisions: the Children's Division with exclusive responsibility for all cases involving children under sixteen years of age (except for children accused of first degree murder); and the Family Division which hears disputes involving nonsupport of wives, children, or dependent relatives. There are 23 judges in the Domestic Relations Court each appointed by the Mayor for a ten-year term. Vacancies are filled by the Mayor for the unexpired portion of the term.

The County Court System

With increasing urbanization, many of the earlier functions of the counties have been transferred to the municipal government. Those functions that remain are principally concerned with the administration of justice. In each county there are two courts presided over by elective judges. The *Surrogates' Courts* have jurisdiction over the probating of wills and the administration of the estates of deceased persons. A Public Administrator is appointed by each Surrogate Court to administer, subject to the supervision of the Court, the estates of persons who died intestate or without relatives competent to administer the estate. The Surrogates' Courts in New York and Bronx Counties each have a Commissioner of Records whose duty it is to examine the arrangement of records and to make copies of documents no longer legible.

The remaining court in each county is called a *County Court* in all counties except New York County, where it is called the *Court of General Sessions*. These five courts have original criminal jurisdiction over all persons indicted by a county grand jury, as well as civil jurisdiction in cases appealed from the Magistrates' Courts. The judges are elected for a fourteen-year term and vacancies are filled by the Governor until the next general election.

In 1941 the office of Sheriff in each of the five counties was abolished and the functions were transferred to a single *City Sheriff* appointed by the Mayor from three names submitted by the Civil Service Commission on competitive examination. The City Sheriff has permanent tenure under the Civil Service Law. The City Sheriff, with his undersheriffs in the five counties, is the agent for executing the civil processes of the courts.

There is a *County Clerk* in each county who is appointed by the Appellate Division of the Supreme Court. County Clerks are custodians of the records and papers of the county and also act as Clerks in each of the five counties.

Higher Courts

While state agencies are not within the scope of this discussion, the New York State *Supreme Court* and its *Appellate Divisions* are an integral part of the administration of justice in the city. Some of the expenses of these courts which serve the city are paid by the city. The Supreme Court in New York State is not the final appellate court unlike most states. Indeed the reverse is true. The Supreme Court is the first state court of unlimited original jurisdiction for more important civil and criminal cases and controversies. Appeal, where allowed, lies to the Appellate Divisions of the Supreme Court and thence to the *Court of Appeals*, which is the highest court in the state.

Cases which do not come within the jurisdiction of the municipal, the county, or the federal court systems are handled by the Supreme Court and the Appellate Division. The Supreme Court First Judicial District and the Appellate Division First Department serve New York County and Bronx County. The Supreme Court Second Judicial District serves Kings County and Richmond County. Supreme Court Tenth Judicial District serves Queens and two other counties on Long Island. The Appellate Division Second Department serves Kings, Queens, Richmond, and several other counties outside the city. Judges are elected for a fourteen-year term and vacancies are filled by the Governor until the next general election.

Mention should be made of the probable simplification of this complex court structure in the near future. In 1953, pursuant to state statute, a Temporary Commission on the Courts was established, consisting of 11 nonsalaried members, of whom there are 7 nonlegislative members appointed by the Governor, and 4 legislative members equally divided between the two houses of the legislature and the two political parties. This Commission submitted proposals for the reorganization of the state court structure to the 1957 and 1958 legislatures. Other proposals were made by the State Judicial Conference; suggestions also came from interested organizations throughout the state. A compromise plan was finally approved by the state legislature, on March 24, 1959, known as the Erwin-Lownsberry Concurrent Resolution. To become effective it must be approved again at the legislative session in 1961 and by the voters at the general election in the fall of 1961. It provides (1) a unified state court system; (2) consolidation of family court matters in one court; (3) effective administration for the business of the courts; and (4) adequately supervised fiscal procedures. Changes in the organization of the lower courts, both civil and criminal, apply primarily to New York City leaving the upstate system as it is at present.

The Federal Courts of the United States also operate in New York State. They have criminal jurisdiction in cases involving violations of federal laws and civil jurisdiction as provided by the United States Constitution and Laws. There are three levels of Federal Courts: the *District Court*, the *Court of Appeals*, and the *Supreme Court*.

New York and Bronx Counties are part of the Southern District of New York State. There are 18 Federal District Judges serving in the Southern District. Each judge is nominated by the President and confirmed by the Senate and holds office for life. The Eastern District embraces Kings, Queens, and Richmond Counties as well as some counties outside the city. There are six Federal District Court Judges serving in this area.

Appeals lie to the United States *Court of Appeals*, a body composed of six Judges nominated by the President and confirmed by the Senate. New York City is in the Second Circuit which includes all of New York State as well as Connecticut and Vermont. The Court of Appeals for this circuit sits part of each year in New York City.

The *Supreme Court* of the United States is the highest court in the United States. Composed of the Chief Justice of the United States and eight Associate Justices, this Court sits in Washington, D.C. Appeals upon matters involving the Constitution of the United States come to it in various ways from both State and Federal Courts. The ordinary route for appeals lies from the Federal Circuit Courts of Appeals or from the highest state court—in the case of New York State, the Court of Appeals.

BOROUGH OFFICERS

Each borough elects a President, who is a member of the Board of Estimate and is executive officer of the borough. In general, the *Borough President* has control over the design, construction, and repair of streets and crosswalks, public roads, surface railroads in public streets, sewers, public comfort stations, grading and excavation of land, removal of incumbrances, use and opening of streets, and highway bridges and tunnels except those across navigable streams. He may appoint and remove at pleasure a *Commissioner of Borough Works*, not under civil service, to whom he may delegate any of his powers. In addition, he may appoint, subject to the Civil Service Law, a secretary and various assistants and clerks.

In each borough there is one or more *Local Improvement Boards*, each having authority over a special district, and composed of the President of the borough and the Council members elected from the borough. The Boards initiate proceedings and hear petitions on assessable improvements. There is one such board in Manhattan, one in The Bronx, eight in Brooklyn, one in Queens, and one in Richmond.

The President of each borough also appoints a varying number of Local School Boards and an Advisory Planning Board, mentioned previously.

STATE AND INTERSTATE AGENCIES WITH SPECIAL LOCAL JURISDICTION

Aside from the departments of the state government which have local offices in the city, there are five independent agencies organized under state law each with special local jurisdiction in New York City.

The *Port of New York Authority*, established in 1922, under an interstate compact between New York and New Jersey, supervises, controls, and develops projects designed to facilitate interstate traffic and improve the Port of New York. It operates the city-owned airports under a lease from the city. It maintains and operates the George Washington Bridge, the Bayonne Bridge, Goethals Bridge, Outerbridge Crossing, the Lincoln Tunnel, the Holland Tunnel, and four freight terminals. Its work is governed by 12 Commissioners, six appointed by the Governor of New York and six by the Governor of New Jersey. Each Governor has veto power over the Commissioners' action. The Board of Commissioners handles all executive duties through an appointed Executive Director.

The New York City *Alcoholic Beverage Control Board* investigates and controls the issuance of licenses for the operation of barrooms and package liquor stores, investigates applicants for licenses, and inspects places where liquor is sold within New York City. The Board is composed of four Commissioners, two of whom are appointed by the State Liquor Authority and two by the Mayor. The Mayor makes his appointments from a list made up of two nominees selected by the Academy of Medicine of New York City, two by the Commerce and Industry Association, and two by the Central Trades and Labor Council of New York City.

The *Waterfront Commission of New York Harbor* is composed of two members, one of whom is appointed by the Governor of New York State, with the consent of the New York State Senate, and the other by the Governor of New Jersey, with the consent of the New Jersey State Senate. This agency, created in 1953, licenses stevedoring contractors, pier superintendents, hiring agents, and port watchmen, and registers longshoremen.

The *Interstate Sanitation Commission* is composed of 15 Commissioners, five from each of the states of New York, New Jersey, and Connecticut. This agency was created by interstate compact for the abatement of existing pollution and the control of future pollution in the tidal waters of the New York metropolitan area. This Commission operates primarily through cooperation and persuasion with occasional orders issued to local units of government.

The *Temporary State Housing Rent Commission* is composed of one member known as the State Rent Administrator, who is appointed by the Governor. Its purpose is to enforce the residential rent control laws under state legislation. Established as a temporary body in 1950, the Commission has been continued by successive acts of the legislature for two-year periods. Business, commercial, and residential rentals in New York City are analyzed by the *Temporary State Commission to Study Rents and Rental Conditions*, which makes recommendations to the state legislature with regard to extent and character of rent controls.

FEDERAL ACTIVITIES IN NEW YORK CITY

Federal government activities in New York City are too numerous to catalog in detail, but several facts are worth noting. New York does not have so many federal regional headquarters as, for example, San Francisco, probably because it is geographically nearer to Washington, D.C. Thus the range of federal activities would seem to be less extensive. In part this is illusory because federal agencies send their personnel into New York City from Washington as needed, in place of maintaining permanent regional headquarters as they do in the more distant cities.

In the long-established federal activities such as post office, customs and immigration, internal revenue, security and exchange regulation, and the armed services, New York City has a heavy concentration of federal personnel. In point of number of persons employed by the federal government, New York City ranks high among the nation's cities.

Finally, and perhaps most important of all, the newer federal programs such as housing and urban renewal, and health, education, and welfare have not only involved the expenditure of large sums of money and required many employees but have had a major impact on the city's life. Federal grants-in-aid for public housing, urban renewal, public welfare of all types and, more recently, highways are playing a major role in remaking the face of the city. Some federal funds come to the city directly and some through the state. They have been the means of stimulating a more intensive attack on the city's slums and other housing problems. Without federal assistance in welfare activities, the city's fiscal problems would be much more difficult. Federal grants for the school lunch program, airport expansion, veteran aid, public health, and port maintenance all contribute to meeting the costs of government within New York City.

MANAGEMENT IMPROVEMENT

Substantial as have been the management improvements in the government of the City of New York during the past decade, the continued growth of the city and the changing living patterns of its inhabitants foretell the need for continued attention to this problem in the years ahead. Older solutions of assigning a function to a single level of government may no longer prove adequate since neither the City of New York, nor the five counties, and to some extent not even the State of New York alone can solve the problems of transportation, water supply, sanitation, air pollution, or urban renewal and housing. Emerging, instead, are new types of intergovernmental cooperation between cities and other local or regional units, and between city, state, and national government. While this movement holds great promise in meeting some of the most important problems of modern living, it also demands efficient and effective government organization. Far from diminishing in importance, sound governmental organization will be even more vital to good metropolitan living in the future.

INDEX

Index

NOTE: Items in the bibliographies appearing at the end of chapters in this report have not been indexed, nor have items in the Appendices.

JACKSON LIBRARY — LANDER UNIV.
JS1228 .S37   CIRC
Governing New York City; politics in the metropoli

3 6289 000366234